MAKERS OF JEWISH MODERNITY

MAKERS OF JEWISH MODERNITY

THINKERS, ARTISTS, LEADERS, AND THE WORLD THEY MADE

EDITORS

Jacques Picard

Jacques Revel

Michael P. Steinberg

Idith Zertal

Editorial Assistant and Photography Curator: Ulrich Schutz

Princeton University Press ■ *Princeton & Oxford*

Coordinating Editors: Jacques Picard, Idith Zertal (University of Basel, Switzerland)

Funded by Fondation Berma, Geneva, Switzerland

Library of Congress Cataloging-in-Publication Data

Makers of Jewish modernity : thinkers, artists, leaders, and the world they made / edited by Jacques Picard, Jacques Revel, Michael P. Steinberg, Idith Zertal.
    pages cm
ISBN 978-0-691-16423-6 (hardcover : alk. paper) 1. Judaism—History—Modern period, 1750– 2. Jews—Intellectual life—19th century. 3. Jews—Intellectual life—20th century. 4. Jews—Intellectual life—21st century. 5. Jews—Civilization. 6. Civilization, Western—Jewish influences. 7. Jewish scientists—Biography. 8. Jewish artists—Biography. 9. Jews—Identity. I. Picard, Jacques, editor. II. Flem, Lydia. Sigmund Freud (1856–1939). Container of (work):
BM195.M35 2016
909'.0492408—dc23   2015025101

British Library Cataloging-in-Publication Data is available

This book has been composed in Stempel Garamond LT Std and Franklin Gothic Std

Printed on acid-free paper. ∞

Printed in the United States of America

10 9 8 7 6 5 4 3 2 1

CONTENTS

V

Introduction

THINKING JEWISH MODERNITY

Jacques Picard, Jacques Revel, Michael P. Steinberg, Idith Zertal

"MODERNITY," CHARLES BAUDELAIRE WROTE IN 1859, "IS THE TRANSITORY, THE fleeting, the contingent; it is one half of art, the other being the eternal and the immovable."[1] As one side of art, modernity is also one side of history, and thus one side of Jewish history. In all these cases, modernity connotes a state of mind more than it indicates a historical period or structural condition. As a catalyst for late-nineteenth-century critical thinking, modernity takes up the promises, limitations, and failures of the Enlightenment as they reconstitute themselves in a postrevolutionary, bourgeois age. Thinking about modernity involves a complex relation to time, in which the past appears as both distant and relevant, the future at once promising and vague.

Makers of Jewish Modernity offers original portraits of thinkers, writers, artists, and leaders who founded, formed, and transformed the twentieth century and laid down intellectual, cultural, and political foundations for the world ahead of us. These forty-three portraits understand intellectual and political biographies in the context of the life-worlds of their protagonists—in other words, in terms of the mutualities of texts and contexts, space and time, thought and action, inheritance and transformation.

Modern Jewish experience forms a dimension of our post-Enlightenment world. The term "Judaism" is, in English, immediately problematic as a noun alongside of which "Jewish" is the adjective. "Judaism" often connotes religion and religious texts and laws rather than a more fluid category of general cultural and intellectual inheritance. A bagel, as the saying goes, is not the Talmud. The more general category of Jewish culture in relation to the world at large is often referred to by the awkward word "Jewishness." There is no simple replacement for the powerful and polysemic German term *Judentum*, which strikes the tone and meaning we would engage here. Moreover, it should escape no one that the word *Judentum*, and its implicit claim of a strong religious as well as secular cultural world, came from the nation that subsequently sought to destroy precisely the powerful hybrid that it had nurtured.

Albert Memmi once introduced a distinction between *judaïcité* and *judéité*, whose sense in French is similar to the one that today undergirds a constitutive tension in English between *being Jewish* and *doing Jewish*: "La judéité est la manière dont chaque Juif vit, subjectivement et objectivement, son appartenance au judaïsme et à la judaïcité. La judaïcité est l'ensemble des personnes juives. Le judaïsme est l'ensemble des doctrines et des institutions juives."[2] Or put in English: "Jewishness is the way every Jew lives, subjectively and objectively, his or her belonging to Judaism and Jewry. Jewry includes all kind of Jewish individuals. Judaism is all of Jewish ideas, doctrines, and institutions." This distinction makes it clear that the English "Jewishness," the French *judéité*, the German *Jüdischsein*, and the Hebrew *Yehudiut* include both *being Jewish* and *doing Jewish*, but they also differ from the latter terms. It thereby may become clear that such qualities as boundaries, varieties, and uncertainties—which are also inherent qualities of modernity—are central to such distinctions.[3] A similar way of self-expression may be found in the Yiddish term *Yiddishkayt* as a fusion of experience, often described as the cultural and sensual marrow of "Jewish soul"—thus including imagination and reason, intellectual and emotional languages, performances and reality, difference and commonality. After all, *being Jewish* versus *doing Jewish* distinguishes between the fact of having been born as a Jew versus other connotations—such as, on the one hand, being designated as a Jew by society, a powerful bureaucracy, or imagined attributions of "anti-Judaism,"[4] and, on the other hand, being Jewish through individual choice and practice, how one's own understanding is realized in daily life, or through ideas, connections, and opportunities forming what today often falls under the glittering term "Jewish identities."

Metaphors, formulas, and classifications never form without preconditions and contexts. They help only to bring to the surface—nothing more—complexities, interrelations, or tensions that we thus hope to comprehend. Into the tension between *being* and *doing* as two metaphors and formulas a third element, or spotlight, now interpolates itself, posing a question without a firm answer, but one that remains endless and multifaceted. This is a question of *thinking*. In its focus on *thinking Jewish modernity*, this book turns away from essentializations of "Jewish thought," "Jewishness," "Judaism," or "the Jewish people," aiming instead to grasp the diverse work of thinkers who have confronted and reimagined the relation between Judaism and the modern world.

Thinking is the concept appropriate to the contributions in this book. As the many readings make clear, thinking is a human practice that endeavors to *imagine* life, to imagine the future and the past, to imagine meaning and performance, or community and society. This includes analytical work but also those affective and performative forms of expression, such as music, art, and poetry, that in turn produce knowledge and meaning. This practice of the imagination is constitutive of the production and performance of what was and is experienced as "Jewish," what is sometimes also called "Jewish" by the world—including the established Jewish world—and sometimes not. All kinds of categorical gaps open here. In such a manner is thinking a way *into* modernity, which in turn is to be interpreted in all its coincidences, contradictions, and uncertainties. Thinking modernity involves also a call—in part implicit, in part explicit—that not only Jewishness but indeed any doctrine or specific identity position, whether construed as "religious," "secular," or "cultural," be understood as highly fluid and contingent. They represent the results of the work of human beings to understand their own time and to enact their own lives in the contexts of specific and limited times and spaces.

This predicament poses considerable challenges. It may remind us overall of the image conjured by Franz Kafka in a posthumously published aphorism: the search for the true way proceeds by way of a rope which is wound tightly just above the ground, and which therefore seems intended more to make one stumble rather than to be traversed. The protagonists in this book—alongside, it is important to note, their portraitists—are witnesses to this balancing act, as they themselves feel their way toward a not-quite-tangible future. To many of these figures it was not so important whether this future would bear the name "Jewish" or some other name, but rather that this way and this balancing act themselves might one day be read as one or more modern Jewish experiences. It is this *conditio humana*—this rope wound tightly just above the ground—that may today be recognized and described as the *conditio Judaica*. The contributions collected in this volume therefore do not present an overview but seek rather to demonstrate the strenuous and abiding effort of tripping and tightrope walking, of being, doing, and thinking, of the forcefields connecting *Jewishness* to *Judaism* to *Jewry*, or *Jüdischsein* to *Judentum* and *Judenheit*, or *judaïcité* and *judaïsm* and *judéité*, or *Yehudiut* to *Yahadut* to *Yehudim*. Achieving one's own life, however, requires a strenuous practice of thinking, and will continue to require it—within the struggle, to use Kafka's terms, among "sin, suffering, hope, and the true way."[5]

■

Judaism (and its analogues in other languages since its epigenetic phrasing and migration from the German *Judentum*) has been understood for the most part as a doctrine of religion, not of philosophy, sociology, psychology, anthropology, or the arts. However, it is important to understand that "religion" itself is a post-emancipatory construct of the nineteenth century derived from previous uses of the term—and, as such, is construed as a social and cultural concept of modern society.[6] This is likewise the case for terms such as "history" (*Geschichte* in German), "science" (*Wissenschaft*), "culture," or "secularization"—once they were condensed into notions and ideas in the time of early Enlightenment to the nineteenth century.[7] The political and intellectual realities in the twentieth and twenty-first century's multilateral topography correspond to a previous change in terms, codes, and linguistic images; this may indeed reflect a centuries-long multisecular shift in Western philosophy since the seventeenth century, a movement from thinking in terms of logic to the episteme and the modern dispute over epistemic definitions. Since Søren Kierkegaard, Jewish and non-Jewish writers alike have filtered their denominational and religious traditions through an epistemic grid—they wanted to strip away the exclusivity of its origin from a particular religious community in order to make the contents of their own intellectual tradition and beliefs philosophically, publicly, and universally understood, a task now appearing globally in the call for dialogue and intercultural understanding.[8] Similarly but in a different context and contrast, the same is true regarding Zionist thinkers.[9] What we have before us, then, is a not always conscious linguistic transcoding of the semantics of "Jewish" itself. What is called "Jewish" shifts here—from the "law" of the Jewish legal system to "culture" and "history," to "philosophy" and national "politics"—while a historicizing and secularizing of Jewish hermeneutics, the *Wissenschaft des Judentums*, is involved with and within these codes.[10] These transcodings often enough go in the reverse direction again, from philosophy and the culture of secular societies to the law of new tribal or ethnic segregations, shaping the debate about the determinability of "Jewish" in various—and even antimodernist—versions of modernity.[11] It is through this shift of concepts, and the emergence of new or rediscovered narratives, that Jews worldwide are required to anticipate, envision, and enact history anew. They are drawn into a political positioning with respect to questions of human rights and minority protection, whether they now like this share of responsibility or not.[12]

The codes of any transformation can generally be read in the shifting episteme (or epistemes) and semantics that arise, from the late nineteenth century to the present day, in the course of the ramifications of syncretism and globalization. More and more people of different backgrounds live ever more closely together, and increasing knowledge seems available to them. The juxtaposition or spectrum between tribal and cosmopolitan modes of life also leads, in Jewish modernity, to different modes of self-awareness—and inescapably to a pluralistic, diversified world of being, doing, imagining, and thinking Jewish. What then constitutes "Jewish modernity" or one of its versions, the different codes and semantics that seem to be claimed as "thinking Jewish," are laid down, established, canonized, restricted, and criticized depending on the perception and projection. Jewish modernity cannot be grasped as a unity, but can first be made visible only as a manifold and often conflictual multiplicity. To sum up, language and epistemic transformations, along with natural philosophy, political thought, social environment, and modes of life, constitute decisive factors supporting the concept best expressed by the varieties of Jewish modernity. Thus one can consider, borrowing from Jacques Derrida, all these ways of life as alternatives, and hence speak of them in the plural as "Judaisms."[13]

Therefore, a term like *thinking* is construed here as a human practice toward the construction of various modernities, paths of imagination, and choices that make sense for both individual and collective expectations of being and acting in the world. No unambiguous definition of *Judaism* can therefore be given. Already in the talmudic intellectual edifice, as Daniel Boyarin and Michael Walzer have shown, a very diverse corpus of biblical interpretation, an "exclusive, divinely sanctioned heterodoxy," can be detected, but no semantic determinability and no unambiguous exegesis of the text of the canonical Scriptures are at hand.[14] This indeterminacy of tradition holds—since Baruch Spinoza—all the more for the discourse of modernity and secular thought, whose episteme is stamped by uncertainties and displacements. The epistemes and semantics that persist when it comes to descriptions of Jewish "religion" generally—alongside such subcategories as "Orthodox," "Haredi," "Reformist," "Liberal," "Conservative," "Reconstructionst," or "Humanist" Judaism—derive from a historical context quite removed from the realities to be encountered in the twentieth and twenty-first centuries.[15] "Orthodox," for example, is a postemancipatory concept under which very different influences are summarized today—anything but a unity of doctrine, this term serves the preservation of privilege and power. The discovery of mysticism, too, as a dimension of Jewish modernity, alongside its popularization in the global media today, is patently contingent on modern plays of images and imagination. The same is the case for masculine and feminine imagery of God, since a redefinition of epistemic construction of sex and gender in Jewish and non-Jewish feminist theology enhances a general understanding that is not limited to "masculine" metaphors.[16] Even allegedly modern concepts, like the metaphor of "blood"—of blood as a mythical medium of differentiation and essentialization as found in the writings of such nineteenth- and twentieth-century Jewish male authors as Martin Buber, Franz Rosenzweig, and Uri Zwi Greenberg—have become deeply questionable today. Cultural ideas about genetics have been, since Ludwig Fleck, debunked by science itself as fictions, after they had previously and for a long time been vehemently asserted as socially relevant.[17]

Among the moderns, the questionable nature of such categories have gone unrecognized by some, have been suspected early on and recognized by others, and were simply ignored or even fought by others still. Mordecai Kaplan, for example, stipulated that both universal values or "ethics" and the diversity of "folkways" were part of "Judaism as a Civilization," and were thus opposed to ideologies of blood and race.[18] Similarly, Franz Boas formulated his rejection of the alleged biological foundations of anthropological hierarchy based on eugenic fantasies of "race" and "color" by emphasizing the significance of language skills for human intercourse.[19] To be sure, the nineteenth and twentieth centuries spawned political and ideological versions of biological or institutional ways of *being Jewish* as well as social and cultural ways of *doing Jewish*, thus bearing witness to the radical diversity among the claims and interpretations of the Jewish past and future. Feminism has added a key strand to this diversity of human and Jewish experiences. The history of modern Western feminist movements and their so-called waves or struggles—including the drive to enfranchisement; women's liberation in social and economic life; the inclusion of Jewish secular women among thinkers, shapers, and pioneering activists of feminism; the prominent place of women in activist Palestinian Zionism and the early state years, including women soldiers and officers; and the rabbinical ordination of women—has included an explicitly Jewish dimension.[20]

■

Jewish modernity possesses a largely European heritage. It negotiates between the universalisms of the Enlightenment and their potentials—opportunities, threats—and of cultural absorption. The emancipation and reclamation of the Jewish Enlightenment has long been considered the decisive moment in the history of diasporic Judaism. After centuries of oppression and persecution, an atmosphere of toleration, philosophical deism, and entrepreneurial inclusion originating in the Netherlands in the seventeenth century, and taken up in a few other places,[21] led to the Jews finally gaining civil status in a certain number of countries during the nineteenth century. They glimpsed the possibility of getting "out of the ghetto"[22] in Western and Eastern European topographies, and of a more or less complete incorporation into the societies constituted within nation-states. But to summarize thus would be to do violence to a process that was far more complex, and whose rhythms and modalities differed profoundly from country to country—from one end of Europe to another, but also from one social milieu to another. The central dynamic, what became the dominant trait of nineteenth-century modernity, was a pressured integration, the predicament usually referred to as "assimilation." Assimilation affirmed the belief that the specificity of Jewish culture was not incompatible with national cultures.

Thus the Haskalah, or Jewish Enlightenment, which accompanied the assimilation movement in the German world during the last decades of the eighteenth century, saw itself as an undertaking of modernization. Inspired by that undertaking, the developing *Wissenschaft des Judentums* tasked itself with applying to history and to texts from the Jewish tradition that historical-philological approach whose rules were at that moment being formalized within German historiography. At the same time, the establishment of academic studies of Jewish and Islamic heritages in Hungary sharpened the correlation between *Wissenschaft* and tradition, as is evident in the scholarly writings of Ignác Goldziher and his educated Southeastern European contemporaries.[23] But again, it is important to not simplify or reduce a movement—the will to leave the cultural ghetto—that was not uniform, for its effects were varied and at times contradictory. Many aspects of Eastern European Jewish communities would continue to be contrasted against the experiences of those in the West. The same is true, in a similar but later and not comparable manner, for Mediterranean Jewish cultures.[24]

In France, the universalism of the rights of man—a heritage of the Revolution of 1789—is generally understood as a guarantee of access into civic equality and into the distinct culture of *laïcité*. With generous intentions, a thoroughly lay policy put Jewish identity in a potentially awkward position. Wasn't Jean-Paul Sartre's *Réflexions sur la question juive*,[25] published in 1946, still controversially understood as some kind of threat to Jewish identity? In Germany, the relative absence of revolution funneled national modernity into the post-Kantian articulations of secularized Protestantism (*Kulturprotestantismus*). Judaism became itself "Protestant" in style and argument, as evident in the practices and aesthetics of the Reform movement. Literal conversion was an option as well, as is obvious in the cases of the descendants of Moses Mendelssohn as well as in paradigmatic voices of all three German Enlightenments: German, Jewish, and German-Jewish.[26] On the other side of the nationally inflected universalisms, Jewish modernity faced and considered the attractions of particularity, including sacred and secular models, as well as the strong hybrids of the sacred/secular dialectic such as nationalism itself. The diverse roles of Jews in these attempts at self-exploration and imagined ethnicity, world-discovery, or relecturing on Jewish traditions allowed for their activity as scholars, artists, critics, political propagandists, and cultural mediators.

World War I, with its millions of dead, its massive destruction, and perhaps even more so the absurd logic that commanded it, was responsible for a profound, pan-European moral crisis. The optimistic century of progress was violently called into question as modern civilizations realized that they, too, were mortal, as Paul Valéry lamented in 1919. "We see now," he wrote, "that the abyss of history is deep enough to bury all the world. We feel that a civilization is fragile as life."[27] This dark prophecy evidently came even truer in World War II, particularly for the Jewish people, as well as others, who were singled out for destruction. Did genocide not place the very means of modernity—"an attempt at social engineering"—at the service of mass extermination, as Zygmunt Bauman has suggested?[28] Generally speaking, the conviction that modern reason is inseparable from barbarism (Walter Benjamin), the assertion that the "dialectic of enlightenment" fuses reason with violence (Max Horkheimer and Theodor Adorno), would henceforth undermine the innermost hopes so long placed in modernity.

Jewish experience lies at the heart of these upheavals. The creation of the state of Israel marks a major shift in its intention to usher in a new future. It also compels the other Jewish communities of the world to rethink their status, their project, as well as their relationships to the new national entity. At the very moment that the trust placed in two centuries of progress is called into question, it becomes necessary to substitute it with other founding values and endow it with other hopes. The reinvention of Jewish tradition will thus have been one of the characteristic features of the twentieth century, although for many of those who undertook to find it in canonical sources, the meaning would now seem unattainable.

Young Gershom Scholem's experience offers a telling example.[29] Born in 1897 to an average, bourgeois, assimilated family in Berlin, he despised the inconsistencies in, and persistence of, Jewish rituals and references now emptied of their meaning. In terms that evoke those of Franz Kafka's *Letter to His Father* (1919), he denounced the contradictions of a family—and its wider milieu—that was capable of preserving superficial attachments to tradition, but not of understanding it, let alone conveying its significance. Thus, in 1913 he chose to immerse himself in an intensive study of Hebrew, the Bible, the Talmud, and canonical Jewish texts, dedicating his life to the belief that it was possible to rediscover a living Judaism, to "revive the dried bones of German Jewry."[30] As striking as it may have seemed, Scholem's experience was in no way isolated. It was shared in various forms by some of the most brilliant German intellectuals of his generation. Franz Rosenzweig, for example, advocated "dissimilation" (as opposed to assimilation), in which he contended that the only way the Jewish people could remain true to themselves would be to recognize the perseverance and tenacity in their long history. Many others endeavored to denounce, with Scholem, the "troubling and tragic illusion" of an ostensible Judeo-German "symbiosis" in which Jews had chosen a fallacious modernity, one that never gained them any recognition in return for having opened themselves up to the dominant culture. But in turning their backs on a model that appeared exhausted, these men did not renounce modernity. Rather, they sought to create different versions that would make room for the specificities of Jewish experience so that their expectations could be fulfilled.

From Hermann Cohen (in the late nineteenth century) to Emmanuel Levinas (in the second part of the twentieth), the immense effort of rereading, questioning, and interpreting serves to decipher the meaning of this tradition for the present. Yet the thread of tradition is also broken for the twentieth century. Such was the lesson of Kafka and Benjamin; and after the Jewish catastrophe in World War II, it was picked up and magnified by Hannah Arendt, Paul Celan, Primo Levi, Jacques Derrida, and others. As Stéphane Mosès writes: "This is to grieve for truth, but at the same time steer clear of absolute shipwreck and the engulfing of everything, including shattered debris. This means recovering and rethinking, in new contexts, the pieces that resurface. In an age that can no longer believe in the truth of tradition, the only way to salvage memory is to tell the story of its disappearance."[31] Is it any wonder, then, that the reaction to the lengthy process of assimilation and secularization that characterized the nineteenth century was the rebirth of a Jewish messianism, whose expressions were multiform, but which still chose to break with the progressivist and cumulative conception of modernity in order to emphasize the possibilities of the present—that which Benjamin calls "now-time" (*Jetztzeit*)—and the promises it conceals, those of a history we do not expect?

The explosive and genocidal twentieth century reshuffled all Jewish options: political, intellectual, religious, social, cultural. In Europe, the fragile identity combinations of the post-Enlightenment world were irretrievable after 1945. Jewish life in Europe finds itself increasingly nonindigenous: Jewish life in France is increasingly North African in its demographic trends; in Germany, where it begins on an appreciable scale only after 1989, it is increasingly Eastern European and recently Israeli. Most generally and globally, and most relevant to the structure of this book, Jewish modernity after 1945 becomes a function of a tri- and even multilateralized world, with centers of gravity in Europe, Israel, and North America. In the United States, the "melting pot" principle, the pragmatist philosophy of pluralism and the emergence of a "post-Christian nation" (Harold Bloom),[32] enabled a relatively stressless alchemy of "Americanness" and "Jewishness" in a mode not available in most European societies or in the Israel of today. Meanwhile, for Jews in Canada, as well as for the country's many other minorities, the new political doctrine of "multiculturalism" has shifted to an ongoing negotiation and management of diversity.[33] Such privilege has claimed a price in a certain moral sentimentality: the tendency, as Peter Novick argued, to claim moral victory from other people's murder or survival and then to shape that moral victory into an existential loyalty to the state of Israel.[34] Israel was in turn able to persuade a majority of American Jewry that it spoke authoritatively and exclusively on behalf of "the Jewish people," the secular replacement of the Jewish religion and one that, for the reason just stated, found compatibility with American identity.

■

Israel, whose political culture in the 1950s denied continuity with its European past and most specifically with Holocaust victimhood, came, by the 1970s, to rely exactly on the latter for its legitimation in general and for the legitimation of its military ideology, politics, and practices more specifically. Furthermore, from a historical perspective, not only did Israel have a European past, but political Zionism has been European from its genesis, and Israel has always perceived itself as a bastion of European civilization in the backwardness of the East, or a "villa in the jungle," as recently put. Drawing on the great revolutions that swept the European continent in 1789 and 1848, shaped by romanticism, nationalism, and socialism, and galvanized by modern political anti-Semitism, Jewish nationalism—in other words: political Zionism—came into its own in the later nineteenth century. The idea of Jewish nationhood was thrust into modern history not by scientists or technocrats, nor by industrialists or social reformers, but rather by theorists and poets—by thinkers, writers, artists, journalists, and educators in Russia and Eastern and Central Europe, who reimagined their own as well as their people's Judaism and Jewishness. By so doing, these protagonists imagined a new era and formed a positive vision for themselves and their people, acting as innovators and conveyors of new ethics and frameworks of life, establishing ideological and political movements in times of crisis and upheaval, transforming the value systems of their communities, and playing a major role in the process of their modernization. A minority discourse within the Jewish world, political Zionism struggled for dominance in a crowded and militant European Jewish arena of assimilationists, national-cultural autonomists, socialist Bundists, folk-diasporists, Orthodox Agudists, Yiddishists, and a plethora of other factions. Ultimately, Nazism and Stalinism led to the demise of this ideological and cultural rage.

It was the early Zionists' aim thoroughly to transform Jewish consciousness as well as the material conditions of Jewish life—to create and invent the Jewish people anew and to reclaim its territorial and temporal space, its language, and its very model of the human being. This mind-bending project was not immune to contradictions. While imagining a totally brave new world and human being, it drew no less on the romantic idea of a return to the distant past, of the restoration of the mythical golden age of ancient Jewish sovereignty in Zion/Palestine. Biblical narratives, tales, and lessons impregnated twentieth-century Zionism and Zionist history, and shaped it. The conquest of the land was thus to be perceived as a replay of the ancient conquest led by Joshua. The very ingathering of the Jews in newly invented Zion would be a replication of the Exodus from Egypt and the return to the land from the Babylonian exile. Indeed, the Babylonian syndrome has defined Zionism all along. Although the Palestinian voluntarist branch of Zionism, in its effort to restore ancient Hebrew domination, declared and established Hebrew as its sole, exclusive spoken and written language, Zionism, and also Zionists/new Israelis from all continents and lands, continued to speak in some seventy distinct dialects, experiencing and expressing at once their profound differences in origin, upbringing, culture, customs, and faiths. Unlike Hebrew literature, Israeli literature and scholarship continue to be written in a multitude of languages.

Israel's later, statist policy of the melting pot would amount to no more than a heroic, yet short-lived, attempt to repress these differences and to level the multitude of hierarchies, shades, and nuances assembled by the Zionist revolution. Socialist and capitalist, liberal and Marxist, religious and atheist, orthodox and anarchist— Zionism, to be sure, had been all of these. While displaying an all-against-all tumultuous and ongoing struggle of ideas and ideologies, all vying for prominence and influence, Zionism has also encouraged strange partnerships. It is, for instance, big, private Jewish money that financed the most original and innovative social and cultural experiments in Palestine/Israel in the first half of the twentieth century: the kibbutzim and other agricultural cooperative sorts of communities. Chaim Weizmann was said to take pride in another uncanny match created by Zionism, represented by those "poor Galician immigrants" who arrived in Palestine with no clothes but with "one hand holding Marx's *Capital*, and in the other, Freud's *Interpretation of Dreams*."[35]

The realization of the Zionist ancient-futuristic utopia (*Altneuland*) required that those poor immigrants and especially their progeny to be born in Zion and become the "New Man" or the "New Hebrew" imagined by the Zionist revolution. The model of the French and other revolutions of recent times, a new interest in the human body, and novel theories of sexuality and eugenics, together with influential Nietzschean ideas, were all borrowed by early Zionist thinkers in their quest for the new Jew. Nietzsche's *Lebensphilosophie* (philosophy of life) and its assertions of vitality, will, power, and myth, along with the dismissal of tradition, equipped abundantly the new discourse of the Zionist thinkers. Nietzsche's "new man" and "superman" (*Übermensch*) served the early Zionists, the followers of Herzl among them, in their imaginings of the Zionist "new man" or the "new Hebrews" as against the inherited archetype of the "diaspora Jew." In the last decade of the nineteenth century, while residing in Bern, Switzerland, Micha Yosef Berdichevsky, one of the most complex and compelling Jewish intellectuals of his time, wrote to a friend: "I am a Nietzschean . . . and know only might, power, power!" The neurologist and social critic Max Nordau, the cofounder, with Herzl, of the World Zionist Organization, coined the term "muscle Judaism" (*Muskel-Judentum*) as a counterpoint to the stereotyped Jewish body, allegedly ravaged by centuries of "degenerate" (*entartet*) life in the diaspora, to which Zionism was for him the only possible political remedy. Zionism meant in this context physical and mental robustness, normalcy, beauty, self-discipline, responsibility, cleanliness, and steady marriage. "The future generation shall not be small and weak, beaten and sickly as is this dwarfish generation," the Russian Jewish publicist Reuben Brainin said, reflecting on this version of modernity. "Rather shall a strong and mighty generation arise, a generation of giants, a generation which shall inculcate new physical strengths and new mental capacities which we never imagined — a generation of the 'superman.'"[36]

∎

Fin-de-siècle, antisemitic Vienna, a crossroad of many trends and trades, offered the stage for the inception of two major modern movements, both emblems of Jewish modernity: Freud's psychoanalysis and Herzl's political Jewish nationalism. Contemporaries and major agents of modernity, Freud and Herzl were intrigued by yet reluctant toward one another's work. One aspired to probe, understand, and heal the individual psyche; the other aimed at the utopian transformation of the collective body, along with the simultaneous regimentation of the individual. While Freud showed dislike for all forms of nationalism and their false myths and promises of salvation, Herzl, hitherto a resolute assimilationist, lost faith in that option and looked for "a permanent shelter for the Jewish people." Freud worried about the identification of psychoanalysis as a "Jewish science." In the foreword to the Hebrew edition of *Totem and Taboo*, with which he was very satisfied, Freud wrote, "The reader of this book [in its Hebrew version] will not easily find himself at the emotional standpoint of the author, who is ignorant of the holy tongue and scriptures, who has moved away completely from the religion of his forefathers — as from every other religion — and who cannot share national ideals."[37] The atmosphere in Zionist Palestine (the Yishuv) was in turn rather inhospitable toward the new school of thought and its practices. The Psychoanalytical Society was founded in Palestine in 1933 by Max Eitington, a close disciple of Freud's, and some of his colleagues from the Berlin Psychoanalytical Institute. And although many Jewish psychoanalysts found refuge in Palestine in the 1930s, twenty years later the Psychoanalytical Society still counted only ten members. "The intensive construction which characterizes this place compels us to make our way without prematurely paying attention to our integration in public life," Eitingon wrote to Freud in 1934. "On the whole we have to do here with the same people with similar problems that we dealt with in the past, as religious Jews and Arabs do not count for psychoanalysis."[38] The Zionist "New Man" appeared to be everyman in the eyes of psychoanalysis.

The newly established material-territorial space of Zionism and Hebrew national-modernism, Palestine and/or Israel, has constituted itself as a political and social subject, acting within history and shaping and changing it in the process. For the first half of the century, or rather until the early 1970s, it was a space of distinct modernity: a place of self-determination, secular rationalism, social experiments, and creative innovation, committed to a vision of justice and equality for all. This revolutionary option of *Tikkun* (mending, or rebuilding) in the life of the Jews was led once again primarily by thinkers, writers, artists, and other cultural agents. The invented Israeli spaces of nation building, social planning, and social engineering in the arts, sciences, architecture, and design, prior to the establishment of the state and well into the second decade of statehood, were mostly imagined, guided, and shaped by European modernism. The city of Tel Aviv, to cite but one example, still reveals one of the densest displays of Bauhaus buildings designed by European Zionist architects in the 1930s and the 1940s. Without belittling the presence and importance of deviationist expressions of nonmodernism or even antimodernism within the Israeli modernist project, one might claim that Western modernism informed and guided the planning, design, and construction of the country, and has been most dominant in giving shape and form to its infrastructures, discourse, print culture, music, and fashion.[39]

The Jewish catastrophe in World War II and the establishment of the Zionist Jewish state in 1948 impacted the Jewish world and displaced the great drama of the Jews and its principal theaters from Europe to Israel and Northern America. The Jewish question, which in Europe seemed for centuries unsolvable, metamorphosed now into the Israeli or Palestinian question, creating a new and so far unsolved tragedy that has largely—if not entirely—displaced the earlier one. The historical proximity of the Holocaust to the achievement of Jewish political sovereignty, together with the decisive role of the former in establishing and shaping the latter, was to yield a special kind of catastrophic messianism, and a new or new-old myth of destruction and redemption, of powerlessness and empowerment, that was removed from both the historical and the political. The connection of Israeli power and power practices of the Jewish state, especially since the occupation of the Palestinian lands in 1967, with the history of total powerlessness and victimhood of the Holocaust has been dialectical. Memory of the catastrophe would invest local circumstances and the ongoing conflict with alien significance, extracting them from their political and historical dimensions, while the discourse created by the ongoing conflict consolidated and reinforced the role of the Holocaust as the constituent myth of the Zionist-Israeli metanarrative.[40]

As a result, the unprecedented and bold—if imperfect—experiment of existential, political, social, and cultural innovation and creativity that tagged the Zionist endeavor as a modern miracle, claiming Israel as its product and drawing into close alliance principal Jewish communities worldwide, now finds itself gradually shrouded and sinking into a self-made new ghetto, even if a high-tech one, of an old-new Arendtian "worldnessness"—a ghetto defined by fears, isolationism, and devastated public spheres where critical thought, free deliberation, and exchange of ideas are persecuted. This ghetto is also driven by a self-perception of victimhood and politics of unaccounted for violence, where children are being taught, once again, to suspect the world and fear their neighbors. "Slowly slowly children learn to hate," writes Meir Wieseltier, a leading contemporary Israeli poet: "It takes some time / two-three years at school—to teach a child to hate / a rather simple matter, to be sure."[41]

■

Modernity—we should, again, better speak of *modernities*, as the term refers to so many and diverse experiences—can be understood, as we have seen, as a border- and contact-zone: as liminal spaces and liminal times, in which rituals of transformation and of renewal and conversion are believed and staged—and this is expressed in a great deal of critique. It is a polyrhythmic sound of different, contradicting voices, a result of its rich diversity.[42] This in turn implies that modernity, long held to be an eminent overcoming, reinterpretation, and even radicalization of fixed-seeming paradigms, contains within itself that heretical moment we have already mentioned. This does not mean that the moderns lived an existence on the edge of society, although some did indeed so live. But often they were part of a bourgeois culture—whether on the left, right, or center of the political spectrum—and would radically alter this culture itself by creating new disciplines or fields within it. Modernity is therefore characterized, too, by entropy, a tendency to cultural upheavals and challenges. In other words, the pioneering moderns were never able to make themselves immune to illusions; they were partially addicted to them.

Our book therefore pays special attention to those critical spirits who both have recourse to oft-forgotten traditions and simultaneously overthrow the fixed rules and conventional ideals of their times. Many of the "moderns" were often destroyers of paradigms that governed scholarship and thinking in the society of an emancipatory century, as they deemed them incorrect owing to their epistemological inconsistencies, or put them in critical perspective whenever the underlying procedures were insufficiently indebted to inductive principles. Modern critique was therefore directed against evolutionism, the reductionist scheme that regarded history and culture as a linear-progressive development from the "simple" to the "complex." Others rejected an ideological version of diffusionism, that is, the assertion that culture would always develop gloriously in a monogenetic way, spreading out like a wave from a central point into different regions of a newly discovered world or even—more modestly—into a certain particular culture called Judaism. Instead, methodological skepticism was directed toward all universal standards or attempts at asserting generalized "laws" or deterministic regularity in describing cultural, social, or historical processes that were said to be unavoidable or eternal.[43] This placed such liberal thinkers in stark contrast to the kind of early-twentieth-century thinking that Marvin Harris described as "neo-Hegelian racist visions of national souls working their way toward ineffable glories."[44]

Our book, in the selection of forty-three essays, acknowledges a multiplicity of foci and locations. It includes a fluid and constantly changing topographical dispersion—Western Europe, Eastern Europe, the Mediterranean, North America, Latin America, and Israel. This makes clear that *Makers of Jewish Modernity* is also to be understood as characterized by global spaces, conditioned through migrations in historical perspective and the liminal possibilities of communication and of today's transfers of knowledge. This tri- or multilateralization—which might be understood as the Jewish variant of globalization—has determined the dramatis personae of this book's editors, authors, and subjects. Its four editors are based in and professionally identified with Switzerland, France, Israel, and the United States. It goes without saying that we have curated the essays that follow for their historical and empirical accuracy. At the same time, we have arranged the choice of subjects and authors, as well as the "marriages" between subjects and authors, according to the present realities of the trilateralized Jewish world. We hope for coherence in terrains of multiple diversity. Readers will find fresh portraits of canonical European thinkers; unusual selections with vexed relationships to Judaism, whether their own or other people's; lesser known or even forgotten figures; contemporary figures whose Jewish relevance may outperform their canonical status; and the occasional portrait of a complete antimodernist, and yet at the same time also an idiosyncratic modernist, like Rav Kook. In some cases, thinkers are portrayed by scholars strongly identified with them; in other cases, the association may be profound but previously unarticulated. We have also striven, it is important to note, for gender balance in the rosters of both subjects and contributors.

The thinkers analyzed and the scholars who write share these convictions and thus a working understanding of modernity as an objective and subjective condition, a condition of both world and self in which the knowledge and transformation of either or both remain essential but elusive human necessities. Modernity and Judaism remain in flux, and the thinking here is strong, free, individual, and indeed idiosyncratic in its voices. These are tense readings, living thinking, intimate dialogues between author and subject—with us as close, active ushers or, rather, "matchmakers." This book is not, to be blunt, a series of encyclopedia entries. We make no claim of exhaustive coverage or of a historical or geographical survey. Our volume is thereby an invitation: Call it alchemy or call it marriage, we have been interested in inspiring a new and unpredictable dynamic between writer and subject, and it will follow that every reader will enter a debate as a third position—as a third thinker and participant in the project.

Notes

1. Charles Baudelaire, "The Painter of Modern Life," in *Selected Writings on Art and Literature* (New York, 1972), 403.

2. Albert Memmi, *La Libération du Juif* (Paris, 1966), 35f.

3. On its emergence, see Shaye J. D. Cohen, *The Beginnings of Jewishness: Boundaries, Varieties, Uncertainties* (Berkeley, Los Angeles, and London, 1999).

4. See David Nirenberg, *Anti-Judaism: The Western Tradition* (New York and London, 2013).

5. Franz Kafka, *Betrachtungen über Sünde, Leid, Hoffnung und den wahren Weg*, in *Sämtliche Werke*, ed. Peter Höfle (Frankfurt, 2008), 1343.

6. This was recognized by Max Wiener, a contemporary of Max Weber; see Max Wiener, *Jüdische Religion im Zeitalter der Emanzipation* (Berlin, 1933).

7. Reinhart Kosselleck, *Vergangene Zukunft, Zur Semantik geschichtlicher Zeiten* (Frankfurt, 1979), 109–29.

8. Jürgen Habermas, "Politik und Religion," in *Politik und Religion: Zur Diagnose der Gegenwart*, eds. Friedrich Wilhelm Graf and Heinrich Meier (Munich, 2013), 298f.; Hermann Levin Goldschmidt, *The Legacy of German Jewry* (New York, 2007), 236–43.

9. See Gideon Shimoni, *The Zionist Ideology* (Hanover and London, 1995).

10. This also holds, by the way, for modern Islamic hermeneutics, which would definitely be taken into account in an analogy to Judaism and in historically situating the context of Jewish Reform in the nineteenth century.

11. Compare Fredrik Barth, *Ethnic Groups and Boundaries: The Social Organization of Cultural Difference* (Oslo and London, 1996). Isaiah Berlin, *The Crooked Timber of Humanity* (London, 1991).

12. On the rise and fall of the international minority protection system, see Congrès Juif Mondiale, *Protocole du Premier Congrès Juif Mondial, Genève 8–15 août 1936* (Geneva, Paris, and New York, 1936); World Jewish Congress, *Unity in Dispersion: A History of the WJC* (New York, 1948); Caroline Fink, *Defending the Right of Others: The Great Powers, the Jews, and International Minority Protection, 1878–1938* (Cambridge, 2006); Erwin Viefhaus, *Die Minderheitenverträge und die Entstehung der Minderheitenschutzverträge auf der Pariser Friedenskonferenz 1919* (Cologne and Würzburg, 1960); Martti Koskenniemi, *The Gentle Civilizers of Nations: The Rise and Fall of International Law (1870–1960)* (Cambridge, 2001); "Genf," in *Enzyklopädie jüdischer Geschichte und Kultur*, ed. Dan Diner (Stuttgart and Weimar, 2012), 2:411–17.

13. Jacques Derrida, "Abraham, l'autre," in *Judéités: Questions pour Jacques Derrida*, eds. Joseph Cohen and Raphael Zagury-Orly (Paris, 2003).

14. Compare Daniel Boyarin, *Den Logos zersplittern: Zur Genealogie der Nichtbestimmbarkeit des Textsinns im Midrasch* (Berlin, 2002), 43; Michael Walzer, *In God's Shadow: Politics in the Hebrew Bible* (New Haven and London, 2012).

15. Some thinkers today therefore plead for a "postorthodox" development, which would take its bearings from the fluid epistemes of religious practice in everyday social life.

16. Using masculine and feminine metaphors for "God" is a vehicle to remind followers that gendered descriptions in theology are beyond gender but have been hermeneutically used many times to legitimate and privilege elitist power and prerogatives. Instead, today in modernity, engendering Judaism became an important contribution to progress *inclusive* Jewish ethics and theology. Judith Plaskow, *Standing Again at Sinai: Judaism from a Feminist Perspective* (New York, 1990), is the first book of Jewish feminist theology ever written. Melissa Raphael, *The Female Face of God in Auschwitz* (Oxford, 2003), is the first full-length feminist theology of the Holocaust. See furthermore Rachel Adler, *Engendering Judaism: An Inclusive Theology and Ethics* (Boston, 1998).

17. Ludwig Fleck, *Erfahrung und Tatsache: Gesammelte Aufsätze* [1927–1960] (Frankfurt, 1983). Also see Eva Jablonka and Marion J. Lamb, *Evolution in Four Dimensions: Genetic, Epigenetic, Behavorial, and Symbolic Variation in the History of Life* (Cambridge, 2005); Paul Gilroy, *Against Race: Imagining Political Culture beyond the Color Line* (Cambridge/London, 2000); Veronika Lipphardt, *Biologie der Juden: Jüdische Wissenschaftler über "Rasse" und Vererbung 1900–1935* (Göttingen, 2008); John M. Efron, *Defenders of the Race: Jewish Doctors and Race Science in Fin-de-Siècle Europe* (New Haven and London, 1994); Caspar Battegay, *Das andere Blut: Gemeinschaft im deutsch-jüdischen Schreiben 1830–1930* (Cologne, 2011).

18. Mordecai M. Kaplan, *Judaism as a Civilization: Toward a Reconstruction of American-Jewish Life* (1934; Philadelphia and New York, 1981), 180. See David Biale, *Not in Heaven: The Tradition of Jewish Secular Thought* (Princeton and Oxford, 2011), 176–180

19. Franz Boas, *Anthropology and Modern Life* (1928; New York, 1962); Boas, "Aryans and Non-Aryans," in *The American Mercury*, New York, June 1934, 219–23.

20. Kalpana Misra and Melanie Rich, eds., *Jewish Feminism in Israel: Some Contemporary Perspectives* (Hanover, 2003); Sylvia Barack Fishman, *A Breath of Life: Feminism in the American Jewish Community* (Hanover, 1993).

21. Jonathan I. Israel, *Radical Enlightenment: Philosophy and the Making of Modernity 1650–1750* (New York, 2001); Yosef Kaplan, ed., *The Dutch Intersection: The Jews and the Netherlands in Modern History* (Leiden and Boston, 2008); David B. Ruderman, *Jewish Thought and Scientific Discovery in Early Modern Europe* (New Haven and London, 1995).

22. Jakob Katz, *Out of the Ghetto: The Social Background of Jewish Emancipation 1770–1870* (Syracuse, 1973).

23. Peter Haber, *Zwischen Tradition und Wissenschaft: Der ungarische Orientalist Ignác Goldzieher, 1850–1921* (Cologne, Weimar, and Vienna, 2006). This also holds, by the way, for modern Islamic hermeneutics, which would definitely be taken into account in an analogy to Judaism and in historically situating the context of Jewish Reform in the nineteenth century. See Ottfried Fraisse, *Ignác Goldziher's monotheistische Wissenschaft: Zur Historisierung des Islams* (Göttingen, 2014).

24. David Abulafia, *The Great Sea: A History of the Mediterrranean* (Oxford and New York, 2011), 562–620.

25. Jean-Paul Sartre, *Réflexions sur la question juive* (Paris, 1946).

26. See Carola Hilfrich, "Lebendige Schrift," in *Repräsentation und Idolatrie in Moses Mendelssohns Philosophie und Exegese des Judentums* (Munich, 2000), 41; David Sorkin, *Moses Men-*

delssohn and the Religious Enlightenment (London, 1996); Willi Goetschel, *Moses Mendelssohn und das Projekt der Aufklärung*, in *German Review* 7 (1996): 163–75.

27. Paul Valéry, "La Crise de l'Esprit" (1919), in *Oeuvres*, I, (Paris, 1957), 988.

28. Zygmunt Bauman, *Modernity and the Holocaust* (Ithaca, 1989).

29. Gershom Scholem, *Von Berlin nach Jerusalem: Jugenderinnerungen* (expanded edition; Frankfurt, 1994); and *Tagebücher, 1913–1917* (Frankfurt, 1995).

30. Gershom Scholem, "Youthful Days with Zalman Rubaschoff" (1963, in Hebrew), quoted in David Biale, *Gershom Scholem: Kabbalah and Counter-History* (Cambrige, MA and London, 1979), 71.

31. Stéphane Mosès, "Judaïsme, modernité normative et modernité critique," in *Un retour au judaïsme* (Paris, 2008), 63 [translated by editors]. See also Stéphane Mosès, *L'Ange de l'histoire: Rosenzweig, Benjamin, Scholem* (Paris, 1992); and Pierre Bouretz, *Witnesses for the Future: Philosophy and Messianism* (Baltimore and New York, 2010).

32. William James, *A Pluralistic Universe* (London, 1909); William James, *The Philosophy of William James*, ed. Horace M. Kallen (New York, 1925); Harold Bloom, *The American Religion: The Emergence of a Post-Christian Nation* (New York, 1992); Jonathan Sarna, *American Judaism: A History* (New Haven and London, 2004).

33. See Ira Robinson, ed., *Canada's Jews: In Time, Space and Spirit* (Boston, 2013).

34. Peter Novick, *The Holocaust in American Life* (Boston and New York, 1999).

35. Ernest Jones's letter to Freud, December 7, 1920, quoted in G. Wittenberger and C. Toegel, eds., *Die Rundbriefe des "Geheimen Komitees"* (Tübingen, 1999), 202. See also Eran J. Rolnik, *Freud in Zion: Psychoanalysis and the Making of Modern Jewish Identity* (New York, 2012).

36. David Ohana, "Zarathustra in Jerusalem: Nietzsche and the 'New Hebrews,'" in *The Shaping of Israeli Identity: Myth, Memory and Trauma*, eds. Robert Wistrich and David Ohana (London, 1995), 38–60. On the New Hebrews, see Doreet LeVitte Harten and Yigal Zalmona, eds., *Die Neuen Hebräer, 100 Jahre Kunst in Israel* (Berlin, 2005). On Berdichevsky in Switzerland, see René Bloch and Jacques Picard, eds., *Wie über Wolken, Jüdische Lebens- und Denkwelten in Stadt und Region Bern* (Zurich, 2014), 201–335.

37. Quoted in: Yosef Hayim Yerushalmi, *Freud's Moses: Judaism Terminable and Interminable* (New Haven, 1991), 14.

38. See Eran J. Rolnik, *Freud in Zion: Psychoanalysis and the Making of Modern Jewish Identity* (New York, 2012).

39. Assaf Cohen and Johanna Asseraf, eds., *Pax Israeliana: Israeli Modernism Index, 1948–1977* (Tel Aviv, 2014). On Tel Aviv, see Maoz Azaryahu and Ilan Troen, eds., *Tel Aviv: The First Century, Visions, Designs, Actualities* (Bloomington, 2012).

40. See Idith Zertal, *Israel's Holocaust and the Politics of Nationhood* (Cambridge, 2005), 167.

41. Meir Wieseltier, *Motza El Ha'iam* (Exit to the Sea) (Tel Aviv, 1981), 2014 [English translation I. Z.].

42. There also exists a readily cited "classical modernity," which is adopted for design, architecture, and cultural criticism. Still others understand modernity as a period that can only be described through the fragmenting of traditions, the decay of bourgeois rules, and the convulsion of iron truths, as they were still believed during the Victorian era. In contrast, again others describe a modernity of an uncompromising self-exploration, and an unconditional, if not radical or defiant, investigation of the inner and outer world, or in the belief in an ingenious conspiracy, or in the glorification of "art for art's sake," or in the fantasies of techno-enthusiasts, or in the projecting of inner fantasies and stereotypes onto society and politics. Even fascism and Nazism have been referred to as "anti-modern modernity." See Peter Gay, *Modernism: The Lure of Heresy. From Baudelaire to Beckett and Beyond* (New York, 2008), 21–51. For today's appropriate account, see Zygmunt Bauman, *Liquid Modernity* (Cambridge, 2000).

43. Modernist thought often accepted Darwin's nonteleological and antimechanistic view of evolution, while strongly rejecting Herbert Spencer's ideas of "evolutionism" and social "progress."

44. Marvin Harris, *The Rise of Anthropological Theory* (New York, 1968), 272. See also Herbert S. Lewis, "Boas, Darwin, and Anthropology," *Current Anthropology* 42, no. 3 (2001): 381–406; and Bernd Weiler, *Die Ordnung des Fortschritts: Zum Aufstieg und Fall der Fortschrittsidee in der "jungen" Anthropologie* (Bielefeld, 2006), 296–365.

Sigmund Freud (1856–1939)

JUDAISM ESSENTIAL AND MYSTERIOUS

Lydia Flem

TRANSLATED BY CATHERINE TEMERSON

WHEN SIGISMUND SCHLOMO FREUD TURNED SEVEN, HIS FATHER, JAKOB, OPENED the family Torah for him. The biblical story he presented for Sigmund to read was from the remarkable bilingual German-Hebrew edition, the *Israelitische Bibel*. The stories in this edition were illustrated and included commentaries by the Reform rabbi Ludwig Philippson in the spirit of the *Aufklärung*, the Judaism of the Enlightenment. This exceptional version of the Bible is subtitled *Den heiligen Urtext*, and for Freud this first book of stories and images was a fundamental, founding text.

From the time he was nine and a half, when his maternal grandfather, Jakob Nathansohn, died, the archaeological engravings from Philippson's Bible served as the backdrop to the only anxiety dream that Freud talked about and analyzed over thirty years later in *The Interpretation of Dreams*, the dream he called "beloved mother and bird-beaked figures." On his thirty-fifth birthday, his father gave him the copy of his childhood Bible, newly rebound, or perhaps bound for the first time, for it is not impossible that Jakob Freud acquired this Bible in its first edition, in fascicules, between 1839 and 1854. He added an inscription in Hebrew to this symbolic gift:

Son who is dear to me, Shelomoh. In the seventh in the days of the years of your life the Spirit of the Lord began to move you [Judges 13:25] and spoke within you: Go, read in my Book that I have written and there will burst open for you the wellsprings of understanding, knowledge, and wisdom. Behold, it is the Book of Books, from which sages have excavated and lawmakers learned knowledge and judgment [Numbers 21:18]. A vision of the Almighty did you see; you heard and strove to do, and you soared on the wings of the Spirit [Psalms 18:11]. Since then the book has been stored like the fragments of the tablets in an ark with me. For the day on which your years were filled to five and thirty I have

put upon it a cover of new skin and have called it: 'Spring up, O well, sing ye unto it!' [Numbers 21:17] And I have presented it to you as a memorial and as a reminder of love from your father, who loves you with everlasting love. Jakob, Son of R. Shelomoh Freid [*sic*]. In the capital city Vienna, 29 Nisan [5]651, 6 May [1]1891.[1]

This Bible with his father's dedication was among the collection of books that Freud brought from Vienna to London in 1939. Aside from this incomplete family copy, there was also a complete second edition of the Philippson Bible that Freud purchased later, probably secondhand since the volumes bear the stamp of a certain Rabbi Dr. Altman, but we do not know the date of acquisition. Freud also owned Luther's translation; he apologized for quoting from it his 1914 paper *The Moses of Michelangelo.*

From Anna Freud's letter of September 24, 1979, to the pastor Théo Pfrimmer,[2] we know exactly what the family Bible consisted of: "It is one very thick but incomplete volume, for it only includes Samuel 2 followed by the book of Kings and the five books of Moses." The Philippson Bible in its entirety consists of three volumes and has a total of 3,820 pages, whereas the volume Jakob gifted to his son had only 1,215 pages; in other words, it included only about one-third of the original text. We can therefore assume that if Freud's father acquired the volume in fascicules, some of these got lost during his travels or when he moved; and there is the added fact that he had them bound by someone who did not know the Hebrew canon.

In addition to the dedication made for his son's thirty-fifth birthday, Jakob Freud had inscribed the death date of his father, Rabbi Schlomo Freud, on the *Gedenkblatt,* and the birth, several weeks later, of Sigmund (his third son, named Schlomo after the deceased). At the top of the same page is Jakob Freud's signature and the date November 1, 1848. Is that the date on which he acquired the Bible, or an indication of how important the acquisition of civil rights by Austrian Jews was for Jakob? Or is it a reference to something else? We do not know. We do know that Jakob's own father, Rabbi Schlomo, left the village of Buczacz for the village of Tysmenitz, no doubt in order to pursue his talmudic studies in a more renowned yeshiva. Jakob's gift was his way of saying that he and a whole line of ancestors treasured the Bible and that he was now placing his son in this tradition and giving him the mission of being worthy of his grandfather and namesake, whose erudition earned him the title "rabbi."[3]

If Jakob already recognized in his son the beginnings of his intellectual success, he also reminded him that he wished to see him rise on the wings of Spirit, within the culture to which they belonged. This was conveyed not only in the content of his inscription, but especially in the language he used—Hebrew, which his son did not know how to read. For Jakob, the Bible was always the organizing frame of reference. According to one of his granddaughters, Judith Bernays-Heller, who stayed with her grandparents in 1892–1893, Jakob Freud spent his time taking walks and diligently reading the Talmud as well as a few other books in Hebrew and German. He probably hoped that his son would follow Philippson's example and broach secular—even taboo—subjects in his writings only to better deepen and emphasize the rich aspects of the Holy Scriptures. We thus have every right to wonder whether Sigmund Schlomo Freud, in reflecting on religion and the Bible all his life—and increasingly, as he grew older, grappling with the paternal figure of Moses and seeking to give it psychoanalytic explanations—was not in fact trying to meet his father's expectations and free himself of a debt to him. It is as though Freud in his own way sought to broaden the ideas of moderate Reform Judaism. But we could also ask why Jakob chose to buy that particular Bible, the Bible born of the Enlightenment, even though he came from Tysmenitz, a small town in Galicia known for its yeshiva and study center but also for its two opposing currents of Judaism: Hasidism and Haskalah.

For at least four generations, the Freuds (whose name seems to derive from the first name of a female ancestor, Freide) lived in the region of Galicia where being Jewish was far from painless. Indeed Jakob Freud and his maternal grandfather, Sisskind Hoffman, who engaged in trade between Galicia and Moravia, were designated by the local authorities as "wandering Galician Jews." In order to have the right to live outside an assigned fixed abode, they had to pay a yearly tax, called the tolerance tax, and periodically renew their request for a residence permit for foreign Jews. Jews had to stay in special inns and did not have the right to live in private housing. In order to prevent Galician Jews from settling in Moravia, the authorities granted the "tolerance" for a period of only six months. The rest of the year, "tolerated" Jews had to travel outside the city or return to Galicia.

Father and Son

Jakob's relief when Jews were granted civil rights in 1848 must have been great. Given these circumstances he was no doubt attracted to the messages of Philippson's Bible, which attempted to bring together traditional Orthodoxy and the Reform movement supporting assimilation. Jakob chose to bring up his son amid the Judaism of the Enlightenment and the movement toward emancipation. Sigmund became interested in Mosaic Law but not in the Talmud, unlike his father, who never ceased reading the latter. An interesting detail, known to us from the content of his library, is that at the end of his life Freud owned a copy of the Babylonian Talmud, edited and translated into German by L. Goldschmidt in 1929.

At age forty-three, Freud published the book that became the bible of psychoanalysts, *The Interpretation of Dreams (Die Traumdeutung)*. Identifying himself with Joseph, he sometimes called it the "Egyptian book of dreams." He offers in this book his commentaries on several of his own dreams. After the "botanical monograph" dream, the Etruscan cinerary urn" dream, the "Three Fates" dream, and many others, as a final personal note before concluding his first great book he recounts the dream "beloved mother and bird-beaked figures" and mentions the Philippson Bible for the first and only time in his entire body of work.

> It is dozens of years since I myself had a true anxiety-dream. But I remember one from my seventh or eighth year, which I submitted to interpretation some thirty years later. It was a very vivid one, and in it I saw *my beloved mother with a peculiarly peaceful, sleeping expression on her features, being carried into the room by two (or three) people with birds' beaks and laid upon the bed.* I awoke in tears and screaming, and interrupted my parents' sleep. The strangely draped and unnaturally tall figures with birds' beaks were derived from the illustrations

to Philippson's Bible. I fancy they must have been gods with falcons' heads from an ancient Egyptian funerary relief.[4]

As of age seven, and certainly at the time when he had this dream, Sigmund often leafed through the Philippson Bible seeking answers to his questions about life and sexuality. Indeed Rabbi Philippson discusses various aspects of sexual life quite openly: sensual pleasure, homosexuality, incest, rape, masturbation, and so on. Beyond the Oedipal emotions his dream expresses, it already works out the renunciation of incestuous fulfillment, supplanting it with an intellectual passion encouraged by his father. Yet it was only in 1935, at age seventy-nine, that Freud acknowledged the decisive importance of that early reading in a note added to his autobiography, like a postscript to a long life: "My deep engrossment in the Bible story (almost as soon as I had learnt the art of reading) had, as I recognized much later, an enduring effect upon the direction of my interest."[5]

Why did he wait until so late in life before mentioning the importance of this biblical reading? Did he become aware of its influence only in his later years, or did he avoid expressing it publicly earlier because it was part of his private, intimate life and he wanted to carve out a position for himself within a Western cultural reality that consistently concealed that part of its heritage passed down from Jerusalem? Was it anxiety due to the rise of Nazism? Was it triggered by the fact that he would soon reach the age when his father Jakob died? Whatever the case, we should point out that the sentence was written in *English*, the language of America, the country that he always assumed was exempt from antisemitism. For in 1935 an American publisher asked if he could republish Freud's text *An Autobiographical Study*, which had appeared ten years earlier in Germany, and include it in a series devoted to medicine in self-portraits. On that occasion, Freud made a few corrections and added this postscript specifically for the American public. Whether an irony of history or a typographer's Freudian slip, the sentence is included in the complete works in English but omitted in the German *Gesammelte Werke* (Collected works) and was only incorporated in a paperback edition of the German text in 1971.

This "acknowledged debt" to the Bible was set down in writing at the same time as he sketched the broad outlines of his intellectual development, mentioning his teacher Ernst Wilhelm von Brücke, his strong attraction to the theories of Charles Darwin, his desire as an adolescent to study law, and, generally speaking, his thirst for knowledge directed more toward human concerns than toward natural objects.

The flurry of publications and meetings around 1935 must have encouraged him to become aware, had he not already been so, of the importance of his father's biblical culture and its influence upon him. In 1933 Freud treated the American poet Hilda Doolittle, H. D., who was born in Bethlehem, Pennsylvania. The childhood memories she recounted surely resonated with him. Before she even knew how to read she enjoyed looking at the Gustave Doré illustrations of the Bible. When she visited Egypt at the time of the Tutankhamun excavations, she saw a living illustration of the Bible that had fascinated her as a child. During that period the Italian translation of *The Moses of Michelangelo* came out and Freud started to write the first draft of his second work on Moses, *Moses and Monotheism*, which he discussed at length with Arnold Zweig, who was in Palestine at the time. He read a great many works relating to the Bible, its exegesis, Israel, and the populations of the Middle East, as well as books on the history of religions. There are about 118 books on these subjects in his library and bibliographies.

The Visible and the Invisible

At the same time that the family Bible, offered by Freud's father, served as an introduction to Jerusalem, it pointed the way to Athens and Rome, the two other sacred places of the West—the "visible" ancient poles of Western civilization. Unlike Athens and Rome, objects of many daytime journeys for Freud, Jerusalem remained his dark continent, his blind spot, his "wife."[6] It was associated with intimacy, with the invisible. As Freud wrote to his future wife Martha on July 23, 1882: "The historians say that if Jerusalem had not been destroyed, we Jews would have perished like so many races before and after us. According to them, the invisible edifice of Jerusalem became possible only after the collapse of the visible Temple." Athens, Rome, and Jerusalem, the visible and the invisible, the outside and the inside, are bound up for Freud with the ambiguous combination of his vengeful ambition and the Oedipal guilt it arouses in terms of both superiority to his father and the transgression of the Jewish heritage that it entails. Freud never resolved these tensions that stemmed from being simultaneously the son of a humiliated Jew and the father of a Western oeuvre. A secular Jew, assimilated into classical and Germanic civilization, he refused the temptation, as Heine put it, to pay the price of admission to European culture: the act of baptism. He lived in the midst of these fertile and subtle contradictions, finding in them a creative power and sensitivity: "The fact that things will be more difficult for you as a Jew will have the effect, as it has with all of us, of bringing out the best of which you are capable."[7]

Both Herzl and Freud, two Viennese Jews, imagine almost at the same time, each in his own way, an answer to the crisis of Jewish identity in their time. And for each of them the answer takes a geographical form. Herzl's solution in *The Jewish State* suggested the geographical concentration of the Jewish people in a single territory and an autonomous entity, whether it be called Uganda, Argentina, or Palestine. Freud's psychoanalysis hypothesis is also formulated as a spatial theory: in each one of us there is an "elsewhere," another kingdom, the unconscious; the psychic apparatus is a space, a topography. The same spatial preoccupation underlay both the Zionist approach and psychoanalytic research at the time of its discovery. The geographical metaphor reveals Freud's personal journeys. To understand the ties that bind him in fantasy to the Promised Land, we must place that mythic land in the symbolic triangle formed by Athens, Rome, and Jerusalem. When it comes to a choice between the visible and the invisible, Freud does not hesitate. Although throughout his life he is tempted by visual seductions, Freud, like Moses, condemns images and always privileges the latent over the manifest, idea over form, the word over the thing, and hence an invisible land to the incarnation of a promise.

Despite all their differences, whether returning a country to the Jews or returning man to the fertile soil of his unconscious, Herzl and Freud both appealed to the power of the dream. For Freud, "The interpretation of dreams is the royal road to a knowledge of the unconscious activities of the mind."[8] For Herzl the royal dream leads to Zion, to leaving the diaspora and finally realizing the promised millennium.

But for Freud, in contrast, only an invisible Jerusalem remains fertile. Thus, even while suffering in Vienna, which he hated "with a positively personal hatred," he yet saw it as his home;[9] he never was in search of a host country other than the one he was exploring on the basis of intimate knowledge of himself. It was the space of the unconscious that he wished to conquer, however high the price might be. On the occasion of his seventieth birthday he confided in his fellow "brothers" of the liberal lodge of B'nei B'rith in Vienna the reasons why he chose to become a member not long before the publication of his *Interpretation of Dreams*. He claimed that the disclosure of his "unpopular discoveries," that is, the depth of human instinct, led to him losing most of his personal relationships at the time: "I felt as though outlawed, shunned by all," he said. "This isolation aroused in me the longing for a circle of excellent men with high ideals who would accept me in friendship despite my temerity. . . . That you are Jews could only be welcome to me, for I was myself a Jew, and it has always appeared to me not only undignified but outright foolish to deny it. What tied me to Jewry was—I have to admit it—not the faith, not even the national pride, for I was always an unbeliever, have been brought up without religion, but not without respect for the so called 'ethical' demands of human civilization. Whenever I have experienced feelings of national exaltation, I have tried to suppress them as disastrous and unfair, frightened by the warning example of those nations among which we Jews live."[10]

Freud is a true diasporic Jew. On the Greco-Roman side of his life there is a claim, an ambition, a wished-for intellectual assimilation. On the Jerusalem side there is a deep emotional attachment that has no need of words. Thus he told his colleagues at B'nei B'rith that his attraction to Judaism had to do with "many dark emotional powers all the stronger the less they could be expressed in words."[11] And toward the end of his life he claimed once again that his sense of being Jewish was made up of something very slight, a "miraculous thing" that is "inaccessible to any analysis."[12] For a man who, in all his works, had sought the latent beneath the manifest so as to put it in words, and whose approach had always been to analyze and explain what up to then had remained inaccessible, the unconscious, these words are a rather fraught statement.

As such an essential yet secular, assimilated Jew, Freud could not remain indifferent to the fate of the Jews in his own time. Jerusalem, in Palestine, became in a way more visible to him. The unfolding Jewish experience in situ preoccupied him quite intensely in the first decades of the last century, yet as always he kept himself ambiguously reluctant, as if observing from afar. Attraction and distance, solidarity and reservations characterize his approach to active Zionism. "Toward Zionism," he wrote in a 1926 letter, "I have only sympathy, but I make no judgment on it, on its chances of success and on the possible dangers facing it."[13] The Promised Land and the adventure taking place at this faraway, unreal site stirred "strange, secret" feelings in him, as he wrote in 1922 to his most intimate disciple, Sandor Ferenczi: "Strange secret yearnings rise in me—perhaps from my ancestral heritage—for the East and the Mediterranean and for a life of quite another kind: wishes from late childhood never to be fulfilled, which do not conform to reality as if to hint at a loosening of one's relationship to it. Instead of which—we shall meet on the soil of sober Berlin."[14]

These childhood wishes that cannot be fulfilled on the shores of the Mediterranean do not refer to nostalgia for a lost fatherland. To Freud, Palestine is a "strip of our mother earth," one that is "tragically mad" and that "has never produced anything but religions, sacred frenzies, presumptuous attempts to overcome the outer world of appearance by means of the inner world of wishful thinking."[15] The land of his ancestors, now being reborn, is maternal for Freud, unattainable—a mother earth, not a fatherland.

He missed the inaugural celebrations of the Hebrew University in Jerusalem in 1925, to which he was invited, owing to his state of health, according to the official explanation. Having agreed to take part in an honorary capacity, he wrote to his Hebrew University colleagues: "A University is a place in which knowledge is taught above all differences of religions and of nations, where investigation is carried on, which is to show mankind how far they understand the world around them and how far they can control it. Such an understanding is a noble witness to the development to which our people has forced its way in two thousand years of unhappy fortune."[16] He had hoped that a chair of psychoanalysis would be created in Jerusalem and offered to his close disciple, Max Eitingon, and his followers in Palestine toiled hard to realize this dream. Neither Freud nor Eitingon saw it happen. The Sigmund Freud Chair of Psychoanalysis would be established at the Hebrew University more than half a century later, in 1977.

Freud's correspondence with Arnold Zweig, who had immigrated to Palestine out of Zionist conviction but found himself deeply disillusioned as soon as he arrived, reveals Freud's approach to the Zionist project in Palestine in all its convolution, as well as the sense that the world had become more ominous for the Jews. He didn't hide his joy in face of Zweig's disappointment: "I know you are cured of your unhappy love of your so-called Fatherland. Such a passion is not for the likes of us," he wrote to his friend.[17] But when Zweig considered the possibility of returning to Germany and asked the advice of his friend back in Vienna, Freud kept him from "the folly of returning to Eichkamp . . . that is, to the concentration camp and death." In another, long letter, he wrote to Zweig: "It is not the first time that I have heard of the difficulties the cultured man finds in adapting himself to Palestine. History has never given the Jewish people cause to develop their faculty for creating a state or a society. And of course they take with them all the shortcomings and vices in the culture of the country they leave behind them into their new abode. You feel ill at ease, but I did not know you found isolation so hard to bear. . . . In Palestine at any rate you have your personal safety and your human rights. And where would you think of going? You would find America, I would say from all my impressions, far more unbearable. Everywhere else you would be a scarcely tolerated alien . . . I really think that for the moment you should remain where you are."[18]

The translation of Freud's books into Hebrew during that period made him happy, and he generously offered any help he could. He wrote a special preface to the Hebrew edition of *Totem and Taboo*, in which he directly addressed the Hebrew-speaking reader "of this book [who] will not easily find himself in the emotional standpoint of the author, who is ignorant of the holy tongue and scriptures, who has moved away completely from the religion of his forefathers—as from every other religion—and who cannot share national ideals, and yet at the same time has never kept his brethren at a distance nor moved away from them, and that if the question were put to him . . . what is there left to you that is Jewish, he would reply: 'A very great deal, and probably the essence of his being, with no desire to change that being.' "[19] He also contributed a preface to the Hebrew edition of the *Introductory Lectures on Psychoanalysis* in which he said, "Readers of Hebrew and especially young people eager for knowledge are presented in this volume with psycho-analysis clothed in the ancient language which has been awakened to a new life by the will of the Jewish people. The author can well picture the problem which this has set its translator. Nor need he suppress his doubt whether Moses and the Prophets would have found these Hebrew lectures intelligible. But he begs their descendants (among whom he himself is numbered), for whom this book is designed, not to react too quickly to their first impulses of criticism and dislike by rejecting it."[20]

Freud was man of many books, yet it is the text of his ancestors that accompanied him from childhood to old age. What was the Bible of Rabbi Ludwig Philippson like?

The Philippson Bible

A true encyclopedia, 3,820 pages long and containing 685 illustrations, the Philippson Bible was bound to fascinate the child Freud. The Leipzig publisher Baumgärtner purchased the most beautiful engravings available at the time in England in 1838; these were mostly archaeological engravings from the British Museum, the *Description of Egypt*, and other sources. He then spoke to Ludwig Philippson about publishing a translation of the Bible with a commentary whose content would be geographical, physical, historical, and theological. Philippson in turn wrote to his brother, Phöbus, who would collaborate on the work: "I suggested adding the Hebrew text as well, because it is only under that condition that the work would be accepted by *all* the Jews. . . . My idea is to create something that does not yet exist."

The Bible was published after sixteen years of work. The first edition was issued in 1854, and later editions were published in 1858 and 1878. A version illustrated by Gustave Doré came out in 1875. In their commentaries, the Philippson brothers stressed the universal character of the Jewish message while striving to preserve its originality as well. Every passage of the Bible is placed in its historical context: linguistics, anthropology, geography, and, above all archaeology are drawn on to prove the historical truth of the Holy Scripture. These commentaries are mainly of a cultural nature. The illustrations allow the biblical text to be visualized while the commentary invites the reader to imagine the places and actions of the men and women of the Bible.

As he glanced through this book of images and words, Freud could daydream while gazing at figures of the Egyptian pantheon, bas-reliefs from Pompeii and Thebes, the Acropolis in Athens, the palace of Nero in Rome, the profile of Alexander the Great, the statue of Diana of Ephesus, a representation of Hannibal crossing the Alps, and the "Man Moses" at the beginning of the volumes—all the places and persons that haunt his writings, dreams, and travels, both imaginary and real. As an adult Freud surrounded himself with dozens of Greek, Roman, Chinese, and especially Egyptian statuettes, like so many incarnations of his childhood visual recollections. A passion for archaeology haunted his dreams; his book collections; the display cabinets and tables in his study; and his heroic identifications with Schliemann, Winckelmann, *Gradiva*'s Hanold, and others. He acknowledged that this "world of dreams" gave him "unsurpassed consolation in the struggles of life." Archaeological metaphors run through the Freudian oeuvre, from *Studies on Hysteria* in 1896 to *Moses and Monotheism* in 1939.

In reading and looking through this Bible, the reader is invited to become aware of the polysemy of the text. The Hebrew text is provided with a parallel German translation; the commentary presents the holy story, and the illustrations serve as a counterpoint to the words. Each page is informed by what amounts to a complex system of signs, codes, translations, and transpositions shifting from one chain of meaning to another. In the same place, Hebrew and German face each other and meet through text and commentary, written material and imagery; one can read from left to right and from right to left, scanning the page in every direction and finding meaning everywhere.

Numerous exegeses are mentioned: the Septuagint, the Vulgate, Abravanel, Rashi. But we also find the names of Protestant exegetes, the Church Fathers, and Greeks such as Herodotus, Aristophanes, Homer, and Plato. Champollion, Goethe, and Spinoza are summoned too, in order to deepen the human understanding of the Holy Scripture. Ludwig and Phöbus Philippson's personal commentaries often display common sense; they like to draw psychological portraits of the biblical figures, fighting any tendency to idealize them. They stress the conflictual nature of human beings and are very interested in dreams. In discussing Joseph, for example, they describe twenty biblical texts that deal with dreams and also mention the Greek conception of the oneiric world. "No one can tear himself away from the mysterious fabric of the world of dreams . . . we have all been affected, at important moments in our lives, by very meaningful [*bedeutungsvoll*] dreams for which we are missing the main thread [Gen. 37:5]."

The Philippsons rarely delve into the strictly theological and spiritual. The authors' intention, it seems, is to let the biblical text speak for itself and invite the reader to contemplate nature, the work of God, and, above all, to reflect, get to know, and understand the world around him, human beings, and life in society. They are driven by a pedagogical project, encouraging both integration into German culture and greater knowledge of the ancestral tradition, language, and faith. They offer a moderate and enlightened Reformism.

Biblical Text and Freudian Text

The father of Ludwig and Phöbus, Moses Philippson, was the first translator of the Hebrew Bible into German. He taught religion and Hebrew at his native Dessau *Franzschule*, a school founded by the Jewish community for the poorest among them. A Jewish intellectual, Moses was among those who paved the way out of the ghetto so that Jews could become integrated into European culture. In 1804 he published a translation of the Proverbs of Solomon with commentaries from the Talmud, and then dedicated himself to a Hebrew-German dictionary. He died at age thirty-nine, leaving his wife and four children. The eldest, Phöbus, taught Hebrew, studied medicine, and went on to publish two periodicals—one on pharmaceutical science, ancient and modern, the other a monthly on popular medicine. For his brother's Bible, he contributed a commentary on the prophets.

As for Ludwig Philippson (1811–1889), he first studied in his father's *Franzschule* and followed the religious teaching of the future rabbi of the Reform synagogue in Hamburg; he also studied the Talmud as well as Greek and Latin. At the age of fourteen, he was admitted into a Protestant secondary school and started writing poems. At the University of Berlin where Hegel was teaching at the time, he took courses in philosophy, natural sciences, geology, law, history, and classical philology, subjects that would all serve in his biblical commentaries. He became interested in politics, defending the civil emancipation of the Jews, and would serve as substitute deputy of the Reform Party in the Frankfurt parliament. As rabbi of the Magdeburg congregation, he introduced German into the religious services but expanded the teaching of Hebrew for young people and gave girls access to a religious education. He brought in organ music but maintained the Jewish calendar and Jewish celebrations. He was the author of many books besides his Bible and also served as editor of *Die Allgemeine Zeitung des Judenthums*, a weekly that outlasted him and continued to be published until 1922.

An exhaustive chronological display would show the constant appearance of biblical quotations in Freud's writings. All the books of the Bible are quoted several times: Genesis, of course, as well as Exodus, Leviticus, Numbers, Psalms, Proverbs, the Song of Songs, and so on. There are also references to the Gospels, especially Matthew. Though there is barely a Freudian text that does not include some—implicit or explicit—allusion to the Bible, it is moments of change or transition that bring him closest to his cultural heritage: in adolescence, when he distances himself from school and the influence of his first teachers; during his long engagement to Martha Bernays; in the midst of the dissensions within the psychoanalytic movement in the years 1911–1914; and very clearly in his writings in old age until the end of his life.

The first biblical allusions known to us are to be found in the correspondence Freud maintained when he was seventeen years old with a classmate, Eduard Silberstein, a Romanian Jew. We read there a quite unexpected statement from 1873: "I am wretched and annoyed," Freud writes, "at the news in your letter that you have received neither book nor letter from me. You see, this letter contained a short essay, a biblical study with modern themes, something I could not write again and of which I am as proud as of my nose or my maturity. It would have refreshed you like balm; one could not tell it was concocted in my den. It was so sensitive, so biblically naïve and forceful, so melancholy and so gay—it's the very devil that it's been lost, it grieves me." And alluding to Samuel 1:23 and Job 38:35, he adds in a postscript: "If you reply on the wings of an eagle, or like a flash of lightning, you will not have done too much."[21]

Later in his correspondence, we discover allusions to Saul, Job, lord "Jeschoua christos," and Ishmael dying of thirst. We see him fluctuate between theism and materialism and take on the philosophical positions of Spinoza, Kant, and Brentano.

One man left a special mark on Freud's Jewish sensibility: Samuel Hammerschlag, his teacher of religion and a friendly supporter with whom he maintained deep ties of friendship into adulthood. Freud even gave two of his children the first names of Hammerschlag's daughter and niece, and in his obituary he said of him: "A spark from the same fire which animated the spirit of the great Jewish seers and prophets burned in him and was not extinguished until old age weakened his powers.... Religious instruction served him as a way of educating towards love of the humanities, and from the material of Jewish history he was able to find means of tapping the sources of enthusiasm hidden in the hearts of young people and of making it flow out far beyond the limitations of nationalism or dogma."[22]

Worried about the length of their engagement, Freud wrote to Martha, "All I can tell you is that had it taken not three but seven years—according to our patriarch's custom [*nach dem Gebrauch bei unserm Patriarchen*]—for my courting to succeed, I would have considered it neither too early nor too late."[23] No doubt "custom" mentioned in tandem with "patriarch" is an expression of his inner turmoil. We can undoubtedly find here a self-identification with Jacob of Genesis 29:20: "And Jacob served seven years for Rachel; and they seemed unto him but a few days for the love he had to her."

Unlike his references to Greek mythology or to the Western canon of poets and playwrights, Freud did not use the Bible as a conceptual instrument, an intellectual tool, or proof of the universality of his unusual discovery; what he knew of the biblical text was part of his private, intimate sensibility. He did not expose his Jewishness to others, though he may have drawn joy and strength from it. And he never disowned it—quite the opposite. Did he harbor a sense of shame linked to the time his father's hat was thrown in the mud by a Christian? He preserved his anonymity three times: twice when writing about Moses, and another time when he ordered from an elderly Jewish printer personal stationery in which his initials were to be intertwined with those of his fiancée, of whom he wrote with a kind of pensive admiration that she, unlike him, was from a family of scholars.

Indeed Martha was the granddaughter of Isaac ben Ja'akov Bernays, who, in his capacity of chief rabbi, was summoned to Hamburg in 1821 and put in charge of building a bridge between the city's Orthodox Jews and Reform Jews. As it happened, the printer grew up not far from this wise man and spoke to Freud about him with the greatest respect. Freud felt proud, no doubt, of being united to such a noble and erudite Jewish family but dared not reveal who he was—that is, the son of an unlucky tradesman. Was the figure of the wise rabbi, the *hakham* of Hamburg, extraneous to the charm Freud attributed to his fiancée? Bernays's portrait, we may add, would never be absent from the living rooms of the various Freud-Bernays households. It is in this letter of July 23, 1882, that Freud alludes to the invisible edifice of Judaism that became possible only after the collapse of the visible Temple. It is on this same occasion that he promises his future wife a home full of joy (*Freude*): "something of the core, of the essence of this meaningful and life-affirming Judaism will not be absent from our home."[24]

Two biblical themes accompanied Freud during his self-analysis: "Jakob wrestling with the angel" and "Moses seeing the promised land from afar." "It will be a fitting punishment for me," he wrote to Wilhelm Fliess on May 7, 1900, "that none of the unexplored regions of psychic life in which I have been the first mortal to set foot will ever bear my name or obey my laws. When it appeared that my breath would fail me in the wrestling match, I asked the angel to desist; and that is what he has done since then. But I did not turn out to be the stronger, although since then I have been limping noticeably. Yes, I really am forty-four now, an old, somewhat shabby Jew [*etwas schäbiger Israelit*], as you will see for yourself in the summer or fall."[25] It is in the biblical passage that recounts Jacob's struggle with the angel that Jacob receives the name of Israel (Gen. 32:29), and as it happens, this is the only time that Freud calls himself "Israelite" rather than "Jew."

Another example of his extensive knowledge of the biblical text is apparent in one of his four Roman dreams, where he sees himself led to a hill from which Rome is shown to him from afar, which he associates with "seeing the promised land from afar" like Moses. On this subject, Philippson, in his commentary, stresses the fact that Moses must "see" the land that he has no right to enter and "appoint a successor." Freud seems not to have forgotten this when he writes to Jung: "We are certainly getting ahead; if I am Moses, then you are Joshua and will take possession of the promised land of psychiatry, which I will only be able to glimpse from afar."[26]

Again in *The Interpretation of Dreams*, Freud relates the following dream: "My wife was giving me a drink out of a vase; this vase was an Etruscan cinerary urn which I had brought back from a journey to Italy and had since given away. But the water in it tasted so salty (evidently because of the ashes in the urn) that I woke up."[27] The Philippson Bible happens to contain three Etruscan engravings, two of which illustrate Jeremiah 16:5–8, a passage that forbids participation in funeral rites. On this occasion, Philippson draws on all his anthropological knowledge as he often does. It is not far-fetched to think that, attracted by the beautiful Etruscan engravings, Freud read this commentary as a child.

In 1913, when his breakup with Jung was complete, Freud immediately reimmersed himself in his cultural heritage and compared his solitary self to the figure of Moses. It was during this period that he wrote *The Moses of Michelangelo*, about the work he went to see and admire regularly in Rome for over ten years. It was also during this period that, for the first time, we find long explicit biblical quotations with precise references. Thus does he add to a note in *The Interpretation of Dreams* a passage from Isaiah 29:8: "It shall even be as when an hungry man dreameth, and, behold, eateth; but he awaketh, and his soul is empty; or as when a thirsty man dreameth, and, behold, he drinketh; but he awaketh, and, behold, he is faint, and his soul has appetite." In his *Moses* he quotes at length from Exodus 32 and adds in parentheses: "(I apologize for my anachronistic use of Luther's translation)." By apologizing is he not addressing his father, who was able to read the Holy Writ in its original language?

The judgment of Solomon in the ninth chapter of *Group Psychology and the Analysis of the Ego*, or the ten commandments commented on throughout *Civilization and Its Discontents*, are just two out of hundreds of examples that can be found, hidden or exposed, in Freud's work and available correspondence. Freud really did read and love the biblical stories; but on the other hand we find no trace of the Talmud. Jewish Orthodoxy and its scholarly tradition, Freud acknowledged, was "this lack in my education" (*dieses Stück meiner Unbildung*); he chose to be intellectually assimilated to Western culture while being intensely attached emotionally, in an essentially intimate way, to Jewish memory.

In order for his name to be printed on the cover of a Western book, a world he was not born into, Sigmund Freud used the scientific tools of his time and classical culture, but it was to the intimate joy of his Jewish memory that he owed his lifeblood and daily consolations. *Schlomo ben Ja'acov* was not an Orthodox rabbi or a Hasid, nor was he an assimilated Jew. Rather, he was a Jew of the assimilation, for whom a few biblical figures, a few Yiddish jokes, a certain solidarity with his people, and a "*je ne sais quoi* up to now inaccessible to analysis" express a fidelity that Freud called both "mysterious" (*that miraculous thing*)[28] and "the essence" (*dies Hauptsache*). Fascinated all his life by the biblical text, which he could not read in the language of his ancestors, the one time, in the entire body of his work, that Freud wrote out a sentence in Hebrew was in his last book, *Moses and Monotheism*: "Schema Jisroel Adonai Elohenu Adonai Echod" (Hear, O Israel: the Lord our God, the Lord is one).[29]

Did he know that these words were not used only in the daily prayer, but were also the last words pronounced by every pious Jew before dying?

Notes

1. Yosef Hayim Yerushalmi, *Freud's Moses: Judaism Terminable and Interminable* (New Haven, 1991), 71 (Bible references added).

2. Théo Pfrimmer, *Freud, lecteur de la Bible* (Paris, 1982), 14.

3. Marianne Krüll, *Freud und sein Vater* (Munich, 1979), 188.

4. Sigmund Freud, *The Standard Edition of the Complete Psychological Works of Sigmund Freud*, 24 vols., trans. and ed. James Strachey with Anna Freud, et al. (London, 1953–1974), 5:583; see also Didier Anzieu's analysis in *L'Auto-analyse de Freud* (Paris, 1975), 389–407.

5. Freud, *Standard Edition*, 20:8.

6. In Jewish mysticism the Shekhinah, the divine presence of God, is said to be God's feminine side; it is also the bride of God or the community of Israel.

7. Letter to Karl Abraham of October 8, 1907, in *A Psychoanalytic Dialogue: The Letters of Sigmund Freud and Karl Abraham, 1907–1926* (New York, 1965), 9.

8. Sigmund Freud, *The Interpretation of Dreams* (1900), in *Standard Edition*, vols. 4 and 5, 608.

9. Letter of March 11, 1900, in *The Complete Letters of Sigmund Freud to Wilhelm Fliess, 1887–1904*, trans. and ed. Jeffrey M. Masson (Cambridge, 1985), 311.

10. Letter of May 6, 1926, in *Letters of Sigmund Freud* (New York, 1960), 367.

11. Ibid.

12. Letter to Barbara Low, April 19, 1936, in *Letters of Sigmund Freud*, 428.

13. Letter to Professor Thieberger, April 25, 1926, cited in Ernst Simon, "Sigmund Freud, the Jew," *The Leo Baeck Institute Yearbook* 2 (1957): 257.

14. Letter of March 30, 1922, in Ernest Jones, *The Life and Work of Sigmund Freud*, vol. 3, *The Last Phase* (New York, 1957), 3:84.

15. Letter of May 8, 1932, in Ernst L. Freud, ed., *The Letters of Sigmund Freud and Arnold Zweig* (New York, 1970), 40.

16. Freud, "On the Occasion of the Opening of the Hebrew University," 1925b, in *Standard Edition*, 19:292.

17. Letter of January 28, 1934, in *Letters of Sigmund Freud and Arnold Zweig*, 45.

18. Letter of February 21, 1936, in *Letters of Sigmund Freud and Arnold Zweig*, 122.

19. Freud, *Standard Edition*, 13: xv. Translation amended, based on other sources.

20. Freud, *Standard Edition*, 15:11.

21. Letter of July 24, 1873, in *The Letters of Sigmund Freud to Eduard Silberstein, 1871–1881*, ed. Walter Boehlich and trans. Arnold J. Pomerans (Cambridge, 1992), 25–26.

22. Freud, *Standard Edition*, 9:255.

23. Letter of June 19, 1885, in Freud, *Standard Edition*, 153.

24. Ibid., 19, 22.

25. Letter of May 7, 1900, in *Complete Letters of Sigmund Freud to Wilhelm Fliess*, 412.

26. Letter of January 17, 1909, in *The Freud/Jung Letters*, trans. Ralph Mannheim and R.F.C. Hull (Princeton, 1974), 196–97.

27. Freud, *Standard Edition*, 4:124.

28. Letter of April 19, 1936, *Letters of Sigmund Freud*, 428.

29. Sigmund Freud, *Moses and Monotheism*, in *Standard Edition*, 23:25.

3

Émile Durkheim (1858–1917)

MODERN SOCIETY AND THE JEWS

Bruno Karsenti

TRANSLATED BY AMY JACOBS COLAS

ÉMILE DURKHEIM'S OWN REMARKS ON JUDAISM TELL US LITTLE ABOUT HIS RELATION to the subject. He was disinclined to examine his own biography or engage in anything resembling self-applied socioanalysis, and his sociological writings show no persistent preoccupation with the matter—not even with the "Jewish question" in the broad sense the term had acquired in the nineteenth century. This impression is not at all belied by what we have of his correspondence. Generally speaking, we have so little "evidence" to go on that further probing, stimulated by the fact that a founder of sociology descended from a long line of rabbis,[1] usually leads to naught but fragile hypotheses or unsubstantiated allegations. Of course there is always the implicit or unsaid, and much can be made of a few incidental touches here and there, such as expertly wielded biblical references or irreproachable family solidarity. We can try to reconstruct a consistent identity based on such things, but the exercise is perilous and in any case superficial; it fails to engage with Durkheim's work, telling us next to nothing about it that we did not already know without taking into account his being Jewish. The art of interpretation requires at least the tact of asking whether what was not said *should* be and whether silence is really a symptom. In Durkheim's case, it seems highly advisable to tread lightly.

But it is quite another thing to consider the problem from without and in more contextual terms. It is fully relevant to resituate Durkheimian thinking—a school of thought that engaged a proportionately high number of French Jews—in a conjoined history of secular Judaism and the development of the social sciences in Europe, particularly in France. From this perspective Durkheim actually becomes a paradigmatic case, and two intersecting hypotheses may be formulated.[2] The exercise should be instructive for both sides of the question, enabling us to discover in Durkheim the very model of a certain attitude toward science at a time when it was organized in Europe as a *vocation*, a term to which its primary practitioners readily laid claim. The notion of "professional calling" is most familiar to us in Weber's

1917 German version, but the French version was already discernible in Durkheim's *Rules of Sociological Method* of 1895, if only in the first rule, "to consider social facts as things"; that is, to radically desubjectify the very type of facts—human and social ones—that might reasonably be assumed acutely subjective.[3] For Weber, an accentuated sense of *Beruf*, of abolishing the subject in the "task" incumbent upon him, was necessarily rooted in Protestantism. In Durkheim's case the theological soil is much more friable, and the religious reference is hard to invoke without forcing it. The fact that the first *Rule* triggered a hostile reaction fanned by considerable antisemitism is obviously not in itself an argument. Nor is Durkheim's intervention in response to the Dreyfus affair. "L'individualisme et les intellectuels," written in reply to Brunetière following the Zola trial, does not contain the slightest apology for Judaism, even the secular variety. In it Durkheim defends freedom of thought from a sociological perspective, explicitly identifying it as a Christian achievement, one further fueled by the French Revolution but requiring a social foundation that could only be provided by sociology. No "Jewish motif"—regardless of the meaning attributed to the adjective "Jewish"—can be discerned in Durkheim's reading here of present or past.

Moreover, the most striking feature of his brief reply to an 1899 survey on antisemitism is his concern not to dramatize the issue. French antisemitism was "superficial" and "passing," in contrast to the German and Russian varieties, qualified as "chronic." What had to be combated was the social discontent brewing in reaction to economic crises, because in uncertain or difficult economic conditions people had a tendency to look for "expiatory victims" and "pariahs" (Durkheim actually preceded Weber in linking this category to Jews).[4] Here again, he placed sociology at the forefront of the battle. But one passage of his reply stands out:

> The Jew's defects are compensated for by indisputable qualities, and though there are better races, there are also worse ones. Moreover, Jews lose their ethnic features extremely quickly—in two generations the thing is done.[5]

If ever there was a passing remark to latch onto (in a minor text written in the heat of the moment), surely it is this one. Jews' extreme aptitude to lose their "ethnic features" (Durkheim's adjective undoubtedly encompasses both biology and culture) thus makes them *extremely* modern subjects—at least potentially, as long as antisemitism does not get in the way. But how do they assimilate in the sense Durkheim uses here? And in what way is that aptitude *extreme*?

Durkheim and the Jewish Durkheimians assimilated through adherence to a scientific project focused not on a particular culture but rather on acquiring knowledge about social phenomena posited in the greatest possible generality. Jews who supported either French or German versions of the "science of Judaism" (*science du judaïsme*; *Wissenschaft des Judentums*) were already rationalists, but the Jewish sociologists of Durkheim's new school were rationalists in a different way: their thinking was not characterized by any special attention to the people they came from. If, then, we wish to relate the identities of scientific thinker and Jew, we shall have to formulate the question differently, scrutinizing the elective affinity between a type of Judaism typical of the late nineteenth century and a disposition to objectivism in the study of social facts. Among Durkheimians, that disposition took the form of a collective undertaking, which explains the forming of an *école*, a distinctively French entity at the time, not to be found in German sociology. It turned out to imply a *mission*—a word used repeatedly in Durkheimian writings and an attitude noted by direct observers of the new discipline's development.[6] It is striking to see sociology, defined in a way that owed more to positivism than to the vicissitudes of *Wissenschaft*, taking new shape and gathering strength at the intersection of three types of motivation: religious, political, and scientific. In doing so, the process did not just substantiate a kind of renewed Christianity, emptied of its theological dimension and transplanted in secular soil (as was the case for Saint-Simon and Comte), but rather occurred in open support of rationalism—to which many Jewish scholars continued to devote themselves with an intensity akin to self-sacrifice without feeling any need to link that devotion to their Jewish identity, let alone to any "essence" of Judaism.

Without having to engage the question of such an essence, we can say that Judaism for Durkheim was obviously itself a social phenomenon. As such it carried more weight than all individual, subjective incarnations of it—*including himself*. And on the basis of this decidedly Durkheimian remark, we can take up the question from a different angle, working to shed light not on Durkheim by way of his putative Judaism, essentialized for the needs of the cause, but rather on Judaism—a historically specific version of it—by way of Durkheim, letting that Judaism come into focus as we consider how he proceeded in his thinking. Once we have taken this detour we can use the postulates it enables us to make about his thought to shed light on the man. The approach is justified if only by the text I will be using to implement it: *Suicide*.[7] In that work, Durkheim examined Judaism in just the way that will be most helpful to us here; there is no need to read between the lines.

It will be recalled that in *Suicide* Durkheim compares the Jewish religion in its modern form to Protestantism and Catholicism to determine what being Jewish implied for the individual's "social integration."[8] The point was to measure the different religions' "preservation coefficients," that is, how well they protected individuals from the "suicidogenetic current" (*courant suicidogène*) leading to what he called "egotistical suicide." That particular current, he explained, was the main factor behind the massive rise in suicide during the nineteenth century in Europe.[9] However, it should be clarified from the outset that Durkheim's general analysis of religious solidarity as a rampart against egotism did not lead him to suggest that such solidarity was adequate therapy. No religious—or family or political—solidarity could assuage the social and moral ill of rising egotistical suicide. The only practicable solution was to build professional solidarity in the form of "corporations." Integration through religion, Durkheim explained, belonged irrevocably to the past, unless a new religion were to appear "permitting more freedom to the right of criticism, to individual initiative, than even the most liberal Protestant sects" (431; 1951, 375).

That eventuality could not be excluded, and in a later work, *The Elementary Forms of Religious Life* (1912), Durkheim would assert much more strongly his sense of the permanence of religiosity. But he would not revise a crucial thesis of his earlier analysis: no existing religious group could claim preeminence in modern times. And there was no point in invoking a Rousseauistic "civil religion" either. "The religion of the future," conscious at last of its social foundation, would not be structured by the dogma of "sanctifying" contract laws;[10] nor could it work to bolster incomplete political solidarity. It was much more likely to have its own function, which would be to generate ideals to be acted on, or else to maintain belief in a power that dominates the subject but in which that subject also partakes, a force that "both supports him and raises him above himself."[11] It was this function that should persist or be given new force. Nonetheless, the forms it would take when "relaunched" would not resemble what religion had been in the past. While each religion had unconsciously contributed in its way to the function of making "the social" perceptible to individuals as both immanence and transcendence, those religions were not good resources for determining new ends or goals. The only seed of the past whose integrative potential could still be developed was the ancien régime–style professional "corporation." It was this form that modern mankind should find a way of resuscitating or redeveloping.

Suicide is commonly thought of as a path-breaking study; some consider it the founding work in the sociology of deviance.[12] But it needs to be clarified that suicide for Durkheim, while a form of deviance, was not exactly a transgression and certainly not a negation of the norm, but instead literally a detour (*déviation*) that implied overstepping limits *from within* moral life or in a way consistent with the flow of moral life: "Every suicide is then the exaggerated or deflected form of a virtue" (263; 1951, 240). The virtues in question could be named; they were "the spirit of renunciation, the love of progress, the taste for individuation"(420; 1951, 366). All three were socially necessary, and it was only when the spirit of renunciation became too "active," when individuation degenerated into "languorous melancholy" or when feeling for progress was exacerbated and gave way to "irritation" or "exasperated weariness," that the virtue was deflected and led to "self-murder."

Suicide, then, if closely read, gives us Durkheim's *ethics*. It is a sociologically substantiated treatise of the virtues. A group's moral constitution derived from a composite set of moral "currents" that could be apprehended by examining their excessive forms, in which they became "suicidal currents." The present was pathological in that egotistical suicide had become preeminent and anomic suicide was catching up to it. These causes of self-murder, themselves caused by a kind of inflation of the respective virtues of individuation and progress—virtues that could not be called "individualist" in themselves because they were operative in every kind of social life, though in varying proportions—had become preponderant compared to the virtue of renunciation for the sake of the group. In this case no one *virtue* had swelled excessively; rather, a single suicidal current was growing and outstripping the others, causing imbalance. That was indeed a sign of disease—a disease for which a sociologically rational therapy could be prescribed, a framework that would allow for reestablishing appropriate proportions of the three qualities and therefore the proper balance.

Durkheim never contemplated rehabilitating the *religious* solidarity of the past, even a considerably rearranged past. But he did believe that action had to be taken to reestablish a balance between the three suicidogenetic currents in a way that would simultaneously impact on each without excessively squeezing any. The professional corporation form seemed to him flexible enough to do this. It was a corps or body that did not balk at progress and in which the individual was recognized for his functional labor. It would regulate individual actions while integrating them into a set of shared goals, a common horizon. Similarly, and ever more insistently as *Suicide* progresses, Durkheim dares to express the idea of a religion of an entirely different type than all that had previously been tried out: a religion of society combined with a cult of the individual. That religion would have an unprecedented type of relationship to science, for free inquiry would be recognized rather than banished, but it would become effective quite differently than in Protestantism. Such hypotheses and prospecting were radically modern. But they were also modern in an unexpected way. It is just at this "nerve center" that we can see the Jewish question resurfacing in Durkheim's thought at the end of the nineteenth century—and taking a remarkable turn.

Jews, said Durkheim, were *strangely* modern. In this respect they might well represent something of both Durkheimianism as a theory of modernity and Durkheim as an individual thinker using that theory to reflect on his own experience. What was to be made of Jews' "preservation" against the observed rise in suicide rates? That protection had to do with the religion's "inferiority":

> Indeed, like all inferior religions, Judaism consists essentially in a body of practices which minutely control every detail of life and leave only a little room for individual judgment. (160; 2006, 166).

This practical solidarity was combined with a factor specific to ostracized minority groups forced to submit to an external influence that actually strengthened its unity—an obvious reference to antisemitism. In the modern situation, however, and as mentioned, antisemitism could be dismissed. It was not structural but instead dependent on the economic situation, and it could reasonably be expected to recede and gradually disappear. The ritual observance factor remained. It did seem to express something essential about Judaism, and it was destined to exist for a long time, independently of the fact that Jews were persecuted and ostracized. "Judaic monotheism" (156; 2006, 163) did not grant much room to "thought and reflection"; it was not "idealistic." On just this point it contrasted with the other two major religions, both of which aspired to "reign over the understanding and the conscience." Catholicism spoke "the language of reason" to demand reason's "blind submission" to faith. This can be called "dogmatic idealism." Protestants gave voice to the protestations of reason, demanding the right of free inquiry for the individual conscience and turning critically on dogma. This can be called "critical idealism." Judaism, meanwhile, kept a low profile and persevered in its mechanical observances, unimplicated in the clash between religions superior to it—superiority being measured by the degree of idealization or spiritualization, namely disengagement from practices that control the body.

However, Judaism's inferiority did not make it an "elementary" religion in the sense that Durkheim used the term in his later study of Australian totemism. It did not even offer a good example of mechanical solidarity, in contrast to the strong integration of archaic societies and civilized society "corps" like the military, in which altruism played a strong role. Indeed, Durkheim hardly mentions Judaism in the section on "altruistic suicide," that is, giving up one's life for a cause that exceeds the individual and is rooted exclusively in the group. Though he does cite the expected reference—Flavius Josephus's account of Masada—he does not attribute quite that meaning to those suicides, presenting them instead as an example of "suicides of the beseiged," an exceptional type of suicide in which the altruistic and anomic currents were combined (326; 2006, 319). Judaism was of course a residual, archaism-tinged phenomenon that persisted in modern societies, but it was also sociologically interesting and amounted to more than a mere vestige of mechanical solidarity.

It is here that the portrait of the Jew becomes more complicated, or rather that Durkheim's definition of Jewish monotheism as nonidealistic becomes enriched with a sociological definition of modern Jews. The Jewish population was now heavily urbanized and intellectual,[13] especially compared to Catholics. Both those features aggravated the likelihood of suicide. Yet in the case of Jews that effect seemed to have been neutralized. The effect of Jews becoming "intellectual" was particularly hard to understand. The fact should have been correlated, as it was for Protestants—who were also more intellectual and urban than Catholics—with increased self-searching and with education fueled by free inquiry. To put it roughly, it should have been possible to ascribe Jewish "intellectualization" to what I have called "critical idealism." But the operative principle here seems different. Above all, it seems quite disconnected from the *inferiority* indicated by the primacy of mechanical observance in Judaism. I suggest the term "disconnected," or rather nonaligned, for in Durkheim's time the connection had not yet been entirely severed: Jews were *in the process* of assimilating and therefore *not yet* assimilated. The two dimensions—intellectuality and mechanical religious observance—simultaneously present in the *modern Jewish individual* were not aligned.

At this stage several questions arise. What is the source of Jewish intellectuality? How does this figure of a Jew living somewhere between Judaism and modernity, an individual who in one part of her- or himself practices without understanding and in the other understands without practicing, cohere as a single being? And what was the status of that figure for Durkheim? Was it pathological?

No, quite the contrary. The Jew's unconsciously split way of being functioned as a rampart—weak, insufficient, yet operative at its own level—against egotistical suicide. As mentioned, the real contemporary pathology as Durkheim saw it was due to egotism, understood as an excessive taste for individuation—and more to egotism than to anomie as the passion for progress. In fact, the pathology could be attributed to the mutual reinforcement of these two currents. Why, then, were Jews engaged in the process of assimilation—that is, people living a kind of life that should have overexposed them to suicide—actually immunized? Durkheim offered the following portrait of this individual:

> Jews seek an education not in order to replace their collective prejudices by rational ideas, but simply to be better armed for the struggle. For them, this is a means of compensating for the inferior position they are accorded by public opinion and, sometimes, by law. And since in itself knowledge is powerless against a tradition that remains in full force, the educated Jew superposes his intellectual life upon his ritual observances without the first interfering with the second. Hence the complexity of his make-up: primitive in certain respects, he is in others a refined and cultured person. He thus combines the advantages of the strong discipline that was characteristic of the small groups of earlier times with the benefits of the intense culture enjoyed by the widely based societies of

the contemporary world. He has all the intelligence of modern people without sharing their despair. (170; 2006, 175).

In this passage, Judaism and science are inseparably intertwined. It is an apology for science by way of a portrait of the modern Jew—which does not mean it is an apology for the modern Jew. Durkheim's figure of the Jew is a composite, structured into two mutually impermeable dimensions. The primitive coexists with the evolved *in the same person.* The dualism of Durkheim's *homo duplex* is sociological here: in one part of his being the Jew partakes of mechanical society, in the other of organic society—at least that striking aspect of organic society that corresponds to the development of intellectuality—without one part affecting the other. This Jew is historically defined: after starting and before completing the assimilation process, he is *still* practicing his religion. He performs the mechanical acts that regulate the details of his life without questioning them intellectually, settling for the integrative benefit they afford him. And "above" this consolidated foundation of mechanical practice, the Jew's mind is free to operate and investigate, exempt from the critical activity that would have been required if he were trying to liberate himself from a shared body of thought. Clearly what the Jew *did not have* amounted to his fundamental advantage in modern life; that is, he was immune to the critical attitude toward dogma. At a deeper level—phylogenetically and ontogenetically—that advantage consists in his "immunity" to the kind of faith that Christianity introduced into history. Because the Jew has not experienced faith as a social determinant of conscience, dogma as a power that constrains the mind to believe in a certain way, he *thinks* in a different direction, as it were, and for different reasons than those that push people to emancipate themselves *spiritually* and thereby to expose themselves to the despair that accompanies that emancipation.

But then what moves the Jew to think, to use his reason, to partake in science? In order for Jews to think, thinking had to become a goal for them. In Durkheim's portrait of Judaism, *that goal is not a specifically Jewish one* but a modern one, which emerged most clearly in modern societies that were developing consistently with their own natures. Durkheim is therefore not an heir to Mendelssohn. His understanding was not continuous with the Jewish Enlightenment: thinking had come to Jews from without. But they "received" it in a specifically Jewish way. For in the case of Jews, two activities might be disconnected that in Protestantism could not be: the activity of criticism, and intellectual activity. Critique had been decidedly favorable to the advancement of science, both in and of itself and because it had transformed scientific knowledge into a recognized social goal. But it operated this way by means of free inquiry, and thus according to a particular sense of what it means to criticize. The main vector in the struggle to get free of dogmatism, prejudice, and tradition had been Protestant. The two virtues implicated in that development—love of progress and a taste for individuality—had now been accentuated to the breaking point, as attested by the increase in suicides. Now Durkheim needed to see whether science itself was responsible for this—whether science bore within it as a kind of essential characteristic the depressive factor that fueled egotism. It was this question, disturbing for modernity as such, that the Jewish case enabled Durkheim to resolve. The heuristic function of the Jews in Durkheim's argument was in fact to *exculpate science*, to protect it from any and all unjust accusations. For Jews were living proof that critique, necessarily subjective and individualizing, had been grafted onto thinking; and while this critique fostered and facilitated thinking, it was not consubstantial with it. Jews were proof that thinking could develop outside the twofold move to attack dogmatic faith and to obtain recognition for the individual conscience as an interpretative and judicative authority. Jews were the historically attested substratum of nonsubjective thinking; that is, thinking in which the task of critique was not apprehended as asserting personal judgments that went against the norms of collective thinking. The fertility of Jewish intellectuality derived precisely from this easing of the task: the nonconnection between thought and critique.

Returning to ritualism, was integration its sole positive effect? When Durkheim spoke of the "advantages of strong discipline," was he thinking of integration alone? Could not practice of a sort whose rules never change constitute a kind of foundation within oneself, ensuring that the group was internally present at the very moment one was freeing oneself from it? This two-story individual seemed disposed to become modern *as a socially disciplined being*—it was this that explained his resistance to suicide. Jewish discipline, then, was not strictly material or limited to bodily movements.

In Durkheim's understanding, belief differed from ritual in the same way thinking differed from movement.[14] And for Jews, as for the Aruntas of Australia, the main aspect of religion was to apply meticulously detailed, inviolable rules in a way that produced the same shared movements. It is difficult to discern in *Suicide* one of the functions of ritual that became essential in *The Elementary Forms*— that of putting the subject into the mental conditions required for experiencing "the impersonal." This function came to light in connection with mimetic ritual, which Durkheim saw as central to primitive sacrificial rites. Such ritual, as he came to understand it, wove a tie among minds in a way that implied moving beyond subjective perception.[15] It is reasonable to assume that Durkheim's description of modern Jews undergoing assimilation in *Suicide* already pointed in that direction. Arnaldo Momigliano was therefore right to say that Durkheim "Judaicized" Australian totemic society, to the point where it came to resemble those small communities in Lorraine "no longer exercised by mysticism or Messianic fervor."[16] The Judaism of Durkheim's self-described "serious, precocious childhood" now appeared to him as mere ritualism, and as such it shaped his conception of elementary religions. In any case, when it came to generating ideals, Judaism's inferiority was manifest and could not be denied. But there is another side to that judgment. Durkheim's idea of the modern Jew—and consequently of himself—led him to appreciate ritualism for its mental effects, which were a kind of external, indirect consequence of its practical structure. Modern Jews (that is, those of Durkheim's time) were simultaneously archaic and *extremely* modern. And in Durkheim's understanding, *being archaic got high marks* not only for its virtue of strengthening ties and consolidating the group but also because archaic ritual pulled thought in the direction of what it did not *contain* (in both senses of the verb: *encompass* and *limit*). As long as ritual implies neither regression (and how could it if Jews were *genuinely* split?) nor a process in which it acquires *spiritual* meaning for the subject practicing it (nothing of the sort happened in Judaism because ritual was inert), it creates a mental state favorable for the development of a different type of thought than thinking governed by personal judgment. Therein lies the unexpected advantage of this particular fossil.

Does this mean that modern Jews were a figure of scientific thinking as entirely positive, *disinterested* thinking? Absolutely not. The disjoining of critique and thinking identified above did not imply disinterestedness in the subjects in whom they had been disjoined. This is why there is no two-part apology—of science *and* Jews. What Durkheim's portrait does contain is a diagnosis of antisemitism as negative stimulus. Jews had a very strong interest in investing in thought, because for them intellectual activity represented a kind of "weapon" in the social struggle they were condemned to wage given the discrimination that had pursued them throughout the history of European societies—discrimination not only in the form of negative public opinion but also legal discrimination. In that struggle, caused by unfavorable external conditions, science was of use to Jews. Conjointly, Jews were of use to science—*as Jews*—and this time for reasons internal to Judaism. Jews served science differently than Protestants or Catholics. The paradox is that despite their vested interest in science, they were doomed, as it were, to practice it in their own disconnected way. They could not practice it in any other way, given that critical subjective probing—precisely the kind that had caused the nonessential, context-governed convergence between thinking and a particular suicidal current—was alien to them.

Jews showed that another way was possible. This in no sense meant that they were the privileged agents of that other way. Once again, objectively practiced science as Durkheim defined it in *The Rules of Sociological Method* was an attainment and culmination of modern thought; in no way was it specifically Jewish. Ridding ourselves of what Durkheim called "prenotions" and combating prejudice were central purposes of fully developed science. In this sense science was of course critical. But though the critical attitude had had to endure the searing break attested to by the history of Christian thought, this did not mean it was riveted to free inquiry as shaped by individuation. The case of Jews, the ease with which they moved and advanced in the area of intellectuality, showed that science could be practiced independently of such conditions. And here we can go further than Durkheim: the case of Jews shows that critique, freed of its subjectivist component, can win recognition for the collective dimension of thought without that dimension being a matter of dogma. In this sense, Jews do indeed have a remarkable aptitude to think sociologically and to participate in science—science as sociology allowed for conceiving it. This aptitude is related to their relative immunity to the suicidal current wherein thought, having become *excessively individualized*, acts as cause in spite of itself.

As we know, that current is egotism—not, interestingly enough, anomie (i.e., deregulation caused by overswelling of the passion for progress). Thinking went off the rails—and came to partake of the modern pathology—by connecting up with individuation through the subjectifying act of critique. The figure of the modern Jew, with his extreme aptitude for assimilation, was an exception when it came to thinking. The Jew's relative immunity to the primary ill—rising egotistical suicide—has thus been understood and demonstrated. But what of his relation to the secondary ill, anomic suicide? Nothing Durkheim says on the subject allows us to answer that question. Yet we have to ask it if we want to further detail the portrait he left us and elucidate its full sociological meaning. Understanding the relation between Durkheim's thought and the historical figure of the modern Jew requires formulating hypotheses on the subject of Jews and anomic suicide.

Once again, the rapidity with which modern Jews assimilated corresponded not only to the general direction of progress but also to their own desire for advancement. The two-story individual was a transitory figure pertaining to Jews still practicing mechanically while fully devoting themselves to an intellectual career. In 1907, in his review of Father Krose's *Die Ursachen der Selbstmordhäufigkeit* (1906), a turn-of-the-century reanalysis of the religious determinations of suicide, Durkheim noted a significant change: "As the Jewish population becomes assimilated to the surrounding population, it is losing its traditional virtues without, perhaps, replacing them with others."[17] The "perhaps" is worth noting. Nonetheless, it was undeniable that Jewish suicide rates had increased. Was this due to a fall in the preserving virtues or, on the contrary, an exaggeration of what was a virtue in some other connection? It is legitimate to formulate the question this way if we take the assimilation process seriously, that is, as a more complex and ambiguous phenomenon than the mere disappearance of Jews. If assimilation was the way of the future—and if the process was not stopped by antisemitism—then it was clear that Judaic practice would decline. It was already doing so, and the benefit in terms of integration was shrinking. It was not that Jews were *criticizing* practical norms for the discipline those norms imposed; rather, practices that were as "mechanical" as Jewish ones, practices that could hold together groups in the process of assimilating, would ultimately fall away in and of themselves when such groups no longer had any external (negative) incentive to maintain their internal cohesion. However, even if we assume that observance was disappearing and that, with antisemitism receding, the need for regressive solidarity would do likewise, some specific feature would subsist in Jews. Their "upper story," the singular intellectuality whose formative conditions I have just specified, would continue to distinguish them within modern society. How would that society react to this from now on?

My point here is that the two dimensions comprising the portrait of the Jew "in the process" of becoming assimilated *have not undergone the same fate*. In the *full assimilation* scenario that we need to imagine, some singularizing feature persists. But it is not a residue of rootedness. What's more, it is not *uniformly* Jewish in that it cannot be derived from some presumed nature of Judaism now reduced to religious or cultural foundation. That enduring feature results from the contingent encounter between a certain religious configuration—being alien to idealism and therefore to a critique of faith—and the modern process, that is, the construction of organic societies and the importance those societies grant to intellectual activity. Moreover—and this is surely the most important point—that feature could not function as a center around which a new membership group could form. It could be found in a certain number of individuals but did not serve to unite them into a substantive, self-conscious group. In sum, and without denying the fact of assimilation and its dissolution of particularized collective identities, it is clear that one Jewish feature—or rather a feature that *fell to Jews* and that each would exhibit individually—would persist after assimilation. It pertains to a way of thinking present in dispersed individuals. And it amounts to a change in rationalism, a curious historical "secretion" that modernity carried on its side and that manifested itself belatedly, once a set of factors had come together in which Judaism as such played a very limited role.

This feature has nonetheless doomed the Jews to progress. According to the topics of *Suicide*, this can mean two different things. The passion for progress, a fundamental virtue of modern societies, implies regulation of activity, and that regulation can be either too strong or too weak. If it is too weak, there is nothing to rein in infinite desire or provide it with purpose; if it is excessive, the future seems "pitilessly blocked" (311; 1951, 239) and the passion for progress shatters against impossibility. Anomic and fatalistic suicides are symmetrically opposed on the count of regulation, just as altruistic and egotistical suicides are opposed on the count of integration. Durkheim dismissed fatalism as a quantitatively insignificant phenomenon: historically, it referred to suicide by slaves and, in his time, "very young husbands" and "the married woman who is childless" (ibid.; 1951, 276). But might fatalistic suicide be relevant for some modern Jews? The question is a fair one once we take into account the possibility of antisemitic opinion growing stronger or becoming instituted as antisemitic law, of its rising once again in Europe and precluding de facto any margin of progress among individuals already engaged in an assimilation process. Being particularly well adapted to intellectual practice precisely because one has chosen it as a "weapon" in the struggle (170; 2006, 177) becomes a factor for despair when that struggle is lost even before it can begin, that is, when acquired aptitudes cannot be converted into social benefits. Negative consolidation—such as the bolstering of internal ties in communities that are discriminated against or persecuted—only works if the assimilation process has not gone beyond a certain point. Once it has, Jews no longer have any other tie to turn to than the one they hope to make with the receiving society. This means that the very people who shared in the intelligence of modern men without sharing their despair can come to that despair by a path other than egotism.

Jews do not feature in Durkheim's discussion of anomie either.[18] There may be a general explanation for this: both anomie and fatalism are problems involving the passions rather than the intellect. The intrinsically unlimited nature of desire— which explained why economic, industrial, and business activities were directly affected by anomie (288; 2006, 284)—had made regulation necessary. Nonetheless, the move to embrace progress through intellectuality does involve passion, particularly when the motivation is to obtain better odds in the social struggle. What does it mean for Jews to progress? Once again, the point is clarified through a comparison of Jews and Protestants. In the Christian world, where Protestants remained, progress implied a critique of dogma. Progressing was an act of emancipation— self-extrication from a collective foundation that remained relevant for the emancipated even after they had extricated themselves. Jews, on the other hand, wage that combat with their eyes trained on the future only. The combat is coextensive with progress itself—progress understood as time that is constantly redeployed as one advances, as one "progresses"—without any reference to a tradition that one has left behind and that might serve to measure the distance covered. We see that the danger of anomie here comes not from antisemitism but rather from the same singularizing feature of the modern Jew that has just been identified. For devoting oneself to progress by practicing criticism—the individual consciousness turning back to or on itself as a reasoning consciousness—is not the same thing as willing progress. Progress here is understood as pure accomplishment of the modern project in an impersonal mode, where the only wager is on history itself, as it were: the indefinite temporal openness of history.

As we saw at the outset, it was because Jews changed so quickly that they appeared to Durkheim *extremely* modern. We now have a clearer idea why. Disburdened of the cumbersome aspect of critique by which thought is related to the thinking subject (in either psychological or transcendental mode, it matters little here), Jews move fast. They have no difficulty considering facts as "things" or analyzing them from the perspective of impersonal reason. But at another level this makes them vulnerable. Entirely projected toward the future, they are the first to fall when history trips up—when "progress" is not progress at all, and science and civilization betray themselves by submitting to the expansionist warring of nations. There can be no doubt that Durkheim invented the concept of anomie and distinguished it from egotism *before* the first signs of World War I, and that he thought of it as something more than social discontent. Anomie is the sociological version of "civilization's discontents." It is just as certain that Jews' extreme aptitude for assimilation—that is, for *intrinsically historical* progress—condemned them to suffer from anomie *specifically*. In this connection, Heine's old line, "Judaism's not a religion, it's a misfortune," seems to acquire new resonance and a rightful place in Durkheim's discourse.

Except that that discourse does not exist. Once again, there is no data in *Suicide* to confirm the hypotheses I have been formulating about Jewish suicide in connection with the singularizing feature of modern Jews that Durkheim did identify. Have I been applying the very method I criticized at the outset, trying to detect what Durkheim left unsaid on the Jewish question in a body of work that hardly lends itself to such interpretation? In the empirical framework initially defined, the demonstration had no right to go so far. *My own questions* about modern Jews are what have dug the aforementioned "hole" in Durkheim's discourse, and it makes little sense to ask why Durkheim did not fill it, let alone reproach him for that.

On the other hand, it is important to note that the history of Durkheimian thought went some way toward filling that hole. In 1930, in a work that returned to the root of Durkheim's suicide problem and related it to new knowledge acquired through the intervening empirical and methodological advancement of social science, Maurice Halbwachs pointed out that the trend in Jewish suicide noted by Durkheim had been entirely reversed. If there was one point on which Durkheim's analysis should be corrected it was that one, Halbwachs insisted. Moreover, Durkheim himself had begun to acknowledge this in his 1907 review of Father Krose's book. The time had come to be clear and direct: suicide among Jews in Prussia had risen to nearly six times what it was, overtaking the rate for Protestants.[19] Durkheim's theory of Jewish "preservation" was an illusion.

Halbwachs thoroughly reorganized Durkheim's suicide question, rejecting the very idea that the religious factor—or the family one—could be isolated or observed in isolation and calling instead for a comprehensive, integrated term such as "lifestyle" or "milieu," in which customs, institutions, practices, and representations would be understood to *interact*. That shift is not of primary interest here, but it is important to note Halbwachs's remark that Durkheim had formulated the suicide problem even less relevantly for Jews than for Protestants and Catholics (regarding the latter groups, Halbwachs nonetheless consented to criticize Durkheim's method). According to Halbwachs, Jews—and if this applied to a large proportion of them in 1930 it already applied to a significant proportion in 1897—could not be ascribed a specific religious identity:

> The extremely rapid multiplication of mixed marriages between Israelites and Christians does not primarily result from the weakening of religious beliefs among them. Rather, such marriages would not be possible at all if Jewish families were forced back upon themselves as much as formerly and did not allow their members more freedom. There is nothing here that cannot be expressed in purely secular terms except for customs of long standing that have some ties to religion. For the purpose of examining the influence of the religious group as such on suicide, then, it would be better to discard the example of the Jews.[20]

And indeed, the rest of Halbwachs's discussion says nothing of Jews. His is an entirely different interpretation of the two-story individual. The "customs of long standing that have some ties to religion" did not amount in and of themselves to a "religious factor." Jews were assimilating very quickly, as attested by the high rate of intermarriage. They were *free* individuals—evermore free. Custom-based ties were doomed to disappear, and when they persisted they were insignificant, meaning they did not have enough impact to enable us to assess the specific affect of the religion on suicide. Durkheim, suggests Halbwachs, misled us on this point, even more than in his comparison of Protestants and Catholics. For Jews, a strictly secular reading was required.

We can wager that this reading was *urgently* required at the time Halbwachs was writing. At the end of the preceding century, Durkheim could write that anti-semitism in Western Europe was "superficial" or "passing." In 1930 no such assumption could be made. For anyone who, like Halbwachs, saw and understood the implications of the rise of Nazism at a time when antisemitism had been steadily flourishing in French public opinion as well, judgments had to be unambiguous, free of any emphasis whose effects might prove incontrollable. Jews were modern— the proof was that they were assimilating at high speed. Durkheim had of course already said this many years before, but it had had a different meaning when he said it. For Halbwachs, to speak of assimilation was to take literally the indiscernible future of "Jews" and not to take into account their singular integration trajectory, in which they could still be discerned as Jews. In speaking of assimilation, it was important to ensure that no specifically Jewish feature subsisted and also to be careful not to point up any specifically Jewish contribution to the destiny of modern democratic societies.

Legal antisemitism, not just that of public opinion, would soon hit so-called civilized Europe, acquiring unprecedented scope and giving rise to unheard-of violence. Halbwachs, the Christian husband of an assimilated Jew, a representative of just those mixed marriages whose multiplication he had pointed out, was arrested by the Gestapo and died in Buchenwald in 1945. There can be no doubt that he had perceived *before* Hitler came to power the urgency of precluding any judging of Jews that would distinguish them from other groups, especially when such judgments were being revised "outside," *while* Jews were in the process of assimilating. For antisemitism too was progressing, and not just quantitatively. It was learning to discriminate ever more finely—just when all evidence suggested there was nothing left to be discriminated. With an admirable mixture of intellectual probity and political acuity, Halbwachs settled the matter: *"it is preferable to leave aside the example of the Jews."* And "the Jews" were already in the sights of Western European societies.

Durkheim and Halbwachs were also separated by the distance between nascent social science and solidly constituted social science, with its own publications and publishers, teaching institutions, tested methods, and attested results. From *The Causes of Suicide* onward, what was no longer visible, for excellent reasons—for the *very best of reasons*—was precisely what Durkheim had articulated about Jews at the inaugural moment, upon the founding of a new discipline forced to carve out its own territory and to determine and formulate the broad lines of its own type of scientificity. The paradox that shifted into the background in the interwar period and was not perceived later was that in Durkheim's thought the initial explanation of the fully developed scientific spirit developed surreptitiously by way of a *continued, maintained* Jewish singularity, a singularity that took shape within the sociological perspective itself and could do so precisely because this perspective meant to be and was thoroughly, unambiguously *secular*.

Jewish singularity was produced by a complex conjoining of historical factors. It emerged at the intersection of (1) a cultural lineage characterized by a backward "life of the mind"; (2) the exercise of free inquiry and critique as inherited from modernity steeped in Christianity; and (3) long-term social conditioning in the form of persecution and ostracism, which explained Jews' particular way of "entering" modernity. The interesting precipitate of these three factors, each of a different nature and status, was modern Jews. It is interesting for science and the history of reason, for Jews represent a paradoxical actualization of that history. And the Jewish human entity in itself is interesting as a kind of casting-against-type, "perpetrated" by history, a conjoining of heterogeneous factors that, through their improbable synthesis, ended up conferring the attributes of the avant-garde on one of the oldest and most archaic of society's distinct groups. This type of modernity was capable of critiquing itself by rising to the level of impersonal, collective thought—a type of thought that, as long as it is not rigidified into new dogma, stands as modernity's highest achievement.

Notes

1. A line of eight generations, the last representative being Moïse Durkheim, the rabbi of Epinal, Émile's father. Neither Émile nor his brother Felix took on this function and profession. Were they deliberately breaking with it? To answer that question we would have to define what they were breaking from, for the family's Judaism changed over the nineteenth century. According to Ivan Strenski in *Durkheim and the Jews of France* (Chicago, 1997), 60–61, the rabbi Moïse Durkheim was in significant ways a "modernizing Jew": the household observed Judaic rules, but not in the orthodox way of the preceding generations. Émile's "serious, precocious" childhood, as he described it, characteristic of those small Jewish communities in Lorraine "no longer exercised by mysticism or Messianic fervor," as Arnaldo Momigliano put it in his astute analysis (*Problèmes d'historiographie ancienne et moderne* [Paris, 1988], 422), was actually fairly permeable to the rationalism Durkheim came to devote himself to. For a genetic, psychoanalytic reading of Durkheim's work through the prism of his relationship with his father, see Bernard Lacroix, *Durkheim et le politique* (Paris, 1981).

2. For a particularly useful analysis on this subject see Victor Karady, "Les intellectuels juifs et les sciences sociales," in *Pour une histoire des sciences sociales: Hommage à Pierre Bourdieu*, eds. Remi Lenoir and Gisèle Shapiro (Paris, 2004), 155–76.

3. Jean-Claude Milner's study of the repercussions of Weber's "Science as a Vocation" on certain German Jews (*Le Juif de savoir* [Paris, 2008]) could be transposed to the case of French Jewish scholars and scientists in the first half of the twentieth century. The Durkheimian movement would be important in such a study and might even constitute a main avenue of investigation. The epistemological point of departure would be *The Rules of Sociological Method*; the study would examine how this text fit into the political-ideological context of the Third Republic.

4. Momigliano recalls that while "Weber introduced the term pariah into scientific study of Judaism," the link between Jews and the term *pariah* (social outcast) was already current in the early nineteenth century (*Contributions à l'histoire du judaïsme* [Paris, 2002], 219).

5. Émile Durkheim, *Textes* (Paris, 1975), 2:253.

6. Compare Hubert Bourgin, *De Jaurès à Léon Blum* (Paris, 1938), 218.

7. Translator's note: There are two English translations of Durkheim's work: *Suicide*, trans. John A. Spaulding and George Simpson (New York, 1951); and *On Suicide*, trans. Robin Buss (London, 2006). For each quotation here, the translation deemed closest to the original French and Bruno Karsenti's argument was chosen; that choice is indicated by translation date—1951 or 2006—following the English quotation and page number in the original French.

8. Commentaries written in the wake of Parsons's *Structure of Social Action* (New York, 1937) are likely to focus on the comparison between Protestantism and Catholicism. In fact, Halbwachs had set the tone as early as 1930, explaining that the case of Judaism was misleading, a kind of *trompe l'oeil*: "For the purposes of examining the influence of the religious group as such on suicide, it would be better to discard the example of the Jews" (Halbwachs, *The Causes of Suicide*, trans. Harold Goldblatt [London, 1978], 169; Halbwachs, *Les Causes du suicide* [1930; Paris, 2002], 194). In the conclusion I consider the meaning of Halbwachs's move to exclude Jews from study of suicide by religious membership.

9. "The kind of suicide that is currently the most widespread and which most contributes to raising the annual figure of voluntary deaths is egotistical suicide" (*Le Suicide* [1897; Paris, 1995], 406; *On Suicide*, trans. Robin Buss [London, 2006], 396). Exclusive focus on the concept of anomic suicide (which was also increasing but was not, according to Durkheim, the *main* cause of the general rise) may lead us to forget this important point.

10. Jean-Jacques Rousseau, *Le contrat social*, bk. 4, chap. 8.

11. Émile Durkheim, "L'avenir de la religion" (1914), in *La science sociale et l'action* (Paris, 2010), 307.

12. See Albert Ogien, *Sociologie de la déviance* (Paris, 1999), 19–20.

13. Durkheim substantiated this statement with Prussian statistics.

14. Émile Durkheim, *Les formes élémentaires de la vie religieuse* (1912; Paris, 1990), 50.

15. Ibid., 511. It is useful to recall that Durkheim arrived at his thesis on sacrifice through a discussion of Robertson Smith's *The Religion of the Semites*. In passing, he draws a parallel between Australian sacrifices and the sacrifices described in the Pentateuch (ibid., 488).

16. Momigliano, *Problèmes d'historiographie ancienne et moderne*, 422.

17. *Journal sociologique* (Paris, 1969), 664.

18. With the partial exception of Masada, a case of mixed anomic-altruistic suicide that Durkheim ultimately classified as "exasperated effervescence" (332; 2006, 325).

19. Halbwachs, *Les Causes du suicide*, 184; Halbwachs, *The Causes of Suicide*, 169.

20. Ibid.

4

Theodor Herzl (1860–1904)

SOVEREIGNTY AND THE TWO PALESTINES

Raef Zreik

THEODOR HERZL WAS NOT A MAJOR, ORIGINAL INTELLECTUAL FIGURE AND SHOULD not be considered as such. Most of his ideas were not new, yet he left perhaps a bigger mark on twentieth-century Jewish life than any other Jewish figure.[1] Herzl was also not a prolific writer, and his heritage remains more political than literary. Nevertheless he wrote three key works: *The Jewish State* (1896) and *Altneuland* (*The Old New Land*; 1902) are his major writings; while the earliest of the three, a play titled *The New Ghetto*, written in the transitional period around 1894, offers a glimpse into Herzl's world and his evolving attitude toward antisemitism. *The Jewish State* is written in a dry but eloquent style and includes his analysis of antisemitism, in which he advances the idea of a Jewish state as the only possible alternative. *Altneuland*, on the other hand, takes the form of a realistic novel, allowing Herzl to imagine cultural and political life in the new society. His vision addresses the nature of relations between Jews and Arabs, Jews and Gentiles, wealthy and poor Jews, and religious and secular elements of society.

Antisemitism and Sovereignty

Born as Benjamin Ze'ev (Theodor) Herzl in 1860 in Budapest to a bourgeois family that later moved to Vienna, Herzl grew up in the spirit of assimilation and acculturation. He studied law before choosing journalism. As many have observed, Herzl's take on antisemitism went through a certain development.[2] In his diary, Herzl mentions his first encounter with antisemitism via Eugen Dühring's book *The Jewish Question as a Question of Race, Morals, and Civilization*.[3] Herzl accepted many of Dühring's stereotypes with regard to the "crookedness of the Jewish nature" and the origins of this nature from within ghetto life.[4] But while Dühring claimed such characteristics to be a function of blood and race and thus incorrigible, Herzl thought that they were a product of history and, as such, could also be repaired by history.

In this early understanding, antisemitism for Herzl was a mere continuation of medieval Christian society's hatred of the Jews. The disappearance of antisemitism,

together with other prejudices associated with the old regime, was therefore a matter of time, as these older attitudes dissolved slowly with the rise of liberalism in Europe and the spread of emancipation. At this early optimistic stage, Herzl saw himself as attached to Austro-Hungarian culture more than to Jewish culture. In *The New Ghetto*, he already evinces a certain revision—a critical attitude toward assimilation and a positive attitude regarding Jewish dignity and self-respect. This play was published before the antisemitic Dreyfus affair, supporting a recent assertion that the incident was not, in itself, the turning point in Herzl's thinking. Rather, his political shift was a continuous, largely autonomous process.[5]

The Jewish State understands the Jewish question as a national problem rather than a religious or individual one. This, in itself, was not a great innovation and was to be found—as Herzl himself testifies—in the works of Moses Hess and Leon Pinsker.[6] Yet, his personal move was a major one. To Herzl, the legal equality that was granted to the Jews remained a dead letter, dissolving in the cry *Juden Raus!* (Out with the Jews!). The Jews could try to be loyal patriots, but their efforts were in vain: at the end of the day, they remained outsiders. The mature Herzl thought that emancipation exacerbated the problem rather than solving it. Prior to emancipation, segregation was assumed, and living in a ghetto was understood and accepted. Emancipation created an illusion—a promise of equality and integration with European societies that could not be fulfilled. Against this background of presumed common citizenship, the separation and rejection of the Jews became palpable. On the part of the Jews themselves, "our enfranchisement came too late. It was no longer possible to remove our disabilities in our old homes."[7] On the other hand, there was no way back to the old status quo: "The equal rights of the Jews before the law cannot be withdrawn where they have once been conceded."[8] Emancipation created a reality with no future and no return to the past. As such, antisemitism is a modern phenomenon and a product of nationalism and emancipation—an attack on the Jews within a liberal society, but in itself an attack on the new liberal regime and its values. It had been not the exception but the rule of European thought in his lifetime.

But Herzl's take on the issue of antisemitism did not, and could not, lead him directly to Zionism.[9] To move to Zionism and to suggest the ideas in the *The Jewish State*, there was a need for further links in the argument.[10] Toward the end of the section in *The Jewish State* that deals with antisemitism, Herzl concluded: "We are one people—our enemies have made us one without our consent . . . distress binds us together. . . . Yes, we are strong enough to form a state. . . ."[11] Herzl was probably the first to use the word "state," though the ideas of nationalism and a territorial solution had been mentioned earlier in the Jewish context.[12] He now opened the section titled "The Plan" with this startling sentence: "Let the sovereignty be granted us over a portion of the globe large enough to satisfy the rightful requirements of a *nation*; the rest we shall manage for ourselves."[13] There is something in the structure of the argument that resembles the writing of a court decision. The verdict comes at the end as a necessary, logically mandated conclusion: If this is the problem, then the solution is a Jewish state with sovereignty over any portion of the globe. But in fact there is no such logical entailment, and the conclusion in favor of the Jewish state does not derive naturally from the fact of antisemitism.

Herzl thought that the Jewish question was an international question and not just a problem of the Jewish people.[14] As such, the solution in the form of a Jewish state had to be a solution to which all nations—European nations—had to contribute. There was a division of labor here, in which land was granted to the Jews by Europe and the Jewish people did the rest. In this sense, Herzl was prophetic: his project would be realized thanks to the Balfour Declaration, the Mandate, and then the United Nations partition plan. It shouldn't come as a surprise that Herzl himself devoted years to convincing the Ottomans and the Germans to grant him a charter, so that Jewish immigration would have the legal support of the great powers; for many years he opposed any Jewish settlement in Palestine that would not be supported by legal documents. For Herzl, the project required the support of Europe, including that of antisemitic countries: "The governments of all countries scourged by anti-Semitism will be keenly interested in assisting us to obtain the sovereignty we want," he wrote, and he was sure that he could recruit money not only from Jews but also from "Christians who wanted to get rid of them."[15] In fact, the idea of a Jewish state in the midst of the Arab world had been suggested and supported by Christian Zionists long before Herzl; the Jewish question and the Eastern question were very much linked.[16] In one of his most quoted statements, Herzl returns the favor to Europe, revealing at the same time a typical colonial mindset: "[W]e should there form a portion of rampart of Europe against Asia, an outpost of civilization as opposed to barbarism. We should, as a neutral state, remain in contact with all Europe, which would have to guarantee our existence."[17] No wonder that in *Altneuland* it is the Gentile Kingscourt who first suggests the visit to Palestine, reminding Lowenberg that it is his Jewish homeland.[18]

Herzl's thinking is grounded in the European terminology of his day. First, his understanding of the nation-state is couched in contemporary European terms, where the concept of sovereignty lies at the heart of a Westphalian understanding of territoriality and the sovereign state. In many ways, Herzl thought to get out of Europe in order to return to it, to exit it in order to join it conceptually and culturally. One can obviously conceive a Jewish nationalism that would not focus on sovereignty and on territory, but it was this European vision of nationalism that connected them both. Second, Herzl mirrors a certain Eastern and Central European understanding of nationalism based on ethnicity, as opposed to the civic model that was developed in the West. Many have noticed that Herzl's understanding of Jewish nationalism and the Jewish state project is a continuation of a long tradition in European thought that conceives of the nation through the metaphors of "blood" and "race."[19]

Finally, and less stressed in the existing literature, there is the problem of a rational priority that hides an implied violence: a mode of argumentation that moves in discrete stages but is structured on levels according to the Kantian faculties of understanding.[20] In this mode of argumentation, one will ask whether, given their experience of persecution in Europe, the Jews deserve to have their own state. At another level of the debate appears the question of *where* to establish the state, how to implement it, and at whose price. There is no trade-off between the two levels of argumentation: the level of principle and that of implementation. The argument moves in one direction, and there is no way to reevaluate the soundness of the first judgment based on its consequences. In many ways this mode of argumentation is deontological and anticonsequentialist. It does not pay much attention to results and consequences: once an action is considered to be just, then regardless of its consequences it must be carried through. One can argue that such an attitude downplays the role of external factors to the actor and allows a high level of self-centeredness. No wonder that Herzl never mentions the Arab Palestinian inhabitants of the land before he reaches his verdict concerning the need to establish a Jewish state.

This, in all likelihood, is the philosophical basis underlying Hannah Arendt's argument of a certain tilt in Herzl's theory that paves the way for revisionist interpretations. In her own words, "the truth of the matter is that Zionist Ideology, in the Herzlian version, had a definite tendency toward what later was known as revisionist attitudes and could escape from them only through a willful blindness to the real political issues that were at stake."[21] It was in fact the revisionist leader Ze'ev Jabotinski who argued that the Zionists had to decide whether Zionism was just or not, and if it was so then they should not shy away from the use of force against any opposition to the Jewish Zionist settlement in Palestine.[22]

The Herzlian State: Between Hobbesean and Lockean Views of Representation

Probably one of the most important and effective ideas in *The Jewish State* is the establishment of a "Society of Jews" as a representative of the "Jewish people" everywhere, by way of the Roman law concept of the *gestor*. Herzl exemplifies the leader who is aware of the importance of the question of representation, and he sets the example of how national movements do indeed create nations, rather than the other way around. In a reality of dispersal, Herzl understood the problem of representation and also was aware that solving this problem meant creating a national movement that would speak on behalf of all Jews. As he puts it: the Society will "treat with governments in the name of our people . . . the Society will thus be acknowledged in its relations with governments as a state-creating power. This acknowledgment will practically create the state."[23] But how did he imagine the creation of this representative body? Here, Herzl opted for a thick understanding of representation, not merely a procedural one. X might represent Y without being appointed by Y, but simply by following up and protecting X's interests; in this sense he represents Y's interest though he does not represent Y's manifested will. X takes on the function of the Roman *gestor*—an institution equivalent to trusteeship. As Herzl put it: "When the property of an oppressed person is in danger, any man may step forward to save it. This man is the *gestor*. He has received no warrant— that is, no human warrant; higher obligations authorize him to act. . . . The *gestio* is intended to work for the good of the *dominus*—the people, to whom the *gestor* himself belongs."[24] The argument is that in the process of struggle for establishing a state, people can't be of one mind, and there is no way to reach agreement or to allow a regular process of election. Thus, no alternative is left but for the *gestor* to act—to appoint himself and to be in charge. Herzl suggested two representative bodies: the Society of Jews and the Jewish company. The first was to have moral and symbolic authority; the other would be tasked with pragmatic and administrative matters.

Clearly this issue of "enforced" representation was vital for the idea and the project. As governments started dealing with a body representing the Jewish people as a people, the Jews as individuals would find a body to identify with, thus transforming the Zionist idea into the Zionist project. An affective identification would develop into a real political program with attendant institutions. In this sense, Herzl's idea proposed one answer to the old "prisoner dilemma" or to the problem of collective, coordinated action: namely, how a group of people with common converging as well as diverging interests can come to work together and create a general common, collective interest. Herzl's solution is located, one could say, midway between Hobbes's Leviathan and Locke's Sovereign. It resembles the Leviathan in its imposition of oneness on the nation. But its Sovereign is a Lockean one, by virtue of having a duty of trusteeship toward the people he claims to represent. I consider this element one of the most important achievements of Herzl's program.

Alongside its power, this strategy has its costs. One cost is that it enforces representation on those Jews who do not share the Zionist worldview, and who have no wish for Zionist leaders to speak in their names. This is even more accentuated in the case of those non-European Jews who had not experienced antisemitism in their home countries and who opposed the generalization of the Zionist narrative as a summary of the modern Jewish experience in its entirety. Oriental Jews are the first to come to mind as rejecting such narratives, though they are not the only ones.[25] Many religious Jews have considered Zionism as imposing a certain interpretation on the Jewish existence that they have not accepted.

The other negative externality stems from the nature of the project as well as from the nature of representation. In a reality of dispersal and divergence in interests, there must be a strong central representative body that can enforce all the necessary coordination. This can be problematic, as it suggests a highly centralized system that renders individuals rather dependent on the central body. Herzl suggests that the Jews liquidate their businesses in their current locations and move to the "new place"; in order to do so, a central coordinating body is required. But as a first move, this liquidation of business is disempowering on the individual level and leaves each individual dependent on the central body that is supposed to take care of his or her needs: "The Jewish company will be prepared to conduct the transfer of the smallest affairs equally with the largest. Whilst the Jews quietly emigrate and establish their new homes, the company acts as the great controlling body which organizes their departure, takes charge of deserted possessions, guarantees the proper conduct of the movement with its own visible and tangible property, and provides permanent security for those who already settled."[26]

In many ways, Herzl disempowered the Jewish individual before reempowering her or him again in the new society. This high-level coordination does not stop here, but continues throughout the entire project—including the acquisition of land and the settlement project itself. These central bodies must know everything during the settlement project: "The local groups will have plans of the towns, so that our people may know beforehand where they are to go, in which towns and in which houses they are to live."[27] The need for collective, centralized action with the new settlers brought Herzl to approve the truck system (the practice of paying a worker's wages in goods instead of money), so that there would be no wages during the first period of settlement.[28] These issues are still with us today in the form of permanent emergency and the ongoing states of exception, representation, centrality, and dependency.[29] Zionism aimed to solve vexing problems for the European Jews, yet along the way it has created many other new problems for the Jewish people in their entirety. To some extent, Zionism has evolved to be in part a solution, in part a problem, and in part a solution of its own problems.

East and West, or Two Palestines

Herzl is a man of his time in terms of East and West and the colonial imagination. He thinks of Zionism partly in terms of a civilizing mission, and in that he resembles many colonialists of the late nineteenth century. As such, his vision sets not only Jew versus Arab but also the West versus the East. The Jews are associated with the West, but not in full, and the Arabs are associated with the East, but again not in full. This is very clear when we compare Herzl's impressions of Palestine between the two visits, as told in *Altneuland*. In the first trip, Palestine makes "a most disagreeable impression" on Lowenberg. The same is true for Jerusalem, which he describes as full of "shouts, smells, tawdry colors, people in rags crowding the narrow, airless streets, beggars, cripples, starveling children, screaming women, bellowing shopkeepers. . . . The once royal city had indeed sunk to the lower depths." There is a widespread eye disease because "of the dirt and neglect," but still the land itself has great potential. Dr. Eichetsman concludes, "and yet the land itself is such a fine land."[30]

Twenty years pass and the place is absolutely a new place. As Dr. Lowenberg remarks, "something very important has happened in our absence." Jews, Gentiles, and Arabs are all transformed, not to mention Palestine itself. The new Palestine is full of harbors and railways. Fast boats race to Europe. Haifa "has become the safest and the best port in the Mediterranean sea," and its citizens are "most sophisticated and well dressed." Haifa looks like the Riviera but "the buildings were modern and far cleaner than there, and the streets less noisy."[31] The city has a rich cultural and musical life and one can choose between different theaters in "German, French, English, Italian, [and] Spanish."[32] The same holds for Jerusalem: "Once Jerusalem was dead, now it was risen again . . . and full of life."[33]

The "Arabs," for Herzl, are Muslims. The only Arab we meet in the novel is Reshid Bey, who is introduced as a Muslim rather than as an Arab. There are, of course, no Christian Arabs in the novel. Shlomo Avineri argues that Herzl saw the Arabs but simply did not foresee the rise of Arab nationalism.[34] Already in the first encounter, David Litwak introduces Reshid Bey as "my friend," almost in a preventive move as to what might appear to many as "his enemy." Reshid is Westernized as well—he has studied at the University of Berlin and even speaks with a northern German accent.[35] His wife is charming and cultivated but does not step outside the house; and Miriam comments that "they are both truly good people."[36] When Reshid is pressed by Kingscourt as to whether the Jewish immigration has damaged and ruined the local population and whether they were forced to leave, he replies: "On the contrary . . . Jewish immigration was a blessing for all of us," and "there was nothing more wretched than the Arab village of *fellaheen* at the end of the nineteenth century . . . the children were naked and uncared for, their playground the street. . . . These people are better off than before. They are healthy, they have better food, their children go to school."[37] Reshid therefore concludes that "the Jews brought us health and wealth."[38] It is quite interesting to note that whereas David and the Zionist came to Palestine precisely because they felt themselves to be members of a nation, not merely a religious group, Reshid Bey still views David mainly as someone belonging to another religious group, not to another nationality that claims self-determination and sovereignty: "I had never a better friend among Muslims than I have in David Litwak. . . . He prays in another house to the same God."[39] In this manner the issue becomes an issue of interfaith coexistence between two religious groups for Reshid Bey. While for David the Jewish question is upgraded to a national question, the Arab question is still conceived as one of religion.

The "privatization" of Reshid opens the way to portray him as a friend. Reshid in the novel is a peculiar figure: he has no relatives, no other Arab or Muslim friends, no community, no history, and no connections, and there are no institutions for his own community. He is absolutely atomized and stripped of his context. Yet it is true that Herzl puts words in his mouth that show Reshid's rejection of the claim made by Steineck that Jewish immigration brought civilization to Palestine: "There were oranges before your time," he asserts.[40]

Nationalism, Liberalism, Colonialism

Some Zionist commentators take Herzl to be a liberal, cosmopolitan, multicultural, and secular thinker, open to the Other.[41] It is true one can find many places in the text that point in this direction. We have already seen that, in terms of culture and religion, the new society celebrates plurality: French, Italian, German, and Spanish theaters; people of all nationalities in the streets; Reshid Bey as a welcome guest at most events; and the scene at the Passover evening bringing together the Russian priest Father Ignatius, Reshid Bey, and Litwak, together with Kingscourt and Lowenberg himself, all in a very colorful and multicultural scene. And when Lowenberg and Kingscourt enter Jerusalem on their second visit, Herzl remarks that "a Christian and a Jew went up arm in arm towards the Holy City."[42]

But the issue is not only a matter of culture. Herzl makes arguments on the political level, where he asserts his take on issues of civic equality and his faith in the equal value of human beings. David—who is clearly Herzl's hero—makes the sweeping argument that "neither I nor my friends make the least distinction between one man and another. We do not ask about anyone's race or religion. It is enough for us that he is human."[43] This issue becomes clear during the discussion between David and Mendel, who is a supporter of Gyere—the fanatically Orthodox religious Jew—regarding the admissibility of non-Jews to the new society. David asserts that "it would be unethical for us to exclude any man, whatever his race or religion from our achievements and as such we have to allow him to join our society as long he accepts our duties."[44] Herzl in this debate juxtaposes David and his party to Gyere and the fanatical supporters of exclusivity who do not want Gentiles to be accepted into the new community. Mendel puts the challenge to David and his party when he argues the following: "Who has sweated to reclaim the land? We, who have grubbed up the stones? We, who have drained the swamps, built the canals, planted the trees? We, who have toiled and sweated till it was all done? We, we and again we . . . when we came here there was nothing, absolutely nothing . . . what we have made with our hands must remain ours, and we shall defend it against all comers. That's all I have to say."[45]

While David feels that Mendel spoke in good faith, he still thinks that he is wrong. David agrees with Mendel to a point; were he to be asked, "who created all this within twenty short years, I shall answer like Mendel: We, we, we."[46] Still, he would allow Gentiles—Gentiles in general, not only Arabs—to join the new society for the reason that the Jews stand on the shoulders of other civilizations and make use of the achievements of other nations. David's speech may not convince Herzl's readers; a question remains. If all of this is "ours," and "we" were the ones who established it, then it is not at all clear why others are entitled to be part of it (especially the Arabs). If it is "ours," then what is the status of the others? What is the status of the Arabs? Are they guests? Do they have equal entitlements? There is a tendency in nationalistic discourse in general and globally to become exclusivist and violent. Though this tendency exists in almost every national project, some critics, such as Hannah Arendt, have argued that the Zionist case is more prone from the start to such a deviation.[47] Mendel might not be the necessary outcome of Herzl's idea of establishing a Jewish state in the midst of the Arab population, but he is clearly not an unnatural or unlikely outcome. That does not mean there is no difference between David and Mendel: of course there is a difference in terms of the role of identity politics *after* the Jews have established their own new society and state, but up to and *before* that point, and in the process of establishing the state, David's entire discourse is one of an exclusive nationalist. What is the point of establishing a Jewish state if it is not for the Jews? And how can one be blind to identity within such a process? How can one establish such a state without the radical demographic intervention that settles the Jews and unsettles the Arabs? David's liberalism stops short at this point. There is a difference between Mendel and David, but there is a continuity between them as well.

Even without these questions, David—and, by extension, Herzl—remains unconvincing. One very good reason to question Herzl's liberalism lies in the fact that he himself has already voted no-confidence in Europe, and has become convinced that the ideal of equality is not achievable there. To Herzl, civic equality in Europe was at best an ideal, and this was in part the reason why he opted for a national solution to the Jewish problem instead of a liberal and universal one, based on individual and civic equality: "Universal brotherhood is not even a beautiful dream. Antagonism is essential to man's greatest efforts."[48] This raises the question of whether Herzl was a nationalist in Europe while he wanted to become a liberal in Palestine, or was it the other way around—to be a nationalist now and later on, after achieving the state, a liberal?

Second, it is not clear what the limits of Herzl's liberalism are. What does he mean when he says that anyone may join the new society—"be he Jew or Gentile, white or yellow or black."[49] The entire point of national self-determination in the political sense of statehood and sovereignty is closing the borders to other groups and nationalities, and homogenizing the body politic. Herzl leaves no room for hesitation as to whom this land belongs: "we founded a new society on *our* dear and ancient soil," he says; and in another place, "look, this is the land of *our* fathers."[50] Here lies an unresolved tension in the whole project. Herzl leaves it to the Zionist praxis to solve the quandary. Herzl did not tell us how demographic changes and new realities in Palestine can take place and form; how the old society will be replaced by a new one and what that entails; or what the relation is between the old society and the new one, between the Jews and the Arabs. In the novel, there is a gap of twenty years between the first visit to Palestine and the second visit, a two-decade blindspot, and this gap did not go unnoticed.[51] This gap, I argue, is the condition of possibility for the Jewish state to emerge: the dirty demographic job that still allows Herzl to maintain his surface liberalism.

There is no magic formula that can make this change on behalf of the Zionists; also, there is potential here for conflict with the local Arab population that the Herzlian state concept shies away from dealing with. Herzl seems to be leaving it to later generations, or perhaps hoping for a miracle, although there is enough evidence in his diaries and in the charter that he was considering ways to depopulate Palestine from its Arab inhabitants.[52] In this sense, it is important to read Herzl's text, but it is as important to read his subtext, in the sense of asking what it would take to make Herzl's vision materialize in reality regardless of his intentions, his justifications, or his subconscious. Still, one can have a glimpse into his mind by going back to his diaries: "When we occupy the land, we shall bring immediate benefits to the state that receives us. We must expropriate gently the private property on the estates assigned to us. We shall try to spirit the penniless population across the border by procuring employment for it in the transit countries, while denying it any employment in our country." And then he adds: "Both the process of expropriation and the removal of the poor must be carried out discreetly and circumspectly."[53]

The Power of Myth, Science, and Religion

When it comes to the role of religion in the public life of the Herzlian state, things get a bit ambiguous. On the one hand, Zionism in general and Herzl in particular could be viewed as departing from Judaism as merely a religion. The entire point of Zionism is the new conception of the Jews not only as a religious group but as a national one. Zionism is a rebellion within Judaism in its refusal to leave salvation to God and in its determination to intervene in history again. It should come as little surprise that several Jewish groups and figures made clear statements against the Zionist project, including Herzl's close friend Rabbi Moritz Guedmann.[54] Steineck—an architect in the novel—criticizes the role of rabbis in establishing the new society when he says about Rabbi Geyer: "He read Zion in the prayer book, but he told the sheep who listened that Zion was not Zion. It was anywhere but here, anywhere in the world but not in Zion. . . . Where was your Geyer then? The same Geyer that incites you . . . was one of the protest Rabbis."[55] This is a hint at the passive role of religious groups in establishing the new society as well as to Steineck's position against theocracy.[56]

The new society is supposed to allow freedom of worship for different religions, without religion playing an official role in public life. This being said, one still cannot ignore the messianic language that Herzl deploys here and there in *Altneuland*. The word "God" is deployed more than once in the text. After David mentions at the Passover evening that "we are the descendants of Rabbi Eliezer, Rabbi Yehoshua and Rabbi Eleazar" and that "we have to have the good will of the nations and their rulers," old Litwak adds, "it was God who helped us."[57] After mentioning the "Had Gadya"[58] so as to explain the miracle of establishing the new society again, old Litwak reminds the audience: "And above all is God."[59]

Herzl's "religious" fervor comes out when he describes Lowenberg's second visit to Jerusalem, together with David. They visit the Temple of Jerusalem on a Friday evening. The site itself is "the holy region of mankind." It is clear that the Temple has been rebuilt: "They now have reached the Temple, which had been rebuilt because the time was at hand."[60] For Lowenberg, Jews had wailed for years—clearly not for stones but for something intangible: "And now Frederick felt this intangible was the newly rebuilt Temple of Jerusalem. It glowed within him, making him proud and free. Here within him stood the sons, returned to God's own ancient people and land, and standing on Mount Moriah as their forefathers had done, they lifted up their hearts with him toward the invisible." Lowenberg wonders: Jews used to pray everywhere around the world and "their invisible God, the Omnipresent, must have been near them everywhere. Yet only here was the true temple. Why was that?" Here comes the answer: "Only when the Jews had both freedom and the feeling of community could they rebuild the house of the invisible and almighty God."[61]

Shlomo Avineri does not attribute much religious significance to these paragraphs, and he reads the rebuilding of the Temple rather in national terms. The destruction of the Temple was not only a religious symbol but also a symbol of the destruction of the Jewish kingdom, and as such it bears rather a political and national significance.[62] Avineri can find some support in Herzl's *The Jewish State*: "Faith unites us, knowledge gives us freedom. We shall therefore prevent any theocratic tendencies . . . we shall keep our priests within the confines of their temples. . . . Army and priesthood shall receive honors. . . . But they must not interfere in the administration of the state which confers distinction upon them."[63]

But the issue is not whether the priests or army "interfere" or not. The concept of "interference" assumes a separation of fields and spheres that divides state from religion and state from the military, as if the latter might "interfere" from outside in the former. But the state could be militarized, with the ideology of war and eternal confrontation becoming the dominant ideology until there is no need for the army to "interfere"—it would simply always be there. The same goes for religion. The question is not whether religious groups dominate the state—the question is whether the whole narrative and ideology of the Zionist state is coherent *without* the deployment of religion. As such, the issue is not whether priests and the army interfere, but whether the state could be imagined without religious and military ideology.[64] Why would priests need to interfere in a country where most Jewish citizens think that the Bible is the best proof of their ownership over the land, and why would the army need to interfere if most of the political leaders think that there cannot be a political solution and there is no escape from resort to force as both strategy and ideology? The question is not what Herzl designs for the state but what the state requires for it to exist—what is implied in the notion of the Jewish state. Religion and force are constitutive of the state, not from without but from within, and as such the issue of interference offers a rather limited category of analysis. *Altneuland* ends with a scene of wonder about the new society and "by what was created." While there were several answers offered by many, the last word was given to Rabbi Shemuel who "rose solemnly and said God."[65] In *The Jewish*

State, Herzl already locates the project of the Jewish state within a religious frame when he writes: " 'Next year in Jerusalem' is our old phrase: It is now a question of showing that the dream can be converted into a living reality."[66] What is that if not a political theology?

Again, Herzl is neither the first nor the last European thinker to deploy religion in his national project. The question has to be if there is something unique in the deployment itself that we do not witness in another national or colonial project. I am not able to answer this question in full here. I can only point to two directions to be followed: one is whether the deployment of religion in Zionism is contingent or intrinsic, in the sense that no Jewish nationalism can become thinkable without the deployment of religion. The second direction takes us in the direction of political theology and the question of divine intervention. There is more than one remark in Herzl's texts that the project of the Jewish state is a mad dream, redolent of the myth and fantasy required to solidify and unite the Jewish people in the diaspora. Herzl clearly found a ready-made tool in the shape of the already-existing religious discourse that points easily to the direction of Palestine. But this instrumentality of religion will become something that haunts Zionism: just as Zionism uses religion, religion can use Zionism for its own purposes. The question here is whether there can ever be a way out from this "theological dilemma."[67]

In summary, the Herzlian state and the image of Herzl's "new society" assume two kinds of liquidation: that of Jewish religious life in exile and that of an Arab collective life in Palestine. The negation of exile parallels the negation of the Palestinian Arabs. On the one hand, the establishment of the Herzlian state seemed to be almost an unthinkable dream, a myth. Herzl believed in the power of passion and ideals to move people.[68] For Herzl, dreams are not very different from deeds, as all deeds were once dreams in the minds of their actors. The project of establishing the state, however, is not just a matter of zealous enthusiasm, but rather it is a scientifc project, planned and thought through.[69] The dream and the myth give the passion while science gives the means to carry out the project. Palestine appears like a virgin land or a clean slate. One can plan it, mold it, and apply scientific technology to it. "The true creators of our Old-New Land," David says, "were the hydraulic engineers." He also adds: "Everything in the farm building, the factories, on the paths and in the fields was arranged according to the last word in modern agriculture science."[70] On the other hand there is the sense of newness — acting in a *terra nullius*, without the need to give much weight as to what is already there. This approach does not add to or alter reality but rather breaks with existing civilization, achievements, and culture in Palestine. In many other ways, Herzl's project also breaks away from the lives of the Jews in exile — thus introducing two breaks and two beginnings.[71] David explains the success of the new society this way: "We founded our New Society, so to speak, without any inherited dead weight."[72]

Beginnings have advantages but also disadvantages, as we know from history — they are sometimes associated with violence, ruptures, and revolutions. Science is associated with reason and with the authority of reason. In this regard, Edmund Burke's critique of the French Revolution, with its abstract reasoning and emphasis on newness alongside its disavowal of tradition, cumulative achievements, temperament, moderation, and good sense of judgment, is well in place here — and perfectly valid.[73] But while the French Revolution spoke in the name of universal freedom and equality, Zionism speaks the language of ethnic religious particularism. In many ways, Herzl's Zionism is a vote of no confidence in the ideals of the French Revolution, and as such it is reactionary. It is a revolution and counterrevolution at the same time.

Notes

1. Amos Elon, *Herzl* (Tel Aviv, 1976) [Hebrew], 15. See also Walter Laqueur, *A History of Zionism* (Tel Aviv, 1974) [Hebrew], 51; and David Vital, *The Origins of Zionism* (Tel Aviv, 1978) [Hebrew], 188.

2. Daniel Gutwein, "The Development of Herzl's Theory," in *Theodor Herzl: Visionary of the Jewish State*, eds. Gideon Shimoni and Robert S. Wistrich (Jerusalem, 1999), 80–98.

3. Jacques Kronberg, "The Construction of an Identity," in *Theodor Herzl: Visionary of the Jewish State*, eds. Gideon Shimoni and Robert S. Wistrich (Jerusalem, 1999), 16. See also Shlomo Avineri, *Herzl* (Jerusalem, 2007) [Hebrew], 80.

4. Laqueur, *History of Zionism*, 77.

5. Avineri, *Herzl*, 81. See also Vital, *Origins of Zionism*, 186–87.

6. Moses Hess, "Rome and Jerusalem (1862)," in *The Zionist Idea: A Historical Analysis and Reader*, ed. Arthur Hertzberg (New York, 1969), 116–39.

7. Theodor Herzl, *The Jewish State* (New York: Dover, 1988), 154.

8. Ibid., 154.

9. Avineri, *Herzl*, 82–83.

10. Herzl, *The Jewish State*, 71, 86. Herzl made two generalizations. One (which at other places he withdraws) is that all nations are antisemitic: "the nations in whose midst Jews live are all either covertly or openly anti-Semitic" (ibid., 86). But this would not suffice to turn Herzl into a Zionist. Herzl has a very pessimistic view of the future, as it does not promise a solution: "Can we hope for better days . . . I say we cannot hope for a change. . . ."(ibid., 86); and "I shall even go as far as to ask those Jews who have most earnestly tried to solve the Jewish Question to look upon their attempts as mistaken and futile" (ibid., 71). Herzl is aware of some arguments made by other Jews that a change is "possible by the means of the ultimate perfection of humanity" (ibid., 91). To this Herzl answers: "Is it necessary to point to the sentimental folly of this view?" (ibid.). Those who rely on this, he writes, are "relying on Utopia!" This makes the picture even bleaker: while the question is national, the problem is widespread, so there is no escape in space; no point to look for other places to immigrate to; and nothing to wait or hope for in the future, so there is no escape in time. The 1895 victory of the antisemitic Karl Lueger as mayor of Vienna rendered Herzl's diagnosis more dire.

11. Herzl, *The Jewish State*, 92.

12. Vital, *Origins of Zionism*, 107.

13. Herzl, *The Jewish State*, 92 (italics mine).

14. Avineri, *Herzl*, 79–90. See also Laqueur, *History of Zionism*, 78.

15. Herzl, *The Jewish State*, 122.

16. Laqueur, *History of Zionism*, 41–43.

17. Herzl, *The Jewish State*, 96.

18. Theodor Herzl, *Altneuland* (Haifa, 1964), 26.

19. Edward Said, "Zionism from the Standpoint of Its Victims," *Social Text* no. 1 (Winter 1979): 7, 18, 58. See also Monica O'Brien, "The Politics of Blood and Soil: Hannah Arendt, George Eliot, and the Jewish Question in Modern Europe," *Comparative Literature Studies* 44 (2007): 97–117.

20. George P. Fletcher, "Symposium on Kantian Legal Theory: Law and Morality: A Kantian Perspective," *Columbia Law Review* 87, no. 3 (1987): 533–58.

21. Hannah Arendt, "Zionism Reconsidered," in *Jewish Writings* (New York, 2007), 46.

22. Ze'ev Jabotinsky, "The Iron Wall," in http://www.jabotinsky.org/multimedia/upl_doc /doc_191207_49117.pdf. See also Avi Shlaim, *The Iron Wall: Israel and the Arab World* (New York, 2000).

23. Herzl, *The Jewish State*, 94

24. Herzl, *The Jewish State*, 138.

25. Ella Shohat, "Sephardim in Israel: Zionism from the Standpoint of Its Jewish Victims," *Social Text* nos. 19–20 (Autumn 1988): 1–35.

26. Herzl, *The Jewish State*, 112.

27. Ibid., 127–28.

28. Ibid., 103.

29. For further insight see Raef Zreik, "The Persistence of the Exception: Some Remarks on the Story of Israeli Constitutionalism," in *Thinking Palestine*, ed. Ronit Lentin (London and New York, 2008), 131–47.

30. Herzl, *Altneuland*, 31–35.

31. Ibid., 44–48.

32. Ibid., 64.

33. Ibid., 182.

34. Shlomo Avineri, "Herzl's Zionist Utopia," in *Cathedra: For the History of Eretz Israel and Its Yishuv* 40 (1986): 194.

35. Herzl, *Altneuland*, 54.

36. Ibid., 75.

37. Ibid., 95.

38. Ibid., 100.

39. Ibid.

40. Ibid., 94.

41. Ibid., 155. See also Anita Shapira, "Herzl, Ahad Ha-'Am, and Berdichevsky: Comments on Their Nationalist Concepts," *Jewish History* 4, no. 2 (1990): 59–69; and Laqueur, *History of Zionism*, 111.

42. Herzl, *Altneuland*, 33.

43. Ibid., 53.

44. Ibid.

45. Ibid., 109–10.

46. Ibid., 112.

47. Arendt, "Zionism Reconsidered," 343–74.

48. Herzl, *The Jewish State*, 153.

49. Herzl, *Altneuland*, 109.

50. Ibid., 52 and 54, respectively; italics mine.

51. Muhammad Khalidi, "Utopian Zionism or Zionist Proselytism? A Reading of Herzl's *Altneuland*," *Journal of Palestine Studies* 30 (2001): 55–67.

52. Ibid., 59, see also Shapira, "Herzl, Ahad Ha-'Am, and Berdichevsky," 61.

53. Theodor Herzl, *The Complete Diaries of Theodor Herzl*, ed. Raphael Patai, vol. 1 (New York, 1960), 88–90.

54. Avineri, *Herzl*, 100.

55. Herzl, *Altneuland*, 108.

56. Laqueur, *History of Zionism*, 81.

57. Herzl, *Altneuland*, 145.

58. "Had Gadya" ("One kid") is an Aramaic song that is recited at the conclusion of the Seder service, held on the first two evenings of the Passover (Pesah) festival in Jewish households. The kid symbolizes the Hebrew nation. According to the dominant interpretation, the song's legend illustrates how the people of Israel were for centuries oppressed and persecuted by all the nations of antiquity, how the oppressors all perished one by one, and how Israel, the oppressed, survived ("Had Gadya," JewishEncyclopedia.com, http://www.jewishencyclopedia.com/articles/6998 -had-gadya). The poem of Had Gadya, which on many levels reflects the idea of redemption, closes the Pesah Seder because it is written in Aramaic, a language that is not understood by the angels, only by God. Therefore even Had Gadya's language stresses that God alone can hear our pleas and deliver us into redemption (Kenneth Brander, "An Analysis of Had Gadya," *Journal of Jewish Music and Liturgy* 17 (1994): 17). The Israeli poet Yehuda Amichai coined the phrase "the terrible Had Gadya machine" to symbolize the vicious cycle of killing of the Middle East peoples ("Had Gadya," in *The Encyclopedia of Jewish Symbols*, eds. Ellen Frankel and Betsy Platkin Teutsch [Lanham, MD, 1992], 66).

59. Ibid., 156.

60. Ibid., 182 and 186.

61. Ibid., 188–89.

62. Avineri, *Herzl*, 167.

63. Herzl, *The Jewish State*, 146.

64. Jacqueline Rose, *The Question of Zion* (Princeton, 2007).

65. Herzl, *Altneuland*, 217.

66. Herzl, *The Jewish State*, 82.

67. Menachem Friedman, "The State of Israel as a Theological Dilemma," in *The Israeli State and Society: Boundaries and Frontiers*, ed. Baruch Kimmerling (Albany, 1989), 165–215.

68. Avineri, *Herzl*, 98. See also Aleksander Bein, *Theodor Herzl: A Biography* (London, 1957), 98.

69. Jeremy Stolow, "Utopia and Geopolitics in Theodor Herzl's Altneuland," *Utopian Studies* 8 (1997): 55–76.

70. Herzl, *Altneuland*, 175.

71. Eyal Chowers, *The Political Philosophy of Zionism: Trading Jewish Words for a Hebraic Land* (Cambridge, 2012), 109–15 and 142–48.

72. Herzl, *Altneuland*, 60.

73. See Edmund Burke, *Reflections on the Revolution in France*, ed. (with Introduction and notes) John G. A. Pocock (Indianapolis/Cambridge, 1790[1987]).

5

Simon Dubnow (1860–1941)
RELUCTANT SECULARISM

Dan Diner

TRANSLATED BY JEREMY GAINES

SIMON DUBNOW IS ONE OF THE MOST EMBLEMATIC FIGURES IN JEWISH HISTORIOG-raphy. Born in 1860 in the Belarusian town of Mstislavl to a traditional Jewish family, he was brought up and educated in the reform period during the reign of Czar Alexander II, which may explain the strong Maskilic leanings in his thought. However, quite notably for Jews of his generation in that time, the essence of Dubnow's outlook changed on several occasions. Starting as an adherent of common Jewish learning, he then became an advocate of Russian acculturation and later moved on to champion a culturally and nationally tinged understanding of the Jews as a people through history.[1] Though cut short by his murder at the hands of the German Nazis in Riga in 1941, his life and work span the period of Eastern European Jewry's access into modernity and its ultimate crisis—namely, from the promise of emancipation to the eve of destruction.[2] Dubnow's ideas express both intellectually and politically a diasporic version of Jewish nationhood, transforming the features of premodern autonomy into internationally enshrined minority rights.[3]

Simon Dubnow's thinking is situated on the threshold between the traditional and the modern, reflecting the passage from one world of ideas to another. His oeuvre contains historical notions still imbued with religious meaning along with increasingly secular ones. The following discussion seeks to highlight this straddling position as it is of utmost significance for his work as a scholar. The central issue is the attribution of a collective identity to the Jews or, more precisely, the semantics of the historical Jewish narrative that come into effect in Dubnow's work, particularly in the changing nomenclature for the historical subject of Jewish narrative—the Jewish people. Taking such a pronounced semantic focus is vital precisely because Dubnow was not only a key figure within the Jewish world—as a historian on the threshold between tradition and modernity—but also because he left a mark as a public figure in Jewish politics in an epoch of transition from multinational empires to ethnically homogenizing nation-states. For Dubnow, then, academic historiography and committed public work went hand in glove, whereas the quality of the Jewish collective manifests itself in three ways: as a transhistorical, religious People of God; as an ethnic and religious diasporic nation; and as a national and cultural minority to be safeguarded by international legal requirements. An additional factor, obviously, is the political moment of Dubnow's oeuvre. He completed his ten-volume *World History of the Jewish People* in the crisis years between the wars, and it was first published in German in the 1920s. It offered specially to German Jews, caught in the maelstrom of Nazi discrimination and persecution in the 1930s, a corpus of historical education, meaning, and collective identification. Thus Dubnow's work became a textual icon of the restoration of their Jewish belonging in dark times.

No less a person than political philosopher Hannah Arendt addressed Dubnow's significance for the Jews' postassimilatory collective transformation during those years of tightening crisis. Her take on the nomenclatures of collective affiliation, in particular the collective designation of the Jews as kinsfolk, a "Jewish people," a term she began to employ increasingly as of the mid-1930s, hinged on two intrinsic meanings: first, the deterioration in guarantees for the protection of individual citizens, a problem that she later addressed outstandingly in the chapter titled "The Perplexities of the Rights of Man" in *Origins of Totalitarianism*; and, second, the decay of the minority regime that guaranteed collective rights (that is, group-rights), which had been internationally protected by the League of Nations. That was alluded to in a letter dated January 1940 and addressed to the lawyer Erich Cohn-Bendit who, just like Hannah Arendt, had relocated to Paris in 1933.[4] However, it is not this predecessor text to Arendt's attention-getting piece on the perplexities of human rights that is of further interest. Rather, it is my intention here to highlight a minor remark of Arendt to be found in that very piece, where she focuses on the culmination at that time of the endemic phenomenon of refugees and statelessness. In that compelling context, she mentions the name of Simon Dubnow, albeit marginally, in a note.[5] Her words contain an instructive reference, however, as they indicate that Arendt associated Dubnow (with whose work she was apparently only vaguely familiar) with what emerged for her as being of the utmost importance, namely, the strong assumption that the Jews were a people—a nation—and a community striving to express itself politically. In any case, she was evidently very impressed by this discovery.

With catastrophe on the horizon, a semantic transformation ensued among German Jews who, because of their emancipation, had felt themselves to be German and fully accepted as German citizens. They began to regard themselves instead as members of a Jewish collective. Thus the "Jewish people," canonized in Dubnow's historiography, would have felt this imposed change in their sense of belonging far more keenly if Dubnow's magnum opus had been conveyed to them in its Hebrew translation.

The first volume of the Hebrew translation of Dubnow's Jewish history was published in 1929 by the D'vir publishing house (then based in Berlin), and the final volume about a decade later among the Yishuv, the Jewish population in British Palestine. The choice of wording for the Hebrew title expresses the sheer semantic power of the argument throughout the work: *Divrei yemei am olam* (The holy chronicles of the eternal people). With the emblematic thrust of the Hebrew title, Dubnow's supposedly secular and national interpretation of the history of the Jews

has a concealed religious twist. This was achieved not only by avoiding the profane loanword *historia*, which is generally used in modern Hebrew, but also by calling to mind the biblical allusion of *divrei yamim*, "the words of the days"—the "holy chronicles," as it were. The essential significance underlying the transformation of the coding from a secular into a religious context through the translation of German (and Russian in the original) into Hebrew can be gleaned from the rendering of the word *Welt* (world) as *olam* (world, eternity). The latter word contains a double meaning: it signifies the "world" in both spatial and temporal terms, that is, the "world" and "eternity." Such a duality in meaning sheds light on a deeply rooted ambiguity in Dubnow's historical writing: it vacillates between the religious, as embedded in tradition, and his secular intent for transformation into a profane historical form.[6]

Language: Hegelian Concepts of "World" and the Power of Names

On closer inspection, we can expect secular words and concepts to be less worldly than commonly considered. This applies to the concept of *Weltgeschichte*, which so obviously has secular connotations. Translated into English, it would retain its descriptive, literal meaning of "world history." For Dubnow, too, it could have signified the topographical, spatial meaning of the world as the universal space for Jewish diasporic existence—its material extension, as he often claimed. A closer look at the semantic meaning of the term and its German tradition, however, could lead us to a quite different significance. Emanating from the Hegelian legacy, or rather from Hegel's conception anchored in "The Philosophy of World History," the term clearly entails the manner of the world spirit's genesis and its forward-directed movement toward freedom, which was later distilled by some of his followers into the concepts of progress and its imperatives. Conceptually derived from patterns of *Heilsgeschichte*, of salvific history, as it were, in line with Karl Löwith's later interpretation,[7] the term implies God's hidden intention, paradoxically clad in the garb of profane design.[8] The term *Weltgeschichte* thus found its way into the iconic aphorism, coined by Friedrich Schiller: "Die Weltgeschichte ist das Weltgericht"[9]— merging the notion of world history with that of Judgment Day.

The term *Weltgeschichte* is deeply steeped in the Hegelian tradition. Its appearance in Dubnow's historical compendium, *Weltgeschichte des jüdischen Volkes*, can be traced back to his familiarity with Russian Jewish social philosopher David Koigen, who advised the historian to make use of that very term.[10] Koigen had arrived in Berlin at the same time as Dubnow. Both were fleeing the Bolsheviks—Dubnow from Petrograd, Koigen from Kiev. In early 1920s Berlin, Koigen published a magazine named *Ethos* as a mouthpiece for his theory of the so-called cultural act, or the cultural self-definition of human beings. Its immersion in Hegelian thought becomes evident from Koigen's own intellectual concern with the Young Hegelians, whom he studied intensively at the fin de siècle—Bruno Bauer, Ludwig Feuerbach, Moses Hess, Karl Marx, and others.[11] David Koigen's orientation was evidently directed to an uncompromising universalism, yet one that was dressed up in Jewish garb.[12]

The choice of the Hebrew title *Divrei yemei am olam*, however, might have been prompted by the intention to create a Jewish counterpart to offset the concealed

Christian roots of the Hegelian nomenclature both at the level of historical thought and in conceptual and metaphorical terms. One can perhaps discern Chaim Nachman Bialik's influence behind the religiously charged Hebrew words that make up the title. After all, Bialik was the editor of D'vir, the publisher of Dubnow's Hebrew edition of *Weltgeschichte*—and Bialik had kept a close eye over the translation. Indeed, it had been Bialik who, years earlier, in 1913, had claimed in an article in the Odessa monthly *Hashiloach* that Jewish authenticity can only be expressed properly in the Hebrew language.

Simon Dubnow—as Shmuel Werses has shown by quoting Baruch Krupnik (Karu), Dubnow's translator into Hebrew[13]—was himself deeply involved in the act of translation. Indeed, Dubnow aspired fervently to ensure that the Hebrew terms used were as ancient, as original, and as accurate as possible. Here Dubnow, the self-proclaimed nationally identified and secular Jew, affirms the reluctant insight put forward at precisely that time by Gershom Scholem in his notoriously emblematic letter of 1926 to Franz Rosenzweig. In his letter, Scholem discussed his intended profane use of the Hebrew language and its hidden sacred imprint—namely, that the language had an "apocalyptic thorn," as Scholem put it.[14] In the original German version of the letter, Scholem proposed: "Sprache ist Namen. Im Namen ist die Macht der Sprache beschlossen, ist ihr Abgrund versiegelt" (Language is Name. In the names, the power of language is enclosed; in them, its abyss is sealed).[15] Such a seal might have been Bialik's purpose in transforming or rather emblematically converting Dubnow's German *Weltgeschichte* into the Hebrew *Divrei yemei am olam*.

Over and above that emblematic transformation of a foundational text of modern Jewish self-awareness into a language imbued with sacred meaning, the choice probably further discloses an insightful view on a semantic undertone that was already ubiquitous in Dubnow's historical oeuvre—an undertone particularly reflected in his use of the notion of nation as a collectivity and a people. It can likewise be detected in the historical concepts evoking the question as to the scope and limit of secular terminologies and the profane in texts masquerading as historical writing—its inherently theological-political moment, as it were. The question of language, of semantics and their proper meaning, is persistently present in Dubnow's historical writings. And the variety of languages that find their way into his oeuvre is legion. Dubnow, who had written his major works in Russian (with the important exception of his *History of Chassidism*, written in Hebrew), went on to master several more languages, and he closely monitored the process of translation. Still, his command of the process of translation didn't prevent the intrusion of historical terms, or concepts rooted in different historical cultures, from imposing their meaning on his proper oeuvre.

Historical Concepts, the Meanings of "Nation," and the Process of Secularization

Historical concepts are charged with a multitude of meanings. In the modern form of writing about history, which describes and interprets social and political life in a narrative mode, one of the most constitutive concepts is the historical subject known as a "people" or a "nation." This concept is semantically highly ambiguous, and the linguistic trajectory is highly complex. It becomes even more complex and compounded in the case of the Jews—a diasporic population, existing outside of a territory and endowed with a long, liturgically infused collective memory. In the realm of Imperial Russia, particularly in the Pale of Settlement, where the bulk of the Jewish population was most densely gathered, the modes of transformation from a religiously regulated to a more ethnically driven collective consciousness—from the meaning of *am Ysrael* (the people of Israel) to that of *ha-am hayehudi* (the Jewish people)—reshaped emblems of belonging and led to semantic changes. Generally this process culminated in a concept of nationhood where the old, traditional, liturgical understanding of the Jewish people melded with the timely notion of Jewish collectivity.

The person and oeuvre of Simon Dubnow is not least a medium of this secularizing transformation of Jewish self-perception and its canonization as history—and indeed, this was the role that Dubnow assigned himself. It is well expressed in his various theoretical and methodological deliberations as well as in his practical advice on the craft of writing Jewish history and its unique sources. It becomes most evident in his early programmatic piece "Let Us Seek and Investigate" (*nahpesa venahkora*), written in Odessa in 1891/1892, the very time of Heinrich Graetz's death, and published in an extended Hebrew version in the journal *Ha-pardes*.[16] In his lifelong, titanic scholarly effort, Dubnow set out to overcome the dichotomy between the premodern Jewish categories, concepts, and semantics, and those of a nascent modernity. This dichotomy was by and large the result of the secularization of lifeworlds and the profanation of text culture. The Jews, who in traditional society lived literally by strictly religious interpretation of a legal text, entered a different world offered by the construction of a mode of crafting meaning referred to as "history." Dubnow proceeded along that universal transformation while generating his eminent synthesis established in his *Essays on Old and New Judaism*[17]—resulting in the novel concept of "historical consciousness."[18] Historical consciousness per se, and definitely not territory, becomes the essence of Jewish collectivity, which is thus, in Dubnow's words, defined as a "spiritual nation" (*nazia tuchovnaya*).[19] The project of that transformation is fulfilled by the historian's mission—a "holy duty," in his words.[20]

Essential to his considerations on the concept of the "Jewish nation" was the traditional institution of community, henceforth secularized—a *kahal* stripped of its previous character based on religious law. *Di heylike kehile* (Yiddish for "the holy community") became conceptually transformed into a secular and culturally anchored *evreiskaya obscina* (Russian for "Jewish community")—the grounding institution, the nucleus of an autonomous, nonterritorial Jewish nation.

The notion of "nation," however, remains highly blurred during this period of upheaval, and stays especially blurred in the Jewish case and in Jewish consciousness from the very outset of its emergence at the threshold from premodernity to modernity, molding the liturgical meaning it embraces with recently emerging terminologies.

The terminological complexity of the concept in the Jewish case in particular is perhaps best exemplified by a highly significant semantic misunderstanding, deeply anchored in common Jewish memory. It focuses on the notorious statement by Count Stanislaus Clermont-Tonnere at the French National Assembly in December 1789, announcing that as citizens, Jews should be granted everything, but as a nation, nothing: "Il faut tout refuser aux Juifs comme nation et tout leur accorder comme individus."[21] In the commonly accepted Jewish understanding of that iconic speech—and especially in Jewish collective memory—it is remembered as a presumptuous rejection of the very understanding of Jewish collectivity. This may have been true to a degree; however, such a perception distorts the contextually bound meaning of Clermont-Tonnere's words. This distortion evokes the complexities of fundamental concepts of collective belonging and their shifts from premodern to modern meanings.

In the days of the French Revolution, in 1789, *nation* (in Latin, *natio/nationes*) was still conceived as an institutional constituent of traditional social order based on estates—a corporation. Not until the revolutionary wars some years later did the concept of nation undergo a change in meaning, directed at the unifying trinity of people, territory, and regime. In Clermont-Tonnerre's speech on the "nation" of the Jews, he obviously referred solely to their status as a corporation. The French Revolution hinges on the idea that the premodern world of corporations (all corporations, without exception) had to be abolished, together with the bulk of associated privileges. This was the principal goal of the French Revolution. Clermont-Tonnerre's iconic sentence on the Jews therefore has to be read as follows: "They should not be allowed to form either a political body or an order within the state." This demand admittedly sealed the fate of premodern Jewish autonomy, which was already declining and eroding at differing velocities under the late absolutist regimes farther to the east.

However, what should supplant that old decaying autonomy—based on the rule of a corporate, vertical hierarchy—that was commensurate with a social and political system that was now horizontally arranged? The emerging fundamental issue of the modernizing world that undermined the ancien régime in general and the Jewish corporate order in particular formed Dubnow's launchpad as a historian and political educator. He set about constructing a historically grounded concept of a Jewish nation against the backdrop of both a forfeited premodern autonomy and the largely hindered—and at best hampered—prospects of civil equality in Imperial Russia. Within this experiential framework, Dubnow embarked on his historiographic enterprise of defining a nonterritorial corporate body infused by emblems of ethnicity, of origin—of *Volk*, as it were. From that paradigm, he proceeded to outline an interpretation of the entire history of the Jews down through the ages and to wed it to a political vision of the future of the Jewish people and its diasporic existence. This he based on the Jews' legally enshrined status as a national-cultural minority based on the idea of group rights and, if possible, enshrined and protected by international law.

Parallel Realities: Transforming Semantics, Semantics of Transformation

The process of transforming the People of Israel (*am Ysrael*), which was largely steeped in religious connotations, into a secularizing collective embodied in the notion of the Jewish people (*ha'am ha-yehudi*) had in fact started long before Dubnow's appearance on the historiographical stage. The secularization—and to some extent, while located farther west, the individualization and confessionalization of

Jewish self-understanding and self-awareness—was indeed advanced by the systematic attempt to give the Jewish culture of the text quasi-profane roots, as practiced by the followers of the *Wissenschaft des Judentums* (Science of Judaism).[22] Leopold Zunz offers a deep insight into the modes of such an alteration. In his essay "Etwas über die rabbinische Literatur" (1818),[23] he set out to transform the traditional Jewish discourse commonly known as "rabbinical literature" into a new textual future, classifying it as "modern Hebrew or Jewish literature." Quite apart from the fact that the concept of "literature" applied here was adopted from the Christian Hebraist tradition, the meaning of the text has become secularized as well. For example, he takes the traditional image of the oil lamp burning for seven days in the Temple, and in the course of the same sentence (in the same breath, as it were) transposes it into the illumination called for by Enlightenment.[24] The imagery of the miracle is taken and mapped anew as a metaphor in the entirely secular world of knowledge. This helped pave the way for the metaphorical transformation of God's finger into the invisible hand, of religious law into profane history.

In his free-thinking years (more precisely, in 1884), Dubnow performed a metaphorical transformation similar to that of Zunz, evoking the parallel existing worlds of Old and New Judaism autobiographically as he compared his grandfather Benzion orally passing on the wisdom of the Talmud and the rabbis to his listeners with Shimen, the grandson, disseminating knowledge to a large audience in writing and by means of the printing press.[25] During those days the wisdom of the Talmud and the knowledge of the young historian were still antipodes in Dubnow's thinking, still Old versus New Judaism.

Less than ten years later the young Dubnow embarked on his ultimate task, namely, synthesizing the two. Actually, he was pursuing the pioneering secularizing thrust of the Science of Judaism, amply reflected in historicizing form in the work of Heinrich Graetz, author of the eleven-volume *Geschichte der Juden: Von den ältesten Zeiten bis auf die Gegenwart* (History of the Jews from the earliest times to the present day). Dubnow set himself apart from the old master historian by relying to a lesser extent *on* the Jewish text and hermeneutics than on the traces of social life left on the margins *of* the text—this was his "sociological conception" of history.[26] In his own words, the project was to secularize religion by embedding it in the idea of the nation.[27]

The idea of a sociological conception of history is not easy to grasp—especially as regards the historical semantics associated with it. Actually, what Dubnow intended was a stance that would enable him to distance himself from the religious, ritual, liturgical, and thus *traditional* meaning of the sacred text—and instead to edge toward addressing its significance as an inventory of the past, informing the historian about the Jews' social, political, and institutional *lifeworlds*. Profane knowledge, inscribed "with a pen of iron and lead" (Job 19:24) in the *pinkassim*, the community registers, became the historian's object of interest, more so than the holy wisdom written traditionally with a goose quill.[28] The information about social life culled from the *pinkas*, however, reflects a form of life still regulated by the holy *kehile* (community) and its semiological worlds, a life still steeped in highly liturgical imagery. Dubnow himself depicted the *pinkas* in a language reminiscent of the description of a relic that cultivates the quality of palimpsest by means of writing, rewriting, and overwriting. And since it is often stored in the *geniza*, the text is impregnated by the aura of the sacred, preserving the past for eternity. In the days of the transition from tradition to modernity, eternity loses its hold on the people, and to this extent it becomes the historian's "holy duty," or so Dubnow claimed, to preserve the remnants of traditional wisdom while converting them into historical knowledge.[29] Not to do so would mean, to quote Dubnow, to "sin against history."[30] Paradoxically or not, the sacred becomes preserved by and in the profane.

For all the claims of secularization, of sociology and the application of social semantics in the construction of the historical imaginary, the contours of the biblical narrative can be sensed at the edges of Dubnow's historical writing, mobilizing religious metaphors that resurface in his discourse. Pharaoh, Amalek, Haman, Chmelnitzky, and other liturgical as well as historically emblematic figures[31] find their counterparts in later events, evoking a cyclical image of history. The early Dubnow—cosmopolitan, or more precisely "heretic" (*apikorsik*) in outlook—cast the religious safeguards aside in line with his guides Auguste Comte and John Stuart Mill,[32] and he identified himself with Baruch Spinoza.[33] In his later, more mature phase he remained firmly in the grip of that hybrid composition so significant to a Jewish conception of belonging in the Enlightened world—that mesh of old and new, of tradition and modernity, of religion and nation. This hybridity can also be read in the features of the semantics ascribed to the Jewish collective singular, which sprang from the secularizing and profaning transformations of the "People of Israel" into the "Jewish people." This semantic also permeates the conceptual domain, guiding historical inquiry. While a liturgical meaning is the primary signification of the "People of Israel," the nomenclature of the "Jewish people" verges on an ethnic dimension prompted by secularization that nevertheless does not entirely break free of the religious semantic connotations. Dubnow's programmatic article "Let Us Seek and Investigate"[34] (note that this was his "spiritual testament," or so he himself said) offers a deep insight into the early emergence of his semantic world, especially the way a nomenclature steeped in religious terminology became bound up with modes of a highly modern speech, in particular when notions of collective belonging were evoked.[35]

Dubnow opens his fundamental text by evoking Grandfather Israel, *yisrael saba* (Midrash Bereshit Rabba), and continues with the People of Israel (*am Yisrael*), the House of Israel (*beit Yisrael*), and the Children of Israel (*bnei Yisrael*).[36] Dubnow admittedly inherited the foundational prerequisites for constructing the Jewish nation from Ernest Renan, adapting them to the case of the Jews along with the three stages of emergence of collective belonging—*regesh ha-mishpaah* (the sense of family), *regesh ha-emunah* (the sense of belief), and *regesh ha-historiah* (the sense of history).[37] Possibly the most important element of Renan's understanding of a nation, as put forward in his famous lecture at the Sorbonne in March 1882 with the emblematic title "Qu'est-ce qu' une nation?" (What Is a Nation?), was its subjective core as enshrined in Renan's concept of the *plebiscite de tous le jour* (the daily, constant political consensus), something Dubnow omits in his usage of Renan's terms.[38] Indeed, the Jewish nation is, according to Dubnow, not political; it is spiritual by definition—a *nazia tuchovnaya*. And however profane its spiritual self-understanding may be, it remains bound to the sacred, irrespective of how close the bond is.

"Social History": Labeling a Sacred Language, Popularizing a Profane Telos

Under the auspices of modernity the sacred remains hidden, encoded, but it is nevertheless present. Its emblems can be detected in semantics that have apparently been completely secularized. Such a tendency can be discerned when examining the evolution of Dubnow's "sociological" approach in the realm of social history more closely. Social semantics, highly related to the zeitgeist at the turn of the twentieth century, strongly penetrate historical writing in the interwar period, with the consequence that the category "the people" was increasingly tinged by the signs of social class. This can be detected in both manifestations of the Jewish left—in Bundist political rhetoric as well as in the Poalist (Labour Socialist) tendencies in Zionism. The concept of the people had become injected with a strong popular meaning.

A conspicuous example of the ongoing dynamics of semantic transformation with the multifaceted concept of the people at its core can be found in the writings of historian Raphael Mahler, one of Dubnow's most outstanding students. As a member of the left Yiddishist Poale Zion and, later, a committed Marxist, he was engaged in a semantic focusing of the concept of the people while simultaneously preserving the basis of Jewish collectivity. By alluding to traditional patterns of the common Jewish conflict over acculturation, Mahler juxtaposes the higher classes (the "bourgeoisie") and their assimilatory and individualist habits with the lower classes (the simple people) and their enduring loyalty to tradition. The latter he describes as the true and thus unspoiled vessel of the nation.[39]

The Bund, however, though Jewish and Yiddishist in stance and self-awareness, laid claim to universal class solidarity over and above collective Jewish constraints as reflected in the notion of the Jewish people. That concept was emerging in the 1880s, apparently suggesting that "the Jewish people" in its modern, more ethnically connoted meaning of *am yehudi* (Jewish people) might have forfeited its previous all-embracing capacity formerly enshrined in the notion of *am Yisrael* (people of Israel). This was probably of particular importance most especially for the Orthodoxy, which was taking on new forms at that time and moving more toward self-awareness as a *confessio* while applying the term *klal Yisrael* to denote its strictly law-observant public, the "Torah-true" Jews.

The increasingly evident differentiation in the meaning of "the Jewish people" reached an interesting juncture in the key year 1897 with the founding of the Bund in Vilna, the convention of the First Zionist Congress in Basel, and the beginning of publication in the journal *Voskhod* of Dubnow's "Letters on Old and New Judaism," which formed the historiographic foundations for a Jewish autonomist, kahalistic-diasporic orientation based on a notion of the Jewish nation and championed by Dubnow as a public figure and historian. In contrast to the Zionist wish to territorialize and the Bundist intention of addressing the so-called Jewish question in a socialist as well as general context, the autonomist orientation relied on guarantees enshrined in the rule of law, founded at best in a liberal order. However, in the wake of World War I, multinational empires collapsed and myriads of nation-states arose, stripping the idea underpinning the autonomist project of its historical multireligious, multiethnic, and multicultural foundations. The only gleam of hope was the minority-rights regime enshrined in the Paris peace treaties.[40] Those rights evinced a number of features analogous to Dubnow's concept of autonomy. But in no case were they meant to grant institutional assurances that could be construed as outlining a scheme of nationality rights, independent of majority-minority ratios, as envisioned in the political agenda put forward by the Austro-Marxists in the days of the monarchy. Read in terms of those ideas, the 1919 minority protection legislation enacted by the League of Nations was only a feeble shadow of what could have been. After all, in some places, such as Lithuania, it proved possible to establish an exemplary Jewish educational system. During his short stay in Kovno in 1922 en route to Berlin, Dubnow was truly impressed by the Jewish institutions he encountered there, possibly a harbinger of things to come, the cradle of a reborn Jewish autonomy.[41]

In Geneva

The League of Nations' approach to dealing with minorities was doomed to failure, and so was the concept of a Jewish nonterritorial autonomy that Dubnow had advocated. In any event, attempts by the political historian to champion a Jewish concept of nation and nationhood beyond mere religion, on the one hand, and a territorially confined nation-state, on the other, bore no fruit. The 1927 Zurich Conference on the Protection of Jewish Rights, an attempt to establish a World Jewish Congress, evoked the notorious controversy between the adherents of the Jewish nation (among them Dubnow), who demanded common Jewish action to safeguard Jewish national rights, and Western Jewish notables as proponents of individual emancipation based on citizenship, who rejected collective Jewish claims. Dubnow ridiculed that understanding as the old politics of assimilation had proven abortive, claiming that the national idea would eventually emerge victorious.[42] As we know in retrospect, such optimism was to be ferociously repudiated by things to come. However, in 1936, when the ultimate Jewish catastrophe in Europe was still not in sight, from his newly established home in Kaiserwald, a Riga neighborhood, Dubnow sent an address to the World Jewish Congress at its founding meeting at Geneva, welcoming its establishment. As a diasporic body, it intended to represent the Jews in their entirety.[43] But what transpired after 1939, and intensified from 1941 onward, was beyond the wildest imagination of all—autonomists, Bundists, traditional and "Torah-true" Jews, and Palestine-centered Zionists.[44] Dubnow's prophecy of the "victory of the national idea" was to come true, albeit in a very different way than he had intended. As a consequence of the catastrophe, and due to the phenomenon of heirless Jewish assets and property resulting from the genocide, a Jewish collective claim had to be raised.[45] That claim could only be made by a subject legally recognized under public international law. In the interwar period, primarily Jewish legal activists of Lithuanian extraction (such as Jacob and Nehemia Robinson), following by and large Dubnow's project of autonomy in the guise of minority rights, championed the construction of a legal entity that could raise collective claims in the name of the Jewish people—both in their writing and in their political commitment as Jewish civil servants of an international Jewish body politic in the framework of the World Jewish Congress.

Hannah Arendt participated in the 1936 Geneva founding conference of the World Jewish Congress, which arose from the *comité des délégations juives*. In

1940, she expressed in her letter to Erich Cohn-Bendit in Paris her joyful support for Dubnow's historiographical construction of a Jewish people—nay, a Jewish *nation*.[46] Later, after the catastrophe, she was paradoxically to provide through her very critique of universal human rights, in the absence of a means of enforcing them, a strong universal rationale for a Jewish collective claim.

Notes

1. See Victor E. Kelner, "Nation der Gegenwart—Simon Dubnow über jüdische Politik und Geschichte,", in *Simon Dubnow Institute Yearbook II*, ed. Dan Diner (Stuttgart and Munich, 2003), 519–44; Jeffrey Veidlinger, "Simon Dubnow Recontextualized: The Sociological Conception of Jewish History and the Russian Intellectual Legacy," in *Simon Dubnow Institute Yearbook III*, ed. Dan Diner (Göttingen, 2004), 411–27.

2. See Anke Hilbrenner and Nicolas Berg, "Der Tod Simon Dubnows in Riga 1941—Quellen, Zeugnisse, Erinnerungen," in *Simon Dubnow Institute Yearbook I*, ed. Dan Diner (Stuttgart and Munich, 2002), 457–72; Grit Jilek, "'Alle Wege sind mir versperrt'—Simon Dubnows Brief aus Riga, März 1941," in *Simon Dubnow Institute Yearbook VI*, ed. Dan Diner (Göttingen, 2007), 339–59.

3. See Anke Hilbrenner, "Diaspora-Nationalismus: Zur Geschichtskonstruktion Simon Dubnows," in *Schriften des Simon-Dubnow-Instituts*, vol. 7 (Göttingen, 2006).

4. Hannah Arendt, "The Minority Question (Copied from a Letter to Erich Cohn-Bendit, Summer 1940)," in *The Jewish Writings*, eds. Jerome Kohn and Ron Feldman (New York, 2007), 125–33.

5. See Arendt, "Minority Question," 126.

6. See Dan Diner, "Ambiguous Semantics: Reflections on Jewish Political Concepts," in *Jewish Quarerly Review* 98, no. 1 (Winter 2008): 89–102.

7. See Karl Löwith, *Meaning in History* (Chicago, 1949), 1–19, 52–59.

8. See Reinhart Koselleck, "Geschichte—V. Die Herausbildung des modernen Geschichtsbegriffs," in *Geschichtliche Grundbegriffe*, eds. Otto Brunner, Werner Conze, and Reinhart Koselleck, vol. 2, *E–G* (Stuttgart, 1994), 647–91; here 682–86.

9. Friedrich Friedrich Schiller, "Resignation," in *Werke und Briefe in zwölf Bänden*, vol. 1, *Gedichte* (Frankfurt, 1992), 168–71; here 171.

10. See Simon Dubnow, *Buch des Lebens*, vol. 3, *1922–1933*, ed. Verena Dohrn and trans. Vera Bischitzky (Göttingen, 2005), 93–94; Viktor E. Kelner, *Simon Dubnow: Eine Biographie*, trans. Martin Arndt (Göttingen, 2010), 475.

11. See David Koigen, *Zur Vorgeschichte des modernen philosophischen Socialismus in Deutschland: Zur Geschichte der Philosophie und Socialphilosophie des Junghegelianismus*, Berner Studien zur Philosophie und ihrer Geschichte 26 (Bern, 1901).

12. See David Koigen, *Der moralische Gott: Eine Abhandlung über die Beziehungen zwischen Kultur und Religion* (Berlin, 1922); *Das Haus Israel: Aus den Schriften von David Koigen*, Bücherei des Schocken-Verlages 8 (Berlin, 1934); Martina Urban, "Religion of Reason Revised: David Koigen on the Jewish Ethos," *Journal of Jewish Thought and Philosophy* 16, no. 1 (2008): 59–89.

13. See Shmuel Werses, "Simon Dubnov Finds His Way through the Language Labyrinth" [Hebrew], in *Writer and Warrior: Simon Dubnov, Historian and Public Figure*, eds. Avraham Greenbaum, Israel Bartal, and Dan Hartuv (Jerusalem, 2010), 87–114; here 107.

14. Gershom Scholem, "Confession on the Subject of Our Language: A Letter to Franz Rosenzweig, December 26, 1926," trans. Gil Anidjar, in Jacques Derrida, *Acts of Religion* (New York, 2002), 226-27; here 226.

15. Gershom Scholem, "Bekenntnis über unsere Sprache: An Franz Rosenzweig zum 26.XII.1926," in Stéphane Mosès, *Der Engel der Geschichte: Franz Rosenzweig, Walter Benjamin, Gershom Scholem* (Frankfurt, 1994), 215–17; here 216; cf. Scholem, "Confession," 227.

16. Simon Dubnow, "Nahpesa ve-nahkora: Kol kore ha-nevonim ba-'am ha-mitnadvim le-'esof homer le-binyan toldot bene yisrael be-polin ve-rusiya [Let us seek and investigate: an appeal to the informed among us who are prepared to collect material for the construction of a history of the Jews in Poland and Russia]," *Ha-Pardes: Osef sifruti* 1 (1892): 221–42. See Simon Dubnow, "Let Us Seek and Investigate," in *Simon Dubnow Institute Yearbook VII*, ed. Laura Jokusch and trans. Avner Greenberg (Göttingen, 2008), 353–82; Laura Jockusch, "Introductory

Remarks on Simon Dubnow's 'Let Us Seek and Investigate,' " in *Simon Dubnow Institute Yearbook VII*, (Göttingen, 2008), 343–52.

17. Simon Dubnov, "Pis'ma o starom I novom evrejstve," in *Voskhod* (1897–1906); Simon Dubnov, *Pis'ma o starom I novom evrejstve* (St. Petersburg, 1907); Simon Dubnow, "Letters on Old and New Judaism," in *Nationalism and History: Essays on Old and New Judaism*, ed. Koppel S. Pinson (Philadelphia, 1958), 73–249.

18. Dubnow, "Let Us Seek," 356, 362.

19. Dubnow, "Second Letter: The Jews as a Spiritual (Cultural-Historical) Nationality in the Midst of Political Nations," in *Nationalism and History*, 100–115.

20. Dubnow, "Let Us Seek," 381.

21. Simon Dubnow, *Weltgeschichte des jüdischen Volkes*, vol. 8, trans. A. Steinberg (Berlin, 1928), 75, 94; Frederic Cople Jaher, *The Jews and the Nation: Revolution, Emancipation, State Formation and the Liberal Paradigm in America and France* (Princeton and Oxford, 2002), 66–69.

22. Ismar Schorsch, *From Text to Context: The Turn to History in Modern Judaism* (Hanover, NH, 1994); David N. Myers, *Resisting History: Historicism and Its Discontents in German-Jewish Thought* (Princeton, 2003), 21–28.

23. Leon Wieseltier, " 'Etwas über die jüdische Historik': Leopold Zunz and the Inception of Modern Jewish Historiography," in *History and Theory* 20, no. 2 (May 1981): 135–49.

24. Leopold Zunz, "Etwas über die Rabbinische Literatur (1818)," in *Gesammelte Schriften von Dr. Zunz*, ed. Curatorium der Zunzstiftung (Berlin, 1875), 1–31; here 5.

25. Simon Dubnow, *Buch des Lebens*, ed. Verena Dohrn and trans. Vera Bischitzky, vol. 1, *1860–1903*, (Göttingen, 2004), 207.

26. Simon Dubnow, "Einleitung," in *Weltgeschichte des Jüdischen Volkes: Von seinen Uranfängen bis zur Gegenwart*, vol. 1, trans. A. Steinberg (Berlin, 1925), xiii–xxxi; Simon Dubnow, "The Sociological View of Jewish History (Introduction to the Weltgeschichte, 1925)," in *Nationalism and History*, 336–53; Dubnow, *Buch des Lebens*, 3:92, 104.

27. Dubnow, *Sociological View*, 353.

28. Dubnow, "Let Us Seek," 360.

29. Ibid., 360, 381.

30. Ibid., 363.

31. On Pharaoh, see: Simon Dubnow, *Die neueste Geschichte des Jüdischen Volkes*, vol. 1, trans. Alexander Eliasberg (Berlin, 1920), 15, 29, 178, 186, 225–26, 244, 253; Dubnow, "Tenth Letter. The Moral of Stormy Days," in *Nationalism and History*, 200–214; here 213. On Amalek, see Dubnow, "Tenth Letter," 200, 204–5, 214; *Simon Dubnow in Memoriam: Essays and Letters*, ed. Simon Rawidowicz (London and Jerusalem, 1954), 447. On Haman, see Simon Dubnow, "Vos derf men ton in homen's tsytn? A briv tsu der redaktsiye fun Afn Sheydveg," in *Afn Sheydveg* 2 (August 1939): 3–7; Simon Dubnow, "What Should One Do in Haman's Times? (A Letter to the Editors of Oyfn Sheydveg)," in Dubnow, *Nationalism and History*, 354–59; 355; Joshua Karlip, "In the Days of Haman: Simon Dubnow and His Disciples at the Eve of WWII," in *Simon Dubnow Institute Yearbook IV*, ed. Dan Diner (Göttingen, 2005), 536. On Chmelnitzky, see Dubnow, "Tenth Letter," 200; Dubnow, "What Should One Do in Haman's Times?," 355; Kelner, *Dubnow*, 170–71.

32. Dubnow, *Buch des Lebens*, 1:140–42.

33. Ibid., 1:177, 186, 199.

34. Dubnow, "Nahpesa ve-nahkora," 221–42.

35. Dubnow, "Let Us Seek," 353–83.

36. Dubnow, "Let Us Seek," 353, 355, 372.

37. Ibid., 354.

38. Ernest Renan, *Qu'est-ce qu' une nation?/What Is a Nation?*, trans. Wanda Romer Taylor (Toronto, 1996), 48–49.

39. Raphael Mahler, "Geschichte Israels in neuester Zeit (1961)," trans. Antje C. Naukoks, in *Jüdische Geschichte lesen: Texte der jüdischen Geschichtsschreibung im 19. und 20. Jahrhundert*, eds. Michael Brenner and Anthony Kauders (Munich, 2003), 80–90; *A History of Modern Jewry, 1780–1815* (New York, 1971); and *Hasidism and the Jewish Enlightenment: Their Confrontation in Galicia and Poland in the First Half of the Nineteenth Century*, trans. Eugene Orenstein, Aaron Klein, and Jenny Machlowitz Klein (Philadelphia, 1985).

40. Carole Fink, *Defending the Rights of Others: The Great Powers, the Jews, and International Minority Protection, 1878–1938* (Cambridge, 2004); Erwin Viefhaus, *Die Minderheitenfrage und die Entstehung der Minderheitenschutzverträge auf der Pariser Friedenskonferenz*

1919: Eine Studie zur Geschichte des Nationalitätenproblems im 19. und 20. Jahrhundert (Frankfurt, 2008); Samuel Moyn, *The Last Utopia: Human Rights in History* (Cambridge, MA, 2010); Jacques Picard, "Geneva," in *Enzyklopädie Jüdischer Geschichte und Kultur (EJGK)* (Stuttgart and Weimar, 2012), 2:411–17.

41. Simon Dubnow, *Buch des Lebens*, ed. Verena Dohrn and trans. Vera Bischitzky, vol. 2, *1922–1933* (Göttingen, 2005), 62–64.

42. Dubnow, *Buch des Lebens*, 3:115–18; Kelner, *Dubnow*, 474.

43. World Jewish Congress, *Protocols of the First World Jewish Congress* (Geneva, Paris, and New York, 1936), 4.

44. Karlip, "In the Days of Haman," 531–64.

45. Nehemiah Robinson, *Indemnification and Reparations: Jewish Aspects* (New York, 1944); Siegfried Moses, *Jewish Post-War Claims*, ed. Wolf-Dieter Barz (1944; Münster, 2001); Martin Dean, Constantin Goschler, and Philipp Ther, eds., *Robbery and Restitution: The Conflict over Jewish Property in Europe* (Oxford and New York, 2008).

46. Arendt, "The Minority Question," 16.

6

Bernard Lazare (1865–1903)

RADICAL MODERNISM AND JEWISH IDENTITY

Nathaniel Berman

At the origin of all life, there is nothing but rot [*pourriture*] and dung [*fumier*] and impurity. Splayed out along a path, under the sun, a rotting carcass swells with splendid life; bird droppings in a dried-out pasture hold the promise of marvelous fruitions. . . . We do not ask ourselves whence they come—or why the flower that is so beautiful plunges its roots into abject slurry.

—OCTAVE MIRBEAU, 1895[1]

Like all governments, you want to beautify the truth, to be the government of a people that appears clean and proper; the highest duty has become for you "not to display national shames." However, I myself am in favor of displaying them, so that one should see poor Job on his dunghill [*fumier*], scraping his sores with the broken shard of a bottle. We will die from hiding our shames, from burying them in deep caves, instead of bringing them into the pure air. . . . Our people is in the most abject mud. We must roll up our sleeves and go seek it where it moans, where it groans, where it suffers. We must re-create our nation.

—BERNARD LAZARE, LETTER TO THEODOR HERZL, 1899[2]

IN THE COURSE OF A WRITING CAREER THAT BARELY SPANNED THE LAST FIFTEEN years of his short life, Bernard Lazare (1865–1903) traversed a gamut of alternatives familiar to those concerned with modernism, particularly its radical strands, and Jewish identity. Indeed, Lazare's work may be viewed as one of the sites of invention of that gamut. His radical modernism included: *avant-garde politics*——ranging from antiparliamentary anarchism, to leftist electoral alliances, to public opinion mobilization, to ethno-anarchist federalism; *avant-garde aesthetics*—ranging from opaque fictions, with an affinity for the mystical and exotic, to a "Social Art" accessible to the masses and aimed at revolutionary change; and *shifting stances on the relationship between politics and aesthetics*—ranging from a vision of elective affinity between radical aesthetics and politics to an insistence on the direct political engagement of intellectuals. His ever-changing constructions of Jewish identity were, perhaps, even more heterogeneous: ranging from overt embrace of antisemitic tropes, to initiation of the campaign to exculpate Dreyfus, to engagement on behalf of Zionism, to fierce rejection of Zionism's "bourgeois" Herzlian form, to a "Jewish nationalism" focused on the collective transformation of subjectivity rather than territory, to adoption of what we might call "cultural pluralism." It would, moreover, be a mistake to order these divergent stances in the form of a linear narrative; rather, we might model Lazare's oeuvre on the unconscious, in which no stage is ever fully abandoned even as it may seem to give way to its successor.

Lazare was born in Nîmes in southeastern France. His family was long-established in the region and well-integrated in bourgeois society, while retaining some anodyne observance of Jewish holidays. Lazare moved to Paris when he was twenty-one, seeking out the avant-garde literary circles often vaguely grouped under the label "Symbolism," and the radical political circles often called "anarchist." He embarked on a prolific writing career, in genres including literary and political essays, novels, short stories, historical treatises, and public manifestos. His public activities involved editing avant-garde reviews, writing for mainstream newspapers, defending anarchists in court and the press, and publicizing the plight of Eastern European Jews.

Those who have tried to comprehend this remarkable figure have adopted a number of strategies to cope with the kaleidoscopic variations in his thought. These strategies have ranged from identifications of discontinuous breaks, to claims of an essential continuity amid surface incongruities, to teleological readings that affirm a linear evolution from immature foreshadowings toward a true (or, at least, final) form. Such attempts to situate Lazare's protean oeuvre within a coherent narrative, however, miss the secret of its enduringly fascinating quality. For it is precisely its unsettled, shifting character that makes Lazare's writings key to thinking about modernity and identity today.

In considering Lazare's work, therefore, I de-emphasize the century-long quest for a verdict on its thematic continuity or discontinuity. For example, I do not seek to decide whether Lazare completely broke with the antisemitic matrix of his early writings or whether traces of that matrix persisted, however transvalued, in his later work; nor, conversely, do I seek to determine whether his early writings contained the "kernel" of later insights that would flourish once his "prejudices" were overcome. Rather, I seek precisely those features of his writing that destabilized his quest for a firm position—both propelling his search for identity and making it impossible for him to rest with any particular construction of it. Such features illuminate a body of work perpetually driven forward, to borrow Julia Kristeva's terms, by an incessant "structuring and destructuring," taking Lazare to "the outer limits" where subjective and social identities are formed and shattered.[3]

In this Kristevan spirit, I argue that a central clue to reading Lazare lies in his continually repeated evocations of social and aesthetic "*pourriture*" (rot) in various guises—decomposition, decay, corruption, defilement, abjection—and his concomitant quest to demarcate boundaries between the pure and the impure. Lazare's texts continually evoke, depart from, and return to the theme of "*la pourriture*" as, alternately, the enemy, catalyst, or even model of human and national identity. An emphasis on this dynamic serves to resituate Lazare in his chosen milieu, the French

political and cultural avant-garde, whose obsession with *"pourriture"* propelled its drive to reinvent identity and aesthetic form.[4]

As Kristeva argues, this drive is inevitably quixotic. The struggle for separation from the abject is a "war" that "fashions" the human being, pre-existing the coming into being of the "I," and yet—or perhaps precisely thereby—rendering human identity "permanently fragile."[5] This struggle is also intrinsically ambivalent, for the abject is both part of the subject (or proto-subject) and that from which it must separate to establish its identity. Such Pyrrhic struggles reach a particular intensity, at both the individual and collective levels, at historical moments when the great cultural vehicles for securing the "proper" boundaries of individual and collective identity—law, morality, religion—lose their taken-for-granted legitimacy.[6] It is in such moments that avant-gardes take up the challenge of abjection as the fulcrum for the creation of new aesthetic and political forms.

The French late nineteenth-century was precisely such a moment. One contemporary observer declared that Symbolism was "the expression of the generation which has arisen since 1870, a generation of the defeated, an anxious and disillusioned generation, with sensitive and subtle nerves, marked by an unhealthy impressionability."[7] During such crises of subjectivity amid social instability, both aesthetic and political revolt exert a sharp fascination.

> So many people hope for nothing other than a total upheaval! . . . This is why we see this collusion between the aesthetes and the anarchist comrades. They take turns with each other at public meetings in declaring their programs to the crowd. The latter gets only one point out of all these motley discourses: that it's a question of destroying something . . . and the crowd disperses to alternating cries of "Long live free verse!" and "Long live anarchy!"[8]

This juxtaposition of aesthetic and political revolt, better known in its early-twentieth-century incarnations, was key to Lazare's milieu. He describes *Entretiens politiques et littéraires*, a journal in which he played a key role, as "a paper of combat: fierce, aggressive, violent in art as in literature and as in politics."[9] Revolt against traditional political and cultural forms, and a concomitant destabilization of identity, both led the young to a plethora of radical movements and rendered precarious their adherence to any one of them. In Lazare's words:

> It is indisputably the youth and its distressing preoccupations which disconcert the solemn people of our time. For what do they reproach these newcomers? First, the range of their tendencies, the tumultuous effervescence of their thoughts, the seemingly contradictory variety of their aspirations. . . . These young men have been, by turns, Impressionists, Decadents, Symbolists, mystics, and, finally, anarchists. This astounding multiplicity, this staggering diversity, this stunning complexity, heightens the surprise of the censors and shocks the straight-edged and conventional banality of their judgment.[10]

However, this explosion of new forms was also accompanied by—or rather, if we take Kristeva seriously, generated by—a continual confrontation with the abject. For example, in the opening epigraph of this essay, the relationship to the abject is expressed in affirmative terms by Lazare's close friend, the anarchist and avant-garde writer Octave Mirbeau. One scholar has even characterized Mirbeau's work as a veritable *"poétique de la pourriture."*[11] To be sure, such a poetics cannot but be pervaded with ambivalence ("the flower that is so beautiful plunges its roots into abject slurry").

However, self-creation through a struggle with abjection also has a much darker side. If the breakdown of tradition leads to a proliferation of new forms, it also generates deep anxiety, often linked to ferocious attempts to subdue heterogeneity. This anxiety—and ferocity—were sharply expressed by Lazare in an 1891 essay, significantly entitled "De la nécessité de l'intolérance." Merging the problematics of the construction of subjectivity with the creation of artistic works in an age in which social consensus has collapsed, Lazare declares:

> The creative artist does not fight for absolute Beauty, nor for infinite Truth, but for the idea that he has constructed for himself of Beauty, the Good, or Truth. Henceforth, he fights for his own existence. It is necessary that he be a sectarian for his own conservation; his intolerance is his safeguard. Would one ask of a human body to accept the introduction of hostile substances, mortal toxins, dangerous microbes? No. Then why ask a spirit to welcome disorganizing principles, to choose poisonous ideas, to consent to theories that are enemies to his substance?[12]

Here, in stark contrast to Lazare's celebration of the proliferation of radical movements, heterogeneity becomes associated with the fatal, disintegrating forces of abjection, forces that undermine the construction of subjectivity and artistic creation. Another passage draws out these implications even more darkly:

> Indeed, every artist, poet and writer truly worthy of the name lives through ideas. . . . [T]hey become an integral part of himself. They are forces which help to bring about his existence. . . . Therefore, every being who lives through ideas . . . must struggle for them, defend them against enemy ideas, and for this he must cultivate hatred against his adversaries. . . . [A literary genre] must be fought by us if it contradicts our thought, and we must resist every work that belongs to it, because it is detrimental to ourselves, because it is fatal and harmful to us, because it acts on our spirit like a poison would act on our vital organs. This is why hate is good. It preserves and purifies. . . .[13]

At first startling, this celebration of "hatred" should not, upon further (Kristevan) reflection, be unexpected in a writer preoccupied with the abject and, consequently, with "purification" as indispensable to the construction of personal and artistic identity.

And yet, ambivalence remains irreducible: in other passages on artistic creativity from the same period, one finds Lazare expressing a stance much closer to that of Mirbeau, as in his celebration of Huysman's *"génie de la pourriture"* (genius of rot), at least of *"la bonne pourriture"* (good rot)(!),[14] which he associates with that writer's knowledge of "unsuspected splendors, unknown powers."[15] This kind of tight association between "high" ("unsuspected splendors") and "low" (*"la pourriture"*) is, of course, something we have come to expect in the avant-garde of the past century. Like Mirbeau, then, Lazare's work may be characterized as an ambivalent *"poétique de la pourriture,"* or perhaps a *"poétique et politique de la pourriture,"* or even, as we shall see, a *"poétique, politique, et judaïque de la pourriture."*

To be sure, as the 1890s advanced, Lazare, in his Dreyfusard incarnation, would increasingly denounce intolerance and hatred. Indeed, in an 1898 essay, he embraces the very aesthetic relativism he so fiercely denounced just a few years earlier. "Groups of individuals," no less than individuals, he declares, have "particular manners" of "expression": "each renders beauty differently, each has a unique plastic sense." And this variety should be celebrated, for "the wealth of humanity consists in these diversities."[16]

At a thematic level, these shifts in position raise the perennial questions about continuity and discontinuity in Lazare's work. At a deeper level, however, these incompatible stances—condemnation of diversity, celebration of diversity—reflect an ongoing struggle with the abject, a struggle whose outcomes were always precarious. Periodizations of Lazare's work (of the kind: "he began as an intolerant antisemite, moved to a particularist Zionism, and then became a tolerant pluralist"), however heuristically necessary, thus tend to prove very fragile. As I have already shown, praise of heterogeneity, together with mockery of its opponents, may be found even in Lazare's earliest texts. Conversely, the construction of identity through a fierce attack on those seen as embodying *la pourriture* features prominently even in his latest texts. This persistent ambivalence can be seen most clearly in his shifting constructions of Jewish identity, to which I shall shortly turn.

Before turning to that examination, I note that, in the English-speaking academy, the name of Bernard Lazare primarily owes its survival to Hannah Arendt. A brief examination of Arendt's interpretation, therefore, is necessary in order to clearly distinguish my own reading. Arendt distills Lazare's position on Jewish identity to a dichotomy between two stances: the "pariah" and the "parvenu." The former stance is that in which the Jew has for centuries been placed by Christian domination. For most of that history, according to Arendt's Lazare, the Jews were "unconscious pariahs," passively and unreflectively accepting their status. After Emancipation, however, the Jews of Western Europe became conscious of their pariah status and faced a choice: either seek to enter non-Jewish society through assimilation, thereby becoming "parvenus," or engage in political action against broad social injustice. For Arendt, Lazare

> knew where the solution lay: in contrast to his unemancipated brethren who accept their pariah status automatically and unconsciously, the emancipated Jew must awake to an awareness of his position and, conscious of it, become a rebel against it—the champion of an oppressed people. His fight for freedom is part and parcel of that which all the downtrodden of Europe must needs wage to achieve national and social liberation. . . . He saw that it was necessary to rouse the Jewish pariah to a fight against the Jewish parvenu. . . . Lazare's idea was, therefore, that the Jew should come out openly as the representative of the pariah.[17]

This interpretation, however influential, is woefully inadequate. At the simplest level, I note that a simple opposition between "pariah" and "parvenu" appears rarely in Lazare's work—though his writing is replete with a series of other stark dichotomies. More importantly, Arendt's interpretation is reductionist: in its frame, the heterogeneities of Lazare's positions, if visible at all, can only appear as constituting a maturation process, that of a young man evolving to a time when he came to "know where the solution lay." Above all, Arendt's interpretation of this self-consciously literary figure is not really a *reading*: in its reduction of Lazare's work to a set of solidified cognitive and normative positions, it looks neither at the textual strategies and libidinal propulsions that drive his incessant proliferation of dichotomies between divergent identities nor at their relationship to his aesthetic positions. Arendt's Lazare is a rationalist voice for justice, the "representative" and "champion" of the oppressed, a man without anxieties about his own identity, but rather, justly disappointed by the failure of his people to follow him. In short, Arendt's Lazare is a man who "knew where the solution lay." I argue that, on the contrary, the compelling quality of Lazare's work is that he was constantly propelled beyond his positions, including his stance on the relationship of the intellectual's "knowledge" to popular politics—an issue central to his shifting stances on Jewish identity.

A tour through those stances must begin with his "early" writings, which, in Lazarean terms, extend from approximately 1890 to 1892. His most concise statement during this period is the 1890 essay, "Juifs et Israélites," and its eponymous dichotomy. These terms appear as quasi-racial categories, the "*Israélites*" roughly identified with Jews who had lived in France for many centuries and the "*Juifs*" with those who came from an "East" that began at the Alsace. The essay asserts that the charges of the antisemites, including Edouard Drumont, the father of modern French antisemitism, are correct—but only if directed against the "*Juifs*" and not the "*Israélites*."

> *Juifs* are those for whom integrity, benevolence, abstinence are merely words or virtues to be used for venal purposes; they are those for whom money is the goal of life and the center of the world. But side-by-side with this contemptible Judaism, rotted by cupidity [*pourri par la cupidité*], filled with hatred for noble gestures and generous wills, there are beings who are completely different, there are the *Israélites*.[18]

This excerpt suggests the virulence with which the early Lazare adopts the worst antisemitic clichés—above all, that of the penchant of the "*Juifs*" to corrupt noble human activities by turning them into opportunities for financial gain. It is particularly significant that he describes "this contemptible Judaism" as "*pourri*," rotten—and that this "*pourriture*" is due to "*la cupidité*." The latter term, if it most often signifies financial greed, has as its core meaning "any keen desire"[19]—and can thus refer to lust for power and sex, as well as avarice. It is this "uncontrollable desire to possess"[20] that, for *this* Lazare, characterizes the "*Juifs*." Lazare even purports to show with particularity how the immoderate desires of the "*Juifs*" pervert each noble profession they have entered. One might say that "*la pourriture*" of the "*Juifs*" lies precisely in the excessiveness of their desire—with the boundary-disintegrating libidinal excess posing the threat to "proper" identity characteristic of all experiences of abjection. Another essay from the same year highlights the abject nature of the "*Juifs*" with more vivid physical descriptions, culminating in a repulsive linguistic hybridity: the "*Juif*" of Eastern Europe is "a dirty, ragged being, with a viscous, repugnant look, speaking a bizarre dialect, a judeo-german jargon."[21]

By contrast with the "*Juifs*," the "*Israélites*" are characterized by moderation, "limited in their desires."[22] They are also true Frenchmen, for Lazare is only concerned with the "*Israélites de France*": the "others are indifferent or alien to me." Unlike the "*Juifs*," who are carried across all boundaries by their unrestrained desires, the "*Israélites*" are rooted in France: "They live peacefully, attached to the soil where they were born," the land of "innumerable generations" of their ancestors. Moreover, unlike the "*Juifs*," they do not stand out and, indeed, have no noticeable identity of their own despite, or because of, their long presence in France: "They have no history, their names are unknown, for they were never mixed up in raucous trials [n.b.: an ironic comment for the soon-to-be ardent Dreyfusard!], shady adventures, sensational plunders." It would thus seem that the only proper Jewish identity is one that is submerged in French identity; any distinct Jewish identity appears to be intrinsically improper. And Lazare limits himself to this modest gloss on Drumont's antisemitism: "it would be fitting for the anti-semites to become rather *anti-Juifs*; finally just, they would be certain, on that day, to have with them many *Israélites*."[23]

If "Juifs et Israélites" is relatively modern in its antisemitism, other writings by Lazare during this period improvise on classic Christian tropes. In one of Lazare's Symbolist fables, "Les Incarnations" (1891), the narrator, an "*Israélite*," meets a mysterious Chinese rabbi in an exotic "Levantine" city. The two discover fellowship in their shared antipathy toward the "*Juifs*." Prominent among their complaints is a heterodox version of the hoary Christian charge of the Jews' stubborn rejection of the Messiah: it is not just Jesus whom the Jews failed to recognize, but a whole series of divine "incarnations," an entire range of messianic aspirants (Serenus, David Al Roy, Sabbatai Zevi, and so on).

Lazare characteristically explains this perennial rejection of the messianic by yet another fundamental dichotomy, the "two messianic currents in Israel."[24] The first, which the fable's protagonists praise, is "the prophetic current, characterized by ferocious hatred of the rich and the oppressors." The second is "this same belief transformed by the thick skull of the opulent and hard Pharisees," those "merchants" who "could not recognize in the pitiable Nazarene . . . the earthly monarch of which they dreamed."

Lazare steadily thickens the exotic air: the Chinese rabbi tells his own tale of an Indian rabbi, whose imprecations against Jewish perfidy are recounted in ever-more virulent prose. They culminate in a terrifying vision of a satanic anti-Messiah, a "little hideous *Juif*, with yellow, dirty hair, bleary eyes, twisted mouth, and bushy beard." This figure "comes out of seedy houses and whispers words to passing prepubescents; he preaches evil, and people listen, seduced."[25] This repulsive figure is, in short, a pimp, who approaches the "palace where gold triumphs"—described so as to allude to those favorite antisemitic targets, the Rothschilds. He is then proclaimed the Messiah by the crowd. The Chinese rabbi concludes, "Israel will only recognize its Messiah when he will manifest himself in the only form accessible to its soul"[26]— which, given the nature of the "little hideous *Juif*," must be a thoroughly abject soul, perhaps the source of all abjection.

Among the telling aspects of this fable is its complex Orientalism. The text seeks to augment its authority, in affirmative Orientalist fashion, by multiplying layers of "easternness": the Levant, China, India. It is thus not their foreignness that is the problem with the "*Juifs*," but their perverse boundary-crossings—territorial, cultural, and aesthetic transgressions: as ever, key hallmarks of the abject.[27]

Lazare's tome, *L'Antisemitisme, son histoire et ses causes*, marks a transitional phase in his writings on Jewish identity. Following Michael Löwy,[28] we can read the second part of the work, written in 1893, as a break with the more clearly antisemitic first part, completed in 1892. In this light, I draw attention to the divergent evocations of purity and impurity in the two parts. In the first chapter, Lazare highlights the role of the fear of defilement, "*la souillure*," in the construction of Jewish identity, particularly its Pharisaic version. This fear led to the promulgation of innumerable purity laws, ultimately leading the Jews to "flee the society of non-Jews."[29] These Rabbinic strictures generated a malignant construction of Jewish identity:

> They withdrew Israel from the community of peoples; they made of it a solitary savage, resistant to all law, hostile to all fraternity . . . stupefied by narrow education, demoralized and corrupted.[30]

It is these features of Jewish identity to which this Lazare largely attributes the fact that the Jews became an "object of horror and reprobation."[31] And it is these features to which he attributes the first persecutions of the Jews in antiquity and, ultimately, modern antisemitism.

Even in this phase, however, Lazare identifies abjection as the fulcrum of the construction of *all* identity: the flight from "*la souillure*" is associated with the construction of Jewish particularism, while "horror and reprobation" directed against the Jews is associated with the construction of antisemitic subjectivity. I note, though, that, at this stage, the initiation of this infernal dialectic is attributed to the Jewish side.

In the second part of the book, the emphasis shifts to the non-Jewish side:

> At the basis of . . . the antisemitism of our time . . . lies the horror and the hatred of the foreigner. This is . . . its permanent motivation . . . which one finds [in the ancient world], in feudal Europe, and in contemporary States animated by the principle of nationalities.[32]

Even in this part of the book, the notion of reciprocal projections of the Other as impure by Jews and non-Jews persists, as well as the indispensability of those projections to the construction of identity: "for the Christian, the *Juif* was the abject being, but for the *Juif*, the Christian was the *goy*, the abominable foreigner, the one who did not fear defilement [*les souillures*] . . . the one through whom Judea suffers."[33]

If, despite my strictures above, I continue to indulge heuristically in some temporal framing of Lazare's career, the second part of *L'Antisémitisme* may be seen as a way station, soon yielding to a complete reversal in his conception of the origins of abjection. In two essays from the late 1890s, the localization of abjection has resolutely shifted away from the "*Juifs*" and toward their two antagonists—non-Jews and rich, assimilationist Jews—and, above all, toward the unhealthy relationship between them. "Le Nationalisme et l'émancipation juive" denounces those assimilationists who, like the Lazare of a few years earlier, seek to divest themselves of the label "*Juif*" and call themselves "*Français de confession israélite*" ("Frenchmen of the Israelite faith")[34] Contrary to his earlier position, Lazare now declares that antisemitic animus is unrelated to Jewish self-isolation—as demonstrated by the fact that assimilationist self-renaming, aimed at denying that Jews are a separate "nation," has done nothing to mitigate the growth of antisemitic "furor."[35] Indeed, it is the Jewish bourgeoisie itself that is now the locus of abjection; they are for this reason rejected by non-Jews and should be rejected by Jews: "It is necessary . . . to extirpate them from us, to reject them as the rot [*la pourriture*] that poisons us, that defiles us [*qui nous souille*], that debases us."[36] Lazare thus now locates the source of "*la pourriture*" not in isolationism but, on the contrary, in assimilationism. Moreover, as befits the identity-disrupting abject, he attributes "*la pourriture*" not to the essence of either Jewish or non-Jewish cultures, but rather to the malignant encounter between them. Largely replacing the terminological opposition between "*Israélite*" and "*Juif*" with that between the "*bourgeoisie*" and the masses, he declares that the "*bourgeoisie juive*"

> rotted [*s'est pourrie*] upon contact with the Christian world, which inflicted upon it the same disintegration that the civilized inflicted upon the savages, to whom they brought alcoholism, syphilis, and tuberculosis. Thus, it is obvious that the so-called superior class of the *Juifs* of the West and, particularly, the *Juifs* of France, is in a very advanced state of decomposition. It is no longer *juive*, it is not Christian. . . . While the Christian bourgeoisie keeps itself standing thanks to the corset of its dogmas, the *bourgeoisie juive*, deprived of its centuries-old supports, poisons the *nation juive* with its *pourriture*. It will poison other nations as long as it does not decide—which we cannot encourage it enough to do—to adhere to Christianity and thus to rid Judaism of it.[37]

It was the monstrous self-reconstruction of the Jewish bourgeois, the "self-amputation"[38] of "de-judaization," that wrought its transformation into "*la pourriture*": "when the *Juif* had ruptured the barriers which separated him from the world, he slowly de-judaized himself and, in addition . . . corrupted himself through contact with Christian society; he lost his own virtues and acquired only the vices of those who surrounded him."[39] In short: "This Jewish bourgeoisie, rich and not Jewish [*cette bourgeoisie juive, riche et pas juive*], is our refuse, our dregs, we must rid ourselves of it."[40] It is their very assimilationist drive that leads them to be the object of non-Jewish scorn: "they are ready for all renunciations, all degradations, to prove that they have abandoned everything that linked them to the past and . . . to their brothers . . . ; they will only succeed in heightening and justifying the contempt they are shown."[41]

Lazare's attack on the monstrous hybridity of "*cette bourgeoisie juive, riche et pas juive*" is neither purely cognitive nor purely normative. This is demonstrated by its association with his ferocious calls for the "extirpation" of "*la pourriture*," rather than a rationalist call for the correction of an error—but also by its proximity in one essay, "Le Nationalisme Juif," to Lazare's celebration of aesthetic pluralism cited above. In this essay, Lazare again vilifies the Jewish bourgeoisie for poisoning the Jewish nation.[42] Yet, a bit further on in the essay, responding to homogenizing versions of left-wing internationalism, Lazare declares (and here I provide the frame of the passage celebrating pluralism):

> Humanity, for them, is an anthropological, political, or economic expression; it should, however, be yet something else: it should be an aesthetic expression. In

order for humanity to not cease to exist, it must, in the first place, maintain its diversity. . . . The wealth of humanity consists in these diversities. Thus, every human group is necessary.[43]

This pluralist vision appears, as I noted above, to stand in direct contrast to his earlier proclamations of the "necessity" of "intolerance" and "hatred" for the establishment of identity. Closer examination of this passage in the context of the essay in which it appears—in which Lazare also reiterates his ferocity toward his enemy, the bourgeoisie—shows a more complex situation. The pluralist vision is not a repudiation of the construction of identity through the "extirpation" of the Other's "*pourriture*." Rather, it represents a consideration of matters from a different standpoint, that of "humanity." Within national cultures, Lazare continues to combat the sources of "*la pourriture*"—which, in the Jewish context, requires ferocity toward the "*bourgeoisie juive et pas juive*." From the standpoint of "humanity," by contrast, he celebrates heterogeneity and cultural diversity.

Lazare stands here in the midst of a paradox that has long marked liberal European thought on the relationship between nationalism and internationalism. This paradox is expressed most clearly by Herder, in whose writing one finds an "abyss"[44] yawning between the perspective of those living within particular cultures and those considering humanity as a whole. On the one hand, cultural particularist "prejudice is good," for it "thrusts people toward their center, attaches them more firmly to their roots, causes them to flourish more fully in their own way. . . . The age that wanders towards the desires and hopes of foreign lands is already an age of disease, flatulence, unhealthy opulence, approaching death!" On the other hand, one should proclaim the universalist truth of cultural relativism, that "the good" is "scattered throughout the earth": "Since one form of humanity and one region cannot encompass the good, it has been distributed in a thousand forms, continually changing shape like an eternal Proteus throughout all continents and centuries."[45] There is hardly a word that would need to be changed to insert these two passages from Herder into Lazare's later writings.

Lazare expresses the relationship between these two divergent perspectives in a number of rhetorical and thematic forms. An attempt to bridge the "abyss" may be found in the assertion, whose paradoxical quality Lazare nonetheless emphasizes, that national liberation is necessary for the achievement of human liberation. Thus, Lazare declares that nationalism is the "condition of individual liberty," that the very definition of the term, "nation," is "the milieu within which the individual can develop and blossom in a complete fashion."[46]

More characteristically, however, Lazare's stagings of confrontations between the "national" and the "human" are marked by an ever-increasing self-awareness, a multiplication of the planes on which the poles of his proliferating dichotomies encounter each other, and an increasing turn to images of the unconscious. The collection of fragments posthumously published as *Le Fumier de Job* (Job's dunghill) is particularly rich in these features. In one passage, he deploys a dream/reality matrix to portray the relationship between French and Jewish identity:

> One day, I awoke from a dream. I had lived in the midst of a people and I believed myself to be of the same blood. . . . The day I awoke, I heard that they were saying I was of another blood, another soil, another sky, another fraternity. I awoke a *Juif* and I knew nothing of what a *Juif* was.[47]

This is not simply a precursor of some Sartrean notion that the antisemite makes the Jew. Rather, Lazare characterizes his self-construction as a Frenchman as a dream in relation to which, if we follow the imagery, his Jewish identity would be the reality—with antisemitism serving merely as the occasion for awakening from the one to the other.

Another passage from the same text, however, defies any reduction to a dream/reality schema, casting the unconscious as itself the key site of conflict among divergent stances toward the "*Juifs*":

> At times, he felt against them a veritable hatred. He was so different from these money-handlers, these merchants with narrow aspirations. . . . [Yet,] he wondered what mysterious atavism was causing to be reborn in him the desires and dreams of the old shepherds of the desert—and this rush of violent words that at times arose to his lips, as to the ancient prophets, destroyers of their own nation. And when he reproached himself for this furor against those of his race, he thought of Jeremiah. . . . At other times, he thought he was not of this nation.[48]

In the first two sentences, we have Lazare's self-portrait as he was a few years earlier: "hatred" as key to identity, here as the mechanism of the construction of his "*Israélite*" self through differentiation from the "*Juifs*." This self-construction does not turn on a movement from dream to reality, but rather on a passionate struggle between identities, requiring "hatred" to differentiate Self from Other. The rest of the passage even more thoroughly confounds any dream/reality schema. The oneiric realm is here not that of a delusional and superficial identity but, on the contrary, that of the most primal identity, that of the "desires and dreams of the old shepherds of the desert." These "desires and dreams" are portrayed as truer, and, in any case, more vital, than the conscious "*Israélite*" self. Finally, further undoing any cognitive understanding of the movement from one identity to another, even his anger against the "*Juifs*" is portrayed as emerging from a collective national unconscious: "this rush of violent words that at times arose to his lips, as to the ancient prophets." This short passage, then, portrays the surfacing from the unconscious of three kinds of passions, independently of the will or reason of the subject: "hatred" for the Jews, identification with them, and quintessentially Jewish prophetic anger at them. Nearly the entire range of Lazare's shifting relationship to Jewishness is thus resituated from the realm of rationally elaborated dichotomies to a storm of conflicting passions in the unconscious, buffeting and overwhelming the subject.

In light of Lazare's self-analysis, we can re-read the passage about awakening from the "dream" of assimilation in a different light. Above, I read this "awakening" as the emergence into Jewish "reality" from the dream of integration into the French nation—and as the sad fact that, although the subject is "really" a Jew, he does not "know" what it means to be Jewish. In this reading, however, it is unclear in what the "real" of his Jewishness lies; neither a Sartrean "gaze of the other" sense nor a racial/essentialist sense seems adequate. In light of the second passage's portrayal of the unconscious as the site of the struggle between conflicting passions, however, we can understand "I awoke a *Juif* and I knew nothing of what a *Juif* was" in a very different way: as the "knowing and not knowing" characteristic of unconscious ambivalence. Hence the imperative to "remake your soul,"[49] rather than simply to become cognizant of its pre-given reality.

We have thus arrived at a very different Lazare than Arendt's man who "knew where the solution lay." We can now understand his central attack on Herzl (the second epigraph to this essay) as a claim that traversing the depths of the unconscious is indispensable for the construction of national, as well as individual, identity. Attending to the later Lazare's attunement to the unconscious, it is important to carefully track the "truth" as it moves from surface to depth in the course of this excerpt:

> Like all governments, you want to beautify the truth, to be the government of a people that appears clean and proper [*propre*]; the highest duty has become for you "not to display national shames." However, I myself am in favor of displaying them, so that one should see poor Job on his dunghill, scraping his sores with the broken shard of a bottle. We will die from hiding our shames, from burying them in deep caves, instead of bringing them into the pure air. Our people is in the most abject mud. We must roll up our sleeves and go seek it where it moans, where it groans, where it suffers. We must re-create our nation .[50]

The "truth" that Herzl wishes to "disguise," to "bury in the deepest caves," is the truth of "shame." It is the truth that the nation is not "*propre*," that it is found in the "most abject mud," on "Job's dunghill." Rather than repressing this truth ever further, one must descend into that place of abjection, deeper than articulate and rational language, where the nation "moans, groans, and suffers." The "re-creation" of the nation will only take place through such a confrontation with abjection. Herzl's fault is to skip this work on the abject national subject, to begin as though identity were already constituted and thus that one could "know where the solution lay." Lazare characterizes this fault with his severest insult, "bourgeois," which for him always bears political, aesthetic, and existential connotations.

> You are bourgeois of thought, bourgeois of feeling, bourgeois of ideas, bourgeois of social conception. As such, you want to guide a people, our people, an unfortunate, proletarian people—but you can only do so in authoritarian fashion, seeking to lead them toward that which you think is best for them. You thus act outside of them, above them, you act as though you were moving a herd.[51]

The "bourgeois" character of Herzl is equated here precisely with his determination to guide the people without descending into the abject mud in which all struggles for identity must begin. Herzl already "knows" what is good for the nation and therefore can operate in a space "above them." Yet without descending into the abject depths, Herzl is leading a nation without a "proper" identity: for only the traversal of abjection can make possible the "re-creation" of the nation—just as an individual must traverse abjection to "re-make his soul."

Such disagreements about the construction of national subjectivity inevitably translate into conflict over concrete political positions. Within the limits of this essay, I can only briefly run through some of these correlations in Lazare's work.

I consider first the pro-*Israélite*/anti-*Juif* Lazare. *This* Lazare's vision was that, once the distinction between the two was made clear, "*Israélites*" would simply be accepted, culturally as well as legally, as ordinary Frenchmen—so that eventually "one would no more recognize an *Israélite* than one would recognize the Visigoth that exists in some Frenchmen."[52] A clear corollary to this position was the rejection of any political "solidarity" between the "*Israélites*" and the "*Juifs*."[53] Having eliminated the "*pourriture*" of the "*Juifs*" from among themselves, the "*Israélites*" would ultimately be able to "disappear, to lose themselves in the mainstream of the nation."[54]

Once he firmly transvalues the *Juif/Israélite* dichotomy, Lazare reverses all of these positions. He now declares that solidarity should exist *only* among the "*Juifs*," significantly embracing both those in France and elsewhere. For *this* Lazare, antisemitism was unlikely to disappear in the foreseeable future, grounded as it was in age-old religious mythology as well as "the horror and hatred of the foreigner." On the affirmative side, this Lazare affirms that Jews are a "nation"—based not on race or religion, but on a commonality of traditions, emotions, literature, and philosophy.[55]

In his "anti-*Juif*" phase, Lazare was clearly writing in the French Jacobin tradition, favoring a homogeneous French nation with no intermediate identities between the individual and the State. In his "pro-*Juif*" phase, Lazare has so departed from this tradition that he can even advocate that supreme Jacobin heresy, the existence of "States within the State." Indeed, he declares:

> I find that there are not enough "States within a State." To be more precise: within modern States, there are not enough autonomous, free, and interconnected groups. The human ideal does not appear to me to be political and intellectual unification.[56]

This position culminates in an ethno-national adaptation of the anarchist vision of society as a federation of autonomous groups:

> Is not one of the familiar conceptions of international socialism—and even of revolutionary anarchism—the federalist conception, the conception of a fragmented humanity, composed of a multitude of cellular organisms? . . . However, currently, it is by virtue of traditional principles that men wish to join together. For this purpose, they invoke certain identities based on origin, a common past, a similar manner of seeing phenomena, human beings, and things, a history, a common philosophy. It is necessary to permit them to come together.[57]

This image of an emancipated society as "fragmented" along ethno-national lines is the fruit of Lazare's amalgam of his anarchism and his "*nationalisme juif*." It implies a rejection of both assimilation and Herzlian statism. We might be tempted to call this position a "multi-cultural" vision of society, although "multi-national" would be more accurate—"culture" being too tepid a word for an identity Lazare insists is that of a "nation." This anarchist nationalism would not be bound to territorial aspirations:

> The *Juif* who says today, "I am a nationalist," does not say in a particular, precise, and clear-cut way, "I am a man who wants to reconstitute a Jewish State in Palestine and who dreams of reconquering Jerusalem." He says, "I want to be a fully free man, I want to enjoy the sun, I want to have the right to human dignity. I want to escape oppression, escape insult, escape the contempt that they want to inflict on me."[58]

As Lazare writes elsewhere, "It is necessary to liberate ourselves and we will thereby help to liberate others. We must revive as a people . . . but provided that this collectivity does not replicate the image of the capitalist and oppressive States in the midst of which we live."[59]

Nonetheless, shortly after the passage in "Le Nationalisme Juif" where Lazare appears to renounce territorialism, he seems to express the opposite view. I note that "Le Nationalisme Juif" was originally delivered as an address to the Association des Etudiants Juifs et Russes, and its published form retains that frame. Foreseeing a time when the oppression of the Jews becomes unbearable, Lazare writes:

> And what solution will they then see before them? The contemptible and vile part, without convictions and without any other motivation than its personal interest, will convert. . . . What will the believers do and what will those non-believers do who will never resign themselves to recantation [*la palinodie*]? They will feel more strongly that they will be free, as individuals, when the collectivity to which they belong will be free, when this nation without territory which is the *nation juive*, will have a soil and will be able to determine itself without constraint.[60]

Rather than a call for a fragmented, multi-national society, Lazare here seems to endorse social and territorial separation—both from the Jewish bourgeoisie and from non-Jewish society.

The essay thus contains both of the polar political responses to the disintegration associated with abjection—an embrace of that disintegration, in the form of anarchist fragmentation, and a call to construct insulated collective subjects through social and territorial separation. This seemingly overt political contradiction is an expression of the irreducible ambivalence intrinsic to the dynamics of the struggle with abjection.

However, as I have noted above, the key characteristic of this phase of Lazare's writing is its self-reflective quality—or, perhaps, what one might call its "dialogic" quality. Thus, immediately after the separationist/territorialist passage, Lazare puts into question whether it is indeed his own vision or rather an artifact of his empathetic dialogue with his audience, an audience that he prophetically admonishes:

> These are your cherished ideas, cherished by all of you who have given me the honor to call me amongst you. . . . You want to be yourselves, is there anything higher and more legitimate? . . . But . . . never forget that you have been the people, as Renan said, that introduced justice to the world.[61]

Ironically, perhaps, the rhetorical strategy that might best describe important parts of "Le Nationalisme Juif" might be precisely the very *"palinodie,"* the classical term for the advancement of theses and their retraction, upon which Lazare heaps scorn in the same essay. It is the public expression of the self-reflective ambivalence that at this time he expresses in his other writing, particularly in *Le Fumier de Job.* As he describes this textual practice in one of the fragments that make up that book: "He who speaks and he who represents the ideas of the book are not always the same."[62] At times, this writing practice, with its self-reflective distinction between authorial and narratorial voices, takes the form of a description of a conflict within his own subjectivity, as in the "Jeremiah" passage cited above. At other times, it takes the form of the representation of different ideal types. At one point, it even takes the form of an epistolary exchange: the *"lettre du nationaliste"* and *"lettre du cosmopolite."*[63]

These fragments pose nearly impossible challenges to any interpreter, since one never knows for sure which to attribute to the author and which to a particular persona he is staging. One can find here textual support for all the incompatible readings that have been given of Lazare: that he rejected Zionism, that he retained an anti-Herzlian Zionism, that he embraced universalism, that he adopted essentialist nationalism, and so on. I argue that these alternatives are variant responses to his perennial struggle with abjection, that they express the fundamental ambivalence of all writings that thematize such struggles, and that Lazare became increasingly self-aware of this ambivalence and protean in his textual strategies. This ambivalence is pithily expressed in this melancholy phrase in *Le Fumier*: "Tragic conflict between his cosmopolitan consciousness and his national consciousness."[64]

The fragmentary nature of the notes published in *Le Fumier* is partly a result, of course, of Lazare's untimely death. However, it is also a result of his increasing self-awareness of the irreducible ambivalence of an individual and a nation struggling to reconstruct identity amid material and spiritual abjection. Indeed, the fragment as Lazare's final textual genre corresponds uncannily to "the conception of a fragmented humanity" as his final utopian social vision. And so I conclude where I began: with the juxtaposition of aesthetic and political radicalism.

Notes

1. Octave Mirbeau, *Les écrivains*, vol. 2 (Paris, 1925), 52. All translations are mine unless otherwise noted.

2. "Letter from Lazare to Herzl," February 4, 1899, in Edmund Silberner, "Bernard Lazare et le sionisme (avec des lettres inedites de Lazare a Herzl)," Appendix X, *Shivat Zion*, vols. 2–3 (1953): 358.

3. Julia Kristeva, *La Revolution du Langage Poétique* (Paris, 1974), 15.

4. See generally, ibid., Part C ("L'Etat et le Mystère"), 359–608.

5. Julia Kristeva, *Pouvoirs de l'horreur* (Paris, 1980), 21.

6. Ibid., 24–25; Kristeva, *La Revolution du Langage Poétique*, 361–62.

7. Ernest Reynaud, *La Mêlée Symboliste* (Paris, 1918), 7.

8. Ibid., 7–8.

9. Bernard Lazare, "L'Avenir littéraire" (1892), quoted in Gaetano Manfredonia, "Du Symbolisme à l'Art Social," in *Bernard Lazare, Anarchiste et Nationaliste Juif*, ed. Philippe Oriol (Paris, 1999), 112.

10. Bernard Lazare, "La Déroute," *La Revue Parisienne* (January 25, 1894), quoted in Manfredonia, "Du Symbolisme à l'Art Social," in *Bernard Lazare, Anarchiste et Nationaliste Juif*, 109.

11. Philippe Ledru, "Genèse d'une poétique de la corruption," *Cahiers Octave Mirbeau* 11 (2004): 24.

12. Bernard Lazare, "De la Nécessité de l'intolérance," *Entretiens Politiques et littéraires* (December 1891): 209–10.

13. Bernard Lazare, *Figures contemporaines; ceux d'aujourd'hui, ceux de demain* (Paris, 1895), ix–xiv.

14. Ibid., 41.

15. Ibid., 7.

16. Bernard Lazare, "Le Nationalisme Juif" (Paris, 1898), 14.

17. Hannah Arendt, *The Jew as Pariah: Jewish Identity and Politics in the Modern Age* (New York, 1978), 76–77.

18. Bernard Lazare, "Juifs et Israélites" (1890), in Bernard Lazare, *Juifs et antisémites*, ed. Philippe Oriol (Paris, 1992), 6.

19. Littré, available at http://littre.reverso.net/dictionnaire-francais/definition/cupidite.
20. Ibid.
21. "La Solidarité Juive" (1890), in Lazare, *Juifs et Antisemites*, 15.
22. "Juifs et Israélites", 6.
23. Ibid., 7.
24. "Les Incarnations" (1891), in *Contes symbolistes*, ed. Bertrand Vibert (Grenoble, 2009), 230.
25. Ibid., 237.
26. Ibid., 239.
27. Kristeva, *Pouvoirs de l'horreur*, 12.
28. Michael Löwy, *Redemption and Utopia* (London, 1992), 188.
29. Bernard Lazare, *L'Antisemitisme, son histoire et ses causes* (Paris, 1894), 11.
30. Ibid., 14.
31. Ibid., 15.
32. Ibid., 404.
33. Ibid., 292.
34. Bernard Lazare, "Le Nationalisme et l'émancipation juive" (1901; a revision of two essays written in 1897), in Lazare, *Juifs et Antisémites*, 168.
35. Ibid.
36. Ibid., 167.
37. Lazare, "Le Nationalisme Juif," p. 7.
38. "Le Nationalisme et l'émancipation juive," 172.
39. Ibid., 171.
40. Ibid., 175.
41. Ibid., 175.
42. Lazare, "Le Nationalisme Juif," 9.
43. Ibid., 14.
44. Damon Linker, "The Reluctant Pluralism of J. G. Herder," *Review of Politics* 62 (Spring 2000): 275. My discussion of Herder adopts Linker's excellent reading.
45. Johann Gottfried Herder, "Yet Another Philosophy of History for the Development of Mankind" [1774], excerpted in Herder, *Against Pure Reason: Writings on Religion, Language, and History*, trans. and ed. Marcia Bunge (Minneapolis, 1993), 44.
46. Lazare, "Le Nationalisme Juif," 10.
47. Bernard Lazare, *Le Fumier de Job* (Paris, 1998), 25.
48. Ibid., 22.
49. Ibid., 24.
50. "Letter from Lazare to Herzl," 358.
51. Ibid.
52. "La Solidarité juive" (1890), in Lazare, *Juifs et antisémites*, 19.
53. Ibid., 16.
54. "La Nationalité française et les Juifs," (1893), in Lazare, *Juifs et antisémites*, 55.
55. Lazare, "Le Nationalisme Juif," 1–4.
56. Ibid., 4.
57. Ibid., 13.
58. Ibid., 12.
59. "Le Prolétariat Juif devant l'Anti-sémitisme," (1899), in Lazare, *Juifs et antisémites*, 140.
60. Lazare, "Le Nationalisme Juif," 15.
61. Ibid., 16.
62. "Les Deux Etoiles d'Israël," in Lazare, *Le Fumier de Job*, 115.
63. Ibid., 117.
64. Lazare, *Le Fumier de Job*, 111.

7

Avraham Yitzhak Ha-Cohen Kook (1865–1935)

REVELATION AND REDEMPTION

Yehudah Mirsky

The old will be renewed, and the new will become holy.
—LETTER FROM RABBI KOOK, OCTOBER 21, 1908[1]

FEW JEWISH THINKERS GRAPPLED WITH THE CLAIMS AND TEXTURES OF MODERNITY as expansively and intensely as Avraham Yitzhak Ha-Cohen Kook, whose passionate encounter with modernity is all the more striking for his coming at it from the deepest recesses of rabbinic tradition. Best known as the founder of Israel's chief rabbinate and the leading theologian of religious Zionism, he was a bold and original religious thinker and mystic. In his striking reading, modernity, far from being at odds with the world's oldest and most authoritative truths, as received through the Bible, Talmud, and Kabbalah, is precisely that which will reveal their essence and bring them to their historical fruition.

Kook's thought-world was filled with bold ideas and intense experiences—arising from sustained reflection on perennial questions of Jewish thought and his multiple, conflicting engagements with the unique circumstances of modern times. It was his opening himself to the many antagonistic currents running through his times that distinguished him from most other thinkers and certainly from his colleagues in the Orthodox rabbinate. For them, modernity was largely catastrophic, and the gains it may have brought in political equality and economic prosperity—decidedly dubious in the Eastern European Jewish heartlands—were more than offset by the internal collapse of Jewish communal structures and wholesale abandonment of tradition.

Some Orthodox rabbis did seek intellectual accommodation with modernity. Rav (Rabbi) Kook, by contrast, positively embraced it—including its rebellions against tradition and, in Zionism and socialism, its radical reinterpretations of Jewish tradition and concepts. These, for him, signaled no less than the messianic advent, when

the world's latent contradictions would become manifest on the threshold of their final resolution in God and God's final resolution within Himself.

A brief essay can adequately compass neither the sheer extent, relentlessness, complexity, and lyric power of Kook's writings nor the twists and turns of his public career.[2] But we can trace broad outlines, offer some observations, and raise further questions.

Kook's historical significance is twofold: the rabbinic institutions he created and, perhaps more importantly, the ideas he left behind. The former represent the rationalizing and bureaucratizing side of modernity, the latter the expressivist-utopian, and in crucial ways the two pull against each other—a tension he hoped to resolve by placing both against a messianic time line, in which the former would be a prelude to realizing the transformative spiritual possibilities of the latter. He sought to resolve them, and sometimes did, by a powerful yet subtle dialectic, which was later shattered with tragic results by his most ardent latter-day followers—above all his son Zvi Yehudah, who in the 1970s emerged as leader of the religious vanguard of the settler movement known as Gush Emunim.

Kook was born in 1865 in what is now Latvia.[3] A youthful prodigy in the Eastern European Jewish mold, he was groomed from a young age for rabbinic leadership. Early on he distinguished himself through a lyric, poetic sensibility and a striking and unfamiliar mix of intellectual prowess, emotionalism, and intense piety, which enthused some of his teachers and peers and alienated others. In the early years of his rabbinic career, begun in a tiny Lithuanian shtetl, he was drawn to Maimonidean rationalism. With time, including a period of intense grief over the death of his first wife, he turned inward and undertook deep introspection and extensive study of Kabbalah. Through the 1890s his thinking steadily expanded toward a richer emotional and spiritual palette. Alongside his command of Talmud and Halakhah, he mastered an extraordinary range of Jewish mystical, philosophical and other texts; read widely in the rich Hebrew and Yiddish periodical literature of the day; and became an autodidact of contemporary philosophy. He also began to keep a spiritual journal that would eventually become the venue of his most profound and consequential writing.

Kook participated neither in the proto-Zionist Hibat Zion nor in the Zionist movement itself, including its religious faction, the Mizrachi. But in the years 1901–1904 he published a series of essays in which he emerged as a supporter of the Jewish national movement as a potential vehicle of cultural and spiritual renewal—pending a profound rethinking by radicals and rabbis alike. Then as later, he was drawn less by the political program of Zionism than by its cultural program, and by the energies and idealism of the young people who were moving Zionism forward. Alongside writing talmudic-halakhic works and sermons, he began two noteworthy, lifelong projects: a commentary on the "aggadic," that is, legal, exegetical, and theological portions of the Talmud; and the spiritual diary mentioned above. Both were a genuine departure from rabbinic conventions (the former for its focus on nonlegal texts, the latter for its unmistakably personal nature) and bespoke a crucial dynamic of those years and beyond—his effort to accept himself. This coming to terms with his own inner truth brought him into contact with a central element of modernity, beautifully characterized by Charles Taylor as "the expressivist turn," an inward turning born out of the conviction that the truth is to be found in one's own sub-jectivity and in the recesses of one's own experience and passions.[4]

Unshakably rooted in traditional rabbinic culture, Kook nonetheless found him-self receptive to and vibrating with the multiple, regularly antagonistic social, cul-tural, and ideological currents swirling around him: contending Hasidic, scholastic, and moralistic trends within Orthodoxy; Enlightenment and traditionalism; na-tionalism and socialist universalism. As he tried to resolve the varied and seemingly contradictory ideas, insights and inclinations within himself, he became increasingly a thinker in the tradition of dialectic philosophy. His efforts to encompass and contain his own complex thought world led him toward a markedly dialectical ap-proach that bore elements of both Western philosophy and the multitiered world view of the Kabbalah.

Kabbalah and an Inclusive Worldview

The organization of the multiple and seemingly contradictory dimensions of be-ing into a unified structure is at the heart of perhaps the most basic of kabbalistic ideas, that of the Sefirot, the ten nodal points of divine energy emanating outward from Eyn Sof—That, or He, Who is Without End, the cosmic source of endless re-newal—which constitute the deep structure of Being. Each Sefirah has its own character and place, from infinity on down, and each has multiple names, through which one comes to understand its cosmic function and its place in scripture and Jewish symbolism.

Via this richly elaborated structure, one can—and Kook emphatically did—grant disparate dimensions of Being their own integrity while seeing them in dynamic tension as parts of a larger whole. While he drew on almost every known school of kabbalistic thought, especially significant for him as for so many others was the creative synthesis known as Lurianic Kabbalah, named after the major sixteenth-century figure Isaac Luria (1534–1572). Luria forged a myth of primordial creation in which God contracted Himself to make space for finitude, leaving behind traces of divine light in "vessels" whose "shattering" scattered sparks of divine goodness and the shells of shattered vessels, which make for the forces of good and evil. It is the task of the Jewish people to restore the sparks to their source and thus heal not only the world but the fissures in the divine, leading to the ultimate repair and resto-ration, *Tikkun*. Moshe Haim Luzzatto, known as Ramchal (1707–1747), translated Luria's mythic doctrines into a philosophy of history in which the conscious realm of good and evil is complemented by an unconscious divine hand that inexorably guides humanity and all of creation to their Tikkun, the world's and God's. With time Kook would see that unconscious redemption at work in the variously con-flicting social and political movements of his day.

Hasidism was another ground of Kook's thought. In Hasidic teaching, the locus of the motions of the divine energies was the inner life of the individual, at some remove from the sacred historiosophy of the Tikkun. Kook, in a characteristically synthetic move, affirmed the ontological status of the vicissitudes of the inner life, while connecting them to the larger process of the Tikkun—which he saw at work in the concrete social and political movements of his time.

His intellectual perspectives on these movements went hand in hand with his developing a deeply conciliatory personal stance that would accommodate them all. He made two large leaps here, one conceptual, the other personal. The conceptual was pluralism, not liberal but metaphysical—the fullness of God's creation requires the fullness of many different and seemingly opposing views. The personal was a rare ability to empathize with people and groups dramatically opposed to all that he, as an impeccably Orthodox halakhist, stood for.

This inclusive metaphysics and empathic personality slowly developed in Eastern Europe. Toward the end of his years there he wrote:

> There are those who erroneously think that world peace will only come from a common character of opinions and qualities. But no—true peace will come to the world precisely by multiplication of all the opinions and perspectives . . . all facets of the larger truth . . . peace [is] the unification of all opposites. But there must be opposites, so that there be those who labor and that which will be unified. . . . Hence peace is the name of God, who is the master of all the forces, all-capable and gathering them all.[5]

Encounter with Zion

In the summer of 1904 Kook moved to Palestine after accepting an offer to become the rabbi of Jaffa and the surrounding colonies, effectively becoming rabbi of the New Yishuv (Jewish collective). The year of his arrival marked the beginning of the period known in Zionist history as the Second Aliyah, the migration wave that also brought a small but influential cadre of young intellectuals and revolutionaries who left an outsized mark on the political and cultural development of the New Yishuv (such as David Ben-Gurion, Berl Katznelson, Yosef Chaim Brenner, and the slightly older worker and thinker, in some ways Kook's secular counterpart, Aharon David Gordon). Kook's encounters with members of the Second Aliyah, and their willingness to sacrifice themselves for the sake of the Jewish people and for the ethical universalism of socialism, combined with the vibrancy of the New Yishuv and the sheer embodiedness of the land, had an electrifying effect on him. In public, he became the leading rabbinic champion of the New Yishuv, thus a target of traditionalist attacks. In his halakhic writings he tried to reach accommodation with the burgeoning realities on the ground, most notably and controversially regarding adapting the biblically ordained Sabbatical year to the exigencies of contemporary agriculture and commerce.

In private, as time went by he wrote more and more furiously and extensively in his diaries, lost in a torrent of thought as he began to train the dialectical worldview that he had developed to understand the complex mix of his own soul and the ideological debates of Eastern Europe through larger historical patterns. His thinking also became explicitly messianic. Thus in his reading, the rebelliousness of the pioneers was no accident but part of God's plan to restore to Judaism a vitality and universal spirit worn thin during centuries of exile.

He referred to the revolutionaries as "souls from the world of Tohu," the chaos preceding the creation of the world in the opening verses of the Book of Genesis, whose revolution reenacts the primordial shattering of creation:

The souls of the world of Tohu are great, very great. They seek much from reality, they seek that which their vessels cannot endure, they seek a very great light. . . . They see themselves imprisoned in laws. . . . Their living ferment does not rest . . . all the more so at the end of days . . . before the birth of a law above the laws. . . . These storms will bring bountiful rains, these dark fogs will prepare great lights, *and from the pitch darkness, the eyes of the blind will see* (Isa. 29:18).[6]

In some ways, these ostensible sinners, "who lovingly join themselves to the affairs of the Jewish people, the land of people and national renaissance," are, in the quality of their souls, even greater than the pious faithful of Israel.[7]

The hermeneutic key to understanding contemporary rebellions against tradition was provided by the famously cryptic statement in the Mishna (Sotah 9:15) that "in the time of the footsteps of the Messiah, chutzpah will swell." And so the youth rebellions result from "thirst for thought, and reason, and with it for richer, more drenched feeling, fresh, and alive," paradoxically tied to the farthest aims of spiritual contemplation:

The chutzpah of the footsteps of the messiah comes from an inner longing for the supreme holiness of silence, and in the end it will come, for Israel is destined to stand closer in than the ministering angels. The sons of the boundary-defying impudent will be prophets of the highest level, higher than Moses, and shining with the splendor of Adam.[8]

The "splendor of Adam" of which he speaks, a kabbalistic term, is in his reading a Nietzschean transvaluation in a sacred key, a return to prelapsarian fusion of matter and spirit, body and soul, which is the deepest meaning of the Land of Israel and the Jewish people as revealed by the dialectical development of Jewish history. Thus, the biblical-prophetic period, raw and vital, is the thesis; the millennia of exilic Halakhah, disembodied and spiritual, is the antithesis; and the final redemption, Israel on its land and at the center of universal regeneration, with the eventual dissolution of the binaries of body and spirit, is the synthesis.

This he laid out in a major essay of 1912 that presented a philosophy of Jewish history structured along a series of mirroring dialectics, theses and antitheses, whose collective synthesis is redemption: Biblical Judaism—Exilic Judaism—Redeemed Judaism; Collective Spirituality—Individual Spirituality—Redeemed Spirituality; Body/Soul—Nation/Ethics—Redeemed Nationhood; God Idea—Religion—God Idea, Redeemed.[9]

The Land of Israel is central to this vision of the ultimate unity of body and spirit, nature and soul, which resolves the historically necessary but ultimately transitory spirituality of exile.

The holiness within nature is the holiness of the Land of Israel; the *shekhinah* which went into exile is the ability to maintain holiness in opposition to nature. But that combative holiness is incomplete, its higher essence must be absorbed into the higher holiness, which is the holiness within nature herself, the foundation of the restoration of the world [*tikkun olam*] and its utter fragrancing. And the holy that is in exile will be joined to that of the land, *and the synagogues and study halls of Babylonia will be reestablished in the Land of Israel* (BT Megillah 29a).[10]

Grasping the import of the Land of Israel in the Jewish mystical tradition clarifies the stakes of his discussions. In the kabbalistic doctrine of the Sefirot, the tenth Sefirah is the meeting place of divinity and the world; it is thus at one and the same time the Oral Torah (created by human interpretation); sovereignty; the Land of Israel; the ecclesia of Israel; and the immanent divine presence, the Shekhinah. This cluster of related mystical concepts was the lens through which he viewed nationalism and Zionism, and those developments shaped his new readings of the Kabbalah. This in turn yielded a different way of looking at the Torah and the commandments. Normative they are in the present, but they are to be understood as preparatory for the Torah of the future, one in which universal ethics will reign, not only between Jew and Gentile but also between man and animal. And just as the tenth Sefirah is the repository for the spiritual energies of all the rest, so too the Jewish people are the repository for the spiritual energies of humanity, the "idealized distillation" of the history, beliefs, and ideals of all nations.

Contemporary nationalism was for Kook the vessel of the internally diverse spiritual life of mankind: "In our time, after the differentiation into nations nobody can receive his spiritual influences outside of the garment of the specific channel of his nation."[11] But in keeping with his dialectical perspective, alongside national feeling, universal love must feature in a God-saturated world. "Love of all creatures must live in the heart and soul, love for every individual, for all the nations."[12] Indeed, the existence of nations is only a way station until the joining of all humanity into a single family.[13]

The imperative of love is not a theological abstraction arrived at on reflection, but something that emerged from his own religious experience: "I love all. I can't not love the created ones, all the nations."[14] Kook was deeply aware of the temptations of national chauvinism, which he ascribes to secular nationalism, joined at the roots to economic injustice, as the two phenomena are twin celebrations of the crabbed and pathetic need to cry "mine, mine, mine."[15]

He had come to see himself as a Zaddik, a figure who, in kabbalistic terms, enacts the dynamics of the ninth Sefirah, the principle of transmission of knowledge and life-giving energies—and, in some Hasidic teachings, who reflects in his own inner life the spiritual vicissitudes of his time. And thus, for him, in a deep sense, Israel is the Zaddik of the world. It experiences the ups and downs of all the nations, absorbing them all into its collective consciousness and restoring them to God.

As is by now clear, Kook was deeply influenced by Hegelianism (itself shaped by some of the Neoplatonic currents that also shaped the Kabbalah), with a significant difference: that for him, it is not the state as such but the nation that is the vehicle for self-realization of the spirit. In one of his few discussions of the state, he dissolved it entirely into the self-realization of each individual Jew, and thus the redemption of the world.

That the state is not the greater fulfillment of man may be said of the regular state, which is little more than a great big insurance company. . . . Unlike the state that is fundamentally Idealistic, graven into its being the higher Ideal which in truth is the greater fulfillment of the individual. This state is truly the higher rung on the ladder of fulfillment, and this is our state, the state of Israel, the foundation of God's throne in the world, whose entire desire is that *God be one and His name one* (Zech. 14:9), which truly is the higher fulfillment.[16]

Kook thus firmly places himself among the idealistic utopians, yet his keen dialectical awareness keeps him rooted in the world of structure or, as he put it, the prophet ultimately being mastered by the sage. How then to function with a simultaneous commitment to messianic utopia and the necessity for working through the medium of time via the means of ideological struggle? This he addresses in an especially important passage in his notebooks, written sometime around 1913, which is perhaps his most arresting analysis of the vicissitudes of modern Jewish identity: "Three forces are wrestling in our camp . . . and their roots lie in the consciousness that probes the expanses of the human spirit." What are they? "The holy, the nation, humanity, those are the three chief demands of which life as a whole, ours and every man's, of whatever form, is composed."[17]

In other words, Jewish identity is a complex amalgam of relationships to one's own people, to humanity and its universal values, and to the sacred (in terms familiar from later sociology, the primordial, civic, and transcendent forms of community and identity). Modernity has operated on Jewish identity like a centrifuge, whirling its component elements away from one another, each becoming the property of a party—nationalism, liberalism, and Orthodoxy, respectively—and they stubbornly refuse to be rejoined, because each fixates on the negative dimensions of the other. Yet all three dimensions are necessary, and each should appreciate not only each others' good sides but also their seemingly bad sides. Ideally, liberals will appreciate that the narrowness of nationalism comes from real love for one's own community, and that the fanaticism of the Orthodox is rooted in a flaming desire for God. Liberals and the Orthodox will see that nationalism's putting solidarity above broader aspirations for universal ethics or transcendence arises from powerful, loving attachments to people and fellow-feeling. Nationalism and Orthodoxy in turn will see that the liberals' preference for humanity over nationalism, or for religion itself, is itself rooted in an ultimately divine ethical perspective. The sacred is the energy that synthesizes all three elements—religious commitment, national identity, and ethical universalism—and a relationship to the All that lies beyond them.

There emerges from Kook's analysis a bold prescription for a complex gesture: to affirm the negative sides of those against whom one legitimately and powerfully struggles. The object of struggle is not to defeat, but to transform, both others and ourselves: "And so the pure Zaddikim don't decry evil, they add justice; they don't decry heresy, they add faith; they don't denounce ignorance, they add wisdom."[18]

Messianism and Antipolitics

The Great War caught Kook in Europe. He had traveled there in July 1914 to attend an Orthodox rabbinic conference, hoping to convince his colleagues to lessen some of their harsher opposition to Zionism. Unable to return home, he spent the war years in Switzerland at first, and then from 1916 onwards he was in London, where he served as rabbi of the city's Eastern European community. During the exile of the war years his love for the Land of Israel grew fierce with longing:

The Land of Israel is no extraneous thing, extrinsic property of the nation, some means towards general unity and maintaining its physical or even spiritual, existence. It is a thing in itself, bound in a living tie with the nation.[19]

He also began to think a bit more concretely about politics, including democracy. The sovereign institutions of the people, when chosen by the people on their land, would, he began to think, have the authority of biblical kings.[20] At the same time, the war deepened the fear of the moral perils of nationalism that had attended even his earliest writings on Zionism. Non-Jewish nationalism and collectivity is premised on alienation, among and within nations, and inescapably leads to violence.[21] Israel's politics must be different, otherworldly, and in a deep sense, a kind of antipolitics: "We left world politics under a duress that had an inner will, until that fortunate time when it will be possible to run a polity without evil or barbarity, the time for which we hope."[22]

Yet in his thinking about the war, matters of geopolitics and statecraft, as ever, interested him hardly at all. The chief impulses of the war, as he saw it, were spiritual; and the chief culprit, he came to think, was Christianity in particular, the principled willingness to render unto Caesar, and the rejection of law in favor of the illusion of love. "*Minut* [lit., "sectarianism," the traditional epithet for Christianity] abandoned the law, planted itself in the imagined attribute of mercy and kindness, which destabilizes the world, and destroys it."[23] He himself grasped and at times identified with antinomian energies—and that accounts in part for his vehemence regarding Christianity.

In the press of wartime, his eschatological reading of world events intensified. Early in the war he wrote: "When there is a great war in the world, the energy of Messiah wakes ... the greater the war, in quantity and quality, the greater the anticipation of the coming Messiah."[24] Sometime in 1915 he wrote: "The world structure currently in the midst of collapse, amidst the dreadful storms of the bloody sword, requires the building of the Jewish nation . . . the disintegrating world structure await[s] a force full of unity and a higher spirit. And all that is to be found in the soul of the ecclesia of Israel. . . . World culture totters, the human spirit is weakened, darkness covers all the peoples, *night covers the earth, and mists, the nations* (Isa. 60:2). And the hour has come . . . Abraham's blessing to all the peoples of the world will begin its work, and on that foundation there will begin anew our building in Eretz Yisrael. The current destruction will prepare a new rebirth, deep and transformative."[25]

Indeed the world crisis was redeemed for him by the Balfour Declaration, which he took as electrifying confirmation of his messianic reading of contemporary history. Many people and thinkers, Jewish and non-Jewish alike, had at the war's outset thought they were witnessing a new springtime of nations, and by the end of four gruesome years they were disabused. But for Kook, aghast though he was at the awful bloodshed, as for the Zionist movement, the war really had brought about a stunning step forward. As always, the national was for him complemented by the universal, and in the midst of the war he reached some of the farthest heights of his universalism:

There is one who sings the song of his self. . . . And there is one who sings the song of the nation, who cleaves with gentle love to Knesset Yisrael as a whole, and sings her song with her, grieves for her sorrows and delights in her hopes. . . . And there is one whose soul expands further beyond the bound of Israel, to sing the song of man. . . . And there is one whose spirit expands and ascends even higher, to the point of unity with all creation, with all creatures and all worlds, and sings with them all. . . . And there is one who ascends above all these songs in a single union, and all sound their voices. . . . The song of the self, of the nation, of man, of the world—all come together within him at every time, in every hour. And this perfection in all its fullness ascends and becomes a sacred song, God's song, Israel's song . . . a simple song, doubled, tripled, fourfold, the *Song of Songs of Shlomo* (Cant. 1:1), *The King to Whom Peace, Shalom belongs* (Shir Ha-Shirim Rabbah, 3:1[6]).[26]

In 1919 Kook returned to Palestine, now as Ashkenazic Rabbi of Jerusalem.[27] He had by then become an indispensable man. The secular Zionist leadership, the fledgling religious Zionist movement, and those traditionalists who sought to cooperate with the Zionists where they could all needed him—his sheer stature as a scholar and pietist, who had articulated a theology that justified the Zionist enterprise, albeit on very distinctive terms, bestowed on each group the legitimacy they needed. Now, in this deeply conflicted arena, his doctrines of tolerance and pluralism were put sorely to the test. Within the Yishuv, the heroic period of ideology gave way to institution building with very concrete stakes in the struggle over the shape of the new society and polity, and Kook was squarely in the middle.

The year 1921 saw the establishment of the modern Chief Rabbinate and Kook's installation as Ashkenazic Chief Rabbi, the new institution's leading figure. What was for the British an extension of established colonial policy of delegating religious services and some legal jurisdiction to local religious authorities was for Kook an opening to institutions that would gradually reshape the law into a new Torah for a redeemed Eretz Yisrael. He hoped to create institutions that would move the historical progression forward, refitting the law and legal institutions for the great changes to come. In his lifetime Kook made very little progress because of his profound limitations as an administrator, the unwillingness of his key rabbinic allies to identify wholeheartedly with Zionist institutions and the new rabbinate, and a chronic lack of funds for the new institution, due in no small measure to his reluctance to cast his lot with any one political party within the Yishuv as a whole.

He confounded his supporters among secular and religious Zionists by his enduring halakhic conservatism—especially his opposition to women's suffrage—and by his principled unwillingness to adopt partisan political positions. More broadly, the broad ecumenism that emerged from his teachings floundered when he tried to put it into practice—the center of gravity in the Yishuv had shifted from ideological exploration to institution building, and in this new situation one simply had to take sides.

But he was most hated by the ultra-Orthodox. The publication in 1920 of a volume *Orot* (Lights), consisting of entries from Kook's diaries woven into coherent essays by his son Zvi Yehudah, and laying out his ideas for all to see, simply drove ultra-Orthodox activists mad with rage, stoked by their fear of his growing public standing. The book was banned, made the target of vitriolic attacks by leading rabbis, and publicly burned. One particular passage showed how far Kook was from conventional rabbinical thinking and ignited a firestorm: "The calisthenics with which young Jews in the Land of Israel strengthen their bodies so that they may be vigorous sons of the nation betters the spiritual strength of the heavenly Zaddikim. . . . This sacred service [of exercise] elevates the Shekhinah higher and higher, like its elevation by the songs and hymns of David the King of Israel in the Book of Psalms."[28]

Yet many (though by no means all) of the rebels and heretics who were the object of Kook's fascination and admiration were unmoved or downright contemptuous of his trying to cast them as players in an esoteric divine drama. The ultra-Orthodox hated them but at least saw them as they saw themselves. As for Rav Kook, though the ultra-Orthodox couldn't fail to acknowledge his vast learning and personal saintliness, they utterly rejected his teachings and authority. The more zealous among them kept up a steady stream of verbal and sometimes physical attacks on him as the embodiment of Zionism's most pernicious assaults on tradition. Ironically, they attributed to him greater closeness to the Zionist leadership than either he or that leadership ever sought or claimed.

He consistently responded to even the most vicious personal attacks against him with extraordinary equanimity and striking nobility, to the point of using his influence to secure funds and other benefits even for some of his most bitter enemies. He himself drew a meager salary and lived in genuine material want.

Dream of Integration

The conflict with the Arabs took him by surprise. Like so many, he had come of age in a time when Jews and Arabs alike were pressing their moral and national claims in the context of the Ottoman Empire, and he had in those years taken pains to assert that the Arabs of Palestine were not the Jews' enemies. After the Great War, those claims were now being pressed by Jews and Arabs against one another, in a conflict that Kook's deeply optimistic and nonapocalyptic messianism had trouble accommodating. (The apocalyptic horror of the Great War, much as it pained him, was, for him, an affair of the Gentiles.) He was deeply shaken by the riots of 1929, during which he had been one of the few senior Jewish leaders on the ground (as most of the Zionist leadership was out of the country) and had been unable to convince the British to take more vigorous action to stem the violence. Yet in a series of subsequent open letters he steadfastly resisted the attempts of the mufti of Jersualem, Haj Amin al-Husseini, to cast the conflict in terms of a holy war.

The 1930s saw increasingly hard-fought conflicts within the Yishuv, as the growing specter of Nazism intensified already-bitter ideological conflicts. These exploded with the murder in June 1933 of the general secretary of the Labor movement, Chaim Arolosoroff, of which Revisionist followers of Jabotinsky were accused. As the inquest and trial dragged on, a number of leading figures, Kook included, became convinced of the innocence of the accused shooter, and Kook threw the full weight of his stature and influence behind an ultimately successful public effort to secure the man's acquittal.

This was a bittersweet triumph—Kook had effectively burned his bridges to the Labor Zionists, whose revolutionary fervor figured so prominently in his worldview—and demonstrated not only the terrible fault lines running through the Yishuv but the ultimate failure of his ecumenism. The last thing he published before his passing in the fall of 1935 was a *cri de coeur* at the death of his dream of integration:

> What has become of us! . . . (Lay aside anger, learn to look one at another, party to party, with the eyes of compassionate brothers, cast together into great trouble, willing to unite for one sacred goal: the common good, its dignity and sacred service . . . *return, and live* [Ezek. 18:32]) [29]

Two distinguished scholars, Isaac Herzog and Ben-Zion Uziel, more adept than Kook at institution building, succeeded him in the Chief Rabbinate after his death. His writings were little studied outside of limited circles of disciples and academic philosophers—the most significant being *Orot*, which Zvi Yehudah augmented in later editions; and *Orot Ha-Kodesh*, a theological magnum opus wrought from his notebooks by his disciple David Cohen, himself a fascinating mix of mystical ascetic and cosmopolitan intellectual. These two works neatly illustrate the complementary sides of Rav Kook's thought and legacy—religious nationalism and a universal philosophy of human culture and religion.

Zvi Yehudah eventually succeeded his father as head of the yeshiva he had founded, which for decades was a respected but marginal institution. That began to change in the early 1960s with the arrival of students who had been reared on Kook's writings and primed to see his charisma at work in his son. For his part, Zvi Yehudah had come to see the Holocaust as God's "radical surgery" on the Jewish people in order to bring them to the Land of Israel. This in turn made the Land of Israel the supreme value, and the apotheosis of all the dimensions of his father's teachings. After the 1967 war, and with greater force in the near-apocalyptic atmosphere following the Yom Kippur War of 1973, Zvi Yehudah's new disciples, with his encouragement, spearheaded the movement to settle the West Bank territories of Judea and Samaria, which had modestly begun under Labor auspices several years before.[30]

As the settlement movement grew so did its celebration of Kook, yet the expressive dimensions of his teachings were almost entirely collectivized and the universalist dimensions nearly forgotten. His sinuous, complicated personal meditations were read as dogma, and the dialectical energy that makes them so thrilling to read was eclipsed by a new political theology.[31] (The personal dimensions of his writings have continued in the nonpolitical realms and fuel much contemporary spirituality and artistic exploration.)

Zvi Yehudah's reading was not without challengers even among Rav Kook's latter-day disciples, most prominently Rabbi Yehudah Amital, founder of Israel's network of yeshivot combining military service with study, and of a leading yeshiva in Gush Etzion. A onetime theoretician of the settlement movement, Amital was the eventual founder of *Meimad*, the closest Israel has ever come to a religious peace movement.[32] While accepting the broad outlines of Kook's perspective, he insisted on the primacy of the moral and universal dimension, certainly over the primacy of the land; and he refused theological justifications (including Zvi Yehudah's) for the Holocaust, which he had experienced in a Nazi labor camp. Amital's alternative attracted much notice but little traction in religious Zionism as a whole.

The acute messianism of the settler movement was descended from the utopian energy, and the reworking of traditional concepts, that marked the Zionist movement as a whole. Kook was not the only messianic Zionist—but while mainstream Zionism had secularized the language of redemption, he kept its religious charge. For him, the secular and religious meaning of those terms existed reciprocally: "In every process in life, the secular-mundane awakes first, and then the sacred must necessarily follow, to complete the renaissance of the mundane . . . woe unto the secular . . . that says *there is none beside me* (Isa. 47:8) and woe unto the sacred that goes to war with the secular, which sucks, unconsciously, on the sacred."[33] This balance was unsettled by Zvi Yehudah, for whom secular Zionism had fulfilled its historical purpose, and was done.

In recent decades the renowned social theorist Shmuel Noah Eisenstadt developed the provocative idea of "multiple modernities."[34] For Eisenstadt, the welter of forces and movements we call modernity is best understood as a collection of open-ended processes, which, amid genuinely new sociopolitical conditions, radicalize tensions within premodern civilization, among them universalism and particularity, pragmatism and utopia, discipline and freedom. These multiple currents of modernity pulse throughout Kook's life and ideas, and a helpful way of looking at his protean life's work is as an attempt to see these multiple and seemingly antagonistic currents as all illuminated from within by a divine light that would with time reveal itself, through the Jewish people, to all humankind. In a mix of insight and empathy, all the more striking for someone of his background, he understood that the rebellions of the age were no catastrophe imposed from without, or depraved rebellions from within, but powerful, if incomplete and insufficiently self-conscious, responses to genuine moral and spiritual dilemmas, and to the multiple antinomies of modernity. Thus he threw himself into the task of reconciling them because within himself he felt them all.

Simultaneously embracing both universalism and particularism with rare vehemence, he saw genuine revelation in the spiritual life of all peoples, and in the very body of Israel, whose unique collective vocation was the salvation of humankind. He affirmed both pragmatism and utopia, or in his terms sagacity and prophecy, and envisioned the rationalization and institutionalization of the rabbinate in keeping with modern forms of administration, while adhering to a conservative interpretation of the law in the here and now as the first step toward a future "prophetic law" that would transcend structure and antistructure both.

The common thread in this entire way of thinking is the dialectic, a principled appreciation of complexity, and the ways in which precisely that complexity, that coincidence of opposites, gives birth, slowly, to whatever it is that we can know of truth. And yet to believe that that transformation is already with us is a dangerous illusion, so one must not abandon the law, even while working to infuse it with the prophetic light streaming toward us from the future.

Postscript on Further Reading

Kook has been the subject of scores of academic volumes, studies, and monographs, almost all in Hebrew. An English-language introduction to his life and thought is this writer's *Rav Kook: Mystic in a Time of Revolution* (New Haven,

2014) and other studies, available at academia.edu. Readers seeking to learn more about Kook's thought in English are advised to consult Yosef Ben-Shlomo, *Poetry of Being* (Tel Aviv, 1990); Zvi Yaron, *The Philosophy of Rabbi Kook* (Jerusalem, 1991); Benjamin Ish-Shalom and Shalom Rosenberg, eds., *The World of Rav Kook's Thought* (New York, 1991); Lawrence Kaplan and David Shatz, eds., *Rabbi Abraham Isaac Kook and Jewish Spirituality* (New York, 1995); and Aviezer Ravitsky, *Messianism, Zionism and Jewish Religious Radicalism* (Chicago, 1996). Other valuable studies in English include those written by Shlomo Fischer, Jonathan Garb, Tamar Ross, and Daniel Rynhold.

Readers looking for his works in English translation should consult the two excellent volumes edited and translated by the late Ben-Zion Bosker, *Abraham Isaac Kook* (Mahwah, NJ, 1978) and *The Essential Writings of Abraham Isaac Kook* (Teaneck, NJ, 2006), as well as Bezalel Naor's bilingual edition of *Orot* (Jerusalem, 2015), which is accompanied by an erudite and insightful introduction and source notes. Another valuable translation of Naor is his *When God Becomes History: Historical Essays of Rabbi Abraham Isaac Hakohen Kook* (Spring Valley, NY, 2003). A very helpful recent volume is Julian Sinclair's translation of parts of Rav Kook's consequential volume on the Sabbatical year (*Shabbat Ha-Aretz* [The Sabbath of the land]), *Rav Kook's Introduction to Shabbat Ha'Aretz* (New York: Hazon, 2014).

Notes

1. Rav Kook, *Igrot Ha-Reayah* (Collected letters of Rabbi Avraham Yitzhak Ha-Cohen Kook) (Jerusalem, 1962), 1:214.

2. The library of volumes by and about Kook is large, and constantly growing. The standard edition of his works, published by Mossad Ha-Rav Kook (The Rabbi Kook Foundation) in Jerusalem, runs to nineteen volumes of essays, letters, halakhic treatises, talmudic commentaries, and other writings—this in addition to other collections of essays and teachings that have long been in print. These have in recent years been supplemented by the publication of many works from manuscripts, most significantly a number of his spiritual diaries in their original forms, especially *Shemonah Kevatzim* (Eight compilations), the eight notebooks written during the heroic period of his theologizing, from 1910–1919. These were the mother lode for the many works culled and edited by Zvi Yehudah (*Orot, Orot Ha-Teshuvah,* and *Orot Ha-Torah* [Lights, Lights of repentance, and Lights of the Torah] among them) and also by David Cohen ("Ha-Nazir"), editor of the theological magnum opus *Orot Ha-Kodesh* (Lights of the sacred). Zvi Yehudah's editorial style skillfully wove essays out of his father's extensive meditations and visions, accentuating the nationalist dimensions and attenuating his more penetrating criticisms of conventional religion. Cohen retained the episodic and aphoristic flavor of the writings in their original form, while presenting them as a comprehensive universal philosophy of religion. Both consistently downplayed the more personal visions recorded in the journals.

The publication of the eight notebooks has gone a long way toward settling the long scholarly debate over whether Rav Kook was to be read chiefly as a philosopher or a mystic (one particularly noteworthy proponent of the latter view is Yosef Avivi). The notebooks' publication has demonstrated the overwhelmingly mystic and kabbalistic tenor of Rav Kook's own thought-world, which does not banish the philosophical dimension but rather embeds it in a richer perspective.

Other notebooks and hitherto unpublished works have been published, sometimes in censored forms, leading to new and heated debates over the shape and meaning of the evolving canon of works by Rav Kook Nearly all of Rav Kook's published works, in his lifetime and after, have been edited, often intensively, by others. For a fascinating discussion of his editors and their milieus, see Jonatan Meir, "Orot ve-Kelim: Behinah Mehudeshet shel 'Hug' Ha-Reiyah Kook ve-'Orkhei Ketavav" (Lights and vessels: A new examination of Rav Kook's circle and the editors of his writings), *Qabbalah* 13 (2005): 163–247. For a very helpful survey of the state of these publications, and of the political and theological stakes of seemingly recondite bibliographic and editorial issues, see Avinoam Rosenak "Hidden Diaries and New Discoveries: The Life and Thought of Rabbi A. I. Kook," *Shofar: An Interdisciplinary Journal of Jewish Studies* 25, no. 3 (Spring 2007): 111–47.

3. A full-length scholarly biography of Kook has yet to be written in any language. For now, English readers should turn to this writer's biography of Rav Kook, mentioned in the postscript above, as well as to Jacob Agus's *Banner of Jerusalem* (New York, 1946), which, though dated, still offers valuable insights and durable interpretations; for a full-length study of his early decades, see Yehudah Mirsky, *An Intellectual and Spiritual Biography of Rabbi Avraham Yitzhaq Ha-Cohen Kook from 1865 to 1904* (Ph.D. diss., Harvard University, 2007). For a brief Hebrew biography see Aryeh Frankel in *Ha-Encyclopedia shel Ha-Zionut Ha-Datit* (The encyclopedia of religious Zionism), 5:89–422 (Jerusalem, 1983); s.v. Kook, Avraham Yitzhaq.

4. Charles S. Taylor, *Sources of the Self: The Making of the Modern Identity* (Cambridge, 1989), 368–90.

5. Rav Kook, *Eyn Ayah 'al Massekhet Berakhot* (Eyn Ayah on Tractate Berakhot) (Jerusalem, 1990), 2:397–98. *Eyn Ayah* is his extensive commentary on the Aggadot contained in the first two tractates of the Babylonian Talmud, which he began in Eastern Europe and worked on for the rest of his life. The nature of its composition makes it an especially valuable source for tracing his evolution over time.

6. Rav Kook, *Shemonah Kevatzim*, 2d ed. (Jerusalem, 2004), 1:135, 43. (The italics here, and throughout, are meant to indicate his quoting or alluding to a biblical, talmudic or other classic text.) *Shemonah Kevatzim*, literally "Eight compilations," is, as noted above, a particularly rich set of Kook's spiritual diaries from the years 1910 to 1919, from which most of his canonical works were culled by his disciples/editors. The writing therein is vast and sprawling, and the editors have numbered the paragraphs within each notebook, such that a citation, such as 1:135, indicates "notebook number 1, paragraph number 135." This passage also appears in the standard edition of Rav Kook, *Orot* (Jerusalem, 1923), 122.

7. Kook, *Shemonah Kevatzim*, 2:21.

8. Ibid., 2:35, 264. This passage also appears in the standard edition of Rav Kook, *Orot Ha-Kodesh* (Jerusalem, 1964), 2:298.

9. Rav Kook, "Li-Mahalakh Ha-Ideiot be-Yisrael" (Toward the progress of ideals in Israel) was first written in 1910, appeared in 1912, and is reprinted in Kook, *Orot*, 102–18.

10. Kook, *Shemonah Kevatzim*, 2: 326–27, 342.

11. Ibid., 2:302.

12. Ibid., 1:807.

13. Ibid., 1:808.

14. Ibid., 2:76.

15. Ibid., 2:267, 285.

16. Ibid., 1:186; Kook, *Orot*, 160; Kook, *Orot Ha-Kodesh*, 3:191.

17. Kook, *Shemonah Kevatzim*, 3:1–3; Kook, *Orot*, 70–72.

18. Kook, *Shemonah Kevatzim*, 2:99.

19. Kook, *Shemonah Kevatzim*, 7:13.

20. Rav Kook, *Misphat Cohen* (Jerusalem, 1985), 337–38. This is one of the many volumes collecting his talmudic and halakhic writings and legal opinions.

21. Kook, *Shemonah Kevatzim*, 7:38.

22. Ibid., 6:101.

23. Ibid., 5:98; Kook, *Orot*, 21.

24. Kook, *Orot*, 13.

25. Kook, *Shemonah Kevatzim*, 5:63–64.

26. Kook, *Shemonah Kevatzim*, 7:112; Kook, *Orot Ha-Kodesh*, 2:444–45.

27. The finest and most extensive discussions of Rav Kook's Jerusalem years are to be found in Menachem Friedman, *Dat ve-Cherah: Ha-Ortodoksiyah Ha-Lo-Ziyonit be-Eretz Yisrael, 1916–1938*, (Religion and society: Non-Zionist Orthodoxy in the land of Israel, 1916–1938), 2nd ed. (Jerusalem, 1988); Yosef Avneri, *Ha-Reayah Kook ke-Rabbah shel Eretz Yisrael, 1921–1935* (Ph.D. diss., Bar-Ilan Universiy, 1989).

28. Kook, *Orot*, 80. The passage was first written in Kook, *Shemonah Kevatzim*, 1:716. Some interpreters have suggested that the particular calisthenics that Rav Kook had in mind were those

of the Jewish self-defense organizations; this is far from clear and even if so would hardly have diminished the shocking nature of this pronouncement.

29. Reprinted in Rav Kook, *Maamarei Ha-Reayah* (Collected articles of Rabbi Avraham Yithzak Hacohen) (Jerusalem, 1984), 365–66.

30. On Zvi Yehudah's teachings and his role in the settlement movement, see Idith Zertal and Akiva Eldar, *Lords of the Land: The War over Israel's Settlements in the Occupied Territories, 1967–2007* (New York, 2007), in particular chap. 4, 197–228. See also Gershom Gorenberg's valuable volume, *The Accidental Empire: Israel and the Birth of the Settlements, 1967–1977* (New York, 2006).

31. For an excellent survey of the trajectory of radical religious Zionism in recent decades and the ways it complicates conventional understandings of "fundamentalism," see Shlomo Fischer, "Radical Religious Zionism from the Collective to the Individual," in *Kabbalah and Contemporary Spiritual Revival*, ed. Boaz Huss (Beersheva, 2011), 285–310.

32. Amital deserves study in his own right. For now, see the biography by Elyashiv Reichner, *By Faith Alone: The Story of Rabbi Yehuda Amital* (Jerusalem, 2011); Alan Brill, "Worlds Destroyed, Worlds Rebuilt: The Religious Thought of Rabbi Yehudah Amital," *Edah Journal* 5, no. 2 (2006), available at http://www.edah.org/backend/JournalArticle/BRILL_5_2.pdf; and Reuven Ziegler and Yehudah Mirsky, "Torah and Humanity in a Time of Rebirth: Rabbi Yehuda Amital as Educator and Thinker," in *Torah and Western Thought: Intellectual Portraits of Orthodoxy and Modernity*, eds. Meir Y. Soloveichik, Stuart W. Halpern, and Shlomo Zuckier (Jerusalem and New York, 2015), 179–217.

33. *Pinkasei Ha-Reayah* (Notebooks of Rabbi Avraham Yitzhak Hacohen), 7:86, 1:451–52.

34. See, briefly, his major essay "Multiple Modernities," *Daedalus* 129, no. 1 (Winter 2000): 1–29.

8

Aby Warburg (1866–1929)

"THINKING JEWISH" IN MODERNITY

Griselda Pollock

Ebreo di sangue, Amburghese di cuore, d'anima Fiorentino.
(Jewish by birth, Hamburger at heart, a Florentine of the spirit.)
—GERTRUD BING, "ABY M. WARBURG," *RIVISTA STORICA ITALIANA*

ABRAHAM M. WARBURG, KNOWN AS ABY WARBURG, WAS A HAMBURG-BORN ART historian whose legacy has only recently been acknowledged.[1] Warburg was a thinker of modernity and an innovative cultural analyst of the centrality of unresolved issues of Jewish emancipation to modernity. For Warburg, a "dissident" from all religious practice and belief (according to the official term created by the Prussian constitution of 1850 that provided freedom of and from religion), it was nonetheless clear that the most profound analysis of culture and history was necessary in order to understand the equivocal and unresolved condition of the Jewish minority in European culture. He felt this ever more urgently as he himself lived through a specifically modern chapter in that history—that of Imperial and Weimar Germany. In that moment, both religious tolerance and civil emancipation rubbed up against an emergent and racist antisemitism that was formally articulated as a populist political program and became an academic, intellectual position, coinciding with the wake of political emancipation and social advancement for many Jewish Germans.[2]

As a Jewish intellectual, Aby Warburg's biography has figured in recent reassessments. Formerly studied as a "spiritual Florentine"—*fiorentino di anima* was his phrase—for his art historical writings on the Italian and Northern Renaissance, he is now also read as a participant in the formation of intellectual modernism in Germany. Warburg is also being appreciated for his active work in the civic and cultural life of the high bourgeois patrician elite of Hamburg. Cultural analysts are reassessing his acute studies of contemporary artistic, cultural, and political developments in Wilhelmine and Weimar Germany and Fascist Italy.[3] Aligned with contemporaries such as Sigmund Freud, Georg Simmel, Max Weber, and Walter

Benjamin—all known to him—Warburg is increasingly taking his place in the study of cultural formations of a liberal, progressive, modernizing, and conflicted Jewish middle class in Germany in those critical years of the early twentieth century. He thus belongs with those contemporaries who variously probed the ambivalences of modernity they themselves intimately inhabited and, in a sense, represented intellectually.

The renewed interest in Warburg, his thought, and his legacy flowers where art history opens onto anthropology and psychoanalysis and fosters a nonaestheticizing form of visual culture studies vigorously contesting canonical art history. In that same space, the field of modern Jewish studies has emerged to probe modernity intellectually and to reconsider modernization through its cultural formations and resulting identities: not Judaism so much as Jewishness, or *judacitié* as Kristeva, writing on Proust, translates the novel, nonreligious self-reflexive positionality.[4] The dual question of the meaning that Warburg, as a cultural analyst, attributed to Jewishness through his study of image culture, and the meaning of modernity for Warburg's own intellectual research into the Jewish question—*the* question, as he himself put it, posed not by Jews and Judaism but by non-Jewish culture—demands complex analysis that cannot be reduced to either biographical and personal or sociological and communal readings.

Warburg was the eldest son of Moritz M. Warburg of Hamburg and Charlotte Oppenheim of Frankfurt. The Warburgs had come in the late seventeenth century to settle in the Hanseatic republic of Hamburg/Altona from Warburg in Westphalia, hence their civic surname. Born into an Orthodox Jewish family, Aby Warburg was also deeply conscious of his geopolitical location in the Hanseatic town of Hamburg, to which he would attempt to make a lasting intellectual contribution. His father, the third generation of a banking family, M. M. Warburg & Co. (founded 1798), paid little attention to Jewish education, although he maintained Orthodox customs in a fully kosher home. Warburg's mother, Charlotte Oppenheim, taught her children Hebrew, along with their Christian governess, who also shared the children's many other language classes.

At the symbolic moment of coming of age Jewishly, the age thirteen, according to a family legend with self-consciously biblical overtones, Aby Warburg renounced his "birthright" as the eldest son due to take his father's place as head of the banking firm. Offering this position to his younger brother Max, Aby asked in return that Max always support his acquisition of books. Scholarship was to be his chosen profession. While the Orthodox family could imagine his studying to become a rabbi or even entering the professions through university training, both leading to some financial independence, Aby Warburg's subsequent estrangement from religion around the age of fifteen directed him to a secular education and a most unlikely field: art history. Yet, in a broader picture, he was symptomatic of a trend. By 1930, Karen Michels has calculated that almost 25 percent of those in the art historical profession in Germany were of Jewish origin, indicating that sociologically Jewish scholars made a contribution to this discipline disproportionate to their population.[5] Warburg's choice of subject thus should be viewed in a broader sociological perspective and history of Jewish-born Euro-American art historians. His specific contribution was, however, distinctive. Charlotte Schoell-Glass has argued that Warburg's entire project must be understood as being always deeply involved with Jewish-Christian relations and how they played out across both images and their cultural production and use. In the cultural environment of both popular and publicly authorized antisemitism this profound concern was not articulated by Warburg in his writings. It can, however, be read as a guiding thread throughout them.[6]

At the point at which Warburg entered the University of Bonn in 1886 (remaining until 1889, during which time he studied with Carl Justi, Herman Usener, Henry Thode, and Karl Lamprecht), art history meant either the study of pagan antiquity and its images; medieval studies, largely Christian in orientation; or the study of the Renaissance, namely Catholic Christian European culture. Worse still, the formation of art history as a discipline, which Germany had dominated during the nineteenth century, was nationalist and geopolitical, forging links between religion, culture, art, and current national identities. In her contribution to Catherine Soussloff's pathbreaking study, *Jewish Identity in Modern Art History,* Margaret Olin shows with painful clarity how implicated the discipline of art history has been in racist narratives underpinning such nationalism. Art history, a modern cultural reflex of the new nation-states, shaped their cultural self-identities by teaching that the spirit of a people finds expression in its arts and architectures. These cultural units of peoples were geographic and linguistic. Territorial rather than cultural, aligned with the emerging nationalisms underpinned or symbolized by still-active religious divisions expressed in historical cultural artifacts, art history sought to use invented cultural tradition as an imaginary mirror of the timeless essence of the nation (*Volk*) that was, only in the modern period, taking on its novel political, hence contingent, form. Thus Olin demonstrates how "nationalism imbued art history with a pattern of aims and categories it shared with modern anti-Semitism."[7] Modern racism becomes implicit in what appears as merely cultural distinctions because it lends "nationhood a basis in biology, while cultural phenomena such as art history were among the diverse conflicting criteria by which nineteenth-century scholars classified people into races and nations."[8] As art historical discourse unfolded on this model, scholars established intimate links between invented concepts of national character and cultural spirit and specific forms of determining climatic and geographical factors, all of which was, however, deeply tied into religious affiliations. Olin thus writes that "[t]he visual was thoroughly bound up in the national by the time German Romanticism promoted the Gothic as a German national style and certain media, such as wood, were cultivated as part of German heritage."[9]

Olin also points out how these nationalist identities needed others against which to set themselves. In thinking about the Germanness—synonymous with spiritual Christianity—of German art, difference played a major role. These differences were not only nationalist, such as defining the German character in art against the French or the Italian, but epochal, such as defining the Germans against the Greeks, Romans, and, in fact, the Jews. Not the contemporary Jews of Europe, but temporally and spatially distanced Jews of Middle Eastern antiquity were summoned onto the stage of a chronologically charted developmental history of art to be placed firmly among the ancients. Olin shows that most of the major art historical surveys of the nineteenth century did acknowledge a category of Jewish art. Yet it was envisaged precisely in order to repeat the Hegelian interpretation that could only locate Jews as ancient Orientals, a negative cipher to an idealized classical antiquity from which

German culture would derive its own succession, now integrated into modern European Christianity.

Linking religion and art was common. In the first *Handbuch der Kunstgeschichte* (Handbook of the history of art) by Franz Kugler, published in 1842, a fully Hegelian and, hence, Christianocentric conception of Jewish art produces it as oriental, fantastic, decorative, and decadent. This orientalist reading was based on nineteenth-century classicizing appraisals of biblical descriptions of the Ark of the Covenant and Solomon's Temple. Christian German authors positioned the Jewish people either as without any art at all or, at best, having had a wild and fantastical culture in the ancient past.

In order to counter these tendencies still present in identitarian cultural politics, Olin makes a significant theoretical move that I wish to borrow to avoid all dangers of identifying a thinker such as Warburg with a fixed idea of Jewishness. If, states Olin,

> one thinks of actions rather than being, of narrative positions rather than ontology, then a work of art can speak in several narrative voices. The question of whether it is Jewish art becomes meaningless, since to say something is Jewish is not the same as saying that it may speak "Jewish" at any given moment or for a given historical listener.[10]

Olin's anti-identitarian model of artworks "speaking Jewish" in various modes enables me to position Aby Warburg's transformative intervention in the emerging culture of art historical scholarship in Germany and Europe as a whole in the last decades of the nineteenth century and the first three of the twentieth. It is not a matter of his being Jewish and this "fact" inflecting his thought. Rather than *speaking* Jewish, itself alerting us to strategic positioning and critical, contextual interventions by artists, Warburg might be understood as an intellectual *thinking* Jewish.

This is not because of an ontology by which we define Warburg as *being* Jewish. Birth, history, and legal status remain critical factors; he acknowledged always that he was *ebreo di sangue*—Jewish by birth/blood. *Thinking* Jewish is strategically dependent on subsequent articulations, choices, and practices in highly specific historical contexts. The idea of thinking Jewish within a modern German or European context makes us pay attention to thought as a strategic activity, a practice, activating certain positions of possibility, difference, and distance as well as probingly investigating the world in which "Jewishness," a lived, shifting individual and collective experience, and "the Jew," a figure of imaginative fantasy and paranoid projection, conflictually operated on a field of images and ideas. Warburg's *thinking* Jewish in his modern moment constitutes precisely a double distancing. Warburg distanced himself from the religious-magical practices and beliefs he experienced as a child in a practicing but nonspiritual Orthodox family. Because of that formation, he could, at the same time, operate at a distance from those beliefs and practices he came to study in art history, specifically through his work on Florentine society and culture in the fifteenth and sixteenth centuries. There he uniquely identified and sought to make sense of the surprising coexistence of devout Catholic Christianity, pagan astrology, and engagement with the imagery of pagan antiquity.

Both late-nineteenth-century Hamburg, subject to modernizations of industrial capitalism and political emancipation, nationalism, and imperialism, and fifteenth-century Florence, the home of early modern banking and urbanized mercantile patronage that combined Christian belief, astrological beliefs, and the embrace of classical antiquity, were moments of structural transition in European economies and societies that have been identified with the uneven emergence of what we call modernity. It was indeed a widely held scholarly assumption in Warburg's time that Renaissance Italy was the cradle of modern man, as evidenced through the flowering of humanism, rationalism, trade, science, and the reengagement with pagan antiquity. Warburg echoed (though he later differed substantially) positions learned from his study of Jacob Burckhardt, the leading proponent of the modernizing thesis about the Renaissance, when he concluded a study of a perplexing assemblage of classicism and astrological symbols in the frescoes of the Renaissance Palazzo Schifonia in Ferrara:

> Our sense of wonder at the inexplicable fact of supreme artistic achievement can only be enhanced at the awareness that genius is both a gift of grace and a *conscious dialectical energy*. The grandeur of the new art, as given to us by the genius of Italy, had its roots in the shared determination to strip the humanist heritage of Greece of all its *accretions of traditional "practice,"* whether medieval, Oriental or Latin. It was with this desire to restore the ancient world that "the good European" began his battle for enlightenment, in that age of *internationally migrating* images that we—a shade too mystically—call the Age of the Renaissance.[11] (my emphasis)

These highlighted phrases mark Warburg's decisive thought, which stressed conscious engagement rather than romantic ideas of genius, whether individual or cultural. Work was needed to transcend practice-encoded beliefs if transformation through conscious work was to produce genuine enlightenment (as opposed to a new illusion of pure rationality). Note too his comments on the international migration of images, which directly opposes the territorialization and nationalization of the study of artistic cultures.

Using a biographical model, some scholars have been tempted to propose a mirroring of Warburg's own mercantile, religious family background in Hamburg in the mercantile but Catholic religious background of the Medici and one Francesco Sassetti, whose funerary chapel and last testament he studied in several key papers.[12] This would make Warburg's work as an art historian a displaced projection from his present onto an Italian past. His art history thus becomes merely a disguised self-portrait. Instead, I suggest that Warburg used the dislocation and difference between past and present, understood as distinct moments in a dialectical history of modernity, to examine, in an archaeological (in Foucault's) sense, the incongruous concurrency of religious or magical thinking and aspirations toward self-conscious rationality. These tensions remained unfinished business within modernity, continuing to pose critical questions of any contemporary cultural analysis of humanity's historical or present cultures. Thus Warburg's method of closely argued, textual, and document-based study of specific works from the past (in lieu of grand metaphysical theorizations typical of contemporary German system-making scholarship) would mirror back to the present of an increasingly antisemitic

German religious-nationalist culture those contradictions that needed to be exposed and transformed if the inherent trend toward blood sacrifice and death were to be averted, even within modernist capitalist and urban societies.

Stated thus, his project sounds melodramatic. Blood? Death? Warburg's thinking Jewish was daringly and deeply perspicacious, and arose out of the disjunction between his desire to access a scholarly life as a cultural historian and his intense consciousness of the conditions in which he tried to live as such in modern Germany—accepted but marked out as "a Jew." Warburg's understanding of contemporary forms of German and European modernity were full of dread and anxiety that the unresolved dimensions of humanity's oscillating psychic structures, fueled by real social, material, and often local changes, could pierce the shell of Enlightenment rationality. We cannot claim him as a prescient foreteller of the catastrophe that would destroy Germany after 1933. Retrospectively, we can see that the attention he paid to the persistent undercurrents in modernity that would generate fascisms worldwide was far more alert than most to the potential within modernity itself for such an eruption of deadly racist violence.

Warburg's originality in thinking Jewish modernity arose from his daring to conjoin then contemporary and emerging anthropological and historical arguments that located the origins of religion and culture in primordial human anxieties, fears, and passions with a totally innovative theory of cultural memory. His theory of memory involved the function of the image in sustaining links and transmitting formulas for emotion from the originating passions through many cultural transformations and overlays. This scholarly operation acquired its energy and urgency from the very reality of the fears he felt personally in the unresolved contradictions of feeling, though not living, Jewish (by choice) in modernizing Europe and the potential he saw for the eruptions of violence that had fueled sacrificial modes of managing collective fears. In my opinion, it was not his own unstable mental condition that made him project onto cultural history a schizophrenic undercurrent in culture, as some have argued.[13] It was rather the recurring schizophrenic polarities revealed by his cultural analysis that threatened a sensitized, personal, but also culturally attentive mental state. Warburg's research cultivated within him a seismographic consciousness attuned to underlying violence in human cultures.

At the end of World War I, Warburg was institutionalized (from 1918 until 1923) for trying to act out uncontrollable fears for his family's safety. He was driven by his own studies of the past and witnessing of the violent present to the view that his family might indeed be murdered by their own compatriots. This sense of potential violence against Jews was not his fantasy. He had systematically built up a collection to document the present, which included many file boxes on ritual murder, including the unsolved Konitz case in 1913 and the terrible Stavrapol pogrom, in which a Christian schoolteacher accused of revolutionary sympathies, hence aligned with "the Jews," had been brutally killed by a frenzied mob "as a Jew" in 1902.

In her study of the central role of antisemitism in the project of Aby Warburg as a cultural analyst, Charlotte Schoell-Glass examines a fragmentary document in the Warburg archives drafted in response to outbreaks of violence against Jews. The document was also examined by Hans Liebeschütz in his essay "Aby Warburg as Interpreter of Civilization." Liebeschütz considers this incomplete document as evidence of one moment when Warburg felt he might have to make " 'a public declaration of his personal commitment' as a Jew."[14] Both authors read this text for a double message.

One direction of the text led to a proposed "psychological survey of German Jews." This was necessary to develop Jewish self-knowledge in the current conditions (anticipating Hannah Arendt's postwar trenchant analyses of prewar Jewish blindness); it was also drawn from Warburg's own experience of Orthodox Jewish life and his struggles as he separated from that tradition (though he was never a complacent assimilationist). He expressed his own distaste for the ostentatiousness of the very wealthy among his own community. "But further experience," writes Schoell-Glass, "had shown Warburg the very conspicuous complacence on the Jewish side was less dangerous than the 'teutonic wrath' hidden behind the pretension of restraint."[15]

Schoell-Glass then proceeds to place this document in the second context of the history and symbolism of the blood libel, which reaches back into archaic sacrificial cults with blood. These archaic traces were, however, grafted, in the Middle Ages, onto the complex and radically different theologies associated with both Passover and Easter rituals, without which the libel makes no sense at all.[16] During the Middle Ages, far from being a folkloric survival, the blood libel was held and spread by intellectuals, notably priests and friars. By the modern era, where it is still current, it is no longer a matter of belief (that could fire up again). Blood libels are spread as calculated manipulations of the slanderous memory for novel, racist antisemitic purposes.

Nonetheless, linking this persistent delusion with a critically refashioned Nietzschean acknowledgment of the dialectic between Apollonian restraint and Dionysian excess, Warburg formed a view that, in the modern context of emerging cults of aestheticized irrationalism, the Dionysiac could unleash disaster and that "the 'breakdown of the *principium individuationis*' could mean: frenzied bloodlust."[17]

The potential was present in certain symbolic and superstitious dimensions within Christianity, which had been given specific imagery and textual forms by that tradition. But superstition also persisted within Judaism as well as in pagan religious formations that, in ersatz postreligious modern forms, also contained such potentialities. This perspective was made possible by linking, as Warburg did in his interdisciplinary university studies, philology, anthropology, the study of ancient religions, and philosophy with art history. Warburg's transdisciplinary modern thought, therefore, becomes so significant and singular precisely because, as a dissident within art history (he radically opposed what he called aestheticizing and formalist art history), he brought all these disciplines and thinking methods back into contact with the image. Furthermore, he theorized visual forms as mnemonic devices.

For Warburg, images retain originary imprints of actualized passion. Like batteries, but in terms of iconic form, they store up such energies that persist through material forms and cultural memory to recharge anew later cultures that seek or need formulas for their own passionate articulations of fear, desire, mourning, or violence. The image hovers, therefore, between the realm of enacted passion and its memory, management, or translation by symbolization.

Starting in art history, Warburg had, however, to deviate from its pacifying aestheticism, its nationalist narrowness, and its foreclosure of the dialectics of fantasy and the symbolic. He had to create a new domain—the untranslatable German term is *Kulturwissenschaft*, which can be loosely rendered as "cultural analysis"— precisely to breach polite and self-occluding boundaries, maintained by the curricular university system, between the study of ancient, older, primitive, early, antique, archaic pasts in human history and the present in the contemporary period. Modernity could not be allowed to delude itself as being more developed and evolved, superior to, or different from preceding moments. Persistence of deeper fundamentals had acquired over time forms or formulas through which such archaic or atavistic feelings had been encoded and might find contemporary expression. Art, understood as image, as *pathosformel*, preserved these formulas over time, as did other cultural forms of narrative, folklore, and oral tradition that constituted cultural memory. These lent their energies to new image cultures.

Warburg's work was not a romanticism of human essence that abolished history and posited, like Jung, eternal and transcultural symbols in a collective unconscious. Nor is it a kind of reductivist comparative anthropology proposing an unchanging common human destiny, making history redundant. Warburg fully acknowledged radical transformations in the material, political, and cultural conditions of human societies, and he assessed their implications through detailed studies of complex cultural formations and minute readings of documents and art practices. In the drama of German Jewish modernity, Warburg saw a history and its cultural memories that would have to be confronted without either complacency or the delusions of both separatists and assimilationists, both racists and the tolerant. The Jewish question, which in prefascist times referred to issues arising from emancipation and coexistence, was not to be solved without understanding it as a matter of *both sides* and of the image-unconscious of all traditions. Thus what "the Jew" represents for the non-Jewish world, so far in excess of, and downright contrary to, any actuality at any point in history, indexes forces and factors utterly unrelated to any particularity of Judaism. This paradox required an entire cultural/historical/analytical apparatus to research.

Hence the gradual formation of what became Warburg's lasting legacy: the Kulturwissenschaftliche Bibiothek Warburg—the Warburg Library of Cultural Analysis—in Hamburg and, since 1933, at the Warburg Library in the University of London that was recently threatened with its own extinction. Warburg's case recalls that of James Loeb (1867–1933), a fellow sufferer from extreme mental illness, who was also the intellectual son of a great banking house. Loeb also ultimately preferred scholarship and patronage to finance and made his mark culturally—not merely through guilty generosity but through conviction in the potential role of music and classical knowledge. Loeb founded and sustained the School of Music in New York (now the Juilliard School of Music), and, most famously, he created and financed the Loeb Classical Library.[18]

Warburg homed in on the most irrational, powerful, and atavistic dimensions of human culture that were expressed in and somewhat contained by the emergence of formalized religion. Hence his later fascination with Christian theologies of trans- and consubstantiation: symbolic displacements of blood sacrifice. In common with the radical thinkers of his time, Warburg understood religion as a relatively late (historically) formulation of much more ancient rituals and practices by which impotent human beings had managed their intense anxieties and fears associated with survival. Religions already were symbolic encodings, aesthetic and cultural formulations of once immediately experienced and acted-out emotions.[19] They created and, in material remnants, bequeathed what Warburg named *pathosformel*—formulations of pathos, suffering, and ecstasy that, as images, were both mnemonic devices and, like a battery, stored-up energy that could be reactivated by reuse of the image formula in a new cultural moment. Images were the key mediators between foundational human passions and historical conditions in which they functioned as reignition.

While sharing with many of his contemporaries the legacies of Darwin in an evolutionary model of human culture, developed most notably by anthropologist of primitive religion Edward Tylor, Warburg was far from plotting a unidirectional, developmental trajectory—from the atavistic, the irrational, and the "primitive" toward the civilized, rational, and even secular. What he drew from Darwin concerned the relation of adaption to survival and the evolution of gesture and expression as indices of emotions.[20] He looked back across human cultural and material history to foster the recognition, much closer to Freudian thought (which he did not, however, embrace), that nothing of any human being's formative processes or stages are erased by later development, because the primary energies and anxieties carve fundamental and determinant patterns within the human mind and its forms of cultural memory. These passions give rise individually and culturally to forms, and ultimately to thought and symbolization. Cultural crises are to be understood, therefore, as the potential loss of symbolization, which means the destruction of the space for thought—the interval for negotiation between pure passionate action and human self-reflection. Thought is not mere rationalism; rationalism is, in Warburg's terms, self-deluding because it fails to grasp the need for constant work on this tension.

For Warburg the powerful psychic mechanisms were always responses to material realities and social conditions that were misread by fantasy. They have to be addressed, not suppressed. Thus modernity, or the long struggle toward it, misleads itself with the simplified legend of evolving rationality—a rationalization if ever there was one. Modernity is not a confident development but the ever-shifting site of unresolved tensions in humanity regarding aspirations toward rational self-mastery and self-knowledge, the appeal of ecstatic self-dissolution, and the dangers of such release. This opposition of the rational and the irrational had been articulated by Nietzsche in *The Birth of Tragedy* (1872), which Warburg briefly studied as a student but dismissed for being ultimately too mythical. Nietzsche aimed to explode contemporary bourgeois complacency and a one-sided identification with the selective model of classical, calm gravity by exposing a deep conflict in the classical world between Apollonian and Dionysian forces. Such a dichotomy was, however, too neat and susceptible, notably in German thought, to potential dialectic resolution: *Aufhebung*. Favoring more contemporary and electrical metaphors, Warburg understood these opposing forces as a polarity; the course of human history constantly oscillated between these poles, needing both, but necessitating cultural and historical analysis as well as readings of their signs in contemporary culture. One face of modernity deceived itself with the false belief that rational self-mastery could in and of itself also master its other, projected out onto others and the distant past. Warburg dedicated his scholarly life to tracking the power and significance of the counterforces that lay within rather than behind, which could and did resurface in what his contemporary Freud would term "acting out" (as opposed to "working through").[21]

Thus the tendency of the new disciplines of anthropology, archaeology, and even philology to propose a developmental or teleological model of human history, thus arriving at the pinnacle of a rational and scientific modern Europe, was a dangerous self-delusion in the sciences of humankind. The mechanism for dealing with what such sciences wanted to disavow was the invention of an other as the locus of all that was to be rejected in the idealized modern self. Hence the anthropologist's "primitive" paralleled the scapegoated, racialized other of contemporary nationalizing (hence, racist) discourse: "the Jew." A Jewish person was thus burdened, irrespective of his or her own singularity and historically formed being, with the externalized marks or rather signifiers of repudiated/unacknowledged otherness within the dominant group. Germanness was, therefore, as much an issue as Jewishness; both culturally misrecognized their mutual dangers through believing in modernity's contradictory myths of progress. Warburg's core concept was *Nachleben*. This means having an after-life, living on rather than mere survival which is, in German *überleben*. For Warburg, *Nachleben* as a cultural phenomenon requires, therefore, a more agitating attentiveness to concurrent forces in both individual psychologies and cultural imaginaries.

It is vital to stress, therefore, that it was both Warburg's familiarity with Jewishness and his principled anti-Orthodox dissidence that provided an Archimedean point outside of Christianocentric European thought. It was this combination, itself historically contingent on modern conditions in Germany, that made him alert to aspects of Christianity's own archaic, sacrificial, and ecstatic components that could be identified as they surfaced in superstition, particularly in the extraordinarily persistent blood libel against the Jews (as we have seen). At the same time, his own "dissidence" or atheism, and profound estrangement from what he saw as emptied Jewish ritualized practice with its own accreted inheritance of superstition and folklore, provided an *interval*, a thinking space or *Denkraum*, that enabled him to recognize these elements, cross-culturally, as representative of common psychoanthropological tendencies rather than essential signs of different religious modes or racialized typologies.

Puzzlingly, Warburg was not a Freudian. Yet Freud's thought illuminates Warburg's groping toward a way of holding together in constant play early formations and later developments—in some kind of evolution to which history testifies—with structural formations and a more archaeological model of subjectivity and culture as a changing scenario that indicates a return of the repressed.

In 1919, Freud published a difficult but influential essay, "The Uncanny" (Das Unheimliche), which is considered to be one of his most important reflections on aesthetics. Freud performs a lengthy linguistic deconstruction of the German adjective *unheimlich*, which reveals itself paradoxically as being at the same time both what is unfamiliar and hence unhomely and as the all too familiar and too homely. Its troubling quality is the return of the latter, after repression. Freud borrows Schelling's definition of the uncanny as "that which ought to have remained secret and hidden but has come to light."[22]

Freud concluded, however, by specifically associating the sensation of the uncanny with two psychological operations. The first related to what he called the "omnipotence of thoughts." Imagining that murderous thoughts could kill, thus that our thinking can affect the world, expresses an infantile fantasy of control akin to rituals and sacrifices of ancient religions attempting to control nature. The second operation indexes repressed infantile complexes, such as fantasies of castration or of intrauterine life, both of which arouse anxiety if and when any trace resurfaces from primal repression. Freud identifies the first operation of omnipotence of thoughts with animistic beliefs that the rigorously atheist or thoughtful adult may overcome. But he shows that such overcoming is not so easy, for the two lines converge. Thus Freud refuses Jungian archetypes or universal tendencies in favor of a psycho-dynamic historical foundation for our tendencies to regress to modes of belief: anxieties and superstitions that, as adults, we should have surmounted. Freud writes:

> Our conclusion could then be stated thus: the uncanny occurs when either infantile complexes which have been repressed are once more revived by some impression, or when primitive beliefs which have been surmounted seem once more to be confirmed. Finally we must not let our predilection for smooth solutions and lucid exposition blind us to the fact that these two classes of uncanny experience are not always sharply distinguishable. When we consider that primitive beliefs are most intimately connected with infantile complexes, and are, in fact, based on them, we shall not be greatly astonished to find that the distinction is often a hazy one.[23]

Thinking Jewish modernity for Warburg, therefore, was not an engagement with the modernization of Jewish thought, aligning Jewish poetry, philosophy, linguistics, history, and theology with the German academic organization of modern knowledge categories, as we find in the formation of *Wissenschaft des Judentums*, the cultural analysis of Jewish civilization undertaken by Jewish intellectuals from the beginning of the nineteenth century. It was not a matter of cleansing Judaism of its embarrassingly primitive archaicisms, such as the Reform Movement in German Judaism had attempted. Certainly it was not a matter of renewing and revising Judaism to defend tradition and ritual against the inroads of modernity, as we find in modern Orthodoxy as a negative retrenchment in the face of a risk of undoing of boundaries through assimilation to Christian and post-Christian modernity. Finally, it was not a turning away from the Jewish question to lose himself as a self-defining monad in that brief moment when civil and political emancipation seemed to offer freedom of movement and thought to the hitherto confined and marked Jewish citizen in modernizing Germany. Warburg was not a deracinated flâneur in intellectual modernity or its urban life.

He knew that above all the question of "the Jew" had to be confronted precisely inside modernity. The moderns seemed unaware of the danger modernity itself posed to the life of this particular minority that was not a newly encountered territorially or temporally remote other, a colonial subject, an indigenous primitive, or a remnant of the past that might die out. As sociologist Zygmunt Bauman has argued, the reason that the case of the integrated, modernizing, educated, commercially vital, and culturally relevant German Jews was so problematic and exemplary is not owing to their absolute difference but rather to the absence of significant difference. The apparent difficulty lay not in their remoteness but in their continuing proximity and seamless approximation. How could Germanness be essentially defined if its attributes were successfully assimilable by non-Christian others? Yet as such close, cohabiting strangers (insisting on their own particularity yet acting as intensely patriotic locals), the Westernizing Jewish communities posed the question modernity found intolerable: ambivalence.[24] According to Bauman, modernity is best understood through a gardening metaphor, clearly managing social formations through proper plants, weeding out the improper. Ambivalence has no place.

The meaning of Warburg's Jewish origins to his significance as a cultural analyst and thinker has been variously interpreted.[25] In his scholarly *Intellectual Biography*, Ernst Gombrich minimized it. Gombrich was immediately critiqued by two scholars, Hans Liebeschütz and Felix Gilbert, who felt Warburg's background and family history needed to be brought into the equation. These and other studies refocus attention on the biography of Warburg, relating it personally and socially to his thought. But such readings tend to be reductive, as if either life or work can be explained simply in relation to the other. Two texts approach the question at the level of his thought, the most influential of which is Charlotte Schoell-Glass's *Aby Warburg und der Antisemitismus: Kulturwissenschaft als Geistespolitik* (1998), translated into English as *Aby Warburg and Anti-Semitism: Political Perspectives on Images and Culture* (2008).

Schoell-Glass refocuses attention from biographical influences to intellectual and political engagement with antisemitism in Germany between the 1870s and 1920s, when a racializing redefinition emerges in both popular and intellectual media and political culture. Her method is itself Warburgian. Warburg insisted that difficult things like cultural beliefs and mentalities, contradictory trends of economic rationalism and irrational superstitions, have to be traced in historical, documentary evidence so as to avoid the mystifying and generalizing metadiscourses typical of some of the German scholars with whom Warburg had studied and whose grand theoretical generalizations undermined their historicity and effectivity. Schoell-Glass thus carefully studies Warburg's thought through a close reading of his own documents, weaving her analysis across letters, scholarly articles, and political pamphlets; above all, she examines the evidence of collections Warburg made of contemporary newspaper clippings, photographs, postcards, reports of incidents, pamphlets, and major publications by leading antisemitic authors.[26] Though not overtly declared by Schoell-Glass, the ceaseless activity she notes from these documentary sources is Warburg's profound and formative study of antisemitism.

A brief scenario taking place in Strasbourg in 1889, and a letter to his mother from that city where Warburg had moved to extend his art historical studies and prepare his dissertation, makes this clear. When he first went to study at a university in Bonn, he was accompanied by an Orthodox companion. They lived in an observant Jewish household to maintain ritual practices regarding food. The poor quality of this food and other factors led to Warburg's abandoning all attempts at maintaining the rules. When his parents suggested he change universities, the better to enable him to keep kosher, he wrote to his parents that he refused to direct his studies according to such obligations. Thus he threw off the last of these. From Bonn in 1887, he wrote:

> When you write dearest Mama, about the things that will go by the board through eating differently, I must tell you that you are doing me an injustice. I

am not at all ashamed to be a Jew, on the contrary I am trying to show others that representatives of my kind are well suited, in accordance with their talents, to insert themselves as useful links in the chain of present-day cultural and political developments; but just because I want to do that I must strive to shake off whatever will not organically fit into my activity. I want to act as I am; I want to be regarded by people for what I am.[27]

From Strasbourg in 1889, however, he writes a letter (later annotated by his son Max Adolph Warburg with the words, "important: whole letter") that shows how this ambition hits the wall of blind prejudice:

I find though at every turn that our so well loved German people, with the blessing of the authorities, chose to see every Jew as above all a foreign interloper with dubious manners, which depresses me. To be sure, I must also emphasize that everybody whom I have come to know better—students or professors—shows me good faith and goodwill, and they are quite a number of rather nice people.

And yet, and yet! The common folk here are dreadful: I cannot go out during the day without once or twice hearing the comment somewhere behind me "Thassa Jew" ["Descht ist a Jud" is the local dialect in the original.] Or as recently—when I go into the Germania, I hear a group of Christian gentlemen entertaining themselves by murmuring and *mauschel*-ing [*mauschein* is to talk Yiddish] as they play cards: of course in such cases you cannot call anybody to account; it has nothing to do with oneself: but *how* such things can happen at all![28]

He then makes the statement:

I often entertain the thought of seeking a practical solution to the Jewish question later: does one have the right to keep life at a distance?[29]

Schoell-Glass offers careful textual analysis of both letters in order to bring out the dialectic between the young Warburg's desire to experience his own singularity as a person—*who I am*—discovered by others in the process of unprejudiced and grounded familiarity. Personality and intellect constitute an identity which is, however, always in suspension as his singularity is disfigured by projection of typology: he becomes not Aby M. Warburg but a Jew, and in a specific way that pits German Christian gentlemen against foreign interlopers with dubious manners. Physically marked by appearance—"Oriental," in Warburg's own words—the Jewish body stifles the recognition of subjective singularity, while the attempt to train the Jewish body into conformity is apparently always betrayed by manners that are but indices of the attempted dissimulation.

Another key scholar to explore Aby Warburg's negotiations of German Jewish modernity, Michael Steinberg, catches the anguish of this physicality of difference by analyzing a collection of postcards of Jews during World War I that Warburg collected. Ostensibly demonstrating German-Jewish solidarity against Russian war atrocities, some postcards represent the very marked differences in size and appearance between the German officers and Eastern European Jewish men in their kaftans, beards, sidecurls, and headwear. In his essay analyzing Warburg's famous lecture, given in 1923, about his trip in 1895 to encounter the Pueblo Indians, notably the Hopi, of the American Southwest, Steinberg juxtaposes one such photograph of Jewish men from Lodz with one titled *Hostile Hopi*. He thus speculates on the striking visual similarity between images collected by Warburg of Polish Jews taken by German army photographers and portraits of Hopi Indians taken by the Reverend H. R. Voth (some of the latter were taken when Aby Warburg was also present during the photography session). Steinberg draws attention to the way the "camera creates primitiveness by recording an asymmetric exchange between, on the one side the observers, a culture of expansion, power and control and professed intentions of liberation and, on the side of the observed, a culture seen, literally, as primitive and transformable."[30]

In this dialectic of primitivism and modernization, Warburg, according to Steinberg, senses a parallel between the Pueblo peoples of the American Plains as viewed by European anthropologists and Polish Jewish communities in Europe's economic backwaters as viewed by Germans. But more significantly, Steinberg suggests, Warburg was also seeing "ritualistic residues present in the practices even of the Hamburg Jewish community."[31] Hence the lifelong anguish that Steinberg recognizes in Warburg's work arises from having to recognize himself within an image of primitivized otherness, while he is neither able to identify with it through some fantasy of the noble savage nor able entirely to disown belonging. Steinberg concludes: "The suffering and greatness of his career and person lie in the failure, or refusal to draw the line."[32]

The 1895 encounter with the Pueblo Indians in person, mediated by Warburg's own and others' photographs, captured a dramatically real encounter between the living persistence and performance (*Nachleben*) of ancient religious modes and modernization. Modernization for the Indians arrived in the form of both missionaries and businessmen, railways, and electricity, all touching the rain dances and magical incantations with wild animals still performed by the Hopi and other peoples of the Plains. Writing about that encounter was the exercise that tested Warburg's ability to rejoin ordinary life after six years in an institution in 1923.

We can stress Warburg's place as a major force in art history or as a figure in public culture in Hamburg. He helped found that city's university and he supported many contemporary artists and cultural ventures. We can also acknowledge the real significance of his breakdown in response to the horrors of World War I and his extraordinary process of recovery by his writing through the 1895 visit in retrospect. Bracketing these activities, the ancient and the modern literally touched them all, sometimes dangerously and often beneficially. On his release from the clinic in Kreuzlingen, Warburg returned to the transformation of his book collection into a public institution and a library. This we must understand not as a personal project.[33]

Performing as exemplary members of the German Jewish haute bourgeoisie, Warburg and his banking family (whose financial acumen secured the means) created one of the most important institutions of twentieth-century modernity's thinking Jewish: an interdisciplinary, transcultural library that dared to place the Jewish question in its historical, cultural, and anthropological context. Thus he created an institution for reflexive cultural analysis. The intellectual and resulting physical architecture of Warburg's library and the kind of thinking it fosters and sustains remain as relevant as ever, even as we still struggle to comprehend the depth and

complexity of Warburg's own challenge to think Jewish in modernity without idealizing a new intellectual hero—and without isolating the mad but brilliant scholar
from his active sociocultural and political engagements. Warburg died in 1929, witnessing in his last months the bizarre sight of what he called the "repaganization of
Rome" when the Pope, yielding the Vatican's territorial and political sovereignty,
signed the infamous Lateran Treaty with Mussolini's fascist state. The last photomontage in the Mnemosyne BilderAtlas was created to demonstrate the power and
relevance of Warburg's mode of cultural reading of the clash of past and present in
the image—catching with Benjaminian insight the shock of the dialectical image of
Christianity's secession to invented fascist militarism, reclaiming the Roman *fasces*
as their emblem.[34]

Notes

1. Ernst Gombrich, in *Aby Warburg: An Intellectual Biography* (London, 1972), minimized
the significance of Warburg's family and religious background. This oversight was criticized in
early reviews and has since been shifted through major scholarship by Michael Steinberg, Charlotte Schoell-Glass, and Matthew Rampley.

2. It has been argued that the issue was in fact intensified by the post–World War I settlement
and territorial losses from Germany, which severed Prussian Jewry from the larger population
of Ostjüden against which the acculturated Prussian Jewish bourgeoisie could set itself. With the
loss of these more visibly and linguistically marked Jewish others, the local Jewish community
inherited what had hitherto been reserved for more obviously foreign elements. This argument
conflicts, however, with Bauman's analysis of the exemplary predicament of the urbanizing German Jewish bourgeoisie, whose success at acculturation played out the dynamic of a host culture's superiority sustained precisely by the aspirations of the outsider to assimilate. Yet, that
could never be permitted since the host's superiority consisted in its irreplicability, and thus Bauman concludes: "The harder they try, however, the faster the finishing-line seems to be receding.
When, at last it seems to be within their grasp, a dagger of racism is flung from beneath the liberal
cloak." Zygmunt Bauman, *Modernity and Ambivalence* (Cambridge, 1991), 71.

3. On Warburg's involvement in civic culture and modern art in Hamburg, see Mark A. Russell, *Between Tradition and Modernity: Aby Warburg and the Public Purposes of Art in Hamburg
1896–1918* (New York and London, 2007).

4. Julia Kristeva, "Marcel Proust: In Search of Identity," in *The Jew in the Text: Modernity
and the Construction of Identity*, eds. Linda Nochlin and Tamar Garb (London and New York,
1996), 140–55. Kristeva is indebted to Hannah Arendt, who also writes at length on Proust in *The
Origins of Totalitarianism* (1951; New York, 1968), 54–89, where she formulates the tensions for
modernizing Jewish communities between the status of *parvenu* and pariah, rendering this novel
form of Jewishness both a vice and a crime in the eyes of non-Jewish societies. Arendt says, "As
far as Jews were concerned, the transformation of the 'crime' of Judaism into the fashionable
'vice' of Jewishness (ineradicable since it was now an essence not a denomination) was dangerous
in the extreme. Jews had been able to escape from Judaism into conversion; from Jewishness there
was no escape. A crime, moreover, is met with punishment; a vice can only be exterminated" (87).

5. Karen Michels, "Art History, German Jewish Identity, and the Emigration of Iconology,"
in *Jewish Identity in Modern Art History*, ed. Catherine M. Soussloff (Berkeley, 1999), 167.

6. Charlotte Schoell-Glass, *Aby Warburg and Anti-Semitism: Political Perspectives on Images
and Culture* [*Aby Warburg und der Antisemitismus: Kulturwissenschaft als Geistespolitik*], trans.
Samuel Pakucs Willcocks (1998; Detroit, 2008). See also Charlotte Schoell-Glass, "Aby Warburg:
Forced Identity and Cultural Science," in Soussloff, *Jewish Identity and Modern Art History*,
218–30. I am deeply indebted to Charlotte Schoell-Glass in writing this essay.

7. Margaret Olin, "From Bezal'el to Max Liebermann: Jewish Art in Nineteenth Century Art
Historical Texts," in Soussloff, *Jewish Identity and Modern Art History*, 20.

8. Ibid.

9. Ibid.

10. Ibid., 33.

11. Aby M. Warburg, "Italian Art and International Astrology in the Palazzo Schifanoia, Ferrara [1912]," in Warburg, *The Renewal of Pagan Antiquity*, intro. Kurt Forster and trans. David Britt (Los Angeles, 1999), 586. The phrase "the good European" is a reference to Nietzsche.

12. Aby M. Warburg, "The Art of Portraiture and the Florentine Bourgeoisie" [1902] and "Francesco Sassetti's Last Injunctions to His Sons" [1907], in Warburg, *Renewal of Pagan Antiquity*, 185–222 and 223–62.

13. Georges Didi-Huberman, *L'Image Survivante: Histoire de l'Art et Temps de Fantômes selon Aby Warburg* (Paris, 2002).

14. Schoell-Glass, *Aby Warburg and Anti-Semitism*, 56; Hans Liebeschütz, "Aby Warburg (1866–1929) as Interpreter of Civilization," *Publication of the Leo Baeck Institute: Year Book* 16 (1971): 225–36.

15. Schoell-Glass, *Aby Warburg and Anti-Semitism*, 57.

16. Originating in Norwich in 1144, the blood libel accuses Jews, strictly forbidden by their own law to consume blood in any form whatsoever, of ritually killing Christian children to use their blood in the making of Passover matzos: unleavened bread composed of flour and water cooked within eighteen minutes of being made. The impossibility of the accusation, from the Jewish point of view, points back to the fantasmatic structure of Christian engagement with blood and sacrifice and its even more ancient roots. "Altogether, there have been about 150 recorded cases of blood libel (not to mention thousands of rumors) that resulted in the arrest and killing of Jews throughout history, most of them in the Middle Ages. . . . In almost every case, Jews were murdered, sometimes by a mob, sometimes following torture and a trial." Walter Laqueur, *The Changing Face of Antisemitism: From Ancient Times to the Present Day* (Oxford, 2006), 56.

17. Schoell-Glass, *Aby Warburg and Anti-Semitism*, 62.

18. For a detailed study of this parallel case, see Andrea Olmstead, "The Toll of Idealism: James Loeb—Musician, Classicist, Philanthropist," *Journal of Musicology* 14, no. 2 (1996): 233–62.

19. Warburg would later, in 1923, draw on the work of the Cambridge Ritual School, notably the work of Jane Harrison, *Themis: A Study of the Social Origins of Greek Religion* (1911; London, 1963).

20. During his brief medical studies in Berlin in 1892, Warburg read Charles Darwin, *The Expression of the Emotions in Man and Animals* (1872).

21. Sigmund Freud, "Errinern, Wiederholen und Durcharbeiten (Weitere Ratschläge zur Technik der Psychoanalyse, II)," *Internationale Zeitschrift für ärztliche Psychoanalyse* 2 (1914): 485–91; "Remembering, Repeating and Working-Through," in *Standard Edition of the Psychological Works of Sigmund Freud*, ed. James Strachey (London, 1958), 12:147–56.

22. Sigmund Freud, "On 'The Uncanny,'" (Das Unheimliche, 1919), trans. Alix Strachey, in *Penguin Freud Library*, vol. 14, *Art and Literature* (London, 1990), 345.

23. Freud, "On 'The Uncanny,'" 372.

24. Zygmunt Bauman, *Modernity and Ambivalence* (Cambridge, 1991).

25. For a review of this question see Schoell-Glass, *Aby Warburg and Anti-Semitism*, 12–24; Felix Gilbert, "From Art History to the History of Civilization: Gombrich's Biography of Aby Warburg," *Journal of Modern History* 44, no. 3 (1972): 381–91; and, most recently, Matthew Rampley, "Aby Warburg, *Kulturwissenschaft*, Judaism and the Politics of Identity," *Oxford Art Journal* 33, no. 2 (2010): 317–35.

26. It is important in passing to note the modernist nature of Warburg's anthropology of the modern: using a newspaper clipping service, he functioned as a kind of psychoanalyst to contemporary culture, drawing from this promiscuous listening to the symptoms registered across the modern media key images, which would later take the form of intellectual photomontage—a form invented by Berlin Dadaists.

27. Schoell-Glass, *Aby Warburg and Anti-Semitism*, 165–66.

28. Ibid.

29. Ibid., 166.

30. Michael P. Steinberg, "Interpretative Essay," in Aby Warburg, *Images from the Region of the Pueblo Indians of North American*, trans. Michael P. Steinberg (Ithaca, 1995), 88–89.

31. Steinberg, "Interpretative Essay," 89.

32. Ibid.

33. For a slightly different and more sociohistorical perspective on the role of Jewish foundations of libraries, see Michael Brenner, *The Renaissance of Jewish Culture in Weimar Germany* (New Haven and London, 1996), 56-59.

34. For an excellent reading of this last plate see Charlotte Schoell-Glass, "'Serious Issues': The Last Plates of Warburg's Picture Atlas Mnemosyne," in *Art History as Cultural History: Warburg's Projects*, ed. Richard Windfield (London, 2001), 183–208; Griselda Pollock, "Aby Warburg and Mnemosyne: Photography as Aide-Mémoire, Optical Unconscious and Philosophy," in *Photo Archives and the Photographic Memory of Art History*, ed. Costanza Caraffa (Berlin, 2011), 73–99.

9

Walther Rathenau (1867–1922)

BILDUNG, PRESCRIPTION, PROPHECY

Leon Botstein

WALTHER RATHENAU RETAINS A PERMANENT PLACE IN HISTORY AS A MARTYR, THE victim of a startling and well-planned assassination in June 1922 designed to destabilize the Weimar Republic. The unanticipated irony was that killing Rathenau, Germany's Foreign Minister and its most prominent Jew in public life, produced precisely the opposite of its intended effect. The assassination triggered a national outpouring of sympathy and support for the Republic and an uncharacteristic (albeit brief) display of unity against the radical right wing responsible for it. The public outcry in response to Rathenau's death helped extend the life of the Republic and bolstered its fragile legitimacy; the reaction stood in marked contrast to the muted response to the killing, less than a year earlier in August 1921, of Matthias Erzberger, the leader of the Catholic Center Party who had been, like Rathenau, a bête noire of the right.

Posterity has, however, not been kind to Rathenau as author and writer. He was more than the commonplace politician who wrote an occasional essay; he harbored serious intellectual ambitions. Those ambitions have left little residue, but during his lifetime Rathenau the author succeeded. His writings established him as a thinker with a wide public and extensive critical reception. He achieved standing therefore not merely as a commanding and powerful figure in the Imperial Germany of Wilhelm II and the Weimar Republic, but as an influential critic of culture and society.

By all accounts Rathenau was cold yet charismatic. For all his fame, he was never a popular personality. He was known best as a giant of industry, a virtuosic organizer of industrial production. He was a key figure in the effort to normalize the relations between Germany and the victors of World War I. Rathenau is credited with the 1922 Rapallo Treaty that bolstered Germany's renewed status in international affairs.

As legendary for his vanity as he was for his fabulous wealth, Rathenau was secretive, self-absorbed, immaculately dressed, a socialite, and a bachelor. He was admired for his exquisite taste in art, architecture, and literature. Since he had been a key figure in sustaining the supply system of raw materials for the war effort in the

early years of World War I, after Germany's defeat his wartime role rendered him controversial, his brilliant patriotic service notwithstanding.[1] In large measure because he was thoroughly urbane and cultivated and also a Jew and rich, he was held in suspicion, particularly by members of the very political elite whose acceptance he craved. His success and visibility as a controversial and tireless polemicist on political, economic, and social issues did little to endear him to his more pedestrian political and commercial rivals.

Indeed, Rathenau's status as the acculturated and assimilated Jew par excellence made him stand apart in his lifetime and posthumously from others in highly visible political roles, both in Wilhelmine Germany and the Weimar years. And Rathenau continues to be remembered as the wealthiest and seemingly most confident and tragic protagonist of the ideal of successful Jewish integration into German society and culture. Rathenau's personal life was marked by relative loneliness as well as the circumstances of a narrative (later construed as illusionary and self-delusional) characteristic of the fin de siècle: the promise of a stable future for the Jews as a constituent element within modern Germany.

Particularly in post–World War II historiography Rathenau has come to be seen as the ideal type of a privileged and thoroughly German Jew who believed in the authenticity of his "Germanness" and who ought to have seen what now, in retrospect, appears to have been so evident (as argued by the Zionists during the 1920s): Jews in Germany would never elude prejudice and discrimination. Their status as pariahs and second-class citizens—no matter their wealth, education, and achievements—was permanent, and denial of that would end in catastrophe. History on the subject of German Jewry prior to the Nazi seizure of power is rather easily written in retrospect.

Given the impressive readership that Rathenau's books and essays attracted during his lifetime, a closer look at Rathenau as thinker and writer appears timely, if only to sharpen and deepen our understanding of the intense debate from the 1890s through the early 1920s on the character and trajectory of modernity and modernism. Rathenau's vantage point was that of someone of political significance who was at the same time looking in, so to speak, from the "outside"—a public figure at the margins of intellectual life and posthumously essentially excluded from serious historical consideration as an intellectual.

Rathenau articulated a philosophically inclined comprehensive interpretation of history and contemporary events. He was the author of three influential books, the last of which, *Von kommenden Dingen* (On things to come), published in 1917, sold more than 70,000 copies, 24,000 of those in its first three months. His first major book, *Zur Kritik der Zeit* (On the critique of the age), published in 1912, had brought him considerable attention; its immediate successor, from 1913, *Zur Mechanik des Geistes* (On the mechanics of the spirit), was his least popular, but, owing to its explicit philosophical scope and ambition, it earned him the greatest measure of intellectual respectability. A five-volume set of "complete works" appeared first in 1918, a reliable sign of his status as an author.[2]

This impressive literary achievement itself ensured that no one ever forgot Rathenau was a Jew; indeed he took some perverse pride in making sure that his Jewishness would not be forgotten. But beyond this almost perverse assertive pride in the mere fact of being a Jew, there was little evident substance in his identity as a Jew. He was certainly not observant. He was neither a formal member of the community nor even a reluctant secular Jew. In his writings Rathenau consistently privileged the inner spiritual experience and substance of an individual's metaphysical beliefs over any membership and participation in organized religion, a social institution for which he had contempt. At the same time, he rejected conversion and was idiosyncratically comfortable with the unambiguous and well-rehearsed facts of his birth and parentage. He took pride that he was linked indelibly to a distinct race.

Precisely because he was so thoroughly assimilated into German culture and mores, Rathenau flaunted his exceptional status as a powerful and influential Jew in politics as proof that individuals, especially in modernity, possessed the autonomy to transcend, through achievement, the seemingly inevitable markings of inherited identity. Therefore, from the very start of his career at the age of thirty as a commentator on public affairs to the end of his life, he argued vociferously against calls on Jews to convert to Christianity.[3] Despite the distance he kept from religion and the Jewish community, he relished his place as a Jew in German public life and the irritation it inspired. And he was unrelenting in his challenges to the premises, claims, and prejudices of legal, political, and economic antisemitism.[4]

In Rathenau's view the assimilation and acceptance of Jews in Germany (whom he understood as a force of change) would help avert the danger that the "German" would cease to evolve and would become ossified, regressive, and obsolete. Ironic as it seems, Rathenau saw himself in relation to the historical destiny of all matters German as a sort of Jewish Parsifal figure, a source of fundamental spiritual renewal demanded by outmoded pre–World War I Prussian aristocratic mores and habits.

A poignant indication of the overwhelming centrality of Rathenau's identity as a Jew, both to himself and others, was Albert Einstein's visit to his home in April 1922, just two months before the assassination.[5] Einstein arrived with Kurt Blumenfeld, the prominent German Zionist (later Secretary of the Federation of German Zionists). Blumenfeld is best remembered as a close friend and correspondent of Hannah Arendt.[6] Einstein sought Rathenau out for two reasons. First, he wanted to persuade Germany's foreign minister to be more sympathetic to Zionism. Second, he sought to convince him that no German Jew—and certainly not Rathenau—could or should serve legitimately as the nation's foreign minister. Einstein's arguments were partly principled and partly pragmatic. In Einstein's view, no Jew was or could ever be sufficiently German—however "Germanness" might be construed—to represent the nation. A Jew—in light of the recalcitrant popularity and political significance of rabid antisemitism—would never be regarded as properly or authentically German. Furthermore, for Einstein, Rathenau's prominence actually placed his fellow Jews in Germany in greater jeopardy than they already were. Einstein and Blumenfeld argued that Rathenau's place in the government would inspire yet another dangerous upsurge of antisemitism.

As Blumenfeld recalled in 1952 (thirty years after Rathenau's death), this remarkable evening encounter—which lasted well into the early hours of the morning—was singularly unsuccessful, although Rathenau confessed in an unguarded moment that in an alternate universe he might have preferred, as a Jew, to realize his political ambitions (which he likened to those of Disraeli) as an Englishman—not on the Wilhelmstrasse but on Downing Street. This concession, however, did not signal any weakening on Rathenau's part in his belief that, his birth and heritage aside, he was in the very truest of senses thoroughly if not ideally German, and certainly as German as anyone else. He rejected the dream of a Jewish national home in Palestine as misguided and economically impractical, a point of view his father, Emil, had held as well. More importantly, for Walther Rathenau being Jewish was neither cultural nor political. It did not mean membership in a dispersed nation. This made true cultural assimilation and the internalization of German patriotism possible.

Blumenfeld recalled Rathenau's awareness that among Jews and antisemites alike he was derided as "Jesus in a tailcoat" (*Jesus im Frack*). Indeed, Rathenau flirted with the image of himself as a Jewish martyr to Germany. In the two years immediately following the German defeat, he feared that he might be brought to trial on account of an unrealized plan he had developed toward the end of the war to force hundreds of thousands of Belgians to work in Germany's industrial sector. He imagined himself becoming Germany's Alfred Dreyfus, the proud upstanding Jew and quintessential patriot who was the victim of a public miscarriage of justice. Dreyfus's pride in his identity as a Frenchman never wavered, despite the gratuitous vilification and unjust treatment he endured.

Einstein and Blumenfeld believed that Rathenau's managerial acuity, ambition, influence, wealth, and literary pretensions all extravagantly embodied the antisemitic stereotypes that inspired the radical and nationalist right-wing agitators during the Weimar era. He was the caricature of Jewish assimilationist ambitions that helped lend plausibility to imaginary conspiracy theories regarding the undue influence of Jews. Indeed, Rathenau's career seemed to prove the myth of an overwhelming, corrosive, antitraditional, and destabilizing Jewish influence in Germany tied to the advances of industrial capitalism. His assassination was a harbinger of the success of the Nazis, and a reminder of the danger inherent in discounting the violence of a minority of radicalized traditionalists within an advanced industrial culture as marginal and extreme.

It is painfully ironic that so few lasting markers of Rathenau's public influence remain, and none linked to his work as a thinker. Rathenau survives in the historical memory much as Einstein and Blumenfeld predicted: as a symbol of the misguided path of German Jewish assimilation. Rathenau's distinguished visitors doubted that rationality and progress would trump right-wing nationalist ideology or that the resilience of a shared collective allegiance to civility in Germany would hold against radical evil. His murder two months after the visit suggested the weakness of civility as a deterrent in the Weimar era; for many it stands as a warning against appeasement when faced with the threat of racialist ideology and populist tyranny. In the context of post-Holocaust historiography of Germany, Rathenau is put forward, rightly or wrongly, as the exemplar of the delusions shared by those privileged, assimilated German Jews who trusted in the permanence, legitimacy, and significance of their status as Germans. Rathenau's *Bildung*, his elegance, and his intellectual prominence bore witness—falsely, it turned out (particularly from Blumenfeld's perspective)—to how tenuous the social promise and stability of Jewish life in Germany were; the continuity of cultural, social, and political antisemitism in German-speaking Europe since well before the Renaissance could not be discounted.

The "Jesus im Frack" epithet was not so wildly off the mark. Rathenau was rather more an exception than an exemplar. There was the unique combination of political prominence and extreme wealth. But most important, the wealth derived from a strikingly visible dimension of the modern: the transformative introduction of electricity into daily life. Through a partnership with the Thomas Edison Company, Walther's father, Emil, obtained the exclusive right to use Edison's patents in Germany. Walther reluctantly succeeded Emil as a captain of industry. Far more than Emil (who cherished personal contact with the Kaiser), Walther craved the public limelight. The combination of Walther's status in the business world as a reformer and modernizer and his insistence on publishing his opinions on economic and social policy as well as foreign affairs turned him into a veritable poster-child for the widespread antisemitic claim that an international network of Jewish finance controlled Germany, if not the world, precisely through the introduction of industrial and commercial innovation.

To make matters worse, Rathenau himself suggested in 1911—in one of his periodic lapses of political and rhetorical judgment—that an elite group of 300 individuals actually controlled the economy of Europe.[7] Much to his surprise (but no one else's), this statement (a prelude to his own idiosyncratic arguments for fundamental social and economic reform) appeared to confirm antisemitic assertions. The fact that the 300 leading bankers and industrialists Rathenau had in mind were not Jews made little difference; that did not prevent his statement from being used as proof of the ideological claim of an international Jewish conspiratorial cartel.

No less controversial to reactionaries were Rathenau's cultural and aesthetic tastes, even though they revealed at best an ambivalent attitude to aesthetic modernism. He was among the first to collect the paintings of Edvard Munch, together with his close friend Count Harry Kessler (Munch painted portraits of them both). His friends were writers (Maximilian Harden and Gerhart Hauptmann prominently among them), and his relatives included Max Liebermann (whose paintings he owned).[8] Rathenau himself was quite talented in painting and drawing and once harbored hopes to make a career as an artist (an ambition Liebermann never took seriously). The portrait of his mother, among other works, testifies to his abilities and rather conservative tastes, as did his designs for his house in Berlin Grunewald and the interiors of Schloss Freienwalde, the former summer home of Queen Frederike Luise that he meticulously restored. They both mirror Rathenau's mistrust of both pre- and postwar aesthetic modernism in the visual arts.

In the end, the most unusual and striking aspect of Rathenau's public persona that augmented his status as the fully acculturated German Jew par excellence—well beyond wealth, studied elegance and refinement, and political ambitions—was his determination as a writer and public intellectual—already at the turn of the century, insistently on the eve of World War I, and most visibly in the wake of Germany's defeat—to chart a path of renewal for Germany to ensure its economic, cultural, and political preeminence.

Rathenau's forays into cultural criticism and philosophy inspired particular resentment. He assumed a prophetic voice. Rathenau attempted a coherent theory of history and a philosophical critique of modern life that accounted not only for the losses and gains over time, but also the threat that the challenges of the present would not be met adequately. He believed his philosophical speculations were derived from a fundamentally accurate conception of human nature and the immanent evolution of humankind. In the three books published between 1912 and 1917 he sought to outline a synthesis of sociological, economic, and psychological analysis with a normative ethical theory of what the meaning of life in modernity should entail, both for the individual and society as a whole.

Rathenau grappled with the central issue that preoccupied his generation: how to resolve the seeming contradictions of modernity in the context of German political and cultural history through the formulation of a valid synthesis between the analytical and the normative. Mechanization, modern capital and industrial organization, and the progress of science, all attributes of rationality, were seen to be at odds with the spiritual, tradition, and the individual, the space which Max Weber termed the realm of ultimate ends. Rathenau's striking success with the reading public rested in the fact that he distilled and simplified the perception of the threat of discontinuity and dislocation rooted in the brutal facts of modern economic and social life. Furthermore, he had something for everyone. Rathenau's rhetorical arsenal overlapped with a startlingly eclectic range of contemporaries, from Max Weber to Eduard Spranger, the influential proponent of *Lebensphilosophie* (a systematic critique of scientific rationality based on the need to displace it with a coherent system of values). Links can be found to revisionist socialism, the critique of historicism, Rudolf Steiner's anthroposophy, the sociology of "understanding" phenomenology, Carl Schmitt's critique of parliamentary democracy and liberalism, and even the ontological musings of Heidegger from the 1920s.

For Rathenau's generation, modernity confronted the individual with the dissolution of consensus and community and the triumph of materialism, skepticism, competition, and criticism over any allegiance to a guiding set of absolute "spiritual" values. What separated Rathenau from others was his ease in offering practical sounding although highly improbable strategies for addressing the challenge. Perhaps unfairly, more than one reviewer observed cogently that original ideas were not to be found in Rathenau's thought. Yet the way he put things together—the diagnosis and cure for the ills of modernity that he put forward—struck a chord with the public. It was only posthumously, beginning in the late 1920s, that as a writer and thinker Rathenau lapsed into obscurity, more even than Spranger, Ernst Troeltsch, or Alfred Kerr. The reason rests in the asymmetry between the close political focus Rathenau maintained on the historical moment and the inflated rhetoric of his prescriptions. Nonetheless, Rathenau displayed a striking and historically prescient vision and showed remarkable independence. He went beyond analysis and speculation, calling for sharp limits to property, and the bridging of class differences through a cultural and social synthesis that combined the industrial imperatives of economic rationality, the power of the modern state, and the need to support a unifying mystical spirituality within a nation.

Rathenau was not content with a pessimistic critique of the modern. Since his ambition was prescriptive, he crafted a philosophical secular theology of history, in stark contrast to Max Weber, who sought to distinguish the empirical analysis of history, economy, and society from the advocacy of social, political, and ethical norms. Rathenau believed that his political agenda—his vision of the society of the future—was rooted in and justified by ethical claims and values derived from a reading of history, human nature, cognitive psychology, and epistemology that assumed a trajectory of progress based in human rational adaptability. He sought to articulate a political philosophy that aligned itself with a philosophy of ultimate ends, values regarding the spiritual dimension of life that could effectively engage the real circumstances and challenges of modernity. The arts remained crucial to this program, since their essential virtues were not relative; as public goods they aided in reconciling the promise of individuality with the economic demands of standardization and the social imperatives of collective justice.[9]

The mix of philosophy, prescription, and prophecy in Rathenau's intellectual project as a writer—as well as his remarkable success and popularity—placed his contemporaries who were "professional" intellectuals in a quandary. Those who praised him in public, such as Stefan Zweig, were seen as self-serving intellectuals only too eager to curry favor with a patron of great wealth and political power. Friends who were writers and intellectuals were often bemused or insincere in their praise and in the end took his writings only half-seriously. Others were offended by what they regarded as the arrogance and impertinence of an industrial tycoon who dabbled without restraint in the writing of social criticism and philosophy.

The pivotal and stable conviction that formed the basis of Rathenau's thought was the belief that he, despite being a Jew by origin, was demonstrably German. The "German" was, after all, synonymous, in Rathenau's view, with a historical mission and destiny: securing the priority of the spiritual, the ethical, and the aesthetic over the material in culture and society. In his first foray into journalism, a controversial 1897 article in Harden's *Die Zukunft*, "Hear O Israel!," he articulated the ideal that he believed he himself had achieved: to become thoroughly German "by nature and education."[10] He called on all Jews to follow in his path.

The significance of being truly "German" was tied to Rathenau's belief in the cultural distinctiveness and superiority of the German race. One of the dangers of modernity and its rapid drift into a world dominated by rational calculation—behavior driven by what Max Weber categorized as *Zweckrationalität*, or, in Rathenau's language, the values of "mechanization"—was the parallel process of the "de-Germanizing" of culture and society. The "German" represented the last best hope, particularly among the elite of humankind, for the spiritual dimension and triumph of the "soul" in human nature over mechanical calculation focused on the accumulation of property.

The "German," in racial, historical, and cultural terms, represented the ethics of "courage" (*Mut*) and "basic principles" (*Gesinnung*). In the "German" rested a historical possibility of counteracting a modernity defined by egotism and vanity—qualities characteristic of the intellectual and calculating world of England and America and the superficiality of the French. The truly "German," if it could be rendered dominant as the defining value system of modernity, represented the hope that an "enthusiasm" of "integrity" (*aufrichtige Begeisterung*), together with "loyalty," could become the basis of a modern society and culture. There would be less idle talking and more judgment, character, and concern for the public good. Opposed to these virtues were the habits of intellect, cowardice, conflict, and naked self-interest.[11]

Access to this state of mind required a process of acculturation and education. In his 1897 essay, much to the consternation of his fellow Jews, Rathenau called on all Jews not to convert but "to assimilate to outside demands" and "cast off" "tribal qualities," by which he meant, much like many conservative antisemites, the cliché-laden "oriental" characteristics exhibited allegedly by Eastern European Jews (*Ostjuden*), who were relatively recent arrivals in Germany. Jews needed to replace these vestigial habits with "more suitable ones." This, Rathenau conceded, would be "without historical precedent." But he had no doubt that the "metamorphosis" of Jews—which would take generations—into Germans would improve the "balance sheet of moral values" in the world. At stake in this transformation was nothing less than the moral and ethical soul of modernity, which he considered at risk in the sense that it was rapidly extinguishing "spirit" (*Geist*) from humankind through an unchecked process of "mechanization." Jews could play a role by assimilating and strengthening the role of the German in counteracting this corrosive mechanization. In Rathenau's account, Marx's notion of the Jew was inverted. Rather than be the model of the exploitative capitalist, the Jew could join in the vanguard of a humanistic, spiritual, and aesthetic revival in the midst of the materialist ravages of modern economic life.

An inflexible dualism about human consciousness pervades Rathenau's thought: the distinction between the spiritual or the creative—a realm that simply "is," "arises," or "becomes," and is "felt"—and the intellectual world of *Erkenntnis*: that is, understanding, logic, law, and science. The latter can be taught easily, whereas the former is a mystical phenomenon and a divine mystery; the spiritual and creative (as in art) lack goals and purpose, whereas the intellectual and the material possess them.[12] Yet the former can be cultivated and transmitted. For Rathenau, accessing the spiritual and the creative defined the task of assimilation and the definition of *Bildung* to which Jews in Germany needed to submit and to which they were uniquely suited.

These ideas described the political mission to which Rathenau was committed; they also captured the mystical character of Germanic virtues. The elite that represented the triumph of a unique transcendent Germanic "spirit" included Shakespeare, Bach, Rembrandt, and Goethe.[13] Their examples and achievements were essential to the task of inserting into modern society and culture the spiritual element of life and nature. The human attribute—the one overriding human quality accessible to all—that signaled for Rathenau the proper presence of spirituality in life was none other than "love." Rathenau believed Jews, through education and acculturation, could enter the vanguard of this mission as Germans, leaders of a new "spiritual" utopia dominated by love and beauty. This basic assumption revealed his construct of the mystical, nonrational realm as fundamentally ordered and balanced, and therefore shaped by modernity rather than a nostalgic mirage. The integration of the virtues of a progressive analytic rationality at which Jews excelled (as noted by antisemites and philosemites alike) into his vision distinguished his philosophical outlook from the more familiar *völkisch* and often racist contemporary discourse about the superiority and character of the "German."

Although Rathenau overtly rejected a well-known parallel line of argument in the ideologies fashioned by proponents of what Fritz Stern famously termed the "politics of cultural despair," uncanny similarities and affinities with them do exist in his thought. Not surprisingly, he accepted the notion of racial distinctions. He shared a dream of creating a community with values that he believed mirrored the special attributes of the German. Consequently, leading proponents of a reactionary German cultural and racial ideology, including Wilhelm Schwaner (the conservative if eccentric journalist and editor, an early favorite of the Nazis who finally fell out with them, and a close personal friend of Rathenau), responded with enthusiasm to Rathenau's ideas. After reading Rathenau's first major book, *Zur Kritik der Zeit*, Schwaner observed, "The dark Jew has redeemed the blue-eyed blonde German!"[14]

But there were two crucial differences. First, following both Karl Marx and Max Weber, Rathenau viewed the achievements of modernity as not only irreversible but also essential. But Rathenau went even further. The characteristics of modernity could be appropriated by the task of a cultural rebirth, and integrated into the more spiritual and just community of the future. His reasoning was philosophical in that it derived from views about the universal character of human nature, and not from a mythic account of historical racial heritage. The elite idealized "German" he so prized was the result of an acquired culture rather than a static racial, biological quality. The spiritual in contemporary life actually had to reflect modernity and progress; it was not part of a racial inheritance. Its character was contingent on history, and its stability was cemented by the passage of time; time and patience were therefore required in order for Jews to become Germans.

Second, Rathenau chose to construe contemporary German antisemitism as capable of being overcome. He understood it in terms of an older form of prejudice, particularly widespread at the turn of the century among Germans with otherwise "liberal" convictions. This "liberal" strain of antisemitism dated from the period between 1790 and 1848. It distinguished between the confessional characteristics of Jews, and their "tribal" and "national" qualities and conceits. It understood the "German" much as Rathenau did, not as a racial characteristic but as an amalgam of accumulated cultural norms. The plausibility of Rathenau's belief that his fellow Jews could become good Germans (as he believed he himself had become) derived from his quite reasonable privileging of one significant line of argument within German antisemitism as the dominant barrier.

Given, however, the prominence of racialist antisemitic thought at the fin de siècle, and with it the popularity of the idea that "Jewish" characteristics in the end could not be eradicated either by baptism, conversion, or acculturation, what explains Rathenau's curious optimism at the prospect of Jews becoming Germans, particularly without conversion? As his decision to conduct his father's funeral without the presence of any official representative of religion suggested, Rathenau held conventional religious belief and adherence in contempt as little more than reductive, sterile images of true spirituality. Like many others, he believed that, in modernity, traditional religious beliefs and therefore Christianity would disappear. Replacing religion would be a higher order of spirituality, defined by a shared secular metaphysical belief system based on the ethics of love and beauty. The traditional theological basis of prejudice would in effect disappear. Furthermore, Rathenau underestimated the overwhelming success and influence of a radicalized and racialist antisemitism that gained its plausibility through a fundamental attack on modernity.

Rathenau's brand of progressive, proto-rational spirituality was ultimately universal and cosmopolitan in character; it was tied to a candid vision of the modern. It had little in common with a romantic nostalgia for a communitarian world before industrialization, capitalism, and urbanization. Despite Rathenau's absorption of more conventional racialist rhetoric, his debt to romanticism was marginal, rendering him blind to a new breed of antisemitism.

The contrast between the two species of German antisemitism, the 1848 form and the late nineteenth-century version, can be located in the arguments made by Richard Wagner in his essay "Judaism in Music" (Das Judentum in der Musik, published anonymously first in 1850 and later issued under Wagner's name in a somewhat revised form in 1869). Wagner's seminal if not quite so wholly original text represented a decisive mid-century shift in German antisemitism toward a race-based argument, one that Rathenau rejected. The contested readings of Wagner's conclusions—his call for the total disappearance of all traces of the Jew—do not set aside the fact that Wagner's attack was immediately understood as denying the fundamental capacity of Jews ever to adapt and become equals to Germans; they would never be fully human. And certainly in Europe Jews would never shed their status as pariahs and parasites and forge a true connection to land and community. Wagner employed the language of spirituality and creativity and the metaphysics of cultural and aesthetic values—the very virtues Rathenau ascribed to Jews—against the Jews. Jews were, at their best, imitative virtuosi who were skilled in abstracting creativity but not sharing its essence. Indeed, the most nefarious Jews were those who "passed" and appeared to be sufficiently "German"; these Jews (e.g., Felix Mendelssohn and Giacomo Meyerbeer) exemplified one negative characteristic of a culture of "mechanization"—the lure of the formal and superficial, and the resultant ease of imitation. Rathenau, like Wagner, was concerned that these trends might potentially overwhelm modern existence, but he nevertheless saw a redeeming spiritual potential in the very aspects of modern life Wagner derided and associated with the Jews.

A poignant example of the pre-Wagnerian and preracialist argument that Rathenau assumed as a representative of German antisemitism can also be found, not surprisingly, embedded in the history of music (the aesthetic realm of Gentile culture in which Jews made their most visible and powerful contribution between 1815 and 1848). In an early essay from 1848, entitled "Über Religionsverschiedenheit" (On religious diversity), Eduard Hanslick (whose Jewish mother converted to Catholicism before her wedding and who would become one of Wagner's most prominent detractors) argued, much like Rathenau would a half-century later, that baptism, and therefore conversion, were not only irrelevant but also fundamentally wrong. Instead, intermarriage, over time, would solve the "Jewish" problem. Hanslick understood (as Rathenau would later) "Germanness" as an acquired characteristic, an aspect of culture and learning, and not of race.[15]

This construct of the German—the desired endpoint of assimilation and acculturation, one shared by several generations from Hanslick to Rathenau and the distinguished Viennese music theorist Heinrich Schenker (notably in the context of the rabid and intense political antisemitic agitation of the 1920s)—baffled and infuriated not only Zionists like Blumenfeld, but also voices on the political left. Kurt Tucholsky, for example, distanced himself from Jews and his own Jewish origins and exploited a great many antisemitic stereotypes to great effect in his own writings. Not only did Rathenau's explicit idealization of the German distance Tucholsky from Rathenau but so did Tucholsky's incomprehension of the Jewish wish to become German. Tucholsky shared no romance about the ideal of the culturally superior "good" German—a delusion he associated with a thin layer of the wealthy within German Jewry.

For Rathenau, what was quintessentially behaviorally and culturally "Jewish" — the traditional characteristics that were premodern and needed to be shed — was, in the sense of Otto Weininger, inferior, and perhaps even diseased and corrupting — the opposite of Germanic courage, creativity, manliness, and character. The alleged link between the Jewish and the homosexual was a commonplace in Rathenau's milieu. Partly on account of rumors about his own sexual proclivities, he discreetly avoided joining a widespread campaign in 1908 to decriminalize homosexuality, only later to advocate for it vigorously in 1922. He tacitly shared the commonplace association of the Jewish with a corrupting femininity, at odds with a genuine genius defined by the masculine. Rathenau's quarrel with his contemporary antisemites derived from his belief that Jews, perhaps in a ratio larger than Germans, could lose their inherited negative attributes and assume their very opposite; thus Jews would emerge as an elite, not only culturally, but also in terms of the physical courage and intellectual prowess required for the future within Germany.[16]

For Kurt Tucholsky, however, all the contemptible distinctions, characteristics, and habits of thought tied to Jews defined something far more widespread than the "Jewish"; they represented rather the bourgeois in general, and the German in particular. It was absurd that Jews should seek the approval of conservative German nationalists, a constituency that hated them, and who were even less admirable than they. Why aspire to assimilate into the worst of the conceits of petit-bourgeois individualism? In July 1922, weeks after Rathenau's murder, Tucholsky pilloried the assimilationist project and rendered a biting caricature of German Jews in his notorious "Wendriner" monologues.

Unlike Tucholsky Rathenau did not share an affinity for a Marxist view of history. He formulated his own guiding framework for assimilation based on the primacy of spiritual values within his extensive philosophical project and was confident in Jewish superiority becoming visible through the process of acculturation. Just as many Jewish advocates believed socialism and communism would solve the Jewish question by making it disappear as a subsidiary but welcome consequence of history so Rathenau also believed the world of the future he envisaged would render the "Jewish question" moot.

Much like Friedrich Naumann and other turn-of-the-century proponents of the model of a "Mitteleuropa," Rathenau saw in the German a civilizing alternative to Russian barbarism to the east, and French superficiality and Anglo-American materialism to the west. He therefore called for radical change within Germany, vociferously attacking the antiquated cultural conceits and practices of the Prussian aristocracy and the barriers they erected, directed not only against the Jews, but also against the middle and working classes.[17] He may have clung to notions of an inherent evolutionary divide between an elite and the masses, and the resultant moral obligation of the superior to guide the inferior, but in 1917, in contrast to most of his conservative contemporaries, he challenged the legitimacy of the German and Prussian state structure and its electoral traditions and advocated a parliamentary democracy.

Rathenau believed that the economic and political consequences of modernity — the division of labor, the triumph of organization and finance, and the technology of industrial production and transportation on the European continent — demanded and made possible a more ethical and economically just society and an unprecedented level of general culture. The instrument of his utopia of spirit and mechanical efficiency was the modern state, whose objectives were to achieve "the most noble example of the amalgamated collective will." These included central economic planning and steps to diminish individual economic possessiveness. Eliminating poverty and addressing humanity's "highest tasks," which were ultimately ethical and aesthetic, remained his highest goals.[18]

Rathenau's vision of Europe's historical destiny took shape before the catastrophe of World War I. His final version of the European future was laid out in 1917, when he recognized the inevitability of a German defeat (his extremely controversial public exhortation to continue the fighting in the autumn of 1918 was motivated by the belief that better Armistice terms could be negotiated). In the 1917 version, he included a prefiguring of the European Union in political and economic terms, including the severe regulation of market capitalism; a top-down, state-driven industrial sector, with worker participation in governance; and restrictions on the accumulation of wealth and its inheritance by individuals.[19] His vision of the future was reminiscent of Rousseau's. It was a project of the fundamental re-education of the citizen in a context that exploited but did not resist history and the legacy of "mechanization." His ultimate objective was one of moral and cultural rebirth and the subordination of the economic and material in politics. This was to be achieved through greater productivity and fair redistribution, all to the benefit of spiritual regeneration rooted in the affect of empathy.

Rathenau's most ambitious philosophical writing, particularly his 1913 *Zur Mechanik des Geistes, oder Vom Reich der Seele*, was animated by a diagnosis concerning modernity that can be properly compared to the verdict of Max Weber. In Max Weber's view the historical process of rationalization in modernity led to the dominance of "purpose" rationality—a close-knit connection between means and ends at the expense of tradition and so-called "value" rational behavior motivated by spiritual ends such as those posited by religion, particularly salvation. For both, modernity witnessed the triumph of a disciplined commitment to the rationalized technical character of social action. A renunciation of overarching nonutilitarian values was demanded; this rendered successful the routinized, differentiated function of bureaucracy. There was no reigning communitarian consensus beyond the realm of improving the competitive success of disciplined individual participation in economic activity. The modern individual faced a collapse of a community and consensus, and a troubling competition of conflicting transcendent values in the conduct of daily life.[20]

Rathenau differed from Weber, however, in his conviction that the very instruments that forged the "iron cage," in Weber's renowned formulation, were also the means of escape from it. It was therefore possible to project into the future a utopian end of history that successfully reconciled the rationality of modern industry and its work ethic with the spiritual, aesthetic, and emotional demands of human nature. What was required was the fashioning of a new communitarian spirit, first within the nation-state and ultimately in international affairs. Rathenau's philosophically grounded prophetic voice and optimism were entirely alien to Weber.

Rathenau's argument was based in the belief (derivative of his reading of Nietzsche) that the spiritual imagination in modernity had lagged behind the material; humanity was still caught in the web of historically outdated ideologies, the bankruptcy of which could be exposed. Rathenau argued his own epistemology. We project a subjective world order on the chaos within the external world. Rathenau absorbed the epistemological skepticism of critics regarding a concrete objective realism within the external world. Nevertheless, the actual plausibility and psychological traction of subjective conceptual projections were delimited by undeniable concrete circumstances of life, particularly economic factors. The consequence of those real factors—the substance of the economic history in the West—had encouraged humans to eliminate the spiritual, and to substitute material ends for spiritual ones, rendering all aspects of life, including the aesthetic realm, as mirror images of a utilitarian and spiritually impoverished world.

Because subjective projection shaped human reality, if the subjective will could be motivated to change, the political and economic realm could change as well. Ideas and beliefs mattered to Rathenau (as they did to Weber) as historical forces. This set him apart from Marxism. Rathenau's vision also diverged from the pessimistic assessment of modernity in the literature of cultural decline, notably in the work of Max Nordau. Rathenau avoided the language of degeneration, since despiritualization—the elimination of the element of the soul—was a consequence of the historically indispensable mechanization of the conduct of life. That mechanization involved a cost, no doubt: the "de-Germanizing" of society and the suppression of its communitarian nature. But this was only a short-term phenomenon. Science, technology, organization, and production created a "deficit" in moral certitude, profundity, idealism, and, above all, faith in "absolute" values. But society, through critical reason, had become an efficient instrument of collective productivity; therefore the very roots of skepticism—the achievements of critical rationality—could be harnessed to make an affirmative spiritual rebirth plausible.

Indeed, the key to this rebirth rested precisely in the recognition of the very limits of the intellect. In Rathenau's view, the intellect had been the engine of the mechanization in modernity. But the intellect was fallible. Although it triumphed in its role as the instrument of human reason in the historical process of mechanization, and greatly suppressed the "soul," the spiritual had not been entirely extinguished. The true power of *Geist* (spirit) could now emerge clearly as the fatal flaw of the intellect became increasingly exposed. The soul, unlike the intellect, is infallible. In a dialectical fashion, just as the intellect seemed to gain in power, its fallibility and limitation became apparent, revealing in modernity the immortality, potentialities, and infallibility of the spirit and soul.

The proof of this contrast between soul and intellect was to be found in the realm of art. Since intuition rather than rational calculation was the source of aesthetic genius, the aesthetic clearly derived from the soul and man's spiritual nature. Therefore beauty—the realization of the aesthetic impulse—was not subject to historical progress and consequently was immune to mechanization. The attempt to mirror goal-oriented materialism in modern art (and therefore radical aesthetic modernism) was, for Rathenau, a failed project. Modern art (by which he meant abstraction and cubism rather than impressionism or expressionism) sought to be self-consciously conceptually original, and therefore merely intellectually individualistic in intent, ignoring the imperative of spiritual infallibility.[21] This made modern art empty—and as strangely uniform and mechanical as art of the intellect. Only an artist such as Rembrandt, who can forget his individuality, temper his intellect, and give himself up intuitively to the "true, the objective, and the absolute," creates art that transcends the individual and fully realizes the soul and spiritual side of humanity.[22]

By suppressing the soul, modern man ignored both nature and love. That neglect needed to be reversed. At the same time, for Rathenau, true genius—the highest human achievement—required a perfect balance of intellect and soul, and therefore intuition. By cultivating our capacity to love—and reconnecting ourselves to nature, our inner spirituality, and the lives of others—the soul in modern man could be reborn. The means toward that rebirth mirrors modern mechanization and is a proper adaptation of history's intellectual and material gains. Rathenau did not advocate a retreat from modernity derived from a romance with a re-imagined past. History required modern man to reassert spirituality first in a mechanized manner, by dividing the spirit into discrete units, and then engaging in combinatorial experiments. The second step would generate reciprocity with the experience of others—a form of spiritual reflexivity. In this uniquely modern manner, adequate to the real material circumstances of contemporary life, the spiritual would experience its own progressive mechanization and rebirth into a modern community of love.

Rathenau developed an epistemological dialectic of spiritual mechanization. Accumulation, integration, and the demand for comprehensibility and order would drive the translation of spiritual experience into symbols. These symbols would exemplify the human capacity to shape reality to match a transcendent metaphysical truth. The real circumstances and experiences in the external world would be reshaped by our conceptual world. Rathenau's mundane metaphor for the dynamic between the conceptual and the real was the orchestra. In real time and space, humans realize the imaginary and spiritual mental projections that constitute the work of a composer. Real sound is commanded and rendered concrete along lines dictated by the metaphysical imagination.[23]

Rathenau's ultimate objective was the realization of the realm of love and the need to build a plausible, collective spiritual human unity. Following loosely the shape of Kant's three Critiques, in *Zur Mechanik des Geistes*, he traversed pure reason and scientific knowledge (as the perceiving spirit), practical reason (the ethics of the spirit), and judgment (the aesthetics of the soul). His conclusion was that the triumph of the intellect through mechanization had been pyrrhic. Although the majority of humanity was enslaved (in the sense of Weber's "iron cage"), the intellect in modernity had destroyed itself. By reducing everything spiritually "holy" to the status of a means to an end, the intellect finally confronted its limits and restored to the soul its basic self-awareness, its sense of truthfulness, and its ultimate ethical priority. Modernity exhausted itself. Humankind was standing before a new beginning, in which all the power of mechanization—the scientific progress, organizational productivity, and intellectual habits and achievements attained in history— emerges as the instrument of the spirit and love, ushering in a new era of the soul, not only for a ruling elite, but for all.[24]

Rathenau's mystical account of history and human experience, as expressed in all of his three major books, was notable for its striking absence of detail, and its reliance on general, abstract arguments and rhetoric. His prose is an uneasy synthesis of the poetic and the philosophical. Yet what distinguishes his writing is the effort at a synthetic reconciliation between the real and the normative—between the harsh facts of modern economic and political life, including exploitation and inequality and its ultimate transcendence within a social order. His utopian vision of a world suffused with spirit and love was not nostalgic, but it was conservative in its embrace of normative ethics and aesthetics and its rejection of radical individualism, subjectivity, and skepticism.

Rathenau's insight—not to reject the evolution of history and the progress of discovery and critical inquiry in modernity, but rather to appropriate them as a starting point for a constructive and necessary historical transition—was distinctive. It made the struggle for a world of the absolute, a unified era of spirituality, love, and peace, plausible. He believed that ultimately humans are capable of transcending the superficial, material aspects of life. Rathenau's elaborate philosophical context therefore offered the project of Jewish assimilation a coherent and logical foundation. Rathenau also sought to respond to a postwar sense of despair, particularly among the young, the very same sense of aimlessness and confusion Max Weber famously confronted in 1919 in a manner that sparked a debate about the methods and purposes of the social sciences.

Among Rathenau's sharpest critics, and perhaps the only continuing source of his fame as an intellectual, was Robert Musil. Despite disclaimers, there is little doubt that Rathenau was Musil's model for the figure of Arnheim, the foil for Ulrich, who was the author's protagonist in *The Man without Qualities*. Musil's Arnheim was of Jewish descent (only on his father's side in the novel), a man of power, money, and intellect. As Musil describes him: "This combination of intellect, business, and good living and learning was absolutely insufferable." Rathenau, transformed into Arnheim, embodied all that was horrific about the educated bourgeois and modern culture and its pretenses, styles, rhetoric, and mannerisms. What troubled Musil the most was the facile degradation of the aesthetic, poetic language, and scientific thought. In Rathenau's hands, the realm of culture was trivialized as a handmaiden of political power and high capitalism. Culture and learning were elevated rhetorically as ultimate markers of spiritual freedom consistent with vulgarity, vanity, and ethical blindness. In the hands of such men, reason and imagination, the pinnacles of human achievement, were trivialized, subordinated, manipulated, distorted, and discredited.

The prestige accorded culture and learning in Rathenau's account was based on the premise that they were civilizing forces, superior to a reluctant, routine adherence to conventional morality; they were weapons against human evil and barbarism. Musil, like Karl Kraus, realized the cruelty and dishonesty of this conceit, particularly after World War I. More to the point, Musil and Kraus pilloried the allegiance of German Jewry to culture and learning as instruments of personal social and political advancement and as effective means to bypass and ignore hate, exclusion, and prejudice. Walther Rathenau represented the worst in the undisciplined embrace of art, science, and culture on the part of men of wealth and power, particularly Jews, in the hope that the cultural could or would influence the character of mores and politics.

In April 1914 Musil wrote a review of *Zur Mechanik des Geistes*, whose title hints at the idiosyncratic character of Rathenau's arguments. Musil diagnoses a lack of "clear thinking." Although the book purported to be about the soul and love, because the actual details of experience were left out, its reader was left with a didacticism that was "devastatingly comical." All "spiritual content is dispersed" since the metaphysics of Rathenau's book were deployed merely as "ennoblement and heraldic speculation," lacking any real connection to life. For Musil such ambitious books needed to be about the world as it is, about "people" and "life." The gap between the ethical and aesthetic and the scientific—the real—had to be bridged with rigor, not rhetoric. Nevertheless, Musil accorded Rathenau a modicum of respect. After all, Rathenau sought to grapple with the vacuum of meaning in modernity, the mystic spiritual experience and its relation to reason, and explored what the consequences of a spiritual construction of life might be like. But the appeal to transcendence and the soul in Rathenau's account did not release thinking from the demands of clarity and precision—the proper dictates of reason.[25]

Early in his career, in 1899—two years after he had published the much-maligned essay "Hear O Israel!" exhorting his fellow Jews to become distinguished but indistinguishable as Germans—Rathenau published five "Talmudic Folktales."[26] Among the five "folktales" are two thinly veiled parables about kingship and its responsibilities, replete with praise for the self-sacrificial character of courageous speech in the presence of power. These two stories were both directed at Wilhelm II. Yet this collection of aphoristic pieces provides the link between Rathenau's construct of Judaism to his later mystical-conservative utopian vision of the restoration of the spiritual in modern life.

Rathenau's version of the wisdom of Ancient Israel centers on how, in the Jewish tradition, the spiritual in the form of ethical conduct is reconciled with a candid and kind recognition of the frailties of human nature. Rathenau's account of the Golem legend underscores the ethics of love and forgiveness, not for pure and idealized individuals but for ordinary mortals as they really are, rather than as we might imagine them to be. In two of the stories he reveals the courage of man in the face of human cruelty and divine wrath and judgment; he stresses the victory of transcendence in the human spirit through love and forgiveness.

It is as if Rathenau, both at the beginning of his career and at the end, sought to locate the contribution of modern German Jewry to solving the human predicament of modernity. That contribution lay in Judaism's profound and infallible spiritual heritage. In Rathenau's vision, the future of the "German" and the European is based in truths articulated by the first and most significant dispersed community in European history, the Jews.

Rathenau's ultimate arrogance, of which he was perhaps only dimly aware (but it did not escape those who sought his murder), was to redefine the German ideal in terms of an ethical and socially just spirituality whose truth centered on a candid love of human nature. This mystical wisdom of love derived from Jewish dispersion and the existential condition of foreignness—those very conditions Rathenau knew were central to the justification of antisemitism in modern European nationalism.

Notes

1. See Walther Lambach, *Diktator Rathenau* (Hamburg and Leipzig, 1918).
2. The citations in this essay come from a posthumously published version: Walther Rathenau, *Gesammelte Schriften*, 5 vols. (Berlin, 1925).
3. See, e.g., Walther Rathenau, *Eine Streitschrift vom Glauben* (Berlin, 1917).
4. See Walther Rathenau, "Staat und Judentum" (1911), in *Gesammelte Schriften*, 1:183–207.

5. Kurt Blumenfeld, "Walther Rathenau," *Hakidmah*, July 11 and 18, 1952.

6. Hannah Arendt and Kurt Blumenfeld, ". . . in keinem Besitz verwurzelt," *Die Korrespondenz*, eds. Ingeborg Nordmann and Iris Pilling (Hamburg, 1995), 65 and 73–75.

7. From an article by Rathenau, "The Next Generation of Businessmen," published in Vienna's *Neue Freie Presse*; cited in Shulamit Volkov, *Rathenau: Weimar's Fallen Statesman* (Yale, 2012), 104.

8. See Walther Rathenau, "Max Liebermann zum siebzigsten Jahr" (1971), in *Gesammelte Schriften*, 4:75–84.

9. See his essay, "Das Grundgesetz des Ästhetik" (1900–1908), in *Gesammelte Schriften*, 4:47–68.

10. An English-language version of the article "Hear O Israel!" can be found online at http://germanhistorydocs.ghi-dc.org/sub_document.cfm?document_id=717 (September 15, 2015).

11. See Walther Rathenau, "Ungeschriebene Schriften," in *Gesammelte Schriften*, 4:199–245; and his *Zur Kritik der Zeit*, in *Gesammelte Schriften*, 1:11–148.

12. See Rathenau, "Das Grundgesetz der Ästhetik," 4:47–86.

13. Walther Rathenau, *Zur Mechanik des Geistes*, in *Gesammelte Schriften*, 2:61 and passim; 2:32f.

14. Quoted in Wolfgang Brenner, *Walter Rathenau: Deutscher und Jude* (Munich, 2007), 337. On Schwaner, see the introduction to Wilhelm Schwaner and Walther Rathenau, *Eine Freundschaft im Widerspruch: Der Briefwechsel, 1913–1922*, eds. Gregor Hufenreuter and Christoph Knüppel (Berlin, 2008), 7–66.

15. See Eduard Hanslick, "Über Religionsverschiedenheit," in *Sämtliche Schriften*, vol. 1, *Aufsätze und Rezensionen, 1844–1848*, ed. Dietmar Strauss (Vienna, 1993), 189–200.

16. This vision appears already in 1897 in "Hear O Israel!"

17. See Rathenau, *Zur Kritik der Zeit*; and Friedrich Naumann, *Central Europe*, trans. Christabel M. Meridith (New York, 1917).

18. See Rathenau, *Gesammelte Schriften*, 2:9–21; 23–46; 288–340; and 3:77–234

19. See Walther Rathenau, "Vom wirtschaftlichen Gleichgewicht" (1908), in *Gesammelte Schriften*, 4:293–305; *Die neue Wirtschaft* (Berlin, 1918); and *Probleme der Friedenswirtschaft* (Berlin, 1918).

20. Max Weber, *Wissenschaft als Beruf (1917/1919); Politik als Beruf (1919)*, in *Max Weber Gesamtausgabe*, vol. 17, eds. Wolfgang J. Mommsen and Wolfgang Schluchter, with Birgitt Morgenbrod (Tübingen, 1992).

21. See Rathenau's 1905 essay, "Von neuerer Malerei," in *Gesammelte Schriften*, 4:263–90.

22. Walter Rathenau, *Gesammelte Schriften*, 2:61.

23. Walter Rathenau, *Gesammelte Schriften*, 2:94–95.

24. See Rathenau, *Zur Mechanik des Geistes*, vol. 2, particularly pts. 1 and 3.

25. Robert Musil, "Anmerkungen zu einer Metapsychik," in *Gesammelte Werke*, vol. 2, *Prosa und Stücke. Kleine Prosa. Aphorismen. Autobiographisches. Essays und Reden. Kritik*, ed. Adolf Frisé (Reinbek, 1978), 1015–19. See also the English translation, "Commentary on a Metapsychics," in *Precision and Soul: Essays and Addresses by Robert Musil*, eds. D. Luft and B. Pike (Chicago, 1995), 54–58.

26. They were first published under the pseudonym "W. Hartenau" by Maximilian Harden and later included in Rathenau's collection *Impressionen* (Leipzig, 1902), 101–20. They can be found in *Gesammelte Schriften*, 4:353–66.

10

Else Lasker-Schüler (1869–1945)

POETIC REDEMPTION

Vivian Liska

> We artists are God's darlings, the children of the Marias of all lands. We play
> with His sublime creations and rummage in His colorful morning and golden
> evening. But the bourgeois remains God's step-son, our reasonable brother, the
> killjoy. He cannot feel at ease with us, neither he nor his sister.
>
> —ELSE LASKER-SCHÜLER, *WERKE UND BRIEFE*

"NOT FROM HERE AND NOT FROM NOW."[1] THE WORK OF THE GERMAN JEWISH POET
Else Lasker-Schüler has often been situated by its critics and readers in a realm
not of this world and outside historical time, in a sphere of eternal poetic truth—a
realm oblivious of the cultural, political, and social realities of her day. Although her
eccentric and exalted poetic imagination seemingly escapes her immediate environment into fairy-tale fantasies peopled by princes and princesses, sheiks and magi-
cians, angels and tricksters, such a description of her work misses its importance
as an artistic as well as existential endeavor of creative innovation. In her work, a
return to age-old religious, primarily Jewish, literary, cultural, and textual traditions
meets a radically modern—or rather modernist—idea of poetry and selfhood. The
inspiration she drew from her Jewish legacy and origins—the founding texts of
Judaism as well as her situation as a German Jew in the first half of the twentieth
century—played a major role in her artistic vision and its profoundly critical stance
toward the Jewish and non-Jewish bourgeois establishment of her time.

As for many other German Jewish authors and intellectuals of the early twentieth century, the spirit of the bourgeoisie was, for Lasker-Schüler, a consequence of
modernity and the Enlightenment gone awry. A continuing emphasis on rationality, pragmatism, autonomy, and progress—at the expense of the imagination, the
passions, and a more immediate sense of proximity to nature and the divine characterizing premodern traditions—had established a narrow and oppressive mode of
existence that left little room for artistic, spiritual, or emotional self-expression. Furthermore, late-nineteenth-century bourgeois social and familial structures imposed
strict gender roles, which confined women to a life that Virginia Woolf famously

described as the "angel in the house." Although Lasker-Schüler did not adhere to any feminist movement and even mocked activists seeking women's emancipation, she transgressed the norms imposed on her by the patriarchal environment of her youth. She has been called the first hippie,[2] as she was married and divorced twice and had a son whose father, she claimed, was a Greek prince. During her Berlin years she lived mostly in cafés and slept on park benches or in cheap hotels. She walked around in colorful, oriental garb and a boyish hairstyle; wore cheap, shiny jewelry; and invented for herself an androgynous, shimmering persona that disturbed even some of her fellow artists and intellectuals.[3] The female angel that repeatedly features in Lasker-Schüler's poems is very different from Woolf's: it is a sensuous and subversive creature, a stranger from an imaginary land, a messenger of divine inspiration and a harbinger of redemption through poetry.

Among German Jews, the bourgeois lifestyle generally went hand in hand with acculturation or assimilation to the non-Jewish environment. In reaction against the Jewish establishment that had left the values and beliefs of its ancestors behind, many German Jewish intellectuals, writers, and poets searched for ways of reconnecting with the Jewish tradition. Most often raised with scant knowledge of this tradition, they developed idiosyncratic visions of an alternative modernity suffused with fragmentary knowledge, often either erroneously or purposely transforming elements of the Judaic textual, ritualistic, and religious heritage. Paradoxically, they became modernists precisely by turning to the past and retrieving from it what Hannah Arendt, speaking of Walter Benjamin's thought, called "corals and pearls,"[4] precious elements of a bygone tradition enriched by centuries of lying submerged at the bottom of the sea, protected from the disenchantment of modernity. Recovering these elements, which the generation of their parents had ignored or discarded, and simultaneously adapting them to the demands and needs of their time, German Jewish modernists generated new possibilities of apprehending both modernity and the Jewish tradition itself. Lasker-Schüler's idiosyncratic participation in this endeavor contributes significantly to her prominence as one of the most important modern Jewish poets in the German language.

Lasker-Schüler was called "the greatest lyrical poetess Germany ever had"[5] and "the true granddaughter of the Psalmists."[6] Although she did not speak Hebrew and wrote exclusively in German, Uri Zvi Greenberg spoke of her as "a great Hebrew poetess who dwells in solitude in Berlin."[7] The importance of her work—not only her poetry, prose texts, dramas, drawings, and paintings but also her live performances and, in some ways, her whole vibrant persona—derives to a considerable extent from the unusual ways in which she combined stories and figures from the biblical tradition and avant-garde poetic forms. One of the most striking manifestations of this amalgamation occurs in her blurring of the boundaries between her multiple and eccentric fictive personae, often based on biblical figures and the real people and events in her personal life. Several of her invented personae—most famous among them Prince Jussuf, based on the biblical figure Joseph—feature in her prose and poetry, drawings, and quasi-fictive letters. These characters serve both as her alter ego and as a means of transcending as well as critically commenting on the lack of intensity and authenticity of her surroundings. Early on, she overstepped the limitations set for her by her situation as a Jewish middle-class woman in Wilhelmine Germany and invented an alternative world of freedom, exuberance, and openness toward the fantastic and the imaginary, the stranger and the outsider, embracing an attitude to life and art critical of the normative, segregating, and monotonous world in which she grew up.

Else Lasker-Schüler was born in 1869 in Elberfeld, a small German city in the industrial region of Wuppertal. She was raised in a largely assimilated Jewish family belonging to the local establishment. She left this milieu after a brief marriage to the physicist and chess player Bertold Lasker and the birth of her son, Paul, in order to join the bohemian artists' circle of Berlin. She soon became one of its most eccentric figures. Her second marriage, to Georg Lewin, the editor of the leading Expressionist journal *Der Sturm* (better known by his pseudonym "Herwarth Walden"), ended after he left her for a Swedish actress in 1911. Beginning with her early writings, her poetry participates in shaping the most diverse modernist styles and modes. Her first book, the poetry collection *Styx* (Styx, 1902), displays a flowery *Jugendstil*, while *Der siebente Tag* (The seventh day, 1905) and *Meine Wunder* (My miracles, 1911) are mainly written in the Expressionist mode. While living in Berlin from 1894 until 1933, she published a collection of semi-fictive letters, *Mein Herz, ein Liebesroman* (My heart, a romance, 1912) and several volumes of poetry. Among them, *Hebräische Balladen* (Hebrew ballads, 1913) contains the most explicitly Jewish references. Her most famous prose volumes written in this period—*Die Nächte Tino von Bagdads* (The nights of Tino from Baghdad, 1907), *Der Prinz von Theben* (The Prince of Thebes, 1914), and *Der Malik* (The Malik, 1919)—evoke an oriental context in the style of *Arabian Nights*, but include indirect references to the Jewish tradition as well. Her plays *Der Wunderrabbiner von Barcelona* (The wonder rabbi of Barcelona, 1921) and especially *Arthur Aronymus und seine Väter* (Arthur Aronymus and his fathers, 1932), which thematize the relationship between Jews and Christians, increasingly respond to the antisemitic climate in Germany in the 1920s and early 1930s. Although they contain a message of hope for possible harmony between the religions, they also convey an awareness of past hostility against the Jews and an even greater fear of a renewal of antisemitic violence. Lasker-Schüler emigrated to Zurich in 1933 after Hitler came to power, then traveled twice to Palestine. On her third trip, in 1939, she was refused reentry to Switzerland and settled in Jerusalem for good. She never felt at home there, never learned Hebrew, and nostalgically longed for a Germany that no longer existed. In the last years of her life she suffered from sickness, poverty, and loneliness. She died in 1945 and was buried on the Mount of Olives.

Lasker-Schüler's consciousness as a Jew was no doubt determined more by the antisemitism of her German environment that eventually forced her into exile than by her family's knowledge of the Jewish tradition. Nonetheless, this consciousness—in all its ambivalence—found its most creative and forceful expression in relation to biblical stories and motifs. These references are present in her work from the earliest writings until poems written shortly before her death. She felt closer to what she called the "wild Jews," repeatedly evoked in her poetry, than to the assimilated Jewish middle-class world she had come from. This aspect of her writings has been interpreted as the product of her fascination with the archaic and the exotic, as well as her remoteness from reality. Looking more closely, however, one can recognize an inclination to anarchic rebellion against the repressive order of her environment and the imaginary creation of an "uncommon community" embracing the "children of the Marias of all lands"—artists, poets, and outsiders whom she considered harbingers of messianic redemption.

Until the 1970s the view prevailed that Lasker-Schüler's poetry was primarily a florid, mystically tinged condensation of religion, love, and art. Margarete Kupper, for example, sums up Lasker-Schüler's worldview as follows: "The pious in prayer, the lover in love, the artist in art break through the crust of the earthly and temporal world and experience paradise and eternity; piety, love, and art are possible ways of redeeming the world, of reconciling God and the world, and of turning the darkened world back into shining Eden."[8] Lasker-Schüler's poetics of redemption, however, hardly corresponds to these spiritualized, conciliatory, and orthodox approaches. In her poetry, the possibility of redeeming the world through piety, love, and art is combined with a destructive dynamic and a mischievous irony in the shape of an often heretical and iconoclastic art. It is primarily in her reworking of Bible stories that she expressed her revolt against bourgeois norms and values, without, however, making a return to traditional faith. Her lyrical representations of biblical figures are part of a literary tradition that takes up the original Bible stories and goes against the grain to both evoke and question values that have, in one form or another, prevailed from biblical times on.

The Jewish modernity of Lasker-Schüler's poetry expresses itself most powerfully in the usage she makes of the Jewish textual tradition in counteracting specific aspects of the bourgeois order, while at the same time transforming this textual tradition in terms of values inspired by her life as an avant-garde poet and bohemian. In her writings, she rejects the Enlightenment ideal of identifying with a homogenizing universality, but at the same time she insists on the necessity of a reconciliation between the religions. She opposes practices of intolerance and exclusion directed against foreigners, instead embracing both pluralism and particularity in all its guises as well as valorizing the stranger, the marginalized, and the outcast. She refuses to adhere to the modern belief in the progress of civilization, and instead fixes her poetic gaze on an imaginary, bygone past and a hoped-for future. Thus she develops a messianic hope of redemption through poetry that includes utopian visions suffused with both religious and erotic intensity. She turns against the realist—transparent and representational—language propagated by Enlightenment thought and the literature of realism. In her deviation from this language—in playful distortions as well as in lofty verses reminiscent of psalms and prophesies—she envisions a remedy against a decaying world. More than mere flights from her own reality, these yearnings for a distant past and a redeemed future are an expression of her critique of her own times.

In one of her most famous early poems, "Mein Volk" (My people), first published in 1905, her awareness of this decay extends to her Jewish origins and leads her to a highly ambivalent yet deeply felt pledge of allegiance to the Jewish people. The intricacies of the poem's multiple meanings capture the full complexity of Lasker-Schüler's dialectic between ancient and modern.

MY PEOPLE

The rock decays
From which I spring [*entspringe*]
And sing my songs of God. . . .

Headlong I rush off [*stürz*] from the way
And murmur deep within,
Distant, alone over the wailing stones
Towards the sea.

I have flowed so far away
From the must, the ferment
Of my blood.
And still, still the echo
In me,
When to the East, awesomely,
The crumbling rock of bone,
My people
Cries out to God.

(*Hebräische Balladen* [Hebrew ballads], 58; transl. modified by VL)

The first stanza develops the tension between old and new, and the ambivalent relationship of the speaking "I" with her people, in a series of words with a double meaning. The rock—both the people of Israel and a biblical reference to God (Psalms 18:32), evoking the eternity, steadfastness, and reliability of the divine—is crumbling. This rock is the origin of the I's existence and the wellspring of inspiration for her hymns to God. "Spring" (*entspringen*) has the double meaning of "stemming from" and "jumping off," suggesting an awareness of a lineage from an old ancestry and, simultaneously, a distancing from it. Similarly, the "rushing off" (*stürzen*) from the path could indicate both a falling off, caused by the decayed state of the rock that no longer provides a steady and secure ground, and a willful decision of the I to leave her origins, which leads her into estrangement and isolation from the original unity of her people and her God. As a result, the I and her song—figured as a poetic brook—is simultaneously isolated in a lonely interiority, alienated from any collectivity, *and* flowing toward the sea, a symbol for undifferentiated universalism that no longer recognizes the particularities of the brook's origin. Both the individualism of interiority and the universalism of the sea are aspects of modernity, which contrast with the particularism of the original rock, *my people* and its God. The speaker's "rushing off" from its origins occurs as the singing I glides "over the wailing stones" (*Klagegestein*). The lament, evoking the Wailing Wall, is inextricably linked to the initial rock and forms the bond between God, his people, and the poet singing her grieving song. Although it remains unclear whether this "gliding over" suggests a proximity with the age-old lament of the Jewish people the poem refers to, or whether it implies a certain indifference to it, there is no doubt as to the I's awareness of the suffering evoked in these verses. It is the suffering of the poet's people and—paradoxically—also her pain of being alienated from it.

The second stanza makes this awareness explicit and resolves the paradox in the image of a collective echo that continues to resound in her. The I, insisting on estrangement from her people, associates with her blood two elements: must and ferment. Both result from ages-long storage of wine; but while *Mostvergorenheit* (rotten must) has a negative connotation of an overripe, no longer healthily vital organism, "ferment" suggests the possibility of new life. Although it is her own blood, the I has distanced herself from both elements. The echo of the community from which she has been alienated, however, remains and, it is suggested, nourishes her song as it calls out "to the East," toward Jerusalem as the locus of redemption. Fusing her people's cry to God about a world in need of salvation with her own lament about her alienation, the poem captures the potentially redemptive inspiration Lasker-Schüler draws from the Jewish tradition even as she depicts her own condition as a modern, alienated poet.

Living with the Other

Debates about Lasker-Schüler often revolve around the extent to which she can be considered a self-consciously Jewish poet affirming her belonging, whether—as her frequent positive references to Mary, Jesus, and the saints suggest—her work is heavily influenced by Christian faith and beliefs or if her attitude to religion is ecumenical, syncretic, or simply confused. Although Lasker-Schüler considered herself a "poet of the Jews,"[9] she despised the self-righteousness of the Jewish establishment and spoke in often violent terms about it. She felt that it had betrayed the original teachings, had become tame and pale, and had lost all sense of transcendence. Her attitude to Christianity is similarly fraught with ambivalence. Her own experiences of antisemitism, and her awareness of centuries of Christian Judeophobia poignantly evoked in *Arthur Aronymus and His Fathers*, kept her at a distance from the Christian creed, in spite of an undeniable attraction to its self-understanding as a religion of love. Her identification with figures from different religious traditions—Judaism, Islam, Christianity, and even Buddhism—has been a matter of contention among scholars of her work. Considered by some an expression of her tolerance and openness, it was seen by others as a mere arbitrary, syncretic mixture of cultural references. Jakob Hessing regards the religious diversity of her self-projections as "a fantastic punishment" of the superficiality of her Jewish environment.[10] However, a closer look at her poetry suggests that her main motivation for this mingling of religious references is a fundamental impulse to cross borders between same and other, as well as a deep-seated sense of solidarity with the stranger.

The poem "Hagar und Ismael" (Hagar and Ishmael) presents an alternative reading of the biblical text, one that sets itself in opposition to the repudiation of Hagar and her son in Genesis. Lasker-Schüler accompanies Ishmael, who in the Bible is called a "wild man" (Gen. 21:20), and his mother, Hagar, the Egyptian maid of Abraham's wife Sarah, into the desert. In the biblical narrative, Ishmael and his mother are cast out by Abraham at the behest of Sarah, the original Jewish mother: "Wherefore she said unto Abraham, cast out this bondswoman and her son: for the son of this bondswoman shall not be heir with my son" (Gen. 21: 10). In "Hagar and Ishmael," Lasker-Schüler grieves for the fate of Ishmael and his mother and indicts those who have expelled them. Her accusation of those who expel the stranger foreshadows her protest against those who will eventually expel her from Germany.

HAGAR AND ISHMAEL

With shells played Abraham's young sons,
floating their little vessels of mother-of-pearl,
then Isaac, anxious, leaned on Ishmael.

And full of sadness sang the two black swans
such somber melodies around their colored world
and Hagar disowned, swiftly stole her son away.
Into his little tears she shed her larger tear,
and their hearts murmured like the holy well
and hurried faster even than the ostrich birds.
The sun blazed on the glaring desert plain
and Hagar and her boy sank down into the yellow fur,
into the sand they dug their negro teeth so white.[11]

(trans. Esther Kinsky)

The relationship between the young brothers is initially peaceful. It is only the decision of the arch-father Abraham—behind which, according to the Bible, lies Sarah's demand—that separates the two and drives Ishmael and his mother into the desert. That Isaac "leaned on Ishmael" emphasizes that the rupture between Abraham's sons does not result from a dispute between them, but is the fault of the father figure and his female ally. Lasker-Schüler does not mention the involvement of Sarah, but with the word "mother-of-pearl" (*Perlmutter*) she nevertheless draws attention to the mother's role. In this context, however, this shimmering, multicolored material takes on another meaning in the subsequent verses. Carried through to the end of the poem is a dichotomy between colorful imagery and black-and-white imagery. The world in which the half-brothers play before the Egyptian maid and her son are expelled is described as colorful, and it is this colorful world that they lose through their forcible separation. The grieving, separated boys become "black swans," and the poem ends with a contrast of black and white. Because of the expulsion of the two foreigners, a world has been lost in which heterogeneous elements can exist together in a colorful and playful way. Lasker-Schüler hallows the unjustly expelled pair: their flight is compared to the running of ostriches, sacred creatures in ancient Egypt. She calls the tears of the banished a holy well. This sadness replaces the flowing waters on which the shimmering boats could float before the cruel decision was made to part the two unequal brothers. Henceforth, the reconciliation of the antagonistic children of Abraham will, in other works by Lasker-Schüler, be projected onto a far-off hope for the future, a messianic realm of universal redemption.

Messianism and Sensuality

A similarly unorthodox rereading of biblical references can be found in many of Lasker-Schüler's religiously inspired love poems. In them, melancholic recollections of past happiness, suffering in the absence of the loved one, and, most of all, the longing for reunion link the individual experience of love to ideas of collective redemption derived from the Jewish tradition. The Song of Solomon is the subtext of a large part of Lasker-Schüler's love poetry. This intertextual relationship is evident in stylistic elements—opaque metaphor, tonality of entreaty, phatic redundancy—and in the basic situation of a pair of lovers singing duets in praise of each other and embracing all things, plants, beasts, and landscapes for their mutual celebration. One constant within these poems is a movement between ecstatic union, on the one hand,

and the enforced and violent separation of lovers, who cling to their yearning for a future restoration of their happiness, on the other. Their love becomes a metaphor for the poetic process of the reunification of what has been separated and hence turns into an eschatological vision. Shulamite, the female protagonist of the Song of Songs, is simultaneously the singer and the one who is sung about as a personification of the Bible itself. She is lover and beloved, who binds erotic desire and hymnic expression in a vision of messianic redemption. This text, unusual in the biblical context, was given a mystical reinterpretation in the rabbinical Midrash. Sensual love was understood in purely metaphorical terms and dissolved in the eschatological dimension. The erotic union of the lovers was entirely swallowed by the pure symbol of the relationship between God and His people. In her poem "Sulamith" (Shulamite), Lasker-Schüler refers explicitly to the Song of Songs, but she combines sensual love and messianic anticipation in a way that does not admit a metaphorical dissolution of sensuality into pure spirituality.

SHULAMITE

O, from your sweet mouth
I learned too much of bliss!
Already I feel Gabriel's lips
Burning on my breast . . .
And the night-cloud drinks
My deep dream of cedars.
O, how your life beckons me!
And I dissolve
With blossoming heartbreak
And I drift away in the universe
Into time
To forever,
And my soul burns away in the evening colors
Of Jerusalem.

(HB, 75)

With its title and its references to the archangel Gabriel, to Jerusalem and the cedars growing there, the poem establishes a messianic vision of redemption. However, this vision remains ambivalent. The poem begins with the recollection of a past experience of love and goes on to describe a process of self-dissolution, of a withdrawal from the reality of time and space, culminating in messianic Jerusalem. In the Bible, Gabriel is the archangel who delivers and interprets the Word of God. He announces to the prophet Daniel the time of the end, the defeat of Israel, and the destruction of Jerusalem, whereupon Daniel breaks into a song of atonement. As a reward for Daniel's contrition, Gabriel appears to him again, "about the time of the evening offering," and proclaims the tidings of the future reconstruction of Jerusalem (Dan. 8 and 9). Lasker-Schüler's "Shulamite" can likewise be read as a song of atonement that is rewarded as evening falls, at the time of the end, with the announcement of approaching salvation.

The picture of Gabriel's lips and the metaphor of the drinking night-cloud in the first lines twice take up the motif of the mouth: step by step, the physical figure of the lover first addressed as "you" is replaced by an abstraction. In the middle of the poem this progression toward abstraction leads to a new invocation of the lover: "O, how your life beckons me!" The mouth of the lover has turned into the more abstract "life." The words "dissolve" (*vergehen*), "drift away" (*verwehen*), and "burn away" (*verglühen*) point to the sense of loss brought about by spiritual redemption: erotic love is forfeited along with the existence of the physical world. The heart blossoms and suffers at the same time. At Gabriel's kiss, it still bore traces of burning passion, but now, when the world's evening falls, it burns up as a purely spiritual soul. The invocation of the messianic state of "worldlessness" (*Weltlosigkeit*) is accompanied throughout by a sense of loss and mourning. In contrast to the orthodox metaphorical sublimation of the Song of Songs, Lasker-Schüler marks the loss that accompanies the transformation from the sensual experience of love to spiritual unification. In the poem, eroticism and spirituality are simultaneously analogous and opposed: Shulamite is not wholly absorbed into the image of a people yearning for God; she remains an erotic lover caught between conflicting longings. Her song constitutes the keynote of Lasker-Schüler's modernist adaptations of the biblical text.

Redemption through Poetry

While her writings concerning Judaism and its relation to other religions can be considered as either ecumenical, affirming the encounter and even the merging of different established creeds, or partaking of an eclectic syncretism—a somewhat arbitrarily and haphazardly mixing of references to various religions—it is the accusation of merely confounding these references in a confusing, incoherent, chaotic jumble of allusions to different traditions that is belied by the role Lasker-Schüler assigns to confusion as a poetic strategy. As an important element of her poetics thematized both in her fictional and reflective writings, it constitutes an important means of subverting established ideas and, beyond that, a potential origin of redemption.

Lasker-Schüler's most idiosyncratic invocation and revision of the Jewish tradition, particularly its vision of messianic redemption with the means of avant-garde poetry, occurs in some of her early prose pieces where these strategies take on a programmatic though often hidden dimension. "Der Grossmogul von Philippopel" (The grand mogul of Philippopel),[12] one of the stories in *The Nights of Tino from Bagdad*, is a bizarre political and poetological parable written in the style of the grotesque. The principal characters in this fantastic story are the Grand Mogul, Minister of the Sultan, and the poetess Tino, Lasker-Schüler's alter ego. The Grand Mogul, who believes that as a result of an insect sting he is no longer able to speak and who is urgently needed for the state affairs of the threatened empire, is to be healed by the poetess. She is to find the legendary magic word that will restore the minister's speech and save the country. Tino becomes the official mouthpiece of the minister and is acknowledged by the Sultan and his entourage. However, she systematically distorts the minister's decisions. The decrees that result from her willful misrepresentations of the ruler's intentions are successful: Tino puts the Grand

Mogul's enemies to flight and brings prosperity to the land. When her deception is discovered, however, she is driven from the palace in disgrace and now wanders through the night as a solitary accompanied by a donkey. In the concluding scene of "The Grand Mogul of Philippopel," a biblical reference is superimposed on the oriental background and transposes this text into a modernist poetics. In the final image of the outcast wandering through the desert, Lasker-Schüler seems to have incorporated elements of the biblical story of Balaam. In that tale, Balaam, a foreign soothsayer, is appointed by the Moabite king, Balak, to curse the people of Israel. Balaam sets out on his donkey, but turns the curse he was charged with into a blessing and so saves the Israelites. To the fury of his enemies his prophecies are successful and change the course of history. According to some traditions, Balaam is a herald of the Messiah. That Lasker-Schüler was at least aware of the Balaam legend, and equates the function of the biblical interpreter with redemption through confusion—in the story a liberating "distortion"—is evident from the correspondences between her 1902 poem "Weltflucht" (Flight from the world)[13] and the later poem "Elbanaff,"[14] which, according to Lasker-Schüler, represents the "translation" of the former poem into a "mystical Asiatic language." The poem is preceded by Lasker-Schüler's comments that her early poems were written in a "primordial language" (*Ursprache*) from the time of Saul, the royal wild Jew. "I still can speak this language which I probably breathed in my dreams. My poem 'Weltflucht' is written in this mystical Asiatic language."[15]

WELTFLUCHT

Ich will in das Grenzenlose
Zu mir zurück,
Schon blüht die Herbstzeitlose
Meiner Seele,
Vielleicht ists schon zu spät zurück,
O, ich sterbe unter euch!
Da ihr mich erstickt mit euch.
Fäden möchte ich um mich ziehen
Wirrwarr endend!
Beirrend,
Euch *verwirrend*,
Um zu entfliehn
Meinwärts.

ELBANAFF

Min salihihi wali kinahu
Rahi hatiman
fi is bahi lahi fassun—
Min hagas assama anadir,
Wakan liachid abtal,
Latina almu lijádina binassre.
Wa min tab ihi
Anahu jatelahu

Wanu *bilahum*.
Assama ja saruh
fi es supi *bila* uni
El fidda alba hire
Wa wisuri—elbanaff!

FLIGHT FROM THE WORLD

I will go back into the endlessness
Back to myself,
The autumn saffron of my soul already
in bloom,
maybe it is too late already to go back,
Oh, I am dying among you!
As you suffocate me with yourself.
I want to spin threads around myself
Ending the tangle,
Leading astray,
Confusing you,
To take flight
Mywards.

(trans. Esther Kinsky; emphasis added by VL)

In "Elbanaff," the "mystical-Asiatic version" of her poem "Weltflucht," of which only individual semantic particles are comprehensible, the eighth and ninth lines are "Anahu jatelahu / Wanu *bilahum*." In the German "translation," the equivalent lines are "Wirrwarr endend! / Verwirrend" (Ending the tangle / confusing): *bilahum* accordingly stands for "confusing." "Anahu" contains the Greek root "ana," which stands for "rearrangement, transformation, reordering." "Anahu jatelahu" thus means ending confusion through—confusion? This correlation also reflects the actions of the poetess *in* the story—her distortion of the decrees of those in power—and the confusing shape of the story itself.

On both levels, confusion/distortion is thus granted a liberating and redeeming function. In the story, the distortion of the language of the rulers by the poetess leads temporarily to a new order, to a utopian state of affairs, in which borders are opened, enemies retreat, and artists move into the palaces. In the narrative mode of the text, there is a correspondence to this distortion in the estrangement of linguistic and narrative conventions that aims at a similar liberation: the undistorted, "realistic" mode of representation is equated with the form of communication of the rulers. Tino/Lasker-Schüler is the poetic rebel who threatens their power by infiltrating and "corrupting" their medium of expression. The modernist poetics sketched here confers a revolutionary and messianic function on the effect of experimental modes of writing. The liberating function of the distortion holds equally for the poetess Tino *in* the story as for Lasker-Schüler's readers. The end of the story associates this rejection of the modernist poet as wanderer without a fixed place and a defined identity with the expelled Jew or the outcast Redeemer: straying and causing confusion, she wanders aimlessly across the earth.

The Disillusions of Jerusalem

After 1933, when she left Berlin, aimless wandering following a violent political expulsion became for Lasker-Schüler a painful reality. Her first trip to Jerusalem would inspire her exuberant account *Das Hebräerland* (The land of the Hebrew), which she wrote upon her return to Europe. In spite of its colorful and exalted descriptions, one can read between the lines a deep ambivalence, suggesting her awareness of a gap between her imaginary projections and the reality of her experiences in this conflict-ridden place. Jerusalem, the city of her poetic dreams and hopes, became for her a permanent exile as she mourned the world she had to leave behind and that was about to be violently destroyed. In the final years of her life, bitterness and disillusionment dominate her writings. The alternative to the bourgeois modernity she had created in her multiple personae and her artistic work was shattered by the historical developments. Poetic self-invention, the valorization of the stranger and the outsider, and reconciliation between religions and cultures had lost all credibility. Her imaginative transformation of the modern world through poetry turned into a mournful lament over a darkening world. Two major works written in this final period, the collection of poetry *Mein blaues Klavier* (My blue piano, 1943) and the play *Ichundich* (I and I, 1961), testify to this disillusionment. In a very different sense than in her earlier writings, her late works reaffirm the Jewish modernity of her poetic achievements. Both works prefigure in many ways the direction postwar German Jewish poetry was to take. *Ichundich*, written in 1940–1941, is a bitter, fragmentary, and chaotic satire set in a hellish Jerusalem. It features predominantly German fictional as well as historical figures, such as Faust, Mephisto, and Goebbels, who are depicted in ways so grotesque and incongruous that they convey the bankruptcy of German high culture as well as the impossibility of poetically coming to terms with the evil and brutality of Nazi Germany. In invoking Goethe, the play voices an accusation against the German *Bildungsbürgertum*, the educated bourgeoisie that let itself be seduced by Hitler and his followers. The shattered idea of reconciliation among different cultures and the broken promise of a union between Germans and Jews made Lasker-Schüler lose her earlier hope of redemption through poetic language. Her former playfully "distorted" verses, once meant to undermine conventional speech and point toward divine redemption, turned into a lament over an irreparable loss. An untitled poem written shortly before her death, published posthumously, starts with the words "Hear, God" and ends on a scream from the soul of the earth in the midst of a heap of corpses.[16] Reversing the traditional "Sh'ma Israel," "Hear O Israel," Lasker-Schüler's longing for proximity and intimacy with God turns into a blasphemously threatening gesture that foreshadows some of the most powerful verses by the German Jewish postwar poet Paul Celan.[17] In "Mein blaues Klavier," the most famous poem of the eponymous collection published in 1943, the instrument of her poetic voice, a piano in the color of the blue flower of German Romantic poetry, stands in the darkness of a cellar "since the world's decay."

> Broken is the keyboard . . .
> I weep for the blue dead
> Ah, dear angel, open to me

—What bitter bread I ate—
Even against the law's decree,
In life, heaven's gate.

(HB, 85)

Not only has Enlightenment modernity failed, its poeticized alternative has been silenced by history as well. Beyond this requiem for poetic possibilities to elevate and transform reality, the poem expresses a death wish, a plea to be delivered from a world become uninhabitable. And yet, even in these verses of resignation there is a rebellious tone, as the I requests to be, while still "in life," admitted to heaven—the most traditionally religious image for the realm of the dead—"even against the law's decree." This appeal with suicidal connotations, preceded by a distorted reference to the Passover tradition of eating bitter herbs and unleavened bread, constitutes Lasker-Schüler's final rebellious transgression of boundaries. Her desire to escape from the here and now is simultaneously a political and metaphysical protest against the historical conditions of her times.

Bibliography

Arendt, Hannah. "Introduction to Walter Benjamin." In Walter Benjamin, *Illuminations*. Trans. Harry Zohn, ed. and intro. Hannah Arendt. New York: Harcourt Brace Jovanovich, 2007, 1–58.

Bänsch, Dieter. *Else Lasker-Schüler: Zur Kritik eines etablierten Bildes*. Stuttgart: Metzlersche Verlagsbuchhandlung, 1971.

Ben-Chorin, Shalom. "Prinz Jussuf in Jerusalem." In *Else Lasker-Schüler: Dichtungen und Dokumente*, ed. Ernst Ginsberg. Munich: Kösel, 1951, 582–90.

Benjamin, Walter. *Gesammelte Briefe*. Vol. 1, eds. Rolf Tiedemann and Hermann Schweppenhäuser. Frankfurt: Suhrkamp, 1995.

Benn, Gottfried. "Rede auf Else Lasker-Schüler." In *Essay-Reden. Gesammelte Werke*. Vol. 1. Wiesbaden: Limes, 1959, 537–40.

Celan, Paul. *Die Gedichte*. Ed. Barbara Wiedemann. Frankfurt: Suhrkamp, 2003.

Kafka, Franz. *Briefe 1913—März 1914*. Ed. Hans-Gerd Koch. Frankfurt: Fischer, 1999.

Kupper, Margarete. *Die Weltanschauung Else Lasker-Schülers in ihren poetischen Selbstzeugnissen*. PhD diss., University of Würzburg, 1963.

Hessing, Jakob. *Else Lasker-Schüler: Ein Leben zwischen Bohème und Exil*. Munich: Wilhelm Heyne Verlag, 1985.

Lasker-Schüler, Else. *Hebrew Ballads and Other Poems*. Trans. and ed. Audri Durchslag and Jeanne Litman-Demeestère. Philadelphia: Jewish Publication Society of America, 1980.

Lasker-Schüler, Else. *Werke und Briefe: Kritische Ausgabe*. Eds. Norbert Oellers, Heinz Rölleke, and Itta Shedletzky. Frankfurt: Jüdischer Verlag im Suhrkamp Verlag, 1996–1998.

Notes

Portions of this chapter previously appeared in Vivian Liska, *When Kafka Says We: Uncommon Communities in German-Jewish Literature* (Bloomington, IN, 2009).

1. Dieter Bänsch, *Else Lasker-Schüler: Zur Kritik eines etablierten Bildes* (Stuttgart, 1971), 50.

2. Yehuda Amichai in his preface to Else Lasker-Schüler, *Hebrew Ballads and Other Poems*, trans. and eds. Audri Durchslag and Jeanne Litman-Demeestère (Philadelphia, 1980), xi. Hereafter referred to as HB (with page numbers for quoted citations).

3. In a letter to Felice Bauer from February 12, 1913, Franz Kafka writes that he "can't stand her poetry" and that he always imagines her "drunk and dragging herself every night from one café to the other." Franz Kafka, *Briefe 1913—März 1914* (Frankfurt, 1999), 88. In a letter to a friend,

Walter Benjamin describes her countenance as "empty and sick—hysterical." Walter Benjamin, *Gesammelte Briefe*, vol. 1 (Frankfurt, 1995), 241.

4. Hannah Arendt, "Introduction to Walter Benjamin," in Walter Benjamin, *Illuminations*, trans. Harry Zohn, ed. and intro. Hannah Arendt (New York, 2007), 51.

5. Gottfried Benn, "Rede auf Else Lasker-Schüler," in Gottfried Benn, *Gesammelte Werke*, ed. Dieter Wellersdorf, vol. 4 (Wiesbaden, 1968), 1102.

6. Shalom Ben-Chorin, "Prinz Jussuf in Jerusalem," in *Else Lasker-Schüler: Dichtungen und Dokumente*, ed. Ernst Ginsberg (Munich, 1951), 582–90; here 588.

7. Jakob Hessing, *Else Lasker-Schüler Ein Leben zwischen Bohème und Exil* (Munich, 1985), 158.

8. Margarete Kupper, *Die Weltanschauung Else Lasker-Schülers in ihren poetischen Selbstzeugnissen* (Ph.D. diss., Würzburg, 1963), 63.

9. Margarete Kupper, ed., *Lieber gestreifter Tiger: Briefe von Else Lasker-Schüler* (Munich, 1969), 263.

10. Hessing, *Else Lasker-Schüler*, 97.

11. Else Lasker-Schüler, *Gedichte 1.1, Werke und Briefe* (Frankfurt, 1996), 208.

12. Else Lasker-Schüler, *Prosa 3.1, Werke und Briefe* (Frankfurt, 1998), 85–89.

13. Lasker-Schüler, *Gedichte 1.1*, 234.

14. Else Lasker-Schüler, *Lyrik. Prosa. Dramen 2.1, Werke und Briefe* (Frankfurt, 1996), 520–21.

15. Ibid.

16. Lasker-Schüler, *Gedichte 1.1*, 265.

17. Compare particularly his poems "Psalm" and "Tenebrae": Paul Celan, *Die Gedichte* (Frankfurt, 2003), 132, 97.

Rosa Luxemburg (1871–1919)

UNIVERSALISM AND PARTICULARISM

Kevin B. Anderson and Peter Hudis

What do you want with this theme of the "special suffering of the Jews"? I
am just as much concerned with the poor victims on the rubber plantations of
Putumayo, the Blacks in Africa with whose corpses the Europeans play catch.
You know the words that were written about the great work of the General Staff,
about Gen. Trotha's campaign in the Kalahari desert: "And the death rattles of
the dying, the demented cries of those driven mad by thirst faded away in the
sublime stillness of eternity." Oh that "sublime stillness of eternity," in which
so many cries of anguish have faded away unheard, they resound within me so
strongly that I have no special place in my heart for the [Jewish] ghetto. I feel at
home in the entire world, wherever there are clouds and birds and human tears.
—ROSA LUXEMBURG, "TO MATHILDE WURM" (1917)[1]

FEW THINKERS IN THE SOCIALIST TRADITION PLACED AS MUCH EMPHASIS ON CON-
sciousness, education, and self-examination as Rosa Luxemburg, the Polish-Jewish
German revolutionary renowned for her intense opposition to authoritarianism and
organizational elitism and for her insistence on the critical role played by spontaneous mass struggles for social transformation. She viewed socialism not as the product of some blind, automatic process but rather as the first historical formation that
would arise from a *conscious* effort to reshape social existence in accordance with
human needs and capacities. For Luxemburg, the revolution that brings socialism
into being "requires self-consciousness, self-knowledge, and class consciousness."[2]
As she summed up the lessons of the 1905 Russian Revolution in *The Mass Strike,
the Political Party, and the Trade Unions*, "The most precious, because lasting,
thing in this rapid ebb and flow of the wave is its mental sediment: the intellectual,
cultural growth of the proletariat, which proceeds by fits and starts, and which offers an inviolable guarantee of their further irresistible progress in the economic as
in the political struggle."[3]

Luxemburg was no less insistent on the importance of consciousness and self-
examination when it came to personal matters. As she wrote to her comrade and

lover Leo Jogiches in 1900, "One must constantly carry out anew an inner review, or inventory, of oneself, in order to reestablish order and harmony. Thus one must constantly deal with oneself in order not to lose sight, at any moment, of the overall proportion of things."[4] She often complains in her correspondence about those who "forget for the most part to go deeper into themselves and experience the full import and truth of what they're writing."[5]

At the same time, few individuals seem to have displayed less self-awareness and consciousness when it came to their Jewish heritage than Rosa Luxemburg. She was born in Zamosc, a Polish town with a considerable Jewish population, and was brought at age three to Warsaw, which at the time had a larger percentage of Jews than any major city in Europe. Yet she never explicitly identified with her Jewish background, which was considerable. Her mother Lina (née Löwenstein), the sister and daughter of rabbis, was descended from a long line of religious scholars, among them Rabbi Jacob Joshua Falk (1680–1756), a talmudist who sharply criticized the class divisions within the German Jewish communities. But although Rosa Luxemburg was raised in a household that was fully aware of its Jewish heritage, one finds hardly a single reference to a Jewish cultural or religious milieu in her writings, including her letters. Although this was not atypical for assimilated intellectuals of her time, her aversion to identifying with her Jewish background outdid her other assimilationist colleagues in the Marxist movement, such as Eduard Bernstein and Leon Trotsky.

That Luxemburg did not acknowledge her Jewish heritage does not mean that it did not impact her in important ways, however. Throughout her career she found herself attacked both inside and outside of the socialist movement for "idealism," "rootlessness," and "theoretical abstraction," characteristics often attributed to intellectual Jews. While it is not possible to determine whether her sense of social justice and compassion for the wretched and the weak derived from her Jewish background, a strong ethical strain is clearly present in Luxemburg's work that can be viewed as entirely consistent with the social justice message of Judaism.

What is one to make of this contradiction within Luxemburg, who makes so much of self-awareness and self-consciousness but appears to appreciate so little her own ethnoreligious background? And how does an examination of that contradiction contribute to the project of rethinking Jewish modernity today?

Internationalism and Gender

Marx's philosophical mentor Hegel famously attacked "abstract universality," as exemplified by those who presented things as a "night, in which, as the saying goes, all cows are black."[6] Hegel's barb was directed against those kinds of Enlightenment reason that he regarded as overly formalistic, conceptualizing human experience via categories that neglected historical or cultural variety and particularity. In short, the universal had swallowed up the particular.

Was Luxemburg's thought burdened with this kind of abstract universalism? And if so, did this impact the ways in which she grappled with the place of the Jews in European society and with her own ethnic background? Before approaching the latter question directly, let us first examine Luxemburg's theorization of

nationalism and gender, two areas in which the issues of universality and particularity were paramount.

From the inception of her political career, Luxemburg was a firm and uncompromising internationalist. Internationalism, for her, was completely incompatible with any form of nationalism, which she viewed as a diversion from the struggle against capitalism. Luxemburg applied these strictures most forcefully to her native Poland, rejecting any and all calls for Polish independence or national self-determination. Poles living in Russian-occupied Poland (as she did in her youth) should fight for the liberation of the Russian Empire, just as Poles in areas occupied by Germany or the Austro-Hungarian Empire should fight to transform those regimes. Any compromise with nationalist politics, she held, would come at the expense of the overall struggle for democracy and socialism.

She was fully aware that this put her at odds with Marx, who had fervently supported Polish independence, even to the point of calling such support the "external thermometer" through which "the intensity and viability of all revolutions since 1789 may be gauged."[7] She was no less aware that it put her at odds with the bulk of the Polish labor movement, which strongly supported national independence. Yet in a striking illustration of her independent will and intellect, she never moved an inch from opposing Polish independence. Instead, she consistently applied her anti-nationalist stance by opposing *all* struggles for national self-determination that (as she saw it) distracted from the struggle for socialism, whether by Czechs, Ukrainians, Lithuanians, Finns, the Irish—or Jews. This does not mean, however, that Luxemburg opposed *all* struggles that took on a national character. When the Greeks on the island of Crete rose up in opposition against the Ottoman Empire in 1896, she supported the insurrection. She did so on the grounds that the Greeks were being brutally subjected to discrimination on the basis of their ethnicity. There was no reason not to support their struggle, she held, because no socialist or workers' movement had yet arisen in the Ottoman Empire. But where such movements had arisen, either in Poland or in the rest of Europe, support for national self-determination was a distraction from the "real" battle at hand.[8]

At the same time, Luxemburg was deeply committed to independent *political* activity on behalf of Polish socialism. She deeply resented efforts by the Second International and the Russian social democrats to interfere with her work in the Polish party that she helped found, the Social Democratic Party of the Kingdom of Poland (SDKP; after it disbanded in 1896, she joined the more longlasting Social Democratic Party of Poland and Lithuania [SDKPiL], founded in 1900). Thus, her insistence on subsuming national struggles under socialist ones did not mean centralization under a single organizational rubric. In this sense her position was the reverse of that of Lenin, who supported national self-determination for Poles, Ukrainians, and other subject peoples within the Russian Empire, while insisting on the dominance of a tightly centralized national party—and later, a Communist International—that would override national and ethnic differences.

Luxemburg is renowned for her prescient criticisms of Lenin's authoritarianism and centralism, some of which predate the 1917 Russian Revolution by more than a decade. For example, in the aftermath of the 1917 Revolution, she famously criticized the revolutionary dictatorship of Lenin and Trotsky, warning her Russian comrades:

"Freedom is always and exclusively for the one who thinks differently."[9] This utterly modern stance has become a rallying cry for the twenty-first-century left.

However, her disputes with Lenin over the "national question" were by far the most contentious aspect of their long and complex relationship. Luxemburg's intransigent opposition to national self-determination has long puzzled commentators, who have attributed it to everything from an exaggerated fondness for German and Russian culture to a misplaced response to reactionary and antisemitic variants of Polish nationalism, with which she was all too familiar. To the contrary, we would like to suggest that Luxemburg's views on nationalism, as well as on many other issues, flowed from an attachment to a basic *philosophical* assumption, namely, that demands for universal freedom and liberation trump particularist considerations. She was by no means insensitive to particularist considerations, whether concerning the struggle for higher wages or even the fight to redress specific national grievances. She held, however, that they needed to be subsumed under the overarching goal of universal human emancipation. Her commitment to political universals, and her diffidence regarding their actualization when individuals commit themselves to particularist interests, grounded her views on a host of issues. In this sense, she would have fallen under Hegel's critique of abstract universalism, as cited above.

Luxemburg's attachment to universalist principles is also reflected in her attitude toward the politics of gender. After moving to Germany, then the center of the largest socialist movement in the world, she threw herself into what were regarded as the central theoretical debates of the time involving reformism, imperialism, and war. She refused repeated suggestions from important male social democrats that she become active in the German socialist women's movement, which she nonetheless supported. She did so on the grounds that it would keep her away from the major theoretical and political debates gripping the socialist movement. Similarly, although she remained active in the Polish socialist movement, she wanted to make her mark in Germany, then the center of European Social Democracy, as an *international* Marxist theoretician addressing the questions facing what she saw as the only "universal" class—the industrial working class.

Luxemburg was well aware that she repeatedly faced opposition, both open and concealed, because of her gender. One leading Socialist, Viktor Adler, referred to her in a letter to August Bebel, the esteemed German socialist who was the author of *Women under Socialism*, as "that poisonous bitch."[10] Yet because of her reluctance to openly define herself as a *woman* socialist, it has often been presumed that Luxemburg's life and work are of little or no interest to feminism. Luxemburg was surely a feminist in her insistence on being heard and taken seriously as both a political leader and a theorist, and she overcame many obstacles along the way.

Moreover, she was more concerned with the specificity of gender than is generally acknowledged by her biographers.[11] She found these issues compelling but insisted on not emphasizing them at the expense of the overall goal of socialist revolution. Thus, throughout her life she encouraged her colleague and friend, Clara Zetkin, who headed the socialist women's movement; Zetkin also edited its publication, *Gleichheit*, and wrote occasionally on women and socialism.

Strikingly, her interest in women's emancipation took on a new emphasis after she was freed from prison in November 1918 and plunged into the effort to steer

Germany toward a socialist revolution. The last months of her life, from November 1918 to January 1919, were a tremendously intense and active period. And yet it was precisely in this period, perhaps the most demanding and difficult of her entire life, that she turned with new emphasis to the issue of women's emancipation. On the very day she was released from prison she asked Zetkin: "Write something perhaps about women, that is so important now, and none of us here understand anything about it."[12] A week later she added, "Actually, at the first meeting of our top leadership we decided, at my suggestion, to put out a women's paper as well. . . . At any rate a women's paper must be produced by us here in Berlin. . . . And it is such an urgent matter! Every day lost is a sin."[13] Shortly before her murder at the hands of proto-fascist officers, she stated, "We here are in the process, among other things, of laying the basis for the work with women and for educational work."[14] It is as if the fire and enthusiasm of revolution, as well as her break from the stultifying atmosphere created by her former comrades in the Second International, released in her a passion to plunge directly into the issues of women's liberation on a new level.

Luxemburg was a universalistic thinker who would let nothing get in the way of proletarian internationalism, the overarching principle to which she committed herself from her youth. It would be just as wrong, however, to conclude that she was uninterested in anything that fell outside of such universalism, as it would be a mistake to suggest that her universalism did not have problematic aspects, seen most clearly in her implacable opposition to national self-determination. She opposed such calls because she thought that the masses would increasingly seek to bypass national particularism as they engaged in the struggle for universal human emancipation. As she wrote of the 1905 Russian Revolution:

> It was visible to everyone here that, for the first time, the whole gigantic proletarian mass of the Russian Empire emerged as *one* working-class in the political arena—without difference of nationality and religion—Russians, Poles, Lithuanians, Armenians, Latvians and Jews, striving for a common, political goal through common action.[15]

Luxemburg was no doubt correct that different national groupings came together to struggle against Russian capitalism in 1905 as part of "one" working class. However, this "oneness" was also internally differentiated, and such internal, national differentiations clearly mattered to large numbers of people. Luxemburg assumed that the achievement of common unity for purposes of action on the part of diverse national groupings pointed toward a transcendence of national identity itself. Yet just as different political parties can unite for common action without surrendering their distinctive theoretical positions, so it is possible for different national and ethnic units of the working class to unite for common action without surrendering their distinctive national identities. This was the Achilles heel of her argument.

Moreover, just as Luxemburg's relative silence on issues of gender and women's oppression did not mean that she was insensitive to the suffering of women, her universalist dismissal of national self-determination did not mean that she ignored the plight of national minorities and oppressed nations. Luxemburg condemned imperialism and repeatedly denounced capitalism's destruction of traditional cultural and communal formations. At a time when many—including not a few socialists—

viewed European imperialism as part of a "civilizing mission," she attacked it unstintingly. This is seen in her writings on Africa, a part of the world she studied carefully. A prominent example is in her *Junius Pamphlet*, written against World War I:

> The "civilized world" which looked on calmly while this same imperialism consigned tens of thousands of Hereros to the most horrible destruction, and filled the Kalahari desert with the mad cries of those perishing from thirst and the death rattles of the dying . . . while in Tripoli the Arabs were bowed to the yoke of capital with fire and sword, their culture and their dwellings razed to the ground—this "civilized world" has only today become aware that the bite of the imperialist beast is fatal, that its breath is infamy.[16]

Luxemburg's internationalism was therefore premised on a *defense* of those suffering from the ravages of imperialist oppression. She held—incorrectly in our view—that the best way to combat this oppression was to ensure that socialists not be sidetracked by calls for national self-determination, since that would presumably forestall the effort to target capitalism itself. But that is a far cry from ignoring either the ravages of national oppression or the dignity of those who rose up to oppose it.

Jewishness and Jewish Identity

As Luxemburg saw it, the only "fatherland" worth promoting was that of the working class, which advances, by its very opposition to capitalism, the negation of all exclusive particularism and nationalism. As her biographer J. P. Nettl argued:

> She was not alone in this. It was an allegiance shared by many of the intellectual émigrés, mostly Jews, who deliberately renounced the attempt to find refuge in any particular nationalism of the present or future . . . the only attainable fatherland was the working class—or, more correctly, the proletarian revolution.[17]

It does not necessarily follow, however, that Luxemburg was therefore "genuinely impervious" to antisemitism, as Nettl also contends.[18] She was all too conscious that her outsider status as a Jew, a woman, and a Pole explained much of the hostility she experienced from members of the German Social Democracy and the Second International. She chose to fight such hostility by claiming her place not as a woman or a Jew but as a Marxist theoretician. She wanted to show that she could outthink and outdebate any of her adversaries, regardless of their gender or ethnicity.

There was of course a deeper reason for Luxemburg's reluctance to explicitly claim her Jewish identity, namely her view that antisemitism was a product of class society that, like so many other problems, would vanish with its abolition. Why focus on antisemitism when it would cease to exist with the abolition of capitalism? Better to concentrate on the overall goal of creating a new society rather than be diverted by expressions of the old one.

There were exceptions to this. During the Dreyfus affair, Luxemburg criticized her usual allies, the more leftist Jules Guesde wing of French socialism. Even though Guesde opposed the military verdict against Captain Alfred Dreyfus, he had refused to join the large Dreyfusard movement so as not to align with liberals or reformists.

While Luxemburg usually castigated the reformist socialist Jean Jaurès, at one point during the affair she praised him as a "mighty figure" that "stands alone" amid the "confusion" of French responses to the affair.[19] Her critique of Guesde's intransigence and self-isolation, which she saw as an overreaction to Jaurès's "opportunism," and which she also made into a more general principle, prefigured her far better known later critiques of Lenin's elitism and organizational intransigence.[20] Another aspect of Luxemburg's writings on the Dreyfus affair distinguished her from the dominant Marxist view of the time, which held that antisemitism was a vestige of the precapitalist past. Instead, as Enzo Traverso notes, Luxemburg saw antisemitism as "one of the aspects of the maturity of capitalism"; he cites Luxemburg's characterization of the affair as imbued with "militarism, chauvinism/nationalism, anti-Semitism and clericalism" at a time when French "bourgeois society" was "declining."[21]

This critique of capitalist modernity grounded Luxemburg's opposition to the two main currents of Jewish nationalism in her time, Zionism and Bundism. She paid relatively little attention to the former, precisely because it had so little to say about the perspective of world revolution. Its particularism and exclusivism, she held, would lead the Jews to engage in ethnic hatred of other minorities. This view was less controversial than it may appear, since it was shared by most politically active Jews of the time, relatively few of whom had committed themselves to Zionism.

Luxemburg's relation to the anti-Zionist Bund is a much more complex matter. She criticized the Bund on the grounds that its emphasis on Jewish cultural identity could undermine the need for a united struggle against tsarism. But she also deeply appreciated its pioneering efforts to reach radicalized Jewish workers by addressing them through their own language and culture. In a 1903 review of a Bundist pamphlet, she praised the Bund for its revolutionary élan and projection of Marxist ideas.[22] Despite her antinationalism, Luxemburg did not therefore deny the Bund a right to its own independent political existence. She could tolerate organizations based on national affiliation so long as they did not promote nationalism. In this regard, her own insistence on the need to maintain the independence of her party, the SDKPiL, shows that rather clearly.

This helps explain the relatively friendly relations between the Bund and Luxemburg, at least before 1907. She openly opposed the chauvinist attack on the Bund by some leaders of the Polish Socialist Party (PPS), who accused the Bundists of "hating Poland," while also denying the widespread existence of antisemitism. And Bundist leaders like John Mill and Isai Aizenshtat much preferred Luxemburg and Jogiches to the PPS. As Nettl notes, while Mill "found both Luxemburg and Jogiches resistant to his early appeals to them as Jews, and firmly opposed to any obligation to a specifically Jewish Socialist movement, he none the less saw them with an eye that at that time was politically and personally neutral, if not benevolent."[23] Luxemburg herself took up Mill's offer to submit several articles to the Bundist paper *Der Yidischer Arbeter* in 1899 and 1902.

Luxemburg and the Bund differed, however, over her insistence that the struggle of Jewish workers in Poland be conducted as an integral part of the labor movement of the Russian Empire as a whole. She opposed the Bund's calls for regional autonomy and its claim to represent Jewish workers within the Empire. Her attacks on the Bund brought out the *centralist* implications of her rejection of "the national question," even though in the very same period she disagreed with Lenin's *organizational* centralism as well. She maintained that the Bund's politics

> are simply the expression of the federative policies which those organizations would like to raise to the level of a principle in relations among socialist groups. It is not only that such a tactic does not represent any kind of step forward on the road to the unification of Social Democrats in Russia; it actually means the opposite, the canonization of the federative principle, which we reject. . . . This mode of operation of the federalist nationalists goes together very logically with their eclectic views on the tasks [of Social Democracy] in general and on the methods of struggle against the autocracy, but these [views] do not go together very well, in my opinion, with the comprehensive political world outlook of Social Democracy.[24]

By 1907, Luxemburg's polemics against the Bund became extremely heated, leading to a near-total break. At the 1907 Congress of the Russian Social Democracy, she attacked the Bund in harsh, inappropriate language: "The Jews from the Bund revealed themselves as the shabbiest of political horse traders [*Schacherpolitiker*].[25] They constantly, after many tricks and dodges [*Winkelzüge*] and radical phrases, ended up holding the banner of . . . opportunism."[26]

Luxemburg's objection to Jewish national self-determination in general, and to the Bund in particular, was grounded in a rather abstract universalistic claim: "The only manifestation of a truly modern culture on a Jewish foundation is the Social Democratic movement of the Jewish proletariat." This *sole* indication of modern Jewish culture, she held, "is itself the manifestation of a culture that is international and proletarian."[27] Clearly, Luxemburg did not deny the existence of Jewish culture. But the only manifestation of Jewish culture that really mattered to her was "a truly *modern*" one. And in her view, the only existing manifestation of a *modern* Jewish culture was found in the socialist movement!

It is hard to imagine a more striking expression of the reduction of Jewish cultural particularity to an abstract universal. Luxemburg held so firmly to the view that universal principles trump particularist values that she failed to even notice the emergence of a number of expressions of Jewish modernity in her time, many of which had little or nothing to do with "the movement of the Jewish proletariat." The irony here is that Luxemburg appears to have been oblivious to the existence of a bourgeois Jewish Enlightenment of which she can be said to have been in many respects the direct inheritor.

At the same time, her argument here undermines the widespread claim that she was a self-hating Jew who despised all efforts to affirm Jewish culture. She instead held that the only basis for *modern* Jewish cultural affirmation was to be found with the socialist movement, which itself disdained any national or nationalist affirmation. The shtetl, she held, was far too "backward" and "primitive" to sustain Jewish culture. This was, in large measure, central to her arguments against the Bund. She even denied that Jews in Poland had any *national* culture at all. But that does not mean that she ruled out the possibility of Jewish cultural affirmation, *so long as it was inextricably tied to and expressive of the universalist demands of the socialist movement.*

As she put it, "For the followers of Marx, as for the working class, the Jewish question as such does not exist, just as the 'Negro question' or the 'Yellow Peril' does not exist."[28] On similar lines, it could be noted, a number of tendencies in the U.S. socialist movement at the time, including important figures like Eugene V. Debs, were arguing in parallel fashion that there was no race question outside of the class question. Luxemburg's denial of any possibility of Jewish cultural identity independent of the overall aims of the socialist movement is therefore by no means exceptional. But it hardly becomes for that reason any more acceptable.

Rethinking Jewish Modernity

Although Luxemburg cannot stand accused of opposing any and all efforts to develop a modern Jewish cultural expression, there is no doubt that she did not make a "special case" out of the oppression of Jews. As Luxemburg put it in the 1917 letter we used as an opening epigraph for this essay, there is "no special place in my heart for the [Jewish] ghetto. I feel at home in the entire world, wherever there are clouds and birds and human tears." The *meaning* of this passage, however, is by no means self-evident. Does it indicate that Luxemburg was simply and solely a victim of self-denial, if not subject to unconscious feelings of "guilt" about being Jewish? Or does the passage have a deeper significance?

We see no evidence from either her published works or private correspondence that Luxemburg suffered, as Robert S. Wistrich contends, from an "unresolved guilt-complex when it came to the pogroms and the need to resist brutal anti-Semitism in practice."[29] As Wistrich himself acknowledges, Luxemburg did not turn a blind eye to antisemitism, especially when it manifested itself within the workers' movement. See, for example, her stinging retort to Andrej Niemojewski, a Polish nationalist who held that discrimination against Jews was consistent with the aims of the labor struggle, a position that influenced some right-wing elements within the Polish Socialist Party:

> Niemojewski . . . is the most rabid ringleader among our opponents. And the main point is that this "Free Thought" publication has suddenly begun preaching against us with the slogan "Down with the Jews!"—and the entire liberal, progressive press has abandoned itself to an all-out orgy of anti-Semitism. Socialists are "Jews," our *Mlot* is an organ of "the Jewish syndicate," we are all agents of "Jewry," and the "progressive" press is overflowing with personal slander and vulgarity. As you see, it is a Dreyfus case in miniature that is happening among us at the present time, and all of bourgeois Poland—progressives, liberals, and free-thinkers in competition with full-blooded reactionaries and the clergy— have formed a single camp to wage class war against us.[30]

That Luxemburg did not devote very many of her writings to antisemitism was due, as we noted, to her belief that it would cease to exist once class society and exploitation were overcome. But this does not mean that she was reluctant to oppose antisemitism when it threatened her universalist goals. That explicit discussions of antisemitism are rare in her work appears to be the result, not of any guilt complex, but of her internationalism, her confidence in the socialist revolution, and her belief that modern antisemitism was an outgrowth of capitalism.

Moreover, in contrast with some claims, Luxemburg did make "allusions" to the widespread antisemitism in the Germany of her time.[31] Shortly after the Bolshevik revolution of 1917, referring to the 1903 tsarist pogrom in Kishinev (now Moldova), she wrote: "As far as pogroms against Jews are concerned, all rumors of that kind are directly fabricated. In Russia the time of pogroms has passed once and for all. The strength of the workers and of socialism there is much too strong for that. The revolution has cleared the air so much of the miasmas and stuffy atmosphere of reaction that a new Kishinev has become forever passé. I can sooner imagine— pogroms against Jews here in Germany."[32]

To be sure, like most of her contemporaries, Luxemburg could not imagine the horrific future awaiting the German Jews (or, for that matter, Stalin's persecutions), but at least the danger was on her radar screen as early as 1917.

Since Luxemburg was clearly aware of antisemitism and did not hesitate to speak out against it at various points, why then did she not reserve a "special place" in her heart for Jewish suffering? Why was she "just as much concerned with the poor victims on the rubber plantations of Putumayo, the Blacks in Africa" as she was with the suffering of Jews? The reason is that she felt compassion for *all* human beings suffering from discrimination and exploitation and refused to compromise that sensibility by privileging the suffering of her own kind. Was her universalism the expression of "abstract concern at a distance for all of suffering humanity," which necessarily ignores "the immediate, concrete misery of the ghetto"?[33] To be sure, Luxemburg's sensitivity to the victims of European colonialism and imperialism was no "abstract concern." There was nothing abstract about the damage being done by imperialism to the technologically underdeveloped world, and it was no distant or abstract matter for Luxemburg to defend those suffering from it. On the contrary, her analysis of how capitalist accumulation and reproduction depends upon the incorporation and destruction of noncapitalist formations in the developing world represents one of her most important theoretical contributions.

Moreover, in her denunciation of imperialism, she was speaking out against practices that would later be used against European Jews, her own kind. As many have argued, the Holocaust represents the application to a European people of genocidal practices carried out for centuries by Europeans against non-Europeans.[34] It is no small matter that the figure whom she most sharply attacked for implementing the genocide of the Herero and Nama peoples of Namibia, General Lothar von Trotha, later went on to lead the racist Thule Society, which had such an important influence on the mind of the young Adolf Hitler.[35]

Luxemburg is actually the last person who can be accused of only being concerned about suffering "at a distance." She would not tire of alluding to antisemitism as part of her analysis of modern militaristic barbarism. For example, in the *Junius Pamphlet*, her most important denunciation of World War I, she compared the nationalist fever that gripped Europe in 1914 to the earlier pogroms in the tsarist empire, referring to "the atmosphere of ritual murder, the Kishinev air," which revealed "capitalist society . . . devastating culture and humanity . . . in all its hideous nakedness."[36] As Michael Löwy has noted, the *Junius Pamphlet*, with its stark alternative of "socialism or barbarism," was where Luxemburg broke with the progressivist logic of contemporary Marxist and liberal thought, foreshadowing the barbarism that was to follow. To Löwy, "Luxemburg's forecast revealed itself to be tragically correct: the failure of the socialist revolution in 1919 led in the final analysis to the triumph of Nazi barbarism and the Second World War."[37]

Despite the shortcomings of Luxemburg's tendency to detach universal principles of freedom and revolution from struggles for national self-determination and national consciousness, her universalist internationalism and her principled opposition to all forms of oppression contain precious dimensions that are well worth preserving and, indeed, developing anew in the twenty-first century. For the view that the suffering of one's own people does not trump consideration for the suffering of others is actually *beautiful* as well as *necessary*. No one needs to make a "special case" of the suffering of his or her own people, because it is culturally accepted and expected that each takes care of his or her own. It requires no great step in moral or ethical valuation to defend one's own family or ethnicity. In fact, it is rather automatic and commonplace. Plato addressed this long ago in Book I of the *Republic*, in presenting Socrates' critical engagement with Polemarchus's definition of justice as "doing good to your friends and harming your enemies." As Socrates shows, that is really no definition of justice at all.[38] Justice exists in order to care for the weaker and less fortunate, just as medicine exists to treat not the healthy but the sick. It can be argued that the world is not in a sickened state today because there is an insufficient concern with the sufferings of one's own tribe or ethnicity. Do we not instead suffer from a deficit of compassion and solidarity with those outside our familial and ethnic orbit? And is not overcoming such a lack of compassion increasingly needed in a globally integrated world, in which events in one part of the world immediately impact those in radically different parts of it?

It is precisely here, when it comes to her universalist humanism, that Luxemburg is connected to one of the most important parts of the Jewish tradition, one well worth rescuing today, when Jewish culture and tradition is threatened not only from without but even more so from within. Is not one of the greatest gifts of the Jewish tradition as a whole, and one that passed directly or indirectly into those who adopted the Marxian conception of human liberation, the notion that *my* oppression makes me *more* instead of *less* sensitive to *your* oppression?

If there is one thing that Rosa Luxemburg cannot be accused of, it is elevating the interests of her own kind above those of humanity—not humanity as some abstraction, but the mass of actually existing individual human beings suffering the ravages of capitalism. In this sense, for all its limitations, her universalism may serve as a corrective to the predominant tendency to posit one's own particularity at the expense of others. After all, it was not her espousal of universalism per se that was the defect in her approach to questions of national and cultural identity, but rather the way she counterposed such particulars to the universal goal of social transformation. If we can rethink the dialectical connection between particular and universal in a manner that overcomes her limitations while preserving some of her most important insights, we will have done a most important service—not only for her legacy but also for dealing with the problems facing us today. It is in this sense that Luxemburg speaks to rethinking Jewish modernity.

Notes

1. "To Mathilde Wurm" (February 16, 1917), in *Letters of Rosa Luxemburg*, eds. Georg Adler, Peter Hudis, and Annelies Laschitza (London and New York, 2011), 375–76.

2. Rosa Luxemburg, *The Mass Strike, the Political Party, and the Trade Unions*, in *The Rosa Luxemburg Reader*, eds. Peter Hudis and Kevin B. Anderson (New York, 2004), 183.

3. Luxemburg, *Mass Strike*, 185.

4. Rosa Luxemburg, "To Leo Jogiches" (July 3, 1900), in *Letters of Rosa Luxemburg*, 138.

5. Rosa Luxemburg, "To Robert Seidel" (June 23, 1898), in *Letters of Rosa Luxemburg*, 65.

6. G.W.F. Hegel, *Phenomenology of Spirit*, trans. A. V. Miller (Oxford, 1977), 9 [16].

7. For a discussion, see Kevin B. Anderson, *Marx at the Margins: On Nationalism, Ethnicity, and Non-Western Societies* (Chicago, 2010), 57.

8. Rosa Luxemburg, "Die nationalen Kämpfe in der Türkei unter die Sozialdemokratie," in *Gesammelte Werke*, vol. 1/1 (Berlin, 2007), 57–68.

9. Rosa Luxemburg, *The Russian Revolution* (1918), in *Rosa Luxemburg Reader*, 305.

10. See J. P. Nettl, *Rosa Luxemburg* (London, 1966), 432.

11. Our mentor Raya Dunayevskaya was the first to bring out the feminist dimension of Luxemburg in her *Rosa Luxemburg, Women's Liberation, and Marx's Philosophy of Revolution* (London, 1982).

12. Rosa Luxemberg, "To Clara Zetkin" (November 18, 1918), *Letters of Rosa Luxemburg*, 480.

13. Rosa Luxemburg, "To Clara Zetkin" (November 24, 1918), in *Letters of Rosa Luxemburg*, 481.

14. Rosa Luxemburg, "To Clara Zetkin" (late December 1918), in *Letters of Rosa Luxemburg*, 489.

15. Quoted in Robert S. Wistrich, *Revolutionary Jews from Marx to Trotsky* (New York, 1976), 81. Rosa Luxemburg, "Politische Bilanz," in *Arbeiterrevolution 1905/06: Polnische Texte*, ed. Holger Politt (Berlin, 2015), p. 71. The article originally appeared in Polish in the SDKPiL publication *Czerwony Sztander*, under the title "Obrachunek Polityczny." See *Czerwony Sztander* no. 25 (April 1905), 2. Like most of Luxemburg's writings in the Polish press, the piece does not appear in the German-language *Gesammelte Werke*. The fourteen-volume *Complete Works of Rosa Luxemburg*, of which Peter Hudis is the general editor, will for the first time make Luxemburg's Polish writings, amounting to several thousand pages, available in English.

16. Rosa Luxemburg, *The Junius Pamphlet: The Crisis in German Social Democracy* (1915), in *Rosa Luxemburg Reader*, 339.

17. Nettl, *Rosa Luxemburg*, 32–33.

18. Nettl, *Rosa Luxemburg*, 33. Elsewhere, Nettl partially contradicts this claim, insofar as Luxemburg's private sentiments are concerned: "Like anti-Semitism, the inferior status of women was a social feature which would be eliminated only by the advent of Socialism; in the meantime there was no point in making any special issue of it. But disinterest in public did not mean private indifference" (672).

19. Rosa Luxemberg, "To Boris Krichevsky" (August 19, 1898), in *Letters of Rosa Luxemburg*, 85.

20. This point is made, albeit rather elliptically, in Nettl, *Rosa Luxemburg*, 240.

21. Enzo Traverso, *The Marxists and the Jewish Question: The History of a Debate, 1843–1943*, trans. Bernard Gibbons (Atlantic Highlands, NJ, 1994), 67.

22. See Rosa Luxemburg, "Krytyka I Bibliographia," *Przeglad Socjaldemokratyczny* 4 (1903): 159–63.

23. Nettl, *Rosa Luxemburg*, 83. Nettl adds that through much of its history the SDKPiL was actually on friendlier terms with the Bund than with Lenin's Bolshevik wing of Russian Social Democracy.

24. Rosa Luxemberg, "To Aleksandr N. Potresov" (August 7, 1904), in *Letters of Rosa Luxemburg*, 169–70. This was written around the time she took issue with Lenin's organizational centralism in *Organizational Questions of Russian Social Democracy*.

25. This could also be translated as "political hagglers." The German word *Schacher* often has antisemitic overtones, as discussed by Allan Megill in his *Karl Marx: The Burden of Reason* (Lanham, MD, 2002), 146–47.

26. "To Clara Zetkin" (June 4, 1907), in *Letters of Rosa Luxemburg*, 242.

27. Quoted in Wistrich, *Revolutionary Jews*, 82.

28. Rosa Luxemburg, "Dyskusja," *Mlot* [The hammer, weekly newspaper of Luxemburg's SDKPiL], no. 14, November 5, 1910. The passage is reproduced in Iring Fetscher's *Marxisten gegen Antisemitismus* (Hamburg, 1974), 147–48. For a more recent collection that includes her writings from the Polish press, see *Luxemburg, Nach dem Pogrom: Text über Antisemitismus 1901/11*, ed. Holger Politt (Potsdam, 2014).

29. Wistrich, *Revolutionary Jews*, 86.

30. Rosa Luxemberg, "To Émile Vandervelde" (October 8, 1910), in *Letters of Rosa Luxemburg*, 295. For discussions of this controversy, in which Jaurès supported Luxemburg by publishing an article in *Mlot* denouncing antisemitism, see Annelies Laschitza, "Rosa Luxemburg—mit Leidenschaft und Vision für eine bessere Welt," in *Spurensuche: Das Vermächtnis Rosa Luxemburgs für deutsche und Israelische Linke*, ed. Angelika Timm (Tel Aviv, 2009), 47–56; Laschitza, *Im Lebsensrausch, trotz alledem, Rosa Luxemburg, Eine Biographie* (Berlin, 1996); Traverso, *Marxists and the Jewish Question*.

31. See Wistrich, *Revolutionary Jews*, 89.

32. Rosa Luxemburg, "To Sophie Liebknecht" (December 24, 1917), in *Letters of Rosa Luxemburg*, 453.

33. Wistrich, *Revolutionary Jews*, 86.

34. In his *Black Skin, White Masks*, Frantz Fanon quotes Aimé Césaire's comments in *Discourse on Colonialism* about the European colonial powers: "'It is Nazism, yes, but . . . before they were its victims, they were its accomplices; . . . they tolerated that Nazism before it was inflicted on them . . . they absolved it, shut their eyes to it, legitimized it, because, until then, it had been applied only to non-European peoples; . . . they cultivated that Nazism . . . they are responsible for it, and . . . before engulfing the whole edifice of Western, Christian civilization in its reddened waters, it oozes, seeps, and trickles from every crack" (Frantz Fanon, *Black Skin, White Masks* [New York, 2008], 71). It is instructive that Fanon, a Black man who held in his *Wretched of the Earth* that "national consciousness, which is not nationalism, is alone capable of giving us an international dimension," also had a great deal to say against antisemitism (Fanon, *Wretched of the Earth* [New York, 2004], 179).

35. Ian Kershaw, *Hitler 1889–1936: Hubris* (New York, 1998), 138–39.

36. Luxemburg, *Junius Pamphlet*, in *Rosa Luxemburg Reader*, 313. For a discussion, see Traverso, *Marxists and the Jewish Question*, 67.

37. Michael Löwy, "Rosa Luxemburg's Conception of 'Socialism or Barbarism,'" in *On Changing the World: Essays in Political Philosophy, from Karl Marx to Walter Benjamin* (Atlantic Highlands, NJ, 1993), 95.

38. See Plato's *Republic*, trans. G.M.A. Grube, in *Complete Works* (Indianapolis, 1997), 976–81.

12

Arnold Schoenberg (1874–1951)

SONIC ALLEGORIES

Ruth HaCohen

ARNOLD SCHOENBERG'S CONTINUOUS ENGAGEMENT WITH THE SONIC COSMOS throughout his life aimed to reshape, reformulate, and rethink its past, present, and future configurations as well as possible interrelations with other worlds and cosmoses. His creative enterprise is thus partially comparable, and linked in nature and scope, with those of three major figures of Jewish modernity: Einstein and Freud, his contemporaries; and Marx, whose legacy was critically felt at the turn of the twentieth century and beyond. All four revolutionaries of Jewish origin, who matured in a gradually modernizing German culture, considered themselves as radical creators in terms of entrenched Christian-European traditions. Though yielding far less cultural resonance than the others, Schoenberg's versatile activities as composer, painter, theoretician of music, teacher, conductor, entrepreneur, writer, dramatist, and political activist bear witness to lifelong, relentless, and uncompromising attempts to explore unfathomed territories and discover new evolutionary paths, while keeping vital connections to worlds of yesterday.

Schoenberg is related to Einstein through the *Quadirivium* lore, which, since Late Antiquity, placed the mathematical liberal arts—geometry, arithmetic, astronomy, and music—under a Pythagorean worldview that conceived of them as various manifestations of world harmony. Despite the seventeenth-century scientific revolution that apparently abolished the numerical foundation of that tradition, astronomy and music, especially in the wider German sphere, would continue to adhere to the underlying metaphysics of preestablished harmonies in the forthcoming centuries. Both Einstein and Schoenberg further distanced their universes from that metaphysics and, at a certain moment, were even compelled to address the motif of chance in their respective worlds. Still, they never completely cut off their work and thinking from the theological roots of certain harmonizing models. Schoenberg, however, with a sharpness untypical of art theorists in his or earlier times, would clearly differentiate the epistemological nature of a formulated art system from that of a scientific one. In his groundbreaking *Theory of Harmony* (1911), he clarifies that "however much [he] theorizes" he is "only presenting comparisons . . . symbols, which are merely intended to connect ideas apparently remote from one another [and] to promote intelligibility through coherence of presentation."[1]

Early on in his career he could find psychoanalytic ideas, whether of Freud or others, of great relevance to his work, however "remote" they appeared from the musical ones he advanced. In the microcosm of the human soul explored by these two Viennese Jews, areas of latent and obscure emotional life loomed large. More particularly, one can find in Schoenberg's work fascinating parallels to what Freud branded, following Jentsch, the *Unheimlich*, as well as to Freud's concept of the melancholic (as opposed to the mournful) and the traumatic—the latter because it intricately connects the individual with an abiding collective.[2] But whereas Freud was preoccupied with modes of theorizing and reconciling disruptive psychic elements, Schoenberg, an expressionist artist, searched for artistic tools to emancipate the repressed elements in life and art. Bearing the stamp of repugnant dissonances, he sought to aestheticize such elements only to the extent that they enhanced the vitality of artistic experience.

Moreover, whereas Freud opted for a vertical-hierarchical conception of the psyche's parts and energies, Schoenberg, in a far less theoretical way, was guided by a conception, quite in vogue at the turn of the century, of a lateral-associable model of the diversified parts of human consciousness.[3] Less bound by the idea of a transcendental ego, his multivocal imagery of inner being adopted an intersubjective-horizontal model of creativity and personal growth.[4] He fathomed his own biography as consisting of *Begegnungen*—encounters with persons of various kinds, such as artists, thinkers, friends, and students—rather than as the linear, solitary trajectory of a genius.[5] Similarly, he deemed the active, and primarily lateral, making of chamber music—the way he himself was initiated into the world of sound—as crucial to the development of a musician. Moreover, his attraction, as a composer, to small ensembles, especially once he drew on the path of New Music (in the mid-1900s), bespeaks the deep significance he attributed to intimately interactive processes in the working-through of human vicissitudes and their symbolic mediators.

However defiant his work and ideas would appear to his Viennese bourgeois audiences, almost from the outset of his artistic journey Schoenberg was well aware of his own status as a middle-class individual, though he was far from being a typical representative of this social stratum.[6] If his oeuvre became the ultimate embodiment of an uncommodified art, it was partially because he almost never gave way to commercial demands. Moreover, his mode of composition was extremely unprofitable, for he did not specialize in certain genres the way, say, Richard Strauss did, but rather sought to ever explore new problems—tonal, dramatic, and compositional—resulting in a collection of condensed, sui generis pieces, some never completed. Schoenberg's uncompromising artistic path meant also a lifelong struggle to secure a living for himself and his families (over the course of his life he married two women, who bore him a total of five children in a time span of about forty years), both in Europe and later in the United States. His creative approach thus rendered him the epitome of "*true* artistic consciousness" in the eyes of the neo-Marxist Frankfurt school leader Theodor Adorno, who may be considered as the harbinger of Schoenberg's cultural reputation beyond the realm of what became a rather closed, if not esoteric, artistic circle. Despite the high pedestal on which he positioned Schoenberg, Adorno never refrained from pointing out undesirable consequences of the dialectics that trapped the composer's way.[7]

Schoenberg did not receive a better Jewish education than either Einstein or Freud (not to speak of Marx). At the age of twenty-four he even converted, in Catholic Vienna, to Protestantism—not an uncommon move among acculturated Jewish intellectuals at the time. Still, his artistic choices and course of life were more significantly bound up with Jewish history than any of these three eminent representatives of Jewish modernity. The fate of Jewish musicians and the entanglement of Jewish sonorities with Christian ones from about the mid-eighteenth century on played a crucial role throughout his career, even at its early stages, when he apparently distanced himself from Jewish affairs and sources. His major choice in life—or was it destiny?—was to become "this notorious Schoenberg . . . because no one wanted to be, someone had to be, so I let it be me," as he sardonically told a superior officer during World War I. In this statement he echoed Luther's famous words, which he eventually gave to the Divine Voice in the opening scene of *Moses und Aron*:[8] "you cannot do otherwise." But later in life the notion of Lutheran predestination became mixed with a precept of the lonely biblical prophet, bound to pay for his bold and provocative messages.[9]

During his life, Schoenberg experienced the major phases of twentieth-century fateful history of the Jews in Central Europe. He lived and was active in two central capitals—Vienna and Berlin—each with its own unique variation on European and Jewish modernity. He sensed the danger of Jews in Europe long before others became aware of the impending catastrophe and, once Hitler came to power, left his high post at the Prussian Academy of Art, anticipating official dismissal. Later he emigrated to the New World—first the East, then the West Coast of the United States. He bore highly ambivalent relations with the rejecting continent, while adjusting himself once more to a radically different polyphony of art, modernity, and Jews. All the while he toyed with Zionist ideas, even before he "converted" back to Judaism (in 1934, in Paris), mixing messianic and pragmatic ideas for saving European Jews if not the Jewish nation as a whole.[10] As for his art, his early encounter with modern artistic configurations cannot be separated from his perception of the complex integration of Jews in modern Europe, yielding, later in his career, aesthetic-theological precepts concerning chance, choice, and the chosen as well as an understanding of the internal connections of cultural agency and legacy.

From *Judenjunge* to *Jeder Junge Jude*: Sonic Assimilation Turned Noisy

"Und . . . daß es ein Komödiant und ein Judenjunge sein müssen, die den Leuten die größte christliche Musik wiederbringen" (And [to think] that it has to be a comedian and a Jew-boy who return the greatest Christian music to the people). Thus said twenty-year-old Felix Mendelssohn to his friend and collaborator Edward Devrient in February 1829, once they succeeded in persuading obstinate old Carl Zelter to let them perform Johann Sebastian Bach's *St. Matthew Passion* in the framework of the Berlin Singakademie.[11] *Ein Judenjunge*, a Jew-boy; at this crucial moment in his budding career, already thirteen years since he was baptized Lutheran, Mendelssohn chose to identify himself with that derogatory epithet, indicating his sense of otherness vis-à-vis the Christian world that even the highly acculturated and protecting environment in which he grew up could not brush away.

Beyond his own sense of self-identity, this phrase ironically marks the inauguration of two interrelated processes: the powerful ingress of Jews into European music and the celebratory reception of Bach's oeuvre—a leading model for the increasing historicizing tendency of the musical world, in which Jews were already playing an important role. Whether they opted to conceal or to highlight their Jewishness in music, for the main part of this period, which terminated abruptly when the Nazis came to power, Jewish musicians in Europe acted, by and large, under the belief that they performed, composed, and listened to music like (if not better than) any other good Christian. In most cases, they shared the belief—no matter how they defined their Jewish allegiance—that the musical arena was open to all and that its abstractness and transcendence marked a new era in the republic of *Bildung* and knowledge, in which Jews became full-fledged citizens. More particularly, they could now "convert" to the ascending "religion of music," leaving behind theological and denominational specificities to bask in what were considered to be the most elevated art forms. Even if they had not received the appropriate schooling, Jews increasingly saw themselves as entitled to contribute further to this cultural capital, as the case of Schoenberg, even more than that of Mahler, attests.

Yet the reception of Jewish musicians in Central Europe was largely infected by noticeable ambivalence. Jews' musical perfidiousness or hypocrisy, as seen through the eyes of a Christian, would surface at certain moments in modern times, to wit: Though Jews might excel in performance, or even the composition of music, actually they hid their noisiness, a living testimony of their obstinate, uncompassionate nature resembling the mercilessness of the Old Testament's God-forsaken people who killed the Messiah and who had resisted, ever since, harmonizing with the true religion—the ideal cosmos.

This accusation, or libel, which goes back to the High Middle Ages in Ashkenazi and related countries, resurfaced at the dawn of modernity to be later elaborated and negotiated in a variety of genres, all through the nineteenth century and beyond.[12] Schoenberg must have been well aware of the spectral presence of this libel, ubiquitous as the phrase *Lärm wie in einer Judenschule* (noise as in the synagogue) was in his native Vienna, and humiliating as it found expression in Wagner's *Judentum in der Musik* and numerous replications.[13] Like other Jewish musicians, young Schoenberg apparently chose to ignore Wagner's lampoon; and also like others, he paradoxically must have believed that the absolute mythological subjectivism expressed so stunningly in Wagner's oeuvres—in the spirit of Schopenhauer's idea of the metaphysical *Urwille*—transcended this particularistic prejudice and should thus be forgiven.

In Schoenberg's immediate environment, there were different reactions to this music libel. Since the establishment of the Israelitische Kultusgemeinde (Vienna Israelite Community) following the Napoleonic wars, a new era was launched for Jews in the imperial city, attracting Jews from the periphery. From the outset, the new community leaders were searching for ways to cast off the old appearance of the synagogue, in particular its actual "noisy" soundscape, replacing it with music and vocalities befitting the new age, modernized Jews, and the image they wished to radiate inside and outside their world. Under the charismatic and highly professional leadership of the eminent composer and cantor Salomon Sulzer, they succeeded beyond expectations. The synagogue turned into a site of pilgrimage for both Jews and non-Jews, though Sulzer himself became gradually aware that the balance—essential for sustaining a modern vocal Jewish community—between harmonization and assimilation into European, if not Christian sonorities, on the one hand, and the more indigenous Jewish musical elements, on the other, would not be easily struck.

Schoenberg did not react to this development directly. Being so musically alert, however, he could eschew neither these renewed vocalities nor the older synagogal sonorities emitted by a host of synagogues established by Eastern European Jews, who streamed into the city at the time in which Schoenberg matured. He must have noticed the nonsimultaneous or "heterophonic chant mumbling,"[14] the specific mixture of speech and song characterizing that soundscape, and perhaps also caught the praying gestures of supplication (Taḥanun) less at home in either Catholic or Lutheran worship traditions. Such sonic qualities would materialize in his works, though seldom with a clear allusion to a Jewish element. And yet his own famous conception of "emancipating the dissonance"—the ultimate slogan of his musical radicalism—though usually explained through pure autonomous musical terms, cannot evade its clear theologico-political implications. An "emancipated" Jew emancipating sonic dissonant elements to the world, from which they were so carefully kept under control for so many generations, proves even more ironic than Mendelssohn's *Judenjunge* act. The *diabolus in musica* and the devil in the religious world thus merged, gradually casting off their inappropriateness.[15] That the music of the school he founded would be banned by the Nazis as "degenerate art" further exacerbated this irony. Moreover, free from beautifying expressive clichés, this very art would poignantly serve attempts to give voice to "dissonant" victims—as in Schoenberg's *A Survivor from Warsaw* (1947).

Schoenberg himself never belonged to a Jewish community, nor to any "singing congregation." From a certain point onward, however, he could not escape the need for a collective, the voice of the many, the "we"—a basis to music as such, as Adorno pinpointed—a need more vehemently felt in the face of the musical isolation to which he had sentenced himself. His attraction to choir music—he would compose throughout his career a variety of pieces, most of which he set to religious or spiritual texts—betrays the wish to establish a community through music. This aspiration addressed a double need: a musical one and a religio-political one, each acutely felt by him. The actual community he created with his students and related colleagues, especially in the framework of the Verein für musikalische Privataufführungen (Society for Private Musical Performances) he led in the aftermath of World War I—a model for many such associations of New Music all through the century and beyond—aimed to achieve the double purpose of creating an artistic home for avant-garde musicians while promoting their work.

Thus, it may not come as a surprise that in 1934, more than a century after the event at the Singakademie, Arnold Schoenberg published a short article titled "Jeder junge Jude" (Every young Jew) a designation connoting in this case no disparaging sense, calling every young Jew to reflect on how "we Jews of the nineteenth century conceived of our course of life"; and how, more particularly, "we were recognized, while still at school, through our foreign outlook, pronunciation, different religion lessons and our achievements, which were better than the average."[16] If this was not respected by non-Jews, he further relates, but rather gave reasons to hide one's Jewishness, then the Jews would either seek to further suppress those "Jewish symptoms," heighten their achievements, or aspire to belong to a top social rank. Schoenberg, who vehemently criticizes this approach in the article, clearly characterizes here several generations of acculturated Jews to which he had so clearly belonged not long before. A sixty-year-old Schoenberg, kicked out of his native environment on account of his Judaism, further discloses in this semiconfessional, spiritually motivated text that all the efforts and sacrifices made by Jews in order to be accepted by the general society were never really successful, betraying, rather, "their chosenness as the people of God."[17]

The sense of chosenness undoubtedly stemmed from Schoenberg's major source of inspiration throughout this life—the Bible, mainly Luther's Bible, though he was attracted, probably early on, to its "older" more than to its "newer" part.[18] Attending a *Realschule*, he skipped the initiation into Greco-Roman classical lore of a humanistic gymnasium, finding in the Bible not only a spiritual guide but also a nexus between his Jewish identity and that of his Christian classmates. Throughout his life, the Bible became an actual source for his oratorios and dramas, musical and others;[19] even his choices of modern poetry can be interpreted in terms of this revered model. This preference put him on a par with many Jewish creators and leaders from the Haskalah movement onward, especially Zionist ones: from Abraham Mapu, David Ben-Gurion, and the poetess Rachel (Blumstein) to Buber, Agnon, and Dahlia Ravikovitch. On the other hand, "the tripartite identity" typical of a Habsburgian Jew (being ethnically Jewish, politically Austro-Hungarian, and culturally German)[20] would result in Schoenberg's case, according to Steven J. Cahn, in a diminished readiness to unify the ethno-religious with legal-political and cultural elements of his existence, once the issue of Jewish identity started to preoccupy him.[21] Cherishing a strong ethno-Jewish identity, he nevertheless would fully integrate in the United States as an American citizen, with his children growing up as Catholics (following their mother). Was this domestic difference a "noise" in his soul or did he conceive it as mere variety, contained within a system? Lacking a traditional Jewish background, Schoenberg would claim that the role of the emotio-communal bond in spiritual upbringing is crucial, and thus better provided by his Catholic wife. The understanding, elaborated in Spinoza's writings, that abstract spiritual commitment needs a concrete religious environment was not foreign to the composer of *Moses und Aron*. [22]

Encountering Art and Modernity in Vienna and Berlin: Detaching Signifiers from Signified

What is it then that compelled Schoenberg to make radical innovations throughout his life? Never resting on his (infrequent) laurels, nor intimidated by critics and hostile audiences—what drove him to probe uncharted territories, believing his greatness would be recognized by *die Tapfere*, the bold and courageous?[23] How, in turn, did he become so appealing to young aspiring musicians, who regarded him as their ultimate teacher and leader? And of special pertinence to the present discussion: Could his series of artistic experiments and masterpieces have originated from a "Teutonic" mind, as Thomas Mann would define Adrian Leverkühn's (his

Dr. Faustus), albeit, in the latter's case, issuing from a "real" pact with the devil? In other words, is there something Jewishly modern about the specific contents of his work, beyond general choices and trends?

The answers I offer to some of these questions, as they arise from within Schoenberg's work and thinking, take as their point of departure a specific nexus of anti-Jewish aesthetics, especially in its later Wagnerian appearance and in modernist art. In its millennia-long aspiration to distance itself from "Judaized" appearances, argues David Nirenberg, Christian aesthetics, or that which replaced it, sought to overcome the particularity of the sign, its preponderance over the signified, by rendering it as transparent to the signified as possible. Richard Wagner, Nirenberg further maintains, was one of the more explicit champions of this approach in modern times, and his art, from early on, attests to his actual effort to merge semiotic entities in harmonized totalities.[24] This aesthetics would find its prime expression at the decade following the first publication of the *Judentum* essay—in his *Tristan und Isolde* (composed between 1857 and 1859)—in which he sought to portray the ultimate coalescence of minds, subjectivities merging in total absorption in *Liebestod* as the culmination of art and life. He aspired to that condition in other works, resorting, as many before him, to the figure of the Jew—noisy, parasitic, melancholic—as an antithesis to this absolute cohesion: the dissonant elements that never resolve.

Intoxicated by the Wagnerian experience, Schoenberg, like many young composers, poets, and artists in fin-de-siècle Vienna, embraced the German composer's legacy but with a difference—a difference that gradually turned into a (Derridian) *différance*. These artists favored artistic "correspondences" (à la Baudelaire), that is, dynamic, transfigurative metamorphoses inhabiting semirealistic realms, rather than *gesamtkunst* totalities prescribed into predestined legendary myths. In the special synthesis he was forming in a work like *Verklärte Nacht* (op. 4, a string sextet, based on a text by Richard Dehmel), the twenty-five-year-old Schoenberg further developed this new aesthetics, in which he combined Wagnerian themes with Brahmsian textures, opting for what he eventually advocated as the aesthetics of "developing variations." Wedding the two adversarial composers within the same score, he portrayed a nocturnal love scene, in which a nameless "Tristan" sings a *Liebesleben* to his pregnant "Isolde" (who in her craving for a child conceived, prior to their meeting, with a man she never loved). In his embrace of her and the expected child, their realistic, modern "love of life" is transfigured into a livable, mature, and moral form of existence. Most of Schoenberg's subsequent works, up until World War I, would grapple with the "reality principle" of intimate relations, which, even at their height, "stream in parallel motion" (*Gurre Lieder*, op. 5), highlighting the mutual opacity of consciousnesses (*Peleas and Melisande*, op. 6), the subliminal, noncoherent, and unconsummated "language of love" (*Erwartung*, op. 17) and, as in the biblical Song of Songs, the elusiveness of the libidinal object (*Songs of the Hanging Gardens*, op. 15). As Walter Benjamin would have it, in Schoenberg's hands the artwork no longer aspired to the conditions of symbol, turning rather into allegorical concatenation, into successions of signs, scripts, runes, and ruins bespeaking the narrative of fall, failure, or fallacy, still subsumed, however, by a nonpessimistic worldview that postulated the emancipatory power of art when true to its calling.[25]

While Schoenberg was not the only one to delve into these uncharted territories, he ever felt the need to devise new vehicles for this exploratory mission, to enable the "breathing of the air of unfathomed planets," as he defined his quest, following Stefan George, in one of the most memorable phrases in his entire oeuvre (String Quartet op. 10, iv). "Free atonality" turned into a major agent in this adventure, as it clustered a whole new mode of musical thinking, stimulating experiments also with painting (especially during 1908–1912)—oil on canvas, pencils on paper— searching unfathomable subjectivities through his own self-portraits. He further distilled them into abstract gazes, while on his musical pallet he blended *Klangfarben* (sound-color) melodies exploring as well new modes of vocal expression.

The epitome of such vocal personae is Pierrot the Lunatic (*Pierrot Lunaire*, op. 21), a wandering poet (or Jew?)—transported from eighteenth-century commedia dell'arte, through the realms of French symbolism, into the imaginary world Schoenberg shaped for him, now inspired by the Berlin cabaret environment. Here he found an outlet for his numerical penchant, and in a series of twenty-one cinematographic *tableaux vivants* this aerial figure would encounter real and fantastic characters and events, to finally head homeward, never to arrive. Pierrot's voice, however, is never heard. A group of cabaret-like instruments set the scenes, while the vocal element—relegated to a song-speaking voice (*Sprechgesang*)—tells Pierrot's fragmentary tale. A *Verfremdung* effect (ante Brecht) is achieved in this grotesque, yet lyrical journey. In the twilight between dream, nightmare, and reality, the work grips its listeners—at its first performance and thereafter—leaving them to search for "interpretation" (à la Freud) of these dreams and apparitions.

The young disciples who gathered around Schoenberg during this creative phase, above all Berg and Webern, were driven by their own entranced experiments with tone, tone-color, and new relations between text and texture, musical unfolding and the dissolution of conventional forms, while seeking the master's advice, approval, and new ideas. In the oasis they created for themselves, they mutually enriched each other with their new works and inventions, to the extent that sometimes even Arnold did not know "who he was."[26] Such intimate, fertile relations also characterized his friendship with Wassily Kandinsky at that period, but it did not survive the wave of antisemitism that flooded Austria and Germany after the Great War.

All those *Begegnungen* and nonintegrated dissonances of life and creation—what do they stand for in this stage of his career? Neither chaos nor even *Lärm*, the way Christians conceived it in relation to a Jewish soundscape. Rather it was an attempt to reach the nameless and to leave it unlabeled, unharnessed, enabling an encounter with the nonmediated, minimally ritualistic "real" through performative, unpatterned gesture.

Chance, Choice, and the Chosen: Closed Systems and Open Texts

From within this universe of floating selves, signs, and sensations there emerged a double and rather contradictory urge, thematically expressed in terms of modern man "relearning how to pray,"[27] and technically in the attempts to anchor composition outside tonal harmony in a system of its own. The thematic road would lead Schoenberg to various "oratorical" texts, most of them his own, from *Jakobsleiter* (Jacob's ladder, a fragment) to his final *Moderne Psalmen* (op. 51c), culminating in the grand operatic midrash of *Moses und Aron* (also a fragment).[28] The technical search would drive him into his "method of composing with twelve tones which are related only with one another,"[29] a groundbreaking innovation, evolving over more than two decades, which brought him both fame and defamation. In the course of that double odyssey,[30] he would gradually reconnect himself to Jewish destiny and lore (with a blatant antisemitic treatment of him and his family in the town resort of Mattsee in 1921 serving as a catalyst).

The twelve-tone (dodecaphonic) system itself, along its set of rules and procedures, granted that each new monadic-like work would base itself on a distinct pitch-row using all twelve tones, and none twice, from which various derivative orders would be obtained. Its conception perpetuated Schoenberg's understanding that the avoidance of older coinage and formulation needs special contrivance. Adorno would interpret this move as an iconoclastic attack on bourgeois idolatrous culture (believing that old musical language was complicit with the Golden Calf, or Mammon) and twelve-tone composition as symbolizing the strictness of ancient Jewish law.[31] In a similar spirit, one may view Schoenberg's move from the loneliness of his expressionist period to the regulative space of twelve-tone procedures as parallel to Rav Joseph B. Soloveitchik's (1903–1993) shift from his existential "Lonely Man of Faith" (1965) to his conception of the "Halakhic Man" (1979) who, like the mathematician, measures the world through his ideal system of laws.[32] Unlike Soloveitchik, however, Schoenberg did not ascribe any transcendentality to his system, nor to any musical or artistic technique as such.

This does not mean that the use of the system was void of philosophical repercussions. Schoenberg's fervent search for a subjective religious element that went alongside his engagement with the intricacies of that "cold," "objective" system entails a conundrum: whereas the twelve-tone system, at least according to Adorno, introduced the factor of chance into composition in unprecedented dimensions, the spiritual-Jewish themes Schoenberg opted for increasingly underscored the motif of the chosen—of the group or person elected by God for their particular mission or destiny. Is this apparent paradox a mere coincidence or does it reflect a deeper historical and cultural meaning? Was Schoenberg himself aware of it?

Between chance and the chosen, I wish to argue, we find choice: human, rather than divine, of those thrown into a world (Heidegger) no longer conceived as the best of all possible ones. In such a world, full of randomness and vice, how does one choose correctly, be it in the moral, religious or artistic spheres? Thus asks Schoenberg in his texts and via his protagonists. The world is given and so is artistic heritage, which continues to impose its modes of thought even after a seeming breakdown. The twelve-tone system is like that: while, for better or for worse, no preconceived scheme coerces it, it is still bound by the twelve semitones of equal temperament, inherited from previous generations. And thus, with all the combinatorial effort to circumvent a possible falling into the "trap" of tonal harmony (an effort relating mainly to the major rule of the system, never to repeat a tone of the row outside its place in the order), one cannot avoid the "chance" eruption of old harmonic elements. On the other hand, the system, rigid as it turned out to be, gradually gave way to the freer hexachordal aggregate structure, allowing for complementary tonal relations. This made it possible to bequeath further agency on individual parts, or voices, which, to begin with, entertained autonomy and independence in line with early counterpoint,[33] avoiding even mimetic relations among them. Felt already in an early dodecaphonic work like the Wind Quintet (op. 26, 1925) and, a few years later, in the chamber opera *Von heute auf morgen* (op. 32, 1929, text by Gertrud Kolisch-Schoenberg, his second wife), written in the spirit of the prevailing *Zeitoper*, the composer uses this vocal independence for ridiculing the genre and its underlying philosophy. The dilemma is real: in an atmosphere of free love and open marriage, what could advocate old loyalties, if these are so much connected with obsolete bourgeois ethics that inhibits one's creativity, sexuality, and emotional vivacity? A feminist awareness exacerbates the dilemma. One must choose, and the choice can be unpopular. But if this choice is assumed by full-fledged personalities undergoing their own emotional probing, loyalty, as the piece set out to demonstrate, turns into profound and committed human attachment.

In *Moses und Aron* (composed mainly through 1930–1932) the dilemma spreads out into the politico-theological sphere, and each of the major protagonists plays its role through a radically different artistic means (speech vs. singing). This aggravates the major aporia: whether a philosophical monotheistic God to whom no (positive) quality can be ascribed, humanly or otherwise (Moses' conception), can play the historical role of a compassionate deliverer, redeeming his chosen (*auserwählte*) people out of "the house of slaves" into a bright future, into "the land of milk and honey" (Aron's belief). As part of his basically nondeterministic approach, Schoenberg lets various conflictual elements work against each other in this dramatic world, avoiding a simple resolution (that may account for his unsuccessful attempt to musically set act 3). And yet, Aron-like, he, Arnold, would set out to save his brethren from the impending disaster that he so strongly envisioned, even being willing to renounce his artistic career for this purpose. Tragically, despite his great efforts, his various initiatives bore no fruitful consequence. Thus he remained within an even more fragmented world, while trying, now in distant California, to make sense of that world, never hesitating to draw his inspiration from existing sources, above all those he himself had developed especially in his expressionist phase. While the grip on his system slackened, his texts—explicitly or implicitly—would interact with that fragmented world, highlighting human vulnerability and anxiety but also determination and a sense of mission.

Within this late phase of his work, dissonances could play a variety of roles, attesting for, pace Adorno, the nonlegal nature of his artistic approach. Within the universes he created or wished to give sound to, there reigned basic incoherence as a modern "human condition," reflecting a variety of norms, interests, sentiments, desires, and ideas, playing against each other and searching for modi vivendi, for oases of partial completions, configurations of togetherness that emerge from below and open up new forms of experience and feeling.

Agency and Legacy

Going through such extreme moments of angst and disaster, the self, as agent, seeks spiritual shelter through the gesture of prayer. Schoenberg composed prayers throughout his oeuvre, but especially in the last years: prayers communal and personal, more or less traditional, in English, Hebrew, and German, and with no words at all; prayers that do not expect response, nor fulfillment, but that, as Franz Rosenzweig contended, are self-rewarding, aiming to mold a collective. The final ones, of 1950—a Hebrew Psalm associated with the Days of Awe ("Mima'amakim"/*de Profundis*) and his personal *Modern Psalm*, which he never completed, are both the expression of an individual who, well aware of his moral and philosophical human situatedness (Heidegger's *Befindlichkeit*), still seeks the Divine. The most crucial words in the latter work, set in soft contrapuntal reverberations, contain the essence of that belief, resonating with pleas of Jews and others who underwent similar ideological and historical ordeals:

> Und trotzdem bete ich, wie alles Lebende betet;
> trotzdem erbitte ich Gnaden und Wunder;
> Erfüllungen.
> Trotzdem bete ich, denn ich will nicht des
> beseligenden Gefühls der Einigkeit,
> der Vereinigung mit dir, verlustig werden.

> And yet: I pray like every living creature
> Prays; yet I ask for mercy and miracles;
> Fulfilment.
> Yet I pray because I do not want to lose
> The sublime feeling of unity,
> Of union with you.[34]

Another aspect of the artist's sense of agency is also bound up with an entrenched Jewish element: Jewish teaching, or Limmud. From the onset of his career and throughout, Schoenberg was an instructor, teacher, and mentor. Originating, perhaps, out of necessity, this work grew into a deeply felt calling and passion, which may reflect the gratitude he felt toward his own mentors/benefactors: Zemlinsky and Mahler. Schoenberg was mainly a private teacher, but he also taught at certain schools and academies, some rather prestigious.[35] He had composition students in Vienna, Berlin, Boston, and Los Angeles. Wishing them to be conversant with the musical wisdom that had developed for hundreds of years in Central Europe, only rarely did he teach them his own methods and compositional modes. For that matter, he continued to work, until his last days, on a variety of "manuals" for students and teachers.[36] Most of his students, or disciples, were extremely devoted to him, despite rare fallings-out on his side (e.g., his break with Hanns Eisler). They would carry his teachings, his care, and his love to their last days, bestowing on him various gestures of honor and keeping his legacy alive. One of the last awards he received was from the Jerusalem Academy of Music, which named him their honorary president. On his side, Schoenberg bequeathed his estate to the National Library of Israel in Jerusalem, a dedication that, however, never materialized.

This is the place to ask what remains of this enormous creative endeavor, besides a significant group of scholars who are fascinated by this formidable creator and his highly challenging oeuvre, and small groups of musicians and connoisseurs who would fervently defend it. Adorno, in 1948, chooses to conclude his essay with the following memorable sentences: "Modern music sacrifices itself to this effort. It has taken upon itself all the darkness and guilt of the world . . . all of its beauty in denying itself the illusion of beauty."[37] He further envisages it dying away, unheard, without even leaving an echo, since "mechanical music" would bury it completely. More than sixty years have elapsed, and these fateful words would sound, to many, false or exaggerated. The impact of this music is still felt in various spheres (more than that of the following "Darmstadt generation"), which even in his own times, especially in the United States, could not be ignored.[38]

Adorno further bemoans: "Modern music sees absolute oblivion as its goal. It is the surviving message of despair from the shipwrecked."[39] While the historical veracity of the first claim is doubtful, I do agree that the message imparted by this entire oeuvre is, indeed, of the shipwrecked, but also of the survivors. As in the grand Leviathan allegory *Moby-Dick*, a survivor from an ultimate shipwreck—call him Arnold—acts as a major agent of memory, wisdom, and reflection. Like Ishmael's narrative, his work reminds one of the unending enterprise of interpretation—of traditions, lores, and destinies,[40] commanding inheritors to carry further the toil and the tale. Again in the realm of allegories, we may ask: Can we claim that Schoenberg's sonic worlds are mainly allegorically Jewish, or is it in the openness and abstraction characteristic of Jewish allegories over millennia that the secret of Schoenberg's modernity, and his perennial relevance, reside?

Notes

1. See Arnold Schoenberg, *Theory of Harmony*, trans. Roy E. Carter, 3rd ed. (London, 1983), 11.
2. As reflected in Freud's *Moses and Monotheism*; see Ruth HaCohen, "Psychoanalysis and the Music of Charisma in the *Moseses* of Freud and Schoenberg," in *New Perspectives on Freud's "Moses and Monotheism*," eds. Ruth Ginsburg and Ilana Pardes (Tübingen, 2006), 177–95.
3. See Hugo Munsterberg et al., *Subconscious Phenomena* (London, 1910); and Ruth Leys, *Trauma: A Genealogy* (Chicago, 2000), chap. 2.
4. In tune with Schoenberg's precepts, psychoanalyst Heinz Kohut—a younger Jewish Viennese émigré and an admirer of Schoenberg—further developed the notion of the relational self.
5. See Joseph Auner, *A Schoenberg Reader: Documents of a Life* (New Haven, 2003), 7–9; and Nuria Nono-Schoenberg, ed., *Arnold Schönberg 1874–1951: Lebensgeschichte in Begegnungen* (Klagenfurt, 1998). See also the outline for his "autobiographical" Concerto for Piano and Orchestra (op. 42, 1942).
6. See his self-portraits that depict him as a decent bourgeois.
7. See Theodor W. Adorno, *Philosophy of Modern Music*, trans. Anne G. Mitchell and Wesley B. Blomster (New York, 2004). This important study was published for the first time in Germany while Schoenberg was still alive (1948).
8. The quotation is brought by Schoenberg in "New Music: My Music" (ca. 1930), in *Style and Idea: Selected Writings of Arnold Schoenberg*, trans. Leo Black, ed. Leonard Stein (Berkeley, 1975), 104.
9. See his public lecture (1937) titled "How One Becomes Lonely," in *Style and Idea*, 30–53.
10. See Alexander Ringer, *Arnold Schoenberg: The Composer as Jew* (Oxford, 1990), 116–49.
11. Eduard Devrient, *Meine Erinnerungen an Felix Mendelsssohn-Bartholdy und seine Briefe an mich* (Leipzig, 1872), 62.
12. See Ruth HaCohen, *The Music Libel against the Jews* (New Haven, 2011).
13. The treatise was first published in 1850, pseudonymously (under "K. Freigedank"), and then fully signed, in 1869.
14. See Boaz Tarsi, "Voices in the Sanctuary: Musical Practices of the American Synagogue," *Conservative Judaism* 55, no. 1 (2002): 71–72.
15. "Diabolus in Musica" was the medieval term for the interval considered most dissonant—the tritone (as between C and F#), which "naturalized" itself gradually in chromatic harmony but still demanded its resolution. For Jews and the devil, see Joshua Trachtenberg, *The Devil and the*

Jews: The Medieval Conception of the Jew and Its Relation to Modern Anti-Semitism (Philadelphia, 2002). Interestingly, Schoenberg will attest: "I was . . . regarded as Satan of modernist music" (*Style and Idea*, 42).

16. Arnold Schoenberg, "Jeder junge Jude," *Journal of the Arnold Schoenberg Institute* 177, nos. 1–2 (1994): 451.

17. Ibid., 454.

18. *Jakobsleiter*, however, a work that Schoenberg composed during World War I, clearly derives from, among other sources, the Book of Revelation.

19. His *biblische Weg*, written during 1926–1927, is a spoken drama. On the role of the Bible in Schoenberg's life see William Kangas, "The Ethics and Aesthetics of (Self) Representation: Arnold Schoenberg and Jewish Identity," in *Leo Back Institute Year Book* 45 (2000): 143.

20. See Marsha Rozenblit, *Reconstructing a National Identity: The Jews of Habsburg Austria during World War I* (Oxford, 2001).

21. Steven J. Cahn, "Schoenberg, the Viennese-Jewish Experience and Its Aftermath," in *The Cambridge Companion to Schoenberg*, eds. Jennifer Shaw and Joseph Auner (Cambridge, 2010), 197.

22. HaCohen, *Music Libel*, chap. 6.

23. "Tapfere sind solche, die Taten vollbringen, an die ihr Mut nicht heranreicht" (brave are those who perform deeds which surpass their courage)—Schoenberg's first movement of his Four Pieces for Mixed Chorus, op. 27 (1925).

24. David Nirenberg, "The Judaism of Christian Art," in Herbert L. Kessler and David Nirenberg, *Judaism and Christian Art: Aesthetic Anxieties from the Catacombs to Colonialism* (Philadelphia, 2011).

25. Adorno ascribes this move already to Mahler.

26. Schoenberg, *Style and Idea*, 484–85.

27. In his famous letter of 1912 to Dehmel, see *Schoenberg Reader: Documents of a Life*, ed. Joseph Auner (New Haven, 2003), 119.

28. See my "Schoenberg's Exodus: A Theological Midrash in Search of Operatic Action," in *Operalibretto: Its Place between Source and Music*, ed. Sabine Lichtenstein (London, 2014).

29. Schoenberg, *Style and Idea*, 218.

30. See Ethan Haimo, *Schoenberg's Serial Odyssey: The Evolution of His Twelve-Tone Method 1914–1928* (Oxford, 1990).

31. In "Sacred Fragment."

32. Soloveitchik and Schoenberg were both in Berlin during the Weimar years, the former writing his PhD on the epistemology and metaphysics of Hermann Cohen.

33. Adorno, *Philosophy of Modern Music*, 91.

34. The translation is by Martin Thurn-Mithoff, from the booklet accompanying the CD Pierre Boulez, *Schoenberg: Das Chorwerk* (Sony Classical, 1990), 86.

35. See Joy H. Calico, "Schoenberg as Teacher," in *The Cambridge Companion to Schoenberg*, 137–46.

36. A nine-volume book titled *Schoenberg in Words*, including all these works, is being coedited by Severine Neff and Sabine Feisst for Oxford University Press (Oxford, forthcoming).

37. Adorno, *Philosophy of Modern Music*, 133.

38. See Sabine Feisst, *Schoenberg's New World: The American Years* (Oxford, 2011).

39. Adorno, *Philosophy of Modern Music*, 133.

40. As powerfully argued by Ilana Pardes in *Melville's Bibles* (Berkeley, 2008).

13

Martin Buber (1878–1965)

THE THEOPOLITICAL HOUR

Christoph Schmidt

TRANSLATED BY SAMUEL HAYIM BRODY

FROM 1932 ON, MARTIN BUBER TRIED TO EXPAND HIS DIALOGICAL THOUGHT PO-
litically and ethically through the idea of theopolitics, which presupposes a dialogical relation to God as the basis for a similarly dialogical constitution of society
beyond domination and violence. This concept of theopolitics not only shifts to the
center of Buber's philosophical-theological reflections, but from it he tries anew to
define the essence of Jewish modernity. Theopolitics[1] is intended to apply "closure"
to the political theology of power and sovereignty,[2] as the reorientation within the
concept already reveals. This concept is guided by the biblical and antimonarchist
politics of Gideon, Samuel, and the prophets, in order to obtain from them a model
for a theologically grounded anarchism of individual and collective freedom, valid
for Jewish history and Jewish modernity. The concept of theopolitics that Buber
establishes is in opposition to any instrumentalization of conceptions of God as
applied to a theory of the authoritarian state, and thereby understands itself from
the beginning as a reaction to the contemporary political context through which the
concept originated: namely, on the one hand, the total crisis of modern secular culture in the political theology of the Third Reich; and, on the other hand, the nascent
Zionist state as a potential horizon of a utopian realization of this concept.

What follows will reconstruct Buber's concept of theopolitics from various historical contexts, that is, first from the historical perspective of the new political
situation in Germany after 1933, which Buber expressed in his controversy with
Carl Schmitt and Friedrich Gogarten in *The Question to the Single One* (Die Frage
an den Einzelnen).[3] He perceives in this political theology a radical inversion of
what he calls the "theopolitical commission" (*Auftrag*). For Buber the new political
situation in Palestine contains, despite the claims of realpolitik, the possibility of
a theopolitics that could lead to a binational Arab-Jewish state. From the perspective of the contemporary political origins of the concept of theopolitics, it is then
demonstrable that Buber's concept of theopolitics develops a complex temporal
structure, which elevates biblical prehistory as a model for understanding moder-

nity and the present, such that it can be grasped at any moment in its very own messianic future-possibility. For example, from the judge Gideon's refusal of the royal crown, which Buber describes as a foundation of any theopolitics in *Kingship of God* (Königtum Gottes), and from the controversy between the prophet Isaiah and King Ahaz of Judah, which he develops in *The Prophetic Faith* (Glaube der Propheten),[4] Buber will explain in sum the sense of theopolitics as a dialectic of power and its critique. The chapter on Isaiah and Ahaz, called "The Theopolitical Hour," had actually been conceived in 1938, the year of Buber's emigration from Germany to Palestine, and thus, given the impact of the political situation at that time, stands biographically between both of these contexts as central for Buber's engagement with modernity. But for Buber at that time, the construction of the messianic moment for the concrete situation of Zionist politics had not yet become real. The establishment of a Jewish state has admittedly frustrated the expectation of binational statehood in the sense of a theopolitical utopia. But Buber's strategy has been transformed into a praxis, bound to the prophetic tradition, of speaking truth to the powers of the state and the Israeli public; it has openly criticized Israeli policy on all key issues, including the refugee problem, expropriation of land, and production of a Jewish-Arab civil society.

The Political Hour

In *The Question to the Single One* of 1936, Martin Buber tries to capture the conception of the contemporary political situation in Germany after 1933, using the example of the constellation of Carl Schmitt and Friedrich Gogarten, as a report, so to speak, on "the humanistic situation after the dismissal of parliamentarianism."[5] He places this rather sketchy controversy regarding two political theologians of the sovereign state in the context of post-Hegelian philosophy, specifically of the philosophical reflection on the Single One (*den Einzelnen*) and on individuality in Søren Kierkegaard and Max Stirner. Buber's *Question to the Single One* thus may be classified, on the one hand, in this existentialist context in order to, on the other hand, indicate by the example of Schmitt and Gogarten the false political consequences of such an orientation to the Single One.

The various understandings of the contemporary political situation in Germany that Buber brings into play may be described as a kind of intellectual-historical parallelogram. The names Stirner and Schmitt denote the anthropological axis, while Kierkegaard and Gogarten denote the theological axis. In each case the first names mentioned (Stirner, Kierkegaard) represent an orientation to the Single One, while the second names (Schmitt, Gogarten) represent the projection of that concept of the Single One into the political sphere.

For Buber, the parallelogram axes of Stirner and Schmitt/Kierkegaard and Gogarten represent a series of fundamental disjunctions: of the individual from society, of power from justice, of the political from the theological, and, also implicit at the margin, of the Christian from the Jewish. Buber's diagnosis emphasizes the separation of politics and theology: "The modern Occident stands on the sanctioned rupture of politics and religion. Politics is inglorious, but powerful; religion is . . . non-binding."[6] While Christianity attempts on principle to distance itself from politics, Judaism stands in a permanent political-theological tension, because

"the prophets of Israel . . . had to confront the king in Jerusalem, as the patron of injustice in the country" with their "religio-political word."[7]

Kierkegaard and Stirner represent for Buber the necessary existentialist turn away from the idealism of the pure, self-creating (*erzeugenden*), sovereign subject and spirit, and thereby a turning toward the concrete-historical existence of the individual:

> A few years before Kierkegaard conceptualized his "Report to History" under the title "The Point of View of My Activity as an Author," in the "Two Notes" [*Beilagen*] of which the category of the Single One found its adequate formulation, Max Stirner published his book about "the unique one" [*den Einzigen*]. This too is a border-concept [*Randbegriff*] like the Single One, but one from the other end.[8]

That is to say, both individuals stand for a configuration of the radical polarization of theology and politics. Kierkegaard points to the rediscovery of the theological beneath the turning away from politics; by contrast, Stirner's practical solipsism denotes the total secularization of the political as the ultimate consequence of a politics emancipated by pure, reckless egoism from any religious and moral reservations.

> This border-picture [*Randbild*] of a German Protagoras is usually underrated: the de-realization [*Entwirklichung*] that responsibility and truth have suffered in our hour has here if not its spiritual origin, certainly its exact conceptual announcement. "The Ego [*Der Eigene*] [. . .] is originally free, for he acknowledges nothing but himself," and "True is what is mine" are pre-formulas [*Vorformeln*] of an icing-over of the soul undreamt of by Stirner in all his rhetorical assurance.[9]

The Hegelian dialectic, which leads away from Being to Idea, from the bloody struggle between master and servant to a society of mutual recognition, initially breaks down due to the radical critique by Stirner and Kierkegaard of the metaphysics of identity and of the totality of theology and politics. However, at the same time, the epochal antithesis between Kierkegaard and Stirner demonstrates the price of the necessary emancipation of this type of individuality from the metaphysical-theological constraining event (*Zwangsveranstaltung*) of the realized identity of Being and Idea, Theology and Politics. Precisely through the division of theology and politics, there arises once more the possibility of an agreement between them, in the form of a real-practical synthesis and a mutual nonintervention pact. The unbridled display of power of the sovereign egoist (Stirner) has nothing to fear from the theological existentialist (Kierkegaard), since while this subject remains at a remove from politics, it nonetheless, in doing so, legitimizes it. Conversely, the theological existentialist in his private adventures of faith has nothing to fear from the absolute power. Stirner's individualism represents itself as the logical consequence of a secularizing politics. With the radical abolition of all theological and ethical remainders, the political must be reduced to only pure will to power, to pure egoism, which, inhibited by no moral limits, can unleash itself unconditionally. The withdrawal of Kierkegaard's Single One from politics declares its counterpart, insofar as the Single One is defined here purely theologically, the social-political dimension having been relinquished. The Hegelian totality of Being and Idea as identity of God and State is here exploited through the excesses of political and theological individuality, only in order to reproduce the totality of the political from an individualist plane.

Against this, Buber himself attempts to reinsert the Single One and existentialist into social relation, so that he appears neither as master over society (Schmitt, Gogarten) nor as pure function of the general and social (Hegel), but rather as the Single One who takes over for society and its critical responsibility. Commonplace existence should not merely posit the negation of Hegelian metaphysics, but rather must prepare its critical (re-)integration into society on the basis of individual responsibility. Buber seeks a form of existentialist individuality that aligns itself with the idea of a true, anarchic community (*Gemeinschaft*), and from there assumes critical responsibility in the real society (*Gesellschaft*), determined (*bestimmten*) by concrete power structures.

His dialectical criticism of excesses (*der Extreme*) places Buber close to a theological existentialism, that is, to Kierkegaard. Indeed, let the "I-can-say," thus Buber, be the condition of the possibility for the theological, but viewed biblically it always remains "the people" as a whole that partners with the divinity, though indeed while always represented through a name-bearing Single One. Like Kierkegaard, Buber finds the archetype for the Single One in Abraham,[10] whose singularity first comes to light through the revelation of God, therefore in that double challenge "to go off" (*sich aufzumachen*; Heb., *lekh lekha*), namely to go once from the native city Ur and then to go to sacrifice the son. The biblical narrative reports about Abraham's radical disengagement from all social bonds, from the world of fathers and sons, but this disengagement from society is not thinkable without the address by God that preceded it, which after all promises the foundation of a new community, in which the dialogical-ethical and that dimension of existence called "political" can realize themselves completely for the first time.

Buber reproaches Kierkegaard for passing over just this social-political dimension of the theological Ur-relation of existence, and with this Creation altogether; thereby he practices a kind of theological egoism, in which the Single One as good as lays claim to God for himself alone. It is interesting, though not relevant to our discussion here, that Buber indicts Kierkegaard much too quickly on the basis of his surface rhetoric, thereby perhaps completely leaving out of the picture the latter's concept of a "contending church" against bourgeois Christianity.[11] For Buber, Kierkegaard's relationship to marriage is symptomatic of that which he identified as his leap beyond creation and community. "In order to come to love," Buber quotes him on his disengagement from Regine Olsen, "I had to remove the object of love." But that is, Buber comments, "to misunderstand God in the subtlest way. Creation is no obstacle on the road to God, it is this road itself."[12] While he raises marriage to the Ur-model of dialogical relation, Buber emphasizes, next to the moment of intersubjectivity, precisely the moment of everyday and intensive controversy with the other. The reference to God will be only in reference to the nearest one (*Nächsten*), but this in a real, effective form of life, in which people deal every day with the mindset, attitude, and lifestyle of the other.

From these sketchy reflections on the constellation of Stirner and Kierkegaard, Buber goes to the second, no less sketchy constellation—Schmitt and Gogarten—

designed to characterize the current political situation. Carl Schmitt's *Concept of the Political* (Der Begriff des Politischen) is the continuation of Stirner's absolute individualism of power "beyond the moral." Foreshadowed in the figure of the ruthless and criminal loner, we find here the projection of Stirner's idea of a self-generation of the I "out of its own Nothing" onto the political sphere. Implicit in this connection is the argument that Schmitt's *Political Theology* (Politische Theologie) of 1922 already no longer defines the sovereign theologically but rather, as he already claims at that time, as "decision created purely out of nothing."[13] Consequently, in *Concept of the Political*, it is explicitly stated that the concept of the sovereign requires no theological grounding, insofar as it would be better served by a correctly understood anthropology of the dangerous nature of man, which is sufficient to ground the conflict with the enemy.[14] In this sense it is not only that famous footnote from *Concept of the Political*, which restricted Christian love of the enemy to the private domain, that thereby completely depoliticized "the theological," but also Schmitt's *State, Movement, People* (Staat, Bewegung, Volk), in which the Führer is defined as sovereign beyond all theological, philosophical, and political traditions as the "unmediated presence [*Gegenwart*] and point of presence [*Präsenz*]," prior to the general failure of "every concept and every picture."[15]

Buber is interested above all in Schmitt's definition of the "pure" political as "decision on friend and enemy," which in an emergency must include the possibility of physical killing. Such a concept of political enmity corresponds to the conception of political life as a duel. "This situation exists, then, when two people perceive an established conflict between them as an absolute one, which can only find its solution in the annihilation of one by the other."[16] Buber's reading, which initially amounts to unargued declarative statements and contrary positions, seeks, wherever Schmitt posits the situation globally, to differentiate; that is to say, to take into consideration Schmitt's distinctions as such. Indeed, Buber accepts the anthropological presupposition of the evil nature of man, insofar as "evil" signifies "far from unproblematic, and dangerous."[17] But he stops short of a radical view of this evil nature as absolute sinfulness; for without this dangerousness, nothing further can be achieved.

But above all, one must distinguish within the concept of enemy between the outer and the inner enemy. While the outer enemy in particular "has no interest in the preservation of the state," the internal enemy — Buber calls him the "Rebel" (*Empörer*) — would be quite interested in the continuity of the state.[18] His goal, rather, is to change the state. Therefore the outer enemy would not ultimately be a political problem, whereas the inner enemy, when he places the existing order in question, first actually thinks/means "the political." Buber establishes this while taking up Schmitt's rhetoric:

> The highest points of concrete politics are not, as Schmitt thinks, "at the same time the moments in which the enemy is caught sight of in his concrete distinctness as enemy," but rather the moments in which an order, in the face of the gravest responsibility of an individual confronting himself with it, demonstrates the legitimacy of its static character, its character (however necessarily relative) of fulfillment.[19]

When theology is humbled directly by the concept of the political, which is to say, pushed back into privacy, this disempowerment succeeds only at the price of

a demonization of the human, which in the last instance is still grounded theologically. The idea of absolute sinfulness for Buber is the condition of possibility as
well as the prevention of the purely political. On the one hand, politics ought to be
emancipated with it from every this-worldly (*innerweltlichen*) messianism; on the
other hand, this politics must, since every critique is already grasped as an extreme
case of rebellion against the order as such, freeze in an absolute stasis.

Buber analyzes the hidden theological substratum of Schmitt's concept of the political through the example of the dialectical theologian Friedrich Gogarten, whose
views are closely related to Schmitt's.[20] While Schmitt actualizes Stirner's doctrine of
the I politically, Gogarten carries out—according to Buber's intellectual-historical
parallelogram—the political consequences of the purely theological grounding of
the individual in Kierkegaard. Both approaches meet on the basis of the doctrine of
the absolute sinfulness of man, from which the existentialist position of Stirner and
Kierkegaard represents itself on the political plane as a laissez-faire (*Nichteinmisc-
hung*) principle, which rests on a positive and full accord (*Einvernehmen*).

The evil nature of man, as manifested in the I-Thou relation between man and
God, declares itself in the insight of the letter to the Romans: "The good that I will,
I do not do, and the evil that I do not will, that I do" (Rom. 7:19). This leads Gogarten to the determining justification of the political as the necessary domination
of the in-itself evil freedom of man. With Romans 13 Gogarten justifies the severe
authority that erected "barriers" against the hatred and being-against-each-other of
man, "so that it doesn't come to the worst and people don't mutually destroy and
consume one another."[21] Faith and the justification by faith thereby always concern
only the individual relationship of man to God, so that this man, when it comes to
the state, takes its power for granted, since it is legitimized by faith in the power
instituted by God against sin.

While Gogarten has explicitly theologically grounded Schmitt's doctrine of the
enemy on original sin, thus revealing for Buber not only the accord between authoritarian politics and individualistic theology, in the sense of a nonintervention
pact by full mutual agreement, but also and above all the complete inconsistency of
both—the political theology of Schmitt as well as the dialectical theology of Gogarten. First, Gogarten shares a problem that already arises from the Pauline teaching,
which understands man as redeemed and unredeemed at once: "from the dialectical
union of both moments, the unredeemedness can break out and act separately. In
the face of human systems, man cannot justifiably be described as absolutely sinful,
since the distance is lacking which alone is able to ground the unconditioned."[22]
But Buber thereby says that politicians must take for themselves this distance by
right and thus absolutize the instance itself, which must be itself relieved of evil.
Therein lies the ultimate political-theological irony: that Gogarten has tried to
ground the relation of the I to God of all things on Buber's dialogical doctrine of
"I and Thou,"[23] in order from there to legitimize Schmitt's political theology with
Paul's understanding of sin and authority. So now Buber shows that the authority
of the state, while it is indeed justified through evil, in Gogarten's sense, must itself
ultimately presuppose a redemption from evil.[24]

The theology of the authoritarian police state not only permits the latent contradictions in Schmitt's attempt to derive the political from the concept of the enemy
to appear in a clear light but also demonstrates its own contradictions, which themselves reveal the same purely political definition of the absolutely evil nature of

man. That is to say, Schmitt and Gogarten recognize the core of man's sin—and modernity with its politics of emancipation is for both the epitome of sin—as abuse of freedom, as autonomy and individualism, which implies the liberating of man from evil and hence the enthroning of the self as God. Thus, when they define political power as divine plenitude, which ought to be removed from the sphere of creation and thereby from the vulnerability to evil, both theories of the political refute themselves. Both do no more than recapitulate the problematic, which they have criticized in emancipatory modernity, on the plane of sovereign power.

In this context, deduced from the basis of thought on a radical crisis of humanity, ethics, and politics, Buber now develops his own conception of the dialectical relations of individual, society, and politics from the biblical conception of "authority" (*Vollmacht*) as an office appointed by God: "The Old Testament knows in the history of the kings of Israel and the history of foreign rulers the degeneration of legitimacy into illegitimacy, and chronicles the decline of 'authority' into 'resistance' [*Widermacht*]."[25] With the divine commission, the possibility is always already given that the particular commissioned one acts against God's commission and betrays the commission. This contravening is for Buber nothing other than the reinterpretation of a commission of God designed for a designated, temporally bounded task (*Aufgabe*) as a perpetual license. Rather than interpreting commission in the sense of a responsibility commissioned by God for society "to set to work," it serves in this case as a sovereign self-empowerment by the commissioned one.

Buber stands with Gogarten on the idea of a dialogue between God and the Single One following the "coronation" of the Authority. But against Gogarten he recognizes this commission not as an appointment over society, but rather for society; and not in the sense of a legitimation of sovereign rule, but rather of the production of a communicating society free from domination, already co-defined (*mitdefinierten*) with the production of the dialogical relation to God. The one called by God should remember the dialogical, temporally bounded commission and must always retire from his task as soon as it is fulfilled.

When Buber defines the commission with Max Weber's concept of charisma, actually as *Charis*, which is to say as a gift in which God himself communicates with the Single One and confers on him the divine commission,[26] therein lies the ultimately "political" inversion of this commission—to appropriate this gift itself as property and through this appropriation to award oneself a special authority, which wants to place itself over society.[27] This inversion of the commission is a function of the inherently evil and dangerous nature of man. However, against such a reification and appropriation of the gift, the power of the rebellious counterinstance (*Gegeninstanz*) of a Single One, who remembers the original commission and in its name claims to suffer, under the reinforced power-hierarchy, its unmediated implementation. This Single One is the "inner" enemy, who confronts the political system in the emergency of the revocation of the divine commission. Buber recognizes the archetypes of these rebels in the biblical case of the prophet.

The Aporia of the Jewish Concept of the Political

Buber is first and foremost a committed Zionist.[28] With Herzl, he perceived in political Zionism the possibility of a radical and fairer organization of Jewish society.

However, early on he asserted against political Zionism that this justice for the Jewish people must not warrant injustice against the Arab people in Palestine.[29] Zionism is for Buber always in danger of betraying its own theopolitical commission, asserting the autonomy of the political against the theological and instrumentalizing the latter for the purpose of domination and power.

The division of theology and politics belongs to the essence of the exilic tradition itself, determined through two long millennia of rabbinic theology. Against this tradition, Zionism revolts with a program of ending the exile in order to reproduce the split on the political side. Ever since the destruction of the Temple seventy years after Christ and the definitive end of the political sovereignty of Israel, the Jewish people had existed as a theocracy, which politically was subject to a non-Jewish sovereign. *Dina de-malkhuta Dina* (The law of the king is the law) runs the rabbinic principle,[30] which acknowledges the non-Jewish authority as a political power as long as the religious-legal autonomy of the Jewish theocracy remains untouched. The idea of Jewish statehood (*Staatlichkeit*) is in principle tied to the appearance of the Messiah, which brings about world peace together with the restoration of the Jewish state. Therefore the political sovereignty of Israel stands inherently under a messianic taboo, so exilic Judaism is a manifestation of a fundamental split of theology and politics. It was in this sense that the neo-Orthodox rabbi and legal scholar Isaac Breuer in 1918 defined the Jewish people as "the messianic nation, which lacks the characteristic for sovereignty [*der Zug zur Souveränität abgeht*], namely the pursuit of political power."[31]

If one wants to speak of a concept of the political *before* Zionism, this is based on a radical separation of religion and politics, of Jewish theocracy and the non-Jewish state. Zionism—defined in the words of one of its radical pioneers, Jacob Klatzkin, as the secularization of Israel and the negation of the Exile[32]—would have been nothing more than the transformation of the theocracy into the state and therefore the suspension of the religious-legal constitution developed in the Exile. While Zionism breaks the messianic taboo, this return to Jewish sovereignty carried out in principle only the reverse separation of religion and politics.[33]

If Zionism is actually supposed to be the negation of the Exile, then that means for Buber that it must behave not only as a geopolitical suspension but rather as a theological commission to overcome the division of politics and theology and to place Zionism under the theopolitical commission. Buber accomplishes a move so basic as to be inspired, by returning to the pre-exilic, biblical sources of Judaism and thereby effectively leaping over the whole exilic history, which is so to speak only a reflection of the Christian division of religion and politics, as symptom of crisis and division. He therefore defines the demand of the day as a radical revaluation of all rabbinic-exilic and all Zionist values, which the reinstatement of political sovereignty also thoroughly attempted to derive from the biblical kingdom of Israel. Buber's theopolitics addresses itself equally against both the rabbinic theocracy and against the biblically grounded Zionist idea of political sovereignty. Buber's reevaluation of all values tends not toward a biblically grounded will to power,[34] but rather toward a theopolitical commission to justice.

Buber sought this commission to justice, playing the part of the charismatic in a time of crisis, and preaching to the Zionist Congresses a Zionism that must renounce any sanctification of national egoism.[35] From here Buber developed his unconditional demand for a rapprochement with the Arab people in Palestine and the idea of a bi-national Jewish-Arab state. Buber wants to actualize biblical theopolitics, that is, the idea of an absolute kingship of God, for political Zionism.[36]

The Kingship of God

Buber conceptualizes theopolitics as the kingship of God in the book of the same title from 1932 using the example of the so-called Gideon passage (Judg. 8:21), as well as Gideon's refusal of the royal crown that the Israelite people offered to him:

> His No, born out of the situation, will apply unconditionally to all epochs and his-torical times. For it leads to an unconditioned Yes, to a proclamation of a King in aeternum. I, Gideon, will not rule over you, my son will not rule over you. Therein is it decided: no man shall rule over you; then it follows: YHVH alone is God him-self and it is he who will rule over you.[37]

Using the example of Gideon, Buber constructs within the biblical history an absolutely original, primal stratum of theopolitics, which is situated even before the emergence of the Israelite kingship. It is an epoch of the absolute unity of the theological-political commission, which alone comprises the charisma, the divine *Charis*, the gift, and derives from this no permanent hereditary title. This pure the-ocracy is the direct kingship of God, whose significance exists precisely in this—that no man shall rule over other men, inasmuch as any man, without supervision of another, can develop his individual freedom in the framework of the community. "There is," Buber writes, "in pre-monarchic Israel no in-itself of sovereignty, since there is no political sphere outside the theopolitical."[38]

This primal time does not form an ahistorical ideal construction, but rather con-stitutes the stage of a "historically locatable will," so that the refusal of the crown itself implies already an inner-dialectical tension, the possible dissociation of the po-litical from the theological, whose reverberation Buber seeks to substantiate by the example of two discernible tendencies of redaction in the Book of Judges: the one, along Gideon's line, antimonarchic, the other monarchic. The monarchist tendency takes on the pure theocracy with the argument, that which passes for theocracy after all is only anarchy. This monarchic countertendency becomes very vivid for Gideon in the short biblical narrative of the man Micha, who establishes his own house of God in order to install and worship his household gods there. The biblical text ex-pounds this incident thusly: "At that time there was no king in Israel and everyone did what seemed right to him" (Judg. 17:6). Theocracy is denounceable as chaotic anarchy, in which man can give free rein to his dangerous, evil nature. Theopolitical freedom must be unmasked as sinful freedom for idolatry. Thereby the beginning of the kingship of God already stands in danger of becoming the foundation of a centralist constitution that requires a terrestrial power and authority to limit man's freedom, which is understood as sinful.

Buber assigns to antimonarchy originality, immediacy, orality with charisma, whereas to the monarchic tendency he assigns the ordered constitution, mediacy, and scrip-turality. This would be evidence for a presentist (*präsentische*) metaphysics. How-ever one wants to assess Buber's characterization of the two tendencies in detail, the point is that the dialectic is reporting, with Gideon himself, only in order to ask to whom the predicate "king" is due.

In the moment when the one appointed by God acting as judge in Israel for his people seeks to consolidate and to institutionalize his own position beyond his commission, the original society itself, which Buber describes as a perfect community of voluntariness, begins to convert itself into an order regulated through law and constitution. Hence for Buber the beginning of injustice is already set insofar as the constitution is necessarily restricted to the members of the community; and it needs the exclusion of others from power, which has infiltrated the law. This consolidation already contains in itself the danger of allotting to the theological commission a specific role within this order, a location, Temple, and cult, so that the "kingship of God" more and more serves only as the legitimation of the self-establishing worldly kingship. By betraying its commission, theopolitics transforms itself into political theology.

But this fundamental alternative placed by Buber between the kingship of God and the kingship of man is in principle the expression of a problematic already laid out in the idea of theopolitics, which somewhat alleviates the suspicion of a simple presentist metaphysics. God stands here for the absolute demand for justice, meaning that any possible realization of this justice cannot satisfy the absolute claim, and must be extended. God *is* the permanent difference between presence and absence, between the absolute and the real, just as man himself is of a double essence and in the particular situation must act responsibly and simultaneously question his own, final action. Still, before there is a theopolitical dissociation, any Single One stands, insofar as he enters into this dialogue, in a double role: to create order at once from duty and impossibility.

Buber elucidates what one may tentatively call the "theopolitical difference," with reference to the sociological concept of charisma, which he explains in connection with the theological concept of the self-revelation of God as EHYEH ASHER EHYEH ("I will be what I will be"):

> Charisma adheres here to charis and to nothing else; there is here no resting charisma, only a floating one; no possession of spirit, only a wandering, a coming and going of ruach (of spirit); no power-certainty, only the currents of its authority, which presents itself and detracts. Charisma adheres here to the charis of a God that reveals himself to Moses as EHYEH ASHER EHYEH.[39]

Thus charis stands, as Buber explains, "over all law," but not in the sense of Weber's pure irrationality or Carl Schmitt's Nothing of sovereign decision; rather, in the sense of a conceptually and legally indefinable absolute demand for justice. The *charis* over the law is in a way the pure law above all law, the pure calling to responsibility.

In this sense Buber interprets the answer of God to the question of Moses as to who he really is—EHYEH ASHER EHYEH—as primarily a conjugation of the first person of that which is predicated in the third person in the Name of God (YHWH). In this interpretation, HAWA or HAYA is rendered as "Being" in the philosophical tradition and urges here the concept of God as one of essence, unity, and identity. Hegel's phenomenology of Spirit is the consummation of this Being-and-identity thinking—which freezes the ultimate meaning of God as a "Happening and Event" where God is thoroughly, inaccessibly omnipresent. At the same time, the self-sacrifice of God in *charis* is understood only in connection with the previously descending word of God EHYEH IMCHA ("I am with you").[40]

The original theopolitics then enters its ultimate radical crisis with the fresh demand of the people put to the prophet—that he may "now place over you a king," a king "like all the other nations have" (1 Sam. 8). This demand leads to the establishment of monarchy in Israel and thereby to the complex dialectic of king and prophet, of power and the demand for justice, which will from now on determine Israelite history. Now the two aspects of the divine commission, the realization and the challenge, arrange themselves in two distinct political bodies. Buber calls the act of usurpation of the royal title through man "theopolitical reduction." In the beginning, it already reveals itself in the transfer of leadership from Moses to Joshua; then with Abimelech, the first Jewish king; and in full form, finally, with King Solomon.[41]

The Theopolitical Hour

From his controversy with Carl Schmitt, Buber took over Schmitt's turn of phrase "the high points of concrete politics" in order to raise the theopolitical intervention against Schmitt's concept of the political. In *The Prophetic Faith*, written as Buber escaped from Germany, Buber defines one such high-point of concrete politics as the "theopolitical hour." It is the case here of Isaiah's appearance against King Ahaz. By this example of concrete theopolitics, the concept is able to demarcate itself specifically as a messianic act.

I ignore the deliberations on the context of the call of Isaiah in the year of the death of King Uzziah (king of the southern kingdom of Judah, 736 BCE), and come straightaway to the historical-political situation at the time of King Ahaz (who reigned from 736 to 725 BCE). Israel, the northern kingdom, has allied itself with Syria for an assault on Judah, the southern kingdom. King Ahaz of Judah wants to manufacture a coalition with Assyria in order to defend against the impending assault of the northern enemies. "In light of the growing danger (2 Kings 16:3), he leads (Isa. 3:27) his son through fire, under which either the real sacrifice of the firstborn or its substitute through symbolic action can be understood."[42] This cultic sacrifice is an indication of his political claim to power.

YHWH now sends Isaiah to Ahaz, in fact with his son, to whom the prophet had given the curious name "She'ar Yashuv," meaning "a remnant turns back [*Rest kehrt um*]."[43] By "the remnant" here is meant any fellowship of the faithful of God, who do not drop away from the kingship of God in times of crisis. Naturally, with these faithful it is a question of a minority, even a remnant.

But what should Ahaz do? Nothing other than "abandon the plan of alliance." With this mission begins Isaiah's struggle against the politics of alliance—first the one with Assyria (against the northern kingdom) and later the one with Egypt (against Assyria, which has by this time grown dangerous). Alliance politics is in the eyes of YHWH and his spokespeople nothing other than a purposeful estrangement from God. So outrageous must the idea initially appear—to secure oneself in the event of a military assault, other than through a coalition—that the theopolitics propagated by Isaiah possesses after all an aspect of realpolitik: that Judah, in the attempt to tamper with the game of the great powers, certainly must forfeit its political independence. Indeed, Isaiah's politics must be understood, as Buber thinks, as a politics of a special type.

The point is not an alternative to alliance politics created by the spirit of peace, but rather something still more fundamental: "In return and rest will be your deliverance; in quiet and calmness [*Gelassenheit*] will be your power" (Isa. 30:15). If Buber were only commenting that "since Samuel's time . . . again and again the unfaithful governor of God and the unauthorized [*unbeauftragte*] advocate of God's rule have faced one another," it would quite directly evade the essence here: "concerning the kingdom."[44] He then marks this controversy as an absolute either-or decision—as the theopolitical hour, in which calmness, against a rushed political action, first reflects upon the true theopolitical commission.

King Ahaz does not rise to Isaiah's speech with submission, since he "will not seek YHWH."[45] This refusal leads to the famous prophecy of the imminent birth of a child—the counter-king (*Gegenkönig*) in Immanuel (8:3). This birth is initially the expression of the failure of Isaiah's commission and therefore forms, so to speak, the Eschaton incarnate. First, the announcement of the "child that is born to us" and "who bears rule on his shoulder" is also for Buber first of all not an allusion to a spiritual counter-king, as in Christianity, but rather of a messianic kingship as "real, political, merely and simply theopolitical" and a "kingship powered with political power to the political realization of God's will for the people and by the people [*für Volk und Völker*]."[46] Second, Immanuel is grasped as a messianic-political figure (*God with us*) who will realize himself the promise of YHVH, who had revealed himself as EHYEH ASHER EHYEH ("I will be who I will be") in the sense of EHYEH IMCHA ("I will be with/by you"). As such, Immanuel is also the Prince of Peace, who begins from the politics of calm of the great primal community of the remnant. Third, it is crucial that Immanuel is "born" also out of the theopolitical difference, a function of the neglected royal commission, and out of the tension of commission and challenge. So far he is eschatological but in a directly existential-political sense. Despite the utopian substance of the image, which has accumulated around the vision of peace, the specifics of the messianic hope lie in the fact that it is renamed "the eternally varying center of the practical hour and its possibility."[47] Fourth, hence "the Messiah" is not given, as Buber says, as a special category in general: "the awaited . . . is the anointed one, who fulfills his commission. More is not necessary." Fifth, the waiting, to which Isaiah seeks to oblige Ahaz, is not directed as an expectation to a former point in time but rather to a possibility already present in this moment, which—under the routine of a politics oriented to power—is derided as outrageous, dangerous, and evil. And sixth, Immanuel, as the Messiah—as a "charismatic prevailing in time"—must also be "born" out of the historical situation.

Buber's theopolitics, conceived from the biblical sources of world history, fulfills itself messianically, and that means that it should potentially fulfill itself in the moment in which the Single One is able to seize, in any present, the possibility of producing the Kingdom of God. In principle, this Single One can be any person; and this Kairos can have already begun with any moment.

After the Founding of the State:
Theopolitics as Act of Prophetic Truth-Speaking

The construction of this messianic moment for the concrete situation of the return to Zion has not fulfilled itself historically. The establishment of the sovereign state of Israel not only destroyed Buber's hope in a theopolitical realization of the binational utopia but also symbolized to him the "greatest crisis" of modern Jewish history, since with it the division between politics and theology typical of the Exile was in fact continued on a Jewish foundation and thus theology was exploited for sovereign politics. This realpolitik departure from theopolitical utopia thus itself represents a "theopolitical reduction," whose meaning is a continuation of assimilation on a national basis—and thus, in fact, of the Exile. Buber actually considered the rhetoric and presentation of the "Jewish majority"—of Jewish statehood as in itself the fulfillment of all the hopes of Zion and the valid overcoming of the Exile—as pure delusion in the euphoric moment of the founding of the State.

If the dissociation between politics and theology and between religious and atheist existentialism, which Buber had diagnosed for the European situation in the epochal constellation Stirner/Kierkegaard and Schmitt/Gogarten, should henceforth replicate itself under Jewish auspices, then it would be valid to formulate a new basis for a theopolitical strategy under the conditions of sovereign statehood. Indeed, Buber repeatedly codified his utopian vision of binationalism in light of his increasing skepticism with regard to its real political possibility; this occurred at the height of the Israeli-Palestinian conflict and before, during, and after the war of independence. As such, to preserve the teaching programmatically before its oblivion, Buber in this codification contrasts his vision again and again with the realpolitik tendency, the political will to sovereign domination with the theopolitical vision of justice, and the tendency to politicize the national conflict with the demand for a politics of depoliticization. "We must fight the hypertrophy of the political from within, standing in the midst of the political sphere."[48]

In this new situation of national euphoria and delusion, Buber drafted a double strategy, which he repeatedly describes as an act of "speaking the truth." It draws on the one hand on prophetic speech, but also appears to stand in connection to the Greek *Parrhesia* (the established right in the Greek polis to speak the truth publicly).[49] Precisely because prophetic speech is silenced with the last prophet, henceforth the "courage of truth" shall be considered to be found before the powers that be, of politics and public opinion, to expose ideological delusion and to name the alternative—theopolitical—option. "We have to show what is false to the powers, our version and our representation in each case, and to demand the just. We have to oppose to falsehood and to the even more dangerous mixture of truth and falsehood the complete human truth."[50]

However utopian, Buber's critical interventions have since then always hit the nerve of the conflict. From the demand for a just solution to the refugee problem, opposition to the military regime in the border areas and to confiscation of Arab soil, and up to his commitment to a just Arab-Jewish civil society, Buber as speaker of the Ichud—the party that he cofounded in 1942 together with Judah Magnes, Ernst Simon, and Henrietta Szold and further emerging from the Brit Shalom of 1925—repeatedly and sharply criticized the factual injustice of realpolitik and its compulsions, in direct controversy with then prime minister David Ben-Gurion. Buber's interventions have thus repeatedly moved the establishment of a just Jewish-Arab civil society to the center of discussion.

We may cite here, as typical of this critical stance, Buber's comment on Ben-Gurion's claim, expressed in an interview with *Le Figaro*, that "the Arabs have it better in Israel than in all the Arab states": "With the establishment of the State of Israel full equality was guaranteed for the Arab population, without any discrimination whatsoever. In the past 18 years, however, the government has missed opportunities and done things which must have aroused in the Arab population the impression that they are second-class citizens."[51]

Martin Buber's concept of theopolitics may in fact be construed as a focus of his theoretical-practical project for a new foundation of Jewish culture. With it he attempted not only to understand the political-theological dialectic of Jewish history from its biblical beginnings up to the political situation of the Jewish state but also to chart a vision of Jewish modernity, which could produce proof of this theopolitics in a concrete political context even in the failure of utopia. Even in the night of the seemingly apocalyptic catastrophe of the destruction of the European Jews, Buber, unlike most Zionist politicians, would not give up that hope. In light of the negative dialectic of the continuing conflict situation in the state of Israel, he had the idea of a nonviolent theopolitics, not only as critical awareness of the fact that this project of Jewish modernity was an "unfinished project" but also through existential faithfulness to the truth this theopolitics invoked as a guide for praxis, which in its claim to speak the truth does not want to be demoralized by conditions of realpolitik.

Notes

1. Martin Buber, *Königtum Gottes* (Berlin, 1932). It is interesting that Erik Peterson, in the twenties, deploys the concept of theopolitics in a similar context against Carl Schmitt's political theology, albeit totally developed from the theology of Paul's letter to the Romans. Compare here Erik Peterson, "Paulus—Der Brief an die Römer," *Ausgewählte Schriften*, ed. B. Nichtweiß (Würzburg, 1997), 15. See also the excellent presentation of Barbara Nichtweiß, *Erik Peterson: Neue Sicht auf Leben und Werk* (Freiburg, 1992).

2. Carl Schmitt, *Politische Theologie: Vier Kapitel zur Lehre von der Souveränität* (1922; Berlin, 1996).

3. Martin Buber, *Die Frage an den Einzelnen* (Berlin, 1936). For Buber's work in general see Paul Mendes-Flohr, *Von der Mystik zum Dialog: Martin Bubers geistige Entwicklung bis hin zu, Ich und Du* (Königsstein, 1979); and Dan Avnon, *Martin Buber: The Hidden Dialogue* (Lanham, MD, 1998).

4. Martin Buber, *Der Glaube der Propheten* (Heidelberg, 1984). For the context of composition, see the foreword to the book (9). Part of the text appeared in Holland in 1940; the book was initially published in 1942 in Hebrew and first published in German in 1950.

5. Trans. note: "Geisteswissenschaftlichen Lage nach der Verabschiedung des Parlamentarismus" is a play on the title of Carl Schmitt's 1923 work *Die geistesgeschichtliche Lage des heutigen Parlamentarismus*, usually translated into English as *The Crisis of Parliamentary Democracy*.

6. Buber, *Die Frage an den Einzelnen*, 121.

7. Ibid., 127.

8. Ibid., 12.

9. Ibid., 13.

10. Ibid., 18.

11. Compare Søren Kierkegaard, *Furcht und Zittern* (1843; Hamburg, 1998), 51: "Faith is just this paradox, that the Single One is greater than the general, that he stands justified over against

this, not subordinated, but rather superior; nevertheless, please note that the Single One . . . becomes the Single One only through the general, which is placed higher than the Single One; thus the Single One as the Single One stands in absolute relation to the Absolute." See also Kierkegaard, *Einübung im Christentum* in his *Gesammelte Werke*, vol. 26 (Düsseldorf, 1955), 202.

12. Buber, *Die Frage an den Einzelnen*, 34.

13. Schmitt, *Politische Theologie*, 69.

14. Schmitt, *Der Begriff des Politischen* (1932; Berlin, 1996): "The methodical connection of the theological and of the political thought-conditions [*Denkvoraussetzungen*] is also clear. But the theological support occasionally mystified the political concepts, since they deferred the ordinary decision into the moral-theological, or at least blended them" (64). Hence it even commends itself to examine "all theories of the state and political ideas from their anthropology" (59).

15. Carl Schmitt, *Staat, Bewegung, Volk* (Hamburg, 1933), 41.

16. Buber, *Die Frage an den Einzelnen*, 79.

17. Ibid., 83.

18. Ibid., 80.

19. Ibid., 82.

20. See Gogarten, *Politische Ethik* (Jena, 1932).

21. Ibid., 107. Gogarten refers in this connection to Gal. 5:15: "If you bite and devour each other, take care that you are not consumed by one another."

22. Buber, *Die Frage an den Einzelnen*, 85.

23. Martin Buber, *Ich und Du* (Leipzig, 1923).

24. Buber, *Die Frage an den Einzelnen*, 89.

25. Ibid.

26. Buber, *Königtum Gottes*, 144. There Buber determines that "the sociological 'utopia' of the voluntary community is nothing other than the immanent side of the direct theocracy." It is not improbable that Buber wants to render his own outline of the kingship of God in concepts something like the sociology of Karl Mannheim (*Ideologie und Utopie* [1929; Frankfurt, 1952]). On Buber's concept of utopia see also his *Pfade in Utopia* (1950; Heidelberg, 1985), and Buber, *Der utopische Sozialismus* (Cologne, 1967).

27. Buber, *Königtum Gottes*.

28. Martin Buber, *Kampf um Israel: Reden und Schriften 1921–1932* (Berlin, 1933).

29. Ibid., 427.

30. Yosef Hayim Yerushalmi, *Diener von Königen und nicht von Dienern* (Munich, 1995); and Nahum Glatzer, *Geschichte der talmudischen Zeit* (Berlin, 1937) have presented the attitude of the rabbis toward their own state and the state of non-Jews after the destruction of the Temple and the Bar Kokhba revolt.

31. Isaac Breuer, *Programm oder Testament: Vier jüdische politische Aufsätze* (Mainz, 1929), 79. But for all that, few Orthodox theologians recognized in the statelessness of nonsovereignty the theological essence of Israel, as did Cohen in *Religion of Reason aus den Quellen des Judentums* (Leipzig, 1919); or Leo Baeck in *Die Pharisaer: Ein Kapitel jüdischer Geschichte* (Berlin, 1934).

32. Jacob Klatzkin, *Probleme des modernen Judentums* (Berlin, 1930), 35.

33. Mathias Acher, *Die jüdische Moderne* (Leipzig, 1896), 35, defines Jewish modernity precisely as a return to sovereignty.

34. Jacob Klatzkin, *Shq'iat ha-hayim* (Berlin, 1925); Micah Joseph Berdichevski, *Nachgelassene Schriften* (Berlin, 1926). For Buber's understanding of Nietzsche, see Paul Mendes-Flohr, "Zarathustras Apostel—Martin Buber und die jüdische Renaissance," in *Nietzsche und die jüdische Kultur*, ed. Jakob Golomb (Vienna, 1998), 225–35.

35. Buber, *Kampf um Israel*, 426.

36. Ibid., 423.

37. Buber, *Königtum Gottes*, 3.

38. Ibid., 140.

39. Ibid., 146.

40. Ibid., 84.

41. Buber, *Der Glaube der Propheten*, 114.

42. Ibid., 172.

43. Ibid., 171: "At the hand of the father the boy represents corporeal, godly protests against the sacrifice of the first-born and likewise the divine warning: now the deciding begins, who belongs to the remnant, who is revealed to me and whom I will save."

44. Ibid., 173.

45. Ibid., 178.

46. Ibid.

47. Ibid., 180.

48. Martin Buber, "Ein tragischer Konflikt?" in Martin Buber, *Ein Land und zwei Völker: Zur jüdisch-arabischen Frage*, ed. P. Mendes Flohr (Frankfurt, 1983), 249.

49. Compare Michel Foucault, *Der Mut zur Wahrheit* (Frankfurt, 2010). Foucault distinguishes four modes of speaking the truth or of veridiction: prophecy, wisdom, teaching, and parrhesia (the latter is that speech by which utterance of the truth risks provoking the anger of the addressees, whether ruler or friend). Foucault emphasizes, however, that this typology admits of mixtures (46). The prophet, as understood by Buber, is actually the Parrhesiast par excellence, insofar as he with his truth-telling is exposed not only to the sanctions of power but also to public opinion.

50. Buber, "Nach der politischen Niederlage," in *Ein Land und zwei Völker*, 324.

51. Buber, "David Ben Gurion und die israelischen Araber," in *Ein Land und zwei Völker*, 373.

14

Albert Einstein (1879–1955)

SOLIDARITY AND AMBIVALENCE

Robert Schulmann

IN APRIL 1918, NOT YET FORTY YEARS OLD AND WITH A BRILLIANT ARC OF ACCOM-plishment in theoretical physics behind him, Albert Einstein paused to reflect on the refuge that the realm of science had until then afforded him. The occasion was a special session of the German Physical Society honoring Max Planck on his sixtieth birthday.[1] Einstein spoke of those who found sanctuary in the temple of science, making quick work of those who gained entry in order to display their virtuosity or pursue a career. The deserving few, like Planck and by implication Einstein him-self, legitimized their presence by a single-minded commitment to a pure love of knowledge. Einstein reinforced the positive imagery with the notion of alienation that he attributed to the philosopher Arthur Schopenhauer: "One of the strongest motives that lead men to art and science is the wish to escape from everyday life with its painful harshness and pitiless dreariness."[2] This refuge serves not only as an intellectual retreat for the worthy individual but also becomes "the center of his emotional life," which in turn crowds out the concerns of daily life and leaves little room for self-examination and introspection.[3] The time and place for evoking these images of sanctuary and escape are significant: Einstein did so against the backdrop of a Berlin beset by privation and bitterness in the fourth year of World War I as well as the four-year mark of his own arrival in the German capital.

After leaving Munich in 1894 as a teenager, Einstein spent his formative years in Switzerland. It was here that his creative powers were nurtured, his groundbreak-ing papers of 1905 were written, and the groundwork for his theory of general relativity was laid. As his reputation in the physics community grew, he developed a sense of solidarity with an international community of scholars and an intellectual commitment to the ideal of scientific cooperation. All the while his camaraderie with a small band of bohemians and outsiders reinforced a sense of personal iso-lation. In the face of lean times and psychological pressures, including the bur-den of a failing marriage and alienation from his sons, he steeled himself during this early period of great scientific achievement with an almost ascetic indifference to everyday concerns. These years were also marked by a profound disregard for questions of ethnicity and religion: "While in Switzerland, I was not aware of my

Jewishness nor was there anything present there which affected or stimulated my Jewish sensibility."[4]

In late 1913 Einstein accepted an appointment to the Prussian Academy of Sciences in Berlin, a position he took up the following spring, just before the outbreak of hostilities.[5] During the war years, he continued to guard jealously his sheltered existence in the "snail shell," replicating in bustling Berlin those conditions of self-absorbed isolation that he had fashioned for himself in Switzerland. Religious indifference persisted as well during these early Berlin years.[6] Even as Germany was facing a radically altered political reality in 1918, Einstein achieved a successful resolution of the foundational problems in his new gravitational theory. While the country grappled with the ghosts of its past and struggled to replace a collapsed political system, he recognized that the ineffectiveness to which intellectuals had been relegated under the Empire could now be overcome. Confirmation of his theory of general relativity in November 1919 reinforced this. The dramatic announcement to that effect by the British Royal Society, the most prestigious scientific body of Germany's recent bitter enemy, conferred upon Einstein an unparalleled worldwide legitimacy, strengthened by popular fascination with the thought of finding certainties in the stars that had proved elusive in a war-torn world. Views on moral and political issues, which had been confined to his correspondence and tentative assertions in the early Berlin years, could now be broadcast to an international audience and carry great weight. It was under these conditions that Einstein's isolation truly came to an end.

Two commitments took pride of place in Einstein's new sensibility: advancing international understanding; and searching for a Jewish identity, coupled with a growing dedication to Zionism. His longstanding belief in internationalism was rooted in recognition of the need for scientific cooperation that knew no national bounds. This enduring conviction nourished a lifelong campaign to support the pacifist movement. Setting out on the Jewish quest, on the other hand, was in large part a belated compensation for Einstein's earlier isolation—an attempt to find emotional resonance beyond the confines of his youthful self-absorption in Switzerland and his first years in Berlin. Consistently impervious since youth to the religious elements in Judaism, he now turned to Zionism's concern for social justice as a guiding principle in defining his public persona and role. For Einstein the intellectual, the Zionist movement afforded ideological purity combined with an emotional link to those with a similar ethnic background.

Another factor reinforced this quest. Unleashed during the tumult of the old regime's demise was a resurgence of venomous antisemitism. Einstein's personal encounters with this virus of racial hatred, projected by vengeful nationalists and the radical right, were minimal.[7] Yet it made his heart bleed, he recounted later, to witness the pervasive discrimination and contempt heaped on the Jewish community in Berlin by the media. "I saw how schools, the satirical press and countless other cultural institutions of the non-Jewish majority undermined the confidence of even the best of my kinsmen [*Stammesgenossen*], and felt that it should not *thus* be allowed to continue."[8]

What heightened his sense of moral outrage was the ugly fact that not only Gentiles engaged in antisemitism. Among Einstein's fellow German Jews, prejudice was frequently directed against their Russian and Polish brethren within the Jewish community. These socially and economically disadvantaged *Ostjuden* (Eastern Jews), numbering about 30,000 in Berlin, represented somewhat more than one-quarter of the total Jewish population of Berlin. Their religious and social traditions, rooted in a shtetl culture, appeared both strange and menacing to their more assimilated German coreligionists. Many *Ostjuden* had fled pogroms in the Russian lands; others had immigrated to perform labor service voluntarily during the war years.[9] Various measures contemplated by the Prussian government to control and even deport them after the war exacerbated the fear of many German Jews that they were the real targets of official displeasure. While protesting the intentions of the authorities, Einstein dismissed the fear of his fellow Jews with the acerbic observation that it was "a Jewish weakness . . . always and anxiously to try to keep the Gentiles in good humor."[10] Jewish antisemitism, he thought, represented nothing less than a degrading ritual of diverting the antisemitism aimed at all Jews onto those least able to defend themselves.

A second element shaping Einstein's newfound solidarity with the most vulnerable of his kinfolk was his concern for the plight of young émigrés in the Eastern European Jewish community of Berlin who sought a higher education. Given Einstein's own financial struggles as a student and his difficulties in obtaining employment after graduation,[11] he identified closely with ambitions that were often thwarted by a cruel *numerus clausus*. In this case, it was aimed at a prospective student's ethnic origin, compounded by his alien status. Maja Winteler-Einstein, in a memoir of her brother's early life, singled out empathy for the lost academic potential of Eastern European youths as decisive in the development of Einstein's Jewish sensibility.[12] By early 1920, Einstein had successfully petitioned the Prussian Ministry of Education to officially recognize courses offered by Berlin university professors outside the framework of the university. This allowed approximately two hundred foreign students, mostly Eastern European Jews, to receive credit toward a degree.[13]

In fact, Winteler-Einstein's memoir is more pointed. She recalls not only the awakening of her brother's Jewish identity but also his increasing advocacy on behalf of Zionism, an allegiance to which only a minority of German Jews adhered at the time. Most bourgeois-liberal Jews in Germany stressed the necessity of assimilation in order to guarantee Jewish civil rights. For Einstein, accommodating the hegemonic culture was tantamount to seeking approval from the Gentile community. It was, he thought, a fatal concession to the normative authority of the antisemite and one that perpetuated humiliation. Only by expressing solidarity with an Eastern European Jewish community, which had maintained authenticity through loyalty to its roots, might assimilated German brethren recapture feelings of communal worth. Zionism afforded this promise. The institutional embodiment of the assimilationist position was the Central Association of German Citizens of the Jewish Faith (Central-Verein deutscher Staatsbürger jüdischen Glaubens), an organization for which Einstein expressed open contempt on a number of occasions. Refusing to attend one of its meetings in the spring of 1920, he condemned it in a particularly vehement fashion in a statement that was published as "A Letter of Confession by Einstein." In the most pungent portion of this letter, he ridiculed the name of the

Central-Verein, pointing out that there scarcely exists "a kind of unbelief by virtue of which one ceases being a Jew." To his mind, the designation contained two admissions: "1. I want nothing to do with my poor Jewish (Eastern European Jewish) brethren, 2. I do not want to be regarded as the child of my people, but rather as the member of a religious community. Is this honest? Can the Gentile have any respect for such pussyfooters?"[14]

The Federation of German Zionists (Zionistische Vereinigung für Deutschland), on the other hand, shared neither its rival's emphasis on civil liberties nor its optimism about integrating the Jew into German society. With an influence that went well beyond its relatively small numbers, the key to its appeal was that it held out the renewal of a sense of pride in the communal loyalties of its adherents. German Zionists were also uncompromising on the issue of antisemitism. Quite simply, they shrugged off calls for self-defense as a distraction from a preferred emphasis on creating a national presence in Palestine.

Zionism's appeal for Einstein was not exclusively ideological. In November 1917, a major effort was launched by the Federation of German Zionists to win prominent new members to its cause after the British government in the Balfour Declaration expressed sympathy with Jewish aspirations in Palestine. Recruiting Einstein became a prime objective.[15] There are at least three variants to the tale of how personal contacts provided the catalyst, though it appears likely that they may all be complementary strands of one narrative thread. One version relates how Einstein was invited by officials of the federation to a meeting on December 19, 1918 to discuss Jewish demands to be put forth at the upcoming Paris Peace Conference. Whether Einstein actually attended is unknown, but his intention to do so was acknowledged a few days later.[16]

A second account describes Einstein, together with a number of other Jewish notables, invited to a dinner party in a private home in Berlin on February 23, 1919 to discuss the founding of an academy devoted to Jewish studies. The attendees were a mixed group of Central-Verein members and Zionists. Among them was the artist Hermann Struck, a confirmed Zionist and devout Orthodox Jew, who was eager to woo Einstein to the cause.[17]

A third strand portrays Einstein attending a lecture given in February 1919 by Kurt Blumenfeld, propaganda chief for the Federation of German Zionists and a co-conspirator in the December 1918 attempt to win Einstein for Zionism.[18] In a meeting with Blumenfeld prior to the lecture, Einstein questioned whether internationalism could be reconciled with the narrower national emphasis of Zionism. However, the conversation seems to have sufficiently piqued his interest that he attended Blumenfeld's lecture. On this occasion, Einstein noted that he had already rejected Struck's efforts to enlist him in the ranks of the religious Zionists, but Blumenfeld's more secular argumentation had banished any lingering doubts he had about Zionism—or as we shall see, perhaps only dispelled them in the heat of the moment.

The phrasing that Einstein used to describe his "conversion" (*Verwandlung*) is instructive, even if the exact words are those recounted by his mentor Blumenfeld many years later: "I am *against* nationalism, but I am *for* the Zionist cause. The reason for this has become apparent to me today. If a man has both arms and constantly asserts 'I have a right arm,' then he is a chauvinist. If a man is missing his right arm, however, he must do all in his power to compensate for the missing limb. For this reason, I am, in my general personal attitude, an opponent of nationalism. As a Jew, however, I support, from this day forward, Jewish-national Zionism."[19] The power of the anecdote lies in its summary of emotional transition rather than a precise historical reconstruction of Einstein's commitment to the Zionist cause.

There are a number of contradictions inherent in the Zionist phenomenon and implicit in Einstein's conversion that require examination at this point. As Einstein's perception of the phenomenon was so central to his *Weltanschauung*, the contradictions and ambivalence also serve to illuminate various aspects of his personal character and political identity. The first, most obvious of these conflicts is the tension between his heartfelt belief that intellectuals had a moral obligation to strive for international solidarity and the tug of Zionist nationalism. Yet as his metaphor of the one-armed man makes clear, Einstein's personal opposition to nationalism was directed more against aggressive chauvinism than against the nationalism of patriots. As he explained to a colleague in the autumn of 1919, "one can be internationally minded, without being indifferent to one's kinsmen."[20] Moreover, Zionism's nationalist coloration was further dimmed in Einstein's eyes by his expectation that Zionism might achieve the internationalist goal of bridging with a common purpose the fragmented Jewish communities of Europe. Ideally, this model of human interdependence might prove even more elastic: "Zionism, which appears to be a nationalistic movement," might not only be relevant for the Jew but also have "a significant role to play for all mankind."[21]

One of the sources of Zionism lay in the völkisch-tinged roots of its German variant with an emphasis on the cultural origins of nationalism. Conceiving of kinsmen as members of the same community, bound not only by common language but also by blood ties, German Zionists veered uncomfortably close to a racialist view of the so-called völkisch group that was by definition exclusivist in nature. A movement based on the principles of blood and soil (*Blut und Boden*), which encouraged a return to the land and its cultivation, proved enormously attractive to a Jewish population that had historically been restricted in its ownership of real property. On the other hand, it was a concept foreign to a convert such as Einstein, whose interests and commitments lay on a purely intellectual plane.[22]

Identification with the less fortunate members of the Jewish community revealed another incongruity: Einstein's rebellion against the mainstream opinion of the Central-Verein was driven in part by his disdain for an establishment that sat in judgment of the powerless. The contempt was deep-seated. As early as 1909, just before receiving his first university appointment in Zurich, Einstein ridiculed the craven attitude of wealthy young Jews, who, in vying desperately for civil service positions, submitted to the lash of authority.[23] With his own apotheosis in late 1919 came the added burden of responsibility to—and perhaps guilt vis-à-vis—those less fortunate. Yet the irony of disparaging authority while increasingly being looked up to as one himself was not lost on Einstein. In an aphoristic aside to a friend in 1930, he claimed that "to punish me for my contempt of authority, Fate has made me an authority myself."[24]

The initial impulse that attracted Einstein to the Zionist cause was his instinctive empathy for the plight of *Ostjuden*, the Jews from Eastern Europe, but he did not share in the slightest their religious inclinations. While feeling an emotional—to some degree romanticized—affinity for the sense of solidarity that the religious communities of Eastern Europe had been able to preserve, he derived more comfort from the sterner rationality of a Baruch Spinoza, who asserted that philosophy could be based on a geometric model. He also accepted Spinoza's rejection of an absolutely transcendent God, believing with him that Nature and God are one and the same.[25] His dismissal of religiosity was sharp-edged and to the point: "I can only view confessional traditions historically and psychologically; I have no other relationship to them."[26] This was in response to a query about his views of the "Redeemer" (*Heiland*), one of four questions posed in December 1922 by a member of the Young Men's Christian Association of Tokyo during Einstein's trip to Japan. Two months later, visiting Palestine on his return voyage, his reaction to Orthodox Jews davening at the Western Wall was brutal: "a miserable aspect of people with a past and no present."[27]

Nothing better illustrates the tensions inherent in the Zionist program and Einstein's attitude toward its goals than the debate on how most effectively to restore Jewish national life. All Zionists agreed that the fatal illusions of assimilation could best be avoided by undertaking tasks in common, and they also concurred that Palestine was the heart of such an enterprise. Yet the question remained how best—and how realistically—these goals might be achieved.

The Balfour Declaration of 1917 had recognized the Zionist aim of a national home for the Jewish people. In setting up a British mandatory authority there three years later, the League of Nations used the same expression: "national home." Much in the development of Zionism over the next thirty years would hinge on the interpretation of this phrase. Two points of departure were dominant in the Zionist camp. One stressed Zionism's spiritual and cultural character; the other, its political nature. Cultural Zionists directed their energies toward a Palestine that would rekindle a sense of self-worth in the diaspora, in which both Palestine and the diaspora would enjoy a "constant reciprocal spiritual relationship."[28] They sought relatively modest funding for gradualist settlement that was committed to the social and economic development of Palestine as a spiritual resource for world Jewry.[29] Political Zionists, on the other hand, wished more or less openly to advance an agenda for the formation of an independent political entity. They dwelled on the importance of mass colonization and ambitious supporting budgets to achieve this goal.

Whether these alternatives are considered as polar opposites or not, it is clear that Einstein viewed Palestine as a universal symbol of Jewish cultural unity rather than as the seedling of a politically independent nation state. During a speech at a Zionist meeting in June 1921, he proclaimed pointedly, if inaccurately, that "the goal which the leaders of the Zionist movement have in mind is not political; rather it is social and cultural." The statement ignored the political ambitions of the World Zionist Organization (WZO) in London and those of its president, Chaim Weizmann.[30] More importantly, it is misleading for two other reasons. First, the positions of the cultural and political Zionists at the beginning of the 1920s were not diametrically opposed. The gradualist immigration program of the former and the large-scale colonization plans of those who were more politically motivated did not seem that far apart at the time. No one could then anticipate the external pressures that would massively increase the influx of Jews into Palestine. One surge spiked in the early to mid-1930s as Nazi persecution in Germany became ever more fearsome,[31] and the refugee numbers in the period after World War II dwarfed all that had come before. After his first (and only) visit to Palestine in 1923, Einstein argued that because of its lack of fertility, Palestine "will become a moral center, but not be able to absorb a large proportion of the Jewish people."[32]

Einstein's blunt assessment also misrepresents his own position. The statement is far less sweeping than appears at first glance. Both in his science and in his public persona, Einstein was a realist, though inexperience in political matters coupled with a devotion to principles rather than specifics led him to make categorical assertions. While always laying the greatest stress on the cultural aspect of the Zionist enterprise, he did recognize the need for administrative, economic, and social organizations to galvanize it into action. The one-armed man would defend his heritage with political measures—"to compensate for the missing limb," in Einstein's phrase. At this early stage of settlement, however, he felt the exercise of power could scarcely endanger the moral purpose that lay at the heart of the enterprise. In response to a friend who in 1921 feared that Jews in a Jewish homeland might in its name perpetrate the same atrocities and crimes as had others in the name of their countries, he wrote: "I confidently believe that the Jews will be restrained from an obsession with power by the small size and dependency of their colony in Palestine."[33]

Jewish solidarity might also be achieved by "drawing nearer [in Palestine] to the social ideal of our ancestors, much as it is laid down in the Bible and at the same time become a haven of modern intellectual life."[34] Respect for biblical tradition would complement the development of a modern society buttressed by a cohesive Jewish culture. Religion too would have its place, but under certain conditions: "I fully realise that the development of the jewish [sic] spiritual life in the direction of a synthesis of the religious and scientific spirit, if resulting in original and powerful production, would be an event of greatest importance for the whole of mankind." Yet "restriction of the freedom of thought would be intolerable . . . and would defeat your own purpose—to further a *free and creative* synthesis of faith and reason."[35] This then was Einstein's ideal: Palestine as a synthesis of tradition and modernity, linking the communal enthusiasm of shtetl Jews with the rational spirit of the secular Enlightenment. The construct could also bridge the differences between cultural and political Zionists, reconcile the fervor of the righteous with the pragmatism of the pioneer, and give the analytic rigor of the intellectual full play.

The unifying element for both cultural and political Zionists was also the centerpiece of Einstein's commitment to the cause—an institution of higher learning, a Hebrew University, that would form internationally renowned research departments in the medical, natural, and human sciences and instill pride and provide a livelihood for young students and their teachers. It would thereby also "contribute to counteract the shameful inclination of many successful intellectuals among the Jews who deny and anxiously hide their group affiliation."[36]

In the autumn of 1919, he was invited to a conference to discuss preparations for the university, the cornerstone of which had been laid by Weizmann on Mount Scopus in Jerusalem the year before. In passing, Einstein was informally also asked to consider a future university appointment. Without acknowledging the overture to teach, he promised to attend the meeting, though a week later he wrote a friend that he would most likely renege, as "such an occasion involves too much chatter and needless fatigue."[37] The conference was postponed, but a more consequential opportunity to demonstrate Einstein's commitment arose a year later.

Concern for adequate funding of the Palestinian colonization effort had long plagued the WZO leadership, in particular financial support for its flagship university. To meet this challenge, Weizmann and his allies in London planned a two-month trip to the United States with hopes of enticing Einstein from Berlin to accompany them. Expectations were high of raising significant funds for the Hebrew University from well-heeled Jewish professional groups and swaying American public opinion in support of the Zionist effort. One major obstacle to the success of such an expedition was the WZO's conflict with its American affiliate (the Zionist Organization of America, ZOA) over the pace of colonization and the sources for its support.[38] To overcome this complication, the WZO recognized the symbolic importance of Einstein's presence in their delegation. A German Jew, he might in the name of an incontestable objective appeal above the heads of the American leadership to the great majority of American Jews who were of Eastern European origin.[39]

Once again, it was Kurt Blumenfeld who was enlisted to recruit him, and Einstein acceded with alacrity to the proposal that he accompany Weizmann, "scarcely giving it more than five minutes of thought."[40] Not all were pleased with his decision. Visits by prominent individuals from former belligerent nations to recent enemies so soon after the war were actively discouraged. When his friend and colleague, the physical chemist Fritz Haber, accused him of disloyalty to the German state in undertaking the American tour, Einstein minced no words in pointing out where his loyalties lay. "Devotion to the political entity Germany would be unnatural for me as a pacifist. . . . In spite of my emphatic internationalism I believe myself always under an obligation insofar as it is in my power to advocate on behalf of my persecuted and morally oppressed kinsmen."[41]

The trip to America during April and May 1921 took on the character of a triumphal procession for Einstein, who was singled out for adulation by large crowds of recent Eastern European Jewish immigrants. He in turn was enthusiastic about them. "My most remarkable experience was that *for the first time in my life I have seen Jews en masse. . . .* In Berlin and elsewhere in Germany I have seen very large numbers of Jews but never Jewish masses. This Jewish public that I have seen in America emigrated from Russia, Poland, and other parts of Eastern Europe. These people still retain a sense of national solidarity that has not been destroyed by atomization and the fragmentation of the individual."[42] He was less pleased about the internecine battle between American and European leaders, and the trip did little to ease ill feeling between the two camps. Though viewing the tour as only a qualified financial success, Weizmann could not resist scornfully pointing out that the Europeans had raised far more money than the ZOA had thought possible.[43]

An opportunity to witness for himself developments in the communal life of Palestine arose soon after Einstein's American adventure. In the autumn of 1921, he accepted an invitation to visit Japan. On its heels came a similar offer from the head of the Palestine office of the WZO to come to Palestine on the return leg of his journey. Einstein's initial decision to travel abroad was reinforced by fears for his safety in Germany. In the first half of 1922, a wave of political assassinations, including that of the Jewish foreign minister of Germany, Walther Rathenau, swept the country, and rumors were rife that Einstein too "belonged to that group of people whom the radical right plans to assassinate." He followed his own advice "to be patient and—travel,"[44] embarking for the Far East in October 1922. Four months later, he set foot in Palestine.

His impression of the country was overwhelmingly positive. For the first time Einstein saw with his own eyes the practical implementation of his vision of a cultural center in Palestine: how the agricultural communes and thriving small towns were creating farmers and laborers out of the largely urban Jewish population of Europe, and how deserts were being irrigated, forests planted, swamps drained, and crippling diseases subdued. He admired the vitality and self-sacrifice invested in schools, technical facilities, and art academies. Commenting on a visit to Tel Aviv, he marveled at "what Jews had accomplished in this city in a short period of time. A modern Hebrew city with a vital economic and cultural life stamped out of the ground."[45] He found public health and agricultural challenges paramount, far more pressing an issue than Arab hostility. "At no time did I get the impression that the Arab problem might threaten the development of the Palestine project. I believe rather that, among the working classes especially, Jew and Arab on the whole get on excellently together. . . . The problem of the rehabilitation and sanitation of the country seems incomparably more difficult."[46] Asked on his departure what remained to be done, he replied: "Collect more money."[47] A less prosaic and far more ambivalent message was conveyed in Einstein's diary notation of the day before: "I am wanted without reservation in Jerusalem and am attacked in closed ranks with this in mind. The heart says yes, reason says no."[48] In a struggle for Einstein's ultimate allegiance, the latter would always prevail.

Forces other than his strenuous refusal to make *aliyah* were at work in the late twenties to reinforce the ambivalence that Einstein divulged to his diary. After the exaltation he felt at encountering Jews for the first time en masse on his tour of America, and his excitement at the technical and cultural accomplishments he witnessed in Palestine, a slow fracturing of his hopes for a Zionist synthesis of heart and reason—for a melding of tradition and modernity—was taking place along three fault lines. All indicated a reassessment of his attitude toward the movement and its leaders. The first was his loss of faith in the direction that the Hebrew University was taking under its American chancellor, a former rabbi who lacked prior administrative and academic experience; the second, his despair at the seeming irreconcilability of Jew and Arab that undermined the moral foundation of the Zionist experiment; and the third, an ebbing of confidence in the Zionist leadership, whose pursuit of political ends increasingly ran roughshod over Einstein's cultural Zionist ideal. The last two fault-lines overlap in that Einstein's indignation at official Zionist attitudes toward the Palestinian Arabs frequently coincided with his dismay at Zionist power politics.

Einstein's dispute with the administration of the Hebrew University was both personal and a matter of principle. Impatient with the intrigues of its first chancellor, Judah Magnes, he further resented what he thought was Magnes's incompetence compounded by his stubbornness. Einstein was above all concerned that the university become an international center of learning and not a provincial backwater.[49] In the face of Magnes's opposition, Einstein fought to retain academic and administrative control in the hands of recognized European scholars, at the same time belittling the intellectual authority of those in Jerusalem.[50] Multiple threats on his part to resign from the governing bodies of the university, as well as actual resignations and reluctant resumption of oversight duties, haunted his relationship with the university in the late twenties. The upshot was that an exasperated Einstein became thoroughly alienated from the very institution that had first attracted him to the Zionist fold.

Disappointment with the Hebrew University paled in comparison with Einstein's disillusionment about the Arab riots of 1929. Accommodation between Arab and Jew was for him the moral criterion for settlement in Palestine, a crucial component of his vision of Zionism as a model of human interdependence that could overcome what he called living "side-by-side separately."[51] Both camps had shown bad faith in the events leading up to the riots. Even as he assigned major responsibility for the massacres to unscrupulous Arab leaders, he faulted as typical the dismissive attitude of a prominent Zionist, who failed to recognize the symbiosis of Jew and Arab and wrote off the conflict as a mere incident, ignoring its economic and psychological roots.[52] His greatest fear was that the Zionist elites' indifference, if not outright contempt, for Arab interests undermined the very foundation of the movement. "Should we be unable to find the way of honest cooperation and honest coming to terms with the Arabs, we will have learned nothing on our two-thousand-year journey of suffering and deserve the fate that awaits us."[53] There is a certain irony in the fact that Weizmann, who was the target of Einstein's admonition, was in the 1930s himself beginning to lose ground within the movement to a more radical faction that chafed at his "gradualist" approach to achieving political Zionist goals.

■

Einstein's physical distance from the fray, ignorance of day-to-day events, and instinctive distrust of politicians caused him to underestimate the power calculus that prevailed in Palestine by the end of the 1920s. His appeal to a spiritualized Jewish community was incompatible with the reality of competing ideologies, Jewish and Arab, in the name of which each side was prepared to justify using force. In a word, though aware of Zionist failings, he misjudged the depth of Arab alienation and of Zionist hard-bitten resolve, believing that there were "no irreconcilable differences stand[ing] in the way of peace between Jews and Arabs in Palestine."[54]

Alienation from the mainstream Zionist movement also sprang from what Einstein perceived to be the growing reliance of his "one-armed man" on military solutions. "However firm [is] the stand we make for the defence of our lives and property," he exhorted the Zionist leader not to forget "that the strength of our whole movement rests in its moral justification, with which it must stand or fall."[55] He stated his opposition to the creation of a Jewish state born of force even more vehemently ten years later. "Apart from practical consideration, my awareness of the essential nature of Judaism resists the idea of a Jewish state with borders, an army, and a measure of temporal power no matter how modest. I am afraid of the inner damage Judaism will sustain—especially from the development of a narrow nationalism within our own ranks, against which we have already had to fight strongly, even without a Jewish state. We are no longer the Jews of the Maccabee period. A return to a nation in the political sense of the word would be equivalent to turning away from the spiritualization of our community which we owe to the genius of our prophets."[56] More reproachful than accusatory, the speech mourns the repudiation of Einstein's ideal synthesis of biblical tradition and a modern community in the name of a mean-spirited nationalism that denies to others the social and economic justice it demands for itself.

Einstein was spending the winter of 1932–1933 at the California Institute of Technology in Pasadena when he learned of Hitler's appointment as chancellor of Germany in late January 1933. Leveling a scathing attack on the regime in the press,[57] he also resigned his position at the Prussian Academy. Loss of German citizenship soon followed, and he never returned to his native land. By April, the Nazis had passed the first of their discriminatory laws according to which Jewish and politically unreliable civil servants and employees were to be excluded from state service. With one eye on German developments, Einstein continued to follow the fate of Jewish settlers in Palestine closely. Disenchantment with Zionist leadership did not imply a loss of faith in the Zionist cause nor in those he thought would most benefit from it. He gave lyrical pride of place to the labor movement in Palestine, extolling men and women of the soil and in the crafts as "an elite consisting of robust, aware, and unselfish individuals."[58] His experience visiting the farm settlements of Degania and Rishon LeZion in Palestine ten years earlier had made a lasting impression. "These workers alone are able to build good relations with the Arabs—the most important political task of Zionism." At all costs the diaspora should support the burgeoning labor movement in Palestine, thereby "effectively combating those narrow-minded nationalistic undercurrents, which today plague the political world in general, and to an attenuated degree, the small political world of the Palestine enterprise."[59]

The magnitude of the refugee problem, brought on by Nazi persecution and the devastating restrictions on admission to Western countries, greatly increased the importance of Palestine as a potential place of refuge in spite of the Arab revolt of 1936 to 1939. Yet under the terms of a British White Paper of 1939, Jewish immigration to Palestine, except for the filling of a minor quota, was to be prohibited after April 1944. Einstein's fury knew no bounds. If the Nazis were the chief villain of the piece, the British were their unwitting henchmen by shutting off the last escape route for a people facing extinction. In testimony before the Anglo-American Committee of Inquiry in January 1946 in Washington, he made no bones about his contempt for the British policy of pitting Jew against Arab. He also caused consternation among the Zionist leadership by reiterating his resistance to the idea of a Jewish state in the strongest terms while calling for a binational solution to the Palestine problem.[60]

Einstein's negative position on the nature of the Jewish homeland was, however, already being overtaken by events. Four years earlier, as Nazi armies advanced to their furthest limit on the Eastern front, the chairman of the Jewish Agency's Palestine Executive and later first prime minister of Israel, David Ben-Gurion, called unequivocally for a Jewish army and the transformation of postwar Palestine into an independent Jewish commonwealth.[61] What had long been an implicit feature of the political Zionist agenda was now out in the open. Though non-Zionist organizations for the first time joined with their Zionist counterparts in advocating the establishment of a state, Einstein resisted the calls for such a political solution. As the full horror of the systematic genocide of European Jews was revealed, however, the psychological dynamic in favor of a Jewish state became irresistible.

Two years later, in April 1948, the state of Israel was proclaimed. Einstein welcomed the development but continued to insist that the new state's supreme moral test was yet to be met: "Our attitude toward our Arab minority is the true touchstone for our moral standard."[62] In the last month of his life, in a message to the world that was never finished and never delivered, he raised a final concern.[63] In the face of a looming conflict with Egypt, which broke out a year after his death, he feared that Israel, in rejecting nonaligned status, would become a pawn in the Cold War. Alliance with the West would only lead to the further militarization of Israeli society and deal a deathblow to Einstein's central Zionist hope that the bitterness of living "side-by-side separately" for both peoples could be overcome.

The Zionist movement held out the promise of a refuge for persecuted and disadvantaged Jews in the diaspora, a refuge that would embody the highest ideals of Jewish social justice. Einstein was attracted by the movement's vision of a cultural center in Palestine and by the sense of communal dignity it was at pains to restore. While his moral commitment to the movement was absolute, collaborative problem-solving and political sparring were alien both to his fundamental nature as an outsider and to his training as a theoretical physicist. He identified the problem concisely on declining the presidency of Israel on the death of Chaim Weizmann in 1952: "All my life I have dealt with objective matters; hence I lack both the natural aptitude and the experience to deal properly with people."[64] On the other hand, his disdain for the political rough-and-tumble should not suggest that Einstein was a political naïf. Unwilling to engage in political minutiae, he tempered his idealism with a hard-headed grasp of political motivations. He was fully aware, for instance, that the Zionist leadership had used him as a decoy on his travels to the United States and to Palestine, and he was prepared to accept being instrumentalized as long as his Zionist ideals were upheld.[65] His prediction of an ever more militarized society reveals a canny appreciation of Israel's political fate, as do his dire warnings about the cost to the new state of shunning its near neighbors while embracing a distant West.

What then of Einstein's hopes for his Zionist ideal of a synthesis of tradition and modernity? His nostalgia for the vital sense of community inherent in the shtetl culture of Eastern Europe, as well as his hope for a modern society in which individual potential might be realized, foundered on the harsh reality of two peoples with equally strong claims to the land of Palestine. The prospects for such a synthesis were also dashed by recent advances in weapons technology and the external realties of the Cold War. The development of the atomic bomb under the leadership of J. Robert Oppenheimer, scientific director of the Manhattan Project, as well as the decision by Israel to reject the principle of nonalignment, turned the fledgling state and the entire Middle East into pawns in a new version of the great power game.

In another context Einstein had written that, in the human sphere, all depended on maintaining the strength of one's convictions while not losing sight of the fact that "these convictions must be based on a clear understanding of the prevailing objective conditions ."[66] In the pursuit of his Zionist ideal, Einstein never lacked conviction, but his failure to assess the objective situation in Palestine betrayed him. And yet his long-range hopes for a symbiosis of Arab and Jew persist to this day.

Notes

1. The title of the talk is "Motive des Forschens," presented on April 26, 1918. It was originally published in *Zu Max Plancks sechzigstem Geburtstag. Ansprachen, gehalten am 26. April 1918 in der Deutschen Physikalischen Gesellschaft von E. Warburg, M. v. Laue, A. Sommerfeld und A. Einstein* (Karlsruhe, 1918), 29–32; republished in *The Collected Papers of Albert Einstein* (hereafter *CPAE*), vol. 7, document 7.

2. "Motive des Forschens," 29. Einstein had, in his early twenties, read and recommended to friends Schopenhauer's "Aphorismen zur Lebensweisheit," a part of the *Parerga und Paralipomena*, which extols solitude (Einstein to Marcel Grossmann, September 6[?], 1901: *CPAE*, vol. 1, document 122; and to Mileva Maric, December 17, 1901: *CPAE*, vol. 1, document 128). This negative aspect is emphasized on an earlier occasion when he spoke of retreating from the incomprehensible, puzzling, and odious external world into the snail shell of his musings: Einstein to Heinrich Zangger, January 11, 1915, in *Seelenverwandte: Der Briefwechsel zwischen Albert Einstein und Heinrich Zangger, 1910–1947*, ed. Robert Schulmann (Zurich, 2012), document 66.

3. "Motive des Forschens," 30.

4. "Wie ich Zionist wurde," *Jüdische Rundschau*, June 12, 1921; republished in *CPAE*, vol. 7, document 57.

5. Prussian Academy of Sciences to Einstein, November 22, 1913: *CPAE*, vol. 5, document 485.

6. There was one striking exception: Einstein's refusal to accept an invitation to observe a solar eclipse in Crimea in August 1914 extended by the Imperial Academy of Sciences in St. Petersburg: *CPAE*, vol. 8, document 7.

7. In February 1920, Einstein had created a stir at the University of Berlin when he sought an open admission policy to his lectures for unregistered students, many of whom were Eastern European Jews (in *Berliner Tageblatt*, February 14, 1920, Morning Edition, 2). Einstein summarized the reaction as having an undertone of antisemitism: "Tumultszenen bei einer Einstein-Vorlesung," published February 13, 1920 in *8-Uhr Abendblatt*; republished in *CPAE*, vol. 7, document 33.

8. A decade later Einstein recalled his shock: Einstein to Willy Hellpach, October 8, 1929, Einstein Archives, 46-656. Einstein's first known use of the term "Stammesgenossen" was in his refusal in 1914 of the invitation of the Imperial Academy in St. Petersburg to witness a solar eclipse; see note 6, above.

9. Accounts of the economic deprivation and continued pogroms against Jews during the civil war in the Soviet Union and the Russo-Polish War reinforced Einstein's awareness of the hapless fate of Eastern European Jews: "Wie ich Zionist wurde." . Einstein's first public statement on Jewish affairs was "Die Zuwanderung aus dem Osten," published in *Berliner Tageblatt*, December 30, 1919; republished in *CPAE*, vol. 7, document 29.

10. Einstein to Felix Frankfurter, May 28, 1921: *CPAE*, vol. 12, document 139.

11. Einstein was dependent on support from his parents and relatives to support his university studies and was forced to accept temporary positions before joining the Swiss Patent Office in 1902. His future first wife, Mileva Marić, believed that antisemitism played a role in denying him "a secure position": Marić to Helene Savić, November–December 1901: *CPAE*, vol. 1, document 125.

12. "Albert Einstein—Beitrag für sein Lebensbild," February 1924, first published in *CPAE*, vol. 1, lx.

13. Konrad Haenisch to Leopold Landau, March 9, 1920: *CPAE*, vol. 9, document 344. The *Jüdische Pressezentrale*, April 23, 1920, duly noted the occurrence under the title "Hochschulkurse für Juden."

14. First published as "Ein Bekenntnisbrief Einsteins" in *Israelitisches Wochenblatt für die Schweiz*, September 24, 1920, though two typed drafts are dated April 5, 1920; republished in *CPAE*, vol. 7, document 37.

15. Kurt Blumenfeld, *Erlebte Judenfrage: Ein Vierteljahrhundert deutscher Zionismus* (Stuttgart, 1962), 126. An even earlier approach was made in spring 1918; compare *CPAE*, vol. 8, document 547; and Ze'ev Rosenkranz, *Einstein before Israel: Zionist Icon or Iconoclast?* (Princeton, 2011), 54–55.

16. The list of demands is contained in an enclosure [Einstein Archives, 45-332] to Zionist Association of Germany to Einstein, December 9, 1918: *CPAE*, vol. 8, document 666. The acknowledgment is in Zionist Association of Germany to Einstein, December 12, 1918: *CPAE*, vol. 8, document 671.

17. *Korrespondenzblatt des Vereins zur Gründung und Erhaltung einer Akademie für die Wissenschaft des Judentums*, vol. 1 (Berlin, 1919), 2–4.

18. This account is drawn from an essay by Kurt Blumenfeld in *Helle Zeit—Dunkle Zeit: In Memoriam Albert Einstein*, ed. Carl Seelig (Zurich, 1956), 75–76; and from Blumenfeld's book, *Erlebte Judenfrage*, 127–28. In the essay, Blumenfeld assigns the date February 1919 to the first encounters with Einstein; in the book chapter, he gives the critical year as 1920. The former year is more likely.

19. Blumenfeld, *Erlebte Judenfrage*, 127–28. The version cited in *Helle Zeit* differs insignificantly from this one.

20. Einstein to Paul Epstein, October 5, 1919: *CPAE*, vol. 9, document 122.

21. *Jüdische Rundschau* 30, no. 14 (February 17, 1925): 129.

22. German wartime labor needs reinforced Jewish romantic nostalgia for working the soil and helped redefine for Zionists the importance of manual labor in the colonization of Palestine: Walter Preuß, "Jüdische Arbeit in Deutschland," *Der jüdische Student* 18 (1921): 151–53.

23. Einstein to Jakob Laub, May 19, 1909: *CPAE*, vol. 5, document 161.

24. September 18, 1930; cited in Banesh Hoffmann and Helen Dukas, *Albert Einstein: Creator and Rebel* (New York, 1972), 24.

25. Einstein had read Spinoza's *Ethics* in his first year in Bern (1902): see the reading list in *Albert Einstein: Lettres à Maurice Solovine*, ed. Maurice Solovine (Paris, 1956), vii–viii. He was deeply impressed by it again during the war (Einstein to Elsa Einstein, September 3, 1915: *CPAE*, vol. 8, document 115); and he summarized his "faith" in response to question no. 3 of "Antwort über Religionsfrage": *CPAE*, vol. 13, document 398. An interesting interpretation of Spinoza and Einstein can be found in the speech of Swiss writer Friedrich Dürrenmatt at the ETH Zurich; compare Friedrich Dürrenmatt, *Albert Einstein* (Zurich, 1979).

26. In response to question no. 4 of "Antwort über Religionsfrage": *CPAE*, vol. 13, document 398.

27. Travel Diary Japan-Palestine-Spain, February 3, 1923: *CPAE*, vol. 13, document 379.

28. The phrase is Stephen M. Poppel's in his *Zionism in Germany, 1897–1933: The Shaping of a Jewish Identity* (Philadelphia, 1977), 97–98.

29. See, for example, the statement in Richard Lichtheim, *Das Programm des Zionismus* (Berlin-Charlottenburg, 1911), 41.

30. Draft version of a speech held at a Zionist meeting on June 27, 1921 in the Blüthner-Saal, Berlin: *CPAE*, vol. 7, document 59 as "On a Jewish Palestine. First Version." The statement is all the more surprising in that Einstein had been exposed to Weizmann's political ambitions for Palestine during his recent fund-raising trip with him to the United States.

31. See *A Survey of Palestine: Prepared in December 1945 and January 1946 for the Information of the Anglo-American Committee of Inquiry* (Jerusalem, 1946), 1:185.

32. Einstein to Maurice Solovine, May 20, 1923: *CPAE*, vol. 14, document 34.

33. Solovine to Einstein, March 11, 1921: *CPAE*, vol. 12, document 93. Einstein answered five days later: to Solovine, March 16, 1921: *CPAE*, vol. 12, document 100.

34. "On a Jewish Palestine, First Version."

35. Einstein to Solomon Rosenbloom, April 27, 1921: *CPAE*, vol. 12, document 127.

36. "Zur Errichtung der hebräischen Universität in Jerusalem." Interview with Einstein in *Jüdische Pressezentrale Zürich*, August 26, 1921; republished in *CPAE*, vol. 7, document 62.

37. Einstein to Michele Besso, December 12, 1919: *CPAE*, vol. 9, document 207.

38. The American leaders, most prominent among them Louis Brandeis and Felix Frankfurter, favored a gradualist approach to the question of settlement in Palestine, with an emphasis on separate investment corporations established for specific commercial projects. They rejected the financial monopoly of the general settlement fund (Keren Hayesod) that was under the control of the WZO. See the article on Horace Kallen in this volume.

39. Einstein to Fritz Haber, March 9, 1921: *CPAE*, vol. 12, document 88.

40. Ibid.

41. Ibid.

42. Published in *Jüdische Rundschau*, July 1, 1921, 371; republished as "On a Jewish Palestine: Final Version": in *CPAE*, vol. 7, document 60; emphasis in original.

43. "The work was vigorously continued after our departure, and the first year's income was about four times the five hundred thousand dollars which Mr. Brandeis had set as the maximum obtainable from the Jews of America": Chaim Weizmann, *Trial and Error: The Autobiography of Chaim Weizmann* (New York, 1949), 272–73.

44. Einstein to Max Planck, July 6, 1922: *CPAE*, vol. 13, document 266.

45. Travel Diary, February 8, 1923: *CPAE*, vol. 13, document 379.

46. Published in Albert Einstein, *About Zionism: Speeches and Letters*, ed. Leon Simon (New York, 1931), 57–60; republished as "Internal and External Effects (1927)" in *Einstein on Politics*, ed. David E. Rowe and Robert Schulmann (Princeton, 2007), 168–69.

47. Frederick Hermann Kisch, *Palestine Diary* (London, 1938), 31.

48. Travel Diary, February 13, 1923: *CPAE*, vol. 13, document 379.

49. Einstein to Felix Warburg, January 1, 1926; photocopy in Einstein Archives 37-729.

50. Einstein to Judah Magnes, September 9, 1925, Einstein Archives 36-895.

51. One of Einstein's practical suggestions for ending the separation was for "all Jewish children to be taught Arabic": Einstein to Hugo Bergmann, September 27, 1929, Einstein Archives 37-768.

52. Einstein to Weizmann, November 25, 1929, Einstein Archives 33-411.

53. Ibid.

54. First published in Einstein, *About Zionism*, 69–71; republished as "Creating a *Modus Vivendi* (August 1929)," in *Einstein on Politics*, 172–73. Weizmann expressed that resolve most keenly in Weizmann to Einstein, April 28, 1938, Einstein Archives 33-443.

55. "Creating a *Modus Vivendi* (August 1929)."

56. "Our Debt to Zionism," *New Palestine* 28, no. 16 (April 29, 1938): 2; republished in Albert Einstein, *Ideas and Opinions* (New York, 1954), and in *Einstein on Politics*, 299–302.

57. *New York World Telegram*, March 11, 1933; republished as "Political Manifesto" in *Einstein on Politics*, 269–70.

58. "Arbeitendes Palästina," ca. 1933; Einstein Archives 28-224. Published as "Working Palestine" in *The World As I See It*, 161–62.

59. Ibid.

60. "The state idea is not according to my heart. I cannot understand why it is needed, It is connected with many difficulties and a narrow-mindedness. I believe it is bad": "Testimony at a Hearing before the Anglo-American Committee of Inquiry on Jewish problems in Palestine and Europe," January 11, 1946, in *Ideas and Opinions*, 118–35; partially republished in *Einstein on Politics*, 340–44.

61. May 6–May 11, 1942, at the Biltmore Conference in New York City. The joint statement issued at the end of the meeting was known as the Biltmore Program and in addition called for unrestricted Jewish immigration to Palestine.

62. Einstein to Zvi Lurie, January 4, 1955, Einstein Archives 60-388.

63. Draft of projected telecast commemorating Israel Independence Day, Einstein Archives 28-1098; republished in *Einstein on Politics*, 506–7.

64. Statement to Israeli ambassador Abba Eban, November 18, 1952, Einstein Archives 28-943; published in Otto Nathan and Heinz Norden, eds., *Einstein on Peace* (New York, 1960), 571.

65. Einstein to Solovine, March 8, 1921: *CPAE*, vol. 12, document 85.

66. "Reply to Sumner Welles' article on the Atomic Bomb and World Government (January 1946)," Einstein Archives 28-719; republished in *Einstein on Politics*, 380–81.

Horace Kallen (1882–1974)

PRAGMATIC MODERNISM

Jacques Picard

TRANSLATED BY JEREMIAH M. RIEMER

IN DEBATES ABOUT RELATIONSHIPS BETWEEN GROUP IDENTITY AND CITIZENSHIP OR the nation and human rights, there is a well-known metaphor that illustrates William James's vision of a "pluralistic universe." In these debates, modern societies are described as an "orchestration of mankind" in which the timbre and tonality of every instrument, based on its substance and form, contributes to a harmonic "symphony of civilization." This musical metaphor illustrates the concept of cultural pluralism, coined and popularized by Horace Kallen in the 1910s and 1920s. Kallen presented the metaphor in an article for the weekly magazine the *Nation*, then later in a chapter in one of his many books, *Democracy versus the Melting Pot: A Study of American Nationality*, which he published out of concern about machinations of the Ku Klux Klan and right-wing nativists.[1]

Today, too, the concept of cultural pluralism and its concomitant musical metaphors are used to initiate the kinds of critical studies that turn to theories dealing with global migration, group identity, ethnic diversity, cultural anthropology, postcolonial studies, and transnational societies. Here Kallen is characterized as the creator or advocate of this concept, as if he himself were always playing several melodies on different instruments. This is Kallen as the thinker who inspired the philosophical movement of ethnic-cultural pluralism and a transnational America; as a prophet of American liberal Zionism; as the destroyer of illusions about Jewish or Christian ideas of chosenness and the opponent of all creeds' sacred missions; as a critic of big business and monopolistic capitalism; and as a post-Marxist, progressive thinker who anticipated communitarianism and an economy based on consumer cooperatives. Not least of all, Kallen embodies a version of Jewishness in which all these different aspects are bundled and fractured as in a prism, so as to bring to consciousness the boundaries between nationalism and pluralism.[2] To put this in terms of a musical metaphor (of the kind Manès Sperber[3] applies to a type of multitalented Jewish artist from Eastern Europe), this American philosopher

cited for his many faces appears like an *homme-orchestre*, a one-man band striking different tones; acting on different stages, mostly out in the open, occasionally in the background; somewhat obstinate and even manipulative, but ultimately pushed aside and soon forgotten as theories of pluralism starting in the 1970s were either radicalized or obscured.

The son of an Orthodox rabbi, Horace Kallen was born in Silesia in 1882 and came to the United States at a young age. He earned his doctorate in 1908 at Harvard, where he studied with William James, and was a protégé of John Dewey and Louis Brandeis. For a brief period he worked at Princeton and the University of Wisconsin, became a professor at the newly established New School for Social Research in New York City, and traveled in Europe and Israel. He died in 1974 in Palm Beach, Florida. That the perils and facets of a fragmented century found their way into his thinking (something that can also be gathered from his voluminous correspondence with academics, intellectuals, and politicians) is testimony to what makes Kallen such a contradictory figure in American Jewish thought. Philip Gleason noticed an "extreme sketchiness" and even "obscurity of language" in Kallen's writings, or sorts of ambiguities that characterize his different versions of modernity.[4] Roughly speaking, we might find here a meaningful distinction between different versions of modernity: a New World modernity as revealed—with different accentuations—in the American ideal of Zionism à la Brandeis and Kallen, in the kind of anthropology Boas aimed against racism, or in the aesthetic criticism and discoveries of the Harlem Renaissance and among European expatriates. And some modernists looked, from out of the apotheosis of bourgeois culture, for an interpretation of society and politics that surfaced in seemingly contradictory formulas concerning aesthetic *Sachlichkeit*, or narratives of "the new man," a new sort of nostalgic monumentality, or the disinhibiting tremors of fascism. These versions of modernity come to light on both sides of the Atlantic, though each was marked by its own peculiar specifications.

Liberal Zionism and the Language of Mythography

As Sarah Schmidt and Melvin Urofsky have shown, it was Horace Kallen who authored Louis Brandeis's Zionist program, presented in Pittsburgh in 1918. "Political and civil equality irrespective of race, sex, or faith, for all inhabitants of the land," was the first major point listed in a series of principles meant to guide the development of the Jewish nation in Palestine. Public access to education and scholarship for all inhabitants, common use of natural resources, and "the cooperative principle . . . applied as far as possible in the organization of all agricultural, industrial, commercial and financial undertakings" are additional items enumerated in Kallen's pragmatic utopia, which contemplated financing whatever was technically and economically feasible in the spirit of cooperative liberalism.[5] A visionary declaration, the Pittsburgh program strove to extend the American ideal to Zionism and believed in the power of this ideal to assert itself. It was about principles of equality and freedom that, as Kallen and Brandeis emphasized, would serve the cause of community building from economic and social welfare perspectives. What Kallen and Brandeis were seeking with their program was, above all, a set of new principles for a practical kind of Zionism. But European Zionists, whether in London and Warsaw or residing in New York, had a rather different view of things. Chaim Weizmann did not accept this kind of Bill of Rights for the Palestine project. Nor did the Jews who had immigrated to the United States, and who still had relatives back in Vilna, Bucharest, or Vienna, have much sympathy for principles like this. "It is sheer bunkum to assert that political and civil equality irrespective of race, sex, and faith, was one of the principles . . . which were the foundations laid down by our lawgivers and prophets for the Ancient Jewish state. . . . Whatever ideas our lawgivers and prophets had, they were not twentieth-century American democrats," is how Leon Simon, the translator of Ahad Ha'am's writing into English, characterized the gap between the European and American Zionists. "We are different, absolutely different; there is no bridge between Washington and Pinsk," Weizmann informed Brandeis. And Menachem Ussishkin added, "You have a goyish head, we have a Jewish heart."[6] Following the rupture between Weizmann and Brandeis in 1921, Kallen, the intellectual mind behind Brandeis's Zionism, left the organization along with his political mentor.

It was obvious that the universal ideal of "equality in difference" was prominent for Brandeis and Kallen and that Jewish nationalism came only second. For that reason they opposed the prevailing paradigm of political Zionism in Europe, which struck them as a nationalistic reproduction of the old ghetto. The failures of Kallen and of the political aspirations of American Zionism Brandeis-style harbor a number of historical ironies. The underlying assumption of liberal pluralism contained in this model was the foundation enabling European Jews who had migrated to the United States to profess a commitment to the Zionist ideal without thereby denying their own self-perceptions as loyal Americans. Kallen himself, after his version of Zionism failed politically, remained true to the ideals of the American Progressives, confined himself to philanthropic activities promoting practical development in Palestine, and commented on political events in a 1921 book.[7] Finally, in his 1958 publication *Utopians at Bay*, he recorded something he noticed on a trip to the young Israeli state—that politics and religion there were neither separated nor even sufficiently disentangled. For Kallen, this lapse seemed like the Fall of Man, as the Israeli Declaration of Independence of 1948 spoke first, at length and in a mythical language, about Jewish history and only toward the end, and very briefly, about civil and human rights. Noticing the contrast with the American Declaration of Independence from 1776, whose telos he saw in the Bill of Rights, Kallen was concerned about the conversion of older Jewish myths into a Zionist semantics, thus representing no real break with history. Furthermore Kallen read in the Zionist interpretation of the Arab question, and the aggressive reaction of Arab leaders, a sequel to the Jewish question in Europe, as yet another chapter in the uninterrupted European philosophy of history going back to Hegel and his epigones. Kallen insisted on an alternative: Just as it makes little sense to talk about *the* Jew, and bearing in mind how diverse Jews are inside Israel, so too it is crucial to remember that there is Arab diversity and no such thing as *the* Arab. "The numbers and varieties of associations that its [Israel's] men and women figure in, are their security against totalitarianism, whether political, theological, or theological-political"—on both sides of the frontlines.[8] That was it, the pragmatist ideal of Israel and its Arab neighbors, as a version of modernity, with egalitarian societies identifying themselves by the democratic pluralism of their cultures.

Coining "Cultural Pluralism"—between the Concave and the Cosmopolitan

Philosophically, the kind of pluralism employed by Kallen arises from the insight that the world consists of independent things that are different from and related to each other. The universe is plural, it coheres, and it does this in more than just one dimension; its reality is distributive, and that is why what matters is not acquiring truth but rather observing its diverse effects and weighing them against the fruits they yield.[9] "Consequences are the essential content of truth, error, and meaning," as Kallen summarizes the view of his mentor William James, known as "pragmatism."[10] Pragmatic philosophy was aimed not only against a Hegelian logic of knowledge and culture, with a teleological dialectics of philosophy of history leading toward a God proclaimed as *Weltgeist* (world spirit); it also amounted to an attempt at interpreting a host of secular revelations, protecting individuals from the disturbing turmoil of religious prophecies and mental irrationalism of the kind that Harold Bloom has described as characteristic of American religion at the end of the twentieth century.[11] For William James, that flight into a positive religiosity or into a substitute secular ideology (including national-theosophical monstrosities and autohypnotic tea parties) was something that should be prevented in the first place. His philosophical project of liberal empiricism reads like a hermeneutics of the numinous, the weird, the monstrous, and the maniacal, capable of gripping both individuals and groups. Yet—in contrast to Nietzsche and Freud—James keeps a window open to a metareligious or transcendental idealism, so as to make the confusing plurality of experiencing the world somewhat more tolerable for people. In this way, by making the concept of truth pragmatic, James inspired a generation of American intellectuals who, as his students (just like the students of John Dewey, his philosophical successor), searched for an answer to the world of modernity that was in a process of fragmentation. They came from different minorities in American society. And it was James's student Horace Kallen who was asked by his teacher before his death, in 1910, to be responsible for the publication of his last book.

Kallen and Alain Locke became acquainted at Harvard and both got scholarships to Oxford, where they arrived in 1907. Their longlasting friendship dates from this period, in spite of the differences in the ways they conceived the concept of pluralism. Kallen regarded the birth of the concept of cultural pluralism as a founding drama surrounding the ritual of the Thanksgiving dinner. He refused to accept a Thanksgiving invitation from the American Club in Oxford as long as Locke was excluded from the club owing to the black color of his skin. The two friends found refuge in Oxford's Cosmopolitan Club along with students from India, Ceylon, and Egypt. Back at Harvard, Kallen intervened against the racist machinations of American students who were opposed to Locke being awarded the Rhodes Scholarship. Locke left Oxford in order to study for a while in Berlin, and in 1911 he took a post at Howard University.[12] His situation—as an avowed Anglophile and loyal black man, as an anti-imperialist and pacifist, and as a cultural cosmopolitan and advocate of an

African American "racialism" in defense of a culture of the New Negro—was and remained delicate.[13] Kallen and Locke articulated the idea of cultural pluralism at the same time, around 1915, with the support of Randolph Bourne.[14] The concepts of pluralism and cultural pluralism, subject as they are to various displacements and alterations, were intermittently forgotten, only to reemerge de novo as a fad during and after World War II.[15] Today, once again, Kallen and other early American pluralists are mentioned as legitimating references in many different disciplines of a multiethnic and postmodernist cast.[16] And when the Jewish intellectual descendants of Horace Kallen express their "multicultural dilemma" and formulate their version of a "return of the exiled" for today, one may certainly suspect what a critic had already said back in 1974: "In the philosophy of cultural pluralism, secular Jews anxious to avoid assimilation discovered a rationale to justify their instincts."[17]

Between 1901 and 1920, fourteen and a half million people came to the United States—Catholics, Jews, and even Muslims, mostly from Southern and Eastern Europe. Forty percent of New York City's residents were foreign-born Americans. So all these early pluralists articulated their personal qualms about social conditions and racist and xenophobic reactions to immigration by searching for a way to answer both the popular "melting pot" formula (advocated by assimilationists) and the attacks launched by avowed racists (like Kenneth Roberts, who opposed assimilation and favored apartheid). Randolph Bourne, a student of Dewey, recognized that pragmatism contained a vital vision of a transnational America, a "cosmopolitan federation of national colonies" requiring that "all our idealism must be those of future social goals in which all can participate, the good life of personality lived in the environment of the Beloved Community."[18] Unlike the kind of monistic rationalizations offered by Kant and Hegel, the philosophy of pragmatism took into consideration the feelings and values of acting subjects and, by extension, of the cultural forms underlying their lives. This kind of message, owing to its cosmopolitan and pacifistic character, should be understood as an act of patriotism. Kallen was pleading—much as he had already done in the version of Zionism he had advocated—for a concept of statehood that distinguished between the idea of nationality and that of sovereignty, and he endorsed Switzerland as a genuinely modern alternative opposed to the tribalization of society that seemed so flagrant in a Europe plagued by nationalist rivalries, hatred, and wars.[19]

In retrospect, having experienced fascism, Nazism, communism, and apartheid, contemporary criticism has figured out how to clearly formulate the legacy of communitarian traditions as something that refers, according to Roberto Esposito, to the way the concept of "community" has drifted off into the realm of the mystical: "All the figures of identity, fusion, and endogamy that the representation of community will assume in modern political thought are nothing other than the unavoidable result of this first conceptual short-circuit. If the *communitas* is the escape or release from the individual subject, its myth is the interiorization of this exteriority, the representative doubling of its presence and the essentialization of its existence."[20] In this regard—the *concave* character of the "beloved community"—even the early pluralists ran up against the double-edged question of political reality as they searched for social and cultural answers to the new dynamics of society's industrialization and orientation toward productivity.

If Kallen's outlook on cultural pluralism from the first decades of the twentieth century had still been a retort to the idea of the melting pot, directed against radical assimilation by people of different heritages as popularized by Israel Zangwill's 1908 play *The Melting Pot*, he later replaced the critique James had once aimed at the "exaggerations" of philosophical monism with a critique of the newly emerging concept of totalitarianism or the totalitarian *Volksgemeinschaft* (the racist Nazi version of "ethnic community"). It was during the 1930s that some European intellectuals—Antonio Gramsci, Arthur Koestler, George Orwell, Elie Halevy, and others—started using the term "totalitarianism" to denote communism, fascism, and Nazism. Kallen did it in 1936 at the latest. We may not find such arguments, indebted to European circumstances, in Alain Locke's thought or writings. His hopes included, as George Hutchinson shows, the variegated and overlapping impulses of the Harlem Renaissance in art and literature, the New York movement that came to be known from 1925 onward under the name "Negro Renaissance" on both sides of the Atlantic.[21] Locke, along with Bernhard Stern in a 1942 book *When Peoples Meet: A Study in Race and Culture Contacts*, had brought together numerous intellectuals who, since the end of the nineteenth century, were turning their attention to the never-ending political topic of pluralism using arguments backed by scholarly authority.[22] He thus displayed, at the height of the war, his cosmopolitan view of a world in peace. This book lacked a chapter from Horace Kallen; it does, however, include one from another German-born Jew, Franz Boas, a leading voice among both Jewish and non-Jewish students of anthropology, who died the same year.

Pragmatism and Boasian Anthropology

There has long been a somewhat shadowy, silenced discussion about the Jewish origins of American anthropology and its identification with Jewish intellectuals. At the same time, it's hardly disputed that the early years of the "youthful" discipline of anthropology owed much to the liberal humanism of its founder, Franz Boas, and his students and followers. They claimed, with the help of empirical means, that no group or community can be superior to any other. The marginality of anthropological studies related to Jews and the fact that a large number of American anthropologists came from Jewish families—but only rarely used what Jonathan Boyarin called "Jewish resources"—were compatible with the prevailing idea at the time, namely, that one should write about "other" cultures rather than focus on one's own. This was also a strategy for acquiring scholarly authority.[23] No less risky was the fact that the young field of anthropology was perceived in political terms as part of Progressivism, prone to be attacked as "Jewish business."[24]

Boas initiated a paradigm shift when he ascribed human behavior to cultural and environmental influences rather than to biological determination.[25] The formation of "racial" groups was, according to Boas, a social rather than a biological phenomenon. Racial classifications generated from social and political motivations.[26] Talk of "race" is usually a question of class, the ascription of "color" a question of language. It is manifested in Karen Brodkin's recollection of her Yiddish-speaking grandparents' world when she characterizes the upward mobility of the second generation during the 1940s and 1950s by using the phrase "How Jews Became White."[27] This position also discredited the metaphor of "blood"—of blood as a mythical medium of differentiation—that could be found in the writings of German Jewish authors, from Heinrich Heine to Franz Rosenzweig. Boas—aware of being Jewish, coming from Germany[28]—formulated his rejection of the concept of race and eugenics policies by emphasizing the significance of language skills for human intelligence.[29] Language, along with the natural and social environment, was one of the decisive factors supporting the concept of culture that Boas argued for in his writings against apartheid, the Aryan and blood myths, and policies of eugenics.[30]

Boas was a destroyer of paradigms that governed scholarship and thinking in nineteenth-century society, as he deemed them incorrect owing to their epistemological inconsistencies, or put them in critical perspective whenever the underlying procedures were insufficiently indebted to inductive principles.[31] His methodological skepticism applied to all attempts at asserting generalizing "laws" or deterministic regularity in describing cultural, social, or historical processes. This placed him in stark contrast to the kind of early-twentieth-century thinking that Marvin Harris described as "[n]eo-Hegelian racist visions of national souls working their way toward ineffable glories."[32] Boas's insistence on the significance of language, culture, environment, and customs for the formation of a society of citizens is something one cannot overestimate. As Herbert S. Lewis has shown, it links Boasian anthropology to the tenets of pragmatism and pluralism and its major elements like diversity and the importance of the individual; rejection of determinisms, contingency, and chance; and, strikingly, James's "pluralistic universe." Pluralists, pragmatists, Boasians—they all accepted Darwin's nonteleological and antimechanistic view of evolution but strongly rejected Herbert Spencer's ideas of "evolutionism" and survivalist social progress.[33]

The mood in these American debates was still a long way from allowing for revision or even abandonment of concepts like race or color, which usually showed up in parallel; for that reason, postmodern critics were shortsighted when they blamed, for example, Boas and his combat against antisemitism for having been "another exploitation of colored people";[34] or Kallen for his saying that "men may change their clothes . . . they cannot change their grandfathers."[35] What proved fruitful for Kallen—in his version of pragmatism—was his link between social classes and justice, which he, in the spirit of the pluralists, associated with the concept of communitarianism and that served, according to him, as a buffer against xenophobia and racism. But Kallen doubted the always-vague vocabulary of culture and heritage. To guide political thinking in a different direction was something that could only be achieved through transformation of economic structures. This aspect of Kallen's thought, marking the transition from the Progressives to the New Dealers, enlisted the concept of totalitarianism used at the New School in the 1930s. In Kallen's problematic interpretation, fascism, Nazism, and communism showed up as "rivals" to a consumer economy and communitarian society, organized on the basis of individual choices in cooperatives.[36] Henry Ford—industrialist, automobile manufacturer, political figure, and a man susceptible to antisemitism and conspiracy myths—struck Kallen as the "archetypal producer," the problematic trendsetter for a new type of market-dominating big business, its monopolies, and its elitist racism. Against any American version of totalitarianism, Kallen picked up those foundations from the Scottish Enlightenment that led once to the formation of new industrial societies: the principles of science and technology. Kallen did not wish to see arts and sciences as the exclusive property of the privileged classes.[37] Far more crucial were the redistribution of resources, profits, and wealth facilitating opportunities to acquire or consume material and immaterial goods such as food, education, art, or health. What was needed, according to Kallen, were an integration of man and machine, a social welfare–oriented democratization of industry, participation in institutions, and thus an organized union to create a different reality—beyond race, blood, and color. Talent was a question of freedom.

In contrast to Marx—whom Kallen regarded as ingenious and a "thoroughly Jewish character"[38]—he substantiated the telos of liberation not on the basis of dialectical materialism but on a collaboration of intellect, technology, and organized interests for education and training and for cooperative forms of life. For this reason he also preferred banks owned by customers—and thus a credit system that would be organized in a co-operative fashion to the greatest extent possible.[39] He associated social change with the essence of communitarian liberalism or what is called "social democracy" in Europe today, which replaces status and class with a multiplicity of contracts, alliances, and numerous forms of cooperation in the traditions of the Scottish and American Enlightenment. The real movement of history could be found in the multiplication of groups that are consumers in cooperatives competing with each other, are aligned against and with each other, and who, as such, become participants in society's means of production. The nucleus of pragmatism should be a "free, responsible, and cooperative individualism" through which a variety of talents could reveal themselves.[40]

Against Chosenness and the Tribal Shrines of Big Judaism

Hence, not only did American "big business" look to Kallen like a false "nuclear dynamic" of capitalism; he had the same critical view of the "worker's economy" in the new state of Israel, which he visited a decade after its establishment.[41] His observations in the book *Utopians at Bay* transposed his American dream of the liberal communitarian welfare state to the state of Israel. Even if he did concede that this "socialist republic of farmers and workers"—embodied in the kibbutz, moshav, and Histadrut—was necessary at first, he remained skeptical about it. Histadrut, that remarkable conglomerate of industrial enterprises and trade unions, of distributors and insurance funds, "in fact cares about work only as a means of earning a livelihood in order to live a life; [but] life is not lived in earning but in spending, not in labor [only], but in the leisure which spends what the labor earns. . . . The 'religion of labor,' as an end in itself, has had for its paradoxical consequence an economy of consumption to which labor is a defective means."[42] Kallen the critic discerned an unfavorable tendency to be always concerned with "what is done for the membership, rather than with and by the membership." He saw similarities between the Histadrut and another institution, that of religious Orthodoxy in Israel. Each had its own leadership, rabbinate, hierarchy, and holy values, and each had a totalitarian grip on people's lives. He issued a strong warning against the consequences of Israel having a "state within a state," one run by the trade unions and another one run by the religious elites—and he employed arguments similar to ones he had used more than thirty years earlier when he depicted the rise of capitalist monopolies in the United States as damaging for social development.

The big unions and big religions were like big business: each gospel had its own shrines and its own courts, and each was always encumbered with a nucleus serving the reproduction of its canonized self.[43] In all, they were Big Judaism, to be criticized as forms of exceptionalism. The first thing Kallen repudiated in his critique was religious Orthodoxy. Not that he was trying to do something like supplant his father, an Orthodox rabbi, but he felt that these old schools of the Jews "make absolutely no concession to their environment but make their [own] environment wherever they go."[44] Kallen also found disturbing the Reform movement's interpretation of Judaism, which talked about Israel's exclusive mission as a "priestly people" and attributed—in the spirit of philosophical idealism—cultural superiority to its interpretation of religion. Kallen's solution to this dilemma of pluralism and chosenness postulated that American Jews should maintain their identity or peculiarity on the basis of cultural diversity and not on the presumption of a missionary-driven sense of superiority.[45] Kallen rejected, as he had already explained in 1910 in the journal *American Hebrew*, any conception of Judaism's exclusive mission or superiority. Notions of a Jewish or Christian or Islamic mission were merely compensatory dogmas serving to confirm competitive religions in their rivalry for mutual superiority or inferiority, or to confirm the necessity of their missions and their claims to hegemony.[46] Kallen's arguments, which undoubtedly owe much to William James and his psychological observation of religious phenomena, are close to Mordecai Kaplan, who in 1934, as an influential rabbi, argued against a theology of superiority and for replacing "mission" with a cultural "vocation" for Judaism: "Judaism is but one of a number of unique national civilizations guiding humanity towards its spiritual destiny. It has functioned as a civilization throughout its career, and it is only in that capacity [of vocational culture] that it can function in the future."[47]

What made Jews different and Jewishness multilayered, but could not justify an ontologically definable certainty about Jewish culture, were hard-to-fathom ingredients taken from conceptions of cultural pluralism, those conceptions having to do with cooperation among minorities who needed to find a way to fill anew the gaps in their selves—something characterized today as the problem of "identity." In Kallen's time we are still a long way from being able to fathom what drives the utterly secular hero of Howard Jacobson's recent novel *The Finkler Question* in the title character's quest for the beloved community: "Talking feverishly about being Jewish [is] being Jewish."[48] For Kallen, however, what mattered was the relationship between private and public ascription. Whether as an ethno-cultural group or as part of a religious movement, the function of a group and the choice of individuals about wanting to count as part of a group required no rationale: "The fiddler has no 'mission' to fiddle, he is no more responsible for his nature than the perfect frog or the lily in the field. He fiddles by instinct, and because this happens incidentally to be also a social service, of use to others, these others protect, reward and honor him."[49] This means, as Daniel Greene has noted about Kallen, that a sense of mission and chosenness is not the actual solution to the so-called Jewish problem. These things are, rather, the actual catalysts of the problem itself.[50]

In the final analysis Kallen arrived at the view that a position banking on the old, tribalistic evocations of the Jewish question, on the struggle against antisemitism, or on the invocation of blood—or compensating for itself via the ideal of chosenness, superiority, or a sense of mission, or even just simply continuing to hope for a mystical fulfillment of a messianic promise—was not acceptable in the modern world and, above all, not very sustainable. Here the human talents that modernity offered were being woefully squandered. For this was merely playing with the old reproductive patterns as they may be encountered in the religiously enshrouded gospel of nationalism in Western—and, no less often, in non-Western—societies.[51] But the critique of these gospels was what constituted modernity and, indeed, what was Jewish about modernity.

Notes

1. "Horace M. Kallen: Democracy versus the Melting Pot: A Study of American Nationality," in *The Nation*, February 18 and 25, 1915, 190–94 and 217–20; published as a book in 1924 under the same title, where the musical metaphor appears on 116–17.

2. Here I emphasize the following articles dealing with Kallen over the last several years: Noam Pianko, "The True Liberalism of Zionism: Horace Kallen, Jewish Nationalism, and the Limits of American Pluralism," in *American Jewish History* 94, no. 4 (2008): 299–329; Daniel Greene, "A Chosen People in a Pluralist Nation: Horace Kallen and the Jewish-American Experience," in *Religion and American Culture, Journal of Interpretation* 16, no. 2 (2006): 161–94.

3. Sperber applied this characterization to Simche Schwarz (b. 1900 Czernowitz–d. 1974 Buenos Aires), sculptor, painter, musician, poet, singer, puppeteer, cabaret artist, and critic; compare my book *Gebrochene Zeit: Jüdische Paare im Exil* (Zurich, 2009), 145–218.

4. Philip Gleason, "American Identity and Americanization," in *The Harvard Encyclopedia of American Ethnic Groups*, ed. Stephan Thernstrom (Cambridge, 1980), 31–58, quoted 43.

5. Sarah Schmidt, *Horace M. Kallen: Prophet of American Zionism* (New York, 1995), 107–46; Melvin I. Urofsky, *Louis D. Brandeis* (New York, 2009), 405–29.

6. Cited in Schmidt, *Horace M. Kallen*, 138; Walter Laquer, *A History of Zionism* (New York, 1972), 477; George Berlin, "The Brandeis-Weizmann Dispute," in *American Jewish Historical Quarterly* 60 (September 1970): 37–69.

7. Horace M. Kallen, *Zionism and World Politics: A Study in History and Social Psychology* (Garden City, NY and Toronto, 1921).

8. Horace M. Kallen, *Utopians at Bay* (New York, 1958), 107.

9. William James, *A Pluralistic Universe: Hibbert Lectures at Manchester College on the Present Situation in Philosophy* (London, 1909); *Pragmatism, and Four Essays from "The Meaning of Truth,"* ed. Ralph Barton (New York, 1955); *Some Problems of Philosophy*, ed. Horace M. Kallen (New York, 1911); *The Philosophy of William James Drawn from His Own Works*, ed. Horace M. Kallen (New York, 1925).

10. Horace M. Kallen, "Introduction," in *The Philosophy of William James* (New York, 1825), 9.

11. William James, *The Varieties of Religious Experience: A Study on Human Nature* (New York and London. 1902); in addition, see Peter Sloterdijk, "Chancen im Ungeheuren, Notizen zum Gestaltwandel des Religiösen in der modernen Welt im Anschluss an einige Motive bei William James," in *William James: Die Vielfalt religiöser Erfahrung* (Frankfurt, 1997), 11–34. Harold Bloom, *The American Religion: The Emergence of a Post-Christian Nation* (New York, 1992).

12. Louis Menand, *The Metaphysical Club: A Story of Ideas in America* (New York, 2001), 389–92. Compare Ira Eisenstein, "Dialogue with Dr. Horace M. Kallen," in *What I Believe and Why—Maybe: Essays for the Modern World* (New York, 1971), 279.

13. He described himself in 1935; see Alain Locke, "Values and Imperatives," in *American Philosophy Today and Tomorrow*, eds. Sidney Hook and Horace Kallen (New York, 1935), 312.

14. It is an open question whether the idea was shaped by their experiences in Europe, initiated by James and Dewey, inspired by Booker T. Washington, or even if it was some distant echo of James Madison's argument that the state and national interests can be incompatible. Moreover, as Isaiah Berlin has shown, there definitely were early modern European precursors who inspired these ideas, including Giambattista Vico, the "true father both of the modern concept of culture and of what one might call cultural pluralism," along with Johann Gottfried Herder. See Isaiah Berlin, *The Crooked Timber of Humanity: Chapters in History of Ideas* (London, 1990), 59.

15. Werner Sollors, "A Critique of Pure Pluralism," in *Reconstructing American Literary History* (Cambridge, 1986), 269; Leonard Dinnerstein and David Reimers, *Ethnic Americans:*

A History of Immigration (New York, 1998). Compare Gerald Meyer, "The Cultural Pluralist Response to Americanization: Horace Kallen, Randolph Bourne, Louis Adamic, and Leonard Covello," in *Socialism and Democracy* 22, no. 3 (2008), online: http://sdonline.org/48/the -cultural-pluralist-response-to-americanization-horace-kallen-randolph-bourne-louis-adamic-and -leonard-covello/.

16. For example, see Jennie Wang, "Tripmaster Monkey: Kingston's Postmodern Representation of a New 'China Man,'" in *MELUS* 20, no. 1, special issue on Chinese-American Literature (1995): 101–14, with a reference to Kallen: "Can a Chinese be an American, and an American have Chinese features? Can a Chinese American writer create a character undeniably American?" (102)

17. Alan Guttman, *The Jewish Writer in America* (New York, 1971), 93.

18. Randolph Bourne, "Trans-National America," in *Atlantic Monthly* 118 (July 1916): 86–97. The concept of the "beloved community" was something Bourne took over from Josiah Royce, a colleague of William James at Harvard.

19. Horace M. Kallen, *The Structure of Lasting Peace: An Inquiry into the Motives of War and Peace* (Boston, 1918–73); and Kallen, "Democracy versus the Melting Pot," 114. See also Jonathan M. Hansen, *The Lost Promise of Patriotism: Debating American Identity 1890–1920* (Chicago and London, 2003), 131–84.

20. Roberto Esposito, *Communitas: The Origin and Destiny of Community* (Stanford, 2009), 15.

21. Alain Locke, "Introduction," in *The New Negro*, ed. Alain Locke (1925; New York, 1968), 3–16; George Hutchinson, *The Harlem Renaissance in Black and White* (Cambridge and London, 1995), especially 63–93. See too *The Cambridge Companion to the Harlem Renaissance*, ed. George Hutchinson (Cambridge, 2007), 2.

22. Alain Locke and Bernhard J. Stern, eds., *When Peoples Meet: A Study in Race and Culture Contacts* (New York and Philadelphia, 1946), reprinted 1949; after the first edition from 1942, there was a revised edition published in 1946.

23. Leonhard B. Glick, "Types Distinct from Our Own: Franz Boas on Jewish Identity and Assimilation," in *American Anthropologist* 84, no. 3 (1992): 545–65; Benjamin Orlove, "Surfacing: Thoughts on Memory and the Ethnographer's Self," in *Jews and Other Differences: The New Jewish Cultural Studies*, eds. Jonathan Boyarin and Daniel Boyarin (Minneapolis and London, 1997), 1–29; Mitchell B. Hart, "Franz Boas as German, American, and Jew," in *German-Jewish Identities in America*, eds. Christof Mauch and Joseph Salmons (Madison, 2003), 88–105.

24. For more on this, see Gelya Frank, "Jews, Multiculturalism, and Boasian Anthropology," in *American Anthropologist* 99, no. 4 (1997): 731–41.

25. George W. Stocking Jr., "The Basic Assumptions of Boasian Anthropology," in *A Franz Boas Reader: The Shaping of American Anthropology, 1883–1911*, ed. George W. Stocking Jr. (Chicago and London, 1974), 1–20.

26. Initially Boas had developed his arguments, encountering mighty opposition from the prevailing biological determinism of the period, within the framework of physical anthropology, in order to undermine stereotypes and prejudices about "race" and its implications. Boas and his German mentor and friend, Rudolf Virchow, subscribed to the Lamarckian tradition of research. On Virchow, see Constantin Goschler, *Rudolf Virchow: Mediziner, Anthropologe, Politiker* (Stuttgart, 2002). On the Lamarckian tradition, see Eva Jablonka and Marion J. Lamb, *Evolution in Four Dimensions: Genetic, Epigenetic, Behavioral, and Symbolic Variations in the History of Life* (Cambridge, 2005).

27. Karen Brodkin, "How Jews Became White," in *Race*, eds. Steven Gregory and Roger Sanjek (New Brunswick, 1994), 78–102. The expression "making white" has been applied to many groups: see, e.g., Noel Ignatiev, *How the Irish Became White* (New York, 1995), esp. 62–91, where the author writes about "how the Party of Jefferson became the Party of Van Buren, and the role it played in making the Irish white."

28. Boas had been a member of the Society for Ethical Culture, inaugurated by Felix Adler in New York, a nondenominational offshoot of Reform Judaism. See Benny Kraut, *From Reform Judaism to Ethical Culture: The Religious Evolution of Felix Adler* (Cincinnati, 1979).

29. Veronika Lipphardt, *Biologie der Juden: Jüdische Wissenschaftler über "Rasse" und Vererbung 1900–1933* (Göttingen, 2008); John M. Efron, *Defenders of the Race: Jewish Doctors and Race Science in Fin-de-Siècle Europe* (New Haven and London, 1994); Caspar Battegay, *Das andere Blut: Gemeinschaft im deutsch-jüdischen Schreiben 1830–1930* (Cologne, 2011).

30. Franz Boas, *Anthropology and Modern Life* (1928; New York, 1962); and Franz Boas, *Aryans and Non-Aryans* (New York, 1934).

31. Werner Kummer, "Franz Boas und die antievolutionistische Wende in Anthropologie, Ethnologie und Linguistik," in *Franz Boas 1858–1942: Ein amerikanischer Anthropologe aus Minden*, ed. Volker Rodekamp (Bielefeld, 1994), 39–54; Bernd Weiler, *Die Ordnung des Fortschritts: Zum Aufstieg und Fall der Fortschrittsthese in der "Jungen" Anthropologie* (Bielefeld, 2006), 296–365.

32. Marvin Harris, *The Rise of Anthropological Theory* (New York, 1968), 272. For more, see Paul Gilroy, *Against Race: Imagining Political Culture beyond the Colour Line* (Cambridge and London, 2000).

33. Herbert S. Lewis, "Boas, Darwin, and Anthropology," in *Current Anthropology* 42, no. 3 (2001): 381–406.

34. For a defense of Boas see Herbert S. Lewis, "The Passion of Franz Boas," in *American Anthropologist* 103, no. 2 (2001): 447–67.

35. Thus John Higham, who readily talks about "white ethnocentrism" and ultimately surfs on the old conceptual continuum of "race" and "color"; compare John Higham, *Send These to Me: Jews and Other Immigrants in Urban America* (New York, 1975), 208. Noam Pianko and Eric Goldstein, by contrast, have undertaken an accurate interpretation of the historical context in that they explain Kallen's ambiguity. Compare citations from Pianko, "The True Liberalism of Zionism," in *American Jewish History* 94, no. 4 (2008): 308.; Eric L. Goldstein, *The Price of Whiteness: Jews, Race, and American Identity* (Princeton, 2006), 171–78.

36. Horace M. Kallen, *The Decline and Rise of the Consumer: A Philosophy of Consumer Cooperation* (New York and London, 1936), 392 and 407.

37. Horace Kallen, *Education, the Machine, and the Worker: An Essay in the Psychology of Education in Industrial Society* (New York, 1925), 5–6.

38. Cited in Schmidt, *Horace M. Kallen*, 26.

39. Initially, to be sure, Kallen and some Progressives had once admired Lenin and early Italian fascism, movements that seemed to be acting in the spirit of Mazzini's Young Italy. See Everett Helmut Akam, *Transnational America: Cultural Pluralist Thought in the Twentieth Century* (Lanham, MD, 2002), 94–95.

40. Quoted in Kallen, *Decline and Rise of the Consumer*, 434–35; quoted in Kallen, *Utopians at Bay*, 211.

41. Much of what he said about Israel in 1958 he had already formulated in 1925. Compare Kallen, *Education, Machine, and Worker*; in addition, *Utopians at Bay*, 207–12.

42. Quoted in Kallen, *Utopians at Bay*, 207–12.

43. Quoted in ibid.

44. Letter from Kallen to I. B. Lipson, cited in Greene, *A Chosen People*, 165.

45. Horace M. Kallen, "Judaism, Hebraism, Zionism," in *American Hebrew*, June 24, 1910; reprinted in Kallen, *Judaism at Bay: Essays toward the Adjustment of Judaism to Modernity* (New York, 1932), 28–41.

46. Horace M. Kallen, "Can Judaism Survive in the United States," in Kallen, *Judaism at Bay*, 177–220, especially 181–84. The argument implicitly buttressed the formation of a new covenant among the public denominations of Catholics, Jews, and secular humanists opposed to the hegemony of Protestants denoted as "white" in the 1920s; on this see José Casanova, *Public Religions in the Modern World* (Chicago, 1994), 170.

47. Mordecai M. Kaplan, *Judaism as a Civilization: Toward a Reconstruction of American-Jewish Life* (1934; Philadelphia and New York, 1981), 180.

48. Howard Jacobson, *The Finkler Question* (New York, 2010), 275.

49. Quotation in Kallen, *Judaism, Hebraism, Zionism*, 35.

50. Cited in Greene, *Chosen People in a Pluralist Nation*, 161–94, esp. 163–71.

51. See William R. Hutchinson and Hartmut Lehmann, eds., *Many Are Chosen: Divine Election in Western Nationalism* (Minneapolis, 1994).

16

Franz Kafka (1883–1924)

WRITING IN MOTION

Galili Shahar

TRANSLATED BY SUSANN CODISH

FRANZ KAFKA LOVED TO TRAVEL. HE WROTE ABOUT MANY OF HIS TRAVELS IN LET-
ters, postcards, and diaries. As for the trips he did not take, he substituted these
with literary sketches and exercises. A trip to the United States was replaced by the
unfinished novel *Amerika* (*The Man Who Disappeared*), and a trip to Palestine was
converted into his love letters to Felice Bauer as well as Hebrew lessons. Traveling for work, recreation, and convalescence thus turned into literary events in his
journals. But to some extent, traveling for Kafka also expressed a central experience
of the new world—the experience of modernity.

Travel and Writing

Kafka traveled mostly through Central Europe. He never, in fact, left the continent of
his birth. He usually traveled by train; he saw the sea three times, and sailed on steam-
ships. Some of his travels took him to large cities—Paris, Zurich, Vienna, Budapest,
and Berlin—and twice he journeyed to Italian resort towns. But most of these trips
brought him to convalescent homes. These were obviously his main destinations
during his illness, which finally caused his death at a sanitarium near Vienna in 1924.

On his trips, Kafka liked visiting the theater and opera, museums, art galleries,
bookstores, casinos, and brothels. He would usually stay in hotels and take his
meals at vegetarian restaurants. Most of his time was spent roaming the streets,
conversing, reading the newspaper, and writing. At sanitaria, he would sometimes
also exercise, swim, or rest while in nature. But in all his travels, he paid attention
to movement, the road, and the landscape flitting through the windows. Kafka's
travel writings, too, hinge on movements and paths, main roads, detours, and paths
of return. His writing is a journey.

A miniature sketch of travel opens Kafka's diaries:

The onlookers go rigid when the train goes past.[1]

This single, solitary line adorns the first page of Kafka's 1909 diary dedicated to travel sketches. Perhaps this line, like other lines and paragraphs in the early pages of the diary, should have been the topic sentence of a story or marked the beginning of a writing experiment. After all, this was Kafka's reason for keeping a diary — literary experimentation. This brief sentence demands further attention despite, or perhaps because of, its initiality or the fact that it never found continuation or completion. Even the line's placement — at the top of the page of the diary — could have hinted at its contents: the motive/the motor, literature's principle of movement. In this embryonic state, the line embodies the encounter between body and script taking place in the realm of the machine — the passing train.

Before we read the line, we must first note the sentence form: it is complete, contained, and final, but at the same time only a part or sliver of a missing work, a remnant of a story not yet written. "The onlookers go rigid when the train goes past" hints at a world of fragments. And the fragment is one of the hallmarks of Kafka's writing: the short story, autarchic, enclosed, sealed like a riddle, but at the same time totally open, waiting to be written. After being severed from its context or, in this case, because it precedes its context, the fragment stands as a shard, a part of a whole, a hint. The first line in Kafka's diary already hints at a poetics that avoids grand, comprehensive images, choosing instead to describe the world from its broken, unfinished side. There is, however, something essential in the fact that much of Kafka's literary legacy consists of collections of isolated sentences, beginnings of stories, aphorisms, and other fragments of prose. Kafka's fragments are not only evidence of difficulties in writing, hesitation, failures, and obsessive periods of erasing, nor are they merely proof of the experimental nature of his literature. Rather, the fragment is an autonomous literary form appropriate in every way to a linguistic consciousness of crisis.

A minor drama lies at the heart of this fragmentary first line, "The onlookers go rigid when the train goes past." The moving train causes the onlookers to freeze, effectively paralyzing them. The onlookers go rigid at the sight of the machine. This brief description seems to epitomize a perspective on the fate of the living body in a technical age in which the movement of a train forces people into a state of shock. The movement of the train creates a sphere of trauma, of suspended consciousness in which time and space freeze and the body goes rigid. The passing train embodies not only the principle of motion but also that of epistemological crisis. The appearance of the train is beyond what can be perceived: the speed, the power, and the immediacy of its appearance impact the criteria of cognition. The sentence structure of the line, "The onlookers go rigid when the train goes past," can thus be understood in light of Walter Benjamin's "dialectic in standstill."[2] It is a sentence constructed as an experience of shock, suspension, and awe, a silent moment of attention in the face of reality. According to this reading, the still and silent state of the subject is not only a psychological condition, a momentary collapse or crisis of the psyche, but rather — ironically — a fertile moment of consciousness. The rigidity, the state in which the subject rests, is the moment the gaze is born. The spectator going rigid is in suspension, but it is precisely the fact that one has been forced to stop that teaches one to look, take notice, critique. Thus Kafka's line implies that taking a critical stance is possible even in the technical era: the awestruck spectator, even if unable to stop the running trains wreaking havoc on the world, embodies a refusal

to go along. The spectator's body turns in on itself in silence, but this silence is louder than the roar of the machine. Kafka's fragments in their brokenness thus also express a motion of opposition or resistance in the new sphere of movement.

The train travel in Kafka's diary justifies further readings. The "passing train," for example, cannot be divorced from a critical review of the concept of territory: the train crosses borders, rides through settlements and territories, leaves one's domicile, and abandons one's homeland, marking deterritorialized paths and routes of *Unheimlichkeit*. The "passing train" is a marker of emigration. Emigrants swept up in journeys in *Amerika* are the offspring of that train trip. Kafka's writing is a journey.

The Body and the Script

Kafka's manuscripts are suffused with motion that is difficult to separate from the technical era's concepts of time and speed. In fact, every set of writing reflects a fundamental tension between motion and rest. The script is fundamentally built on a play of signs, exchanges, and new combinations of letters. But in Kafka's world, the syntax of writing has internalized the movement of the train, and perhaps this is one of his literary innovations: the creation of the concept of a script that matches modernity's laws of motion.

The relationship between travel and script is, in Kafka's world, embodied by the traveler. This figure inherits the fate of the Wandering Jew, familiar from Christian folk tales of the new era. According to legend, the Jew was cursed with wandering because he jeered at the suffering of Christ on his way to the crucifixion and refused Christ's request to rest at his doorstep. The curse supposedly became the lot of all Jews, wandering the world hither and yon, never finding any rest, for denying the Messiah.[3] The traces of this legend can be discerned in the biography of the traveler in "A Country Doctor," doomed to travel naked ad infinitum, without even a nightshirt, as if his journey were a return to humankind's natural state. Among Kafka's travelers, the hunter Gracchus stands out: an unwilling mariner, the patron of seafarers, sailing for 1,500 years in a ghost ship, after falling from a cliff in Germany's Black Forest. The hunter, cast from the land of German folk stories, has since then wandered through all nations of the world without ever finding any rest. He has neither a place of his own in this world nor a portion in the world to come. His background is familiar to all, and now, says the hunter to his interlocutor, he is even discussed in the newspapers and elevators, and his story is being disseminated with hitherto unknown speed via telegrams and trains.[4] Gracchus embodies the concept of movement reflected in nature's cycles and sidereal motion, internalized in the life of commerce, soldiers' parades, and history books. His movement now revolves in the machines of the modern era. To understand this traveler, a biographical hint may be necessary. Kafka took the hunter's name, Gracchus, from the Italian, in which the word refers to a kind of blackbird, crow, or raven. In Czech, the word *kavka* is a jackdaw, a small species of crow. Thus, the hunter, the eternal seafarer and emigrant, bears the writer's surname—the name of the father.

We sought allusions to the principle of the journey that engenders Kafka's bodies of writing in the "passing train." Traveling by train generates states of silence in which Kafka draws tiny portraits of travelers and spins new yarns of emigrant life.

It is not coincidental that Kafka used to copy travelers' likenesses in his travel diaries alongside descriptions of the landscape, perspectives, and concepts of motion. Many of these sketches are begun at the railway station and in the cars where he discovers the traveler's body. He then describes that body, the face that goes with it, poses, gestures, items of clothing, the traveler's slips of the tongue and whispers. Kafka often encounters Jews among the travelers. The Jewish traveler is a body whose portrait, languages, and story he joyfully copied into his travel journals as if they were preliterary plans, drafts of a picaresque novel. A few of his travel sketches seem to indicate an internalization of anti-Jewish figures and stereotypes common in fin de siècle Europe. Antisemitic figures were part of his literary dramatization paraphernalia. Still, one must not overemphasize their place in fashioning Kafka's philosophical or literary world or forget the ambivalent character of the Jewish travelers. Other travel sketches show a generous measure of curiosity, empathy, and sense of closeness to his fellow Jewish travelers. On a journey to Milan in the summer of 1912, Kafka discovers the figure of "a young Italian woman whose otherwise Jewish face becomes non-Jewish in profile."[5] Her father, "a man with a hooked nose," is seated next to her. Kafka, in describing the young woman's nose, adds that "hers was 'curved gently' and was therefore 'more Jewish.'" The "Jewish nose" Kafka discovers on this trip is physiognomic evidence but also a metonymy for the body of literature born on the road.

In other travel sketches, Kafka rewrote tiny humoresques and parodies about Jews gathering in train cars. He imagines finding among them well-known figures and terrible manners, and listens avidly to their stories. In Paris, for example, Kafka meets a Jewish goldsmith, newly arrived from Krakow. "He has long, curly hair," and "very bright eyes, a gently curving nose."[6] The Jewish traveler describes the new world, the fantasy called "America." But, as Kafka notes, he speaks an odd German: "His German was disturbed by an English pronunciation and English expressions."[7] The Jew from Krakow is a traveling body whose history, jokes, and language output exemplify the birth of a subgenre of travel prose: a literature of characters speaking garbled German.

In Kafka's travel sketches, the Jewish travelers still appear by name and description. Kafka notes their points of departure and countries of birth, the cities they come from, the languages that swirl through the train cars. But in the literary works, and in the chapters in *Amerika*, the traveler leaves his origins behind. Karl Roßmann, the novel's protagonist who gets caught up in journeys through the new continent, is happy to get rid of his past. He has been cast out of his family, his passport lost. Finally, when he is accepted into the Nature Theater of Oklahoma, he goes so far as to change his name. The traveler gets a taste of freedom. So writes Kafka in his diary:

> Sit in a train, forget the fact, and live as if you were at home; but suddenly recollect where you are, feel the onward-rushing power of the train, change into a traveler, take a cap out of your bag, meet your fellow travelers with more sovereign freedom, with more insistence, let yourself be carried toward your destination by no effort of your own, enjoy it like a child, become a darling of the women, feel the perpetual attraction of the window, always have at least one hand

extended on the window sill. Same situation, more precisely stated: Forget that you forgot, change in an instant into a child traveling by itself on an express train around whom the speeding, trembling car materializes in its every fascinating detail as if out of a magician's hand.[8]

The journey is not only the movement of being released from a place but also a movement of dismissal from debts and duties. The traveler leaves his sins behind, forgetting for a long time his obligations and origins. Like Karl Roßmann, the carefree traveler journeying with his immigrant friends at the Nature Theater of Oklahoma through America, this traveler too sits in a "trembling car" of an express train and "forgets that he forgets."[9] His memory vanishes as, finally, does his name, and he ceases being a man of guilt. Kafka's travel notes, which begin with sketches of frozen bodies, and express an ambiguous self-reflection of being Jewish, sometimes continue as a movement of freedom from one's origins and the withdrawal of all charges until the birth of a new attention. This movement is well documented in the text "The Wish to Be a Red Indian" from the collection *Contemplation*:

> If one were only an Indian, instantly alert, and on a racing horse, leaning against the wind, kept on quivering jerkily over the quivering ground, until one shed one's spurs, for there needed no spurs, threw away the reins, for there needed no reins, and hardly saw the land before one was smoothly shorn heath when horse's neck and head would be already gone.[10]

This fragment does not seem to display a racing horse riding through the lines, but rather an express train. Another example of this movement being imprinted in the syntax of Kafka's writing is found in "Up in the Gallery," which belongs to Kafka's circus prose. This is a story made of two long, breathless sentences that refuse to stop; it tells of the adventures of a horse rider in the ring and reveals to the reader the same movement of script in the technical era—the era of the trains. The acrobat, like the traveler, is a body-script embodying movement, hovering, and tremors. But what used to be the exclusive province of the acrobat—the absolute motion, the human leap of death—is now the task of the machine.

This relationship is made beautifully apparent in "First Sorrow," also part of Kafka's circus oeuvre.[11] The story describes a trapeze artist who insists on remaining on his trapeze, suspended from the ceiling of a variety theater day and night. When traveling from one city to another, the trapeze artist would sleep on the luggage netting in the train's luggage compartment, thus preserving his unique weightless motion that seems to exist beyond gravity. One day, he loses his equanimity during a train journey and, for the first time, sinks into despondency. It is during the train ride that the entire advantage of the athletic body is effaced; the acrobat's feats are now doomed to be forgotten. What use is the acrobat's body in the age of the rapid machine? The story of the acrobat would seem to contain yet another parable about the dialectic of Enlightenment,[12] an explanation of the destructive move of modernity, written this time in the world of circus artists as a fable about the waning of the human body in the technical era. In the story of the trapeze artist, as in the story of the former ape in "A Report to the Academy," Kafka spins a modern tale about the sacrifice of athleticism and the birth of the machine myth. Like the hunger artist, in whom no one takes any interest anymore and whose days of fasting pass in vain and disappear from the calendar until his body is finally eradicated, so too do the acrobats mourn the death of the body's artistry.[13]

We learned that the journey by train establishes a new perspective at the core of Kafka's literature. The "passing train" is the machine rewriting the order of things and drawing new outlines in the world of nature. In its passage, familiar landscapes are rewritten as telegrams. Nature itself becomes a message: a short, quick burst, coming and going in the blink of an eye. Riding the train is an allegory of the technical world as such. The train affords new routes, excavates chasms, and bridges valleys. The ride is an opening ceremony, kicking off the question of existence in the modern era.

The following citation from the fragment "The Nature Theater of Oklahoma" also testifies to the horizons of the journey in Kafka's literary world:

> The first day they travelled through a high range of mountains. Masses of blue-black rock rose in sheer wedges to the railway line, even craning one's neck out of window, one could not see their summits; narrow, gloomy, jagged valleys opened out and one tried to follow with a pointing finger the direction in which they lost themselves; broad mountain streams appeared, rolling in great waves down to the foot-hills and drawing with them a thousand forming wavelets, plunging underneath the bridges over which the train rushed; and they were so near that the breath of coldness rising from them chilled the skin of one's face.[14]

A Blackbird: The German, the Jewish

In a 1911 diary entry Kafka treats a new compromise of travel in the age of trains. In it he discusses the travel records of the German author Johann Wolfgang von Goethe:

> Goethe's observations on his travels [are] different from today's because made from a mail-coach, and with the slow changes of the region, develop more simply and can be followed much more easily even by one who does not know those parts of the country. A calm, so-to-speak pastoral form of thinking sets in. Since the country offers itself unscathed in its indigenous character to the passengers in a wagon, and since highways too divide the country much more naturally than the railway lines to which they perhaps stand in the same relationship as do rivers to canals, so too the observer need do no violence to the landscape and he can see systematically without great effort.[15]

Goethe's travel journals were written around the year 1800 in the age of the mail-coaches, which made their way over dirt tracks at a speed that never exceeded 7 kilometers an hour and covered at most 20 to 25 kilometers per leg before being forced to stop and rest.[16] The speed of the mail-coach allows a "pastoral form of thinking" to occur, one that Kafka compares to the "rapid observation" of the era of trains. The mail-coach and steam engine are means of transportation that not only create utterly different modes of travel and contact with nature but also utterly different conditions for observation and writing.

The comparison with Goethe's diaries, letters, and autobiographical essays recurs time and again in Kafka's writing. Goethe is one of the great symbols of German literature: a poet, playwright, essayist, critic, and memoirist whose work shaped modern German language and poetry. His diaries, especially his *Italian Journey*, generated a distinct new literary genre. Goethe's influence extended to Kafka, who wildly admired his predecessor and viewed him as his literary forefather. At the same time, Kafka was also keenly aware of the heavy yoke of his literary ancestry and had plans to write an essay on "Goethe's terrible nature."[17] Kafka's special bond to Goethe's work (to German classicism and European literature in general) is revealed by a brief comment in a diary entry from late December 1911. The entry begins with a comment on "the literatures of the minor nations," such as Jewish and Czech literature flourishing in Eastern and Central Europe and trying to pave their own way in the shadow of the "great literatures"—that is, Russian and German. Minor literature, writes Kafka, is "the diary of a nation," a work that provides a community with an identity, a sense of confidence and pride. Furthermore, such literature expresses "political carefulness." Minor literature is defensive in the face of a hostile environment, withdraws to its borders, and internalizes the stranger only through reflections. Minor literature presents the antithesis between fathers and sons in a delicate manner and describes national failures with forgiveness. Minor national literatures, Kafka goes on to say, are well preserved, because the communities commit themselves always to study them.[18] Minor literatures do not have great talents, but this is precisely the reason they are more vital than the literatures that exist in the shadow of great writers. Small nations, Kafka writes, accord their own writers greater honor and yearn for books, magazines, literary schools of thought, and debates.[19]

But suddenly, in the middle of the diary entry devoted to small national literatures, which touches also on Jewish literature and language, Kafka is swept into a description of "a circumcision in Russia." The rendering of the ritual induction into the "Jewish body" (through circumcision) succeeds the description of the "Jewish writing" (as minor literature). Kafka describes the bed where the new mother lies with her infant: her room is bedecked with slates inscribed with kabbalistic formulae to protect the mother and child from evil spirits. Every evening, a dozen or so children come into the room, stand around the bed, and together chant the Shema prayer ("Hear, O Israel, the Lord our God, the Lord is one"). The circumcision itself is attended only by relatives and friends. The mohel (ritual circumciser), Kafka goes on, usually a red-nosed drunkard with bad breath, concludes his work with an oral gesture—the sucking of the circumcised member.[20] The description of the Jewish body's circumcision is parallel to the form of a minor literature: in both cases, Kafka speaks of enclosed spheres of communities defending themselves in a hostile environment using written systems, whether symbols, words, or prayers. The circumcision, too, the marking of the Jewish body, is an act of writing: the Jewish body is written with the mohel's knife. The mohel, like the ritual scribe and the secular writer, is also a "word" (*milah*) artist.[21]

Kafka describes in his diary the act of minor writing, but it is one that stands in relationship to world literature, the literature of Goethe. He says:

Goethe probably retards the development of the German language by the force of his writing. Even though prose style has often traveled away from him in the interim, still, in the end, as at present, it returns to him with strengthened yearning and even adopts obsolete idioms found in Goethe but otherwise without any particular connection with him, in order to rejoice in the completeness of its unlimited dependence.[22]

Goethe is one of those tremendously gifted writing geniuses who creates an important literary tradition and thereby places an unbearable burden on the shoulders of the coming generations. Goethe is also the name of an era, a culture, and a literary tradition on whose paths Kafka, too, tried to define his way: his memories of Goethe, Goethe's literary works, his autobiographical *Poetry and Truth*, his diaries and theories—all come up time and again in Kafka's own writing. Reading Goethe's diaries is among Kafka's inspirations for his own autobiographical thinking and writing, and some of the comments on Goethe's diaries or travel journals serve as transitions to thoughts about Jewish existence.

From the comment about Goethe, appearing after the story of circumcision in Russia and the birth of the Jewish body, Kafka goes back to the biographical essay and talks about one of his actual ancestors:

> In Hebrew my name is Anschel, like my mother's maternal grandfather, whom my mother, who was six years old when he died, can remember as a very pious and learned man with a long, white beard.[23]

The comment on Goethe is where Kafka returns to rewrite his own Jewish autobiography. From the story about the dead grandfather of German literature and culture, Kafka segues into talking about his own dead Jewish grandfather, Amschel (which Kafka renders with a small error as Anschel), who embodies Jewish learning.[24] But the name of the distant forebear contains another drama: the Jewish grandfather is named Amschel, sounding much like *Amsel*, German for blackbird. Just like the name Kafka that alludes to the Czech *kavka*, the jackdaw, his Jewish name also resonates with that black, raucously cawing, winged creature. The Jewish ancestor's name, too, contains the potential for flight. Indeed, in the lines that conclude the diary entry for December 25, 1911, we finally find Kafka's free prose. The lines are short and yet enfold a first movement toward original prose, a literature breaking free of its origins:

> To run against the window and, weak after exerting all one's strength, to step over the window sill through the splintered wood and glass.[25]

The leap from the window is a recurring motif in several of Kafka's diary entries and in some of his stories. It is one of the fundamental movements in his work that can be seen as a path of escape or move of liberation and the start of a new journey. In this essay, the movement through the window marks the birth of an original type of prose that leaps from canonical literature and national fields.[26] In a liberated gesture of writing, Kafka realizes the potential of motion inherent in the name of his ancestor Amschel (Amsel, a blackbird) and composes the fundamental characteristic of his literary work—a movement like a bird in flight.

In June 1912, Kafka traveled with Max Brod, his friend and future literary executor, to the city of Weimar where Goethe had lived for some sixty years. Kafka commemorated this visit in his travel diary. On their way, Kafka and Brod stopped off in Leipzig where they met with some members of the German expressionist movement who lived in the city, including the playwright Walter Hasenclever and the critic Kurt Pinthus. Kafka also met there the publisher Ernst Rowohlt and his partner Kurt Wolff who specialized in publishing avant-garde literature. The meeting ended with a promise: to publish Kafka's first book, a short story collection titled *Meditation*, at the earliest opportunity. The journey to Leipzig thus heralded Kafka's entry into the world of German books. In Weimar, however, he had to cement his identity as a writer entering the court of Goethe's literature. His visit and ramblings through the labyrinths and detours around Goethe's home and grounds, and his visit to Schiller's house and the archive there, reflect Kafka's brand as a wanderer in the field of German literature. Kafka writes his impressions outdoors, on the doorsteps of German literature's residences. He stays in Weimar not as a native but as a stranger, not as a resident but as a guest for the night. But it is precisely and ironically through the wandering that Kafka stakes out a fascinating path in modern literature, a path made out of caesuras, retreats, and hesitations.

But there is more. The Weimar chronicles, Kafka's visit to the capital of German literature, ends with a train ride to the Jungborn Sanitarium. That trip would take him through Halberstadt, a town with a large Jewish community. In the train car, Kafka meets familiar figures:

> Trip from Halle with four Jews from Prague: two pleasant, cheerful, robust, elderly men, one resembling Dr. K., one my father, but much shorter; then a weak-looking young married man, exhausted by the heat, and his dreadful, stoutly built young wife.[27]

So on his way to the sanitarium, Kafka is again brought face-to-face with his heritage. Amusing Jews from Prague arouse in him mixed memories of his father. When he arrives in Halberstadt, Kafka takes a room for the night at a hotel and goes out for a walk. In the park he encounters children heckling the Jews and immediately notices a Jewish inn whose gate is adorned with Hebrew lettering. A guest—a local Jew—is just leaving. Kafka relates:

> I walk behind a Jew who came out of the hotel and spoke to him. After nine. I wanted to know something about the community. Learned nothing. Looked too suspicious to him. He kept looking at my feet. But after all, I'm a Jew, too [*Aber ich bin doch auch Jude*].[28]

Kafka fails to earn the trust of the local, an Eastern European Jew who refuses to answer Kafka's questions about the life of the local Jewish community. Kafka arouses suspicion. The local examines his body, especially his feet, as if evidence of the traveler's identity may be found there. The feet?—one may ask. But this is precisely the part of the body that holds the traveler's secret. After all, it was the scar on Odysseus' foot that revealed his identity at the end of his journey. It was Oedipus' swollen feet that were part of his identifying marks, and it was the open, stinking wound on Philoctetes' foot that encompassed his entire being as an exiled body. In the antisemitic medical discourse of Europe, the "Jewish foot" was scientifically observed in-depth as if it—the "crooked foot of the Jews"—was a marker of the withered body and sickly soul of the stranger still unfit for the civic and military functions of the modern era.

From Halberstadt Kafka made his way to Jungborn Sanitarium where he stayed about three weeks, until the end of July 1912. The Naturopathic Institute in Jungborn was more than an ordinary sanitarium: it was an enormous resort village built by Adolf Just in 1896 on the "return to nature" principle, and involved the outdoors, nudism, exposure to the sun, clean air, vegan food, hygiene, relaxation exercises, and physical activity. Similar retreats sprang up throughout Europe at the turn of the century, and were an expression of bourgeois society's attempt to heal itself of the diseases of the technical era—the wasting body, pollution, breathing difficulties, traumatic neuroses, and other disorders—viewed as a byproduct of life in an urban environment.

At first, it was difficult for Kafka to find a place for himself among the patients in Jungborn, most of whom were Protestant tourists from German and Sweden. The sight of the naked, mostly old male patients aroused "no particular delight" in him.[29] In the coming days, he participated in relaxation exercises, physical training classes, ball games, and agricultural work, and listened to lectures on mending the body. But Kafka's attempts at healing failed. Already on the second day, he fell ill with a stomach ailment, and the following day he twisted his ankle while working in a field. At night, he suffered from insomnia; his swollen foot throbbed as a high fever spread through his body. Goethe appeared to him in a dream, and Kafka listened to his declamations with great enjoyment.[30]

The attempt at farming was disastrous for Kafka. It was as if it told him of his lack of fitness for the kind of territorial tasks that were adopted at the time by groups of pioneers in Palestine. Kafka found comfort instead in the appearance of a new friend, a German official from Breslau, a certain Dr. Friedrich Schiller, a man proud of his atheism. Together, they wandered down trails in the woods; visited a carnival, dances, and a local fair; and passed many hours discussing Christianity, journeys, and the nature of friends.[31] The fact that Kafka's new acquaintance bore the name of the great eighteenth-century German poet, whose Weimar house Kafka had visited just a few days before, shouldn't be all that surprising. We have already noticed that Kafka's travel diaries are full of curious coincidences, literary fantasies, and mundane facts. In his diary, Kafka interwove the figure of Dr. Schiller as a doppelganger, companion, and interlocutor. He thus adorned his diary as a slight literary memory, a memoir of his journey to Weimar.

Literature and the Minor

Kafka's travel diary from the summer of 1912 documents the birth of the writer. Once back in Prague, Kafka begins fixing the manuscript for the short story collection *Meditation*. This small collection includes short works that had already been published in local magazines as well as some new pieces, including several miniatures he had written in his diaries. Many of these pieces are written in a "dialectic in standstill": brief snapshots or gestures containing eternal motion. Indeed, many of the stories in the collection deal with travel, motion, the wish to get on the road. So, alongside "The Wish to Be a Red Indian," which in a single breath lays out the story of a jockey on the back of a horse galloping over quaking ground, the piece "Reflections for Gentlemen-Jockeys" provides advice to jockeys rushing past that they best beware of victory, which brings man only sorrow and regret. The jockey, like the acrobat and the traveler, is a dynamic body, a body whose essence is movement. His virtue lies in hovering above ground, being lifted off the ground, and the tremors of the journey. The bachelor in "Unhappiness" rushes back and forth in his room as if his rug were a horseracing track and horses harnessed to a wagon were waiting for him in the alley. The desire to travel, to be caught up in motion, is the lot of the character observing the world in "The Street Window," whom, even against his will, "the horses below will draw . . . down into their train of wagons and tumult, and so at last into the human harmony."[32]

The wish to be moving is unconsciously muttered also by the protagonist of "The Tradesman," who points out the virtues of processions and ships sailing to distant shores and praises the figure of a "beautiful lady who drives past"[33] before returning home alone. Travel is also the subject of the short segment "On the Tram," which relates the musings of a tram passenger whose thinking has become addicted to the sense of motion. Like the traveler who, in the opening line of Kafka's diary, freezes in place when the train passes, the tram passenger's world also becomes a picture in which the author inscribes—like in his diaries—the precise figure of a girl who doesn't respond to his courting: the pleats of her skirt that seem to have frozen, the tight blouse, the palm of her hand, a brief description of "her nose, slightly pinched at the sides,"[34] and finally a sketch of the small ear that refuses to hear his pleas. The fragment is a fine example of the still-life sketch technique: the drawing of bodies caught in repose in train cars. This motion also shapes the world of the speakers in "Passersby," dedicated to thought that lingers in the middle of the night, as opposed to the anonymous, inexplicable motion that cannot be stopped. The motion leaves its mark also on "The Way Home," in which a bachelor's march from the past to his empty future turns into a "tempo machine" banging into streets, doors, tables, and beds of loved ones cowering "in the scaffolding of new buildings."[35]

It is in this collection that Kafka investigates the concept of motion and learns how to transpose it to poetic situations, apparent first and foremost in the fragment form. Notable for its fundamental tension between home and street, destination and road, rest and motion, the very notion of territory is in doubt in many of its stories. The place itself is a locus of questions.

The Machine: Literature and the Law

Kafka's work testifies to an era of new machines. The train, steamship, airplane, automobile, telegram, telephone, and alarm clock created a new medium in which the conditions of the possibility of consciousness and language were redefined. Human relationships were reinvented and reshaped in the spheres in which the machine exerted its influence. Kafka was aware of the machine's realms of influence thanks to his work as an officer of the Worker's Accident Insurance Institute for the Kingdom of Bohemia in Prague, where he was hired to work in the technical department in 1908. As part of his work, Kafka visited factories, mines, and other labor sites throughout Bohemia and participated in professional conferences where he regularly met with industrialists, factory foremen, and workers. A large part of his work was dedicated to analyzing and categorizing insurance documents and writing work accident reports. Kafka's years at this company, even if it is customary to think of them as a dark, horrid wasteland and a burden on his literary creation, were also very productive. The documents he read, the reports he dictated, the protocols and essays he wrote—all of these gave form and content to his literary work. Not only his literary musings about the law, documented in several of his works, such as "The Problem of Our Laws" and *The Trial*, but also his stories featuring machines (first and foremost "In the Penal Colony"), can be reread in light of the documents from his office-clerk years. This was the time Kafka investigated the tremendous implications of technology for society and the human perception of reality: studying the disasters wrought by machines on the human body and documenting the disfigurement occurring in their sphere of influence informed and enriched his literary work.

The main subject of Kafka's official writing was work accidents. Many of the texts he took part in writing catalogue risks in industrial plants, safety regulations, and accident prevention. Other writings of his are devoted to the issue of mandatory insurance and the fate of war invalids. The first striking feature of these essays is their anonymity: Kafka's official literature was published anonymously in his company's yearbook. The chapters he wrote concerning, for example, "The Scope of Mandatory Insurance at Construction Sites" (1908), "Protection against Work Accidents with Wood Working Machines" (1909), "Risk Types in Wartime" (1916), and work accidents at quarries (1915), were published without the author's name. Likewise, his contributions to essays about traumatic neuroses and the establishment of a sanitarium in Rumburg-Frankenstein (1916), published by the Bohemian German press, appeared without his name attached. The essays in his company's yearbook were usually the result of teamwork, involving different writers, clerks, editors, and translators. That way Kafka experienced the possibilities of collective writing—writing expropriated from the realm of the individual, writing from which the author's name is expunged and swallowed up by the anonymous corpus. Kafka's official writings are nameless and, in this sense, seem to represent the alienated, faceless, and identity-less aspect of the technical era. All of this bears also the stamp of bureaucratic discourse: when writing as an insurance official, Kafka used technical and legal jargon. The official writing thus provided Kafka with insight into the literary horizon of alienation. Bureaucratic writing creates anonymous, identity-less, generic linguistic figures. Something from the depth of this writing experience is evident also in the anonymous figures of Kafka's literary works: the protagonists of his late novels, who bear no surnames, are not only subjects of loneliness and humiliation but also open, collective, multivalent markers.

In the years he worked at the insurance institute, Kafka experienced the destructive side of progress. The world of technology opened up before him as a sphere filled with dangers, accidents, and traumatic neuroses. This experience is evident in the essay "Protecting against Work Accidents in Quarries" (1914) to which Kafka contributed. The text begins with an introduction about the human factor in accidents and expands on means of protection against accidents in quarries. About a particular granite quarry in Bohemia he visited before penning the report, Kafka writes that it looked like "an abandoned, desolate field of ruins." He takes note of the flimsy quarry structure, the heaps of waste dotting the landscape, the unsecured tracks and railway cars, the boulders looking ready to tip over, the uncontrolled discharge into water sources, and other environmental failures. It is no coincidence, note some of Kafka's readers, that the end of *The Trial* is portrayed by the narrator as "a small, abandoned, desolate quarry." There, in the rubble-strewn field of modernity, is where Josef K. will be murdered by his companions. The final scene of *The Trial* is evidence of the form and contents Kafka borrowed from the granite quarry in Bohemia for his literary world. The clerk's hopes for somehow fixing the world of industry have been exchanged for a literary nightmare about a murder at a quarry. Furthermore, are we not allowed to see the quarry in *The Trial*, with its heaps of rubble and stone, as an allegory for Kafka's literary legacy, left behind like a field of fragments, broken, gaping, incomplete texts?

The law occupies as well a special place in Kafka's writing. It is the closed, unexplained world of the law and its arbitrariness that irritates Kafka in his official essays. The insurance laws of the Kingdom of Bohemia, writes Kafka in the essay "The Scope of Mandatory Insurance at Construction Sites," are abstract, ambiguous, almost unreadable legal formulas in which only a few are conversant, and even they are usually prevented from interpreting the laws or applying them. The laws of the kingdom allow for contradictory interpretations on the scope of insurance and where it applies. In the legal world, writes Kafka, there is inconsistency and incoherence, so that it is not "principle" but "happenstance" that plays the determining role. In the essay "Including Private Automobiles in the Law of Mandatory Insurance" (1908), Kafka comments on a new regulation of the insurance laws, saying it is unclear and leaves "room for free interpretation," and also that it is improperly enshrined in the law and does not match the proper order.[36] The new law does not yet include the necessary distinction between types of workers in the field of transportation, does not propose an appropriate category for types of vehicles, and imposes a policy of double insurance fees on drivers. The law is revealed as a flawed, illogical text needing endless amendments and interpretations. Kafka's stance on the law is clear: he demands the broadest possible inclusion of mandatory insurance. This, according to his essay's opinion, is the desirable interpretation of the law and only it can impose some order in the insurance field. This was a conclusion regarding the law that Kafka spared his literary output, where the question remains both closed yet infinitely open, just like "the gate of the law" where "a man from the village" stood in his story "Before the Law". In both cases Kafka draws the figure of a person existing within the law's sphere of influence. The laws are empty, arbitrary; their wording is nebulous and unintelligible; they become riddles and enigmas, valid, absolute, yet completely meaningless. The paradox of the law that Kafka tried to resolve in the daytime in his office was transformed at night into his literary enigmas.

This, finally, is also the enigma of the machine writing the verdict and executing it on the bodies of the accused of *In the Penal Colony*. The machine of the penal colony serves the law, whose writing is said to be indecipherable, looking like a "labyrinth of lines crossing and recrossing each other, which covered the paper so thickly that it was difficult to discern the blank spaces between them."[37] These charts, created by the former government of the colony, are the puzzles in which the verdicts of the accused are embedded. The penalties of the colony, similar to the insurance laws of Bohemia, are arbitrary: they are at once valid and meaningless. In both cases, the laws are unreadable. The verdicts stem from legal writing that is completely closed off, inaccessible, and self-contradictory, which none can decipher. The machine therefore becomes the medium of pure, unjustifiable, and incomprehensible violence. This feature of the law is finally revealed in the work accident experienced by the officer who makes himself the last victim of the machine. After setting up his verdict, the machine starts its work, but very soon it breaks apart with great clamor: the upper part splits off and the wheels fly off their axis and scatter in every direction. The work of the machine is interrupted, and instead of writing the verdict on the officer's body it sticks him with all its needles, without rhyme or reason. And so, purely by accident, the "secret of the machine" sees the light of day. By analogy, this is how the insight about the hidden, destructive essence of the technical era is born in the world of literature.

Unlike Kafka's official writings and essays on machines and the law, in which he tried to bridge the vast legal gulfs he perceived, his literary work throws off the yoke and illustrates slip-ups, incidents, work accidents, and other bodily catastrophes, thereby revealing the arbitrary, opaque nature of the law that cannot be penetrated. Finally, Kafka takes that machine apart too, at which point the conditions allowing metaphysical interpretations of his work also fall apart. Kafka's (literary) machine produces fragments and torn signifiers; its symbols are multivalent. The machine copies, reproduces, and disseminates worldviews and traditions: it carries messages, news, and telegrams from the past. Kafka's machine inherits what was once the oracle's fate—the word of man's destiny.

Epilogue

Kafka's diary begins with the description of a train journey. Any writing that begins with travel is, at every level, conscious of motion. The journey marks the twisty road, the special path taken by the Jewish author in the space-time continuum of modernity. While the journey is subject to technical definitions of time and space and is thus made up according to the outlines of law, the travel reveals, in its turn, countermovements, delays, stops, accidents, detours, and standstills. In this sense, Kafka's journey may also mark a way to understanding the Jewish journey of the modern era: a detour that comes to cross the main roads of Western culture. And the travel is also one of the ways to come back through the gates of this literature that, still, refuses to open all the way.

Notes

1. Franz Kafka, *Tagebücher*, vol. 1, 1909–1912 (Frankfurt am Main, 1994), 1:11.
2. Benjamin develops the notion of "dialectic in standstill" as part of a discussion of the dramaturgical function of the gesture in epic theater. See Walter Benjamin, "Was ist das epische Theater? (I)," in *Versuche über Brecht: Texte, Briefzeugnisse, Aufzeichnungen* (Frankfurt am Main, 1981), 19.
3. On the figure of the wandering Jew in European folk literature, see George K. Anderson, *The Legend of the Wandering Jew* (Providence, 1965), 1–37. For more, see R. Edelmann, "Ahasuerus: The Wandering Jew: Origin and Background," in *The Wandering Jew: Essays in the Interpretation of a Christian Legend*, eds. Galit Hasan-Rokem and Alan Dundes (Bloomington, 1986), 1–10.
4. Fragment to "Jäger Gracchus," in Franz Kafka, *Beim Bau der Chinesischen Mauer* (Frankfurt, am Main 1994), 96–100.
5. Franz Kafka, *Diaries*, trans. Martin Greenberg (London, 1949), 256.
6. Ibid., 263.

7. Ibid.

8. Ibid., 172.

9. Ibid.

10. Franz Kafka, "The Wish to Be a Red Indian," trans. Willa and Edwin Muir, in *The Complete Stories* (New York, 1983).

11. Franz Kafka, "Erstes Leid," in *Ein Landarzt* (Frankfurt am Main, 1994), 249–252.

12. Using this notion—the dialectic of Enlightenment—Theodor Adorno and Max Horkheimer explain the destructive element inherent, in their opinion, in Enlightenment culture, which begins with a critique of mythology. The Enlightenment, Adorno and Horkheimer argue, falls into new myths of power and domination embodied in compulsive repetition of legalistic thought and suppression of the body. See Max Horkheimer and Theodor W. Adorno, *Dialektik der Aufklärung* (Frankfurt am Main, 1997), 9–49.

13. Walter Bauer-Wabnegg, *Zirkus und Artisten in Franz Kafkas Werk: Ein Beitrag über Körper und Literatur im Zeitalter der Technik* (Erlangen, 1986). The author tries to discover the sources of Kafka's circus literature and clarify its horizons in relation to the question of the representation of the body in art in an era of technological change. The book also points to the fact that Kafka's circus stories are devoted to documenting the fall of the art of the body since new forms of representation—photography, telephone, telegraph—came into the world and started to supplant the natural place of the body.

14. Franz Kafka, *America*, trans. Willa and Edwin Muir, in *The Penguin Complete Novels of Franz Kafka* (New York, 1983), 638.

15. Kafka, 29.9.1911, in *Diaries*, trans. Joseph Kresh (New York, 1976).

16. Hartmut Schmidt, "Die Kunst des Reisens: Bemerkungen zum Reisebetrieb im späten 18. Jahrhundert am Beispiel von Goethes erster Italienreise," in *Goethe in Italien: Ein Ausstellungskatalog*, ed. Jörn Göres (Mainz, 1986), 9–14.

17. Kafka, 31.1.1912, in *Diaries*.

18. Kafka, 25.12.1911, in *Diaries*.

19. Kafka, 27.12.1911, in *Diaries*.

20. Kafka, 25.12.1911, in *Diaries*.

21. The Hebrew phrase for circumcision is *brit milah*, lit., "the covenant of the word."

22. Kafka, 25.12.1911, in *Diaries*.

23. Ibid.

24. Kafka's maternal great-grandfather was Adam Porias (1794–1862), and his Yiddish name was Amschel.

25. Kafka, 25.12.1912, in *Diaries*.

26. On possibilities of liberation marked by moving outward from rooms or enclosed spaces and other paths of escape in the sphere of Kafka's writing—by means of morphing into animal shapes—see Gilles Deleuze and Félix Guattari, *Kafka: Toward a Minor Literature* (Minneapolis, 1986), 16–17.

27. Kafka, *Diaries*, 300–301.

28. Ibid., 301–2.

29. Ibid., 305.

30. Ibid., 304.

31. Ibid., 305–7.

32. Franz Kafka, "The Street Window," trans. Willa and Edwin Muir, in *The Complete Stories*, 384.

33. Franz Kafka, "The Tradesman," trans. Willa and Edwin Muir, in *The Complete Stories*, 385–86.

34. Franz Kafka, "On the Tram," trans. Willa and Edwin Muir, in *The Complete Stories*, 389.

35. Franz Kafka, "The Way Home," trans. Willa and Edwin Muir, in *The Complete Stories*, 387.

36. Franz Kafka, "Einbeziehung der privaten Automobilbetriebe in die Versicherungspflicht," *Amtliche Schriften* (Frankfurt am Main, 2004), 178–80.

37. Franz Kafka, "In the Penal Colony," trans. Willa and Edwin Muir, *The Complete Stories*, 148.

17

David Ben-Gurion (1886–1973)
THE POLITICIZATION OF THE JEWS

Yaron Ezrahi

ALMOST UNIVERSALLY, THE BIRTH OF NEW STATES OR REGIMES IS A BLOODY AFFAIR. Democracies evolve when, following the violent revolutionary stage, the hegemonic government moves to tame the revolutionary violence and subordinate the use of force to the law. Usually these two phases require profoundly different types of leaders and leadership styles. Among founders of modern states, David Ben-Gurion belongs among the very few examples of a revolutionary leader who both became head of a state he founded and presided over it (in Ben-Gurion's case, for almost fifteen years). As a revolutionary leader Ben-Gurion succeeded in gaining power and establishing authority in a voluntary and politically fragmented society of settlers and immigrants living under foreign rule. He then led the achievement of independence; internal organization of the new state, cabinet, and parliament; wars; international relations; and recognition of the state by world public opinion.

In this feat of institutionalizing charisma and approximating utopia, Ben-Gurion had to radically transform himself, his leadership style, his rhetoric, his actions, and his people. Many of his decisions in the course of this process of converting a prestate revolutionary power into a legally controlled, postrevolutionary state power, constrained by the principles of a social-democratic republican nation-state, have affected the political history of Israel ever since. In this process Ben-Gurion moved on from his leadership roles as a trade unionist and Zionist into a set of new roles as prime and defense ministers, a parliamentarian, a head of the hegemonic government party, a military strategist who directed the war of independence, and the chief diplomat of the new state. In addition he invested his energies in growing a voluntary community of Jews into a modern democratic-republican polity of law-abiding citizens united by a civic state culture. This objective was and remained only partially successful, considering the difficulties he faced: turning immigrants from nondemocratic countries, independent ideologically partisan pioneers, and survivors of Nazi concentration camps into democratic, public-regarding citizens.

It is easy, therefore, to agree that, as the founder of the state of Israel, David Ben-Gurion is undoubtedly one of the most historically memorable Jewish figures of the twentieth century and the most important Jewish statesman in modern times.

It is quite another matter, however, to discern and understand the traits of the man, reconstruct the circumstances and context in which he acted, and assess the qualities of leadership that made Ben-Gurion a central figure in the epic moment of the creation of the state of Israel. This essay is not a historical account of Ben-Gurion's evolution from Zionist activist to founder and then leader of Israel. My intention in the following is rather a brief inquiry into the core elements of his extraordinary leadership and his singular contribution to the political modernization of the Jewish people while avoiding the pitfalls of both apologetics and backshadowing.[1]

Shaping Herzl's Vision of the Jewish State

In retrospect it appears that Ben-Gurion's unique role in the genealogy of the state of Israel was to further develop Theodor Herzl's great vision of a Jewish state—to deepen its grip on the collective imagination of Jews of the prestate Yishuv and the diaspora as a realistic, achievable dream and then to lead his people in enacting this collective political imaginary and translating it into political reality. In other words, Ben-Gurion was the crucial link between a Jewish political utopia and the actual political modernization of the Jews. He took the idea of a Jewish state, led its transformation into the collective political imagination, and then promoted its actual performance into existence.[2] As the leader of this monumental transformation, Ben-Gurion focused on both the modes of collective consciousness that enable a voluntary society to evolve into a sovereign modern state and the means necessary to materialize the political foundations of modern Jewish existence.

The distinguished cultural historian of nationalism, Benedict Anderson, who demonstrated the role of the creative collective imagination in converting usually idealized visions of a primordial past and bonds to the fabric of national consciousness and solidarity, wondered how we can explain the readiness of "millions [of] people to willingly die for such limited imaginings . . . [and] why people are ready to die for such limited inventions and generate such colossal sacrifices?"[3] My answer to this query is that, regardless of the incoherence of the collective imaginary of a nation or the validity of its claimed historical foundations, people are willing to die in defense of a collective story that gives meaning to their group and to each individual's life and death. The fear of meaningless life, of storyless existence, is apparently greater than the fear of dying meaningfully, or as a hero, in a shared epic narrative.

No one has known this "secret" truth better than a leader like Ben-Gurion, who experienced disorientation and despair at moments when he imagined the possible meaningless of life and death and responded to that despair with intense, almost obsessive activism. At about the age of forty, feeling lonely one night while on a boat on the way back to Palestine after one of his many missions abroad, he poured into his diary gloomy reflections on the meaninglessness of human life, juxtaposing the beauty of the night on the sea with the night of his heart, thinking "that everything will pass and disappear when eternal coldness and loss will prevail without an end or purpose. What is the meaning of our being," he continues to ask, "what is the meaning of our meaningless momentary existence? Who will answer?—the grave," he concludes, "is the only answer, the only purpose."[4] Waves of European existential and philosophical pessimism were, of course, part of the cultural climate since the

end of the nineteenth century. Not a few intellectuals expressed their agonizing doubts concerning the worthiness of life and the possible futility of hoping for significant progress in the human condition. Obviously Ben-Gurion was not an exception among Jews or other reflective people who experienced a crisis of meaning during that period of upheaval. But he probably was exceptionally unique in his response to it. Given his extraordinary resourcefulness and the opportunities presented by the historical situation, is it too much to assume that for Ben-Gurion the horror of meaningless life and death could perhaps be transcended by an immortal deed like the founding of a state?

Ben-Gurion realized that such a monumental accomplishment required a revolutionary shift in collective Jewish consciousness even before Jews possessed any territory or had an army, and before the Holocaust or waves of mass immigrations to the land. Inspired by Herzl's vision of a Jewish state and by contemporary socialist and nationalist European movements, often jointly with his political rivals Chaim Weizmann and Ze'ev Jabotinsky, he progressively conquered the imagination of the Jewish people and won the commitment of masses of Jews to the often controversial project of establishing a Jewish state in 1948. Following decades of Zionist agitation, and at the very moment when the long history of Jewish persecution and narratives of holy Jewish victims were meant to be replaced by the narrative of Israeli warriors—a transition inevitably fraught with dangers, pitfalls, breaks, and discontinuities, especially with the advent of the genocide of the Jews—it was mainly Ben-Gurion who had the courage and fortitude to navigate the collective consciousness of his people. By means of his powerful speeches and writings he sought to motivate Jewish youth to give themselves to this new, costliest mission: realizing the ideal of a "sovereign Jewish commonwealth" and the earthly aspirations of their people.

In advancing the dream of statehood Ben-Gurion must have had a profound intuition of the relations between fantasy and reality or, more precisely, of how a collective political imaginary can be translated into a political reality and how to lead a people through the arduous odyssey of converting a desired fiction into an actual fact. In May 1939 he revealed his thought that the strategy to guide the collective effort to create a state consisted, among other things, of the ability to ignore reality in order to change it, thus enacting a desirable illusionary until it came to pass. Confessing to his diary, he wrote, "We need to behave as if we [not the British, YE] have the mandate over the land of Israel, and we have to behave as if we are the state in the land of Israel . . . until we will become the real state."[5]

Part of the greatness of Ben-Gurion as a leader was precisely his intuition when and how "as ifs" could be realized in the political world and how to shape the resources of legitimation and power to institutionalize the collective imaginary of a Jewish state. This talent included his sense of how to trigger behavior that enacts a collective political imaginary of a desired, yet still nonexistent condition; how to generate collective, performative conduct to create institutions that gradually come to approximate the dreamt-of social order; and, no less important operationally, how also to contrive military behavior that projects a much greater force than was actually available to the Israelis. In other words, Ben-Gurion understood the working of the mechanism of self-fulfilling (political) prophecy and its potential as a means of political creativity.

Enacting the Zionist Utopia

Isaiah Berlin has been widely quoted as saying that "the Jews have too much history and not enough geography."[6] Ben-Gurion, trying to correct this imbalance, did not reject the central place of history in Jewish consciousness but recognized the importance of harnessing Jewish history and literature to the project of territorialization. He had a clear view of the necessity of materializing the foundations of modern political Jewish existence, supplementing or replacing the spiritual and metaphysical cement of traditional Jewish diasporic communities with material elements through which a modern state is made and sustained. These elements were territory; military force; a demographic infrastructure for a Jewish state; and, finally, the political power to make, and the institutional procedures to legitimate, the leadership and its often difficult controversial decisions. This transformation required privileging a palpable political present as the normative temporal site of meaningful action over both the past and an abstract future. In order to accomplish this goal, Ben-Gurion relied heavily on his powers to mobilize and inspire prestate Israeli youth to risk joining a military and facing the prospect of imminent war to enable and protect the possession of territory. His repeated appeal to Jewish youth as a principal missionary agent of the Zionist revolution was a powerful expression of the call for a historical shift of focus from what the Zionist ideological perspective regarded as traditional ancestral wisdom to a present-oriented collective and individual self-creation—from the immemorial Jewish preoccupation with timeless sacred texts to a new focus on action and contemporary enterprises. Ben-Gurion kept linking the dreams of the young with their fearlessness in pursuing them, while criticizing the passive, apolitical Orthodox religious culture of "unemancipated" Jews.

Motivated by the urgent necessity of making the Land of Israel a center of Jewish military, political, social, and economic powers, Ben-Gurion used his public speeches to translate the epic Zionist narrative into a heroic, present-oriented program of action. He must have intuited that it is necessary to transform Jews, who throughout their history of persecution were willing to sacrifice their lives for *Kiddush Hashem*— the sanctification of God—into Jews willing to sacrifice their lives for their state, embarking on a risky new path of self-determination in their territorial homeland, thus shifting from regarding themselves as defenseless victims to heroic freedom fighters. Ben-Gurion was deeply aware of the crucial Zionist transformation of the Jewish understanding of the relations among freedom, sacrifice, death, and meaning. He believed that a modern Jewish state would depend on the willingness and ability of Jews to cope with, and overcome, new kinds of dangers. In the flurry of angry letters and speeches in response to the White Paper of 1939, in which the British government under Neville Chamberlain restricted Jewish immigration to Palestine, Ben-Gurion repeatedly stated that "only by means of warships and automatic machine guns would the British Government be able to overcome the resistance of Jewish youth and the pioneers of Israel and block the way to the homeland."[7]

In making a Jewish state, Ben-Gurion relied on pioneers and Jewish workers with the ideology and enthusiasm to cope with the hardships of settling desolate land and cultivating agriculture in a country not blessed with water resources; on entrepreneurs ready to take the risks of industrialization in a country poor in natural resources and skilled manpower; and on mass immigration to empower the state economy and secure a stable Jewish political majority.

Along with trust in the military prowess of Israeli youth, Ben-Gurion's stress on the value of labor and the centrality of workers was another element in his vision of materializing the Jewish condition.[8] For him as well as for other Zionist leaders, Jewish physical labor was a central part of the emancipatory Zionist ideal advanced in reaction to the Jewish confinement to bourgeoisie commercial and financial culture. Jewish farmers and workers were widely regarded therefore as embodying the values of the "new Jews" who would build the new country. As a leader of the federation of workers' unions in the prestate period (Histadrut, 1921–1935), and a socialist Zionist critic of Jewish religious and middle-class cultures, Ben-Gurion cultivated and expanded the socialist ethos of Jewish laborers as a cornerstone of his vision of a society of workers/citizens/soldiers who would fashion, run, and defend the new state. As Zeev Sternhell has pointed out, ultimately, however, Ben-Gurion often subordinated the values and organizations of Jewish workers, and even of civic democratic principles, to the project of buildling a nation-state. Despite his commitment to the principles of equality and freedom inscribed in the Declaration of Independence, in practice nationalism often took precedence over both socialism and democracy.[9] Perhaps the most consequential example is his willingness, during the first years of nation building and state formation, to sacrifice the rare opportunity to pass a constitution for the new state to the political convenience of reducing tensions with Haredic (ultra-Orthodox) factions, as well as his own reluctance to formally limit his highly centralized powers as a prime minister.

The Civic Education of the Jewish People

The revolutionary materialization of Jewish life, which involved territorializing the Jews, physicalizing Jewish force in the military, massive immigration to secure a Jewish majority in a corporalized body politic, and an evolving national economy, was bound to require an equally revolutionary transformation of Jewish social and political consciousness and the inculcation of civic democratic political culture. Such a change posed a series of unprecedented and sometimes unsolvable problems: How to modernize the political consciousness of Jews within the completely new framework of an armed territorial Jewish polity, regulated by law, while preserving the virtues of the prestate voluntary civil community? How to negotiate the relations between a Jewish majority and an Arab minority? What should be the place of Jewish traditional religious education in a secular Jewish society? And how to coordinate the relations between liberal and socialist economic principles—and their implications for social structure and the vision of a just society?

Ben-Gurion recognized the acute difficulties in converting a multitude of diverse, often contesting voices into the unified voice of the state and avoiding the fragmentation of the new polity into irreconcilable political factions. In other words, he had to confront the dilemma of how to socialize politically inexperienced Jews, many of whom were never exposed to, or had been alienated from, democratic values and practices, into a republican culture of cooperative, public-regarding citizens.

In pursuing this objective Ben-Gurion revealed his extraordinary rhetorical powers as a national pedagogue. Already during the twenties and thirties, when he emerged as the leader of the workers' party Mapai and the federation of trade unions Histadrut, he repeatedly attempted to project his vision of an idealized Jewish polity. It consisted of a combination of semi-messianic, highfalutin rhetoric; hyperbolic moral arguments; and a stress on the education and cultural cultivation of workers, immigrants and Israeli-born youth. Ben-Gurion recognized that this monumental enterprise would depend on the ability to evolve a common civic ethos from the voluntaristic Yishuv community, which would give birth to the authoritative, collective official voice of the state. This would be a new, powerful voice in modern Jewish life, a voice that by virtue of its inclusivity could transcend the partisan voices of various political and ideological factions, including the traditional voice of the rabbis, and become a supreme new source of power and authority in Jewish life. Ben-Gurion started, therefore, to cultivate that ethos of statehood long before the creation of Israel in May 1948, generating a powerful rhetoric that combined elements of biblical messianic language with the high principles of republicanism, socialism, and even liberalism. Perhaps in his most ingenious move to reorient Jews in this revolutionary transformation he devised the concept of *mamlakhtiyut*, combining elements of both an inclusive civic ethos of a democratic and a republican state.[10] As the leading national statesman-pedagogue and strategist presiding over this monumental transformation of the relations between Jews and power, and despite his own ardent advocacy of secular education and a secular army, his extensive references to the Bible, and to heroic chapters in ancient Jewish history, he had the double contradictory imports of both strengthening and weakening secular civic, secular nationalist, and religious-nationalist education. He was motivated by the intuition that the powers of the biblical imagination as well as of warranted or mythologized historical memories would inspire Jews unexposed to democratic-republican values and practice. Thus he chose to translate the civic-republican ethos of the state to the Hebrew term *mamlakhtiyut*, with a strong connotation and linguistic affinity to the term *mamlakha*, meaning "kingdom," with implications of a unified political entity under God or a chosen leader. He must have intuited that the legacy of the deep monarchic political sensibilities of traditional Judaism among both observant and unobservant Jews, mostly from nondemocratic countries, would connote *mamlakha* (kingdom) rather than *mamlakhtiyut* (civic statism).

Admittedly quite a number of Israeli intellectuals who accused Ben-Gurion of cultivating a cult of the state (statism) were disturbed by this employment of a mixture of messianic rhetoric and the glorification of the state, which was typical of authoritarian leaders like Robespierre, Lenin, and Mussolini who sought to focus revolutionary generations, burdened by enormous human suffering and losses, on a redemptive future. The Hebrew University philosopher Nathan Rotenstreich and historian Jacob Talmon were worried that Ben-Gurion's veneration of statehood by his advocacy of *mamlakhtiyut*, his frequent use of messianic biblical imagery, and his control of military power as both a prime minister and a minister of defense would encourage fascist-like political authoritarianism, the repression of the voluntary springs of a Jewish democratic society, and, in light of his own aggressive leadership style, also a personality cult.[11] Undoubtedly at that crucial historical moment of early state formation, this warning had an important restraining function. Decades later it became relevant again due to the revival of waves of undemocratic popular desire for strong leadership. Nevertheless in the early years of Israel, Ben-Gurion, as other leaders in hard times, must have intuited the necessity of optimism, of both faith in a future that would justify the heavy sacrifices in the present and the centralization of political power needed to cope with acute current difficulties. Rotenstreich, Talmon, and other critics, whose criticism reflected the grim recent memories of the experience of European Jews under fascism and authoritarian socialism, underestimated the acute need for a state founder to preside over the formative stages of a state just born and to exploit all available cultural and rhetorical ammunition to empower his authority to extract, mobilize, inspire, and legitimate individual and collective energies needed for nation and state building. For that he needed also all his powers of persuasion to render historically powerless Jews into Jews capable of shooting to kill on the battlefield. Obviously, at this formative historical moment, such a need to advance *mamlakhtiyut* did not amount exactly to a cult of statehood, nor did an inspiring messianic rhetoric warrant the fear of a dangerous political trend toward antidemocratic authoritarianism.

In trying to maintain the optimism and hopes of the revolutionary generation, Ben-Gurion had to confront the spread of postwar pessimism influenced by the legacy of earlier waves of pessimism that had swept the Russian and Russian Jewish intelligentsia who were inspired by Friedrich Nietzsche, Arthur Schopenhauer, and others. This influence penetrated to modern Hebrew literature, indicated for instance in the writing of Yosef Haim Brenner.[12] Ben-Gurion expected Israeli novelists like S. Yizhar to write a celebratory epic of the political emancipation of the Jews, and he did not hesitate to violate cherished liberal values by admonishing Israeli historians, writers, and poets for their failure to glorify the great deeds of the age.[13] So while *mamlakhtiyut* as a version of civic statism could be abused to serve as a façade of authoritarian leadership, it was conceived by Ben-Gurion to enable governance in a deeply divided society of a notoriously unruly people.[14]

Unyieldingly advancing this imaginary of *mamlakhtiyut*, Ben-Gurion succeeded in elevating it to the level of an influential collective norm that implicitly denounced partisan party, sectoral, or arbitrary individual actions in matters of public interest. He demanded that on vital matters of collective freedom, security, and welfare, political activists, ministers, top civil servants, educators, and ordinary citizens should speak and act in a nonpartisan, public-regarding way and focus on the inclusive interest of the state. Considering the syncretic political fabric of the Zionist movement as a fragile coalition of five rival Zionist visions of the new state, Ben-Gurion framed this civic statism as an integrative focus of loyalty and solidarity, resistant to all attempts to wholly subordinate the state and its ethos to the particular interpretation of Zionism according to socialism, liberalism, nationalism, and modern-Orthodox and Haredic Judaism.

Ben-Gurion vigorously applied the code of *mamlakhtiyut* to three crucial components of the newly born state: the army, the government, and the educational system. He enlisted the rationale of *mamlakhtiyut* in the sense of "reasons of state" and "public interest" to carry out one of the most important and risky decisions during the early formative years of the Jewish state: dismantling the prestate Jewish paramilitary militias of the various Zionist factions in order to create one people's (*mamlakhti*) army under civil authority. Building on the skills and experience of these factional prestate paramilitary organizations, while simultaneously disbanding them in order to consolidate Jewish military power in a common people's army based on the principles of parliamentary democracy, demonstrated Ben-Gurion's confidence in the power of civic-republican Zionist culture to uphold the privileged authority of the state beyond any particular factional Zionist ideology—but also without excluding any. He must have believed that a collective Zionist narrative that cuts across local ideological or political factionalism can invest the lives of Israeli Jews with sufficient meaning to motivate hundreds and, later on, many thousands of young Israelis to fight to defend it. Ben-Gurion's approach to the founding of a Jewish military force was challenged by the inspiring Revisionist right-wing approach of Vladimir Jabotinsky. In this view, Jabotinsky advanced a narrower, more aggressive, yet still appealing alternative nationalist conception of converting Jews into soldiers by means of a militaristic cult of Jewish force, induced by military rituals and symbolism, rather than by the social-democratic ethos of citizens-soldiers. That alternative illuminates both the magnitude of the challenge faced by Ben-Gurion and his considerable achievement in building a democratic republican army. As we shall see below, however, following the 1967 war this character of the Israeli army did not remain uncontestable.[15]

Similar to his effective employment of "reasons of state," of *mamlakhtiyut*, to dismantle the prestate ideologically affiliated militias, Ben-Gurion used *mamlakhtiyut* to empower his radical educational reform, dismantling the Israeli sectoral system of education divided by competing ideological schools in order to replace it by a system of public schools. Except for the sector of Haredic education, which was wrongly excluded from the mandatory introduction of the core of civic public education on the grounds that religion is beyond ideology and politics, Israeli Zionist secular and modern religious public schools (*mizrahi*) were instructed to provide general modern education beyond partisan ideological and political orientations. This very controversial move was significantly successful during the first two decades of statehood. But eventually, especially since the establishment of the coalition between right-wing and religious parties following the 1977 elections, the respect for the separation of general and universal civic education from ideologically partisan nationalist education began to erode through pressures for reideologization. This trend was influenced by the illegal, and therefore anticivic, culture that enveloped the unofficial, partly covered government-supported project of settling the occupied territory.[16] This trend was reinforced further by the persistent growth of antisecular and uncivic education in strictly Orthodox schools as well as the poverty of general public and civic education in both secular and religious public schools. Buttressed by the atmosphere created by the wars that followed, these developments increasingly facilitated the false yet popular equation of civic with nationalist education, manipulatively or unknowingly misconstruing civic *mamlakhtiyut* as loyalty to the nation-state.

The First Modern Jewish Statesman

If Theodor Herzl was the great prophet of Zionism, the visionary of the Jewish state, and Chaim Weizmann was the most prominent modern Zionist diplomat until the reversal of Britain's support for a Jewish home in Palestine with the publication of its second White Paper,[17] Ben-Gurion was the first modern Jewish statesman, the founder and first leader of Israel as a modern Jewish state. He deserves this status not only by virtue of his remarkable role in founding the new state but also for the enduring example of the extraordinary scope, versatility, and resoluteness of his statesmanship.

In many respects, his rhetoric and mode of acting were inspired by both Lenin and Churchill. From Lenin he learned the often lethal practice of using the power of idealism to legitimate brutal violence, the example of effective authoritarian political centralism, and the use of a party organization to project and deploy his power. From Churchill he learned the power of inspiring and guiding a nation at war. When applied to the1948 war, these powers helped contain the massive Israeli losses and eclipse the tragic losses and suffering of native Palestinians who paid the price.

As both the principal shaper of the collective political imaginary of the new Jewish political universe and the key agent of its enactment, the leader who took upon himself the risks and responsibilities of bringing a Jewish state into being, Ben-Gurion had the advantages and liabilities of an armed visionary. His greatness as a leader consisted, among other things, of his ability to sustain this dualism and excel in the pragmatic, cold, and even cruel application of Jewish political and military power as well as the skillful, often ingeniously creative and effective guidance of the Jewish political imagination, demonstrating a virtuosic ability in managing the images, symbols, propaganda, and public moral rationalization of the new state.

Because *mamlakhtiyut* was devised as an apolitical civic ethos, Ben-Gurion was quick to effectively exploit it to politically empower himself and apply it to combat his radical partisan adversaries on both the left and the right. With the establishment of the state, Ben-Gurion began institutionalizing the voice of the state as the official voice of Israel. As the principal spokesman of the state and government, Ben-Gurion did not hesitate to appropriate this official voice of the state in order to discipline and delegitimize rival political voices as private, personal, or sectarian. In a speech before officers of the newly established Israeli army, who included some resentful former commanders of the very prestate militias he dismantled, Ben-Gurion asserted in response to one such critical officer: "I agree with [you] that your opinion has the same right to be heard as mine but there is one difference. The one who speaks in the name of the state already persuaded the people . . . the opinion of an authorized representative of the state is not an individual opinion and . . . it is therefore the opinion that decides the matter."[18]

The challenge Ben-Gurion faced in building up and sustaining the authority of an impersonal, unified official voice of the state in the cabinet and the Knesset was no less hard. In order to draw a collective official voice from a politically fractured community and a strenuous coalition of contesting ministers, it was not sufficient to depersonalize that voice through democratic elections and the creation of a cabinet and the Knesset. In addition to such institutional means, it was necessary to develop the kind of leadership that can even temporarily neutralize, include, and integrate conflicting voices. Shaul Shenhav has traced the strategies and the authority by which Ben-Gurion imposed in the early cabinets of the state the political-constitutional code of "collective responsibility" in order for the cabinet to speak with one coherent voice as well as to effectively confront the voices of the opposition.[19] As one would expect, it was very difficult to protect the coherence and stability of the narratives and policy statements produced by a coalitional cabinet in the very politically divided Knesset committees and the plenum. Shenhav points out to the combined use of persuasion and secrecy in preparing the grounds for public debates on controversial issues in the parliamentary plenum. Probably even more important was Ben-Gurion's leadership and political power in generating and sustaining cabinet and Knesset majorities. This was often achieved by his particular strength in combining and integrating fragments of the diverse traditions and ideologies of the various political groups, including references to socialist principles, Zionist goals, "reasons of state," military considerations, moral arguments, the Bible, and other classical Jewish sources. He also employed economic considerations, for example, in defense of his policy of soliciting reparation payments from post-Nazi Germany.

Consistently with his effort to enlist historians to glorify the enormous sacrifices and suffering of the time, Ben-Gurion repeatedly attempted to historicize the present—to frame the politics of the moment as a climax in the epic historical narrative of the Jewish people. The idea that monumental Jewish history is unfolding in the present implied the classical democratic demand that because democratic politics is both made by, and accountable to, the living, not to the dead and the unborn, it is mandatory that the living regard it as their own enterprise, that they participate and assume responsibility for the decisions and choices taken by the elected leadership, as well as be ready to make the necessary sacrifices to carry them out.

Undoubtedly Ben-Gurion's ability to project his longstanding vision of the establishment of a Jewish state as an act of collective self-creation, as the sociopolitical embodiment of Jewish values and ideals, faced a profound crisis once the monumental tragedy of European Jewry during the Holocaust eclipsed the focus on the emancipatory redemptive meaning of the rise of a Jewish state. The urgency of rescuing surviving Jews and the involuntary migration of refugees lacked the aura of voluntary ideological immigration of would-be pioneers that inspired the early pre–World War II immigrants and Jews, such as Albert Einstein, who considered that "Palestine is not primarily a place of refuge for the Jews of Eastern Europe but the embodiment of the re-awakening of the corporate spirit of the entire Jewish nation."[20] If Ben-Gurion's ideals of a vibrant civic society of creative workers, soldiers, and intellectuals distinguished him and his circle from the "catastrophic Zionism" of the Zionist right, the switch from an idealistic voluntary immigration to a forced rescue of human beings broken in concentration camps required a painful adjustment.[21] In this process Ben-Gurion went through several phases: silence, ambivalence, and an effort to exploit the catastrophe and suffering of survivors as a weapon against the British government and to advance the creation of the state. When the dimension of the mass extermination of European Jews became widely known at the end of 1942, Ben-Gurion displayed a mixture of despair and deep personal absorption with rescue operations. Shaken by the Holocaust, he was less preoccupied with the tragedy of individual Jews than with the disastrous collective implications for creating a national home for the Jewish people. In December 1942, he wondered desperately if "the annihilation of European Jews is the very end of Zionism, because we would not have the very people with whom we have planned to build the Land of Israel."[22] Yet, as one would expect from a revolutionary man of action like Ben-Gurion, he very quickly came back to assert that a self-paralyzing despair was not an option.

What stands out as a factor in Ben-Gurion's political efficacy during the pre-state period of the Yishuv is his calculative yet belligerent aggressive leadership style and his political acumen in eliciting support for his programs and decisions by shifting between alternative forms of decision making according to his political convenience, thus moving back and forth between the councils of his workers' party (Mapai), the Union of Israeli Workers (Histadrut), the Jewish Agency of Palestine, and the World Zionist Organization. This tactic culminated in the decision taken on May 12, 1948 by the temporary quasi-governmental body "The People's Administration" (Hamoatza Hazmanit, created to govern during the transition period to the first elected government), in which Ben-Gurion succeeded in achieving a majority for endorsing the declaration of independence that followed two days later.

The public career of Ben-Gurion demonstrates, in addition, his great political talent in creating institutions and using them to extract powers to influence decisions, actions, and behavior. This ability, which had been already revealed in his conduct as a Zionist leader, the head of the Histadrut, the union of workers, and head of his Mapai party, culminated in the founding of the state of Israel and his uses of the new state bureaucracy. He recognized how the force that the Israeli anthropologist Don Handelman calls "bureaucratic logic" could be employed to augment political power by depersonalizing and depoliticizing it in institutional-legal terms.[23]

Ben-Gurion realized that the respective logics of managing force and managing persuasion rarely converge—that in matters of state, an emotional and moral response is often a bad guide. As a person of a very hot temper, a leader whose anger often frightened and paralyzed his rivals, it was often difficult for Ben-Gurion to be as cool as he advised himself and others to be. Nevertheless, to some people in his close circle and distant environment he appeared as a calculative, cold-hearted leader. In a rare revealing letter to his son Amos, dated May 10, 1937, he had addressed this question about the relations between logic and feelings in politics. "Political questions are not a subject for feelings," he wrote. "One must consider only: what is desirable and good for us, what is the way to achieve our goal and which policy strengthens or weakens us." Then he went on to disclose a dimension of his operational code: "I obviously dislike the division of the land," he writes, referring to the UN partition plan. "Yet the matter is beyond our control . . . but according to the partition we are getting more land than is under our control although much less than we deserve or want. But the question remains: can we get more without partition? Would we feel better. . . . For us the present state is fatal. We want a change . . . and the critical issue is: will the establishment of a Jewish state (on only a small part of the land) advance or block our efforts to turning the entire land Jewish. . . . I assume that even if the creation of a partial Jewish state requires a partition now this is just the beginning, not the end. Such a state will become a powerful lever for our historical efforts to redeem the entire land."[24]

This small section in his confessional letter reveals important features of Ben-Gurion's leadership as a decision maker: his pragmatic realism and his tendency to focus on clearly defined short-term goals while concealing his more long-term, maximalist, and therefore more controversial ones. Ben-Gurion intuited already during the years before World War II that the enormous powers required in order to create a sustainable state were multiplied by even a small start that would bring about only a fraction of the dreamed-of land under Jewish control. Even a small state "in hand," the tiny piece of land proposed by the UN partition plan of Palestine, would be better than the present situation. This recognition relates to his understanding of the instrumental potential of even a small Jewish state not only for advancing political, diplomatic, and military goals but also as a principal source of meaning and identity. Therefore, for Jews in the Yishuv and in diasporas across the world, the state would be a trigger for the readiness to make necessary commitments for realizing other parts of the dream. In many respects, this vision was increasingly confirmed before, during, and following World War II.

As revealed throughout his career as a leader, Ben-Gurion's "operational code," his arsenal of strategies, consisted, among other things, of confrontational responses to his domestic and international adversaries (demonstrated for instance in his aggressive, belligerent responses to the White Paper in May 1939: "We will fight the White Paper of the British Government as if there is no war against Germany and join England in the struggle against Germany as if there is no White Paper"). His frequent recourse to militant confrontational language and his radical decisions added another dimension to understanding his efficacy as a leader. It pierced ambiguous and uncertain situations with a disarming clarity of purpose that persuaded many of his associates and audiences that he saw and intuited things beyond their grasp. Another aspect of this militant style of leadership was his brinkmanship, manifest in repeated threats to resign if his opinion was not accepted.

As a statesman Ben-Gurion showed time and again his uncanny sense of timing. He anticipated, for instance, that since after the war the great powers would move to redefine a new world order, no time should be wasted in preparing the grounds of Zionist influence in America. The anticipated shift in the weight ascribed to America relative to Britain in the postwar period also served his tactical political interest to reduce the influence of Weizmann, who drew much of his power in the Zionist movement from his connections with top British political leaders, connections whose value declined drastically following the White Paper that dramatized the retreat of the British government from its earlier commitments in the Balfour Declaration. In his handling of the Biltmore Plan of 1942, Ben-Gurion was a zealous, mission-oriented leader, totally self-mobilized to use all available rhetorical and political resources to achieve a goal he set and then to relentlessly carry it out. The sheer force of his intensive energy made it difficult to resist him. Another particularly effective political strategy was Ben-Gurion's frequent insistence on the necessity of deciding or acting immediately. This pressure for immediacy left his rivals no time to rally an opposition or take responsibility for the risky delays that resulted from stopping him.

Ben-Gurion's Legacy

Obviously the state of Israel is the single most important and potentially most enduring legacy of David Ben-Gurion. I say "potentially" because, as of this writing, it is hard to predict the future shape and regime of this political entity: a state located in an extremely tumultuous region still without agreed-on boundaries, without a constitution, and profoundly destabilized by a controversial occupation well into its fifth decade. Admittedly this is not exactly the state left by Ben-Gurion when he retired from his last (ninth) government in 1963. Still, many of his decisions and choices as the leader of Israel, both as a "state in the making" and as a sovereign state for nearly fifteen years, had, and are still having, profound effects on the political life of the country.

The creation of Israel has launched millions of Jews in Israel, and indirectly also Jews of the diasporas, into an uncharted future, an uncertain adventure in modernity. Nobody could anticipate in May 1948 the consequences of creating a Jewish army in a secular state, uncommitted to the separation between state and religion; the result of massive waves of immigration from the Arab countries and Eastern Europe; the impact of a series of wars since 1948; and, finally, the impact of massive settlement in territories occupied in the 1967 war for Israeli society and the Arab-Israeli conflict. Without getting into the complex issue of relating the attribution of causes to the attribution of responsibilities, it is clear that despite Ben-Gurion's republican, social-democratic civic rhetoric, his centralized mode of governing as well as the implicit monarchic connotations of his concept of *mamlakhtiyut*, facilitated decades later the dangerous constitutional experiment of replacing Israel's democratically radical electoral system of proportional representation with a system of personality focused on direct election of the prime minister. This system, which was in force between 1992 and 2003, regulated three national elections. The massive criticism of the electoral system of the direct election of the prime minister had, in many ways, echoed the warning made, during the time of Ben-Gurion, by professors Nathan Rotenstrich and Jacob Talmon against the propensity for a cult of strong leadership in Israel. Also, the aura of tolerance and inclusivity that guided Ben-Gurion's compromise with Israel's small Haredic parties has dissipated over time with the realization that it paved the way decades later for disproportional growth in the demographic and political power of the Orthodox and Haredic sector to consistently tip the delicate balance between right and left political blocs in favor of the right. Moreover, it has dramatically enhanced the power of Haredic parties to block processes of secularization so dear to Ben-Gurion; to feed the non-working class of the Haredic sector by draining the national budget; to create a separate, large-scale educational system completely insulated from democratic civic education; and, finally, to allow an implausibly large number of Haredic and strictly Orthodox youth to avoid military service.

One of Ben-Gurion's concessions to the Israeli religious sector, combined with his own authoritarian instinct, led him to miss the unique moment when the newly born state could adopt a constitution. In the course of time, repeated attempts to enact a constitution have drowned in the contests of ordinary politics, becoming less and less politically feasible. This omission implies that so far the powers of the Israeli governments are not properly constrained and regulated by a constitutional legal frame sufficiently immune from day-to-day political pressures. In contemporary Israel, the law is not satisfactorily protected from politics, and politics is not sufficiently bounded by the law. At the same time Israel's Declaration of Independence, signed by Ben-Gurion and his associate state founders, and then publicly read by him on May 14, 1948, persisted in projecting the double commitment of the newly born state to be both a home for the Jews and a democracy. While Israeli governments and political groups have a dismal record of respecting the freedom and equality of underprivileged Israeli citizens, the declaration kept its power as an authentic foundational document that has been repeatedly invoked by Israeli citizens to defy and criticize these violations.[25]

As a prime minister, Ben-Gurion consistently showed greed for territorial expansion. There is unambiguous evidence that before and immediately following the

Sinai War of 1956 he hoped to annex the entire Sinai Peninsula, which was an Egyptian territory. Humiliated by the necessity of complying with the demand of the great powers to withdraw from the conquered territory, Ben-Gurion must have experienced a stinging lesson on the limits of power. This certainly was an important station on his way to reassessing the policy of territorial expansion. As an elder statesman, he went further in that direction: following the spectacular military victory of the 1967 war, he expressed a strong objection to the occupation and favored returning all the territories except for Jerusalem. In other words, his legacy on the issue of Israel's borders is mixed. Both those who advocate keeping occupied territories beyond the 1967 Green Line and those who support withdrawal can rely on his attitudes in different periods.

Ben-Gurion's legacy in foreign policy was the imperative of relying on the support of a great power. Recognizing the emergence of the United States as the most significant world power following World War II and its potential role in accepting a Jewish state in Palestine as a legitimate component of the new postwar world order, he was quick to shift the Israeli orientation from Britain to the United States.

Gaps between the visions and policies of Ben-Gurion are in many ways more instructive than the unanticipated consequences of his decisions, some of which are discussed above. They indicate, among other things, the necessary tensions between the two roles of a leader: to inspire his people to act, cooperate, and endure and to create policies and make harsh, often unpopular decisions. Ben Gurion took very risky and politically costly actions that, despite great uncertainties, were deemed more instrumental for protecting the sovereignty and security of the country than more convenient alternatives. Ben-Gurion was conscious of such complex requirements of effective leadership. Above all he was a remarkably resolute decision-maker. Although his decisions were often the result of a group process of deliberation, they were mostly the consequence of an agonizing, lonely personal struggle. Once they had been made, however, he moved with all his powers to unyieldingly carry them out. This was demonstrated in historic decisions he took, such as passing his Biltmore Plan for the creation of an independent Jewish state (1942) and adopting it as the supreme mission of the Jewish people, fueling the resistance to the British White Paper; declaring the independent state of Israel in May 1948; accepting reparations from postwar West Germany (1952); and deciding to go to war against Nasser's Egypt in 1956.

Since the time of Ben-Gurion, many Israeli leaders across the entire political spectrum claimed to follow his legacy. In retrospect, the sight of Ben-Gurion's numerous self-appointed heirs illuminates his historic achievement in embodying and containing rather than resolving or whitewashing the contradictions and dilemmas inherent in the Zionist movement and the project of the Jewish state in Palestine. As such, beyond the great controversies provoked by this contentious creator of the state of Israel, he projects a rare brand of leadership that dwarfs most of the Israeli political leaders that rose to power after him.

Notes

1. On "backshadowing" see Michael Andre Berenstein, *Forgone Conclusions: Against Apocalyptic History* (Berkeley, 1994).

2. On the performative political imagination see Yaron Ezrahi, *Imagined Democracies: Necessary Political Fictions* (Cambridge, 2012).

3. Benedict Anderson, *Imagined Communities: Reflections on the Origins and Spread of Nationalism* (London, 1991), 7.

4. Michael Bar-Zohar, *Ben-Gurion: A Biography* (Tel Aviv, 2005), 96.

5. Shabtai Teveth, *The Jealousy of David: The Life of Ben-Gurion*, vol. 3 (Tel Aviv, 1987), 322.

6. Oliver Leaman, *Judaism: An Introduction* (London, 2011), 31.

7. Teveth, *The Jealousy of David*, vol. 3, 321.

8. Zeev Tzahor, *The Vision and the Account: Ben-Gurion between Ideology and Politics* (Tel Aviv, 1994) [Hebrew].

9. Zeev Sternhell, *The Founding Myths of Israel* (Princeton, 1988).

10. For an extensive illuminating study of *mamlakhtiyut*, see Nir Kedar, *Mamlakhtiyut: David Ben-Gurion's Civic Thought* (Jerusalem, 2009) [Hebrew].

11. Michael Keren, *Ben-Gurion and the Intellectuals: Power, Knowledge and Charisma* (De Kalb, 1983), 130–51.

12. Menachem Brinker, *Nietzsche's Influence on Hebrew Writers in the Russian Empire* (Berkeley, 1994); Hamutal Bar-Yosef, "De-Romantisized Zionism in Modern Hebrew Literature," in *Modern Judaism* 16, no. 1 (1996): 67–79.

13. Keren, *Ben-Gurion and the Intellectuals*, 130–51.

14. Tzahor, *Vision and the Account*, 77.

15. On the decline of the ethos of the citizen-soldier following the occupation in the later decades of Israeli statehood, see my "Soldiers' Violence and the Dialectics of Citizenship and Victimhood in Contemporary Israel," in *Democratic Citizenship and War*, eds. Yoav Peled, Noah Lewin-Epstein, Guy Mundlak, and Jean L. Cohen (London and New York, 2011), 132–43.

16. Idith Zertal and Akiva Eldar, *Lords of the Land: The War over Israel's Settlements in the Occupied Territories, 1967–2007* (New York, 2009).

17. The White Paper of 1930, by British colonial secretary Lord Passfield, was a formal statement by the British government limiting official Jewish immigration to Palestine. It was interpreted by the Yishuv Zionist leadership as a retreat from the Balfour Declaration in 1917 in which Britain was committed to the founding of a Jewish national home in Palestine.

18. Kedar, *Mamlakhtiyut*, 122.

19. Shaul Shenhav, "The Voice of the State: The Israeli Government's Shaping of the State Narrative in the Early Years of Israel," unpublished PhD diss., The Hebrew University of Jerusalem, 2003 [Hebrew].

20. Cited in Isaiah Berlin's "Einstein and Israel," in *Albert Einstein: Historical and Cultural Perspectives*, Centennial Symposium in Jerusalem, eds. Gerald Holton and Yehuda Elkana (Princeton, 1982), 285.

21. Idith Zertal, *From Catastrophe to Power: Holocaust Survivors and the Emergence of Israel* (Berkeley, 1998).

22. Teveth, *Jealousy of David*, vol. 3, 441.

23. Don Handelman, *Nationalism and the Israeli State: Bureaucratic Logic in Public Events* (New York, 2004).

24. I am indebted to Eyal Chowers and Zeev Tzahor for calling my attention to this reference in David Ben-Gurion, *Letters to Paula and Children* (Tel Aviv, 1968) [Hebrew].

25. Note the use of the Declaration in the massive antigovernment demonstrations in the summer of 2011.

18

Franz Rosenzweig (1886–1929)
ON THE IDEA OF DIASPORA

Peter E. Gordon

> The day Zionism produces the Messiah my *Star of Redemption* will be
> superfluous. But so will all other books.
> —FRANZ ROSENZWEIG, DIARY ENTRY (APRIL 12, 1922)

WHAT DOES IT MEAN FOR THE MODERN JEW TO LIVE IN THE DIASPORA? MUST EXILE be understood as a temporary condition from which the Jewish people hope eventually to be redeemed? Is the Zionist aspiration—to effect nothing less than a "negation of exile"—the very fulfillment of an ancient promise? Or might one imagine the inversion of this idea, the proposal that Jewish existence simply *is* and *cannot be otherwise than* an existence in exile? And if one considers the latter, would it not seem to follow that Zionism would be not the negation of exile but rather the negation of Judaism itself?

More than half a century after the establishment of the modern state of Israel, it may seem either perverse or merely utopian to imagine the latter possibility. But it should at least be acknowledged that Jewish modernity comes in many forms and persists today with a multiplicity of allegiances and identitarian beliefs, not all of which have been ready to embrace the Zionist option as preferential, let alone definitive. Among the many philosophical and political-theological alternatives that have been articulated in lieu of the territorialist conception of modern Jewish identity, perhaps the most fascinating is that developed by the German Jewish philosopher Franz Rosenzweig in the earlier decades of the twentieth century. This essay offers a brief reflection on Rosenzweig's theological and political understanding of exile as the privileged condition of Jewish life.

Born in 1886 into the comfort of a bourgeois family in the Hessian town of Kassel, Rosenzweig did not originally dedicate himself to questions of Judaism. In the years immediately preceding the World War I he undertook studies in both philosophy and history at the University of Freiburg with the prestigious German intellectual historian Friedrich Meinecke. For his doctorate he submitted a formidable work on the development of Hegel's political philosophy, which was published in

265

1920 as *Hegel and the State*. But a series of exchanges with Eugen Rosenstock (a philosopher and historian of Jewish origin who had earlier converted to Christianity) brought Rosenzweig to a spiritual crisis, which reached its denouement only after he attended Yom Kippur services in 1913 and thereafter resolved to remain a Jew and devote the remainder of his life to the development of a Jewish philosophy. Already in the midst of the war Rosenzweig began to draft the framework for what he would eventually describe as his "system of philosophy," a formidable tripartite work of theological and metaphysical speculation that appeared in 1921 as *The Star of Redemption*. Even before its completion Rosenzweig felt that it would be his life's work and that his remaining days would be merely "posthumous." Shortly afterward he was diagnosed with amyotrophic lateral sclerosis, a neurological disease of progressive paralysis that slowly robbed him of all motor functions and confined him to his home. Notwithstanding his difficulties, Rosenzweig sustained a prodigious energy as a founder and teacher at the Frankfurt Lehrhaus (an institute for adult Jewish learning) and as a translator—first of the poems of Jehuda Halevi and then as a cotranslator of the Hebrew Bible into German. The latter was a monumental task that he undertook in partnership with Martin Buber, but it remained unfinished when Rosenzweig passed away in December 1929.

The Star of Redemption contains Rosenzweig's original and highly provocative reflections on the character of Jewish life. But it is not only an exercise in Jewish philosophy; it is concerned in equal measure with Christianity and also addresses general questions of metaphysics, history, politics, and aesthetics. Both Judaism and Christianity are fastened to an ambitious metaphysical-historical framework or "world-picture" (the book's original subtitle), which portrays the dynamic temporal interaction of three cosmic elements—God, world, and human being—that are purported to be the building blocks of reality. Within this framework Rosenzweig explores both Christianity and Judaism as the two privileged systems of social belonging that allow for legitimate, if divergent, modes of religious experience. Christianity is portrayed in *The Star* as the religion of linear history, which actively forges its path toward redemption by means of world-transformation. Judaism is the religion of eternity-in-time, which absents itself from history so as to concentrate its fullest attention upon the God whose unique favor it can already claim. These two aspects of redemption correlate with two concepts of time. For Christianity, time is a line such that historical existence becomes the necessary theater in which moral-political agency moves the believer progressively toward salvation. For Judaism, time is a circle such that mere history is evacuated of all redemptive significance. The Jewish community dwells in history but is not of history. Indifferent to the struggle for terrestrial permanence and drawing nourishment only from its own piety, the Jewish community lives in an anticipatory condition of peace toward which other nations must continue to strive.

It is most of all this portrait of Jewish apoliticism and historical indifference that explains why *The Star of Redemption* has seemed to many readers an antiquated and even offensive work. Especially for its readership in modern Israel, the book has aroused a plausible objection that its portrait of the Jewish condition is unrealistic and perhaps even irresponsible, insofar as it denies to the Jews the political agency prerequisite for defending themselves against their historical enemies.[1] Some have observed that Rosenzweig died before the rise of Nazism and was thus spared from

witnessing the true costs of the Jews' indifference to political history. They have concluded that the two transformative events of modern Jewish history, the Holocaust and the creation of the state of Israel, have rendered Rosenzweig's philosophy more or less obsolete. But it is worth noting that these objections forge the tools for their own legitimacy. They appeal to a prior decision in favor of historical-political facts, which they award the power of refutation even when levied against a philosophy that denies their significance. One may be tempted to conclude that between an ideology that finds its warrant in politics and one that denies the possibility of such a warrant, there can be no common measure. It is therefore worth investigating the more precise contours of Rosenzweig's argument so as to reckon with his theologically inspired indifference to Zionism and the deeper conception of Jewish identity that serves as its ultimate justification.

The Star of Redemption may be profitably read as a bold affirmation of the Jewish diaspora.[2] Whereas the origin legends of other nations typically make reference to territorial provenance, "the earliest legends about the tribe of the eternal people are not based on indigenousness [*Autochthonie*]."[3] It is true that Adam ("the father of mankind") sprang from the earth itself, but even this truth demands qualification because it describes his physical substance alone and not the spirit by which he was given life. But Adam was not yet Abraham: "the father of Israel" developed his identity not in unity with the earth but "came from the outside." The story of Abraham "begins with God's command to leave the land of his birth and go to a land God will point out to him." For Rosenzweig, this primitive event of *dislocation* remains logically prior to and more essential than any claim of territorial location: "Thus in the dawn of its earliest beginnings, as well as later in the bright light of history, this people is a people in exile, in the Egyptian exile and subsequently in that of Babylonia." The condition of exile is not merely a curse from which the Jews hope one day to recover. It is instead an essential feature of the Jewish condition, and it remains so even when the Jews dwell in the holy land that was first promised to them.[4] Rosenzweig amplifies this claim in the following remarkable passage:

> To the eternal people, home is never home in the sense of land, as it is to the peoples of the world who plough the land and live and thrive on it, until they have all but forgotten that being a people means something besides being rooted in a land. The eternal people has not been permitted to while away time in any home. It never loses the untrammeled freedom of a wanderer who is more faithful a knight to his country when he roams abroad, craving adventure and yearning for the land he has left behind, than when he lives in that land. In the most profound sense possible, this people has a land of its own only in that it has a land it yearns for—a holy land. And so even when it has a home, this people, in recurrent contrast to all other peoples on earth, is not allowed full possession of that home. It is only a stranger [*nur ein Fremdling*].[5]

According to *The Star*, the Jewish experience of exile is therefore not merely an affliction to be overcome. It is instead a kind of ontological-communal distinction due most of all to the fact that the Jews simply do not require a metaphysical grounding in land. Any such territoriality would be supererogatory. Thanks to the intensity of their proleptic experience of God, they find that profane time "has no power" over them and "must roll past." Isolated from the "bellicose temporality" of political history, the Jewish people can "produce its own time" and "provide the warrant of its eternity."[6] It is this nonterritorial guarantee of its endurance that explains why the Jews are not permitted to imagine that the holy land is a secure possession.

It is also this suprahistorical existence that obviates the Jewish struggle to secure permanence through territorial conflict. This, claims Rosenzweig, distinguishes them in the starkest way from the other nations of the world that strive to realize the illusion of eternity through territory. Such nations seek eternity in "the solid ground of the earth [*im festen Grund der Erde*]." Territoriality is therefore a species of erroneous foundationalism, a misguided attempt to secure permanence in time by means of physical dominion: "Their will to eternity clings to the soil and to the reign over the soil, to the land." This results in a confusion between temporality and territoriality. The difficulty is that such a bid for foundationalism through land will always prove self-defeating and will never achieve the genuine security of a foundationalism in God. From these observations Rosenzweig derives a dramatic conclusion. Whereas the nations of the world experience the stark contradiction between profane identification and their sacred mission, the Jews withdraw themselves entirely from the violence of profane identification: "Because the Jewish people is beyond the contradiction that constitutes the vital drive in the life of the nations—the contradiction between national characteristics and world history, home and faith, earth and heaven—it knows nothing of war."[7]

> As against the life of the nations of the world, constantly involved in a holy war, the Jewish people has left its holy war behind in its mythical antiquity. Hence, whatever wars it experiences are purely political wars. But since the concept of a holy war is ingrained in it, it cannot take these wars as seriously as the peoples of antiquity to whom such a concept was alien. In the whole Christian world, the Jew is practically the only human being who cannot take war seriously, and this makes him the only genuine pacifist.[8]

This argument is no doubt surprising, but it is important to acknowledge that it is not motivated by political or historical observations. The Jews' condition as a nonterritorial people is not a *cause* but rather a *consequence* of a studious piety that remains altogether beyond the disorder of the world:

> The power of world history breaks against this quiet life which looks to neither side [*An diesem stillen, ganz seitenblicklosen Leben bricht sich die Macht der Weltgeschichte*]. World history may claim, again and again, that its newest eternity is the true eternal. But, over and against all such claims, we see the calm and silent image of our existence [*das ruhige, stumme Bild unsres Daseins*].[9]

One may hasten to dismiss this image of Judaism as a retreat into naive apoliticism. But Rosenzweig recognizes that the Jews' quiescence does not render them immune to the violence of their surroundings. His unusual portrait of the Jews as a calm community in the midst of the storm provides an equally unusual explanation for their persecution: resentment. "The true eternity of the eternal people," he writes, "must always be alien and vexing to the state, and to the history of the world."[10] But if antisemitism stems from resentment, this does not challenge but merely justifies the Jewish retreat from politics. Rather than proposing that the Jews assume a mimetic response of defensive nationalism against the nationalist violence of their persecutors, Rosenzweig suggests instead that the Jewish community should sustain their apoliticism even if it has the consequence of leaving the Jews exposed to persecution. This is because Rosenzweig cleaves to the religious value of quasi-Stoic inaction (comparable in certain ways to the ancient practice of ἀταραξία, the Stoic cultivation of undisturbedness) and he deems this of infinitely greater significance than any possible advantages that might be derived from political action.

Although Rosenzweig is in many ways a philosophical modernist, his argument for Jewish uniqueness must strike most readers as an astonishing remnant of traditionalism. For unlike both assimilationists and Zionists, Rosenzweig cleaves to the doctrine of Jewish chosenness and even amplifies its significance. It is indeed one of the more perplexing features of *The Star* that it extols the Jews for their inaction, not because it regards this inaction as a political virtue but rather because such inaction serves as a religious sign of their election. Indifference to politics is therefore also an affirmation of difference: it distinguishes the Jews as a people untouched by history itself. Whereas it is the fate of all other nation-states that they take up the sword to carve "hours of eternity on the bark of the growing tree of life," the Jews are "the eternal people" and as such do not concern themselves with the tree's surface. "Untroubled and untouched" (*unbekümmert und unberührt*), they devote themselves only to eternal life. Ultimately this means that the Jews exist in a condition of self-sustaining temporality—"outside of a time agitated by war." They can therefore exist beyond the confines of the historical arena for which peace remains only a dream. Because the Jewish nation "has reached the goal which it anticipates in hope, it cannot belong to the procession of those who approach that goal through the labor of centuries." For the Jewish nation, any concern for "the labor, the deed, and the struggle for the sake of the world has died off." The holiness of the Jewish nation therefore "incapacitates it from devotion to a still-unholy world." The Jewish people "lives in its own redemption."[11]

Rosenzweig's affirmation of Jewish apoliticism and his correlative indifference to Jewish territorialist aspirations is clearly evident if one consults his correspondence. In 1917 Rosenzweig confided to his friend Gertrud Oppenheim that he felt no greater warmth for the Zionists than for those who preached assimilation. The assimilationists endorsed the wholly unadmirable goal of turning world Jewry into little more than a nation of "petty civil servants . . . artists . . . or God forbid, German peasants." The Zionists would attain the very same goal if they managed "to found their Serbia or Bulgaria or Montenegro in Palestine." The second prospect aroused far greater alarm:

> I don't think that the first danger is serious, for in this Europe replete with history the past cannot be simply dismissed; we have to swim with the current. But the second danger holds a serious threat. . . . It is for this reason that Hermann Cohen, with absolutely trustworthy instinct, hates the Zionists. He once said to me something he has never put on paper (nor ever, for think how the Verein, and the Central-Verein and the Verband would react!): "These bums want to be *happy*!"—There's the *rub*! Verein, Central-Verein, and Verband have precisely

the same wish, yet Cohen senses that it will never be fulfilled; in the case of the Zionists he feels that they *will* be happy, eventually.[12]

As we have already seen from the argumentation developed in *The Star of Redemption*, Rosenzweig's hostility to Zionism had less to do with political concerns than with his religious conception of the diaspora. He therefore took exception to the Zionist idea (chiefly associated with Ahad Ha'am) that Jewish life in exile would remain dependent for its longevity on the vitality of a Jewish center in Palestine or to the more drastic conclusion that Jewish existence in the diaspora would simply come to an end. His argument against Ahad Ha'am involves a conscious inversion of the relation between center and periphery:

> The Zionists will be lost once they lose touch with the Diaspora [*Und deshalb werden die Zionisten verloren sein, wenn sie die Fühlung mit der Diaspora preisgeben*].... Their contact with the Diaspora is the only thing that makes them hold fast to their *goal*, which means, however, that they must be homeless in time and remain wanderers, even there [*d.h. aber heimatlos in der Zeit zu werden und auf der Wanderschaft zu bleiben, auch dort*]. Ahad Haam's conception of Zionism is thus quite (unconsciously) correct; only by realizing its connection with Berlin, Lodz, or, someday, if you like, New York, Valparaiso, and Tobolsk, will Palestine remain Jewish and also make life in the Diaspora really possible.[13]

In a letter of December 1917 to his parents, Rosenzweig revisited the same argument, warning that "[i]f Zionism were to gather all the Jews into Palestine there would be no Jews left after two hundred years."[14] The fundamental flaw in the Zionists' efforts, according to Rosenzweig, lay not with practical questions of settlement or political issues of encouraging migration; it sprang from their very conception of Jewish identity as allowing for territorial attachment. His objection applied not only to the maximalists' claim that the diaspora would disappear but also targeted Ahad Ha'am's cultural-Zionist conception of the Jewish homeland as a "spiritual center" to an enduring diaspora. For cultural Zionism "desires to create a Jewish *center* (this it knows) and this center (this it doesn't know) will be governed by considerations of the 'periphery,' and not, as it hopes, the other way around." It followed that Zionism represented merely "one more root gripping the earth."[15]

Rosenzweig believed that the exilic character of Jewish identity remained a more or less inviolable principle across all of Jewish experience and as far back as the biblical era itself. Both the prophets and the Pharisees maintained an attitude of "distance" (*Distanz*) toward their own states and the states of the diaspora, respectively. As Rosenzweig explained, the proper attitude to be cultivated was "distance" rather than "negation" or, in other words, a studied policy of "nonidentification" (*Nichtidentifizierung*). To his cousin Hans Ehrenberg, Rosenzweig complained that "[t]he nineteenth century destroyed both these forms of objectivity (the Pharisean in practice and the prophets in theory) by falsifying into cosmopolitanism what, in reality, was a revolutionary criticism of their own state." He was convinced the Zionists would find it necessary to revive "the attitude of prophetic criticism" among themselves. But he worried that it might prove far more difficult to reestablish the stance of "Pharisean distance [*pharisäische Distanz*]" among the Jewish communities of the diaspora, "which [he hastened to add] persists even in Palestine."[16]

Rosenzweig developed a similar line of criticism in his review of the Hebrew translation of Spinoza's *Ethics* by the Zionist writer Jacob Klatzkin, who celebrated "a nationalism that denies the Jewish heritage any claim whatsoever on the new generation about to assume it." For Rosenzweig it seemed clear that Klatzkin's "extremist theory" was born in "the experimental laboratories of European nationalism."[17] What Rosenzweig failed to acknowledge was that most forms of European nationalism celebrated rather than rejected their grounding in prior traditions of nonstatist cultural identification. But even those forms of cultural Zionism that acknowledged their continuity with a diasporic heritage committed the basic error of assuming the cultural priority of the newly established center to its periphery. For Rosenzweig the true relation was the reverse: the homeland would continue to draw its spiritual nourishment from the diaspora.

> Thus a spiritual center such as we have in mind in regard to Palestine can be seen at a great distance and so become representative for all Jewry. But if it is to be a real center, it must depend on the periphery and the laws governing it so long as there is a periphery. To express it plainly and drily to the point of blasphemy: the spirit of this spiritual center cannot grow in the direction of pure, uninhibited nationalism avid for its own development, no matter how much it would like to; just because of its focal character it must constantly keep in sight the periphery which can never be governed by pure nationalism but will always be constrained to regard the national as a function of the religious.[18]

This objection followed not from any pragmatic concerns regarding the future success of the Zionist movement but rather from an underlying conception of what it meant to be Jewish. Zionism would only survive if it remained cognizant (even within Palestine) of the essentially diasporic character of Jewish identity. In a 1921 letter to Rudolf Hallo, Rosenzweig summarized this thought with startling brevity: "To be a Jew *means* to be in exile ['Jude sein *heißt* im "Golus" sein']."[19] Significantly, Rosenzweig writes "exile" according to the Ashkenazic pronunciation ("Golus"), resisting the spelling in modern Hebrew (*Galut*) that had become customary amongst his Zionist contemporaries.

From the inquiry above it may be tempting to label Rosenzweig an anti-Zionist. But the prefix "anti-" as applied to what is essentially a political ideology fails to specify the nuance of his true position.[20] As we have seen in *The Star of Redemption*, Rosenzweig's posture toward Zionism and the broader question of Jewish territoriality is supported by principles deeper and more complex than mere political opposition, which might imply an allegiance to a different but no less political ideology. The difficulty with this reading is that it fails to take seriously the depth of Rosenzweig's apoliticism.[21] It would be more accurate to describe his stance as that of religiously inspired indifference: a species of quietism rather than antipathy.[22] The principles that animate this quietism are religious but they are also— surprisingly—universalistic. For even while Rosenzweig subscribed without apology to the idea of Jewish election, he nonetheless interpreted this idea in a way that supported principles of universalist humanism, principles that, in his view, a Jewish nationalism of the mundane variety could only betray.

The universalistic strain of his thinking comes clearly into view once we turn to the important 1920 open letter to Eduard Strauss ("Bildung und kein Ende") that

Rosenzweig drafted as a programmatic statement for the establishment of the Free Jewish Lehrhaus in Frankfurt.[23] In this essay Rosenzweig lays out a series of arguments and insights that should guide the creation of the new institution. One of his major themes is the primacy of "the Jewish human being [*der jüdische Mensch*]," about which Rosenzweig hastens to explain that "[t]his term should not be taken in its (ostensibly loose) meaning, which is actually a very narrow one." It is especially important to recognize that it does not bear the "petty-Jewish sense [*kleinjüdischen Sinn*] that has been assigned to it by exclusively political or even exclusively cultural Zionism." Rosenzweig instead explains that he intends the phrase "in a sense that though certainly including Zionism goes beyond it [*der gewiß jenen zionistischen mit umgreift, aber außer ihm noch viel mehr*]." For the phrase "the Jewish human being" does not imply that there is a distinction in kind between Jews and other groups: "No dividing walls should rise here [*keine Scheidewand woll sich hier aufrichten*]."[24] There follows a long passage that contains a blunt corrective to Jewish nationalism and a stunning affirmation of universalist humanism:

> Just as Jewishness does not know limitations inside the Jewish individual, so does it not limit that individual himself when he faces the outside world. On the contrary, it makes for his humanity. Strange as it may sound to the obtuse ears of the nationalist, being a Jew is no limiting barrier that cuts the Jew off from someone who is limited by being someone else. The Jewish human being finds his limitation not in the Frenchman or German but only in another human being as unlimited as himself: the Christian or pagan. Only against them can he measure himself. Only in them does he find individuals who claim to be and are as all-embracing as himself, above and beyond all divisions of nationality and state, ability and character (for these too divide human beings from one another). His Judaism must, to the Jew, be no less comprehensive, no less all pervasive, no less universal than Christianity is to the Christian human, or paganism to the pagan humanist.[25]

Rosenzweig's affirmation of a humanity beyond all division grows out of his idea that nationalist distinctions (such as Frenchman or German) introduce limitations into the human community, whereas distinctions of religion (such as Christian, Jew, and pagan) allow for the disclosure of an "unlimited" humanity. Discourses of nationality and state retain their appeal only to the "obtuse ears of the nationalist."

But the question can hardly be avoided: How could Rosenzweig reconcile his apparent universalism with his affirmation of Jewish difference? In *The Star of Redemption* the author only rarely permits himself expansive gestures of humanism such as in the passage above. He is far more concerned to assert the strong distinction of the Jews against all other peoples of the world. As we have seen, this distinction operates on the higher plane of theology—the Jews live already in the light of God's favor, whereas all other peoples remain caught in the gap between mundane struggle and religious aspiration—that would seem to disallow any prospects of humanistic universalism. A common strategy for reading this apparent contradiction is to observe that *The Star of Redemption* embraces a variation of "mission theory."[26] It describes the Jewish people as a particular charged with the power of signifying the universal: an eternity in the midst of time. All other peoples of the world are expected to look to the Jews for the light that illumines the way to redemption. But it remains unclear how this theory resolves the difficulty: if the Jews stand for a universalism that has not yet arrived, then the humanity they are said to share in common with other nations is compromised in the present by a metaphysical privilege reserved for themselves alone.[27] It seems we are left with the perplexity of a theory that endorses a universalism for which it lacks conceptual justification.

But even if Rosenzweig did not arrive at a satisfactory explanation for his universalist commitments, we should nonetheless recognize that at its core his philosophy was animated by the urge to sustain the dogma of Jewish distinction without permitting this idea to express itself in the violence of political theology. Rosenzweig's solution was to affirm Jewish election but only within the confines of a religious phenomenology that resisted any possible realization on the plane of political history. His idea of the diaspora was meant to be a religious idea purged of all political effects, but by the logic of its own apoliticism it laid the groundwork for a critique of modern Jewish territoriality and affirmed the primacy of exile.

Rosenzweig's philosophical affirmation of the diaspora may strike us as distinctively modern insofar as it bears the obvious imprint of apocalyptic and utopian tendencies that were widely shared among the Central European thinkers who came to maturity after World War I.[28] But this does not mean that Rosenzweig's thinking represents a radical departure from Jewish tradition. Modernism (in aesthetics as in philosophy) often involves an appeal to the primitive or a call for the restoration of forgotten origins.[29] This holds for Rosenzweig's case as well: one need not judge his argument as a mark of heterodoxy since the affirmation of diaspora is a commonplace in Jewish sources themselves. It is worth recalling that the idea of diaspora has remained almost from the beginning a site of ideological and theological contestation. The term itself derives from the ancient Greek διασπορά ("scattering" or "dispersion") and is found in passages from the Septuagint where it typically (but not always) corresponds to the Hebrew expression *Galut* ("exile").[30] The Greek noun form gained currency only when it was taken up by the Hellenized Jewish communities of Alexandria, most notably in the writings of both Philo and Josephus, for whom it named the condition of exile in Babylon (or elsewhere). This condition was generally understood as a divine curse that the Jews had brought upon themselves through their disobedience and impiety. Across centuries of semantic transformation the term *Galut* has persisted as the preferred name for the dispersal from which the Jews hope to be redeemed.[31] In the modern period, Zionist discourse (even in its secular form) modified the term without separating itself from this commonplace meaning, although the promise of national redemption passed divine to human agency: the establishment of the Jewish state was frequently understood as a "negation of the exile" (*shelilath ha-Galut*).

But even while we acknowledge the authoritative power of this tradition, it deserves notice that Judaism also bears within itself a countertradition, according to which exile carries a more expansive and metapolitical significance. According to the Lurianic Kabbalah, for example, even God suffers the affliction of cosmic exile.[32] This striking idea, that exile is not merely a political or territorial difficulty for the Jews alone but rather a predicament that touches the innermost nature of the divine, tends to modify (if not invalidate) the modernist political aspiration of overcoming exile by means of human agency. Nor is this merely a rarefied theory unknown in the modern era. For certain sectors of the ultra-Orthodox community, the auto-emancipatory ideology of modern Zionism has always been and remains illegitimate even today.[33]

The countertradition thus introduces an important note of dissent into the discourse of political nationalism and the interpretation of Jewish history on which it is founded. As Amnon Raz-Krakotzkin has observed, the cosmological conception tends to reinforce the view that Jewish exile is not an affliction to be undone but rather a constitutive feature of Jewish identity itself. Such an interpretation challenges a deeply established view of the Jewish exile as only an intermediary stage in the unfolding drama of Providence—a view that derived much of its original authority from Christianity. In the modern era, the constitutive theory of exile continues to stand as an important alternative. Its basic understanding of history (as a dispersal rather than a unity) runs counter to the most significant Enlightenment-derived philosophies of historical progress and the historicist logic that animated the historical discipline in its formative years.[34] But, more specifically, it represents an important challenge to the Zionist view that territorial settlement in Palestine marks the beginning of the Jews' "return to history."[35] If one were to follow Raz-Krakotzkin's countersuggestion that Jewish history be written from the "exilic" perspective, the resultant narrative might bear some resemblance to Rosenzweig's inverted conception of center-and-periphery.[36] Ironically, however, such a historical narrative would represent both a realization and a betrayal of Rosenzweig's thought—a realization of the idea that the Jews are a people of exile, but a betrayal of the idea that in exile there can be no such thing as Jewish history at all.

The actuality of Franz Rosenzweig is not infrequently contested by those who associate Jewish modernity chiefly with the Jewish "return to history" and the political event they consider its foremost sign: the establishment of the state of Israel.[37] But if one sustains the thought that there is not one but multiple Jewish modernities, then it would prove necessary to retain a conceptual space for an alternative, whereby the idea of a return to history would not stand as the privileged marker of modern Jewish life. Against this idea one might entertain the paradoxical thought—Rosenzweig's thought—that what is most modern in Judaism is also what is most unmodern. It is the conception of a life in exile from both the modern *and* the unmodern—an exile from history itself.

Notes

1. For a general survey of responses, see Michael Oppenheim, "The Relevance of Rosenzweig in the Eyes of His Israeli Critics," *Modern Judaism* 7, no. 2 (May 1987): 193–206.

2. On Rosenzweig and exile, see the remarks in Amos Funkenstein, *Perceptions of Jewish History* (Berkeley, 1993), 291–95. See also Rivka Horwitz, "Franz Rosenzweig and Gershom Scholem on Zionism and the Jewish People," *Jewish History* 6, no. 1 (1992): 99–111.

3. Franz Rosenzweig, *Der Stern der Erlösung*, 4th ed (Frankfurt, 1993); in English as *The Star of Redemption*, trans. William Hallo (Notre Dame, IN., 1985), hereafter SE, followed by the English translation (E). Quoted here from SE, 333; E, 300.

4. Ibid.

5. Ibid.

6. SE, 331–32; E, 299.

7. SE, 366; E, 329.

8. SE, 333–34; E, 331.

9. SE, 371–72; E, 334–35.

10. SE, 371; E, 334.

11. The quote "lives in its own redemption" is from SE, 364; E, 328.

12. Rosenzweig's letter to Gertrud Oppenheim, dated May 1, 1917, translated in Nahum Glatzer, *Franz Rosenzweig: His Life and Thought* (New York, Schocken, 1953), 53–55. The passage is worth quoting in full: "Do you want to know my exact position? Ever since the emancipation Jewry has been split into two main bodies: the assimilationists and the Zionists. Both are paths, directions, and as such unassailable. But both are in danger of changing from paths through the universe to streets leading to a certain house. That is to say, both are in danger of attaining an attainable goal. The assimilationists by becoming, instead of brokers, lecturers, journalists, bohemians, and usurers—that is, the Jewish brains that again and again arouse the nations' hatred—petty civil servants (as is now being urged), artisans (which was urged as early as 1800, e.g., the Humanität in Cassel, the Gans-Heine ethical Kulturverein of 1820 in Berlin) or, God forbid, German peasants. The Zionists will attain that goal by managing to found their Serbia or Bulgaria or Montenegro in Palestine."

13. Ibid. N.B.: Glatzer often omits (without indication) certain passages from the German texts he cites. He does so here, and I have indicated the omission with an ellipsis. German quotations from Letter 159, "Unter Mitwirkung von Ernst Simon: Ausgewählt und herausgegeben von Edith Rosenzweig," in Franz Rosenzweig, *Briefe* (Berlin, 1935), 198–203.

14. Letter 205 (18.12.1917), Ernst Simon und Edith Rosenzweig, HRSG, in Rosenzweig, *Briefe*, 270.

15. Rosenzweig, letter to his parents, December 18, 1917, as quoted in Glatzer, *Franz Rosenzweig*, 64.

16. Letter 490, An Hans Ehrenberg (5 May, 1927), in Rosenzweig, *Briefe*. English modified from Glatzer, *Franz Rosenzweig*, 353–54.

17. "Neuhebräisch? Anläßlich der Übersetzung von Spinozas Ethik (1925)," in Franz Rosenzweig, *Kleinere Schriften* (Berlin, 1957), 220–27; quote from 221.

18. Rosenzweig, "A Review of a Translation into the Hebrew of Spinoza's *Ethics*," quoted in Glatzer, *Franz Rosenzweig*, 264ff. In German in *Kleinere Schriften*, 220–27.

19. Letter number 306, An Rudolf Hallo, in Franz Rosenzweig, *Briefe* (Frankfurt, 1921), 398.

20. For certain biographical aspects to Rosenzweig's attitude toward the Zionist movements of his time, see Paul Mendes-Flohr, "Rosenzweig and the Kameraden: A Non-Zionist Alliance," *Journal of Contemporary History* 26, nos. 3–4 (special issue, "The Impact of Western Nationalisms: Essays Dedicated to Walter Z. Laqueur on the Occasion of His 70th Birthday") (September 1991): 385–402.

21. Rosenzweig further clarifies his stance toward Zionism in a letter to Hans Ehrenberg (April 19, 1927): "Theory is invariably only a line. The roads of life deviate more or less, to right or left, from the beeline of theory. That line indicates only the general direction; anyone who insisted on walking the straight line could not move from the spot. Nevertheless, the beeline is still the right one; the road to the left and the road to the right . . . are in reality as little negotiable as the beeline, and are moreover theoretically false simply because there are two of them. What I came to an understanding of in 1913 and wrote down in 1919, in the third part of the Star of Redemption is the beeline. Everything I have done, including the very act of writing down and publishing, as well as all that followed: Academy, Lehrhaus, the founding of a home, the Judah ha-Levi book, the Bible, all this lies to the right of the beeline and can as little be construed in its details from the beeline as what the Zionist does to the left of it. To the right lies the Diaspora, to the left present-day Palestine. It would be a good thing if at least the leaders on both sides could see the beeline. Only a very few do, and rather fewer on the right than on the left." Quoted in Glatzer, *Franz Rosenzweig*, 157–58.

22. Stéphane Mosès also characterizes Rosenzweig's attitude toward Zionism as a species of "quietism." In earlier years Rosenzweig expressed himself without qualification against the ideology of political Zionism whose active restoration of Jewish national sovereignty struck him as a denial of Judaism's genuine mission. But in later writings Moses detects a subtle shift toward an appreciation of the nationalist idea—an interpretation that in my view overstates the nature of Rosenzweig's transformation. On this argument, see Stéphane Moses, "Franz Rosenzweig in Perspective: Reflections on His Last Diaries," in *The Philosophy of Franz Rosenzweig*, ed. Paul Mendes-Flohr (Hanover, 1988), 185–201, esp. 163–95.

23. Franz Rosenzweig, "Bildung und Kein Ende: Wünsche zum jüdischen Bildungsproblem des Augenblicks insbesondere zur Volkshochschulfrage" (Frankfurt am Main, 1920), reprinted in Rosenzweig, *Kleinere Schriften*, 79–93; translated in fragmentary and incomplete form in Glatzer, *Franz Rosenzweig*, 214ff.

24. Rosenzweig, *Kleinere Schriften*, 80–81; quoted from Glatzer's translation, *Franz Rosenzweig*, 214–15.

25. Quoted from Glatzer, *Franz Rosenzweig*, 215; Rosenzweig, *Kleinere Schriften*, 81.

26. See, e.g., Leora Batnitzky, *Idolatry and Representation: The Philosophy of Franz Rosenzweig Reconsidered* (Princeton, 2009).

27. On this point see my argument in Gordon, *Rosenzweig and Heidegger: Between Judaism and Jewish Philosophy* (Berkeley, 2003).

28. On these tendencies see the perceptive remarks in Michael Löwy, *Redemption and Utopia: Jewish Libertarian Thought in Central Europe. A Study in Elective Affinity* (Stanford, 1992); David Biale, *Gershom Scholem: Kabbalah and Counter-History* (Cambridge, 1979); and Anson Rabinbach, *In the Shadow of Catastrophe: German Intellectuals between Enlightenment and Apocalypse* (Berkeley, 2001).

29. On Rosenzweig and "modernism as archaism" see Gordon, *Rosenzweig and Heidegger*.

30. An excellent linguistic survey is Ladislav Gusta, "Diaspora: The Past in the Present," in *Diaspora, Identity, and Language Communities* (Studies in the Linguistic Sciences) 31, no. 1 (Spring 2001): 291–97.

31. David Roskies, *Against the Apocalypse: Responses to Catastrophe in Modern Jewish Culture* (Cambridge, MA, 1984).

32. Gershom Scholem, "Isaac Luria and His School," 1941; reprinted in *Major Trends in Jewish Mysticism* (New York, 1946), 244–86.

33. Amnon Raz-Krakotzkin, "Exile in the Midst of Sovereignty: A Critique of 'Shelilat Hagalut' in Israeli Culture" (Hebrew), *Theory and Criticism* 4 (Fall 1993): 23–55; Daniel Boyarin and Jonathan Boyarin, "Diaspora: Generation and the Ground of Jewish Identity," in *Critical Inquiry* 19 (1993): 693–725.

34. The locus classicus for this critique is of course Walter Benjamin, "On the Concept of History," in *Illuminations* (New York, 1969). For general remarks on antihistoricism in modern Jewish thought, see David Myers, *Resisting History: Historicism and Its Discontents in German-Jewish Thought* (Princeton, 2009).

35. It is even possible (Krakotzkin suggests) that the Zionist view represents a projection into Jewish history of a Christian historical understanding of time as governed by divine grace: "[F]rom the Jewish point of view," he writes, "the adoption of this concept of history was a renunciation and even a negation of the Jewish belief that the world is in exile and an acceptance of the Christian view according to which the world was progressing through an era of Grace, now in a secularized form—a new kind of a 'rational' grace." Amnon Raz-Krakotzkin, "Jewish Memory between Exile and History," *Jewish Quarterly Review* 97, no. 4 (Fall 2007): 530–43; quote from 536. The exilic aspect of Jewish identity is also an important theme in Jacob Taubes, *Occidental Eschatology* (Stanford, 2009); see esp. 17–18.

36. For historiographical trends that may validiate this perspective, or, at least, offer an implicit challenge to the primacy of the Zionist narrative, see Todd M. Endelman, "The Legitimization of the Diaspora Experience in Recent Jewish Historiography," *Modern Judaism* 11, no. 2 (May 1991): 195–209.

37. See Oppenheim, "Relevance of Rosenzweig in the Eyes of His Israeli Critics."

19

René Cassin (1887–1976)

HUMAN RIGHTS AND JEWISH INTERNATIONALISM

Samuel Moyn

RENÉ CASSIN IS BEST KNOWN AS ONE OF THE DRAFTERS OF THE UNIVERSAL DECLA-ration of Human Rights of 1948. Born in 1887, Cassin achieved momentary global renown when he was awarded the Nobel Peace Prize in 1968. Yet it is only in recent years that Cassin has been lavished with international scholarly attention, as affili-ates and observers of human rights as a global hope and a global movement have searched for their predecessors—not least "founding fathers" like Cassin, who, under Eleanor Roosevelt's wise direction, put critical norms down on paper in the shadow of war and genocide.

Biographical studies of Cassin may be indispensable in understanding his signifi-cance, yet they are only a point of departure.[1] Cassin was also, of course, a modern Jew—and I would like to reflect in this essay on how he fits into the long-term his-tory of modern Jewish politics. In what follows, my suggestion is that Cassin's im-portance comes into most profound relief when he is considered as a renovator of the tradition of modern Jewish internationalism. But the term "internationalism" needs more explanation as a basis for the following discussion.

As historians of the modern world have shown, internationalism emerged after 1850 as a triple phenomenon: a new space, a new consciousness, and a new activity. These need to be carefully distinguished, for the space of interdependence and com-petition among modern nation-states could exist without forcing any conscious-ness of that space, let alone any programs to respond to it or reform it. And such programs, when adopted, were themselves various. The goals of bureaucrats stan-dardizing units of measurement differed from the agendas of royal families pursu-ing cross-border marriages, just as academics pursuing cooperation in scientific re-search were rather different in their aims from socialists in Karl Marx's International Workingmen's Association singing the "Internationale" as their anthem. Yet all presupposed the same transforming global space, and sometimes they wanted to shift its transformation in a new direction. The same was true of Jews beginning in the same period. For Jews, as for everyone, it is not so much the breakthrough to cosmopolitan internationalism as different versions of it in contention that matters. And this was not least because—as the very name implies—internationalism most

frequently remained tethered to nation-states it proposed to knit together, and which few reformers hope to transcend radically or altogether.[2]

As a notable committed to an elite defense of the Jewish people globally, Cassin inherited many precedents for his post–World War II pursuits from his predecessors in propounding a Jewish internationalism. But he did not continue the existing versions without interruption. In fact, the recent scholarly recovery of the origins of nineteenth-century Jewish internationalism helps establish room for much novelty in subsequent developments, such as Cassin's activism. If Cassin's twentieth-century internationalism proved less appealing compared to other versions forged by fellow Jews in his own time, it was reborn as the dominant present model of internationalism—and not simply for Jews alone.

■

According to historian Yosef Hayim Yerushalmi, Jews have had a persistent tendency to seek a "vertical alliance" with the highest powers in the places in which they find themselves—a tendency that survived the modern revolution in which political sovereignty passed from kings to peoples. Yerushalmi saw this strategy of promoting Jewish interests and, not infrequently, protecting Jews as coming to rest in the modern state, including in France, where Jews were by the late nineteenth century *Fous de la République*—that is to say, among some of the highest and most dedicated servants of the Third Republic, the regime under which René Cassin was born.[3] No one, so far as I know, has suggested that the vertical alliance also obtained above the modern state once the twentieth-century dream of supranational authority came to be dreamed—but I believe Cassin's case is a helpful one for determining the extent to which it was possible to transcend a vertical alliance with the state.

Growing up in the Third Republic, child of a Sephardic father from southern France and an Ashkenazic mother from Alsace, Cassin adopted the commonplace values of French Jewry in the era. Though members of both branches of his family were religiously observant, René's father, Azaria, styled himself a freethinker, renaming himself Henri and causing such strained relationships with his wealthy in-laws as to deprive his wife of her dowry. Cassin's parents in fact divorced in 1911, when he was in his mid-twenties. As a result, Judaism for the young Cassin primarily meant affiliation with the project of Jewish emancipation, tested though ultimately confirmed by the saga of the Dreyfus affair. Cassin was seven years old when Alfred Dreyfus was first condemned, and nineteen when he was finally exonerated. Thus he was formed politically in the heated controversy through which the "Judeo-republican" ideology of modern French Jewry was reforged and even strengthened.[4] A few years later, Cassin married a Catholic woman he met as a student.

His path to the law professor he eventually became was interrupted by World War I, in which he served and was wounded. Historians Antoine Prost and Jay Winter have convincingly emphasized how fundamentally Cassin was a product of his experience in World War I—especially as he became a leading figure in the associational defense of wounded veterans. In the interwar years in which he had no connection to or interest in Jewish affairs, he pursued the cause of veterans not simply at the level of the French state but also in the activities of the new League of Nations, including the International Labour Organization, which first exposed him to processes and networks of governance beyond the nation. His work on behalf of veterans connected him to the larger causes of peace and disarmament, familiar from the era's internationalism. But the idea of the rights of man so crucial for French Jewry had not yet made its transit upward to describe the moral and political ideals of international organizations or of any internationalist movement. Far more important was the ideal of peace through law: when in 1924 Édouard Herriot came to power and appointed Cassin to the French delegation to the League of Nations, Cassin spoke grandly in a major speech of a world of federated states all subordinated to "a superior moral rule: law."[5]

The absence of a concern for international human rights for so long, even in the career of someone who was to become so closely associated with them, is striking. The Dreyfus affair had prompted the creation of the French Ligue des droits de l'Homme, twenty years before civil liberties unions were formed in the Anglo-American sphere. But, like them, the Ligue concerned itself almost exclusively with the promotion of rights in domestic and imperial spaces. In any event, Cassin did not come to human rights through the Ligue, though he had some relationships to it. And prior to World War II, there was no sign that he would play the major role he did in elevating human rights to an international level and connecting them to the international politics of the Jewish people. In these years, to the extent it was detectable at all, Cassin's own Jewish identity consisted in being the ferocious defender of republican values. Rarely, he also reflected on the effect of the antisemitic gaze that, until World War II changed everything, he easily shrugged off. Before turning to his wartime and post-Holocaust innovations, therefore, it is useful to recall how Jewish internationalism had been forged by others in the nineteenth century before events led Cassin to transform it.

Jews were emancipated not into the world but into states, which sooner or later became nation-states. This was also true—in fact, above all true—in France, where the *droits de l'homme* of the French Revolution were defined from the first by the political goal of the constitution of the nation. In the beginning, the revolutionary appeal to rights was not in the service of the *constraint* of the state, from within or without, but in the name of the *constitution* of the state. As in America before, in France the political goal of invoking natural or "human" rights was violent insurrection for the sake of the foundation of a new polity. Nevertheless, this fundamental fact about modern Jewish history—the indispensable linkage between the emancipation of a minority and the creation of the nation-state as a normative political form—hasn't received much explicit attention. Instead, the main approach to emancipation has been to study how it differed in character and timing from nation-state to nation-state.[6] This historiography takes for granted, in other words, the very forum that international human rights law and movements would strive to denaturalize in the latter part of the twentieth century.

As a result, internationalism—defined as the constitution of a Jewish political subject across borders for the sake of collective agency or mutual defense—is only now receiving the scrutiny it deserves. True, premodern and longstanding networks of rabbinic authority ran athwart of frequently shifting lines of dynastic territories and interstate arrangements, and there were early forms of transnational charitable solidarity. But, as Abigail Green has best shown, it was only toward the middle of the nineteenth century that, along with the emergence of the social and technological infrastructure of all internationalisms, a Jewish version emerged. In the first place, an international Jewish public coalesced as a new sort of Jewish press monitored the vicissitudes of Jewry everywhere. When antisemitic outbursts happened in one place, they became the concern of "international Jewry," imagined as a new entity and with notable leaders like Moses Montefiore. Eventually, the formation of the Alliance Israélite Universelle (AIU) in 1860, though strongly marked by its French origins, is unintelligible apart from the creation of what one might dub the "transnational Jewish public sphere." In the second place, a far-flung new philanthropy emerged, tracking a similar geography from America in the west to the Russian Empire in the east, and extending from Continental Europe in the north into the Ottoman Empire to the south (that empire surely became the object of most political concern, as well as much philanthropic activity).[7]

The emergence of Jewish internationalism in the nineteenth century was transformative in a number of ways. Its unintended contribution to the conceptual possibility of a modern antisemitism denouncing "international Jewry" is obvious; it remains a troubling fact that its rise as an ideology and practice corresponded to the creation of an antisemitic fantasmagoria of global Jewish control. While some have claimed that the collective Jewish assertion in the new internationalism paved the way for Zionism, its unexpected legacy for the formation of later national consciousness is easily overestimated. Not only did internationalism not lead to nationalism, but it persisted alongside it in complex ways. As Green has put it, "The boundaries between religion and nation have remained fluid, but nationalism has never fully displaced religious internationalism in the Jewish world."[8] It goes too far, however, to suggest that Jewish internationalism, with its philanthropic and humanitarian commitment to ameliorate the lives of suffering coreligionists in imperial spaces and the Ottoman Empire alike, amounted to a "human rights" agenda.[9]

Extending prior investigations of how closely relief for Jews through the Alliance Israélite Universelle tracked imperial interests in the French case, Green plausibly shows how in the even more important British case Jews like Montefiore were able to pursue transnational Jewish solidarity, in part because they were active in an empire in which liberal economics and beneficent humanitarianism provided universalistic rationales for imperial expansion. But in the Great Britain of Lord Palmerston, the fact that Jewish relief dovetailed so neatly with an emergent humanitarianism did not blunt the priority of public discourse around "commerce, Christianity, and civilization." Jews cannily exploited these public commitments to bring the British state into their agenda of remediating the plight of Jews in Eastern Europe and, especially, Muslim lands. As a result, the collective rights of Jewish minorities could function as a distinctive object of foreign policy. Indeed, so successful were Jews in applying this pressure that "even when British interests were not at stake, British agents in Muslim lands took up the Jewish cause out of disinterested humanitarianism."[10] All the same, it obscures much to straightforwardly conclude that this imperial context promoted the rise of a politics of international human rights: Cassin's twentieth-century Jewish internationalism before its time.

Ideologically, there was no general language of international human rights in the nineteenth century—which may seem strange until it is recalled how centrally, for Jews and others, the language of *droits de l'homme* referred to emancipation within the nation-state. What would become in the twentieth century an eventually widespread language of individual entitlements "beyond borders," pursued by civil society activists and monitored by governments, remained overwhelmingly cabined to the domestic sphere (and it was of declining significance there due to the loss of prestige of naturalistic and metaphysical notions after their brief moment of Enlightenment and revolutionary visibility). It was no small thing to disentangle "rights" and "citizenship," which may account for how little liberal values were deployed in the international sphere in the age of empire, by Jews as by others. Instead, while notions of minority and collective rights enjoyed some circulation, it was humanitarianism that provided the cultural formation and conceptual framework through which downtrodden Jews were addressed in Jewish internationalism—especially since, in colonial spaces and the Ottoman sphere, the salience of rare episodic political crisis like the Damascus Affair gave way to a generalized humanitarian concern in which Jews targeted their coreligionists as civilizationally backward and socioeconomically deprived.[11]

The institutional perspective confirms the ideological one. By and large the political and philanthropic agenda of nineteenth-century internationalism took shape around Jewish notables—characteristically wealthy Jews like Gerson von Bleichröder or Moses Montefiore. After 1860, the Alliance Israélite Universelle came into existence, followed later by cognate groups like the German Hilfsverein der deutschen Juden. But the Alliance's mainly charitable and educational operations left it highly dependent on the French empire, including the informal French empire. Absent any supranational institutions, concern operated through civil society outreach or at most pressure on states in hopes of bilateral policy outcomes favoring remediation of crises involving Jews or the collective rights of Jews under foreign rule. It was only toward the end of the nineteenth century that, in places like southeastern Europe, the lineaments of a truly international approach to Jewish depredations were faintly visible. And these only took a quantum leap at the Versailles conference, due to the agitation of Lucien Wolf and the Comité des délégations juives (later, since 1936, the World Jewish Congress), with the creation of a minorities regime intended to protect Eastern European Jews living under fragile new sovereigns thought too immature to govern minorities responsibly.[12] What this meant is that while Jews certainly learned to harmonize the interests of Jews abroad with the humanitarian policies of their states, they had no supranational authority through which to act, nor an international regime to construct around the formulation or promotion of new norms. In short, if the human rights agenda of twentieth-century vintage is collapsed into a prior humanitarian internationalism of nineteenth-century origins, much is lost.[13]

■

In other words, the vertical alliance still culminated in states even in the new international system of the nineteenth century. In the first try at international organization above the state, the League of Nations, it was collective minority rights, that creature of nineteenth-century Jewish internationalism, that Jews first tried to transfer upward. But famously, in part because it turned out that Adolf Hitler could abuse the system and claim the rights of Germans in the east were being trampled, that approach fell into disrepute.[14] Cassin, who had had no connection to Jewish politics in the interwar period, proved a key figure in proposing a new internationalism based on individual rights.

The year of the fall of France was significant enough in interrupting Cassin's trajectory that his longest piece of autobiographical writing is devoted entirely to it.[15] After leaving France, he joined the Free French in London and worked tirelessly and along many dimensions for Charles de Gaulle, becoming a prominent Frenchman in general and Jewish circles alike. It was in the midst of the war that Cassin turned to *les droits de l'homme* as the principles most at stake in the conflict. He still did not have that perspective on the eve of the fall of France, when he penned an essay on the "Leviathan-State" that probably remains his most intellectually stirring work, going beyond the technical spirit of his prewar professorial career without lapsing into the summary and frequently platitudinous character of his postwar officialdom. There, he actually criticized the interwar proposal of one or two jurists to draft an international declaration of rights—for it did not go far enough in recognizing the true problem, which was the hypertrophy of the state![16]

But this is not to say that "international human rights" immediately became Cassin's obsessive focus. In fact, in spite of looking hard, Cassin's biographers have found few mentions of the idea in the midst of his wartime activities. Pioneeringly, he made a public declaration at St. James Palace on the importance of a peace based on international human rights in the fall of 1941.[17] The enthusiasm he expressed for the notion thereafter was due essentially to the fact that President Franklin Delano Roosevelt began to use the phrase "human rights"—novel in English at that time—as a new potential principle of world affairs in the midst of his other wartime rhetoric.[18] Cassin, for his part, seems to have taken the concept much more seriously in its traditional role, working with a planning committee occupied with constitutional design for a postwar French state. As a secondary item on the agenda, however, it is true that his interwar dream of international law and his concern with aggressive states made it possible for him to join others who were toying with transferring rights upward to international organizations.[19]

The war was also the occasion of Cassin's reaffirmation of the meaning of human rights at home for the French Jewry of which he increasingly saw himself a part and even a leader. Participating in Free French propaganda efforts, Cassin spoke on the BBC in April 1941 directly to French Jews to remind them that the Free French stood for the state that emancipated them before any of their coreligionists—even as "in the France that calls itself free, the work of the Abbé Grégoire and the Declaration of the Rights of Man are trampled underfoot."[20] (The Abbé Grégoire had been the chief promoter of Jewish emancipation during the French Revolution.) Cassin also worked hard to ensure that the restoration of the French Empire envisaged after the war—one of his main official assignments—would come without loss of the special privileges that the Crémieux decree had accorded Algerian Jews in the nineteenth century.[21] It thus seemed a moment of going beyond the state only in a certain sense, for the French and French-Jewish cause in view of the Leviathan state consisted in the first instance in reestablishing the liberal nation-state that had served Jews so well.

Nevertheless, with the war over, Cassin decided against taking the ministerial position that Charles de Gaulle offered him, opting for the Conseil d'État instead, which he reasoned would give him the time and latitude to internationalize human rights. At the crucial moment, between the Dumbarton Oaks agreements of 1944

and the San Francisco conference of 1945, during which human rights were introduced on condition of their reduction to ornaments on a great power settlement,
Cassin advised on French policy, urging more room for human rights in the final-
ization of the United Nations Charter. But his duties on the Conseil d'État meant
he missed the San Francisco negotiations, where international human rights were
ultimately given only a rhetorical role in world organization.[22]

A year later, once the United Nations Economic and Social Council—to which
human rights had been assigned—began to meet, Cassin was made a member of the
"nuclear commission," so called because it was the nucleus of a new Commission
of Human Rights whose first task was to draft an international bill of rights. The
events that followed, and Cassin's role in them, have received a huge amount of
attention, since the two years of Cassin's involvement with Eleanor Roosevelt led
to the climactic adoption of the Universal Declaration of Human Rights on December 10, 1948.[23] While Cassin won the Nobel Peace Prize alone, it is now known
the drafting of the declaration was a highly cooperative affair. Cassin made the most
decisive contribution in organizing articles culled from constitutions around the
world and writing the basic version of the document's preamble.

■

Even as other internationalist Jews like Hersch Lauterpacht dissented from the
reduction of the newfangled idea of international rights to symbolic ornamenta-
tion of a great power settlement, Cassin's hard work from 1946 through 1948 helped
make the Universal Declaration possible. If this were all he had done, he would
have been an internationalist Jew, but not a Jewish internationalist. As his Jewish
self-consciousness grew, Cassin also took on a new role in the Jewish world in these
years. At de Gaulle's invitation, Cassin accepted leadership of the AIU in 1943, a
position that—unlike his other assignments—he held until his death.

The internationalism of Jewish organizations was, in these years, shifting in the
direction of "human rights," in ways that were to open new pathways, both ideological and institutional, after the war. In the United States, the American Jewish
Committee (AJC) had taken the lead in wartime to promote the identification of
the Jewish cause with the new idea of human rights, and Cassin was certainly disposed to do the same.[24] Cassin's Alliance, too, did not simply incorporate the new
language, but made a pronounced shift toward the view that Jewish self-defense
was best pursued through general defense of principle, first of all by treating the
Jewish fate in the world war then ending as part of the general suffering of humanity.[25] During wartime Cassin entered debates about prospective policy toward war
crimes. As part of an inter-Allied commission, Cassin proposed that it would be
best to subsume the pursuit of justice for Jews, in what was not yet known as the
Holocaust, under the desire to reckon with the general threat to humanity the
Nazis represented. Once the strategy of defending Jews through constructing an
international human rights regime crystallized among kindred organizations like
the AIU and AJC, Cassin instigated the creation of a Consultative Council of Jewish Organizations (CCJO), so named because it assumed consultative status as a
nongovernmental organization for purposes of United Nations advocacy.[26]

Cassin's work to create and reform institutions like the United Nations and, re-
gionally, the European Court of Human Rights, on which he came to serve as judge,

reflected a large step beyond prior Jewish internationalism. Ideologically, it was no longer a matter of finding ways to align Jewish interests with the high-minded rhetoric on civilization of imperial powers like France and Great Britain, so as to encourage their foreign policies to incorporate Jewish defense. Jewish internationalism went beyond mere harmonization with hegemonic norms of Christian states of the nineteenth century to forging new norms above states and institutionalizing them. Most clearly, Jewish internationalism was no longer simply a matter of the noblesse oblige of notables of the nineteenth century. It also went far beyond even first institutional steps like those of the AIU, which remained a French organization even under Cassin's leadership, in an era during which the creation of the state of Israel and decolonization led to a crisis of its educational mission in the Mediterranean basin (including Palestine). The League of Nations, it is true, had introduced fledgling international institutions that Jewish parties exploited to the fullest. But Cassin, like other Jewish internationalists after World War II, not only incorporated the new ideological language of international human rights. He also shifted to a strategy in which the institutional advancement of universal human rights regimes in general seemed the best embodiment of Jewish defense in particular.

These were all brand-new elements in Jewish internationalism, which made it distinct from its nineteenth-century predecessor. And while others who were Jews made the same move, notably international lawyers like Paul Guggenheim and Hersch Lauterpacht, Cassin's presidency of the Alliance makes his evolution especially pivotal for understanding the evolution of Jewish internationalism as a whole.[27] It is important to record that these innovations in Jewish internationalism did not mean that Cassin's Jewish identity, while becoming more explicit, transformed altogether. Cassin's sister and her husband, along with twenty members of his extended family, had been arrested, deported, and killed in Auschwitz late in the war. The Holocaust presumably informed Cassin's own commitment to human rights deeply, and that of other Jews involved with the concept, even if there is no cause to extrapolate from their cases to think that human rights were generally a response to Jewish death (which went unmentioned in the debates in the United General Assembly and in public around human rights).[28] All the same, the internationalization of human rights that Cassin championed for general and Jewish purposes did not lead him to profess more interest in Judaism as a religion or to frame more than a reactive conception of Jewish identity. In his April 1941 message to French Jewry, he noted that "some solidarities sleep in times of prosperity in order to reawaken spontaneously when crisis comes."[29] When Jean-Paul Sartre gave a lecture before the AIU on the basis of his *Anti-Semite and Jew* in June 1947, Cassin heaped high praise on him for responding so vigorously to mass death. In effect Cassin, if not Jews generally, fit Sartre's model of the Jew stimulated by antisemitic hatred—there could hardly be a clearer example of such a model.[30] Cassin could lead the AIU in its mission to emancipate backward Jews in the Mediterranean through education, and engage in international defense of his people against antisemitism. But his existential interest in Judaism or even Jewishness remained minimal, and when as a widower he remarried shortly before his own death, it was for the second time to a Catholic Frenchwoman.

■

But if, in my account, Cassin stands for the novel attempt to go beyond vertical alliance with nation-states to what one might call "vertical construction" of new norms and institutions above, it must be added that his attempt to do so by and large failed—at least in most respects.

For one thing, the 1940s were primarily the age of nationalist rather than internationalist victory, for Jews and most everyone else. Just as in wartime he prioritized the legal reconstruction of the French nation-state, after the war Cassin did not allow his devotion to liberal values to disturb his generally tolerant attitude toward the French Empire, even as it moved to violent counterinsurgency during the Algerian war—which Cassin was involved in legally approving—in a last-ditch effort to avoid dissolution.[31] (In recognition of his fervent devotion to France, Cassin became the first Jew buried in the Pantheon, where his body was moved ten years after his death, and the Algerian conflict forced him into a revealing choice between his statism and his universalism.) Even at the level of international institutions, typically speaking as a representative of France, Cassin did not favor the interference of international human rights with colonial governance—let alone support the inclusion of the earlier and much more globally appealing notion of postcolonial self-determination as a human rights norm (which it eventually became).[32]

Just as much as the persistence of French nationalism that had generally accompanied French *droits de l'homme* for its votaries, the achievement of a long-sought Jewish state, which Cassin also fully supported from the 1940s in spite of his own prior allergies toward Zionism, complicates any notion that a new Jewish internationalism broke through in the era. Cassin had passed through Palestine in 1930, as he recalled receiving an honorary doctorate from the Hebrew University in 1968, and eventually came to insist that the historic mission of the AIU did not conflict with the Zionist project. In fact, he assigned deep meaning to the accident that the state of Israel and the Universal Declaration date to the same year. He responded to the post-1948 Palestinian refugee crisis in the language of humanitarianism rather than in that of human rights. If he was, moreover, not particularly clairvoyant about the disastrous consequences for all concerned of the Israeli occupation after 1967, it was because he did not fully understand what it meant to be loyal to the 1940s assumptions he had pioneered about the interdependence of Jewish and human rights rather than because he rejected those assumptions. In his speech on Mount Scopus, in fact, Cassin insisted that the fate of Israel, like that of world Jewry as a whole, would ultimately be synonymous with the fate of international human rights as a project on behalf of all: "*Never* will Jews in particular obtain real equality," he told his listeners, "until the totality of human rights are respected for everyone."[33]

Given his stances on Algeria and Israel, Jewish internationalism thus offered a supplement rather than an alternative to nationalist assumptions—even for Cassin. But it is perhaps even more important to observe that international human rights provided only one *version* of Jewish internationalism in the era and since. If one were to identify the version of supranational consciousness that most affected modern Jewish history, it would be neither the elite humanitarianism of the nineteenth century, nor the international human rights of the twentieth, but various versions of leftism, which eventually became identified with the communist project in the twentieth century. In real time in the 1940s, including as a response to Jewish death in wartime, communist antifascism seemed in ascendance, not international human rights, which were to remain rather obscure for a long while. Insofar as Jews, like others, voted with their feet, it was nationalism, along with other versions of internationalism, that were triumphant in the 1940s.

In fact, in general as for Jews, aside from a few pioneers like Cassin, it was only decades after World War II, due to the crisis of the first choices in the 1940s of nationalism and communism, that "international human rights" became a visible and plausible option.[34] Alongside the sheer appeal and popularity of the competition, the stillbirth of human rights in international institutions explains why. Just as Cassin was helping draft the Universal Declaration, it was decided that the UN Commission on Human Rights could not entertain complaints of violations, which rendered it essentially irrelevant. And while this later changed, the transformation of the General Assembly of the United Nations through the accession of new states, almost quadrupling the number from those approving human rights in 1948, became a source of depression to Cassin as to many other Jewish observers. Cassin kept faith in the United Nations forum till the end—notably at a twentieth-anniversary conference in Tehran in 1968, in which he stuck out like a sore thumb in the era of anticolonialist reinterpretations of his cherished concept.[35] But these developments have otherwise convinced most Jews that the UN is to be avoided as a place where, in an infinitely repeated opinion, hypocritical states denounce Israel from on high even as they ignore their own worse despotisms.

After decolonization, nationalism lost its romantic appeal, and as the Cold War continued, communist internationalism failed too, on the terrain of ideology and then in reality. At first to achieve a neutral space, then as a weapon in the final stages of the Cold War, human rights emerged as a powerful public idea through new nongovernmental organizations (NGOs). Unlike Cassin's CCJO and others, these new NGOs, and Amnesty International above all, reclaimed international human rights from the United Nations and provided new spaces for civil society activists to join hands across borders in the pursuit of various moral causes. As rival internationalisms died, human rights came to the fore, especially in the 1970s, when in a last act before his passing Cassin joined the international campaign around Soviet Jews, which played some part in the new prestige of international human rights at the time and in the years since.

That campaign shows that the original, nineteenth-century form of Jewish internationalism persisted, no matter what else happened in the twentieth century. From its Zionist impetus to its achievement of a social movement in the West in the 1960s, the cause of the Soviet Jews arguably received a massive boost when it was redefined after 1970 as a matter of international human rights. Cassin attended an epoch-making conference in Uppsala, Sweden in June 1972, at which the right to leave and to return was recalled from the Universal Declaration and presented as a nonnegotiable norm of international politics. Writing in a March 1973 op-ed in the *New York Times*, Cassin agitated for this right, and it found its way in the United States into Senator Henry "Scoop" Jackson's lawmaking on the issue.[36] The episode suggests how much depended on the more traditional version of Jewish internationalism, with pressure on the foreign policy of a powerful state like the United States (and through it the Soviet Union) determining the success the campaign enjoyed. But the campaign also featured appeal to the international human rights norms and laws that it helped canonize publicly, which were, in turn, critical to the plausibility of defining Jewish defense as a human rights issue.

Ironically, the emigration of Soviet Jews to Israel and the United States seemingly closed the long era of Jewish internationalism. With the Holocaust and the effect of the creation of the state of Israel on Jewry in the Mediterranean basin, the massive shift of Jewish geography in the direction of secure residence in the friendly nation-states of Israel, the United States, and Western Europe is practically complete, leaving no large threatened communities as objects of persistent internationalist concern.

All the same, the norms of international human rights seem here to stay, both in providing terms of appeal in debate among Jews and beyond around the state of Israel (notably in response to its continuing occupation policies), and in defining the moral terms of the highest hopes of Jews along with many other globally minded citizens. Jewish internationalism as a worldview has fewer causes today than in any other era in modern history, but it certainly left behind many Jews who are internationalists. A space opened up for vertical ideals above the nation-state by Jews, in part for the sake of Jews, now serves mostly others, even when large numbers of Jews identify with its norms or even devote their lives to their promotion. In Cassin's hands, the vertical alliance ascended, at least aspirationally, to the level of the globe, and with all humanity as its end, not Jews alone. Cassin laid out this legacy perhaps most clearly himself: "Would it not be the most suitable revenge for the Jewish people for all the evil it has suffered to allow the whole world to benefit from the rights of man it has already acquired?"[37]

Cassin's revision of modern Jewish internationalism in the direction of international human rights ultimately shaped the world this way most of all: defining the aspirations of many people, Jewish and non-Jewish, who see no other way to conceive of the terms of global betterment after the collapse of nationalism and communism. International human rights may have failed ideologically and institutionally in Cassin's hands and during his life: he died on the brink of their massive prominence in world affairs. But so long as their ideological hegemony remains secure today, even as their institutionalization faces serious limitations, Cassin's transformation of Jewish internationalism will require attention.

Notes

I am grateful to the volume editors, especially Jacques Picard and Idith Zertal, for their suggestions for revision, and to Jay Winter for thoughtfully correcting my text in spite of several friendly disagreements in interpreting René Cassin's significance.

1. Most recently, Antoine Prost and Jay Winter have published an admiring biography of this figure—the third book-length appreciation Cassin has earned in the few decades since his death in 1976, and a wonderful basis for reflection. In this essay, I rely substantially on these books: Gérard Israël, *René Cassin (1887–1976): La guerre hors la loi, Avec de Gaulle, Les droits de l'homme* (Paris, 1990); Marc Agi, *René Cassin, Prix Nobel de la Paix, père de la Déclaration Universelle des Droits de l'Homme* (Paris, 1998); and especially Antoine Prost and Jay Winter, *René Cassin et les droits de l'homme: Le projét d'une génération* (Paris, 2011), now in English as *René Cassin and Human Rights: From the Great War to the Universal Declaration* (Cambridge, 2013). Subsequent citations are from the French edition. See also Marc Agi, *René Cassin, fantassin des droits de l'homme* (Paris, 1979), his earlier intellectual survey.

2. On internationalism generally, one can consult F.S.L. Lyons, *Internationalism in Europe, 1815–1914* (Leyden, 1963); and Martin Geyer and Johannes Paulmann, eds., *The Mechanics of Internationalism: Culture, Society and Politics from the 1840s to World War I* (New York, 2001).

3. Yosef Hayim Yerushalmi, *"Diener von Königen und nicht Diener von Dienern": Einige Aspekte der politischen Geschichte der Juden* (Munich, 1995); for the notion of *Fous de la République*, see Pierre Birnbaum, *The Jews of the Republic: A Political History of Jews in France from Gambetta to Vichy*, trans. Jane Marie Todd (Stanford, 1996). Hannah Arendt, to whom Yerushalmi

records his debt, famously covered similar themes in *The Origins of Totalitarianism*, 3rd ed. (New York, 1973).

4. See, e.g., Michael R. Marrus, *The Politics of Assimilation: A Study of French Jewry at the Time of the Dreyfus Affair* (Oxford, 1971).

5. Cited in Israël, *René Cassin*, 54. See also now Bruno Cabanes, *The Great War and the Birth of Humanitarianism, 1918–1924* (Cambridge, 2014), chap. 1.

6. Pierre Birnbaum and Ira Katznelson, eds., *Paths of Emancipation: Jews, States, and Citizenship* (Princeton, 1995).

7. See Abigail Green, "Nationalism and the 'Jewish International': Religious Internationalism in Europe and the Middle East c. 1840–c. 1880," in *Comparative Studies in Society and History* 50, no. 2 (2008): 535–58; Lisa Moses Leff, *The Sacred Bonds of Solidarity: The Rise of Jewish Internationalism in Nineteenth-Century France* (Stanford, 2006).

8. Green, "Nationalism," 555.

9. Abigail Green, "The British Empire and the Jews: An Imperialism of Human Rights?," *Past & Present* 199 (May 2008): 175–205.

10. Ibid., 198.

11. See Abigail Green, *Moses Montefiore: Jewish Liberator, Imperial Hero* (Cambridge, 2010), where humanitarianism is pervasive but "human rights" are not (though elsewhere Green has a tendency to treat them synonymously). Leff, *Sacred Bonds* actually includes an index entry for "human rights discourse."

12. See Carole Fink, *Defending the Rights of Others: The Great Powers, the Jews, and International Minority Protection, 1878–1938* (Cambridge, 2004); Mark Levene, *War, Jews, and the New Europe: The Diplomacy of Lucien Wolf, 1914–1919* (Oxford, 1992).

13. For a different narrative claiming the continuity of Jewish concern for human rights (and a continuity from minority to human rights), see Nathan Feinberg, "The International Protection of Human Rights and the Jewish Question (A Historical Survey)," in *Israel Law Review* 3, no. 4 (October 1968): 487–500.

14. Mark Mazower, "Minorities and the League of Nations in Interwar Europe," in *Daedalus* 26, no. 2 (1997): 47–64.

15. René Cassin, *Les hommes parti du rien: Le réveil de la France abattue, 1940–1941* (Paris, 1975).

16. René Cassin, "L'État-Léviathan contre l'homme et la communauté humaine," in *Nouveaux cahiers*, April 1940, reprinted in René Cassin, *La pensée et l'action* (Paris, 1972), 70. This piece, published originally in the Christian personalist journal of Denis de Rougemont, provides much evidence that Christian thought was the main source of Cassin's rhetoric, especially his invocation of the "dignity of the human person" against the totalitarian state, a Catholic dichotomy in origins that Cassin began by thanking Pius XII warmly for introducing to world affairs in his encyclical Summi Pontificatus. For personalism, see my "Personalism, Community, and the Origins of Human Rights," in *Human Rights in the Twentieth Century*, ed. Stefan-Ludwig Hoffmann (Cambridge, 2010).

17. Samuel Moyn, *The Last Utopia: Human Rights in History* (Cambridge, 2010), 52.

18. Prost and Winter, *René Cassin*, 280n, criticize giving Americans priority, saying that "the dossiers of the Free French and Cassin on this subject during the war" contain much evidence on the origins of international human rights. Perhaps; but their own biography fails to discuss those dossiers, immediately moving several years ahead to 1945, suggesting that Cassin may simply have been too busy during the war to pursue the issue.

19. See Prost and Winter, *René Cassin*, 204–9.

20. This message, "Israélites de France," is reprinted in Cassin, *Les hommes*, 480–81.

21. Agi, *René Cassin*, 167–72.

22. Ibid., 181, 188–89.

23. See especially Mary Ann Glendon, *The World Made New: Eleanor Roosevelt and the Universal Declaration of Human Rights* (New York, 2001); and Johannes Morsink, *The Universal Declaration of Human Rights: Origins, Drafting, Intent* (Philadelphia, 1999).

24. American Jewish Committee, *Declaration of Human Rights* (New York, 1944); see now James Loeffler, "The Particularist Pursuit of American Universalism: The American Jewish Committee's 1944 'Declaration of Human Rights'," *Journal of Contemporary History* 50, no. 2 (October 2014): 274–95.

25. See Prost and Winter, *René Cassin*, 377.

26. On the CCJO, see my *Last Utopia*, 122–25.

27. See Jacques Picard, "Zwischen Minoritätenschutz und Menschenrecht—Paul Guggenheims Rechtsverständnis im Wandel, 1918–1950," in *Jahrbuch des Simon-Dubnow-Instituts* 4 (2005): 111–30; Elihu Lauterpacht, *The Life of Hersch Lauterpacht* (Cambridge, 2010)—a good point of comparison for the further reason that Lauterpacht famously poured cold water on the achieved human rights enterprise of the 1940s.

28. See Prost and Winter, *René Cassin*, 318n.

29. Cassin, "Israélites de France," 480.

30. I assume this is what it actually means to say, as Prost and Winter do, a bit romantically: "Ce sont les racistes et les tueurs qui ont révélé son identité juive" (378). See my *Origins of the Other: Emmanuel Levinas between Revelation and Ethics* (Ithaca, NY, 2005), 208–9, where Cassin's introduction of Sartre is recounted. Compare François-Joachim Beer, "René Cassin et le judaïsme," in *La pensée et l'action*, 287.

31. None of Cassin's hagiographers give this material its due, but see Prost and Winter, *René Cassin*, 330–34 for a creditable step forward.

32. See Moyn, *Last Utopia*, 96; and some parts of Glenda Sluga, "René Cassin: *Les droits de l'homme* and the Universality of Human Rights, 1945–1966," in Hoffmann, *Human Rights in the Twentieth Century*.

33. Cassin, "Discours de Jérusalem," in *La pensée et l'action*, 159, 161 (emphasis in original). See Prost and Winter, *René Cassin*, 381–87, 393–98, for a subtle discussion of this issue.

34. See my *Last Utopia*, which makes this general argument.

35. See Roland Burke, "From Individual Rights to National Development: The First UN International Conference on Human Rights, Tehran, 1968," in *Journal of World History* 19, no. 3 (September 2008): 275–96.

36. Sidney Liskofsky and Karal Vasak, eds., *The Right to Leave and Return: Papers and Recommendations of the International Colloquium Held in Uppsala, Sweden 19–20 June 1972* (New York, 1976); René Cassin, "For a Right to Leave and a Right to Return," *New York Times*, March 23, 1973; Gal Beckerman, *When They Come for Us, We'll Be Gone: The Epic Struggle to Save Soviet Jewry* (Boston, 2010).

37. Cited in Beer, "René Cassin et le judaïsme," 286.

20

Shmuel Yoseph Agnon (1888–1970)

BAPTISM BY FIRE

Ariel Hirschfeld

TRANSLATED BY AVNER GREENBERG

THE NEW HEBREW LITERATURE, WHICH EMERGED ONLY IN THE MID-NINETEENTH century, demanded far more than the writing and publication of prose and poetry. A Jewish author who sought to write a Hebrew novel in the 1850s found himself amid a peculiar, unique culture, consisting of at least two and often four tongues: Hebrew and Aramaic, the languages of religion, rite, and learning; Yiddish, the language of the community, in which the everyday was lived; and, for many, languages of the surrounding Gentile world—Russian, Lithuanian, Polish, and so forth. Yet, albeit this polyglossia, this culture—Jewish culture—had no secular literature of its own.

Hebrew and Aramaic were the timeless, universal tongues of Jewish culture, in which educated Jews were knowledgeable, and this prepared them for their role in the creation of a new Hebrew national language—the Hebrew of modern literature. We may already here point to the fascinating difference between European nationalism, in which language was linked to the locus of the land, and Jewish nationalism, which was founded upon a language that was "disembodied"—existing in time but, for the most part, without a space. This attribute was not entirely lost even when Hebrew literature eventually became correlated with a single locus—the Land of Israel.[1]

Avraham Mapu (1806—1867) was the first to create a foundation, a specific locus, for modern Hebrew prose, fashioned from deep connections among language, genre and place. His *Ahavat Tsion* (Love of Zion, 1853) is one of modern Hebrew literature's most stirring achievements because it created, seemingly out of nowhere, a site of cultural independence. European literature served as a dominant and obligatory model for modern Hebrew literature, and from this point onward the relation between them no longer took the form of a passive acquisition of forms, styles, and literary norms. Instead, it developed into an alert negotiation that was informed by a radical movement toward the literary sources scattered within the long textual

history of Judaism, thus marking a theological and cultural differentiation between Judaism and European culture.

Following Mapu's literary revolution, modern Hebrew prose was transposed to the concrete reality of Jews living in the towns of Eastern Europe. This step was taken, about half a generation after Mapu, by S. Y. Abramovich (1835–1917), better known by the nom de plume Mendele Mokher Sefarim (Mendele the bookseller). Mendele's literary exemplars were Miguel de Cervantes, Johann Wolfgang Goethe and the eighteenth-century English writers—especially Henry Fielding and Laurence Sterne. His confident literary treatment of the Jewish shtetl's reality—which for him was a contemporary social, economic, and psychological milieu—and the novel Hebrew style he created in order to describe this reality were major innovations. Because it was shrouded in sanctity, Hebrew, and especially biblical Hebrew, was not used in everyday Jewish life and was thus ill-fitted to represent actual spoken language. In order to solve this problem, Mendele Mokher Sefarim based his work on the language of the Mishnah (oral law) and on the Hebrew of *Hazal* (our Sages of Blessed Memory)—the ancient secular Hebrew—rather than on biblical Hebrew. Biblical Hebrew had been posited as the "classical" model, facilitating a stylistic differentiation and stratification between "high" and "low" Hebrew. This was supplemented by the introduction of Aramaic, which was regarded by Mendele as a sort of ancient equivalent to Yiddish, as a third voice intended to reflect both the distortions and vibrancy of everyday speech. While this resulting style demanded a virtuoso command of Hebrew, it became the obligatory model of modern Hebrew literature for over two generations, and it is this style that was later adopted by S. Y. Agnon—the greatest modern Hebrew writer.[2]

Shmuel Yosef Agnon was born into the Czaczkes family in the town of Buczacz, Galicia. His spiritual world rested upon a firm Jewish foundation, notwithstanding the fact that his knowledge of European literature was acquired in his childhood (he became acquainted at an early age with the works of Goethe, Schiller, and Shakespeare as well as those of Jewish authors of the Haskalah). The breadth of his knowledge of the Jewish literary corpus—ranging from the Bible to the latest literary publications of his lifetime—was truly astounding. By virtue of both his *heder* (primary religious school) education, and private studies with his father (a fur trader and ordained rabbi), he knew the Bible, the Mishnah, and the liturgies by heart. At the age of eight he was already writing poetry and prose, in both Hebrew and Yiddish, and seriously studying German. His acquaintance with contemporary European literature began with a reading of fin-de-siècle impressionist literature, such as the works of Knut Hamsun and Bjørnstjerne Bjørnson, which were in turn followed by a reading of the great works of nineteenth-century realism.[3]

During the twelve years he spent in Germany, where he married (in 1920) and his two children were born, he naturally experienced a great affinity with European modernism, which was at the time highly vigorous in all fields of art. Yet this affinity was not the earliest source of Agnon's modernism. Clear signs of modernism were already evident in his early writing, and his very first works reveal an intense tension between the traditional and the contemporary. For Agnon, modernism was not some lofty ideal toward which one should strive so as to feel at home in the world of contemporary Western literature, nor was it an external aesthetic code derived and propagated from the centers of Western culture. To him modernism was, above all, a subversive element that confronted tradition. This subversive element had coursed through his veins ever since his youth. Because he believed that every literary norm was intertwined with some theological or political system, his literary iconoclasm was immediately linked to the theological and political totality of Judaism. In Agnon's works, Jewish tradition itself underwent a modernist baptism by fire.

The absorbing drama of Agnon's relationship with European literary modernism originated from his deep emotional attachment to the various forms of Jewish literature, systematic knowledge of the field, and ongoing study thereof. A highly visible example of this tension is Agnon's way of referring in his stories to the traditional eschatological Jewish narrative, that is, to the tale of redemption.

This is how Agnon begins the novel *Tmol Shilshom* (*Only Yesterday*), which relates the tale of the second *aliyah*, the wave of immigration to Palestine in the early twentieth century: "Like all our brethren of the Second *Aliya*, the bearers of our Salvation, Isaac Kumer left his country and his homeland and his city and ascended to the Land of Israel to build it from its destruction and to be rebuilt by it."[4] Agnon's "we" denotes the people of Israel in its entirety, and had it not been for the expression "our salvation," one might suppose that Agnon was speaking on behalf of the second *aliyah* immigrants. Yet, the expression "the bearers of our Salvation" makes it clear that the story addresses far broader dimensions, reaching beyond the domain of history to the realm of myth and belief—to the Jewish narrative of the final redemption and the coming of the Messiah. The sentence contains additional allusions to the ancient Jewish tale, which rested in the past upon the creation and the choice, on the divine promise, on the building of the temple, and on its destruction. One cannot but recall the opening verse of Genesis 12:1: "The Lord had said to Abram, 'Leave your country, your people and your father's household and go to the land I will show you' "; in Agnon's story quoted above, he uses the words, "to build it up from its destruction." The very choice of words reveals the story—the story of the destruction and the beginning of the exile.

At first glance these expressions in *Tmol Shilshom* appear to be suffused with the optimism, flowery language, and religious pretensions that characterized the Zionist movement at the time. It is as if these words were delivering the Jewish people from exile, possessing a divine dimension that transcended history—transforming the historical course of the Jewish people, like a gigantic hand descending from heaven and leading a "people" to its land—rather than being a product of social human action, an idea, and a bitter, worldly political struggle. Yet, when one reaches the end of the novel, it becomes apparent that it contains not a jot of the rhetoric of Zionist propaganda (other than a few caricatures at its expense) and, in fact, expresses a profound allegiance to the significance of a practical Zionism—which, in a sense, also belongs to the Jewish narrative of redemption, albeit not in a direct and simplistic manner that equates the Zionist second *aliyah* with the final redemption.

The novel's Zionist protagonist, Isaac Kumer, neither cultivates the land nor makes the desert bloom. Instead of meeting the challenges of Zionism, he works as a painter and returns to the old Jewish world of Jerusalem, to the Me'ah She'arim quarter, where a stray dog bites him, and he is infected with rabies. Before he dies the whole country is beset by a severe drought, and Jerusalem suffers an epidemic.

Just as in the denouement of Sophocles' *Oedipus Rex*, the protagonist's death brings rain and solace to the city. *Tmol Shilshom* is thus an alarming modern tragedy; the victim fails to comprehend his mistake. His suffering is incomprehensible, and both the novel's world and verbal texture do not offer any logical nexus between the protagonist's death and the fate of the city, the polis.

Upon the completion of the story of Isaac Kumer, who "failed the test" of the pioneer, the final sentences of *Tmol Shilshom* reinvoke the tone of voice and speech register of the opening sentence and its redemptive language. The novel relates a story that is not merely incompatible with the simple, optimistic vision of redemption; instead, it evokes and narrativizes a world that is utterly estranged from the contemporary Zionist notions of correction and liberation, which it thus questions and undermines. Nonetheless, the redemptive narrative provides the frame within which the story and the historical era it reflects are contextualized—this is the broad panorama within which *Tmol Shilshom* is contained.

This demands an interpretation, and I shall suggest here only two fundamental directions in which it might be carried out: the narrative of redemption is either an ironic framework, presenting an idea that the novel refutes and derides; or it constitutes the novel's central theme, namely a depiction of the throes of redemption—the tragic stages of suffering that the nation will undergo on its path to redemption. In other words, the notion of redemption is inherently a hubris, which has brought and will bring again a tragic fall on the way to its realization. In any event, one cannot ignore the fact that this Israeli fable, which plays out in recent history and evokes the physical, cultural, and political reality of Palestine circa 1910 so precisely, is enveloped by and emerges through the redemptive narrative.

This voice of the redemptive narrative pervades the story, and this is clearly Agnon's intent. As Isaac approaches Jerusalem for the first time, he is traveling by carriage between the hills: "A wind came and started blowing. It shook the dust and flapped at the rocks. The air began to change, and a still small voice was heard like the voice of wailing in the mountains."[5] The pair of biblical references (Kings I 19:12; Jer. 9:18 and 31:15) that surface in the narrator's account of the approach to the city creates a sphere charged with emotion and meaning. This is a divine voice and it speaks the language of the diaspora: "For a voice of wailing is heard out of Zion: How are we undone! We are greatly confounded, because we have forsaken the land, because our dwellings have cast us out" and "Rachel weeping for her children." It is as though Jerusalem is enveloped within a sphere of speech, for when Isaac approaches the city for the first time:

> Isaac looked before him and his heart began pounding, as a man's heart pounds when he approaches the place of his desire. . . . Before him, the wall of Jerusalem suddenly appeared, woven into a red fire, plated with gold, surrounded by gray clouds blended with blue clouds, which incise and engrave it with shapes of spun gold, choice silver, burnished brass, and purple tin. Isaac rose up and wanted to say something. But his tongue was hushed in his mouth as a mute song.[6]

This is the language of ancient Hebrew liturgy as used in the ecstatic poetry that describes God's throne. Thus, at the moment that Jerusalem reveals itself, it appears not merely infinitely "fair," but is observed through words derived from the world of the loftiest sanctity at a moment of transcendence, words belonging to a divine vision.

When Isaac arrives at the Wailing Wall on the anniversary of his mother's death, the narrator crafts a sight that by way of inversion suggests the portrayal of the temple in its heyday. Set against the Levite's Song of Ascents (*shir hama'alot*) in the Psalms, Agnon composes here "the song of descending ascents," all the while fascinatingly playing with the meaning of the word *ma'alah* (step, ascent, degree, or virtue). It is also worth recalling that the path to the Wailing Wall indeed comprises a series of steps since it is located in the valley of the cheese makers:

> On every single one of the stone steps on the way to the Western Wall are flocks of paupers, cripples, and blind men, some have no arms, some have lame legs, some have swollen necks, and are swollen with hunger and some are shriveled with despair, and there are other invalids and diseased people, fragments of people whose Creator left them in the middle of His work and didn't finish their creation, and when He left them, He left His hand on them and increased their torments. Or their Creator did finish them and strict justice struck them. And every step down had a sorrow greater than the last one. When you have descended all those stairs, you see a bundle of rags. You think they're rags, but they are a woman and her daughter, and it's not clear if the daughter is younger than her mother, but it is clear that they have the same calamity of hunger. Their eyes look straight ahead, but it's not the eyes that seem to be looking, but the pus in the eyes. Those remnants of bodies lie before our precious Temple that was destroyed, a place where Holy-One-Blessed-Be-He heard every prayer and every supplication of any child of Israel and filled his request, and now that it is destroyed, they pray and supplicate and request and the prayer isn't heard. And if it is heard, it achieves only half, a person's soul is saved but his body isn't.[7]

This brilliant and horrifying play on the symbol of *ma'alot* generates an impression that is the inverse of exaltedness: the precise order of the descent, which presents a symmetry of defects and maladies culminating in the vision of the blind mother and daughter, is a grotesque negative of the temple; it is a realistic portrayal of the Wailing Wall area at the time and also a powerful symbol of the destruction of the Jewish people. Placed at the exact center of the novel, this picture is a concentrated expression of the intermediate stage of the Jewish narrative that stretches from the creation to redemption. While the messianic story and its promise of redemption are indeed referenced, the impression of destruction, the lack of affinity to the deity, and the affront to both the human and divine images are stronger elements.

The iconic image of the blind mother and daughter, who have no hope of escaping their calamity, is the holiest symbol of the destroyed temple—personifying a far more general condition. Set against the powerful impression of purpose created by the tale of redemption—leading from the onset toward a solution, the *historical* condition of the people, even at the height of the Zionist endeavor—it appears to be disintegrated, abandoned, and directionless. Yet, the issue of the Jewish people's historical position is nonetheless addressed by means of the tale of redemption, albeit by way of a contradiction: Agnon locates the actual story within the eschatological narrative by means of a raucous, modernist contradiction—a tattered, directionless, and utterly absurd reality. More than anything else, the figure of the dog Balak signals the conclusive elimination of the literary concept of causality. The classical tragic ending is merely a thin veneer for an appalling reality that defies comprehension. When seen in this light, Zionism itself appears to be a traditional, obsolete legend that cannot withstand the stychia of actual historical forces.

Tmol Shilshom is not the only one of Agnon's stories whose world is rendered through the tale of redemption. In fact, almost all of his stories refer to decisive moments within this story, thereby generating a pervasive duality of narratives. The straightforward tale—the center of the new story—is placed within a broader narrative, that is, the Jewish redemptive narrative. Before discussing this structure, we should consider the first story that Agnon published in Palestine—"Agunot" (Forsaken Wives)—from which he took his nom de plume, Agnon, and which he regarded as the ceremonial-symbolic beginning of his writing career. Our interest lies in its plot, which is presented in the story's opening paragraph:

> It is said: a thread of grace is spun and drawn out of the deeds of Israel, and the Holy One, blessed be He, Himself, in His glory, sits and weaves—strand on strand—a prayer shawl all grace and all mercy, for the Congregation of Israel to deck herself in. Radiant in the light of her beauty she glows, even in these, the lands of her exile, as she did in her youth in her Father's house, in the Temple of her Sovereign and the city of sovereignty, Jerusalem. And when He, of ineffable Name, sees her, that she has neither been sullied nor stained even here, in the realm of her oppressors, He—as it were—leans toward her and says, "Behold thou art fair, my beloved, behold thou art fair." And this is the secret of the power and the glory and the exaltation and the tenderness in love which fills the heart of every man in Israel. But there are times—alas!—when some hindrance creeps up, and snaps a thread in the loom. Then the prayer shawl is damaged: evil spirits hover about it, enter into it, and tear it to shreds. At once a sense of shame assails all Israel, and they know they are naked. Their days of rest are wrested from them, their feasts are fasts, their lot is dust instead of luster. At that hour the Congregation of Israel strays abroad in her anguish, crying, "Strike me, wound me, take away my veils from me!" Her beloved has slipped away, and she, seeking him, cries, "If ye find my beloved, what shall ye tell him? That I am afflicted with love." And this affliction of love leads to darkest melancholy, which persists—Mercy shield us!—until, from the heavens above, He breathes down upon us strength of spirit, to repent, and to muster deeds that are pride to their doers and again draw forth that thread of grace and love before the Lord. And this is the theme of the tale recounted here.[8]

The story of God weaving a prayer shawl (*talith*) from a "thread of grace and mercy" that extends from the deeds of Jews and is intended for the congregation of Israel, who shall cover themselves with it while God shall speak the words of the lover from the Song of Songs—"Behold thou art fair, my beloved"—is a chapter of the tale of redemption that is given here in an allegorical manner derived from the teachings of the Sages (*midreshei hazal*). The fifth chapter of the Song of Songs serves here as a subtext in the construction of the allegory. The episode in this chapter, in which the "lover" slips away from his beloved's home, and in which she in turn wanders about at night until the guards tear off her veil, is the episode of the rending of the *talith*—the episode of a historical present that is far removed from redemption. The interesting part in this tale is that the rending of the *talith*—an episode replete with obstacles, shame, and aimless wandering—is not analogous to the destruction of the temple and to the exile. Rather, it refers to the subsequent unfolding of a process of corruption and subversion among the people that severs the continuity of the thread that constituted the cloth of the *talith* (or wedding canopy) that extends from God to the people. That is to say, Agnon signifies here an additional chapter of the tale of redemption that is not linked with events of a mythological stature, such as the destruction of the temple, which in turn serves to posit redemption as even more remote, and suggests that this eternal Jewish story is now poised on the brink of an irrevocable rupture.

This chapter of the rending, added to the tale of redemption, is among the leaps of genius made by the young Agnon on his way to becoming a Hebrew writer. It cannot be assigned to some distinct moment of crisis in Jewish history (e.g., Sabbateanism; the rifts among Hasidim, Mitnagdim, and Haskalah; or conflicts between Zionism and secularism) because it is not a historical moment, but rather a literary condition: the rupture is the present moment whenever it might be. In other words, a tale of mythological stature can, by its very exalted nature, be set only in the past, whereby the authentic perspective of an actual view of the world, which demands realism (as opposed to idealism), undermines by its very nature a generalizing superior perspective. Thus this kind of tale can see human reality, both Jewish and general, in such a complexity that it precludes containment within a linear, focused, purposeful, and religious narrative, such as the tale of redemption. The young Agnon realized that there was a profound, revolutionary upheaval generated by modern Hebrew literature within Jewish culture, which did not necessarily arise from its attachment to Zionism. Rather, this change resulted from an obligation to confront the greatest achievement of Western literature in the century that preceded Agnon—realism. In turn, a profound deliberation of realism reveals that it encompasses elements that deny any suggestion of causality or directionality in one's perception of human activity and history, thereby making it essentially secular and modernistic.

Realism is the concept of "truth" that Agnon required and to which he was committed above all other values. Agnon did not regard his concept of truth as something secular, but saw it instead as an embodiment of the divine—in the complex and radical sense in which Agnon understood this concept. Even the most disintegrated, secular, and worldly "present" is, in his eyes, a manifestation of the divine, not because it is wondrous or sublime but rather because it is random, chaotic, boundless, and incomprehensible. This rupture is the Agnonic modernist signal, signifying the rift between the present and the past.

This rupture is thus something that occurs in the present and constitutes the symbolic embodiment of the historical present within which the story "Agunot" takes place. Moreover, this introduction invites the reader to read the work as a continuation of the allegory of the story of redemption on a new level—not on the level of a sweeping generalization, as in the introduction, in which a fleeting moment from the Song of Songs grasps the historical present in its totality, but rather in a more detailed and intricate manner. Thus it is likewise understood that the narrative's protagonists and its course both symbolically and allegorically represent the rending of grace and mercy that connects the people with God, that is, the rending of the tale of redemption itself. The "nakedness" in the rending is also a departure from the protective power of the coupling between the Jewish people, as the Congregation of Israel, and the lover, that is God. This tale, then, is not merely about Jews residing in the world and in history but is part of the Jewish story in the singular—a story that should be understood as the story of the relationship between the people and God. Of course, this is not to say that one should search for some figure that represents God and so forth, but rather that one should regard the stories as two distinct spheres that depict reality and that are superimposed on one another.

In this manner, Agnon created an intricate, singular literary state; a concept of a peculiarly Jewish story; and a story whose Jewishness is not manifested in a single language or some literary tradition of national Hebrew prose. This tradition was rather poor, discontinuous, and lacking in distinctiveness, but it resides in the link to an existing, ancient, and all-embracing narrative—which indeed exists as the story of the Jewish people. On the other hand, Agnon created here an exquisite literary opportunity, in which the "rupture"—the historical circumstance within which the new story fits—is in any event a chaotic and exposed condition that is capable of absorbing foreign elements, "evil spirits" of various sorts, and can serve as a conduit for an immense profusion of literary forms. For in this manner, every story will be connected to the one Jewish story by a relation that is simultaneously an affinity and a rupture. In this way Agnon made it clear that modernism itself was an event that was occurring within Judaism and possessed a specifically Jewish significance.

We should finally discuss the two words with which the story begins: *Muva bekhtavim* (It is written). Written evidence is, of course, the established mode of proof and argument in all the numerous branches of Jewish literature. The written is the basis of all interpretation and is the foundation of the literary structure that evolved historically. Thus, the written is that which comes *first*; it is prior in time and foremost in value, thereby understood as being *more comprehensibly written* than that which was written after or about it. It is as if it were engraved in the hard stone of time. To the Sages (*Hazal*), the written was the Bible, but for the sages of the Middle Ages, *Hazal*, too, became the written, and to those that came later all these predecessors appeared as the written—up to the present day, when Agnon and the national poet H. N. Bialik are now considered to be the written. This mechanism, whereby the prior is elevated in spiritual authority until the ancient becomes supreme, is a universal cultural mechanism. But the special attitude toward the written as something that signifies writing, and the sign that indicates it—"as is written" (*kakatuv*)—is particularly Hebrew and is bound up in the annals of Hebrew as the intertwined development of language and belief. The written is a foundation. It is like a fixed edifice of the world; it is a place.

Beginning "Agunot" with "It is written" is both a principled and ceremonial gesture. The young Agnon hereby announces that he is founding his work on the ancient Jewish structure of study and proof, in which the new text presents itself as both a pale version of the former and as emanating from it. But this opening statement is not simple: the tale of God weaving the cloth of the prayer shawl, which is subsequently torn due to "a hindrance, God forbid," is not to be found in the written! Although it is composed in a style derived from the language of the Midrash (homiletic interpretation), and although it masks itself as a traditional story based on the template of the Jewish redemptive narrative, it is by no means a traditional story as it contains strange discrepancies uncharacteristic of the stories of the Midrash. It is an Agnonic story par excellence. In a sense this is a false citation, but this is not the point, since this citation is nonetheless true to the spirit of the kabbalistic-Hasidic tale of redemption. Rather, the point is that Agnon creates an autonomous structure that contains its ancient origins as internal foundations, and in so doing he transforms the standing of the Hebrew writer vis-à-vis the ancient textual authority. Thereby he maintains that this authority is itself a work of creation, emanating from the author no less than from the written. In this manner the metahistorical Jewish story, the redemptive narrative, is comprehended as a story that is still changing; it is a story that is still being created, which constitutes some sort of "thread" between this world, the human world, and the eternal world of redemption.

Sefer HaMa'asim (*The Book of Deeds*) is one of Agnon's most daring modernist breakthroughs. The plots of these stories are not subject to the premises of realism: the dead enter the world and interfere with the living; the tenses become confused and jumbled, undermining the sense of continuity; and, most importantly, the conventional concepts of cause give way to twists that appear puzzling, frightening at times, and always alien and strange. Agnon commingles various kinds of representations, shifting between them rapidly and without warning, and both their continuity and endings are vastly different from what one would expect from a realistic story. Many have termed these stories as "surrealistic"; others have regarded them as dreams written. However, the label "surrealistic" is inappropriate here because the stories do not seek to appear as a stream of associative writing that is entirely devoid of "understanding"; thus, conceiving them as written dreams explains nothing.

One of the elements that Agnon addresses in *The Book of Deeds* is the way in which a modern human being relates to traditional concepts of time: that is, both by the conventional measurement of time and by the concepts of sacred time. The "entering of the day"—the onset of sacred time—exceeds, in the stories of *The Book of Deeds*, the space of regular time signals. This moment is not merely the signifier of some ritual and deed, but it is rather a substantial alteration of the temporal texture, as if time was a substance with relative mass. Furthermore, the manner in which narrative events are related to each other undergoes profound changes. The design of sacred time in these stories is doubtlessly influenced by its shaping in the Hasidic tales, which impart to it an aura of sanctity and the magical atmosphere of a fable. Yet, the construction of these stories around sacred time is a lot more complex than the mere presence of the signifiers of a romantic ambience; in fact, it is directly related to the stories of the Sages.

Most of the stories in this book take place on the threshold of holy days—Sabbaths, Passover, Rosh Hashanah, and Yom Kippur. Their openings signal the threshold of sacred time:

I was busy all year round. Each day, from early morning until midnight, I would sit at my desk and write . . . since New Year's Eve was upon us I thought to myself, a new year is in the offing and I have left many letters unanswered; I shall sit myself down and reply to them and enter the new year without obligations. ("The Orchestra")

Or another passage:

> The house was prepared for Passover. The walls appeared white as snow and the floor shone like marble. . . . [A]nd we too were prepared for the festive occasion. Had it fallen upon us that instant it would have found us ready. Having searched for leaven we sat down to the meal. Before we had put spoon to mouth we succumbed to sleep and dozed, since we had not slept the entire week. ("The House")

Agnon fashions here the onset of sacred time as a fundamental transformation of the laws of reality. He does not announce the principle involved, but rather presents it as a reality that embodies a novel set of rules.

In the story "HaNerot" ("The Candles"), a man is searching, in actuality, for the precise moment in which sacred time begins. The story opens with the words "After midday on the Sabbath eve," and from this moment it is apparent that the Sabbath is approaching. The story is studded with time signifiers, yet time's linearity, which is supposed to continuously bring nearer the moment of onset along a predictable and irreversible vector, disappears in a strange manner and is replaced by time fragments that disturb the linear perception that should establish the definitive arrival of sacred time:

> The house was prepared and awaited the Sabbath. Yet its occupants busied themselves with mundane matters. . . . as I stood reading the light of day faded. . . . I raised my head and noticed that all the neighboring houses were lit by the Sabbath candles and the people of the house were displeased. I wondered why these houses had been lit so early, before the holy day was at hand, in any case I must hurry. . . . [S]ome person leaned toward the window and looked out, withdrew his head and said "naharayim.".[9] The word naharayim [two rivers] is in truth inappropriate here, but I take it to be an antithetic allusion to darkness: This person, that is, had weighed his words so as to spare me humiliation. I became alarmed and went to the sea. . . . [A]nd many people stood among the puddles shining in the light of the sun that had set.[10]

The disappearance of the perception of a linear continuum, which safeguards the story's protagonist's orientation in time and would have pinpointed in a conventionally established manner the moment of the onset of sacred time, is bound up in this story with an entire cluster of disturbances in other dimensions. The story's opening signals a plan of action: "After midday on the Sabbath eve I set aside all my chores, gathered white garments and went to the bath."[11] The action refers to time and to its quality as sacred time: the bathing is an act of purification performed in anticipation of its coming. We have here a dual movement, in time and also in another dimension, a moral and an emotional one. And here, at this moment: "Mr. Haim Apropos came upon me. . . . I bowed my head and greeted him. He greeted me in return and said: 'You are on your way to pray with the Kabbalists.' I nodded to him in affirmation. And even though I had said nothing, I had, after all, lied. I had not intended to lie, but could not bring myself to contradict him. I felt embarrassed, as I always do when I meet Mr. Apropos, since I knew that he did not approve of me, perhaps because I had set my eyes on his daughter although she is not meant for me."[12]

Mr. Haim Apropos's peculiar name suddenly disturbs the flow of the realistic story since it is an allegorical sign—symbolizing something essentially different from what is apparent—and, as an allegorical sign, it is particularly complex. "Apropos" means "by the way," but Haim Apropos is far more than a person who is incidentally encountered. He is the possibility of life "by the way"; he is simultaneously a condition and an otherness. That is, this meeting ("came upon me"—a motion that emanates from the "world") disturbs the dual motion found at the beginning of the story, the motion in space and time, and the motion towards a moral rectification—the purification. The narrator is revealed to be entangled with Mr. Apropos. He lies because he dares not disengage from the being of this by-the-way fellow, concealing the lie and then revealing it all the more, and this revelation carries with it a further entanglement: a guilty embarrassment about the lust he felt for Mr. Apropos's daughter, who is not intended for him.

There is no awful sin that is revealed in the encounter with Haim Apropos. The constellation of relations that is revealed here is a life constellation in all of its complexity. Apropos's first name is "Haim" (life), and in what follows it becomes apparent that indeed in front of our eyes the ideal of an entire life is fashioned— with its differences of outlook, religion and belief; its imperatives of morality, style, falsehood, and truth; the desire to make peace; and also the ill-fitting, embarrassing, uncalled-for lust. The contact with Apropos has irreparably hindered the dual motion of time and soul toward the sacred time. Instead of the desired smooth motion toward the Sabbath, we are faced with a chaotic journey that appears as a fractal of motions and submotions distancing the protagonist, the I, from any comprehensible concept of direction and purpose.

The following paragraph, as well as the rest of the story, is a consequence of this encounter, which can be understood as an inner encounter between a person and himself and a growing awareness of the complex and problematic presence of the component of "life" within the "I." This component cannot be contained within the simple directional movement of external time and the rules of the precepts (*mitsvot*) that are bound with it. The revelation of the allegorical element subverts the entire perception of reality, exposing it to an expanding cluster of inner realities. This is the working of sacred time, the time of judgment, which comes nearer and nearer and is always on the threshold of arriving. Yet, this divine condition occupies a position that is different from the one it occupies in the traditional story. It is not a tangible change in the world that occurs with the onset of the holy day but rather a spiritual, inner motion within a space that exists far beyond the onset of sacred time. The threshold condition of the holy day is the fissure, the disturbance, through which is revealed everything that stands opposite to the stable concepts of sacred time: a world whose dimensions are expanding to the point at which its interiority reveals the sea that blocks all motion and that undermines the mechanisms of perception themselves. The bridge, the extension of the path over the water, is trembling.

It is fascinating to observe the sea's dual standing in the story. At the beginning it is merely an instrument for bathing and purification that represents the entry into sacred time and a moral test that precedes it, that is, it is both a worldly instrument with a realistic presence and a symbolic and ritualistic instrument like a *miqveh* (Jewish ritual bath). Further along the journey, the sea's status changes: it loses its simplicity as both the signifier of a place ("the sea raised itself and the water stood as a wall") and the signifier of a ritual. The sea emerges as the innermost being of the "apropos life" of the "I" and as the pinnacle of the inner journey, but at the same time it is experienced as the external, active manifestation of sacred time following its entry into the world. The movement toward the sea is therefore the movement toward the Sabbath, and the confrontation with it is akin to a confrontation with sacred time and its divine quality. From this it becomes apparent that it is actually the tortuous inner path—painful and incidental in its entirety—through which the sacred element with all its divine power is revealed. That which was once a means eventually becomes the end, and that which was a limited symbol, in speech and in deed, becomes an infinite symbol, dangerously powerful, all-disturbing and all-devouring, incomprehensible and yet meaningful. Standing on the trembling bridge is a consciousness of exposure, an almost total nakedness of thought, poised on the verge of wordlessness. But it is nevertheless a stand vis-à-vis the sea.

The final word of the story—"trembling"—is essential to its internal movement, being the sign of the disturbance in all dimensions of perception. It follows that the story tears down and annuls the sign of the ending and the purpose that underlies the concept of narrative and the human agency within it—and therefore also the dividing lines between land and sea, between sacred and mundane time, between the essential interiority and the incidental (apropos) exteriority—replacing it with a "trembling" sign that is all movement, a bridge stretching into infinity that shudders, complementing the motion forward with movements of collapse and retreat. This is not a harmonious merging in the manner of tragedy or an ascent to heaven, because the symbolic sign itself (the bridge, the path, the instrument) is destabilized upon contact. This is a symbol that incorporates its own nullification without interfering with the flow that occurs within it. The word "trembling" is associated with the religious awe that at this very moment becomes an intense experience, as in its origin: "with horror and with awe and with trembling and with sweat" (Berakhot 22:1).

The ending of the story with the opening symbol, which destabilizes even the act of symbolization itself, does not contest the ancient literary and religious perception but rather supplements it with a critical dimension that in fact reinforces it. The standing on the trembling bridge is a powerful literary rendition of the condition of awe; it is a standing in the presence of God, which embodies, using a startling but effective verbal instrument, the collapse of perception and wordlessness in the face of the inconceivable infinity of the all-mighty. "The Candles" thus ends by breaking through obstacles and establishing an immediate contact with the divine meaning of sacred time as embodied in space.

Agnonic modernism is expressed in the constitution of relations between traditional (both Jewish and Western) literary and poetic elements and innovative modes of storytelling through a radical subversion of the concept of causality and an undermining of the concept of world and narrative continuity. Agnon wrote a series of modernist tragedies that form the apex of his oeuvre, including such works as the novella *And the Crooked Shall Be Made Straight*, the novel *A Simple Story*, and the stories "The Forsaken" and "The Two Sages Who Were in Our City," as well as many others. In these tragedies the friction between the tradition of classical literature and the innovative modes becomes patently apparent.

This much is clear: for Agnon, modernism was a syndrome associated with the subversion of Jewish traditional life and faith, and with the ruin that befell the Jewish communities of Central and Eastern Europe from the late nineteenth century up to European Jewry's final devastation in the Holocaust. His two monumental works—*A Guest for the Night* and *A City and the Fullness Thereof*—deal with the anatomy of Jewish community life in the town of Buczacz, Agnon's Galician place of birth. The former work, for which he was awarded the Nobel Prize for Literature in 1966, addresses the destruction of community life during World War I, while the latter is a chronicle of this community from its founding in the late Middle Ages to its demise in the catastrophe inflicted by the Nazis. In these two works Agnon's art of storytelling reaches its pinnacle, and in them his most audacious modernist breakthroughs occurred. One clearly senses that the literary modernism that pulsates through both these works originates from within the fabric of Jewish life itself, and that this is not a mere stylistic attribute but rather an essentially Jewish event. The experience of the rift between the present and the past and tradition, and the acute awareness of the past as a complete world that cannot be changed, occurred within and emanated from the life of Judaism.

Like several other great authors of Hebrew literature who were his contemporaries, such as Yosef Haim Brenner and A. N. Gnessin, Agnon was not influenced by "strong" or hegemonic literature but rather stood at the forefront of Western modernism as it unfolded. He contributed to it his own innovations through an initiative that was not based on the position of a minority. The fact that Agnon's innovations did not become as well known as those of Kafka, for instance, does not stem from a difference in originality and importance but rather from Agnon's deep dependence on Hebrew and its immensely rich depth and resonance. The special intertextual quality of modern Hebrew literature cannot, in fact, be translated into any other language, and from this it follows that Agnon's literary greatness is destined to remain confined to Hebrew.

Notes

1. See Benjamin Harshav, *Language in Time of Revolution* (Stanford, 1993).
2. See Robert Alter, *Hebrew and Modernity* (Bloomington, 1994).
3. See Gershon Shaked, *Geschichte der modernen hebräischen Literatur* (Frankfurt, 1996), 127–50.
4. S. Y. Agnon, *Only Yesterday*, trans. Barbara Harshav (Princeton, 2000), 3.
5. Ibid., 195.
6. Ibid., 196.
7. Ibid., 367.
8. S. Y. Agnon, *Twenty-One Stories*, ed. Nahum N. Glatzer and trans. Baruch Hochman (New York, 1971), 30.
9. The word *naharayim* has several connotations. Here it would appear to mean "light" or "brightness"; and it is understood by the narrator to indicate "darkness" by way of antiphrasis, and to imply a reprimand.
10. S.Y. Agnon, *Samukh ve-nir'eh, Sipurim im sefer ha-ma'asim* (Tel Aviv, 1968), 117. The quotations were translated by Avner Greenberg from the Hebrew original.
11. Ibid.
12. Ibid.

21

Walter Benjamin (1892–1940)

ANTI-APOCALYPTIC WORLD POLITICS

Astrid Deuber-Mankowsky

TRANSLATED BY CATHERINE DIEHL

IN HIS METHODICAL ENDEAVOR TO DO PHILOSOPHICAL JUSTICE TO THE DIGNITY OF transitory experience, Walter Benjamin created concepts—in a sense, following Gilles Deleuze—that have challenged philosophy and thought up to the present day. This is not only true for his concept of history but also for his concept of the "artwork in the time of its technological reproducibility"; for a politics "whose method is called nihilism," as well as for that of "second technique" (*Technik*); for contemplative versus distracted perception; for the concept of a "happiness thoroughly colored by time"; for the concept of the gestural; for the concept of rendering legible the technical media of photography and film and of phantasmagoria as an ideal (*Wunschbild*); and for the concept of the aura. The list could be continued, but the concept of Jewish modernity will not appear on it. Although Benjamin indeed referred to philosophical interpretations of Jewish sources, he nevertheless developed his critique of violence in the context of the demand for a cosmopolitics that could not be reduced to a "portion of mankind." Benjamin's reflections on modernity, however, cannot be separated from his reflections on capitalism. But his reflections on capitalism and accompanying critique did not arise from a reading of Karl Marx but from the tension between his understanding of Jewish traditions of thought and his critical engagement with Max Weber's thesis of secularization. For precisely this reason, there is hardly a text better suited to serve as a point of departure for the question of the relationship between modernity and Judaism in Walter Benjamin's thought than the fragment "Capitalism as Religion."[1] This short note from 1921 clarifies something that has received scant attention in the interpretation of Benjamin's theory of modernity: that Benjamin was concerned with the question of capitalism long before he drew on Marxism and before his 1924 meeting with Asja Lacis, who introduced him to communism and, in 1928, to Bertolt Brecht. Benjamin's theory of modernity originated from his critical relationship to contemporaneous sociological discussions concerning the relations among capitalism, secularization, religion, and economics and was thus informed by questions treated in those discussions.[2]

Capitalism as Religion

At the turn of the twentieth century, the founding fathers of sociology—Werner Sombart, Max Weber, Ferdinand Tönnies, and Georg Simmel—were engaged in a search for more complex sociological and historical explanations of the emergence of capitalist modernity than those provided by the mechanistic theory of base and superstructure. They found them in the interplay between the history of religion and economic formations. Max Weber's thesis, first published in 1904–1905, that the spirit of capitalism developed from the ethics of Protestantism and, in particular, from Calvinism, is well known.[3] Not so well known, but no less important for understanding the contemporary context of Benjamin's note, is the counterthesis to Weber's linkage of Protestantism and capitalism upheld by Werner Sombart, the sociologist and author of the classic *Modern Capitalism* (1902), in his 1911 study *The Jews and Modern Capitalism*. Drawing on Weber and simultaneously critical of him, Sombart maintained that all the elements (*Momente*) of Protestant Puritanism relevant to the development of the spirit of capitalism in fact derived from an intellectual circle around the Jewish religion. Unlike Weber, who was continually critical of anthropological theories of race, Sombart explained the emergence of capitalism on the basis of the supposed national character of the Jews and thereby explicitly referred to anthropological models and theories that served both epistemically and intentionally in the construction of a "race." During the runup to World War I, Sombart's theses triggered a vigorous debate within the Jewish community concerning German-Jewish relations, a debate in which the twenty-year-old Benjamin was compelled to take a position.

In a lecture course on "The Future of the Jews" held in the winter of 1911–1912, Sombart once again publicly presented his theses concerning the Jewish contribution to the emergence of capitalism and, based on this, his understanding of the national Jewish movement of Zionism. As was already the case with his books and an earlier lecture series, Sombart received approbation from the side of the Zionists. The reason for this was that Sombart took the existence of a Jewish people to be self-evident. In the eyes of the Zionists, he thereby acknowledged the fact of a Jewish nationality and identity and legitimized Zionism and its goal of restoring to the Jewish people an ancestral space and home (*Raum*). In contrast, liberal-minded and anti-Zionist Jews—whose leaders included the well-known neo-Kantian philosopher Hermann Cohen—condemned Sombart's nationalism and antisemitism. It was unacceptable to them that, by invoking the "otherness" of the Jewish people, he justified legal discrimination, in particular exclusion from public office. The discussion culminated in the so-called *Kunstwart* debate, which was prompted by the publication of Moritz Goldstein's essay "The German-Jewish Parnassus" in the German nationalist journal *Kunstwart* (Guardian of art) in March 1912.[4]

The debate provided Benjamin with an occasion for entering into an exchange of letters with Ludwig Strauß, an acquaintance of the same age who adhered to a moderate form of cultural Zionism. As Benjamin emphasized, this exchange was of "programmatic significance"[5] for him and led him to clarify his relationship to Judaism and Zionism. For Benjamin, who up to that point had known of Judaism as "in fact only anti-Semitism and an undefined piety,"[6] national Zionism, which he called "Palestinian Zionism,"[7] was not an option. Only the "cultural Zionism that sees Jewish values *everywhere* and works on their behalf"[8] held out to him the promise of a tenable standpoint. Crucial, for Benjamin, was a *universal* concept of humanity, which he—going against convention—did not connect with Christianity and Christian values but rather with Judaism and Jewish values. In this sense, he wrote to Strauß that the "best Western European Jews" were not free but were "indebted" to the "literary movement" and to "internationalism."[9] For the young Benjamin, the concept of a cultural consciousness that "forbids us *in ideality* from ever restricting the concept of culture to some *part* of humanity"[10] was linked to the international literati. He answered the question of his political persuasion by noting that only "the present-day current literary Jew" was important to him and added, providing proof of his insight into the abyssal nature of national Zionism, that "insofar as Zionism leads this type, which at bottom it must in fact fight, to self-consciousness, it is (within the complex of the political) welcome to me in some way. That is, I pay my dues, especially since I know, that this money also serves the Russian Jews."[11]

Jewishness and Germanness stood, for Benjamin, in a relationship full of tension but they did not mutually exclude one another, similar to how Jewishness and Christianness are not mutually exclusive so long as both follow those universal values that Benjamin connects with the "literary movement." He thus inserts the idea of the literati into the history of Christianity when he writes: "I will not say anything more about the member of the literati (as idea) than that he is called upon to be for the new social consciousness what the 'poor in spirit, the downtrodden, the humble' were to the first [i.e., early] Christianity."[12] Benjamin's programmatic positioning with respect to Zionism and Judaism took the antisemitic figure of the literary Jew as its point of departure, in order to strengthen it as an ethical concept of universal humanity that would not annul differences and would not exclude weakness and fragility. The question of national, confessional, or ethical belonging is less relevant in this regard than the ethical scope of the concepts and ideas theoretically linked to each historical and philosophical tradition. He followed this programmatic position, even if along circuitous paths, up through the composition of his notes for "On the Concept of History," shortly before his suicide in France in 1940 while fleeing from the National Socialists.

Capitalism as a "Parasite of Christianity"

In the fragment "Capitalism as Religion," composed nine years later, Benjamin does not mention Werner Sombart. Against the backdrop of the debate triggered by Sombart at the time of Benjamin's engagement with the Youth Movement (*Jugendbewegung*), we can assume that the question of capitalism remained connected, for Benjamin, with the history of Judaism and Christianity. In 1920, the new edition of Weber's study, *The Protestant Ethic and the Spirit of Capitalism*, was published in the two-volume edition of his *Collected Essays on the Sociology of Religion* (*Gesammelte Aufsätze zur Religionssoziologie*), which Benjamin possessed. In this edition, Weber had already extensively criticized Sombart's theses in long footnotes. Indeed, already in the second sentence of his fragment, Benjamin draws on Max Weber's thesis that capitalism developed from the ethics of Protestantism.[13] He positions himself by going farther than Weber in maintaining that capitalism is not, as Weber thought, "a formation conditioned by religion" but that it is a "purely cultic religion."[14]

Capitalism is distinguished from traditional religions in that it possesses neither a "specific body of dogma" nor a theology and, consequently, unlike in traditional religions, there is no doctrine or law to be interpreted; instead, "things have a meaning only in their relationship to the cult."[15] Unlike Weber, who understood the relationship between Christianity and capitalism as *genealogical*, Benjamin thus defines the relation between capitalism and Christianity—pursuant to his initial thesis that capitalism is not secular but possesses for its part a "religious structure"[16]—as *parasitic*.[17] What does he mean by this? In biology, the organism designated as the host is indeed damaged by the parasite, but the life of the parasite nevertheless depends on the survival of the host organism. Transferred to Benjamin's comparison, this means that Christianity is indeed weakened, injured, and altered but that Christianity is not, as Weber suggests, historically surpassed by the capitalistic rationalization of the conduct of life. Weber indeed admits the capitalist conduct of life with its "restless pursuit" of monetary gain appears irrational "from the viewpoint of human happiness," but he nevertheless emphasizes at the same time that now there is "generally no correlation between the conduct of life and religious principles."[18]

Benjamin Franklin's autobiography served Weber as a paradigmatic example of the capitalist mode of life—in particular the public letter at the beginning of the book, which Franklin addressed to his son in order to instruct him in the correct conduct of life. Franklin impressed upon his son, first, that money is time; second, that credit is money; and, third, that money has a "prolific, generating nature," since money begets money and its "offspring can beget more."[19] Bearing this in mind, the son should be a good payer, punctual, dutiful, and moderate, and never forget that whoever loses five shillings not only loses this sum but everything that he could have earned through its use in industry. The reference to the accumulation and self-accumulation of capital suffices for Franklin to give his son all his advice for a promising future and a mode of life oriented to success. In this regard, Franklin was not, according to Weber's argument, referring to religious tradition in order to bestow an ethics on the capitalist mode of life.

Weber famously tried to explain the irrationalism of the capitalist conduct of life through secularized man's emotional tie to his profession. Not so Benjamin: in the moments diagnosed by Weber as irrationalism, he saw the continuity of the religious within capitalism. His argument is as simple as it is pragmatic: "capitalism serves essentially to allay the same anxieties, torments, and disturbances to which the so-called religions offered answers."[20] In this regard—and this is the claim of Benjamin's that has the richest consequences—capitalism, as an "essentially religious phenomenon," at the same time relies upon the history of Christianity so that, as he declares, the history of Christianity "is essentially that of its parasite—that is to say, of capitalism."[21] He strengthens this provocative thesis with the statement, found a few lines later: "The Christianity of the Reformation period did not favor the growth of capitalism; instead it transformed itself into capitalism."[22]

Nietzsche and Baudelaire

In summary, as I would like to emphasize, Benjamin follows in each point Weber's analysis, according to which the religious historical process of the disenchantment of the world and the arrangement of the capitalist conduct of life corresponds to the Calvinist theory of grace.[23] In particular, he follows him in drawing those consequences that this (according to Weber) "harsh doctrine of the absolute worthlessness and remoteness from God of all mere creatures" for the believers' conduct of life: "the inner isolation of the individual, loneliness and disconsolateness, "a fundamental rejection of every kind of culture of the senses."[24] Benjamin follows nearly word for word the subsequent passage in which Weber depicts the "pathos-laden inhumanity of life," according to which "every creature was separated from God by an unbridgeable gulf": "In what was for the people of the Reformation age the most crucial concern of life, their eternal salvation, man was forced to follow his path alone toward a destiny which had been decreed from eternity. No one and nothing could help him."[25] Benjamin puts it as follows, with respect to the religious movement of capitalism that he sees worked out for the first time in the nineteenth century with Friedrich Nietzsche: "God's transcendence is at an end. But he is not dead; he has been incorporated into human existence. The passage of the planet 'Human' through the house of despair in the absolute loneliness of his trajectory is the ethos that Nietzsche defined. This man is the superman, the first to recognize the religion of capitalism and bring it to fulfillment."[26]

Ignoring Nietzsche's own sharp critique of Christianity, Benjamin locates the ethos of Nietzsche's philosophy in the tradition described by Weber of the Protestant secularization of asceticism and interprets its extension as a "paradigm of capitalist religious thought."[27] The decisive criterion for Benjamin is that the "thought of the superman transposes the apocalyptic 'leap' . . . into an apparently steady, though in the final analysis explosive and discontinuous intensification."[28] Benjamin is playing here on the idea that the heavens could be broken open by an "intensified humanity"[29] — an allusion to the biblical ecce homo, the man who has become God, following whose example, according to Benjamin, the *superman* must grow through the sky without possessing the possibility of turning back (*Umkehr*), of cleansing, or of repentance. Modernity demands — this is the idea behind it — that human beings have superhuman powers. This idea appears, among other places, again in Benjamin's first study on Charles Baudelaire in which Benjamin exposes the "hero" as the "true subject of *la modernité*" — which means that one needs a "heroic constitution to live the modern."[30] He adds that in this *modernité* suicide should not be understood as "resignation" but as "heroic passion."[31] He comments upon this with the laconic remark: "The resistance that modernity offers to the natural productive élan of an individual is out of all proportion to his strength. It is understandable if a person becomes exhausted and takes refuge in death. Modernity must stand under the sign of suicide, an act which seals a heroic will that makes no concessions to a mentality inimical toward this will."[32]

The Capitalist and the Vulgar Marxist Cult of Work

Benjamin's reference to Weber's religious-historical study becomes particularly evident in his depiction of the religious idealization of work as a central effect.[33] One could read the sentences in which Weber depicts the process in the course of which the "tireless labor in a calling" became the "best possible means" to gain certainty of grace directly as an illustration of Benjamin's contention that "capitalism is the celebration of a cult *sans rêve et sans merci*."[34] This cult without armistice or grace, which, according to Benjamin, knows no day that is not a feast day—a day on which, to put it otherwise, one does not work—is none other than the secularization of asceticism by the cult of work described so forcefully by Weber. When, in his fragment, Benjamin designates capitalism as a cultic religion, he is not referring to the fetish character of commodities but, instead, to the "sanctification of life" through fulfillment of one's duties and to the systematization of the ethical conduct of life, which, as Weber laconically puts it, might "almost assume the character of a business enterprise."[35]

The critique of the capitalistic cult of work not only remains central for Benjamin's critique of capitalist modernity—for instance, when he mobilizes the figures of the dandy, the flâneur, or the scavenger (*Lumpensammler*) for this critique—but also forms the center of his sharp critique of the politics of social democracy in his theses in "On the Concept of History." Benjamin begins with the Gotha program, which defined work as the "source of all wealth and all culture."[36] Here, as he writes, "the old Protestant work ethic was resurrected in secularized form."[37] He cites Josef Dietzgen's comparison of work with the "savior of modern times" and calls the concept of work that underlies it "vulgar-Marxist."[38] His critique of the social-democratic celebration of the capitalistic cult of work parallels his critique of beliefs in technical progress and the necessary domination of inner as well as outer nature arising from it. For Benjamin, all three moments reveal social democracy as the inadvertent and unwitting executor of the cultic religion of capitalism. It is clear that Benjamin's harsh critique of the orientation toward work in the concept of history and in the program of politics also holds for Marxism. Benjamin not only distances himself from the banalizing theory that the cultural superstructure reflects the politico-economic substructure, where this means the real relations of work and ownership; he also separates himself from the conception of a historical-dialectical materialism that reduces the course of history to the development of the relations of production, explaining and predicting it in the manner of a natural event. Against the theory of base superstructure, he maintains that the superstructure does not reflect the substructure but that it is its expression, "precisely as, with the sleeper, an overfull stomach finds not its reflection but its expression in the contents of dreams, which, from a causal point of view, it may be said to 'condition.'"[39] For him, the fetish character of the commodity is not so much the objective appearance of the characteristics of its work as an expression of the "mythical fear" to which, as Benjamin notes in the *Arcades Project*, humanity is delivered as long as phantasmagoria has a place in it.[40]

To this mythical fear that, Benjamin believes, haunts the history of humanity, along with ideals and phantasmagorias as its primordial history, he opposes a historical materialism that derives its revolutionary potency from the hopes and wishes of those who cannot redeem them. In this historical materialism, far removed from any historical materialism that would identify the working class with all the oppressed, Benjamin grounds the connection between Marxism and messianism. Here, the difference separating Benjamin not only from Marx but also from Weber begins to bear weight. Benjamin does not understand modernity and capitalism as a process of rationalization that, in the course of its historical realization, would wipe out all religions to an equal degree. Rather, he regards the process of rationalization from its reverse or underside and recognizes capitalism from this perspective as a cultic religion that is, on the one hand, universal and hegemonic and, on the other hand, at once part of the religious history of Christianity. Benjamin holds firm to the designation of capitalism as a religion, not least for the reason that it allows him to use the formulation and take the position of a "member . . . not gainfully employed," one who was "irreligious or had other beliefs,"[41] thereby assuming at the same time a standpoint if not of the outside then of critique. From the outside, he made reference to Jewish figures of thought concerning time and happiness, of turning (*Umkehr*) and of forgiveness, of celebration and of hope, which he rendered seminal for a theory of the critique of violence.

Turning and Remembrance

Benjamin had drawn the methodological conclusion from his determination of the parasitic relation of capitalism and religion that capitalist modernity must be systematically investigated with respect to this relation, and he remained, if often only implicitly, no less consistent in his adherence to this axiom. This holds particularly for the later texts that arose in the context of the *Arcades Project* and are thus decidedly dedicated to the history of modernity, such as the studies on Baudelaire or the theses in "On the Concept of History." At the same time, Jewish messianism with its concepts of fulfilled time, hope, delay, turning, and remembrance became the point of reference for the critique of capitalist modernity. At this juncture, the following passage from a letter that Benjamin wrote during the summer of 1939 from Paris to Theodor Adorno may suffice as evidence. In it, Benjamin comments upon the changes that, following Adorno's extensive critique, he had undertaken to his text on Baudelaire.[42] The text was conceived as part of a planned book with the title *Charles Baudelaire: A Poet in the Age of High Capitalism*: "I will permit my Christian Baudelaire to be borne aloft to heaven by Jewish angels alone. But arrangements are already in hand to let him fall during the last third moment of Ascension as if by accident, just before his final entrance into glory."[43] Above all, Benjamin had in mind here Baudelaire's heroism and the Christian-apocalyptic and gnostic traits found in him, as well as his proximity to the literature of decadence.

Second, I would like to cite the sentences in the last section of the theses in "On the Concept of History," which Benjamin formulated in 1940, the year of his death. Benjamin's turn to the past and the demand he formulates there for remembrance appear like an answer to Franklin's letter and the orientation spelled out therein for the conduct of life with regard to a calculable future that depends only on the speculative self-accumulation of capital. In place of speculation on the future and the apocalyptic certainty of the imminent end of history pervading modernity—which Benjamin understood as the perverted *reverse side* of capitalist speculation on the future—he puts expectation. In place of time that one can count and *on* which one can count, he puts the intensive, infinitesimal, and undetermined openness of the moment. And in this precise turn of phrase, he makes reference to the Jewish tradition, which holds fast to the idea that the Messiah is still to come:

> We know that the Jews were prohibited from inquiring into the future: the Torah and the prayers instructed them in remembrance. This disenchanted the future, which holds sway over all those who turn to soothsayers for enlightenment. This does not imply, however, that for the Jews the future became empty

homogeneous time. For every second was the small gateway in time through which the Messiah could enter.[44]

The reference to the Jewish tradition does not result from religious or national reasons but from the interest in a methodological procedure that allows change, renewal, or even revolution to be thought otherwise than through heroic intensification and apocalyptic "expansion of despair, until despair becomes a religious state of the world in the hope that this will lead to salvation,"[45] as is characteristic of the religious movement of capitalism.

Free Humanity's Search for Happiness

Now, rather than referring to biology, one can also start from the history of the word itself in order to interpret Benjamin's designation of the relationship between capitalism and Christianity as parasitic: "parasite" derives from the Greek *pará* and *sitos* and means "eating beside one another." The concept was originally used in ancient Greece for respected officials who partook of the sacrificial meal along with the priests and the gods. This connection to the history of the sacrificial cult at the same time illuminates a reflex of that understanding of the enlightenment which is found in the sentence Adorno quotes from Walter Benjamin in *Negative Dialectics*: "As long as there is still one beggar around, there will still be myth."[46] The origin of this sentence itself once again leads beyond Benjamin to one of his most important sources, along with his conversations with Gershom Scholem, for Jewish traditions of thought: the writings of the neo-Kantian philosopher Hermann Cohen.

Benjamin had already referred to Cohen in his epistolary exchange with Ludwig Strauß, and he cites Cohen's concept of myth as a complex of guilt in his essays "Fate and Character" and "On the Critique of Violence," both from 1921. In the eleventh chapter of the book *Religion of Reason*, posthumously published in 1919, with which Benjamin was likewise familiar, Cohen treated the transformation of sacrifice in the historical displacement of myth by religion. The question why the Prophet Ezekiel, like all the prophets, condemned the worship of idols yet did not abolish sacrifice finally leads Cohen to a discussion of the relationship of state and community, as well as that of state and religion.[47] The chapter cited bears the title "Atonement." Cohen focuses the question on the relationship between sacrifice and justice and that between sacrifice and cult. The sacrifice is indeed, through its imprisonment to myth, subjected to fate and thereby to lack of freedom and to injustice; it thus awaits its abolition. Nevertheless, as Cohen offers for consideration, the question arises at the same time whether it is not, for its own part, capable of transformation and whether in this transformed form it could have a historical right to existence.

In his famous study *The Gift*, Marcel Mauss described the historical background for this transformation of sacrifice. Mauss shows there that the transformation of the sacrifice historically involved its binding to the concept of justice and its orientation toward the human being. The transformation of the sacrifice into alms also involved, according to Mauss, the constitution of a community that defined itself by its perception of its social responsibility with respect to the poor:

> Alms are the fruits of a moral notion of the gift and of fortune on the one hand, and of a notion of sacrifice, on the other. Generosity is an obligation, because

Nemesis avenges the poor and the gods for the superabundance of happiness and wealth of certain people who should rid themselves of it. This is the ancient morality of the gift, which has become a principle of justice. The gods and the spirits accept that the share of wealth and happiness that has been offered to them and had been hitherto destroyed in useless sacrifices should serve the poor and children. In recounting this we are recounting the history of the moral ideas of the Semites. The Arab *sadaka* originally meant exclusively justice, as did the Hebrew *zedaqa*: it has come to mean alms. We can even date from the Mishnaic era, from the victory of the "Poor" in Jerusalem, the time when the doctrine of charity and alms was born, which, with Christianity and Islam, spread around the world. It was at this time that the word *zedaqa* changed in meaning, because in the Bible it did not mean alms.[48]

The historical connection that Mauss draws among sacrifice, justice, and alms corresponds to the meaning that Cohen gives to the discovery by the prophets of the poor as other and thus as fellow human beings. Decisive for Cohen is that poverty is neither attributed to the poor as guilt nor accepted as fate. In consequence, a society can be regarded as enlightened when it takes social responsibility upon itself and makes the abolition of poverty a common goal.

For Benjamin, precisely this prospect of a collective elimination of poverty—in the sense of a dissolution of the sacrifice by a form of justice that is brought to fruition in the gift—undermines capitalism, with its orientation toward the accumulation of capital as its highest rational criterion. In its parasitic adaptation of reformed Christianity, on the one hand it makes poverty appear to be self-inflicted and, on the other, makes alms seem like a futile waste that should be replaced with pedagogical measures on behalf of work. As a cultic religion it is distinctive in being the first religion whose cult is in no manner penitential but, as Benjamin emphasizes, "universally guilt-inducing" (*universal verschuldend*).[49] Benjamin plays here on the ambiguity of the German word *Schulden*, which means both monetary debt and moral guilt. *Universal verschuldend* (universally indebting or guilt-inducing) means—and here one can also refer to Weber's study—that the capitalist religion holds its believers captive in a closed circle of moral guilt and economic debts, which, as Benjamin Franklin impressed upon his son and readers, are also at the same time credits. With this, however, capitalism excludes that precise form of justice that, for Benjamin, represents the condition for a free humanity that may seek its happiness.

Nihilism, Messianism, and Anti-apocalyptic World Politics

The short note "Capitalism as Religion" was composed in 1921 and belongs in the context of works on politics, criticism, and violence. These are themes that had concerned Benjamin since his conversations with Ernst Bloch, whom he met through Hugo Ball shortly after the end of World War I during his Swiss exile in Bern in the spring of 1919. The works that originated in connection with the meeting with Bloch and that have survived include the essay "Fate and Character";[50] "On the Critique of Violence," which was published in the newspaper *Archiv für Sozialwissenschaft und Sozialpolitik* in August 1921; and the unpublished "Theological-Political Fragment."[51] Parallel to this, Benjamin continued his work on his translations of the *Tableaux Parisiennes* by Baudelaire and composed the essay "The Task of the Translator," which he conceived of as the foreword for the 1923 publication of a book of translations. He wrote a large part of a sonnet dedicated to his dead friend, the poet Fritz Heinle. He also developed the concept for a planned but never-realized journal, *Angelus Novus*, in memory of his friend, who had taken his life in the summer of 1914 when he was only twenty years old.

The essay on Goethe's *Elective Affinities* was designed as a larger work. Here, Benjamin continued his engagement with literary modernity and proposed a philosophical concept of art criticism whose task did not consist in the reflexive intensification of the work of art, as in the Romantic concept of criticism,[52] but, to the contrary, in the destruction of the appearance of totality—or, as Benjamin, borrowing from Hölderlin, put it, in the inscription of a caesura and of the demonstration of the expressionless as "critical violence."[53] He concludes the essay with the following four lines from Stefan George's volume of poems, *The Seventh Ring*—of which two had already been prefixed to the third part of the essay—and adds a short commentary that shows the relation to the fragment "Capitalism as Religion." The lines read:

> Before you wage the battle of your star,
> I sing of strife and gains on higher stars.
> Before you know the bodies on this star,
> I shape your dreams among eternal stars.

"Those lovers [Ottilie and Eduard in Goethe's *Elective Affinities*]," Benjamin comments on the lines, "never seize the body. What does it matter if they never gathered strength for battle? Only for the sake of the hopeless ones have we been given hope."[54] These two sentences express a decisive critique and rejection of the affirmation of the heroic constitution, which, according to Benjamin, not only determines George's aesthetics but also those of his predecessor, Charles Baudelaire, who is the central figure in the works that Benjamin composed in the context of a project of a prehistory of modernity in the thirties. George, who himself invoked Baudelaire at the beginning of his career, stands—as Benjamin would write at the conclusion of the 1933 essay "Stefan George in Retrospect," written on the occasion of George's death—"at the end of a spiritual movement which began with Baudelaire."[55] This movement is decadence.

At the same time, the concluding sentences of the essay on *Elective Affinities* exhibit the aspects that link the concept of art criticism to the concept of the critique of violence that Benjamin was developing at the same time in his texts on the thematic realm of law, politics, and violence: they concern the reevaluation of human life in its transitoriness by a paradoxical-seeming condensation of happiness and destruction. In a 1917 note on the "Program of the Coming Philosophy," Benjamin poses the question of the "dignity of an experience that was transitory"[56] to philosophy. It is this question that refers him to the Jewish tradition or, more precisely, to particular ways of reading the Jewish tradition. I would like to point here to Hermann Cohen's interpretation of atonement and of turning-away (*Umkehr*, in Hebrew *tschuwa*) from the previously cited chapter of the *Religion of Reason*. Cohen interprets this turning-away as a renunciation of death and orientation toward life.[57] Thus, in his depiction, this movement of turning-away captures the very essence of God. As Cohen explains, this itself changed in the prophecies of the prophet Ezekiel, according to which the saying that "the fathers eat sour grapes and the children's teeth are set on edge" (Ezek. 18.2) is no longer valid. "Punishment is not the infallible sign of his rule," Cohen writes, "rather he has pleasure in the sinner's turning-away from his ways. God, therefore, has no pleasure in his death, but rather in his life."[58] The life in which the Jewish God takes pleasure is not redeemed life but mutable and temporally conditioned human life.

The meaning that Cohen grants to the experience of turning-away and of atonement is accompanied by a reassessment of and new appreciation for human weaknesses and for vulnerable and precarious life.[59] Instead of a source of pain, the experience of weakness and of error becomes the point of departure for the possibility of change and transformation. "The turning-away [*Umkehr*] provides," as Cohen writes, "man with this new life, which, to be sure, can last only in the bliss of a moment. But this moment can and should repeat itself unceasingly: it should never grow old, and it must and can constantly rejuvenate and renew itself."[60] Cohen describes here a rhythm of human life characterized by interruption, in which change, happiness, and renewal are bound to the experience of human weakness. This process, characterized by the interruption of moments, turning-away, penance, and renewal represents an alternative to the "steady, though in the final analysis explosive and discontinuous, intensification"[61] that the religious movement of capitalism demands from humanity in the thought of the superman.

If Walter Benjamin confesses to a world politics "whose method can only be called nihilism," then this nihilism does not stand in the service of the self-annihilating apocalyptic intensification that he recognizes as the sole form of hope in the movement of the capitalist religion; rather, he constantly takes up a critical stance toward it and toward the heroism inherent to it. In his note "World and Time," composed during the same period, this is stated firmly: "My definition of politics: the fulfillment of an unimproved humanity."[62] The "world politics whose method can only be called nihilism" is not oriented toward despair but toward the "idea of happiness."[63] But the idea of happiness realizes itself, for Benjamin, in "free humanity's search for happiness." This formulation once again makes clear that Benjamin holds fast to the idea of enlightenment—world politics is nothing other than cosmpolitanism—and that he binds the idea of enlightenment to the idea of a Jewish messianism. Even if, as he writes in the first sentences of the "Theological Political Fragment," nothing historical could endeavor on its own accord to refer to the messianic, nevertheless the philosophy of history is, for Benjamin, conditioned by a mystical conception of history in which the messianic and the search for happiness of a free humanity refer to one another in a counterstriving disposition (*gegenstrebige Fügung*).[64]

Notes

1. In Walter Benjamin, *Selected Writings*, eds. Howard Eiland and Michael Jennings, 4 vols. (Cambridge, 2003), 1:288. [Trans. note: all translations are my own. I have, however, provided references to published translations where available.]

2. In 2003, Dirk Baecker devoted an entire essay collection to Benjamin's fragment; however, most of the contributions did not seriously pursue questions concerning the meaning of the difference between Judaism and Christianity in Benjamin's critique of Weber's secularization thesis.

See Dirk Baecker, "Einleitung," in *Kapitalismus als Religion*, ed. Dirk Baecker (Berlin, 2003), 7–17. An exception is provided by Werner Hamacher's contribution, "Schuldgeschichte. Benjamins Skizze 'Kapitalismus als Religion'" (77–121) (translated as "Guilt History: Benjamin's Sketch 'Capitalism as Religion,'" trans. Kirk Wetters, *diacritics* 32, nos. 3–4 [2002]: 81–106), which, in the context of the concept of turning (*Umkehr*) not only explicitly refers to the connection between Benjamin's fragment and Hermann Cohen but also explores this connection in more depth. At important places in his contribution in *Kapitalismus als Religion*, "Schwarzer Freitag: Die Diabolik der Erlösung und die Symbolik des Gildes" (121–44), Joachim von Soosten, a theologian from Bochum, also discusses Benjamin's thesis that capitalism is a parasite of Christianity.

In his essay "Capitalism as Religion: Walter Benjamin and Max Weber," *Historical Materialism* 17 (2009): 60–73, Michael Löwy shows that Benjamin's fragment builds directly on Max Weber's study *The Protestant Ethic and the Spirit of Capitalism* and that Benjamin turns Weber's analysis into a powerful anticapitalistic argument. Löwy places Benjamin's fragment in the tradition of romantic anticapitalism.

3. Max Weber, *The Protestant Ethic and the Spirit of Capitalism*, trans. Talcott Parsons (New York, 1930). Weber published the first edition of the study in two parts in the *Archiv für Sozialwissenschaften und Sozialpolitik* in 1904–1905. In 1920, soon after Weber's death, a revised version appeared in the two-volume edition of his *Gesammelte Aufsätze zur Religionssoziologie*. Benjamin's notes are based on this edition.

4. For extensive discussion, see Astrid Deuber-Mankowsky, *Der frühe Benjamin und Hermann Cohen. Vergängliche Erfahrung, Kritische Philosophie, Jüdische Werte* (Berlin, 2000), 282–99.

5. Walter Benjamin, *Gesammelt Briefe*, eds. Christoph Gödde and Henri Lonitz (Frankfurt, 1995) (cited hereafter as GB), vol. 1, 1:74.

6. GB 1:72.

7. Ibid.

8. Ibid.; emphasis is in original.

9. Ibid., 63.

10. Ibid., 77; emphasis is in original.

11. Ibid., 83.

12. Ibid., 64.

13. Walter Benjamin, "Capitalism as Religion," in *Selected Writings*, 1:288.

14. Ibid.

15. Ibid.

16. Ibid.

17. Ibid., 289.

18. Max Weber, *The Protestant Ethic and the "Spirit" of Capitalism and Other Writings*, trans. Peter Baer and Gordon Wells (New York, 2002), 23.

19. Weber, *Protestant Ethic*, 9.

20. Benjamin, "Capitalism as Religion," 288.

21. Ibid., 289.

22. Ibid., 290.

23. Michael Löwy has already established this convincingly. See Löwy, "Capitalism as Religion," 63–64.

24. Weber, *Protestant Ethic*, 74.

25. Ibid., 73; 73–74.

26. Benjamin, "Capitalism as Religion," 289.

27. Ibid.

28. Ibid.

29. Ibid.

30. Walter Benjamin, "The Paris of the Second Empire in Baudelaire," in *Selected Writings*, 4:44.

31. Ibid., 45.

32. Ibid.

33. Weber, *Protestant Ethic*, 75 Michael Löwy also refers to this passage. See Löwy, "Capitalism as Religion," 64.

34. Weber, *Protestant Ethic*, 77; Benjamin, "Capitalism," 288.

35. Weber, *Protestant Ethic*, 85.

36. Benjamin, "On the Concept of History," in *Selected Writings*, 4:393.

37. Ibid.

38. Ibid.

39. Walter Benjamin, *The Arcades Project*, trans. Howard Eiland and Kevin McLaughlin (Cambridge, 1999), 392.

40. Benjamin, *Arcades Project*, 939.

41. Benjamin, "Capitalism as Religion," 290.

42. See the corresponding extensive remarks of the editor of the *Gesammelte Werke*, vol I.3, 1064.

43. Theodor Adorno and Walter Benjamin, *The Complete Correspondence, 1928–1940*, trans. Nicholas Walker (Cambridge, 1999), 317.

44. Benjamin, "On the Concept of History," 397.

45. Benjamin, "Capitalism as Religion," 289.

46. Benjamin, *Arcardes Project*, 400; and Theodor W. Adorno, *Negative Dialektik* (Frankfurt, 1980), 203. [Trans. note: This line is not included in the English translation but see Theodor W. Adorno, *Minima Moralia: Reflections from Damaged Life*, trans. E.F.N. Jephcott (New York, 2000), 199.]

47. Hermann Cohen, *Religion of Reason: Out of the Sources of Judaism*, trans. Simon Kaplan (New York, 1972), 177.

48. Marcel Mauss, *The Gift*, trans. W. D. Halls (New York, 1990), 17–18.

49. Benjamin, "Capitalism as Religion," 288.

50. Benjamin wrote the essay in 1919, when he was still in Switzerland. It appeared in 1921 in the journal *Die Argonauten* (The Argonauts).

51. In addition, one might mention the two short notes, "The Meaning of Time in the Moral World" and "World and Time."

52. The Romantic concept of art criticism was the theme of Benjamin's dissertation, completed in 1919.

53. Walter Benjamin, "Goethe's *Elective Affinities*," in *Selected Writings*, 1:340.

54. Ibid., 355–56.

55. Walter Benjamin, "Stefan George in Retrospect," in *Selected Writings*, 2:711.

56. Walter Benjamin, "Program of the Coming Philosophy,"in *Selected Writings*, 1:100.

57. Cohen, *Religion of Reason*, 193.

58. Ibid.

59. Ibid., 205 .

60. Ibid., 204.

61. Benjamin, "Capitalism as Religion," 289.

62. Walter Benjamin, "World and Time," in *Selected Writings*, 1:226.

63. Walter Benjamin, "Theological Political Fragment," in *Selected Writings*, 3:305.

64. Ibid.

22

Peretz Markish (1895–1952)

MODERN MARXIST AND YIDDISHIST

David Shneer and Robert Adler Peckerar

> And all of a sudden, Markish interrupted in his bass voice that in moments of passion became a heroic tenor: "We shall host a literary event that will make the whole of Warsaw tremble. On a Saturday morning, when all the old pious Jews in every synagogue are praying to God—we, the young Jews, shall offer our own hymn in our synagogue to our god."[1]
>
> —MELECH RAVITCH

IN HIS MODERN-CLASSIC REFLECTION ON JEWISH HISTORY AND MEMORY IN *ZAKHOR: Jewish History and Jewish Memory*, Yosef Hayim Yerushalmi famously links the entry of Jewish life into modernity with the emergence of Jewish historiography. "The modern effort to reconstruct the Jewish past," Yerushalmi writes, "begins at a time that witnesses a sharp break in the continuity of Jewish living and hence also an ever-growing decay of Jewish group memory. In this sense, if for no other, history becomes what it had never been before—the faith of fallen Jews."[2] This rupture, the theoretical break in what was understood as a continuous progression of Jewish life, divides modern Jews from their past, and with it comes a consciousness of the Jewish past. According to this theory of rupture, the catalyst, if not the direct agent, for creation of Jewish modernity is the abandonment of traditional faith for secular historical consciousness.

Many Jews were abandoning traditional faith in the nineteenth and early twentieth centuries, and nowhere was this process of becoming modern more complicated than in the Russian Empire. After all, this was a place that was still ruled by a tsar, that had never had legal emancipation or instituted citizenship, and in which Jews continued to maintain a separate existence in ways unheard of in places like England, France, and Germany. One would be hard-pressed to find another place on earth where, as late as 1897, 97 percent of Jews listed a Jewish vernacular, Yiddish, as their native language. Although a small segment of Russia's Jews were becoming modern through urbanization and secularization, for most in Russia, becoming modern was a conscious choice—an act of breaking with one's past.[3] Peretz Markish,

who was born in 1895 in the heart of Volhyn province, was one of those consciously breaking with history.

How and when does a young Jew from the sticks become modern—can we even begin to pinpoint the moment? Could it be when he made his seemingly secular break, leaving his position in Berditchev as a *meshoyrer*, a synagogue chorister, after his Bar Mitzvah to part ways with the world of religion?[4] Or was it five years later, when the rupture with tradition widened as he abandoned his traditional Jewish antimartial masculinity to enlist in the tsarist army at the start of the Great War? Perhaps it was when he continued his militaristic stance during his time in Ekaterinoslav amid the turmoil of the Russian Civil War? In these brazen acts, the young Markish not only picked up a weapon to defend his country but also his fellow Jews during the worst wave of antisemitic violence to ravage the region in centuries. And not coincidentally, it was at this time that he began his career as a Yiddish poet self-consciously reflecting on Jewish life. He published an untitled poem in the provocatively named journal *Kempfer* (Fighter), which appeared in Ekaterinoslav in 1917.

Or, in accordance with what was "truly modern" in Russia after 1917, did Markish have to move beyond Yerushalmi's postmaskilic sense of Jewish historical presence and embrace historical materialism, devoting himself to the revolutionary overturning of history? It is this Marxist sense of *Umwälzung* (upheaval), both in the figurative sense of a cataclysmic shift in power and in the literal upending of language, that Markish began to express in his earliest published poetry of 1917–1919. His work was steeped in a curious mixture of rhymed, isosyllabic quatrains and the radical poetics of Vladimir Mayakovsky–styled Futurism. In this postrevolutionary moment, Markish not only embraced a particular Marxist modernity but also became its chief representative in Jewish literature through the medium of Yiddish poetry.

> fargosn hot a veykhe finsternish di velt
>   shoyn bizn kop . . .
> farendikt der farnakht zayn goldn bentshn
>   shtil un—op . . .
>
> Un altsding shvaygt un hert,
>   i mentsh, i ferd . . .
> Nor a vintl blondzhet un redt tsu vent
> un shtume vintmil makht tsum himl
>   epes mit di hent . . .
>
> Then a tender darkness flooded the world
>   Right up to its head . . .
> The dusk finishes its golden blessing
>   —Quiet, now it's done . . .
>
> And everything hushes and hears
>   Both man and steed . . .
> Only a breeze rambles and speaks to the walls

And silent windmills wave their hands saying
  Something to the skies . . .

In this early, untitled poem, Markish, echoing the prayers that end the Sabbath on Saturday evenings, evokes the traditional tropes of Jewish liturgical poetry for revolutionary purposes. He draws from both the Hebrew *havdola* prayer, with its forceful separation of sacred from profane and light from darkness, and the traditional women's Yiddish blessing, the *Got fun avrom* (God of Abraham). Markish overturns the conventions of Jewish prayer; his new liturgy does not usher in a peaceful "good week," as "God of Abraham" does, but rather depicts the coming night as an onslaught in which the evening twilight is looted by the forces of darkness. Despite all of the violent action in the poem, not a sound is made and there is no mention of a divine, dividing power, but rather the night stealthily subsumes the twilight. The poem fuses the traditional and the modern, the sacred with the profane. Alongside the Hebrew liturgical strains, Markish weaves quotations of John Keats's "Ode to a Nightingale," with the futile image of Don Quixote and with his horse and windmill, all in a poetic style reminiscent of Mayakovsky's 1915 "Oblako v Shtanakh" (Cloud in trousers). Perhaps more remarkable than the imagery or politics of his early poetry was this young modern's choice of language—Yiddish.

A central feature of Markish's emergence as both a figure and a representative of the modern moment is his decision to write in Yiddish. Writing in one's native language may, on the one hand, seem like a perfectly "natural" choice for a poet. Yet, this naturalness proves to be decisively deceptive for Jewish writers, perhaps even more so when considering the choice of Yiddish. Writing in Yiddish, which importantly was neither universally called "Yiddish" at the time nor even considered a language by many of its speakers, was a particularly complex and highly fraught move on the part of any writer, let alone a "modern" one. Traditionally, to write in Yiddish meant to write with an embodied audience in mind, often a feminized audience. Although Yiddish literature has existed alongside Hebrew literature for at least seven hundred years, the use of these literatures in Jewish culture was strictly regulated.[5] Yiddish was used for low-status genres and for edifying prose aimed at those who did not have access to the Jewish canon from which Jewish law was generated. Such literature was intended, in the oft-repeated prologue to early modern ethical literature, for "women and for men, who are like women in not being able to learn."[6] As far as Yiddish poetry and liturgy, the primary genre in which such literature was created in traditional Ashkenazic Jewish culture was the *tkhine*, a Yiddish supplicatory prayer for women to read while Jewish men prayed from a more formalized liturgy in the Siddur, or canonical prayerbook.[7] From the sixteenth-century explosion of Yiddish literature, with the advent of printing presses and Jewish publishing houses, through the nineteenth-century emergence of the maskilim, who wrote Yiddish "with a bitter taste in their mouths," the use of Yiddish as a self-consciously *literary* enterprise—as opposed to an entertaining or edifying one—was simply not possible.

To write in Yiddish for literary posterity, and to imagine volumes of these works kept on readers' bookshelves, was already a clear break from the prescribed role for Yiddish within the traditional Jewish cultural network—the interlocking, interrelated social and linguistic system that Itamar Even-Zohar termed a "polysystem."[8]

As Benjamin Harshav, who later developed Even-Zohar's polysystem theory, describes, from the Middle Ages onward Jewish life in Europe was grounded in a complex, distinct trilingual culture that operated in Hebrew, Aramaic, and Yiddish, with each of these languages possessing "a separate library of texts, a separate educational system, an ethical movement, and a separate conceptual world," but together making up a culture that completely lacked aspects of a territorial or statist power. According to Harshav, "the definition of Jewishness in the Religious Polysystem was *legal* and *essentialist*: a Jew was defined by *being* a Jew and was included in the whole network; whereas in the new Jewish Secular Polysystem it is *voluntary* and *aspectual*."[9]

One of the biggest problems of the advent of modernity, along with the displacement of the traditional cultural polysystem, was a linguistic one. Simply put, could modern culture be Jewish but take place in non-Jewish languages? For some writers, following the earlier maskilim, the answer was decisively in favor of the abandonment of the languages of the traditional system. But to others–perhaps the characteristic response of the new moderns–the choice to write in Hebrew or Yiddish, was a project intimately linked with modernity. Even though there were major exceptions to the politicization of Jewish language choice, the decision to write in Hebrew or Yiddish also became associated with particular worldviews: for example, Hebrew and political Zionism and Yiddish and the left (Bundism and communism). And even though all writers in the modern polysystem were typically multilingual and able to read and write in Hebrew and Yiddish as well as in German and Russian, among a host of other local languages, as the major worldviews of the twentieth century evolved the formerly intertwined linguistic cultural systems separated. Therefore, when Markish chose to write Yiddish poetry in the biggest revolutionary moment in Russian history (and for many in world history), he was performing a self-consciously radical act. He made the Revolution a modern Jewish event. And at the same time, by choosing the "lowly" Yiddish instead of the "queen" Hebrew, he was making a modern statement by elevating the popular at the expense of the elite.[10]

Markish became a published writer in the wake of war and two revolutions. He published his first volumes of poetry in 1919, when language was, as in the title of Benjamin Harshav's book on the subject, "in time of Revolution."[11] By giving one of his first volumes of poetry the title *Inmitn veg* (Midway), he was referring to the process of overturning history but signifying that Russia was only in the middle of that process. As important was the name of the publishing house that put out his book, significantly named in Russian *Mayak* (The beacon), although spelled in Jewish letters.[12] In contemporaneous reviews of Markish's work, the prolific literary critic Shmuel Niger used nearly every possible synonym for "modern" to describe Markish, characterizing his poetry as iconic of the here and now. Writing in 1922 about Markish's four 1919 volumes, Niger said, "He is no revolutionary who wishes to overturn the world; rather he, himself, is the overturned world; he alone is the glowing ember that the wind has carried off from a wildfire. He is not only the poet of the present moment [*fun der hayntiker tsayt*]—for the poet of *his* time is a poet for all time—Markish is a *record of that moment*."[13] Niger traces out the strands of contemporary Russian and German poetic artistic movements as they are woven together into Markish's text; he sees the form, technique, and imagery of the German Expressionists and hears the voice of Mayakovsky and, even more prominently, of Aleksandr Blok. Niger insists that the influence of Blok is most explicit in *Inmitn veg*, a volume that begins with a long prose poem cycle entitled "Draystn" (Thirteen). Just as Blok evokes Christian messianic images and references to the apostles in his famed "Dvenadtsat'" (Twelve), in Markish's gory "Thirteen," the poet invokes the estimated thirteen million war dead (the number is repeatedly multiplied by powers of ten throughout the poem) to conclude with kabbalistic significance:[14]

mir zaynen draytsn khurbns!
mir zaynen draytsn hundert toysnt milyon.
mir zayen umonheybdik—
undzere sharbns flakern—draytsn kroynen.
—keser!
Mir zaynen—draytsn!

We are thirteen remains!
We are thirteen hundred thousand million.
We are never-starting—
Our skulls gleam—thirteen crowns
—KETHER
We are—thirteen!

The continuous chain of metaphorical extensions ends with the transformation of the thirteen decomposing corpses that begin the work into the topmost point in the kabbalistic sefirot, or emanations, which Markish introduces as *umonheybdik* (lit., never-starting), the antithesis of the *Eyn-sof* (never-ending, or infinite). The thirteen skulls become the *kether*, or crown, the source of Cordovero's thirteen attributes of mercy. In reaching such a conclusion, "Thirteen" reads like a Yiddish, particularly Jewish sequel to Blok's apocalyptic, revolutionary "Twelve."

For someone so clearly invested in the Russian Revolution, why would Markish not write in Russian, the language of the Revolution? The easy answer is that he wasn't good enough to earn a reputation among the lights of radical Russian poetry like Mayakovsky and Blok. And that may well be true. But for Markish, Yiddish would not just be a safe linguistic universe in which to write. It was also the most modern of modern *Jewish* choices. In the same year that several volumes of his poetic works appeared, the Soviet state, centered in Russia but expanding to include Ukraine, Belorussia, and elsewhere, named Yiddish the official language of Soviet Jews. On the one hand, this was simply an act of normalizing Jews' relationship in the brotherhood of nations that would come to define the Soviet Union, an entity officially established in 1924.[15] But it was also a way of making the Bolshevik Revolution Jewish by overturning the Jewish linguistic hierarchy.[16] For someone like Markish, there was never a separation between a political and a cultural revolution. By choosing Yiddish, Markish was taking his place in the Soviet Revolution in the most Jewish way possible.

In the aftermath of the pogroms in Petliura's independent Ukraine in 1919–1920, Markish wrote his first major *poema*, or long-form formal poem, *Di kupe* (The heap),[17] in a clear break from the accepted poetics of Yiddish poetry in the early decades of the twentieth century—not so much for its radical secularism but for its use of revolutionary poetics to respond to anti-Jewish violence. After all, this was no traditional Jewish lamentation. In terms of apocalyptic themes and gory imagery, the poem was nearly identical to "Thirteen," published *prior* to the specifically Jewish massacres in Ukraine. Several years later, in an appreciation of Markish's poetic oeuvre, the Soviet literary critic I. M. Nusinov rejected the claim that the Yiddish readership would have been astonished or shocked by the "blasphemy" of Markish's work: "Neither Markish nor his readers believe in god any more—and so god [in the work] was for the most part an act of staging," he wrote.[18] He claimed that Jews were "*inmitn veg*," on the path toward the abandonment of faith and tradition and an embrace of social reality in the face of unprecedented violence. Markish's fully secular, modern articulation of violence breaks with the redemptive eschatology that embedded the pain of loss into a yearning for the Messiah through lamentations and martyrology. Moreover, according to Nusinov, Markish produced work that did not revel in an outdated, nationalist mode of threnody, a poetry of mourning composed or performed as a memorial to the dead, but rather wrote in a productive social vein.

In the year 1920, Markish moved from Soviet Ukraine to Moscow where he worked for the Communist Party's Yiddish-language newspaper, *Der Emes* (The truth), as a contributor and translator. While in Moscow, he lived in an apartment that served as the salon for Moscow's growing Yiddish cultural community.[19] Several Moscow-based writers put out the Yiddish literary journal *Shtrom* (Current) from 1922 until 1924. But by then, Markish was gone: in late 1921, he had left for Warsaw. In the post–World War I, post–Civil War, and post-pogrom era, when millions of Jews were on the move from the devastated heartland of *yidishland*, Markish was simply one more peripatetic Jew. But he made Warsaw, the largest Jewish center and most vibrant Yiddish literary center in the world, his (always temporary) home. In fact, he himself helped make Warsaw the ground zero of modern Yiddish literature. From there, he maintained his personal and professional contacts with colleagues back in the emerging Soviet Union and with friends throughout Europe. But unlike other exiled Yiddish writers like David Bergelson, who settled in Weimar Berlin and earned money writing for the New York–based Yiddish daily press, Markish didn't regularly earn his bread publishing in the Yiddish dailies. Instead, he bet on radical poetry and modern aesthetics.

Upon arrival in Poland, Markish joined the Ringen avant-garde literary group, and he also helped found other publications. Like most Yiddish writers, Markish didn't associate himself with a single ideology, such as expressionism or futurism. The closest he ever came was during his Warsaw years, with the publication of his 1922 expressionist manifesto *Estetik fun kamf in der moderner dikhtung* (The aesthetics of struggle in modern poetry). The presentation of this manifesto at a public performance rocked the Yiddish literary world. Markish's literary manifestos from this period show how he saw literature as a new secular liturgy.[20] In the same year, he helped found the expressionist journal *Albatros* and the group *Khalyastre* (Street Gang). In addition to his work with avant-garde magazines, Markish also cofounded the influential journal *Literarishe Bleter* (Literary pages) in 1924, making himself a central figure in its Yiddish literary scene. But Markish was rarely settled in this period. From 1921 to 1926, he demonstrated his commitment to internationalism by constantly traveling, spreading the gospel of modernity to Yiddish-speaking audiences throughout Europe. Poet and critic Melech Ravitch once said, "[O]ne could rarely find Peretz Markish in Warsaw on a Friday night. He usually traveled across the country with his fiery word waterfalls, with his blazing geysers, with his lectures, all of which had many titles but one theme: 'Warsaw, Moscow, New York, Jerusalem,' 'The Past, Present and Future of Yiddish Literature.' "[21] Markish was the wandering poet-prophet of the revolutionary moment, but he saw Russia and the Revolution, even while in Warsaw, as the center of his creative universe—as the source of his own sense of being modern. In his 1922 essay collection on aesthetics called, typically, *Farbaygeyendik* (Passing by), he wrote that contemporary Yiddish poetry, like socialist revolution, originated in Moscow and radiated out from there. Linking his own modern project to the work of his contemporaries across national and linguistic boundaries, who were also experimenting with language, his early work shows a pronounced engagement with international modernism. For Markish, like Mayakovsky, there is no poetics without revolutionary politics. From Markish's earliest work and perhaps through his entire career, we can see the strains of Mayakovsky's 1918 "Open Letter to the Workers," in which he proclaimed that "The revolution of content—socialism—anarchism—is unthinkable without the revolution of form—futurism. . . . No one can know what immense suns will light the life of the future. Perhaps artists will transform the grey dust of the cities into hundred-colored rainbows. . . . One thing is clear to us—the first page in the newest history of the arts will have been written by us."[22]

Markish makes the Mayakovskian radical break with poetic form and abandons the confines of traditional metrical systems and rhyme in many of the poems in his earliest collections of 1919.[23] At the same time, this revolution in form was realized in various ways. In other work Markish shows a particular attraction to a different stream of the Russian Silver Age literature: the distinctive Symbolism of Blok and Osip Mandelshtam. He often directly emulates the rhythms and rhyme of Blok and Mandelshtam and even the eccentric metrical systems of Andrei Belyi. For Markish, the importation of the Russian versification systems of his contemporaries into Yiddish poetry was—like the act of writing an engaged, modern Yiddish poetry itself—a revolution in form. Although the Mayakovskian shattering of formal aspects of versification may seem more "radical" or "modern" than the creation of a body of Yiddish poetry that resonated with formal Russian verse, adopting classical verse form to modern Yiddish stood in stark contrast to the longstanding, official uses of Yiddish in *tkhines*.[24] Setting Yiddish poetry free of its historical confines was not only a revolution in form and content but also a far-reaching assertion of the poetic and, following Mayakovsky, *political* possibilities of the Yiddish language.

The opening poem to his 1919 volume *Shveln* serves as a poetic credo for the volume and aptly thematizes the radical transformation of modern culture while using the forms of classical verse.[25] In this case, it is in the form of a deconstructed sonnet (perhaps even a decadent "limping sonnet," or *sonnet boiteux*, à la Paul Verlaine), filled with futurist imagery and style. Markish provides the rudiments of the form: fourteen lines, (nearly) regular iambs, consistent—although alternating—rhyme. He also takes on the typical apostrophic posture of the Petrarchan sonneteer while thematically engaging another Western poetic tradition, the *aubade*, the song of lovers taking leave of each other at daybreak.

ikh zegn zikh mit dir
fargeyendike tsayt,
ikh ken dikh nit, fargangenhayt,
ir kert nit mir,—
ikh hob zikh aykh gekholemt! . . .

Un du ver bist, mayn tsukunft,
farvaksene in groye hor?
kh'geher nit dir,
du kholemst zikh mir nor!

kh'bin dayner, 'nishtiker atsind',
blind!
un blinderheyt kh'bin raykh!
mir shtarbn beyde glaykh
un vern glaykh geboyrn!

I take my leave of you
Passing time,
I don't know you, Past,
You don't belong to me,—
I dreamt you! . . .

And you who are, my Future,
Grown old in grey hair?
I don't belong to you,
But you dream of me!

I am yours, insignificant "Now,"
Blind!
And blindly I am rich!
We both of us die the same
And the same are born![26]

Markish's parting address in the opening stanza is not to an embodied woman
but rather to a different type of female addressee, "Passing Time," a grammatically
feminine substantive in Yiddish. In the same stanza, Markish thematizes the moment where the speaker transitions from the intimacy of the bedroom, using the
intimate "du," to the estranged distance of the formal "ir." And as if to emphasize
his engagement with the Western canonical tradition, the poem closes with a near
quotation from John Donne's poem "The Canonization": "We die and rise the
same, and prove / Mysterious by this love."

From the perspective of many of his Warsaw colleagues, Markish's move back to
Moscow in the summer of 1926 seemed like a permanent goodbye, a writer choosing "the other side." From the perspective of Soviet colleagues, and likely for Markish himself, his move heralded his homecoming and his commitment to the building

of Soviet Yiddish culture. The Soviet Union he left in 1921 was a chaotic, wartorn world of poverty and famine. By 1926, a more defined Soviet literary and political culture had begun to take shape with the Communist Party playing a larger role in cultural production. Markish adjusted quickly to his new environment, although writers who had never left the Soviet Union always reminded him of his self-imposed "exile" in Warsaw. In February 1927 in Moscow, several Soviet Jewish cultural groups sponsored a celebration welcoming Markish back to the Soviet Union. His speech was a declaration of his continuous connection to Soviet culture, even during his five years in Warsaw: "I am not a guest here, because I never went anywhere. I never broke with Moscow, and I never allied myself with any other place."[27] Markish became part of the Soviet Jewish literary establishment and one of its leading figures. He published extensively in the Kharkov literary journal *Royte Velt* (Red world), and less extensively in the Minsk literary journal *Shtern* (Star) and the newspapers *Der shtern* (The star) and *Oktyabr* (October).

If the tumult of the Revolutionary era was dominated by a new Yiddish poetry and the obsession with the manifesto, by the late 1920s Yiddish prose became the most important medium for producing Soviet Jewish literature. This shift in genres reflected a more general movement away from the experimentation of the 1920s toward a more rigid definition of Soviet literature in the 1930s that came to be known as socialist realism. Soviet Yiddish writers began producing literature in this new model, a move to realism in a socialist key, one that portrayed Soviet life through the prism of triumphalism and heroism. Having experimented with prose in *Inmitn veg*, Markish's own literary career reflected this more general shift, as evidenced by the 1929 publication of his first novel, *Generations* (*Dor oys, dor eyn*), which centered on a Jewish family living during the Revolution. If "modern" is defined as a secular sense of time and history, then Markish remained modern until the day he died. But if being modern also means breaking with one's expected path in life, which he did when he left the synagogue behind and joined the Russian army, then Markish stopped being modern only when he became embedded in a Soviet state literary system. Perhaps it was in the establishment of socialist realism, of an aesthetics tied to a state political structure, that marked the beginning of the end of Markish as a modern.

Ironically, although Markish established himself as an important Soviet Yiddish writer, his standing in the non-Yiddish Soviet intelligentsia was no less strong. According to Gennady Estraikh, Markish was embroiled in caustic internal debates among various Yiddish literary cliques, and several times he was bitterly criticized in the press. But at the same time, his reputation as an important *Soviet* (and not specifically Yiddish) author was sealed, as he became one of the most translated contemporary Yiddish writers.[28] Not unlike Isaac Bashevis Singer, the Warsaw-born, New York–based Yiddish writer who won the Nobel Prize for Literature as an American writer via English translations of his Yiddish works, in the 1930s several volumes of Markish's work came out in Russian, including translations of his two novels: *Generations*, in Russian *Iz veka v vek* (1930); and *Eyns af eyns* (One on one), in Russian *Vozvraschenie Neitana Bekkera* (1934).[29] With the 1934 establishment of the Soviet Writers' Union that served as the umbrella organization for all professional writers in the Soviet Union, Markish quickly rose to a position of political power.

The 1930s were a challenging time for a writer with such a radical literary reputation and such a foreign biography as Markish. He was appalled to see his friends disappearing in the Gulag. After the arrest, in May 1934, of Osip Mandelshtam, poet Anna Akhmatova wrote: "Among the men, only one visited [Osip's wife] Nadya—Peretz Markish. On that particular day, though, many women visited her."[30] The emphasis is clearly that Markish was the only man brave enough to visit Mandelshtam's grieving wife. Yet in January 1935, as Melech Ravitch recalls, Markish demonstrated a knee-jerk Soviet suspiciousness when Ravitch, Markish's old Warsaw friend, unexpectedly arrived at his doorstep in Moscow with an Intourist chaperone in tow. Upon opening the door, the first words Markish uttered, even before greeting his old friend, were to the chaperone: "Are his papers in order?"[31] At this moment, in the disappointed eyes of Ravitch, the brave, brash writer of the Revolution showed himself to be a poet ingrained in the bureaucracy of the Soviet state, a status made official in 1939, when he was awarded the Order of Lenin, one of the highest state honors.

Markish put his poetic voice in service to the state shortly after Germany broke its nonaggression pact with the Soviet Union and invaded on June 22, 1941. Two months later, on August 21, 1941, together with a group of Soviet Jewish cultural and political leaders, Markish appealed to "the Jews of the world," in particular to their "fellow Jews [*brider yidn*]" in the United States, to pressure their government to enter the war against German fascism. Among the three speakers recorded for the short propaganda film that circulated widely, Markish was the sole Yiddish voice. He reminds his audience that "only *here* in the Soviet Union, after years of persecution, have Jews found a haven and a homeland that healed the wounds of centuries of massacres like a devoted mother."[32] The 1941 speech is not simply a desperate wartime appeal, but rather a reminder of a not-terribly-distant past, only two decades earlier, when choosing to write in Yiddish was to be a participant, if not a leader, in the enterprise of Soviet Jewish nation-building. But by 1941, Markish's Yiddish speech did not resound with the same challenge to existing power structures or his obsession with being in the moment of revolution as his work of the late teens and early 1920s did. If modernity is about being on the cutting edge, by the time Markish was using Yiddish as part of the Soviet war project and in the service of the state, he was no longer modern.

During the Great Patriotic War, after Nazi Germany invaded the Soviet Union, Markish wielded considerable cultural and literary authority. From 1939 to 1943 he served as the chair of the Yiddish section of the Soviet Writers' Union, and in 1942 he finally became an official member of the Communist Party, a step that in 1942 could only be seen as an expected act of patriotic duty. Throughout the war, he was a member of the board of the Jewish Anti-Fascist Committee (JAFC). Despite his many administrative roles, he wrote prolifically in this period. His early wartime work was published in small pamphlets by the *Emes* (Truth) publishing house and, on occasion, the major Russian press. After the JAFC's newspaper *Eynikayt* (Unity) began appearing in June 1942, Markish was one of its regular contributors. He wrote frequently about Soviet Jews and their destruction. His work repeatedly alludes to the Jewish literary canon, but not to lamentational literature like many other Yiddish writers responding to the Holocaust. Instead, like his Zionist contemporaries, Markish searched for Jewish heroes, martyrs, and vengeance-seekers to craft a counterhistory to traditional Jewish responses to catastrophe. Markish's wartime "Dem yidishn shlakhtman" (To the Jewish warrior) emphasizes Jewish heroism and battle-readiness, rather than Jewish suffering.[33] It is also the poem in which he introduces the image of the biblical avengers, Shimon and Levi, who wipe out an entire town in response to the rape of their sister Dinah. Rather than reading these two brothers ambivalently, as Jewish tradition did, Markish suggests that they are models of Jewish behavior. As he writes near the end of the short essay: "The crying earth of the city of Odessa, and the cry from the bloodied Lukianov cemetery [in Kiev], for the communities ritually slaughtered [geshokhtene]. . . . You, Jewish soldier, will not part from your gun, just as your grandfathers refused to part with their holy book. . . . A city for every slaughtered child! A city for every raped sister. Now go, Jewish Red Army soldier, take revenge, and may the pain never be depleted from your heart until Berlin lies in ruins like Shechem, until the blood of your graves is repaid."

If in his early work Markish rejected the traditional Jewish polysystem and exploded the whole idea of lamentation and martyrology, during the war he went further by excavating a secular Jewish literary history in the Bible. Such a literature responds to violence not by reveling in its horror but by turning it into a call for revenge. In the case of Markish's work from Inmitn veg to Dem yidishn shlakhtman, he mines tradition in order to subvert it. In his earlier poetry, he does this by showing that violence does not bring on messianic redemption. His later work excavates a Jewish textual history of revenge to suggest that the possibility for redemption is only in human hands. The characters that the traditional Jewish literature rejected, in this case Shimon and Levi, are made heroes in Markish's work. He continued to believe in the union of pen and sword: the power of the written word to inspire and of the sword to ensure a Jewish future against perennial enemies. Markish emphasized that this particular chapter in history marked an end to Jewish passivity. As he wrote to the writer Joseph Opatoshu in 1945, "Our literature will now have to re-evaluate the notion of kidesh-hashem [Jewish martyrdom], as an eternal national category, which, in fact, helped fascism annihilate our people."[34] Like the Jewish national poet-prophet Chaim Nachman Bialik, who, in 1903, lashed out against traditional Jewish (particularly male) passivity in City of Slaughter, Markish criticized the traditional kidesh ha-shem as an explanation of the massive Jewish destruction at the hands of the Nazis. Although Jewish martyrdom traditionally meant mass suicide to avoid falling into the hands of the non-Jewish enemy, Markish valorized dying in the act of armed resistance.

One of Markish's most powerful late works was his illusive (and allusive) poem "Sh. Mikhoels—a ner tomid bam orn" (Sh. Mikhoels—A memorial flame at his coffin), his literary response to the murder of Solomon Mikhoels in January 1948 in a staged car accident in Minsk. Mikhoels's death, which signaled the start of the antisemitic "Anti-Cosmopolitan" campaign, was followed by a full state funeral featuring many Soviet political luminaries. Markish was pained by the murder of Mikhoels, who for all intents and purposes was the symbol of Jewish culture in the Soviet Union, and his public, poetic response was subversive. Chana Kronfeld argues that Markish's poem, with its clever use of biblical references, subtly implicated the regime in Mikhoels's death. If Markish's patriotic use of Yiddish during the war put his status as a modern in jeopardy, this final ode to a departed friend was a return to countering the status quo and challenging authority.

Markish's condemnation of the murder of Mikhoels exposed Markish to accusations of being a Jewish nationalist. Perhaps, this was well earned since he had rallied the Jewish nation, which at the time was in the interest of the Soviet Union. But with the end of the war, in the eyes of Stalin and his inner circle, the expression of Jewish nationalism, especially after the founding of the state of Israel, was no longer acceptable. Yiddish cultural institutions were closed down, and in late 1948 and 1949 many Yiddish cultural activists and members of the JAFC were arrested. On January 27, 1949, Markish himself was arrested. In 1952, he and several other members of the Jewish Anti-Fascist Committee were convicted of anti-Soviet activity, espionage, and bourgeois nationalism. In his final statement before the court, Markish pleaded for his life and summed up his work: "The entirety of my life and literary work and activity have been a battle against backwardness in literature. All of my books were brimming with this struggle."[35] His words, tragic and true, rang hollow, and ultimately futile in the courtroom where his perverted staged trial was held. On August 12, 1952, Markish was executed by the regime he served so loyally.

Rehabilitated after Stalin's death, his poems were again published in 1957, not in the original Yiddish but in Russian translation. But by the 1960s, as Estraikh has argued, the Great Patriotic War became the great unifying symbol of the Russian motherland; therefore, censors would only allow Markish's work to appear in the original Yiddish to keep the specifically Jewish story of the war limited to a Yiddish-reading audience. His novel of wartime Jewish heroism during the Warsaw Ghetto Uprising, *Trit fun Doyres* (Footsteps of the generations), which he wrote immediately after the war, was published posthumously in 1966 in the Soviet Union. Unlike mainstream American audiences, who were eagerly purchasing copies of Leon Uris's popularizing historical novels such as *Exodus* (1958) and *Mila 18* (1961), the Soviet Russian-reading public could read about the ghetto uprising only in Yiddish or in the wildly popular, but underground, *samizdat* version of *Exodus* circulating in the late 1960s. According to the state, the Soviet reading public wasn't ready for a 500-page novel about the uprising and its Jewish protagonists.

Epilogue

There is a presumption in Jewish historiography that, by definition, a believing communist can't be a Jewish modernist. The anticommunist strain in the criticism of Markish developed early in his own career and persists to this day. Perhaps this is a result of lingering Cold War attitudes to the Soviet Union and anything connected with it. Indeed, in the 1920s and 1930s, the Soviet Union was both a profound modern social and political experiment and home to one of the largest Jewish communities in the world. This puts Markish at the center of Jewish modernity. His presentist approach to literature is part of what makes him modern, and in many ways, he was ultimately a Russian and then a Soviet poet of the modern in Yiddish. Anticommunist critics often assert that Markish's modernness comes to an end when he moves back to the Soviet Union in 1926. Yet, if Jewish modernity is defined by being cosmopolitan, then Markish ceases to be modern, not in moving back to the Soviet Union, but when he stops moving altogether and strikes permanent roots in Moscow. If Jewish modernity is based on a break with dogma, then Markish begins to lose his status as modern when he becomes a part of the state literary apparatus. But if being a modern Jewish writer demands an aesthetic revolution against literary tradition, then despite his rootedness and his deference to the state, Markish remains the quintessential modern Jewish writer.

Notes

1. Melech Ravitch, "A kurtse geshikhte fun a dinamisher grupe fun dray yidishe poetn in varshe in 1921–1925," in *Warszawska awangarda: Antologia*, ed. Karolina Szymaniak (Gdańsk, 2005), 266–301 (269, 276, 278).

2. Yosef Hayim Yerushalmi, *Zakhor: Jewish History and Jewish Memory* (Seattle, 1982), 86.

3. On the creation of a modern Russian Jewish community, see Benjamin Nathans, *Beyond the Pale: The Jewish Encounter with Late Imperial Russia* (Berkeley, 2002). See also Eugene Avrutin, *Jews and the Russian State: Identification Politics in Tsarist Russia* (Ithaca, 2010).

4. Melech Ravitch, "Di geshalt fun Peretz Markish," in *Eseyen*, eds. Melech Ravitch and Yossl Birstein (Jerusalem, 1992), 63.

5. See, e.g., Shmuel Niger, *Di yidishe literature un di lezerin* (Vilna, 1919); or his *Di tsveyshprakhikeyt fun undzer literatur* (Detroit, 1941); and Naomi Seidman, *A Marriage Made in Heaven: The Sexual Politics of Hebrew and Yiddish* (Berkeley, 1997).

6. Chava Weissler, *Voices of the Matriarchs: Listening to the Prayers of Early Modern Jewish Women* (Boston, 1998)

7. Devra Kay, *Seyder tkhines: The Forgotten Book of Common Prayer for Jewish Women* (Philadelphia, 2004).

8. Itamar Even-Zohar, "Polysystem Studies," special issue of *Poetics Today* 11, no. 1 (1990).

9. Benjamin Harshav, *Language in Time of Revolution* (Berkeley, 1993).

10. Seidman, *Marriage Made in Heaven*.

11. Harshav, *Language in Time of Revolution*.

12. Peretz Markish, *Inmitn veg* (Moscow, 1919).

13. Shmuel Niger, "Perets Markish: algemeyne kharakteristik" (1922), reprinted in Shmuel Niger, *Yidishe shrayber in sovet-rusland* (New York, 1958), 232. Emphasis in original.

14. The 13 million figure also appears in other avant-garde works, such as Erwin Piscator's *Das politisches Theater*.

15. David Shneer, *Yiddish and the Creation of Soviet Jewish Culture* (New York, 2004).

16. See Kenneth Moss, *Jewish Culture and the Russian Revolution* (Cambridge, 2009).

17. Peretz Markish, *Di kupe* (Warsaw, 1921). The Kultur Lige publishing house and cultural network was established in Kiev in 1918, but moved much of its operation to Warsaw with the Bolshevik takeover of Ukraine in the fraught period 1920–1921. See Shneer, *Yiddish*; and Moss, *Jewish Culture*.

18. "Nit Markish un nit zayne leyner gloybn mer nit in got—deriber iz der got . . . geven der iker an instsenirung." I. M. Nusinov, "Fun natsionalen troyer tsu sotsialnmut," *Di Royte velt* 5, no. 8 (August 3, 1929): 95.

19. For address lists of the Yiddish writers, see Gosudarstvennyi arkhiv rossiiskoi federatsii, f. 2306, op. 22, d. 73, l.1; and RGASPI, f. 445, op. 1, d. 29, l.49.

20. Karolina Symaniak, "The Language of Dispersion and Confusion: Peretz Markish's Manifestos from the *Khalyastre* Period," in *Captive of the Dawn: The Life and Work of Peretz Markish (1895–1952)*, eds. Joseph Sherman, Gennady Estraikh, Jordan Finkin, and David Shneer (Oxford, 2011), 66–87.

21. Melech Ravitch, *Dos mayse-bukh fun mayn lebn* (Buenos Aires, 1962), 374.

22. Vladimir Mayakovsky, quoted in Peter France, *Poets of Modern Russia* (New York, 1982), 172.

23. On the history of use of the concepts of "modernity" and "modernism," so complicated in literary terminology particularly in the Central European context, see Hans Ulrich Gumbrecht, "Modern, Modernität, Moderne," in *Geschichtliche Grundbegriffe: Historisches Lexikon zur politisch-sozialen Sprache in Deutschland*, eds. Otto Brunner, Werner Conze, and Reinhart Koselleck (Stuttgart, 1978), vol. 4; or the English translation in Hans Ulrich Gumbrecht, *Making Sense in Life and Literature*, trans. Glen Burns (Minneapolis, 1992), 79. An exemplary study on the complexity of the concept of "modernism" can be found in Astraður Eysteinsson, *The Concept of Modernism* (Ithaca, 1990).

24. A similar attempt to create Yiddish verse in tightly constructed poetic forms was also undertaken by the American Yiddish poet A. Leyeles (the pseudonym of Aaron Glanz, born in Włocławek in 1889). Leyeles, who began publishing in the American anarchist organ *Fraye arbeter shtime* (Free worker's voice), published in New York a volume of poetry in 1926, *Rondos un andere lider* (Rondeaux and other poems).

25. As per the editorial notes in the anthology *A shpigl oyf a shteyn*, Benjamin Harshav, Chone Shmeruk, Abraham Sutskever, and Mendel Piekarz, eds., (Tel Aviv, 1964). Where possible, we have tried to use the original publication of the poems; however, we were unable to procure an original copy of *Shveln*.

26. English translation adapted from Jordan Finkin's original in his "Markish, Trakl, and the Temporaesthetic," *Modernism/modernity* 15, no. 4 (November 2008): 795.

27. This description of the Markish celebration comes from a letter from Shlomo Niepomniashchy to Daniel Charny, February 7, 1927. YIVO, RG 209, File 57.

28. Gennady Estraikh, "Anti-Nazi Rebellion in Peretz Markish's Drama and Prose," in Sherman et al., *Captive of the Dawn*, 172–85.

29. On Markish's early novels, see Harriet Murav, "Perets Markish in the 1930s: Socialist Construction and the Return of the *Luftmensch*," in Sherman et al., *Captive of the Dawn*, 114–26.

30. Anna Akhmatova, "Listki iz dnevnika: Vospominaniia ob O.E. Mandel'shtame" as found on http://ahmatova.ouc.ru/vospominanija-o-mandelshtame.html.

31. Melech Ravitch, *Mayn Leksikon* (Montreal, 1945), 1:126.

32. "Bratiia evrei vsego mira," or "An Appeal to the Jews of the World" (USSR, 1941), 6 min., black and white. Russian, Yiddish, and English with English subtitles. Available from the National Center for Jewish Film, Brandeis University.

33. Peretz Markish, "Dem yidishn shlakhtman," *Eynikayt*, August 31, 1943, 7.

34. Markish as quoted in Estraikh, "Anti-Nazi Rebellion."

35. Joshua Rubenstein and Vladimir Naumov, *Stalin's Secret Pogrom: The Postwar Inquisition of the Jewish Anti-Fascist Committee* (New Haven, 2005), xx.

23

Gershom Scholem (1897–1982)
MYSTICAL MODERNISM

David Biale

AT THE END OF HIS MAGISTERIAL LECTURES ON JEWISH MYSTICISM, GERSHOM SCHOlem concludes the chapter on Hasidism with the following story:

> When the Baal Shem had a difficult task before him, he would go to a certain place in the woods, light a fire and meditate in prayer—and what he had set out to perform was done. When a generation later the "Maggid" of Meseritz was faced with the same task he would go to the same place in the woods and say: We can no longer light the fire, but we can still speak the prayers—and what he wanted done became reality. Again a generation later Rabbi Moshe Leib of Sassov had to perform this task. And he too went into the woods and said: We can no longer light a fire, nor do we know the secret meditations belonging to the prayer, but we do know the place in the woods to which it all belongs—and that should be sufficient; and sufficient it was. But when another generation had passed and Rabbi Israel of Rishin was called up to perform the task, he sat down on his golden chair in his castle and said: We cannot light the fire, we cannot speak the prayers, we do not know the place, but we can tell the story of how it was done. And, the story-teller adds, the story which he told had the same effect as the actions of the other three.[1]

The story had its origins in the works of Israel Ruzhin ("Rishin" in Scholem's orthography), who famously eschewed kabbalistic lore for a more pastoral style of leadership.[2] The flowering of the Hasidic tale as a central pedagogical tool, one that the story demonstrates to have its own theurgic power, was part and parcel of a shift in Hasidism from its early theoretical teachings to the more populist approach pioneered by the Ruzhiner Rebbe.

Scholem first heard this tale from the great Hebrew writer Shmuel Yosef Agnon, who may well have understood it as a warrant for secular storytelling as well. But does the retelling of this story share in its magic? For Scholem, the story seems to signify the relationship of the secular historian to his religious sources, a dialectical continuity by which a modern recounting of the past partakes in the sacred power of that past without surrendering the historian's secular commitments. The modernity of the historian is thus a product of his ability only to tell the tale, since the woods and the prayer remain inaccessibly distant in time and place.

In the following discussion, I will argue that this dialectical relationship to the past constitutes Scholem's view of modernity. It needs to be stated at the outset that, for Scholem, as indeed for all modern thinkers, "modernity" is not a static given but, instead, something to be constructed and defined. It is therefore, in some sense, an individual process for each thinker. At the same time, there are certain tropes in Scholem's work that resonate with other constructions of modernity and thereby connect them to a wider sphere of meaning. If the modern age, as Max Weber famously argued, is an age of "disenchantment," does Scholem's modernity invoke such an age? As Joshua Landy and Michael Saler have argued more recently, the "reenchantment" of the world is equally characteristic of modernity.[3] The magical can coexist in some way with the secular or, perhaps put differently, the secular produces its own form of the magical. Did Scholem subscribe to this view in which the modern age reconstructs something of the enchantment—or mysticism—of the Middle Ages? Put differently, how secular was Scholem?

As Robert Alter has pointed out, words like "rupture," "chaos," and "nihilism" appear frequently in Scholem's vocabulary, a patently modern lexicon that he applies to apocalyptic and antinomian impulses in Jewish mysticism.[4] For example, he famously called messianic apocalypticism an "anarchic breeze" that blows through the "well-ordered house" of halakhic Judaism.[5] Thus, what is often assumed to be characteristically modern—the sense of revolutionary change—becomes in Scholem's hands the key to understanding the premodern or, more precisely, that which in the premodern incubates modernity. Modernist terms illuminate the religious tradition just as the religious tradition casts a long shadow over the modern.

At the same time, though, Scholem strikes a decidedly negative stance with respect to other aspects of modernity, especially bourgeois rationality. His full-throated attack on the nineteenth-century *Wissenschaft des Judentums* is aimed precisely at those earlier historians' apologetic rationalism.[6] Judaism, in their view, had to appear modern, defined as rational and dignified, in order to be *salonfähig*, ready to be welcomed into European society. This rationalist version of modernity excluded the mythic, the irrational, and the demonic. Scholem's desire to recover these forgotten or suppressed dimensions of Judaism was therefore aimed against the nineteenth century's construction of modernity. However, his turn to the irrational was anything but reactionary since Scholem was neither a kabbalist nor a Hasid; he had no desire to turn back the clock and become a medieval Jew.

This stance becomes explicit in one of Scholem's most halting, even awkward, essays, "On the Possibility of Jewish Mysticism in Our Time."[7] The hesitation he expresses repeatedly in this essay stems from the tension he evidently felt between the desire to find mysticism in the modern age and his own secularist inability to identify with it. He declares explicitly that he does not believe in the Torah of revelation and cannot therefore partake in the kabbalist's conviction that the Torah has an infinity of divine meanings (in other places, however, he seems to embrace precisely this view).[8] He also states that Jewish mysticism as a public endeavor, that is, as an enterprise that produces a public literature, has virtually ceased to exist in modern times. Even those genuinely spiritual or religious figures, the Rav Avraham

Yitzhak Ha-Cohen Kook and Rabbi Arele Roth, were not kabbalists proper, but rather expressed their individual spirituality in terms remote from the Kabbalah. If the Kabbalah was a vital force in premodern Judaism, it had become thoroughly marginalized and uncreative in the modern period.

In the same context, Scholem dismisses the Hasidic leaders of the twentieth century as merely perpetuating their dynasties; the creative age of Hasidism was limited, at best, to the eighteenth century when the movement emerged. And even then, Hasidism was not particularly innovative with regard to the Kabbalah but rather translated the earlier Lurianic Kabbalah into a popular, psychological movement.[9] This dismissal of any originality in post-eighteenth-century Hasidism was surely one of Scholem's blind spots as a scholar, but it accords with his secularist definition of modernity.

The essay "On the Possibility of Jewish Mysticism in Our Time" was written in 1963. But as early as the 1920s, he took a similar position in his vehement attacks on Oskar Goldberg (1887–1952).[10] Goldberg, who came from an Orthodox background, developed a bizarre theology focused on the five books of Moses interpreted in terms of numerological magic. Following the Kabbalah, Goldberg held that the Pentateuch is based on the letters of the Tetragrammaton. Since all of the laws and rituals of the Torah are, in effect, the name of God, the Hebrews activated the metaphysical reality at their "center" by means of these rituals. By virtue of this magical procedure, the Hebrews became the most metaphysical of all peoples. All subsequent biblical and Jewish history represented a fall from this "reality of the Hebrews" (the title of Goldberg's 1925 magnum opus). As opposed to polytheistic religions, whose gods were rooted in material reality, only the God of the Hebrews enjoyed a pure metaphysical reality. Goldberg's goal was to recapture this magical essence in the modern world, which, in his view, had become mired in polytheistic materialism. Interestingly, Thomas Mann based the metaphysical ideas in the first part of his *Joseph and His Brothers* on Goldberg's work, but he later satirized Goldberg as "Dr. Chaim Breisacher," the purveyor of a Nazi-like magical racial theory, in his *Dr. Faustus*.[11]

In the 1920s, the Goldberg circle tried to entice Scholem to join their ranks since they were fascinated by Kabbalah but had little access to its texts. Scholem rebuffed these advances, in part in reaction to Goldberg's hostility to Zionism, but also because he rejected Goldberg's ahistorical metaphysics that sought to recreate the primordial "reality" of the Hebrews. This kind of reenchantment was utterly foreign to his sensibility. When Goldberg's *Die Wirklichkeit der Hebräer* appeared in 1925, Scholem attacked it as "Jewish Satanism."[12]

The importance of Goldberg for defining the role of magic and mysticism in Scholem's version of modernity cannot be overestimated. References to Goldberg's book occur repeatedly in his essays and letters.[13] Scholem's resistance to Goldberg seems to have arisen from his rejection of the possibility of a true mysticism "in our time." Goldberg's odd synthesis of magical metaphysics with a biological (even racial) definition of the Jews was utterly remote from what we shall see to be Scholem's far less mythic understanding of the Jewish people in the modern era. And, as we shall also see, in Scholem's view, Goldberg's transplantation of Kabbalah into modernity shared much with the nihilistic vestiges of Sabbatianism, which might explain why he called it satanic.

Thus, for Scholem, even those who adhere to some form of traditional religion have lost touch with the creative forces that he identified—against the *Wissenschaft des Judentums*—with mysticism. Little wonder that he addressed the "possibility of Jewish mysticism in our time" with an evident lack of conviction. If, as he argued in the first lecture of *Major Trends in Jewish Mysticism*, mysticism is the third stage in the history of a religion (the first being the direct experience of God and the second the institutionalization of religion), then the capacity of mysticism to recover the immediacy of the first stage had run its course by modern times. Put differently, the modern age is defined precisely as that which comes *after* the age of mysticism.

In his own way, Scholem thus seems to subscribe to what has been called the "secularization theory" associated with Max Weber and Peter Berger, according to which the modern world represents a rupture with the world of religious tradition.[14] It is really only since Scholem's death in 1982 that this theory has come under repeated assault as religion reemerged in Judaism, as well as in Christianity and Islam, as a force to be reckoned with.[15] The modern—or some might say, postmodern—manifestations of religious fundamentalism are clearly products of modernity, even as they reject modernity. This dialectic is notably missing in Scholem's account.

But it would be too simple to define Scholem only as a secular historian observing medieval mysticism from the distance of his professorial perch. We know from his diaries and letters that the young Scholem flirted with religion, entertained briefly the possibility of Orthodoxy when he was a teenager, and even fancied himself the Messiah.[16] His secularism is shot-through with religious imagery. Indeed, in the essay on Jewish mysticism in our time, he labels anyone who writes about Jewish mysticism without personally embracing divine revelation to be a "religious anarchist": "All of us today may to a great extent be considered anarchists regarding religious matters . . . the fundamental fact that a religious understanding of Jewish continuity today goes beyond the principle of Torah from heaven."[17] Why religious anarchism and not secularism? For Scholem, the very connection to the religious tradition that characterizes the unbeliever who does not sever himself utterly from that tradition is religious in nature, even if anarchistic in intent.

It was this idea of religious anarchism that animated Scholem's attraction to the writings of Franz Kafka, which he labeled on more than one occasion "canonical."[18] By this he seems to have meant that, like the way the kabbalists read the Bible as infinitely interpretable, so one should read Kafka as containing such an infinitude of meaning.[19] He expressed this view best in a letter to the German publisher Salman Schocken in 1937 on his reasons for studying Kabbalah:

> Years of highly stimulating thought had brought me to a rationalistic skepticism concerning the object of my study, coupled with an intuitive affirmation of those mystical theses that lie on the narrow boundary between religion and nihilism. I found the fullest and unsurpassed expression of this boundary in the writings of Kafka, which are themselves a secularized description for a contemporary person of the feeling of a Kabbalistic world. Indeed, at a later stage this led me to look on them as possessing an almost canonical halo.[20]

If nihilism and anarchism are symptomatic of modernity, they exist in some complex, uneasy relationship with religion. And it was Kafka who captured that relationship, or what Scholem calls the "narrow boundary between religion and nihilism."

This relationship between religion and nihilism maps onto the relationship between the premodern and the modern in Scholem's historiography. As is well known, he was deeply fascinated by the phenomenon of antinomianism, the paradoxical doctrine of redemption through sin (in rabbinic parlance: "the commandment that is fulfilled by its transgression").[21] This doctrine found its most extreme and pervasive expression in the Sabbatian movement, the messianic outbreak associated with the Turkish Jew, Shabbatai Zvi, from 1665 to 1667. After Shabbatai Zvi declared himself (or was declared) the Messiah, he began to perform strange, antinomian acts such as eating forbidden foods and turning the fast of the Ninth of Av into a feast day. Following his forced conversion to Islam in 1667, those who continued to believe in him as Messiah interpreted his conversion as an act of holy antinomianism, a descent into the depths of evil in order to rescue the sparks of the Messiah's soul that were trapped there. Some of the more radical of the movement's followers imitated the putative Messiah by themselves converting to Islam and later, in Poland, to Christianity. As Scholem demonstrated in his great essay, "Redemption through Sin," the Polish Frankists (the followers of Jacob Frank, an eighteenth-century Sabbatian) threw off all religious constraints and descended into a kind of nihilism.

In the last pages of that essay, Scholem argues that the doctrine of "the holiness of sin" paved the way to modern secularism:

> The hopes and beliefs of these last Sabbatians caused them to be particularly susceptible to the "millennial" winds of the times. Even while still "believers"—in fact, precisely because they were "believers"—they had been drawing closer to the spirit of the Haskalah all along, so that when the flame of their faith finally flickered out they soon reappeared as leaders of Reform Judaism, secular intellectuals or simply complete and indifferent skeptics. . . .
>
> Those who had survived the ruin were now open to any alternative or wind of change; and so, their "mad visions" behind them, they turned their energies and hidden desires for a more positive life to assimilation and the Haskalah, two forces that accomplished without paradoxes, indeed without religion at all, what they, the members of "the accursed sect," had earnestly striven for in a stormy contention with truth, carried on in the half-light of a faith pregnant with paradoxes.[22]

The spirit of the modern age—rational, skeptical, secular—incubated in the womb of the paradoxical, the antinomian, and the mythic. Sabbatianism, that most extreme and irrational of all premodern Jewish doctrines, dialectically produced its very opposite.

Scholem's dialectical argument for the production of modernity out of the medieval anticipates a host of more recent interpretations that see the origins of secularism in Western religious traditions.[23] Amos Funkenstein, for example, used the term "secular theology" to describe this relationship.[24] According to his argument, the proponents of Enlightenment rationalism and the scientific revolution adopted the medieval scholastic divine attributes—God's omniscience, omnipotence, and providence—and invested them with earthly meaning. The desacralization of the world was thus accomplished with the tools of theology.

But what became of the demonic forces of apocalyptic, antinomian messianism? In his analysis of Hasidism, Scholem introduced the idea of "neutralization."[25] Rather than suppressing Sabbatianism altogether, he claimed, eighteenth-century Hasidism neutralized its messianic energies by redirecting and channeling them into this world. Although less explicit about more secular movements, it would appear that he believed that the Haskalah, Reform Judaism, and Zionism all engaged in forms of neutralization of the messianic. Of the latter, he writes at the end of his essay on "The Messianic Idea in Judaism":

> Little wonder that overtones of Messianism have accompanied the modern Jewish readiness for irrevocable action in the concrete realm, when it set out on the utopian return to Zion. . . . Born out of the horror and destruction that was Jewish history in our generation, it is bound to history itself and not to meta-history; it has not given itself up totally to Messianism. Whether or not Jewish history will be able to endure this entry into the concrete realm without perishing in the crisis of the Messianic claim which has virtually been conjured up—that is the question which out of his great and dangerous past the Jew of this age poses to his present and to his future.[26]

Zionism is not messianism, but it harnesses messianic energies in the process of entering the realm of history, the "concrete" realm. Since messianism demands a world outside of history ("meta-history"), the harnessing of messianism for a non-messianic, political task is a highly dangerous enterprise. It requires neither suppression nor succumbing, but rather neutralization.

In a now-famous letter to Franz Rosenzweig, Scholem expressed this view in terms of language. As a youth, he had embraced the Hebrew language, which he taught himself. Upon his immigration to Palestine in 1923, he mostly went over to writing in Hebrew and only returned to German after World War II (with the exception of *Major Trends in Jewish Mysticism*, first written in German and translated into English, as well as a number of other essays). But he was acutely aware of how the rebirth of Hebrew as a vernacular could never be fully secular and that it therefore concealed within it the dangers of messianism:

> They [the speakers of modern Hebrew] think that they have turned Hebrew into a secular language and that they have removed its apocalyptic sting, but it is not so. The secularization of the language is merely empty words. . . . We live with this language as on the edge of an abyss. . . . A language is composed of names. The power of the language is hidden within the name; its abyss is sealed therein. After invoking the ancient names day after day, we shall no longer be able to hold off their power.[27]

The letter to Rosenzweig is shot through with Scholem's modernist vocabulary—"abyss," "apocalyptic sting"—a vocabulary that draws its power from religious sources. What Scholem fears is that a language that is so bound up with apocalyptic associations can never become fully secular. It must conjure up the sacred in which it originated, a sacred that may lead to its destruction.

What exactly did Scholem mean by this dire warning? What danger did he envision for Zionism? In what way does the religious echo of the Hebrew language threaten its modern, secular manifestation? For an answer, we must turn to Scholem's politics from the period of World War I through the 1920s. The answer will define better the nature of Scholem's modernity, namely what it included and what it excluded. A cultural—or, perhaps, anarchistic—nationalist, he rejected more conventional political nationalism. Of course, both these positions—nationalism and the critique of nationalism—are peculiarly modern phenomena, and Scholem lined up very decisively on one side of the barricade.

No understanding of Scholem's position on nationalism is possible outside the crucible of World War I, the first catastrophe that modern nationalism visited on Europe in the twentieth century. As Scholem has described it in his memoirs, he was one of the few to uncompromisingly oppose the war from its very outset.[28] His opposition was initially mediated through his brother Werner, who belonged to the radical wing of the Social Democrats. But an equally important influence was Gustav Landauer, the German Jewish anarchist whose thought is critical for an understanding of Scholem's own nonsocialist politics, a politics one might call "anarchistic Zionism."[29]

Although Scholem attended a few meetings of the minuscule antiwar movement in 1914 and 1915, his antiwar activity took place primarily within the Zionist movement to which he already belonged. Zionism, for Scholem, meant the conscious rejection of European politics, just as it did the rejection of the bourgeois culture of the German Jews. Only by leaving Europe could the Zionists escape what he called the "dogmatism" of modern nationalism. Escape to Zion meant an attempt to create an anarchistic community, possibly modeled on the thought of Landauer, in which the patriotic pieties of the European setting would have no place. His later hostility to the desire of the political Zionists to create a "nation like all the nations" was rooted in this experience of what it meant to be a nation in the second decade of the twentieth century. As he wrote to Walter Benjamin in 1931: "I do not believe that there is such a thing as a 'solution to the Jewish Question,' in the sense of a normalization of the Jews."[30]

Scholem's decision to undertake his lifelong study of the Kabbalah was also a product of the war years. Authentic Jewish sources seemed to offer an alternative to the petrified Judaism of assimilated German Jews who had revealed their ultimate cultural bankruptcy by supporting the war. The mystical or irrational seemed the most promising answer to the enervated rationalism of bourgeois German and German Jewish culture. Yet Scholem's affirmation of the irrational in Jewish history was not without qualification. Interest in the irrational had already found its chief spokesman among young Central European Jews in Martin Buber. But Buber had enthusiastically supported the war up to mid-1916, connecting his *Erlebnismystik* (mysticism of experience) of the time with the *Erlebnis* of the war. Scholem formulated his own opposition to the war against Buber's mysticism: *Erlebnis*, he argued, is "nothing but a chimera, the Absolute turned into idle chatter."[31] Mystical enthusiasm was just as dangerous as bourgeois rationalism when drafted into nationalist service.

Scholem's own approach to Jewish sources must be understood against this background. He attempted to chart a third course between the rationalism of the *Wissenschaft des Judentums* and the irrationalism of Buber. As opposed to Buber, he

sought an approach to mysticism that did not collapse historical distinctions between the mystic and the historian, or between the premodern and the modern,
while still seeking to capture something of the vitalism that he believed inhered
particularly in the irrational. In this position, Scholem was at once a child of the
vitalistic counterculture of turn-of-the-century Europe but also its critic, a kind of
"anti-Nietzschean Nietzschean," if one may reduce this culture to one name.[32] He
wished to harness history for the Jewish national renaissance, but he recognized the
danger that a historian could easily become the servant of aggressive nationalism, as
was the case for many German nationalist historians.

This third course in historiography was to characterize his political activity as
well, once he came to Palestine in 1923. It was in this period of activity, which lasted
roughly until the Nazis came to power, that the nexus between Scholem's historical
work and his political position becomes most clear. In the late 1920s and early 1930s
Scholem was an activist in Brit Shalom, the group of intellectuals around the Hebrew University who represented the singular, if largely ineffectual, contribution of
a Central European sensibility to the political culture of the Zionist Yishuv.[33] Brit
Shalom advocated limitations on Jewish immigration and a binational parliament
as ways of coming to a political compromise with the Arabs. After the rise of the
Nazis in 1933 and the mass flight of German Jews to Palestine, Scholem, like many
others, could no longer easily accept voluntary restrictions on immigration. With
the Arab riots of 1929 and the violence and general strike of 1936, he abandoned
any hope of a political settlement leading to binationalism. Many years later, he
claimed that from this point onward the course of history leading to the 1948 War
of Independence and the establishment of a Jewish state was largely determined.[34]
In his political statements and letters from those years, one finds a recurring pessimism and despair about the prospects for Zionism to realize the program he wished
for it.

Scholem's own pessimism was prompted chiefly by the rise of the right-wing Revisionists in the 1920s and 1930s. He saw in the Revisionism of Ze'ev Jabotinsky a
Jewish version of the imperialistic nationalism he had rejected in Europe. In 1926,
in his first political declaration in Palestine, he joined with five other members of
the new Brit Shalom to denounce Jabotinsky's call for a Jewish legion and to reject
Jewish militarism and concepts of heroism and national honor. He condemned
what he called the "imperialism" of the Revisionists, arguing in pessimistic terms
that seem all too relevant today:

> If the dream of Zionism is numbers and borders and if we can't exist without
> them, then Zionism will fail, or, more precisely, has already failed. . . . The Zi-
> onist movement still has not freed itself from the reactionary and imperialistic
> image that not only the Revisionists have given it but also all those who refuse to
> take into account the reality of our movement in the awakening East.[35]

The colonial power, he asserted, created the conditions that would inevitably lead
the indigenous population to demand self-determination.[36] The Zionists must anticipate this development and come to terms with Arab nationalism rather than
assuming the Revisionists' version of nationalism, which was, in reality, no better
than other forms of European colonialism.

Equally dangerous to Zionism as the Revisionists' secular nationalism was modern mysticism. In 1934, Scholem attacked the anti-Zionist Orthodox writer Isaac Breuer, who had constructed a mystical alternative to Zionism:

> [J]ust as [Zionism] will not find its salvation, its *tikkun*, in the wild apocalypticism of the Revisionists, it must not give way to a politics of mysticism which uses the most profound symbols of our inner life to usurp a power which others have fought for and have sacrificed themselves to firmly establish—which uses these symbols to subjugate a way of life . . . the adherents of that politics have followed with nothing but excommunications, maledictions, and hate.[37]

The extreme nationalists of the Revisionist movement and the Orthodox anti-Zionists were unwitting allies in their attempts to wrest power from the moderate secular Zionists. By appropriating kabbalistic symbols, Breuer was turning what Scholem considered the source of Jewish vitality in the premodern age into a weapon of oppressive Orthodoxy in modernity.

In his attack on Breuer, Scholem labels the politics of the Revisionists "wild apocalypticism." Secular these nationalists may have been, but they shared with earlier Jewish apocalyptics a politics that could never achieve anything in this world. For that reason, he rejected the association of Zionism with messianism, especially of the Sabbatian type. As he wrote in 1929:

> I absolutely deny that Zionism is a messianic movement and that it has the right to employ religious terminology for political goals. The redemption of the Jewish people, which as a Zionist I desire, is in no way identical with the religious redemption I hope for in the future. . . . The Zionist ideal is one thing and the messianic ideal another, and the two do not meet except in the pompous phraseology of mass rallies which often infuse our youth with a spirit of new Sabbatianism which must inevitably fail. The Zionist movement has nothing in common with Sabbatianism.[38]

In this invocation of Sabbatianism, Scholem explicitly connects his historical work with his politics. This particular statement comes just a year after he completed his first study of Sabbatianism, an essay on Abraham Cardozo. In that essay, he concludes in almost identical language:

> The messianic phraseology of Zionism . . . is not the least of those Sabbatian temptations which could bring to disaster the renewal of Judaism. . . . As transient in time as all the theological constructions, including those of Cardozo and Jacob Frank, may be, the deepest and most destructive impulse of Sabbatianism, the hubris of the Jews, remains.[39]

The messianic impulse consists in the desire to realize the final redemption within an unredeemed world, a kind of hubris that can only result in catastrophe. And Scholem ironically invokes the title of Oskar Goldberg's book, which had appeared three years earlier, a hint that Goldberg's own form of nonmessianic magic was as dangerous to the Jews as apocalyptic messianism: both tended toward nihilism.

The consequence of apocalypticism in politics may be paradoxical. In a fragment found in his *Nachlass* titled "Why Did We Become Zionists," he writes that "the more Zionism turned apocalyptic," the more it perpetuated the exile.[40] Those who had searched for redemption in Zionism, by which Scholem means the renewal of the Jewish people, now found themselves trapped in what they had tried to escape. The *Tikkun* of Zionism (the term itself, from the Lurianic Kabbalah, is messianic) lies paradoxically in abandoning such messianically freighted language. Or, in the terms we encountered earlier, Zionism must *neutralize* the messianic by channeling its revolutionary energies into a this-worldly project.

For Scholem, politics and religion must be kept separate because religion injects a demand for the absolute into politics. This view remained consistent throughout his life. In an interview shortly before his death,[41] he referred to the "fatal attraction" that the Jews have always had to messianism and argued that the contemporary Gush Emunim (the settler movement in the territories occupied by Israel in 1967) is like the Sabbatians, although perhaps even more dangerous because their messianism has political and not only spiritual consequences. He evidently saw these Orthodox messianists as combining the worst of the Revisionists' politics with the worst of Breuer's mysticism.

For all the secularism of Scholem's politics, he was acutely aware of the role that religious motifs must play in nationalism. He did not believe it possible to create a national revival without awakening these vitalistic, but equally dangerous, forces. His ambivalent attempt to build a Jewish nationalism that drew its vitality from religious symbols, but was itself secular, is characteristic of modern nationalism. As Eric Hobsbawm has pointed out, modern nationalism typically takes on such ambivalence: it sees religion as a challenge to its own monopoly on the loyalty of its citizens, but it also uses religious icons to further its own secular goals.[42] Scholem's position seems to reflect this inherent tension: Zionism could never be an entirely secular movement, a movement to "normalize" the Jewish people, yet the religious symbols it necessarily invoked constituted a profound threat to its political goals. Put differently, Zionism as a *modern* political movement could not be a simple product of medieval Judaism, but neither could it divest itself entirely of its religious origins. The modern is always grounded dialectically in the premodern.

Critics of Scholem from Baruch Kurzweil to Eliezer Schweid have accused Scholem of embracing a latter-day Sabbatianism; they see his historiography as glorifying the demonic and the irrational in Jewish history.[43] Such a reading is seriously off the mark. To be sure, Scholem held no brief for those nationalist historians who wished to construct a monumentalist history for Zionism. As he wrote in his famous attack on *Wissenschaft des Judentums*:

> We came to rebel but we ended up continuing [in the same path]. . . . All these plagues have now disguised themselves in nationalism. From the frying pan into the fire: after the emptiness of assimilation comes another, that of nationalist excess. We have cultivated nationalist "sermons" and "rhetoric" in science to take the place of religious sermons and rhetoric. In both cases, the real forces operating in our world, the genuine demonic remains outside the picture we have created.[44]

The nationalist historians searched only for the positive and heroic elements in Jewish history in order to create a myth of the nation. The picture of Judaism could not be complete without the demonic. Scholem must have considered his work to constitute the historiographical equivalent of the "anarchic breeze" with which apocalyptic Kabbalah, in his account, aired out the stuffy house of halakhic Judaism. In

Nietzschean terms, his was the "critical history" that came to unsettle and subvert the monumentalist pieties of the nationalist historians.

Yet to portray the demonic in history did not mean to identify with it. Despite Scholem's obvious attraction to the Sabbatians and the Frankists, as well as to all the other subterranean movements in Jewish history, the political function that he saw for his work was as a cautionary tale. The demonic is a vital element in that history, perhaps even *the* element of vitality, but it must be neutralized lest it lead to catastrophe. Note well: neutralized but not eliminated, for the term "neutralization" in Scholem's vocabulary, like "sublimation" in Freud's, means to channel and control the explosive energies of the irrational.

If it is to avoid catastrophe, Zionism must neutralize the demonic in the form of apocalyptic messianism. For Scholem, this meant to capture the subterranean energies that had earlier surfaced in the Kabbalah and Sabbatianism and bring them down to earth in a pragmatic politics. This, then, is the role of Scholem's historiography in the parlous atmosphere of nascent Jewish nationalism: not to construct a useable past for a militant and aggressive nation, but to sound a warning out of history to which a genuine "counternationalism" might be a response. This counternationalism meant the rejection of all apocalyptic politics in favor of what Scholem took to be the true task of Zionism: the regeneration of the Jewish people through the creation of a secular Hebrew culture.

To be sure, a "secular Hebrew culture" sounds like a contradiction in terms because, as Scholem noted in his letter to Rosenzweig, the very return to Hebrew had to awaken religious energies. For Scholem, "secular" in this context means precisely the same as "neutralization": the redirection of the mystical to the pragmatic task of building a new nation. Moreover, a secular Hebrew culture for Scholem was pluralistic, a culture that included all the contradictory possibilities inherent in Judaism, from the rational to the irrational. In this view, Zionism is less a specific ideology in itself than the inclusive framework in which conflicting ideologies might compete: a kind of deliberately antidogmatic nationalism.

Scholem's attitude toward modern nationalism reflects his uneasy relationship to modernity generally. He rejected those elements of modernity, such as the assimilationism of the bourgeois German Jews, that denied or suppressed the vitality of Jewish history. But he equally rejected those modern forces that sought to rehabilitate that vitality in the form of militant nationalism. If the correct approach to modernity meant, for the Jews, the Zionist "return into history," that return was continually threatened by the return of the apocalyptic, the barely repressed demonic of premodern Judaism.

And so we return to the Hasidic story with which we began. That we do not know the place in the forest, how to start the fire, or the prayer now appears in a more positive light. Those religious acts threaten to overwhelm our modernity and are best left in the recesses of history. But if we did not know the story, we would be cut off from that history and all its hidden vitality. To tell the story—the quintessential act of the historian—strikes the proper balance between that which must remain in the past and that which we need for the present.

It is this balancing act that characterizes Scholem's secular theology. In the letter to Salman Schocken, mentioned earlier, he described the challenge of a secular historian studying the Kabbalah. Using the modernist language we have now come to expect, he speaks of venturing out into an abyss, the "wall of history." This wall appears as a mist that hangs around the "mountain of facts," an obvious allusion to Mount Sinai. These facts, like Kant's "thing-in-itself," are impossible to grasp and thus "history may seem to be fundamentally an illusion, but an illusion without which in temporal reality no insight into the essence of things is possible. . . . Today, as at the very beginning, my work lives in this paradox, in the hope of a true communication from the mountain."[45] The mountain will never speak, and so the historian is left only with history—with those sources that hang like a fog around the mountain.

The imagery here is at once kabbalistic and modernist, but the dilemma is profoundly modern: the silence of God. Like the seeker after the Law in Kafka's famous parable, the historian remains at the first door, unable to discern divine revelation or even if it exists. The sources of the tradition that he or she studies remain hidden and only their decayed remnants come to hand. But as fragmentary and elusive as these sources may be, modernity would be devoid of all meaning if we were to abandon their historical study, the secular enterprise that is the dialectical stepchild of tradition.

Notes

1. Gershom Scholem, *Major Trends in Jewish Mysticism* (New York, 1941), 349–50.
2. Israel of Ruzhin, *Knesset Israel* (Warsaw, 1906), 23. On Israel of Ruzhin see David Assaf, *The Royal Way: The Life and Times of Rabbi Israel of Ruzhin*, trans. David Louvish (Stanford, 2002).
3. Joshua Landy and Michael Saler, eds., *The Reenchantment of the World: Secular Magic in a Rational Age* (Stanford, 2009). See also Michael Saler, "Modernity and Enchantment: An Historiographical Review," *American Historical Review* 111, no. 3 (2006): 692–716.
4. Robert Alter, "Scholem and Modernism," *Poetics Today* 15, no. 3 (Autumn 1994): 429–42.
5. Gershom Scholem, *The Messianic Idea in Judaism* (New York, 1971), 21.
6. Gershom Scholem, "Reflections on Modern Jewish Studies (1944)," in Scholem, *On the Possibility of Jewish Mysticism in Our Time*, ed. Avraham Shapira and trans. Jonathan Chipman (Philadelphia, 1997), 51–71.
7. Scholem, *On the Possibility of Jewish Mysticism*, 6–19.
8. See "Revelation and Tradition as Religious Categories in Judaism," in *Messianic Idea in Judaism*, 282–303.
9. See in particular Scholem, *Major Trends in Jewish Mysticism*, lecture 8.
10. On Goldberg, see Manfred Voigts, "Einführung," in Oskar Goldberg, *Die Wirklichkeit der Hebräer*; and Voigts, *Oskar Goldberg: der mythische Experimentalwissenschaftler* (Berlin, 1992). See also Gershom Scholem, "Oscar Goldberg," in *Encyclopedia Judaica*. 16. vols. (Jerusalem, 1971), 7:705.
11. See Gershom Scholem, *Walter Benjamin: The History of a Friendship*, trans. Harry Zohn (Philadelphia, 1981), 98.
12. See his letter to Ernst Simon, December 22, 1925, in Gershom Scholem, *A Life in Letters, 1914–1982*, ed. and trans. Anthony David Skinner (Cambridge, 2002), 148. He also claims to have written an equally vituperative letter to Walter Benjamin and Leo Strauss on Goldberg.
13. Scholem, *Walter Benjamin*, 95–98; Gershom Scholem, "Die Theologie des Sabbatianismus im Lichte Abraham Cardoses," in *Judaica*. 3 vols. (Frankfurt, 1968), 1:146; and Gershom Scholem, "Ein verschollener jüdischer Mystiker der Aufklärungszeit," *Leo Baeck Institute Yearbook* 7 (1952): 261.
14. Peter Berger, *The Sacred Canopy: Elements of a Sociological Theory of Religion* (Garden City, 1967).
15. See, among other recent works, Peter Berger's own self-revision in his edited volume, *The Desecularization of the World: Resurgent Religion and World Politics* (New York, 1999). And, more recently, David Martin, *On Secularization: Towards a Revised General Theory* (Burlington,

2005); Talal Asad, *Formations of the Secular: Christianity, Islam, Modernity* (Stanford, 2003); David Scott and Charles Hirschkind, eds., *Powers of the Secular Modern: Talal Asad and His Interlocutors* (Stanford, 2006); Vincent P. Pecora, *Secularization and Cultural Criticism: Religion, Nation and Modernity* (Chicago, 2006); Charles Taylor, *A Secular Age* (Cambridge, 2007); and Mark Lilla, *The Stillborn God: Religion, Politics and the Modern West* (New York, 2007).

16. See Michael Brenner, "From Self-Declared Messiah to Scholar of Messianism: The Recently Published Diaries Present Young Gershom Scholem in a New Light," *Jewish Social Studies* 3, no. 1 (Autumn 1996): 177–82; and Benjamin Lazier, *God Interrupted: Heresy and European Imagination between the Wars* (Princeton, 2008), part 3.

17. Scholem, *On the Possibility of Jewish Mysticism*, 16.

18. On Scholem and Kafka, see Robert Alter, *Necessary Angels: Tradition and Modernity in Kafka, Benjamin, and Scholem* (Cambridge, 1991); and Moshe Idel, *Old Worlds, New Mirrors: On Jewish Mysticism and Twentieth-Century Thought* (Philadelphia, 2010), 118–20.

19. See Gershom Scholem, "My Way to Kabbalah," in Scholem, *On the Possibility of Jewish Mysticism*, 23.

20. "A Candid Letter about My True Intentions on Studying Kabbalah," in Scholem, *On the Possibility of Jewish Mysticism*, 3–4. I was the first to publish this letter in David Biale, *Gershom Scholem: Kabbalah and Counter-History* (Cambridge, 1979), 215–16; my English translation, 74–76.

21. On antinomianism as a theme in Weimar Jewish thought, see Lazier, *God Interrupted*.

22. Gershom Scholem, "Redemption through Sin," in Scholem, *Messianic Idea in Judaism*, 141.

23. A far-reaching attempt to ground modern secularism in the very origins of monotheism is Marcel Gauchet's *Le désenchantement du monde: Une histoire politique de la religion* (Paris, 1985) [French]; English version, Gauchet, *The Disenchantment of the World: A Political History of Religion*, trans. Oscar Burge (Princeton, 1997). For an application to Jewish sources of these kind of dialectical arguments about the roots of secularism in the religious tradition, see my *Not in the Heavens: The Tradition of Jewish Secular Thought* (Princeton, 2010).

24. Amos Funkenstein, *Theology and the Scientific Imagination* (Princeton, 1986). Hans Blumenberg formulated this relationship somewhat differently by arguing not so much for a dialectical progression as for modern ideas occupying the places vacated by medieval theology. See his *The Legitimacy of the Modern Age*, trans. Robert M. Wallace (Cambridge, 1983). A similar, recent argument to Funkenstein's is Michael Allen Gillespie's *The Theological Origins of Modernity* (Chicago, 2008).

25. See in particular, Gershom Scholem, "The Neutralization of the Messianic Element in Early Hasidism," in Scholem, *Messianic Idea in Judaism*, 176–202.

26. Gershom Scholem, "The Messianic Idea in Judaism," in Scholem, *Messianic Idea in Judaism*, 25–26.

27. Gershom Scholem, "Thoughts about Our Language," in Scholem, *On the Possibility of Jewish Mysticism*, 27–28. For a recent analysis of this letter, see Galili Shahar, "The Sacred and the Unfamiliar: Gershom Scholem and the Anxieties of the New Hebrew," *Germanic Review* 83 (2008): 299–320.

28. Gershom Scholem, *From Berlin to Jerusalem*, trans. Harry Zohn (New York, 1980). See further my *Gershom Scholem: Kabbalah and Counter-History*, 60–65.

29. On Landauer, see Eugene Lunn, *Prophet of Community: The Romantic Socialism of Gustav Landauer* (Berkeley, 1973).

30. Letter to Walter Benjamin of August 1, 1931; translated into English in Scholem, *Walter Benjamin*, 169–74.

31. Alluding to Jerubbaal (Judge 6:32; Samuel 12:11). See my *Gershom Scholem: Kabbalah and Counter-History*, 64n45. On Scholem's views of German and Jewish nationalism, see my "Gershom Scholem between Jewish and German Nationalism," in *The German-Jewish Dialogue Reconsidered*, ed. Klaus Berghahn (New York, 1996), 177–88.

32. For an analysis of Scholem as a follower of Nietzsche (despite his claims in *From Berlin to Jerusalem*), see Steven E. Aschheim, *Scholem, Arendt, Klemperer: Intimate Chronicles in Turbulent Times* (Bloomington, 2001), 16; and Lazier, *God Interrupted*, part 3.

33. See Dimitri Shumsky, *Ben Prag le-Yerushalayim: Tsionut Prag ve-ha-ra'ayon ha-medinah ha-du-leumit be-Erets Yisrael* (Jerusalem, 2009). The following section of this essay is drawn largely from my *Gershom Scholem*, chap. 8

34. See David Biale, "The Threat of Messianism: An Interview with Gershom Scholem," *New York Review of Books*, August 14, 1980, 22.

35. Gershom Scholem, "The Final Goal," *She'ifoteinu* 2 (August 1931): 156 [Hebrew].

36. In Gershom Scholem, *Od Davar*, ed. Avraham Shapira (Tel Aviv, 1989), 65.

37. Gershom Scholem, "The Politics of Mysticism: Isaac Breuer's *Neue Kuzari*," in Scholem, *Messianic Idea*, 334.

38. "Three Sins of Brit Shalom," in *Davar*, December 12, 1929, 2 [Hebrew].

39. Scholem, *Judaica*, 1:146.

40. Scholem, *Od Davar*, 92. The same idea that Zionism had failed as a result of its own success can be found in his letter to Walter Benjamin of August 1, 1931.

41. Scholem, "Threat of Messianism."

42. Eric Hobsbawm, *Nations and Nationalism since 1780: Programme, Myth, Reality* (Cambridge, 1990), 67–73.

43. Baruch Kurzweil, *Ba-ma'avak al Arkai ha-Yahadut* (Tel Aviv, 1969), 99–243; and Eliezer Schweid, *Judaism and Mysticism according to Gershom Scholem*, trans. David Avraham Weiner (Atlanta, 1985).

44. Gershom Scholem, "Reflections on the Science of Judaism," in *Devarim be-Go*, 2nd ed. (Tel Aviv, 1976), 402 [Hebrew].

45. Scholem, "A Candid Letter," 4.

24

Leo Strauss (1899–1973)

PROTESTANT JUDAISM AND ITS ISLAMIC REMEDY

Leora F. Batnitzky

IT ALMOST GOES WITHOUT SAYING THAT RELIGION'S PRIVATE OR PUBLIC STATUS IS a central concern today, not only for faith traditions but also for national and international politics. We need but note the continuing controversy over the implications of France's infamous headscarf affair,current American public policy debates about abortion and gay marriage, arguments about the Muslim Brotherhood's role in an emergent Egyptian democracy, or ever-present disputes about the meaning of Jewishness in the state of Israel to recognize that the relation between religion and the modern nation-state is far from resolved. But the question of religion's place in state politics is older than it may seem from these contemporary debates. As Leo Strauss argued, the very notion that religion belongs to the private sphere is a modern idea, which only developed in tandem with the rise of the modern nation-state. If this is the case, then today's questions about religion's private or public status are but continued reverberations on one of the most definitive problems of modernity: "Liberalism stands or falls by the distinction between state and society or by the recognition of the private sphere protected by the law but impervious to the law, with the understanding that, above all, religion as particular religion belongs to the private sphere."[1]

For Strauss, thinking about Jewish modernity disturbs the modern definition of religion as private faith. This is because thinking about Jewish modernity requires consideration of whether and how Judaism—which has historically been largely a religion of practice and public adherence to law—can fit into a modern, Protestant conception of religion as a private matter of individual belief, what Max Weber described as the "inward emotional piety of Lutheranism";[2] or what Hermann Cohen, to whom we will turn below, called "the inwardness of personal faith."[3] Through his work on premodern Jewish rationalism, and the thought of Maimonides in particular, Strauss sought to expose the historical, philosophical, theological, and political shifts that required Jews to define Judaism within the Protestant rubric of religion. But the tension between religion as a private sphere protected by the law yet impervious to the law was not for Strauss of mere academic or narrowly Jewish interest. Rather, he linked this tension to an analysis of the rise of modern tyrannies and the unprecedented evils that they are able to perpetuate. According to Strauss the private

sphere, "protected by the law but impervious to the law," fosters prejudice, including the murderous prejudices of modernity such as antisemitism. The legacy of Protestant Judaism, then, is essential for understanding the modern political constraints that allow for freedom of religion as well as the pernicious aftereffects.

Beyond its analytic import, Strauss's diagnosis of the legacy of Protestant Judaism is remarkable for two reasons. First, Strauss anticipates a number of contemporary criticisms of simplistic and ahistorical conceptions of secularism and religion.[4] Second, while Strauss's name is often evoked (for better or for worse) in contemporary discussions of American neoconservatism, Strauss was actually devoted to revitalizing Islamic philosophy, as opposed to Christian thought, for the very sake of the future of Western civilization. As we will see below, Strauss maintains that Islamic philosophy offers a remedy for the legacy of Protestant Judaism. To explore these issues, the first section of this essay focuses on Strauss's claims about the modern category of religion. The second section turns to Strauss's claims about secularism, and the third considers the centrality of Islamic philosophy to Strauss's project of rethinking Jewish modernity and its Protestant inheritance. Finally, the conclusion briefly discusses Strauss's views on Judaism, Islam, and Christianity in the context of contemporary academic discussion of the categories of religion and politics.

Questioning the Category of "Religion"

To begin to consider Strauss's view of the legacy of Protestant Judaism, we must first recognize that Strauss was not the first German Jewish thinker to identify modern Judaism with Protestantism. Hermann Cohen especially stressed Judaism's affinity with Protestantism, arguing that "with reference to the scientific concept of religion I am unable to discover any distinction between Jewish monotheism and Protestant Christianity."[5] He was particularly attracted to this conception of Protestantism because he regarded it as a religion *of the individual*: "This is the real sense of the new faith: an emphasis on the personal, and therefore immediate sense of subjective responsibility of the religious conscience. This conscience does not take refuge in the protection and power of the Church."[6]

While he saw his own project as departing significantly from Cohen's, Franz Rosenzweig also affirmed an identity between Judaism, especially modern Judaism, and Protestantism: "All modern Jews, and German Jews more than others, are Protestants."[7] Rosenzweig's trouble with Cohen did not stem from questioning the equation of Judaism with Protestantism but rather from the epistemological premises of that equation. Like his liberal Protestant contemporaries, such as Ernst Troetsch, Cohen posited a confluence between revelation and modern philosophy (and neo-Kantianism in particular). And especially like his neo-orthodox Protestant contemporary Karl Barth, Rosenzweig rejected the possibility of any such convergence, which he suggested, in his 1914 essay "Atheistic Theology," amounted to a denial of the "hard mark of the divine that actually entered into history and is distinct from all other actuality."[8]

Strauss's rejection of Protestant Judaism begins where Rosenzweig's thought ends. The importance of Rosenzweig's philosophy for Strauss is the recognition of the necessity of thinking about God as wholly transcendent. Strauss dedicated his book *Spinoza's Critique of Religion* (1930) to Rosenzweig's memory. As he would articulate more clearly in his 1965 preface to the English translation of *Spinoza's Critique of Religion*, Rosenzweig's attempt to take revelation seriously marked the *possibility* of showing that Spinoza's seemingly devastating critique of religion failed. We will turn to the details of Strauss's conception of Jewish revelation further below, but for now we need but note that with Rosenzweig, and against Spinoza, he insisted on recognizing the revelatory basis of Judaism, even if one could not believe in God's revelation. As he put it in a lecture late in his life, "I believe, by simply replacing God by the creative genius of the Jewish people, one gives away, one deprives oneself—even if one does not believe—of a source of human understanding. . . . Now I do not wish to minimize folk dances, Hebrew speaking, and many other things—I do not want to minimize them. But I believe that they cannot possibly take the place of what is most profound in our tradition."[9] What is most profound, for Strauss, in the Jewish tradition is a belief in a transcendent God who has revealed, and continues to reveal, himself to the Jewish people by way of the Torah.

By taking God's revelation and transcendence seriously, Rosenzweig's and Barth's theologies exposed the lie at the heart of the modern criticism of religion: "The reawakening of theology, which for me is epitomized by the names of Karl Barth and Franz Rosenzweig, seemed to make it necessary for one to study the extent to which the critique of orthodox—Jewish and Christian—theology deserved to be victorious."[10] For Strauss, Barth and Rosenzweig rightfully rejected the modern idea that scientific knowledge is the only form of and standard for truth. Yet while he credited Rosenzweig and Barth for making him rethink the modern critique of religion, Strauss argued that their approach to theology was still embedded within the prejudices of modern philosophy, and subject to the same fate as modern philosophy, despite their attempts to overcome precisely these prejudices. At bottom, the early-twentieth-century reawakening of theology did not revive reason's critical potential but left reason behind. As such, argued Strauss, this reawakening of theology did not ultimately provide any resources for theological, philosophical, or political rationalism.[11]

With his second book, *Philosophy and Law* (1935), Strauss maintained that a return to rationalism required reconsidering medieval thinkers and their approaches to philosophy and revelation. Julius Guttmann had considered this subject in depth. Strauss began his own work on medieval rationalism by attacking Guttmann, despite the fact that Guttmann at the time happened to be his supervisor at the Academy for the Science of Judaism (Akademie für die Wissenschaft des Judentums) where Strauss was working as an editor of Moses Mendelssohn's papers,. According to Strauss, Guttmann had argued that " 'philosophy of religion' is actually the original achievement of medieval philosophy."[12] Against this view, Strauss points out that within the historical context of medieval Jewish rationalism, the law existentially preceded the possibility of philosophizing. This fact is not merely historically important but also philosophically significant, as Strauss suggests in the first sentence of the first chapter *of Philosophy and Law*: "There is no inquiry into the history of philosophy that is not at the same time a *philosophical* inquiry."[13]

Guttmann, in keeping with his own neo-Kantian model, understood medieval Jewish rationalism primarily in modern epistemological terms, that is, in terms of "science," in this case what was known as the historical science of Judaism (*Wissenschaft des Judentums*).[14] Strauss contended that it is only because Guttmann began with a modern conception of philosophy that he could understand medieval Jewish rationalism in terms of "philosophy of religion." In a footnote, Strauss concisely summed up his argument against Guttmann: "We do not deny . . . that the problem of 'belief and knowledge' is the central problem of medieval rationalism. Our quarrel with Guttmann is only about the meaning of 'belief' here, and it seems to us more precise to say 'law and philosophy' rather than 'belief and knowledge.'"[15] The phrase "law and philosophy" represents the complex but necessary relation between prescientific and scientific knowledge. "Belief and knowledge," on the other hand, represents the attempt to fuse two sources of truth into a scientifically respectable whole that Guttmann called "philosophy of religion."

According to Strauss, once revelation is understood primarily as revealed law, and not as philosophical knowledge, it is necessary to rethink, from a modern perspective, the medieval Jewish and Islamic conceptions of both philosophy and revelation. While Strauss's focus in *Philosophy and Law* was on the status of Jewish, or religious, law, he looked back from medieval Jewish and Islamic philosophy to Plato. Focusing on the significance of Plato's *Laws* and its Islamic reception, Strauss suggested that the classical conception of law concerns and anticipated the tense yet necessary relation between philosophy and law in medieval rationalism:

> The necessary connection between politics and theology (metaphysics) . . . vouches for the fact that the interpretation of medieval Jewish philosophy beginning from Platonic politics (and not from the *Timaeus* or from Aristotelian metaphysics) does not have to lose sight of the metaphysical problems that stand in the foreground for the medieval philosophers themselves. And this procedure, so far from resulting in the underestimation of these problems, actually offers the only guarantee of understanding their proper, that is their human, meaning. If, on the other hand, one begins with the metaphysical problems, one misses . . . the political problem, in which is concealed nothing less than the foundation of philosophy, the philosophic elucidation of the presupposition of philosophizing.[16]

Although philosophy can clarify the meaning of the law, philosophical activity cannot produce the law. Instead, the law is the prephilosophical context of and framework for philosophy. As Strauss put it, "*freedom depends upon its bondage*. Philosophy is not sovereign. The beginning of philosophy is not the beginning simply."[17]

It is important to note that Strauss's theoretical account of the nexus between politics and theology in premodern Judaism is historically accurate. In the premodern era, a Jewish individual was defined legally, politically, and theologically as a member of the Jewish community. While premodern Jewish communities were answerable to and existed only by permission of external authorities, premodern Jews governed themselves; and individual Jews were subject to the Jewish laws of their local communities, which often varied greatly from one another. Jewish communities from the rabbinic period forward were not fully sovereign but neither were their external political authorities. This meant that Jewish communal leaders all had to negotiate their relation to external authorities not just from the perspective of the Jewish community's relation to an outside power but also from an internal point of view, meaning from within the Jewish community. While the extent of the rabbis' political power in the rabbinic period remains historically ambiguous, what cannot be doubted is that the rabbis claimed political authority for themselves.[18] So too, it cannot be doubted that Jewish leaders increasingly exercised a significant amount of political power over the members of their communities.

Salo Baron's 1928 description of the political structure of medieval Jewish communities remains the most concise summary of pre-modern Judaism's political status:

> Complex, isolated, in a sense of foreign, it [the Jewish community] was left more severely alone by the State than most other corporations. Thus the Jewish community of pre-Revolutionary days had more competence over its members than the modern Federal, State, and Municipal governments combined. Education, administration of justice between Jew and Jew, taxation for communal and State purposes, health, markets, public order, were all within the jurisdiction of the community-corporation. . . . Statute was reinforced by religious, supernatural sanctions as well as by coercive public opinions within the group. For example, a Jew put in *Cherem* [excommunication] by a Jewish court was practically a lost man, and the *Cherem* was a fairly common means of imposing the will of the community on the individual. All this self-governing apparatus disappeared, of course, when the Revolution brought "equal rights" to European Jewry.[19]

The political functions of the premodern Jewish community, which included, as Baron shows, the administration of justice between Jew and Jew and the enforcement of sanctions on its members, were the province of Jewish law and were often practically executed by and always theoretically justified by rabbinic authorities.

Let us return to Strauss's comment, quoted at the beginning of this essay, that "[l]iberalism stands or falls by the distinction between state and society, or by the recognition of the private sphere protected by the law but impervious to the law, with the understanding that, above all, religion as particular religion belongs to the private sphere." As mentioned above, while working on *Philosophy and Law*, Strauss was editing Moses Mendelssohn's papers. It was Mendelssohn who had created the very category of Jewish religion by separating Judaism from politics and the individual Jew from the corporate Jewish community. As he put it, the purpose of the Jewish community "is collective edification, participation in the effusion of the heart, through which we acknowledge our gratitude for God's benefactions."[20] As a political corollary to this philosophical point, Mendelssohn vehemently opposed the idea that the Jewish community should retain its autonomy in matters of civil law, stressing that Jews should receive civil rights as individuals and not as a corporate entity. Mendelssohn especially rejected the Jewish community's claim, still maintained in his day, to the right to excommunicate. As he put it, Judaism "as religion, knows of no punishment, no other penalty than the one the remorseful sinner voluntarily imposes on himself. It knows of no coercion, uses only the staff [called] gentleness, and affects only mind and heart."[21]

Along with detaching Jewish religion from politics, Mendelssohn also separated Jewish revelation from the eternal truths of reason: "Judaism boasts no exclusive revelation of eternal truths. . . . The voice which let itself be heard on Sinai on that great day did not proclaim, 'I am the Eternal, your God, the necessary, independent being, omnipotent and omniscient, that recompenses men in a future life according to their deeds.' This is the universal religion of mankind, not Judaism."[22] In contrast to the universal religion of humankind, which he equates with morality, Judaism, Mendelssohn argues, is a historical, temporal truth that makes demands only on Jewish people and not on society and morality at large. By the beginning of the nineteenth century, the liberal society that Mendelssohn envisioned had in large part come to pass. The political agency of the Jewish community was dissolved and Judaism became a religion. So too, philosophers and theologians alike agreed that biblical revelation could not be understood in scientific or philosophically defensible terms but must be relegated to individual faith.

Scholars continue to debate whether Mendelssohn was a covert deist who rejected the possible veracity of divine revelation, whether he was a sincere believer whose rational defense of Judaism makes sense within his historical context, or whether his arguments are in fact philosophically defensible.[23] These debates are of course beyond the scope of this essay. What is important for our purposes, however, is that Strauss vehemently questioned the types of theological and political claims that Mendelssohn, and many after him, made about Judaism and modern society. Once again, Strauss, against Spinoza and with Rosenzweig, insisted on recognizing the revelatory basis of Judaism. But to do so meant that revelation had to be conceived in political, not merely epistemological, terms. In this way, Strauss tried to understand Jewish law as premodern Jews may have understood it.

Here we can appreciate that Strauss's thought, already in 1935, anticipates a number of themes that Talal Asad, among others, has developed only recently. Simply stated, at the core of Strauss's mature thought is a criticism of a modern notion of religion that focuses on the epistemology of belief. Long before Asad noted that the equation of religion with belief "is a product of the only space allowed to Christianity by post-Enlightenment society, the right to individual belief," Strauss suggested precisely this. So too, long before Asad noted that "the suggestion that religion has a universal function is one indication of how marginal religion has become in modern industrial society as a site for producing disciplined knowledge and personal discipline," Strauss had pointed out that the modern focus on the metaphysical problem of belief at one and the same time eclipses what had been religion's political work of, to use Asad's terms, "producing disciplined knowledge and personal discipline."[24]

Asad's concise statement of his goal in *Genealogies of Religion* is helpful for further appreciating the broad shape of Strauss's project: "to problematize the idea of an anthropological definition of religion by assigning that endeavor to a particular history of knowledge and power (including a particular understanding of our legitimate past and future) out of which the modern world has been constructed."[25] Strauss's interest was not in anthropology but in what he called the "sociology of philosophy." Nevertheless, Strauss aimed to describe the particular history of knowledge and power that led to the profound moral and political crises of the twentieth century. Strauss called this problem the "theological-political predicament of modernity," by which he meant to diagnose what he contended were the devastating philosophical, theological, and political consequences of the early modern attempt to separate theology from politics. However, Strauss in no way favored a return to theocracy or, like his contemporary Carl Schmitt, a turn toward political theology. Instead, Strauss attempted to recover classical political philosophy not to return to the political structures of the past but to reconsider ways in which premodern thinkers thought it necessary to grapple and live with the tensions, if not contradictions, that, by definition, arise from human society. For Strauss a recognition, not a resolution, of the tensions and contradictions that define human society is the necessary starting point for philosophically reconstructing a philosophy, theology, and politics of moderation, all of which, he claims, the twentieth century desperately needed.

Strauss argues that the key to medieval rationalism is a respect for the dialectical tension between theory and practice, which he also understands as the tension between philosophy and law. As he put it to Eric Voegelin in a letter of 1950: "the root of all modern darkness from the seventeenth century on is the obscuring of the difference between theory and praxis, an obscuring that first leads to a reduction of praxis to theory (this is the meaning of so-called rationalism) and then, in retaliation, to the rejection of theory in the name of praxis that is no longer intelligible as praxis."[26] While the details of and controversies surrounding his interpretation of Maimonides are beyond the scope of this essay, Strauss's central claim about Maimonides bears directly upon his statement to Voegelin. According to Strauss, Maimonides was able to properly balance the relation between praxis, obedience to the law, and theory—what Strauss calls the mystery of the law's origins,—not by conflating them but by keeping them in continual dialectical tension. For Strauss, Maimonides' refusal to resolve the tension between law and philosophy (between praxis and theory) expresses Maimonides' moderate claims both for what philosophy can produce on its own (it cannot produce the law) and for what revelation can claim to know absolutely (it cannot provide certain knowledge of the mystery of its origin).

Strauss's attention to esotericism is rooted in a philosophical interest in "a golden mean which is neither a compromise nor a synthesis, which is hence not based on the two opposed positions, but which suppresses them both, uproots them by a prior, more profound question, by raising a fundamental problem, the work of a truly critical philosophy."[27] The "absolute problem" at the heart of esotericism for Strauss concerns the self-sufficiency of reason or, put another way, the inescapable and necessary tension between theory and practice. The theological-political predicament of modernity stems from the modern commitment to the self-sufficiency of reason that, Strauss argues, results in reason's self-destruction. Esotericism is a means toward preserving the limits of philosophy and revelation (or law) vis-à-vis one another. The law comes up against its own limitations in the quest to articulate the philosophical foundations of the law. But at the same time, philosophy comes up against its own limits in recognizing that the philosopher is always already within society (or the law) and for this reason dependent upon the law.

Questioning Secularism

We can now turn to the implications of Strauss's thought for thinking about secularism. At first glance this might seem an odd claim since Strauss rarely uses the term "secularism," and when he does he is often critical of it as a term.[28] Yet rather than detracting from appreciation of Strauss as a thinker about secularism, Strauss's ambivalence about the term "secular" provides an important clue to what he contributes to contemporary conversations about secularism. The term "secular" for Strauss implies an extinguishing of the possibility of religion because its use is premised on the notion that the truth claims of religion no longer have validity beyond the purview of individual belief. For this reason, "secularism" properly understood reflects not a response to preexisting religion, as many proponents of the secularization thesis would have it, but rather the very invention of the modern idea of religion as belief divorced from politics. Strauss makes this point in connection with his critique of Weber's arguments in *The Protestant Ethic and the Spirit of Capitalism*. In Strauss's words: "Weber took it for granted that the cause must be sought in the transformation of the theological tradition, i.e., in the Reformation. The utmost one could say was that he traced the capitalist spirit to the corruption of Calvinism . . . Weber overestimated the importance of the revolution that had taken place on the plane of theology, and he underestimated the importance of the revolution that had taken place on the plane of rational thought."[29]

Once again, according to Strauss, it is the modern denial of the dialectical tension between theory and praxis that marks "the revolution that had taken place on the plane of rational thought." Whereas in the seventeenth century Hobbes, like Spinoza would after him, depreciates prescientific knowledge in the name of science, Heidegger, in the twentieth century, depreciates scientific knowledge in the name of historicity. Modern rationalism thus implodes upon itself: what starts as a modern quest for delineating scientific standards in the name of certain knowledge leads to the conclusion that there are neither such standards nor such truths. For our purposes, we need not focus on the particularities of Strauss's reading of Hobbes (or on his subsequent reading of Machiavelli and others) but only on the trajectory that his intellectual history of political philosophy takes as he diagnoses the theologico-political predicament.

The structure of Strauss's account of the history of modern political philosophy parallels the structure of his account of the history of philosophy. Just as modern philosophy begins with an overinflated sense of reason that privileges theory over practice and ends with a radical historicism that denies any meaning to reason outside of history, so too, Strauss suggests, modern political philosophy begins with the attempt to make the human being wholly part of nature as defined by science and ends by denying any notion of nature altogether.[30] For Strauss, these trajectories come together in the coincidence of Heidegger's philosophy and his political misadventures:

> The crucial issue concerns the status of those permanent characteristics of humanity, such as the distinction between the noble and the base. . . . It was the contempt for these permanencies which permitted the most radical historicist in 1933 to submit to, or rather to welcome, as a dispensation of fate, the verdict of the least wise and least modern part of his nation when it was in its least wise and least moderate mood, and at the same time to speak of wisdom and moderation. The biggest event of 1933 would rather seem to have proved, if such proof was necessary, that man cannot abandon the question of the good society, and that he cannot free himself from the responsibility for answering it by deferring to History or to any other power different from his own reason.[31]

At its most extreme, the theologico-political predicament is illustrated by the complicity of intellectuals in the Nazi genocide.

> Liberal democracy had originally defined itself in theologico-political treatises as the opposite of . . . "the kingdom of darkness," i.e., of medieval society. . . . [The German Jews] were given full political rights for the first time by the Weimar Republic. The Weimar Republic was succeeded by the only German regime—by the only regime that ever was anywhere—which had no other clear principle except murderous hatred of the Jews.[32]

Strauss does not mean to imply that National Socialism was inevitable.[33] Rather he means to investigate why there was no adequate rational, moral response to the rise of National Socialism. It is here that the modern crises of philosophy, theology, and politics meet. Neither modern political philosophy nor theology had the critical resources to respond to the disintegration of the liberal state, the very political structure that was touted as "the opposite of . . . 'the kingdom of darkness,' i.e., of medieval society."

Let us return to Asad's goal, which is "to problematize the idea of an anthropological definition of religion by assigning that endeavor to a particular history of knowledge and power (including a particular understanding of our legitimate past and future) out of which the modern world has been constructed." As we have seen, within the context of his own project, Strauss has a similar aim. Strauss seeks to show that the modern idea of religion as private belief is not only predicated on the depoliticization of religion but also, and perhaps more profoundly, on the philosophical discrediting of prescientific knowledge (what Socrates called "opinion") as the moral and political underpinnings of society. The prevailing modern Western idea that first came "religion" and then came "secularism" is thus fundamentally mistaken according to Strauss. In Asad's more contemporary terms, "if the secularization thesis seems increasingly implausible to some of us this is not simply because religion is now playing a vibrant part of the modern world of nations. In an important sense, what many would anachronistically call 'religion' was always involved in the world of power. If the secularization thesis no longer carries the weight it once did, this is because the categories of 'politics' and 'religion' turn out to implicate one another more profoundly than we thought, a discovery that has accompanied our growing understanding of the powers of the modern nation-state. The concept of the secular cannot do without the idea of religion."[34]

The Islamic Remedy for Protestant Judaism

As we have seen, Strauss anticipates a number of more recent criticisms of simplistic and ahistorical concepts of the "secular" and hence of the "religious." Strauss and Asad agree that the modern idea of religion as a private sphere, separate from politics, cannot be separated from the rise of the modern nation-state, and that the formations of modern religion and modern liberalism are the distinct legacy of post-Reformation Christianity. Perhaps most surprisingly, however, they agree that the key to appreciating these two points is the different historical and political legacies of Islam and Christianity. Let us briefly turn to the centrality of Islam for Strauss's claims about both religion and secularism and then back to Asad's claims.

Criticizing a modern notion of religion that focuses on the epistemology of belief, Strauss strongly opposed what he saw as a particularly Christian view of revelation and religion in order to suggest that modernity's intellectual ills stem in large part from the legacy of Christian theology. Strikingly, it was on the basis of the Islamic, as opposed to the Christian, reception of classical political philosophy that Strauss turned to reconsider the meanings of philosophy, revelation, and politics. Strauss's very attempts to move beyond modern philosophy and the modern concept of religion as private belief are predicated on a distinction between the Jewish and Islamic conceptions of revelation, on the one hand, and the Christian conception, on the other. As he put it in his seminal essay on "Persecution and the Art of Writing": "For the Christian, the sacred doctrine is revealed theology; for the Jew and the Muslim, the sacred doctrine is, at least primarily, the legal interpretation of the Divine Law (*talmud* or *fiqh*) . . . The precarious position of philosophy in the Islamic-Jewish world guaranteed its private character and therewith its inner-freedom from supervision. The status of philosophy in the Islamic-Jewish world resembled in this respect its status in classical Greece."[35] Strauss problematizes the Christian view of revelation as doctrinal knowledge that must be believed.

From his early to his mature writings, Strauss contends that the making of revelation into knowledge in scholastic theology ultimately led to modern philosophy's far too overreaching claims, with dire consequences for the possibility of modern rationalism. Strauss goes much further than Asad in distinguishing between Christianity and Islam as such. While Asad maintains that the "separation of religion from power is a modern Western norm," he also notes that such separation diverged from the position of the historical Church: "The medieval Church was always clear about why there was continuous need to distinguish knowledge from falsehood (religion from what sought to subvert it), as well as the sacred from the profane (religion from what was outside it), distinctions for which the authoritative discourses, the teachings and practices of the Church, not the convictions of the practitioner, were the final test. Several times before the Reformation, the boundary between the religious and the secular was redrawn, but always the formal authority of the Church remained preeminent."[36]

Although he sought to call into question the claims of Protestant modernity, Strauss seemed able to view Christianity only in Protestant terms. Indeed, his references to Christian theologians are almost exclusively to Luther, Kierkegaard, and Barth. And when Strauss does write about Thomas Aquinas, for instance, he not only criticizes him but also links him to the ultimate rise of "secularism." In *Natural Right and History*, Strauss ties Aquinas's thought to the demise of the authority of law in the modern world: "According to Thomas . . . natural reason creates a presupposition in favor of the divine law, which completes or perfects the natural law . . . the ultimate consequence . . . is that natural law is practically inseparable from natural theology. . . . Modern law was partly a reaction to this absorption of natural law by theology."[37] Elsewhere Strauss explicitly connects scholasticism to what he regards as the failure of modern philosophy: "I do not deny, but assert, that modern philosophy has much that is essential in common with Christian medieval philosophy."[38] As one interpreter sums it up, Strauss "quietly agreed with Machiavelli's criticism of Christian scholasticism for having openly promulgated a teaching . . . that led men to aspire to transcend their need for *law*."[39]

Strauss's criticism of Christian theology, and especially Aquinas and scholasticism, is perhaps surprising given the enthusiastic reception of Strauss by many Catholic thinkers in his own day as well as today.[40] Indeed, Strauss's Catholic reception, especially in the United States, often goes hand in hand with the embrace of Strauss by American neoconservatives. Ironically, far from defending Christian civilization and natural law, Strauss recommends returning to the wisdom of Islamic philosophy as an antidote to the legacy of Christianity and its child, Protestant Judaism.

But what kind of remedy does Islamic philosophy offer Protestant Judaism? Here again we come up against a particular interpretative irony with regard to Strauss. Despite the contradictory appropriations of Strauss as a problem solver of various sorts (conservative or otherwise), Strauss's enduring intellectual legacy may be better understood as one of posing questions about the vexing theologico-political puzzles of modern life, rather than one of providing solutions.[41] As Strauss succinctly put it, "the problems are always more evident than the solutions."[42] From Strauss's perspective, Islamic philosophy is an antidote to Protestant Judaism only insofar as it begins to dismantle our basic assumptions about what "religion" is. Islamic philosophy allows us to better see the problem of Protestant Judaism but it does not offer us any solutions.

Conclusion

So how do Strauss's arguments help us think about modernity and Jewish modernity in particular? If the comparison between Strauss and Asad brings to the fore the limits of Strauss's conception of Christianity, this comparison equally reveals the absence not just of Strauss from contemporary conversations about the constructions of "religion," "politics," and the "secular," but even more so the glaring omission of Judaism from these conversations. Much as he emphasizes the historical constructedness of the category of religion, Asad seems in the end to imply by way of omission that the story of how Judaism became a religion is irrelevant to investigating the category of religion. We need but note the subtitle of his *Genealogies of Religion: Discipline and Reasons of Power in Christianity and Islam*. In keeping with this exclusive focus on Christianity and Islam, some scholars and political commentators have highlighted the tension between a modern concept of religion as private experience and the centrality of law in Islam, which is concerned not with private, internal experience but public, external standards of behavior. Some have even gone so far as to suggest that this difference represents an ultimate clash of civilizations whose ramifications are being played out in the violence of contemporary global politics. Simple distinctions between purported Christian and Islamic civilizations are highly problematic for multiple reasons. Such claims implicitly deny the multifaceted and at times contradictory strands that constitute what we might call "Christianity," "Islam," "the West," and "the East." But purported divisions between Islamic and Christian civilizations, and between "East" and "West," also wholly ignore Judaism and Jews as constitutive and dynamic dimensions of what we might call "Christianity," "Islam," "the West," and "the East."

Strauss provides an important corrective to recent conversations about religion and politics in which Islam and Christianity are pitted against one another. He reminds us that the tension between religion as a private sphere protected by the law, yet impervious to the law, is not one that we have become aware of only at the end of the twentieth century. Rather, as the Jewish experience shows, for better and for worse, the tensions arising from the demand that "religion as particular religion belongs to the private sphere" are intrinsic to Jewish and Protestant modernity themselves.

Notes

1. Leo Strauss, *Spinoza's Critique of Religion* (Chicago, 1965), 6.

2. Max Weber, *The Protestant Ethic and the Spirit of Protestantism*, trans. Talcott Parsons (New York, 2003), 113.

3. Hermann Cohen, *Jüdische Schriften*, ed. Bruno Strauss. 3 vols. (Berlin, 1924), 2:212.

4. See, e.g., Jonathan Z. Smith, "Religion, Religions, Religious," in *Relating Religion: Essays in the Study of Religion* (Chicago, 2004), 179–96; Talal Asad, *Genealogies of Religion: Discipline and Reasons of Power in Christianity and Islam* (Baltimore, 1993); and Charles Taylor, *A Secular Age* (Cambridge, 2007).

5. Hermann Cohen, cited in Uriel Tal, *Christians and Jews in Germany: Religion, Politics, and Ideology in the Second Reich, 1870–1914*, trans. Noah J. Jacobs (Ithaca, 1975), 60.

6. Ibid., 208.

7. Franz Rosenzweig, "Introduction," in Cohen, *Jüdische Schriften*, 1:xxviii.

8. Franz Rosenzweig, *Franz Rosenzweig: Der Mensch und sein Werk: Gesammelte Schriften*. 4 vol. (Boston and The Hague, 1974–1984), 3:690.

9. Leo Strauss, *Jewish Philosophy and the Crisis of Modernity*, ed. Hart Green (Albany, 1997), 34.

10. Leo Strauss, *Leo Strauss Gesammelte Schriften*, vol. 3, *Hobbes' politische Wissenschaft und zugehörige Schriften—Briefe*, ed. Heinrich Meier (Stuttgart, 2001), 7–8.

11. Ibid., 30–31.

12. Leo Strauss, *Philosophy and Law*, trans. Eve Adler (Philadelphia, 1995), 55.

13. Ibid., 41, emphasis added.

14. Julius Guttmann, *Die Philosophie des Judentums* (Munich, 1933).

15. Strauss, *Philosophy and Law*, 141n24.

16. Ibid., 78–79.

17. Ibid., 88, emphasis in the original.

18. On the rabbinic issue, see Catherine Hezser, *The Social Structure of the Rabbinic Movement in Roman Palestine* (Tübingen, 1997).

19. Salo Baron, "Ghetto and Emancipation," *Menorah Journal* 14 (1928): 519.

20. Moses Mendelssohn, *Gesammelte Schriften Jubiläumsausgabe* (Berlin, 1929–84), 8:21.

21. Moses Mendelssohn, *Jerusalem: Or on Religious Power and Judaism*, trans. Allan Arkush (Hanover, NH, 1983), 130.

22. Ibid., 97.

23. For an articulation of each of these positions, see Allan Arkush, *Moses Mendelssohn and the Enlightenment* (Albany, 1994); David Sorkin, *Moses Mendelssohn and the Religious Enlightenment* (Berkeley, 1996); Michah Gottlieb, *Faith and Freedom: Moses Mendelssohn's Theological-Political Thought* (New York, 2010).

24. Asad, *Genealogies of Religion*, 45–46.

25. Ibid., 54.

26. *Faith and Political Philosophy: The Correspondence between Leo Strauss and Eric Voegelin, 1934–1964*, trans. Barry Cooper (Columbia, MO, 2004), 66.

27. Leo Strauss, "Some Remarks on the Political Science of Maimonides and Farabi," trans. Robert Bartlett, *Interpretation* 18, no. 1 (Fall 1990): 4.

28. See, for instance, Strauss's long footnote in his chapter on Weber in Leo Strauss, *Natural Right and History* (Chicago, 1953), 60–61n22; as well as his "The Three Waves of Modernity," in *An Introduction to Political Philosophy* (Detroit, 1989), 81–98.

29. Strauss, *Natural Right and History*, 61.

30. For a concise statement of this point in regard to Hobbes, see Leo Strauss, *What Is Political Philosophy?* (Chicago, 1959). 176n2.

31. Strauss, *Spinoza's Critique of Religion*, 26–27.

32. Ibid., 3.

33. Ibid., 1.

34. Talal Asad, *Formations of the Secular* (Redwood City, CA, 2003), 200.

35. Leo Strauss, *Persecution and the Art of Writing* (Chicago, 1952), 18–19.

36. Asad, *Genealogies of Religion*, 39.

37. Strauss, *Natural Right and History*, 163–64.

38. Karl Löwith and Leo Strauss, "Correspondence Concerning Modernity: Karl Löwith and Leo Strauss," *Independent Journal of Philosophy* 4 (1983): 107–8, 106; emphasis in the original.

39. Clark A. Merrill, "Leo Strauss's Indictment of Christian Philosophy," *Review of Politics* 62, no. 1 (Winter 2000): 98, emphasis added.

40. See, for instance, Douglas Kries, "On Leo Strauss's Understanding of the Natural Law Theory of Thomas Aquinas," *The Thomist* 57, no. 2 (1993): 216; as well as John Finnis, *Natural Law and Natural Rights* (Oxford, 1980), 8.

41. Similarly, despite the often-contradictory ways in which he has been interpreted, Strauss does not offer definitive arguments against historicism, definitive arguments for or against revelation, or definitive arguments for a return to "nature." Rather, in all these cases, one might argue, Strauss has merely begged the question. Strauss historicizes philosophy in order to make an argument for timeless truth. His rational defenses of both the possibility of revelation and philosophical rationalism are made on the basis of a critique of reason's self-sufficiency. Finally, Strauss's claims about a return to "nature" rest not upon arguments for "nature" but rather on arguments about the consequences of not having a conception of "nature."

42. Strauss, *Natural Right and History*, 122.

25

Yeshayahu Leibowitz (1903–1994)

A BELIEVER'S VOYAGE

Avi Sagi

TRANSLATED BY BATYA STEIN

YESHAYAHU LEIBOWITZ OCCUPIES A SPECIAL PLACE AMONG TWENTIETH-CENTURY Jewish thinkers. Widely known in Israel as a one-man opposition, he tirelessly warned against ethical flaws in the state of Israel's political conduct. Beginning in the 1950s, and particularly after the 1967 Six-Day War, Leibowitz claimed that immoral nationalist values were gaining ground in Israel, a process culminating in the transformation of religion into a tool for empowering the state and its institutions. To many he was, in Heidegger's terms, the voice of conscience that awakens us to ourselves and compels renewed thinking. This was indeed a wondrous paradox. Leibowitz was an unusually dogmatic thinker. Even when he did change his views, he never admitted having done so—an issue at the focus of the current discussion— and invariably presented a solid, rigid outlook. He consistently presented his stance as an inevitable truth, be it in the realm of values or in the realm of religion. Leibowitz's discourse with his readers was invariably conducted through what Richard Rorty called an "abnormal discourse": "normal discourse . . . is any discourse (scientific, political, theological, or whatever) which embodies agreed upon criteria for reaching agreement; abnormal discourse is any which lacks such criteria."[1] Leibowitz's theoretical assumptions enabled only abnormal discourse, since he emphasized the voluntaristic, nonrational dimension of value decisions. So what is the point of this discourse? How can we explain the enormous effort he devoted to the clarification of his views? When I asked him about it, he answered: "I say what I have to say, not in order to persuade but because that's what I have to do. . . . The prophets also said what they said because they had to." It is this statement and this determination, rather than open dialogue, that are the core of this discourse. This discourse, then, is either a means through which the individual—in this case Leibowitz—clarifies his own views to himself or it is an expression of a sense of (prophetic?) mission, whereby speech is an irrepressible necessity.[2] Nevertheless, despite and perhaps because of this form of discourse, he inspired new thinking.

At least in its public image, Leibowitz's thinking since the creation of the state of Israel has been founded on several unbridgeable antitheses: religion and state, religion and morality, values and needs, theocentrism and anthropocentrism, body and soul, and so forth. These antitheses became the foundation of a unique religious outlook, without precedent in Jewish thought. Beyond the polemics he was involved in, Leibowitz was an iconoclast struggling to destroy gods and demons in both secular and religious contexts. It is indeed doubtful whether there has been another iconoclast like him since Maimonides, who was Leibowitz's hero.

My aim here is to go beyond this rigid static semblance to locate the underlying dynamic in Leibowitz's world. I will argue that the external cloak of a dogmatic doctrine conceals a deep tension in Leibowitz's religious world, which turns his thought into the voyage of a believer who seeks to create a religiously meaningful outlook at the core of modern life.

Ernst Simon published in 1952 an influential piece titled "Are We Still Jews?"[3] In this article, he drew a distinction between "Catholic" and "Protestant" religions. A "Catholic" religion encompasses the whole of life for the individual and for society; it does not acknowledge the legitimacy of autonomous domains that are not subject to religion. By contrast, a "Protestant" religion focuses on the individual and on the individual's connection to God and recognizes life realms unconditioned by religion and typically secular. Simon holds that historical Jewish religion is "Catholic," since Halakhah pervades the whole of life and focuses on society rather than on the individual. Yet, argues Simon, a religion facing the reality of modern life must be restructured to fit the "Protestant" model because, faced with secularization, "Catholicism" has failed. Entire areas of economic, social, and military life are typically secular, and the religious attitude toward them is always a delayed response.

Simon points to two Jewish circles as representative of "Catholic" religiosity: one is the circle of extreme Haredim (ultra-Orthodox Jews) known as Neturei Karta (Guardians of the City), and the other is the one that constellated around Yeshayahu Leibowitz. The Neturei Karta resolved the tension between a secular modern society liberated from religion and total religious demand by renouncing the secular world and opting for religious self-enclosure. The circle around Leibowitz chose the reverse option, seeking to assuage the tension by attempting to restore Jewish totality through a religious-Zionist revolution. Its followers would apply religion to all domains of life by renovating halakhic legislation and reshaping Jewish society under the guidance of Halakhah. Placing Leibowitz's thought within a "Catholic" model of religion could appear unfounded, given that he is the classic "Protestant" thinker. His thought is focused on the individual and compartmentalizes human life, drawing a sharp distinction between religious life and political, moral, social, and scientific contexts.[4] This common perception of Leibowitz, however, reflects the success of his attempt to obscure his early thinking, which had indeed been marked by a demand for religious totality.

During the 1930s, Leibowitz was a prominent leader of young religious-Zionist activists and particularly of the Brith Halutzim Dati'im (Covenant of Religious Pioneers, known by its acronym BAHAD), who established the first religious kibbutzim. The need to implement the Torah in all realms of life was a foremost concern of his thought and, in a kind of manifesto, he wrote in 1930: "We declare that the building of the Land of Israel is the task of Judaism at present. The very building of our land and our people is for us one of the Torah's essential roles."[5] The religious revolution he promoted was meant to shift the world of Torah and Halakhah from private realms—the home, the synagogue, and so forth—to the public-political realm, a shift centering on the difference between life in the diaspora and life in the Land of Israel. Only in the Land of Israel can the Torah be all-encompassing. Leibowitz held that "our Zionist definition teaches us that the blame should not be sought in the Torah but in our historical status, which had precluded activation of the enormous power latent in the Torah. In this situation, we must redeem the Torah with our own efforts."[6] To realize the Torah in the public-political domain, then, renews and redeems the Torah that, in exile, had been impoverished and confined to private life.

This is the dominant trend in Leibowitz's writings until the early 1950s. In *Torah and Mitzvoth in Our Time*, a book that reflects Leibowitz's views up until then, he ceaselessly strives to fashion Israel as a Torah state. The term "Torah state," which is usually ascribed to Haredi circles, is central to Leibowitz's early thinking and is expressed, for instance, in the title of one of the book's chapters, "Education for the Torah State."[7] Rather than a Haredi notion, then, the concept of the "Torah state" epitomizes the religious-Zionist revolution that strives to renew Halakhah so as to facilitate its implementation in a sovereign state. Simon justifiably understood that Leibowitz's stance at the time implied preparing a platform for "the rule of religion in the state."[8]

Leibowitz's "Catholic" position, however, is fully modernist, given the special status it ascribes to the individual. The weight and responsibility for fashioning life in the world are shifted from God to humans; moreover, the status of the Torah in the real world is made contingent on the human ability to create a society where the Torah could be fully realized. The kind of society that Leibowitz spoke of is one denoted by the term *Gemeinschaft*. This term, denoting a social group whose members are tied to one another by emotional and value dispositions, was widespread in contemporary sociological thought and deeply influenced youth movements in Germany. Leibowitz used the term to describe future Jewish society in Israel. In a scathing critique of German Orthodoxy, he writes:

> Orthodoxy . . . ignores the fact that proclaiming the "sovereignty of Torah" is doomed to remain only lip service unless accompanied . . . by a commitment to fight for a social and cultural Jewish national "*Gemeinschaft*" in a closed system. Only a "*Gemeinschaft*" can be the basis for the Torah as an overarching value of Jewish culture and education, and as an element shaping the entire human being.[9]

As a modernist thinker, Leibowitz held that the hero of the human drama is the society, not the individual, and the basic challenge is therefore to fashion a community. However far-fetched this might seem, at this stage of his thought Leibowitz was extremely close to Buber, who repeatedly stressed the role of the *Gemeinschaft* and presented it as the challenge of practical Zionism. But contrary to Buber, who held that it is in the community where the individual meets the absolute, Leibowitz, as a halakhic man, held that the community is the arena for realizing the Torah given at Sinai.

But the Jewish national *Gemeinschaft* also establishes a domain for creating a synthesis between the Torah and the spectrum of cultural values borne by the modern individual. Leibowitz determinedly states: "We are partners to general (European) culture; we view this partnership as a *fait accompli*, and neither wish nor can be liberated from it."[10] The future society that Leibowitz strives for, then, is modern not only in the sense of being a product of the individual's sovereign endeavor but also, and mainly, in the sense of being a mediating ground between the world of tradition and the range of European cultural values. Already at this stage of his thought, Leibowitz is clearly not a romantic seeking to establish a utopia detached from the real life of concrete people; he, together with his friends from the Brith Halutzim Dati'im, join the Zionist project and seek to found a society that synthesizes Torah and life.

Following his arrival in Palestine, and as a committed intellectual, Leibowitz began to take part in the processes of building the society. He translated his initial stance into a decisive demand for the renewal of Halakhah, which was required because Halakhah in the diaspora had not functioned in the public realm. In legal terms, Halakhah had not developed public law and had dealt only with laws binding on the individual. But these laws could not provide answers to the problem of the Sabbath in a sovereign state, which, in his view, was not only a "political-social" question:[11]

> The problem of the Sabbath sets a precedent for all the manifestations of the actual religious crisis that Judaism confronts in the State of Israel. . . . The main danger it faces is the helplessness and impotence of official Judaism and its public representatives to enter into a real struggle for it. . . . Religious Judaism has no clear notion of the contents and real meaning of the Sabbath laws in an independent state of the Jewish people in the present. . . . The possibility of a struggle for the Sabbath as a public and political institution depends on submitting a constructive plan for providing public services, for sustaining all realms of the economy, and supplying the public's needs on the Sabbath according to the Torah.[12]

Leibowitz sought to renew the creativity and legislative authority of Halakhah. He held that Halakhah is a human creation and can therefore be renewed and adapted to contemporary reality.[13] Simon, then, was not exaggerating when he claimed that Leibowitz belonged to the group of thinkers who ascribed a messianic dimension to the state of Israel: if it is proper to change or issue halakhot in order to adapt Halakhah to the state, the implication is that the religious value of the state is absolute and overrides Halakhah as well. Simon, as noted, wrote his programmatic article in 1952, prior to the dramatic turnabout in Leibowitz's thought, and his critique offers clues as to the radicalism of Leibowitz's early thinking. In the 1930s and 1940s, Leibowitz fashioned his philosophy as a sociopolitical thinker whose main perspective was to amend the individual and the society.

No wonder, then, that Leibowitz's religious stance at this time does not rely on metaphysical or theological foundations. Living in the midst of the Zionist-pioneering Orthodoxy in Germany, he was not concerned with theological questions and focused on issues of social planning and the fitting halakhic norm. At the second stage of his thought, metaphysics and theology will be identified as the challenges facing believers. At this stage, however, Halakhah is not only a normative system to be realized in a total life domain but also a closed system that fulfills a dual role: it separates and distinguishes believers committed to Torah and *mitzvoth* from the world of secular values, and it delineates the borders of their religious world. Leibowitz, then, changes course in the mid-1950s toward a "Protestant" view of Jewish religion. The change is extreme. The religious hero is now the individual, who is commanded to fashion a closed religious world that is neither open to nor draws on the outside world. Religion is a set realm, defined by the walls of Halakhah, and outside it is the secular world that includes morality, politics, science, and society. Within it, humans are subjects of Halakhah who constitute their existence through absolute compliance with God's command, as opposed to an outside secular world constituted by absolute human sovereignty.

Leibowitz tried to blur this shift from an approach focusing on the community to one focusing on the individual. In an early article, "Education for Torah in Modern Society," published in 1943, he had written:

> To be a religious Jew is a role that is not confined to the molding of a specific personal character and the organization of personal life, but an obligation to prepare for the giant role of setting up a religious society . . . the regulation of society and state matters, the establishment of the Torah state.

Following the turnabout in his position, when the article appeared in a later collection, he added a note: "At present [1975], more attention should be devoted to the meaning of shaping the individual's life in a collective context."[14] This shift from the community and the society to the individual is not a mere change of emphasis but a new direction. The individual is now the protagonist of the religious drama, which will focus on the relationship with God and no longer on the shaping of politics and society. The supreme manifestation of this shift comes to the fore in a voluntary religious decision—faith: "I . . . do not regard religious faith as a conclusion. It is rather an *evaluative* decision that one makes, and, like all evaluations, it does not result from any information one has acquired, but it is *a commitment to which one binds himself.*"[15] Like Kierkegaard before him, Leibowitz argues that faith is a "leap," a free act. The content of this act, however, is the renunciation of a self-perception that places the subject at the center and a readiness to take on "the yoke of the Kingdom of Heaven, the yoke of Torah and Mitzvoth."[16] Only this distinction between the act and its contents ensures that the centrality of the subject will not be translated into the complete subjectification of religious life. Making the normative system the object of the act of faith also ensures Leibowitz's new revolutionary foundation—the absolute transcendence of God.

In his early thought, Leibowitz had devoted no attention to this theological problem. Now, however, he presents a radical religious position whose intuitions are close to those of Maimonides. God is not a "personality,"[17] and relating to God or experiencing God's presence is impossible. As a modern "Protestant" thinker, Leibowitz accepts the complete secularization of the world and its voiding of any religious meaning. God is entirely transcendent and the world is ruled by a set order, which can become known through science and human experience and need not be explained through theological assumptions. The only possible relationship between God and humans is through Halakhah: "There is no other content to the faith in God and the love of God than the assumption of the yoke of the Kingdom of Heaven, which is the yoke of Torah and Mitzvoth."[18] Religious individuals orient their consciousness toward their halakhic obligations rather than toward God. The believer "makes an effort to direct his religious consciousness to himself as recognizing his duty to his God. That is the practice of the men of Halakhah."[19] Humans, who are absolutely sovereign, retreat and make room for the halakhic obligation and assume its yoke, but even when doing so they do not become obedient subjects since Halakhah is given to humans. The telos of Halakhah is indeed to worship God, but humans are those who realize it. God's "voice" has been removed from the halakhic discourse, which humans conduct according to their own discretion and their own interpretations. Leibowitz repeatedly contrasts the worship of God with its antithesis—humans worshipping themselves. He interprets the notion of "Torah for its own sake" as meaning that human beings are not the telos of the Torah, and he draws a distinction between demanding and endowing religions. An endowing religion

> is a means of satisfying man's spiritual needs and of assuaging his mental conflicts. Its end is man. . . . A person committed to such a religion is a redeemed man. A religion of Mitzvoth is a demanding religion. It imposes obligations and tasks and makes of man an instrument for the realization of an end which transcends man.[20]

This dichotomous formulation is necessary given that the distinction between the two types of religion is predicated on the assumption that humans are the protagonists of the human and halakhic drama. Within the modernist anthropocentric life domain, a theocentric kingdom is established. Beyond the person's enlistment as an obligated, committed being, this kingdom is inaccessible. Humans live in a world without God in both their concrete and their religious realities, and although God is presented as the telos of the religious act, humans will never reach communion with the divine. For Leibowitz, the attempt at communion is idolatry because it assumes God's presence in the world. These, then, are the parameters of a radical religious view that claims God is unknown and estranged from both the world and humanity. The recognition of this estrangement is the true climax of religion.

The revolutionary implications of this religious approach are obvious. Not only has the world been emptied of God but, in a deep sense, Leibowitz endorses a religious version of the "death of God." According to this version, God becomes irrelevant to life in the real world, and Halakhah is the only domain through which we relate to God. But even in these circumstances, the relationship with God does not break through the walls of human immanence and is manifest, above all, in the human readiness to establish within the natural empirical realm a domain that transcends it. Self-transcendence, though not the actual goal of the religious act, nevertheless epitomizes it. Like Kierkegaard, Dostoevsky, Sartre, or Camus, Leibowitz understood that in a world empty of the divine where humans live as free beings, they are doomed to alienation from the world and even to a rift with it. For Leibowitz, the alienation and the rift are the core of the religious stance:

> The religious experience is, as such, the crisis of man. . . . Faith is the opposite of human harmony. From a faith perspective, man neither does nor can reconcile himself to the natural reality, even though he is part of it and cannot transcend

it. . . . But the religious man differs from the one who has not assumed the yoke of the Kingdom of Heaven . . . he does not accept the fact that he is part of the natural reality and that he cannot transcend it.[21]

Transcendence, then, is a symptom of religious life. Believers reject their subservience to natural reality. For Leibowitz, the question of whether this goal is attainable is entirely irrelevant—this is an infinite, Sisyphean goal whose importance is not conditioned by its realization. The paradox of believers' lives is evident in their readiness to live in circumstances that may be beyond their ken: "Could it be that worshipping God is not part of human nature—and the meaning of 'nature' is simply what cannot be transcended? And yet, it is incumbent on man 'to be strong as a lion'—to make a supreme effort to do what cannot be done."[22] The paradox or the absurd of Camus, which Leibowitz greatly admired,[23] now become the heart and the test of religious life. Only one who is ready to withstand the crisis caused by the imprisonment within religious life is a true worshipper of God, and that "constitutes his religious perfection or 'redemption.'"[24]

A comparison with Leibowitz's earlier "Catholic" stance will help to grasp the full extent of his turnabout. The Catholic view of Judaism assumes harmony between the person and the world, which is the arena for implementing the Torah. Specifically, the social-political domain is where the Torah will be redeemed from its self-alienation as a system that cannot be fully realized. His Catholic position also compels Leibowitz to make a utopian assumption about the world. Social reality can be amended, and the hero of the human drama is not the individual but the society that amends the world on the basis of the Torah. This amendment will be accomplished with the emergence of the Torah state, which will regulate human behavior.

This totalization of social life premised on the Torah does not lead Leibowitz to claim that believers are estranged from the values that surround them. Leibowitz seeks to fashion a society that integrates all the networks of meaning affecting human behavior, an attempt summed up in Samson Raphael Hirsch's adage of "Torah with *derekh eretz*." This harmony between the individual and the world and between the Torah and life is predicated on an idealism that affirms concrete action, and Leibowitz did indeed work throughout his life to realize the idea. Beginning in the mid-1950s, Leibowitz formulated a "Protestant" view that completely reversed his early approach and rejected the possibility of harmony between humans and the world. Believers are meant to experience estrangement between their lives as people committed to Torah and *mitzvoth*, and their lives as real people living in other contexts of meaning. The protagonist of this drama is the individual, since the social structuring, the *Gemeinschaft*, is a form of social organization concerned with itself and with the set of contacts and attachments created within it. Believers, by contrast, are required to transcend this context and assume the Sisyphean task of divine worship, no longer concerned with the amendment of society but with the amendment of their own religious consciousness. They seek to transcend their real existence and create a religious kingdom at the very core of human life.

In order to anchor this new approach in Jewish tradition, Leibowitz had to retrace the parameters of the religious outlook itself. Jewish tradition, as manifest in Halakhah, had never viewed detachment from concrete secular life as a religious task. As a normative system meant for society and not only for the individual, Halakhah seeks to "amend the world in the Kingdom of the Almighty."[25] Halakhah shows interest in human beings, their values, their needs, and their wishes, and the meta-halakhic principles that convey this approach are quite explicit: "The Torah cares for the people's money" (TB Menahot 76b; Yoma 39a, and elsewhere); "its ways are pleasant" (Prov. 3: 17), the concept of *tikkun olam*, and many more. Halakhah has a dual goal: to amend human life, relating to human beings as real entities, and the worship of God. The early Leibowitz had acknowledged this, but the "Protestant" Leibowitz rejected it and portrayed Halakhah as a system that separates the individual from the real world, embodies transcendence, and has one single purpose—God's worship.

The dramatic difference between the two approaches comes to the fore in the attitude to the state of Israel and to the meaning of Zionism. In his early Catholic approach, Leibowitz had claimed that the state is crucial to the realization of the Torah. From this perspective, Zionism has a distinct religious meaning:

> In religious-Zionism, religion assumes a religious meaning different from one that had been common among our ancestors and rabbis. It is not the same religion as that of religious Jews who are not Zionists . . . there is a fundamental difference between us and them concerning religiosity. According to our approach, religion applies to areas and to problems that, according to their feelings—and possibly also according to their understanding—are not ruled by the Torah.[26]

As the concretization of Zionism, the state enables a totalization of Halakhah and is therefore imbued with a religious meaning that creates a distinction between Zionists and non-Zionists. In his later approach, Leibowitz retreated from this position. The state ceases to be a holy space and becomes a territorial state, which is extremely perilous precisely because absolute rather than exclusively functional value is ascribed to it. Those who attribute religious theological standing to the state are guilty of idolatry:

> The people and their land are the elements that the spokesmen of religious Judaism cloak in a mantle of religious holiness. This is the religiosity of Korah— "all the congregation are holy." . . . Sanctifying the people and their state as a substitute for the worship of God—that is the line that leads from Korah to the contemporary rabbis of the National Religious Party. . . . Concerning the value contents of the Jewish people and of Judaism, both the secular and the religious publics are going though a process of spiritual and mental decay.[27]

Beside his caveat about the value of the state, Leibowitz changes his Zionist approach—he remains attached to Zionism, but discards its theological-religious meaning. The meaning of Zionism is now functionalist: "I have been a Zionist my whole life. . . . We tired of Gentiles ruling over us. That is the meaning of Zionism." Leibowitz, who apparently sensed the change in his approach, proceeds to define the limitations of Zionism in a way that completely discards his early stance: "Neither a fair society, nor existential security, let alone the realization of the essence of Judaism, the Torah and the Mitzvoth . . . none of this depends on a state or on political national independence."[28]

"Catholic" Leibowitz presents a total view of religion, whereas "Protestant" Leibowitz presents a compartmentalized view of life: one defined compartment is that of religious life, which creates a closed, monadic world. Outside it is a world of real people, where no difference prevails between believers and nonbelievers:

> Religious man differs from secular man only in the fact that, in his life, besides the secular matters common to everyone, are activities and behaviors that do not originate in natural reality but are meant for the sake of Heaven—the will to worship God by observing the Torah and the Mitzvoth. Thereby, he sustains islands of holiness in the sea of secular reality.[29]

The compartmentalized view of Jewish religion could be interpreted as a recognition of neutral life domains that, although devoid of religious meaning, do not threaten religious life. The above passage would appear to suggest so. The lives of religious individuals involve additional networks of contexts, but in their shared network, secular and religious people are no different. Through this "Protestant" compartmentalizing approach, however, another approach emerges, closer to Lutheran or even Calvinist beliefs. Leibowitz's statement further on in this passage contradicts its beginning:

> There is no approach more typically idolatrous than one perceiving holiness in natural reality, or in certain natural objects, in natural events, and in actions that people perform for motives inherent in their nature. This is typical idolatry because it turns the world as is into God. The basic foundation of the religious approach is the separation of the sacred from the profane. That hint of a trace in human existence, which is meant for the sake of Heaven, only that is the holy.[30]

A demystifying reading of this text directs attention to what the text hides.[31] In the current context, it is a plausible assumption that the text hides the constant temptation, including among believers, to ascribe absolute meaning to the world or to aspects within it. Hence, the political-social world is not merely a neutral domain for the believer but one of threat or, in Paul Tillich's terms, of the demonic:

> The demonic is the Holy (or the sacred) with a minus sign before it, the sacred antidivine. . . . The demonic is a meaning resistant thrust which assumes the quality of the Holy. . . . The Holy in the original conception does not distinguish between the divine and the demonic. As soon, however, as the cleavage in the religious consciousness identifies the demonic as demonic, the concept of the Holy is identified with the divine.[32]

The complex relationship between the demonic and the divine is constituted through the consciousness of the believer resorting to this dialectic tension. Thus, Leibowitz persistently juxtaposes here and in all his writings the contrast between idolatry—the demonic—and the observance of Torah for its own sake, or between holiness as a description of a situation—the demonic—and holiness as a description of an unattainable ideal as the true worship of God. What had been neutral—the state, human values—henceforth become demonic realms involving temptations dangerous to religiosity. Believers do not live in compartmentalized realms but in life realms that often threaten the religious world. They are supposed to establish God's kingdom at the heart of the demonic city.

A classic expression of this tension is the increasing emphasis on the demonic temptation within ethics. From a compartmentalized perspective, Leibowitz could have confined himself to the claim that ethics is part of the secular world, given that it does not reflect the worship of God. Instead, he made ethics a domain of temptation and risk to the believer: "Those who pray daily recite from the Shema, 'and that you seek not after your own heart'—the negation of Kant. What follows, 'and your own eyes,' is a negation of Socrates. The reason is immediately provided: 'For I am the Lord your God.' "[33] To go after the heart and the eye, which represent the two ethics, is to follow temptation. The believer must overcome this temptation in the name of faith. Ethics, then, is not a neutral realm but one of lure and peril. Many areas of our life are foci of friction with religious belief, and this confrontation reflects the believer's standing in the world. Believers must endure the tension between the divine and the demonic. This basic scheme reflects a new approach; thus, replacing a compartmentalization separating the holy from the profane is a dialectic between the holy and the demonic. Luther set up the tension between God and Satan by stating, "with regard to God . . . he has no 'free will,' but is a captive, prisoner and bondslave, either to God or to the will of the Satan."[34]

Luther too had assumed that, in day-to-day life, free will is captive to and enslaved by Satan.[35] According to Calvinist tradition, however, it is our duty to be at the heart of secular life and contend with the tension between the demonic and the divine. There is no middle neutral domain, and this is the view that Leibowitz endorses. He is a modernist, and this approach is intensified in his attitude toward secular culture. At the third stage of his thinking he holds, like Tillich, that religion is always contending with the tension between the secularization and the demonization of life.[36] Elsewhere, Tillich critically analyzes Karl Barth's approach and states: "Barth suddenly realized that culture can never be indifferent toward the ultimate. If it ceases to be theonomous, it first becomes empty, and then it falls, at least for a time, under demonic control."[37] This analysis is valid regarding Leibowitz as well. The radical expression of this unique view is evident in his approach to the sacrifice of Isaac. Leibowitz is one of the very few thinkers who turned this story into a paradigm of Jewish existence. Jewish tradition, which viewed Abraham as a paragon, refrained from endorsing this story as a model of exemplary Jewish life.[38] Leibowitz's exegesis of Abraham combines elements from Hegel and Kierkegaard. Like Hegel, he held that Abraham represents absolute estrangement from the world; nevertheless, this estrangement is manifest within the real world, precisely as Kierkegaard claims in *Fear and Trembling*. The religious person, as represented by Abraham, is a hero who assumes a stance of freedom that does not yield to the world's demonic temptation, even when he stands in its midst.

In sum, Leibowitz's thought gradually shifts from a Catholic position to a compartmentalizing Protestant position, and from that to a Lutheran-Calvinist one—amid the struggle between the divine and the demonic—both within religious life and in the tension between religious and secular life.

What drove these shifts? Unquestionably, a partial explanation is the resurgence of the state of Israel. Leibowitz had hoped that the state of Israel would create an opportunity for the renewal of the Torah in the public arena. Like many followers of religious Zionism, however, he recognized that the state of Israel is a secular state that, by its very nature, cannot allow the implementation of the Torah state.

Parallel to his recognition of Israel's secular nature, he discerned that the state becomes an absolute value that replaces the worship of God as a value. Inklings of this view appear in his programmatic piece "After Kibiyeh." He wrote this article following a retaliation operation that the Israeli Defense Forces (IDF) conducted against the village of Kibiyeh in Jordan, which had purportedly been a starting point for infiltrators who killed Israeli citizens. In this operation, conducted in October 1953, about sixty villagers were killed, most of them women and children who were noncombatants, and about forty houses were destroyed. Leibowitz, like many others, was shocked by these results and held that the IDF operation was not only a terrible moral mistake but expressed something deeper:

> There is, however, a specifically Jewish aspect to the Kibiyeh incident, not as a moral problem but an authentically religious one. We must ask ourselves: what produced this generation of youth, which felt no inhibition or inner compunction in performing the atrocity. . . . The answer is that the events at Kibiyeh were a consequence of applying the religious category of holiness to social, national, and political values and interests . . . the concept of the absolute which is beyond all categories of human thought and evaluation—is transferred to the profane.[39]

His critique of the absolutizing process only intensified over time. In later articles, Leibowitz pointed out that this process affects not only the state but also the people and their symbols.[40] This criticism reached a height after the Six-Day War. Henceforth, not only are the state and the people holy, but "their military victories and their conquests also become matters of holiness."[41]

But this explanation is only partial, since it fails to deal with the religious revolution generated by Leibowitz. Had Leibowitz merely wanted to contend with the problem of absolutizing the state and with the absolutization of the secular, expressing reservations about the Catholic conception on this question would have sufficed. But Leibowitz did not stop at this point, and he completely changed his religious outlook in several regards. First, he changed his conception of God. At the Protestant stage of his thought, Leibowitz adopts a theology that views God as absolutely transcendent. This approach is opposed to Jewish tradition, which views God as simultaneously transcendent and immanent. Except for Maimonides, who became Leibowitz's hero, this approach is seldom found in Jewish sources and led him to radical conclusions that contradict Jewish tradition, which views humans as involved in a relationship with God, addressing God as "Thou." According to Leibowitz, this mode of address makes no sense since God is entirely transcendent. Second, Leibowitz develops a purist theory of Halakhah, whereby Halakhah is unrelated to reality, neither contingent on it nor activated by it.[42] This purism establishes a closed normative field, unrelated to real life. This conception is alien to the spirit of Halakhah and is entirely Leibowitz's invention. Finally, Leibowitz offers a new religious anthropology, stating that the only standing of humans before God is that of obedient subjects who are meant to renounce their world and values in the name of their duty to God.

This radical revolution cannot be a result of Leibowitz's changed attitude toward the state of Israel. In my view, to assume that Leibowitz changed his religious views because of his displeasure with the course of events that he witnessed seems improper. This is a causal, Marxist explanation whose starting point does no honor to the man and assigns no significance to his views. It also leaves a gap between the explanation and his actual position.

According to another explanation, the absolutization of the state and of the people enables Leibowitz to identify a fundamental problem in the religious position: religious impulses and intuitions may materialize in demonic modes. This "demonic impulses syndrome" easily leads from the demonic within the religious realm to the demonic outside it; the religious obligation does not, as such, protect from the demonic, and a person can therefore become entrapped in it and expand it beyond religious life. Leibowitz explicitly conveyed these insights in one of his central texts, where he warns against unworthy religious impulses:

> The intention to worship God could become a stumbling block if a man's intention is to avoid performing the duty that is incumbent on him and, instead, find a way to satisfy his own feelings and impulses, even if these feelings and impulses appear to be pure. These matters are of interest to us as well . . . pointing to the turning of human impulses into matters of holiness, including such impulses as nationalism, love of the state, love of the land, love of the people and so forth, which are meant to satisfy needs and interests—all these, as noted, are "illicit fire."[43]

The demonic is explained as "illicit fire," as forbidden religious pathos, and is itself prohibited as idolatry. Precisely because Leibowitz stressed the closeness between the divine and the demonic, he sensed the enormous power attached to idolatry. And indeed, there is no greater iconoclast in Jewish thought, particularly in the modern one.

The study of idolatry, meaning the study of the demonic and its sources, generates a change of consciousness in the divine realm as well, given that, as noted, the demonic and the divine are two sides of one phenomenon. The study and criticism of the demonic lead to the demand for a purist religious stance in theological, transcendent, and anthropological-religious domains. The realization of this consciousness is concretized at the third stage of Leibowitz's approach, which I have called "Lutheran-Calvinist."

This clarification explicates the transition from the "Protestant" to the "Lutheran-Calvinist" position. But how to explain the transition from the "Catholic" to the "Protestant" stance? One could obviously assume that this transition endorses Simon's call to adopt the Protestant model of religion, following the failure of the Catholic approach. Contrary to Simon, however, Leibowitz did not endorse Protestantism ex post facto but turned it into a religious ideal. Why, then, did he choose such a radical course?

Reconstructing all the twists and turns of Leibowitz's thought is hard, if not impossible. All the factors noted above certainly contributed in some measure to these shifts but, beyond all of them, I wish to make a claim based on a matter of principle. Leibowitz is a modernist believer who wishes both his religiosity and his endorsement of modern values to be endowed with meaning. The "Catholic" stage reflects the initial, somewhat naïve perceptions of Leibowitz and many of his pioneer friends that modernism and the new options opening up to the Jewish people enabled the realization of traditional Judaism. At this stage, in the early decades of the twentieth century, the tension between religious commitment and modernity had not yet taken shape, since life experiences had not brought Leibowitz and his companions face to face with the dialectic and complexity of this encounter. The "Protestant" stage combines the discovery of the tension between the two poles and the need to contend with them in new ways, and it is precisely this stage that leads him to the "Lutheran-Calvinist" one. If we attempt to see him as a systematic philosopher, we might focus on the analytical and philosophical criticism of his works and identify their vulnerable angles. But this disposition might miss the essence that propels his work. Leibowitz is an intellectual seeking to blaze a trail between the foundational components of his world—Jewish religion in its Orthodox construct on the one hand, and his modernist world on the other. His work must be read as a description of a believer's riveting and complex human voyage in the modern world. Even if some of his approaches are unsubstantiated, the dynamism of his thinking and all its intricacies remain fascinating and intriguing.

Notes

1. Richard Rorty, *Philosophy and the Mirror of Nature* (Princeton, 1979), 11.
2. For further discussion, see Avi Sagi, ed., *Yeshayahu Leibowitz: His World and His Thought* [Hebrew] (Jerusalem, 1995).
3. Ernst Simon, "Are We Still Jews?" [Hebrew], in *Are We Still Jews?* (Tel Aviv, 1983), 9–46.
4. Avi Sagi, *Tradition vs. Traditionalism: Contemporary Perspectives in Jewish Thought*, trans. Batya Stein (New York, 2008), 43–60.
5. J. Leibowitz, "Thoratreuer Zionismus," *Zion* 2, no. 5 (1930): 64.
6. J. Leibowitz, "Ein Versuch Zur Klaerung," *Zion* 2, nos. 10–11 (1930): 143.
7. See Yeshayahu Leibowitz, *Torah and Mitzvoth in Our Time* [Hebrew] (Tel Aviv, 1954), 53–67. In a later book that includes all his writings until 1976, Leibowitz changed the title of this article to "Education for Torah in a Modern Society." See Yeshayahu Leibowitz, *Judaism, the Jewish People, and the State of Israel* [Hebrew] (Jerusalem, 1976) (henceforth *Judaism and People*). This change corroborates my claim that the later Leibowitz tried to blur his early "Catholic" approach.
8. Simon, "Are We Still Jews?," 35.
9. J. Leibowitz, "Zur Tarbuth Frage," *Choser Bachad* 2 (1932): 1–2.
10. Ibid., 2.
11. Leibowitz, *Judaism and People*, 108.
12. Ibid., 109.
13. On this issue see, at length, Sagi, *Tradition vs. Traditionalism*, 135–54.
14. Leibowitz, *Judaism and People*, 45.
15. Yeshayahu Leibowitz, *Judaism, Human Values and the Jewish State*, trans. Eliezer Goldman et al. (Cambridge, 1992) (henceforth *Judaism and Values*), 37 (emphasis in the original).
16. Ibid.
17. Yeshayahu Leibowitz, *The Faith of Maimonides*, trans. John Glucker (New York, 1987), 70.
18. Leibowitz, *Judaism and Values*, 44–45.
19. Ibid., 76.
20. Ibid., 14.
21. Yeshayahu Leibowitz, *Faith, History, and Values* [Hebrew] (Jerusalem, 1982), 57.
22. Yeshayahu Leibowitz, *On Pirkei Avot and on Maimonides* [Hebrew] (Jerusalem, 1979), 107.
23. Avi Sagi, *Jewish Religion after Theology*, trans. Batya Stein (Boston, 2009), 67–98.
24. Leibowitz, *Judaism and Values*, 70.
25. These words are from the end of the *Aleinu*, which concludes the three daily prayers.
26. Leibowitz, *Torah and Mitzvoth in Our Time*, 62.
27. Leibowitz, *Faith, History, and Values*, 195.
28. Ibid., 209.
29. Ibid., 142.
30. Ibid.

31. On the demystifying mode of reading and its contrast with the demythologizing mode, see Paul Ricoeur, *The Conflict of Interpretations* (Evanston, 1974), 389.

32. Paul Tillich, *What Is Religion?* (New York, 1973), 85–87.

33. Leibowitz, *Judaism and Values*, 207.

34. See Martin Luther, *Selections from His Writings*, ed. John Dillenberger (New York, 1961), 190.

35. Ibid., 188.

36. See Paul Tillich, *Systematic Theology*, vol. 3, *Life and the Spirit: History and the Kingdom of God* (Chicago, 1967), 98.

37. Paul Tillich, *The Protestant Era*, trans. James Luther Adams (Chicago, 1957), 61.

38. On this question, see the extensive discussion in Avi Sagi, "The Meaning of the *Akedah* in Israeli Culture and Jewish Tradition," *Israel Studies* 3 (1998): 45–60.

39. Leibowitz, *Judaism and Values*, 189.

40. Leibowitz, *Faith, History, and Values*, 195.

41. Ibid.

42. Sagi, *Tradition vs. Traditionalism*, 135–54.

43. Yeshayahu Leibowitz, *Seven Years of Discourses on the Weekly Torah Reading* [Hebrew] (Jerusalem, 2000), 472.

26

Theodor W. Adorno (1903–1969)

AUSCHWITZ AND COMMODITY FETISHISM

Moshe Zuckermann

TRANSLATED BY STEPHANIE GALASSO

WAS THEODOR ADORNO A JEWISH THINKER? THE QUESTION DOES NOT REFER TO whether Adorno was a Jew by Orthodox Jewish stipulations. That he was not, as his mother was not Jewish. His father, on the other hand, was a Jew, whereby Theodor Adorno, despite his Catholic christening, was also of Jewish descent. He himself however testified that Adolf Hitler—not his father—had "made him into a Jew."[1] Considered thus, the question is one of a certain heterogeneously informed "having-become-Jewish" (*Jude-geworden-Sein*), a fate shared by many Jews of assimilated descent, especially in Germany. One is apt to glimpse a "Jewish fate" therein. After all, all Jews of modernity saw themselves confronted by the question of how they were Jews, insofar as they did not "define" themselves by religion. Their "identity" arose *ex negativo* so to speak—as a reaction to antisemitism, which confronted them from the non-Jewish context of their existence. That holds also for Zionist-oriented Jews, when one considers that political Zionism evolved in no small part from a reaction to the diasporic existence of Jews, which was itself carried out in repression. It holds most certainly for the Jews who indulged in assimilation and then had to discover that antisemitism made this self-determined distance from Judaism impossible. Even Jews who thought they could rise up in the actually existing socialism of the Soviet stripe had, on more than one occasion, to be disabused of this conviction. For both socialist as well as bourgeois societies proved not to be free from crude antisemitic diatribes and repressions.

What, then, is Jewish in the thought of a Jewish thinker? The answer to this question is less trivial than its appearance would have it. For the question concerns itself not with tautology—the sheer coincidence that if a thinker is Jewish, his thinking must also necessarily be Jewish. That so many thinkers and intellectuals of European modernity were Jews—that is to say, of Jewish descent—begs the question: Is there something about the existence of these thinkers qua Jews that aligned their thinking in a specific (hence, Jewish) way? Here, too, there is no easy answer. If it is not a matter of outright religious components of Judaism, and with that also those components that were interpreted secularly and transported verbally, the question arises of whether that which, content-wise, cannot be attributed to the thought of a Jew may be apostrophized as Jewish thought. In order to bring home the importance of this question, it should be emphasized that the Jewish Enlightenment (Haskalah), begun at the end of the eighteenth century, which was accompanied by the effort to overcome the old Orthodox Judaism and its prescribed way of life, to break out of the ghetto, and to integrate itself (if not assimilate itself completely) to the burgeoning bourgeois society, gave rise to a specific symbiosis of the Jewish with the non-Jewish. This symbiosis found its expression chiefly phenomenologically — that which had previously brought about the reception of numerous non-Jewish material and verbal attributes into the life of the Jew in the ghetto and shtetl now found its reflection in a firm disposition. One wanted to strip oneself of the exclusively Jewish in the sense of a consciously chosen acculturation. This effort yielded both the attribute of the "German Socrates," which was even applied to the Jewish philosopher of religion Moses Mendelssohn, as well as the subsequent ideology of "the Mosaic belief of the German citizen." That the former student of the Talmud could have been brought into connection with the spiritual incarnation of Hellenism corresponded to the compromised adherence to Judaism, which itself arose under the conditions of the tendency to consider that same religion hollow from the perspective of a secular, bourgeois self-image. Nevertheless, it must be pointed out that in the course of bourgeois assimilation, as well as in light of the spiritually secular emancipation, the religious components increasingly faded or, as in the case of many Jewish thinkers, was consciously cast off as a practiced religion.

If this context occupies such a meaningful status in the transformation of the spiritual direction of Jewish thinkers, in that the specifics of this orientation reveal themselves precisely in their symbiosis with the non-Jewish (that is, in the cultural sphere of Jews in their respective societies of residence), it raises the question of whether context-generated elements milled themselves into the thought of Jews, and if one might claim of them that, entirely in this respect, they might be Jewish. If, for example, the repressive situation of the Jew in his or her non-Jewish societal context gave rise to the effort to conquer this situation, it would seem an emancipatory view of society may have arisen from this context — an emancipatory view that could be brought into connection with Jewish-messianic ideas of redemption that had a religious connotation, but no longer a religious intention. Such constellations one might think to recognize in the thought of, for example, Karl Marx, Ernst Bloch, or Walter Benjamin. That is not to suggest that intellectual works of all modern Jewish thinkers were informed by (thoughts of) emancipation — Jews, not least in Germany, were also involved in the establishment and the solidification of conservative systems of values — rather solely that that which is emancipatory in the spiritual approaches of those Jewish thinkers to whom one ascribes an emancipatory quality most likely springs from their conscious (or also latent) efforts to remove the repressive aspects of their social situation as Jews. Strictly speaking, they were emancipatory: the firm conservatism of Jews had the goal of emphasizing their own efforts at assimilation in order to promote acceptance throughout their non-Jewish surroundings — to preserve the fruits of acculturation that had already taken place. As I have said, critical thought that aimed at radical change in society had to do with the repressive situation of Jews in the bourgeois constellations of society

that were already infiltrated by emerging modern antisemitism. In both cases it was, at the same time, a matter of a settlement with the "Jewish question" that was served to Jews by non-Jews—to which the strategies of assimilation, socialism (the liberation of Jews by way of societal liberation of all people in general), or of Zionism (the nationalistic solution of the "Jewish problem"), strategies themselves created by Jews—offered themselves as possibilities.

If one then takes Adorno's dictum, *Hitler made me into a Jew*, a saying comes to mind from his thoughts on the genocide of Jews in the twentieth century, which became popular not by accident: "Hitler imposed a new categorical imperative on people in the state of their unfreedom: to orient their thought and actions such that Auschwitz never repeats itself, that nothing similar might happen."[2] This statement is exalted as the origin of discussion regarding Jewish dimensions in Adorno's thinking, namely in light of what he himself considered the cause of his having-become-Jewish. The view proffered here, that the immanence of this thought was intimately twinned with its origin in an innovative way, could be considered Adorno's own in a sense.

Disinterest and the Semblance of a Debate about Nomenclature

In a radio broadcast given in 1966, Adorno claimed that every debate about ideals of education are "futile and insensible" in comparison with a central objective of education that Auschwitz should not recur: "[Auschwitz] was the barbarism against which all education goes. One speaks of the threatening backslide into barbarism. But it is not a threat, Auschwitz *was* that backslide; barbarism further persists as long as the conditions that brought about that backslide essentially continue. This is the whole horror." He goes on: "The societal pressure continues to weigh heavily despite all invisibility of distress today. It pushes people to the unspeakable, which culminated in Auschwitz on a world-historical scale."[3]

A few years ago it became fashionable to reproach the thought of Adorno on account of its being out of date. This way of thought, it was said, fed on the specificity of biographical experience that should long ago have been historicized: the darkly desperate worldview immediately following World War II should be traced back to his own damaged life, to the influence of a decidedly lifesaving, yet traumatic, existential experience of emigration and uprooting. Indeed if you grant this strand of later reflections its historical authenticity, it is at the price of the overall picture's being subordinated to individual experience, or at the very least its taking priority through its connection to individual experience. The emphasis of Adornian desperation appears from such a perspective pathetic, even ideological, because particulars are taken as universals. What should one do with such a way of thinking in a time that supposes itself to have deposed everything ideological?

Furthermore, immanent deficiencies are held against Adornian philosophy (if it is accepted as a philosophy at all). By subjugating the history of civilization to a transhistorical argument, it dehistoricizes historical specificities, thus withholding changes being made visible through historical inclination, which take shape in a vastly more differentiated fashion than it appears in timeworn structural forms and patterns. Still more: since the transhistorical inclination is traced from time immemorial, all the way to modern late capitalism, as an unfolding consequence of constantly more complex and impenetrable mechanisms of hegemony (a consequence that leads to a conception of a highly developed, totally administrated world), there comes a feeling of historical aporia whereby critical theory maneuvers itself into the dead-end street of knowledge. Peter Sloterdijk's polemically oriented exclamation in 1999 against Jürgen Habermas, that critical theory is dead,[4] might subliminally have something to do with the—certainly unthinking—need to cut through the putative Gordian knot of this critical tradition of thought once and for all.

In question certainly is what in particular, over and above this specific intention, should be killed off. Adorno himself suggested in his own time, in another context, that an "ancient bourgeois mechanism that the Enlightenment thinkers of the eighteenth century knew well . . . pro[ceeds] renewed and yet unchanged: the suffering with regard to a negative circumstance, this time as a result of a blocked reality, turns into a rage against the one who expresses it."[5] A field of tension arises between negative reality, its critical concept, and the willingness to confront this perennially defended concept. There are two ways of circumventing it. On the one hand, *disinterest* toward the critical and always-repeated, whereby *interest*—consciously or unconsciously—refuses the actually prevailing. On the other hand, the *nomenclature* wrests oneself free from the actually prevailing, in that one renames it. The indifference coming from disinterest does not thereby require explanation. It is more likely the case that it requires a scientifically self-sacrificing, conceptual shift.

In his introductory remarks at the 16th German Sociological Congress, which aimed at a macrotheoretical discussion of the position of developed societal systems, it was not by chance that Adorno conveyed the following: one "not familiar with the situation of the controversy in the social sciences could be led to suspect that it's a matter of a fight over nomenclature; specialists are plagued by the vain concern of whether the current period should be called late capitalism or industrial society."[6] If, for that matter, it would be different today for one very familiar with this controversy in the social sciences, is a matter to be doubted. Topical codewords such as "globalization," or "civil society," "consumption society," "media society," or even "hedonistic society," index a genuine need to grasp conceptually the obvious transformations that have passed through modern societies around the world in the last few decades. However, they mask no less the fact that that which, in theory, could be dismissed as obsolete has not changed any of the fundamentals. Despite all the renaming, capitalism, along with its inherent mechanisms of domination, exploitation, and manipulation, has by no means been eliminated. Rather, it simply creeps into a euphemistically modified, rubber-stamped discourse that, in the course of this debate of nomenclature (which indeed could hardly still be called a debate today; the actual balance of power in the objectifiable international scene had noticeably affected the agonal theoretical discourse), proves itself to be ideology of the highest degree.

Adorno made incisive reference to this in the aforementioned talk, which is now over forty years old. He thoroughly underscored the objectifiable transformation in the realm of the means of production and thought, beyond which one may not let oneself be bullied into the succinct disjunction of late capitalism or industrial society. He insisted above all that dominance is further exerted on humanity throughout the entire economic process, save that its objects have "for a long time been not only the masses, but also the commanders and their following. According to the old theory, they largely became functions of their own apparatus of production." And if the immiseration thesis had not already proven to be true to the letter, "so still in the no less frightening sense that unfreedom, the dependence of one on the consciousness of an Other, whom one serves, spreads itself out over humanity."[7] Certainly according to the standard of living and consciousness, "class differences become, in the decisive western states, way more visible than in the decades during and after the industrial revolution,"[8] and still, "people [are] what they were after Marxian analysis around the mid-19th century: appendages of the machinery, no longer merely the workers who have to adapt themselves to the quality of the machine that they serve, but far beyond that, metaphorically compelled to fashion themselves as rolling wheels of the mechanism of society, and to model themselves after it, without reservation, and even in its most intimate incitements. Today, as before, things are produced for the sake of profit."[9] Above all, then, it was for Adorno a matter of what he called the "primacy of structure," namely that "concepts such as exchange society have their objectivity, express a compulsion of the general behind the individual circumstance; a compulsion that in no way allows itself to be sufficiently translated into operationally defined circumstances."[10]

Guilt, Barbarism, Lies, Trash: Auschwitz as Culminating Point

On this basis, one can outline Adorno's statement about perennial barbarism *after* Auschwitz a bit more precisely: Auschwitz is comprehensible as a "backslide into barbarism" that has already taken place, but which, as it has actually happened, and as a chronic possibility of paroxystic return, can no longer be brushed off. The reason for that lies in the fact that the structural conditions that historically brought about Auschwitz as the culminating point of an entire tendency, as such—as *structurally* determined constellations, that is—have by no means been overcome, rather they are always persisting. It is therefore in no way a matter of extraordinary conditions, rather one of those conditions that are arranged in the tendency of their own actual sociohistorical logic. That they do not now appear as a threat pregnant with catastrophe, and have even become, as with poverty, "invisible," may not hide the fact that they continue to have an effect on societal pressure that "pushes people to the unspeakable that culminated in Auschwitz on a world-historical scale." In its real historical formation, the monstrosity of Auschwitz may appear to be a state of exception, yet not a tendential potential of actual history.

With that, though, the specifics of Auschwitz are glimpsed. That which was already indicated in Horkheimer's and Adorno's *Dialectic of Enlightenment*—immediately after World War II—is formulated twenty years later in Adorno's *Negative Dialectic* as follows: "With the murder of millions through administration, death has become something that was never before to be feared in such a way. There is no longer the possibility that death enters one's life as something that coincides at all with its course. Since in the camps the individual no longer died, but rather the specimen, death must also affect those who avoided these measures. Genocide is the absolute integration that prepares itself everywhere where people are made into the same— razed, as it was called in the military—until one literally exterminates them, deviations from the concept of the utter nothingness that they are."[11] Adorno's deep desperation about culture's inability to achieve anything against this tendency toward integration (let alone against "absolute integration"), finds its succinct expression in the following: "All culture after Auschwitz, along with all the urgent critique of it, is trash. While it was restoring itself after that which had happened without resistance in its own landscape, it turned entirely into the ideology that it had been potentially ever since it, in opposition to material existence, claimed to breathe a light into it that was denied it by the separation of the spirit from bodily labor."[12] From this situation, arising after Auschwitz and by its nature aporetic, there is obviously no real exit: "Whoever pleads for the preservation of a radically guilty culture turns himself into an abettor, while he who denies himself this culture immediately promotes the barbarism as which culture masks itself. Not even silence emerges from the circle; it only rationalizes the distinct subjective inability with the status of objective truth and thereby, once again, degrades truth into lies."[13]

From this perspective, Adorno conceives of Auschwitz as the culminating point of a comprehensive civilization process, which manifests itself in the "totally administered world" of modernity as the increasing obliteration of the individual. What is intended is the modern world, which had its historical basis precisely in the Enlightenment's "promise of happiness," in the ideal of the individual and the autonomy of the subject, but also the world that shattered these hopes: not only did its socialist-communist attempts at emancipation quickly develop into totalitarian-authoritarian mechanisms of dominance, and not only did the murderous potential of capitalism sporadically assume the repressive form of a "führer" and fascism; rather also the logic inherent to modernity from its inception (the peculiar connection of rational Enlightenment optimism and the beneficial technological development of "material life forms") was shaken to its very foundation in light of the Holocaust. The dialectic of Enlightenment (as a concrete overturning of progress into the most extreme repression, that is to say as a rigorous instrumentalization of a technology that had promised prosperity, all for the purpose of a diametrically opposed destruction and extermination) was, from then on, no longer merely a hypothetical possibility, but had become a real event, a concrete manifestation of a civilization with abilities, achievements, and powers aimed against itself. It was, then, indeed the avowed (instrumentally) rational, institutional achievements of modernity (industry, bureaucracy, and administration) that had actually originally enabled the magnitude of this monstrous extermination—the triumph of the dialectical motive of "overturning quantity into quality." In this sense, Adorno postulates: "What the sadists announced to their victims in the camps: tomorrow you will meander into the sky as smoke from this furnace, refers to the indifference of the life of each individual, toward which history is moving itself: even in his formal freedom he is as fungible and replaceable as under the steps of the liquidators. Because the individual in the world—whose law is the universal, individual advantage—has nothing other than this Self that has become indifferent, is the implementation of the old familiar tendency which is, at the same time, the most horrifying; so little is led out of that as out of the electrically charged barbed wire enclosure of the camp."[14]

Despite this aporia, which results from this historical tendency of an "indifference of the life of each individual," Adorno however did not content himself with its finding, but insisted, as mentioned, on the so-called new categorical imperative, even such that people themselves, "in the case of their unfreedom," orient their thinking and behavior such "that Auschwitz does not repeat itself, that nothing similar should happen."[15]

It is obviously Adorno's task to think about a culture that bears in mind the unspeakable: after Auschwitz. In this case the following weighty moments stand out: Adorno's perception of the events distinguishes itself through a universally oriented attitude. He speaks of the people's fundamental "position of unfreedom," of a situation of existing that is, in essence, repressive and alienated. Accordingly, he also conceives of the "conditions" that could yield the monstrosity as historico-socially determined: as a further oppressive "societal pressure" and an ever-persisting adversity whose outer appearances have nevertheless become less visible in the era "after Auschwitz." It is then this position that allowed for the "backslide into barbarism" to turn into a historically concretized—that is to say already achieved—manifestation as well as into the permanently threatening possibility of its return, unable to be brushed off. Auschwitz already *was* the backslide into barbarism; consequently it became a paradigm of a "breach of civilization" that ran counter to the unwaveringly trusting optimism of progress at the heart of the Enlightenment. The singularity of the event is, viewed thus, to be thought of as something general, as an absolute culmination point of a permanent threat positioned on a "world-historical scale." The fact that, as Adorno expressed, "in the camps the individual no longer died, but rather the specimen," and consequently that the Nazi genocide staged the "absolute integration," is therefore to be understood as a symptom of a world-historical development and, further, also as the universal diagnosis of a civilization constantly bearing the potential for a backslide into barbarism. Hence the charge—the so-called new categorical imperative—that that which has been singularly set by Auschwitz as a yardstick never repeats itself, that nothing approaching or similar to this yardstick occurs. Apart from the huge question of which society should be built such that a backslide into barbarism is eliminated once and for all, another demand is made here of humanity "in the case of their unfreedom": to orient their thought and actions constantly against murderous oppression and the systematic creation of ever-new victims. In this sense, of course, Adorno in later years heavily revised—if not altogether retracted—his famed dictum on the impossibility of lyric poetry after Auschwitz. "The perennial suffering," as it goes in the *Negative Dialectic*, "has as much of a right of expression as the martyred has to bellow; for that reason it would be false to no longer allow poetry to be written after Auschwitz."[16]

Critique of the Culture Industry

And it is now in connection with this socio-historical question of the possibility of lyric poetry after Auschwitz that another category of Adorno's thinking finds its central junction: the category of the culture industry. Taken by itself there's nothing "Jewish" about it; it's also not thought of or intended as such. But insofar as Adorno seeks to recognize in art in general the appearance of the emancipatory in the "universal context of delusion," and thus preserves, unbroken, thoughts of freedom itself in the situation of all-grasping barbarism, this motive reflects a moment that is apostrophized by Walter Benjamin (admittedly in a different context) as a "weak messianic force."[17] The current consideration is directed toward this central theme in Adorno's thought.

The category of the culture industry in the classical theory of the Frankfurt provenance, so it is often said, survived above all because the critical sting was normatively taken out of it. While people began, in French poststructuralist discourses that achieved notoriety in the United States, to overthrow cultural hierarchies and to deconstruct traditional measures of value in aesthetic evaluation, and while, beyond that, the patina of the politically correct imposed itself onto the analytical work of postmodern indifference, the underlying emancipatory emphasis of theory of the culture industry was disposed of more and more. Hence, even today, mere talk about the manipulative machinery dulling the consumer's mind in the culture industry, in conformity with the system, is quashed as "elitist," that is to say it is laughed off as "anachronistic." The triumphal procession of commercial mass culture in the last few decades manifested itself not least of all in the fact that its operators, as well as its clientele, no longer need to care about critiques of it. In contrast, the critique itself is subject to critique, in that one maligns it—with ideological shiftiness—as antidemocratic pretension and smart-alecky arrogance.

The culture industry as a category of thought suffered the same fate as many of the other meaningful categories of the old Frankfurt School, with those of the authoritarian character and the critique of capitalism leading the way. This finding gains importance in the context discussed here insofar as the praxis of the culture industry cannot be thought without capitalism's orientation toward profit, nor without the eagerness to conform that is found in the authoritarian character. Now the question certainly arises of to what extent these categories themselves have historically safeguarded their significance. For if the external authority has, since the early modern period, indeed lost prestige, the individual's conscience has increasingly taken its place. Moreover, if the "individual conscience" is to be conceived of as the elongated arm of societal transformation, this transformation prompted a liberalization of the established forms of controlling and conditioning individuals, and the individual conscience forfeited its earlier bourgeois function of being the "strict tyrant." Then the question is raised as to what the status is of authority figures in today's Western societies; that is to say, if the classical concept of the authoritarian personality type can be maintained as the matrix of modern societies, or even, as it was postulated at that time, as "the human foundation of fascism."[18]

What should primarily be kept in mind is that the changed world scene since the collapse of Eastern European communism has done nothing to change the essence of capitalism, merely that it has now claimed the whole "playing field"—on a global scale—for itself. Talk of "globalization" serves above all as a discourse of nomenclature motivated by neoliberalism; a discourse whose primary function amounts to nothing more than an ideological whitewashing of an objective, global barbarism, through which large portions of humanity (actually or potentially) go to ruin. At the same time that "cultural" globalization is involved medially in the Western ideology of equality: multicultural identity politics as a stand-in for the discussion of (much less the combat against) structural causes of worldwide mass-suffering. Beyond that, it should also be kept in mind that, within developed Western societies, the logic of capitalism produces further structural calamity. Not only does the immensely climbing prosperity in no way benefit all of its members; not only is there in these societies horrendous, increasing poverty with the collapse of traditional social welfare; rather the condition of the means of production, itself historically gained, does not make a difference in the now objectively possible reduction of alienated labor. On the contrary, structural unemployment is maintained such that it perpetuates competition on the job market and alienated labor itself becomes, mutatis mutandis, exalted to the desired goal. The xenophobia that has markedly increased in recent years, the virulent ethnic prejudices and crude racism, point to a clear affinity to these structurally conditioned contradictions.

It is precisely here that I should point out the unequal, "more democratic," and, hence, less visible (and, as such, barely identifiable) form of the authoritarian: the authoritarian subjugation under the globalized diktat of the culture industry. For Adorno this concept functions still as an intentionally polarized contrast to the (as always problematic in itself) concept of autonomous art. The concept of the culture industry, he explained, was in his time deployed as a conscious replacement for "mass culture" in order to eliminate at the outset an interpretation led by interest, "so that it was a matter of something that could appear to be a culture spontaneously rising from the masses themselves, in order to [eliminate] the contemporaneous form of the people's art [*Volkskunst*]." The culture industry, he explained, takes "the familiar" and couples it with a new quality: "In all areas products are more or less methodically introduced and are tailor-made for the consumption of the masses and, in large part, determine this consumption themselves. The individual areas resemble each other's structures or at least fit together. They form, almost seamlessly, into a system." The decisive point here consists in the fact that the culture industry is systematically structured in such a way that it causes a "willful integration of customers from above." Beyond that, the culture industry forces together the "domains of high and low art that had been kept separate for millennia," and to their mutual detriment at that: "The high loses its seriousness through speculation surrounding its effect; the lower through civilizing repression of the obstreperous resistance that was inherent to it as long as societal control was not yet fully developed." While the culture industry manipulatively speculates about the "conscious and unconscious state" of the masses, these become "not the primary, rather the secondary, the discounted, the appendages of the machinery" — "the customer is not, as the culture industry would like to believe, King, not the subject, but rather the object." In other words: "The culture industry misuses the concern for the masses in order to double, to secure, and to strengthen its mentality as given and unalterably assumed. Any opportunity for this mentality to be changed is thus, without exception, foreclosed. The masses are not the measurement, rather the ideology of the culture industry; as little as this latter could exist if it did not align itself with the masses."[19]

Let it be well understood: the fact that the products of the culture industry are produced according to the principle of their exploitation and "not after [their own] content and its inherent design," that the entire cultural-industrial praxis, so to speak, "utterly [transfers] the profit motive onto the immaterial entity" should by no means hide the fact that these appearances are not totally new; their first signs became much more visible ever since those immaterial entities, "through their autonomous character" as wares on the market of their creators, began to serve as a way of earning a living. What is nevertheless "new" about the culture industry is the "immediate and unveiled primacy of the precisely-calculated effect of its most typical product." That is, the significant meaning that it places on the reception it wants for its products—a smooth, essentially uncritical reception at that—through its ever-growing and ever more massive clientele of consumption: "The autonomy of artworks, that, to be sure, hardly ever reigned purely and was constantly infiltrated by contexts of impact, is being tendentially eliminated by the culture industry."[20] If works of art were (*waren*) always already also, but not only, wares (*Ware*), then the products of the culture industry are always nothing other than wares.

The Omen of the Digital

Adorno's conception of the culture industry is noticeably inspired by the emancipatory function of art. As such, the culture industry presents itself to him as an instance of steadily expanding cognitive contamination. Despite its foresight, his analysis certainly appears a bit "outdated" today; not, however, on account of the "revaluation" of culture/industrial mass culture driven from all sides—for example, in postmodern postulation on the suspension of *high* and *low*—rather because, quite to the contrary, the excesses of the culture industry and the incalculable expansion of its domains of impact, as well as the massive unfolding of the culture industry's means of production, circulation, and consumption, have, in the mean time, taken on dimensions that place everything that Adorno (in the age of the relatively nascent development of radio and television) could imagine into the shadows.

Adorno's argument required radicalization. For if it is true that we—as the American cultural critic Michael Denning claims—have reached "the end" of mass culture, if the debates in which mass culture is determined to be an "Other" have survived because there's nothing *outside of* mass culture; if mass culture is rather "the one element that we all breathe";[21] if the culture industry steers itself toward the widespread commercialization of all areas that institutionally transmit "reality" and thus toward the product-informed (*warenförmig*), reified control of our everyday perception, and if the quota mechanisms thereby become oriented toward the total integration of ever-greater portions of the public into the globalized force field of relentlessly increasing consumption; and if, at the same time, the apparatus of integration's repressive repercussions strive to mask the ever more narrowly adjusted individual with a seemingly emancipatory ideology of a democratic "liberalization of the market," of a pseudoliberal "democratization of consumption," of "free will," and of an ostensible "free choice"—*then* the culture industry no longer functions as a diametric antithesis of autonomous art, but rather as *the* form of perception and interaction in the entire domain of the sphere of action in globalized late capitalism. The deceptive underlying principle of the culture industry's structural logic has mutated into an all-encompassing formative principle of the objective defamiliarizing morphology of modern societies. "False consciousness" no longer means an ideological superstructure that reflects the base, but refers instead to an economically determined ideology of that which Adorno apostrophizes as the aforementioned "universal context of delusion," which has become praxis. The communication of Auschwitz through Hollywood films such as "Schindler's List" is, seen this way, only an aspect of the culture industry. One no less significant aspect is that "the story of Auschwitz has become a material, a raw material, with which one can just as easily make something political as make a campaign donation,"[22] as Detlev Claussen has formulated. It is here not only a matter of the normalization of the unspeakable through the inflationary use of a concept, nor only a matter of making the monstrous banal through discussing it to death, rather—less noticeably—it is also a matter of the consciously staged debate about the planned sparking of publicized sensation. As demonstrated in the case of the Goldhagen debate in the United States, in the Memorial Debate in Germany, or in the antisemitic polemic in Israel, today any publicly led, demanding controversy can deteriorate into praxis of the cultural industrial ideology. It is simply a question of the quantity of soured quality and, to be sure, of the quantity of "democratically" expressed opinions on the topic, of the number of made-for-TV discussions on talk shows and polemicized blog posts, respectively, and of the scope of the product-informed fetishization— all of which are evidence of the fact that, since the dominant "After Auschwitz" culture transformed Auschwitz into a product for consumption, whose value was materialized in the form of Hollywood's Oscar trophy (and assorted other reifying practices of Holocaust memorialization), barbarism is no longer a question of praxis that reflects ideology; rather, as already shown, it is an ideology that has become praxis itself.

What is authoritarian about that is the formation of new instances of authority: the increasing devotion to the flood-like deluge of media culture, along with its characteristic formations: the cults of celebrity and idol worship and a fan mentality; the voyeuristic gawking of talk shows, in which freaks and low lives flaunt their pathetic misery and are hailed according to how drastically their violence erupts, how inarticulate their inability to communicate manifests itself; the modern-day audience at a gladiatorial battle that projects its own life onto the ones fully debasing themselves; and the mechanical readiness to expose oneself to increasingly professional seductions toward consumption, to commercialized fashion, to the sensational. Whether it be art, entertainment, political events, or natural catastrophes, whether it's murder or starvation, the pulling of the lotto numbers or the resignation of a secretary—everything deteriorates, according to the structures of presentation, perception, and exploitation, into a digitally transferred product. Death in Africa has an economically translatable prime-time value; it is consumed as an object and has a length of efficacy that is measured by the next item, the next sensation, and the following entertainment program.

What is authoritarian is the fetishized devotion to a comprehensive virtualization of life that, if not "from above," is at least prepared "behind the curtain," which even mutates TV weather reporters into cult figures. If the family, according to Adorno, still follows "the customs of its own social, ethnic, and religious group,"[23] then nothing fundamental has changed under the omen of the digital. Certainly what remains to be researched is to what extent the said "customs" take shape with the aid of standards set by television family series and digital media. Hence, it also remains to be researched to what extent "economic factors" of the cultural industrial media world influence the "conduct of parents toward their child."

Whether fascism in its conventional sense is thereby encouraged cannot be further explicated here. That will only be provable once the objectifiable historical conditions for its renewed acquisition have been developed. In as much as authoritarian structures of character are regarded as the "human foundation" of fascism, one can proceed with the knowledge that traditional authoritarianism has survived in modern societies, and thus the danger of fascism that plagued Adorno and Erich Fromm is obliterated—or somehow only appears to have been obliterated? Hence one would certainly be even more entitled to ask if this authoritarianism has found its (un)worthy successor precisely in the immanent logic and structure of the culture industry.

Adorno as a Jewish thinker? If he is, then it must certainly not be in the sense of that which is deemed "Jewish" in Israel and elsewhere today; absolutely not in the sense of that which is politically, militarily, and socially practiced in Israel. In as much as Judaism is bonded with the tradition of a humanism born out of a long history of suffering, a humanism that seeks the societal emancipation of humanity and hence the overcoming of all human victimhood; a humanism that views the individual experience of suffering as a theoretical and historically active challenge to praxis, then Adorno should very certainly be classed with this tradition even if it's because he was "made into a Jew" by Hitler. Whether he would have found himself at home in the Jewish state—that is to say, in the political construct that today sets about to define itself as a "Jewish state"—is something to be doubted. His Judaism arose out of need and has nothing to do with the Jews who instrumentalized the historically Jewish experience of suffering on the level of the nation-state, and with a relationship to the Other determined by ideology, in order to bring about and strengthen unintentional-intentional, ever-greater suffering, rampant repression, and racist everyday life. Theodor Adorno's thinking is diametrically opposed to such a praxis. And, in that regard, he is Jewish.

Notes

1. Dorothea Fazumovsky, "Credo, Kanon, Theorie und Praxis," in *Adorno-Portraits: Erinnerungen von Zeitgenossen*, ed. Stefan Müller-Doohm (Frankfurt, 2007), 280. Translations of all quoted source material are the translator's own.

2. Theodor W. Adorno, *Negative Dialektik* (Frankfurt, 1982), 35.

3. Theodor W. Adorno, "Erziehung nach Auschwitz," in *Erziehung zur Mündigkeit* (Frankfurt, 1971), 88.

4. Peter Sloterdijk, "Die Kritische Theorie ist tot," in *Die Zeit* 37 (1999): 35f.

5. Theodor W. Adorno, "Resignation," in *Kritik: Kleine Schriften zur Gesellschaft* (Frankfurt, 1971), 147.

6. Theodor W. Adorno, "Spätkapitalismus oder Industriegesellschaft?," in *Gesellschaftstheorie und Kulturkritik* (Frankfurt, 1975), 158.

7. Ibid., 164.

8. Ibid., 158f.

9. Ibid., 165.

10. Ibid., 161.

11. Compare E. B. Ashton: "Genocide is the absolute integration. It is on its way wherever men are leveled off—'polished off,' as the German military called it—until one exterminates them literally, as deviations from the concept of their total nullity" (362); in Theodor W. Adorno, *Negative Dialectics*, trans. E. B. Ashton (New York, 1973), 355.

12. "In restoring itself after the things that happened without resistance in its own countryside, culture has turned entirely into the ideology it had been potentially—had been ever since it presumed, in opposition to material existence, to inspire that existence with the light denied it by the separation of the mind from manual labor" (ibid., 367).

13. Ibid., 360.

14. Ibid., 355.

15. Ibid. (see note 11).

16. Ibid., 355.

17. Erich Fromm, *Die Furcht vor der Freiheit* (1941; Frankfurt, 1983), 147.

18. Ibid., 144.

19. All quotes in this paragraph are from Theodor W. Adorno, "Resümé über Kulturindustrie," in *Ohne Leitbild: Parva Aesthetica* (Frankfurt, 1970), 60f.

20. Ibid., 61.

21. Michael Denning, "The End of Mass Culture," in *Modernity and Mass Culture*, eds. James Naremore and Patrick Brantlinger (Bloomington and Indianapolis, 1991), 267.

22. Detlev Claussen, "Das politische Denken wird ersetzt durch Konfessionen," in *Perspektiven* 31 (1997): 27.

23. Theodor W. Adorno, *Studien zum autoritären Charakter* (1950; Frankfurt, 1973), 7.

Mark Rothko (1903–1970)

BEYOND ABSENCE

Ulrike Gehring

TRANSLATED BY PATRICK HUBENTHAL

FOR MARK ROTHKO, MODERNITY FIRST BEGAN TO TAKE SHAPE IN 1941, WHEN HITLER's plans for the systematic murder of the Jews were becoming known in America, and the Jewish artist of Russian descent banished figural references from his imaginal world. The subject, conjured by artists for more than two thousand years, lost not only its meaning but also, in Rothko's case, its iconographic existence. This change in Rothko's work was a process that unfolded over three stages. First, the motifs of everyday New York life were replaced by abstract, mythological scenes. In 1943, severed extremities and fossil fragments began to summon up the infernal war that claimed millions of lives and, in the mind of the artist, also abetted the murder of God. Then, after 1945, these fragmentary forms gave way to an impenetrable emptiness formed from color alone.[1] Yet this emptiness engenders content and meaning in its very nonobjectivity; it is not at all empty. Why that should be so will be the subject of this study, along with the question of the responsibility Rothko's works, in their openness to interpretation, ascribe to the viewer.

Inventing Modernity in American Art

Marcus Rothkowitz was born in 1903 in Dvinsk, Russia (now Latvia), the fourth child in an Orthodox Jewish family. As a sign of their acculturation, his parents spoke Russian, while the children were taught in Yiddish and Hebrew. Under the increasing pressure of tsarist pogroms, the family emigrated to the United States in 1913. Marcus studied psychology and philosophy at Yale University before enrolling in classes at the Art Students League of New York.[2] He took American citizenship in 1938 and two years later changed his name to Mark Rothko.[3] In New York, Rothko moved primarily in Jewish intellectual circles, a fact crucial to an understanding of his art.[4]

In 1935, he and Joseph Solman formed a group of artists known as The Ten, which was soon absorbed into the larger circle of Abstract Expressionism.[5] With

Rothko and Barnett Newman among its members, as well as Adolph Gottlieb, Elaine de Kooning, Franz Kline, Lee Krasner, Helen Frankenthaler and Morris Louis, Abstract Expressionism was a movement that found political expression through the journal *Partisan Review*. The fact that all members of The Ten were Jews, along with many of the editors and publishers of the *Partisan Review* and critics such as Clement Greenberg, Harold Rosenberg, and Susan Sontag—all frequently found in its pages—points to significant similarities as well as key differences among those New York–based Jewish thinkers from the Great Depression through the McCarthy years. Rothko remained an outsider as well as an insider to this community. This may explain why Rothko resisted religious interpretations of his paintings all his life. Unlike Newman, who rarely missed an opportunity to call attention to his Jewish ancestry and its influence on his nonrepresentational art, Rothko categorically denied any such influence.[6] His Orthodox Jewish upbringing and the antisemitic experiences of his childhood kept him from identifying with the "comfortable, assimilated image of Jewish-American life."[7] Rothko never designed a synagogue or its furnishings, as Newman did in 1963. Instead, he accepted a commission for fourteen wall-scale paintings for a consecrated Catholic chapel in Houston (figure 1). The concern that the symbolic significance of the place would be projected back onto his nonrepresentational color fields was evidently less compelling to him than the fear of producing an art that would be identified as "Jewish" by his interpreters.[8] This suggests that the artist's biography and his personal statements, the products of his art and the contradictory interpretations of his critics, should all be carefully weighed against one another, as it is precisely in the balance that critical insights into Rothko as a protagonist of modernism may be found.

If one judges by Rothko's works, rather than his remarks about himself, then the grounds for religious hermeneutics are certainly there. Such an interpretation is supported by nameless paintings such as *Untitled (1941–42)* as well as by *Gethsemane* (1945) and *Entombment II* (1946). From his surrealist phase, they show dismembered limbs, their hands and feet pierced by nails and piled in boxes. While a birdlike form with outspread wings can still be made out in *Gethsemane*, stiffening into the shape of a cross, in *Entombment II* the same chimera has mutated into a wraithlike hieroglyph. Anna C. Chave[9] and Matthew Baigell[10] read this figure in the context of Jewish burial rituals or Christian representations of the Pietà: "The horizontal body is present, but a mysterious, transparent form hovers around the heads of the vertical figures, a form that does not appear in earlier versions. It is likely, then, that Rothko intended the transparent form to represent the souls of the six million Jews who were murdered and not properly buried according to Jewish practice. . . . This painting is arguably the most original and most profoundly Jewish response by an American artist to the Holocaust in terms of cultural memory and religious observance."[11] Here Baigell is in accord with Rothko's statement that no artist aware of the Holocaust could paint unmutilated figures.[12] Whether these cipherlike creatures truly "represent" the murdered Jews, however, or stand instead for an emptiness left behind by the six million dead, can be seen in Rothko's later compositions, the vast majority of which after 1947 have no titles, only numbers. "The progression of a painter's work," Rothko stated, "will be toward clarity: toward the elimination of all obstacles between the painter and the idea, and between the idea and the observer."[13]

Figure 1. Mark Rothko, Rothko Chapel, 1971, Houston, Texas. Interior view with West triptych and Northwest-North triptych paintings.

Light beyond Colors

Rothko's painting *No. 27* is divided into three tiers of color on an ultramarine blue ground (figure 2). Atop the bottom block of washed-out black-brown lies a narrow ivory stripe beneath a blue band twice its width. The contrasting zones are separated by narrow strips the same color as the ground. The black seems to recede, creating the effect of depth, while the light white thrusts forward. A broad brush has been used to blur the contours of the inner shapes, so that the objects' edges fade into a diffuse colored light.[14]

This light has its origins in a special glazing technique Rothko developed in the late 1940s, using a medium based on solvents rather than oil, which lends an exceptional transparency to both oils and acrylics. By adding turpentine, Rothko thinned the binder so much that the pigment particles separated from the film, spreading unevenly over the canvas and only barely continuing to adhere to its surface.[15] On the physical level, the pigment density of the glaze is so minimal that light striking the canvas penetrates the transparent layers of paint to various depths before being reflected. Where there is no pigment, or nearly none, it falls on the light-colored canvas unfiltered, causing the surrounding pigment particles to glow as though backlit. While viewers may not be able to reconstruct the process of the painting's

Figure 2. Mark Rothko, *No 27*. 1954.

creation, they will certainly register the remarkable luminescence of its unfathom-
ably deep color spaces.

The impression of depth is reinforced by Rothko's layering of more than ten
glazes of varying colors. The result is that indeterminacy of surface so typical of
Rothko, since each glaze possesses different qualities of absorption and reflection.
This is especially clear in the light stripe across *No. 27*, where white mixes with yellow (the color "nearest the light," according to Goethe[16]) to create a liminal shade
that comes quite close to sunlight. Thus Rothko shifts the emphasis from the pure
brightness of light (white) to the atmospheric quality of its color (yellow-white).
The same is true of the other two rectangles in *No. 27*, each of which derives its
luminance from the light-colored paint layer below.

But what sort of light is this? It is a colored light that has nothing to do with the
light in which the American Luminists of the late nineteenth century bathed their
landscapes. Color-field painting is not based on any naturalistic concept of light,
since the light source that illuminates its motifs is not part of its imaginal world.
Rothko liberates light from its functional ties and employs it as an autonomous
chromatic luminosity.[17] Viewers nonetheless associate this sensation with their

experiences of natural light due to learned patterns of perception, through which unfamiliar stimuli are always interpreted in terms of comparable familiar stimuli.

However, such concrete associations are generally detrimental to the interpretation of Rothko's work, as demonstrated by Robert Rosenblum's analysis of his 1954 painting *Light, Earth and Blue*[18] or Dorothy Seiberling's commentary on a work from 1949, *No. 3/No. 13 (Magenta, Black, Green on Orange)*.[19] In a 1959 issue of *Life*, Seiberling compared Rothko's color field to a blurry sunset photographed from a moving train. While the two motifs may be similar in formal terms, what they convey is not the same. Rothko's colors are not depicting a landscape, nor does his light imitate any experience of light from nature. It originates solely in the light-generating apparatus of paint and canvas. "The result," writes Matthias Bleyl, "is not an image of the world, but rather a world of its own; not reducibility to what already exists, but rather new existence."[20] The origin of Rothko's imaginal light is not nature, but rather pigment. It is not naturalistic; it is an abstract light, its source identical to the world of color it illuminates. Its distinguishing feature is indeterminacy.

It appears indeterminate because of the uncertainty surrounding its origin, the mystery of its manifestation, and the magical glow of the diaphanous picture plane. By causing the light to materialize precisely where the canvas begins to optically dissolve, Rothko achieves a suspension described by Gottfried Boehm as the "paradox of 'flat depth.' "[21] If viewers stop consciously seeing and let the eye wander, an empty and boundless spatial continuum opens up before them. But since emptiness provides just as much room for the evocation of transcendental experiences as for the confirmation of sought-for realities, there have been plenty of attempts to interpret Rothko's imaginal light as a sacred moment. Authors such as Hubert Crehan have connected it with the biblical image of the parted heavens and the awareness of an "immanent radiance."[22] As obvious as this divine-light approach may seem, it arises from the associations of viewers inclined to religious interpretations. Like many Jewish or Christian readings purporting to be the one and only explanation, such claims to exegetical prerogative place unacceptable limits on the openness of Rothko's work to interpretation.

On Jewish Metaphors and the Absence of Color and Form

Motivic, technical, and literary references can all be adduced in support of a "Jewish" reading of Rothko's art. Let us begin with the year 1961, when the French art critic Michel Butor professed to have discovered a Jacob's ladder motif in the rhythmic succession of Rothko's broad bands of color and dividing lines.[23] Though contested in the literature, this comparison has been endorsed by Dominique de Menil, who emphasized its metaphorical nature, explaining the paintings' ladder-like ascent in terms of a reality that strives upward and points to something beyond itself.[24] For Werner Haftmann in 1971, the focus was less on rungs than on blocks of color, enwreathed by flowing veils of color, like the holy of holies lying hidden behind curtains in the Temple in Jerusalem.[25] The curtain motif was also taken up by Edward van Voolen, who in 2006 compared Rothko's Chapel paintings to lengths of fabric "separating the Holy of Holies in the desert Tabernacle or the Jerusalem Temple from the rest of the sacred spaces" (figure 1). Thus "these mysteriously dark paintings create a sense of awe, hinting to a divine presence, perhaps even to the invisible abstract God of Judaism."[26] Chave and Baigell take a different approach, linking the contrast of light and dark to the Apollonian and the Dionysian and sub-sequently interpreting Rothko's dark paintings as comments on the Holocaust.[27] For Baigell, the oblong blocks of color recall open graves, the mass graves of murdered Jews: "The large rectangular forms Rothko used in his mature works are rather de-rived in some measure from the large open graves that he saw only in photographs after the war."[28] All three references put forward to explain Rothko's color fields— the Jacob's ladder, the curtain motif, the open graves—are premised on an abstract understanding of the image. But since Rothko specifically rejected this sort of ex-trapictorial reference, Aaron Rosen's haptic parallel is ultimately more convincing. For Rosen, "the velvety sheen of so many of Rothko's late canvases" can evoke "the *parokhet*, the curtain which veils the scrolls of the Torah in the synagogue's ark."[29]

Irving Sandler and Robert Pincus-Witten propose an approach that is simulta-neously theological and iconoclastic in using the monotheistic proscription of rep-resentation to explain Rothko's renunciation of figurative painting, thereby im-puting to Jewish culture a historically unsubstantiated hostility to images.[30] The aniconism ascribed to Judaism, which also lies at the root of the misconstruction of the "artless Jew," provides no basis for distinguishing between the prohibition of idolatry and the production of art. Even the Scholastic philosopher Maimonides did not apply the dictum against idolatry to art itself, but specifically to the problem of the representation of God by human means, as Moshe Halbertal and Avishai Margalit have stressed.[31] Rothko does not submit to some injunction against images, nor do his paintings keep silent about invisible idols. Rather, they tell of a historical truth that Rothko was unable to represent in any other way.

The metaphor the artist sets in opposition to the Holocaust is light. Light be-comes his central formal element and motif. All concrete references to a reality outside the image pale in its diffuse radiance. Form is subsumed into matter, which is why the emptiness in Rothko's paintings gives an impression of spiritual fullness that is more than merely optical.

Rothko's "black on gray" paintings from 1969–1970 were his final series (figure 3). Originally conceived as small works on paper, the sketches were soon transferred to canvases that far exceed their viewers in scale. Commenting on this tendency, Rothko said: "I paint very large pictures. I realize that historically the function of paint-ing large pictures is painting something very grandiose and pompous. The reason I paint them, however—I think it applies to other painters I know—is precisely be-cause I want to be very intimate and human. To paint a small picture is to place your-self outside your experience, to look upon an experience as a stereopticon view or with a reducing glass. However you paint the larger picture, you are in it. It isn't something you command."[32] All twenty-five paintings in the series are horizon-tally bisected in the same way: black rectangle above, gray-brown rectangle below. These two blocks of color are isolated by a sharp dividing line infiltrated in only a few places by the underlying hue. The vibrant pigments of the classic works have vanished, supplanted by an opaque black film overlaid, toward the bottom, with a chalky gray. The resemblance of this gray block to fresco is due to a quick-drying acrylic paint applied with a broad brush.

Once the viewer's eye has comprehended the simple structure, it invariably at-tempts to assign the line a semantic meaning. Rothko, however, rejected any inter-pretive approach that embraced the presumption of a horizon line "as if one were gazing over the edge of a planet into the void."[33] Instead, he maintained that "he had

Figure 3. Mark Rothko, *Untitled*. 1969.

inverted dark and bright, to avoid conventional interpretations of landscape."[34] The black, therefore, represents not darkness but rather, in its two-dimensional (non-spatial) opacity, the absence of all other colors. The same is true of the uncolored area below, from which all the colored parts of the spectrum seem to have been eliminated. Every attempt to define its colors more precisely leads to the realization that the tints used here are not colors at all—or at least none from the middle of the spectrum. These are noncolors from the outer edges where light and darkness meet: gray-brown, black-brown, ash brown, gray-green. That they come from the palette of the great colorist who originated color-field painting in the early 1950s only becomes comprehensible when one looks more closely at the internal distinctions Rothko uses to give that spectral nothingness a specific appearance.

In the way they eluded easy reading and rebuffed both religious interpretation and the supposed landscape-with-horizon, the black-on-gray paintings represented a challenge to art criticism. Its response was swift. Rather than go along with Roth-ko's experiment in pictorial emptiness, interpreters such as David Anfam, Anne Seymour, and Diane Waldman settled on a biographical explanation.[35] Positing a connection between the artist's color choices and his state of mind at the time of the paintings' creation, they interpreted the dark colors as a mark of his worsening health. The black-violet Chapel paintings, completed not long before Rothko took his own life in 1970, were seen as the logical conclusion and confirmation of this theory. In the literature, these paintings are universally portrayed as the consum-mation of his artistic development, a development that ends not, as in the case of Ad Reinhardt, with the discovery of maximum reduction, but with an unavoidable personal tragedy.[36] This oversimplified reading is contradicted by Rothko's bright pastel works on paper from 1968–1969 as well as his last painting, an unfinished composition in brilliant red. Rothko's colors neither reflect the artist's mental state nor derive from nature. If he nonetheless saw them as conveying meaning, it was because they elicited an individual emotional response in the viewer, enabling a per-ception of the general in the specific and not, conversely, the specific in the general.

In the late 1960s, Rothko himself began to limit the range of possibilities offered by the elimination of the object, banishing light and color from his pictures. In com-positional terms, he reached a zero point where no further simplification was pos-sible. Whereas Reinhardt considered this point to be the end of painting, Rothko sought a beginning, a state of painting before painting. That state can best be com-pared to a vacuum in which neither form nor material exist, an emptiness in which all manifestations of shape and substance seem possible. This implies that the black-on-gray paintings present a secular state that should not be equated to the Creation myth from the book of Bereshit (Genesis) or reduced in any such way. Yet that was precisely the aim of a 1966 J.M.W. Turner exhibition at the Museum of Modern Art referenced by Barbara Novak and Brian O'Doherty,[37] who placed Rothko's color-less paintings in the tradition of Turner's 1843 paintings *Shade and Darkness—the Evening of the Deluge* and *Light and Colour (Goethe's Theory)—The Morning after the Deluge—Moses Writing the Book of Genesis*.[38] In their view, the two artists are united by a dissociation of light and color, a separation of form and material, and the resulting conflation of the means of representation (paint) and its subject (light/darkness). By this reading, Rothko's paintings reveal the creation of a new order out of chaos. Light emerges from darkness, and color emerges from light. Because the paint embodies these elements rather than depicting them, the viewer becomes a wit-ness to an imaginal Creation in which the parting of light and dark is just taking place.

Matthew Baigell takes a similarly creationist approach to Barnett Newman's red color fields when he presumes that "Newman imitated God by creating something out of nothing."[39] Renee Ghert-Zand subscribes to this theory as well, representing untitled paintings by Rothko and by Newman as allusions to kabbalistic teaching—specifically to the theosophic concept of *Tzimtzum* in Lurianic doctrine, according to which "God began the process of creation by contracting God's infinite light."[40] The rebuttal to this argument is that Rothko's color fields are not protolandscapes that need only be sorted by the elements they contain.[41] Rothko's emptiness is not trying to be an interpretation of the biblical or the kabbalistic Creation narrative; it genuinely wants to be regarded as empty. The artist is not concerned with the mythical "miracle of the temporal beginning," as Hermann Cohen described it;[42]

rather, he is taking up the thinking of Hannah Arendt and her references to the Augustinian distinction between *principium*, the origin of the world, and *initium*, the origin of humanity.[43]

Creation of the Void versus Creatio Ex Nihilo

In the colors black and gray, Rothko found the perfect vehicle for expressing the absence of light and color with the tools of painting. Using only the sensation of color, he was able to approach a state of painting before painting, which viewers register on a level prior to linguistic articulation or conceptual categorization. Thus the actual creative act takes place not in the painting, but in the receiving eye of the beholder.[44]

It is Rothko's ability to imagine the void without preconceptions, and without relation to existing theological concepts, that makes him truly modern. He brushes aside all those Scholastic fears that persist into the present, whose horror vacui describes a godless state before the Creation: a nothing whose emptiness is dispelled only by the work of God. By contrast, Rothko dares to imagine nothingness—precisely from a perspective of Jewish thought—as something that exists yet is also, paradoxically, constantly on the verge of coming into being. His dark paintings materialize the idea of an empty infinity in which both art and the world exist in an uncreated state. That is why he declared, in a 1943 letter to the *New York Times*, cowritten by Adolph Gottlieb and Barnett Newman: "There is no such thing as good painting about nothing."[45]

An analogy between artistic and theological acts of creation may indeed be noted in relation to the process of creating: Both the conception of Rothko's nonrepresentational imaginal worlds and the Creation of the world as the work of God occur without precondition—*creatio ex nihilo*.[46] The sole cause lies in the medium or material brought forth by the image or world. When Rothko, in depicting a world outside the image, succeeds in drawing our attention to this *terminus ante quem*, his paintings provide an intimation of something that cannot be rationally comprehended. Though he still faces the limitations of paint and canvas, his paradoxical supposition that neither the created nor the uncreated is required as the material of creation suggests a midrashic explanation of the Hebrew word *bara*, which is used in the first verse of the Bible to describe the Creation out of nothing.[47]

On an art-theoretical level, Rothko's color fields meet several of the demands presented in Newman's 1948 essay "The Sublime Is Now": to trace out images that depart from the European art-historical tradition; and to command a visual vocabulary that can be understood independently of preconceptions or cultural background. This enables viewers to maintain their optical neutrality and face the images directly, without prejudice or foreknowledge.[48] Dominique and John de Menil were responding to precisely this demand when they desanctified the Houston chapel where Rothko's paintings have hung since 1971, converting it instead to interdenominational use. As their foundation's bylaws state, it is now "a holy place open to all religions and belonging to none."[49] Just as the building's shape, an octagon inscribed in a Greek cross, resists definitive attribution, the blue-black painted panels refuse denominational categorization. To some Jewish viewers, however, they may present an offer—an invitation to linger in front of them, to study them, to quietly and independently plumb their depths, to imagine them as Midrashim.

Figure 4. Mark Rothko, *Untitled (Red, Orange)*.

For all the vehemence of Rothko's repudiations of Jewish influence, especially on his late work, that influence shines through all the more clearly in his nonobjective fields of color. Although he never wanted to be a Jewish artist, "being Jewish," in the form of "thinking Jewish," is perhaps the central thread that runs throughout his development as an artist. It is the one constant he denies to avoid being co-opted and to keep his work from being cut off from modernism. His fear was unfounded. Rothko was not only the first American artist to think modernism through to all its conclusions; he also paved the way for it, starting in 1941. The most significant evidence for this is his work's openness to interpretation, which the viewer has no choice but to tolerate. By asking more questions than they answer, his paintings reveal their most enduring quality—one that can be seen as deeply Jewish.

Rothko's modernity was radical, but it took place within the confines of painting. Breaking out of those confines would be left to other artists such as James Turrell, who, in his large-scale installations from 1967 onward, completed the separation of color/light and light-generating apparatus.[50] From a distance, both artists' color fields seem much the same in the immaculate velvetiness of their surfaces. Coming closer, one sees that Turrell's color is no longer bound to any surface, materializing instead as a veil of light in the space behind. Since this optical vis-à-vis cannot be identified by eye alone, viewers inevitably reach out toward it, attempting to ascertain its tactile qualities. As their hands penetrate the light-veil without resistance, its spatial reality is revealed. The monochrome surface turns out to be a rectangular opening through which the viewer is seeing into another space, the "sensing space." If one steps closer to the windowlike aperture, so that its framing architecture disappears from view, the formless light is transformed into a red room that then dissolves into an insubstantial fog. One finds oneself surrounded by a dimensionless nothingness, in the face of which object-oriented vision shades into a daydream-like seeing. Theoretically, this is where the process of perception reaches its logical conclusion. In reality, the circle is not complete until the viewer, leaving Turrell's space, turns around and again has the sensation of looking at a monochromatic painting that now seems just as substantial as it did at first glance.

Although one is now aware of the image's spatiality, one can no longer see it. The installation appears to be something it actually is not, thereby raising a question: Why do we perceive a plane of unformed color as an image, when in fact it is not an image? Simply by recalling a painting, it conveys an impression of familiarity, presenting to the viewer an image that conforms to the conventions of a picture on display in a museum. Unlike Rothko's paintings, these images effectively do not exist; rather, they are the product of our perception. With them, Rothko's long-cherished dream of a pure luminous color, uncoupled from pigment and freely existing in space, has at last come true.

Notes

1. Matthew Baigell divides Rothko's work into three phases: the mythological phase (1941–1943), the archaeological-biological phase (1943–1945) and the nonfigurative phase (from the mid-1940s onward). See Matthew Baigell, "Jewish American Art and Artists in the Twentieth Century," in *The Cambridge Companion to American Judaism*, ed. Dana Evan Kaplan (Cambridge, 2005), 389.

2. It is intriguing that the young Rothkowitz, as a descendant of Eastern European Jews, studied at Yale in a time when enrollment restrictions and so-called Jewish quotas at elite private colleges provoked anxious reactions—at stake was the American ideal—among American Jews. See Henri L. Feingold, *A Time for Searching: Entering the Mainstream, 1920–1945* (Baltimore, 1992), 23. The restrictions faced by Jews in various clubs, hotels, hospitals, fraternal orders, and neighborhoods were even harsher than those in universities; see Hasia R. Diner, *The Jews of the United States, 1654–2000* (Berkeley, 2004), 207–13.

3. James E. B. Breslin, *Mark Rothko: A Biography* (Chicago, 1993), 125.

4. For a critical biography of Rothko, including his role within the New York School and his influences on poets, philosophers, and other artists, see two books by Dore Ashton, *The New York School: A Cultural Reckoning* (Berkeley, 1992) and *About Rothko* (Cambridge, 2003).

5. Other members of The Ten—of whom there were actually only nine—included Ilya Bo-lotowsky, Ben-Zion, Adolph Gottlieb, Louis Harris, Ralph M. Rosenborg, and Louis Schanker. Their aim was "to protest against the reputed equivalence of American painting and literal painting." *Historical Dictionary of Surrealism*, ed. Keith Aspley (Lanham, MD, 2010), 426.

6. "Having been subjected to a rigorous Orthodox Jewish education prior to his immigration to the United States at the age of ten, Rothko was probably the best Jewishly-educated of his painter colleagues, while avoiding the pretentious pseudo-intellectual Jewish pronouncements of Barnett Newman." Tom L. Freudenheim, "Was Judaism a Color on Rothko's Palette?," *Jewish Journal*, November 9, 2006, http://www.jewishjournal.com/arts/article/was_judaism_a_color_on _rothkos_palette_20061110/.

7. Aaron Rosen, "Finding Rothkowitz: The Jewish Rothko," *Journal of Modern Jewish Studies* 12, no. 3 (2013): 479–92.

8. Sheldon Nodelman, *The Rothko Chapel Paintings: Origins, Structure, Meaning* (Austin, 1997), 79–143.

9. Anna C. Chave, *Mark Rothko: Subjects in Abstraction* (New Haven, 1989), 149.

10. Baigell, "Jewish-American Art and Artists," 389.

11. Ibid.

12. Breslin, *Mark Rothko: A Biography*, 209.

13. Mark Rothko, "Statement, 1949," in *Abstract Expressionism: Creators and Critics*, ed. Clifford Ross (New York, 1990), 170.

14. In 1932, Ernst Michalski coined the term "ästhetische Grenze" (aesthetic boundary) to describe the contrast, in mimetic art, between the structured space of artifice and the unstructured space of the natural world. See Ernst Michalski, *Die Bedeutung der ästhetischen Grenze für die Methode der Kunstgeschichte* (Berlin, 1932), 10. The illusory space of color-field painting robs this distinction of meaning, since the aesthetic boundary no longer appears to be identical to the picture plane, instead pushing forward during the process of reception. The two spatial regions, once clearly separated, seem to mix, causing the optical interpenetration of the expansive, inversive space of color and the physical space of picture and viewer.

15. Dana Cranmer, "Painting Materials and Techniques of Mark Rothko: Consequences of an Unorthodox Approach," in *Mark Rothko, 1903–1970* (London, 1987), 192.

16. Johann Wolfgang von Goethe, *Theory of Colours*, trans. Charles Lock Eastlake (Mineola, 2006), 168.

17. Ulrike Gehring, *Bilder aus Licht: Zum Bildbegriff von James Turrell im Kontext der amerikanischen Kunst nach 1945* (Heidelberg, 2006), 103–12.

18. Rosenblum placed Rothko's images in the Romantic tradition of European landscape painting, seeing parallels to the work of Caspar David Friedrich in their dimensionless spaces of color, their vastness, their mysterious, hazy light, and their low, unbroken horizons suggesting the boundary between sky and water. See Robert Rosenblum, "The Abstract Sublime," *Art News*, February 1961, 38–41.

19. Dorothy Seiberling, "Abstract Expressionism," pt. 2, *Life*, November 16, 1959, 82–83.

20. "Es entsteht dadurch kein Abbild von Welt, sondern eine eigene Welt, nicht Rückführbarkeit auf schon Existentes, sondern neue Existenz." Matthias Bleyl, "Über die ästhetische Evidenz konkreter Kunst," in *Wallraf-Richartz-Jahrbuch*, vol. 45 (Cologne, 1984), 325.

21. Gottfried Boehm, "Die Wiederkehr der Bilder," in *Was ist ein Bild?*, ed. Gottfried Boehm (Munich, 1994), 33.

22. Hubert Crehan, "Rothko's Wall of Light: A Show of His New Works at Chicago," *Arts Digest*, November 1, 1954, 19.

23. Michel Butor, "Les mosquées de New York ou l'art de Mark Rothko," *Critique* 173 (October 1961): 843–60.

24. "Like Jacob's ladder, it leads to higher realities, to timelessness, to paradise. It is the fusion of the tangible and the intangible; the old hierogamy myth—the marriage of heaven and earth." Quoted in Breslin, *Mark Rothko: A Biography*, 484.

25. Haftmann compares the inner fields to gates: "But the gate did not open. It was as though it were caught by a darkening plane of light that again veiled the opening." He is also reminded of "hangings, opaque curtains which veiled something, or of an awning or a screen." Werner Haftmann, "Mark Rothko," in *Mark Rothko*, trans. Margery Schaer (Zurich, 1971), n.p.

26. Edward van Voolen, *My Grandparents, My Parents and I: Jewish Art and Culture* (Munich, 2006), 136.

27. Chave, *Mark Rothko: Subjects in Abstraction*, 180.

28. Matthew Baigell, *Jewish Artists in New York: The Holocaust Years* (New Brunswick, NJ, 2002), 102.

29. Rosen, "Finding Rothkowitz," 479–92.

30. See Kalman P. Bland, "Anti-Semitism and Aniconism: The Germanophone Requiem for Jewish Visual Art," in *Jewish Identity in Modern Art History*, ed. Catherine M. Sousloff (Berkeley, 1999), 41–66; Kalman P. Bland, *The Artless Jew* (Princeton, 2000); and Jacques Picard, "Aphrodite zu Besuch bei Raban Gamaliel: Über Bildverbot, Kunstproduktion und Körperlichkeit," in *Wie schön sind deine Zelte, Jakob, deine Wohnungen, Israel! Beiträge zur Geschichte jüdisch-europäischer Kultur*, ed. Rainer Kampling (Frankfurt, 2009), 79–98.

31. Moshe Halbertal and Avishai Margalit, *Idolatry*, trans. Naomi Goldblum (Cambridge, 1992), 38–66.

32. Mark Rothko, "Statement, 1951," in Ross, *Abstract Expressionism: Creators and Critics*, 172.

33. Oliver Wick, "'Do They Negate Each Other, Modern and Classical?' Mark Rothko, Italy and the Yearning for Tradition," in *Rothko*, ed. Oliver Wick (Milan, 2007), 25.

34. Brian O'Doherty, "The Dark Paintings 1969–1970: Rothko's Endgame," in *The Art of Mark Rothko: Into an Unknown World*, ed. Marc Glimcher (London, 1992), 140.

35. David Anfam, *Mark Rothko: The Works on Canvas* (New Haven, 1998), 86; Anne Seymour, *Beuys, Klein, Rothko: Wandlung und Prophezeiung* (Stuttgart, 1988), 13; and Diane Waldman, "Mark Rothko: The Farther Shore of Art," in *Mark Rothko, 1903–1970: A Retrospective*, ed. Diane Waldman (New York, 1978), 67.

36. Stephanie Rosenthal, ed., *Black Paintings: Robert Rauschenberg, Ad Reinhardt, Mark Rothko, Frank Stella* (Ostfildern, 2006).

37. The exhibition, mounted by the artist and curator Lawrence Gowing, included two Rothkos. See Lawrence Gowing, *Turner: Imagination and Reality* (New York, 1966).

38. Barbara Novak and Brian O'Doherty, "Rothko's Dark Paintings: Tragedy and Void," in *Mark Rothko*, ed. Jeffrey Weiss (Washington, 1998), 279.

39. Baigell, "Jewish-American Art and Artists," 390.

40. Renee Ghert-Zand, "The Jewish Sides of Rothko, Mondrian and Pollock," *The Times of Israel*, July 1, 2013; http://www.timesofisrael.com/the-jewish-sides-of-rothko-mondrian-and-pollock. On the contrary, Annalee Newman insists: "Barnett Newman used titles such as *Zim Zum* as metaphors"; see Annalee Newman, "Barnett Newman and the Kabbalah," in *American Art* 9, no. 1 (1995): 117. See also Christoph Schulte, *Zimzum: Gott und Welturbsprung* (Berlin, 2014), 414–24.

41. Novak and O'Doherty, "Rothko's Dark Paintings," 279.

42. Hermann Cohen, *Religion of Reason: Out of the Sources of Judaism*, trans. Simon Kaplan (Atlanta, 1995), 69.

43. Hannah Arendt, *The Human Condition* (Chicago, 2013), 177. I will not elaborate here on Emanuel Levinas's opposition to this line of thought.

44. Novak and O'Doherty, "Rothko's Dark Paintings," 269.

45. Breslin, *Mark Rothko: A Biography*, 193–95.

46. Gershom Scholem conceived the Creation out of nothing as an expression of the absolute freedom of a Creator capable of establishing an existence that is not Himself; see Gershom Scholem, "Schöpfung aus Nichts und die Selbstverschränkung Gottes," in *Über einige Grundbegriffe des Judentums* (Frankfurt, 1970), 55.

47. It seems no less paradoxical that the symbolic richness we now call "tradition" has only been brought into being by the many subsequent interpretations and reinterpretations of the Creation out of nothing. These include the Midrashim: talmudic stories that require one to draw an imagined boundary between oneself and the work, by means of which the process of reflection and exploration takes place. This applies not only to theology and its exegeses, but also to art and its theories and criticism.

48. Barnett Newman, "The Sublime Is Now," in *Art in Theory, 1900–2000: An Anthology of Changing Ideas*, eds. Charles Harrison and Paul Wood (Malden, 2003), 580–82.

49. Susan J. Barnes, *The Rothko Chapel: An Act of Faith* (Houston, 1989), 126.

50. In addition to Turrell, one might also mention another light artist, the New Yorker Dan Flavin, although his work centers less on light than on the fluorescent lighting tube as an object. Because the light source is always visible in his installations, his pieces are closer to minimal paintings than to Rothko's ephemeral color fields. See Gehring, *Bilder aus Licht*.

28

Elias Canetti (1905–1994)

A DIFFICULT CONTEMPORARY

Galin Tihanov

ELIAS CANETTI'S PLACE IN THE WESTERN CANON SEEMS UNASSAILABLE YET NOT unproblematic. At the heart of this peculiar status is Canetti's own evolution from a high modernism, displaying, especially in *Die Blendung* (1935), some avant-garde features, to a realism that in the decades after World War II looked increasingly out of date and place. Despite recent attempts to recover or discern postmodernist dispositions and techniques in Canetti's *Die Stimmen von Marrakesch* and his three-volume autobiography, these remain works alien to the postmodern spirit of narrative skepticism, nor do they exhibit any affinity with modernist experimentation. Unlike some of his contemporaries, who chose various versions of realism more or less from the start of their careers (Heimito von Doderer with his social realist novels, Ernst Jünger with his at times allegorical realism), Canetti practiced realism *after* his own modernism.[1] There might be a logic to this transition, insofar as he believed that this "modern realism"—understood as more than a bundle of artistic devices—should be the guiding method of contemporary writing. Canetti claimed—not unlike Hermann Broch, who thought the novel to be the art form best suited to communicate the "disintegration of values" (*Wertzerfall*) in the interwar world—that the task of realist literature was to convey the reality of a "split" (*gespaltene*) and no longer homogenous future.[2] Measured by this standard, even *Die Blendung* could be seen as a work with a realist substratum, despite the salient birthmarks of modernism, expressionism, and *neue Sachlichkeit* (New Sobriety) recognizable in its narrative fabric. Be that as it may, Canetti's abandonment of modernism and the avant-garde in favor of realism in the 1960s meant a very conscious self-removal from the contemporary scene of aesthetic innovation, a journey back into the past, coinciding with, and perhaps facilitated by, his determination to retrace his own roots in his autobiography. Not by chance does he repeatedly tell us that his great examples, in terms of style, come from writers poised between the realist and the romantic: Stendhal and Gogol. This elected affinity with aesthetic modes hailing from the nineteenth century chimes with what strikes the reader of today as an unmistakeably conservative outlook. His shunning of the division between the political left and right, of communism and fascism alike, and his unspoken but transparent endorsement of liberal values, at the heart of which is his reexamination and uneasy revalidation of individualism in the face of the seemingly unstoppable growth of mass culture and the utopian charge of living-in-the-crowd, all appear to be an outward manifestation of self-professed neutrality, of timeless wisdom, promoting an underlying and very clear intellectual commitment to a conservative agenda. This fiercely asserted neutrality stands for independence of judgment, for the ability to attain and uphold equilibrium; but it also stands for the perpetuation of a larger set of cultural and social circumstances and a proclivity to uphold the status quo.

Canetti's reputation rests above all on his novel *Die Blendung*, translated into English as *Auto da Fé*,[3] and his essayistic treatise *Crowds and Power* (1960); his autobiographical prose, his essays, and his slender book on Kafka are still a source of fascination for many, while his plays interest solely the specialist. *Die Blendung* ("Blinding" would be the literal translation) is a novel that was written in the early 1930s but remained largely unnoticed until its 1965 republication, when the publication of *Crowds and Power* had already made Canetti visible as an intellectual. The novel has thus often been read retrospectively, under the shadow of the treatise, as a narrative about the complex negotiation of individual (mental) space vis-à-vis a rising tide of vulgarity; of crowd-like instincts; and of roguery, deceit, and encroachment on one's privacy in pursuit of material wealth and power. This, coupled with the undertone of misogyny, so instantly recognizable in the novel, has given rise to accusations of elitism and detachment from reality, even when Canetti clearly documents the untenability of the delusional condition that he refers to as "head without world" (*Ein Kopf ohne Welt*).

Canetti's novel has a deeper cultural subtext that has not yet been heeded or appreciated in sufficient measure, despite the fact that the novel has enjoyed enormous critical attention. *Auto da Fé* is a satire on the humanistic ideals of universalism. It is a counter-Enlightenment novel that punishes the hubris of believing in pure reason and boundless humanity. Unnoticed so far has remained Canetti's subtle mockery of the idea of "world literature" (*Weltliteratur*), a notion coined about half a century before Goethe by Schlözer and Wieland but given currency by the Weimar sage in the final years of his life.[4] Especially relevant here is Schlözer's usage. Having returned from St. Petersburg after a long stay there, August Schlözer (1735–1809)[5] was appointed Professor of Russian literature and history at Göttingen (1769). It was while holding this Chair that Schlözer, whose spectacular—from today's perspective—range of scholarly interests mirrored the common standards of the age, published a volume on Icelandic literature and history (1773), in which he concluded that medieval Icelandic literature was "just as important for the entire world literature" (*für die gesamte Weltliteratur ebenso wichtig*) as the Anglo-Saxon, Irish, Russian, Byzantine, Hebrew, Arabic, and Chinese literatures.[6] Schlözer's notion of "world literature" reflects the Enlightenment's exploratory drive and ambition to expand the pool of available cultural evidence. This entailed inclusion of that which had previously been regarded as peripheral or simply nonextant. The revision of the Eurocentric cultural model that was to become the ultimate—not immediate—outcome of this process underpins our modern idea of "world literature," in which the Western canon is but a constituent part of a larger and much more diverse repertoire.[7]

Enlightenment and Romanticism constituted in this regard a continuum, in which the exotic and unfamiliar gradually populated literature and the arts, often confronting the artist with the question of how to portray difference so that it becomes comprehensible, while retaining its irreducibility to Western cultural norms. Only slightly later than Schlözer, Herder's *Volkslieder*, in the first version of 1778–1779, comprised samples of oral poetry from as far afield as Peru; the second edition, *Stimmen der Völker in Liedern* (1807), extended this curiosity to Madagascar. It is important to realise that the prism through which Schlözer observed the growth of literature was that of the individual peoples of the world: in Schlözer's view, "world literature" is a cumulative, aggregate entity, whose completeness is a matter of augmenting the list of nations whose literatures are represented in the catalogue of cultural wealth. An appreciation of cultural difference, in the collective agency of the people/nation, was thus on the agenda as an extension of the notion of solidarity with an—empirically attestable—wider humanity. But despite all this, Schlözer was less concerned with promoting a dialogue between these literatures, and their dynamic interaction hardly claimed his research ambitions.

Canetti's *Auto da Fé* cannot be grasped outside this framework of a boundless humanity that offers its cultural gifts to the discerning and appreciative European. Not by accident is Peter Kien, the main character in the novel, a sinologist—Chinese literature having been recognized as a constituent part of "world literature" by both Schlözer and Goethe—who tells Eckermann of his delight in reading a Chinese novel. "Keine menschliche Literatur war ihm fremd" ("No branch of human literature was unfamiliar to him," 15): this is how Kien is introduced to the reader early on, with an added remark on his knowledge also of Sanskrit (no doubt a jibe at the Romantic preoccupation with ancient India), Japanese, and the Western European languages. Kien, in other words, is a philologist par excellence, a model scholar of "world literature" in its enticing totality. The fact that he carries "another," invisible library in his head is a confirmation of his internalization of culture. He has not succumbed to the recent fads of superficially praising Japanese and Chinese art, which had been so much a part of European middle-class demeanor since the late nineteenth century; instead, he walks around as a veritable encyclopedia of Chinese and other Eastern cultures, to which he relates with genuine understanding and informed restraint.

And yet Kien himself gives the lie to this humanistic embrace of otherness. "Literature" to him is the sum total of dead manuscripts and old inscriptions rather than the living word of, say, a novel. For Kien, novels furnish pleasure at a prohibitive cost; they "crack open" the otherwise monolithic personalities of their readers by enticing them into sympathizing with characters who hold dear values that may well differ from their own. This turns the novel into a rather dangerous genre, an instrument of unhinging and dislocating the reader from a space of moral certitude into a zone of unfamiliarity, dizziness, and perilous self-reliance. For that reason, just as in Plato's Republic, Kien believes that literature, exemplified in his mind by the novel, should be "prohibited by the state" (37). Canetti thus ultimately parodies the humanistic idea of culture—and the Enlightenment notion of "world literature" as one of its indispensable manifestations.

The novel parodies not just Enlightenment beliefs;[8] it also abounds in subversive references to clichés of Romantic provenance. One little-noticed example is the special attention Canetti pays to the cultural mythology that had accrued around the color blue. In Novalis's famous *Heinrich von Ofterdingen*, blue stands for an ever-receding ideal, a dream as difficult to turn into reality as it is to wake up from. In the 1960s, Anna Seghers in *Das wirkliche Blau* (True blue) gives the color a new semantic aura; it now begins to symbolize the just social order that communist class struggle aspires to, thus translating the Romantic utopia into lived reality. But earlier than Seghers, in the 1930s, Canetti revives the Romantic myth of the color blue with a rather dissonant suggestion of cruelty, menace, and violence. Blue—now degraded from Novalis's ideal realm of longing to the brutality of the everyday—is, to recall, the color of Therese's skirt, which comes back to haunt Kien: "Scarcely has he thus expelled everything blue from the room when the walls begin to dance. Their violent movement dissolves in blue spots. They are skirts, he whispers and creeps under the bed. He had begun to doubt his reason" (362). It is vital to trace in this passage the transformation of blue from an index of serenity into a harbinger of madness. The Romantic is thus resurrected and estranged in the same breath: insanity makes a return conjoined with a swath of misogynist associations attached to blue. That Canetti must have had in mind precisely the Romantic genealogy of blue as a zone of longing and unreachable perfection transpires in a later passage, in the penultimate section of the novel, where blue is stigmatized as "the colour of the uncritical, the credulous, the believers" (420); ironically, Kien himself is an example of this attitude, blinded as he is by his dedication to a world of knowledge detached from reality.

These are not the only parodic gestures in *Auto da Fé*. The novel is equally poised between asserting and undermining the tenets of the European avant-garde. Cultural memory looms large as a central theme in the novel; Peter Kien and his library are indeed cast as repositories of cultural capital, knowledge, and tradition. At the same time, in the spirit of the German *neue Sachlichkeit* (New Sobriety), the novel confronts the reader with a coldly detailed and fascinatingly grotesque examination of the relationship between knowledge and life, culture and the everyday. The lofty and the quotidian clash in a novelistic composition built on the tension between a "head without a world" and a "headless world." *Auto da Fé* is a novel about the failing mediation between these two conditions; it thrives on an unmistakably parodic radicalization of the avant-garde directive to reject cultural tradition. Kien, as if following Marinetti's call to burn down and do away with libraries and museums, sets his prized book collection on fire. But in a significant departure from the Futurist recipe for cultural rejuvenation, in which Marinetti envisaged the destruction of museums and libraries as a release of creative energy previously suffocated by the baggage of tradition, Kien's decision to set on fire his own library—and also himself—is a confirmation of the elitist cultural ethos of High Modernism, now filtered through loud Nietzschean laughter. Kien burns his books so that they don't fall into his brother's hands (recognizable here is Kien's paranoia of suspecting everybody, including his brother, of seeking to "extract a will" or to simply lay hands on his greatest asset). With this, Kien reasserts himself as a relentless believer in high culture, a hero who manages to save his books from becoming the property of an unenlightened bourgeois. This sacrificial gesture allows him to reoccupy center stage as a defender of, and humble servant to, tradition (against Futurism's calls to throw away tradition). By negating himself as an individual, he attains radical self-fulfillment as the guardian of a threatened cultural status quo (against Futurism's calls for radical innovation).

To appreciate the depth and subtlety of *Auto da Fé*, we must see it in the context of Canetti's renewal of, and challenge to, the Central European Jewish literary patrimony, especially the work of Kafka. Canetti has often acknowledged his fascination with Kafka (in his essayistic work and also in his little book of 1969, *Der andere Prozess*, translated into English as *Kafka's Other Trial: The Letters to Felice*, 1974), but nowhere so vividly as in his novel. Beneath the surface, *Auto da Fé* is a novel about metamorphosis and transmutation. George, Peter Kien's brother and a famed psychiatrist, lives through a Kafkaesque moment when he observes one of his patients: "he saw himself as an insect in the presence of a man" (369). What is more, the doctor is said to be in possession of a very special power: he can change his patient back from his adopted persona (a gorilla in this case) into the disinherited brother of a banker (370). The theme of metamorphosis, more often than not tragically colored, runs through the entire novel; George Kien is just as much enveloped in this discourse as is Fischerle. Yet Canetti gives this journey of transformation a different spin. Unlike Kafka, he is not interested in the labyrinth of institutions that instill in us quiet despondency vis-à-vis the impenetrable machinery of authority. Canetti's sovereign territory is the absurd—not the absurd that flows through the invisible channels of institutional authority but rather the absurd that is begotten in the fold of failed interpersonal communication. *Auto da Fé* is riddled with (sometimes hilarious) misunderstandings that attribute to the other features he or she does not possess. Canetti, who believed that Kafka never surpassed *The Metamorphosis* (so "great and perfect" was this work of poetic imagination),[9] has himself written a novel of metamorphosis: desired and imagined, yet misrecognized and ultimately failed. Peter and Therese constantly misrepresent and misrecognize each other. Peter, readers of the novel will recall, begins to envision his own self as having mutated from scholar to murderer. Fischerle, equally, dreams himself into the glory of a world chess champion, to mention just one of his many imagined transformations. The world Canetti's protagonists inhabit is a figment of their displaced consciousness; most of the time they misread their environment and their fellow human beings. Peter Kien, in particular, attributes to Therese, Fischerle, and just about anyone else he encounters (but not to his brother) gallantry and honorable intentions. Kafka is here met by Cervantes, in a great modern story of fantasized but frustrated metamorphosis, and of chivalry—grotesque, cruel, and residually romantic at the same time (witness the noble battles Kien wages to protect his books, and his insane philanthropic gestures).

Canetti is sometimes accused of endowing Peter Kien with misogynist features. This remains an uncomfortable reality, but I believe one could make sense of it precisely in the context of Canetti's appreciation of Kafka. "Of all writers," Canetti maintained, "Kafka is the greatest expert on power" (*Kafka's Other Trial*, 80). For Canetti, "fear of a superior power is central to Kafka"; the mode of resistance to such a power is "transformation into something small." Reinterpreting Kafka's novella against the grain of its own plot (in which Gregor Samsa faces the monstrosity of his metamorphosis into a large insect-like creature), Canetti restores smallness as a technique of "removing oneself" from the potential consequences, or temptations, of power: "[o]ne becomes very small, or one changes oneself into an insect" (*Kafka's Other Trial*, 35)—"smaller, quieter, lighter, until one disappears" (*Kafka's Other Trial*, 36). Marriage, however, is not an auspicious institution in this respect. No situation, Canetti concludes, is less favorable to this "withdrawal," to the voluntary removal and thus also to resistance to the effects and seductions of power—through becoming "very small"—than marriage: "One must always be there, whether one wants it or not, for part of the day and part of the night—one's own magnitude corresponding to that of one's partner, a magnitude which may not change; otherwise it would be no marriage at all" (*Kafka's Other Trial*, 35). Even if there were some room for smallness in marriage, it is "usurped by the children," whose upbringing requires multiple employments of power and manifestations of authority. We should recall at this point that Kien's aversion to Therese develops within their marriage. It is the institution of marriage that confronts him with the horror of being constantly prevented from living his previous life of *withdrawal* from reality, and thus also of *evasion* of power. Before Foucault, Canetti weaves together power and sexuality and examines them in the framework of a marriage that divides rather than unites the protagonists. It is through marriage that Kien is thrown into the field of power that he had been evading so successfully in his earlier life (or so he imagined). And it is in marriage that Therese's appetite for power—financial and sexual—grows in a way irreconcilable with Kien's own philosophy of life.

It is again with reference to Kafka that I suggest we could attain a more nuanced understanding of Canetti's choice to cast Peter Kien as a sinologist. The mockery of the idea of "world literature" is an important pointer, but there appears to be more behind Canetti's decision. In Chinese philosophy (a lifelong fascination for Canetti) he discovered an apposite parallel to Kafka's art of "transformation" into "something small" (*Kafka's Other Trial*, 89), of disappearance into self-imposed insignificance as resistance to, or evasion of, power. In this sense Kafka, Canetti asserted unhesitatingly, was "the only writer of the Western world who is essentially Chinese" (*Kafka's Other Trial*, 94). Canetti invoked his conversations in London with Arthur Waley, the self-taught Orientalist and translator of *Monkey*, Chinese poetry, and the Confucian classics, as confirmation of his opinion. But the killer proof seems to have come from a passage in a postcard Kafka sent to Felice from Marienbad in which he avowed: "indeed I am a Chinese" (quoted in *Kafka's Other Trial*, 97), with all the ramifications of such a statement that Canetti then chose to read into Kafka's brief text: "[s]ilence and emptiness . . . receptivity of everything animate and inanimate—these are reminiscent of Taoism and of a Chinese landscape" (*Kafka's Other Trial*, 98).

Chinese philosophy and culture in Canetti's novel should not be taken at face value: Canetti deliberately skewed, misread, and manipulated his sources,[10] but the end result was a caricatured emblem of cultural harmony and a deliberately debased ideal of "world literature," emptied, as we have seen, of its core notion of diversity and difference. Part and parcel of this parodying of "world literature" is the very motif of the "battle of the books," a topos in European literatures that goes back to Cervantes and Swift.[11] Revealingly, in order to enhance their endurance in the new "war" regime, Kien reorders his books with their spines turned to the wall, introducing anonymity and obliterating any trace of difference. The novel, then, is a celebration not of the uniqueness of singular cultures, nor indeed of their supposed interaction; rather it is a reconfirmation of skepticism vis-à-vis the very possibility of cultural dialogue.

The idea of transformation (*Verwandlung*) is also the cornerstone of Canetti's other major book, *Crowds and Power* (*Masse und Macht*, 1960). Often accused of not engaging with Marx, Freud, and other trendsetters in analyzing power, Canetti would rebuff his critics by pointing to the need to dehistoricize and depsychologize the way we think about power. Freud would come under particularly persistent attack in Canetti's later interviews, for Freud's psychoanalysis was based on the recognition of the death drive, something Canetti never accepted. In fact, Canetti's entire theory of power rests on the opposite instinct: the survival instinct that underwrites domination and transforms the survivor into someone who accumulates and seeks to augment his power by rejoicing and celebrating the survival of an ever-increasing number of people. Totalitarian regimes, Canetti believes, are born out of the allure of survival, taken to the extreme by fallible human individuals whose ambition in life is to walk over a sea of dead bodies—of humans survived by them.[12] War, therefore, is the most manifest and efficient instrument of power; it endorses and actualizes the ability of power-holders to send others to their death and survive them.

Canetti's treatise is a very uneasy mixture of a phenomenological, timeless approach to power (that has enraged many, especially on the political left) and an equally rich and intriguing hypothesis that seems to anchor power—and especially the rise of totalitarianism—in the vicissitudes of German history. Although he often had to confront the skepticism of those who believed (not always without reason) that his narrative was strangely sanguine vis-à-vis the disasters of Nazism and World War II, Canetti does offer his version of the events that indelibly marked twentieth-century history. Versailles and the prohibition of universal military service in Germany are seen as "the *birth* of National Socialism" (212).[13] Begotten in the days of August 1914 and sealed through the Treaty of Versailles (211), National Socialism offered a substitute for the missing opportunity to participate in that archetypal German crowd formation, the army: "Every single German could become a National Socialist. He was probably even more anxious to become one if he had not been a soldier before, because, by doing so, he achieved participation in activities hitherto denied him" (212). The problem with all this is that a specific, in Canetti's view, crowd formation (the army) is indeed seen in an archetypal light, largely lifted beyond the historical framework of economic, political, and ideological factors. Earlier in his book, Canetti produces a telling parallel between the army and the forest as emblems of German mass identity: "The crowd symbol of the Germans was the *army*. But the army was more than just the army; it was the *marching forest*. In no other modern country has the forest-feeling remained as alive as it has in Germany. The parallel rigidity of the upright trees and their density and number fill the heart of the German with a deep and mysterious delight. To this day he loves to go deep into the forest where his forefathers lived; he feels at one with the trees. . . . For the German, without his being clearly aware of it, army and forest transfused each other in every possible way. . . . He took the rigidity and straightness of trees for his own law" (202). Canetti's take, then, is a strange amalgamation of historical interpretation (Versailles) and archetypal symbolism; for the latter, he seems indebted to a long tradition of conservative German glorification of the forest (often of postromantic provenance), which one finds in Werner Sombart and, with growing frequency, throughout the 1930s. In his 1903 book *Die deutsche Volkswirtschaft im neunzehnten Jahrhundert*, Sombart, foreshadowing Heidegger's much later essay "Why Do We Remain in the Provinces?," indulges in painting a picture that doubles on some unmistakably Romantic motifs that survive in Canetti's treatise: "The old German culture as it was still basically maintained in the beginning of the nineteenth century had actually derived from this ideal of a forest; the murmuring brook, the rustling oak tree are synonymous with the German soul, which in those very days when our imagination travels through the German countryside created the romantic notion of the magic *blaue Blume* [blue flower]. The sensitive, the fragile, the feelings of dread, the deep sentimental disposition and whatever else differentiates the Germans from all other nations: Its primary cause lies in the forest, in the untended wild grown forest, where the birds sang in the bushes during springtime, where fog moved across clearings in the fall."[14]

The symbol of the forest is not Canetti's only debt to the political discourse of German conservatism. In his taxonomy of the "double crowd," one of the axes of differentiation is that between "friend and foe" (73), no doubt a clear, if silent, reference to Carl Schmitt's (in)famous theory of the political in his *Der Begriff des Politischen*. A further trace of this conservative discourse is Canetti's distinction between the crowds of the living and the invisible crowds of the dead (73); here he reproduces Edmund Burke's and, in Germany, Adam Müller's well-known definition of the nation as a bond between the dead, the living, and those yet to come. Canetti does not expand on this in the book, but in a later conversation with Rupprecht Slavko Baur (May 1971) he offers an insightful elaboration. In the past, Canetti submits, the reign of the great world religions meant that our existence was largely regulated by the invisible mass of the dead, the ever-growing sea of predecessors that governed the affective economy of our lives. But today we live in a new, "peculiar condition" where the notion of posterity, the power of those yet to be born, begins to co-shape the present. This historical distinction is, in a move typical of Canetti's treatise, swiftly eroded by claiming that the invisible mass of the dead and that of the still unborn are potent factors that have always been at work simultaneously in every human being. From here, Canetti swerves again to offer a broad-brush typology of ideologies: in nationalism, he avers, decisive is the sense of the invisible multitude of the dead—we live by the example of our forefathers (the "fatherland" is the land of our *fathers*), our lives are regulated by the force of tradition and duty, not least to their memory. In socialism, on the contrary, the emphasis is on the invisible cohort of those yet to be born: the notion of sacrifice in the name of a brighter future rules life under socialism. There should then be historical constellations in which the two ideologies, resting as they do on the ever coexisting "nuclear sentiments" (*Kerngefühle*) associated with the invisible crowd of the dead and with that of the still unborn, could grow together to form a whole.[15] This is Canetti's breathtakingly speculative hypothesis of how National Socialism became possible in the first place. Canetti here joins his illustrious contemporary Hannah Arendt in essaying to understand totalitarianism and National Socialism. Unlike Arendt, he has little to say about the deterioration of the traditional nation-state as the guarantor of rights, which leads to the characteristic disregard for humanity displayed by totalitarianism. Canetti seems to interpret totalitarianism as a symptom of the self-imposed malaise of democracy.

In *Masse und Macht* (221) he disparagingly talks of parliamentary life as a crowd phenomenon, in which the crowd has descended into a quasi-war confrontation without real peril, and thus also without real stake (this itself is a recurring theme in the Weimar conservative political discourse, not least Carl Schmitt's). Whatever the diagnosis he opts for, the simultaneous affective mobilization of the past and the future, which Canetti points to, can indeed be attested in the ideology of National Socialism. He also appears to be right when singling out the flexibility of this ideology: "through shifting emphasis," nationalism and socialism alternate in strength and prominence as the master components of this baleful ideology.

Canetti's treatise, as already mentioned, has attracted significant criticism over the years (Adorno comes to mind among Canetti's distinguished contemporaries),[16] yet it continues to exude a beguiling sense of breadth and visionary suggestiveness. Sometimes its recipes for social amelioration sound naïve. In an interview with Karl Diemer from 1973 Canetti recommends, for example, echoing Marx's critique of the division of labor (but without acknowledging Marxism; Canetti always sought to distance himself from it), that in order for power to be distributed more evenly and for hierarchy to be dispersed and softened, we all have to embrace different professions, leaving behind the habit of concentrating on, and excelling in, a single occupation. Canetti himself believes this to be a revolutionary thought "that turns the world upside down" (*weltumstürzender Gedanke*).[17] Nor can Canetti be trusted in his anthropological posture; after all, what he does throughout the book is to marshal secondhand evidence, garnered from other writers' accounts of events. As Ritchie Robertson has noted, Canetti works with a strained combination of "culturalist and biologistic models,"[18] plausible at times, incongruous at others. What consolidates and holds together his narrative of power is a thick layer of relentlessly recurring representations of frozen habitus, torn away from the realities of an evolving and striving society steeped in historically locatable antagonisms.

But it is often precisely this representation of timeless habitus distilled from a stupendous mass of anthropological and religious sources that invites the reader to follow Canetti's "basic idea" (*Grundeinfall*), the condition sine qua non, in his words, for a successful drama, novel, or essay. That "basic idea" in the case of *Crowds and Power* is the identification of the fundamental fear of being touched, which the mode of being offered by the crowd overcomes. The crowd is here cast in a utopian light (Canetti is certainly also aware of its menacing potential). It produces equality by erasing boundaries and effacing hierarchies: "A head is a head, an arm is an arm, and differences between individual heads and arms are irrelevant. It is for the sake of this equality that people become a crowd and they tend to overlook anything which might detract from it" (32). Most importantly, the new communal body engendered by the crowd begets courage rather than apprehension: "Suddenly it is as though everything were happening in one and the same body. . . . The more fiercely people press together, the more certain they feel that they do not fear each other" (16). This "reversal" of fear is one of the great themes of *Crowds and Power*. Canetti is, of course, alert to the danger that the "discharge" of the crowd could be replaced once more by inequality and hierarchy; the remedy he envisages in order for the moment of bliss to persist is *repetition* (18) through growth: "the crowd always wants to grow" (32). Unbeknownst to Canetti, in the 1940s and 1950s another thinker, the

Russian Mikhail Bakhtin, in his ideologically controversial book on Rabelais, was celebrating the power of the communal body to grow and surmount "cosmic fear" through grotesque acts of discharge.[19] Like Canetti, Bakhtin analyzes the collective body, whose identity is shaped not by drawing a boundary between the self and the other but through the experience of transgressive togetherness. Significantly, laughter and eating are vital topoi in both Canetti's and Bakhtin's narratives of collective bodily courage. The whole of the Rabelais book is centered on those human features that, while exclusively human, manifest themselves without tragically separating humans from the totality of the universe. For Bakhtin it is the laughing human body that becomes the emblem of this longed-for harmony between culture and nature.

What really matters in all this is the fact that both Canetti and Bakhtin, through their portrayal of the communal body of the crowd (or the "people," in Bakhtin's case), abandon the classic humanistic notion of man, celebrating instead the basic functions of the body that make it indiscernible among other bodies. The deeper man sinks into the abyss of the organic, the brighter the redemptive star of utopia shines above him; deprived of individual dignity, he appears to be granted in exchange a guarantee that his every breath and every strain of his muscles will inevitably produce culture and freedom in the warm embrace of community. In this respect, *Crowds and Power* is diametrically opposed to *Auto da Fé*: the utopia of life in the crowd, before it descends into the dystopia of anarchy and aggression, is the ultimate rebuttal of Kien's elevated (and intensely tested) sense of individuality, which appears to survive, time after time, the multiple trials of deindividualization in his encounters with the world outside.

All this seems to be suggestive of the wider significance of the grotesque in Canetti, both in *Crowds and Power* and in his novel. For Canetti the grotesque is not just an aesthetic category; it is a more encompassing mode of conceiving and interpreting the world. The grotesque becomes for him a vantage point from which a different version of humanism arises, a humanism that is no longer bound to a belief in the individual (pace *Auto da Fé*) and is no longer underpinned by an embrace and promotion of the virtues of measure, proportion, or reason (which *Auto da Fé* has also destabilized and critiqued). This is a humanism that manages to incorporate and process in the same breath not just the utopian but also the "darker side" of humanity,[20] the aggressive and unpredictable modes of action characteristic of the crowd. The grotesque, in other words, sponsors in Canetti a humanism without subjectivity (or at least without subjectivity understood in the classic identitarian sense). This is an odd humanism, decentered, cold, revolving not necessarily around the individual but rather around the generic abilities of the human species to resist and endure in the face of cataclysms. Canetti is among the most gifted and persuasive exponents in the twentieth century of that particular strain of humanism without unqualified belief in the individual human being at its core, a distant cosmic love for humanity as the greatest survivor. This new brand of decentered, indeed dislocated, humanism without subjectivity is what aligns Canetti with Ernst Jünger. In their later work, they both exhibit a factual, empirical fascination with nature and biology underpinning an abiding curiosity for the elusive metaphysics of human existence. Jünger's fascination with butterflies (shared by Nabokov, another exponent of what I have termed "dislocated humanism"), and Canetti's excitement over the invisible crowd of the devils imagined as *bacilli* (53), are highly suggestive of this new epistemology of the human in their work.

In both *Crowds and Power* and *Auto da Fé*, Canetti offers his responses, sometimes tantalizingly and only obliquely, to modernity and some of its underlying problems and defining crises.[21] His reflections on Jewishness, too, have to be interpreted as a facet of this sustained, if not always direct, engagement with modernity. In *Crowds and Power*, Canetti avails himself of the stereotypical image of Jews as resilient wanderers. He attempts to explain the fate of the Jewish people in Nazi Germany by establishing a controversial link between inflation and antisemitism. In this passage of *Crowds and Power* Canetti is at his most acute as a critic of Nazism. His explanation is, however, open to objections: "In its treatment of the Jews National Socialism repeated the process of inflation with great precision. First they were attacked as wicked and dangerous, as enemies; then they were more and more depreciated; then, there not being enough in Germany itself, those in the conquered territories were gathered in; and finally they were treated literally as vermin, to be destroyed with impunity by the million" (219–220). The claim that antisemitism and the extermination of the Jews was a mere replication of inflation as a "crowd experience" (220), shifted onto the Jews, appears to be mired in psychologism and to neglect the historical dynamics of antisemitism after 1933; it also verges on naturalizing antisemitism as a healing strategy—admittedly the wrong one—which assists the recuperation of a nation that had been collectively traumatized by the experience of inflation. Of course, it would be implausible, nay absurd, to see in Canetti an intellectual who seeks to extenuate or blur the evils of antisemitism by insisting on understanding them. Canetti has given ample evidence, not least in his autobiography, especially in its first volume, *The Tongue Set Free*, of his deep-rootedness in Jewish culture. His daring to write of Jewishness in a way that at times mobilizes parodic energies and subversiveness—to the point where even his explanations of antisemitism become potentially insightful and precariously flippant at the same time—stems, it seems to me, from his resolve to probe into inherited (and uncontested) claims to cultural identity, all the way to the logical conclusion of their dissolution. To understand this daring, we also need to keep in mind the fact that Canetti gained his first direct experience of antisemitism relatively late, only in Vienna (which he recollects in *The Tongue Set Free*), after the formative years of what he remembered to be a rather comfortable childhood in Ruschuk (now Rousse) and the difficult but still safe time he spent in Manchester. Born in Ruschuk to a family of Sephardic Jews who had been settled there at least since 1869,[22] in his autobiography Canetti glorifies the town as a place of genuine multiculturalism, of easy interaction between various ethnic groups and mutual curiosity. After the liberation of Bulgaria from Ottoman rule (1878), Ruschuk became the site of the first cinema screening, and the first Bulgarian bank and insurance company were set up there. The Danube connects the town to Central Europe, upriver to Budapest and Vienna, the city on which Ruschuk liked to model itself architecturally (all differences in scale considered). Ruschuk offered Canetti a space for observation in which he registered the daily encounters between Balkan and Central European manners, tastes, and aspirations. Pictured by Canetti as a paradise on earth, Ruschuk did not arouse mystical longings or feverish visions of social justice and restored Jewish pride; as Dagmar Lorenz incisively remarks, the experience of Hasidic Jews, Jewish Socialists, or Zionists is nowhere to be found in Canetti's writings.[23] Canetti returned to Ruschuk only once after that, in the summer of 1924, as if to take stock of his own life so far: "anything I subsequently experienced had already happened in Ruschuk."[24]

Note, in this context, the way in which Canetti talks about language. Ruschuk afforded the very young Canetti a glimpse into a polyglot environment marked by the effortless coexistence of Bulgarians, Jews, Turks, Greeks, Albanians, Armenians, Romanians, Russians, Gypsies: "on any one day you could hear seven or eight languages."[25] This plurality of languages will have material consequences for the mature Canetti. German, his language as a writer, is only his fourth language, after Ladino (the language of the family in Ruschuk), Bulgarian (the language of the servants and of the children he plays with), and English (the language he learns as a boy in Manchester). German is not presented by Canetti as an identity marker, certainly not in the sense of group identity; even in exile in England, Canetti continues to write in German, thus signaling his determination not to be seen as just another (German-) Jewish exile who has abandoned the language of Hitler. Instead of being a badge of identity, for Canetti German is, above all, a secret, a language spoken initially by his parents when they wanted to communicate without being understood by the children. Thus language is not a way of assuming and solidifying an identity, it is a way of partaking of a secret, to which one needs to be admitted (not least as a precondition of becoming a writer). What is more, the acquisition of German is portrayed as a particularly painful process: "it was a belated mother tongue, implanted in true pain."[26] That pain is then followed by happiness and bliss, but the constitutive feature of this entire process is denaturalization (by experiencing intense pain) through language. This estrangement (denaturalization) through language is at the heart of Canetti's cosmopolitanism; it is the reason why—while living as a writer exclusively in the cosmos of the German language—Canetti is never indifferent to the prospect of a thriving rather than failing polyglossia. He is ambivalently poised in relation to this old dream: sometimes extolling it (in his autobiography), sometimes interpreting it skeptically, even ironically (in his novel). *The Tower of Babel* (by which title his novel was translated into French, and also in the first American edition) is doomed in Canetti's narrative not as much as a project of polyglossia, but rather as a project of heteroglossia: it is the different discourses within a seemingly single yet socially stratified and irreconcilably divided language that are bound to remain in a state of mutual isolation and hostility. If anything, it is heteroglossia—the linguistic condition of modernity with its relentless social differentiation—that corrodes the entire edifice of polyglossia: the Tower of Babel crumbles not because it cannot be constructed within an individual (Kien has successfully mastered a stupendous number of languages and all branches of "human literature"), but because individuals find it impossible to communicate with one another in what is meant to be their only (and shared) language (German, in the case of the novel).

The novel starts on an optimistic note: the young Frantz Metzger, innocent, smart, and open to the world, wants to travel to India and China, mentioning with bated breath, and secret hope, the Great Wall of China that no one yet seems able to climb over. A journey is about to begin that should push back boundaries and cross cultural frontiers as a matter of course. Yet this beautiful start is frustrated by mistrust on the part of Kien (including later considerations of class and social status),[27] who in turn is mistrusted and misunderstood by others in the novel. The

Great Chinese Wall between the characters never disappears. One wonders whether its mention at the beginning is not another open reference to Kafka, whose allegory of universal discourse and its intrinsic difficulties permeates his story "The Great Wall of China" (published posthumously in 1931, just a few years before the publication of Canetti's novel). Kafka, we recall, insisted on the Wall being a necessary foundation for the Tower of Babel; he welcomed the redeeming power of the fragmentary (the Wall is never completely built in his story), which enables a salutary notion of totality without totalitarian implications.

When discussing Canetti's attitude to Jewishness, and to cultural identity more generally, we should also think of the way in which Canetti refers to himself in the many speeches of gratitude during his long career: he never talks of himself as an Austrian, German, English, Swiss, or even Jewish writer; rather, he consistently chooses to describe himself according to the city whose culture he shares: a citizen of Vienna, of London, Zurich, Berlin. On his chair in the hall of the Nobel laureates, no country name appears: only the name of Rousse, his native town.[28] It is this refusal of identification through race or nation that puts to the test his ability to discern in the Holocaust, especially against the monumentally timeless backdrop he elects to operate with in *Crowds and Power*, a unique event. (A reference to the collective traumas of another nation would not do here: as we have seen, Canetti's own attempt to discuss the Holocaust in *Crowds and Power* in terms of national identities and national crises [German inflation and the consequent infliction of diminishment and suffering upon the Jews] failed.) Nowhere is Canetti's deep probing of Jewishness as a frozen label of identity more captivating, disturbing, and irreducibly complex than in his novel. Fischerle, the hunchback Jew, is depicted as repulsive rather than attractive; the parodic tone is here unmistakable. But at the same time he is portrayed as an epitome of vigor and energy, and as a dreamer. Oscillating between a case of Jewish self-hatred and a glorification of Jewish resilience, Fischerle is a wonderful example of Canetti's ultimate determination to retain a playful distance from any notion of identity (to confuse things further and introduce another parodic demobilization of identity, Fischerle erroneously takes Kien for a Jew).

Canetti thus emerges as our contemporary, albeit a difficult one: he hovers between cultural individualism and fascination with the life of the crowd; he is caustic, noncommittal, refusing to be bound by identity-based thinking, forever determined to interrogate sacrosanct categories of belonging, declining the comfort of established ideologies (be it Socialism or Zionism). And at the same time he is wryly humanist in his inimitably grotesque and intensely dislocated manner, a writer at the close of High Modernism who begins to lift the curtain that reveals the ordeals of our own age.

Notes

1. On the "return" of realism in the midst of, and after, European modernism, see Devin Fore, *Realism after Modernism* (Cambridge, 2012).

2. See Canetti's essay "Realismus und neue Wirklichkeit" (1965), in Canetti, *Das Gewissen der Worte* (Munich and Vienna, 1975), 66–71.

3. References are to the English translation, *Auto da Fé* (London, 1981), with page numbers supplied in parentheses in the main text.

4. On this, see Galin Tihanov, "Cosmopolitanism in the Discursive Landscape of Modernity: Two Enlightenment Articulations," in *Enlightenment Cosmopolitanism*, eds. David Adams and Galin Tihanov (London, 2011), 133–52, esp. 142–43.

5. On Schlözer's life and career, see most recently Martin Peters, *Altes Reich und Europa: Der Historiker, Statistiker und Publizist August Ludwig (v.) Schlözer (1735—1809)* (Münster, 2003).

6. The quote is from Wolfgang Schamoni, "'Weltliteratur'—zuerst 1773 bei August Ludwig Schlözer," *Arcadia* 43, no. 2 (2008): 288–98, here 289; it was first adduced in Sigmund von Lempicki, *Geschichte der deutschen Literaturwissenschaft bis zum Ende des 18. Jahrhunderts* (1920; Göttingen, 1968), 418.

7. On current debates around the meaning of "world literature," see especially David Damrosch, *What Is World Literature?* (Princeton, 2003); John Pizer, *The Idea of World Literature* (Baton Rouge, 2006); Dieter Lamping, *Die Idee der Weltliteratur: Ein Konzept Goethes und seine Karriere* (Stuttgart, 2010); and Franco Moretti's influential articles collected in his *Distant Reading* (London, 2013). See also Elke Sturm-Trigonakis, *Global playing in der Literatur: Ein Versuch über die neue Weltliteratur* (Würzburg, 2007); Alfons K. Knauth, "Weltliteratur: Von der Mehrsprachigkeit zur Mischsprachigkeit," in *Literatur und Vielsprachigkeit*, ed. Monika Schmitz-Emans (Heidelberg, 2004), 81–110; and Ottmar Ette, *Literature on the Move* (Amsterdam, 2003; the German original was published in 2001 under the title *Literatur in Bewegung: Raum und Dynamik grenzüberschreitenden Schreibens in Europa und Amerika*). For a stimulating account that still foregrounds a residually Eurocentric model, see Pascale Casanova, *The World Republic of Letters* (Cambridge and London, 2004; French ed. 1999). For a recent critique of "world literature," see Emily Apter, *Against World Literature* (London, 2013). For an intervention that builds on Damrosch, Moretti, Casanova, and others, but also attempts to go further, see Alexander Beecroft, *An Ecology of World Literature: From Antiquity to the Present Day* (London, 2015).

8. On Canetti's implicit dialogue with Western philosophy in *Die Blendung*, see especially Katrin Schneider, *Viele Philosophen sind des Dichters Tod: Elias Canettis "Die Blendung" und die abendländische Philosophie* (Heidelberg, 2010).

9. Elias Canetti, *Kafka's Other Trial* (London, 1974), 20.

10. See Chunjie Zhang, "Social Disintegration and Chinese Culture: The Reception of China in *Die Blendung*," in *The Worlds of Elias Canetti: Centenary Essays*, eds. William Colling Donahue and Julian Price (Newcastle, 2007), 127–49, here 148–49. For more on China in Canetti's novel, see Alexander Košenina, "'Buchstabenschnüffeleien' eines Sinologen: China-Motive in Elias Canettis Gelehrtensatire *Die Blendung*," *Orbis Litterarum* 53 (1998): 231–51 (with a good bibliography of earlier scholarship).

11. On this, see Achim Hölter, *Die Bücherschlacht: Ein satirisches Konzept in der europäischen Literatur* (Bielefeld, 1995).

12. See in this respect Canetti's attempt to explain Hitler as a phenomenon of power and survival, in "Hitler, nach Speer" (1971), in Elias Canetti, *Das Gewissen der Worte* (Munich and Vienna, 1975), 163–89, esp. 172–74.

13. All references, with page numbers in parentheses, are to Elias Canetti, *Crowds and Power*, trans. Carol Stewart (London, 1981).

14. Werner Sombart, *Economic Life in the Modern Age*, eds. Nico Stehr and Reiner Grundmann (New Brunswick, NJ, 2001), 195–96.

15. Elias Canetti, *Aufsätze, Reden, Gespräche* (Munich and Vienna, 2005), 275.

16. See his conversation with Canetti of March 1962, in which Adorno seeks to confront Canetti on his disturbing lack of interest in history and to warn him that images and notions of reality (rather than reality itself) are insufficiently solid ground on which to build theories (cf. Canetti, *Aufsätze, Reden, Gespräche*, 140–63).

17. Canetti, *Aufsätze, Reden, Gespräche*, 296–97.

18. Ritchie Robertson, "Canetti and Violence," in *The Worlds of Elias Canetti: Centenary Essays*, eds. William Colling Donahue and Julian Price (Newcastle, 2007), 211–24, here 224.

19. Mikhail Bakhtin, *Rabelais and His World*, trans. Helene Iswolsky (Bloomington, 1984).

20. I paraphrase here the titles of Walter Mignolo's well-known books *The Darker Side of the Renaissance* (1994) and *The Darker Side of Western Modernity* (2011).

21. Michael Mack, for example, has read *Crowds and Power* as a response to the Holocaust; see Michael Mack, *Anthropology as Memory: Elias Canetti's and Franz Baermann Steiner's Responses to the Shoah* (Tübingen, 2001).

22. Penka Angelova and Veselina Antonova, "Die Geburtsstadt von Elias Canetti," in *Elias Canetti, 1905–2005, der Ohrenzeuge des Jahrhunderts*, ed. Penka Angelova (Rousse, 2006).

23. Dagmar Lorenz, "Introduction," in *A Companion to the Works of Elias Canetti*, ed. Dagmar Lorenz (Rochester and New York, 2004), 1–21, here 5.

24. Elias Canetti, *The Tongue Set Free*, trans. Joachim Neugroschel (London, 1979), 4.

25. Ibid.

26. Ibid., 70.

27. Dagmar Lorenz has pointed out that throughout Canetti's writing, beginning with *Die Blendung*, "Austrian dialect as well as Yiddish-accented German, both associated with the lower classes and popular culture, are used in a derogatory manner and ascribed to more or less despicable characters" (Lorenz, "Introduction," 4).

28. Svoboda Alexandra Dimitrova and Penka Angelova, "Canetti, Roustchouk, and Bulgaria: The Impact of Origin on Canetti's Work," in *A Companion to the Works of Elias Canetti*, ed. Dagmar Lorenz (Rochester and New York, 2004), 261–87, here 275.

29

Emmanuel Levinas (1905–1995)

TRADITION AND ITS OTHER

Raphael Zagury-Orly

ALONG WITH THE NUMEROUS ENCOUNTERS BETWEEN JEWISH THOUGHT AND philosophy—one can think here of the relation between Aristotle's philosophy and Judaism in Maimonides, between the eighteenth-century European Enlightenment and the Haskalah, between critical philosophy in Kant and Jewish ethics and religious thought in Hermann Cohen, and so on—Emmanuel Levinas inaugurated a new relation and another encounter. After all, until Levinas, philosophers, and consequently Jewish philosophers, have always conformed to synthesizing strategies in order to grasp the relation between Judaism and philosophy: either by including the Judaic revelation in the deployment of philosophical universality; by subjugating philosophical rationality to a Judaic revelation; or, again, by simply maintaining their mutual exclusion. Levinas seeks to think otherwise on the tradition of both philosophy and Judaism by consequently awakening them to their "unthought" and "unsuspected" relation, offering for both their utmost possibility.

This new relation between Judaism and philosophy is steeped in Levinas's longstanding critical debate with phenomenology. It is thus through phenomenology that Levinas perceived a radically new approach to Judaism and consequently to the relation between Judaism and philosophy. Before explicating the many nuances and intricacies of Levinas's understanding of phenomenology and the renewal it reveals of Judaism, and how this understanding redefines entirely the relation between Judaism and philosophy, it is important to mark the meaning of both phenomenology and Judaism in Levinas's writing. One need only examine Levinas's extensive bibliography to validate this point. Indeed, Levinas published canonical texts that belong to the phenomenological/philosophical tradition and offered numerous commentaries and studies, widely known as the *Talmudic Readings*, of Jewish thought. Although these seem to form two distinct and separate canons within Levinas's writing—and although he himself, on many occasions, distinguished his phenomenological/philosophical writings from his talmudic commentaries[1]—they in fact incessantly call to one another, request and require each other, or, to use a Levinasian concept, "desire" each other. Hence, any comprehensive understanding of Levinas's thought necessarily requires an interpretation of the signification, the development, and the deployment of this relationship for this thinker who famously claimed to "give Judaism its philosophy."

Phenomenology and Judaism: An Exceptional Encounter

For Levinas the relation between phenomenology and Judaism is not a simple synthesis of two distinct modes of thought. He did not seek to reconcile phenomenology with Judaism as if both stem from the same origin and require being brought back to their common source. His entire philosophical project did not claim a single, self-identical, wholly appropriable foundation for both phenomenology and Judaism, nor did it assert the need for their speculative reconciliation where phenomenology and Judaism would be comprehended in an Absolute Idea where they would both combine, merge, coalesce, and ultimately speak the same language. He sought rather to think the relation between phenomenology and Judaism by firstly marking the *law* of their difference and then, consequently, the singularity of their encounter. Through both, as he saw it, is elaborated an "in-between" that incessantly *undoes* their accordance by engaging between them an unprecedented dialogue. This is a *dialogue*—if we are to maintain this word—where both phenomenology and Judaism cannot contain each other and are each summoned to speak *otherwise* than as they would have spoken *on their own*. This Levinasian dialogue calls for an explication.

Philosophy and Judaism have had and continue to have a curious relation. Between mutual rejection and attempts to find their synthesis or symbiosis, an infinity of nuances can translate this relation. Yet Levinas was certainly the philosopher who reinterpreted this relation by entirely redefining it, hence furnishing for Judaism its philosophical language, and inversely by awakening the Hebraic in the philosophical. By this he did not mean to claim that philosophy and Judaism say the same thing. On the contrary, he rather stressed the difference between philosophy and Judaism—without ever appealing to an anti-philosophical stance—an appeal toward which Levinas was highly suspicious, if not resolutely hostile. To claim the difference between philosophy and Judaism meant for him the need to clarify what in Judaism authorizes, conditions, and engages philosophical conceptuality *and* at the same time suspends, interrupts, and questions it in a radical way. Judaism, according to him, in fact announced and awakened the very concepts that constitute philosophical thought—concepts such as love, forgiveness, sacrifice, reconciliation, and confession, which cannot be dissociated from the encounter between Greece and Christianity—an encounter radicalized and deepened by what is perceived as German thought, which deployed itself around these very concepts through an assured negation of Judaism.[2]

However—and this is a key point in Levinas's analysis of the relation between philosophy and Judaism—Judaism has always restrained itself from that which it authorized and deployed, the philosophical tradition. According to Levinas it has always exercised a profound suspicion toward the philosophical concepts it nonetheless rendered possible. Without constraining Judaism to the closed sphere of its own texts and doctrines, Levinas sought to think philosophically on Judaic restraint as to the philosophical. Indeed, the Levinasian effort aims to disclose in Judaism the very possibilities of questioning Greece and Christianity, two of the other pillars

of Western thought. Judaism in his thought is not reduced to being the hidden source of the philosophical. Levinas is highly attentive to this possible drift into the proper, the originary, and the fundamental, which he questioned throughout his work. By redefining this relation between philosophy and Judaism, he claimed that neither of them can be said to have an immaculate and pure origin, thus seeking to command both Judaism and philosophy to incessantly redefine themselves beyond their supposed determination.

Why was it necessary for Levinas to think the possibility for a relation between Judaism and philosophy, a relation that searches for another source of meaning beyond their traditional determinations? Levinas's recourse to Husserlian phenomenology and its undeniable overcoming by Heidegger's fundamental ontology can serve here as a possible answer to this. The appeal to phenomenology, and also to the very founders of the "method," is not entirely exterior to Levinas's biography. We know that, in 1928, he registered as a student at the University of Freiburg where he enrolled in Edmund Husserl's seminar, one that would be Husserl's last university seminar. In this seminar Levinas already made himself a sort of a name by giving an outstanding presentation. A year later, he took Martin Heidegger's inaugural university course. Earlier, in 1923, while a student at the University of Strasbourg, the young Lithuanian Jew, who had emigrated to France a few years before, befriended Maurice Blanchot, who would later become a renowned writer, philosopher, and literary theorist. Both students were very enthusiastic and showed great interest in the "new method" coming from the other side of the Rhine. In 1929, the philosophical seminar organized and held yearly in Davos had been swept by the momentous debate between Heidegger and Ernst Cassirer on the interpretation of Kant's first Critique. Levinas attended and participated in this seminal encounter between the neo-Kantian, epistemological interpretation presented by Cassirer and the phenomenological rereading of Heidegger. By 1930, Levinas published his doctoral dissertation, *The Theory of Intuition in Husserl's Phenomenology*, and the following year, in collaboration with Gabrielle Pfeiffer, he translated into French Husserl's Sorbonne Lectures, the *Cartesian Meditations*. Indeed, already in his very early publications, the young Levinas had leveled against both his teachers, Husserl and Heidegger, a formidable questioning out of which is exerted an *ethics* owing to both Judaism and philosophy by projecting them both toward an inextinguishable responsibility for the Other.

This ought not to mean that Levinas simply retrieves a concept or an idea from either lexicon to subsequently advance them in a determined interpretation. Rather, he properly *reinterprets* both Judaism and philosophy by forcing each to speak in the language of the other. Hence, when philosophy speaks its own language, that of "truth," it is already supposing the Judaic, that is, the idea of an irreducible "justice." "Truth supposes Justice,"[3] says Levinas in his *Totality and Infinity* (published originally in 1961). In the same gesture, he claims that Judaism, far from simply constituting itself by its own affirmation, awakens the philosophical, an awakening that is always a double movement of suspension and expansion, interruption and extension of the Judaic, that is, its betrayal and deployment, an unfaithfulness and its development.[4] It is as if the Judaic permitted the philosophical to deploy itself by incessantly inscribing in this deployment its suspension, its interruption, and its disruption, which Levinas also interprets as an "overflowing" of the philosophical by the Judaic.

In this sense, the relation between philosophy and Judaism becomes for Levinas the relation between "truth" and "justice," where both truth and justice form not a dialectical movement of codefinition but rather an incessant working of "supplementarity." By "Truth supposes Justice," Levinas means—contrarily to what the entire philosophical tradition, from Plato to Heidegger, had affirmed—that where truth unveils itself it stems not from its own self-appropriation as comprehension, intentionality, or recognition but rather as inspired by that which is *other* for it, radically foreign to it. Inspired by an irreducible justice commanding, not the work of a justification, but the incessant drive to project truth beyond itself into that which truth can never completely appropriate or reappropriate, Levinas reverses the very foundation of philosophical rationality. Thus justice is no longer understood as a justification or complement to truth, but as its irreducible supplement. Justice *interrupts* and *deploys* truth at once and simultaneously. It is precisely this movement where Judaism and philosophy, without ever coinciding one with the other, call to one another and where Judaism is understood as a *language of justice* in which and from which proliferates the philosophical idea of truth. This antecedence of justice— that Levinas associates with the precariousness of the ethical commandment *Thou shall not kill*—is the pivotal idea of Levinas's thought. It is as if the question of justice by and through its precedence to meaning and truth opened the very possibility for philosophy to deploy itself. In this sense, the Levinasian meaning of "Truth supposes justice" is that justice *inhabits* truth, or again, that justice *guards* and *safekeeps* truth. The idea of justice is not reducible to comparison, to evaluation, or to assessment and remains irreducible to the manner in which it has been traditionally defined in the history of philosophy. Levinas's idea of justice thus stands irreducible to its appropriation by philosophical comprehension, and orients the entire philosophical thinking beyond itself and toward the incomparable uniqueness of each singularity, of each singular individual outside of the structure of commonality, community, or recognition. It is from this understanding of the antecedence of justice over and beyond truth that one must interpret the famous Levinasian phrase, which opened his own philosophical project beyond Heidegger's fundamental ontology: "To be or not to be—is perhaps not the question."[5]

Reading Judaism Phenomenologically

Levinas inherited from Edmund Husserl the phenomenological method that rests on two main principles: (1) the possibility for the subject to remove, to extract, or to step back from its naive engagement in the world, in which it passively receives phenomena, and thus to reduce phenomena to their intentionality; and (2) the possibility for the transcendental subject to constitute the horizon of intentionality from which phenomena are given as such. These two transcendental principles structure the method that reveals for the subject its fundamental quality: its infinite task of grasping phenomenality by constituting its intentionality. And yet, Levinas does not remain in the safety of this phenomenological affirmation. Extraordinarily, he insists on the necessity of surpassing the centrality of the subject and the axis of its constituting force by calling for a *beyond* the phenomenological, saying repeatedly that the subject must not simply be viewed as that entity in which and from which intentionality is constituted, thus requiring subjectivity to be exposed to that which overflows its own power and capacity, that is, its autonomy or selfhood.

This exposition of the subject is not a negation or a repudiation of the phenomenological understanding of subjectivity; rather, it is an act of furthering and deepening, a radicalization of one of the phenomenological subject's main motifs: its *passivity*. This passivity understood as exposition defines the radicality of the Levinasian subject. It marks within the subject an infinite receptivity, that is, a receptivity beyond its predetermined capacity to receive, beyond the intentional horizon constituted by the transcendental subject. It is thus exposed to the radically Other, to all that this subject had traditionally defined as appropriable, conceivable, or determinable. It is in the phenomenological tradition yet also through a critical examination of Husserl and Heidegger, as well as in key talmudic readings of the Bible, that Levinas discovered this openness of the subject, *beyond* its capacity to receive, toward an infinite Otherness that no reason can contain or grasp and that projects the subject onto an insatiable responsibility. *The Temptation of Temptation*,[6] written in 1966, offered a totally new way of reading the texts of the Jewish tradition and created a link between Judaism and philosophy. In his talmudic reading Levinas redefined his understanding of the relation between Judaism and philosophy by requiring them to *supplement* each other beyond dialectics in order to mark that philosophy is the movement by which is expounded the deployment of truth, while Judaism is that which awakens in this very deployment the incessant interruption of its totalization. This is why philosophy for Levinas is pointing toward knowledge, whereas Judaism guards philosophical truth from completing itself in the Hegelian absolute and speculative totality.

The title *The Temptation of Temptation* claims that philosophy ought not to be left to its own perseverance, insistence, and, ultimately, as if it were tempted by its own temptation, but needs its Other, Judaism, to guard and safe-keep it from its own exhaustion. Beyond knowledge and faith, Judaism perpetually awakens philosophy to its repeated and incessant task, namely, deploying itself as truth. The antecedence of justice that awakens philosophy as deployment of truth, however, does not mean that truth remains one-dimensional, strictly ordered by the Same or structured as Sameness. Rather, this antecedence of justice beyond truth opens to the possibility incessantly reiterated for philosophy to surpass its own determination as truth. The idea of justice, which Levinas singles out in Judaism, marks thus an "irreducible otherness"[7] in regards to philosophical truth but never its negation. Quite the contrary: it awakens truth to its unforeseen possibilities. Which means that the "event" of justice, irreducible to the classical motives of ontology (origin, source, foundation, ground, etc.), sometimes also called by Levinas the "trace,"[8] marks the instant where philosophy is exposed to deploy itself without ever accomplishing itself and thus is commanded to always remain open to its own "displacement," that is, to its own unthought possibilities. In this sense, philosophy is incessantly called to reformulate itself otherwise than according to its predetermined destiny.

The Temptation of Temptation exemplifies the phenomenological style of argumentation and description by importing key phenomenological concepts and applying them to his interpretation of the talmudic text. Concepts such as "passivity," "intentionality," "exposition," and so forth are mobilized in a resolute effort to open toward a novel rereading of the traditional ideas of the talmudic text. The radicality of this phenomenological reading, however, lies in the constant and persistent effort to break and shatter traditional oppositions, dualities, and contradictions by supplementing them and to force these to produce a wholly other meaning. This wholly other meaning—always beyond traditional oppositions or their possible synthesis as well as resolutely differing from the intentional horizon of phenomenality (Husserl) and the co-belonging movement of the meaning of Being (Heidegger)—opens to the possibility of a subjectivity incessantly responding in an infinite responsibility to the calling of the Other. This infinite responsibility reveals both the irreducibility of the Other and a subjectivity wholly oriented and riveted to the Other before any affirmation of its own autonomy and ownmost freedom. It is here that Levinas has brought a novel formulation of the ethical as First Philosophy[9]: an ethics that no longer draws nor extracts its determination from a principle or a foundation recognized by a self-reflexive subject but rather entirely summoned by what he labels an "enigma"—the enigma of the otherness of the Other. This enigma—at once awakening subjectivity and impossibilizing its autoconstitution— ought however not to be seized as a "hidden origin" or a "first cause." Moreover, it ought not be filled or fulfilled, accomplished or comprehended by faith or a mystical enlightening. Levinas, let's say again, never operates a "theological turn" or "return to theology."[10] The "enigma of the Other," he says, is exerting a relation to a "past" (as "passing of the other" before being a temporal determination), which as such was never embodied, never presented, nor could ever be reappropriated in a "presentification" or a "presentified" form. In this sense, all attempts to transform Levinasian ethics into a determined form of theology, be it Judaic or Christian, is not only a weakening of his thought but a profound misuse of his philosophy.

Exile and Return

The Levinasian rereading of the philosophical tradition is characterized by a profound and radical questioning of the notion of place. In this regard he is completely rethinking one of the main ideas of the history of philosophy—from Plato to Heidegger—namely that thinking is always and already inscribed in and founded on a substantial ground.[11] As if the spatial categories would always and already catch up with traditional philosophical thought. Or, again, that the categories of "fatherland," "home," "domicile," "dwelling," "soil," and so on were the synonyms of the classical ideas of identity, selfhood, substance, essence, and Being. Drawing from Heidegger, Levinas understands the history of metaphysics as the search for the ground from which all manifestation can occur. This search is for Levinas a return to the origin, that is, a recognition of the place from which thought is stabilized, justified, and ultimately and necessarily universal and true. Hence his comparison of the history of philosophy to the voyage of Ulysses, eventually returning to his "home," that is, to his just and natural place in the universe. Having exposed himself to the multiple vicissitudes of thinking, the philosopher always returns to the place from where reigns the originary universality of thought.

Ulysses as a highly philosophical figure embodies the Greek ideal of the Good Life and personifies the accomplished life that finds itself in harmony with the totality. In this sense, the history of philosophy is the course of an incessant series of detours, which ultimately discovers what was always and already *there*, namely the origin of thought itself. It is because Levinas never reduces the history of philosophy to a static idea of self-identity or sameness. The history of philosophy is always read by Levinas as the profound and perpetual movement between the same and the other where both are recognized as the essential components of rationality. In this sense, it would be false to claim, as is often advanced in what we can call here "postmodern scholarship," that Levinas is simply a thinker of the Other, of exile or of a "nomadic ethical stand," opposed to a philosophy that would then be associated simply with belonging, with the return to the "for and in itself." Rather, Levinas is striving to think the incessant derangement and disturbance of the simple opposition between exile and dwelling, between extraction from a place and attachment to a soil.

In order to orient thinking toward its infinite "expropriation" outside of itself into an undetermined "non-place" ("non-lieu")[12] irreducible to either its determination according to the order of a "return to itself"[13] or the structure of "losing itself," labeled as a "detour from itself," Levinas does not simply devote thought to the binary opposition of "autochthony" and "foreignness." He is much too aware of the vicious trap of transforming and establishing exile and the absence of a homeland into yet another substance, another program, or, in his own word, another "paganism." Between the appropriation of place and the extraction from place, he seeks to think toward *another* order—more ancient than any oppositional and thus inevitably hierarchical understanding of place. If Levinas belongs to the Judaic tradition that abhors the nostalgia and lyricism of place ("home," "origin," "identity," etc.), the insistence on a pure exilic nature is not, for the same reason, a seal of greater authenticity. Accepting neither *exile* nor *dwelling*, Levinas seeks a possibility in thought for a subjection to a Law under which all or any place—the desire for a place and the inscription in a place—is forever worked and traversed by its expropriation. Such is the task that Levinas urges us to think: not to call a place one's own, but in calling one to a place at the same time also stripping this place from any possible ownness. Wishing thus to avoid a systematic, quasi-methodical "logic" of exile or the permanence of a nonreturn as a program of identification with or recognition of a place, Levinas urges thought to an infinite "dislocation in all location," of "exile in the place," and of "otherness in the same."

The dynamic of the relation between Judaism and the history of philosophy is structured according to Levinas in the confrontation between two founding figures, Abraham and Ulysses. This relation has often been portrayed as a simple opposition between a figure of pure exile, on the one hand, and a figure of the simple return to the self on the other. Yet Levinas sees the relation between Ulysses and Abraham as much more complex. Not only because it would be much too reductive to simply envisage Ulysses as that mythical figure who returns home after the Trojan War, thereby symbolizing the necessary movement of Greek rationality always returning to the affirmation of the Same. And not only because it would be equally reductive to portray Abraham as that biblical figure who departs from his home toward another foreign land, thereby parting with his home, his family, and his language and thus marking the Judaic trait of separation and difference. These characterizations are far too limited, and their relation far too oppositional, to explain the mutual injunction we receive from both Ulysses and Abraham.

Indeed, Levinas thinks the radicality of each figure as if each were commanding the other; as if Abraham was exposed to the Odyssean calling of returning to the home and, inversely, as if Ulysses was exposed to the Abrahamic commandment of parting with the home. Levinas does not settle for a dialectical resumption of these figures. He elaborates a wholly other modality for them, the Ulyssean and the Abrahamic, and consequently understands their relation as an infinite movement where both figures are, one by the other, suspended and consented. Thus the Ulyssean figure recalls the Abrahamic figure to his responsibility as regards the return, and the Abrahamic figure calls for the Ulyssean not to remain trapped in the logic of a return and thus to a simple identity. In this sense, both Ulysses and Abraham "complete" each other by radically differing from each other and by marking the need that each supplements the other. The figure of Ulysses "completes" the Abrahamic figure by testifying for the latter the necessity of "return." And inversely, the figure of Abraham "completes" the Ulyssean figure by incessantly bearing witness for the latter to the need for transcending the closure of return. This "completion" is thus opening that way toward a mutual supplement, the exercise of a reiteration that, far from accomplishing one by the other, produces in each figure a necessary exposition of the one to the other and thus an excess commanding each to produce itself always otherwise than by the deployment of its own self-identification or predetermined definition.[14]

Difficult Humanism

Levinas's relation to modernity, and consequently to humanism, still remains to be defined as we reach closure. Let us therefore say that his approach to the question of humanism transgressed the simple alternative between humanism and antihumanism or between freedom and nonfreedom. Neither simply "humanist" nor "antihumanist," Levinas elaborated a philosophical understanding of this debate on world and body as a complex sphere. Levinas has always been deeply suspicious with regard to any position that claims for a "natural ground," a "predetermined identity," or toward a theory based on the idea of a direct and immediate link or relation between man, soil, and blood.

The answer to the question of why Levinas needs to redefine humanism, which is founded on the idea of man as rational and discursive being and on the notions of recognition and intersubjectivity according to a universal and equitable moral Law, might be found, I would suggest, in the dedication of his book *Otherwise Than Being* to all peoples exterminated in the Nazi death camps. This dedication is followed by the assertion that they were *all* victims of the *same* antisemitism—as if to say that traditional humanism, the one precisely founded on the idea of a human rationality, which stipulates that all human beings are rational by nature, could not protect who it said to protect and, instead of protecting, proceeded to engage in a brutal and entirely irrational selection between humans, asserting some worthy while others were unworthy of living, choosing some to life, others to perdition. Rationality was instrumentalized by a brutal and destructive regime that claimed the necessity of a vital space for one identifiable people, whose identification was the object of a series of laws and jurisdiction. The Other was therefore targeted, marked, entrapped, excluded, and ultimately exterminated. From the ashes of traditional humanism, from its failure to save those it was deemed to protect, Levinas took it upon himself, very early in his philosophical career, to redefine the question of humanism and rationality altogether. His core question regarding the task of redefining humanism was: How are we to ensure that rationality does not turn against itself again? How are we to submit rationality to the impossibility of forgetting the otherness of the other? How are we to think another humanism, one not simply or bluntly founded on the profound metaphysical assertion of "sameness," but one that incessantly responds to the call of the Other as other, the Other that we all are in the singular face of each other?

"Negating the primacy which, for the signification of being, would return to the human, free goal of itself, is true beyond the reasons it gives itself."[15] The passage here quoted, from *Otherwise Than Being*, gathers in a concise and condensed manner a radical reflection on the relation between humanism and antihumanism. Levinas states it quite clearly, namely, antihumanism is defined as that modality by which the subject is stripped from that which founds it as an autonomous subjectivity. Thus it is only riveted to being a passivity entirely drawn to embodying the expression of its "milieu," "environment," "situation," and so on. However, by accepting the necessity to problematize the centrality and sovereignty of the subject, Levinas reposes anew the question of humanity in man: How can the subject break with the "milieu," the environment, the social structures and backgrounds without engaging it into a fatality and a resolve that would constitute its very abolition? What Self is here at stake when this Self is not its own source or origin and if it is not simply to sink itself into the pure and simple negation of itself? Can we not liberate a form of "passivity" that, far from losing itself into the pure movement of neutrality, advances into a responsibility?

This form of passivity in the subject sets off a responsibility for the Other and thus opens to an entirely other definition of humanism: *a humanism of the other*. What stands at stake is, in fact, the subject to be thought as "infinite responsibility" and as a freedom that arises out of a certain experience of loss and inconsistency. That is, from an exposition to the otherwise than its own and proper Law: the Law of the Other, a more humane law than the law that humanism furnishes for man and that never reverts to the abandonment of all laws in favor of an overbearing necessity of neutrality.

The sentence "Humanism must be denounced only because it is not sufficiently human,"[16] which concludes Levinas's essay "Humanism of the Other," calls up the biblical scene of the donation of the Law at Mount Sinai. It is in this scene that the frame of this wholly other humanism, beyond traditional humanism, is given. The donation of the Law leaves Moses only capable of "seeing" in this gift what can be translated as the "back" (*Ahoraim*) of God but that could also be conveyed, which Levinas clearly points out,[17] as "Otherness" (*Aher*) itself. This second translation means ultimately that the Law can only be given where its donation as such is not seen, remains thus veiled, retracted, and withdrawn from its givenness. The Law commands, but its commandment is irreducible to presence or representation. The Law is thus beyond presence and representation. Rich from this interpretative reading of the donation of the Law as revelation, Levinas approaches the figure of the Other, and furthermore the donation of the Other's face, as ethically commanding beyond visibility or recognition. Levinas repeats it throughout his work: the face of the Other is not seen but *heard*; it does not appear, but *speaks* and *commands*.[18] This means that the Other's ethical commandment is given as an unrepresentable Law—that is, as a "revelation" that is always singular, unique, unforeseen, and consequently cannot be reduced to a recognizable and presentable expression. From that point Levinas exerts what he calls an "imposition," which overflows the order of presence and the representational modality of the knowing subject, overturning it to an opening, beyond its autonomy, to the irrepresentable as such, the Other, and transporting it toward an infinite responsibility. This called-for responsibility offers the possibility of an infinitely responsible humanism *beyond* its traditional definition, which rests on and is grounded in the idea of a mutual recognition and dialogue of autonomous and willful subjects.

The infinite responsibility that befalls on the ethical subject is infinite precisely because it is not contained or containable in any possibility of autodetermination. In other words, the ethical subject does not, and cannot, possess for itself the required or necessary time needed to respond to the call of the Other. His responsibility precedes any self-given time of decision, constitution, determination. Levinas thus thinks of another, more ancient, in fact "immemorial" subjectivity, preceding the autonomous modern subject, which would not respond through his assessing judgment to the Other's calling but rather would be taken, torn, snatched, pulled before any self-determination or moral order and thus remain always and already oriented responsibly toward the Other. Levinas redefines thus subjectivity, and a humanism for the Other, beyond the classical humanism by allowing us to hear in subjectivity the *subjection* of the subject. It is important to be attentive to this last inclination in Levinas's redefinition of subjectivity. In truth, the *subjection* that Levinas allows to resonate beyond the classical subject, far from simply fixating it as a passivity in the face of an exterior law, exposes it to another mode of responsibility, one whose event opens it to a *prophetic temporality*.[19] One can refer here to the end of *Otherwise Than Being* where Levinas—astonishing the philosophical consciousness— refers to the prophetic figure of Ezekiel as "the psychism of the soul: other in the same; and all the spirituality of man—prophetic."[20] Quoting Ezekiel 8.3, "taken by the hair," he thereby searches to signify a wholly different structure of temporality, a *prophetic* structure that he situates at the unseen and unrepresented core of the ethical subject.

How is this structure of temporality different from the temporal appropriation of philosophical consciousness? It is the figure of the prophet whose temporality, perpetually awakened by the Other's calling, can never be appropriated by it and time can never belong to it. The prophetic figure is called to *respond* before it possesses the time to grasp the call and calculate the adequate response. Here the Other is never standing in front of the prophetic subject, but lies "beyond" presence, already passed and always excepted from any grasp. And the prophetic subject is summoned and invoked to a responsibility that is never temporally determined or ordered. Which means that the responsibility of the prophetic-ethical subject is always without justifiable grounding, and thus already infinitely present *for* the Other. Without *terminus a quo* and without a proper beginning point, the ethical responsibility is turned toward the Other, which it can never wholly and fully gratify. And this is because its temporality is always torn between an *after* it can never reappropriate and a futurity always *to come*. It is from this prophetic temporality in subjectivity that Levinas rethinks the very idea of humanism, stretching it beyond its classical ground, its recognition, and the possibility of rational dialogue. For this wholly other idea of humanism expresses an infinite responsibility for the unrecognizable and unrepresented otherness of the Other.

Infinite responsibility of the prophetic subject is perhaps the most telling phrase in Levinas's philosophy. It marks a profoundly Judaic trace in the philosophical notion of subjectivity, for it marks the incessant and unrepresentable calling of the Other to an infinite responsibility for the Other. A Judaic trace that is also a radical reversal of philosophical determination—a reversal that inscribes in philosophical thinking the impossibility for it to maintain itself as it is and thus forces it to incessantly redefine its own presuppositions without however negating these. What Levinas thus succeeded in opening in thought and for thinking is the possibility to be at once entirely conservative of traditional philosophical values whilst perpetually calling for these to expropriate themselves beyond their simple and fixed meanings or intentions.

Notes

1. See here Jean-Francois Lyotard's famous interpellation of Levinas in *Autrement que savoir: Emmanuel Levinas*, eds. Guy Petitdemange and Jacques Rolland (Paris, 1988), 78.

2. On anti-Judaism in the history of philosophy, see Levinas, "Hegel et le juifs," in *Difficile Liberté* (Paris, 1984); Joseph Cohen and Raphael Zagury-Orly, "Hegel, les Juifs et nous," in *Les Temps Modernes*, 608, (March/April/May 2000).

3. Emmanuel Levinas, *Totality and Infinity*, trans. A. Lingis (Pittsburgh, 1969), 90.

4. Emmanuel Levinas, *Otherwise Than Being, or Beyond Essence*, trans. Alphonso Lingis (Kluwer, 1978), 5–9.

5. Levinas, *Otherwise Than Being* , 3.

6. Emmanuel Levinas, "The Temptation of Temptation," in *Nine Talmudic Readings*, trans. Annette Aronowicz (Bloomington, 1990).

7. This expression "irreducible otherness" has been misinterpreted and erroneously misused. It ought to be thought, as Levinas repeatedly marks it, in that it opens to a *relation* beyond and with the question of Being. In this sense, "irreducible otherness" signifies that event which simultaneously inaugurates an otherness to being (i.e., to the very forms of the meaning of being; truth and identity), incessantly severing its permanency while producing the very possibility for it to say itself always and already beyond its limits (or at least the limits it is giving itself in its history).

8. Emmanuel Levinas, "The Trace of the Other," trans. Alphonso Lingis, in *Deconstruction in Context*, ed. Mark Taylor (Chicago, 1986).

9. Emmanuel Levinas, "Ethics as First Philosophy," in *The Levinas Reader*, trans. Sean Hand (Blackwell, 1989).

10. We are here resolutely critical of the thesis, advanced by Dominique Janicaud in *Phenomenology and the "Theological Turn,"* trans. B. Prusak (New York, 2000).

11. We are aware that for Heidegger the question of the meaning of Being and the entire project of the fundamental ontology as it is laid out and explicated in *Being and Time* is a radical interrogation of the primacy of ground and foundation in the history of philosophy. This primacy is, according to Heidegger, the essential explication for the forgetfulness of the meaning of Being in the development and deployment of "onto-theology." Consequently, and quite understandably so, Levinas does not charge Heidegger's ontology on this ground. Rather, and in many ways, Levinas acquiesces to the Heideggerian critique of foundation. Furthermore, Levinas grasps with incomparable sharpness the Heideggerian "thematization" of Being as *presencing*, that is the "place" from which arises the possiblity of presence. However, Levinas questions Heidegger's placement of the co-belonging between Being and meaning in order to liberate another

source, irreducible to such ontological placing, for meaning—that is, for another meaning itself not graspable by Being. The place *without* place of Justice depends on this liberation toward another source of meaning, another source irreducible and heterogeneous to Being.

12. Levinas, *Otherwise Than Being*.

13. Stéphane Habib and Raphael Zagury-Orly, "Ce qui ne revient pas au même," *Journal of Jewish Thought and Philosophy* 14, nos. 1–2 (January 2007).

14. On the Judaic figure in the history of philosophy, and more particularly on the nondialectical and deconstructive reading of the relation between Judaism and Hegel, see Joseph Cohen, *Le spectre juif de Hegel* (Paris, 2007).

15. Levinas, *Otherwise Than Being*, 250.

16. Ibid., 227.

17. Levinas, "Revelation in the Jewish Tradition."

18. Levinas, *Totality and Infinity*, 79–81.

19. See Levinas, *Otherwise Than Being*, 352.

20. Ibid., 353.

30

Hannah Arendt (1906–1975)

BEING IN THE PRESENT

Martine Leibovici

TRANSLATED BY DAVID NOWELL-SMITH

> We Jews are inclined to have an inverted historical perspective; the more
> distantly removed events are from the present, the more sharply, clearly and
> accurately they appear. Such an inversion of historical perspective means
> that in our political conscience we don't want to take the responsibility for the
> immediate past and that we, together with our historians, want to take refuge in
> periods of the past, which leave us secure in terms of political consequences.
> —HANNAH ARENDT, "PRIVILEGED JEWS"

ONLY AN ACT THAT IMPLICITLY REPLIES TO THE QUESTION ASKED OF EACH NEW-
comer on earth—"Who are you?"—is one that is truly human, asserts Hannah
Arendt in *The Human Condition* (1958).[1] In certain circumstances, however, particularly in "dark times," an act of speaking would need to render explicit in its
reply the precise meaning of the humanity that thus revealed itself. This was what
Arendt did when she received the Lessing Prize awarded by the free city of Hamburg in 1959. A German city was honoring her, and she had to accept the award by
appearing in public and revealing who she was, something she did by recounting
a part of her personal history. The woman being honored that day made a point
of underlining her belonging to those Jews who had been hunted out of Germany.
This link was not exterior to her existence; it was a constitutive feature of her subjectivity. To answer the question "Who are you?" sometimes requires recognizing
the reality of the world in which one exists. Thus, Arendt says, "for many years I
considered the only adequate reply to the question Who are you? to be: a Jew." By
that, she continues, she was simply taking "into account the reality of persecution."[2]

Born in Hanover in 1906 into an assimilated Jewish family, and trained in the
German philosophical tradition, Arendt took the road to exile in the summer of
1933. This departure was not due to a predisposition for adventure: she had been

singled out for persecution not for who she was as a person, nor for acts she had committed, but because she came from a group referred to as "Jewish." In stating that she was "a Jew," Arendt assumed her origins, but this reply also had a political significance, to the extent that Arendt's response was accompanied by her determination to act. It was the Zionists, with whom Arendt had links in Germany, who gave her this opportunity, even if she was somewhat critical of their analysis. Yet, for the young philosopher that she was at the time, such a determination to act was inextricable from an urgent need for understanding. Thus, against the winds and tides of an exile that had initially led her to France, Arendt undertook an ambitious program of research. The result was the publication in 1951 of *The Origins of Totalitarianism* in the United States, where she had found refuge in 1941 after having fled the French internment camp Gurs, in which she, along with other "enemy aliens," had been imprisoned by the French government. It was in 1951 as well that, after having been stateless for eighteen years, she became an American citizen.

Leaving aside in her theoretical reflection the task of thinking Being qua being, and even the critical dialogue with texts from the philosophical tradition, Arendt reacted to events, intervened in debates taking place within the Jewish world, and collected what documentation was available at the time. While grappling with a broad range of nonphilosophical material, she continued at the same time to reflect on theoretical texts. First of all, she asked why it was in Germany that the total exclusion of Jews from the life of the nation had been possible, and from there she subsequently grasped the emergence of totalitarianism from the perspective of the unresolved problems of the modern world. In this respect, Arendt does not provide a theory of Jewish modernity as such. If one can nevertheless attempt to reconstruct the configuration of her thinking on this subject, then it may be seen that Arendt never isolates it from the theoretical and political questions that preoccupy her regarding the world in general.

The majority of German Jews didn't assume the view that there are circumstances where one must reply "a Jew" to the question "Who are you?" Yet, from Arendt's point of view, this position provided a way out of the disorientation Jews were undergoing at the rise of Nazism, which marked them as its target precisely where they seemed most assimilated. This disorientation remained even after emigration: in order to feel accepted in the country where they had ended up, they would claim to have left Germany by their own choice, as though their departure were unrelated to the fact they were Jewish.[3] In a way Arendt's sensibility is close to that of many young Jews born between 1890 and 1910 in the German-speaking world, who rebelled against the liberal ideology of their bourgeois families. Established in the wake of World War I, the Weimar Republic, which had for the first time introduced equal rights for all citizens, had confirmed liberal Jews' belief in progress: thanks to the powers of reason, humanity would move from darkness into light. In this period of cultural and intellectual Jewish renewal, many of its radical tendencies were articulated within the resurgent debate about theological-politics. Arendt's attitude, by contrast, remained resolutely nontheological throughout, proceeding by way of an interpretation of strictly historical and political phenomena.

Arendt's understanding of Jewish modernity is animated by a double intention. At the moment when Nazi totalitarianism produced a political crystallization around the Jewish people, transforming them into political pariahs and threatening them with unprecedented destruction, Arendt sought first to understand how the Jews had recently entered European history through the movement of emancipation, what the configuration of this world had been, and what forces—public as well as covert—were at work. But she also focused on what their responses had been and how they had acted and thought within the entanglement in which they found themselves. According to Arendt, European Jews—German Jews in particular—found it perhaps more difficult than others to free themselves from the political categories of their thought. It was as though they had made a pact with the modern world that was in fact a pact with *Aufklärung*, the German Enlightenment movement, which alone was capable of providing them with the right arguments to defend their claim to equal rights.[4] At the same time, the conception of history underlying this intellectual current (*die Aufklärung*) was ill-equipped to deal with a world forged by the "storm of steel" of World War I. Regarding the Jews, the modern problematic of emancipation had also set forth a system of contradictory injunctions that brought the Jews face to face with insoluble subjective dilemmas whose full effects were felt as the nineteenth century progressed. In this context, a new figure—the Jew as pariah—had nevertheless emerged, which Arendt considered to be the clearest elaboration of the predicament in which Jews found themselves in modern times, a poetic and political predicament more than a philosophical one.

The Modern World and the Modern Age

The speech act from the Hamburg address is nevertheless most singular. If Arendt ascribes the need for a self-presentation as Jew to the past—*for many years I considered*—it is because this need corresponds to a political present that is no longer that of 1959 and not applicable to all contexts. In political terms, for a woman who fully considered herself, in Gershom Scholem's words,[5] a daughter of the Jewish people, Jewishness was not a substantial identity that determined all the positions she took. The use of the past tense indicates that the Jewish question does not present itself in the same way before and after Hitler. That is not to say that antisemitism had disappeared, but that it no longer held the central place it had in the 1930s. Of course, as Arendt directly experienced during the Eichmann trial, the Shoah had not ceased to cast its shadow upon postwar generations. But the present of the 1950s and 1960s required an effort of deciphering that had to take into account the new configuration of the world after World War II, in which the events in Europe were not as central as before. It was the first atomic explosions that had, politically, given birth to the modern world—that is, among other things, to the Cold War—such that the antagonism between the United States and the USSR now served as its spinal column.[6] After Hitler, she specifies, "there is no Jewry left,"[7] and Arendt does not believe a new political crystallization around the Jews to be on the agenda: on the one hand, Jewish assimilation in America was never presented in the same terms as in Europe; on the other—despite whatever deep-seated reservations Arendt might have had with respect to the project, adopted by the Zionists in 1942, of founding a nation-state—the state of Israel was now a fact. This means that somewhere in the world there exists an institution that is not communitarian but political and as such is therefore responsible, constructing a new kind of relation with the Jews of the diaspora. Nevertheless, by presenting herself in postwar Germany as having once had to reply "a Jew" to the question "Who are you?," Arendt indicates firstly that in 1959 it is not yet time for her to appear as a mere citizen of the world, given that this public appearance is taking place in a site where the accounts with the past have not yet been settled and the new Germany must still assume responsibility for settling them; but she also signals, with her use of the past tense, that she knows how to distinguish between epochs.

The *modern world*, which had resulted from the series of catastrophes that arose from out of World War I, nevertheless prefigured the world after 1945, as though, after the military victory over totalitarianism, the political problems of modernity that totalitarianism had claimed to resolve were found in the same state in which they had been left. From a political point of view, this concerned the decline and fall of the nation-state, which at a spiritual level corresponded with the rise of nihilism.[8] By calling this world "modern" Arendt is aligning it with an epoch whose appearance she dates back to the turn of the eighteenth century, and which she calls the *modern age*. This age she describes as "rising with the natural sciences in the seventeenth century, reaching its political climax in the revolutions of the eighteenth, and unfolding its general implications after the Industrial Revolution of the nineteenth." At the same time, the modern world is characterized by "new problems and perplexities" for which the tradition of political thought that comes out of Plato, and which had already been shaken by the modern age, was no longer adequate.[9]

The Jews' entry into the history of the modern world happened at the precise moment of the "political climax" of the modern age. To attribute it to this moment is not to refuse to take into account the numerous exchanges and influences between Jews and their environments before the eighteenth century—something well documented by historians of Judaism—but to consider that the process of emancipation had dealt a new hand, with new aporias, in the history of the Jews. This process entwined together a social problematic (to be posed in terms of assimilation) with a political problematic (to be posed in terms of emancipation), which explicitly engages the concept of equality issuing from the philosophy of natural right and the Enlightenment.

In the name of an idea of human beings as universally endowed with reason, emancipation bestowed upon the Jews the same rights that other citizens already enjoyed. But the reverse side of this acceptance, as has widely been observed, was that recognition of a "private," that is, confessional, Judaism led to the old Jewish "nation" being effaced. "Private" here does not mean clandestine, as during the times of the Marranos. Israelites can assemble in daylight in their synagogues, provided they situate themselves politically as citizens of the nation they live in. However, the persistence of a group who were defined as Jews, what was once called "a people," remains out of bounds in postemancipation European society, lacking either a mode of political representation within the problematic of strict equality between citizens, or integration into a society now broken up by the conflict between social classes. At the social level, then, the Jews found themselves in a void, without status, as the new sociopolitical structure lacked a definition for their type of sociality. This impossibility will remain in spite of emancipation and will give sustenance to that classical motif of political antisemitism: the hidden Jewish group allied to the state.

In whatever way it is initially implemented, the idea of equal rights borders on the idea of similarity. Equality as a human and citizen is always accompanied by an exigency to assimilate into society, something to which Jews for the most part reacted favorably, even though it left them in an almost impossible situation. Emancipation means that Jews will enter the society that receives them *one by one*, individual by individual. But, insofar as this political equality cannot be extricated from a social pressure to assimilate, only he who is like the others is considered really equal. For the Jew this means: not like a Jew. But to not be like a Jew implies that there is a trait of "Jewishness" that individuals might continue latently to possess. The contour of this identity thus becomes increasingly mysterious, not only for the society that welcomes the Jews, which can no longer identify Jews visually, but also for assimilated Jews themselves, who are enthusiastic in their adoption of the cultural norms of this society. The persistence of such a mystery gives new sustenance to the age-old suspicion of and hostility toward the Jews. Arendt calls this kind of relation "social anti-Semitism" insofar as it should be interpreted less as the persistence of Christian anti-Judaism than as a mode of functioning specific to modern societies. The portrayal of this mystery as a "race" then endows it with the veneer of consistency. The pressure to assimilate therefore gives rise to a discrimination that helps construct a strange group, whose members are united neither by nationality nor by religion but by specific attitudes and affective and psychological reactions that together are taken to constitute "Jewishness." Judaism is no longer that millennium-old tradition that kept on going in a largely hostile environment, nor is it the memorializing of a complex diasporic history far broader than a narrow account in terms of persecution; rather, it is reduced to an exclusively interior, personal problem.[10]

It is against these insoluble aporias that the political reply "a Jew" to the question "Who are you?" resounds, in one gesture insisting both on her singularity as an individual and on her belonging to an oppressed group that Arendt persists in calling "the Jewish people." In this, it provides a striking illustration of how, underlying Arendt's theorization, we always find a reflection on her own position in the world. In the same way, she always recognized in Zionism the merit of having pointed out what emancipation, within the conditions of modernity, denied when it presented the entry of the Jews into the modern world purely in terms of the integration of individuals. To struggle against oppression, to form a people, which for Arendt means to become politically organized, to take one's measure of responsibility in world affairs—such was the gauntlet that modernity had thrown at the Jews and that the Zionist movement had taken up. However, as far as the Jews were concerned—and here we return to the framework provided by the distinction between modern age and modern world—the whole question was to know whether the categories of thought that corresponded to the mutations in the modern age—and which Zionism adopted in its turn—continued to allow them to understand their situation in the modern world.

The Pact between the Jews and *Aufklärung*

Yet the integration of individuals that was advocated by emancipation took its inspiration from a magnificent realization: Jews are humans. In each, reason is single and whole, each is capable of thinking by him- or herself, of subjecting to critical examination anything that presents itself to the mind with the stamp of authority or is deemed to be self-evident in advance. The encounter of Jewish intellectuals and Enlightenment philosophy was, for Arendt, love at first sight, leading these intellectuals to abandon Judaism without a second thought. This disavowal of religious practice and belief might seem germane to the lucid observation of the real. However, more generally, being confronted with reality does not in itself produce understanding. Having lost faith in the religious interpretation that had provided the framework for their access to the world, the emancipated Jews found themselves so to speak at a loss, deprived of guidance for interpreting events and confronting the reality of facts.[11] Yet Moses Mendelssohn, the emblematic figure of the pact between the Jews and *Aufklärung* at the apogee of the modern age, deliberately refused to abandon Judaism and attempted to show that its central tenets were truths established by reason, whilst at the same time affirming that the divine Law, which had been revealed to the Jews' ancestors, had been transmitted as a historical truth from generation to generation up until the modern Jews, who were required to observe this practice out of fidelity to their fathers. If the truths of reason are accessible to all autonomously, the historical truths, of a lesser value, were dependent on being witnessed by an other, and were consequently more fragile. In somewhat lapidary fashion, given the complexity of Mendelssohn's thought and action, Arendt concludes that by fixing themselves to the mast of universal reason the Jews became indifferent to the world and history, something that was the case no less for the cultivated Jew than for the oppressed Jew in the ghetto. At least this latter still had frames of reference that allowed him to make sense of events, even if it was not a historical sense. In fact, the turn took place with the generation directly after Mendelssohn. Whereas for him the distinction between reason and history made it possible to salvage the Jewish religion, his inheritors relied on reason in order to devalue the historical truths, whilst at the same time attempting to get rid of religion itself.[12] This is not to say that Arendt is particularly attached to the Jewish faith, but she is interested in the political consequences of abandoning it; while the Jews' millennium-old stance of withdrawal sometimes gave way to a critique of the non-Jewish milieu from a Jewish perspective, this ceased entirely with emancipation. While the spiritual heritage of the Jews was increasingly monopolized by the rabbis, the periods before emancipation were now subjected to renewed scrutiny: they were now considered merely as dark times of persecution, whose prejudices would eventually be stamped out by the Enlightenment, or, building on the historical consciousness of the early nineteenth century, as a field for arid scholarship, according to the perspective that Arendt, following Scholem, had adopted on such questions.[13]

But not all Jewish philosophers—far from it—abandoned Judaism. On the decline of the modern age, did Hermann Cohen not lift anew Mendelssohn's torch while taking Kantian critique as his starting point for a reconsideration of the state of reason? And did he not lead a courageous and public struggle throughout his life against antisemitism? As with Mendelssohn, did not his fidelity to Judaism lead to an obstinate resistance to assimilation? Without giving attention to the theoretical effort through which Cohen proceeded to a reconstruction of Judaism in order to extract its rational core, Arendt examines certain arguments of his from the point of view of whether they are capable of providing Jews with categories of thought adequate to understand the meaning of the present. Whilst the problematic formulated by Mendelssohn at the apogee of *Aufklärung* led to an indifference with respect to a world embedded in history, Cohen's is based on an erroneous conception of history. For Arendt, Cohen is a representative figure not so much of assimilation—by now an irreversible fact—but of assimilationism, overinterpreting this fact and endowing it with a deeper meaning on the basis of an idealized vision of the recent history of Jews in Europe. All the restrictions on the equality of Jews in Germany, still in place despite the 1871 new law of emancipation, and all the more evident if one compares them to the rights of Jews in France, must, Cohen argues, be measured in terms of what really mattered: the Jews' cultural and historical deep-rootedness in Germany. Perhaps the Jewish-German symbiosis wasn't yet entirely visible, but history, affirms Cohen, was moving in that direction. In emancipating the Jews in its own manner, the Prussian state had recognized what was most important, namely, the Jewish religion's entitlement to equal rights. It had created an essential relation with that for which the Jews were the emblematic messengers: monotheism as it is outlined in the biblical text that Cohen wishes to consider exclusively from a moral perspective. In so doing, the state elevated itself to the possibility of entering into history as a moral state, the veritable role that had established it as a beacon of world politics. Thus the sole duty of modern Jews was "the preservation of monotheism." And he concludes: "regarding other miscellaneous details I have no interest whatsoever."[14] By striving, as Cohen had done philosophically, to deepen the meaning of the Jewish religion, the Jews would understand the profound identity uniting monotheistic faith with the German spirit. In so doing, Cohen, unlike Mendelssohn for whom history carried no truth whatsoever, inherits an approach that had become an intrinsic feature of German culture via Hegel and his followers.

Arendt asks, however if, by identifying Judaism with such a noble mission, is one not, in fact, evading history? Is one not turning away once more from the present and its events? The main problem with this approach is always the same: it does not allow Jews to situate themselves in the world. By searching too hard for hidden depths and by portraying Jewish integration in terms of ideas that would subsequently be embodied by real people, one remains unaware that in reality the Jews integrated into neither a culture nor even a people. A people is always constituted by differentiated groups, social classes, and the Jews enter necessarily into one or several social spheres where conflicts already exist. To integrate into a section of society thus always means to be in opposition to others. According to Arendt, the nature of the relations between Jews and their environment must be questioned. In the 1930s, such a proceeding was crucial in order to identify the nature of the threat, and in which specific terms hostility toward the Jews was formulated, even if they had made so many pledges of adopting the codes and values of the societies they lived in. To these questions, Zionism itself had no adequate reply, as it postulated that antisemitism had always been the very basis of Western societies. By contrast, society had to be analyzed in its differentiations and not as a uniform entity. Thus, insofar as the understanding of the present implies relating it not to an immemorial past but to the most recent past, contingency must be acknowledged and have its place. In this respect the meaning of emancipation had not been to render manifest a consubstantial and unrecognized identity between Jews and non-Jews, but to transform Jews with a Jewish past into citizens of different countries, each of which had a different past. The dispersal for Arendt is not anymore the religious concept of *Galut*, but a delineation of a certain position of the Jewish people in the world, dividing it from now on according to the new national partitions and inserting the Jews in an unprecedented manner within European history, thus rendering more and more problematic the ancestral notion of a people.

The Pearl Diver

Ich bin doch, Gott sei's geklagt, ein Epikäures, dem noch viel mehr Dinge abgesehen, als dass er keine Tefillin legt—abgesehen vom weiblichen Geschlecht.

[I am after all—God be blamed—an Epikaeuris, lacking much more than not wearing a Tefillin—let alone being of the female sex.]
—HANNAH ARENDT TO GERSHOM SCHOLEM, JANUARY 14, 1945

Is such a strictly secular approach tenable at all? Does it not flow simply from an ignorance veiled as originality? Hasn't Hans Jonas succeeded in synthesizing both the greatness and limitations of Arendt's work with regard to Judaism in saying that "Hannah was a conscientious Jew, without really knowing anything about Judaism—she is what is called an *am ha-aretz*. But she was also a 'defiant Jew' [*Trotzjuedin*]"? And this "*am ha-arazut* [ignorance of Jewish things], which [her] friends [had] known about for a long time," did it not end up "playing dangerous tricks on" her during the Eichmann trial?[15] It is true that Arendt was not very sensitive toward the problematics of revelation and redemption emanating from the Jewish traditional heritage. It was first and foremost the Western philosophical tradition that served as her frame of reference. But does this necessarily constitute a definitive obstacle in her attempt to interrogate Jewish modernity? Or better: does this not also introduce utterly new ways of thinking, born out of the inextricable character of the hardships of Jewish existence in the postemancipation era, and favoring deciphering of interpretative possibilities offered by the modern world?

To confront these difficulties Arendt could rely on resources bequeathed to her by Kurt Blumenfeld, a friend of hers and the president of the *Zionistische Vereinigung für Deutschland* from 1924 until his departure for Palestine in 1939. The starting point of Blumenfeld's Zionism was neither Jewish suffering nor even antisemitism, but an existential attitude that he defined as the refusal of self-mystification.[16] It is certainly Blumenfeld whom Arendt is thinking of when she asserts that Jewish nationalism arises out of a moral impulse, which amounts to a "protest against a life that in any case must be paid for with a broken back."[17] To refuse the poisoned bond of gratitude that the emancipators always asked of Jews in return for their accession to citizenship was to regain one's dignity and preserve one's freedom of conscience by never putting one's trust a priori in any state, even one that had once brought emancipation. Moreover, when she reconsiders the recent Jewish past, Arendt does not encounter only stances like Hermann Cohen's. She also discovers the experience of certain Jewish intellectuals who were pure products of emancipation: coming from wealthy assimilated families, they were not seen as pariahs in the same way as were Eastern European Jews who immigrated to Western Europe; nor were they parvenus, insofar as, unlike their fathers, they had not chosen to accumulate further wealth within society.[18] They enjoyed, however, direct access to Western thought without ever passing through a Jewish education. Men of culture, they embodied those "new specimens of humanity" predicted by the Enlightenment— whose ideals, moreover, they shared. But "if they were worth their salt, all became rebels."[19] Living, like Walter Benjamin, at the peak of discomfort, distanced from both Jewish and non-Jewish milieus, they were not ready to disguise this situation with generalities of different isms. What Arendt says about Benjamin might be applied to all of them, including herself:

> What was decisive was that these men did not wish to "return" either to the rank of the Jewish people or to Judaism and could desire to do so—not because they believed in "progress" and an automatic disappearance of anti-Semitism or because they were too "assimilated" and too alienated from their Jewish heritage, but because all traditions and cultures as well as all "belongings" had become equally questionable to them.[20]

In order to find their way in such circumstances they no longer had recourse to the tradition of their people. They too were animated by a moral impulse, by pride, by will for truth, and by revulsion toward deception and denial. They did not reject emancipation but focused on what it promised—a humanity in which all humans are treated with respect—in order to make out of it a twofold critical stance: toward the world they came from and the world of their destination. This situation afforded positive possibilities of knowledge, engaging a reformulation of the traditional Jewish relation to the past, and endowing the present with a new meaning.

When one approaches, as Arendt does, the works that arose out of these moral impulses, one discovers what she calls a "hidden tradition," the Jew as pariah. The notion of tradition is certainly playing on the reference to the Kabbalah; but such wordplay indicates merely that Orthodox Judaism is not Judaism as a whole, for, while taking distance from the liberal consensus shared by a large part of assimilated Jews, what is at stake here rejects any kind of integration into the tradition of Jewish heterodoxy that just as much as orthodoxy constitutes a modality of biblical interpretation. Thus, the hidden tradition can be called "tradition"—somewhat paradoxically—only insofar as it is not traditional. From one author to the next, there was no organized transmission, no institutional support. Rather, it would appear that, as the same conditions inhered from one generation to the next, between the nineteenth century and the first half of the twentieth century, Jewish individuals were confronted with the same impasses. In order to reach the same conclusions they did not have to consult one another: each reached them by him- or herself. The tradition of the pariahs is a tradition of individualities that were not bound by any consciously sustained continuity. The relation between these individuals is one of a shared mode of response, more artistic and political than philosophical.

Attempting to regain a common bond with their people, the authors of this hidden tradition eventually invoked its immemorial traditions, but did so in a free and detached manner. Heinrich Heine (1797–1856), German Jewish poet, literary critic, and inventor of the *Schlemihl* and "lord of dreams," is one example. Don Isaac Abravanel, who we can suppose represents Heine himself, is the Spanish knight from the *Rabbi of Bacharach* who comes from the "House of Israel." In love with joie de vivre, he calls himself "a heathen" and feels at home neither with the "melancholy self-tormenting Nazarenes," nor with the "dry and joyless Hebrews." The subtext of the work is a massacre of Jews, the threat of which had reached Germany in the beginning of the nineteenth century, with the first riots against Jews accompanied by the rallying cry of "Hep! Hep!" Thus Don Isaac Abravanel/Heine cannot stop himself coming back to wander through the Jewish quarter. It is not however prayer or nostalgia that lures him "to the tents of Jacob," but the food, the tasty memories of "carp with brown raisin sauce" and of "steamed mutton with garlic and horse-radish, fit to raise the dead, and the soup with dreamily swimming dumplings."[21] For Heine the return to tradition is impossible; it is through poetry that he attempts to give Judaism the right to reside in the German language, hence his exploration of Jewish themes that he nevertheless treats with freedom and humor, connecting them to Greek themes, speaking for instance of Apollo as a "big divine *Schlemihl*."[22] If Heine returns to Jewish legends, he constructs a new configuration through poetic language's capacity for condensation, which allows him to bring together the most contradictory elements in a unique form. This process creates an ironic effect by virtue of which Heine brings about, within German cultural forms, the gaiety and insolence of the pariah, that ironic regard on the world that ridicules hierarchies whilst at the same time introducing Yiddish expressions into the German language.[23]

A century later, when Kafka evinces a fascination for Jewish theater or aims to rehabilitate Yiddish over German, it is not in order to accomplish a return—now impossible—to the traditions of the Jewish people. And even if, as has often been done, one might interpret his work from the perspective of his relation to the Law or to messianic themes, these only inform his text in a cryptic manner, dissociated from the traditional modes of transmission. Like Günther Anders, Arendt distances herself from this kind of reading. Nevertheless, she argues that, even if K. is never explicitly qualified as Jewish, the situations and embarrassments he encounters are typical of Jewish life. K. is excluded from society, but takes seriously the promises of emancipation, that is to say the entitlement to equal rights. First he follows the injunction to assimilate, which impels the Jew to claim his rights as a human being while agreeing to become indistinguishable, that is, by breaking his ties with other Jews. But Kafka seems to say that we should take at face value the notion that the assimilation of the Jews would be far easier if only they did not insist on regrouping among themselves. What then becomes of K., the abstract individual, with no identifiable qualities, who wouldn't resign himself when faced with injustice nor consider the rights he is entitled to as privileges granted by the powers that be? These rights are universal, hence K. could have been joined in this struggle by the villagers; he could have established a bond with them. And yet he ends up understanding that, the more he claims his rights, the more distinct from the villagers he becomes, for he is the only one to do so: "K. appears strange to them not because, being a stranger, he is deprived of human rights, but because he comes and asks for them."[24] By never flinching from the inextricable embarrassments characteristic of Jewish life, Kafka can thus construct through the sheer force of his imagination and thinking a model of experience in which ingredients taken from reality are found in purified form. He reveals the structure of the modern world and the perils that threaten it. Very much like Benjamin, he does not have the sensation of standing at the threshold of a new era for which he is the prophet; the components, whose mechanisms he has so succinctly understood, are but those of the present world.

Kafka's K. nevertheless remains a solitary figure, that of the "man of good will." It is Bernard Lazare who has employed the word "pariah" to designate the modern Jew, in spite of emancipation, and termed himself as a conscious pariah. He is the only one, Arendt writes, who tried "to forge the peculiar situation of his people into a vital and significant political factor."[25] The right to be Jewish that Lazare asserts against antisemites takes for its basis an idea of the individual as a free being, which is at the heart of the rediscovery of politics in modernity, and this will be as well Arendt's notion of politics: "the meaning of Politics is freedom."[26] Henceforth the pariah is expected to consider oppression as indignity to him as a human. At the source of his rebellion lies the shame of having to act as an acquiescent victim, not only of the social order as a whole but, correlatively, of the structure of the Jewish community as it was reconstructed after emancipation. According to Arendt, Lazare was the first Jew to denounce the double dependency of Jewish life: on the hostile forces of the surrounding world on the one hand, and on the wealthy, prominent members of the community on the other. For Lazare, the pariah is no longer a victim but rather is the oppressed responsible for his oppression, not because he collaborates, but because he understands that his acquiescence is required for the oppression to function—that this world order depends on him and so he is not foreign to it. In rallying Jewish nationalism, Lazare makes manifest the reality of the Jewish people, against emancipation, but in its wake. Yet this rallying is done in the name of freedom, in the name of having achieved emancipation rather than denying it. For Lazare true freedom for the Jews can only consist in the freedom to be a people, to "live as a people." Here being-for-freedom of man is in solidarity with the idea of plural humanity, constituted by a diversity of human groups that Lazare wishes "autonomous and freely interrelated."[27] Freedom is as much a question of a people's relation to all other peoples—among whom the Jewish people must stand side by side, neither oppressed nor the oppressor of another people—as of the end of any kind of oppression within an individual people.

Through the interposition of the figure of the pariah, Heine, Kafka, and Lazare managed to return to their Jewish origins in a creative gesture by which they bequeathed to humanity a new elaboration of Jewishness whose meaning was universal. In this respect the figure of the pariah is a touchstone not simply for the Jews. Forged out of their experience within modernity, it indicates at the same time and indissolubly a universal type of crucial importance for apprehending humanity as a whole, and casts light on the status of individuality in the modern world, whether of subjects or of peoples.

At the moment when in 1945 Arendt rediscovers the diverse meanings that the figure of Jew as pariah had taken, she has the impression that the tradition that she is reconstructing no longer has any relevance, but that it is precisely the reason why it must urgently be saved, for multiple amnesic factors threaten to bury it. These include: the conformism of official Jewish history only retaining authors writing in Yiddish and Hebrew in its tradition; the Nazi crusher, which had stamped out the political foundations of European Judaism, including the relevance of the choice between pariah and parvenu (all parvenus were transformed anew into pariahs, the people as a whole being the political pariah of Europe); and, finally, another factor of forgetting related to the problems encountered by Jews living in Israel after the establishment of the state, both insofar as there was no longer a European Jewry in the sense that there had been before the war and as that very establishment of the state had been accompanied by an interminable conflict with the Palestinian people. As early as 1944, Arendt had identified the political origins for the persistent denial of justice in this regard in her article "Zionism Reconsidered." Concerning the hidden tradition, Arendt's inspiration comes from Benjamin. Her figures belonging to the past, they can be perceived only "as an image which flashes up at the instant when it can be recognized and is never seen again."[28] To counter all these factors of oblivion requires witnessing, salvaging, and diving again for this hidden tradition, like the diver who brings up the pearls buried deep in the sea. Once gathered and placed side by side, the pearls do not form a whole, nor are they already bound together as links of one tradition that preserves continuity between generations. None of the authors of this hidden tradition constituted a point of reference for the others, as would be the case in a tradition in the conventional meaning of the term. The pearls are rediscovered one by one, retaining their singularity. It is their exhibition next to each other that puts in relief their affinities and makes manifest their shared configuration. And it is Arendt who—in the present—constitutes into a tradition works that did not know of each other's existence; it is she who in a way once more binds together the family ties.

Notes

1. Hannah Arendt, *The Human Condition* (Chicago, 1958), 178.

2. Hannah Arendt, "On Humanity in Dark Times" (1959), in *Men in Dark Times* (New York, 1968), 17.

3. Hannah Arendt, "We Refugees," in *The Jewish Writings*, eds. Jerome Kohn and Ron H. Feldman (New York, 2007), 264.

4. Hannah Arendt, "Original Assimilation: An Epilogue to the One Hundredth Anniversary of Rahel Varnhagen's Death," in *The Jewish Writings*, 39.

5. Hannah Arendt, "A Letter to Gershom Scholem, 24 July 1963," in *The Jewish Writings*, 466.

6. Arendt, *Human Condition*, 6.

7. Hannah Arendt, Letter to Kurt Blumenfeld, January 9, 1957, in Hannah Arendt and Kurt Blumenfeld, *". . . in keinem Besitz verwurzelt": Die Korrespondenz*, eds. Von Ingeborg Nordmann and Iris Pilling (Hamburg, 1995), 174.

8. Hannah Arendt, "Bertolt Brecht: 1898–1956," in *Men in Dark Times*, 228.

9. Hannah Arendt, "Tradition and the Modern Age," in *Between Past and Future: Six Exercises in Political Thought* (1961; New York, 1993), 27.

10. On all these points see the first section of Arendt's *The Origins of Totalitarianism* (1951; rev. ed. New York, 2004).

11. Hannah Arendt, "*The Jewish State*: Fifty Years After, Where Have Herzl's Politics Led?" in *The Jewish Writings*, 378.

12. Hannah Arendt, "The Enlightenment and the Jewish Question," in *The Jewish Writings*, 9.

13. For more on this see Arendt, "Enlightenment and the Jewish Question"; and Hannah Arendt, "Anti-Semitism," in *The Jewish Writings*, 50.

14. Hermann Cohen, "Ein Bekenntnis zur Judenfrage," *Jüdischen Schriften II* (Berlin, 1924), 18.

15. Hans Jonas, *Memoirs* (Waltham, MA, 2008), 61 and 180.

16. Kurt Blumenfeld, *Erlebte Judenfrage* (Stuttgart, 1962), 44.

17. Arendt, "Anti-Semitism," 22.

18. Hannah Arendt, "Zionism Reconsidered," in *The Jewish Writings*, 356.

19. Arendt, *The Origins of Totalitarianism*, 64.

20. Hannah Arendt, "Walter Benjamin: 1892–1940," in *Men in Dark Times*, 190.

21. Heinrich Heine, "The Rabbi of Bacharach," in *Jewish Stories and Hebrew Melodies*, trans. Charles Godfrey Leland, updated by Elizabeth Petuchowski (New York, 1987), 19–80, 75–76.

22. Heinrich Heine, "Yehudah Ben Halevy," in *Jewish Stories and Hebrew Melodies*, 83–109, 105.

23. Hannah Arendt, "The Jew as Pariah: A Hidden Tradition," in *The Jewish Writings*, 281.

24. Hannah Arendt, "Franz Kafka: Appreciated Anew," in Susannah Young-ah Gottlieb, ed., *Hannah Arendt: Reflections on Literature and Culture* (Stanford, 2007), 94–110, 100.

25. Arendt, "Jew as Pariah," 286.

26. Arendt, *Was ist Politik? Fragmente aus dem Nachlass*, ed. Ursula Ludz (Munich and Zurich, 1993), 28.

27. Bernard Lazare, *Juifs et antisémites*, ed. Philippe Oriol (Paris, 1992), 140–46.

28. Walter Benjamin, "Theses on the Philosophy of History," in *Illuminations*, ed. and intro. Hannah Arendt, trans. Harry Zohn (New York, 1968), 255.

Arnaldo Momigliano (1908–1987)

JUDAISM PAST AND PRESENT

Silvia Berti

OVER TWENTY-FIVE YEARS AGO, WHEN I FIRST MENTIONED TO ARNALDO MOMIG-
liano my idea of publishing a one-volume selection of his writings on Judaism,[1] few
people would have recognized in this strong sense of belonging the most intimate
source of his relationship with the past—the primum mobile of his work. This is not
a question of affirming that Momigliano is essentially a historian of Judaism or of its
contemporary interpreters and theorists. A statement of the kind would go against
all the evidence and deconstruct all the connotations that Pierre Vidal-Naquet's
adjective *momiglianesque* intrinsically conveys. What the anthology (selected in
agreement with Momigliano himself) was foregrounding was the way in which
the lines of his thought on Judaism gradually built up an accurate and detailed
self-portrait, besides throwing light on his studies overall and the deeply rooted
motivation behind them.[2]

Today this is widely accepted, and not simply as regards his intellectual biography. Life, doctrine, and *métier d'historien* all converge in a very original approach
to the problems of Judaism in the modern world today. Central to his position is
an insistent and mandatory defense of historical truth and truthfulness, with which
his commitment to what may be termed the "ethical experience" of Judaism is so
closely interconnected that it is difficult to speak of unless all its discrete components are read as an entirety.

Arnaldo Dante Momigliano (1908–1987) was one of the great twentieth-century
historians, and left an indelible mark on both European and American culture. For
more than sixty years his influence was felt far beyond the field of ancient history,
his chosen area of specialization, particularly as regards intercultural relations in
the Hellenistic and Roman world and the related historiography. Anyone who
came in contact with him in individual or academic discussions, above all younger
scholars, was immediately aware of his prodigious intellectual energy, a second
nature in him, forcing his interlocutor to confront more extensive issues and test
them against the most rigorous analytical enquiries. Momigliano studied at Turin
University under Augusto Rostagni and Gaetano De Sanctis, graduating in 1929.
He then moved to Rome to work with the latter, who had supervised his thesis. In

1933 he accepted the Chair of Greek History that De Sanctis himself had had to vacate on refusing to swear loyalty to the fascist regime (1931). In 1936 he moved back to Turin to lecture in Roman history, but after the Race Laws were enacted in September 1938 he was forced to leave and go into exile. These were difficult months in which, besides the horror of racial persecution, he was subjected to the unexpected and unbearably painful scission of the double Italian-Jewish identity in which he had been raised, and which was nourished by its enthusiasm for the ideals of the Risorgimento and for the opening of the ghettos. This also marked the beginning of an anxious search for an academic post abroad. Momigliano explored all avenues in American academia,[3] but initially with no success despite the very vocal support of such figures as Benedetto Croce and Giovanni Gentile and intellectuals of the caliber of De Sanctis, Rostagni, Luigi Russo, and Lionello Venturi. The opening came, unexpectedly, from Britain, and with the help of Hugh Last he was able to move to Oxford in 1939. Despite a sense of isolation and initial language difficulties, through his work at University College (1951–1975) and at the Warburg Institute, where he taught and held seminars for almost twenty years (1965–1983), Momigliano gradually began to create a position for himself in a world and culture on which he was to have a strongly transforming power, especially in the field of historiography. For the last twelve years of his life, after retiring from University College, he held seminars and courses at the University of Chicago in the spring and fall. This was probably the place where his teaching, study, and chosen way of life came together most productively, and it was in Chicago that he formed the friendship with Edward Shils that lasted to the end of his life. When he finished his term of seminars in Pisa, every February, it was with an amused and satisfied smile that he would leave as his contact address "the Quadrangle Club."

The components feeding into a lifelong project of this extent must inevitably be many and considerably different. It is to the ethical nucleus of the Jewish tradition, however, that Momigliano refers in the very moving preface to *Pagine ebraiche* written from the hospital of the University of Chicago a few weeks before he died (inexplicably not republished in either the ninth or the tenth of his *Contributi*). This preface is a vivid recreation of his all-embracing and rigorous upbringing in a fiercely intellectual and intensely devout Jewish household. He describes the two fundamental figures in his development, Amadio and Felice Momigliano. Amadio, his grandfather's brother, was a very fine biblical scholar specializing in talmudic and particularly kabbalistic studies (a contributory factor in his relationship with Elia Benamozegh, the mystic rabbi of Livorno), who introduced Arnaldo as a child to the study of Hebrew texts. They were in close and continuous contact: from 1914 to 1924, the year Amadio died, Arnaldo's family was living in his grandfather's house. In an interview that he gave me in March 1987, only recently published, Momigliano stated: "We had two apartments, one above the other, and met frequently during the day; every evening he read the *Zohar*. It was he who taught me Hebrew; he wrote me a complete grammar, which I kept for years."[4] Felice, Momigliano's cousin, on the other hand, was a socialist and dedicated scholar of Renan, of prophetism, and of Mazzini; he read Spinoza to the eleven-year-old Arnaldo and instructed him in a more open form of reformed Judaism: "I remember Felice Momigliano would arrive, and we would have him read Spinoza."[5]

Momigliano inherited, absorbed, and always retained these two very different ways of interpreting and practicing the Jewish tradition, although less as the unresolved conflicts they potentially were than as heuristic elements in his ongoing critical and exegetical study of Judaism, where his method was continually to pose new questions rather than to find conciliatory solutions. The two elements in this very productive comparison-contrast between what we might hesitantly define as "Jewish modernism" and the observance of tradition share an element of constancy that, while not resolving the contrast, would seem to constitute the fulcrum of his reflection: the consideration of Judaism as an axiomatic ethical experience, essentially comprising "the first monotheistic and ethical religion in history, the religion of the prophets of Israel" on which, he writes, "to this day our morality depends."[6] It may be objected that biographical notes such as the above have little to contribute to the view of Jewish modernity Momigliano constructed over the years. This is not the opinion of the present writer. In a recent, seminal essay to which we shall return, Moshe Idel too compares Momigliano's idea of Judaism with that of Scholem and of Rosenzweig and attributes theoretically structuring weight to the education and example he received from Amadio.[7]

Numerous other autobiographical testimonies and passages from essays poured into the posthumous *Ottavo contributo* confirm the thesis posited in *Essays on Ancient and Modern Judaism*, like the following one:

> I was born in a house full of books: Italian books, Hebrew books, French books, Latin and Greek writers either in the original or in translation. Jewish was our tradition, and indeed my house had the reputation of a patriarchal Jewish house. . . . The need to put order between the Jewish and the Italian side of ourselves daily conditioned our life, besides filling our reading and our conversation. Having been introduced to Spinoza and modern Bible criticism long before I was a Bar-Mitzva, there was no serious conflict between reason and faith, rather a question of evaluating the components of the multiple civilizations of which I was a conscious heir. In a sense, in my scholarly life, I have done nothing else but try to understand what I owe both to the Jewish house in which I was brought up and to the Christian-Roman-Celtic village in which I was born.[8]

Ten years earlier, the synthesis, which is presented here in autobiographical terms of reminiscence, had read as an intellectual assessment when, in a letter to Sebastiano Timpanaro, on July 30, 1967, he writes: "If I had to define what I have been interested to find out in the study of history so far, I would say roughly three things: the influence of Greco-Roman and Jewish historical thought on subsequent historical thought; the organisation that the ancient political and social structures gave or didn't give to themselves to stabilize peace and to ensure freedom of decision and of discussion; the position of the Jews and of Jewish civilisation in the ancient world and after."[9] The assessment is shrewd and anticipatory in foregrounding the Jewish question as a conspicuous part of the whole (interestingly, as regards the historiographical issue too).

However, the horizons widened considerably beyond the pillars of tradition. Momigliano was raised in a family environment that left no doubt as to how the birth of Christianity and the encounter between Greek and Hebrew civilizations constituted the definitive turning-point in our history.[10] This intellectual experience then became historiographical knowledge under the guidance of Gaetano De Sanctis, and a magisterial conceptualization of the idea of Hellenism in his interpretation of the work of Johann Gustav Droysen.[11]

If Momigliano quickly realized that lacking from Droysen's reconstruction of the encounter between Greek and oriental culture in the early days of Christianity was any trace of the Hebrew component, it was because all the urgency and disquiet of his historical enquiry was concentrated on precisely this point. Many years later he was to speak of it when revisiting his early writings from an autobiographical slant: "above all, Hellenism meant to me the period when the Jews were confronted with Greek civilization."[12] He added that he took precisely *this* Droysen "as a viaticum, starting from a Jewish household in a Piedmont village."[13] The problem of Judaism's function in the modern world, which Momigliano had dealt with well before the Shoah, in an essay published as early as 1931,[14] for him meant above all a historical enquiry as to how it had survived the centuries of the clash/encounter with other cultures and other governmental and religious organizations. In considering such a crucial issue, Momigliano pondered the relationship between document and historical truth, reviewed the intellectual biographies of Jewish scholars of the classical world, and questioned, without repudiating it, the fertile historicist tradition in which he had been educated. What all these passages particularly evince is his personal relationship with Judaism united with his specific philosophical inclination, the latter quality noted by Croce with his habitual perceptive succinctness. In a cover letter of December 18, 1938 backing Momigliano's application for a position in America or Britain after his dismissal, as a Jew, from Turin University, Croce wrote: "He combines philological expertise and philosophical intelligence in a rare union."[15]

This was confirmed by Carlo Dionisotti, his friend from 1925 onward. Speaking of Momigliano's readings of Immanuel Kant, he emphasizes "the conjunction, characteristic of his whole work, of a preoccupation which is both philosophical and religious."[16] It was this particular fusion of philosophical, religious, and ethical interests, with his exceptional flexibility and intellectual curiosity, which opened up a dialogue with the more radical intellectual experiences of contemporary Judaism: those of Gershom Scholem, Walter Benjamin, and Leo Strauss.

Indicative of all his historiographical essays is an underlying autobiographical trait, which became more insistent in his last years as his own life and that of Jewish culture and tradition interpenetrated still further. Hence the charged significance of his work on the history of religions, on the relations between philology and the comparative method, and on language and myth in the history of historico-religious studies. His profiles of Müller, Usener, Schwartz, Wilamowitz, and Wellhausen, written in 1982, are also portraits of German cultured society of the period, as well as a revelatory *mise au point* of classical scholarship in Germany.[17] It is certainly no coincidence that the two historiographical studies that, in the present writer's opinion, are insuperable in Momigliano's oeuvre concern two philologists, or more precisely two creators of philology who were closely involved with the religious question: Jacob Bernays and Hermann Usener.[18] Like them, Momigliano felt with urgency the need for truth/fulness (in this quasi-philosophical sense), which is intrinsic to philological enquiry[19].

His choice of the "form" of his enquiries is equally significant. Imposing and exhaustive monographs and general histories were rejected (at least after the 1930s, the main production of which however were two essays) in favor of the fragment, the essay, and the specific analysis: "a more honest history," as he liked to put it. But equally striking in these detailed analyses is the constant presence of the historical question: the insuperable ability to invest single facts, concerning even the smallest detail, with the significance of a problem anchored to a resounding need for truth. This probably derives, in part, from the British academic training he acquired later in life; but I would adduce this attention to detail, this exegetical quality of Momigliano's work, where an exquisitely analytical mentality is predicated on a universalizing tension, as evidence also of his profound links with the interpretive method of the rabbinical tradition.

In a rare passage in which he speaks of himself and the motivation behind his research, the value of documentation emerges fully: "I am a Jew myself and I know from my own experience what price Jews had and have to pay to be Jews. I am not collecting facts for academic purposes when I try to understand what moved the Jews to refuse assimilation to surrounding civilizations. But I could choose to give an answer to this question in religious and moral terms. If instead I choose to clarify my ideas on this matter in historical terms . . . I subordinate myself *ipso facto* to what the specific evidence . . . will tell me. . . . Whatever ideological considerations guide my research, I shall be judged by my use of the evidence."[20] This underlining of the importance of documentary analysis in historical research, while particularly insistent after World War II, is already well in evidence in earlier work. In an important essay from his youth, when Croce's influence on him was particularly strong, an anticipatory note can be heard of his taste for erudition and natural philological inclination: "The evocation of the single fact is magisterial since . . . it is always dominated by the need for precise comprehension."[21] He is speaking of Gibbon, but the words are almost a prefiguration of what was to become his own method and historiographical style. In this sense it was Gibbon who furnished the model: like him, Momigliano decided to be both *érudit* and *philosophe*. A celebrated essay, "Ancient History and the Antiquarian" (1950), makes explicit this intention of combining philosophical history and the antiquarian method: "This remains the aim which many of us propose to ourselves."[22]

This strong commitment to the value of evidence and the antiquarian method, esteemed not simply as an evolutionary stage in the historical method but as a goal in itself, and structurally essential in historical research on account of its autonomy, inevitably conflicted with Croce's idea of philological history. Although himself the most erudite of scholars, Croce famously leaned toward a decided theoretical undervaluing of erudition in the work of the historian. Philological history forms part of his list of pseudo-histories; it lacks *das geistige Band*, the spiritual nexus: it is merely *richtig* but not *wahr*, correct but not true.[23] The divergence between Momigliano and Croce is accentuated in an essay from 1955. First, a distinction is made between the ascertaining of facts and evidence and the act of interpretation: "The true difficulty in the historian's trade consists, it seems to me, in the relationship existing between establishing the facts and interpreting them."[24] On another, no less weighty question, however, Momigliano analyzes a number of Croce's celebrated theses and expresses increased dissent: "I see no reason why I have the right to pronounce moral judgment on my contemporary, the mayor of Pocapaglia, but not on the Athenian archon Themistocles. We have been brought up to consider judging the mayor of Pocapaglia equivalent to seeking to improve him . . . while no purpose would be served by judging the archon of Athens, who has been dead for centuries and whose possible actions are now over. But in truth few of us judge our contemporaries to improve them; we judge them, as we judge the men of the past, to affirm our own convictions, posit values, and establish solidarity with some individuals and distance ourselves from others. We wish to orientate ourselves in the world . . . and thus judge as we are judged." Further on he reiterates: "We judge Moses, Socrates or St. Paul . . . because their actions are still morally important for us too."[25] He is clearly referring to the pages in which Croce maintains that, as a logical and not practical consciousness, "history should not apply the qualifications of good and evil to the facts and the people it studies."[26] This criticism of historicism puts Momigliano squarely on "Gibbonian"—or, equally, enlightenment—ground, in its reaffirmation of the right to moral judgment. Moreover, in an important essay, "Historicism Revisited," Momigliano turns a critical eye on a further characteristic of historicism: relativism. Influenced also by Leo Strauss,[27] his friend and colleague at the University of Chicago, who relegated Weber and historicism to the (moral) meagerness of a perspective that considered it could jettison value judgments, Momigliano repositioned the work of the historian in terms that distanced themselves from historicism while maintaining solid ethical and theoretical presuppositions. In tones that echo a series of passages in *Natural Right and History*, Momigliano writes: "Either we possess a religious or moral belief independent of history, which allows us to pronounce judgements on historical events, or we must give up moral judgment. Just because history teaches us how many moral codes mankind has had, we cannot derive moral judgment from history."[28] And like Bernays, having received and nurtured a set of ethics and a faith, Momigliano "had no need to look to history for one."[29]

If the ethical-religious foundation remained intact, actually intensifying in his later years, the mediation between faith and reason was from his earliest works represented by history. This historicization, which studies the different forms of religious experience on a par with other historical manifestations, is however predicated on a firmly rooted principle that would seem to contradict it: "Even the notion of transforming history by studying history implies a meta-historical faith."[30] Indeed, the complexity, which includes the different phenomena as historically determined without subordinating its foundations to diachrony and history, and thus the risk of reducing them to amorphous relativism, comprises one of the supreme and indelible points of Momigliano's teaching.

While his point of departure continued to operate as a constant in Momigliano's work, it was in concrete historical research that he exercised the ancient obligation of memory. I well remember his comment to me during a discussion of Yosef Hayim Yerushalmi's questions as to the relations between Jewish memory, history, and historiography: "Historical thinking which looks at these things seriously is a form of religious life."[31] Beyond its intrinsic value, such a personal response was also implicitly referring to the fact that "the Jews are the only people of antiquity in whom a reflection as to their historical destiny lay at the centre of their spiritual life: a part of their religion."[32]

On the one hand, then, is Jewish religious life, which found its position, secularized, within historical thought; on the other, the idea—not actually new in twentieth-century Jewish thinking—that observance of the law and due meditation on the Jewish past and destiny are one and the same process.

A historicist and antihistoricist position would then seem to coexist in Momigliano, as Moshe Idel perceived with great acumen.[33] The real issue is a consensus as to what this means. In agreement with my point as to Leo Strauss's importance for the development of Momigliano's antihistoricist position, Idel reinforces Momigliano's antihistoricism by comparing a number of his statements with others expressed by Scholem and Rosenzweig in order to hone the dialectics of the relationship between historicity and ahistoricity in Jewish history. Momigliano considered Scholem the greatest contemporary historian of Judaism;[34] he was certainly in a position to appreciate Scholem's exceptional skills in retrieving and interpreting the many facets of the mystical tradition that before his work was largely unknown (and even where known, largely disparaged: see the classic example of Heinrich Graetz, whose rationalism deemed the kabbalists "irregular" when they were not out-and-out scoundrels). He equally admired the acuity Scholem brought to bear on the whole Jewish question, in search of the element that had kept Judaism vibrant through the centuries, resisting all assimilationist tendencies. What he rejected was Scholem's solution: the search for the mystic foundation of Halakhah, and the acknowledgment of Zionism as the redemptive force of the whole of Jewish history, an idea in which a messianic inheritance and Zionism as an actual historical movement converge. The solution was highly individualistic, and for Momigliano indicated a tendentially anarchic personality,[35] dangerously akin to his objects of study, Sabbatai Zevi and Jacob Frank, and impossible to transmit, not least because, as he wrote in an essay from 1986, "within Judaism, messianism finds its limits in the statement constantly reaffirmed by major thinkers like Saadya Gaon, Maimonides (d. 1204), and Chasdai Crescas (fifteenth century) . . . that the Torah, the Law, remains valid for the messianic age also; in fact, it is strengthened by the joy of a contemplative life under the Law. . . . The anomic impulse is repressed by normative Judaism practically until the nineteenth century; anomie was brought back into fashion by G. Scholem in the twentieth century."[36]

Idel suggests that Momigliano's antihistoricist stance was influenced by Rosenzweig's position on the ahistorical character of Jewish history, which considers all its phases as simultaneous, a hypothesis that for the present writer is not entirely persuasive for a number of reasons. First, because this would involve the idea— which, indeed, Idel sustains—that "Momigliano is inclined to envisage Judaism as a phenomenon that transcends history."[37] Second, it is improbable that in aiming at an autonomous position with respect to the radically historicist culture in which he was raised, Momigliano would embrace an idea of Judaism like Rosenzweig's, distorted by the heavy weight of Hegelian idealism (see Momigliano's judgment of the more Hegelian aspects of Droysen's work as interpretative weaknesses). When asked, in the interview mentioned above, for his opinion on Scholem's violent rebuttal of Rosenzweig's theories, Momigliano replied, including himself in his answer: "He must have felt that there was an element of falseness in Rosenzweig's work. A great man, most certainly. But this uniting of Hegel and the Jewish world: what are we to make of it? They just don't go together."

This in no way undermined his explicit admiration for the strenuous intellectualism of Rosenzweig who, had he lived longer, would in Momigliano's opinion have been "the only scholar capable of challenging Scholem's interpretation of Judaism."[38] An identical intellectual trajectory of admiration for him mixed with sharp criticism is also to be found in Strauss and Scholem. Strauss dedicated his book on Spinoza to Rosenzweig, while observing that the *Stern der Erlösung* constituted a philosophical system rather than a reflection on Judaism (a similar position to Momigliano's);[39] Scholem considered him a genius,[40] but deplored his determined efforts to maximize the idea of *Deutschjudentum*, and "the way he saw Judaism as a kind of pietistic Protestant church."[41]

It is difficult, however, to believe that for Momigliano Judaism transcended history, and that he applied to the study of his own tradition confessional criteria he would not have applied to other religions; certainly, it would be more difficult to demonstrate it. Any number of statements can be adduced against the idea, not least the following, devoid of all equivocation: "Let me admit from the start that I am rather impervious to any claim that sacred history poses problems which are not those of profane history. . . . It must be clear once and for all that Judges and Acts, Herodotus and Tacitus are historical texts to be examined with the purpose of recovering the truth from the past."[42] And indeed the scholar who at twelve was *au fait* with Spinoza and Renan could hardly write otherwise.

This profession of faith in the historical method, necessarily placing Jewish history on a par with that of the other nations with which, over the centuries, the Jews had found themselves cohabiting, was clearly the expression of a consciously secular awareness: an awareness that denied legitimacy to the notion of Judaism's ahistorical character, thereby simultaneously excluding an internalist reading of Jewish history. Momigliano of course knew more than most to what extent the study of the Torah and its interpretations had been a structuring element of Jewish tradition through the centuries, but he was also aware that the ongoing, vibrant Jewish contribution to the history of civilization was equally due to their ability to absorb values and ideas from other cultures. This is probably the point on which he takes most serious issue with Scholem who, despite having more than once rejected the possibility of defining an "essence" of Judaism, insisted on interpreting the essential points of rupture in Jewish history, such as the Sabbatian crisis after Sabbatai Zevi's apostasy, as exclusively confined to the Jewish world. For his part Momigliano remained loyal to the lesson of Eduard Meyer, whom he was already reading as a student under De Sanctis: a vision of the ancient world that went beyond Greece and Rome to consider Persia, Judea, Mesopotamia, and Egypt as elements in an interplay of cultural, religious, and institutional refractions. Years of pondering the historiographical results of Meyer's work immunized him permanently against the illusion of interpreting Jewish — or indeed any other — history by following exclusively the immanent lines of its development. On the other hand, Scholem and Momigliano are closer in position in emphasizing the religious dimension that separates them both from mere orthodoxy and secularization: Scholem always rejected both terms in the orthodoxy-atheism polarization while roundly declaring that he failed to understand what being Jewish meant if it excluded the ethico-religious dimension.[43]

A review of the different points in Jewish history that particularly concerned him reveals very clearly that in the clash/encounter with other cultures, the Jews had remained Jews in their determination to remain faithful to the Law, and not to be assimilated to other faiths and their related historic-juridical cultures; this is not, of course, to imply that their faith remained unmodified by these contacts, as variously conflictual as they were fruitful.

Two classic examples to emerge forcefully from Momigliano will suffice here. If it is true that what preserved religious unity and reestablished the devotion to the Law was the outcome of the revolt of the Maccabees, thereby avoiding the cultural victory of a profoundly hellenized Judaism such as that of Flavius Josephus was to become, considering Moses more a legislator than a prophet, it is equally true that the debt toward the Greek concept of *paideia* helped to form the Jewish ideal of a life dedicated to study and focused on the teacher-student relationship.[44] As he wrote in a significant passage, part of Jewish intellectualism derived from the close interrelation of piety and study. Thus while in the Athenian and Roman models, "thinking about religion usually made people less religious, among Jews the more you thought about religion the more religious you became."[45] To return, then, to the question of the simultaneous coexistence in Momigliano of a historicist and an antihistoricist position, it is perhaps possible to state that while the study of Judaism, like any other historico-religious entity, necessarily requires historicization, the "metahistorical faith" he brought to bear in interrogating past civilizations, Judaism included, depended on his relationship with "the religion of the prophets of Israel."[46] Hence his decision to dedicate his *Ottavo contributo* "to the memory of Amadio Momigliano (1844–1924) who taught me to study and love the tradition of the Fathers Ps.1:2; 146:8–9,"[47] while as early as 1958 he had thought of the following words for his own epitaph: "His faith was that of a free-thinker, without dogma and without hatred. But he loved with a son's devotion the Jewish tradition of the Fathers." And how closely his inexhaustible requirement for truth was linked to his commitment to that tradition is stated directly: "the battle between true and false, fought out by the Greek historians, is still our battle, though we need to fight it with the more general and profound historical awareness inherited not from Herodotus and Thucydides but from the Old Testament."[48]

Momigliano's insight into the questions posed by twentieth-century Jewish intellectuals is considerable, yet he failed to address the issues of Zionism, the Shoah, or the ways in which the founding of the state of Israel reconstituted a political and state entity originally lost with the destruction of the Second Temple. That Momigliano chose not to live and teach in Israel is a fact, and perhaps not only because, living and studying between London, Chicago, and Pisa, he felt more in sympathy with the cosmopolitan intelligentsia of the diaspora. Like Benjamin, Strauss, and Rosenzweig, he did not follow Scholem's and Goitein's example, and did not go to Jerusalem. And again like Benjamin, who as late as 1936 published an anthology titled *Deutsche Menschen*, a searing elegy to a lost and much-lamented Germany,[49] Momigliano nurtured his own, inner Germany, the Germany of great philologists and scholars of the ancient world, many of whom were Jews. For all the empathy someone like Momigliano—brought up in the cult of the Risorgimento, which liberated Italian Jews from the ghettos—would necessarily have felt for the idea of Jewish national emancipation,[50] it is difficult to believe that he could have failed to perceive how the very degeneration of the nationalist ideal led to the devastation of Europe under fascism and Nazism. Once the primacy of the nationalist principle has been established, it is conceptually impossible to deny others access to it, and history bulges with ideals degenerated into their opposites, as Momigliano was certainly well aware.

At this point the example of the ancient world returns paradigmatically, in the ways Judaism kept itself vibrant and faithful to itself while interacting with a number of the adjacent cultures. It could also be added that a great historian's work on the past acts as backlighting, as it were, for the moral anxieties and intellectual preoccupations of the present rather than prophesying about the future. It also stands as reminder and admonition that the Nazi extermination of millions of Jews— among which were eleven members of his family, including his parents—"would never have taken place in Italy, France, and Germany (not to say more) had there not been a centuries-old indifference on the part of the peoples of these countries toward their Jewish fellow citizens": an indifference that was "the ultimate result of the hostility of the churches, which viewed 'conversion' as the only solution of the Jewish problem."[51] The idea, so deeply rooted in the Christian world, that Jewish destiny lay in conversion, denying Jews the right to remain Jews, had left Europe defenseless and culturally incapable of reacting against the exterminating will of the Nazis.[52] A short, only recently published text, left on a note pad, moves along the same lines and is still meaningful to us: "The main obstacle that a Jew encounters in Western Europe, after all, is that of not being a Christian . . . [Judaism] is a tradition that as such seems worthy to be preserved and developed in competition with, along with and even as a possible alternative to Christianity. For the reason that it requires less faith, but more study, than the Christian religious tradition, it is worthy of consideration."[53]

It would be impossible to end this piece without mentioning the much-debated question of Momigliano's presumed compromise with fascism.[54] The issue is a painful and disturbing one, and greater intellectual honesty (among his critics) might have spared his memory. It is not a question of ignoring or, worse, of concealing documents that might destabilize and create unease, but of contextualizing and understanding them. The first of these documents is a card from 1928 that Riccardo Di Donato found among Momigliano's papers attesting to his membership in Turin University's GUM (Gruppo Universitario Musicale), founded in 1921, which slowly moved into the force-field of the fascist GUF.[55]

In my opinion the best and most contextually conscientious response to the tragic moment in history that Momigliano was forced to steer his course through is given in Carlo Dionisotti's writings. A lifelong friend from undergraduate days, no one was better positioned to evaluate his actions. Dionisotti indignantly states that "the accusation against Momigliano of concealing his immediate Fascism, or at least of endorsing it very early on,"[56] the putative proof of which is the membership card giving him access to performances at the Teatro Regio in Turin, is quite simply unfounded. Had he had fascist leanings, there was nothing to stop him directly and openly becoming a member of GUF or, after the age of twenty-one, of Partito Nazionale Fascista.

Putting into context also means bearing in mind what is already a well-known fact, not least from Giorgio Bassani's novels: that fascist sympathies were common among Italian Jews, particularly in Ferrara and Piedmont, partly the consequence of an extreme form of patriotism and nationalism within an acquired Risorgimento *ethos* that blinded them as to the true authoritarian, illiberal, and very quickly antisemitic nature of the fascist dictatorship.[57] This was the case in Arnaldo's family, including his parents, unquestioning supporters of the the "fascio" in Caraglio, his native town in the Cuneo area. An important exception was his beloved cousin Felice, a socialist and admirer of Mazzini. Many of his fellow university students such as Leone Ginzburg, Aldo Garosci, and Massimo Mila, equally embracing Gobetti and Croce, joined the antifascist front. Momigliano concentrated exclusively on his studies, and held no explicit political position: neither fascist nor antifascist, he was, as he was later to say, a *NONFASCIST*.[58] The only political consideration of the period (in a comment on Croce's *Storia d'Italia*) was on liberalism and on the level of political theory: "Every revival of liberalism is conditioned by its capacity to transform itself into a party of the people. . . . Formulating and developing this new liberalism may be a sound way of preparing for the future, albeit distant."[59] Once again, we see detachment from the present and, certainly, no trace of fascism. Events were closing in, however. In 1931 his mentor Gaetano De Sanctis refused to swear the oath of loyalty to fascism requested by Giovanni Gentile, and he immediately lost his Chair in Greek history. Momigliano joined the PNF on November 6, 1932, the condition for taking the post himself when it was offered by Rome University in March 1933. The choice still seems inconceivable to us today, yet it was the only way to continue his studies and, paradoxically, preserve his mentor's intellectual heritage. It was certainly taken with De Sanctis's blessing; years later De Sanctis wrote to him: "You have the knowledge to continue and indeed improve on my work in the teaching profession and in books, and make a real contribution to the study of antiquity."[60]

There were, it is true, few—unfortunately very few—individuals who immediately and unhesitatingly embraced open opposition to fascism. As, needless to say, I wholly sympathize with those few, including close members of my family, who chose militant antifascism and therefore exile, I trust that no one will be induced to read my observations as a legitimation of those who joined the PNF as a means of staying safely in Italy. The explicitly antifascist choice of those who opted for direct political engagement and opposition, however, cannot be retrospectively required from those who, like Momigliano, were obeying above all "an imperious vocation of scholars and maestri"[61]. Once again, Carlo Dionisotti makes a just and balanced observation: "I have no doubt at all that he reluctantly took out membership of the Fascist Party, but I equally have no doubt that in his situation it was the inevitable and irreproachable thing to do. Born for the intellectual life, and not the political, Momigliano simply tried to adapt to conditions he was unable to change."[62] In the same way the letter Momigliano wrote to Bottai in 1938, setting out the fascist virtues of his family (himself included), which it is very hard to read without moral and even physical distress, surely testifies, however, to an extreme and desperate attempt to escape the consequences of the Race Laws. It does *not* constitute a proof of any fascist faith on his part.[63]

To summarize: (1) there exist no papers or letters of Momigliano's in which he expresses philo-fascist inclinations or beliefs, nor did he ever write in regime publications; (2) his scholarly work contains no trace of fascist leanings, not even in the darkest years of the regime (which for a scholar of Roman history would have been all too easy); (3) no one could reasonably suppose that the flagbearers of antifascist culture and enforced emigrants like Lionello Venturi and Gaetano Salvemini would have given their support in his favor [64] (to procure him a university post in the United States) if they had considered him in any way politically compromised.

The problem, then, is not Momigliano's presumed but unproven fascism. The more cogent question to ask is what exactly Italian academic culture of the 1930s must have been if only 12 professors out of 1,250 felt able to abjure the oath of loyalty to the regime requested by Giovanni Gentile.[65] Even more seriously, we have to wonder at the paucity of voices, even among the militant antifascists who had emigrated, raised clearly in denunciation of the national shame of the Race Laws.[66] These are the wretched, lacerating issues Italian history throws up, which still require attention and analysis.[67]

Notes

1. See Arnaldo Momigliano, *Pagine ebraiche*, ed. and intro by Silvia Berti (Torino, 1987). The Italian title conveys the intimate quality of his meditations, less perfectly rendered in the more academic title of the American edition, *Essays on Ancient and Modern Judaism*, ed. and intro. Silvia Berti (Chicago and London, 1994), from which all present quotations are taken.

2. See my "Introduction" to Momigliano, *Essays on Ancient and Modern Judaism*, vii–xxiv. Along the same lines, see the recent contribution by Tessa Rajak, "Momigliano and Judaism," in *The Legacy of Arnaldo Momigliano*, eds. Tim Cornell and Oswin Murray (London and Turin, 2014), 89–106.

3. See the documentation collected by Annalisa Capristo, "Arnaldo Momigliano e il mancato asilo negli USA (1938–1941): 'I Always Hope That Something Will Be Found in America,'" in *Quaderni di storia* 63 (January–June 2006): 5–55.

4. Silvia Berti, "Conversando con Arnaldo Momigliano," in *Pagine ebraiche*, new edition (Rome, 2016), 294. See also "The Jews of Italy," *New York Review of Books*, October 24, 1985, reprinted in *Essays on Ancient and Modern Judaism*, 133. On Amadio, see Alberto Cavaglion, "La corrispondenza famigliare di Amadio Momigliano (1844–1924) con una lettera inedita di Arnaldo Momigliano," in *Materia giudaica*, 15–16 (2010–2011): 111–19.

5. Silvia Berti, "Conversando con Arnaldo Momigliano," 296. See, particularly, Momigliano's personal recollections in the preface to *Essays on Ancient and Modern Judaism*, xxv–xviii, and the short essay on his cousin, in the same volume, 144–47. On Felice, see Alberto Cavaglion, *Felice Momigliano (1866–1924): Una biografia* (Napoli, 1988).

6. Momigliano, preface to *Essays on Ancient and Modern Judaism*, xxvii–xxviii.

7. See Moshe Idel, "Arnaldo Momigliano and Gershom Scholem on Jewish History and Tradition," in *Old Worlds, New Mirrors: On Jewish Mysticism and Twentieth-Century Thought* (Philadelphia, 2010), 17–30 (previously appeared in *Momigliano and Antiquarianism: Foundations of the Modern Cultural Sciences*, ed. Peter N. Miller [Toronto, Buffalo, and London, 2007], 312–33).

8. See Arnaldo Momigliano, "After-Dinner Speech on the Occasion of the Award of the Degree of D.H.L.H.C. at Brandeis University, 22 May 1977," in *Ottavo Contributo alla storia degli studi classici e del mondo antico* (Rome, 1977), 431–32.

9. Quoted in Riccardo Di Donato, "Arnaldo Momigliano from Antiquarianism to Cultural History: Some Reasons for a Quest," in *Momigliano and Antiquarianism*, 68–69.

10. Further elucidation is given in the above-quoted interview (note 4): "In my home it was taken for granted that this was the decisive moment: the emergence of Christian culture and the contact of Greek with Hebrew culture. It may raise a smile but, literally, these were things I knew at the age of ten. . . . They are things we simply can't think of today, but I read Renan at about the age of eleven."

11. See Arnaldo Momigliano, "Genesi e funzione attuale del concetto di ellenismo" (1935), in *Contributo alla storia degli studi classici e del mondo antico* (Rome, 1955), 165–93.

12. Arnaldo Momigliano, review (1969) of Benedetto Bravo, *Philologie, Histoire, Philosophie de l'Histoire: Etudes sur J. G. Droysen, historien de l'Antiquité* (Varsovie, 1968), in *Quinto contributo alla storia degli studi classici e del mondo antico*, 2 vols (Rome, 1975), 2:902.

13. Ibid.

14. Arnaldo Momigliano, "Un'apologia del giudaismo: il "Contro Apione" di Flavio Giuseppe," in *Terzo contributo alla storia degli studi classici e del mondo antico*, 2 vols. (Rome, 1966), 1:513–22, reprinted in *Essays on Ancient and Modern Judaism*, 58–66.

15. Capristo, "Arnaldo Momigliano e il mancato asilo negli USA," 32.

16. Carlo Dionisotti, "Commemorazione di Arnaldo Momigliano," in *Arnaldo Momigliano e la sua opera*, in *Rivista storica italiana*, 2:350 (reprinted in *Ricordo di Arnaldo Momigliano* [Bologna, 1989], 11). The eighteen-year-old Momigliano had written to him: "I am unable to vanquish that sense of transcendence which I feel so often" (ibid.). The whole monograph issue of *Rivista storica italiana* dedicated to Momigliano is extremely interesting, as is the volume in his memory *The Presence of the Historian: Essays in Memory of Arnaldo Momigliano*, ed. Michael P. Steinberg, *History and Theory* (Beiheft, 1991).

17. The essays are included in the collection *Tra storia e storicismo* (Pisa, 1985).

18. See Arnaldo Momigliano, *Jacob Bernays* (1969), in *Quinto contributo*, 1:127–58, reprinted in *Essays on Ancient and Modern Judaism*, 148–70; Arnaldo Momigliano, *Hermann Usener* (1982), in *Tra storia e storicismo*, 145–67. On these issues, and on Momigliano's increasingly complex views on historicism, compare Silvia Berti, *Autobiografia, storicismo e verità storica*, in *Arnaldo Momigliano*, 297–312.

19. This quotation, putting philology on a par with the religious sense, sounds again as Momigliano's self-portrait: "Since Bernays was a philologist like himself, Usener probably recognized a shared religious experience beneath their mutual philological interests." See Momigliano, *Hermann Usener*, 167.

20. Arnaldo Momigliano, "The Rhetoric of History and the History of Rhetoric: On Hayden White's Tropes" (1981), in *Settimo contributo alla storia degli studi classici e del mondo antico* (Rome, 1984), 54.

21. Arnaldo Momigliano, "La formazione della moderna storiografia sull'Impero romano" (1936), in *Contributo*, 107–64. It is interesting to note that as early as 1936 his reading of Bernays influenced his analysis of Gibbon (ibid., p. 137n100).

22. Arnaldo Momigliano, *Storia antica e antiquaria* (1950), in *Contributo*, 67–106.

23. Benedetto Croce, *Teoria e storia della storiografia* (Milan, 1989), 32–33.

24. Arnaldo Momigliano, "Il linguaggio e la tecnica dello storico" (1955), in *Secondo Contributo alla storia degli studi classici e del mondo antico* (Rome, 1960), 371.

25. Ibid., 370–71.

26. Croce, *Teoria e storia della storiografia*, 95–96.

27. Arnaldo Momigliano, "Ermeneutica e pensiero classico in Leo Strauss" (1967), in *Quarto Contributo alla storia degli studi classici e del mondo antico* (Rome, 1969), 117–28, reprinted in *Essays on Ancient and Modern Judaism*, 178–88. On Momigliano-Strauss relations, see my introduction to the above, xix–xxii.

28. Arnaldo Momigliano, "Historicism Revisited" (1974), in *Essays in Ancient and Modern Historiography* (Middletown, CT, 1977), 365–73, reprinted in *Sesto contributo*, 2:23–32. Momigliano also directly acknowledges his appreciation of Strauss's antihistoricism: "From his chair at the University of Chicago L. Strauss has delivered a penetrating criticism of historicism in favour of the restoring of natural law"; compare "Lo storicismo nel pensiero contemporaneo" (1961), in *Terzo contributo*, 1:272.

29. Momigliano, *Jacob Bernays*, 179.

30. Momigliano, *Historicism Revisited*, 370. For the German-Jewish discussion on historicism, see David N. Myers, *Resisting History: Historicism and Its Discontents in German-Jewish Thought* (Princeton and Oxford, 2003).

31. Again in Berti, "Conversando con Arnaldo Momigliano," 305. Compare the very similar words in a passage quoted by Peter Brown: "in its turn the liberal mind is religious in examining the evidence." See Peter Brown, "Remembering Arnaldo," *American Scholar* 2 (1988): 252.

32. Arnaldo Momigliano, "Prospettiva 1967 della storia greca" (1968), in *Quarto contributo*, 57.

33. Idel, "Arnaldo Momigliano and Gershom Scholem," 18–20.

34. Arnaldo Momigliano, "Gershom Scholem's Autobiography," in *Essays on Ancient and Modern Judaism*, 190.

35. See Arnaldo Momigliano, "Jewish Stories and Memoirs of Our Times," in *Essays on Ancient and Modern Judaism*, 141.

36. See Arnaldo Momigliano, "Preliminary Indications on the Apocalypse and Exodus in the Hebrew Tradition," in *Essays on Ancient and Modern Judaism*, 93.

37. Idel, "Arnaldo Momigliano and Gershom Scholem," 21.

38. Momigliano, "Gershom Scholem's Autobiography," in *Essays on Ancient and Modern Judaism*, 192.

39. Leo Strauss, "Preface to Spinoza's Critique of Religion," in *Liberalism Ancient and Modern*, 237.

40. Gershom Scholem, *From Berlin to Jerusalem* (New York, 1976), 50.

41. "With Gershom Scholem: An Interview," in Gershom Scholem, *On Jews and Judaism in Crisis: Selected Essays*, ed. W. J. Dannhauser (New York, 1976), 20. On Scholem, see at least David Biale, *Gershom Scholem: Kabbalah and Counter-History* (Cambridge, MA, 1979). Scholem's rejection of the whole idea of a useful German-Jewish encounter is well known. For a discussion of it, see Silvia Berti, "A World Apart? Gershom Scholem and Contemporary Readings of Seventeenth-Century Jewish-Christian Relations," in *Jewish Studies Quarterly* 3 (1996): 212–24, where previous bibliography is quoted.

42. Arnaldo Momigliano, "Biblical Studies and Classical Studies: Simple Reflections upon Historical Method" (1980), in *Settimo contributo*, 289, reprinted in *Essays on Ancient and Modern Judaism*, 3.

43. A significant illustration of his philosophy is in "With Gershom Scholem: An Interview," 32–35.

44. On this point Momigliano's and Bickerman's positions seem to converge; on Bickerman, see Albert I. Baumgarten, *Elias Bickerman as a Historian of the Jews* (Tübingen, 2010); on Momigliano, 193–205.

45. Arnaldo Momigliano, "Religion in Athens, Rome and Jerusalem in the First Century B.C.," in *Ottavo contributo*, 296.

46. See note 6.

47. The first of the two psalms states: "But his delight is in the law of the LORD; and in his law doth he meditate day and night."

48. Momigliano, "Prospettiva 1967 della storia greca," 58.

49. In his epilogue to the anthology Adorno wrote that "it arose against the annihilation of the German *Geist*." See Walter Benjamin, *Deutsche Menschen: Eine Folge von Briefen* (Frankfurt, 1977), 126.

50. In one passage, Momigliano looks back with the utmost respect and affection to the old Italian Zionists he had known in his youth, like Dante Lattes and Alfonso Pacifici, while remarking that "their choice was not so simple." See "The Jews of Italy," in *Essays on Ancient and Modern Judaism*, 133.

51. Momigliano, preface to *Essays on Ancient and Modern Judaism*, xxvii.

52. This point is cogently examined in what is still today the best study of Momigliano: Peter Brown, "Arnaldo Dante Momigliano (1908–1987)," in *Proceedings of the British Academy* 74 (1988): 405–42.

53. Arnaldo Momigliano, "Pensieri sull'ebraismo" (1979), in *Decimo Contributo alla storia degli studi classici e del mondo antico* (Rome, 2012), 365–69 (368–69).

54. For a brilliant and original discussion of the issue see Michael P. Steinberg, "Momigliano and the Facts," in *Judaism Musical and Unmusical* (Chicago, 2008), 141–65 (154–58); see also the more recent, well-argued analysis of the question in Pierpaolo Lauria, "Studi recenti su Arnaldo Momigliano: Per una discussione critica," in *Bollettino di storiografia*, no. 14 (2010): 27–48.

55. See Riccardo Di Donato, "Materiali per una biografia intellettuale di Arnaldo Momigliano," in *Athenaeum* 83, no. 1 (1995): 213–244, after the publication of which William V. Harris's violent attack came out: "The Silences of Momigliano," *Times Literary Supplement*, April 12, 1996, 6–7.

56. Carlo Dionisotti, "Momigliano e il contesto," *Belfagor*, 52, no. 6 (1997): 637. See also Carlo Dionisotti, "Momigliano: Quella tessera non può infangarlo," *Il Corriere della Sera*, December 4, 1997, 31.

57. On the complex relationship between the Italian Jews and the fascist regime see Meir Michaelis, *Mussolini and the Jews: German Italian Relations and the Jewish Question in Italy* (Oxford, 1978); Renzo De Felice, *The Jews in Fascist Italy* (New York, 2001; first published in

Italian in 1961); Alexander Stille, *Benevolence and Betrayal: Five Italian Jewish Families under Fascism* (New York, 1991).

58. His words are cited in Dionisotti, *Ricordo di Arnaldo Momigliano*, 97.

59. Letter from Momigliano to Dionisotti, dated August 1, 1928, quoted in Dionisotti, *Ricordo di Arnaldo Momigliano*, 81–82.

60. De Sanctis's letter, dated December 30, 1937, is cited in Leandro Polverini, "Momigliano e De Sanctis" in *Arnaldo Momigliano nella storiografia del Novecento*, ed. Leandro Polverini (Rome, 2006), 20.

61. Dionisotti, *Ricordo di Arnaldo Momigliano*, 18.

62. Dionisotti, "Momigliano e il contesto", 643.

63. See Giorgio Fabre, "Documenti. Arnaldo Momigliano: materiali biografici/2", *Quaderni di storia* 53 (2001): 309–20. As anyone who has any familiarity with the archive documents of prisoners or political internees knows, explicit statements of fascist loyalty were required even to obtain access to a family member in prison. Ignoring this aspect of the question, Luciano Canfora and Ernesto Galli della Loggia found it preferable to discredit Momigliano by accusing him openly of being a convinced Fascist: see Simonetta Fiori's interview to Luciano Canfora, "Ministro mi creda sono un fascista," *La Repubblica*, March 16, 2001, 46. For an intelligently argued reply, see Alexander Stille, "Attenti a come si parla di storia," *La Repubblica*, April 5, 2001, 48–49.

64. See Capristo, "Arnaldo Momigliano e il mancato asilo negli USA," 50–51.

65. On the issue see at least Helmut Goetz, *Il giuramento rifiutato: I docenti universitari e il regime fascista* (Florence, 2000); and Giorgio Boatti, *Preferirei di no* (Turin, 2001).

66. Four names come to mind: Francesco Saverio Nitti, Giuseppe Di Vittorio, Emilio Lussu, and Franco Venturi. See Giuseppe Di Vittorio, "In aiuto degli ebrei italiani!," *La voce degli italiani*, September 7, 1938, reprinted in "1938, non tutti vollero tacere," with two notes by Silvia Berti and Alberto Cavaglion, in *pagine ebraiche*, mensile di attualità e cultura dell'Unione delle Comunità Ebraiche Italiane, no. 3, (March 2010), 27.

67. See, however, the relevant contributions of Eugenio Garin, "Fascismo, antisemitismo e cultura italiana," in *Conseguenze culturali delle leggi razziali in Italia*, Atti del Convegno (Rome, May 11, 1989), Accademia nazionale dei Lincei (Rome, 1990), 9–24; Annalisa Capristo, "Gli intellettuali italiani di fronte all'estromissione dei colleghi ebrei da università e accademie," in *Annali dell'Istituto Italiano per gli Studi Storici* (Naples, 2012/2013), 1039–65; Mario Avagliano and Marco Palmieri, *Di pura razza italiana: L'Italia ariana di fronte alle leggi razziali* (Milan, 2013).

Simone Weil (1909–1943)

A JEWISH THINKER?

Maud S. Mandel

HOW DID SIMONE WEIL, FRENCH PHILOSOPHER AND SOCIAL ACTIVIST, THINK JEWISH modernity? This question is vexing. Despite having been born into a prosperous family of Jewish origin and never converting, Weil did not consider herself Jewish by race, religion, culture, or national affiliation. She is best known for her posthumously published works, *Gravity and Grace*, *The Need for Roots*, and *Waiting for God*, which analyze the individual's relation to God and the state and trace the spiritual shortcomings of modern society. Weil is understood by many as a Christian mystic whose profound rejection of the Hebrew Bible prevented her from ever fully embracing the Catholic Church, which she saw as corrupted by its historical link with Judaism and its unwillingness to accept the wider sources of divine revelation. While viewed as Jewish by the racial logic of the Vichy state, Weil rejected the designation. As she wrote to the Vichy minister of education in October 1940: "I don't know the definition of the word Jew; this subject has never been part of my program of studies. . . . Does this word designate a religion? I have never entered a synagogue and I have never witnessed a Jewish religious ceremony. . . . Does this word designate a race? I have no reason to suppose that I have any sort of tie, either through my father or my mother, with the people who lived in Palestine two thousand years ago. . . . Having pretty much learned to read by reading French writers of the seventeenth century, such as Racine and Pascal, if there is a religious tradition that I consider as my patrimony, it is the Catholic tradition. The Christian, French, Hellenic tradition is mine; the Hebrew tradition is foreign to me; no text of a law can change that for me."[1] Indeed, she was a self-declared antisemite, who repeatedly denounced Judaism and its historical legacy.[2]

And yet despite Weil's self-declared distance from her Jewish origins, numerous scholars, philosophers, and critics have struggled to place her within twentieth-century Jewish history. Indeed, if Weil's "thinking Jewish modernity" was, as we will see, rather spotty, those seeking to understand Jewish modernity have "thought Weil." In other words, rather than dismissing Weil as so ignorant of Judaism and Jewish history as to render her pronouncements beyond consideration, many scholars have insisted on her relevance to Jewish modernity. Thus, according to Thomas Nevin, who subtitles his intellectual biography of Weil "Portrait of a Self-Exiled

Jew," although Weil worked hard to distance herself from her Jewish origins, "a Jew she was, not in any racial sense (which we have learned to regard as spurious) or in a religious sense (Judaism is more than a religion, and her upbringing was nonobservant) but in a historical sense." For Nevin, although Weil "rejected and resented" the constraint of her Jewishness, "much that is most positive in both her life and her writing suggests an *anima naturaliter judaica* [an inherently Jewish soul]."[3]

To draw such conclusions, however, most of Weil's recent critics have been forced to speculate wildly over her motivations and distort her views.[4] Indeed, while Weil had profoundly critical views on ancient Judaism, for the most part Jewish modernity did not interest her very much, and when her attention was so drawn, her views were more conventional (if distasteful to many) than her critics suggest. As I will argue, if Weil is read as a product of her age rather than as a product of the post-Holocaust world, her perspectives on Jewish modernity reflect the views of one subset of highly integrated French Jewish citizens who came to see Jewish identity as a burden and an anachronism. While many came to repudiate those ideas in subsequent decades, Weil's death in 1943 made her forever a product of the prior age.

■

Weil's biography helps historicize the origins of her thinking on Jewish modernity. Weil was born in 1909 into a comfortable, nonpracticing Parisian Jewish family.[5] Her mother, whose family left Galicia for France via Belgium in 1882, had grown up in a prosperous, secular household, her father's forays into writing Hebrew poetry notwithstanding. Weil's father, Bernard, came from a family of Alsatian merchants with stronger links to Jewish tradition. As an adult, however, he distanced himself from his roots, adopting agnostic and even atheist views. Thus despite the regular presence of her pious paternal grandmother, who lived in Paris, purportedly followed Simone's mother into the kitchen to ensure adherence to proper dietary laws, and insisted that she would rather see her granddaughter dead than married to a non-Jew, Simone Weil had little exposure to Jewish culture or community in her early years.[6] Indeed, she had never seen a devout Jew praying until 1942 in a refugee camp and only entered a synagogue once in her life.[7]

Her youth was marked by a tight-knit nuclear family life, intense intellectual stimulation, and a competitive if close relationship with her brother André. While attending the prestigious Lycée Henri IV—at which she studied with Alain (Émile Chartier), the influential educator and philosopher—and the École Normale Supérieure, Weil became a pacifist (a position she held until World War II) and left-wing activist. Certified to teach philosophy, Weil held several posts in provincial schools, while filling most of her time with trade union meetings, writing for syndicalist papers, and defending the working classes, ultimately taking a leave from teaching in 1934 to become a factory laborer. Frail and plagued by migraines, Weil was forced to leave the factory several months later. Nevertheless, the experience, which she found profoundly dehumanizing, proved significant in shaping her views on the place of labor in society. In addition, the experience transformed Weil's thinking on Christianity.[8] While vacationing in Portugal shortly after leaving the factory, Weil was deeply moved upon overhearing local villagers singing hymns.

The music convinced her that Christianity was the religion of slaves, an affinity she felt she shared after her debilitating experiences in the factory. In 1937, a moment of religious ecstasy in the Basilica of Santa Maria degli Angeli—the church in which St. Francis of Assisi had prayed—led her to pray for the first time. During a subsequent visit to the Benedictine abbey of St. Solesmes, Weil experienced an even more powerful revelation on reading a poem by the seventeenth-century poet George Herbert, consolidating her mystical connection with Christianity.

Weil's spiritual mysticism—deeply engaged with Christianity but also informed by a wide study of world religions, her ascetic lifestyle, and her political activism—shaped the rest of her life. Although continuing to teach, Weil took numerous leaves of absence due to poor health and a desire to pursue her political passions, even enlisting in the Spanish Civil War (until an accident forced her departure). Following France's fall to the Nazis, Weil left Paris with her parents, arriving eventually in Marseilles, where she worked with the Resistance until the family departed for New York in May 1942. Much of her subsequent writing focused on explaining France's loss to the Nazis and on how to rebuild a just postwar society. Also while in Marseilles, she befriended Father Perrin, a Dominican friar, and through discussions with him and Gustave Thibon, a farmer, royalist, and writer, Weil further articulated her relationship to Catholicism. Never willing to convert, Weil maintained her love of Christianity while criticizing the Church for many conceptual failings, including its ongoing link to the Hebrew Bible. As Richard Bell argues, her faith "spread across and beyond a single tradition," leading her ultimately to make a case "for a broadly based spirituality consistent with her view of God's relation to nature and the human condition."[9]

After accompanying her parents to safety in New York, Weil obtained permission to join the French Resistance in England. Hoping to lead a mission into occupied France, Weil was instead put to work assessing reports from the French Resistance. Despairing over her marginality, she worked long hours and voluntarily starved herself—a lifelong pattern of denying herself basic necessities—ultimately dying in a sanatorium at Ashford in Kent, England in August 1943.

Throughout her writings, Weil repeatedly denounced Judaism and its historical legacy, moral blindness, tribal collectivism, idolatry, and brutality—in short, for a host of failings. She thus reduced Judaism to a unidimensional caricature while simultaneously excusing or ignoring similar flaws in other religious traditions that she celebrated. As she noted in her famous analysis of the *Iliad*, "[The Hebrews] considered their beaten foes repellent to God himself and damned to atone for crimes; this made cruelty permissible, even mandatory."[10] In other words, due to their belief in their "chosenness," the ancient Israelites felt justified in doing violence to their adversaries. As a result, the Hebrew Bible was a history of murder and massacre, a testament to justified extermination, crime, barbarity, and a host of other evils from fraud to prostitution to incest. Moreover, the crimes in the Hebrew Bible were not limited to ancient times but served as a framework for all subsequent evil. Thus, "the curse of Israel weighs heavily on Christendom. The atrocities, the Inquisition, Capitalism, all came from Israel (and still does to a certain extent)." Totalitarianism—the worst evil of Weil's time—was likewise a legacy of ancient Israel.[11] In this schema, all modern evil had had emerged from Jewish hands:

The Jews—that handful of uprooted individuals—have been responsible for the uprooting of the whole terrestrial globe. The part they played in Christianity turned Christendom into something uprooted with respect to its own past. The Renaissance attempt at a re-rooting failed, because it was of an anti-Christian inspiration. The trend of "enlightenment"—eighteenth century, 1789, laicization, etc.—increased this uprooting to a still infinitely greater extent with the lie about progress. And uprooted Europe went about uprooting the rest of the world by colonial conquest. Capitalism and totalitarianism form part of this progressive development of uprooting; the Jew haters, of course, spread Jewish influence. The Jews are the poison of uprooting personified.[12]

Rehearsing some of the central themes of contemporary antisemitic discourse, Weil thus blamed Jews not only for capitalism and colonialism but also for antisemitism itself.

Thinking Weil

Beginning in 1948, after the posthumous publication of excerpts from Weil's notebooks, *Gravity and Grace*, which brought the full extent of her critique against the Jewish tradition to widespread attention for the first time, scholars and philosophers began grappling with her views. A survey of this literature suggests how reassessments of Jewish identity in the post-Holocaust age have distorted these readings by attributing to Weil a consciousness that only emerged decades after World War II. Interestingly, her *initial* critics—while deeply shaped by recent events—rarely placed Weil in that context and instead sought to *engage* her ideas on their own terms.[13] Some, such as Armand Lunel, did this by hypothesizing whether her initial confidant and editor, Gustave Thibon, rearranged and thereby overemphasized Weil's misgivings on Israel in the published notebook excerpts.[14] Most others, however, refused to allow Weil's distorted views of Jews and Judaism to stand. Emmanuel Levinas thus challenged Weil's arguments by underscoring fundamental flaws therein: first, her assertion that "the origins of Good are foreign to Judaism, while Evil is specifically Judaic"; and second, her claim that Good is "an absolutely pure idea, excluding all contamination or violence."[15] Rejecting her characterization of ancient Judaism as lacking a conception of transcendent justice and challenging her conception of Jewish deracination, Levinas argued that Weil's misreading of the Hebrew Bible left her blind to Judaism's humanity. Like Levinas, Hans Meyerhoff's 1957 essay, "Contra Simone Weil," engaged Weil as an interlocutor despite her death fifteen years earlier. Rooting her thinking in Gnosticism and ignorance, Meyerhoff argued that the very elements that disgusted Weil, including the "purity of [Israel's] monotheism gradually cleansed of all traces of magic and idolatrous imagery," or "perhaps the most creative of all ideas of religion, that which is born of the tension between the faith that the world is not redeemed and the resolve that it be redeemed by man's works and love," were "Israel's great and lasting contribution" and the basis for Meyerhoff's assessment "that it is worth being a Jew in a Christian world."[16] For Meyerhoff, Weil was a "living" interlocutor—that is to say, a thinker whose ideas were to be refuted, presumably because they still reflected a relevant ideological perspective within the Western landscape. Martin Buber's analysis of Weil is likewise critical in this regard. The number of times Buber uses the phrase, "it is not true," before challenging Weil's particular views on Judaism points to his engagement with the *content* of her ideas. Thus, for example, he writes, "When [Weil] referred to the God of Israel as a 'natural' God and to that of Christianity as a 'supernatural' God, she failed entirely to understand the character of the former."[17] Here and throughout his essay, Buber tells us why Weil was wrong.

By the early 1970s, however, analyses of Weil's Jewish writings began to shift. Instead of addressing the merits of her arguments, scholars began exploring the context in which they were written. These works can be broken into three loose categories: Weil as self-hating Jew, Weil as catastrophe Jew, and Weil as post-Holocaust Jew. As we will see, while all approach Weil's relationship to Judaism and Jewishness from different vantage points, all three are intimately enmeshed with the question plaintively posed by Weil's niece in a recent memoir: "So, if you were informed [of the deportations of Jewish families], why, why from the depths of your own despair . . . why did you not have a thought, a word, for all those Jewish babies, crazed with terror, cruelly separated from their mothers?"[18] In other words, recent analyses of Weil's relations to Jews and Judaism have often been deeply enmeshed with the Holocaust. Such texts assume, without stating so outright, that the Holocaust served as an immediate and dramatic turning point in the way European Jews thought of themselves. The fact that Weil did not make this turn disturbs her critics, and their analyses seek to explain this evident failure.

Weil as Self-Hating Jew—Beginning with Paul Giniewski's 1978 *Simone Weil ou la haine de soi* (Simone Weil or Self-Hatred), numerous authors have condemned Weil for her antisemitism. While some have sought to contextualize her attitudes in wider psycho-historical explanations linked to her anorexia and celibacy, most have used the category of self-hatred to criticize her stance on Jews and Judaism.[19] Giniewski, for example, on the one hand, placed Weil's violent anti-Jewish stance in psychological terms, asserting that she was "repelled by the part of herself of which anti-Semites made her ashamed" and that "like many victims, instead of turning against her executioner, she espoused his hatred." On the other, he made clear his disgust for her choices, noting that her outreach to others in need never included fellow Jews: "[O]ne hopes maybe to see her take an interest in Jews in distress (including her own parents) trying to find a place on a boat, a visa on their passport that will make the difference between life and death at Auschwitz. No." Giniewski later accuses Weil of condoning "ethnocide" in a report she wrote that called for the postwar assimilation of French Jews while she was working for the Free French in London. The report, he concludes, "would have been actionable according to the severity with which post-Liberation French courts looked at such matters."[20]

Here Giniewski's work reflects much of the literature that analyzes Weil according to self-hatred frameworks. In such assessments, Weil's anti-Judaism is to be understood rather contradictorily, on the one hand as a personal psychosis emerging in response to the antisemitic times in which she lived and, on the other, as a political stance that *should* have diminished or reversed due to the same factors. She is, in this construction, both a victim of a psychological disorder and a willful parrot of French and German oppressors. As Arthur A. Cohen notes: "At the moment when the Jewish people were being destroyed for being Jews, Simone Weil—loathing her Jewish origins and the Jewish literature of ecstatic covenant, exile and suffering—was herself passing through the identical Jewish experience, though she could not acknowledge it, though she lacked every instrument of interpreting to herself that her own willful assumption of pain and suffering had much in common with the saints and sages of Israel."[21] Here, Weil's "self-hatred"—both repellent and tragic—is read through the lens of wartime violence and anti-Jewish persecution across time, and her failing is the inability to see the paradox in which she was trapped.

Weil as Catastrophe Jew—While not all analysts use self-hatred to understand Weil's relationship to Jews and Judaism, the Holocaust looms large in other approaches as well. For Thomas Nevin, Weil—like Henri Bergson, Walter Benjamin, and Primo Levi—was a "catastrophe Jew," Jean Améry's term for those who came to claim loyalty to their ethnic origins because of the persecutions of World War II.[22] The problem here, of course, is that Weil never made a similar move, leaving Nevin to seek evidence where there is none of Weil's "transformation." While trying on the one hand to historicize Weil's views in the context of Vichy antisemitism, Nevin simultaneously hunts for evidence that her views on Jews were not uniformly negative. Since such "evidence" is scant indeed, Nevin speculates whether she was "perhaps feeling in some atavistic way the pull of the heritage she so insistently had denied to Vichy," and whether, for example, her silence on deportations reflected a newfound awareness of how wrong she had been, a perspective that she "could not bear" to express "even in her notebooks."[23]

Given that Weil's writings do not in any way grapple with the anti-Jewish violence of her world, Nevin's assertions read as a highly speculative attempt to vindicate his subject, a perspective that also leads Nevin to assert that core aspects of Weil's political philosophy, such as her treaties on uprootedness and justice, emerged from her (unconscious) engagement with her Jewish heritage. As he writes in just one example of this thinking: "Though exiled in her own country she exemplified par excellence the cosmopolitan reach of freethinking Jewish culture. . . . It is as though existence itself were one great Talmudic lesson for her to learn, and she brought all the avidity requisite to the learning."[24] For Nevin, Weil's engagement with universal justice and charity was similarly embedded in her Jewish heritage, which after his careful grounding of much of her thinking in twentieth-century French history falls short and can only be understood as part of Nevin's larger project to save her for history. As he writes elsewhere, "our attention is necessarily informed by awareness of Weil's time and her pathetic status as a 'catastrophe Jew.' Her words must be taken seriously and not hermetically sealed off as though there has been no Chelmno, no Treblinka, no Auschwitz." [25] What Nevin misses here is that Weil's conceptual map did not include these places. Rather, it is *Nevin* for whom Chelmno, Treblinka, and Auschwitz resonate, ultimately providing him with perspectives on Jewish history that were meaningless to Weil.

Similar orientations undergird Rachel Feldhay Brenner's *Writing as Resistance*, which compares Simone Weil with Edith Stein, Anne Frank, and Etty Hillesum under a shared rubric of anti-Nazi Resistance writing. In Brenner's telling, all four women suffered from Nazi anti-Jewish policies, and all four responded as the post-Enlightenment humanist Jews that they were. The problem with this framing is that—as Brenner is well aware—Weil never acknowledged her Jewishness as a relevant category in her anti-Nazi struggle, which, for her, was enmeshed in

French patriotism. Moreover, Weil never gave any indication that she saw herself in Nazi anti-Jewish violence. Thus when Brenner writes, "as long as possible, the four women were trying not to permit *the horror of the Final Solution* [emphasis mine] to reduce their existence to a struggle for mere physical survival," she employs categories that were unknown to Weil. Furthermore, like Nevin, Brenner consistently speculates on Weil's unconscious motivations.[26] In one example, Brenner explains why Weil never formally converted to Catholicism (a choice others have convincingly attributed to Weil's strong doctrinal differences with the Church and an unwillingness to join any collective). "Could it be," Brenner speculates, "that, despite her vehement anti-Jewish sentiments, the fear of committing an act of cowardice when other Jews were suffering was the reason for her refusal to be baptized?" Such speculations then lead Brenner to conclude that we can understand Weil's decision not to be baptized "as an act of resistance" and her decision to cut herself off from Catholic and Jew alike as a " 'catastrophe' of self-inflicted estrangement," a distortion of Améry's concept that renders it meaningless in Weil's case.[27] Having failed to force her four authors into ill-fitting conceptual categories, Brenner finds herself ultimately mystified by their choices: How, she wonders, did they continue to occupy themselves with issues of emotional maturity, moral accountability, and intellectual honesty "even in circumstances of inexorably approaching violence and death?"[28] Here we see Brenner's convoluted logic in full, as she makes clear that she expects her four authors to have understood the context in which they were living as we do. While not condemning Weil, Brenner's analysis is as anachronistic as those blaming Weil for moral blindness.

Weil as Post-Holocaust Jew—The urge to use post-Holocaust conceptual categories is explicit in Richard Bell's analysis of Weil's thinking about Jews and Judaism. For Bell, Weil was much less concerned with fleeing her Jewishness than she was with wanting to be regarded as a human being, a position he contextualizes as part of a wider post-Holocaust philosophical struggle with the absence of God. While not discounting her striking anti-Judaism or her failure to react with compassion to suffering Jews, Bell argues that Weil's attack was targeted at "the use and abuse of a will to power and the absence of any 'spiritual life' or discernable 'inspiration' toward the good."[29] For Bell, Weil's "reasons for saying she is Catholic no more make her a Christian than her denials release her from being a Jew."[30] Rather, Bell argues, Weil's understanding of "what it is to be a religious person [are] . . . in some ways . . . compatible with 'being a Jew' as expressed by some post-Holocaust Jewish thinkers."[31] Most notably, he underscores her "compassion-based morality" that brought her moral philosophy and post-Holocaust Jewish morality into dialogue: "Both emphasize practice, the practice of love and justice, of praise and compassion. Both are keenly aware of human suffering and affliction in the face of God's absence. Yet curiously, both find God in the neighbor, as the true Other, and both also find their true humanity there."[32] Like Levinas, "Weil finds 'unsurpassable proximity to God' through love and justice toward her neighbor."[33] For Bell, then, Weil "had moved past both Judaism and Christianity as both seemed manifest to her in the world."[34] This, in Bell's view, is where Weil's so-called post-Holocaust philosophy met up with that of one of her most severe critics, Emmanuel Levinas, as both struggled to understand the suffering of the innocent. The problem with this particular post-Holocaust framework is that Bell cannot root Weil's philosophy in anti-Jewish attacks, since Weil never made those connections. While Bell has certainly uncovered surprising philosophical links between Weil and Levinas, by conceptualizing the issue around responses to God's absence during the Holocaust, Bell's essay misleads, suggesting a "before/after" framework that did not reflect Weil's thinking in the 1940s.

Weil and Thinking Jewish Modernity

Thus far I have argued that post-Holocaust frameworks have distorted the historical Weil. Whether conceptualizing Weil as a self-hater, a resister, or a philosophically prescient thinker, recent approaches to Weil's thinking have been unable to disentangle her from perspectives that emerged following World War II, as scholars began to rethink Jewish modernity in light of the Holocaust. As work on the immediate postwar years has shown, however, for many Jews such shifting perspectives did not emerge immediately after the war. Or rather, while some European Jews quickly understood the Nazi persecutions as a challenge to their very place in European society, it was also common—at least initially—for Jews (and others) to respond to events in ways that reflected their prior perspectives on Jewish life. As I have argued elsewhere, while mid-twentieth-century French Jews responded to Vichy persecution in a variety of ways, not all saw recent events as a radical break from prior ways of understanding themselves or their place in the national community. If, several years after the war, French Jews looked back on the period as one of profound rupture, it took time for such perspectives to coalesce.[35]

Weil was thus hardly alone in "failing" to repudiate all her prior thinking about Jews and Judaism during World War II, particularly if we remind ourselves that she died in 1943, when news of the genocide was widespread but few had fully understood its ramifications. As numerous scholars have made clear, her perspectives on ancient Judaism, many of them penned in the early 1940s, were exceptionally harsh. And yet, as Todd Endelman and Michael Stanislawski have argued, if we contextualize Weil's thinking—during a period in which many thousands of those of Jewish heritage chose to distance themselves from their origins, and in which at least some Jews opted for conversion either out of conviction or as a radical form of assimilation—her violent rejection of that heritage seems less shocking.[36] As Stanislawski writes, "In this context, Weil's abhorrent comments regarding Judaism seem without doubt more like repeated clichés [*clichés maintes fois rabbatus*] than like unique forms of a particularly violent anti-Semitism. She simply repeated, too carelessly certainly, the most commonplace and hackneyed themes that circulated in certain Christian circles, according to which Judaism was reduced to a sectarian communalism and to a set of arbitrary laws, and which put forward the image of a jealous and malicious God, devoid of the essential love of the God of the New Testament and his son."[37] Stanislawski seeks neither to justify nor to excuse Weil's views, which he describes as "virulently anti-Semitic," but rather to contextualize her in the period from which she emerged.

By adopting a similar framework—one that places Weil in her own intellectual context—we can finally return to the question: How did Weil think Jewish modernity? First it is worth recalling that Weil wrote very little about living Jews or Jewish practice. Certainly, as we will see, her aggressive critique of ancient Judaism had implications for modern Jews, as the "individual incarnation—from ancient times to the contemporary era—of the evil principle from which they came."[38] Moreover, as noted above, Weil saw modernity itself, or rather all that was evil within modernity, as a legacy of ancient Judaism. As Gustav Thibon remembered, Weil was "fond of saying that Hitler hunted on the same ground as the Jews and only persecuted them in order to resuscitate under another name to his own advantage their tribal god, terrestrial, cruel, and exclusive."[39] In 1976, Father Perrin likewise remarked, "She thought that if Israel had the same strength as the Nazis they would have had the same attitude."[40]

Yet despite her extensive reflections on this legacy, she rarely spoke about Jewish modernity. Her notable interest in the oppressed peoples in her midst—particularly industrial laborers and colonial subjects—did not extend to Jewish refugees struggling to find a safe haven as antisemitism spread throughout Europe, nor did she take a stand against Vichy antisemitism except in the letter cited above, when she argued that Vichy laws should not apply to her. In short, contemporary Jewish life rarely captured her attention.

Her two major pronouncements on the subject have thus been the subject of much scrutiny. The first of these was a 1942 letter to her brother and his non-Jewish wife in which she urged the Catholic baptism of their baby, Sylvie, by arguing she would never regret such a choice unless she later converted "to fanatical Judaism." However, if she eventually desired to marry a Jew, atheist, or Buddhist, she would not be faulted for her parents' decision to baptize her, while "if a more or less anti-Semitic piece of legislation grants advantages to baptized half-Jews, it would be agreeable for her, probably, to enjoy these advantages without having done anything cowardly."[41] When her brother objected by arguing that a Protestant baptism would accomplish as much without immersing Sylvie in the rituals of Catholicism, Weil responded that a future Catholic spouse would either not recognize a Protestant baptism or his parents might object, whereas a Catholic baptism would leave all doors open.[42]

Notable here is Weil's pragmatic approach to conversion. While her own distaste for Judaism is self-evident in her reference to "fanatical Jews," the familial communication has little to do with forwarding an anti-Jewish agenda and rather reflects a rather widespread view among highly assimilated European Jews that baptism offered certain protections. Indeed, for most Jewish converts to Christianity and for the large majority who opted to baptize their children, the choice reflected neither spiritual nor doctrinal decisions but instead a belief that Jewishness was an impediment to their professional and social aims. As the last and most radical step in a long line of assimilatory behaviors, baptism also offered hope that they or their children could finally escape antisemitism.[43] Weil's letter to her brother suggests that she shared similar views on the plight of modern Jews. Catholicism would open doors for her niece Sylvie, even if authorities continued to see her as a "baptized half-Jew." In this construction, Jewishness was only a relevant religious category with regard to marital choices. Otherwise it was an impediment to be overcome—a quasi-racial category (as the reference to "baptized half-Jews" suggests) best addressed through radical assimilation.

Weil's second explicit instance of "thinking Jewish modernity" came in 1943 when she was working for the Free French in London after being asked to respond to a proposal from the right-wing resistance group, the Organisation Civile et Militaire (OCM), addressing the position of non-Christian minorities in postwar France. The proposal rejected a racial basis for Jewish identity, but it still chastised Jews for their distinctiveness, called for their conversion, and promoted various professional restrictions such as a ban on Jewish migration and the deportation of foreign Jews. Weil's response—undoubtedly her most developed reflection on Jewish modernity—has dismayed many subsequent readers in that she agreed with the report's premise that "the existence of such a minority does not constitute a good; so the object must be to provoke its disappearance." While she emphatically rejected what she saw as the OCM's implicit goal "to set up a crystallized Jewish minority as a ready preserve with a view to future atrocities," she endorsed a project of radical assimilation, calling for mixed marriages and a Christian education for future generations of Jews. [44]

Here, as in Weil's earlier writings on Judaism, Jews were criticized for their deracination and their "irreligion" (since the national idolatry at the basis of Judaism rendered the religion meaningless with the nation's destruction). Moreover, Weil accepted the premise that since most Jews could not grasp "authentic spirituality," they should be limited from taking positions of public instruction. In conclusion, she defended non-Jewish minorities, such as Spanish or Russian refugees, noting that while the latter came from real countries, Jews were "a band of fugitives. . . . In dissolving the Jewish milieu without brutality, they will not be deprived of a country but prepared to have one for the first time." [45]

Here, as in Weil's proposal for her niece's baptism, radical assimilation was understood as a response to the "Jewish problem." Not only would antisemitism diminish—Weil saw negative French reactions to Jewish predominance in French culture as legitimate—but also Jews would fully join the national community. Significantly, she saw it as essential that these processes occur naturally, since any "official recognition of this minority's existence would be very bad because that would crystallize it." Her hope was thus that parents would refrain from informing their children of their Jewishness and that "at the end of two or three generations the only ones to remain conscious of being Jews would be fanatical racists. At this time the problem would be to find a criterion to pick them out so as to deprive them of French nationality." [46]

Such a radical solution to the "Jewish problem," while deeply upsetting to post-Holocaust analysts of Weil's thought, did not reflect any revolutionary new thinking on Weil's part. Nor was it a particularly shocking response to Jewish modernity. In 1893, no less a figure than Theodor Herzl recommended widespread Jewish baptism and intermarriage as a solution to European antisemitism. This move preceded by only three years the publication of *Der Judenstaat*, his next effort at solving the same problem. Nor was Weil the only French Jew to be calling for Jewish conversion and intermarriage in the 1940s. After the war ended, the French Jewish writer Jean-Jacques Bernard became a public proponent of radical assimilation despite his own wartime internment and that of his father, the dramatist Tristan Bernard. Converting to Catholicism shortly after the war, Bernard called on French Jews to assimilate to demonstrate their love for the nation as a reflection of their bond with their fellow citizens. [47]

Bernard's views created significant controversy, an indication of his distance from mainstream thinking about postwar Jewish life. Yet Bernard's writings, penned only a handful of years after Weil's own call for radical assimilation, point to the way Weil's vision of Jewish modernity fit into a wider, if marginalized, field. Radical assimilation was for Weil, Bernard, and others who chose a similar path a way to address both antisemitism and the excesses of Jewish "separatism." While disturbing in hindsight and even to many of her contemporaries, Weil's response to the problem of Jewish modernity was hardly shocking for its time; indeed, for her, it offered an *alternative* to the Nazis' genocidal violence. As no less an intellectual luminary than Jean-Paul Sartre made clear in his famous essay, *Réflexions sur la question juive*, published in Paris in 1946, ambiguity toward Jewish difference continued to mark postwar French intellectual circles following World War II even among those most critical of antisemitism.[48]

For many of Weil's critics, her response to the OCM report was the worst in a litany of her outrages against her people. As noted above, Giniewski labels her plan a call for ethnocide that would have been prosecutable in postwar France. To him, Weil consistently reflected a virulent antisemitism that culminated in a desire for "a veritable bloodless final solution to the Jewish problem: the disappearance of the Jews."[49] While Giniewski is certainly correct that Weil saw no use for Jews or Judaism, his willingness to place her proposals in the same context as those of the Nazis points to the way he (and others) have blurred the line between the violence of World War II and a range of other solutions to the Jewish problem, which, however distasteful, often had more in common with radical Republican visions of erasing differences than they did with genocidal violence.

When placed in the context in which she came of age (and in which she died), Weil emerges as one of a number of highly integrated European Jewish-born thinkers who came to see Jewish modernity as an impediment to the evolution of a democratic society and as the source of numerous social problems. While some thinkers came to reject these views even during the war itself, it took others longer to move away from deeply held ways of thinking Jewish modernity. We can never know how Weil *would* have come to understand Jewishness had she lived a full life or absorbed an empirical understanding of the Holocaust. Condemning her or distorting her perspectives by insisting on how she *should* have seen the problem, however, does little to shed light on the complex ways that Jews came to terms with their world as it was changing around them.

Notes

1. Simone Pétrement, *Simone Weil: A Life*, trans. Raymond Rosenthal (New York, 1976), 390–92.

2. Paul Giniewski, *Simone Weil ou la haine de soi* (Paris, 1978), 30.

3. Thomas R. Nevin, *Simone Weil: Portrait of a Self-Exiled Jew* (Chapel Hill, NC, 1991), xi.

4. For a critique of previous literature on Weil as ahistorical, see Michael Stanislawski, "Simone Weil et Raïssa Maritain," *Cahiers du Judaisme* 11 (2001–2002): 97–107.

5. Two overviews of Weil's life, Pétrement's *Simone Weil: A Life* and Jacques Cabaud, *Simone Weil* (New York, 1964), established the initial parameters of her biography. More recent assessments include Robert Coles, *Simone Weil: A Modern Pilgrimage* (Woodstock, VT, 1989); Gabriella Fiori, *Simone Weil: An Intellectual Biography*, trans. Joseph R. Berrigan (Athens, GA,

1989); Francine du Plessix Gray, *Simone Weil* (New York, 2001); and David McLellan, *Utopian Pessimist: The Life and Thought of Simone Weil* (New York, 1990). A helpful biographical summary can be found in J. P. Little, ed. and trans., *Simone Weil on Colonialism: An Ethic of the Other* (Lanham, MD, 2003).

6. Pétrement, *Simone Weil*, 3. Without contesting that Simone and her brother were removed from Jewish culture and community, Sylvie Weil, *At Home with André and Simone Weil*, (Evanston, 2010), 170, questions "the quaint family fiction which consisted of persuading themselves and others, that as children, they were unaware that they were Jewish." Moreover, Simone's parents were concerned that she might convert to Catholicism. According to her brother, "Being baptized was the most unpleasant thing that could happen to a person in a family with a Jewish background—they (the family) would certainly have expressed their opposition to it." Cited in Sylvie Courtine-Denamy, *Three Women in Dark Times: Edith Stein, Hannah Arendt, Simone Weil* (Ithaca, NY, 2000), 10.

7. Courtine-Denamy, *Three Women in Dark Times*, 8.

8. Weil later claimed that she had held a "Christian conception," of the world since childhood, but as Todd Endelman, *Leaving the Jewish Fold: Conversion and Radical Assimilation in Europe and America from the Enlightenment to the Present* (Princeton, 2015), chap. 6, argues, this was a self-fashioning that only occurred after she had found Catholic ritual in her late twenties.

9. Richard Bell, "Simone Weil, Post-Holocaust Judaism, and the Way of Compassion," in *Simone Weil: The Way of Justice as Compassion* (Lanham, MD, 1998), 170.

10. *Simone Weil's "The Iliad or the Poem of Force": A Critical Edition*, ed. and trans. James P. Holoka (New York, 2003), 68.

11. Simone Weil, *La pesanteur et la grace* (Paris, 1948), 190.

12. Simone Weil, *Notebooks*, trans. Arthur Wills, 2 vols. (London, 1956), 576–77.

13. One exception was the writer and Jewish activist, W. Rabi, "La conception weilienne de la création: Recontre avec la Kabbale juive," in *Simone Weil: Philosophe, historienne et mystique*, ed. Gilbert Kahn (Paris, 1978), 141–54, who linked his critique of Weil to having lived through "the greatest catastrophe of our history." This perspective led him to contextualize Weil's failings in a wider Jewish absorption of antisemitic stereotypes and in "the weakness and spiritual emptiness" of French Jewish life.

14. Armand Lunel, "Simone Weil et Israël," *Revue de la pensée juive* 4 (July 1950): 46–52

15. Emmanuel Levinas, "Simone Weil against the Bible," in *Difficult Freedom: Essays on Judaism* (Baltimore, 1990), 134. Levinas was aware of the problems of "discuss[ing] matters with a dead woman" (133). And yet he proceeds to "speak of her . . . and speak against her," as if a living interlocutor.

16. Hans Meyerhoff, "Contra Simone Weil: The Voice of Demons for the Silence of God," in *Arguments and Doctrines: A Reader of Jewish Thinking in the Aftermath of the Holocaust*, ed. Arthur A. Cohen (New York, 1970), 82.

17. Martin Buber, "The Silent Question: On Henri Bergson and Simone Weil," in *In the Writings of Martin Buber*, ed. Will Herberg (New York, 1956), 312.

18. Weil, *At Home with André and Simone Weil*, 130–31.

19. For Weil and self-hatred, see George Steiner, "Sainte Simone: The Jewish Bases of Simone Weil's *Via Negativa* to the Philosophic Peaks," in *No Passion Spent* (New Haven, CT, 1996), 171–79. For a psycho-historical reading of Weil's anti-Jewish declarations, see Coles, *Simone Weil*, 43–62. For an analysis that links her anti-Jewish views with her attitudes toward food and sex, see Rachel Feldhay Brenner, *Writing as Resistance: Four Women Confronting the Holocaust* (University Park, PA, 1997); and Gray, *Simone Weil*.

20. Giniewski, *Simone Weil*, 12, 35,40, 43, 47.

21. Arthur A. Cohen, "Simone Weil, Prophet Out of Israel," in *Arguments and Doctrines: A Reader of Jewish Thinking in the Aftermath of the Holocaust* (New York, 1970), 50–51.

22. Jean Améry, *At the Mind's Limits: Contemplations by a Survivor on Auschwitz and Its Realities*, trans. Sidney Rosenfeld and Stella P. Rosenfeld (Bloomington, IN, 1980). For Améry's own criticisms of Weil, see "Simone Weil—jenseits der Legende," *Merkur* 33 (1979): 80–86.

23. Nevin, *Simone Weil*, 241; 244.

24. Ibid., 303–4.

25. Ibid., 259.

26. Brenner, *Writing as Resistance*, 21.

27. Ibid., 64.

28. Ibid., 22; 24.

29. Richard Bell, "Simone Weil, Post-Holocaust Judaism, and the Way of Compassion," in *Simone Weil: The Way of Justice as Compassion* (Lanham, MD, 1998), 172.

30. Ibid., 176.

31. Ibid.

32. Ibid., 185.

33. Ibid.

34. Ibid., 186.

35. Maud S. Mandel, *In the Aftermath of Genocide: Armenians and Jews in Twentieth Century France* (Durham, NC, 2003).

36. Endelman, *Leaving the Jewish Fold*, chap. 6; Stanislawski, "Simone Weil et Raïssa Maritain."

37. Stanislawski, "Simone Weil et Raïssa Maritain," 99.

38. Ibid.

39. Cited in Cohen, "Contra Simone Weil," 72.

40. Cited in Giniewski, *Simone Weil*, 39.

41. Cited in Coles, *Simone Weil*, 46.

42. Weil, *At Home with André and Simone Weil*, 38–39.

43. Todd Endelman, "Welcoming Ex-Jews into the Jewish Historiographical Fold" and "The Social and Political Context of Conversion in Germany and England, 1870–1914," in *Broadening Jewish History: Towards a Social History of Ordinary Jews* (Oxford, 2011), 83–114.

44. Citations of this report come from Nevin, *Simone Weil*, 244–47. Also see Giniewski, *Simone Weil*, 44–48.

45. Nevin, *Simone Weil*, 244–47.

46. Ibid.

47. Mandel, *In the Aftermath of Genocide*, 107–10.

48. Jean-Paul Sartre, *Réflexions sur la question juive* (Paris, 1946). For a discussion of Sartre's discomfort with Jewish difference, see Max Silverman, "'Killing Me Softly': Racial Ambivalence in Jean-Paul Sartre's *Réflexions sur la question juive*," in *Antisemitism and Philosemitism in the Twentieth and Twenty-First Centuries: Representing Jews, Jewishness and Modern Culture*, eds. Phyllis Lassner and Lara Trubowitz (Newark, DE, 2008), 47–62.

49. Giniewski, *Simone Weil*, 48.

33

Isaiah Berlin (1909–1997)

UNPRETENTIOUS PASSION

Yuli Tamir

"IT IS ONE OF THE MARKS OF WRITERS OF GENIUS THAT WHAT THEY SAY, MAY AT times, touch a central nerve in the minds and feelings of men who belong to other times, cultures and outlooks, and set up trains of thought and entail consequences which did not, or could not, occur to such writers, still less occupy their minds."[1] These words, which open Berlin's essay on Giambattista Vico and his time—"Vico and the Ideal of Enlightenment"—provide an accurate description of Berlin's own writings. As time passes, Berlin's philosophy becomes more and more relevant. True, his work never created one coherent whole, but such a whole would have been an antithesis to Berlin's intellectual project: trying to teach individuals how to be moral agents in an age marked by uncertainty. We know the limits of our understanding, we know we often err, and our good intentions can lead to horrific consequences—and yet we must act, live a moral life, try to do the best we can. As uncertainty becomes more and more predominant in our lives, the desire to find shelter in some reassuring ethical theory that provides guidance and solace grows rapidly. This may explain why history didn't come to an end while religiosity and ideological extremism are on the rise.

Berlin's writings allow us to understand some of the most challenging psychological, social, and political processes we are witnessing. Theoretical and ideological struggles, he believed, never come to an end, and if they do it is only because we blunder, misunderstand our moral options, sacrifice our integrity, and compromise values we should have held dear. Ours is a life of permanent puzzlement, of questions never to be fully answered, and answers never to be fully approved and verified.

Very few scholars will point to Romanticism as the root of this contemporary state of mind. Yet for Berlin Romanticism was a necessary steppingstone that has shaken the placidity offered by monolithic ideas and beliefs and sent us all trembling into an age of uncertainty.

The Result of romanticism, then, is liberalism, toleration, decency and the appreciation of the imperfections of life; some degree of increased rational self-understanding. This was very far from the intentions of the Romantics. But at

the same time—and to this extent the Romantic doctrine is true—they are the persons who most strongly emphasized the unpredictability of all human activities. They were hoist with their own petard. Aiming at one thing, they produced, fortunately for us all, almost the exact opposite.[2]

One can still hear Berlin giving one of his BBC lectures on Romanticism and reaching a victorious crescendo in this last paragraph, which ends the lecture and leaves him, and us, breathless.

"The Sources of Romanticism" are not only insightful lectures on Romanticism but a rebellion against the spirit of a political and intellectual age that has put much effort in drawing theoretical boundaries, defining and distinguishing different schools of thought, and emphasizing departmentalization and specialization, thus missing what Berlin so clearly saw: great ideas travel across different spheres of human creativity—from art to the opera to novels and poetry—and leave their mark on their critics as much as on their followers.

His open-mindedness to different intellectual influences, to the hidden dialogue between conflicting ideas, alongside his firm belief that monism is the root of extremism and that taking ideas to their ideological end leads to calamity, made Berlin relevant to an age characterized by the need to find a bearable balance among conflicting ideas, needs, hopes, fears, and disappointments. He produces, as Nicholas Kristof beautifully describes it, "a philosophy for adults in an uncertain world."[3]

In the introduction to his celebrated *Four Essays on Liberty*, Berlin clearly defines the essence of his own credo:

> [N]egative and positive liberty are not the same thing. Both are ends in themselves. These ends may clash irreconcilably. When this happens, questions of choice and preference inevitably arise. Should democracy in a given situation be promoted at the expense of individual freedom? Or equality at the expense of artistic achievement; or mercy at the expense of justice; or spontaneity at the expense of efficiency; or happiness, loyalty, innocence at the expense of knowledge and truth? The simple point which I am concerned to make is that where ultimate values are irreconcilable, clear-cut solutions cannot, in principle, be found. . . . If the claims of two (or more than two) types of liberty prove incompatible in a particular case, and if this is an instance of the clash of values at once absolute and incommensurable, it is better to face this intellectually uncomfortable fact than ignore it, or automatically attribute it to some deficiency on our part which could be eliminated by an increase in skill or knowledge; or what is worse still, suppress one of the competing values altogether by pretending that it is identical with its rivals—and so end by distorting both.[4]

The irreconcilability embedded in Berlin's philosophy explains his concern with three human conditions—coping with social and moral uncertainty, exercising freedom, and taking responsibility—all essential for facing a world characterized by a series of unprecedented upheavals.

Berlin witnessed two world wars. His hometown Riga was Latvian when he was born in 1909; was occupied by the Germans in 1917; regained its autonomy in 1918; and was occupied by the Russians in 1940, and by the Nazis and then by the Soviets in 1944. For such a man nothing could be definite, and the worst can certainly happen (though none of the turbulence of his homeland or his people harmed him personally—Berlin used to say he had lived a happy life in the midst of a horrific century). Thus all we can do is to concede the insecurity and tensions embedded in our reality and search for some untidy compromises that will allow us to do the best we can, trying to make a virtue of necessity.

Moral Ambiguity

The most important lesson for an age of uncertainty is to be found in the closing paragraph of Berlin's most important essay, "Two Concepts of Liberty," from his *Four Essays on Liberty* of 1969:

> It may be that the ideal of freedom to choose ends without claiming eternal validity for them, and the pluralism of values connected with this, is only the late fruit of our declining capitalist civilization; an ideal which remote ages and primitive societies have not recognized, and one which posterity will regard with curiosity, even sympathy but little comprehension. This may be so; but no skeptical conclusion seems to me to follow. Principles are no less sacred because their duration cannot be guaranteed. Indeed, the very desire for guarantees that our values are eternal and secure in some objective heaven is perhaps only a craving for the certainties of childhood of the absolute values of our primitive past. "To realize the relative validity of one's convictions," said an admirable writer of our time, and "yet stand for them unflinchingly, is what distinguishes a civilized man from a barbarian." To demand more than this is perhaps a deep and incurable metaphysical need; but to allow it to determine one's practice is a symptom of an equally deep, and more dangerous, moral and political immaturity.[5]

In this paragraph Berlin proves that his philosophy is grounded in a deep command of the basic human need for approval, reassurance, and certainty. Berlin understands that much of our psychological attempts are dedicated to creating an illusion of certainty: repressing our doubts and hesitations, silencing inner and outer voices of criticism. He wants us to be able to face our inner doubts and keep our minds fresh and alert—and when necessary openly reflect on and reexamine our values—yet he also wants us to be undeterred by our reservations. Maturity, Berlin argues, is the ability to accept the possibly transient and contextualized nature of one's ideals and still fight for them fearlessly. Historical uncertainty, he argues, is not the same as skepticism. The skeptic questions the validity of his or her values here and now, while the civilized person understands that one cannot think outside one's own historical context, that one cannot fully understand the processes of validation acceptable for remote ages: from the primitive societies of the past to future societies whose nature we cannot imagine.

We cannot but live and act in a historical sociocultural context, and given this context we must define our values and pave our moral path. Contextualization sows in us seeds of doubt and teaches us intellectual modesty; we cannot transcend our limitations, and we are therefore imperfect. Only God, if he exists, is omniscient; we are always shortsighted, caught within our limited sight and understanding.

Great philosophical questions, Berlin argues, transcend time and place. "The questions Plato asked can still be, and indeed are asked today. . . . These major ideas, outlooks, theories, insights, have remained the central ideas of philosophy. They have a certain life of their own which is trans-historical."[6] Yet eternal questions do not necessarily generate eternal answers. Philosophical periods are thus constructions of our imaginations, a means to structure a stream of ideas that runs across time and space.

It is unclear whether Berlin's position can be classified as modern. In response to the question of whether he considered himself a modern philosopher, Berlin responded:

> I don't know what that means. Empirically minded yes! I cannot sum up all my beliefs in two words, but I think that all there is in the world is persons and things and ideas in people's head—goals, emotions, hopes, fears, choices, imaginative visions and all other forms of human experience. *That is all I am acquainted with, but I cannot claim omniscience.* Perhaps there is a world of eternal truth and values which *the magic eye of the true thinker* can perceive—surely this can only belong to an elite to which I fear I have never been admitted.[7]

For Berlin then the modern mind is empirical, skeptical, and aware of its own limitations. We must therefore live the lives of modest believers who, to rephrase Yeats, are nevertheless full of passionate intensity. That's the nature of civility, the guide for a proper human behavior.

Freedom and Responsibility

The above discussion that emphasizes the importance of intellectual modesty explains why freedom is such an important aspect of a philosophy for adults in an uncertain world. It is quite clear that Berlin's theory demands that we shall constantly be making decisions; evaluating the compatibility of our values, goals and circumstances; and making ourselves capable of explaining why we have endorsed one untidy compromise over another.

This, psychologically speaking, is a challenging state of mind, but it saves us from making the most dangerous mistake of all: taking ideas, attractive as they may be, to their logical ends. Someone remarked, Berlin writes in one of his last essays, that in the old days men and women were brought as sacrifices to a variety of gods: "[F]or these the modern age has substituted new idols: isms. To cause pain, to kill, to torture are in general rightly condemned; but if these things are done not for any personal benefit but for an ism—socialism, nationalism, fascism, communism, fanatically held religious belief, or progress, or the fulfillment of the laws of history—then they are in order."[8]

In all isms true values are embedded, but they are pursued to the point of absurdity, or worse still of an oppressive single-mindedness. Our freedom as individuals demands that we shall act in a well-balanced way. Whenever asked "how much" of each value should we pour into our ideological hodgepodge, we should say: the right amount; just the right amount. The moral rule then is "make your own judgment"; it's your moral duty. Make a decision, revisit it time and again in order to make sure that you have used the right amount of each important element, and then follow your decision wholeheartedly.

When I had the opportunity to interview Berlin in an Israeli newspaper and asked for moral guidance, he kept pointing to practical considerations. I was making an idle attempt to find the perfect answer, a moral code that can guide the society, he told me; he was looking for a bearable compromise, a livable compromise. "When worthy principles collide, one must choose. How do we know what is morally fair and desirable? You should consider the matter, analyze it, think, explain, and evoke relevant examples."[9] Having no recipe book that describes how to create the "good men" or the "good society," it is up to us to make our society better.

This is why freedom is so important. It gives us the space to think and act, and calls for active participation. Freedom is absolutely essential for those who reject the idea that there is one true answer that could be revealed in a moment of enlightenment rooted in either pure reason or religious revelation.

> If I know the true answer and you do not, and you disagree with me, it is because you are ignorant; if you knew the truth, you would necessarily believe what I believe; if you seek to disobey me, this can be so only because you are wrong, because the truth has not been revealed to you as it has been to me. This justifies some of the most frightful forms of oppression and enslavement in human history, and it is truly the most dangerous, and, in our century in particular, the most violent, interpretation of the notion of positive liberty.[10]

It is quite impossible to determine whether Berlin's enthusiasm for negative and positive freedom was a reflection of his disbelief in one eternal truth, or whether he saw the freedom to make decisions and act upon them, and the moral responsibility that follows, as being so fundamental to our humanity that he felt bound to highlight moral incompatibilities. Be that as it may, the two were tightly entangled in his philosophy.

In his discussion of determinism, Berlin openly admits that he is not sure whether the refutation of determinism is indeed possible, yet he argues that determinism undermines our belief in freedom in ways that shatter our conception of human morality. The whole of our common morality, which is anchored in concepts like obligation and duty, right or wrong, moral praise or blame, reward and punishment, will have to change as it presupposes responsibility, and responsibility entails freedom. If determinism was true, Berlin argues, then aesthetics will replace morality.

Honorable or dishonorable conduct, pleasure-seeking and heroic martyrdom, courage and cowardice, deceitfulness and truthfulness, doing right against temptation—these would become like being good-looking or ugly, tall or short, old or young, black or white, born of English or Italian parents: something that we cannot alter, for everything is determined.[11]

Our humanity then demands that we shall adopt a moral theory that forces us to express our distinct qualities. Berlin thus warns us from attempting to achieve freedom by liberating ourselves from our desires, retreating into an inner citadel, effacing ourselves before forces that oppress us. Ascetic self-denial, he argues, "may be a source of integrity or serenity and spiritual strength, but it is difficult to see how it can be called an enlargement of liberty."[12]

A Godless Jew?

Given the centrality of freedom for Berlin's moral philosophy, nationalism and belonging raise an interesting dilemma. Being born to a certain nation is a matter of fate—a deterministic aspect that is hard (if not impossible) to escape. Berlin's own Jewish origin was imposed on him, never chosen, yet he found there are many ways of being a Jew: he understood his Jewishness as a cultural, national, and romantic affiliation, not a religious one. He carried this identity proudly and never tried to hide it or reject it. Berlin understood the Jewish urge for a homeland and supported Zionism, but he was never ready to exchange Oxford for Jerusalem.

Religion, he argued, is a matter of faith, not fate. He wished he could lay claim to having religious feelings or experiences, writing:

> Ever since I persuaded myself that a personal God—an old man with a beard—the Ancient of Days—or anyhow some kind of an individual conceivable in human terms—was unlikely to exist, I have never known the meaning of the word God; I cannot even claim to be an atheist or an agnostic—I am somewhat like a tone-deaf person in relation to music—I realize that others are deeply inspired by it, and I respect that, and I have great sympathy for religious ceremonies and works and poetry: but God?[13]

Berlin then was a sentimental Jew, a national-cultural Jew but not a religious Jew. This explains why it is difficult to see Berlin as a Jewish philosopher or as a Jewish intellectual; he was an intellectual and a Jew. He had interest in other interesting Jews: Karl Marx and Benjamin Disraeli, Moses Hess, Chaim Weizmann, Lewis Namier, and Felix Frankfurter, because he was attracted to remarkable individuals in general, not because of their Jewish origins, and certainly not because of their contribution to Jewish philosophy.

Without the Holocaust it is quite possible that Berlin and his milieu would have leaned toward assimilation, or at least anti-Zionism; that like Edwin Montague, he would have "button-holed his friends in various drawing-rooms in London, and asked them vehemently whether they regarded him as an oriental alien and wanted to see him 'repatriated' to the Eastern Mediterranean."[14]

In his analysis of Jewish history (mostly in his essay on Weizmann), Berlin acknowledges that in the twentieth century Jews were forced to accept the inevitable burden of their origins. Many believed that opting out was an option: Jews did assimilate, though some were forced by others to face the identity they rejected, and others found out that even without external interventions the process of detachment could never be completed. One of Berlin's favorite jokes was about a Jew who decided to convert. Once the process is completed, he applies to be admitted to the local golf club. The clerk interviews him: Name? "John Smith." Profession? "Advocate." Religion? "A Gentile."[15]

Like morality, identity is a sphere where no one can be passive. Whatever one does reflects a choice: to live in the diaspora; to immigrate to Israel; to speak English, Yiddish, Hebrew; to follow the religious commands, whether all of them, some, or none. One can flirt with different identities, choosing different aspects of these identities as central to one's conception of the self and rejecting others, thus creating something that was, like Berlin himself, a mélange. Identity then is the material our choices are made of; it carries the mark of our ancestors but also of our own choices. Freedom and determinism keep interacting in our lives, making us who we are.

Meaningful Choices

Paraphrasing Joseph de Maistre, one may say that Berlin met in the course of his lifetime Englishmen, Frenchmen, Israelis, and Russians; but man he had never met. Berlin, then, could not have written an abstract theory of justice, grounded in individuals stripped of their particularities, like his great contemporary, John Rawls. For Berlin individuals could not be "mutually disinterested" or "envy free," placed in a hypothetical original position. They were deeply contextualized, and it was this contextualization that gave their life meaning and allowed them to make free and meaningful choices.

Talking about identity in Oxford during the fifties and sixties was quite unpopular. Philosophy was all about humanity: rational, universalized, and decontextualized principles that transcend time and place. Identity (like sexual preference and marital status) was an embarrassing fact about oneself that should make no difference—a personal matter that could be mentioned in passing but should not shape one's way of thinking.

Owing to his Jewish and Russian roots, his war experience in Washington, and the deep shame he felt about not trying to discover the horrific fate of Jews in Auschwitz,[16] as well as his emotional meetings with Anna Akhmatova and other Russian intellectuals, Berlin was sensitive to questions of national, linguistic, and religious identity that many of his colleagues ignored. He recognized the anxiety that accompanies the demand to disguise oneself or reject one's own culture, tradition and language: an inescapable *state of being* for those who can neither come to terms with who they are nor shed their identity and acquire a new one. Such individuals, Berlin argues, remain:

> betwixt and between, unmoored from one bank without reaching the other, tantalized but incapable of yielding, complicated, somewhat tormented figures, floating in midstream, or, to change the metaphor, wandering in a no-man's-land, liable to waves of self-pity, aggressive arrogance, exaggerated pride in those very attributes which divided them from their fellows; with alternating bouts of self-contempt and self-hatred, feeling themselves to be objects of scorn or antipathy to those very members of the society by whom they most wish to be recognized and respected. This is a well-known condition of men forced into an alien culture, by no means confined to the Jews; it is a well-known neurosis in an age of nationalism in which self-identification with a dominant group becomes supremely important, but, for some individuals, abnormally difficult.[17]

To the Jews, Berlin recites the warning of the great Zionist thinker Moses Hess: "You may don a thousand masks, change your name and your religion and mode of life, and creep through the world incognito so that nobody notices that you are a Jew. Yet every insult to the Jewish name will wound you more than a man of honor who remains loyal to his family and defends his good name."[18]

Those who deny their identity, he argues, forfeit everyone's respect, for there is nothing worse than "flying under false colors."[19] This is a claim concerning the importance of authenticity, of being able to be oneself. Authenticity, says the Canadian philosopher Charles Taylor, "is not the enemy of demands that emanate from beyond the self; it supposes such demands."[20] More precisely, it supposes membership in a "meaning-giving" group.

An important aspect of contextuality is the role played by language: "[M]en necessarily think in words or other symbols; their feelings and attitudes are . . . incorporated in symbolic forms—worship, poetry, ritual . . . the entire network of belief and behavior that binds them to one another, can be explained only in terms of common, public symbolism, in particular language."[21] The need to belong to a cultural community, then, is not merely a psychological urge to live in the comfort of what is familiar, nor does it spring solely from the need for continuity—for finding a place for oneself in the endless chain of being—but is an epistemological need for systems of meaning that will allow one to interpret the world and understand it, and a creative need for means of expression.

Membership in meaning-giving communities, Berlin argues, be they religious, ethnic, racial, cultural, or gender groups, is constitutive of how individuals define themselves. Human character is "shaped by, and cannot be understood apart from, those of the group, defined in terms of common territory, customs, laws, memories, beliefs, language, artistic and religious expression, social institutions, ways of life . . . factors which shape human beings, their purposes and their values."[22]

Self-determination thus inevitably involves cultural and social dimensions. When I ask myself who am I (Berlin writes) and answer: "an Englishman, a Chinese, a merchant, a man of no importance, a millionaire, a convict—I find upon analysis that to possess these attributes entails being recognized as belonging to a particular group or class by other persons in my society, and that this recognition is part of the meaning of most of the terms that denote my most personal and permanent characteristics."[23]

Those who hide their identity are doomed to live a schizophrenic life, being forced to be a Jew at home and a "man" in the street. In order to be full-fledged citizens they are required to identify with some other group or movement that seems to be free from the defects attributed to their original group, forced to "acquire a new personality, and that which goes with it, a new set of clothing, a new set of values, habits, new armor which does not press upon the old wounds, on old scars left by the chains one wore as a slave."[24] Jews who take off their traditional garments in order to become "men"; businesswomen dressed in men's suits; immigrants changing their name, "forgetting" their mother tongue, taking off their turban, kaffiyeh, or yarmulke; black people who take great pains to straighten their hair; or homosexuals who try to play the role of the perfectly heterosexual man or woman—all are intimately acquainted with the pain associated with efforts to dissolve into what is considered the "ideal type.".

Respecting an identity is a way of preserving an option, the absence of which could be painful, at times unbearable.[25] The politics of identity is therefore an important component of the struggle for freedom; for without having a set of meaningful options to choose from, freedom loses its allure. There is then a short distance between the politics of identity and the politics of recognition, and Berlin covers it with no hesitation. In the second part of "Two Concepts of Liberty," he demonstrates a penetrating understanding of how the human need for status and recognition makes individuals deserving of self-governance.

The lack of freedom about which individuals or groups complain, he argues, amounts, as often as not, to a lack of proper recognition. Human beings desire to secure for themselves not only a set of liberties but also a recognition of themselves as being members of particular groups, as well as an affirmation of the uniqueness and worthiness of these groups. But most of all, what oppressed classes or nationalities demand "is recognition (of their class or nation, or color or race) as an independent source of human activity, as an entity with a will of its own, intending to act in accordance with it (whether it is good or legitimate or not), and not to be ruled, educated, guided, with however light a hand, as being not quite fully human and therefore not quite fully free."[26]

Not only do individuals see their personal freedom as dependent on their group's ability to be self-governing, they also see their self-esteem as closely linked to that of their group. Consequently, they regard offenses against and humiliations of their group as a personal injury, and they take pride and satisfaction in the group's success and prosperity. Shame, Berlin argues, is an expression of a collective feeling motivated by care. In criticizing Israel's policies in the 1980s, Berlin remarks: "Many Jews in the Anglo-American world felt ashamed by Israeli actions during the Lebanon war.[27] They would not have felt this way if they wouldn't have identified, to a large extent, with Israel. British, Frenchmen, and Americans who are not Jews may have objected to these actions but were not ashamed. 'We are ashamed by actions done by those we hold dear not by strangers. If we feel ashamed by Israel's actions it is because we think that Israel was not meant only for Israelis, but for the whole of the people—for the whole of the Jewish people.' "[28]

Tying together personal identity and national identity, Berlin argues, at the heart of modern politics lies "a great cry for recognition on the part of both individuals and groups and in our own day, of professions and classes, nations and races."[29] The desire for recognition, he concludes, is surely "one of the greatest forces that move human history."[30]

To Berlin's credit it is important to note that he was one of the very few great thinkers of the late twentieth century to have had a prescient understanding of the importance of identity and nationalism as a political and cultural phenomenon. He ends his essay "Nationalism: Past Neglect and Present Power" with the following words: "It would not, I think, be an exaggeration to say that no political movement today, at any rate outside the Western world, seems likely to succeed unless it allies itself to national sentiment."[31] Nationalism, he remarked in the early 1960s, a period in which most Anglo-American philosophers anticipated the emergence of a postnational world order, remains the strongest force in the world today.

And yet like many other liberals Berlin had an ambivalent relationship with the idea of nationalism; he endorsed some versions of it while rejecting its malignant and fanatic forms. These types of nationalism, he observed, were often stimulated by social and political injustice. Peoples that have been victims of oppression, aggression, and humiliation lash back like bent twigs at their oppressors, developing a defiant self-esteem and a violent self-consciousness that ultimately turns into burning nationalism and chauvinism.

For Berlin, then, zealous nationalism is the product of an injured pride. A wounded nation can develop "an anxiety to learn from the superior culture or nation, so as to emulate it and reach equality ... [or alternatively it can develop] resentful isolationism—a desire to leave the unequal contest, and concentrate on one's own virtues, which one discovers to be vastly superior to the vaunted qualities of the admired or fashionable rival."[32] The distance from the latter kind of response to the most arrogant and violent forms of nationalism is short.

Soberly analyzing the transformation of abstract universal rationalism into xenophobic, ethnocentric nationalism, Berlin sees the dangers embedded in attempting to sanctify either of these forms of thought. Like any other absolute truth, the proposition "my nation is superior to all others, and must therefore rule the world," which lies at the root of arrogant, expansionist nationalism, must be inherently false.

Different flowers in the human garden should be allowed to grow side by side; different cultures can coexist in creative harmony, Johann Gottfried Herder optimistically, maybe naively, argued. Like all those who experienced the horrors of the last century, Berlin was much less optimistic. He knew nationalism more often than not leads to conflict and disharmony. Nevertheless, he believed that a mild form of nationalism can capture both: the need for belonging and the importance of personal and collective choice.

He therefore endorsed the early form of Zionism, which he saw as an expression of a liberal, if not Herderian, kind of nationalism. The originators of Zionism, he argued, had a cultural mission. Even those Zionist leaders, who, like Herzl, wanted to go beyond cultural Zionism and advocated the establishment of a *Judenstaat*—a state of the Jews—dreamed of a liberal democracy that respected individual rights, guarded the rights of minorities, and secured the separation of state and religion. Theodor Herzl's pluralistic, polycentric form of nationalism—expressed so clearly in defining the purpose of Zionism as becoming "a nation, among nations, governed by the law of nations"—was the perfect example of the kind of nationalism Berlin supported.

Berlin's sympathy with nationalism, then, is a sympathy with the nationalism of the Risorgimento and the European revolutionaries of 1848: the cultural, liberal form of nationalism espoused by Giuseppe Verdi and Georges Clemenceau, Ahad Ha'am, Herzl, and Weizmann. Hence, even though Berlin never produced a theory of nationalism of his own, it is quite clear that had he produced one it would have been guided by Weizmann's principle: the principle of "minimum injustice." This theory of liberal nationalism balances the needs of individuals and communities— the human aspiration for freedom, recognition, and equality, alongside the need for roots. There will always be those harmed by the implementation of national aspirations, and their pain should be acknowledged and respected; yet it cannot nullify the importance of the national act itself. If he was a Palestinian living in Israel, Berlin told me, "I would have objected to the presence of Jews. I am afraid we cannot allow the Palestinians to fulfill their wishes, but their frustration is totally logical and reasonable."[33] What kind of a state should Israel be like, I asked him, a liberal democracy? He answered: "This is what the fathers of Zionism believed in and that is what they have attempted to create. I ask for no more, a kind of untidy liberal democracy. Untidy because when one starts tidying up repression emerges; someone is unjustly oppressed. Suppressing self-expression is undesirable in every country and certainly in an Israel that has a new, heterogeneous society surrounded by diversity."[34] Berlin advised Israel to be an imperfect, human kind of state, the only kind that could fit the "crooked timber of humanity."

The Zionist claim, Berlin argues, is grounded not merely in cultural demands but also in existential ones. Jews need a place where they can live a normal life without fear of persecution or discrimination. Twentieth-century history proved just how desperately they need one. A homeland for the Jews solves the problems not only of those Jews who would immigrate to Israel but of diaspora Jews as well. The establishment of Israel provides Jews with much-desired national recognition and allows each Jew to choose whether to become a citizen of Israel or to remain in the diaspora. Once such a choice becomes real, Jews can consider themselves free and equal members of humanity.

In *Personal Impressions*, Berlin ends his essay on Albert Einstein and Israel with the following words of support for Israel and for Zionism:

> That Einstein, who tolerated no deviation from human decency, above all on the part of his own people—that he believed in this movement and this state and stood by it through thick and thin, to the end of his life, however critical he was at times of particular men or policies—this fact is perhaps among the highest moral testimonials on which any state or any movement in this century can pride itself. Unswerving public support by an utterly good (and reasonably well informed) man . . . may not itself be enough to justify a doctrine or a policy, but neither can it be dismissed; it counts for something; in this case for a great deal.[35]

This is not empty praise for either Einstein or Israel, but an expression of a deep belief that decent, relevant, proper ideas are those that pass the judgment of decent, relevant, well-informed thinkers.

Thinking and acting is a human matter, justified and judged by people. We need then to urge people to think, allow them the freedom to act, and reassure them that the lack of eternal moral validity is no justification for human passivity. In this sense Berlin's philosophy is indeed a philosophy for adults in an uncertain world. It seems to me that this is all we can ask for and all we can get.

Notes

1. Isaiah Berlin, "Vico and the Ideal of Enlightenment," in *Against the Current* (London, 1979), 120.
2. Isaiah Berlin, *The Roots of Romanticism* (London, 1999), 147.
3. Nicholas Kristof, "On Isaiah Berlin," in *The New York Review of Books*, February 25, 2010, 27.
4. Isaiah Berlin, *Four Essays on Liberty* (Oxford, 1969), xlix–l.
5. Ibid., 172.
6. Ramin Jahanbegloo, *Conversations with Isaiah Berlin: Recollections of an Historian of Ideas* (London, 1992), 25.
7. Ibid., 32; italics added.
8. Isaiah Berlin, *The First and the Last* (London, 1999), 57.
9. Yuli Tamir, "An Interview with Isaiah Berlin," *Ma'arive* 26, no. 2 (1987).
10. Berlin, *First and the Last*, 66.
11. Ibid., 72.
12. Berlin, "Two Concepts of Liberty, in *Four Essays on Liberty*, 140.
13. Michael Ignatieff, *Isaiah Berlin: A Life* (New York, 1998), 41.

14. Isaiah Berlin, "Chaim Weizmann," in *Personal Impressions* (London, 1980), 37.

15. The term "Gentile" (from Latin *gentilis*, via the French *gentil*, female *gentille*, meaning "of or belonging to a clan or tribe") is used by English translators for the Hebrew *goy* and *nokhri* in the Hebrew Bible and the Greek word *éthnē* in the New Testament.

16. "I never heard about Auschwitz until the end of 1944," he told Ramin Jahanbegloo: "I only discovered the full horror of the Holocaust very late. . . . [L]ife in the embassy [was] too protected. I still feel guilt"; Ramin Jahanbegloo, *Conversations*, 20.

17. Isaiah Berlin, "Benjamin Disraeli, Karl Marx, and the Search for Identity," in *Against the Current: Essays in the History of Ideas*, ed. Henry Hardy (London, 1980), 255.

18. Isaiah Berlin, "The Life and Opinions of Moses Hess," in *Against the Current*, 233.

19. Ibid., 236.

20. Charles Taylor, *The Ethics of Authenticity* (Cambridge, 1991), 40–41.

21. Isaiah Berlin, *Vico and Herder: Two Studies in the History of Ideas* (London, 1976), 165.

22. Berlin, "Nationalism: Past Regret and Present Power," in *Against the Current*, 341.

23. Berlin, "Two Concepts of Liberty," 155.

24. Berlin, "Benjamin Disraeli, Karl Marx, and the Search for Identity," 259.

25. In the hypothetical case that no one cares about the disappearance of an identity because no one wishes to identify with it, its loss may be an aesthetic one but not a moral one.

26. Isaiah Berlin, "Two Concepts of Liberty," 156–57.

27. This is a reference to the massacre in the refugee camps by the Christian militia that Israel did not stop (and some say promoted).

28. Yael (Yuli) Tamir, interview with Isaiah Berlin, June 26, 1989.

29. Berlin, "Two Concepts of Liberty," 157.

30. Isaiah Berlin, *The Sense of Reality: Studies in Ideas and Their History* (London, 1996), 252.

31. Berlin, "Life and Opinions of Moses Hess," 355.

32. Berlin, "Benjamin Disraeli, Karl Marx and the Search for Identity," 256.

33. Tamir, interview with Isaiah Berlin, June 26, 1989.

34. Ibid.

35. Isaiah Berlin, "Einstein and Israel," in *Personal Impressions*, 155.

Nathan Alterman (1910–1970)

POETRY NATIONAL AND POLITICAL

Hannan Hever

TRANSLATED BY LISA KATZ

I

For four decades, until his death in 1970, Nathan Alterman was a prominent Hebrew writer, a participant-observer at the center of the dramatic development of the Zionist political entity in Palestine-Israel. Born in Warsaw in 1910, Alterman immigrated in 1925 to Palestine (Eretz Israel, the "Land of Israel" in Zionist terminology). In 1929 he traveled to France to study agronomy, returning to Palestine in 1932. Upon his return, he began to write columns, feuilletons, and topical poems for Hebrew-language newspapers. But the core of his literary output was his lyric poetry, collected in five volumes published during his lifetime: in practice, its influence determined the poetic standard of Hebrew verse for many years.

At first he invented himself as an indigenous intellectual of the Yishuv, the pre-state Jewish community in Palestine, and afterward as an intellectual of the Israeli state. To a great extent, Alterman is one of the chief formulators of the Jewish national imagination, with its profound contradictions that accompanied the process of political territorialization and involved continuous, violent conflicts with the Palestinian natives of the land.

Even in his first poem, "Be-shetef ir" (In an urban flood), published in 1931 in the literary weekly *Ktuvim* (Scriptures), Alterman emphasizes his profile as a native local intellectual. At the start, the poem emphasizes his symbolist poetics, praising the music produced by a popular singer in a European city, apparently Paris: "An island throng in an urban flood / instruments swaying. / Golden forges song / between red lips."[1] But paradoxically, Alterman demonstrates his appreciation of the great European capital by setting it in opposition to "my land"—"my hardened land an exposed face / my air—a broken organ."[2] His land, of course, is Palestine, Eretz Israel, the Land of Israel, as it was signified in Jewish cultural consciousness. The main political role of this local, native anchoring is to create an unobjectionable image of the Jews as "natives" with the right to rule over Palestine despite Arab

493

opposition. And so in "Be-shetef ir," as in many of his other poems from the 1930s, Alterman constructs a native subject that justifies and permits the Zionist project by denying the violence of Jewish settlement in Palestine.

But the colonial construction of the native is based on a paradox. On the one hand, the purported native is a child of the earth and of nature, as if he had always been present due to the eternal link of the Jewish people to the Land of Israel and will forever remain. But on the other hand, this native is also the herald of the fresh revolutionary innovation of the birth of the New Hebrew that was in opposition to the exilic Jewish identity. This nativity, which means both a constant presence *and* a homecoming, seems to make the violent conquest of land redundant. But the paradox in having to justify Jewish existence in Palestine exposes Alterman's difficulty in constructing a local identity for himself, severed from Jewish identity in the diaspora, making it impossible to conceal the colonial dimension of the settlement of the Jews from the diaspora in Palestinian territory.

From this native paradox, Alterman's writing in the 1930s developed within the framework of the neo-Symbolist school led by the poet Abraham Shlonsky, who was the main figure in the creation of the literary avant-garde in Palestine. This school's innovation challenged the poetics of Chaim Nahman Bialik, who lived in Palestine from 1924 on. Considered the great national poet, Bialik was identified with diaspora writing, and the neo-Symbolist school defined native poets as the saviors of Jewish culture from diasphoricism, leading toward the creation of a modernist Hebrew identity. At the same time, the modernists did not abandon the facet of a native "eternal" continuity of a Jewish presence in Palestine since the biblical beginnings of the Jewish people. This link to a continuous Jewish presence contributed to Alterman's strong ambivalence, which identified him as a Hebrew "native" who never actually parted with his diasporic Jewish identity.

Members of this literary school were immigrants from Eastern Europe who were active starting in the 1930s in Tel Aviv, the first Hebrew city, whose cafes and Bauhaus architecture provided the greenhouse in which modernist Hebrew culture developed. They adopted neo-Symbolist poetics, drawing on Russian and French Symbolism and its musicality, as well as its nonmimetic figurative language, distancing their poetry from the political. They practiced poetry as a profession and were not associated with political parties or movements. This distancing of themselves from politics stemmed from a desire to write national poetry acceptable by the entire political spectrum. However, starting in the second half of the 1920s, in particular against the backdrop of the worldwide financial crisis, the pioneer—who worked with his hands, realizing the Zionist dream with his body, and who had been the main subject of Hebrew poetry since the second *aliyah* (the wave of immigration from 1904 to 1914)—lost his undisputed place in the consensus, where he had been accepted by the right and left as the avant-garde of the Zionist movement at large.[3] In order to create a local, national Hebrew culture through a central poetic voice that would not be identified with and exploited politically by any one of the Zionist groups, whose mutual hostility arose in the wake of Jewish-Arab violence in 1929, Shlonsky and his colleagues imagined an autonomous Hebrew cultural arena, in which they sought to follow the vague, elitist European tradition of art for art's sake; and in its name they rejected accusations of the incomprehensibility of their verse.

Nathan Alterman's significant breakthrough in the Hebrew cultural scene in Palestine came about with the publication of *Kohavim ba-hutz* (Stars outside) in 1938. In the book's collection of poems, he distances himself from a concrete place and time, characteristic of his topical newspaper verse, and also from the popular songs he wrote for the satirical Broom Theater. However, in a seemingly magical paradox, the first responses to the book in fact underscore its local authenticity; the book's colorful universality was perceived as a genuine Eretz-Israeli expression.

Alterman chose to open the book with a powerful rendition of the Eretz-Israeli native subject, whose organic and unmediated link to place distinguishes him from both Zionism and Judaism:

> Still the tune you abandoned in vain returns
> and the road still opens all down the line
> and a cloud in its sky and a tree in its rain
> still await you, passerby.
>
> [. . .]
>
> your hands empty and your city far off
> and more than once you worshipped on your knees
> a green grove and a woman's laughter
> and a treetop with rainy eyelids.[4]

Alterman depicts the native as a vagabond, wandering in an expanse subject to his gaze. But the literary path he takes here in the wake of Abraham Shlonsky follows antimimetic poetics; it does not specifically identify the reality depicted in the poem, thus creating the Eretz-Israeli landscape as the default setting for the Hebrew reader.

In his programmatic 1938 essay, "Sod ha-markhaot ha-kfulot" (The secret of the quotation marks), Alterman formulates neo-Symbolism's relevance to current events by defining the Zionist revolution in Palestine in which, when the nation attempts "to turn symbols into reality, all reality turns into a symbol."[5] As far as Alterman the neo-Symbolist is concerned, the aim of poetry is to be evocative. For this poetry, names "are the **face** of things and not symbols, the **voice** of things and not their labels."[6] And so, he argues, during the dramatic days of the realization of Zionism, poetry must distance itself from big, empty words and put quotation marks around the word "Zionism." In this way Alterman calls for a cautious approach, which relates to current events but at the same time shies away from florid representations.

This indirect Symbolist manner—in which native poetry signifies reality in order to control it—is revealed in the opening poem of his book *Kohavim ba-hutz*. A wide-open expanse, through which the vagabond wanders accompanied by a Symbolist melody, is one in which a cloud and a tree await him to define the space and take charge. Like Baudelaire's flaneur in Paris, about whom Walter Benjamin wrote, Alterman's rambler turns the Palestinian landscape into artificial nature. He approaches it with a mixture of national affinity and universal foreignness,[7] whose twofold stance of connection and distance embodies the paradox of the native—

continuous renewal alongside the ancient attachment of one who has always been there.

The first poem in *Kohavim ba-hutz* has the native setting out on the road, in an atmosphere saturated with the music that accompanies wandering. But Alterman, in his indirect fashion, while mobilizing music in the service of the Zionist enterprise in the ambivalent manner of a native, reveals great sensitivity to the dangers involved in the modernist link between musical aesthetics and fascism. Alterman objected to the poetry of Uri Zvi Greenberg, who represented a staunchly messianic political position in Hebrew culture in Palestine at the end of the 1930s—a fascist formulation that Benjamin called the aestheticizing of politics. In the poem "Me-ever le-mangina" (Beyond the melody) in *Kohavim ba-hutz*, Alterman expresses his repulsion with the political and messianic use of music made by fascism. Instead, his poem sides with the worker culture of socialist Zionism, whose mistrust of political messianism led to the elevation of agricultural labor and the slow and gradual building of the national home.

II

When World War II broke out on September 1, 1939, Nathan Alterman was living in Tel Aviv. Reports about the start of the war fed into his regular journalistic writing in poems called "Regaim" (Moments), which appeared in the newspaper *Ha-aretz* (The land) from 1934 to 1942, and afterward in his weekly column "Ha-tur ha-shvee-ee" (The seventh column) in the daily *Davar* (Word) from 1943 to 1967. When Germany invaded Poland, the dilemmas of European Jews and collective fears about their fate surfaced in the Hebrew cultural scene in Palestine, and were openly exposed and expressed in the writings of Shlonsky, Alterman, and others.

Thus, violence and death became the main topics that Hebrew poetry of the time was drawn to. Local neo-Symbolism maneuvered itself into national discourse, creating—through the literary symbol—the imagined national community meant to cope with the violence directed toward it. In Alterman's 1941 *Simhat Anni-eem* (Joy of the poor), neo-Symbolism's cautious plans for keeping its distance from current events, and its great sensitivity to them, were disrupted by the violence of World War II. Alterman even attacked his neo-Symbolist colleague, poet Leah Goldberg, who had written an essay in which she declared that in being faithful to the aesthetics of neo-Symbolism, which tended toward pacifism and opposed violent poetry even when defying the forces of evil, she refused to write war poetry even when war had broken out. In the name of the Symbolist school's aesthetic principles, Alterman criticized her for testing a poem's legitimacy and quality with thematic criteria, arguing that "a poem calling for war could be 'pure literary gold.'" Alterman understood that in this new crisis-ridden situation, in order for humanistic poetry to write about the violence of war, it would have to reconsider the linguistic conditions that allow for such literary work.

As early as March 1939, Alterman wrote, "Words, always a human image, always bearing an obligation to human thought, retreat before events that breach the boundary of human comprehension."[8] But after the war started, Alterman, the native intellectual, who published the pacifist poem "Al tit-noo le-hem rovim"

(Don't give them rifles) in 1935, began now, in light of the war, to view violence as a necessary, collective tool in the war against evil, which was aimed first and foremost, from his point of view, at the Jews.

The poems in the 1941 volume *Simhat Anni-eem* tell the story of the love between a woman and a dead man who returns from the grave. He surrounds her with suffocating concern and protects her from the enemies besieging her city. The dead man's love is a symbol of collective existence that transcends the individual's death, while the fighting woman who saves her son, Hagoor ("the pup"), the son of the dead man, signifies collective redemption. The individual's readiness to sacrifice his life for the general good raises a series of moral collective values such as loyalty, revenge, and hope. Within this "culture of death," the individual is willing to die for these values, giving up his (threatened) life—"haim al kav haketz, shlemim veh-hazakim" (life on end's edge, whole and strong)—for the collective. The justification of violence also appears, for example, in the section "Nofelet ha-ir" (The city falls), in which a fatal, deadly rebellion is portrayed as a source of joy in the hope for redemption.

It appears that more than any other publication, the balladic cycle of poems *Simhat Anni-eem* contributed to Alterman's positioning as the main national spokesman of Hebrew poetry during World War II. Indeed, immediately after its publication in 1941, throughout the war, and for many years afterward, the book had an unshakable position as the most prominent text representing, establishing, and shaping the collective world of national values during the period of an existential threat to collective existence.

The poem's Symbolist dualism—current, actual nationalism alongside an abstract, apparently ahistorical representation—strengthened its symbolic effect. The image of the living dead is at its core an ambivalent representation, meant to solve the fundamental contradiction between the individual's commitment to life and his obligation to the collective, to the nation. The metaphor of the living-dead man solves this contradiction by blurring the borders between the worlds of the dead and the living.

This oxymoron is based on an unmistakable masculine tradition, whose main cultural sources are the biblical stories of Isaac, saved from sacrifice, and Jesus, crucified and resurrected. This is a sacrificial tradition in which the end of life is transcended. It exchanges an absence of significance in an individual's bodily death for an alternative significance, either a religious or an exalted national one. The nation too is a dead body that has been resurrected. It suffers but is not extinguished; it is an entity that death is a part of and yet cannot defeat.[9] Alterman seeks to cope with the linguistic crisis brought on by the war—to contain the violence and to overcome it with counterviolence—by producing a higher, consoling authority in the Symbolist poetics of music, melodies, and singers: the very act of poetry, and the language of the transcendental literary symbol that includes, according to Benjamin, a narrative of redemption.

Despite the strong universal aspect of the cycle of poems, it is filled with traditional Jewish allusions, which strengthen Mordechai Shalev's argument that *Simhat Anni-eem*'s central drama is the struggle between Zionism and Judaism,—establishing Zionism through rejecting Judaism.[10] In the wake of this claim, it may be said that Zionism, seeking realization in Palestine, formulates the outlines of its indigenous subject but does not manage to completely cut it off from the Jew, who it wishes to protect from the violence afflicted on him in the diaspora.

III

In contrast with *Simhat Anni-eem*, written from a native Palestinian stance looking at the loss of the Jewish diaspora, in *Shirey Makot Mitzraim* (Poems of the plagues of Egypt, 1944), Alterman expresses a dramatic change in his national point of view. The main cause of this change was his awareness, which permeated his poetic work, that the violent events of World War II deviated from the traditional Jewish martyrology, and were actually an unprecedented genocide. On November 23, 1942, the Jewish Agency published an official announcement about the methodical extermination of European Jewry, and four days later, on November 27, Alterman published "Me-kohl Ha-amim" (Of all the peoples), in which he protested the world's silence at the annihilation of the Jews in Europe, mocking the idea of the chosen people, the teleological and redemptive foundation of Jewish national history.

This poem marks a radical turning point in Alterman's work. In contrast with the redemptive, symbolic overcoming of violence in *Simhat Anni-eem*, basically situated locally in Palestine, *Shirey Makot Mitzraim* powerfully expresses a profound awareness of the crushing defeat of the Jewish people in Europe, in which Alterman sees the total destruction of the Jewish nation's powerful image of itself.

At the height of the Holocaust, a year after the Warsaw Ghetto uprising and its horrifying end, Alterman abandoned this self-image and wrote *Shirey Makot Mitzraim* as a biblical allegory, presenting Jewish experience in the 1940s as an analogy to the Exodus and the plagues visited upon Egypt. But the real surprise in this book is that the Egyptians—and the comparison made between them and the Germans can be neither denied nor obscured—are, paradoxically, the ones who appear as the suffering victims. In light of the genocide perpetrated on the Jewish people in Europe, Alterman completely abandons his stance as a native who rejects the diaspora, and makes room for a Jewish position, exilic in nature, with no homeland and therefore devoid of the power structures of a sovereign national entity occupying its land. It is the total Jewish destruction experienced by Alterman that allows him to distance himself as much as possible from the particular position of the national sovereign entity, taking the radical position of a universal intellectual who shows sensitivity even to the fate of the innocent Germans hurt by the war:

> Because the weapon is just,
> while forever bleeding,
> he leaves behind, like the taste of salt,
> the tear of the sinless.[11]

This reading[12] of the poems in *Shirey Makot Mitzraim* points to the possibility that they were written with total identification with the annihilation of the Jews, while abandoning the pretension that a native land could save the Jews in the European diaspora. "No, there is no rescue!" Alterman cited the poet-partisan Abba Kovner, relinquishing the arrogant native stance that despised the diaspora and blamed the Jews who remained in Europe for their disaster, imagining that it was within the power of the diaspora to save them.

In contrast to the blurring of borders between the lands of the dead and the living, and a redemptive narrative produced by the symbol of the living-dead figure in *Simhat Anni-eem*, *Shirey Makot Mitzraim* makes a sharp distinction between these worlds. Alterman does not offer an intermediary between the living and the dead as a transcendental figure leading up to a mythical one that unites the two. Instead, this book takes an antimythical stance that examines the concrete and the physical rather than the metaphysical and national process of the living turning into the dead. Instead of using a symbol, Alterman writes a mechanical and arbitrary allegory that expresses the lack of continuity between death and life. This cycle of poems creates an allegorical reality, a reality characterized by Benjamin as one that expresses the hopeless world of the dead and rejects the symbol, which functions as an organic continuum that the victim from the world of the dead conveys to the living world of national memory.

Even after the Holocaust, Alterman returned to the Jewish stance of *Shirey Makot Mitzraim* and battled with the native Zionist view pitting the ghetto fighters and the partisans—seen as those who preserved the Jewish tradition of heroism in the spirit of the Jews of Palestine—against the members of the Judenrat, portrayed as their complete opposite and those who betrayed their people.

IV

At war's end Alterman recanted and returned to the hegemony and sovereignty of nationalist Symbolist poetry, harnessing his work to the fight for national independence. From May 1945 to May 1948, Alterman became the central literary spokesman of Jewish settlement in Eretz Israel in its struggle with the British Mandate for the right to illegal Jewish immigration (Heb. *aliyah*, "ascent"), and the establishment of a Jewish state. Poems such as "Reply to the Italian Ship's Captain after a Night of Arrivals" (of illegal underground immigrants, "ma'apilim," from another Hebrew word denoting ascension), reverberated powerfully in the Yishuv. At this stage Alterman was considered an intellectual of the "state to come," and had abandoned his stance as a native intellectual of the nationalist community, which had already placed the sovereign project of the nation-state on its agenda.

In 1948, at the height of the War of Independence, Alterman published a selection of poems from his newspaper column in a book. These poems, perceived by the public as editorials, were proof of Alterman's mobilization in the service of nationalist values and in effect brought about his crowning as the national poet. Alterman's most famous response to the 1948 war is the poem "Magash ha-Kesef" (The silver platter), published a short time after the UN decision to partition Palestine. While the military clash between Jews and Arabs was just beginning, Alterman had already written the poem about its end:

And the land grows quiet. The reddening eye of the sky
slowly disappears
over smoking borders.

And a nation will stand torn-hearted but breathing . . .
to receive the miracle
unlike any other . . .

It will prepare for the ceremony. It will rise under the moon
before dawn, dressed with holiday and fear.
    then will emerge
a girl and a boy
and slowly march before the nation.[13]

Such exaggerated anticipation is comprehensible when it becomes clear that Alterman, at this point, is preparing the national subject for the horrors of war.[14] Alterman returns here to the living-dead symbol, which appears later in the poem in a description of the girl and boy for whom "there is no sign that they're alive or [have been] shot." Once again, Alterman's literary symbol comprises an inclusive response to violence and its consequences while determining that the slain, the individual dead, continues to live in the realm of national collective memory.

In his newspaper poetry, as the state intellectual, Alterman usually concealed Israel's military failures as well as war crimes and immoral acts committed by the Israeli army. Therefore, it is no surprise that when Alterman, exceptionally, attacked the members of Lehi and the Irgun, right-wing Jewish nationalist groups, for the massacre at Deir Yassin on April 9, 1948, he did so in the name of the national consensus, which he depicts as innocent.

V

Ir ha-Yonah (City of the dove), published in 1957, represents Alterman at the height of his role as intellectual of the state in a series of poems that comprise an epic about the battle for independence in the 1948 war and massive immigration in the first years of independence. In this encounter of the neo-Symbolist with the state, Alterman chooses to represent the abstract general essence of the state and its political armor-bearers, such as "people," "realm," and "movement," and in particular "the moment," by erasing their figurative meanings. The "moment" of emergency, which transforms ahistorical time in the diaspora into national, historical time, is represented by Alterman as a real entity, like the dove he chose for the book's title: "And the moment like a city in which / each law is made in public / the face of a dove and the thrust of its sword / are the image of its divided face."[15] The dove, symbolizing the state that is run in exemplary fashion, appears in Alterman's work as an image based on violence; abstract, governmental order is based on the violence of sovereignty, taking power because it, in the words of Carl Schmitt, is the one to declare the state of emergency and suspend the rule of law.

In contrast with the cyclical, ahistorical concept that dominated *Shirey Makot Mitzraim*, in *Ir ha-Yonah* Alterman turns to an eschatological, messianic outlook regarding Jewish existence in the Jewish state: "time" or "the moment" messianically gleam through the quotidian, secular nature of the state[16] and mark a dramatic transformation in the so-called sacred history of the Jewish people who have now created their own state.

In charge of this realm is David Ben-Gurion, the prime minister, who Alterman views as the ruler of the kingdom: the one who, Schmitt argues, because of his authority to declare a state of emergency and suspend democracy, is analogous to God by virtue of his acts and therefore governs the realm with the force of political theology. In *Ir ha-Yonah*, Alterman adopts this messianic position of authority for Ben-Gurion to a great extent, and uses it, much the way he did in his October 1956 ode "To David Ben Gurion," as the theological foundation of Ben-Gurion's role as ruler and sovereign.

Alterman's sweeping support of Ben-Gurion peaked during the 1960s, when Ben-Gurion's tarnished leadership and authority were being challenged politically and morally. Ben-Gurion criticized democratic institutions and resigned from the party that he had founded and personified for many decades. Even though Alterman's identification with Ben-Gurion damaged his reputation as an intellectual who expressed the national consensus,[17] he continued to support him and consider him a leader who embodied the idea of statism and was therefore not fully subject to democratic decision-making.

Ben-Gurion's messianic statism was at its base an etatistic concept, in effect close to fascist patterns of government. Alterman's poetry of accolade and praise is characterized by an aestheticizing of politics. Alterman mobilized the fascist enthrallment of his enthusiastic writing about the Israeli military industry, and brave soldiers, in the style of Marinetti's manifesto of futurism, in service of the state's need for the absorption of immigrants into a melting pot.

Alterman's neo-Symbolism, which in the 1930s defined the Zionist revolution in Eretz Israel as one in which, when the nation makes an effort "to turn symbols into reality all reality turns into a symbol," developed in *Ir ha-Yonah* into an outlook that may be linked with fascism. On the occasion of Ben-Gurion's seventy-fifth birthday in 1961, Alterman wrote: "I know that concepts such as 'nation' and 'movement' and so on, are too general, too 'political,' too social, and yet there are times, and this is one of them, when they cannot be distinguished, in meaning and abstraction, either from life itself and the basic forces of life, or from poetry and high thought."[18] A state in the abstract, in which "all reality [turns into] a symbol," is, in Alterman's eyes, a mechanism whose violence is justified, existing beyond morality, like an official governmental order that exists in the abstract, separate from the actual one who proclaims it.

However, from the first, when Alterman begins to tell the heroic tale of illegal immigration, it contains a clash between the natives and the Jewish refugees. He is threatened by the refugees and so he terms them "rabble" whose necks must be broken by the native Jews in Palestine. From this cruel Zionist point of view, he describes them as the new natives of the realm, born of the destructive violence that eradicated the Jewish refugee identity. And so, in the end, the encounter of the native Jews with the refugees creates a violent upheaval in representation, forging a new image for both the natives and the refugees, embodying the abstract quality of the state as reality in all senses. But Alterman is also aware of the process and not only its consequences. Unlike Ben-Gurion, whose un-Zionist concept of statehood completely severed the connection between the sovereign Jewish political entity and the Jewish nation—that is, between the natives and the Jews—Alterman hesitated. In his poem "Leyl Tmura" (A night of change) in *Ir ha-Yonah*, as well as the long poem "Tsalmay Panim" (Icons of faces), one finds criticism of the price the Jewish people paid for entering into a nationhood established as a kingdom.

Responses to *Ir ha-Yonah* were for the most part tepid. Many saw the book as a regression from lyrical poetry to politically mobilized work glorifying the new Israeli state. Nathan Zach, the most prominent member of the younger generation of poets, the Statehood Generation, intensely joined the critics. In his fierce struggle against the older generation, Zach attacked the work of its chief representative, Nathan Alterman, for literary and moral reasons. In his article "Thoughts on Alterman's Poetry," published in the leading literary journal of the younger generation *Achshav* (Now) in 1959, Zach criticized what seemed to him the irresponsible use Alterman made of figurative language in a mainly decorative way, creating a total estrangement from concrete human experience. Alterman, argued Zach, had lost the poetic connection to experiential human time, using a mechanical and monotonous meter in its place. This attack was added to earlier criticism by Mordechai Shalev of *Shirim al Eretz Hanegev* (Poems about the land of the Negev [Israel's south]), published in 1950 and later included in *Ir ha-Yonah*. Shalev's main argument was that Alterman had failed to represent the Israeli landscape because of his foreignness and lack of an intimate connection with it, both noticeable in his figurative language.[19] But more than anything, both Shalev's and Zach's criticism point to a Zionist stance admonishing Alterman as someone who approaches the local landscape as an immigrant, a foreigner and an invader, someone who exposes Hebrew poetry's colonialist approach to Palestine in poetry that remains Jewish and is unable to position itself in the Palestinian expanse as native poetry.

Alterman's version of statehood was extremely radical. So much so that it sought to ingest the seamen's rebellion of 1951, supported by the left wing of the Mapam Party and the Communist Party and suppressed by the army, as a legitimate governmental phenomenon. He justified protests by Mizrahim, Jews of Muslim descent, such as the disturbances in Wadi Salib in Haifa in 1959, from a clearly governmental point of view that the state must remain neutral with respect to citizens' ethnic identities. Out of his total devotion to the state as an institution, Alterman also defended the democratic right of Arab Knesset member Tawfik Tubi to serve as an Israeli parliamentarian without apology: "Now's the time to decide once and for all: among the delegates of [our] home [in Heb., also "parliament"] / Tubi sits *by order of the regime*!"[20]

VI

In 1965, Alterman's final book of poems, *Hagigat Kaytz* (Summer celebration), was published. The book tells a continuous story through an abundance of characters, in a conspicuous mix of genres: poetry and prose, lyric and epic, satire and fable, some in the spirit of medieval maqama, the originally medieval prosimetric Hebrew literary genre including rhymed prose. In a restaurant in a suburb of the city of Stambol, on a blistering hot summer evening at the end of the 1950s, a party is taking place honoring the local bank's anniversary. During the party the employees wish to present the bank manager with a silver cup; it is, however, the inheritance of Tsiva Tshuva, a new immigrant from Morocco, that he had intended as a wedding present for his daughter, Miriam Helen. On the lower floor of the restaurant, a fight is underway among underworld thugs, including Misha Bar Hassid, a safecracker and long-time resident of the town. Misha attempts to save Miriam Helen from the pimp Woldarsky, who is threatening to slash her face if she does not give in to his pressure to work as a prostitute.

Here too, as in *Ir ha-Yonah*, the abstraction of state and nation exist as a reality on all levels. In *Ir ha-Yonah*, Alterman could not depart from gray and ordinary materiality through acceptance and recognition, and therefore, in order to make the abstraction of the state real to itself, to concretize it, he required state violence. In contrast, in *Hagigat Kaytz*, violence is present as a memory, but in a moment of enlightenment, "everything connects." After an electrical failure, which suspends all activities, violence is prevented and the silver cup is returned to Tsiva. The Jews, immigrants from different diasporas, and the underworld criminals blend into a state that blurs the discrimination against Mizrahim. In this way Alterman attempts to bridge the gap between the essence and abstraction of state and nation and the individual elements that comprise them. This merger of Jew and native creates a new image of the Jew:

> Because there is a nation life within the life
> of the man and the life of the woman
> and there isn't much you can renew
> or deny about these things.

> There is a Jewish light and there is
> a Jewish darkness and things
> like time and place, and suddenly one takes on
> a Jewish icon different from others.[21]

Alterman develops his approach to the form of the correct representation of life in the kingdom in "Shir Hearat Shulayim" (Footnote poem), where he offers the middle way of *Hagigat Kaytz*, moving lightly and with a smile between concrete and abstract writing. In contrast with the humorless, epic tone of *Ir ha-Yonah*, Alterman developed a light, carnivalistic, humoristic burlesque approach in *Hagigat Kaytz* by blurring the borders between lofty and mocking language.[22] On Israel's seventeenth anniversary, Alterman viewed the state as a stable and secure entity that was no longer in need of overt violence, and therefore the position of the state intellectual could be humoristic and lighthearted. In the first half of the 1960s, Alterman reestablished the figure of the native, now living naturally in his country without conflict, who mediates with this light tone between his eternal nature ("and there isn't much you can renew or deny about these things.") and his sudden reappearance in Jewish history in a new guise ("and suddenly one takes on / a Jewish icon different from others").

Here, too, fears and subversion lurk underneath the surface of peaceful, smiling stability.[23] But in the foreground, Alterman reestablishes the tone of *Hagigat Kaytz*, bringing his lyric poetry closer to the work he published in newspapers and thus enabling him to write his updated version of statism, in which the Jew and the native blend together in what he portrayed as the inclusive existence of the Israeli melting pot. In the 1950s, he had sharply opposed selective immigration that discriminated against Mizrahim (for example, in his famous poem, "Ritsato shel ha oleh Danino" [The immigrant Danino's run] in the name of statism, which was supposed to be neutral in relation to a citizen's ethnic identity). But in the first half of the 1960s, in contrast, Alterman gave a more conciliatory version, denying the state's discrimination against Mizrahim: although the Mizrahim are sent to a remote, godforsaken town, without the aid of absorption workers, the story has a happy ending when a doctor tells them he has decided to remain with the frightened immigrants in their town.

VII

All of this turned upside-down in the wake of the June 1967 war. From Alterman's point of view, the occupation of territories in the West Bank and Gaza, and the possibility of settling them with Jews intensively, widened the gap (which, he demanded, should be filled) between the Jewish nation and its territory. Alterman, one of the founders of the Greater Israel Movement following the 1967 war, which sought to impose Israeli sovereignty on all the territories occupied during the war and rejected any peace initiative involving withdrawal, now faced a new political reality. In contrast with *Hagigat Kaytz*, in which he reconciled himself with Israeli reality, whose defects and injustices he portrayed with a conciliatory smile, now Alterman the Zionist found himself in a revolutionary and critical position, criticizing the sovereign Israeli state. In effect, he demanded that the state be released from the laws of government and operate according to other, loftier laws in order to quickly settle the territories and impose Israeli sovereignty on them. The new reality created by the occupation changed, from Alterman's point of view, the distinction between diasporic Jews and native Israelis and produced a dramatic challenge that demanded massive Jewish immigration. In "Mul metsiut sh-ain-la-ach" (Facing a reality like no other), an essay published just after the 1967 war ended, Alterman presented his position about the geopolitical advantage created by the war, whose main principle was presented as a three-stranded thread. He pointed to the gap the war created between the Jewish people, the Land of Israel, and the state of Israel, writing, "The state and the land are now one entity, and what's missing for the historical joining is *the Jewish people*. Only they can weave, together with what has been gained, the three-stranded thread that will not be cut."[24] Alterman, the supporter of statism, who remained attached to its theological foundations with a metaphysical, in effect religious faith in the right of the Jewish people to the Land of Israel, nurtured on its purportedly sacred history, nonetheless believed that the Palestinians in the territories were to be granted full citizenship (but not national) rights. In order to fulfill Jewish claims of democracy, Alterman sketched a vision of mass Jewish immigration that would allow for the preservation of a Jewish majority in the area between the Jordan River and the Mediterranean Sea, and turn the Jews into natives in a dramatic national process.

In his final book, *Ha-maseha Ha-aharona* (The last mask), published in 1968, Alterman wrote a biting satire about the condition of Zionism, in which he returned to the gravity of the statist abstractions of the symbols in *Ir ha-Yonah*, arguing that, after 1967, Zionism was just a hollow, fraudulent mask. In this, he echoed Ben-Gurion, who had argued as early as the 1950s that if Zionism meant no immigration to Israel and the continuation of Jewish life in the diaspora, then he could no longer be a Zionist. In the less than a decade that separates *Ir ha-Yonah* from *Ha-maseha Ha-aharona*, the national poet moved from praise and thrilled admiration of the utopian struggle to establish a state, to the dystopian view of the satirist who in effect predicted, right after the military victory of 1967, the end of Zionism.

Notes

1. Nathan Alterman, "Be-shetef ir" [In an urban flood], *Shirim* [Poems], *1931–1935* (Tel Aviv, 1984), 13. [All translations of poetry were made by the translator of this chapter, Lisa Katz.]

2. Ibid., 15.

3. Hannan Hever, *Paitanim VeBiryonim* [Poets and zealots] (Jerusalem, 1994).

4. Nathan Alterman, *Shirim Shemikvar* [Poems from time pasts] (Tel Aviv, 1972), 7.

5. Nathan Alterman, *Bamaagal* [In the circle] (Tel-Aviv, 1975), 29.

6. Ibid. Emphasis is in original.

7. Dan Miron, *From the Worm a Butterfly Emerges: Young Nathan Alterman—His Life and Work, Part One: 1910–1935* (Ramat Aviv, 2001), 127–29.

8. Nathan Alterman, "Olam Veh-Hipucho" [A world and its upside down], in *Bamaagal*, 36.

9. Hannan Hever, *Suddenly the Sight of War: Nationalism and Violence in the Hebrew Poetry of the 1940s* (Stanford, 2016), 41–42.

10. Mordechai Shalev, "Who's Afraid of the 'Joy of the Poor'?," *Alpaim* [Two thousands] (1992): 5–6.

11. Alterman, *Shirim Shemikvar*, 231.

12. Hever, *Suddenly the Sight of War*, 75–137.

13. Nathan Alterman, *Hatur Hasviee* [The seventh column] (Tel Aviv, 2003), 357.

14. Dan Miron, *Essays about Literature and Society* (Tel Aviv, 1991), 145.

15. Nathan Alterman, *Ir ha-Yonah* [The city of the dove] (Tel Aviv, 1978), 8.

16. Dan Miron, Arbid Panim ba-Sifrut ha-'lvrit bat Yamenu [Four faces in the Hebrew literature] (Tel Aviv, 1962).

17. Dan Laor, "Alterman and the 'Affair,'" in *Alterman and His Work*, eds. Menahem Dorman and Aharon Komem (Sde Boker, 1989), 90.

18. Nathan Alterman and David Ben Gurion, *Bein Meshorer Lemedinai* [Between a poet and a stateman], ed. Menachem Dorman (Tel Aviv, 1986), 50.

19. Mordechai Shalev, "Alterman's Rhymes of the Land of the Negev," *Sulam* [Ladder] 1, no. 2 (September–October 1950): 18–20.

20. "Ha-nezifa Betufik Tubi," *Davar*, November 11, 1949, reprinted in *Hatur Hashevee*, vol. 1 (Tel Aviv, 1972), 278.

21. Nathan Alterman, *Hagigat Kaytz* [Summer celebration] (Tel Aviv, 1973), 76.

22. Ruth Kartun-Blum, *The Jester and the Shadow* (Tel Aviv, 1994), 19.

23. Kartun-Blum, *Jester and the Shadow*, 131.

24. Nathan Alterman, "Mul metsiut sh-ain-la-ach," reprinted in *Ha-chut Ha-meshulash* (Tel Aviv, 1981), 37.

35

Saul Bellow (1915–2005)

ATHENS AND JERUSALEM

Steven Jaron

SAUL BELLOW ONCE RECOUNTED A CONVERSATION HE HAD WITH A YOUNG BELZER Hasid, who happened to be seated next to his wife in an airplane. This Hasid was one of some two hundred ultra-Orthodox Jews who had boarded the plane at Heathrow en route to Israel for the *brit mi'lah*, a circumcision, of the Belzer Rebbe's firstborn son. They wore "broad hats and beards and sidelocks and dangling fringes," which Bellow readily recognized from his childhood. "At the age of six, I myself wore a tallith katan, or scapular, under my shirt, only mine was a scrap of green calico print, whereas theirs are white linen. God instructed Moses to speak to the children of Israel and to 'bid them that they make them fringes in the borders of their garments.' So they are still wearing them some four thousand years later."[1]

The Hasid asked Bellow if he spoke Yiddish, to which he replied affirmatively, and just as quickly told him that he could not possibly sit next to a woman. Bellow changed places with his wife. Not wanting to offend the Hasid, Bellow asked the flight attendant for a kosher meal. There weren't enough for the many Hasidim, the flight attendant told him. When the chicken arrived, the Hasid was indeed disturbed by seeing a Jew eat *treiph*, nonkosher food, and he duly proposed a sandwich his wife had prepared. Bellow again obliged. After *Minchah*, the afternoon prayer service, had ended, Bellow told the Hasid that his wife, a mathematician, would be lecturing at the Hebrew University of Jerusalem. But the Hasid, speaking sincerely, did not know what a mathematician was. Nor did he know what a physicist was; he had never heard of Einstein. Bellow was quietly bewildered. At Ben-Gurion airport, the Hasid and Bellow silently gave each other a final glance. "In me he sees what deformities the modern age can produce in the seed of Abraham. In him I see a piece of history, an antiquity."[2]

The "deformities" wrought by the "modern age." A "piece of history." The contrast could not be greater; the difference between the Hasid and Bellow could not be more obvious. Or so it would seem. Is this so? Did not Hasidut, the movement founded in the middle of the eighteenth century, come to define itself in contradistinction to Haskalah, the Jewish Enlightenment? If the Hasidim traveling to attend the circumcision of their master's son are themselves children of the Haskalah—even if unintentionally and in reaction to it—Saul Bellow is himself an offshoot of Judaism's antiquity, a biblical template rooted in the author's mind.

So too is the central modern drama, the generational conflict between father and son. Tommy Wilhelm, the hero of *Seize the Day* (1956), is the screen name of a young man who has failed in his career as a movie actor in Los Angeles and returns to New York to see his father, Doctor Adler, a distinguished internal physician, now retired. At the Hotel Gloriana on Manhattan's Upper West Side, the staff readily recognizes him. "'Aren't you Doctor Adler's son?' 'Yes, but my name is Tommy Wilhelm.' And the doctor would say, 'My son and I use different monickers. I uphold tradition. He's for the new.'"[3] The father thereby disqualifies the son, and with great efficiency. But Bellow does not leave the father-son rivalry there; he draws out its complexity. When Old Rappaport asks Tommy if he has a seat reserved in the synagogue for Yom Kippur, Tommy says, "No." He considers how he should nevertheless say a prayer for his mother from time to time: "His mother had belonged to the Reform congregation. His father had no religion." His father, then, despite his uttering to the contrary, stood outside tradition. He was an atheist; it fell to Tommy to pay a man to recite a prayer for his mother, herself poised as a Reform Jew between tradition and modernity, at the cemetery. "Now he reflected, in Dad's eyes I am the wrong kind of Jew. He doesn't like the way I act. Only he is the right kind of Jew."[4] Bellow inverts the allegiance to the past, but the son is inevitably vulnerable to a feeling of guilt in relation to the father so long as there remain notions of "right" and "wrong."

The quarrel between the ancients and the moderns, in its mid-twentieth-century guise, is likewise central to *Mr. Sammler's Planet* (1970), set in the late 1960s. A pivotal moment in the narrative is when the Polish-born Anglophile Artur Sammler, a survivor of the Holocaust, is jeered during a lecture he had been invited to give on prewar Bloomsbury politics to a group of Columbia University students. A lecture? No, Mr. Sammler, expecting to talk to a handful of students in the calm intimacy of a seminar, is brought to an overflowing amphitheater that more resembles a revolutionary meeting. Mr. Sammler retains his composure and will speak on the topic—specifically, according to his young Columbia friend and organizer, Lionel Feffer, the "British Scene in the Thirties." But for Mr. Sammler, it is a matter of "the mental atmosphere of England before the Second World War."[5] The language each uses incarnates their respective intellectual frames and highlights their differences: the British versus the American, a "mental atmosphere" versus a "scene." Their "planets" do not seem to belong to the same solar system or, if they do, the life forms present are qualitatively distinct and incompatible. The students are uncomprehending and shout, "'[W]hy do you listen to this effete old shit? What has he got to tell you? His balls are dry. He's dead. He can't come.'"[6]

Yiddish, the Middle Language

Solomon Bellows, or Saul Bellow as he became known, was born on June 10, 1915, in Lachine, Quebec, to Russian Jewish immigrants. He died on April 5, 2005, in Brookline, Massachusetts. As an adult he was not a practicing Jew; nevertheless, upon his death he was buried in Brattleboro, Vermont, in accordance with the traditional Jewish rite. In 1918 Saul Bellow moved with his family to Montreal. Then in

1924 the Bellows settled in Humboldt Park in Chicago, living among other Jewish families and Polish immigrants and their American-born children, depicted as part of the bleak backdrop of *The Adventures of Augie March* (1953) or the urbanity of *Humboldt's Gift* (1975). Bellow's Chicago, like his Montreal, offered up the residue of Eastern European Jewish life, and it was what he perceived as the foreignness of this milieu that led him to study anthropology, a modern discipline to which he thought Jews were naturally attracted. "Among the founders of the science were Durkheim and Lévy-Bruhl, Marcel Mauss, Boas, Sapir, Lowie," he wrote. "They may have believed that they were demystifiers, that science was their motive and that their ultimate aim was to increase universalism. I don't see it that way myself. A truer explanation is the nearness of the ghettos to the sphere of Revelation. . . . Exotics going out to do science upon exotics. And then it all came out in Rabbinic-Germanic or Cartesian-Talmudic forms."[7]

In the mid- and late 1940s Saul Bellow began contributing fiction to *Partisan Review* and essays, reviews, and fiction to *Commentary* and other magazines. A succession of novels followed, including *The Adventures of Augie March*, *Henderson the Rain King* (1959), and *Herzog* (1964). He was awarded the Nobel Prize for Literature in 1976 following the publication of *Humboldt's Gift*, which drew from his friendship with the poet and essayist Delmore Schwartz and, by some accounts, that with John Berryman, who had dedicated *77 Dream Songs* (1964) to Bellow, alongside his own wife. Bellow held many academic appointments in various universities and was professor and chairman of the Committee on Social Thought at the University of Chicago where he worked with Edward Shils (a partial model for Artur Sammler) and, later, Allan Bloom. He contributed the foreword to Bloom's *The Closing of the American Mind* (1987), uniting with its author in his conviction that higher education was dangerously undermining students' intellectual and moral development. Bloom's friendship with Bellow and his death were fictionalized in *Ravelstein* (2000), Bellow's final novel.

Saul Bellow grew up speaking Yiddish at home and French at school. Russian could be heard and Hebrew was also taught. English, the language he wrote his books in, was acquired relatively belatedly. Yiddish was the middle or intermediary language from and around which others turned. As a youth, he translated, with his schoolboy friend Isaac Rosenberg, T. S. Eliot's "The Love Song of J. Alfred Prufrock" into Yiddish, though he later attributed the work to Rosenberg alone. Bellow called the translation "a startling X-ray of those hallowed bones, which brings Anglo-Saxons and Jews together in a surrealistic Yiddish unity, a masterpiece of irreverence."[8] Yiddish was a language of the people, of the mass of European Jewry, the Ashkenazim, which through the pathways of assimilation became paradoxically a language accessible only to the privileged. In the early novel *The Victim* (1947), Kirby Allbee, the drunkard Gentile, chides Daniel Harkavy for singing old spirituals and ballads: "It isn't right for you to sing them. You have to be born to them. If you're not born to them, it's no use trying to sing them."[9] Allbee then encourages him, mockingly, to sing something belonging rather to the Jewish repertoire, a psalm. But Harkavy, an assimilated American Jew, doesn't know any. "Then any Jewish song," provokes Allbee. "Something you've really got feeling for. Sing us the one about the mother."[10] Allbee cannot say precisely just which song about the mother he is referring to; perhaps he had heard a recording of it at some unnamed time. Nor does the narrator indicate what song he is requesting. Does the reader understand that Allbee is asking for "My Yiddishe Momme," doubtless in the late 1920s version sung in English and Yiddish by Sophie Tucker, with its nostalgia for childhood in an East Side tenement overseen warmly by the singer's long-gone Jewish mother? The point is that Harkavy cannot even sing "My Yiddishe Momme."

Yiddish expressions were deployed as a shibboleth, comprehensible only to the initiated and used thereby with exclusive, "instinctive snobbery."[11] While Bellow could also use other languages including French, Spanish, German, Latin, and, of course, Hebrew, Yiddish belonged to a distinct linguistic category, even in relation to Hebrew, which implied a kind of theological erudition. Yiddish was "genteel"; if you spoke it (or, at least, though less favorably, understood it), it was because, after all, you belonged to the family.

Trepverter (lit., "stairways"; fig., "afterthoughts"), for instance, a key Yiddish word found early on in *Herzog*, summarizes the depth and breadth of the protagonist's bitterness and sense of injustice and incomprehension. Describing Moses Herzog's mental breakdown, the narrator says: "At first there was no pattern to the notes he made. They were fragments—nonsense syllables, exclamations, twisted proverbs and quotations or, in the Yiddish of his long-dead mother, *Trepverter*— retorts that came too late, when you were already on your way down the stairs."[12] Bellow may indeed have known the word from childhood, but he could also have come across it—or, rather, its notion—while reading Diderot (a decisive forerunner, along with Dostoevsky, Flaubert, and Dreiser) when he writes of *l'esprit de l'escalier*: when, descending the stairway from the *étage noble* to the street level, the retort comes to mind too late; you are already out the door and can no longer riposte, leaving yourself with a sense of unexpressed anger and regret to mull over in silence. Be that as it may, the meaning of the Yiddish as a reflection of Herzog's desperation is used in the opening pages of the novel, where it might otherwise go unnoticed by a reader seeking to advance along in the narrative.

Those unfamiliar with Yiddish or, worse, those who misused it, were especially loathsome to Bellow. As Herzog's wife is on the verge of leaving him, Herzog confides his despair to his friend Gersbach. At this point in the novel, Herzog does not yet know that she is carrying on an affair with none other than Gersbach (even though Gersbach's own wife does). Herzog, idealizing his physiognomy, sees in his eyes those of a "prophet, a *Shofat*, yes, a judge in Israel, a king."[13] In contrast to this noble idealization, Gersbach vulgarly tells him: "'The bitch is testing you. You're an important professor, invited to conferences, with an international correspondence. She wants you to admit her importance. You're a *ferimmter mensch*."[14] "Moses, to save his soul, could not let this pass. He said quietly, '*Berimmter*,'" correcting Gersbach. "'*Fe—be*, who cares. Maybe it's not so much your reputation as your egotism. You could be a real *mensch*.'"[15]

No translation of *berrimter* (famous, well-known) is given; the narrator, or Herzog, or perhaps Bellow himself withholds it and thereby places the reader onto the same inferior level of carelessness and ignorance as deceitful Gersbach. When Gersbach tells Herzog that he "could be a real *mensch*," irony is added to humiliation since the carefree misusage implies Gersbach's falsehood, his treachery and shallowness. Herzog's dismay at Gersbach's linguistic nonchalance is but a prelude to his bitter rage when he learns of the betrayal.

An Incidentally Jewish Writer

The Judaism of Bellow's childhood, which for him was characterized as timeless but whose biblical characters were intimately familiar, formed a core sense of being and provided a distinct perspective on the goings-on and commerce of life beyond home. "My childhood was in ancient times which was true of all orthodox Jews. Every child was immersed in the Old Testament as soon as he could understand anything, so that you began life by knowing Genesis in Hebrew by heart at the age of four. You never got to distinguish between that and the outer world."[16] As a student, he sensed certain non-Jews' belittlement of him as unwavering: the message they imparted was that English would forever remain beyond his mastery, that "as a Jew and the son of Russian Jews I would probably never have the right *feeling* for Anglo-Saxon traditions, for English words."[17] Even in college, he said, the people who told him this were not necessarily disinterested friends. "But they had an effect on me, nevertheless. This was something from which I had to free myself. I fought free because I had to."[18]

Saul Bellow was thus skeptical about considering himself a Jewish writer, preferring to see himself as a writer who was incidentally Jewish. "I have never consciously written as a Jew," he said. "I have just written as Saul Bellow. I have never attempted to make myself Jewish, I've never tried to appeal to a community, I never thought of writing for Jews exclusively. I never wanted to." And yet it was impossible for him to see himself as anything but Jewish. "I think of myself as a person of Jewish origin—American and Jewish—who has had a certain experience of life, which is in part Jewish. Proportions are not for me to decide. I don't know what they are: how much is Jewish, how much is Russian, how much is male, how much is twentieth century, how much is Midwestern."[19]

But if Bellow's fiction draws variously on problems such as the Old World versus the New World, the vagaries of achieving success in America, mourning and memory, or survival and bearing witness, it cannot be called, for this reason alone, "Jewish." If indeed it may be, it is due to its aesthetic quality—to its tendency to *pilpul*, a talmudic analysis that is at once sharp-edged and seemingly irrelevant, even absurd. A character such as Moses Herzog, acting out of a compulsion to understand the sources and trajectories of modern anxiety, is not much unlike Joseph in the early novel *Dangling Man* (1944), though Joseph's "feeling of strangeness" takes on the form of "not quite belonging to the world, of lying under a cloud and looking up at it."[20] Herzog's decidedly impassioned analysis (he is his own case study) rather reflects the talmudic method: "Herzog had been overcome by the need to explain, to have it out, to justify, to put in perspective, to clarify, to make amends."[21] And yet Herzog is not yeshiva-trained; he is fully an agent of American culture (a sometime lecturer and researcher whose expertise is Romanticism), all the while retaining residually this characteristic feature of traditional Judaism. What, in fact, distinguishes *Herzog* as a work of Jewish fiction? If any criterion exists, it is the necessary quality of Bellovian ambiguity and cross-fertilization, the refusal to maintain an artificially pure cultural state of either/or, of this or that, which effectively signals his fiction's particular Jewish modernity.

Childhood Judaism was coupled in Bellow's mind with a sense of survival—not exclusively in the form of the contemporary antisemitism he might have found in

Lachine or Montreal or Chicago but, rather, that found in the New Testament he read as an eight-year-old patient suffering from peritonitis and pneumonia during a six-month stay at the Protestant Royal Victoria Hospital. Authorized visits were rare, and his parents could not see him at the same time. He read whatever was available to him, mainly comic books and a children's edition of the New Testament. He knew that he was in danger of dying, as other children around him disappeared during the night, and this feeling was for him existentially determinative. He called this fundamental life event a *primitive fact*. "I felt forever after that I had been excused from death and that I was, as gamblers in Chicago used to say in those days, when I was ten or so, playing on velvet—ahead of the game."[22] Survival, he added, implied a sense of debt: something was owed on account of surviving and in time he would come to pay for it, a recurrent theme in his novels. The narrator of *Herzog* relates how, as an eight-year-old in the children's ward of the Royal Victoria Hospital, a Christian woman had taught him the Sermon on the Mount: "Consider the lilies of the field, they toil not, neither do they spin, yet Solomon in all his glory was not arrayed. . . ." She told him further, "Suffer the little children to come unto me."[23] In *Humboldt's Gift* Charlie Citrine refers to this precise primitive fact-event: "I grew up in Polish Chicago, I went to the Chopin Grammar School, I spent my eighth year in the public ward of a TB sanatorium. . . . Kids hemorrhaged in the night and choked on blood and were dead. In the morning the white geometry of made-up beds had to be coped with. I became very thoughtful here and I think that my disease of the lungs passed over into an emotional disorder so that I sometimes felt, and still feel, poisoned by eagerness, a congestion of tender impulses together with fever and enthusiastic dizziness."[24] Or, more concisely, Chick in *Ravelstein*: "At the age of eight I had had to recover from peritonitis complicated by pneumonia."[25]

The memory of this "primitive fact" exerted its relentless hold throughout Bellow's adult life. Artur Sammler, a Lazarus figure who had taken refuge during World War II in a mausoleum, having survived a firing squad of Polish partisans with whom he had previously fought in the Zamosht forest (his wife was among the murdered), could have very well uttered these thoughts of Herzog: "You have to fight for your life. That's the chief condition on which you hold it."[26] Or this passage from a letter written by Herzog, linking survival to the death camps and the era that produced them: "We are survivors, in this age, so theories of progress ill become us, because we are intimately acquainted with the costs. To realize that you are a survivor is a shock. At the realization of such an election you feel like bursting into tears. As the dead go their way, you want to call them, but they depart in a black cloud of faces, souls. They flow out in smoke from the extermination chimneys, and leave you in the clear light of historical success—the technical success of the West."[27]

The Inexhaustible Human Complexity

The natural world of Jewish life was challenged when the Bellows moved to Chicago. "First I translated from the Old Testament into my inner life, then I translated from books I read at the public library, again into the inner life. In the first instance this had the approval of Judaism, that is, mainly from my family. In the second form it could only be fantasy. You had to be wary of what was in truth both stirring and ennobling but at the same time dangerous to reveal."[28] Bellow's father, in the United States, fell to the appeal of assimilation, what he called "Americanism": equality before the law and the progress of democracy (as de Tocqueville saw it) complicated (in Bellow's novels)—at times tragically, at others, comically—by the single-minded drive, with implied or explicit vanity, for material or intellectual or spiritual success. "At the table he would tell us, this really *is* the land of opportunity; you're free either to run yourself into the ground or improve your chances."[29] Bellow described this conflict as one between "Jewish life and street life."

Fiercely opposed to determinism, Bellow believed that the individual could and must overcome the influence of his immediate environment in order to realize his own purpose. "For as a Midwesterner, the son of immigrant parents," he wrote in the foreword to *The Closing of the American Mind*, "I recognized at an early age that I was called upon to decide for myself to what extent my Jewish origins, my surroundings (the accidental circumstances of Chicago), my schooling, were to be allowed to determine the course of my life."[30] At the same time, one's environment, the starting-point of one's life, were fundamental; fundamental but not decisive. "I couldn't say why I would not allow myself to become the product of an *environment*. But gainfulness, utility, prudence, business, had no hold on me."[31] Bellow held that the act of writing could have a transformative effect on one's personality. In a letter to John Cheever, he insisted that the "'given' of social origins'" was "superficial"[32] and he praised Cheever for being "engaged, as a writer should be, in transforming yourself." Writing was thus thought of as an instrument of self-realization, as a means to metamorphosizing and enlarging the self.

Further in the foreword to Bloom's book, Bellow reflected on the futility of trying to pinpoint him in terms of identity or influence. "European observers sometimes classify me as a hybrid curiosity, neither fully American nor satisfactorily European, stuffed with references to the philosophers, the historians, and poets I had consumed higgledy-piggledy, in my Midwestern lair. I am, of course, an autodidact, as modern writers always are." On the other hand, "American readers sometimes object to a kind of foreignness in my books. I mention Old World writers, I have highbrow airs, and appear to put on the dog."[33] Bellow could never conceive of himself as being placed into any rigid, self-limiting category. In his novels he sought to depict the individual character in its varied dimensions and struggled against the reduction to a system or ideology, fully understanding that any representation was itself reductive.

His constant enemy was fatuity in thought and expression, and he steadfastly considered his responsibility as a writer as nothing less than the attempt to wrest the individual from the clutch of culture's potential destructiveness. Literature was the weapon chosen to carry out this struggle. It would draw the reader closer to what was most essential in his or her being. He spelled this position out early on in his contribution to the *Commentary* symposium on "The Jewish Writer and the English Literary Tradition" (1949), writing, "Great things always give pain; they can never be taken smoothly. Can we read *Lear* without the pains of parents and children? Or Job without the pain of the evil that man doesn't bring upon himself?"[34]

The 1976 Nobel Lecture shows a combative but optimistic Saul Bellow arguing against the evaporation of individual character called for by the likes of Alain Robbe-Grillet. While telling his audience that he did not wish to pursue a polemic, his will to argue, to provoke, perhaps, proved to be stronger than himself and he attacked one of the "leaders" (Robbe-Grillet) of the aesthetic program known as *choseisme*, "thingism." Agreeing with Robbe-Grillet, he admitted the common truth that culture had evolved into new forms, but parted company when Robbe-Grillet asserted that character in the novel remained of mere historical interest, like a "mummy." "Can anything as vivid as the characters in their books be dead?" he asked. "Can it be that human beings are at an end?" For Saul Bellow, individuality could not be entirely "dependent on historical and cultural conditions." No matter how persuasively and seductively literary critics, historians, psychologists, philosophers, and social scientists presented their arguments in favor of this concept, the depth and breadth of human character and relations remained inexhaustible, he stated. "I suggest that it is not in the intrinsic interest of human beings but in these ideas and accounts that the problem lies. It is the staleness and inadequacy of the ideas that repel us."[35] He called for looking into "our own heads," fundamentally, without the help of a *preestablished* critical perspective, as there was no order that could possibly account for individual complexity and no "leader," any leader, could purport to decide what was important and what was not in the analysis of culture.

Contempt for modern society preceded his Nobel Lecture. "This society, like decadent Rome, is an amusement society. That is the grim fact," he wrote at the beginning of the 1970s. But art—literature, the poem—had the capacity, and therefore ought, to purge the "amusement society" of its excess, its corruption, and attend to the moral health of "the heart of humankind." He drew here from R. G. Collingwood's *The Principles of Art* in support of his argument: the artist was a prophet who disclosed the secrets of the human heart; he must assume the role of, and bear the responsibility for acting as, the community's "spokesman." The argument is well known, its account is "very old," he wrote, but in modern times this truth was seldom expressed: "No community altogether knows its own heart: and by failing in this knowledge a community deceives itself on the one subject concerning which ignorance means death. . . . The remedy is the poem itself. Art is the community's medicine for the worst disease of mind, the corruption of consciousness."[36]

While in Stockholm, Bellow pondered the essential transformation that modern consciousness had undergone during World War I with its irreversible eruption of human destructiveness. "The unending cycle of crises that began with the war has forged a kind of person, one who has lived through strange and terrible things and in whom there is an observable shrinkage of prejudices, a casting off of disappointing ideologies, an ability to live with many kinds of madness, and an immense desire for certain durable human goods—truth, for instance; freedom; wisdom."[37] He thus argued that there was something of a "refining process" at work on the mind, and it has not stopped even in times of crisis, in our own time. "Looking into Proust's *Time Regained*, I find that he was clearly aware of it. His novel, describing French society during the Great War, tests the strength of his art. Without an art that shirks no personal or collective horrors, he insists, we do not know ourselves or anyone else." And he added, "Only art penetrates what pride, passion, intelligence, and habit erect on all sides—the seeming realities of this world. There is another reality, the genuine one, which we lose sight of. This other reality is always sending us hints, which, without art, we can't receive. Proust called these hints our 'true impressions.' The true impressions, our persistent intuitions, will, without art, be hidden from us, and we are left with nothing but a 'terminology for practical ends which we falsely call life.'"[38]

Death and Jewish Humor

The central preoccupation of Saul Bellow's art was the depiction of the human condition, its tragedy and comedy, its absurdity and brilliance. Its setting was most often urban—the American city, New York or Chicago, the seat of European immigration where democracy animates the political mind of its citizens. Humor by turns is a literary mode, and joke telling, making others laugh, was thought of as a mitzvah—a decidedly Jewish position. "What we were laughing about was death, and of course death does sharpen the comic sense,"[39] says Chick of his friend Abe Ravelstein, dying of complications from AIDS.

The death theme, the dying or departed character, received Bellow's most sustained, and perhaps greatest, treatment. This doubtless originated when he saw the children dying from tuberculosis as an eight-year-old in Montreal. But death could not be prepared for, and more to the point it was the most challenging subject to represent. Bellow recalled a joke—drawn from La Fontaine's fable "Death and the Woodman"—his father, a natural storyteller, would tell about an old man, the last of his family, who lived all alone in the forest. Too sick and feeble, the old man could hardly gather firewood, or do anything else. "One cold day . . . he spread the rope on the snow and laid his fuel on it and tied a knot but he was too weak to lift the bundle. . . . He lifted his eyes and called to Heaven. '*Gott meiner*. Send me Death.' At once he saw the Angel of Death coming toward him. And the Angel said to him, 'You sent for me, what do you want?' And the old man thought quickly and said, 'Yes, as a matter of fact I did. I can't get these sticks up on my back and wonder if you'd mind giving me a hand.'" "So, you see," Bellow's father would instructively add, "when it comes to dying, nobody is really ready."[40]

Bellow believed that Jewish humor defied any effort to understand it. Referring to an essay by Hymen Slate that appeared in *The Noble Savage* in 1961, he admitted that at least "laughter, the comic sense of life, may be offered as proof of the existence of God. Existence, [Slate] says, is too *funny* to be uncaused." We laugh because "*Chaos* is exposed."[41] "'Remember me when I am in my grave, Augie, when I will be dead!'" Grandma Lausch, a boarder at the Marches, commands Augie, shaken; first in her tentative immigrant's English and then, seizing him (accidentally) by the arm, in Yiddish: "'*Gedenk, Augie, wenn ich bin todt!*'"[42] Charlie Citrine, the narrator of *Humboldt's Gift*, contemplates the moral debt he feels toward his deceased friend, the poet Von Humboldt Fleischer: "On esthetic grounds, if on no others, I cannot accept the view of death taken by most of us, and taken by me during most of my life—on esthetic grounds therefore I am obliged to deny that so extraordinary a thing as a human soul can be wiped out forever. No, the dead are about us, shut out by our metaphysical denial of them."[43] And later: "I felt that Humboldt, out there in death, stood in need of my help. The dead and the living still formed one community."[44]

Between "Jerusalem" and "Athens"

The political and creative drive from a position of cultural marginality moving toward its center, characteristic of the outsider struggling to enter in and maintain his hold, largely defines modern European Jewry in the face of the Enlightenment.

Saul Bellow's writing reflects the movement from tradition toward modernity and depicts the drama of its actors in all of their aspirations and contradictions and in how their personalities are at once shaped by emancipation and contribute to its progress. And yet they retain a measure, at times but a hint, at others a large dose, of Jewishness, of marginality (Augie March speaks of "kitchen religion" or superstitious beliefs). Grandma Lausch "never went to the synagogue, ate bread on Passover, sent Mama to the pork butcher where meat was cheaper, loved canned lobster and other forbidden food," yet "she was not an atheist and free-thinker."[45] On the contrary, she "burned a candle on the anniversary of Mr. Lausch's death, threw a lump of dough on the coals when she was baking, as a kind of offering, had incantations over baby teeth and stunts against the evil eye."[46] Or again, in *Mr. Sammler's Planet*, the European-born protagonist is described as a child of the Haskalah. Elya Gruner, Artur Sammler's American nephew, is always eager to learn something about the European-Jewish roots of the family in the old country. He wishes to know how traditional they were and who frequented the synagogue. "Ah, the synagogue. Well you see, Elya, I didn't have much to do with the synagogue. We were almost freethinkers. Especially my mother. She had a Polish education. She gave me an emancipated name: Artur."[47] Not entirely freethinking, but "almost"; and it is the "almost" that is spoken most meaningfully, if but whisperingly, in assessing the meeting with modernity. When Uncle Sammler learns of Elya's death, he prays to God to forgive his nephew, despite his personal weaknesses and, perhaps, immorality, for "he did meet the terms of his contract";[48] that is, the *brit ha'kodesh*, the holy covenant, established from the time of Abraham onward between Jew and God. The force of the divine covenant takes priority over, though by no means annuls, the Rousseauean social contract, in particular when confronted with death.

Confessing to Cynthia Ozick in 1987 on the question of why so few Jewish writers in America ("a repulsive category!" he told her),[49] and himself in particular, had not early on taken on the subject of "the terrible events in Poland," he recalled that, "Growing slowly aware of this unspeakable evasion I didn't even know how to begin to admit it into my inner life. . . . I can't even begin to say what responsibility any of us may bear in such a matter, in a crime so vast that it brings all Beings into Judgment." Bellow regretted that so little consideration was given to what he called "intercession from the spiritual world." But then, he conceded, there did not seem to be "anybody here capable of being moved by powers nobody nowadays takes seriously." Why the resistance? What prevented them? "Everybody is so 'enlightened.' By ridding myself of a certain amount of enlightenment I can at least have thoughts of this nature. I entertain them at night while rational censorship is sleeping. Revelation is, after all, at the heart of Jewish understanding, and revelation is something you can't send away for. You can't be ordered to procure it."[50]

The emancipated Jew, in Saul Bellow's works, is drawn toward "Athens," to use Leo Strauss's term, having left, or rather having tried to leave, "Jerusalem." Not specifically Athens, the polis, and not specifically "Jerusalem," the seat of the Temple; but how, in the mind of the Jew faced with modernity, they function as modalities of thought and feeling: "Biblical wisdom," not "Greek wisdom," argued Strauss. "According to the Bible, the beginning of wisdom is the fear of the Lord; according to the Greek philosophers, the beginning of wisdom is wonder."[51] The modern Jew, it would seem, must choose between the two. And yet, faced with this dilemma, Leo

Strauss observed, the Jew was already beset, now in despair and fear, now in excitement and hope, with a sense of wonderment. "By saying that we wish to hear first and then to act to decide"—as opposed to, as Exodus 24:7 sets out, "All that God has spoken, we will do [na'aseh] and we will hear [v'nishma]"—"we have already decided in favor of Athens against Jerusalem."[52] For the Jew living within the tradition, piety, revelation, and obedience to the law precede and take precedence over understanding, rationality, and knowledge, whereas for the emancipated Jew, the contrary is operative. The terms Leo Strauss distinguished are indeed stark.

In the final novel, Chick says of Abe Ravelstein, the fictionalized Allan Bloom, a student of Leo Strauss in Chicago: "I don't intend to explain here the erotic teachings of Aristophanes and Socrates or of the Bible. For that you must go to Ravelstein himself. For him Jerusalem and Athens were the twin sources of civilization."[53] But Chick does not count himself as a disciple of Ravelstein; he is too old and, as such, "Jerusalem and Athens are not my dish. I wish you well with them." And in fact, though Saul Bellow felt that Allan Bloom was among his dearest friends in later life, he could not accept Strauss's assertion that "[b]y saying that we wish to hear first and then to act to decide, we have already decided in favor of Athens against Jerusalem." For Bellow, the two terms of the paradigm were not as diametrically opposed as Strauss would have them seem but could, through self-transformation in writing, settle one upon the other, although, admittedly, not always altogether comfortably. "Jewish life," then, was not wholly antithetical to "street life." Traces of the Jew's spiritual seat could be effaced, though not entirely; only "almost." Echoes of *yiddishkeit* would remain; one could in fact cling to certain aspects of it and sense it grafted onto the "philosophy," combining thereby to produce a distinct contribution—at once perplexing and dreadful, humbling and painfully witty—to contemporary culture.

Notes

1. Saul Bellow, *To Jerusalem and Back: A Personal Account* (New York, 1976), 1–2.
2. Bellow, *To Jerusalem and Back*, 5.
3. Saul Bellow, *Seize the Day* (New York, 2001), 14.
4. Ibid., 86–87.
5. Saul Bellow, *Mr. Sammler's Planet*, (London, 1972), 35.
6. Bellow, *Mr. Sammler's Planet*, 36.
7. Saul Bellow, "Cousins," in *Collected Stories* (New York, 2001), 212.
8. Saul Bellow, *It All Adds Up: From the Dim Past to the Uncertain Future* (London, 2007), 265.
9. Saul Bellow, *The Victim* (London, 2008), 34.
10. Ibid., 35.
11. Saul Bellow, *Herzog* (London, 2003), 67.
12. Ibid., 5.
13. Ibid., 66.
14. Ibid., 68.
15. Ibid.
16. Gloria L. Cronin and Ben Siegel, eds., *Conversations with Saul Bellow* (Jackson, 1994), 29.
17. Ibid., 63.
18. Ibid.
19. Ibid., 90–91.
20. Saul Bellow, *Dangling Man* (New York, 2006), 17.
21. Bellow, *Herzog*, 4.
22. Cronin and Siegel, *Conversations*, 251.

23. Bellow, *Herzog*, 26, 27.

24. Saul Bellow, *Humboldt's Gift* (New York, 2008), 65.

25. Saul Bellow, *Ravelstein* (London, 2000), 226.

26. Bellow, *Herzog*, 22.

27. Ibid., 83.

28. Cronin and Siegel, *Conversations*, 253.

29. Ibid., 256.

30. Saul Bellow, "Foreword," in Allan Bloom, *The Closing of the American Mind: How Higher Education Has Failed Democracy and Impoverished the Souls of Today's Students* (London, 1987), 13.

31. Ibid.

32. Saul Bellow, *Letters*, ed. Benjamin Taylor (New York, 2010), 386.

33. Bellow, "Foreword," 14–15.

34. Saul Bellow, untitled contribution to "The Jewish Writer and the English Literary Tradition," *Commentary* 8, no. 4 (October 1949): 366.

35. Bellow, *It All Adds Up*, 90, 91.

36. Saul Bellow, "Culture Now: Some Animadversions, Some Laughs," *Modern Occasions* 1, no. 2 (Winter 1971): 178.

37. Bellow, *It All Adds Up*, 93.

38. Ibid.

39. Bellow, *Ravelstein*, 14.

40. Saul Bellow, "Introduction," *Great Jewish Short Stories*, ed. and intro. by Saul Bellow (New York, 1963), 11.

41. Ibid., 12.

42. Saul Bellow, *The Adventures of Augie March* (London, 2001), 36–37.

43. Bellow, *Humboldt's Gift*, 142.

44. Ibid., 411.

45. Bellow, *The Adventures of Augie March*, 11.

46. Ibid., 12.

47. Bellow, *Mr. Sammler's Planet*, 69.

48. Ibid., 252.

49. Bellow, *Letters*, 438.

50. Ibid., 439.

51. Leo Strauss, "Jerusalem and Athens: Some Preliminary Reflections" (1967), in *Jewish Philosophy and the Crisis of Modernity: Essays and Lectures in Modern Jewish Thought*, ed. and intro. Kenneth Hart Green (Albany, 1997), 379–80.

52. Ibid., 380.

53. Bellow, *Ravelstein*, 15.

Primo Levi (1919–1987)

MEMORY AND ENLIGHTENMENT

Enzo Traverso

PRIMO LEVI'S LIFE WAS VERY PECULIAR. UNLIKE MANY OTHER SURVIVORS OF THE Nazi camps (mostly Eastern and Central European Jews), he changed neither his living place nor his language after Auschwitz. Contrary to the cliché depicting the modern Jewish intellectual as a figure of exile and a linguistic nomad, he was a striking example of a Jewish writer deeply rooted in a national society, language, and culture. We could almost speak of physical roots, if we simply recall the words with which he evoked his family home in Turin, where he was born on July 31, 1919, and where he committed suicide on April 11, 1987. Presenting himself as an "extreme example of sedentary life," he wrote that he had become encrusted in his apartment as seaweed "fixes itself on a stone, builds its shell and doesn't move any more for the rest of its life."[1]

He considered himself completely Italian—in many interviews he underlined that it was impossible for him to separate his Jewishness from his Italianness—and showed an extraordinary affection for his city. He passionately described the streets, the river, and the surrounding mountains of Turin, as well as the austere and industrious character of its inhabitants. In the first chapter of *The Periodic Table*, a book of short stories, he retraced his ancestors' journeys to Piedmont from Spain and France (Provence) in the early sixteenth century. This little community had its own jargon made of a strange mixture of Spanish, Hebrew, and Piedmontese dialect that he liked to present as a kind of Mediterranean, less illustrious, lesser Yiddish.[2] In 1976, he portrayed his city with the following words: "I am very linked to my little fatherland [*patria*]. I was born in Turin; all my ancestors were Piedmontese; in Turin I discovered my vocation, I studied at University, I have always lived, I have written and published my books with a publisher very rooted in this city despite its international reputation. I like this city, its dialect, its streets, its paving stones, its boulevards, its hills, its surrounding mountains I scaled when I was young; I like the highlander's and country's origins of its population."[3]

In his novel *The Wrench* he told the story of Faussone, a skilled worker in Turin, describing with empathy a culture made of a body of technical and practical

knowledge, wisdom, and customs passed down through several generations of industrial workers. It was not easy to draw a living portrait of such a pragmatic culture sustained by men (rarely women) with a strong social identity and pride in their work, but Levi was able to resurrect the richness, colors, and nuances of their spoken tongue.[4] In short, he was a *rooted* writer, who needed a deep anchorage in a particular social, cultural, national, and even regional background in order to express the universality of his themes and messages.

Levi was not yet twenty years old in November 1938 when the fascist racial laws were promulgated. Like the great majority of Italian Jews, he was terribly shocked by them. Until that time, antisemitism had never been a feature of Mussolini's fascism. The peninsula's Jews, mostly belonging to the middle class, were deeply integrated into Italian society, where they didn't appear as a separated community. Many Jews, like Levi's father, had joined the Fascist Party, generally motivated by practical reasons rather than political conviction. Without engaging in any political action, Primo Levi belonged to the University Fascist Group (GUF), which organized athletic activities among students (for example, excursions through the mountains outside Turin).[5] In accordance with new antisemitic laws that excluded Jews from all public careers but allowed students already enrolled to finish their studies, Levi graduated in chemistry from Turin University in 1941.

The antisemitic turn of Italian fascism drew Levi into politics, in particular toward the movement Giustizia e Libertà, which drew inspiration from Piero Gobetti and had a certain influence among students. The Jewishness of some of the movement's leaders—including its founders, the Rosselli brothers—gave an impetus to political repression identifying Jews with antifascism.[6] At the end of 1943, when the armed Resistance against the German occupation forces started in Northern Italy, the fascist police arrested Levi in the mountains of Aosta. Inexperienced, he had participated in several propagandist actions like distributing leaflets but not yet in armed ones. Easily identified despite his false papers, he had neither the physical appearance nor the spirit of the warrior. In *The Drowned and the Saved* he frankly admitted that his career as a partisan had been very "brief, painful, stupid and tragic: I had taken a role that was not mine."[7]

He was quickly sent to the transit camp of Fossoli, near Modena in central Italy, where all Jews were concentrated. After the Germans took over the camp in February 1944, all inmates were deported to Auschwitz. There, he was no longer Primo Levi but *Haftling* n. 174517. He stayed in Auschwitz for eleven months, until the arrival of Soviet troops in January 1945. Belonging to the small group of prisoners assigned to the infirmary, he avoided immediate execution when the Nazis left the camp. Most Italian and Libyan Jews deported in the same convoy with him had already been killed; other friends whom he had met in Birkenau did not survive the "death march" following the camp's evacuation. As he frankly explained, his survival in Auschwitz was fortuitous, simply a matter of luck. He was young and knew a little German. A chemist, he passed an exam and was assigned to the Buna-Monowitz factory laboratory, where IG Farben had planned to produce synthetic rubber. He was in touch with Lorenzo Perrone, a volunteer worker from Piedmont in the Third Reich, who gave him an extra soup ration each day for several months— enough food to save his life in the conditions of Auschwitz. Thanks to Perrone, he could also write a letter to his family and receive news from his mother (who was alive and in hiding near Turin).

Levi always rejected the temptation to turn victims into heroes. He refused to present the survivors as the "best," those who put up the most relentless resistance to oppression. As he explained, it had been his deliberate choice to write *If This Is a Man* by adopting "the calm and sober language of the witness, not the complaining voice of the victim, nor the angered tone of revenge."[8] Spreading over several decades, a span of time in which both the status of survivors and their self-perception as witnesses deeply changed in Western societies, the writings of Levi present a remarkable continuity in defining the function and potentialities of testimony. He refused to judge and accepted playing his role as a witness with great humility: "[T]he history of the the Nazi camps has been written almost exclusively by those who, like myself, never fathomed them to the bottom. Those who did so did not return, or their capacity for observation was paralyzed by suffering and incomprehension."[9] In other words, the "drowned" (*sommersi*) who had been swallowed up by the gas chambers could not come back to bear witness.

So it was only as a survivor, as an inmate among hundred of thousands who were deported to the Nazi extermination camps, that Levi related his experience after returning home. First, in 1946, he published a precise account of the organization of the Monowitz camp, written with the collaboration of another deportee, Dr. Leonardo Debenedetti, for the scientific journal *Minerva Medica*.[10] Then he decided to tell his personal experience in a literary form. To write about life and death in the *Lager* was a kind of existential duty for him, something like an irrepressible need, a work of mourning or cathartic therapy. He used to quote the verses of *The Rime of the Ancient Mariner*, Coleridge's famous poem, which perfectly describes Levi's state of mind at the end of the war: "Since then at an uncertain hour / That agony returns: / And till my ghastly tale is told / This heart within me burns." (These verses would become the epigraph opening his last book.)[11]

He wrote *Survival in Auschwitz* in a few months—as explained in its introduction—"looking for an interior liberation." The writing of this book had been for him "an equivalent of a confession or of Freud's divan."[12] There, adopting a spare, sober, and rigorously objective style, he described Auschwitz as "a gigantic biological and social experiment."[13] Totally empty of pathos, his book was astonishingly remote from the antifascist rhetoric and hyperbolic indictment of Nazism that characterized most of the works on the concentration camps at the time. Nourished by classical references from Dante to Homer, Levi's work did not correspond to the neorealist style of new writers like Vittorini, Calvino, and his namesake Carlo Levi, who became internationally known in 1947 thanks to *Christ Stopped at Eboli*.

After having been rejected by the more prestigious Einaudi, *Survival in Auschwitz* was first published in 1947 by Da Silva, a small publishing house in Florence. It won critical praise (in particular from the young Italo Calvino) and a modest readership. Nevertheless, it was almost immediately forgotten in the first postwar years, like other testimonies about the concentration camps. Fascism was over and people were busy rebuilding the country and their lives; they looked to the future, not the past. Both disappointed by this silence and appeased by his book's publication, Levi did not write any more for nearly ten years. He worked as a chemist in a small factory that specialized in paint production, where he rapidly rose to become the director. Married in 1947, he had his first child the following year; his work and family absorbed his life.

In 1958, thanks to a new, partially rewritten edition published by Einaudi, his book enjoyed a significant success, won a literary prize, and reached a large readership. In the following years it was also translated into the main Western languages. Publicly recognized, Levi could come back to literature. He continued his work as a chemist until he retired in 1975, but all his free time was devoted to writing. In 1963 *The Truce* appeared; it was a picaresque account of his trip through a Central Europe devastated by the war, from Auschwitz to Turin, a journey he depicted like an odyssey of almost ten months. Until his death, Levi regularly published a variety of stories and articles on different subjects concerning current events, mostly in the Turin newspaper *La Stampa*, as well as short story collections inspired by both his memory and his scientific knowledge.

In 1982 he published *If Not Now, When?*, which is doubtless the most classic of his fictional works, going beyond autobiographical narration. This historical novel tells the story of a group of Eastern European Jewish partisans who, carrying out armed struggle against Nazism, survived the Holocaust.[14] Having lost everything, they decided, after crossing a continent in ruins, to immigrate to Palestine. Far removed from Zionist mythology, this novel doesn't describe the partisans as a victorious army but as marginal and humble heroes, survivors of a destroyed community, whose choice was inspired by both realism and resignation. They were not optimistic and proud pioneers of a new state but a group of vanquished men and women desperately fighting for their dignity. They continued on their path, impelled much more by the atavistic reflex of an eternal wandering than by the nationalistic ardor of the builders of a redemptive fatherland.

This remarkable venture into the field of fictional narrative preceded Levi's last essay, *The Drowned and the Saved* (1986), which was published one year before he committed suicide. Here he developed a new form of writing, both autobiographical and analytical, with the aim of revisiting the memory of Auschwitz—many figures and places from *Survival in Auschwitz* resurface in *The Drowned and the Saved*—illuminated by forty more years of reflection and research.[15] In this book his lived experience became the starting point for a sad and deep meditation on the place of the Holocaust in history, as well as on the image of humanity revealed by the Nazi camps.

Auschwitz has been an incurable wound for all survivors who are condemned to remember. Unlike later generations, for whom remembering is essentially a conscious choice, for the survivors it is an existential condition. Levi was able to transform it into a foundational experience that reshaped his whole life. It was through Auschwitz, he explained, that he had discovered his writer's vocation and also, in the deepest sense, his Jewishness. The eleven months he spent there were an inexhaustible reservoir of recollections, images, and sensations, a set of unique experiences from which he could constantly draw material for his literary creations. At the same time, Auschwitz confronted Levi with unavoidable questions concerning the Jewish condition. It was at Auschwitz that he encountered, in a tragic and unexpected way, the diversity of Jewish existence. In fact, he discovered there the Yiddish language, as well as the national dimension of Eastern European Judaism, so different from the assimilated Judaism of Italy.

This meditation on the experience of deportation and genocide gradually oriented him toward a search for Jewish history and tradition. The most authentic expression of this discovery and appropriation of a Jewish world largely alien to him is probably *If Not Now, When?*, the novel in which he tried to draw the profile of a civilization—Yiddishkeit—at the moment of its historical eclipse. The astonishment he doubtless experienced on discovering the existence of a Jewish national community was expressed in his novel, we could say, in reverse. Levi described the incredulity of Polish Jewish partisans on meeting Mediterranean Jews: "[H]ow can you imagine a Jew in a gondola or at the top of Vesuvius?"[16]

Defining himself as a "returned Jew" (*Ebreo di ritorno*), Levi began to appropriate a spiritual and cultural inheritance that had not been part of his intellectual formation. We can see the traces of his attempt in many figures and biblical themes that haunt some of his novels and stories. Auschwitz was thus at the origin of his recovered Jewishness, even if the latter never took the form of a religious identity. Levi's human and intellectual journey remained enclosed in a rigorously secular, assimilated, and rationalistic realm, remote from any kind of religiosity or mystical patterns. Death camps confirmed for him the atheist choice he had made when he joined the antifascist Action Party at the age of twenty-three. He considered the Holocaust as the definitive and irrefutable evidence that God does not exist. The question of faith is mentioned once in *Survival in Auschwitz*, when he spontaneously and violently denounces the pious old Jew who loudly thanked God on the night he escaped from the gas chambers: "Kuhn is out of his senses. . . . Can Kuhn fail to realize that next time it will be his turn? Does Kuhn not understand that what has happened today is an abomination, which no propitiatory prayer, no pardon, no expiation by the guilty, which nothing at all in the power of man can ever clean again? If I was God, I would spit at Kuhn's prayer."[17]

This is perhaps the only passage where he slides into pathos, abandoning the internalized moral indignation of the rest of the book. During a conversation with the Catholic writer Ferdinando Camon, Levi reaffirmed this conclusion in very lapidarian terms: "There is Auschwitz, and so there cannot be God. I don't find a solution to this dilemma. I keep looking, but I don't find it."[18] In *The Drowned and the Saved* he confessed that only once, before a selection, he had felt tempted to pray, but had immediately rejected such an "obscene" and "blasphemous" temptation.[19] But this secularized frame of mind left him terribly vulnerable, like other deported intellectuals, to the violence of the camp, depriving him of all sources of spiritual and psychological resistance. He remembered that the political and religious inmates—in particular Orthodox Jews and organized communists—could use their belief as a defense. They explained the Nazi camps as a moment in their political struggle or as a test of their faith. Secularized and skeptical intellectuals, by contrast, were spiritually naked and alone before the violence of Nazism.

Levi was neither a Zionist nor a "non-Jewish Jew," according to Isaac Deutscher's classic definition. He always defended a diaspora-focused vision of Jewishness as a component of a pluralistic European culture. In the first chapter of *The Periodic Table*, he compares Jews to a very particular gas, argon, the only one that is able to preserve its own character while mixing with other chemical elements.[20] He was not indifferent to the existence of Israel—he supported it during the Six-Day War in 1967[21]—but he felt that he was too Italian to have any kind of patriotic allegiance to Israel. In his eyes, the Jewish "normality" had always been the diaspora. Even if he accepted the legitimacy of a Jewish state, he never considered it a necessary and inevitable form of Jewish existence. Above all, he expressed a kind of natural distrust toward nationalism, including Jewish nationalism. In 1982, he strongly criticized the Israeli army's invasion of Lebanon, denouncing the "bloody arrogance" of its leaders and condemning Begin as a "fascist."[22]

In Italy, Levi embodied the merging between Holocaust and Resistance, between Jewish and antifascist memories of the war. Counting himself among the "saved," he often emphasized the "duty of witnessing" carried out by Holocaust survivors. They not only *could* not, they *would* not forget and wanted the world not to forget, because they knew that the death camps were not an accident of history.[23] In other words, the memory of the Holocaust did not belong exclusively to one group (the survivors) or to one community (the Jews). Instead of erecting a private cult of suffering and memory, bearing witness had to take place in the public sphere, in order to build a collective historical consciousness. Victims' recollections had to be incorporated into the memory of the society as a whole. By challenging the oblivion that swallows up the past without elaborating it and therefore ratifies injustice, memory can play a redemptive role. If subjective *recollection* is the substance of Levi's writings, collective *memory* is their essential purpose.[24] Such a dialectic between recollection and memory—we could reformulate it, borrowing Walter Benjamin's words, as a relationship between lived experience (*Erlebnis*) and collective remembrance (*Eingedenken*)[25]—is the only one capable of carrying out the redemption of the past, of saving from oblivion the vanquished of history. Even if recollection will die with the survivors, memory can become a permanent element of social and historical consciousness. In other words, memory is an ethical choice, far beyond the simple reaction to a suffered traumatic experience, which implies a pedagogical dimension.

Of course, the redemptive potentiality of memory does not mean the possibility of repairing what has occurred. After the gas chambers, Levi wrote in *The Truce* (1963), "nothing could ever happen good and pure enough to rub out our past," because "scars of the outrage would remain within us forever." In his words, the offense had been "incurable," spreading "like a contagion," and it was "foolish to think that human justice can eradicate it." What happened, he writes in his conclusion, "is an inexhaustible fount of evil; it breaks the body and the spirit of the submerged, it stifles them and renders them abject; it returns as ignominy upon the oppressors, it perpetuates itself as hatred among the survivors, and swarms around in a thousand ways, against the very will of all, as a thirst for revenge, as a moral capitulation, as denial, as weariness."[26]

With calmer words, delivered from such pathos and anger, this judgment is reaffirmed in *The Drowned and the Saved*, where it significantly coexists with Levi's emphasis on the ethical *duty* and the pedagogic function of testimony in the public sphere (he spent many years meeting schoolchildren and students in Turin's various colleges). In Levi's writings, memory does not appear as a Hegelian *Aufhebung* overcoming the contradictions of history; its function is ethical and cognitive, not allowing repair or reconciliation. The redemptive role of memory—interwoven with reason—lies in its contribution to the knowledge of the past in order not to repeat it, but the wounds of history cannot be healed. Hurbinek, the child he evokes in *The Truce*, is dead in March 1945, "free but not redeemed."

This is a political posture in which some observers found the signs of a "civilized liberalism" that not only rejected the theological vision of memory as a living proof of Providence but also overcame the juridical conception of witnessing as a neutral enunciation of the truth in front of a judge and a jury, who were the only ones authorized to interpret and attribute a meaning to the recollected events.[27] Both a moralist and a skeptical rationalist, Levi was compelled to recognize the human roots of evil and the tragic sense of existence—Auschwitz as a "Hobbesian Hell"—but did not abandon his belief in the potentialities of reason and the virtues of education. The Holocaust had transformed him into a melancholic *illuminista*, not into a Nietzschean or a political existentialist.[28]

Auschwitz had shown, in the most tragic way, what humankind was capable of. Like Hannah Arendt, Levi didn't describe the perpetrators as sadists, perverse and ultimately "sick" beings. They were "normal" people, a fact that deepened even more the mystery of Auschwitz.[29] That awareness permanently accompanied the inmates' lives and sometimes generated a feeling of "shame" (*vergogna*): the shame of the victims who had understood the human character of the crime they suffered. As he wrote in *The Drowned and the Saved*: "It was not possible for us nor did we want to become islands; the just [*i giusti*] among us, neither more nor less numerous than in any other human group, felt remorse, shame and pain for the misdeeds that others and not they had committed, and in which they felt involved, because they sensed that what had happened around them and in their presence, and in them, was irrevocable. Never again could it be cleansed; it would prove that man, the human species—we, in short—had the potential to construct an enormity of pain."[30]

Levi's emphasis on the ethical and political virtue of remembering doesn't exclude a rigorous and severe examination of the limits of bearing witness. Survivors carried only the part of truth condensed in their experience and could not set themselves up as judges of history. Many traps threatened the survivors' recollections: not only the passage of time that erased or modified their memories, but also the very nature of remembering, which is intrinsically subjective, sectorial, and limited. In other words, remembering is both indispensable and insufficient. The condition of the inmates did not allow them to achieve a global vision of the reality of the camps. They saw only a little fragment of the complex and gigantic machine that destroyed them—Auschwitz was both a work camp and an extermination camp, with a population of many tens of thousands of people—and an "enormous edifice of violence" oppressed them permanently. Only the Nazi authorities mastered the segmented and hierarchical organization of such a death factory. Moreover, the recollections of former deportees sometimes "changed" as their reflections, knowledge, and experiences accumulated after the war. Many survivors modified their religious and political points of view in the postwar decades, rethinking their experiences through a new prism of interpretation. Their memory did not change, but its meaning was no longer the same.

According to Levi, witnesses' recollections required critical examination instead of being cultivated as a sacred relic. He never theorized an epistemological hierarchy between history and memory. He simply emphasized, on the basis of his own experience, the constraining boundaries of individual memory. Sometimes he radicalized this approach, defining the "saved" as mere representatives of the "true" witnesses, the "drowned," who are dead and cannot testify. As he wrote in *The Drowned and the Saved*: "We, the survivors, are not the true witnesses. This is an uncomfortable notion of which I have become conscious little by little, reading the memoirs of others and reading mine at a distance of years. We survivors are not only an exiguous but also an anomalous minority: we are those who by their prevarications or abilities or good luck did not touch bottom. Those who did so, those who saw the Gorgon, have not returned to tell about it or have returned mute, but they're the 'Muslims,' the submerged, the complete witnesses, the ones whose deposition would have general significance. They are the rule, we are the exception."[31]

The "drowned," inmates who had been selected for gassing, cannot testify. Levi explored here an intrinsic contradiction of all survivors' narratives, what Shoshana Felman described as the conflict between the necessity and the limits of bearing witness.[32] The act of remembering approaches the truth insofar as it describes a process of destruction that, according to its architects, had to remain an event without a subject. The extermination camps had been conceived as an anonymous crime in which not one single perpetrator but rather many actors played a part; the responsibility was so diluted that it became elusive, indefinable. The SS controlled the camps, but the functioning of the killing machine was assigned to teams of workmen, the *Sonderkommandos*, who were recruited among the inmates themselves. The victims largely accomplished the tasks of execution. In other words, victims executed other victims. The members of the *Sonderkommandos* brought the Jews into the gas chambers, transported the corpses into the crematoriums, and burned them there. Levi defined this perverse system as the "gray zone" (*zona grigia*) that obscured the boundaries between the two sides, the persecutors and the victims. The victims were forced to act as a cog in the machine that would annihilate them, in a process that wiped out the traces of the crime as it was perpetrated. A killing machine should have neither a subject nor witnesses. This is why Levi affirmed that the history of Nazism could be interpreted as a "war against memory."[33]

Because of their drastic and severe character, some passages in *The Drowned and the Saved* gave rise to misunderstandings of Levi's thinking about memory. For example, in his book *Remnants of Auschwitz: The Witness and the Archive*, the philosopher Giorgio Agamben suggests that the "gray zone" would be a space in which perpetrators and victims became interchangeable, and depicts the "Muslim" (*Muselmann*)—the inmate reduced to a state of "bare life" (*nuda vita*)—as the proof that Auschwitz would be "impossible to bear witness to" (*intestimoniabile*). Developing an interpretation as sophisticated as debatable, Agamben suggests that in the "gray zone," "victims become executioners and executioners become victims."[34] Yet, with such an assertion he simply forgets that Levi always distinguished the two camps: in the "gray zone" the perpetrators forced the victims to turn against themselves, but this did not mean that the victims became perpetrators or that all difference between them disappeared. This is why Levi defined the invention of the *Sonderkommandos* as "National Socialism's most demonic crime."[35] Likewise, his emphasis on the "Muslim" as the "integral witness" was not meant to show the impossibility of bearing witness but only to emphasize the limits of recollection as carried on by survivors. In a few simple and concise words, he drafted a portrait of the "Muslim" as the spectral figure of the inmate who, psychically destroyed and physically exhausted, could no longer master his body,[36] but he didn't forget that the great majority of the victims of the death factories were not "Muslims." The core of Auschwitz was industrial killing, not the production of the "bare life."[37]

The death camps were part of history, human beings had created them, and so they had to be understood by human beings. Levi did not like the inflation of rhetorical formulas about the unspeakable, incomprehensible, and incommunicable features of the Holocaust. The idea of a *normative* impossibility of understanding Auschwitz seemed to him a form of obscurantism. Even if Auschwitz remained a "black hole" (*un buco nero*),[38] in front of which rational thought revealed its aporias, this was not a good enough reason to abandon any attempt at knowing, penetrating, analyzing, and explaining it. In other words, Levi never considered the Holocaust a sacred mystery or an enigma without solution. To instill the idea in younger generations that piercing the shadowy realm of the Jewish genocide was a priori impossible, he thought, was to foster a dangerous form of skepticism, perhaps a form of obscurantism.

According to Levi, the genocide of the Jews remained in many respects a unicum in history: "At no other place or time has one seen a phenomenon so unexpected and so complex: never have so many human lives been extinguished in so short a time, and with so lucid a combination of technological ingenuity, fanaticism, and cruelty."[39] He criticized apologetic interpretations of Nazism, especially that proposed by the German conservative historian Ernst Nolte who, reverting to a convenient comparison with communism, reduced Auschwitz to a "reaction" and "copy" of the Gulag. In spite of being one of the first Italian critics to have recognized the value of Alexander Solzhenitsyn's works, Levi thought that industrial extermination was a singular feature of Nazism. In the Soviet camps death remained a "byproduct," not the goal of the system.

At least, Auschwitz remained in Levi's mind a no man's land of human understanding. He did not reject current historical interpretations of the Holocaust—his last book is impregnated by a permanent dialogue with historiography—but considered them "restrictive, measureless, disproportionate compared to the events they should explain."[40] However, the "black hole" of Auschwitz didn't justify a philosophical posture proclaiming the defeat of rational thought.

It is not difficult to recognize behind this position a form of rationalism that Levi had inherited from his scientific education, a rationalism that had guided his carrier as a chemist and became a permanent feature of his mind. One of the lines describing the diagram that opens his personal anthology, *The Search for Roots* (1981), is called "the salvation of understanding" (*la salvazione del capire*).[41] It is marked by four names indicating, from antiquity to the twentieth century, the history of the scientific and rational thought that had inspired his intellectual journey: Lucretius, Darwin, Bragg, and Clarke. As Levi stressed during his conversations with Italian physicist Tullio Regge, he was attached to a "romantic" vision of science: a science "with a human face," he said, that was nearer to the joyful explorations of the Enlightenment philosophers than to a neopositivistic view of history.[42] In his few science fiction stories he warned against Promethean—and totalitarian—projects for dominating nature and annihilating humankind by means of modern technology.

This critical faith in science and rationality also defined Levi's relationship with the Italian left. His humanistic socialism belonged to a social democratic and Gramscian tradition, particularly rooted in Turin, focusing on the redemptive role of work. He believed that the association of the producers could build a liberated society, oriented not toward profit but toward general happiness. That was his vision of socialism. He could not accept the critique of work as a source of alienation and the vision of communism as a process of liberation *from* work that was developed by New Left Marxism. His hero was Faussone, the skilled worker who loves his job, not the rebellious workers of the 1969 FIAT strikes. He could in some cases support the far left, as in the 1985 elections when he endorsed the candidacy of his friend Bianca Guidetti Serra, but he never trusted its culture.[43] The conflict had already been visible some years before, when he published *The Wrench*, and it was sharpened later when the anarchist poet Sante Notarnicola compared modern industrial plants to a concentration camp.[44] Levi untiringly explained the obvious differences between Auschwitz and FIAT plants, convinced that such misunderstandings derived from the ignorance of postwar generations. (Furthermore, these misunderstandings reproduced the difficulties of his relationship with his two children, both of whom were involved in revolutionary movements.)

Levi's scientific background nourished a kind of humanistic rationalism that inspired his will to understand Europe's past, and especially the events in which he had been so tragically involved. No wonder that, defending such a tenacious attempt to comprehend, Levi did not feel much affinity with Kafka. More precisely, he loved the Prague writer, and even accepted Einaudi's offer to translate *The Trial*, but his incursion into Kafka's world only revealed Levi's distance from him all the more clearly.[45] When his new translation was published, the critic Cesare Cases noted that an "alien" optimism had been transplanted into this dark novel.[46] Defending, like every good *illuminista* of the old school, the emancipatory function of Reason, Levi could not share Kafka's resignation in face of a world depicted as an impenetrable enigma.

Furthermore, rationalism needs clarity, a feature that always distinguishes Levi's writings. From this point of view, Paul Celan, the great Romanian lyricist exiled in France, was his antithesis. Levi very much appreciated "Todesfuge," in his opinion the only one of Celan's poems to escape a disturbing form of subjective and cryptic hermeticism.[47] Levi did not like the word "incommunicability" (*incomunicabilità*), a "linguistic monster" that was in fashion during the seventies. Maintaining that human beings are "biologically and socially" predisposed to communication, he concluded that "to refuse to communicate is a failing."[48] In his opinion, clarity was the logical corollary to this natural vocation for communicating, and therefore a writer inclined toward dark metaphors and coded aphorisms could not be a good writer. Levi's style was linear and elegant in its objective and bare simplicity. Clarity did not mean poverty. He mastered an extensive literary tradition, from Dante to Conrad, but the classical references he drew on in his books never became artificial obstacles to reading them.

Levi's obstinate trust in the virtues of human reason was the deepest source of his anthropological optimism. In many articles and interviews, he declared that Auschwitz—"the greatest crime in the history of humanity"[49]—could be used to introduce ethics into history and to improve human relationships. "To my short and tragic experience of being deported," he wrote in 1976, "another one, more complex and longer, was superposed, that of writer and witness. The result was clearly positive, because such a past enriched and consolidated me. . . . Living, writing and meditating on my experience I have learnt a lot about men and their world."[50] Such optimism inevitably opposed him to Jean Améry, the author of *Jenseits von Schuld und Sühne*, another Auschwitz survivor with whom he had established an indirect and difficult dialogue through a common German friend, Hety Schmitt-Maas. Améry accused Levi of being a "forgiver" (*Vergeber*). Levi denied the allegation, but at the same time confessed that he could not share the Austrian-Belgian writer's "resentment" (*risentimento*), adding that he never had been haunted by hatred.[51]

Levi was not a forgiver. In the last pages of *The Truce*, he described the Germans he saw in Munich in October 1945 as a mass of "insolvent debtors."[52] However, his answer to Améry in *The Drowned and the Saved* does not completely coincide with the statement on guilt and forgiveness that he had expressed earlier. Levi's uncertain approach to this delicate matter is revealed by his correspondence with Dr. Ferdinand Meyer, one of the German chemists at the I. G. Farben laboratory of Buna-Monowitz in Auschwitz. After the war, through a concatenation of circumstances that he described in several books, Levi got back in touch with Meyer. Seriously ill, the latter asked insistently for a meeting with him before dying, with the clear purpose of asking to be "forgiven." The meeting did not take place, but their correspondence reveals Levi's embarrassment. In a first letter dated March 1967, he wrote to Meyer that he recognized as legitimate for "any civilized man" the need to master or overcome the past (he used the canonical German formula, *Bewältigung der Vergangenheit*).[53] Yet in his second letter the tone changed: "I would like to help you come to terms with your past," he wrote, "but I doubt that I am able." Meyer asserted that he had chosen the prisoners for the chemical laboratory, which implicitly meant that he had been their savior. Responding, Levi emphasized that he could not "thank" Meyer. "The word," he wrote, "sounds rather foolish and rhetorical in the context."[54] Some years later, in *The Periodic Table* (1975), where Meyer appears as Dr. Müller, Levi presented "mastering of the past" as a German euphemism for reconciliation with the past and "redemption of Nazism."[55] Nevertheless, in evoking his correspondence with Meyer, he accepted the principle of forgiveness. To forgive and even love one's enemies is possible, he wrote, "but only when they show unequivocal signs of repentance, in other words when they cease to be enemies."[56]

Yet, after 1979 Levi abandoned his disposition to forgive. In an article titled "A monstrous guilt," contemporary with other texts on Faurisson and French *négationnisme*, the movement of Holocaust deniers, Levi clearly defended the necessity of continuing legal prosecution of Nazi crimes, even many decades after they happened. To forget them would mean to forgive them, he wrote, and that would clash with a fundamental principle of justice, because Nazi crimes could not be judged as ordinary crimes. "Nazi Germany," he wrote, "perpetrated such crimes that they broke up the legal system built in all civilized countries in order to judge 'ordinary crimes.'"[57]

Levi did not indict the German nation as a whole. He indicated that, using terror as an instrument of domination against its opponents, the Nazi regime tried as much as possible to hide the reality of the extermination camps. Consequently, the "will to kill" cultivated by Nazism could not be attributed to all Germans. But the reality of the Jewish genocide could not be completely hidden; most people knew and did nothing. That was the kernel of German "collective crime" (*colpa collettiva*).[58] Levi used this concept with many precautions. In *The Drowned and the Saved*, he defined Germans as "a mass of 'invalids' surrounded by a core of ferocious beasts. Almost all, though not all, had been cowardly."[59] Curiously, Levi did not quote the best-known and most controversial book on this subject, *Die Schuldfrage* (1945), by the philosopher Karl Jaspers, who had tried to distinguish different aspects of German guilt (penal, political, personal, and "metaphysical" guilt). Like the German philosopher, he raised the problem of our *historical responsibility* for the past.

In short, Levi could not forgive his persecutors but did not share Améry's "resentment." Both of them recognized that they had been incapable of expressing joy when they were liberated in Auschwitz. Stripped of any material and spiritual resource, they could not express any such feeling. But after this common admission, their paths diverged. According to Améry, Auschwitz's violence had broken human beings' faculty to communicate, making them strangers to the world. Levi, on the contrary, could still see, among the skeletal figures of the death camps, "a remote possibility of good."[60]

Like Jean Améry, Levi committed suicide. On April 11, 1987, he threw himself down the stairwell of his Turin apartment building. Curiously, he chose the same death as his grandfather, Michele Levi, who had jumped out of a window in 1888. In 1978, Améry's suicide did not surprise Levi. Unlike ordinary suicides, particularly difficult to penetrate because they originate in the suicide's own private reasons, Améry's had been theorized in a book and in a certain sense announced in advance. In a sensitive obituary published by the Turin newspaper *La Stampa*, Levi explained that since his deportation to Auschwitz Améry had forever lost his trust in humanity.[61] That was not Levi's own attitude. The number marked on his arm ("my name when I had no name"[62]) was ineffaceable, but it had not eliminated his will to live. In 1987, at the end of a long and deepening depression, Levi's suicide took his readers and many of his friends by surprise. In spite of their philosophical discrepancies, we can suppose that Améry and Levi's choice of taking their lives had, among its causes, the deep and incurable wound opened at Auschwitz forty years before, a wound that, as W. G. Sebald wrote, had deprived them of the necessary resources for overcoming "the crisis of soul."[63]

Notes

1. Primo Levi, "L'altrui mestiere" (1985), in *Opere II*, ed. Marco Belpoliti (Turin, 1997), 633; Primo Levi, *Other People's Trades* (London, 1986).

2. Primo Levi, "Il sistema periodico" (1975), in *Opere I*, ed. Marco Belpoliti (Turin, 1997), 741–56; Primo Levi, *The Periodic Table* (London, 1985).

3. From an interview in 1976, quoted in Gabriella Poli and Giorgio Calcagno, *Echi di una voce perduta: Incontri, interviste e conversazioni con Primo Levi* (Milan, 1992), 236.

4. Primo Levi, "La chiave a stella" (1978), in *Opere I*; Primo Levi, *The Wrench* (London, 1987).

5. Ian Thomson, *Primo Levi* (London, 2002), 73.

6. Renzo De Felice, *Storia degli ebrei italiani sotto il fascismo* (Turin, 1993), 138–58.

7. Primo Levi, "I sommersi e i salvati" (1986), in *Opere II*, 1098; Primo Levi, *The Drowned and the Saved* (New York, 1988), 136. On the circumstances of his arrest, see Thomson, *Primo*

Levi, chap. 9. On Primo Levi's experience as a partisan, see now Sergio Luzzatto, *Partigia: Una storia della Resistenza* (Milan, 2013).

8. Primo Levi, "Appendice a *Se questo è un uomo*" (1976), in *Opere I*, 175.

9. Levi, "I sommersi e i salvati," *Opere II*, 1002; Levi, *Drowned and the Saved*, 141.

10. Primo Levi, "Rapporto sull'organizzazione igienico-sanitaria del campo di concentramento per ebrei di Monowitz (Auschwitz—Alta Slesia)," in *Opere I*, 1339–60.

11. Levi, "I sommersi e i salvati," in *Opere II*, 995; Levi, *Drowned and the Saved*, 7.

12. Ferdinando Camon, *Conversations avec Primo Levi* (Paris, 1991), 49.

13. Primo Levi, "Se questo è un uomo" (1947), in *Opere I*, 83; Primo Levi, *Survival in Auschwitz* (New York, 1996), 87 (first translated in English as *If This Is a Man* [London, 1959]).

14. On this book, see in particular Paola Valabrega, "Primo Levi e la tradizione ebraico-orientale," in *Primo Levi: Un'antologia della critica*, ed. Ernesto Ferrero (Turin, 1997), 263–88.

15. Pierre Vidal-Naquet, *Réflexions sur le génocide: Les Juifs, la mémoire et le présent III* (Paris, 1995), 187.

16. Primo Levi, "Se non ora, quando?" (1984), in *Opere II*, 254; Primo Levi, *If Not Now, When?* (London, 1986), 67.

17. Levi, "Se questo è un uomo," *Opere I*, 126; Levi, *Survival in Auschwitz*, 130.

18. Camon, *Conversations avec Primo Levi*, 74–75.

19. Levi, "I sommersi e i salvati," *Opere II*, 1106; Levi, *Drowned and the Saved*, 118.

20. Levi, "Il sistema periodico," *Opere I*, 741.

21. Thomson, *Primo Levi*, 332.

22. Primo Levi, *Conversazioni e interviste 1963–1987* (Turin, 1997), 297–98.

23. Levi, "Appendice a *Se questo è un uomo*," *Opere I*, 185.

24. See Risa Sodi, "The Memory of Justice: Primo Levi and Auschwitz," *Holocaust and Genocide Studies* 4, no. 1 (1989): 92.

25. Walter Benjamin, "Über einige Motive bei Baudelaire" (1939), in *Illuminationen* (Frankfurt, 1977), 185–229.

26. Primo Levi, "La Tregua," in *Opere I*, xxxviii; Levi, *The Reawakening* (New York, 1995), 16–17.

27. Frederic Homer, *Primo Levi and the Politics of Survival* (Columbia and London, 2001), 199–219. On Levi's conception of memory, see Robert S. C. Gordon, *Primo Levi's Ordinary Virtues: From Testimony to Ethics* (New York, 2001), 54–72.

28. Frederic Homer defines this attitude as a form of "optimistic pessimism" (*Primo Levi and the Politics of Survival*, 180–96).

29. Levi, "I sommersi e i salvati," *Opere II*, 1152; Levi, *Drowned and the Saved*, 202.

30. Levi, "I sommersi e i salvati," *Opere II*, 1057–58; Levi, *Drowned and the Saved*, 86.

31. Levi, "I sommersi e i salvati," *Opere II*, 1055–56; Levi, *Drowned and the Saved*, 83–84.

32. Shoshana Felman, "In an Era of Testimony: Claude Lanzmann's *Shoah*," *Yale French Studies*, no. 79 (1991): 39–81.

33. Levi, "I sommersi e i salvati," *Opere II*, 1013; Levi, *Drowned and the Saved*, 31.

34. Giorgio Agamben, *Quel che resta di Auschwitz: L'archivio e il testimone* (Turin, 1998), 31, 15; Agamben, *Remnants of Auschwitz: The Witness and the Archive* (New York, 2002), 17.

35. Levi, "I sommersi e i salvati," *Opere II*, 1031; Levi, *Drowned and the Saved*, 51.

36. Primo Levi, "Se questo è un uomo," in *Opere I*, 86; Levi, *Survival in Auschwitz*, 90.

37. For an interesting critique of Agamben's interpretation of Levi, see Philippe Mesnard and Claudine Kahan, *Giorgio Agamben à l'épreuve d'Auschwitz* (Paris, 2001).

38. Primo Levi, "Buco neero di Auschwitz," (1987), in *Opere II*, 1321–24.

39. Levi, "I sommersi e i salvati," *Opere II*, 1005; Levi, *Drowned and the Saved*, 21.

40. Levi, "Appendice a *Se questo è un uomo*," *Opere I*, 196.

41. Primo Levi, "La ricerca delle radici" (1981), in *Opere II*, 1367.

42. Primo Levi and Tullio Regge, *Dialogue 10/18* (Paris, 1994), 34. On this aspect of Levi's thought, see Cesare Cases, "Sodio e potassio: Scienza e visione del mondo in Primo Levi," in *Primo Levi as Witness*, ed. P. Frassica (Florence, 1990), 21–30.

43. Thomson, *Primo Levi*, 457.

44. Thomson, *Primo Levi*, 407. On the reception of *The Wrench*, see Ernesto Ferrero, "La fortuna critica," in *Primo Levi: Un'antologia della critica*, 339–47.

45. Primo Levi, "Tradurre Kafka" (1983), in *Opere II*, 939–41.

46. Thomson, *Primo Levi*, 434.

47. Levi, "La ricerca delle radici," *Opere II*, 1513.

48. Levi, "I sommersi e i salvati," *Opere II*, 1059; Levi, *Drowned and the Saved*, 89. See also Levi, "L'altrui mestiere," *Opere II*, 676–81.

49. Levi, "I sommersi e i salvati," *Opere II*, 999; Levi, *Drowned and the Saved*, 14.

50. Levi, "Appendice a *Se questo è un uomo*," *Opere I*, 200.

51. Levi, "I sommersi e i salvati," *Opere II*, 1098; Levi, *Drowned and the Saved*, 110.

52. Levi, "La Tregua," *Opere I*, 392.

53. Quoted in Thomson, *Primo Levi*, 326.

54. Ibid., 330.

55. Levi, "Il sistema periodico," *Opere I*, 932.

56. Ibid.

57. Primo Levi, "Una colpa mostruosa" (1979), in *Opere I*, 1258.

58. Levi, "I sommersi e i salvati," *Opere II*, 1000; Levi, *Drowned and the Saved*, 15.

59. Levi, "I sommersi e i salvati," *Opere II*, 1125; Levi, *Drowned and the Saved*, 169

60. Levi, "Se questo è un uomo," *Opere I*, 118; Levi, *Survival in Auschwitz*, 111.

61. Primo Levi, "Jean Améry, il filosofo suicida" (1978), in *Opere I*, 1249.

62. Primo Levi, "Quel treno per Auschwitz" (1979), in *Opere I*, 1285.

63. W. G. Sebald, "Jean Améry und Primo Levi," in *Über Jean Améry*, ed. Irene Heidelberger-Leonard (Heidelberg, 1990), 119. On this question, see Jared Stark, "Suicide after Auschwitz," *Yale Journal of Criticism* 14, no. 1 (2001): 93–114.

37

Paul Celan (1920–1970)

THE WORD PROSCRIBED

Arnau Pons

TRANSLATED BY CATALINA GIRONA

ONCE THE EXTERMINATION, DIRECTED SPECIFICALLY AGAINST THE JEWS, HAS TAKEN place, how do you react when you yourself are and wish to be a Jewish poet in the German language? Poetry would not be the same once Paul Celan had confronted this issue. And it is most certainly this turnabout, or rather this complete inversion in his poetry, which lends it its modernity and force. This modernity, in any case, is not based as much on a virtuous practice of the art of decomposing—as visibly occurs in e. e. cummings, for instance—as on the deep causes and consequences of such a turnaround. The breaking of lyrical forms and the dissolution of poetic content aim to question the very nature of poetry, its reason for being, and its responsibility. The war and the camps, deportations, and mass assassinations were not just a political and historic event but also a profoundly theological and cultural occurrence. Celan asks himself how poetry, with its sublimations and myths, could have contributed. And it is by *undoing* texts of literary tradition and putting them through the screen of a language forged with constancy and mastery that his poems uncompromisingly evaluate the involvement of literature in the atrocities of Nazism. The poet used the subversive force inherent in poetry to carry out a radical change in his perception of his own writing, which he would thenceforth conceive of only through a constant questioning. Hence, if his poetry is subversive, it is so first and foremost through the poetry itself—and this is why it has been distinguished and rightly interpreted as *counter-poetry*.[1] Although there are precedents for this approach in the history of literature, Celan clearly took it to an extreme through the principle of historicization to which he subjected his art. The camps—with their thousand-year *Reich*—had changed everything, and to begin with, his relationship with the language that had accommodated him.

> Only one thing remained reachable [*Erreichbar*], close and secure amid all losses: language. Yes, language. In spite of everything, it remained secure against

535

loss. But it had to go through its own lack of answers, through terrifying silence, through the thousand darknesses of murderous speech. It went through. It gave me no words for what was happening, but went through it. Went through and could resurface, "enriched" [*angereichert*] by it all.[2]

The language itself, language alone, is not just handed down. It comes with a full baggage of texts, and one must therefore choose the relationship to establish with it. When describing the language of his poems, Celan takes the opposite stance to Heidegger, asserting: "Certainly, it is never the language itself, language per se, at work, but always an 'I' speaking from a particular angle of inclination of its existence."[3] With his language, the poet "endeavors to gauge the domain of what is given and what is possible." These statements demand a reading entirely opposed to one seeking universal truths deposited in the language of poets. In fact, what Celan is saying is that first an experience is lived and then a particular position is taken up toward a language, precisely due to that experience, which has marked it forever. His immersion in German literature and his first poems closely accompanied the experience of the deportation of his parents and the persecutions that had begun. He moved to Paris to study medicine toward the end of 1938 after having witnessed the Nazi pogrom called *Kristallnacht* in Berlin. Once back in Romania at the outbreak of the war, he escaped the roundups and survived in a labor camp. But his poems cannot be said to make explicit reference to events; when this is the case, it is rather as an exception and involves a mere description of the experience. His poems are often positioned before a text in order to contradict it, though he also makes use of paintings or films, while some poems analyze a specific event or even bear witness to a meeting or dispute. In other words, each of his poems is built in the face of an obliged otherness—nearly forced by the poem—since the poem needs it in order to be constituted.

> The poem wants to head toward some other, it needs this other, it needs an opposite. It seeks it out, it bespeaks itself to it. Each thing, each human is, for the poem heading toward this other, a figure of this.[4]

Celan's poetry is not enigmatic in the sense of cultivating mystery or esotericism; it does not delve into the unfathomable or aspire to portray the unspeakable. If in *The Meridian* he states that "today, the poem . . . displays . . . a strong tendency to fall silent," it is due to the lack of attention, the indifference, and the inability to be read with which it is often met, and not only because of the difficulty arising from the words chosen, the major jumps in syntax, the accentuation of ellipses, or the enigmas of the pronouns the author puts into play. There is always something apparently concealed for the reader to discover in the light of a new reading. It is a critical light. The German language is illuminated from within in the sense of *Aufklärung*, in accordance with this emancipating movement.

Sprache, Finster-Lisene,

kumi
ori.

Speech, dark-buttress,

kumi [arise]
ori. [shine][5]

That to which the poem refers is particular and historically determined, just as the language that analyzes it is precise and particular.[6]

Every poem is thus the crystallization of a position taken, a verdict or an inquiry, and hence contains the otherness that allows it to be in contradiction of that position. It is the result of a "desperate dialogue." And it is thanks to this confrontation that the poet finds himself in the poem he's writing—an encounter that is never a withdrawal to an isolated, exclusive, or self-righteous position, but rather the requirement and affirmation of a will for truth and resistance that demands he take his distance toward the Other, "under the sign of a radical individuation." The result is none other than the creation of a singular language, and it is this singularity—its separation within the language, against this language—that makes it decipherable, legible.

Each poem will thus unite the acute accent of the present with the grave accent of history, with a view to two dates, and will harbor the memory of these two temporalities: that of the otherness, which the poem seeks and names; and the date of the Wannsee Conference, January 20, 1942, when (and where) the concrete details of the Final Solution were established. Celan says as much in *The Meridian*:

> Perhaps we can say that every poem is marked by its own "20th of January"? Perhaps the newness of poems written today is that they try most plainly to be mindful of this kind of date? But do we not all write from and toward some such date? . . . Even in the here and now of the poem—and the poem has only this one, unique, momentary present—even in this immediacy and nearness, the otherness gives voice to what is most its own: its time.[7]

As if in sign of agreement, Celan finds the date, January 20, again at the beginning of *Lenz*, Büchner's unfinished story of the tragic destiny of Reinhold Lenz, a contemporary of Goethe. *Lenz*, Büchner's fragment, also bears two temporalities inscribed within it: that of the historic Lenz and that of Büchner, who makes the former walk through the mountains on a January 20, obstinately walking upside-down from time to time, such that, for Celan, he becomes the figure of inversion. Indeed, "a man who walks on his head," he adds, "sees the sky below, as an abyss." Poetry would be possible after Auschwitz on the basis of this "topsy-turvyness," this inversion. But Celan also finds poetry in Lucile—a character in Büchner's *Danton's Death*—and, more specifically, in her "act of liberty," in her cry, "Long live the King!," a "counter-word" (*Gegenwort*) that should not be interpreted as a declaration in favor of the ancien régime, since it is a rebel word that evinces "the presence of that which is human" and the "majesty of the absurd." The inversion of poetry thus does not seek the blue of the sky (religious beliefs). Rather, this blue becomes the very color of the void, of an abyss, of a nothingness that contains nothing mystical or philosophical at all, but which is what the human, the creature, stands upon—"he as an 'I.'" It is precisely through inversion that any form of political utopia becomes a *u-topia* (non-place). Historic events brought about the destruction of all these utopian movements. And now Celan places the human in this light: *im Lichte der U-Topie*,[8] which is thus not the light of the ideal "non-place" of utopian revolutions, but the light radiated by the very place of negation.

The poetic obscurity comes as much from the many and varied references as from the use of a language rebuilt through a persistent resemantization of words — which take on a precise meaning, different to the one they have in ordinary language. Some nearly always have a fixed meaning, as, for instance, *Herz*, the heart, which keeps alive the memory of what has passed; *Seelen*, the souls of the dead; *Stein*, the gravestone of the poem, just as *Stern*, star, which establishes paronomastic relations with *Stirn*, forehead, which signifies resistance, like the verb *stehen*, to stand; *Gebet*, prayer, which designates the poem, along with *Fluch*, curse or oath, when it has combative connotations; *schwimmen*, to swim, which always has sexual and at the same time poetic connotations, like the verb "to row," *rudern*; *Aug*, the eye, the organ of language; *Gelb*, the yellow of the star of David; *Rauch*, smoke, always associated with the chimneys of the gas chambers; *Sand*, the sand, which displays the words with which the poems are written; and *Name*, the name as *mot juste*. However, meanings can also be renewed or vary according to the context.

The concepts Celan used to define the poem, such as a "handshake" (*Händedruck*)[9] or a "message in a bottle" (*Flaschenpost*),[10] indicate the possibility of a perfect concordance between the meaning of the text and its reception. The reduction of interpretative pluralism is, in a sense, implicit. The "hands" are the organs of writing and possess the technique and the art of execution; moreover, they tell what is true. This veracity is none other than the poetic adaptation to the historic event. The "handshake" thus implies the reader's acknowledgment of this truth clarified through poetry. By the same token, the idea of the bottle thrown into the sea with a message inside does not leave the poem to the fortune of a new, yet to be articulated reading, but rather to the hope — certainly exceptional or uncertain — that its meaning be grasped someday on the shores of memory — "the shore of the heart."[11]

∎

Despite its considerably demanding nature, Celan's poetry paradoxically continues to be among the most widely read, commented on, and translated literary works of the second half of the twentieth century — as if its difficulty implied extraordinary openness and fertile pluralism, or as if readers could draw from each poem the phrases they needed to assert their discourse. Hence it has become fertile ground for lively conflicts of interpretation, in which nearly all the trends in literary theory have entered into confrontation. Indeed, a great deal of time had to pass before Celan was truly read. At first, this inability to read his poetry arose from an obstinate refusal to consider the central weight of history in his work.[12] The extermination camps were *apparently* only evoked in certain specific, isolated poems. The rest of Celan's poems remained uncharted territory given up to speculation or the establishment of supposed filiations, whether with German figures (Hölderlin, Heidegger, Rilke, Meister Eckhart) or Jewish ones (Spinoza, Freud, Buber, Benjamin, Scholem). The approach focusing on Jewishness — with constant references to the Jewish religion — arose somewhat later, serving as a counterweight.[13] But in either case, the interest that his work elicited was oriented more toward the poet himself, turning him into a sort of Jewish Hölderlin of the twentieth century—or, more recently, as the poet par excellence of the Holocaust, with a fundamentally inadequate terminology and sensibility—rather than toward the meaning of the poems themselves, several of which have been singled out by critics, who have at times subjected them to such fragmentation or decontextualization that they could be quoted as formulas or aphorisms. A case in point is the final strophe of the poem "Ashglory": "No-one / bears witness for the / witness."[14] Celan is not evoking the solitude or isolation of the concentration camp witness. The "no-one" designates an instance, as in Kafka's *Excursion into the Mountains*. When the term appears, it refers to the poet, who is always at the service of the history of that annihilation. Only this "no-one" can succeed in carrying out the poetic and analytical ambition that would be beyond the witness.[15]

Many of the comments that have been generated relating to his later poems, perceived as more opaque, have associated the complexity of Celanian language with the nonmeaning of the fathomless fracture caused by the impossibility of representing or comprehending Auschwitz. And his verses, so artfully disjointed, so sarcastic and combative, have been understood as an impotent stammering or the painful expressions of someone on the verge of losing the faculty of speech, and which supposedly manifest the guilt of having survived.

It is the reader who must identify in each poem, or even in each strophe, the play of pronouns being implemented. Hence, the "you" is never indeterminable (at once poet, reader, and God), as has often been claimed.[16] In Jean Bollack's interpretations, the "you" of the poem is often an emanation of the poet himself, in the manner of an internal otherness.[17] One then witnesses a dissociation of the subject and, consequently, a dialogue by the poet with his alter ego, as if there had been a distribution of roles between an "I" insofar as history (Paul Antschel) and a "you" insofar as poetry (Paul Celan). The historic subject always precedes the other in time and is situated outside of the language of poetry and its accesses, an "I" ready to exercise contradiction, to alter or comment on the writing of the "you," which is always new and is regenerated in each poem. One can moreover read how Celan analyzes this dissociation, the "you" being given by the language. It is thus a "you" "without death," which embodies a potential otherness such that it can contain other "yous."

Es gab sich Dir in die Hand
ein Du, todlos,
an dem alles Ich zu sich kam.

It gave itself into your hand:
a You, deathless,
on which every I came to itself.[18]

Celan thus integrates the issue of discourse on the Other into the creative process. His innovation is the adoption of an external point of view from which to observe the composition of each poem, as if watching himself write and maintaining a distance from what he's writing, as if reading himself constantly yet not allowing himself to be drawn in by the poetry he has written, with a sort of reflexivity that has perhaps never been exercised with such intensity. If anything distinguishes him, it is not the analysis of the act that gives rise to the poem—which can be found in Mallarmé and which constitutes the reflexivity of poetry—but rather that this operation is done solely in the light of the extermination. His poetry is not, therefore, "original," but rather secondary. It intervenes at a secondary stage, through a thorough reexamination. It is intellectual and critical instead of lyrical. It does not "poeticize." First of all, and in quite a natural manner, it is critical of poetry itself. But not only that; it analyzes all languages, even its own, before it begins to make innocent and spontaneous use of language. It de-composes from the moment it starts composing. It never avoids any ruptures.

It is important to refute the false filiations, in this case of a dialogic, Jewish type, that have always been ascribed to Celan. According to Levinas, Celan is also open to the Other, to the detriment of the Heideggerian Being.[19] For Celan, however, it is never the figure of the Other as understood by Levinas: an Otherness totally external to ourselves that demands infinite responsibility and commitment such that it draws us infinitely towards it. It is always a neutral Otherness (*das Andere*), which, in contrast to the othernesses of Levinas and Buber (whose reciprocal and fundamentally religious dialogism is based on the primordial "I-You" pair), can be either a thing or a person, and which, in addition, tends to be contingent—encountering it gives rise to the solitude of the poem "in the secrecy of the encounter" (*im Geheimnis der Begegnung*).[20]

Nevertheless, Celan's language does seem to display inherently Jewish traits. Celan and Kafka shared exceedingly strong ties to letters, and both of them had a way of *living* literature. Writing fashioned their lives. They also shared a relentless exteriority and an ironic, free relationship with Judaism. Indeed, for Celan, "*Becoming Jewish*: it is becoming the Other."[21] But at the same time, "It is not in speaking of irritation, but in remaining unshakably itself that the poem becomes irritating—and becomes the Jew of literature."[22] The word "Jew" would come to designate a form of humanization that is attained by assuming the exclusions and twists of history. Hence, in texts and dedications, Celan ironically champions the hooked nose (*Krummnase*),[23] or in his poems uses words expressing awry, twisted, or oblique shapes, against the straightness of history. The polemical dimension refers to the past, but also to the adversities of the present tied to that past. He was the real "Yid," the persecuted one, because of his poems, with which he struggled against all forms of oblivion.[24] Without the attacks and the slander, without the periodically reopened wound of the plagiarism accusations,[25] he might not have found the strength to remain aloof and passionately defend his point of view, from which he construed a critical poetry based on contradiction. *The No-One's Rose* (1963) is one of these high points of the art of bellicosity and at the same time a profound reflection on contemporary Jewish identity. He saw himself as a combination of the "Jewish warrior" and the "Sagittarius," shooting his arrow-poems.[26] It was not Nazism that led him to gain a deep or problematic awareness of his Jewishness—as it was with Hannah Arendt or Peter Szondi—nor to *return* to Judaism—as was the case with Nelly Sachs—and it certainly was not what made him Jewish, Jewish in a negative sense as with Jean Améry, or, paradoxically (and not dialectically), a non-Jewish Jew such as Adorno. He had acquired an experience of Jewishness through his childhood, which he had maintained and reaffirmed. And he reinvented this identity through poetry, while defending an East that he always displaced even further East, all the way to Mandelstam's Siberia.[27] Hence, the word "Jerusalem," in the *Courtyards of Time* (*Zeitgehöft*) poems, expresses a citadel in poetry and also the site of an erotic encounter with an acquaintance from his youth in Czernowitz, Ilana Schmueli, on his trip to Israel in 1969. It will be his last (and all too brief) amorous encounter before committing suicide.

As a youth, he had grown interested in movements of emancipation and anarchism, as well as in the revolutionary utopias of Rosa Luxemburg and Gustav Landauer. It was this poetic and political anarchism, to which he was always true, that made him incompatible with the communitary and falsely conciliatory forms of religion. This led him to struggle always for recognition of difference, whether that of the Jews among the Germans or his own, as a poet, among the Jews. This difference bore an implicit uniqueness: that of the inalienable freedom of being and thought. "I lay on the stones, back then, you know, on the stone tiles; and next to me the others who were like me, the others who were different and yet like me, my cousins. They lay there sleeping, sleeping and not sleeping, dreaming and not dreaming, and they did not love me, and I did not love them because I was one, and who wants to love One when there are many?"[28]

The history of modernity, which led the Jews towards emancipation, created the conditions allowing a nonreligious view of the world. At the same time, historic events gave rise to conditions allowing a radically critical reading of literature. Paul Celan (Antschel), the only son of a Jewish family living off a small lumber trading business, had to take Hebrew lessons on his Zionist father's insistence, while his mother represented for him the enchantment of poetry and the love of the German language and culture. He himself followed the path of the Haskalah, which led him to a voluntary assimilation and a form of modernity that he found expressed in such authors as Baudelaire, Rimbaud, Apollinaire, and Büchner.[29] Whereas in youth he chose the openness allowed by poetry, he never refrained from an intense dialogue with all the productions of German Judaism and Jewishness, always attentive to the innovations contributed by Jews such as Heine, Else Lasker-Schüler, and, above all, Kafka. But he also accused the most Judaizing German Jews, such as Buber, Scholem, or Nelly Sachs, of remaining in essence too German to be in the position of expressing what is true.

For him, poetry becomes "the fateful uniqueness of language,"[30] a form of uniqueness of language linked to destiny. It is this fateful nature that distinguishes it from other forms of written expression. His lasting memory of the death of his parents in a Nazi concentration camp in Mikhailivka, Ukraine, reaffirmed his decision to continue to be the poet he had been until then in the language that had rendered the annihilation possible, and to be so through to the ultimate consequences—it was, after all, the German language that his mother had handed down to him, choosing a culture that a great many Jews who were more or less assimilated and committed to the Enlightenment felt their own and defended proudly and passionately over other languages and cultures at the periphery of the Austro-Hungarian Empire.

Thus an essential factor to consider when reading Celan is the milieu in which he grew up, the ever so singular city of Czernowitz, capital of Bucovina, "a land where both people and books were alive," where one could hear and read, aside from the official Romanian language, Ukrainian, German, and Yiddish, and which would later be annexed to the Soviet Union—although Celan learned Russian before the end of World War II, and experienced only the first two years of Romania's "Sovietization."[31]

The extraordinary history of "Judeo-German symbiosis" left a rich heritage in numerous domains, in which the most diverse positions were expressed, from those closest to Celan's own, such as Heine, Kafka, or Carl Einstein, to the most contestable or conservative, and from atheists, apostates, and libertarians to the most extreme of German nationalists—the list could go on and on. Many of these people were the object of Nazi slander or persecution because of their difference or their innovative or subversive spirit. They were Jews like himself, associated with Germany, or rather madly or desperately attached to Germany. And this is why they were pursued and assassinated so relentlessly. What Hitler brought to the gas chambers was, in a way, a vast sphere of critical thought. Celan was not going to cease to perceive himself as the result of this strange coexistence:

> I am Jewish. Whereby I would also like to point out that I by no means consider myself a representative of Judaism, let alone its advocate. I simply am Jewish. For I have lived this Jewishness. And it is through this living—with the written word as an integral component–that I have gone there where, according to my language, I have always been and where I am always at home: Germany.[32]

Each poem thus becomes an act of resistance. Whereas exile and refuge in the United States and the urgency of political theory led Arendt to write in English as well, Celan, who had grown up in Romania and lived in Paris more than half his life, could not change languages.[33] In a way, through her death and her unconditional espousal of the German culture, his mother had bequeathed him with a poetic mission that he always strived to fulfill.[34] He considered these historical and personal origins as an investiture. It was only in the mother tongue that deconcealment could be effected: the crimes had been carried out during a period of exaltation of German cultural values, and these same values would later serve to conceal or neutralize the truth in the name of which he was writing. By the same token, the German language had become for him, in contrast to Arendt, the ultimate place where the violence and exclusions remained engraved, as did the violence of the silences, the omissions, not only during the perpetration of the crimes but also afterward. And this concerned in the first place the life and works of Heidegger—the philosopher who ascribed a fundamental role to memory and poetry. Celan replies to him in a tone both serious and ironic at the beginning of his Bremen Address:

> The words "denken" and "danken," to think and to thank, have the same root in our language. If we follow it to "gedenken" [to remember, commemorate], "eingedenk sein" [to keep in mind], "Andenken" [remembrance, token] and "Andacht" [devotion] we enter the semantic fields of memory and devotion. Allow me to thank you from there.[35]

The poem "Todtnauberg" bears witness to the poet's visit to the philosopher at his cabin, and a walk they took in the Black Forest.[36] The landscapes of his walk with Heidegger described by Celan are haunted with the crimes and tortures of the extermination camps. The plant, Eyebright (*Augentrost*), in the first line makes a reference to afflictions of the eye, which for Celan is the organ of language.[37] He had read Walter Benjamin's commentary on Goethe's *Elective Affinities*, which placed the Odilienberg monastery, consecrated to the patron saint of those with eye maladies, in the Black Forest.[38] Benjamin analyzed Goethe's aversion to death and graves. The passage on concealment of cemeteries in *Elective Affinities*, which Jean Bollack associated with a verse in "Todtnauberg,"[39] would corroborate that Celan associates Goethe's avoidance with Heidegger's via Benjamin. These literal associations reveal that Celan is, in fact, more German than any other German writer when he attempts to detect in the sounds, words, images, and metaphors of the German language the origin of the crime, as well as anything that can be associated with it, including the deletion of history from literary texts.

> German poetry is going in a very different direction from French poetry. No matter how alive its traditions, with most sinister events in its memory, most questionable developments around it, it can no longer speak the language which many willing ears seem to expect. Its language has become more sober, more factual. It distrusts "beauty." It tries to be truthful. If I may search for a visual analogy while keeping in mind the polychrome of apparent actuality: it is a "greyer" language, a language which wants to locate even its "musicality" in such a way that it has nothing in common with "euphony" which more or less blithely continued to sound alongside the greatest horrors.[40]

With this clairvoyant reply, the poet was already preparing the reader for the abstraction and austerity of *Speech-Grille* (*Sprachgitter*, 1959). It was also a response to the misunderstandings and criticism that his first two poetry volumes, *Poppy and Memory* (*Mohn und Gedächtnis*, 1952) and *From Threshold to Threshold* (*Von Schwelle zu Schwelle*, 1955), had provoked, in particular his most renowned poem, "Death Fugue." He had been accused of aestheticizing the Nazi barbarity and of a pathos worthy of Goebbels, whereas the poem simply says, in its own intoxicating rhythm, that the event of the extermination camps was assisted by a virtuous exercise of the German language, and that there can thus be a profound relationship between the mastery of art and collective assassination.

The line, "Death is a master from Deutschland," places an entire heritage under attack, from Goethe's *Faust* to Bach's fugues; an entire tradition is questioned here and abolished. Not because writing poetry after Auschwitz would be a barbarous act, to take Adorno's dictum, which remains valid when applied to a certain type of poetry, but because the poetry before Auschwitz traces a path leading up to this. Celan writes from the perspective of music in order to show its effects. The operation has a magical aspect: the dead come back to tell us that what's playing is what had killed them. They second the poet. The gold of Aryan alchemy, cooked in the crucible of Auschwitz to become a head of blond hair and thus a poetic object, is mixed with the ash of the hair from the dead Jewesses in the camps. And this is what the poem, in its stunning musicality, makes the language itself say; a poem that also addresses the mother as "you" just when it describes her death by a bullet to the back of the head, thus becoming the grave she never had.

"Death Fugue," published in 1948, finds its logical continuity in the last poem of *Sprachgitter*, "Stretto,"[41] the musical term designating the end of a fugue, in which two or more voices follow upon one another and overlap. Having shown the functioning of the great organs of German tradition, Celan dialectically addresses Adorno, the philosopher of new music:

Ein
Stern
hat wohl noch Licht.
Nichts,
nichts ist *verloren.*

A
star
probably still has light.
Nothing,
nothing is lost. [42]

Ingeborg Bachmann, the daughter of a Nazi Austrian, a German poet par excellence and a polemical and conflictive love of Celan's, cites this same stanza in one of her Frankfurt lectures. According to her, the *Sprachgitter* poems were "disturbing," yet also "reliable" (*verläßlich*) because the poet carries out "an extremely harsh revision of the relationships between words and the world."[43] They were unsettling for what they said and how they said it. Celan would meet his wife, Gisele de l'Estrange (meaning "stranger" in ancient French), from a French aristocratic family whose history went back to the times of the Crusades, not long after he had put an end to his relationship with Bachmann, the foreign, non-Jewish woman and celebrated young poetess who apparently could not give him the support he needed, both in poetry and life, against the hostility of the literary world. Perhaps Bachmann was expressing a silent malaise in the face of a rigor she considered excessive, which troubled her and would eventually lead her to stop writing poetry. This difficulty accounts for the numerous objections with which Celan's work met among his contemporaries and critics of the most diverse tendencies. He was recognized as having a certain talent, yet he was criticized for the gratuity of such genitive metaphors as "mills of death" (i.e., death mills, *Mühlen des Todes*), which was actually a euphemism used in the Eichmann milieu to designate the camps.[44] He was also considered to display an overdependence on French poetry, if not an excessive influence of Surrealism. All in all, his poetry was criticized for a lack of grounding in reality, for being intoxicated with words, hermetic and solipsist, and for an absence of political engagement with the present.[45] The craftsmanship of his poems was also associated, not without a grain of antisemitism, with his origins.

Although Celan was not a direct witness like Primo Levi, Jean Améry, or Yitskhok Katzenelson, all of his texts have an eminently historical character. Even if their apparent obscurity would seem far removed from the concern for clarity of testimonial literature, their power of incision and penetration arise from a radical effort to comprehend what had happened. In one of his most renowned, widely commented poems, "Tenebrae" (from *Sprachgitter*), the word *Herr* (Lord) is correlated with domination (*Herrschaft*), to the extent that religion and Nazism are juxtaposed and even intertwine just at the point of the agony in the gas chambers.

Nah sind wir, Herr,
nahe und greifbar.

Gegriffen schon, Herr,
ineinander verkrallt, als wär
der Leib eines jeden von uns
dein Leib, Herr.

We are near, Lord,
near and at hand.

Handled already, Lord,
clawed and clawing, as though
the body of each of us were
your body, Lord.[46]

Celan refers to Hölderlin's hymn, *Patmos* ("Near / and difficult to grasp is God. / But where danger is, grows / as well that which saves"), and the story of the crucifixion (the Tenebrae service) to show how problematic these texts become if read from the viewpoint of the victims—and when they are set against testimonies describing death by gas.[47] This poetry does not perpetuate the mysteries of negative theology (Auschwitz as a new Golgotha) but rather revokes the texts concerned—including the very notion of the eclipse of God in the camps. To reduce images and metaphors to the absurd, as Paul Celan invites us to do in *The Meridian*, is to shatter all these figures to reveal what is inside. "Tenebrae" thus denounces the deadly capacity of "images": "We have drunk, Lord. / The blood and the image that was in the blood, Lord," a reflection that the poet takes up again in other texts and by which he brings out the effects of the language of religion or of poetry.

Celan attains the summit of causticity in the poem "To One Who Stood before the Door,"[48] in comparing the alchemical homunculus in Goethe's *Faust, Second Part*, who emerged from a glass retort, to an emaciated Treblinka survivor who emerges, chittering, out of the muddy boot of a *Wehrmacht* soldier. Here, the poet asks the celebrated Rabbi Löw of Prague, as a connoisseur of monster creation, to help the manikin to separate his fingers like the *Kohanim* so he can bless the German nation. The Rabbi Löw becomes, in a sense, a sort of golem at the service of the poet in the German language. It is an apotheosis, a blasphemous ending that speaks of the extinction of Judaism and the outcome of a long and bizarre literary hybridization (from Jakob Grimm and Achim von Arnim to E.T.A. Hoffmann and Gustav Meyrink). It is a visionary poem that foreshadows the theological appropriation of the extermination—with the use of the term "Holocaust," which is, after all, redemptive, as well as the ritualization of memory in Europe. What have the Jews become, after those events, but these lame beings that a hostile tradition has made of them? They are not only victims but also creatures that will forever reflect a murderous culture. Celan thus shared with Hannah Arendt the idea that a European Jewishness had disappeared after Hitler: "I am perhaps one of the last who must live out to the end the destiny of Jewish intellectuals in Europe."[49]

Shortly before the 1967 war, Celan wrote the poem "Near, in the Aortic Arch," published in the last poetry volume to appear in his lifetime, *Threadsuns* (*Fadensonnen*, 1968):[50]

Nah, im Aortenbogen
im Hellblut:

das Hellwort
Mutter Rachel
weint nicht mehr.
Rübergetragen
alles Geweinte.

NEAR, IN THE AORTIC ARCH,
in bright blood:
the bright word.
Mother Rachel
weeps no more.
Carried across
all that was wept

All of the matriarch Rachel's weeping during the exile of her children (Jer. 31:15), an exile that ends, according to Zionism, with the creation of the state of Israel, is transferred to his poetry. Does not the foundational poem "Aspen Tree" (Espenbaum), written in 1945 and published in *The Sand from the Urns* (*Der Sand aus den Urnen*, 1948), say: "My quiet mother weeps for everyone"? It is thus the poet's own mother who weeps, and she weeps for all the dead. The light of the Shekhinah to which the 1967 poem alludes ("*Ziv*, that light"),[51] which emanates from the community of the dead, must be silently unleashed into the coronary arteries, that is, in poems, in the organ of memory:

Still, in den Kranzarterien,
unumschnurt:
Ziw, jenes Licht.

Quiet, in the coronary arteries,
unbound:
Ziw, that light.

The alphabet of this language captures this blinding radiance and makes the blood become light to indicate what shed it. Language is illuminated from alpha to omega (*Ao–rtenbogen*). These are all of Celan's As and Os: "Arnica, Augentrost" and "Orchis und Orchis," in the poem "Todtnauberg," or "das A und das O" in the poem "Huhediblu," from *The No-One's Rose* (*Die Niemandsrose*, 1963). The art of deconstruction is at the service of the rhythms of the heart.

And while the Six-Day War was raging in the Middle East, Celan wrote to his friend, the poet Franz Wurm: "Israel should live, and therefore everything should be mobilized. But the thought of a concatenation of wars, with the bargaining and haggling of the 'high and mighty' while people are killing one another—no, that I cannot think out to the end."[52] A few years later his own survival tale will come to its end. Perhaps his fatigue, his lifelong combats against the silences, the concealments, as well as the hollow celebrations obscuring in his eyes the meaning of the Jewish catastrophe, or some other motives that will forever remain unknown, led him on the night of April 19–20, 1970, to take his own life in the River Seine, under Pont Mirabeau, in Paris.

Notes

1. Jean Bollack, *Poésie contre poésie: Celan et la littérature* (Paris, 2001).

2. Paul Celan, "Bremen Speech" (1958), in *Collected Prose*, trans. Rosemarie Waldrop (Manchester, 1999), 34.

3. Paul Celan, "Antwort auf eine Umfrage der Librairie Flinker, Paris (1958)," in *Gesammelte Werke in fünf Bänden* (Frankfurt am Main: Suhrkamp, 1986, hereinafter *GW*), vol. III, 167ff.

4. Paul Celan, *The Meridian*, trans. Pierre Joris (Stanford, 2011), 9.

5. Paul Celan, "Du sei wie du" [You be like you], in *Lichtzwang* [Light-compulsion]; *GW II*, 327; John Felstiner, trans., *Paul Celan: Poet, Survivor, Jew* (New Haven, 1995). Here, Celan uses an excerpt from Isaiah that appeared in a sermon by Meister Eckhart , and at the same time compares it with the transcription of the original Hebrew text.

6. Celan rarely puts the reader on the right path toward this comprehension. See Peter Szondi's pioneering comment on the poem "Du liegst" in which the assassination of Rosa Luxemburg and Karl Liebknecht is compared to the Berlin Christmas and the story of the Eden Hotel: Peter Szondi, "Eden," in *Celan-Studien*, ed. Jean Bollack (Frankfurt, 1972), 113–25.

7. Paul Celan, *The Meridian: Collected Prose*, trans. Rose Marie Waldrop (New York, 2003), 47, 50; *GW III*, 196, 199.

8. Ibid.; *GW III*, 199.

9. "Only true hands write true poems. I see no basic distinction between a handshake and a poem," Brief an Hans Bender (1961), *GW III*, 177.

10. Paul Celan, "Bremen Speech," *GW III*, 186.

11. Ibid.

12. The most significant example, for the major repercussion it has had, is Hans-Georg Gadamer's interpretation in *Wer bin Ich und wer bist Du? Kommentar zu Celans "Atemkristall"* (1986), in *Ästhetik und Poetik II: Hermeneutik im Vollzug* (Tübingen, 1993).

13. John Felstiner, *Paul Celan: Poet, Survivor, Jew*.

14. "Niemand / zeugt für den / Zeugen," Paul Celan, "Aschenglorie" [Ashglory], in *Atemwende* [Breathturn], *GW II*, 72.

15. This use of "no-one" is, moreover, present in *The Odyssey*: via a play on words, Odysseus becomes Udeis, i.e., No-one. The passage had been commented upon by Horkheimer and Adorno in *Dialektik der Aufklärung*, and Celan's exemplar bears the marks of intense reading.

16. Hans-Georg Gadamer, *Wer bin Ich und wer bist Du?*, 385: "even in the case of the Christian Commandments of Love, it is not clear to what point God is one's neighbor or one's neighbor God. The You is as much I and as little I as the I is I."

17. Jean Bollack, "La mainmise sur le sujet." *L'écrit: Une poétique dans l'œuvre de Celan* (Paris, 2005), 3.

18. Paul Celan, "Die Silbe Schmerz," in *Die Niemandsrose*, *GW I*, 280. English version slightly modified from Felstiner's translation in "The Syllable Pain" from *The No-One's Rose*, in *Selected Poems and Prose of Paul Celan* (New York, 2001), 201.

19. Emmanuel Levinas, "Paul Celan: De l'être à l'autre," in *Noms propres* (Montpellier, 1976).

20. Paul Celan, *Der Meridian*, *GW III*, 198. The words should be broken down to their resignifications: *Ge-heim-nis* (*heim*: at home) and *Be-geg-nung* (with that which is *gegen*, i.e. that which is against, counter-).

21. "Verjuden: Es ist das Anderswerden." From *Der Meridian*, in *Tübinger Celan-Ausgabe*, henceforth cited as *TCA*, Note 417, 130.

22. Ibid., Note 418, 131.

23. "The one with a hooked nose. A twisted tongue. Misshapen—." Ibid., Note 407, 130.

24. This is the meaning of the (modified) quote that Celan borrowed from Tsvetaeva (in Russian): "All poets are Yids" (*GW I*, 287); it is an "all" that excludes.

25. *Paul Celan—Die Goll-Affäre: Dokumente zu einer 'Infamie,'* ed. Barbara Wiedemann (Frankfurt, 2000).

26. *Paul Celan—Gisèle Celan-Lestrange: Correspondance (1951–1970)*, eds. Bertrand Badiou and Eric Celan. 2 vols. (Paris, 2001). There are allusions to poems as arrows, as well as to Sagittarius or the archer: Celan was born on November 23, 1920.

27. Paul Celan, "Sibirisch" [Siberian], *Niemandsrose* [The No-One's Rose], *GW I*, 248.

28. Paul Celan, "Conversation in the Mountains" [Gespräch im Gebirg], in *Paul Celan, Collected Prose*, 21. The same experience is analyzed from another perspective in "Engführung" [The straightening], in *Sprachgitter* [Speech-Grille], *GW I*, specifically on 198.

29. Celan defined himself as a "goyischer Yid" in a conversation with Ilana Schmueli. This idea also underlies the verse: "I sing before strangers" (ich singe vor Fremden), in the poem "Nachtstrahl" [Night ray], in *Mohn und Gedächtnis* [Poppy and memory], *GW I*, 31.

30. Paul Celan, "Antwort auf eine Umfrage der Librairie Flinker, Paris (1961)," *GW III*, 175. For the English version, see "Reply to a Questionnaire from the Flinker Bookstore, Paris 1958," in *Collected Prose*, 15–16.

31. Celan translated several major Russian twentieth-century poets such as Mandelstam, Yesenin, Blok, and Khlebnikov. With them he positioned himself vis-à-vis contemporary German poets, marking a difference, a Judeo-Slavic identity. The figure of Mandelstamm (in the spelling used by Celan) is central to *The No-One's Rose*.

32. Paul Celan, Letter to Siegfried Lenz (Paris, January 30, 1962), in *Paul Celan—Die Goll-Affäre*, No.157, 558

33. During his first two years in Bucharest, after the war, Celan wrote a number of poems in Romanian.

34. His mother becomes at once his initiator, muse, and sister. See, for instance, "Es fällt nun, Mutter," one of his early poems (from *Das Frühwerk*), or "Schwarze Flocken" and "Nähe der Gräber" in *Der Sand aus den Urnen* (1948), or "Espenbaum," reprinted in *Mohn und Gedächtnis* (1953) along with "Der Reisekamerad," and above all "Radix Matrix," in *Die Niemandsrose* (1963). Among his unpublished works: "Mutter, Mutter" and "Wolfsbohne" (in *Die Gedichte aus dem Nachlaß*).

35. "Bremen Speech," *Collected Prose*, 33.

36. In *Lichtzwang* [Light-compulsion], *GW II*, 255.

37. In *Sprachgitter* [Speech-Grille] (1959), the poem "Schliere" already alluded to a "cloudiness" in Heidegger's eye (*GW I*, 159).

38. Walter Benjamin, "Goethes Wahlverwandtschaften," in *GS I·1*, 123–202, 186ff.

39. Jean Bollack, "Le Mont de la mort," in *La Grèce de personne* (Paris, 1997), 357ff.

40. *GW III*, 167. For the English version, see "Reply to a Questionnaire from the Flinker Bookstore, Paris 1958," in *Collected Prose*, 15–16.

41. Paul Celan, "Engführung," *GW I*, 195–204.

42. Ibid., 204. For the English version, see *Poems of Paul Celan*, trans. Michael Hamburger (London, 1995), 151.

43. Ingeborg Bachmann, "Über Gedichte," in *Frankfurter Vorlesungen: Probleme zeitgenössischer Dichtung, Werke IV* (Munich, 1993), 216.

44. See the poem "Late and Deep" ("Spät und Tief"), in *Poppy and Memory* (*GW I*, 35). The polemic is analyzed by Bollack in "Pierre de cœur," an essay expanded in conjunction with Arnau Pons in the Spanish version ("Piedra de corazón," [Madrid, 2001]).

45. Werner Wögerbauer, "L'apprenti sorcier," *Revue germanique internationale* no. 4 (1995), 157–77; and "L'engagement de Celan," *Études germaniques* 55, no. 3 (2000), 595–613.

46. Paul Celan, from "Tenebrae," in *Sprachgitter* (1959) (GW 1:163), translation by Michael Hamburger, *Poems of Paul Celan* (London, 1995).

47. Jean Bollack, Jean-Marie Winkler, and Werner Wögerbauer, "Sur quatre poèmes de Paul Celan: Une lecture à plusieurs. Bollack, Winkler, Wögerbauer," *Revue des Sciences Humaines* 223 (1991), 146.

48. Paul Celan, "Einem, der vor der Tür stand," *Die Niemandsrose*, *GW I*, 242. English version by Felstiner.

49. Unpublished letter from August 2, 1948, from Celan to a relative in Israel, cited by Bianca Rosenthal, "Quellen zum frühen Celan: Der Alfred-Margul-Sperber-Nachlaß in Bukarest," *Zeitschrift für Kulturaustausch* no. 3 (1982), 230. See also Arendt's letter to Kurt Blumenfeld (9/1/1957): Hannah Arendt/Kurt Blumenfeld, *Correspondance*, French trans. J.-L. Evard (Paris, 1998), 229.

50. "Nah, im Aortenbogen," *Fadensonnen* [Threadsuns]; *GW II*, 202. Translation based on Felstiner with slight changes. Felstiner dedicates a long comment to this poem in *Poet, Survivor, Jew*, 236–41, which can be compared to Bollack's analysis in "Juifs Allemands: Celan, Scholem, Susman," 196–99.

51. According to Scholem, "Ziw" is the light emanating from the Shekhinah.

52. Paul Celan, Letter No. 47, from June 8, 1967, in *Briefwechsel* (Frankfurt, 2003), 71.

Clarice Lispector (1920–1977)

A WOMAN OF SPIRIT

Nelson H. Vieira

> Spirit spirit spirit spirit spirit spirit spirit. In the final analysis, what is spirit? It's what I feel inside my non-self. More. It's a word morphologically sparkling and audacious, like the flights of birds. Spirit—and then it takes off.
>
> —CLARICE LISPECTOR

CLARICE LISPECTOR'S LITERARY REPUTATION IN BRAZIL AND ABROAD MARKS HER as a *hors concours* writer, considered to be the preeminent female literary voice in Latin America. The challenge that Jewish modernity posed to Lispector resembles one evident in other cases, while at the same time presenting issues particular to Brazil and Latin America. In other words, Lispector, as a Brazilian writer of Jewish ethnicity, was compelled to discover a covert mode of devising a literary response to the crisis of Judaism in view of modernity's onslaught and to her own struggle with what Leo Strauss called "the exposedness and the hopelessness of life which cannot be eradicated by any progress of civilization."[1] Lispector accomplished this literary sleight-of-hand not as a referential Jewish writer, but as a universal writer whose Jewish childhood and experience in part provided a code for living that was conflicted between affect and reason, belonging and alterity, immanence and transcendence, while at the same time zeroing in on an ethical mode of dealing humanely with the idea of an inscrutable and unreachable divine power. Consequently, I will argue here that Lispector's focus on the incomplete character of language as the unlimited linguistic resource for her spirited quest toward the unknowable reenacts paradigmatically Jewish hermeneutics' relentless search for an explanation of God's absence and silence: "Listen to me, listen to the silence. What I tell you is never what I tell you but something else" (SL 8). Also, Lispector intuits language's poststructural fluidity and its limitless sentience in order to grapple with the existential complexities representative of the modern human condition of despair and the modern Jewish crisis of loss. Furthermore, the arguments presented here will also focus on her persuasive reading of Spinoza, among other thinkers, as a guidepost for living

but especially how her equitable position on alterity and metamorphosis led her toward transcendently inspired human epiphanies, propelled linguistically by an earthly form of what Emmanuel Levinas calls "ethical transcendence."[2]

There exists a vast corpus of critical bibliography on all aspects of Lispector's total oeuvre in Portuguese and many other languages. All of her major novels and several short story collections have been translated into English.[3] There also exist the Hebrew translations of two significant works, the 1977 novella *The Hour of the Star* and the earlier 1960 story collection *Family Ties*. There are three biographies (Ben Moser in English and Portuguese and Nádia Battella Gotlib and Teresa Cristina Monteiro Ferreira in Portuguese) that describe to varying degrees the influence of her Jewish ethnicity and upbringing.[4] However, these biographical interpretations, including also Gotlib's massive *Clarice Fotobiografia* (2008),[5] do not dialogue for the most part with the vast critical and theoretical literary bibliography written by scholars who generally have avoided her Jewish perspective.[6] One notable exception is Berta Waldman's many publications on Lispector's fiction. Waldman's most recent, *Entre Passos e Rastros: Presença Judaica na Literatura Brasileira Contemporânea*, includes five major insightful essays on Lispector's Jewish perspective.[7] Critical publications, along with the numerous reeditions of Lispector's novels and stories in the original Portuguese, and recently a new retranslation project in English, attest to the impressive reception of Lispector as a national and international literary figure.

The focus for this study, however, is to establish a literary dialogue between Lispector's narratives and the viewpoints of other Jewish writers and thinkers in order to address her perspective on Jewish modernity. Above all, this study will aim to demonstrate how, as a diasporic Jewish Brazilian and an intense thinker on the human condition, she developed a literary approach with a universal vision that also incorporated Jewish particularities. Her narratives also draw upon Christian references and symbols, given that she was addressing a multicultural Brazilian yet primarily Christian reading public. Interestingly, these readers frequently participated in other religious practices as well, such as spiritualism, Afro-Brazilian voodoo, and other alternative cults. These fascinated Lispector in her efforts to understand Brazil's myriad cultures and peoples.

Born en route as her refugee family fled the Russian pogroms, Lispector continuously wrestled with the issue of belonging, as can be seen by the eagerness with which she applied to become a naturalized Brazilian when she reached adulthood. Pleased to belong to Brazil and to Brazilian literature, she nonetheless expressed in her fiction and essays the sentiments of estrangement that had shaped her childhood experience, intensified profoundly by the early loss of her mother.[8] Her famous essay "Belonging" intimately evokes this sentiment in universal terms that obliquely manifest Hillel's famous Golden Rule from the Babylonian Talmud: "That which is hateful to you, do not do to your neighbor. This is the entire Torah; the rest is commentary—go and learn it."[9] The talmudic code of being responsible for others, a form of ethical reciprocity, becomes a leitmotif throughout Lispector's writing, stemming undoubtedly from an early matrilineal and later patrilineal Jewish orientation, and not necessarily based upon her having actually read the Talmud. According to Levinas, this responsibility for others is the substance of subjectivity or how the self is transformed in relation to others.[10] "Belonging" movingly captures Lispector's sense of ethical alterity:

> If I experienced this human hunger [for belonging] in the cradle, it continues to accompany me throughout life, as if predestined. So that I feel pangs of envy and desire whenever I see a nun: for she belongs to God. . . .
>
> An intense desire to belong often comes from my own inner strength—I wish to belong so that my strength will not be useless and may serve to strengthen some other person or thing. (DW 148–49)

Lispector's commitment to otherness and her sense of responsibility will be treated in-depth in the following discussion of her novel *The Passion according to GH* (1964) and the novella *The Hour of the Star* (1977). In the former, Lispector rereads Kafka's *Metamorphosis* (1912) and presents a different take on otherness, estrangement, alienation, and redemption. Lispector's actual reading of Jewish writers and thinkers has been confirmed by the notes she wrote in the books of her personal library.[11] Of these thinkers, Baruch Spinoza's philosophy repeatedly appears in her narrative fiction, sometimes referentially, sometimes not, showing her considerable knowledge of and challenges to his philosophy.[12]

Lispector's "discussion" with Spinoza appears specifically in her 1944 first novel, *Near to the Wild Heart*, a novel primarily interpreted critically as a feminist coming-of-age story of feminine defiance, which interestingly preceded Simone de Beauvoir's *Le Deuxième Sexe*.[13] However, suspicious of rubrics and not wanting to be labeled, Lispector later declared that she was not a feminist. This negation stems above all from her preoccupation with the all-encompassing human condition of both males and females but is also derived from a general desire to avoid "ghetto" writing, feminist as well as Jewish. This stance translates into her embrace of modernity's push toward universality while at the same time going back to sources (biblical and philosophical) that contributed to her development as an artist of compelling views on ontology, existence, otherness, and language, therein explaining the thrust of her wide appeal.

In *Near to the Wild Heart*, the inquisitive protagonist Joana behaves from childhood in an exceptionally free-spirited way, beyond basic moral principles, beyond good and evil (Spinoza), in her pursuit of an independent existence and direction. In doing so, she rejects a conventional sense of morality that dictates limits for individuals, especially women, thereby instilling in her character a heretical proclivity that as a young girl earns her the epithet of "viper," an indirect allusion to Eve. At the end of the novel, her eventual breakout journey of full independence toward the unknown leaves in its wake a husband, a lover, and a deterministic society's prescribed way of life. In her relationship with her lawyer husband and his very organized and ordered behavior, Joana represents adherence to nature akin to Spinoza's philosophy, which her husband, Otávio, intellectually paraphrases in an article he is writing on Spinoza but ironically cannot affectively or psychologically apply to his own personal way of living: "Imagination is so essential to man—Joana once more—that his entire world finds its *raison d'etre* in the beauty of creation and not in its utility, not in being the result of a series of objectives conforming to his needs" (NWH 112). Seeking the consolation of order, which he finds with his mistress Lídia, he becomes rattled when he discovers amid his notes a page written by Joana: "The beauty of words: the abstract nature of God. Just like listening to Bach" (NWH 114). This imaginative phrasing does not sit well with Otávio's temperament and is accentuated by the novel's narrative craft of using third-person with interior monologue and occasional pockets of first-person point of view to enable Lispector to present Spinoza's ideas from the distance of the perplexed and intellectual husband who is ill equipped to apply Spinoza's philosophical nuggets to his own circumscribed existence.

With deft irony, Lispector shows how difficult it is for a conservative man to grasp Spinoza's radical thinking via the utilitarian husband who represents modernity's push toward progress, science, conformity, conclusions, and materialism. The novel also captures Joana's bond with nature, sensually manifested by her body's communion with the natural elements and the instinctual animal world—all of these framed by her belief in self-realization in this world and not beyond. Similarly, another female narrator, from the novel *The Stream of Life*, appropriates Spinoza's vision with her particular sensuous spin on life: "I transmit to you not a message of ideas but rather an instinctive voluptuousness of what is hidden in nature and that I sense. . . . Nature is all-encompassing: it coils around me and is sexually alive, just that and nothing more: just alive. I too am savagely alive—and I lick my snout like the tiger after it has devoured the deer" (SL 16–17). Moreover, Spinoza's critique of the rabbinical and authoritative Judaism of theological beliefs is echoed in Joana's full embrace of nature within this world. On a deep structural level, *Near to the Wild Heart* evokes the modern crisis of Judaism via some characters who cling to the safe codes of religion and conformity while the main female protagonist, through her absorption of Spinoza's philosophy and its ethical precepts, opts for a form of freedom that acknowledges the existential plight of women and men in the modern world. Joana's rebellious acts show parallels to Spinoza's own "heretical" spirit and history, such as when he was condemned by the high rabbinical community of Amsterdam—but here, in Lispector's novel, they are made all the more profane by their female voicing.

The modern celebration of Spinoza's philosophy, according to the modern Jewish philosopher Leo Strauss, rests with Spinoza's understanding—new for his time—of "nature" and God. Strauss argues that this celebration stems from "Spinoza's assumed merit about mankind and only secondarily about the Jews" but also "his assumed merit about the Jewish people and only secondarily about mankind."[14] Moreover, Strauss sees Spinoza as only an "heir of the modern revolt" since modern thinking as articulated by Descartes, Bacon, and Hobbes already prescribed that man be the master and owner of nature, with science and philosophy ascribing essentially to the nontheoretical. As Strauss interprets the significance of Spinoza for modern man, he points to Spinoza's restoration of the traditional idea of contemplation: "one cannot think of conquering nature if nature is the same as God. Yet Spinoza restored the dignity of speculation on the basis of modern philosophy or science, of a new understanding of 'nature.' He thus was the first great thinker who attempted a synthesis of pre-modern (classical-medieval) and of modern philosophy."[15] Strauss also asserts that Spinoza believed that the highest form of knowledge was intuitive knowledge (such as that manifested by Joana), knowledge not of one divine substance or God, but of individual things or events. Ergo, the seductive power of this perspective for a diaspora-experience writer such as Clarice Lispector. Additionally, in relation to our earlier reference to the role of universalism in modern Jewish thinking, Strauss also emphasizes the following: "The knowledge of God as presented in the first part of the *Ethics* is only universal or abstract; only the knowledge of individual things or rather events qua caused by God is concrete."[16]

Strauss indicates that Spinoza's take on contemplation and reasoning also features the process of man's attempting to figure out the conundrum of existence, "forming the idea of man, as a model of human nature. He [Spinoza] thus decisively prepares the modern notion of the 'ideal' as a work of the human mind or as a human project, as distinguished from an end imposed on man by nature."[17] Lispector's novels, especially *The Passion according to GH*, represent attempts at "figuring out" what woman/man is all about. Moreover, Strauss defends Spinoza on another point against some aspects of Hermann Cohen's mordant critique because Spinoza did indeed recognize "the universalism of the prophets"[18] Therefore, our underlining the universalism in Lispector's approach to writing via her readings of Spinoza suggests her discovering for her own ontological way of thinking, as a hybrid living in the Jewish diaspora of Brazil, the approach of universalism and its viability for modern Jewish thinking, a strategy she incorporated at the expense of overt Jewish referential narration.

The Lispector family produced three women, each accomplished, two writers and one artist, owing much to their father's support and his belief in education. A reader of Torah and Talmud, Pinkhas Lispector nonetheless had to make a living in commerce in order to finance his daughters' educational future.[19] The artistic accomplishments of these three sisters point, after their mother's death, to an enlightened patrilineal emphasis upon education given the family's financial struggles for settlement in the New World, which introduced a different mode of living far from the shtetl mentality and oppression of the Old World. Furthermore, the complex social codes and hazards for women (and men) in Brazilian society inspired many of Lispector's narratives and stories, uncovering the sociocultural obstacles women consciously and unconsciously were forced to confront. This struggle is mapped out poignantly in her first major short story collection, *Family Ties* (1960), and later in two others—*The Foreign Legion* (1964) and *The Stations of the Body* (1974). Insightful and significant for illustrating the struggle of coping with social changes from tradition to modernity, these stories, as far as Jewish features or motifs are concerned, are surpassed by the novel *The Passion according to GH* (1964) and the novella *The Hour of the Star*, which become symbolically two of Lispector's oblique responses to Jewish modernity.[20]

The novel's New Testament, evangelically driven title evokes the Passion of Christ, but for Lispector, passion here also refers to the passionate human spirit. In addition, the narrative incorporates metaphorically Brazilian sociocultural codes and cults such as Afro-Brazilian Yoruba religion and arts. Nevertheless, *The Passion according to GH* is primarily inspired by biblical sources and above all by Franz Kafka's trenchant tale of condemned otherness depicted in *The Metamorphosis*. In Kafka, the rigid and staid Gregor Samsa is transformed into a beetle overnight, thereby becoming society's other who disintegrates bodily and spiritually given his family's materialist expectations. On the other hand, Gregor's metamorphosis enables him, for the first time, to express human instinctual feelings within his insect carapace, which he was unable to do as the dogged financial provider for his family.[21]

In Lispector's narrative, however, the upper-middle-class GH (only her initials are known) lives very comfortably and self-indulgently in a penthouse facing the sea. Her outlook changes when she begins to enter the zone of alterity. She expects to clean out her recently departed black maid's tiny room, but she finds it unexpectedly tidy. Inside she encounters a wall drawing of three simple, vacuous figures, a statement on GH's ontological emptiness, as well as a cockroach, the lowest form of representative otherness. Realizing, as she stares at the roach, her mistake in treating her black maid as an invisible subaltern, GH is primed for another realization via a repulsive yet seductive act: her sacrilegious ingestion of the white ooze coming from the insect's body, which out of panic she has crushed. Interpreting the white ooze as the material vitality of life, the placenta of birth, plasma, or the semen of life, "the crude, raw glory of nature" (PAGH 56), not as the body of Christ symbolically represented by the Christian Eucharist wafer, GH profanely defies the ceremonial communion with the Christian God as well as the Judaic prohibition of eating an impure animal as ruled in Leviticus 11:13. As she commits this double heresy of creed and law, GH decries the merciless limits of existence with an absent God, a realization leading her to explore via an exhaustive semantic itinerary of language what can never be known or reached. This ultimately leads to the silencing of her inadequate language but not before she reaches a communion with the "real" in opposition to the divine: "But on the human plane that would have been destruction: living life instead of living one's own life is forbidden. It is a sin to go into divine matter. And that sin has an exorable punishment: the person who dares go into that secret, in losing her individual life, disorganizes the human world" (PAGH 136). Ironically, by recognizing the impossibility of delving into representing or naming the divine, GH recognizes the Judaic biblical prohibition against divine representation by concentrating on the here, the alive, and the real of the primary world. Furthermore, in a parody of the "Hail Mary" prayer, GH implores:

> "Pray for me, my mother, for not transcending is a sacrifice, and transcendence used to be my human effort at salvation, there was an immediate utility in transcendence. Transcendence is a transgression. But staying within what there is, that forces me not to be afraid!"
> And I am going to have to stay within what there is. (PAGH 74)

By deciding to stay within nature by eating the impure, GH acknowledges biblical history in what is undoubtedly a Jewish metaphor of *Galut*: "—eating of living matter would expel me from a paradise of adornments and lead me to walk forever through the desert with a shepherd's staff. Many have been those who have walked in the desert with a staff" (PAGH 64). Prior to her digestive act, GH is anguished over how she still clings "to the remainders of her old culture" (PAGH 66), that is, her self-indulgent, delusional modern mores; this is also a covert allusion to the crisis of Judaism. Moreover, her exploration of language and alterity undergoes a passionate, but nontranscendent, metamorphosis that will take GH toward a new perceptual pathway, one germane to an intensity of language's semantic infinity that approximates a form of spirituality.

In doing so, Lispector enacts a seminal Brazilian aesthetic, known as "literary can-nibalism," *antropofagia*.[22] In this case, Lispector undergoes a deglutination of Franz Kafka and Judeo-Christian thinking to open up a discourse of alterity as a mode of "altered" perception and existence. With this act by GH, Lispector evokes a pas-sionate ascendency toward an ethical solution for grappling with modern life—a transformation originally linked to Judaic law—but one definitely beyond medioc-rity, beyond the daily "civilizing" social commitments and egological limitations that bind and blind individuals. In their struggle to attain self-knowledge amid the anxiety and difficulty of a God-less modern life, both Kafka and Lispector draw from the animal/insect world; but for Kafka his employment of the animal world became "his prize embodiment of human truths that evade the grasp of analysis."[23] In universal terms, both texts struggle with understanding the modern human con-dition, and both employ the viewpoint of the other to achieve perceptions that challenge the unyielding limitations of rigid tradition as well as modern man's egological existence away from affect and caring. However, Lispector in addition appropriates biblical properties and law, which she repeatedly defies in order to accentuate and celebrate the indefatigable quest forward, toward the unknown and an inscrutable God. In short, while criticizing traditional Judaism and modernity's hopeless solutions, she nevertheless engages basic tenets of Judaism's cultural ide-ology and Halakhah.

GH's impulse forward also entails a going-forth intuitively out of ego toward the other, which she also implies in her 1973 novel *The Stream of Life*: "What saves you then, is to write absent-mindedly" (SL 14). Writing "absent-(mind)edly" signifies writing by boldly plunging forward without ego and preconceived knowledge—in order to know "what" to see instead of merely seeing what one already knows, to paraphrase Abraham Joshua Heschel in *Man Is Not Alone*.[24] Similarly, as an imag-ined interlocutor of Lispector, Levinas believes that an egological approach (i.e., of writing mindedly), associated with much Western intellectual thinking, is chal-lenged by an ethical one of acting upon, surrendering to our responsibilities, even before we know what we are doing. In *Nine Talmudic Readings*, Levinas criticizes this egological way of thinking: "we do not want to undertake anything without knowing everything. . . . We want to live dangerously, but in security, in the world of truths."[25]

In *Totality and Infinity*, Levinas's "ethical transcendence" constitutes "otherwise than being" and furthermore implicates language as the open passageway toward the potential divine "knowing" and an ethical form of perceptual transcendence beyond the self, and eventually toward social solidarity including that for one's own sake:

> To recognize the Other is therefore to come to him across the world of pos-sessed things, but at the same time to establish, by gift, community and univer-sality. Language is universal because it is the very passage from the individual to the general, because it offers things which are mine to the Other. To speak is to make the world common, to create commonplaces, [laying] the foundation for a possession in common.[26]

The linguistic universal path via the openness to the free play of signifiers (Der-rida) and, for Levinas, leading to ethical social transcendence toward the Other, also infers an interdependence toward "repair" that considers the I and the other as a mutually beneficial "we." At the very end of GH's discourse, she acknowledges the following: "I finally extended beyond my own sensibility. The world interdepended with me—that was the confidence I had reached: the world interdepended with me" (PAGH 173). This interdependence can also be viewed as what Levinas calls "respect," which for him is the condition for ethics.[27] Above all, this process is to be a two-way street of interdependence in which the other in turn directs me and consequently enables me to follow the ethical path.

Despite GH's quest toward ethical transcendence, the reader questions the sustainability of GH's overt consciousness or intense epiphany, despite her apparently passionate and momentous sincerity, since there exists in the narrative no evidence of her actually "performing" ethically toward others, despite having her retrospective narrative end with an overwhelming epiphany. Although she has reached awareness and has experienced a perceptual transcendence, will she act upon her newfound consciousness? Nonetheless, GH's allegorical struggle inside the maid's room-as-desert actually takes place amid living matter—not with a transcendent and personal God, but with an impersonal power within life, like the neutral, the placenta, the plasma, the silence, the "it," and the now. From this point on, GH refers to the divine as "the God," common and impersonal, but the god of today, not of the heavens. In this way, it becomes clear that for Judaism language is the man-made bridge for establishing a human link to God, since the conception of God and the human quest are based upon the incessant reinterpretation of the text. GH fully embraces, albeit with anguish, the limitations of life to the point of ingesting its nature, while Kafka's Gregor is totally destroyed by modern life.

GH's encounter with the primal other, the "barata," gradually strips her of her inauthentic self. Intention and self-salvation no longer become the major forces driving GH's self. Instead new meanings and "altered" perspectives surface: "It is the silence of the cockroach looking. The world looks at itself in me. Everything looks at everything, everything experiences the other; in this desert things know things. Things know things as much as this . . . this something that I shall call pardon" (PAGH 58). Here, one wonders if Lispector is pardoning humanity or a divine power.

In comparing Lispector with Kafka, it becomes evident that Lispector's sense of modernism (let alone modernity) strives for a textuality that enables the individual to read "between the lines" of life. A comment by Andreas Huyssen, in his discussion of different modernisms, seems particularly appropriate at this juncture for appreciating Lispector's stance:

> It is no longer the modernism of "the age of anxiety," the ascetic and tortured modernism of a Kafka, a modernism of negativity and alienation, ambiguity and abstraction, the modernism of the closed and finished work of art. Rather, it is a modernism of playful transgression, of an unlimited weaving of textuality, a modernism all confident in its rejection of representation and reality.[28]

So while Kafka's modernist text enacts the inexpressiveness of the alienated self or other, Lispector's text self-consciously embraces and exposes in the foreground an awareness of this inexpressiveness or, as she coins it, "the unsayable." Lispector seems to imply that if God is unsayable, perhaps so is life itself, since representation is deeply questionable today, at least in literature. The textually conscious or metafictional focus upon language itself differentiates Lispector's text from Kafka's with regard to the theme and problematics of expression and silence. As GH states near the close of the novel: "Oh, but to reach silence, what a huge effort of voice. My voice is the way I go to seek reality" (PAGH 169). In Kafka, the way to reality is *shown* to be a ghastly nightmare.

In the famous and often-cited passage in Lispector's novel on how language is used to approach the impossible—the inexpressive plight of the human condition—"the unsayable," the frustration with language reverberates, as we found in Kafka and his subsequent discovery of the evocative powers within metamorphosis as a process for *dramatizing* inexpressive revelation. However, with Lispector we have an open discussion about the elusiveness, but not negation, of language as the very means for approximating the inexpressive: "Language is my human endeavor. I have fatefully to go seeking and fatefully I return with empty hands. But—I return with the unsayable. The unsayable can be given me only through the failure of my language. Only when the construct falters do I reach what it could not accomplish" (PAGH 170).

Lispector's self-conscious attention to language addresses its phenomenological attribute as trajectory and juxtaposes this process as part of the human condition. Furthermore, as GH continues to explore this way of thinking she touches upon the need to avoid the search for power for she realizes that power can lead to blindness and disintegration: "Insistence is our effort, desistance is the prize. One gets the prize when she has experienced the power of building and, in spite of the taste of power, prefers desistance. Desistance has to be a choice. To desist is the true human moment. And it alone is the glory proper to my condition. Desistance is a revelation" (PAGH 170).

Using words like "deheroization," "dehumanization," "depersonalization," and "desistance" to explain her breaking out of her ego-centered shell or carapace, GH undergoes a momentary metamorphosis, a "turning over of her form" as a possible ethical mode for living.

In her penultimate narrative, Lispector creates an overt homage to her Judaic background by drawing upon the *Book of the Maccabees* to write a modern midrash on the crisis of Judaic modernity that inverts the ancient story of victorious resistance. Recognized as a narrative with a sociological message, not typical of her writing, a critique she endured in socially conscious Brazilian literature that harbored a naturalist bent, this novella is a first for many reasons. Purposely a novella of loose ends in form and content, *The Hour of the Star* (1977) on the one hand questions narrative's or language's ability to represent faithfully the subaltern, the marginalized other, in this case dramatized in the figure of the inept, poor, uneducated, and displaced, but resistant or steadfast, Macabea (from "Maccabees"), who is forced to migrate from the impoverished northeast of Brazil to the modern southern metropolis of Rio de Janeiro, a city replete with the false gods of pop culture to which she hopelessly aspires.[29] On the other hand, Macabea's story also serves as a between-the-lines allegory for the crisis of Judaism's struggle with modernity.

Ignorant of the historical and cultural significance behind her name, Macabea resists the tribulations of modern life by persistent, dogged survival despite her precarious financial and sociocultural "frailty." On yet another level, this modern midrash is narrated by a bourgeois, cynical male writer, a conscious disguise for Lispector herself, indicated in the various titles offered in the dedication by the fictional narrator/author "alias Clarice Lispector" (HS 7). While this literary cross-dressing inserts doubts about who is really narrating the story, the novella also inserts doubt about any authorship, divine or otherwise. This doubt is further exploited at the moment Macabea is about to be run over by a car, right after being told by the fortune-teller, Madame Carlota, that she will have a long and happy life as if listening to the word of God—"as if she were listening to a fanfare of trumpets coming from the heaven" (HS 76). Madame Carlota's mistaken prediction about Macabea's imagined transformation is trenchantly steeped in socioeconomic and biblical irony when the narrator states: "Transformed, moreover, by words—since the time of Moses the word had been acknowledged as being divine" (HS 79). At the beginning of his narrative, as the pretentious narrator discusses his own motive for writing, he sarcastically states: "As I write—let things be known by their real names. Each thing is a word. And when there is no word, it must be invented. This God of yours who commanded us to invent" (HS 17). Here the implied critique relates to the abandonment of man by God.

With the freedom to doubt, Lispector's audacious attempt to capture the alterity of the other via the lower-class protagonist Macabea, without condescension, is "narrativized" via her own masked face-to-face with Macabea and by debunking the masculine writer/narrator. As this narrator fails to surpass his own self, he ultimately becomes the introspective but overdetermined voice/text through which Lispector's palimpsestic own voice emerges as she deconstructs the motives for the violence and injustices that the male narrator and society inflict upon Macabea. As a multilayered narrative, this construct resembles what Leo Strauss understands as reading "between-the-lines," that is, his own reminiscence on and conviction of Maimonides's "esotericism," which sought to reach various registers of readers, enlightened and nonenlightened. One of Lispector's early chronicles (1964) captures Maimonides' esotericism, a concept very similar to her style of "oblique" writing: "Since one feels obliged to write, let it be without obscuring the space between the lines with words" (FL 114).

In trying to reach out to the other, beyond her own ego as a female writer, Lispector chooses to have a masculine narrator/writer (less sentimental, as she wryly and ironically states in her preface) tell Macabea's story. By opting to evoke Macabea, Lispector's other, via a male narrator, Lispector's choice simultaneously discloses her own "depersonalization" as a writer/narrator as she enacts an aesthetic move toward an ethical transcendence of responsibility that the reader intuits in the flickering spark of life we sense within Macabea's frail existence and via the author's camouflaged linguistic presence. Macabea's fragile and marginalized existence is eventually stifled, crushed, and doomed by the male narrator since, given his belief in her socioeconomic destiny, he is ultimately compelled to place her on a collision course toward death. In *Totality and Infinity*, Levinas reminds us that "Pluralism implies a radical alterity of the other whom I do not simply *conceive* by relation to myself, but *confront* out of my egoism" (121). The male narrator is incapable of following this principle.

In *The Hour of the Star*, behind the mask of the male narrator, Lispector is attempting the difficult task of confronting the other by acting beyond her own "egoism" in trying to avoid condescension to the subaltern or pandering to the poor. There exists no "salvation" for Macabea because, as a human, the male narrator cannot be her "absolute" savior. He behaves as a limited, self-centered being. Consequently, Lispector adheres to the biblical ban on man behaving as an absolute power. This prohibition is carried out by man's mistaken attempt to control meaning in light of language's instability, this process being in tandem with the conception of God as unnamable and unreachable since there always exists an unknown meaning, a nonpresence, a blank space that is yet to be filled. According to Torah and Talmud, this has always been the plight of the human condition from time immemorial, but for Jewish modernity this plight is couched in more universal terms, manifested "esoterically" in voices like Lispector's.

Clarice Lispector's literary vision, evoking Levinas's philosophical conceptualizations, adds to an understanding of how the transcendence of the self toward a better world evokes the ethical spirit of a woman writer like Lispector, who was already exploring in 1944 the profound complications of alterity that in terms of social responsibility was ahead of its time for Brazil's entrenched patriarchal society. All the more reason to appreciate Levinas and his stance on alterity and its application to Lispector's work.[30]

In conclusion, Clarice Lispector's stance on Jewish modernity reminds one again of the decidedly modern Jewish thinker, Leo Strauss, who was "committed to learning from the past while not attempting to revive it."[31] In his "Preface to Spinoza's Critique of Religion," Strauss makes a distinction between fidelity to tradition and "literalist traditionalism" and quotes Hermann Cohen on this topic, which is linked to Lispector's rethinking Jewish modernity via a universalism that does not fully reject the past: "Within a living tradition, the new is not the opposite of the old, but its deepening: one does not understand the old in its depth unless one understands it in light of such deepening; the new does not emerge through rejection or annihilation of the old, but through its metamorphosis or reshaping."[32] Lispector's modernist reshaping of Jewish modernity is emblemized through the universal concept of metamorphosis as articulated via a passionate and spirited journey through the labyrinth of language, in which she celebrates life without neglecting the precepts of Torah.

Notes

1. Leo Strauss, *Jewish Philosophy and the Crisis of Modernity: Essays and Lectures in Modern Jewish Thought*, ed. Kenneth Hart Green (Albany, 1997), 172. Although Clarice Lispector's personal library contained works by Jewish philosophers (see below), I have not encountered any reference to her having read the work of Leo Strauss. However, as a modern Jewish thinker, Strauss calls to my mind Lispector's approach to Jewish modernity.

2. See Emmanuel Levinas, *Totality and Infinity: An Essay on Exteriority*, trans. Alphonso Lingis (Pittsburgh, 1969).

3. Works of Clarice Lispector in English (hereafter referred to by abbreviations): DW—*Discovering the World*, trans. and intro. Giovanni Pontiero (Manchester, UK, 1992); NWH—*Near to the Wild Heart*, trans. Giovanni Pontiero (New York, 1990); FL—*The Foreign Legion: Stories and Chronicles*, trans. Giovanni Pontiero (Manchester, UK, 1986); HS—*The Hour of the*

Star, trans. Giovanni Pontiero (New York, 1992); PAGH—*The Passion according to GH*, trans. Ronald W. Sousa (Minneapolis, 1988); SL—*The Stream of Life*, trans. Elizabeth Lowe and Earl E. Fitz, foreword Hélène Cixous (Minneapolis, 1989).

4. Benjamin Moser, *Why This World: A Biography of Clarice Lispector* (Oxford, 2009); Nádia Battella Gotlib, *Clarice: Uma vida que se conta* (São Paulo, 1995); Teresa Cristina Montero Ferreira, *Eu sou uma pergunta: Uma biografia de Clarice Lispector* (Rio de Janeiro, 1999).

5. Nádia Battella Gotlib, *Clarice Fotobiografia* (São Paulo, 2007).

6. In addition to Waldman (see note 7, below), other Brazilian and Brazilianist critics who have focused on her Jewish perspectives are Renata M. Wasserman, Nádia Battella Gotlib, Yudith Rosenbaum, and Nelson H. Vieira. See Nelson H. Vieira, "Beyond Identity: Clarice Lispector and the Ethical Transcendence of Being for the Other," in *Returning to Babel: Jewish Latin American Experiences, Representations, and Identity*, eds. Amalia Ran and Jean Axelrad Cahan (Leiden, 2012), 179–94; and Olga Borelli, *Clarice Lispector: Esboço para um possível retrato*, 2nd ed. (Rio de Janeiro, 1981).

7. Berta Waldman, *Entre passos e astros: Presença judaica na literatura brasileira contemporânea* (São Paulo, 2003).

8. Her essays or *crônicas* (chronicles) were translated in 1992 as *Discovering the World* from the original Portuguese compilation, *A descoberta do mundo* (Rio de Janeiro, 1984).

9. Replicated partially in Barry W. Holtz, ed., *Back to the Sources: Reading the Classic Jewish Texts* (New York, 1984), 11.

10. Emmanuel Levinas, "The Ego and Totality," in *Collected Philosophical Papers*, trans. Alphonso Lingis (Boston, 1987), 25–45; and *Otherwise Than Being or Beyond Essence*, trans. Alphonso Lingis (Pittsburgh, 1998).

11. In the summer of 2008, I spent two months at the Moreira Salles Institute in Rio de Janeiro, doing research on Lispector's own book collection, which had been recently released by her family and donated to that institution. My initial findings disclosed numerous titles on philosophy and various religious ideologies both Jewish and Christian. A considerable number of these texts were written by Jewish thinkers and writers such as Baruch Spinoza, Martin Buber, Michael Bruckner, Alberto Dines, Franz Kafka, Arnold Zweig, and Stefan Zweig. Her collection also revealed her interest in Jean-Paul Sartre and his thesis on the Jewish question. To date I have found no direct link between her and Emmanuel Levinas, even though they were both in Europe during the 1940s and 1950s. Nor have I found any record of her having read Leo Strauss. Nonetheless, my reading of her work indicates strong parallels between her ethical approach to the other and the views of alterity as manifested in writings by Levinas. Publications by Hélène Cixous (*L'Heure de Clarice Lispector* [Reading with Clarice Lispector], 1989) on alterity and gender; Joseph Ballan, "Divine Anonymities: On Transcendence and Transdescendence in the Works of Levinas, Celan, and Lispector," in *Religion and the Arts* 12, no. 4 (2008): 540–58; and other scholars have addressed an affinity between the writings of Levinas and Lispector.

12. Baruch Spinoza, *Ethics, including the Improvement of the Understanding* (New York, 1989).

13. Simone de Beauvoir, *Le Deuxième Sexe* (Paris, 1949).

14. Leo Strauss, "Preface to Spinoza's Critique of Religion," in *Jewish Philosophy and the Crisis of Modernity*, 154–55.

15. Ibid.

16. Ibid., 155.

17. Ibid., 156.

18. Ibid., 163.

19. See both the above-mentioned biographies by Nádia Batella Gotlib and Benjamin Moser for comprehensive pictures of Lispector's upbringing and her life.

20. On Modernity and Judaism see Rabbi Marc D. Angel, "Rabbi Joseph B. Soloveitchik: Judaism and Modernism," in *Conversations: The Journal of the Institute for Jewish Ideas and Ideals* 12, (http://.Jewishideas.org/marc-d-angel/rabbi-joseph-b-soloveitchik-judaism-and-moderni); Arnold M. Eisen, "Rethinking Jewish Modernity," in *Jewish Social Studies* 1, no. 1 (1992): 1–21; Manfred Gerstenfeld (interviewer), "How Modernity Changed Judaism: Interview with Rabbi David Ellenson," in *World Jewry* 36 (2008) (http://jcpa.org/article/how-modernity-changed-judaism-interview-with-rabbi-david-ellenson/); Zvi Grumet, ed., "Judaism and Modernity: Realigning the Two Worlds," *Perspectives on Jewish Education* 4 (2006): 5–48; Amos Oz and Fania Oz-Salzberger, *Jews and Words* (New Haven, CT, 2012); Bernardo Sorj, *Judaism for Ev-*

eryone . . . without Dogma, trans. Bernardo Sorj, Alexandra Forman, and Timothy Thompson (Momence, IL, 2010).

21. Peter Stine, "Franz Kafka and Animals," in *Contemporary Literature* 22, no. 1 (Winter 1981): 58–80.

22. As a modernist theory created by the Brazilian writer, Oswald de Andrade, in his *Manifesto antropófago* (1928), this famous essay proposed a return to Brazil's primitive origins and a palpable existence of life in contrast to European cultural and aesthetic values by suggesting that Brazilian artists undergo a "cultural devouring" in order to create something new and autonomously Brazilian, from the digestion of the foreign. Not a copy but a type of metamorphosis via ingestion.

23. Remark by W. B. Yeats, mentioned by Peter Stine in his *Franz Kafka and Animals*. Lispector's use of animals in her narratives also serves as a means for mirroring human sentiments that are felt but often ungraspable.

24. Abraham Joshua Heschel, *Man Is Not Alone: A Philosophy of Religion* (New York, 1951).

25. Emmanuel Levinas, *Nine Talmudic Readings* (Bloomington, 1990), 34.

26. Levinas, *Totality and Infinity*, 76.

27. Levinas, *Otherwise Than Being*.

28. Andreas Huyssen, *After the Great Divide: Modernism, Mass Culture, Postmodernism* (Bloomington, IN, 1986), 209.

29. Concepts of steadfastness and falseness as folkloric principles are maintained by Brazilian Northeastern culture and manifested in the chapbooks of popular troubadours (*literatura de cordel*). See Candace Slater, *Stories on a String: The Brazilian Literatura De Cordel* (Berkeley, Los Angeles, and London, 1982). These terms are also developed in the context of Lispector's writings; see Nelson Vieira, *Jewish Voices in Brazilian Literature: A Prophetic Discourse of Alterity* (Gainesville, FL, 1995), 143–44.

30. Levinas's views on alterity appear in the following quote: "All thought is subordinate to the ethical relation, to the infinitely other in the other person, and to the infinitely other for which I am nostalgic." Levinas, "The Proximity of the Other," in *Alterity and Transcendence*, trans. Michael B. Smith (New York, 1999), 97–98.

31. Strauss, *Jewish Philosophy*, 45, 65.

32. This quote from Kenneth Hart Green's introduction to Strauss, *Jewish Philosophy and the Crisis of Modernity*, refers to Strauss's "return" to Maimonides in the context of Hermann Cohen's critique of Spinoza.

Juan Gelman (1930–2014)
THE BEREAVED BIRD

Pablo Kirtchuk

> hope fails us often
>
> grief, never.
>
> that's why some think
>
> that known grief is better
>
> than unknown grief.
>
> they believe that hope is illusion.
>
> they are deluded by grief.
>
> —JUAN GELMAN, "THE DELUDED," PARIS, 1983–1984

THERE IS A BIRD FLYING ACROSS ALL OF JUAN GELMAN'S POETRY.[1] ITS PRESENCE IS so palpable that one hears its wings flutter and sees its colors embellish the air. It sings even when it wails. That bird is the poet. It is hope, grief, joy, imagination, journey, freedom. Above all it is elevation. Hebrew calls this bird *tzippor hanefesh* (the bird of the soul). The bird is the soul.

> one day this happened:
> bird with tenor voice who loveloved her much
> before being completely devoured
> planted a tiny tree in her soul
> [. . .]
> it would not let her sleep
> it would not let her live and when mecha vaugham died
> the bird that bird
> left again taking flight from the tree.[2]

The bird, as one can see, may be an autonomous entity, with no need for a determinant—not "a" or "the" bird, just bird—but it also may be an eagle, a sparrow,

a cormorant, a nightingale, a parrot, a rooster, a hen, and even the sweet humming-bird as in an unpublished poem for a newborn girl: "anahí / está ahí / a todo dice que sí / es entre flor y colibrí / sí" (anahí / she is here / to everything she readily agrees / she's between flower and hummingbird / here). [3]

A bird is to be found also in the poem that summarizes Gelman's poetics, representing poetry itself. Here is how Gelman says it:

> Poetry is not a bird
> And it is.
> It is not a lung, air, my shirt,
> No, nothing of all that. And all of that.
> [. . .]
> Poetry is a way of living.
> Look at the people at your side.
> Do they eat? suffer? sing? cry?
> Help them fight for their hands, their
> eyes, their mouth, for the kiss to kiss and
> the kiss to give away, for their table,
> their bread, their letter a and their letter h,
> for their past—were they not children?—
> for their future—will they not be children?—
> for their present, for the piece of peace, of
> history and
> happiness that belongs to them,
> for the piece of love, big, small, sad,
> joy, that belongs to them and is taken away
> in the name of what, of what?
> Your life will then be an innumerable
> river to be called pedro, juan, ana, maria, bird, lung, the air, my shirt
> violin, sunset, stone, that handkerchief, old waltz
> wooden horse.
> Poetry is this.
> And afterwards, write it. [4]

Unexpectedly, or perhaps very much expectedly when speaking about such an unexpected poet, this poem, "End," that lays down with maturity, confidence, and plenitude his view regarding "making" poetry, [5] was written by a man in his twenties, and it closes the poet's inaugural book, *Violín y otras cuestiones* (Violin and other questions), published in 1956, first in a series of dozens of poetry books to come. Both initiating and programmatic, it contains in a nutshell the essence of Juan Gelman's subsequent work and life, his way of being in the world, as a poet, and considering himself responsible for it. "Poetry is this. / And afterwards, write it." Thus poetry is not philosophy: A can be and not be A at the same time. Poetry is not imprisoned in categories of time, space, or species. Childhood is not past, it is part and parcel of adulthood: the wooden horse is present, and one can touch the poet within the child. Poetry does not address solely the uncanny, the glorious, or the heart but that which makes the everyday of everyman: handkerchief, air, shirt, lung, stone. And above all, it is made by, for, and with everyday people who bear everyday names: pedro, juan, ana, maría, people who eat, suffer, sing, cry, and kiss, who have a history, hands, eyes, and a mouth; a piece of joy, happiness, love that are rightfully theirs and of which they are deprived. The poet himself is first and foremost a person, whose name is included in the list. Which includes, also, sunset, violin, an old waltz; moreover the people's feelings, organs, history, and names must be looked at in order to have poetical existence, and poetry has to be written. Only when they pass through the poet's looking glass do those non-A's become A's, and only once they're written do they become poetry, which, in turn, is not a bird if it does not look at them; it becomes one if it exposes the magic that is latent in those everyday things and writes them. Poetry is in the eyes of the beholder, if and only if he or she beholds.

Poet and Poetized

That is Juan Gelman's secret: that there is no secret, for the poet and the poetized that, sometimes, are one and the same interact and depend on each other. They make each other. This explains his verses that, as he evolves, become questions addressed to the reader; his deconstruction and reconstruction of grammar and vocabulary in ways both surprising and self-evident; his colloquial register; his rejection of capital letters and of comparisons, comparisons that are inherent to reason and thought. In the universe Juan Gelman inhabited with Gabriela Mistral, Miguel Angel Asturias, Gabriel García Márquez, Pablo Neruda, Octavio Paz, and Mario Vargas Llosa, the Latin American winners of the Nobel Prize for literature since 1945, and with the continental inhabitants, born from the marriage between Spanish and pre-Colombian cultures and *peoples*, life is not divided into opposed and discrete realms. Animals, flowers, violins, stones, shirts, joy, grief, his lost son and compañeros are not discrete entities but aspects of one and the same reality. "Magic/fantastic realism," as goes the Western term for this literature, is neither: it is comprehensive realism. It comprehends immaterial aspects not constrained by physical and biological limits of space, time, or species. It includes their relationships: all aspects of reality interact and dialogue. That is what makes it coherent. It is lucid realism, too. For it won't let reason occult the light that emanates from things: the continent's literary boom is due to writers who created out of that lucid comprehensive realism. Juan Gelman was Latin American not only by birth, language, and affinity, but first and foremost by his being in the world: an urban poet whose alma mater, the metropolis of Buenos Aires, is washed over by the Río de la Plata, the Paraná's magnificent mouth, "an innumerable river."

Finally, if "End" is prophetic, "Epitaph," the first poem in Gelman's inaugural book, *Violín* (1956), invites us to look at the poet's beginning, which is already pregnant with a life in its fullness, at his paradoxical résumé of a creation yet to come, of a life yet to be lived:

A bird lived in me.
A flower traveled in my blood.
My heart was a violin.

I loved and didn't love
But sometimes
I was loved. I also
was happy: about the spring,
the hands together, what is happy.

I say man has to be!

Herein lies a bird.
A flower.
A violin.[6]

"Man has to be!" It is by his epitaph that Gelman introduces himself: a man, always and each and every day, an obligation, a responsibility, a celebration. As if he had set sail in a direction from which he would never diverge. And so it was. The man who would die fifty-eight years after having published his own epitaph that defined his future poetry remained faithful to the youth he was:

when you went past my window may
with autumn on your back
and flashed signals with the lamp
of the last leaves

what was your message may
why were you sad or in your sadness gentle?
i never found out but there was always
a man alone in the street among autumn's golds
well i was the boy
at the window may
shielding my eyes
when you went past

and come to think of it
i must have been the man.[7]

And a man must resist: "Poetry is resistance against a world that becomes more and more cruel, terrible, dehumanizing; the extraordinary thing is that poetry comes from the bottom of time and keeps on living."[8]

Political Engagement

I'm going to kill you
defeat.[9]

Poetics and politics are engraved in Juan Gelman's work and life to the point that it is hardly possible to address one without the other. Yet the way he looks at the world, affects it and is affected by it, is that of a poet. Political adversaries who, even after his death in January 2014, deemed him a dangerous terrorist agreed he was an outstanding poet. A poet who expanded the limits of language, transformed the world, and brought about the demise of a general by the sheer power of his words is indeed a rare thing in a place where, "as everybody knows, the generals have for generations been liquidating the poets," as the writer and journalist Eduardo Galeano put it.[10]

■

Juan Gelman's parents emigrated from the Ukraine to Argentina in the wake of the defeat of the 1905 revolution in which his father had taken an active part. He returned to the newborn Soviet Union when the revolution of 1917 succeeded. The violence displayed by the proletariat's dictatorship, and especially Trotsky's banishment, first from the Soviet Communist Party and then, in 1928, from the country, made Gelman's father set sail to Argentina for good. Juan was born there two years later in the Jewish neighborhood of Buenos Aires Villa Crespo. This home was a gift, for they spoke Yiddish but also Russian and Ukrainian, along with the vernacular Río de la Plata Spanish. His father taught him to read when he was three years old. "As a teenager I made translations into Spanish from Yiddish and Russian poetry, which my brother Boris knew by heart. I used to turn around in the kitchen, thinking of the proper rhyme, until my mom would tell me with great concern: 'Juan, te vas a volver loco!' meaning 'Juan, you'll go nuts!' "[11] Later he would translate Evgueni Yevtushenko, Bertolt Brecht, and Guido Cavalcanti. In high school he learned French and English, thus being able to read Charles Baudelaire and Edgar Allan Poe, each one in his respective language. Thanks to Yiddish, he would get along in German. All of those languages nourished his poetic creation and his political ideas as well: reading romantic Alexander Pushkin along with anarchist Mikhail Bakunin, nostalgic Yitzik Manger as well as visionary Dov-Ber Borokhov,[12] bourgeois Federico García Lorca but also shepherd Miguel Hernández, each of them in the original, would leave nobody unaffected.

Over the years he learned to admire the author of Psalms or the gatherer of sycamore fruit who became the herald of the people's cause (Amos 7:14); he cherished Ibn Gabirol, Samuel Hanaggid, Ibn Ezra, Ibn Shaprut, and signed poems with the names of all those Jews from antiquity through the Middle Ages to our day. Despite their many differences of background and values, he had high esteem for Jorge Luis Borges as well, even if the latter considered the military junta in its first days a necessary evil for putting an end to chaos. In August 1982, however, with the publication of Borges's "Juan López y John Ward," against the Malvinas (Falklands) War (triggered by the junta's invasion into the islands, combined with Margaret Thatcher's intransigence), which denounced the war's absurdity; and later with his 1985 elegiac-satirical poem "Milonga of the Dead One," which mourns the soldiers sent to their death "with a Catholic prayer book and weapons quite as antique," Gelman pardoned and embraced the old patrician poet.

■

The year of Juan Gelman's birth, 1930, marked a coup d'etat that deposed Argentinian president Hipólito Irigoyen, inaugurating more than half a century of political instability. When Ramón Mercader assassinated Lev Trotsky in Mexico on

Stalin's order in 1940, the ten-year-old Gelman was appalled: he evokes it some seventy years later: "A photo taken a few days after the Russian Revolution's triumph shows the Military Staff with Lenin at the center, then a ladder, then Stalin. The ladder replaced Trotsky, erased from the photo."[13] In 1945, starting his studies at the best high school of the country, Colegio Nacional Buenos Aires, Gelman joined the Communist Party, where he founded in 1955, with other communist youths who wrote political and popular poetry, El Pan Duro (Hard Bread), a cooperative group dedicated to the publication and distribution of their work. It was El Pan Duro that would publish his first poetry book, *Violín*.

Influenced by the success of Fidel Castro and Ernesto "Che" Guevara in Cuba, Gelman began in 1959 to distance himself from the official line of the Argentine Communist Party but was imprisoned in 1963 as a communist along with other activists. Once out of jail Gelman left the party, considering it too soft. With other colleagues he founded the group Nueva Expresión (New Expression) and the publishing house La Rosa Blindada (The Armored Rose), which published and distributed left-wing pamphlets rejected by the orthodox Communist Party. The terms "New Expression" and "The Armored Rose" may well apply to all of Gelman's poetical and political work ever since.

In 1967, under the impact of the murder in Bolivia of compatriot, medical doctor, and revolutionary leader Che Guevara, Gelman joined the Fuerzas Armadas Revolucionarias (FAR), later to merge with the kindred group Montoneros. As an officer in this movement, he was in charge of the link with fellow movements in Europe and with its media and authorities, keeping them informed of the violations of human rights committed by the far-right-wing government headed by Juan Perón's second wife Estela and her strongman López Rega, who, through the paramilitary organization Triple A (Argentine Anti-Communist Alliance), murdered a number of opponents.

In his role as go-between for the Montoneros, Gelman was in Rome on March 24, 1976, when the military took power and launched a bloody dictatorship that would only step down seven years and 30,000 assassinations later—among the dead, Gelman's own son, Marcelo Ariel. One of the junta's first decrees was to prohibit Gelman's return to Argentina. Thanks to Gelman's activities in Europe, several leaders, including France's François Mitterrand and Sweden's Olof Palme, publicly condemned the junta that year.[14] In 1979 Gelman was expelled from the Montoneros and condemned to death after publicly accusing its leaders of making absurd and dangerous decisions, such as sending activists back to Argentina with the obligation to wear a Montonero outfit at public places, which meant a sure death.

Gelman's exile took him to places like Rome, Paris, Vienna, Managua, Mexico, and New York, where he worked as a translator with UNESCO and wrote for newspapers. When democracy was restored in Argentina in 1983 he was considered a potential participant in crimes committed by Montoneros and was not allowed to return. Writers Eduardo Galeano, Alberto Moravia, Juan Carlos Onetti, Octavio Paz, Augusto Roa Bastos, and Mario Vargas Llosa protested publicly, and in 1988 the order of capture was suspended but with no rehabilitation. A year later Gelman was given amnesty by Argentine president Carlos Menem with other activists but along with military criminals as well. Gelman rejected the amnesty, declaring, "I am being traded for the murderers of my son and of thousands of other youths who are now my sons."[15] The decree forbidding his return was abolished only in 2003 when his friend and fervent reader Nestor Kirchner was elected president.

Combat on Paper

> We'll force the future to come back.[16]

Gelman decided to become a journalist after a short period of chemistry studies at the Buenos Aires University. He worked for the Argentinean political magazines *Confirmado* (from 1966), *Panorama* (1969), and *Crisis* (1973–1974); and for the newspapers *La Opinión*, whose cultural supplement he directed (1971–1973), and *Noticias*, where he was editorial director (1974). All were opposed to the governments that ruled Argentina in their time. But his name is mostly associated with the daily *Página 12*. He worked there for twenty-seven years, displaying on its pages his passions, hatreds, political and moral battles, and tastes.

Página 12 was founded in 1987 by a quartet: Jorge Lanata (then aged twenty-six); Ernesto Tiffenberg; Fernando Sokolowicz;[17] and Horacio Verbitsky (surnamed El perro, "the hound"), who would serve as an investigative journalist. The last three are Jewish. The daily is considered to be one of the best in the Hispanic world, whose influence spreads far beyond its rather limited readership. For many years Gelman wrote cultural papers, and in later years the back-cover essay, generally devoted to international matters. His papers were always duly documented, by sources selected so as to support the journalist's—and the newspaper's—viewpoint; and they were critical of the United States' political-cum-economic values and policies. Often he called it "El Imperio." In 2003, referring to the American invasion of Iraq, he wrote: "There are 23,415 liquid tons of sarin gas, mustard gas and nerve gas VX, stocked within the boundaries of the U.S. territory, but it is improbable that the U.S. will invade itself in order to destroy those weapons."[18] Yet he made a distinction between the U.S. regime and the American people, whose dynamism, generosity, and poets—Walt Whitman and e. e. cummings[19] in particular—he admired.

In the American sphere Gelman included Israel, whose existence was problematic for this Jew who considered Judaism as all-embracing and universal, the opposite of a national(ist) enterprise. As far as he was concerned Zionism entailed a regression into a Gentile-like state, in all the senses of the word "state." Over the years he wrote obsessively against Israel's nationalist character, militarist practices, and its military occupation of Palestine, defending openly and loudly the Palestinian cause.[20] Yet if we use his own method we must conclude that he was fascinated with both the United States and Israel, the two most frequently mentioned foreign countries in his papers, even when they were not the issue at stake.

Gelman's work in *Página 12* did not debunk the generals while they were in power, as the journal was founded four years after the junta stepped down from the political scene. But the generals still had the support of parts of the armed forces, the Church, and some members of the upper and upper-middle classes. Gelman's constant and in-depth work condemning the junta made a decisive contribution to turning Argentina into the first, and for a long time the only, country on the continent to judge, condemn, and imprison its dictators for life, consolidating democracy. The personal price he had paid and his rejection of presidential amnesty turned him into a moral authority who exerted an undeniable influence on public opinion.

Under Foreign Rain

> I am a monstrous plant. My roots are thousands of miles from me.[21]

Juan Gelman's civil courage earned him the Hispanic world's admiration and gratitude upon his death in 2014. His poetry earned him every possible award, including the Premio Cervantes, the Hispanic Nobel, in 2007; but first they brought upon him banishment and ostracism, that οστρακισμός which is, has always been, the unforgiving punishment inflicted on people who represent a threat to the powers that be. What greater tribute can politicians render to a poet than the punishment that Augustus inflicted on Ovid, the Roman Empire's outstanding poet, by deporting him "because of a poem and a mistake," to a remote, isolated corner of the Empire? So hard is the ordeal that Jeremiah (22:10) says: "Do not weep for the dead and do not regret him, wail instead for him who is going away and shall never see his homeland again." In a poem written and inspired by the Hebrew poets from al-Andalus, Muslim Spain of Islam's classical antiquity—the Christian Middle Ages—Juan Gelman sees the ordeal of exile as inferior only to the repudiation of a lover:

> they turned me out of the palace
> i didn't care
> they exiled me from my country
> i wandered over the face of the earth
> they deported me from my language
> it followed me
> you kept me away from you
> my bones are burning out
> living flames scorch me
> i am banished from myself.
>
> yehuda al-harizi, 1170–1237; toledo—provence—palestine.[22]

In another poem he speaks about the language as his last refuge, his real homeland, his skin, heart, his utter himself, all things that can be taken away from a human being only by killing him. "they took my books from me," he thus wrote in a poem in prose, "my bread, my son, they wore down my mother, threw me out of the country, assassinated my little brothers, tortured my compañeros, undid them, broke them. Nobody pulled me out of the street where I am weeping besides my dog. [. . .] What military motherfucker can take away my great love for those May twilights, when the bird of being hovers to the falling night?"[23] Is this the reason why upon the abolishment of the decree forbidding his return, in 2003, when Kirchner was elected president, Gelman chose not to return to Argentina and settled instead in Mexico with his second wife Mara Lamadrid, an Argentinian exile like him? Was love stronger than longing? Did freedom make longing bearable? Was it missing his son that made the return more unbearable than longing? Or was it, even if unknowingly, the Bakhtinian understanding that being away, *ailleurs*, at the margins, gives one a uniquely privileged insight about the world?

Dibaxu (Underneath, 1994) contains poems in Judeo-Spanish. Provoked by exile, it was the expression of Gelman's quest for historical roots, badly needed once he was deprived of his geographical ones. Strictly speaking there is an anachronism there, as the poets he evokes lived in Spain before its Catholic kings Isabel and Fernando with their Portuguese counterparts expelled the Jews from the Peninsula; yet for Juan Gelman they symbolize the Jewish fate in the (Hispanic?) world, that is, creativity rewarded by exile.[24] *Salarios del Impío* (1993) bears on exile, as does his exile journal, "Bajo la lluvia ajena" (1993), short prose texts that relate the estrangement generated by exile and the ways to fight it.[25]

According to Juan Gelman, there are three homelands: Life, Childhood, and Language.[26] Accordingly, his texts on, from, and against exile are so many interrogation marks: What is exile? What is it for a Jew? Can anybody be considered in exile on the soil where he was born? Can anybody relate to his mother tongue as if it were a foreign language? Can the music, the food, the landscapes familiar to one from birth and even beforehand be thrown over by fiat as artifacts imposed by history, which one should get rid of? Paradoxically—or not—Juan Gelman's rejection of Zionism too is the rejection of exile. It is his hometown that is his home and his town. No Jerusalem, however celestial, could ever replace *la gran aldea*, "the great hamlet" Buenos Aires; no country, no matter how biblical, could ever be an acceptable substitute for native Argentina, and the tango—*gotán* in lunfardo, porteño slang—is more moving than any cantata, even Johann S. Bach's. Another Juan, Cedrón, composed one to Gelman's lyrics, "La Cantata del Gallo Cantor" (The Cantata of the Crowing Rooster), sung by Paco Ibáñez to honor the sixteen political prisoners killed in 1972 by the Argentine police in Trelew, Patagonia, inaugurating state terrorism that would last for a decade. Both Juans' music and lyrics combined in several concerts and CDs.

Limits of the Soul

> Words are like the air: they belong to everybody. [. . .] Sure, murderers and victims use the same words, but I never read the words utopia, or beauty, or tenderness in police descriptions. [. . .] The Argentinean dictatorship burnt *The Little Prince*. [. . .] They were right to do so because the book is so full of tenderness that it would harm any dictatorship.[27]

Latin American Spanish is a hybrid, a composite language, enriched by a myriad of words from Quechua, Guaraní, and many other Amerind tongues: pampa, macana, cancha, jacarandá. It also displays morphological and syntactic borrowed mechanisms—adverbs and demonstratives admit diminutive suffixes, gerunds may replace conjugated verbs, and discursive particles abound, yielding conversation lively and affective—and all that is reflected in Gelman's work. Nouns change gender, take quantifiers, and conjugate as if they were verbs; demonstratives admit diminutives; word order is turned upside-down. To the opposite of the received opinion, Juan Gelman does not abolish the limits of language, but those of grammar and vocabulary. He applies extant affixes to categories they are not meant for initially; he displaces words from their initial syntactic category to other extant categories; he changes the gender of a word to the other extant gender. He does not import new bricks to the game, just deconstructs the extant bricks and combines them otherwise, which demands a thorough knowledge of those bricks, similar to the chemist's about the structure of molecules, atoms, and subatomic particles. Not in vain did Juan Gelman study chemistry at the university. Only one who knows the law inwardly and outwardly can break it at will without being indicted. Moreover he does not break rules only for the sake of breaking them but in order to make the limits of his language correspond to those of his soul.[28] If Ludwig Wittgenstein's limits of his language were the limits of his world, the limits of Gelman's world were larger than those of his language's grammar and vocabulary. It is thus only consequent that he should push further the latter's. His research is formal only in appearance; in earnest it is spiritual and meant to provide him with adequate forms to say what needs to be said. Santiago, Ernest Hemingway's Old Man, speaks of the Sea as a she-being, "La Mar," while all of his fellow fishermen merely consider "el mar" as a masculine noun. This is justified by Spanish grammar, if only on diachronic and etymological grounds. Juan Gelman's inventions are poetically justified. In German writing "die Welt" is normative. In Spanish writing "la mundo" is sending a love letter to the she-world. "Hijar," namely, "to child" (= to beget), from "hijo/a" (i.e., "child"), is as straightforward as its English symmetrical "to father": "ah mother the one they childed / as always."[29] And if "hijar" is possible then, tragically, "deshijar," namely "to unson" or "to unchild," are too. Some of his book titles render Juan Gelman's Spanish inventions: *De atrásalante en su porfía* (2009) (From backforwards in his perfidy); *El emperrado corazón amora* (2011) (The bitched heart is alove); and *Mundar* (2007) (To world).[30]

A poet who readily comes to mind in this context is e. e. cummings. He began with a classical style—"Thou aged unreluctant earth who dost / with quivering continual thighs invite."[31] Then he gave up capitals and normative English—"now is a ship // which captain am / sails out of sleep // steering for dream."[32] In *Violín* Juan Gelman uses the peninsular Spanish second-person plural form "vosotros" with its corresponding conjugation, as well as capitals where they are due; as he evolves, he uses the colloquial Argentine forms "vos" for second-person singular and "ustedes" for second-person plural, conjugated as a third-person plural. Both poets justify the etymology of "poet" in Greek ποιετησ, which means "maker" and "builder." In his foreword to his book "is 5" [*sic*], cummings hints to that, stating: "If a poet is anybody, he is somebody . . . who is obsessed by Making. . . . It is with roses and locomotives that my poems are 'competing' . . . with elephants, and with El Greco." El Greco worked in Toledo. *Dibaxu*, mentioned above, reveals Juan Gelman's debt to his predecessors in Jewish Spain as well as his identification with their present-day descendants who, inasmuch as they speak or at least understand the equivalent of Yiddish in Medieval Spain are, like him, Jews bathing in Hispanic waters.[33]

Names and Identities

> he escaped from himself as from a prison cell[34]

Exile can be interior. If one's inner homeland has no frontiers, a way to free oneself from this interior exile is to dynamite the inner prison walls beginning with one's name. Choosing other names is assuming other choices. Some heteronyms are Julio Greco and José Galván: they bear Gelman's initials while sounding Hispanic. Maybe Juan Gelman too, who loved everyman, wished he bore everyman's name. *The Poems* of *Sidney West*, allegedly translated from English, reveal the poet's fascination with the dynamism and freedom that suffused the spirit of the United States, best expressed in the nineteenth century by the injunction "Go West!" On the other hand he execrated the United States' quest to control the southern part of the Americas, namely Latin America, which also harkens back to that period and U.S. president James Monroe's doctrine of 1823. This ambivalence he resolved by attributing that book to a poet by the name of Sidney West. The poems are some three dozen "lamentos" for characters called gallagher bentham, david cassidy, and roy hennigann.

> where it says "if we were or we were / as human faces"
> (page such and such verse whatever) it is as the ox that ploughed there
> not rotted by pain or fury
> disguising much of the time in solitude
>
> ah sidney west! here ends (hopefully)
> [. . .]
> what tiny bit round this man
> and what animal within
>
> [. . .]
>
> and so when west with his first love
> headed for sidney sailor
> sidney the last in history
> spun with west as a water wheel's donkey
>
> [. . .]
>
> until his feet grow wings please.[35]

Juan Gelman's taste for heteronyms speaks of his affinity with Fernando Pessoa, that is, "John Person," the Portuguese poet who wrote under identities galore. "Person" comes from Greek προσοπον, "mask." In French *personne* without a determiner means "nobody," but in Juan Gelman's subversive spirit a mask is one's true personality and "nobody" can mean "several": "there once was a Portuguese poet / with four poets inside him / he lived a worried life working for the public administration and / where do you see a portuguese civil servant earning enough to feed four mouths."[36]

The book's translators, Katherine M. Hedeen and Victor Rodríguez Núñez, would say the following about Gelman's exercise: "West is among the best imaginary poets not only of Whitman's native land, allegedly his as well, but of all possible lands."[37]

Wonderland

> Here in Europe time is successive, nobody wears the suit he wore
> tomorrow, and nobody loves the girl he will love yesterday. . . . No
> crackpot interrupts . . . the blind who don't say "see" and see.[38]

Eduardo Galeano, the friend and colleague to whom Juan Gelman dedicates his *Notas* (1979),[39] authored the emblematic *Las venas abiertas de América Latina* (Latin America's open veins), whence it becomes clear that in this part of the continent the term "Native American" is rather nonsensical. The Spaniards did not eliminate the Indians; instead, they used them, abused them, and above all mingled with them, and with their women they begot Latin Americans, who are not Native Americans nor European but both. "Fiction" from Latin "fingo," namely, "I feign," is not a Latin America–compatible term; here reality is vaster and deeper than its visible aspects, subject to constraints of time, space, livelihood, humanness, and so on. The Peruvian anthropologist Carlos Castañeda, studying at UCLA, had to cross the border to Mexico in order to receive the *Teachings of Don Juan* (1968). Gelman was born and bred in Don Juan's universe. Another factor that contributes to the continent's specificity is Nature's imposing dimensions. When there is snow at the extreme south of the country and a desert at its other extreme 2,500 miles north, when vast parts of the land are crowded with cattle, alligators, jasmines, birds, llamas, fish, and waterfalls, Man turns modest. In Latin America, Culture is not opposed to Nature. Its superior force too is echoed in Juan Gelman's poetry as the force of nineteenth-century North American Nature and Indian identity are in Longfellow's. In our day, only in Latin America do the three factors—Western culture, Indian cultures, and untamed Nature—interact. Gelman chanted the continent's beauty and mystery in poems like the one dedicated to Aimé Bonpland, who came with fellow explorer Alexander von Humboldt, was confined for ten years in Paraguay and then stayed there first with his Guaraní lover, who bore him two children, then with his love from Argentina, who gave him four children more, and with other loves too—Aimé he was, indeed. This poem echoes the continent by its dimension (101 verses), scenery, and the opposition between the new world and the old one: the Orinoco versus the Seine; the rainforest fauna with its crocodile, tiger, ape, and boa versus the city's fauna, a cat that fishes; the sweetness of Nunu's sweet multiple breasts versus the hardness and paucity of Bonpland's world; bonfires versus cathedrals; the Indians' emotion versus the Frenchman's reason. Bonpland decides to stay: he learns the "sweet Indian languages" and in them he asks brothers crocodile, tiger, ape, and boa to retrieve Nunu. This poem echoes Atahualpa Yupanqui's "La pastorcita perdida" (The lost shepherd girl), in which a *k'olla*, a Quechua Indian from Bolivia, asks the wind and the Puna or High Andean plateau to give him back his love, stolen by the bad cold night. Gelman goes further, as it is a European who talks to natural elements, showing that, along with his love, he has wedded Latin America itself. This poem represents the immigrants and their offspring including the poet. Its cinematographic quality makes the reader feel in the midst of the forest and its inhabitants with the Indian woman Nunu, namely, Latin America, who conquered the European man's heart:

> and here the Frenchman Bonpland botanist
> looked for asclepias lirolensis
> [. . .]
> he found instead the unknown
> faces or looks of love
> the Indian woman Nunu of the zambos
> near the Orinoco's mouth.[40]

"When I was nine, I fell in love with a girl from my neighborhood [. . .] I wrote her a poem. She wasn't impressed, but I gained poetry." And "the Lady" is what he called poetry.

> The woman was like the word never
> [. . .]
> the woman settled in my left side.
>
> Watch out watch out I'd scream watch out
> but she possessed me like love, like the night,
> and the last signals I made that autumn
> settled down quietly under the surf of her hands.
>
> Sharp sounds exploded inside me,
>
> rage, sadness, fell down in shreds,
> the woman came down like a sweet rain
> on my bones standing in the solitude.
>
> She left me shivering like someone condemned
> and I killed myself with a quick knife-thrust,
> I'll spend all my death laid out with her name.[41]

A typically Gelmanian inversion of the doxa: it is the woman in the guise of rain who possesses the man, like Zeus and Danaë. And death, thanks to love, is life. Incidentally, this poem sheds light on the title of his book "Under Foreign Rain": rain waters one's land, save when it falls on a foreign land. Love is stronger than fear, persecution and exile; no dictatorship can destroy it forever:

> dark times
> filled with light
> the sun spreads sunlight over the city split by sudden sirens
> the police hunt goes on
> night falls and we'll make love under this roof
> our eighth
> in
> one month
> they know almost everything about us
> except this plaster ceiling we make love under.[42]

No need for a psychoanalyst to determine that in every loving, mature man there lies the unconditional love of a mother. Gelman's relationship with women was a consequence of the reciprocal affection that linked him to his mother, just as Kafka's loathing of authority resulted from the resentment generated by his father. Gelman's *Carta a mi madre* (Letter to my mother) is indeed the exact reverse of Kafka's *Letter* to his father. Gelman's is a poem/book to the parent of the opposite sex, in which he declines the filial love of a son who grew up to be a responsible, fighting, and loving adult thanks to a loving mother.

you kept me as long as your body could contain me
[...]
was it fine for us, together like that, me swimming in you blindly [...]
was I always reproaching you for pushing me out into the world
is that my real exile? [...]
does love make deals in the dark
and will I comb once more your lovely hair?[43]

Has Gelman's ability to love and express love helped him surmount the worst ordeal a human being can be exposed to, and survive the tragedy of his life? "unsoning you so much / unsoning me," he wrote in 1979–1980, in one of his most poignant texts as well as one that is wildly free, linguistically speaking, as the lament goes on:

looking for you in your softitude
I step my father lonely of you
passes the secret voice you weave
patient
as unsouling of my being
[...]
what country do you bleed
for me to bleed fleshly
where are you
saddest in your warmness?"[44]

On August 24, 1976, Gelman's son Marcelo Ariel and pregnant daughter-in-law María Claudia "disappeared." Marcelo's corpse was found thirteen years later in a barrel full of cement with a bullet in the back of the head and stigmata of torture. María Claudia was murdered two months after giving birth. It was a minister of the Vatican who, in 1978, informed the bereaved father that the newborn had been given away for adoption: the pope was kept informed of the junta's crimes. "The Church sanctified massacre, one bishop even said: Where there is bloodshed, there is redemption," Gelman would write years later.[45] The tender poet able to address *urbi et orbi* such a bold accusation, in a country whose constitution obliges the president to be Catholic, must have been a tough guy, the same who served in jail on account of his opinions and as an officer in an armed revolutionary movement. Many poems he wrote after losing his son are tainted with the colors of unfathomable grief and infinite anger, never despair.

Sleep my son between sheets of grappa
I will protect you if it takes the whole bottle
[...]
a glow in the night for the hangmen
is your face my son a glow
and I live and die by it these days
my son in the night of the hangmen
i believe in the clarity of the groans in
the clarity of the light that falls from the sobs
the clarity that falls from the beaten flesh
tortured killed the clarity

that falls from your face of the glow
in this long night and the bed where I lie
between sheets of iron
without sleeping.[46]

In his "Open letter to my unknown grandson or granddaughter," written and published in 1995, while scanning the earth to find his disappeared grandchild, he says: "I'd like to talk to you about [your parents] and to have you tell me about yourself. To be able to recognize in you my own son and to let you find in me what I have of your father: both of us are his orphans."[47] With the help of writers, artists, political people, and friends from all over the world, Gelman searched for Macarena during a quarter-century. He met her on March 31, 2000, at the intervention of the president of Uruguay; she had been given for adoption to an Uruguayan police-man's family. Her surname is now Gelman, and as of October 2014 she is a Member of the Uruguayan Parliament. Here is a poem by her father, Marcelo:

The black sheep
grazes in a black field
on the black snow
under the black night
near the black town
where I cry
clad in red.[48]

Many of Juan Gelman's poems since 1976 evoke his murdered friends, poets and writers Paco Urondo, Rodolfo Walsh, and Haroldo Conti as well as other artists, intellectuals, scientists, and laypeople. All would have liked his voice to be heard on their behalf, on their graves. All considered him the one who wrote the poems they would have liked to have written:

walking on my bare knees
through a field of broken glass
walking on my naked soul
through a field of broken compañeros

whom neither the twilight nor the sea
that washes over any man will wash
i don't know what's washing over them now
quiet at last
unafraid

of death
killed by bullets or cyanide
by their own or another's hand
dead all the same
rotting

under the earth in this land
that took them in [. . .]

urge

us on to victory sons.[49]

Juan Gelman had reasons more than enough to say, like e. e. cummings, "manunkind." Yet he was a believer: "Dear Paco, I am remembering years back, when we were fixing lunch in your pad [. . .] years later [. . .] fewer were dying natural deaths [. . .] afterwards they killed you. [. . .] You told me once that you were going to live to be eighty and I believed you. And I still believe you."[50]

For him, tango poets like Homero Manzi, Homero Expósito, and the others were mystics, for they chanted pain caused by loss of a beloved being: a land, a lover. A son. Juan Gelman endorsed his own catastrophe along with his homeland's, with infinite rage and dignity. He never forgot nor forgave, because forgiveness belongs to the victims only, he said, and the dead speak no more. He chose life, and passion, never losing hope and faith, in "the piece of peace, of / history and / happiness that belongs to them, / for the piece of love, big, small, sad, / joy," of his first days as a poet, all those things that belong to us, to him (see above, "End"). He was not a Paul Celan, Stefan Zweig, or Walter Benjamin, all of whom he read; he did not commit suicide "although at times I'd like to be where you are, " he wrote to a dead friend, but resisted his hangmen and his sadness; he did not mourn a past forever gone but swore to bring back the future. "Desire never fades away," he quoted René Char, and added: "Each poem is the realization of desire that keeps on being."

Notes

1. The epigraph is from Juan Gelman, "The Deluded," in *Unthinkable Tenderness*, ed. and trans. Joan Lindgren (Berkeley, 1997), 167. Gelman does not use capitals in poetry save in his early work (see below). Ellipses in brackets [. . .] indicate that one or more words of the poem/text have been omitted from the quotation.

2. Juan Gelman, "lamento for mecha vaugham's uterus," in *Los Poemas de Sidney West*, 1969; English version *The Poems of Sidney West*, trans. Katherine Hedeen and Victor Rodríguez Núñez (Cambridge, 2008), 39, 41.

3. The Guaraní name Anahí, meaning "little member of the family," evokes both the flower "alhelí" and the hummingbird "colibrí." This poem was written by Gelman when my first daughter Anahí was born in 2001. I had translated and published a number of Gelman's poems into Hebrew.

4. Juan Gelman, "End," *New York Times*, January 20, 2014. Starting with the words "Poetry is a way of living," the translation is by Ilan Stavans; the four lines preceding them were translated by me.

5. Making instead of writing poetry draws from the meaning of "poet" in Greek, ποιετησ as maker.

6. "Paréntesis," trans. Robin Myers, in Luis Naón, *Paréntesis / Parenthesis*, No. 6. Folios Collection, MUAC, Museo Universitario Arte Contemporáneo, UNAM (Mexico City, 2013).

7. Juan Gelman, "Another May," from *Cólera Buey* [Wrath ox], 1964, in *Dark Times Filled with Light*, trans. Hardie St. Martin (Rochester, 2012), 33.

8. Juan Gelman, "poesía es resistencia frente al mundo," http://www.festivaldepoesiademedellin.org/es/Diario/10.html.

9. Juan Gelman, "Note I," from *Comentarios* [Commentaries], 1982, in *Unthinkable Tenderness*, 23.

10. Eduardo Galeano, "The Poet's Search and Hope," *Pagina 12*, November 14, 1999. The general, Eduardo Cabanillas, was in charge of the torture and extermination camp, where thousands of Argentine citizens were tortured and assassinated during the junta rule.

11. Conversation with Juan Gelman, Herzliya, Israel, Spring 2001.

12. Yitzik Manger, 1901–1969, was a popular Yiddish playwright and poet; Dov-Ber Borokhov, 1881–1917, was a Marxist-Zionist thinker, who called for the inversion of the social pyramid in Jewish society.

13. *Pagina 12*, December 9, 2008.

14. The United States, which sustained the junta, set up, among other things, both "Plan Cóndor," an alliance among Latin America dictatorships, and the "Escuela de las Américas" in Panama, where repressors were trained.

15. *Pagina 12*, November 10, 1989, reproduced by Horacio Verbitsky in *Pagina 12*, January 15, 2014.

16. "Sucederá," *Mundar* (To world), 2007, and interview in *Clarín*, September 30, 2007.

17. Under the dictatorship he had founded the Jewish Movement for Human Rights.

18. *Pagina 12*, May 11, 2003.

19. This is how Cummings himself used to write his name.

20. Not all the Gelmans shared his opinions. His elder sister Teodora settled in Israel. Gelman's *Carta a mi madre* [Letter to my mother] is dedicated to Teodora. On his way to Israel for her funeral in 2001, Gelman made a fuss on political grounds aboard the plane, was detained by the police upon landing, and was eventually released with the help of local poets.

21. "Bajo la lluvia ajena" [Under foreign rain], XVI, from *Interrupciones II*, 1993, in *Unthinkable Tenderness*, 72.

22. "Com/posiciones" [Com/positions], from *Com/posiciones*, 1986, in *Dark Times Filled with Light*, 157.

23. "Bajo la lluvia ajena," III, in *Unthinkable Tenderness*, 60.

24. Folk author, composer, and singer Atahualpa Yupanqui and singer-interpreter Mercedes Sosa were among the Argentine exiles.

25. "Bajo la lluvia ajena," I, in *Unthinkable Tenderness*, 57. A football fan, Gelman was honored in 2004 with the Supporter of Honor Award by the Jewish football club of Buenos Aires, Atlanta, nicknamed "Los Bohemios," on the occasion of the club's centennial.

26. Interview in *El País*, Madrid, April 15, 2009; conversation recorded by *France Culture*, Paris, in 2012, reproduced in January 19, 2014, http://www.franceculture.fr/emission-ca-rime-a-quoi-hommage-a-juan-gelman.

27. *El País*, Madrid, December 7, 2012.

28. Conversation in *France Culture*, 2012, reproduced, 2014 http://www.franceculture.fr/emission-ca-rime-a-quoi-hommage-a-juan-gelman.

29. Juan Gelman, "lament for john bentham," in *Poems of Sidney West*, 121.

30. Translation mine. While translating I try to create the equivalent to the effect obtained in the original, which implies some innovation in English.

31. e. e. cummings, *Complete Poems 1904–1962*, ed. G. Firmage (New York, 1994), 3.

32. Ibid., 9.

33. Juan Gelman: "Sephardic is the language spoken by Mio Cid. I love its diminutives, candor, a certain type of syntactic construction; it is the most exiled part of the language." See http://www.festivaldepoesiademedellin.org/es/Diario/10.html.

34. Juan Gelman, "Errata," in *Poems of Sidney West*, 129.

35. Ibid.

36. "Yo también escribo cuentos" [I, too, write stories], from *Los Poemas de José Galván*, 1981, in *Unthinkable Tenderness*, 102.

37. *New York Times*, January 15, 2014.

38. "A César Fernandez Moreno," "Bajo la lluvia ajena" XX, in *Unthinkable Tenderness*, 77.

39. *Unthinkable Tenderness*, 23–29.

40. Juan Gelman, "El Botánico," in *Fábulas* (Buenos Aires, 1971) (my translation).

41. Juan Gelman, "Gotán," from *Gotán*, 1962, in *Dark Times Filled with Light*, 21. "Gotan" means "tango" spelled backward.

42. Juan Gelman, "Things they don't know," from *Hechos y Relaciones* [Facts and relations], 1980, in *Dark Times Filled with Light*, 70.

43. Juan Gelman, *Carta a mi madre*, 1989, in *Unthinkable Tenderness*, 177–80.

44. Juan Gelman, "Poem VI," Carta Abierta [Open letter], Paris-Rome 1979–1980, in *Interrupciones I* (Buenos Aires, 1988) (my translation).

45. On September 12, 2008, some clergy were killed and others were put in jail and tortured, such as the priest Liuzzi of Posadas, whose sister's demand of the local bishop to help her retrieve his remains was plainly rejected. Personal conversation, August 20, 2014.

46. Juan Gelman, "Sheets," from *Hechos y Relaciones*, in *Unthinkable Tenderness*, 18.
47. Written for *Pagina 12* and published on April 12, 1995; *Unthinkable Tenderness*, 181.
48. http://www.republica.com.uy/juan-gelman-leyo-poemas-escritos-por-su-hijo-marcelo.
49. Juan Gelman, "Nota III," *Comentarios*, 1982; *Dark Times Filled with Light*, 75.
50. Juan Gelman, "Dear Paco," 1980; *Unthinkable Tenderness*, 78–79.

Jacques Derrida (1930–2004)
JUDEITIES

Joseph Cohen

Early on, and for a long time I have trembled, I still tremble, before the title of this conference (questions addressed to me! And concerning judeities!) and never has the privilege of a conference apparently addressed to me intimidated, worried, or flustered me this much, to the point of leaving me with the feeling that a grave misunderstanding threatened to make me forget how much I feel, and will always feel, out of place in speaking of it; out of place, misplaced, decentered, very far from what could resemble the thing itself or the center of said questions, the multiple questions oriented towards plural judeities and whatever could be implied by this word, judeities, in the plural, to which I shall return. Is it really to me, at the back of the class, in the last row, that such questions must be addressed or destined? On the matter of judeity or Judaism, the insufficiency, the inadequacy, the failure (all mine, and of which I have not finished speaking) are graver and, I fear, more significant than a simple incompetence, an incompetence and a lack of culture, to which, by the way, I at the same time also confess. But I will have to explain myself, and so I must at least respond, precisely, I must answer for all these faults and failures. I must do so, and I owe it to you; I must answer for them to you, before you, all of you who are here, before those who remarkably honour me by partaking in this experience, assuming its meaning with courage and generosity, while alone I would never have even imagined its possibility.

—JACQUES DERRIDA, "ABRAHAM, THE OTHER"

IT IS WITH THESE TREMBLING WORDS THAT JACQUES DERRIDA OPENED HIS KEYNOTE address at the conference "Judeities: Questions for Jacques Derrida," held in Paris in December 2000.[1] This conference posed the question of the relation between Judaism (i.e., between the plurality and multiplicity already and always working through Judaism itself, hence the term "judeities" in the title chosen for this conference) and Jacques Derrida's thought. The conference not only addressed the presence or absence of Jewish culture and history, thought, and references in Derrida's philosophical writing but also pretended to confront and pursue the following interrogation: In which sense did Derrida's philosophical writing and engagement stem—or not—from *his* Judaism? Or again: What effect, if any, did *his* Judaism have on *his* thinking and writing, and furthermore on *his* philosophical and political engagements? To these questions must be added one that is not entirely indifferent to the former philosophical interrogations: the relation between *his* Judaism and *his* biography. The conference aimed, in this manner, to pose the following question: According to which law and from which "place" does Derrida's Judaism work through, write itself, speak within, awake, and inform *his* philosophical thought?

To pose the question in this way meant to expose Derrida *himself* to that which was already within him and yet foreign to him, to that which was closest to himself and yet given to him from afar. Or again, to that which was most profoundly inscribed within him and yet most radically unknown, secret, or obscure to him. The doubled distinctiveness and profound indeterminacy of Derrida's own "judeity" does not allow, nor is it capable of, justifying a clear-cut position. It retracts all statements where a determined and categorical "identity" could be confirmed. This is why, in the same keynote address, Derrida engages a radical "deconstruction" of Jean-Paul Sartre's distinction between the "authentic Jew" and the "inauthentic Jew."[2] In this he did not simply condemn the possibility of such affirmations, but rather deployed within each of these, and as inherent to their very meaning, the manner in which their very formulations are always reductive of what they intend to affirm.

In this sense, Derrida's writing incessantly seeks to reveal in which manner affirmations are always and already *unthought* when they are grasped from and according to the possibility of their own formulation. This "deconstructive" reading of subjectivity through the deconstruction of affirmations and claims is not removed, according to Derrida, from a resolute turn toward the historicity and genealogy of one's identity. This is why, as Derrida often underlined it, the question of "judeity" remained for him an irreducible source that needed to be both guarded and safeguarded as well as that which must not, in order to honor this guard and safeguard, be reduced to a simple affirmation. "Judeity" must remain both here and there, close and afar. It must remain undeterminably undecided, must be inherently *aporetical* and thus always command a "double bind" between the possible and the impossible affirmation of "being a Jew." In this sense, "judeity" meant, for Derrida, at once being "the last and the least of the Jews,"[3] that is, radically exposed to the unending, ambiguous, and undetermined "logic" of living the *most* and the *least* faithful Judaism.[4]

This unending, ambiguous, and undetermined "logic" is not reducible to any type of dialectical comprehension nor to any reconciliation of the difference it propagates, reiterates, and deploys. For this "superlative logic" is not one of simple contradiction. It *exappropriates* all and any form by which one can determine an identity as such (be it cultural, political, religious, etc.) in that it engages a *supplement* grafting each affirmation or proposition by an ungraspable and unforeseen *excess* of meaning derailing and provoking, within the very possibility of affirming or proposing, an uncontrollable increment of *otherness* incessantly extracting and retracting itself from the horizon of any possible hermeneutic of comprehension. Derrida explained and deployed this superlative logic in a 1990 interview with

Elisabeth Weber, published in a volume of collected discussions titled *Questions au Judaïsme*.[5] In this interview, Derrida's claim, "I am the last of the Jews," can and must be understood *both* as "I am the least Jewish and thus I am a bad Jew" as well as "I am the end of Judaism, that is, the death of Judaism that is also its only chance of survival, the last who can say it; the others don't deserve to say it, they've forfeited the right, because to say 'I am a Jew' one should perhaps say how hard it is to say 'I am a Jew.'" A little further on, he acknowledged that "in everything I may do or say, there is a 'Of course, I am a Jew!' or 'Of course, I am not a Jew' . . . which is a way of living simultaneously the condition of the Jew." Hence for Derrida, to be divided and ultimately exiled from Judaism is, today, the very nature of Judaism itself: "[T]he more one says 'My identity consists of not being identical with myself, of being alien, concongruent with myself,' etc., the more Jewish one is." It is thus "possible to say . . . the less one is a Jew, the more one is a Jew." This is why Derrida can hold that "those Jews who proclaim an actual circumcision, a Jewish name, Jewish descent, Jewish soil, Jewish sun, etc., are not by definition better placed than others to speak on behalf of Judaism. . . . There is 'Of course I am a Jew' and 'Of course, I am not a Jew' . . . both together, that is the condition of the Jew."

In this manner, Derrida reveals at the heart of Judaism, of being-Jewish, a "superlative logic" and an incessant "supplement" of otherness in "judeity" itself. To name this movement, Derrida often had recourse to the figure of the "marrano":[6] "the least is the most, the least is the paradoxical condition of the most, a certain experience of perjury is the painful and originary enduring of faithfulness."[7] And Derrida pursues the *exemplarity* of this superlative logic at work in and through the aporia of "judeity" by insisting on its orientation to think always "more than one" "judeity," a "faithfulness to more than one": "the theme of perjury is among those to which I have stayed the most faithful, and here I would have to speak . . . [of a] faithfulness to more than one remaining this impossible and necessary chance that one would have to be 'worthy of inheriting.'"[8] This "faithfulness to more than one," for Derrida, seals and marks that all affirmations are haunted by innumerable references (languages, histories, cultures, places, etc.) that cannot be subsumed under one determination or fused into one comprehension. They incessantly export themselves from any ground that could determine what they signify. This export beyond all or any possibility of grounding, however, far from simply rendering affirmations meaningless, reinforces and maximizes what they affirm—in truth, *all* affirmations become the safeguard of a perpetually reiterated *difference*, whereby "what is said" is instantly inhabited by *other* yet unsaid (ultimately unsayable) propositions and whereby history as such becomes the incessant deployment of infinite traces of irreconcilable and irreducible plural and multiple meanings. Derrida's "judeity" is to be thought through this infinite deployment of irreconcilable and irreducible traces of plural and multiple meanings. And not only because "judeity"—its history, its thought, its culture, its languages, and so on—always recalls its inherently diverse multiplicity but also because "judeity" is always and already thought as an *event to come*, as that which incessantly orients one's own identity toward an unforeseen *other*, toward *another yet unthought and always unpredictable future* than the one that could define it. Derrida names this "quality" of "judeity" a "responsibility *without* limits" or a "hyper-ethical, hyper-political, hyper-philosophical," "*calling*": "I speak to myself, then, I address to myself an apostrophe that seems to come to me from the site of a responsibility without limits, that is to say hyper-ethical, hyper-political, hyper-philosophical, a responsibility the ferment of which—'you understood it immediately,' I said to myself—burns at the most irredentist core of what calls itself 'jew.'"[9]

Born in Algeria as a French national due to the Crémieux decree,[10] Derrida was, along with his entire family, stripped of his French nationality in 1940 in accordance with the anti-Jewish measures implemented by the Vichy collaborationist government. Consequently, in 1941, Derrida was excluded from the French Lycée of Algiers, and had to attend the Ben Aknoun Lycée, run by the Jewish community, for two academic years. He returned to the French educational system in 1944 after the liberation of France and the abolition of anti-Jewish laws implemented by the French transitory government. Losing his French nationality in 1940 in what could only be perceived as an aleatory event had a profound and lasting traumatic effect on Derrida's thought. As he stated on many occasions subsequently, it was through this experience that he was first confronted with institutional antisemitism. But, and inevitably linked to this confrontation with antisemitism, it was also in being deprived of his nationality and his citizenship that the young Derrida felt what he would later think of as the "expropriation of identity." Through this experience the young Derrida understood all or any affirmation that could pretend to define and fixate an authentic identity as purely arbitrary. Being cast out of his national identity and thus forced to enroll in a Jewish community institution—an unhappy experience, by his own avowal—provoked in him a strong suspicion toward any or all forms of nationalism or/and communitarianism. Neither able to fully recognize himself as a French national, nor entirely comfortable with his Jewish religious distinctiveness, Derrida would, early in his life, reflect on the *impossibility* of asserting one's own self-identity.[11] Thus, already at a young age he would experience what he later coined as the differentiated traces of multiple identities within one's own subjectivity. Of course, it would be misguiding to affirm that the core of what Derrida would later call "deconstruction" is entirely defined through this experience. However, one can justifiably claim that through this experience, Derrida's thought was undoubtedly shaped to assert that one's own identity—be it political, religious, linguistic, cultural, or other—can only come to mind as an unpredictable and unforeseeable *event* whose origin is never as such knowable, fixed, or fixated, nor is it ever determinable as such.

The question that needs to be posed here could be formulated in this manner: is Derrida a "Jewish thinker" and, if so, in which manner? And furthermore, on which grounds and according to which justifications can one affirm this claim? Or, on the contrary, is this appellation entirely inappropriate for the thinker of "deconstruction," that is, for the thinker who persistently and incessantly showed the *impossibility* of categorically naming and determining the source, and consequently the resolute identity, of one's thinking and writing?

It is often said in scholarly publications that Derrida is a "Jewish thinker." Many notable interpreters of his philosophy have asserted this thesis. Often these interpreters take the necessary precautions by claiming a "convergence" with Jewish thought or even Jewish mysticism rather than asserting a direct "influence." These precautions are in truth necessary—Derrida has stated, more than once, both orally and textually, that Judaism, and consequently Jewish thought and religion, remained foreign to him. Born of Jewish parents, Derrida was not brought up in an observant Jewish family. His knowledge of Jewish traditions, culture, history, and religious practices was, in truth, minimal. As a young man growing up in French-ruled Algeria, as he wrote in his 1990 essay *Monolinguism of the Other: The Prosthesis of the Origin*: "the inspiration of Jewish culture seemed to succumb to an *asphyxia*; a state of apparent death, a ceasing of respiration, a fainting fit, a cessation of pulse."[12] As an adult as well, he was unable to learn the Hebrew language (despite often having attempted to do so) and carried a deep ignorance of Jewish traditional texts.

Although this question needs to be posed from the outset, it remains, for Derrida, *not yet* properly formulated. The binary form of its formulation testifies that the very question is presupposing unspecified, unexamined, and unclear positions and thus that it is unable to honor its own-most orientation and what it seeks to deploy or reveal. It would, of course, be inaccurate to label this question "false." But nonetheless, according to Derrida, the binary form of this question is structurally determined by what could be called a "teleology of the question," that is, a poised and assured reflexive movement stretching from the question to its resolution and in which the question has already composed the contours of its resolution as much as the resolution confirmed the expected orientation of the question. The question and its resolution is structured by the necessity to circumscribe within a definite meaning the "essence" of what is questioned, and, by this prestructured necessity, is only emptying that which it pretends to unravel. The very modality of this question is structured by an intentional *logic* of signification that voids it from that which it seeks to expound. For Derrida, hence, the very modality of this question is determining a set of fixated rules by which only what is predetermined by it can satisfactorily offer a meaningful resolution. Fundamentally, thus, this question is essentially shaped by an ontological presupposition—it seeks to resolutely define the source, the ground, the origin of one's, here Derrida's, philosophical writing. It seeks to answer the "*what is . . .*" of Derrida's philosophy. And in this sense, it seeks to explicate the clear and certain "truth" of Derrida's philosophical project and orientation. For this question is entirely structured by an "either/or" presupposition aiming at determining an unquestionable identification: *either* Derrida is a Jewish thinker *or* contrarily he is not a Jewish thinker. In this sense, the very binary structure of this alternative voids precisely that which the question nonetheless pretends to expound. However, for Derrida, the question of "identity," and a fortiori of *his* "judeity," *cannot* be settled by such a binary alternative. Wholly otherwise than within the binary form of this alternative, Derrida insists on the *impossibility* to resolutely confirm nor absolutely inform an identity as such. Why? Because this binary structure necessarily engages, through its very formulation, an *exclusion* and thus a *reduction*. It *excludes* and *reduces* other yet *unthought* possibilities. The question of "identity" requires, in this manner, a *wholly other writing*, a *writing* that is already open to the infinite and ungraspable multiplicities of difference working through all assertions of identity. Consequently, Derrida's writing incessantly searches for this *wholly other writing*, one that never reduces the plurality of differences and that never asserts one specific source or identifiable origin of one's own-most identifiable identity. Which means: a *wholly other writing* actively testifying, without reducing to any sole affirmation, the plurality and multiplicity of "judeities" working through *his* "judeity." This *writing* is thus capable of piercing through the binary, "either/or" structure of the question and where are "traced" without exclusion and reduction the infinitely demultiplied and irresolute, unthought, and undetermined possibilities of *being* Jewish.

The question needs thus to be *entirely* reformulated. It requires to open itself *beyond* itself. It needs thus to open itself toward the infinite and irresolute multiplicities of "judeities"—those precisely that can never be contained in that which pretends to fix and fixate them. In this sense, the question that must be formulated is as such *impossible* to phrase, for it demands to question that which remains always retracted and incessantly distances itself from any possibility to seize or grasp it, to aim or comprehend it. As we have seen, all forms of questioning already, according to Derrida, categorize and determine an intention or a meaning, and thus reduce the innumerable traces of that which is questioned. In this particular case, it reduces the infinite, innumerable traces of "judeities" into one definite concept. This idea, by which is refused all possibility to name, to categorize, to define that which is sought, echoes a kabbalistic idea to which Derrida will return, in his 1987 commentary on Scholem and Rosenzweig's correspondence on the future of the Hebrew language, titled *The Eyes of Language: The Abyss and the Volcano*.[13] In Derrida's words:

> There is a power of language, therefore, at once a *dynamis*, an enveloped virtuality, a potentiality that can be brought or not to actuality; it is hidden, buried, dormant. This potentiality is also a power [*Macht*], a particular efficacy that acts on its own, in a quasi-autonomous manner without the initiative and beyond the control of speaking subjects. Scholem will not cease to develop this theme in his works on the name of God, Jewish mysticism, and above all on the Kabbalah. This is indeed an explicit motif in certain trends of the Kabbalah. The magical power of the name produces effects said to be real and over which we are not in command. The name hidden in its potency possesses a power of manifestation and of occultation, of revelation and encrypting [*crypte*]. What does it hide? Precisely the abyss that is enclosed within it. To open a name is to find in it not something but rather something like an abyss, the abyss as the thing itself. Faced with this power, once we have awakened it, we must recognize our impotence. The name is transcendent and more powerful than we are.[14]

The idea by which language itself is structured echoes here kabbalistic thought, and most particularly the ideas of the *Eyn-Sof* and of the *Tzimtzum*, the "In-finity" and the "originary retraction" of God through which is given the world (and the world is always equated with the word and the text). Derrida's approach of language echoes these kabbalistic ideas, for these mark the impossibility for a name, or a concept, to subsume and envelop that which is named or conceptualized. Derrida's entire philosophical writing revolves around this claim, kabbalistic in nature: a name produces unknown and unpredictable effects in that it names *nothing per se* at the very moment it is naming. And hence there is *no* transcendental "signified" but only an "abyss," that is, an originary creative absence. In this sense, to name is thereby *impossibilized through its possibility*. Derrida's own-most "judeity" remains here, and through this impossibility to name it as such, intimately *secret*. And furthermore, this secrecy is sealed and preserved, kept and in safekeeping, maintained as such and as "judeity" itself by the structural impossibility to ever name it as such. Derrida's "judeity" remains thus impossible to name *and* impossible not to name: a pure secret in that it is at the same time "named" *and* "not named." In this sense, for Derrida, what remains secret is therefore not something hidden away from view or smothered, repressed, or restrained; it is absolutely exposed *and* through this exposition absolutely concealed. For the source of its exposition remains impossible to determine per se. It is thus exposed to the point where its very exposition obliterates its exposition. It is in this manner that Derrida claims in *The Dissemination* that concealment is the condition of possibility *and* impossibility of presentation, explaining it in the following terms: "The disappearance of the truth as presence, the withdrawal of the present origin of presence, is the condition of all [manifestation of] truth. Nontruth is truth. Nonpresence is presence. *Differánce*, the disappearance of any originary presence, is *at once* the condition of possibility *and* the condition of impossibility of truth."[15]

This movement by which the possibility of naming is voided by inscribing within it an irreducible impossibility, and thus by revealing in which manner possibility itself exhausts and negates that which it actualizes, is a profound "emptying out" of the traditional philosophical concept of "truth.". For Derrida, the assuredness and sovereignty of the concept of "truth" is infinitely deconstructible. This infinite deconstruction of the philosophical determination of "truth" is profoundly linked to Derrida's own relation to "judeity." Why? Because it marks a radical suspicion in regards to *all* forms of definite, decisive, resolute affirmations and furthermore puts into question the very justificatory power associated with affirmative judgments or claims. What Derrida inscribes thus is a perpetual and incessant *questioning* of affirmations by engaging a radical *doubt* of all possible resolution and justification of any affirmative power. The perpetuation of the *question* and the reiteration of *doubt* is thus a task that, through *writing*, incessantly calls for thought to open and liberate itself from all or any predetermined significations. What is most relevant however in this deconstructive engagement of infinite questioning and suspicion is the confrontation Derrida establishes between Hegel, the philosopher of the Totality of speculative knowledge in the dialectical system of Absolute Truth, *and* the figure of the Jew, understood as the bearer of an *otherness* irreducible to the dialectical logic. But instead of simply opposing Hegel's philosophical totality—understanding all too well that an opposition to the dialectical system of absolute Truth was inherently untenable and would only advance, serve, and pursue the totalizing grasp of this very system—Derrida seeks, within Hegel's writing, that which unpredictably and undecidedly performs an entirely *other* effect than the one Hegel had set out to accomplish. This "deconstructive questioning and suspicion" becomes thus a "deconstructive dismantling" of philosophical systems and their pretension to comprehend the "truth as the whole of all that is," which seeks to reveal how philosophical writing itself falls prey to an inherent, unsurpassable, and irreducible "double-bind" capable of opening it, against itself, to a wholly *other* thought. Working at once *within* and *beyond* philosophical thinking, this wholly *other* thought is labeled by Derrida an "event."

The "event" is not outside the deployment of Hegel's system. Nor is it exterior to philosophical writing and the method that assures and determines its essence in the deployment of its inherent "truth." Rather, Derrida marks the "event" as the point by which Hegel's system, and thus all philosophical writing as such, exhausts itself in its own development.[16] Certainly, there is a strong Nietzschean influence in this reading of Hegel's systematic philosophy. However, the figure Derrida sees as bearing and deploying the "event," the figure thus that at once dismantles and opens to a wholly *other* source of meaning than the speculative comprehension of "Truth as the whole," is that of the Jew. It is most particularly in *Glas* where Derrida marks this figure as both *within* Hegel's system and already piercing *beyond* it.[17] To do so, of course, Derrida rereads Hegel's interpretation of Judaism—an interpretation that is heavily marked by an anti-Judaic Christian presupposition. Following both the letter and the style of Hegel's *The Spirit of Christianity and Its Fate*, Derrida under-mines the Hegelian negation of Judaism to reveal in which manner Judaism escapes the grasp of the Hegelian totality. This escape is however not a simple evasion out of the Hegelian totality. Rather Judaism escapes the Hegelian totality by projecting it in a radical and inescapable, for it is untenable, "double-bind." Ultimately, Derrida demonstrates how the negation of Judaism called for by Hegel is both *necessary* in the affirmation of the entire Hegelian edifice and *impossible* to perform by that very construction. Judaism is thus at once necessary and impossible. And thus Judaism exemplifies the point where Hegel's philosophy is brought by its own affirmation to a paradoxical aporia: the negation of Judaism is that which both engages *and* voids the Hegelian speculative totality of absolute meaning. The key point, how-ever, of Derrida's rereading of Hegel is not only to show in which manner Hegel's philosophical construction of totality, while negating Judaism, ultimately requires it, demands it, and needs it but also that Judaism itself, by the paradoxical aporia it inflicts on Hegel's system, pierces through it and opens it toward an entirely *other* "logic" than the one culminating in the assertion of philosophical "truth" as absolute knowledge. This is an entirely *other* "logic" that does not privilege the affirmation of "self-identity" nor the counteraffirmation of the "difference of alterity," nor their dialectical reconciliation, but rather breaks out toward the incessant reiteration of an *undecidability* between "identity" and "difference," between the "self" and the "other"—an undecidability beyond any or all dialectical reconciliation. This *other* "logic" is not riveted to the idea of expounding the culminating reconciliation of a truth capable of merging opposites but rather aims at thinking the "event" of a "justice" *preceding* the philosophical essence, deployment, and development of an all encompassing and reconciling "truth."

Derrida's rereading of Hegel is, in this manner, oriented by a *wholly other idea* than the one proper to the Jena philosopher. As we have just seen, Hegel, for Der-rida, represented the thinker who made it his philosophical task to *reappropriate* difference in order to systematize and consequently identify otherness in an abso-lute self-comprehension of "all that *is*." The very modality of what Hegel calls the "speculative" is the reappropriation of difference within a reconciliatory "truth" of "all that *is*" culminating in the possibility for thought to recognize this movement as the very deployment of Spirit as History. For Derrida, this very deployment, *by having* determined the essence of "truth" and expressed its absolute actualiza-tion, prompts the question: *What is left of truth in the absolute determination of its essence?*

This question does not mean that Derrida's philosophical "deconstruction" is reducible to a simple quest for a space *beyond* the determination of "truth" ending up in a simplistic form of relativism. Quite the contrary! Indeed, Derrida always stressed this point: "deconstruction" is not a gesture that would simply consist in *stepping beyond* the essence of metaphysics by a negation of its meaning and signification, history and concepts. "Deconstruction" is not reducible to the desire of transgressing and destroying the conditions of possibility of truth in the effort to "do away" with "truth." Such a claim is the furthest away from what Derrida called "the Law of deconstruction." Rather, "the Law of deconstruction" opens to a certain *wake* of "truth," and thus to a certain "safeguard" of its "limits. However — and this is where this commandment is not expressed in any form of stable definition — Derrida insists that the "Law of deconstruction" calls for a "wake" and a "safeguard" of "truth" and its "limits" from a *wholly other event* than the one that has determined the conditions from which one can found or ground the "truth." Hence, while recognizing in the movement of "truth" the incessant surpassing of itself, the incessant quest of a further and more appropriate ground for itself, Derrida audaciously suggests that "a certain passage *beyond* truth does not seem impossible."[18] The shift is subtle. For what Derrida is here marking is that "truth" itself, by its own movement and through its own historical deployment, could *perhaps* export itself outside of itself, expropriate itself from itself and thus that it could suddenly breach its own movement and contravene its own modality to the point where, far from affirming an ultimate foundation, would be disclosed not a regime of *un*-truth but a "space" entirely *other than truth*. As if "truth" were to suddenly project itself *otherwise* than according to its own-most essence and expropriate itself where it could no longer ground its own essence. Or again: as if "truth," its own-most unity and identity, were to derail away from what it is toward an *otherness* irreducible to what its meaning or intentionality means and signifies. It is perhaps here that would lie what could be called "the *promise of deconstruction*." A *promise* inherent to the dismantling turn "truth" could *perhaps* take — that is a *promise* signaling toward that which may or could *arrive otherwise* than legitimized by the frontiers and the circumscription of "truth."

What could this *promise* mean? Where could it carry thinking? And toward which horizon — if one can still speak here of "horizon" — could it lead us? What could a *promise* that would not be determined by "truth," but by the *other than truth*, signify? Derrida signals this *promise* by a proposition that appears in the lecture "Force of Law." The proposition is retrieved from Emmanuel Levinas's *Totality and Infinity*. This *promise* emanates from a *reversal* of what the history of philosophy has repeatedly determined: the primacy of "truth." Derrida, retrieving here Levinas, inscribes a further displacement in this primacy and, contrarily to what the history of philosophy has always marked, insists on "*truth supposes justice*." What does this reversal mean? How can we understand this *turn* in the history of philosophy, which has always understood "justice" as justification and consequently as founded in the possibility of asserting a justificatory "truth"? How are we to understand a "justice" that *precedes* "truth" and is thus irreducible, extracted, and removed from justification as well as from its foundation in an expressible "truth"?

Firstly, this proposition does not to mean that "justice" serves as a novel and rediscovered foundation for "truth." "Justice" is not, for Derrida as well as for Levinas, understood as the *condition of possibility* of "truth." This *turn to justice* is not a simple *turnover* from "truth founding justice" to "justice founding truth." Rather, this proposition marks an *alteration* of the "logic of supposition and conditionality" as it voids the very possibility of stipulating a foundational ground of conditionality. Hence, this proposition marks that "justice" *precedes* "truth" without "justice" composing and constituting the foundation of "truth." For Derrida, hence, what is engaged by the proposition "*truth supposes justice*" is a *de*-foundation of "truth" into a groundless and ungrounded "event." "Justice," for Derrida, will thus be thought as a groundless and ungrounded "event" by which "truth" *occurs*, but in which "truth" does not find its stable and fixed condition of possibility. This is precisely—second point—why one ought to think "truth" as always and already *deconstructible*. Which means: "truth" is exposed to its own dismantling—a dismantling where what it asserts as its own-most essence is already expropriated beyond itself into the impossibility of affirming it as such. This *aporia* working through the "essence of truth" does not mean that there is *no possible truth* or no *possibility for truth*. Rather, it means that the very possibility of truth is *preserved*, *guarded*, and *safeguarded* by the impossibility for truth to ground itself in the fixed determination of its own-most essence. Truth in this sense, for Derrida, does not lie in a hidden structure waiting to be revealed by an act of interpretation or a hermeneutic of comprehension. Rather truth is always and already voiding the very possibility to seize or comprehend itself, ground or found itself as such. And consequently, this impossibility ought not to mean Derrida is proposing here a form of "un-accomplishment" for thinking and thus a perpetual search for truth—although this "un-accomplishement" would also be a consequence of "deconstruction." It means rather that truth is always *to come* from a *futurity* that remains already impossible to categorize or determine. For Derrida, the "un-achievement" or the "un-accomplishment" as "task" or "development" is *still* a modality of actualization and thus marks fixed determination for and of futurity. Rather, according to Derrida, what is preserved is the radical and unpredictable, irreducible, and *wholly other otherness of futurity*. This *otherness of futurity* opens toward a *differing* of temporality where what comes is always and already *other* than that which arrives. It is precisely this "paradoxality" that must be thought, according to Derrida: futurity is to come as always other than what effectively arrives or could arrive.

This "paradoxality," working at the heart of the "Law of deconstruction," marks that the history of philosophy is not *bound* by or to truth. History is not here thought as the deployment of truth. For this very history reiterates and deploys itself, according to Derrida, precisely where the order of truth is already and always suspended to an *other* than what could be named in accordance with the determination of truth. In this sense, the "Law of deconstruction" seeks for the *other* of truth that Derrida deploys by reference to what he marks as the *indeconstructibility of justice*. What is meant by this *indeconstructibility of justice*?

It marks that "truth" is *not* the primary affair of deconstruction. That is, deconstruction does not aim at revealing a unitary and fixed, determined and recognizable "truth" about a context or a text, about a situation or a factuality. Deconstruction works *otherwise* than according to the possibility of determining the conditions of possibility of "truth" as such. It seeks rather to *open* toward that which is *irreducible* to the unitary determination of "truth." That is, it seeks to perpetually undermine conditionality and the inherent limitations, fixity, mastery that conditionality imposes by incessantly thinking *before* any given and thus by always predetermining its "truth.". Deconstruction thinks thus the *undetermined unconditionality of that which is conditioned as such.*

It is from this *unconditionality*, which by definition remains unnameable, that we can approach Derrida's "judeity." A "judeity" which thus would be inherently plural and multiple because undetermined and unconditional. In this sense, Derrida incessantly marks undetermined and unconditional "judeities" irreducible to what is named "Judaism" but from which "Judaism" can also appear as such in History. In this sense, Judaism is a *given* which comes from an abyssal and unknowable "event" remaining impossible to determine as such and of which there cannot be any identifiable ground or foundation. Which means: "Judeities" always and already *other* than what is presented and actualized under the name "Judaism." And this is precisely why Derrida calls for *yet another Abraham*: "There would be *perhaps* yet another Abraham, not only he who received another name in his old age and, at ninety-nine, at the time of his circumcision, felt, by the blow of a letter, the letter *H* right in the middle of his name; not only he who, later, on Mount Moriah, was called twice by the angel, first "Abraham, Abraham", then, a second time still, from the height of the heavens, as Scripture tells us. There would be perhaps not only Abram, then Abraham, Abraham, twice."[19]

This *other* Abraham can be understood as *wholly other* than what the name Abraham has signified in Judaism (as well as in Christianity and Islam). This *other* Abraham, this Abraham always to come from a coming that has never been as such present and will never reduce itself to presence, that is and will always remain unexpected and unforeseen. It is a wholly *other* Abraham: other than any possible Abraham that is, one that *perhaps* would be impossible to name and determine, recognize or identify. An Abraham so other than any possible Abraham that it could *perhaps* never resemble any figure, nor take on any form nor any name. For this wholly other Abraham remains inherently, undecidedly, unconditionally multiple and demultiplied. He remains other to any and every possibility of even affirming itself in one collected or recollected "identity." In this sense, this wholly other unnamed and unnameable "Abraham" would and could only come as that which is *to come* or again as an impossible "event." But this impossibility of its eventuality is precisely that which it must endure to any possible and actual Abraham to come in our history. It is precisely this impossible "event" of a wholly other unnamed and unnameable Abraham that Derrida urges us to think in "thinking judeities." Certainly Derrida urges us to think within these multiple and plural "judeities" those that, in our history, have determined themselves and taken on the name Judaism as he never would recommend to not think what our history has known under the name Abraham, but also and at the same time what is urged of us (also to think what our history has named) is to carry thought beyond and before what has been and continues to be thought in order to *imagine* wholly *other* yet undetermined and unnamed "judeities," other yet undetermined and unnamed Abrahams—precisely the plural and multiple other "judeities" and other Abrahams that are as such impossible to name and determine, to circumscribe or categorize. In this sense, Derrida urges of us to think not the truth of what is or has been thought but a certain *justice* toward the infinite multiplicity and plurality of *other* yet unthought and yet unthinkable "judeities," *other* yet unthought and yet unthinkable "Abrahams" before and beyond their actualization in a determined and nameable "identity": a justice thus to the *other* "judeities" and the *other* "Abrahams" *before and beyond* what has, in our history, defined the "essence" of Judaism and the figure of Abraham.

But there is a *risk*. Derrida often marked this risk, which is also the risk of all deconstructive thinking. This risk works through and haunts this hyperbolical "justice" *beyond* and *before* truth, works through and haunts the thought of an "event" always *to come* as the plurality and multiplicity of "judeities" and "Abrahams" *beyond* and *before* the actualized historical name of Judaism and the known biblical figure of Abraham. What is involved in this risk? It is the following: the possibility that to think the plurality and multiplicity of unnamed and unrecognizable "judeities" and "Abrahams" *beyond* and *before* Judaism and Abraham could, perhaps, also mean to *think wholly otherwise than* Judaism itself and an Abraham entirely other than the one who was named as such. It could mean to think Judaism more *judaically* than it has ever been thought but it could also mean to *no longer* think Judaism. *But this risk is also the most radical chance of thinking the very possibility of Judaism.* As if to think the multiplicity and plurality of unthought and yet unknown and unknowable "judeities" was the only chance of thinking Judaism itself. For the risk is never to be dissociated from the chance. As if the question which remained *for* Derrida and *his* "judeity" was: What will be the future to come for Judaism? This question cannot succumb to any sort of teleology nor can it be solved by an either/or structure of questioning. Its undecidability haunts Judaism itself. That is, it marks always and already the impossibility for Judaism to close itself on itself and signify itself only from that which it is for itself. Which means: the multiple and plural "judeities"—and its inherent risk for Judaism—incessantly keep Judaism possible. And they incessantly keep Judaism coming—in multiple and demultiplied possibilities. This possibility is always haunted and worked by its inherent impossibility, but such is the risk of thinking Judaism—the risk to no longer think Judaism in the name of Judaism. This risk undecided as chance and this chance undecided as risk were formulated in the concentrated closing remarks of Derrida's keynote address to the Judeities conference: "That there should be yet another Abraham: here, then, is the most threatened jewish thought, but also the most vertiginously, the most intimately jewish one that I know to this day. For you have undersood me well: when I say 'the most jewish,' I also mean 'more than jewish.' Others would perhaps say 'otherwise jewish,' even 'other than jewish.'"[20]

Notes

1. The opening epigraph is from Jacques Derrida, "Abraham, the Other," in *Judeities: Questions for Jacques Derrida*, eds. Bettina Bergo, Joseph Cohen, and Raphael Zagury-Orly (New York, 2007), 4.

2. See Jean-Paul Sartre, *Anti-Semite and the Jew: An Exploration of the Etiology of Hate* (New York, 1995).

3. Derrida, "Abraham, the Other," 13. See also Jacques Derrida, "Circumfession," in Geoffrey Bennington and Jacques Derrida, *Jacques Derrida* (Chicago, 1993), 154.

4. On the ambiguity of this deconstructive "logic" and its rapport to faithfulness and unfaithfulness, see Joseph Cohen and Raphael Zagury-Orly, "A Monster of Faithfulness," in *Judeities: Questions for Jacques Derrida*, 155–74.

5. Jacques Derrida, "Un témoignage donné . . . ," in *Questions au judaïsme*, ed. Elisabeth Weber (Paris, 1996), 73.

6. Derrida, "Abraham, the Other," 13.

7. Ibid., 14.

8. Ibid.

9. Ibid., 13.

10. The *Crémieux decree*, named after Adolphe Crémieux (born in Nïmes in 1796 and died in Paris in 1880; French Minister of Justice in 1848 and from 1870–1871), was adopted in 1870 and stipulated that all Jews residing in French-ruled Algeria were authorized by law to become French citizens.

11. See Elisabeth Roudinesco, *For What Tomorrow . . . : A Dialogue with Jacques Derrida* (Palo Alto, CA, 2004). See also Derrida, "Abraham, the Other," 28.

12. Jacques Derrida, *Monolinguism of the Other: The Prosthesis of the Origin*, trans. Paul Mensah (Stanford, 1998), 53.

13. Jacques Derrida, "The Eyes of Language: The Abyss and the Volcano," in *Acts of Religion*, ed. Gil Anidjar (New York, 2002), 191–227.

14. Ibid., 226–27.

15. Jacques Derrida, "Dissemination," in *Dissemination* (Chicago, 1981), 168.

16. For a deconstructive reading of Hegel's philosophical system and speculative dialectic, see my *Le Sacrifice de Hegel* (Paris, 2007).

17. See Jacques Derrida, *Glas*, trans. J. P. Leavy and R. Rand (Lincoln, NE and London, 1986). For a deconstructive reading of Hegel's interpretation of Judaism, see also my *Le spectre juif de Hegel* (Paris, 2005).

18. Jacques Derrida, *Aporias*, trans. Thomas Dutoit (Stanford, 1993), 2.

19. Jacques Derrida, "Abraham, the Other," 34.

20. Ibid., 34–35.

41

Philip Roth (1933–)

WRITING THE AMERICAN JEWISH CENTURY

Sidra DeKoven Ezrahi

THE FICTIONS OF PHILIP ROTH DEBUTED IN THE MIDDLE OF WHAT HAS VARIOUSLY been called the "American Century" or the "Jewish Century." In profound ways they represent the amalgamation of the two—or what I prefer to call the "Jewish-inflected American self." I am defining "Jew-*ish*" in Roth's work as originating historically in the second and third postwar decades and generically in satire. He satirized the speech-intoxicated, God-saturated idiom of urban and suburban humans who happened to be Jews meeting the speech-intoxicated, God-saturated idiom of urban and suburban humans who happened not to be Jews.

The virtues of a long creative life include directional changes. Roth, who was born in 1933 and raised in Newark, New Jersey, came of age in a moment defined by a subtle shift in the American premises of modernity and by extraordinary ethnic and religious porousness. The satire that Roth perfected in the decade from 1959 to 1969 was enabled by the evolution of inventiveness and self-inventiveness as a postwar version of the ever-new enterprise that is America. At the same time, and almost obscured by the comic mode in which they were performed, his early fictions capture a unique "theological" moment in which religious sensibilities converged to unite Christians and Jews in an urban congregation. By the end of the century, however, these impulses had given way to something far more sinister and insular in Jewish culture and in American culture, a process that was, in turn, reflected in generic shifts in the late work of this writer who has been both a barometer and a beacon of his time and place.

I will not attempt to recapitulate here the myriad attempts, friendly and hostile, to define Philip Roth's Jewish project.[1] The moment is long past, and well documented, when this young writer, following on the heels of—and enabled by—Henry Roth, Delmore Schwartz, Daniel Fuchs, Saul Bellow, and Bernard Malamud, loudly announced the advent of the first generation of native-born American Jews, even as he himself balked at the label "Jewish writer." Isaac Bashevis Singer, who had had his own English debut in 1953 through Saul Bellow's masterful translations, was the poster child for what Roth was *not* doing. In an interview for *The Paris Review* in 1968, Singer both dismissed and reinforced the conundrum: "To me there are only Yiddish writers, Hebrew writers, English writers, Spanish writers.

The whole idea of a Jewish writer, or a Catholic writer, is kind of far-fetched to me. But if you forced me to admit that there is such a thing as a Jewish writer, I would say that he would have to be a man [*sic!*] really immersed in Jewishness, who knows Hebrew, Yiddish, the Talmud, the Midrash, the Hasidic literature, the Cabbala, and so forth. . . . If in addition he writes about Jews and Jewish life, perhaps then we can call him a Jewish writer, whatever language he writes in. Of course, we can also call him just a writer."[2]

The whole idea of a Jewish writer . . . is kind of far-fetched to me. Roth's readers, who came of age (and aged) along with the author and his characters, can hear him riff on that statement, wondering if "far-*fetched*" is a Yiddish word. The point is that *hearing* it that way makes it Jewish and, more important, makes it quintessentially American; the ears have it in America's chorus of accented voices. What Roth's generation lacked in Jewish literacy, they made up for in Jewish orality—and American freedoms.

What Singer does not acknowledge, although he was the beneficiary of its larger implications, is that "the American Adam" can make a virtue of not knowing "Hebrew, Yiddish, the Talmud, Midrash, the Hasidic literature, the Cabbala and so forth"; that his birthright is not bartered at the price exacted from his Eastern or Central European counterparts; and that his freewheeling pen may add a significant American shelf to the Jewish library. The reasons for this may be manifold, but they boil down to one: "only in America" is the question of identity up for grabs. And, one might add, only in America can that transaction be carried out in the comic mode.

The Newness of This New World

America has always been, at least for people of the white persuasion,[3] the country most hospitable to the fictions of self-invention—the place where invention and self-invention are foundational principles. It is also the country that most reveres the material world: facts on the ground; the surface itself, not the treasures and traces buried in its depths. Facticity rhymes with self-invention when human acts of manufacture produce things or objects that have the same ontological weight as the facts of nature.[4] The celebration of the natural and of the manufactured world in Emerson, Whitman, and Dickinson spilled into the twentieth century and into the critical realism of Theodore Dreiser, John Updike, and Joyce Carol Oates. Young Jewish writers (e.g., Bellow & Co.) were seasoning their fiction with ironic distance and wit, but it was Philip Roth who, nearly single-handedly, would nudge the fictions of "real life" into a fully realized, Jewish-inflected comic mode.

Looking back on his own career at the celebration of his eightieth birthday in Newark, New Jersey on March 19, 2013, Roth chose to recount a number of details from his life that peppered some six decades of his fiction. He told his audience:

In my defense . . . I should insert here that remembering objects as mundane as a bicycle basket was a not insignificant part of my vocation. The deal worked out for me as a novelist was that I should continuously rummage around in memory for thousands and thousands of just such things. Unlikely as it may seem, a passion for local specificity—the expansive engagement, something close to fascination,

with a seemingly familiar, even innocuous, object like a lady's kid glove or a butcher shop chicken or a gold-star flag or a Hamilton wristwatch . . . [-a passion] for the hypnotic materiality of the world one is in, is all but at the heart of the task to which every American novelist has been enjoined since Herman Melville and his whale and Mark Twain and his river: to discover the most arresting, evocative verbal depiction for every last American thing. Without strong representation of the thing—animate or inanimate—without the crucial representation of what is real, there is nothing. . . . It is from a scrupulous fidelity to the blizzard of specific data that is a personal life, it is from the force of its uncompromising particularity, from its *physicalness*, that the realistic novel, the insatiable realistic novel with its multitude of realities, derives its ruthless intimacy.[5]

In the first decades and again in the late middle decades of the twentieth century, Jewish-accented prose converged with the "scrupulous fidelity to the blizzard of specific data that is a personal life" and with the comedy of American self-invention to affirm what is also profoundly modern (in the sense of being perpetually in-the-moment): America as by definition the embodiment of "the new." In the preface to his republished classic, *The Puritan Origins of the American Self*, Sacvan Bercovitch wrote: "The newness of this New World defied, indeed reversed, the common-sense meaning of new. . . . [In other colonial histories, one finds] that New France, New Spain, and New Amsterdam were new in the sense of replica, imitation, or offspring. Even when they condemned the effects of conquest, they promoted the social structures and belief systems of the 'parent country.' [Cotton] Mather, on the contrary, describes a venture destined to supersede a corrupt Old World. . . . *His* New England opens a new stage in world history."[6]

Here Comes Everybody Jewish

It is not that the Jews in the literature we are considering do not live in an echo chamber with voices from the "parent country." But it is the people themselves, and not an inherited culture or cult, that nourish their narratives. At the turn of the twenty-first century, Roth addressed a class of Columbia University students who were reading *Operation Shylock*, which had been published in 1993. Responding to the inevitable interrogations about the autobiographical basis of his fiction, Roth positioned himself implicitly as a writer who is both rooted and cosmopolitan, though (unlike Singer) it is primarily his characters' ethnic identity—loosely defined—that roots him in the same way that, for example, Joyce's characters are rooted: "Every Jewish exigency, pain, and antagonism flows through 'Roth,'" he told the students, referring to the narrator/character who is often mistaken for the author himself. "In *Finnegan's Wake*, there is the character Humphrey C. Earwicker, who sleeps with absolutely everything flowing through his mind, and Joyce uses the initials H.C.E. as 'Here Comes Everybody.' Well, in *Operation Shylock* you have 'Here Comes Everybody Jewish.' Leon Klinghoffer. Jonathan Pollard. Menachem Begin. Meir Kahane. All these names were passing through the collective Jewish brain at the time, and I wanted to get inside the Jewish mind."[7]

One might note that a major difference between Joyce and Roth is the fluidity of identity in America as compared to Ireland, about which more below. What is common to the fictions of these two writers is the exuberant flaunting of communal norms and the price exacted for such transgressions in the public forum. David Remnick, who accompanied Roth to the Columbia classroom in preparation for a profile of the author, comments that from the beginning of his career, Roth's "project" was "much the same" as it would be in mid-career, when he wrote *Operation Shylock*: "writing about Jews."[8] When his stories began to appear in 1958–1959—first in *The Paris Review*, *The New Yorker*, and *Commentary*; then as a collection in *Goodbye, Columbus*; and, ten years later, as a strident psychoanalytic monologue in *Portnoy's Complaint* (1969)—the ethnic minority that had been granted pride of place in the postwar and post-1948 years as the culturally hungry, sharply ironic, but always morally sincere remnants of a martyred people or as valiant young nationalists fighting for their collective existence found themselves exposed as humans with bodies, erotic fantasies, lots of appetite, and the dirty laundry that is the physical evidence of appetite. Just when that cohort of Jewish writers had succeeded in creating what was coming to be regarded as a compelling "regional" literature, defining the cultural landscape alongside the fictions of the American South and the cities of America's Midwest and Eastern Seaboard,[9] just when Jewish intellectuals like Irving Howe, Alfred Kazin, the Trillings, and the Bells were engaged in earnest conversation about the nature and permeability of the boundaries of Western Civilization, their fine intelligence going so far as to embrace the naughty shenanigans of the young author of *Goodbye Columbus*, Roth would put the whole project at risk by publishing his most transgressive novel— about which more later.

But the view from the end of the last century affords Remnick a longer perspective upon a career that outlived all that, shifted gears several times, and was, in retrospect, licensed by many ambient voices—Faulkner's as well as Bellow's, the cognoscenti at the University of Chicago as well as the housewives and Hebrew school tyrants in Newark, New Jersey. But most importantly, Roth exploited the permission granted his own generation, defined by Remnick as "steeped in America, in its freedom and talk, its energies and superabundance."[10]

The Talking and the Shouting

> There is a certain place where . . . every window is a mother's mouth bidding the street shut up, go skate somewhere else, come home. My voice is the loudest.
>
> —GRACE PALEY, "THE LOUDEST VOICE," 1959

The license was in the first place verbal (and here again the parallels with Irish orality and transgressive speech are inviting) and in the second, comic—what Remnick calls "verbal robustness, people talking, being terrifically funny."[11] In an earlier interview, with Hermione Lee (1984), Roth referred to Nathan Zuckerman, the narrator/character who appears in many of Roth's fictions and has often been identified as the author's alter ego. "Zuckerman's struggle with Jewishness and Jewish criticism is seen in the context of his comical career as an American writer, ousted by his family, alienated from his fans, and finally at odds with his own nerve endings," Roth said. "The Jewish quality of books like mine doesn't really reside in their subject matter. . . . It's a kind of sensibility that makes, say, *The Anatomy*

Lesson Jewish, if anything does: the nervousness, the excitability, the arguing, the dramatizing, the indignation, the obsessiveness, the touchiness, the playacting—above all the *talking*. The talking and the shouting. . . . The book won't shut up . . . won't leave you alone. I knew what I was doing when I broke Zuckerman's jaw. For a Jew a broken jaw is a terrible tragedy. It was to avoid this that so many of us went into teaching rather than prizefighting." [12]

Roth was not alone in this jawspace, but neither was there much of a crowd—in fact, there was only one other fiction writer. Perhaps because she was a woman breaking into the men's club, Grace Paley's voice was louder and more worried and her ears sharper and more easily distracted. Born in 1922 and raised in the Bronx, Paley claims her "other ear" was recruited "to remember the street language and the home language with its Russian and Yiddish accents, a language my early characters knew well, the only language I spoke. Two ears, one for literature, one for home, are useful for writers."[13]

Paley's medium was domestic comedy that would be translated by the alchemy of kitchen and conscience into political action—while raising the children and divorcing or recombining with their fathers. Roth's comedy was evolving into something else: social satire with speech itself as its medium, a hyperbolized transcription of ambient speech that collided or coincided with voices from the radio and from the library. Many of Roth's fictions are narrated by "talking heads" whose own stories are more or less central to the development of the narrative. There hardly exists a narrative authority in Roth's work outside of the heads—and speech patterns—of his characters. Speech is the primary trace of identities that were otherwise fully negotiable.

Acts of Impersonation

"I am an American, Newark born," is the way a Philip Roth character might have paraphrased Augie March's inaugural leap onto the literary stage in the eponymous novel by Saul Bellow. But these authors, like most of their characters, are also Americans, *Jewish*-born. What multiple particularities enabled and what Roth realized to the fullest was not a clash of identities but an amalgamation of cultural possibilities. American identity emerged in the second and third postwar decades as a meeting ground of cultures that were themselves in flux—although the process began, of course, well before World War II. "America, I love you. If I didn't hear an accent every day, I'd think I was in a foreign country," says Molly Goldberg in her own Yiddish-and-Bronx-accented speech, which was amplified from 1929 to 1946 through hundreds of thousands of Philcos in homes like that of Herman and Bess Roth.[14] When Augie appeared in 1953, paving the way for Eli (the fanatic), Neil (the romantic), Sgt. Nathan (defender of the faith), Ozzie (the theologian), Epstein (the philanderer), and finally Alex (the neurotic),[15] American identity was already being performed in fiction as a series of hyphenated but nonessentialized possibilities: Jewish-American, Italian-American, Chinese-American, and Spanish-American. (African-American has taken longer, and indelible traces of the ongoing struggle are exposed in Roth's late novel, *The Human Stain*, which preceded Barack Obama's election by only eight years.[16]) But this process depended on two other forces that had converged in the years of Roth's apprenticeship: the reaffirmation of an American landscape that had been deeply affected, but not physically devastated, by World War II, and the reclamation of an heirloomed Jewish comedy.

If the first generation of postwar Jewish writers had produced a torrent of morally earnest cultural gestures, tinged by European melancholy or pathos as well as redemptive American empathy (Edward Lewis Wallant, *The Pawnbroker*; Malamud, *The Assistant*) and neurotic Jewish energy (Bellow, *The Victim*), the task for the next generation of ambitious, self-ironizing Jewish writers was not only to make their parents laugh again—at the world and at themselves—but to recover inherited comic impulses from under the ruins of the European Jewish catastrophe. They didn't have far to dig to find the sources that had fed Jewish comedy in America in the first half of the century: before Charlie Chaplin had been inducted into the honorary Jewish Hall of Fame by Hannah Arendt,[17] even before the Marx Brothers and the Borscht Belt comedians, Sholem Aleichem had arrived in New York in 1914 and transformed an Ashkenazi Jewish tic into an American muscle. Taking the practice that he had perfected in his European fictions of affirming a God-superintended universe—teleology as comedy—by turning history on its head, Sholem Aleichem authorized a particularly American brand of Yiddish humor that celebrates the surface world. In the novel *Motl Pesi dem Khazns* (Motl the Cantor's son), published serially between 1907 and the author's death in 1916, American technology—the subway, the elevated—and economic promise—from pushcart to department store—replace the *luft gesheftn* of the shtetl. Jewish comedy thus moves from an act of faith and wishful thinking to a celebration of the created and the manufactured universe. And, anticipating and enabling his successors, Sholem Aleichem performed this celebration mainly through speech acts.[18]

Starting over for these Jews meant that a lack of familiarity with the abandoned culture was not, then, a liability, despite the nostalgia that would come later. Unlike the immigrant generation, who had actively to jettison their cultural baggage to embrace this new identity, their children were raised in this amnesiac condition defined as an invitation to a costume ball. Invention and inventiveness stretch in the comic mode to radical acts of mimicry and impersonation. America is the place where, as Motl, the eternal nine-year-old, says, "every day is Purim."

No one took advantage of the comic opportunities of self-invention, of unencumbered encounters with the ambient cultures, more than Philip Roth. Even when Nathan Zuckerman is the anchor, his longevity embraces many twentieth-century Jewish incarnations, among them the young writer serving his apprenticeship at the feet of a Great Arbiter of the Great Books and falling in love with the woman he presumes to be the Greatest Martyr of all (Jewish) time, Anne Frank (*The Ghost Writer*); the brash young writer nearly crushed by the titans of literary criticism (*The Anatomy Lesson*); and the "secret sharer" and recorder of another man's drama (*The Human Stain*). Finally, in *Exit, Ghost*, Nathan, himself aged and physically compromised, is reunited, briefly, with his "Anne Frank" (Amy Bellette) who is even more heir than he to the depredations of the flesh. There are other characters who tip over from impersonators into impostors—in the comic mode ("Philip Roth" in *Operation Shylock*) and in the tragic mode (Coleman Silk in *The Human Stain*). "My hero," the Real Philip Roth explains to Hermione Lee, "has to be in a state of vivid transformation or radical displacement. 'I am not what I am—I am, if anything, what I am not.' . . . Nathan Zuckerman is an act. It's all the art of impersonation, isn't it? That's the fundamental novelistic gift. . . . Concocting a half-imaginary existence out of the actual drama of my life *is* my life. There has to be some pleasure in this job, and that's it. To go around in disguise."[19]

The Urban Congregation

As it turned out, something even bigger was at stake than the pleasure of disguise: in 1959, Philip Roth's and Grace Paley's inaugural stories transformed the American theater of impersonation into an urban congregation. In "The Conversion of the Jews" and "The Loudest Voice," respectively, they brought the conciliatory tools of comedy into sacramental space. Both narratives convert elementary schools into cathedrals where new inclusive sacraments are forged of old and mutually exclusive materials. And both focus on the studied naiveté of the child whose faith surpasseth dogma.

In Paley's story, the venue is a red brick public school, the official religion Protestant, and the dominant "demographic" Jewish. Shirley Abramowitch, who has the Loudest Voice, recites Jesus's lines in the school Christmas pageant in which the Savior, Marty Groff, "wearing his father's prayer shawl," is strung up to die but wrenches free, supplanting the sacrificial-redemptive narrative of Crucifixion and Resurrection with a comic narrative of Christian-Jewish reconciliation.[20]

In Roth's "The Conversion of the Jews," it is Hebrew school that serves as the unlikely venue for the sacramental act. Rabbi Binder tries to inculcate Jewish skepticism of Christian dogma in the minds of pre–Bar Mitzvah boys who would rather be outside playing baseball. One little boy, however, is listening, and when the Rabbi emphasizes the absurdity of Immaculate Conception, Ozzie Freedman objects: "If God could create the heaven and the earth in six days, and He could *pick* the six days He wanted right out of nowhere, why couldn't He let a woman have a baby without having intercourse?" Rabbi Binder accuses Ozzie of impertinence and summons his mother to a meeting. At the next class, Ozzie tries to coax Rabbi Binder's theology into a more capacious place: " 'Then, Itz,' " he tells his friend, " 'then he starts talking in that voice like a statue, real slow and deep, and he says that I better think over what I said about the Lord . . .' Ozzie leaned his body towards Itzie. 'Itz, I thought it over for a solid hour, and now I'm convinced God could do it.' " Finally, when all his scholastic strategies have been exhausted, Ozzie shouts at Rabbi Binder: "You don't know anything about God!" for which he gets a smack on the face—and runs up to the roof of the school. At the *denouement*, when all the congregation—his fellow Hebrew school pupils, Rabbi Binder, Yakov Blotnik, the janitor with the mark of Auschwitz on his arm, his mother and the municipal fire department—are assembled in the courtyard below to see if he will jump; when his mother shouts up to him, "Ozzie, come down. Don't be a martyr, my baby" and the pupils chant in chorus, "be a Martin, be a Martin!" Ozzie forces everyone to their knees. He has them proclaim the following doxology: "Tell me you believe God can do Anything." Then: "Tell me you believe God can make a child without intercourse." And finally, the catechism: "You should never hit anybody about God."[21]

The "Conversion of the Jews," with its rich resonances from Jewish lore, Christian dogma, English poetry and, most significantly, the accommodative legacy of *Conversos* who were among the first Jewish settlers in New Amsterdam,[22] becomes, like "The Loudest Voice," a tale less of conversion than of *convergence* of Jews and Christians, transforming the supersessionist narrative into one of comic amalgamation. When she gets ready for bed, after successfully declaiming her lines in the school pageant, Shirley Abramowitch gets down on her knees. "I made a little church of my hands, and said, 'Hear O Israel . . .' Then I called out in Yiddish, 'Please, goodnight, good night. Ssh.' My father said, 'Ssh yourself,' and slammed the kitchen door. I was happy. I fell asleep at once. I had prayed for everybody: my talking family, cousins far away, passersby, and all the lonesome Christians. I expected to be heard. My voice was certainly the loudest."[23]

The urban congregation that Roth and Paley forged out of the good materials of midcentury America[24] will be realized in the streets a few years later when Abraham Joshua Heschel and Martin Luther King join hands and march on Selma in the name of human freedom and dignity.

A Moment of Infinite Possibility

Sacramental moments matter, but they do not last. What happened next in the American Jewish Century as written by Philip Roth was that the comedy of impersonation and acts of spiritual convergence tipped over into full-fledged satire. In order for satire to work, characters have to be sufficiently grounded in their identities to be distillable as familiar stereotypes. This begins in the novella *Goodbye, Columbus*, where Neil Klugman and the Patimkin family, whose daughter Neil is courting, like their tennis courts and their well-stocked refrigerator (sans herring in cream sauce!), are caricatured versions of icons well-planted on the landscape of nouveau riche America. As are the lawn rocks that suburban Jews paint pink in "Eli the Fanatic," or the kvetchy communitarians who expect tribal favors in "Defender of the Faith." But these are nothing compared to the satiric bite of *Portnoy's Complaint*— which ostensibly parodies the Jewish family and Jewish angst but whose real work, as Bernard Avishai argues, is the parody of the psychoanalytic conversation itself— and whose real object of satire is the analysand Alexander Portnoy himself.[25] "As a result of his fearlessness and bravado," Remnick writes, "of his aversion to a pious literature of virtue and victimhood, [Roth's] public reputation began with scandal, distortion, and a wound. It was a modest scandal at first, and then became the sort of full-scale storm that may well be looked back upon as a curious relic."[26]

Most of the studies of Roth's fiction over the years have indeed focused on the *scandal, distortion, and wound* that the author inflicted on his readers and that they in turn inflicted on him through their gatekeepers: rabbis, of course, mothers and women generally,[27] but also some of his most respected colleagues and former supporters, chief among them Irving Howe.

Satire, which was not widely performed in twentieth-century America, is the very thing that Howe, in his devastating "reconsideration" of Roth's work in *Commentary* in 1972, insisted Roth was not doing. "The nature of good satire," Howe wrote, is "not at all to free oneself from the obligation to social accuracy. . . . If it can be shown that the targets of the satirist are *imprecisely located* or that he is *shooting wild*, the consequence may be more damaging than if the same were shown for a conventional realist" (emphasis mine). (It is highly unlikely that Howe, who holds Jonathan Swift up as the satirist who defines the genre, can have forgotten "A Modest Proposal," which shot more wildly and was more imprecisely located than the most acerbic of Roth's stories.) Howe then goes on to argue that Roth falls short even within the purview of Jewish satire, "a substantial tradition extending in Yiddish from Mendele to Isaac Bashevis Singer and in English from Abraham Cahan to Malamud and Bellow."[28] This is a rather unfortunate list of largely lugubrious writers who occasionally venture into the comic mode; the only one who really qualifies as a satirist is Mendele Mokher Seforim (S. Y. Abramovitch), whose biting satires compete with Roth's not only for their sting but also for the fury they evoked in their readers.

The likelihood that Aristophanes was taken to court, despite his wealthy patrons, and the documented evidence that Swift was roundly attacked on many occasions add some perspective to the symbolic gallows on which Roth was strung up in numerous journals and synagogues in America. The most famous opprobrium of *Portnoy's Complaint* came from Jerusalem, where Gershom Scholem compared the novel to the Nazi propaganda machine that would be eventually used (again!) as "testimony" in a worldwide trial of the Jews.[29] The second was Howe's: "The cruelest thing anyone can do with *Portnoy's Complaint* is to read it twice," he writes in "Roth Reconsidered"; "the controlling tone of the book is a shriek of excess, the jokester's manic wail." But perhaps the most telling sentence in Howe's screed was this: "Some literary people . . . could almost be heard breathing a sigh of relief, for it signaled an end to philo-Semitism in American culture, one no longer had to listen to all that talk about Jewish morality, Jewish endurance, Jewish wisdom, Jewish families. Here was Philip Roth himself, who even seemed to know Yiddish, confirming what had always been suspected about those immigrant Jews but had recently not been tactful to say."[30] Howe here ignores all the young Jewish readers and "literary people" who, finally given the license to laugh again—at the world and at themselves—were breathing the deepest sigh of relief.

As if to nail home the point that those who miss the satire may end up in the bull's-eye, Roth's response came in the form of a thinly disguised roman à clef in which Nathan Zuckerman is a young writer who has just published the novel *Carnovsky* and Milton Appel is the famous critic who, in the journal *Inquiry* (!), writes the "unkindest review of all." Zuckerman, by turns devastated and furious, retorts: "He doesn't find me funny . . . well, I never set myself up as Elie Wiesel." Impulsively calling his nemesis on the phone, Zuckerman says to him: "I'm a 'case,' I have a 'career,' you of course have a calling. Oh, I'll tell you your calling—President of the Rabbinical Society for the Suppression of Laughter in the Interest of Loftier Values! Minister of the Official Style for Jewish Books Other than the Manual for Circumcision."[31]

Roth's satiric writing continued well into the next decades. Between the 1960s and the 1990s, through *The Counterlife* (1986) and *Operation Shylock* (1993), Roth became America's—and American Jews'—most trenchant satirist. He also, willy-nilly, led the postmodern conundrum over fact and fiction by providing mischievously contrived counterlives and counterhistories.[32] Yet something changed profoundly as the writer matured. Clifton Spargo goes so far as to claim that Roth actually internalized Howe's criticism and reinvented himself as a writer of realistic fiction and, in his late narratives, as "perhaps the most accomplished American novelist of his generation."[33] And he has won all the prizes—including the National Book Award (1960, 1995), the Pulitzer Prize (1997), and the Man Booker Prize (2011)[34]—that reward such prominence. I would go even further to argue that after Roth's satire had done its work, liberating something deep in the American Jewish psyche that desperately needed to be liberated, he was indeed free to move into other realms and modes of American fiction. Although satiric elements persist in all his late novels, the vision has veered toward the tragic and even beyond. But it was the country itself that was moving, along with its Jews, away from that magical moment of infinite possibility.

Tragedy and Beyond

By the end of the century, the comedy had run its course. The acts of impersonation that each of Roth's early characters had engaged in were indeed masquerades after which, presumably, they would return to (a more complex version of) who they were: Eli trying on the clothes of the Orthodox Holocaust survivor in Woodenton is not about to join a yeshiva in Boro Park ("Eli the Fanatic"); Ozzie chanting the doxology of the Virgin Birth is not about to take communion; even Alex will, we must believe, walk out of his analyst's office and reclaim his battered but responsible adult identity as Assistant Commissioner of Human Opportunity for the City of New York (*Portnoy's Complaint*). The only character who is stuck with his assumed identity is Coleman Silk, a light-skinned African American passing as a Jew—which, in this case, means passing as a white man.[35] Finally, Coleman Silk and the Jewish satire of impersonation tip into tragedy and Silk pays the ultimate price.

Indeed, if we look more closely at Roth's late novels—what have been called his "American Trilogy" (*American Pastoral* [1997], *I Married a Communist* [1998], and *The Human Stain* [2000])—we can see that they actually constitute a generic shift from satire to tragedy. It seems that Roth had found parallels to the turbulence of the end of our millennium in the tragic dramas of fifth-century B.C.E. Athens and in the tragic fictions of nineteenth-century America.

By turning to tragedy, Roth also seemed to round out the twentieth-century history of the American novel, updating the project that Theodore Dreiser had undertaken a hundred years before. In 1892, as a young journalist, Dreiser had observed "a certain type of crime in the United States that proved very common. It seemed to spring from the fact that almost every young person was possessed of an ingrown ambition to be somebody financially and socially."[36] Although, unlike Clyde Griffiths in Dreiser's *An American Tragedy* (1925), Coleman Silk doesn't murder anyone in order to achieve his social position, *The Human Stain* is, in nearly all its elements, a latter-day appropriation of classical tragedy in which the "major act" of the protagonist's life becomes what Silk himself calls "something enormous," triggering the eventual "intersection" with "fate."[37] *The Human Stain* announces itself explicitly as tragedy: opening with an epigraph from Sophocles' *Oedipus the King*, the novel is set on the campus of a college called *Athena*, and the main character, Coleman *Brutus* Silk, is a professor of *Latin* and *Greek*. And that is only the beginning.[38]

And yet something does not quite fit. There is a point late in this novel that invites the question: *How should this novel end?* Of course the careful reader knows how it must end, because exigencies of form and convention, and all the Sophoclean breadcrumbs that the narrator has strewn along the path, dictate that the two main characters, Coleman Silk (now a seventy-one-year-old disgraced dean) and Faunia Farley (a thirty-four-year-old illiterate cleaning woman), who had found an unlikely joy in each other's presence, will meet a sudden and violent death. "The tragic hypothesis," writes Thomas Pavel, "presents the image of a universe in which the possible chains of actions are drastically limited: compactness and closure meet the tragic heroes."[39]

So, if the struggle between fate and freedom, between closure and porousness, is between Athens and New York, has Athens finally won? Or is Coleman playing Oedipus just another grand act of impersonation as egregious as a black man passing for white? Maybe this American tragedy is itself a parody of the cathartic grandeur and cohesion of Greek drama, signifying something else? Maybe in "retiring" his comic muse, Roth was signaling, on the cusp of the millennium and the eve of the collapse of the Twin Towers, a profound resignation to the *inexorability* rather than the open-endedness of history, to what Nathan Zuckerman, the narrator, calls the "stranglehold of history that is one's own time . . . the terrifyingly provisional nature of everything"? And maybe in so doing, Roth—and Nathan—were making a horrible pronouncement on the civilization that they had been chronicling (and celebrating) for half a century. This connects us again to the role of Jews in Roth's fiction.

Roth's stories and novels had always inhabited that comic realm where life was a series of endlessly possible inventions. The tragic genres "affirm the authority of existence and proceed in a mimetic mode that elevates what *is*," writes Terrence des Pres, whereas "the comic spirit "proceeds in an antimimetic mode that mocks what is. . . . [The tragic] quiets us with awe. Laughter revolts."[40] From his earliest naughty appearances on the scene, Roth was read as the revolting writer who had exploded Jewish pieties and exposed and shaped the Jewish comedy of the American twentieth century. But that may have been the means and not the end of his literary project. Given the protean character of the Jews themselves as they made their way from pushcarts on Delancey Street to terminals on Wall Street, they had provided the perfect canvas on which endless flights of fancy could take place, the perfect site for fiction. But there was another place on the Jewish map that defied fiction.

Operation Shylock and the crazy "diasporist" manifesto at its center—the plan of the impostor "Philip Roth" to resettle all the (Ashkenazi) Jews of Israel in Europe to spare them the murderous wrath of the Arabs—were as much about *real* versus *imagined space* as they were about territorial options for solving the Jewish problem. But this was also the premise in the other fictions that had Israel as one of their geographic-existential poles: *Portnoy's Complaint, The Counterlife.* Life in the diaspora is life in fiction; life in Israel is life in "fact." Americans, as we have seen, revere facticity *in its plasticity.* In the diaspora you could create an infinity of counterlives, whereas Israel—like the Hebrew language—is REAL.[41] In the early stories in *Goodbye Columbus* and in *Portnoy's Complaint*, history as comedy is endless promise, endless beginnings; *Portnoy's Complaint* ends, after all, with the psychoanalyst Dr. Spielvogel speaking his only line: "Now vee may perhaps to begin, yes?" In *Operation Shylock*, the diaspora-based writer or narrator can still "slip silently out of the plot," Houdini-like. In *The Human Stain*, however, *as in Israel*, the inexorability of the tragically real renders this impossible.

As the century waned, it became clear that Roth was painting on something larger than a Jewish canvas, that tribal loyalties and even the Israel/diaspora divide had become background or local color for something more consequential. If Coleman Silk wants to become a Jew, it is because the Jew has become a mainstream American—though with enough of an edge to make him interesting.

Toward the end of *The Human Stain*, as fate closes in on them, Faunia dances for Coleman, her elderly lover. "Keep dancing," Coleman tells Faunia. "How can we know the dancer from the dance?" asked W. B. Yeats in "Among School Children" (1928). There is, in fact, a lot of Yeats in late Roth, who is in this moment, like his Irish predecessor, a "sixty-year-old smiling public man." Yeats's "Sailing to Byzantium" ends with: "Consume my heart away; sick with desire / And fastened to a dying animal / It knows not what it is; and gather me / Into the artifice of eternity."[42]

When Faunia finishes dancing, the "artifice of eternity" ends and the clock of tragedy starts up again. However, it is not the catharsis of hubris but expiatory acts of sacrifice and purging that come into play here. In the novel's epigraph and the last chapter, the "purifying ritual" invites blind Nemesis to work its way through to a hideous end.

Actually, even at this point there are several possible endings that this story tries on, like a Haydn symphony—including a comic version. But the reason the story can't go on is that Roth himself seems to have lost faith in what comes next, in what Nathan calls "America's story, the high drama that is upping and leaving"—*faith in the plot itself*. Capitulation to the "rite of purification," primitive precursor of tragedy, amounts to relinquishing the most precious American resource, *the future tense*—a loss of faith in America, whose very self-definition is embedded in time as a meliorative process, an open-ended plot.

The novella *Nemesis*, which appeared in 2010, reinforces this move by explicitly naming this unknowable agent of human fate (here in the form of the polio bacillus). Unlike the moral freedom of former acts of impersonation, Nemesis has fateful consequences for the unwitting protagonist and all who come in contact with him.

Is it the times or a writer's particular time that bring such dire pronouncements? Indeed, like America, Roth in his comic mode was the perpetual child or, at most, the precocious or whining adolescent. "America was created for children," said Sholem Aleichem's Motl, in that moment early in the last century when everything seemed possible.[43] That is no country for old men.

The ultimate emblem of this relinquishing of the future while gesturing to the artifice of eternity is the frozen pond covering the river's flow at the end of *The Human Stain*. Coleman's sister Ernestine begs her brother Walt not to excommunicate Coleman, but to see him "historically . . . as part of something larger." Instead, Walt "froze everything in time. And that is never a good idea," she tells Nathan. [44]

Nathan is on his way to the Silk family home when he sees the vehicle of Vietnam veteran Les Farley, who is ice fishing after—Nathan is certain—having killed his ex-wife Faunia and her "Jew." At the edge of the frozen field, Nathan admits that he is "unable to just keep on going," and so he ends with a static pastoral scene that effectively effaces the plot.[45]

Les on the hilltop is, then, the "artifice of eternity" as the foreclosure of history. The inexorable work of Nemesis supplants the open-endedness of comedy, the utopian vision that drives dystopian satire and even the cathartic vision of tragedy. This millennial move mimics a sinister development in the contemporary Hebrew political imagination that has moved from the comic-utopian faith in an eternally deferred messianic future to apocalyptic anxiety that would hasten the Messiah and reinstate sacrificial, cultic worship ("purifying rituals") and exclusive claims to territory and truth.

All we are left with is the ecstasy of the present moment frozen in time, this one dance, one picture of a solitary fisherman atop an Arcadian mountain in America. It is a lot. It is the ultimate consolation of every art form, though the story must always exist in time and unfold with some of life's desperate promise and sorry logic. But, even if his last fictions are cameos of a "dying animal," Philip Roth has done his work, which is now seared in our flesh.

■

For invaluable readings of earlier drafts of this essay, I wish to thank Bernard Avishai, Chana Kronfeld, Natalie Zemon Davis, Paul Bochner, Susannah Heschel, the Simon Dubnow seminar in Leipzig (January, 2010), Mati Senkman, and Idith Zertal.

Notes

1. *Philip Roth Studies* publishes a semiannual journal (since 2004) of critical work on Roth; as of 2011, there are over 700 items in the critical bibliography compiled by this journal, including 61 PhD dissertations, 426 journal articles, 188 chapters in books, 22 monographs, 30 edited collections, and a number of bibliographies.

2. Isaac Bashevis Singer, "The Art of Fiction No. 42," interview by Harold Flender, in *The Paris Review* 44 (Fall 1968): 53–73.

3. I use the word advisedly, since Jewishness, coded as "whiteness," is the "persuasion" that Coleman Silk chooses. On "identity" in America, see the work of John Higham and Werner Sollors.

4. See Bill Brown, "Thing Theory," *Critical Inquiry* 28, no. 1 (Autumn 2001): 1–22.

5. Philip Roth, *Philip Roth at 80: A Celebration* (New York, 2014), 53–54.

6. Sacvan Bercovitch, *The Puritan Origins of the American Self* (New Haven, CT, 2011), x. Emphasis in original.

7. David Remnick, "Into the Clear: Philip Roth Puts Turbulence in its Place," *The New Yorker*, May 8, 2000, 76–89.

8. Ibid.

9. Irving Howe called this "body of writing [inspired by the immigrant generation] a regional literature [comparable to] southern writing." Howe, *World of Our Fathers* (New York, 1976), 585–86.

10. Remnick, "Into the Clear."

11. Ibid.

12. Interview with Hermione Lee, *The Paris Review*, http://www.theparisreview.org/interviews/2957/the-art-of-fiction-no-84-philip-roth. Nathan Zuckerman had already appeared in several stories before the interview with Lee, and made a few more appearances afterward, sometimes as the dominant center of consciousness and sometimes as a background voice. His last sighting was in *Exit, Ghost* (2007), which anticipated his demise. For a reader's farewell to Nathan, see Miriam Jaffe-Foger, "Eulogy: Nathan Zuckerman, 1933–2007," *Philip Roth Studies* 5, no. 2 (Fall 2009): 281–82.

13. Grace Paley, "Two Ears, Three Lucks," in *The Collected Stories* (New York, 1994), x; see also Sidra DeKoven Ezrahi, "Jew-*ish*: Grace Paley's Prose of the City and Poetry of the Country," *Contemporary Women's Writing* 3, no. 2 (2009): 144–52.

14. See Donald Weber, "Gertrude Berg and the Goldbergs," in *The Other Fifties: Interrogating Mid-Century American Icons*, ed. Joel Foreman (Urbana, 1997), 144–67.

15. The first five were in the collection *Goodbye, Columbus*; the last is Alexander Portnoy in *Portnoy's Complaint*.

16. Clearly Roth is drawing on the entire twentieth-century history of African-American writers including Hughes, Ellison, Baldwin, and Morrison, without whom he could not have written *The Human Stain*, any more than John Updike could have written *Bech: A Book* (1970) without American Jewish antecedents. The specific history of black-Jewish impersonations goes back at least as far as Al Jolson in blackface (1927).

17. See Hannah Arendt, "The Jew as Pariah: A Hidden Tradition," *Jewish Social Studies* 6, no. 2 (April 1944): 99–122.

18. Sidra DeKoven Ezrahi, *Booking Passage: Exile and Homecoming in the Modern Jewish Imagination* (Berkeley, 2000), 116–30.

19. Interview with Hermione Lee, *The Paris Review*.

20. Paley, *Collected Stories*, 39–40.

21. Philip Roth, *Goodbye Columbus* (1959; New York, 1987), 140–42, 146, 155, 157–58.

22. See the resonances of the *akeda* (the Binding of Isaac) in the enacted scene as well as in the name of the teacher (Mr. *Bind*er); see also Theoharis C. Theoharis, "For With God All Things Are Possible: Philip Roth's 'The Conversion of the Jews,'" *Journal of the Short Story in English* 32 (Spring 1999): 2–6.

23. Paley, *Collected Stories*, p. 40. See Sidra DeKoven Ezrahi, "America as the Theatre of Jewish Comedy: From Sholem Aleichem to Grace Paley," *Studia Judaica* 13 (2005): 74–82.

24. For other expressions of what I call "the urban congregation," see the end of Henry Roth, *Call It Sleep*; Saul Bellow's Herzog, who experiences the "funeral of exhausted objects" (*Herzog* [New York, 1964], 175); and toward the end of the century, E. L. Doctorow, *The City of God*.

25. Bernard Avishai, *Promiscuous: Portnoy's Complaint and Our Doomed Pursuit of Happiness* (New Haven, CT, 2012).

26. Remnick, "Into the Clear."

27. In her interview with Roth in *The Paris Review*, Hermione Lee speaks gingerly in the name of "some feminists": "What do you feel about . . . the feminist attack on you?" And then, by way of explanation without claiming ownership of this position, she elaborates: "the force of the attack would be, in part, that female characters are unsympathetically treated . . . that nearly all the women in the books are there to obstruct, or to help, or to console the male characters." Interview with Hermione Lee, *The Paris Review*. For a feminist critique of impersonation and the "ludic mimicry" that is essentially "phallogocentric," see the work of Luce Irigaray and Judith Butler.

28. Irving Howe, "Philip Roth Reconsidered." *Commentary*, December 1972, http://www.commentarymagazine.com/article/philip-roth-reconsidered/.

29. Gershom Scholem, *Haaretz*, June 6, 1969.

30. Howe, "Roth Reconsidered."

31. Philip Roth, *Zuckerman Bound: A Trilogy and Epilogue* [includes *The Ghost Writer*, 1979; *Zuckerman Unbound*, 1981; *The Anatomy Lesson*, 1983; *Epilogue: The Prague Orgy*] (New York, 1985), 484, 475–76, 573.

32. This becomes explicit in the touching memoir *Facts* (1988), which is prefaced with a letter to Nathan Zuckerman—who is, of course, Roth's creation but also his designated interlocutor.

33. "How Telling: Irving Howe, Roth's Early Career and the Dialectic of Impersonation" in *The Anatomy Lesson*," *Philip Roth Studies* 5, no. 2 (Fall 2009): 253.

34. Roth is also a significant literary impresario; the series he edited, *Writers from the Other Europe*, featured, among others, a number of Jewish writers from Central and Eastern Europe, including Josef Roth, Bruno Schulz, Osip Mandelshtam, and Joseph Brodsky.

35. See Brett Ashley Kaplan, "Reading Race and the Conundrums of Reconciliation in Philip Roth's *The Human Stain*," in *Turning Up the Flame*, eds. Jay L. Halio and Ben Siegel (Delaware, 2005), 172–93.

36. Yoshinobu Hakutani, "Preface," in Theodore Dreiser, *Selected Magazine Articles*, vol. 1, *Life and Art in the American 1890s* (Madison, N.J, 1985).

37. Philip Roth, *The Human Stain* (Boston, 2000), 139.

38. See Sidra DeKoven Ezrahi, "The Tragical-Comedy of Impersonation: Jews, America, and the Twentieth Century," in *Jewish Studies at the CEU* 4 (2004): 53–61; Elaine Safer, *Mocking the Age: The Later Novels of Philip Roth* (Albany, 2006), 117–33.

39. Thomas Pavel, *Fictional Worlds* (Cambridge, 1989), 134.

40. Terrence Des Pres, "Holocaust *Laughter*?" in *Writing and the Holocaust*, ed. Berel Lang (New York, 1988), 217–20.

41. Philip Roth, *Operation Shylock* (New York, 1993), 315. See also Ezrahi, *Booking Passage,* 221–33; and Gerard O'Donoghue, "Philip Roth's Hebrew School," *Philip Roth Studies* 6, no. 2 (Fall 2010): 153–66.

42. "The dying animal" is of course the title of one of Roth's short novels.

43. Sholem Aleichem, letter to Chaim Nahman Bialik. Quoted in Sidra DeKoven Ezrahi, *Booking Passage*, 122.

44. Philip Roth, *The Human Stain*, 360–61.

45. Ibid.

Dahlia Ravikovitch (1936–2005)
POETRY, POWER, POWERLESSNESS

Chana Kronfeld and Chana Bloch

"I AM ALWAYS ON THE SIDE OF THE DEFEATED," DAHLIA RAVIKOVITCH SAID IN A 1991 interview about her poetry, echoing Walter Benjamin's appeal to write the history of the vanquished.[1] Ravikovitch explores the devastating consequences of unequal power relations for the individual and for society; her focus is on the self in a state of crisis, refracting the state of the nation. While she is best known for her poems about the twists and turns of the human psyche and the passionate tension between eros and thanatos, she also addresses questions of ethics and social justice with analytical precision, always informed by a profound engagement with Jewish textual tradition. Her early work articulates the asymmetries of power in poems about fathers and daughters, men and women, kings and their subjects. The later work focuses more intently on the precarious position of women and, with increasing directness, the plight of Palestinians under the Israeli Occupation. Indeed, power and powerlessness is the binary opposition at the core of her poetic worldview, an opposition she consistently destabilizes.

Whether admired or vilified for her peace activism, Ravikovitch has been universally acknowledged as one of the great Hebrew poets of our time. Her first book of poems, *The Love of an Orange*, published in 1959, immediately established her as one of the leading poetic voices of the post-1948 Statehood Generation, alongside her elders, Yehuda Amichai and Natan Zach. She is the author of ten books of poetry, several collections of short stories, and children's verse, as well as translations of English poetry and children's classics by women.

No other contemporary Hebrew poet, with the exception of Amichai (1924–2000), the best known of the Statehood poets, has been so warmly embraced by Israelis. Her poems have been integrated into all facets of Israeli public life. Influential for several generations of Hebrew poets, and particularly empowering for younger women writers, her work has long been a staple of the Israeli school curriculum and, increasingly, the subject of scholarly research. Despite the oppositional stance of her poetry, Ravikovitch received all the major Israeli literary awards, culminating in 1998 in the Israel Prize. Her work has been translated into twenty-one languages.

Ravikovitch was born in 1936 in Ramat Gan. When she was six, her father was run over by a drunken soldier in the British army. Without telling Dahlia about his death, her mother moved the family to a kibbutz, where she learned of the tragedy two years later from taunting classmates. The early poem "On the road at night there stands the man" enacts the compulsion to visit and revisit the scene of childhood trauma.[2]

> On the road at night there stands the man
> Who once upon a time was my father.
> And I must go down to the place where he stands
> Because I was his firstborn daughter.
>
> Night after night he stands alone in his place
> And I must go down and stand in that place.
> And I wanted to ask him: Till when must I go.
> And I knew as I asked: I must always go . . .
>
> . . . .
>
> Not one word of love does he speak to me
> Though once upon a time he was my father
> And even though I was his firstborn daughter
> Not one word of love can he speak to me. (*Collected Poetry*, 55–56)

Although "On the road at night" clearly sets forth a personal narrative, the poem is also a psychological exploration of the workings of trauma and, ultimately, a philosophical statement about the limits of language.

The loss and displacement of Ravikovitch's early years shaped her social sensibilities and informed all her writing; indeed, her emotional vulnerability always engendered an ethical imperative. "If I didn't know despair myself, I wouldn't be able to feel the tears of the oppressed," she said.[3] The public was well aware that Ravikovitch struggled with clinical depression; thus when she died suddenly in 2005, it was assumed that she had taken her own life, an assumption refuted by the pathologists' reports.

Her fragile health and reclusiveness did not deter Ravikovitch from becoming deeply involved in the cause of Palestinian human rights (and political causes in general). She often joined demonstrations against forced evacuations, land confiscation, and the mistreatment of women and children in the West Bank. She spoke out on television and in print, condemning the messianic nationalist settlers, and didn't hesitate to confront Israel's leaders directly.

The poems in Ravikovitch's first two books, *Love of an Orange* (1959) and *Hard Winter* (1964) employ traditional forms and an archaizing language, resonant with biblical and liturgical echoes, alongside experimental verse that invokes surrealist parable, avant-garde opera, and folk genres. Modernism for her always involves the bold juxtaposition of the archaic and the avant-garde, the Jewish and the non-Jewish. From 1969 on, with the publication of *The Third Book*, Ravikovitch renounces some of the rhetorical riches of her early style for a charged plain speech that draws more heavily on modern Hebrew diction and colloquial idiom. Nevertheless, even in this spare later poetry, she continues her critical dialogue with traditional Jewish sources.

Common to both the early and the late work is a radical intertextuality that invokes and rewrites sacred Jewish sources, from the poetic books of the Bible through diverse postbiblical genres—rabbinic legalism and kabbalistic incantation, midrashic parable and liturgical poetry. For the contemporary non-Israeli reader, it may be difficult to understand why so secular a poet would draw so heavily upon the traditional Jewish bookcase. This is not an issue for an Israeli audience, since secular rewritings of the sacred have become the norm in modern Hebrew literary culture, in no small part owing to poets like Amichai and Ravikovitch. Amichai, a lapsed believer, constructs a systematic countertheology, recasting the God of his Orthodox childhood as a literary character in his poems. In Ravikovitch's work, with one important exception, "The End of the Fall,"[4] God is reduced to appearances in ironic quotations, expletives, and exclamations.

Throughout her oeuvre, she is drawn to rare and arcane biblical expressions whose emotive import is strong even when their exact meaning remains mysterious. These ancient locutions paradoxically offer her a way of making her language new. A masterful example is her use of *hapax legomena*, words or expressions that appear only once in the Bible, as in "The Love of an Orange," the title poem that opens Ravikovitch's first book, a fable about the passion of an orange for the man who devours it.[5] The poem ends:

An orange did love
The man who ate it,
To its flayer it brought
Flesh for the teeth.

An orange, consumed
By the man who ate it,
Invaded his skin
To the flesh beneath.[6]

The word we have translated as "flesh" (*barot*) appears only once in the Bible in this form, in Lamentations 4:10, in one of the most horrific biblical scenes where women are reduced by famine to eating their own children during the siege of Jerusalem. The grisly suggestion of cannibalism this word conveys in the poem amplifies the tension between love and death, eros and thanatos, which is Ravikovitch's main theme. Paradoxically, by the end of the poem, at the very moment when the orange is being devoured, it is granted agency and power over "the man who ate it." The biblical *ba be-* (lit., "came into," which we translated as "invaded") can suggest both sexual and military penetration. The poem ends with a forceful role reversal of the powerful and the powerless in which the submissive orange, as it were, has the last bite.

Biblical poetry offers Ravikovitch a model for the modern lyric in which the political is inseparable from the personal and the ethical from the aesthetic. While her use of biblical allusions is often critical and even irreverent, she is determined to rescue traditional Jewish texts from the hands of religious zealots and sloganeering politicians and to recover from within Judaism a secular ethical compass. Even so, she takes issue with many tenets of the patriarchal biblical and rabbinic value sys-

tem. Her poetry critiques the sexual violence expressed in the prophets' metaphor
of the Nation-as-Woman (e.g., God's punishment of the "Whore of Zion"), and its
devastating latter-day uses in the discourse of conquest typical of various "civilizing
missions" and settler colonialisms. Similarly, she condemns the insistence of Jewish
texts on Israelite exceptionalism as well as the binary oppositions separating pure
from impure, Jew from Gentile, self from other.

But Ravikovitch embraces many of the socioethical precepts of traditional Judaism, exhibiting an impressive erudition in the rabbinic texts, which till recently women
were forbidden even to touch and which by now have become unfamiliar to most
secular Jews. Her nuanced engagement with Jewish texts is perhaps linked to her
maternal history. Her mother was the granddaughter of Rabbi Shmuel Hominer,
a founder of the ultra-Orthodox neighborhood of Me'ah She'arim in Jerusalem in
1874. Though secular herself, the mother was a graduate of a religious teachers' college and taught Jewish studies for many years. In a late poem, Ravikovitch refers to
the socioethical precepts that were always vital for her mother as the "Ethical Teachings of the Jews." The critical voice and class sensibility of these precepts resonate
for her with the egalitarian ethos of the Yishuv, and later the Israel, of her childhood.

Ravikovitch often chooses to adopt the voice of those prophetic texts that warn
against doing violence to the vulnerable. Informing her entire poetic outlook is Jeremiah's exhortation:

Act with justice and righteousness, and deliver from the
hand of the oppressor anyone who has been robbed. And do no
wrong or violence to the alien, the orphan, and the widow,
or shed innocent blood in this place. (Jer. 22:3, NRSV)

As she points out in an explication of her famous early poem, "Oshek" (a term in
biblical ethics expressing moral outrage at the violent oppression of the underprivileged), the ethical and the aesthetic are always mutually implicated in their very opposition. While the aesthetic is associated with vulnerability, violence is associated
with the ugly:

In the final analysis, what I am trying to do, perhaps, is to expose wrongdoing or
ugliness . . . in order to illuminate the contradiction between them. . . . Wherever
the poem ["Outrage"] deals with brutality, I end with a focus on beauty. And
where the image is one of beauty, I bring the focus back again to the brutal.[7]

While early reviews labeled her a "keening poet," a traditionally female role, recent feminist studies have emphasized her persona as a female prophet of wrath.[8]
For a woman poet to speak in the wrathful and uncompromising voice of Jeremiah
or Isaiah is no simple matter, given the gender politics of Jewish cultural history.
Prophecy, one of the chief biblical models for Hebrew poetry, is paradigmatically
the domain of the male spokesman of God. The poet-as-prophet was a standard
trope of premodernist Hebrew poetry, mediated by Russian romanticism and associated especially with Chaim Nachman Bialik, the "national poet" of the Hebrew
revival period (1881–1920s). For Ravikovitch to claim the privileged stance of the
prophet as her own, and what's more, to do so without accepting its authorizing
divine source, amounted to a powerful feminist gesture.[9]

Both in biblical and in modern Jewish culture, the literal female subject is rarely allowed to speak for the collective, except when the woman is a figure for the nation. From the very first, however, Ravikovitch's poetry insistently establishes female subjectivity not only as the voice of a vulnerable individual consciousness but also as a locus for expressing collective concerns. As early as 1963, in an essay with the mock-traditional title "Women's Wisdom," Ravikovitch uses the example of Emily Dickinson to challenge "the assumption that a woman's world is frail and restricted by nature."[10]

"Clockwork Doll," from her first collection, is the poem most frequently singled out as the paradigmatic example of Ravikovitch's feminism *avant la lettre*. This is a closely rhymed sonnet in which the perfect outer form, like that of the mechanical doll, contrasts powerfully with an irreparable inner brokenness. The poem literalizes the stereotype of the "doll," referring to a pretty young woman, only to grant her the sorry fate of Humpty Dumpty.

In the later poetry, Ravikovitch's critique of patriarchy increasingly includes an account of women's collusion with their own social marginalization. Typically, these poems highlight the link between gender and class. In "Cinderella in the Kitchen" (*True Love*, 1987), she calls into question the passive ideal of womanhood fostered by fairy tales, a genre she herself found seductive early on. Her Cinderella finds an alternative to Prince Charming in the "infinite treasure [that] filled her imagination" (*Collected Poetry*, 179). Yet without social change, her "freedom of mind," such as it is, serves only to reinforce her inertia:

And she clenched her fists and said:
I'm going off to war—

Then dozed off in bed. (*Collected Poetry*, 178–79)

Ravikovitch resists the nationalist and religious construction of the matriarch Rachel as a figure for the (male) national subjects, based on Jeremiah's allegory of the grieving Mother of the Nation, and portrays her instead as a flesh-and-blood mother. It is against this background that we must read the allusions to various literal characters named Rachel who appear throughout Ravikovitch's poetry, linking and at times conflating the matriarch of Genesis with the Hebrew women poets Rachel Morpurgo (1790–1871) and Rachel (Bluvshteyn; 1890–1931) to create a literary and national matrilineage of refusal and resistance. This matrilineage culminates poignantly in a de-allegorization of the Nation-as-Woman in the poems "But She Had a Son" and "What a Time She Had"[11]—dedicated to, and spoken in the voice of, Rachel Melamed-Eytan, the working-class mother of a fallen soldier, who declares:

I am Rachel your mother
of clear mind and free will,
I will not be comforted.

Few critics have noted the connections among the critiques of gender, class, and politics, connections that are a central principle in Ravikovitch's poetic worldview. The difference between the early and the late poetry, we argue, is not simply in the transition from a personal to a political poetry, but rather in the specific ways in which the poetics and stylistics of the political are articulated. One of the concerns that unifies Ravikovitch's early and late political poetry, and that associates her with the poetic mission of Amichai, is a determination to purify the language and to resist what is referred to in colloquial Hebrew as the "word laundry," the abuse of language for political gain. She is perfectly aware of the dangers of this mission. "Like deep-sea divers," she wrote, "most poets lead a high-risk life because they are compelled to listen with such scrupulous attention to the very essence of words."[12]

Ravikovitch's political poetry, even when it resorts to direct statement, is always linked with literary form. Both the early and the late work are marked by the lyric's modes of indirection, among them dense intertexuality, layered figurative language, and rhetorical distancing devices. All of these allow the political to work, as Adorno has famously suggested, through a "negative mimesis" and as "content that articulates itself in formal structures."[13] To examine Ravikovitch's political poetry through thematic analysis or by focusing exclusively on direct statement would be reductive. It is her verbal art that scrutinizes "the smudges left behind . . . by the fingers of power," as Adorno proposes in his early essay "Notes on Kafka."[14]

In the early work, the world represented in the poem encodes the political as remote from the here-and-now; the later political poems, usually referred to as "protest poems" but poignantly renamed by her as "*J'accuse* poetry," increasingly establish a critical distance between the values of the implied author and the position of the poem's speaker(s), who represent(s) the collective voice of the public and whom she clearly ironizes and condemns.[15] For Ravikovitch, artistic indirection does not imply political or ethical wavering: it is simply the way the poetic makes the political legible.

In her first four books (1959–1976) the distancing devices are sometimes genre-based—the Jewish parable (*mashal*), allegory, and fairy tale. Sometimes the distance is stylistic (e.g., archaisms). In other cases, the political is encoded through a literal distancing of the poetic world: the poems are set in ancient times or are located in faraway places. A particularly cogent example of geographic distancing that is unmistakably political is the dystopian Brechtian "How Hong Kong Was Destroyed," set in a surreal apocalyptic Hong Kong, "hanging like a colored lantern on a hook at the edge of the world."[16] In this poem the "rotting bodies" of the "little prostitutes" are a metonymy not only for the disintegrating body of the modern metropolis, but also for "the earth" (Heb., *ha-aretz*, which is both "planet Earth" and a common locution for Israel, here specifically post-1967 Israel): "The earth [/Israel] seethes and explodes, / seethes and explodes." Thus, a critique of modernity, gender, and class implicitly becomes a critique of the Occupation as well.[17]

The simile describing the prostitutes' clients provides perhaps one of the most radical political moves in Ravikovitch's corpus, though it takes the form of a complex allusion to Scripture: "Already at dusk the first guests arrive / like a thorn in the living flesh." The simile, "like a thorn in the living flesh," implying that the women's sexual exploitation is akin to torment and death, is a sacrilegious portmanteau of allusions to the Talmud and the New Testament, combining the rabbinic saying, "The worm is as grievous to the dead as a needle in the living flesh" (Tractate *Berakhot* 18:72), with 2 Corinthians 12:7, "there was given to me a thorn in the flesh." In the first stages of Hebrew and Yiddish modernism, Christological allusions were embraced as a transgressive avant-garde move. While these first modernists used

Christological motifs and structures in their rebellion against tradition, Ravikovitch takes the blasphemy down to the finest points of nuance and texture: she forms a hybrid of two forbidden texts—the Talmud, traditionally forbidden to women, and the New Testament, forbidden to Jews altogether.

Most of the political poems in the early oeuvre employ temporal, historic distancing as a way of encoding references to the political present. "The Coming of the Messiah,"[18] which dramatizes the seductions of charismatic leadership and its dangers for ordinary human beings, has been read as an allegory set in the seventeenth-century diaspora, when Jewish masses were captivated by the promises of the so-called false Messiah, Sabbatai Zevi;[19] here, however, the analogy between the messianic Sabbatean expectations of seventeenth-century Jews of Europe and Asia Minor and the messianic impulse of normative Zionism is merely implied. Similarly, "Horns of Hittin" (1969), a cautionary tale about the then-new Israeli Occupation of Palestinian lands, tropes on the conquests of the Crusades, a fraught political symbol in the Middle East: "How cruel and naive those Crusaders were. / They plundered everything."[20] When it was first published, this poem was immediately seen as provocative. In an interview with Bloch in 1989, Ravikovitch remarked that Yehoshafat Harkaby, a leading Israeli Defense Forces (IDF) general and military historian, read this poem as a warning that the attempt to conquer another people could prove suicidal for the conqueror.[21]

The tension between past and present gives voice to the political in "The Hurling,"[22] where the title evokes Isaiah's *taltelat gaver*: "The Lord will hurl thee up and down with *a man's throw*" (Isa. 22:17, Soncino Bible), as a heightened metonymy for national uprooting and exile. The poem begins and ends with contemporary references to Israeli border guards and the muezzin in pre-1967 Jerusalem; the two middle stanzas, however, present a parable on class, gender, and ethnic tensions in Jerusalem during Solomon's reign. In the apocalyptic vision that closes the poem all the king's power and all the king's wealth cannot forestall the coming disaster.

The late 1970s marked a major turning point in the ways Ravikovitch articulated the political. This was a period of great upheaval in Israeli society, when Menachem Begin's right-wing Likud Party rose to power for the first time, routing the Labor Party. An economic crisis ensued when, at the instigation of Milton Friedman, the government abruptly converted the economy to stock-market-driven capitalism. This was followed in short order by Israel's incursions into Lebanon, culminating in the 1982 invasion. The crisis in the national sphere contrasted sharply with the personal joy and fulfillment this period held for Dahlia: the birth in 1978 of her only son Ido, the "true love" in the title of her 1986 book of poems. The confluence of these events made Ravikovitch's sensitivity to the oppression of the weak even more palpable; henceforth, motherhood, feminism, and peace activism became inextricably linked for her.

Ravikovitch's poetry from this point on, usually referred to as the "late work," is marked by an urgency to express the political with increasing directness and bluntness, a tendency that is most pronounced in the posthumous collection *Many Waters* (2006). During this period, all of Israeli literary and cultural production was undergoing a paradigm shift away from a focus on the individual subject and his or her universalist recoil from the topical, associated (correctly or not) with the humanist neoliberalism of the Statehood Generation. Ravikovitch's "new poetry" played a crucial role in creating the conditions of possibility for a return to political poetry.

By the early 1980s Ravikovitch was in the unique position to lend literary and ethical legitimacy to this return and infuse it with a heightened gender-awareness. She was the only female poet of the Statehood Generation to have achieved a central place in the canon and to have become an influential model for younger female and male writers alike. Having recently become a mother for the first time at age forty-one, she had just attained what is the culturally sanctioned condition in Israeli society for a woman's right to speak out on matters of war and peace.

At a conference for Israeli and American Jewish writers in Berkeley in 1989, we asked Ravikovitch about the new turn in her poetry. "Until the 1982 Lebanon war," she said, "I managed somehow to go on living inside a bell jar" (invoking Sylvia Plath's novel). "But then suddenly, all at once, when the invasion started, the bell jar shattered. Now there's no divide between personal and political. It all comes rushing in." In a 2004 television interview she elaborated: "Because I hold an Israeli passport, I have a share in all the wrongs that are done to the Palestinians. . . . I want to be able to say that I did all I could to prevent the bloodshed."[23]

Ravikovitch's focus on abuse is accompanied by a keen awareness of the ethical responsibility of the writer. In this period she explores the parallels between the plight of the Palestinians, the suffering of Jews in the diaspora, and the constraints on women in patriarchal society, all the while resisting identity politics. Thematically the turn in her work is marked by the inseparability of concerns with war, woman, and child. That, indeed, is what unites her two books from this period. In the 1986 *True Love*, following the first Lebanon war, a section of explicitly feminist poems is followed by one devoted to political protest poetry; in the 1992 *Mother and Child*, published after the first Intifada, poems about an Israeli mother losing her son in a questionable military operation ("But She Had a Son," "What a Time She Had!") are followed by a poem about a pregnant Palestinian woman whose fetus is "killed in his mother's belly / in the month of January, in the year 1988, 'under circumstances relating to state security,'" in the euphemistic lingo of IDF spokespersons.[24]

There has always been a strong temptation to read Ravikovitch's political poetry—and her poetic project as a whole—in reductive biographical terms. The emphasis on mother and child in Ravikovitch's work, however, should also be seen as a meaningful poetic and political move. It is clear that the convergence of motherhood, the political and economic upheaval of the late 1970s, and the first Lebanon war deepened the connection between gender, class, and political consciousness in her thought. But biographical circumstances do not fully account for two of the telling moves in Ravikovitch's late poetry. First, she blurs the boundaries between self and other in her principled refusal to see any type of identity as fixed and monolithic. Second, she intensifies her dialogue with traditional Jewish texts in a "hyper-Judaizing" of its resonances, almost to the point of returning (though with reinforced irony) to the intertextual *Mussivstil* of her first book.[25]

The urgency, indeed the despair, that gripped Israeli intellectuals on the left in the 1980s explains their public call to retreat from the aesthetic to an engagé poetry of direct statement. Yet such a position disregards the inseparability of political protest from verbal art in the work of Ravikovitch, if not in lyrical poetry tout court.

What's more, it paradoxically ratifies the very bourgeois individualist presuppositions that it struggles against, namely that political poetry is mere harangue and that true poetry must be apolitical (i.e., collaborate willy-nilly with the status quo).

Indeed, the directness of political statement in *True Love* and *Mother and Child* does not stand in contrast to the aesthetic; rather, the political is enabled by the poetic and is imbricated in it. It is articulated through an intertexual collage as well as a complex metaphorics and a layered stylistics. In this respect, Ravikovitch's late political poems are every bit as rhetorically rich and expressive as her most personal or early poetry.

Ravikovitch sardonically titles the section of her 1986 volume *True Love* devoted to political poems "Issues in Contemporary Judaism,"[26] using a technical term (*sugiyot*) for a talmudic disputation. Her choice to model her poetic account of the Lebanon war, the Sabra and Shatila massacres, and the oppression of Palestinians in the Occupied Territories on the logic of rabbinical argument may seem at first glance to be merely satirical; however, it also has the effect of invoking the authority of Jewish law as an ethical criterion by which Israeli militarism may be judged.

One of the most intertextually complex political poems in this section is "Beheaded Heifer," a poem that has elicited conflicting interpretations. In an interview with us,[27] Ravikovitch explained that it is based on an actual incident in which a yeshiva student was shot in the Hebron marketplace and left to die because no one knew his identity; the Jews assumed he was a Palestinian, and the Palestinians, a Jew. In the poem, once his yarmulke has fallen, it takes no more than a few steps until he is "not a Jew, / not an Arab anymore," as Ravikovitch drily observes, calling into question the identity tags that create divisions among the living. Thus the inability to distinguish friend from foe, self from other becomes a deliberate rhetorical strategy thematizing the manipulated populace's confusion and fear of border-crossing that makes many yearn for clear separations between self and other.

The title ritual of the poem described in the final stanza quotes verses from Deuteronomy 21:1–9, a symbolic rite of expiation for the guilt of an untraced murder:

> If one be found slain in the field
> if one be found slain on the ground,
> let your elders go out and slaughter a heifer
> and scatter its ashes in the stream.

Ravikovitch's striking omission of the best-known verse of this biblical passage—the elders' pronouncement "Our hands have not shed this blood," which is followed by the conclusion, "And the blood shall be forgiven them"—signals her refusal to absolve her community and the nation's leaders from direct or indirect responsibility. Pontius Pilate and Lady Macbeth cast their long shadow backward on the text.

One of the last poems published in Ravikovitch's lifetime has the polyvalent title "Mi-zimrat ha-aretz," which we render as "The Fruit of the Land." In biblical Hebrew, which is insistently present in the poem, *zimra* can mean "produce, bounty" and "power, might," though in modern usage it means "singing." The poem's effect depends on the metaphor of Israel's military might as its bumper crop. The different meanings of the word *zimra* combine in a cacophony of voices—all ironically distant from the values of the implied author—mouthing a chorus of boasts and clichés about the bounty of the land:[28]

> and we've got crates of napalm and crates of explosives,
> unlimited quantities, cornucopias,
> a feast for the soul, like some finely seasoned delicacy.

Ravikovitch reenacts the drama of Israel and Palestine through a mostly female cast of characters and by invoking the central Jewish topos of the Nation-as-Woman. One of the most powerful examples of the workings of Jewish intertextuality in gendering the political is the poem "Lullaby,"[29] where a Palestinian mother and grandmother lament the violent death of the family's father after he was beaten by Israeli soldiers in the presence of his teenage son. This lament is intoned by the Palestinian women to the rhythms of the Yiddish cradle-song, which has often served as a vehicle for Jewish national lament. As is often the case in the traditional Yiddish lullaby, the mothers speak of themselves in the third person, and their address is directed at the child:

> Mama and Grandma
> will sing you a song,
> your shining white mothers
> will sing you a song,
>
> . . . .
>
> will sing in Jabalya's cordon of gloom.
> There they sat, clinging together as one:
> Papa wrecked, coughing up
> blood from his lung,
> his son of fifteen embracing his frame
> like a steel hoop girding
> his father's crushed form
> —what little remained.
>
> . . . .
>
> Rachel is weeping aloud for her sons.
> A lamentation. A keening of pain.
> When thou art grown and become a man,
> the grief of Jabalya thou shalt not forget,
> the torment of Shati thou shalt not forget,
> Hawara and Beita,
> Jelazoun, Balata,
> their cry still rises night after night.

It is difficult to imagine a more trenchant example of "*J'accuse* poetry." But the poem's political work is not exhausted by its protest-laden content. From the genre affiliation asserted in the title to the biblical allusion in the last line, the poem works through a distinctly Jewish intertextual network, which for the Israeli reader compels identification with and thwarts the dehumanization of the Palestinian victim.[30]

In the opening lines Ravikovitch sutures together three prototypical texts of Hebrew culture in pre-Statehood Palestine, now associated in Israel with nostalgia for the pioneering days.[31] Once these texts have been grafted onto the Yiddish cradle-song form, it will have become very difficult for the Israeli reader to see the speaker(s) as "other." At this very moment the line "Jabalya's cordon of gloom" appears, making it unambiguously clear that the speakers are located on the outer margins of national and class otherness, in the Palestinian refugee camp near Gaza City. Thus it is precisely in the tension between the Palestinian context and various evoked formations of Jewish popular and literary culture that Ravikovitch's intertextual collage intensifies the women's sense of loss, horror, and grief.

Following this, through a bold and surprising allusion in the second stanza to "Rachel mourning for her sons" (Jer. 31:15), Ravikovitch reconstitutes the lullaby as lament, while appropriating for the Palestinian national narrative the Jewish textual tradition that sees Rachel as the mother of the Jewish nation-in-exile. In the description of the father's torture by Israeli soldiers in the presence of his son, this central topos of the Jewish diasporic lament becomes the Palestinians' national story: the analogy between these two, through the keening words of their women, recounts both the Jewish and Palestinian allegories of displacement and loss. That the Israeli Occupation is now in the role of the historic exilers of Israel—from the Babylonians to the Romans—is an inescapable conclusion from the intertextual mapping of Rachel's lament onto that of the Palestinian women. These Palestinian Rachels address not only their teenage son and grandson but also, metonymically, the younger generation of the Palestinian nation, commanding them to remember and not to forget, intoning a catalogue of names of villages and refugee camps (a prototypical rhetorical practice in the Israeli culture of commemoration).

For the Israeli reader, these intoning repetitions also constitute a chilling ironic reversal, for the traumatic Palestinian command to remember reiterates verbatim the command to the Israelites to "remember what Amalek has done to you" (Deut. 25:17), which ends with the injunction, "thou shalt not forget." Thus, the torture and deprivation described in the poem inescapably turn the Israelis into the Amalek of Palestinian national memory. The catalogue of names that must not be forgotten also recalls, of course, Psalms 137, the locus classicus of the Jewish poetics of deterritorialization.[32] Iteration of names in the style of the Jewish lament (kina) follows as well the convention of the Arabic elegy (rith'a),[33] carving the Arabic into the Hebrew through the mediation of the Yiddish. The poem ends on the one biblical allusion that does not distinguish between self and other, "For their cry has risen many a night," evoking both the outcry of the enslaved Israelites in Egypt (Exod. 2:23) and the outcry of the Philistine city of Ekron: "And the cry of the city went up to the heavens" (1 Sam. 5:12).

During times of historical strife, it was common to rewrite the Yiddish lullaby as a collective lament and an expression of terror and grief. That Ravikovitch is invoking the specific Yiddish model becomes indisputable in light of the poem's first published version, which was titled "A Lullaby Translated from the Yiddish." This version appeared in a special feminist issue of the journal *Politika*, about a year and a half after the beginning of the first Intifada.[34] Both lament and lullaby are, of course, traditionally female genres. But Ravikovitch, who did not speak Yiddish, takes this gendered use of genre one step further: the torture and suffering related here by Palestinian mothers and grandmothers are typical of the "feminized," "diasporic" Jewish discourse, which—like Yiddish itself—is the Israeli's excluded "other."

It is no accident that women—mothers, grandmothers, and Rachel the symbolic mother of the nation—serve here as agents of poetic transmission, whose voice gives expression to traumatic national memory and constructs a solidarity between Palestinians and diasporic Jews. This is not to say, however, that some essentialized female position is identified in Dahlia Ravikovitch's poetry with immanent blamelessness and victimization. In a poem sarcastically titled "The Poetics of Applying 'Moderate Physical Pressure,'" published in her posthumous volume, *Many Waters*, a horrific Abu Ghraib–like torture is perpetrated by an Israeli female soldier on the Palestinian man she is addressing.[35]

In Ravikovitch's best-known political poem, "Hovering at a Low Altitude," an ethical condemnation of the female speaker vitiates any essentializing idealization of a woman's voice. More than any other poem by Ravikovitch, "Hovering" has come to represent the return to an ideologically engaged poetry of protest in the Israeli literature of the late 1970s.[36] "Hovering" presents two female characters and a man who, though offstage almost till the end, fills the space of the poem with his ominous presence. At the center of the scene is an innocent young shepherdess, presumably Arab, who is about to become a victim of rape and murder; and hovering surrealistically overhead is an Israeli woman, the poem's speaker, who watches from a safe distance, repeating "I am not here," "I haven't seen a thing." Using the first person, Ravikovitch presents her poetic persona as implicated in her culture's denial, thereby enabling us to confront our own.

The title, "Hovering at a Low Altitude," uses army Hebrew in the style of military briefings or news bulletins. In the context of the early 1980s, the phrase would typically refer to low-flying helicopters in hovering formations, patrolling over Southern Lebanon. Here, however, it is the female speaker who is hovering, floating mid-air as in a Chagall painting, thus compelled to see what is happening below. But the title is also a brilliant double-take: in Hebrew slang, "to hover" (*le-rachef*) means to be politically and emotionally detached. *Richuf* is a Tel Aviv state of mind, an Israeli version of "cool" that allows people to dissociate from the political "situation" (*ha-matzav*):

> I've found a very simple method,
> not so much as a foot-breadth on land
> and not flying, either—
> hovering at a low altitude.

As Robert Alter writes: "The image of low-altitude hovering over an atrocity is an ... effective emblem of the situation of the ordinary Israeli, knowing but choosing not to see certain terrible acts perpetrated by other Israelis, or even in the name of the nation; more generally, it is a parable of the moral untenability of detached observation in any political realm."[37]

The poem has generally been taken to be a direct response to the first Lebanon War since it first appeared in an anthology of antiwar poems published in the wake of the 1982 Israeli invasion. The landscape, however, doesn't quite fit—there are no ice-capped mountains to the east of Israel—nor does the time line of the poem's publication history match that of the June war.[38] Ravikovitch herself indicated that she was initially visualizing the situation in Afghanistan or Iran, and that for her the girl in the poem was "not only Arab," though "the Palestinian question was nevertheless on my mind while I was writing."[39]

"Hovering" brilliantly dramatizes the dilemma of witnessing. Reading the poem through its ethical charge means refusing either to locate its referents at a "comfortable" distance in Central Asia or to regard it simply as a universalist humanitarian condemnation of injustice. The poem thematizes and condemns precisely such attempts to escape the here-and-now ("I am not here") when rape and murder are taking place right before one's eyes. Given that Ravikovitch chose to publish the poem in the context of the 1982 Lebanon War, one is compelled to read it in the light of the Israeli reality of the late 1970s and early 1980s. How can the speaker—as woman, as Jew, as ethical subject—persist in passively observing every detail of the rape and murder of a young (Arab) shepherdess (in the mountains of Lebanon) from a close distance ("a low altitude")? That is to say, metonymically, how can one stand idly by as horrors are perpetrated just a "hover" away from Tel Aviv—without becoming party to the responsibility for those crimes? Furthermore, how can the poet aestheticize such violence, in the very process of making it the subject of the poem, without implicating herself?

This ethical probing is profoundly intertwined with the poem's Jewish intertextual practices. Ravikovitch asks quite a lot of her reader here: first, to identify and reject the biblical metaphor of the nation as licentious woman ("She doesn't walk with neck outstretched / and wanton glances. / She doesn't paint her eyes with kohl"—see the descriptions of the Whore of Zion in Isa. 3:16–17, Jer. 4:30, and Ezek. 23:40); and then to infer from this also a rejection of the patriarchal move of blaming the victim ("she asked for it"). Ethically and politically explicit though it is, "Hovering" is thus far from being a one-sided *J'accuse*. Through a series of radical uses of lexical ambiguity, metaphor, and a critique of the biblical topos of the Nation-as-Woman, Ravikovitch rejects any possibility of obscuring the crime, or the wider analogy it implies, between sexual and national violence. In the process, the young girl is constituted as a subject, just as the speaker, and her audience, risk losing their humanity.

The perpetrator, described only as "that man," is identified synecdochically at the end of the poem through his "hard hand." While this horrifying detail is part of the literal description of the crime, it is clearly also a citation of the IDF idiom for the "iron fist" policy of suppressing Palestinian resistance. The narrative of rape and murder in the poem, therefore, inseparably links gender and national politics. Through the biblical allusions, Ravikovitch draws our attention to the literal and figurative sexual brutality of (the discourse of) religious obedience, as well as that of conquest, colonialism, and occupation-as-rape of the subaltern, feminized land—a discourse that has historically been legitimized by this gendered biblical metaphor. The verse from Isaiah quoted here ends with an appalling sexual punishment inflicted by God on the head and genitalia of the Nation-as-Woman, an ending that is rarely translated into English. It literally reads: "And God will afflict with leprosy the crown of the head of the Daughters of Zion, and Yahweh will empty their vaginas / make gonorrhea pour forth from their vaginas."[40]

"Hovering at a Low Altitude" has become a model for the new Israeli political poetry, not despite but precisely because of its figurative and intertextual complexity.[41] The process of radical biblical intertextuality that we have observed in Ravikovitch's oeuvre cuts two ways, as in the poetry of Yehuda Amichai. On the one hand, Ravikovitch rescues meaning, and a code of conduct, from the sacred Jewish sources, by which she wishes us to judge contemporary institutions of army and state. On the other, she also subjects those sources, and their modern nationalist appropriations, to a relentless critique. This bilateral engagement with the textual archive of her culture makes Ravikovitch at once profoundly modern and unabashedly Jewish—a secular woman prophet for our times.

Notes

1. Interview with Sima Kadmon, *Ma'ariv*, February 2, 1991, 22–23. For incisive discussions of this and other aspects of Ravikovitch's poetry, see *Sparks of Light: Essays about Dahlia Ravikovitch's Oeuvre*, eds. Hamutal Tsamir and Tamar S. Hess (Tel Aviv, 2010) [Hebrew]. Henceforth, *Sparks of Light*.

2. Dahlia Ravikovitch, *Kol ha-shirim*, eds. Giddon Ticotsky and Uzi Shavit (Tel Aviv, 2010), 19. English translation in *Hovering at a Low Altitude: The Collected Poetry of Dahlia Ravikovitch*, trans. Chana Bloch and Chana Kronfeld (New York, 2009), 55–56. Henceforth, *Collected Poetry*. All subsequent citations of Ravikovitch's poems are from these volumes.

3. To Ayelet Negev in "Dahlia Ravikovitch Talks (About Everything)," *Yedi'ot Acharonot*, March 1, 1996, 22–28 [Hebrew].

4. *Kol ha-shirim*, 99; *Collected Poetry,* 119–20.

5. Ravikovitch is alluding to the title of Prokofiev's avant-garde comic opera, *The Love for Three Oranges.*

6. *Kol ha-shirim*, 11–12; *Collected Poetry*, 49–50.

7. In Idith Zertal, "'Poetry—A Disembodied Soul': Interview with the Poet Dahlia Ravikovitch," *Dvar Ha-Shavu'a*, July 8, 1966. [Hebrew].

8. See Mordechai Shalev's early essay, "Dahlia Ravikovitch: Keening Poet," in *Ha-Aretz*, April 2, 1969 and June 13, 1969 [Hebrew]. Shalev revised this essay for Tsamir and Hess's volume *Sparks of Light* (2010), 109–36.

9. See Hess, "A Poetics of the Fig Tree: Feminist Aspects in the Early Poetry of Dahlia Ravikovitch," *Mi-kan* 1 (2000): 27–43 [Hebrew]; and Tsamir and Hess's introduction to *Sparks of Light* (2010).

10. *Amot* 6 (1963): 96 [Hebrew].

11. *Kol ha-shirim,* 230–33; *Collected Poetry,* 212–14.

12. In "David Avidan: Just the Man in the Poem," May 1995 [Hebrew], after the death of poet David Avidan.

13. Theodor Adorno, *Aesthetic Theory* (London, 1984), esp. 327.

14. Theodor Adorno, *Prisms* (Cambridge, MA, 1981), 256.

15. See interview with Karpel in *Ha-Ir* (1986). [Hebrew]

16. *Kol ha-shirim*, 93–94; *Collected Poetry*, 113–14.

17. For a detailed reading of this poem and of Ravikovitch's political verbal art in general, see Chana Kronfeld, "Political Poetry as Verbal Art in the Work of Dahlia Ravikovitch," in Tsamir and Hess, *Sparks of Light* (2010), 514–43.

18. *Kol ha-shirim*, 22–23; *Collected Poetry*, 59–60.

19. Hamutal Tsamir, "The Dead and the Living, the Faithful and the Uprooted: Dahlia Ravikovitch, Keener and Prophet—A Reading in 'Waiting for the Messiah,'" *Mi-Kan* 1 (2000), 44–63 [Hebrew].

20. *Kol ha-shirim*, 103–4; *Collected Poetry*, 122–23.

21. See our "Dahlia Ravikovitch: An Introduction," *Prooftexts* 28 (2008): 268–69. Ravikovitch added that the poem was understood in this way by Arab readers as well, and that it was translated into Arabic by Mahmoud Darwish and published in *Al Ahram* in Cairo.

22. *Kol ha-shirim*, 54; *Collected Poetry*, 85–86.

23. "Upon First Reading," Israeli Educational Television, 2004, [Hebrew].

24. *Kol ha-shirim*, 230–34; *Collected Poetry*, 212–15.

25. *Shibutz*, the traditional Jewish stylistic device of inserting *tesserae* of biblical quotations to enhance the authority and beauty of the text.

26. *Kol ha-shirim*, 198–213; *Collected Poetry*, 189–99.

27. March 28, 1989, Berkeley, CA.

28. *Kol ha-shirim*, 300–301; *Collected Poetry*, 263–64.

29. *Kol ha-shirim*, 241; *Collected Poetry*, 219–20.

30. See Kronfeld in Tsamir and Hess, *Sparks of Light* (2010) for the specifics of the poem's engagement with the Yiddish cradle song, especially the famous "Rozhinkes mit mandlen" (Raisins and almonds).

31. "Nigun atik" (old tune), both a nostalgic folk-song (and dance) and a 1957 gothic poem by Nathan Alterman; and "Zemer nugeh," a poem of yearning "for that which has been lost" by the poet Rachel (Bluvshteyn).

32. On diasporic deterritorialization as the norm in Jewish literature, see Sidra DeKoven Ezrahi's *Booking Passage: Exile and Homecoming in the Modern Jewish Imagination* (Stanford, 2000).

33. Thanks to Margaret Larkin for this insight.

34. July 27, 1989. This was first discovered by Ofra Yeglin in 2005 in an essay reprinted in Tsamir and Hess, *Sparks of Light* (2010), 161–72. The posthumous edition of Ravikovitch's work wisely includes this earlier version as a separate entry. See *Kol ha-shirim*, 334–35.

35. *Kol ha-shirim*, 293–94; *Collected Poetry*, 261–62; the title invokes the language of the Israeli Supreme Court, establishing what is permissible in interrogating Palestinian detainees. The expression is generally used as a sarcastic euphemism for torture.

36. *Kol ha-shirim*, 179–81; *Collected Poetry*, 174–76. See special section on this poem in *Reading Hebrew Literature*, ed. Alan Mintz (Hanover, NH, 2003), 213–45; and in Tsamir and Hess, *Sparks of Light* (2010), 514–65.

37. Foreword to Dahlia Ravikovitch, *The Window: New and Selected Poems*, trans. Chana Bloch and Ariel Bloch (New York, 1989), xii.

38. Hanan Hever and Moshe Ron, eds., *There Is No End to the Battles and Death: Political Poetry in the Lebanon War* (Tel Aviv, 1983), 90–92 [Hebrew]. The poem was actually written before the war.

39. In conversation with Chana Bloch, Berkeley, CA, March 28, 1989.

40. See, for example, the exegesis by Amos Chacham, in *Knowing Scripture: Isaiah* (Jerusalem, 1984) [Hebrew].

41. For a detailed discussion of these and other inverted allusions in the poem, such as to Psalms 121, to the popular song "The Little Shepherdess from the Gulch," and the citations of IDF Hebrew to anchor it in the Israeli here and now, see Chana Kronfeld in Mintz, *Reading Hebrew Literature* (2003) and Tsamir and Hess, *Sparks of Light* (2010).

Joel and Ethan Coen (1954– /1957–)
FINDING RABBI MARSHAK

Daniel Herwitz

THERE IS A PARTICULAR PERSPECTIVE FROM WHICH RELIGIONS MAY BE EXAMINED in modern times: how modern religions deal with those ultimate human concerns that are most impervious to time, change, and progress. Death is now accountable by biochemistry but it still packs a wallop. Modern medicine can pinpoint disease to genetic configurations. But this does not reduce the sense of unfairness when it is a family member who has the gene and comes down with something terminal at a young age. Why me, Job asks God, staggering, bloated with boils, in anguish, his property destroyed and family extinguished. Today Job could be a refugee, an impoverished child, an abused woman, or a young adult stricken with some mortal disease petitioning from Yemen, Iraq, China, Zimbabwe, New York, or Washington. Inequality has never been more telling than it is in the second decade of the twenty-first century. For those working the derivative markets there are peace, prosperity, personal trainers, second homes on tax-sheltered islands, and youth-preserving procedures done in private clinics. For them entire law firms are put on twenty-four-hour call when divorce rears its (inevitable) head. At the same time so many other people are treated *as* derivatives.

Ultimate questions about human life are raised around trauma, dislocation, and massive inequality but are also—as the history of philosophy has suggested—basic to the way human beings try to make sense of their experience: of what it is to dwell on earth in the presence of evil, knowing one will disappear soon enough. Meditation on such matters is as old as the sources of religion, as obsessive as the origins of philosophy. Nothing is more human than to petition life with unanswerable questions; these are signs of human wonder, seriousness, anxiety, and uncertainty. The philosopher Martin Heidegger went so far as to claim that we become authentic *only* by raising these questions. Only then does death come to frame life in the right way. The search for answers may be quixotic, but can lead to a deepening of human purpose. There is comedy in this: this predicament or liability of humans to rise to their most serious, most human aspects when they gape at life in the hope of answers to questions that surpass, as Immanuel Kant put it, the very bounds of (their) reason. There is also terror. "Where were you when I created the world," God asks Job. "Why should you expect to understand my work, when I am the transcendental God?" God's response (which I have somewhat improvised) puts Job in his place, but also teaches him a lesson, deepening his spirituality and humility. Explanation, God means Job to understand, comes to an end.

I

The petition to God is perennial to religious life, yet the power of religion to address the petition has shapeshifted dramatically in modern times. Science has caused religion to frame its response differently to those seeking the solace of the next life. Religion has gone on the defensive, become more adamant, or conversely it has tried to find some kind of intellectual/spiritual rapprochement with the lessons of science. Religion has also given way to therapeutic intervention; death always feels easier and tastes better on the analyst's couch, especially with the help of diazepam (Valium).

This loss of authority in modern life by religion has been offset by various ways in which religion has gained in authority. A rabbi is by name and vocation a teacher, but his/her project is not simply to teach the wisdom of the ancients, instruct the young, or stand humbled and in awe before the power of God. The rabbi or priest is in the modern world also a conduit for a new kind of *secular* project, which is claimed to be rooted in religious origin, that is, heritage/history, and which can under certain circumstances acquire (for the good, bad, or ugly) the force of a calling, cause, or destiny. Heritage is that scripting of history into a group's origin and destiny, and for the modern Jew, as is well known, Zionism has taken on the heritage role: return to the Holy Land, claimed as "ours" by virtue of "our" biblical past, our long and uneasy years in the diaspora, our bond between land, religion, and people. After World War II, Zionism became the essential project for many if not most religious Jews (and many secular ones). Israel became *the* secular/spiritual project of postwar Jewry—that and the memorialization of a vanquished, vanished world of the European past. *Never again* the cry rang, commuted into resolve. Resolve became support for the Jewish state. A prayer for the safety of Israel was written into Reformed and Conservative American Jewish prayer books. If the rabbis in the postwar American temples have experienced a loss of authority since the days of their Orthodox shtetl past, if freedom of opportunity and diminishment of antisemitism in postwar America, along with assimilation, intermarriage, and other Americanizing traits, have weakened the authority of the rabbis and the temples, the rabbis and the temples have gained in authority in America and elsewhere through their shepherding of pain into Zionist resolve. That and in virtue of their appearing in the guise of an old-world heritage, which has taken on (for the American Jew) auratic value (the fiddler on the roof).

At the same time as the American Jew was moved by old-world/prewar heritage and Zionist resolve, American Judaism became by the 1960s a comfort zone, an insular world of rhinestone temples and suburban station wagons. If you asked many Jews at that time why they showed up for Sabbath service and had their children Bar or Bas Mitzvahed, they would have spoken of great and terrible things: the ruinations of the twentieth century, the defiant power of Israel, and the lingering power of *tradition*. A good bit of the time, however, they simply schmoozed their way through life at the temple while getting ahead in America, engaged in life's

usual intensities and banalities, raising families, mourning loved ones, betting on mah-jong, or booking flights to Miami Beach. This is not simply a stereotype (although it is certainly that). The attitude extended I think to the rabbis (some anyway) who became a strange graft of authority derived from old-world immigrant awe; post-Holocaust resolve; and American flatness, complacency, and gung-ho, combined with the usual male-centered claims on authority. Were one to make a film that subdued the element of Judaic destiny and sustainability (the story of the Holocaust, the state of Israel, and the commitment of the Jewish religion to both), and instead highlighted the temple as a place of dope-smoking Bar Mitzvah boys, dessicated Hebrew teachers, and men driving cream-colored Buicks between religious services and steam baths at the YMCA, trading anecdotes, golf clubs, and leather goods and bonding in broken Yiddish, postwar American Judaism might be reframed to bring out the oddness, the comedy in the graft. The rabbi would be there in all his authority but *not* to speak of heritage and secular destiny, *not* to pronounce on the Holocaust, Israel, or the sustainability of the Jewish people; rather, his role is to play out suburban dramas around divorce, tenure, and television. Such a film might highlight the historical nuttiness of the moment (the 1960s) even more sharply by telling the story of a serious individual whose divorce, tenure, and television leads him to posing ultimate questions in the manner of Job. There is nothing like the perennial question to illustrate the historically specific nature of the temple's response.

II

This film has been made and it is called *A Serious Man* (written, directed, and produced by Joel and Ethan Coen, 2009). The film rewrites the Book of Job for the suburban Middle American temple of the 1960s. There is no Israel, Holocaust, or psychoanalyst in the film, although I do think the way the rabbis act in part depends on a kind of authority generated by the Holocaust and Israel (which the Coen brothers do not highlight). There is a lot of heritage, a fair amount of old-world immigrant awe, and a way of playing all this out through a suburban American sensibility that lends the film its character. "We're Jews," Larry Gopnik's sister tells him as he sits with her by a tree, downhearted (he is the film's stand-in for Job). "We've got that well of tradition to draw on." And by tradition she means something like *heritage*. But no one in this suburban middle-class community seems to understand this heritage. Larry Gopnik (Michael Stuhlbarg) is in the middle of being divorced by his wife Judith (Sari Lennick), who tells him she needs a GET because otherwise her lover cum intended, Sy Abelman (Fred Melamed), says she'll be "agunah." "A GET," Larry repeats uncomprehendingly, as if she has said something from Mars. A Jewish writ of divorce, she tells him. We never find out what being "agunah" is and they certainly don't know, but it carries the portent of something ancient, Hebraic, profound, which is how the Hebrew language is for this group. No one understands it, the Bar Mitzvah boy recites it; this language carries the weight of some vast remnant that has lost its meaning in translation. (In point of fact "agunah" means "chained", as in a woman "chained" to her marriage.) In an opening scene of the film Danny sits in Hebrew class, the teacher so old he can hardly move, so boring Danny makes it through only with the help of his transistor radio plugged into one ear, listening to Jefferson Airplane. The teacher confiscates the radio.

Sy Abelman talks softly, as if at a wake. He believes himself sympathetic but is in fact predatory. With funereal unctuousness he hugs Larry (whose wife he has stolen), asking, "How *are* you?" as if Larry has just come down with something terminal (which may not be far wrong). His real purpose is to shore up Judith while she tells Larry to leave the house and go stay in a motel. The ever-passive Larry moves into the Jolly Roger, a local pasteboard motel, which is part of the suburban aluminum-sided landscape in which they live, they of this suburb of Formica kitchens, astroturf lawns, and motels with swimming pools. Larry takes a despondent room there with his brother Arthur (Richard Kind), who keeps Larry from sleeping because he snores. When not snoring, Arthur drains the cyst on his neck and works on his illegible book called the "Pentabulum," which carries the aura of the Kabbalah, the I Ching, the Tibetan Book of the Dead, all combined into the ravings of a madman. The Pentabulum rings of special access to divine meaning. Arthur's book is of a piece with the bizarre and hilarious story one Rabbi Nachtner (George Wyner) tells Larry about a dentist who discovers a secret script on the teeth of one of his patients and is determined to decipher it (to no avail). These portents of forgotten lore are like the Hebrew language itself and the Judaic heritage: awe-inspiring, incomprehensible, insane, and comic. Larry is a physicist, and early in the film we see him demonstrating the Heisenberg uncertainty principle to his class: the proof that one cannot simultaneously and with precision determine the position and momentum of an electron. Secret scripts all, this universe of things and people, ancient and modern.

Later in the film Larry will discover that Arthur's Pentabulum is in fact a virtuoso plan for how to cheat at poker. Arthur is arrested for sodomy and solicitation. Meanwhile Larry's tenure appears endangered because he has failed a Korean student who has given him a bribe without his being aware of it. He cannot find a way to return the money. Poison-pen letters are sent to the tenure committee, which Larry believes are from the Korean student's father but turn out to have been from Sy, who is killed in a car accident en route to the country club halfway through the film. Judith bludgeons Larry into paying for Sy's funeral.

The themes of heritage and of evil run through the film from its opening sequence, a Dybbuk story in black and white and in Yiddish. A Dybbuk is an evil being who in this case enters the home to wreak damage, and in a guise that is not easy to determine. In a completely artificial opening sequence one Velvel (Alan Lewis Richman) unwittingly invites such an evil being into his shtetl hovel, and the Dybbuk (Fyvush Finkel) is stabbed by Velvel's wife Dora (Yelena Shmuelenson). The sequence is drenched in the feel of old movies, as if old movies were in America the closest thing to prehistory and heritage. This opening sequence then immediately gives way to the film's present (the 1960s), turning from black and white to color, changing texture from grainy to translucent. Larry is in a doctor's office getting a chest X-ray (his yearly physical exam). The doctor smokes (yes, this is the 1960s, and the Coens do not miss a beat). The cut between *then* (Yiddish, black and white) and *now* (Americanese, color) juxtaposes old with new, inviting the theme of oceans crossed, time traveled, immigrations processed, suburbs gained, meanings lost. This gap is revealing, but also the product of artifice, a construct of Hollywood-style camera techniques and an American consciousness that treats the old country as ancient history (black and white), while constantly finding itself liable to receive (as if through telepathy) its secret, indecipherable, bizarre messages. These messages are at once absurd, irritating, and mesmerizing for their suburban recipients.

Jewish modernity in this postimmigrant suburban world of the 1960s therefore carries a double attitude toward the past. The past is affirmed through the authority of heritage, that compendium of talmudic and/or secret kabbalistic scripts that, inexplicable as they are, exalt the rabbis and the rituals (Bar Mitzvahs, Hebrew learning, etc.). But the past is also treated like stale bread, a thing past its sell-by date, an anachronism. The Coens' characters do not know who they are with respect to the Jewish culture that is their own. They are captivated and bored, agonized and dissociated, anxious and prosaic. Larry clings to scientific explanations (he is a physicist), but the kind of explanation he unfolds is that confirming uncertainty (the Heisenberg principle). He is desperate for an explanation of all that is happening to him but also passive, uncomprehending, unresponsive, almost an idiot savant. Significantly he lacks the ability to get angry. Larry is pained, but his affect is also flat, as if he isn't entirely there.

III

Flatness is a distinctive, one might say *definitive* American trait, which the Coens have spent their lives studying/parodying in the medium of film. They storyboard a landscape of humans speaking in processed, prefabricated language, humans who are also convinced that their blended lifestyles are singular and original. Convinced that they resolutely follow their own drummers, this parade of Coen brothers' characters live through prefabricated sources, and flatten out into a kind of Velveeta cheese. Alternately they think like food processors, digesting bits of circulated language with an excitable, resolute incoherence that passes for individuality. Coen characters mostly cannot distinguish between creativity and consumption. They are comics and consumers of *F Troop* and other TV programs, little GI Joes. These denizens' haunts are the bowling alley, mini mall, gym, Seven-Eleven store, and occasionally the Russian embassy or jail. They live where the cowboy, gangster, music man, wild one, and other artifacts of the American genre industry come to you in an audience of suburbanites downing coke and popcorn. The Coens' favoring of highly storyboarded movies increases the sense of artifice, unreality, and preprocessed formatting. Theirs is an America storyboarded halfway between genre and comic book.

Theirs is the America of Jeffrey Lebowski, aka the Dude ("El Duderino if you're not into the brevity thing"). The first time we meet the Dude (Jeff Bridges) in *The Big Lebowski* (directed by Joel Coen, written and produced by Ethan Coen, 1998), he is shopping at his local Ralph's supermarket for milk (he needs the milk for the white Russians he drinks). The Dude is wearing a bathrobe and either tennis or boxer shorts. On a TV in the supermarket George Bush Sr. declares war on Iraq with his trademark platitude: "This aggression will not stand." He is speaking of Saddam. Halfway through the film the Dude repeats what Bush Sr. says—"This aggression will not stand"—but in a situation that is so unlikely as to parody Bush Sr. himself (whose ideas of good governance and American morals are a collection of sound bites and ideologies), while also bringing out how language circulates (from TV to the Dude). The Dude, ever deluded, believes this prefabricated currency is in his mouth absolutely original (as if he were some Thoreau beating to his own drummer). This delusion makes him one of a genre, the genre being in this film Los Angeles proper. The film is itself a circulation of old genres and instances that storyboard into a graft as hilarious as the way people speak. In particular it is (loosely) based on Raymond Chandler's famous mystery *The Big Sleep*, especially the movie version of 1946 (based on the original 1939 novel) directed by Howard Hawks and written by William Faulkner, Leigh Brackett, and Jules Furthman and starring Humphrey Bogart and Lauren Bacall. The Dude is as daft as Bogart is canny. He is stoned (not hard-boiled) and wanders around in a fog. At no point does he have the slightest idea what is happening. The plot in which he is embroiled is as complex and unresolved as the Hawks film. Mistaken for a millionaire who also has the name of Jeffrey Lebowski, the Dude finds himself hired by this millionaire (played by David Huddleston) to recover his wife Bunny (Tara Reid). She has apparently been kidnapped. The millionaire spouts self-righteous Norman Vincent Peale talk of American virtues (featuring himself and in contempt of the Dude), while his wife is a pink-nailed, bikini-clad bimbo who offers the Dude sex for money. One of the nihilists is hanging around in their pool. Soon the Dude receives information in opera seria form that she's been kidnapped. The adolescent, addled Dude (himself an abiding flashback to the 1960s) recruits the help of his bowling friend Walter Sobchak (John Goodman) to recover her (with ransom money). Also sometimes involved is their third bowling partner, the amiable and idiotic Donny Kerabatsos (Steve Buscemi). Walter is a Polish Vietnam veteran, a character minted of uniquely maniacal currency. His meticulous obsession with rules and mores ("Asian-American is the preferred nomenclature") gives him the patina of rationality (by encoding him in America's craze for regulations and political correctness); however, he is a nutcase who cannot drop any pursuit until havoc is wreaked. The man cannot stop. And so he manages to totally mess up the delivery of the ransom money to said kidnappers, thus precipitating one of the nuttiest detective stories ever penned, involving a cast of landlords starring in their dance quintets, porn producers, incapacitated TV writers and their Hispanic nurses, and a stepdaughter of the millionaire (played by Julianne Moore) who paints from the body, literally spraying canvas while being hoisted naked above it courtesy of a machine into which her body is strapped. Later she sleeps with the Dude in order to get pregnant from a man she knows will have no interest in the baby. The Dude blunders his way through this collection of scenes in a drug-induced haze, hardly caring, just liking the idea of something to do besides bowling, enjoying the fantasy of himself as detective (as if in a TV commercial for one). You are what you perform.

The uniqueness of each character is a matter of how they make their way through the department store of American sound bites and identity types, picking and choosing, then amalgamating in accord with some unique, incomprehensible principle of concatenation. The Coen brothers have said they originally conceived this movie as a set piece for John Goodman, and he's got a number of the best lines in the film. Walter, a converted Jew, finds out that his bowling team is scheduled to "roll" on a Saturday and explodes: "I don't cook, I don't drive, and I don't fucking roll on the Sabbath. Shomer fucking Shabbas!" He is the tough/angry vet in the flak jacket, more Orthodox than the Orthodox Jew (when he so desires). The Dude tells Walter that the three emaciated Germans who keep showing up in odd places are "nihilists." Walter replies: "Fuck me! One thing you can say about National Socialism: at least it was an *ethos*." Here Walter speaks as the deep moral analyst of modernity and evil. Later still the Dude says the nihilists have put a ferret in his bath, which almost bit off his "Johnson." Walter responds (now the strict commissioner of rules), "Having a ferret within city limits contravenes state law." He is a combination know-it-all and paratactic logician (always offbeat). This inability to digest information except in accord with one's own addled drummer (composed from all manner of sound bites) links Walter to Larry in *A Serious Man*.

By some fluke Walter and the Dude do however manage to (more or less) solve the mystery through traversing a landscape of Los Angeles rollers, each parading in the guise of omnipotent certainty if not amiable lunacy. The German nihilists have faked the kidnapping in order to extort money from the millionaire, who is probably also in on it for financial reasons (his self-made success is a front, he is a failure in debt). Walter and the Dude confront the millionaire with the truth. It is important to note that this millionaire is in a wheelchair, the result of a war injury in Korea; as he says, "A Chinaman took my legs from me in Korea and yet the loss of my legs did not prevent me from getting up and achieving!" Walter, who always goes too far, decides he's lying about that too and lifts him from the chair to force him to reveal that he can walk. He cannot. The scene is dead-on (about Walter), riveting, and absolutely appalling. A "battle" with the nihilists follows in which Walter bites one of their ears off (another has already lost a toe). Donny dies of a heart attack—mostly to allow the ending of the film to occur. It ends on a beat of flatness: Carrying Donny's ashes in a Ralph's supermarket coffee container to the cliffs above the sea (Walter is too cheap to pay for a proper receptacle), Walter tosses them toward the water in a paean to their friend, only to have said ashes blown back over the Dude because Walter has tossed them into an opposing wind. "Oh fuck it," Walter says. "Let's go bowling."

In *Raising Arizona* (1987), the plot hinges on the theft (and eventual return) of a baby, one of the "Arizona quints" or quintuplets. Hi (Nicholas Cage) and Ed (Holly Hunter) have met at the moment of arrest, and more than once: Hi is a repeat offender (petty theft with short-term jail sentences); Ed is a policewoman, thrice decorated. When they (now married) find that they cannot have children, nor adopt (on account of his checkered past), and when they get news of the Arizona quints (five babies born to one Nathan Arizona and his wife), they conceive (to stretch a word) the plot of stealing one of the babes for their own. After all, with five how much will it be missed? All manner of zany hilarity breaks out around this act of theft, with the five infants crawling about the second floor of the Arizona house creating chaos while Hi tries (successfully) to whisk away the fifth (the "best one," he tells his wife Ed proudly). As he introduces the infant to their Tempe, Arizona prefabricated home, he enters their TV room saying this is the room for "relaxing with the family unit." Naturally he gets the grammar of this wrong since the baby is part of the family unit, not a thing that relaxes "with it" as if with a pet. That Hi uses this arcane turn of phrase, more appropriate to social science or policy reports, shows the *Americanus bubus*'s desire to connect to circuits of speech that carry (in his mind) special authority and power, as if to an electric current. Hi's buddies show up at the house and make this desire even more clear. They have just escaped from prison and Ed (who is a policewoman) asks them: "You mean you busted out of jail?" "No ma'am," one replies. "We released ourselves on our own recognizance." The other man breaks in: "What Evelle here is trying to say is that we felt that the institution no longer had anything to offer us." They have twisted circuits of speech in a way that turns confinement into freedom of opportunity (free choice). Once the institution no longer serves, they leave it (as if it were a university or church). In this semantic idiocy the illusion of their freedom and independence is confirmed.

In the interests of space let *The Big Lebowski* and *Raising Arizona* stand in for other Coen films, almost every one of which offers a unique twist on (1) how the prefabricated aluminum siding of language circulates with complete confidence, cheerfulness, and resolve; (2) how bits of language and belief are grafted together with equal aplomb into a unique, incomprehensible logic by each character, which is their self-performance, their right of citizenship if you will, and also legitimated by references to their source (in George Bush, TV, magazines, whatever); and (3) how these characters exist and act in situations in which everyone else is also concatenating reality in equally nutcase ways, producing total anarchy within the social order.

IV

The amazing thing about *A Serious Man* is how these features extend not only to Larry but to the rabbis. Their authority derives from religious heritage and postwar secular resolve, but they speak with the grain-fed cheerfulness of the *Americanus bubus*, grafting logic from all quarters (tradition, ritual, and suburb) into something even funnier because it is also combined with their penchant for Judaic irony. As he sinks into Job's mire, everyone tells Larry Gopnik he has to talk to Rabbi Marshak. The rabbi is wise, venerable, of the old country; everyone believes he is the real spiritual thing. But Larry cannot get to this man. Marshak won't make appointments, except with Bar Mitzvah boys; he won't take calls; and finally, when a desperate Larry pleads with Marshak's secretary that he simply must speak to the rabbi, she limps into Marshak's office on arthritic bowed legs only to return with the remark: "The rabbi is thinking" (meaning unavailable for consult). Now this is a direct transcription from a famous scene from the life of Martin Heidegger, in which people hike their way up the Alps to meet the great man only to be told by Heidegger's faithful wife: "Er denkt" (he's thinking; ergo, you will disturb him). (Ethan Coen got a philosophy degree from Princeton University before joining his older brother in Hollywood to work on scripts.) This aura of authenticity surrounding the great man is where religion, the sublime, and modernity fuse in a Kafkaesque plot, since Gopnik never gets to see the rabbi. (At least God reveals himself to Job, if only to put Job in his place.) Marshak is the last remnant of the old Europe of the shtetl rabbi, an artifact with sagging skin, the heavyset wisdom of the old country. He is the last living remnant from steerage and held in appropriate awe.

Instead Gopnik meets Marshak's two younger colleagues. The first, Rabbi Scott Ginzler (played by Simon Helberg), listens to Larry's tale of woe and then goes into a riff about parking lots whose point is to say, more or less, *Who knows God's ways they are strange and mysterious, but still isn't life wonderful, just look outside my window at the parking lot, what a beautiful parking lot on such a beautiful day.* This disquisition places the young rabbi steadfastly in the land of Americana, in love with its vast expansion of space, its oversized Buicks, anything at all outside his office window. Gopnik literally does not know how to react, especially to the resolute cheerfulness with which the speech is delivered as if the rabbi is offering breakfast cereal to the desperate, believing it will lessen malaise. This is more than the Yiddish shrug (who knows, who can tell?); it is American optimism writ large, the commercial break peddled as vintage wisdom. Were Rabbi Scott Ginzler transposed back into a novel by Voltaire, he would be Pangloss.

Gopnik's consult with the second rabbi happens at the urging of his sister: "We're Jews," she says. "We've got that well of tradition to draw on. Have you talked to Rabbi Nachtner?" From Nachtner we get the most bizarre moment of the film, the story of the teeth that goes so nicely with the Pentabulum, the Torah, and the dazzling mathematical script of Heisenberg's proof. Naturally, this story does not help either. Moreover, Larry's lawyer suggests Nachtner tells *everybody* this story, it's his generic tale, like some shtick from the Catskills. From Nachtner, as from Ginzler, the Judaic skepticism about God (Who can know, who do you think you are to presume to understand the ways of God, better to take things as they are, in all their uncertainty, and by the way I love every minute of it), fuses with the breakfast of champions to "cerealize" Judaism. Were the film to have stopped at this point, it would present the postwar American rabbi as simply ludicrous, with a capacity for response and a digest of tradition offered with a cheerfulness that make you unsure if they are responding from the pages of the Book of Job or selling cars. So much for how the authority of the postwar rabbi plays itself out when it turns from the great matters of the day (the Holocaust, Israel) to the more mundane matters of suburban existential pain.

Which brings us to Rabbi Marshak, whose authority is that of a leftover sage from the old country, a last remnant of black and white cinema (in Yiddish). Marshak is the sage you never get to meet anymore than you would meet Moses on the mountaintop. He is in the past, at the temple by courtesy of rapidly receding time. This makes his presence auratic. Marshak shares with the Bible a sublime power to compel awe that comes from his old-world unavailability. Were Gopnik actually to talk to him, he might well disappoint. Since Marshak's power to inspire depends on his absence he can't *help* you. This seems to me the basic principle of Judaism as the Coen brothers frame it: Judaism is the religion that can't help you, but on the other hand it doesn't offer the illusion of a rose garden where you would sit with the angels of the Lord in a state of beatitude watching the world through a flat-screen TV in the afterlife. What it's got are parking lots and encrypted teeth. There is honesty in this, along with the skeptical stance of: *I've really no idea, I can't answer your question even if you are suffering and on the brink of disaster.* There is also absurdity, because a parking lot doesn't offer any extra help to those who have already parked, as Gopnik presumably has when he goes to the temple to see the rabbis.

However, this is not the full story because *someone* gets to see Rabbi Marshak even if it isn't Larry Gopnik: his son Danny and the other Bar Mitzvah recipients.

When Danny steps into Marshak's study, the tenor of the movie shifts. The rabbi speaks little and slowly. He is not a man of (American) run-on platitudes. His is the severe intensity of the Old World, terrifying, stale, but also surprising. The rabbi quotes the Jefferson Airplane song that is on the tape in Danny's transistor radio (that radio has ended up in Marshak's keeping). The words to the song begin, "When the truth is told," and go on from there. Marshak then returns the radio to Danny with the words: "Be a good boy." Either he has said nothing, or a great deal. It is a moment when the film seems to hover at the gates of reversal, to break through (or almost) to something more authentic, even while retaining an ironic stance on this anachronistic old man. The key is: he says little and *does* something (returns the radio). And in spite of the fact that Danny is so high on the day of his Bar Mitzvah that he can hardly make it to the altar to recite his Torah portion when he does recite, this is enough to produce a transitory reconciliation between Judith and Larry. The profound things in life do not happen in words, especially in the words of the American suburb. The profound things, or almost profound things, happen in the manner of signs, gestures, inscriptions, deeds, and also rituals. So maybe Judaism isn't completely useless even in contemporary times?

A Serious Man ends on an ominous note. We are at Danny's Hebrew school. The students, including Danny, are outside. A tornado approaches and they are told to take safety in another building. While the old Hebrew teacher fumbles to find the right key to the door, Danny is mesmerized by the gelid discoloration in the sky, fast approaching. Cut now to Larry's doctor, who calls Larry to say he should come immediately to discuss his chest X-ray. Unlike Job, Larry is not taught any lesson in the film that would deepen his humility or spirituality. The film ends in a state of existential danger.

V

The film explores the role of a half-illegible heritage in a contemporary suburban world and the role of the rabbis in its transmission. It does not explore that part of the postwar Jewish heritage that pertains to the Final Solution and the state of Israel (mission, destiny), although as I suggest these events are critical in framing the authority of the rabbis Larry Gopnik meets — or does not meet. Probably there is a good artistic reason for this absence of context: it would kill the comedy, deflect from the preposterous hilarity of a Book of Job in which heritage meets parking lot. The Coen brothers are filmmakers first. Their characters have to jump off the page. Their story and storyboarding must remain taut to the point of zaniness. They exaggerate to draw out their picture of America. Moreover their work is as much about Hollywood genres as it is about anything else.

One might then reasonably ask if their picture of 1960s suburban temple life strikes home, if it is fair and accurate given the comic exaggeration, storyboarding, and genre-bending? Fictional films are hardly exact mirrors of the social reality they picture. Their point is to veer off with a certain slant that brings home the portrait. Here the slant is highly storyboarded exaggeration. Is it, however, exaggeration to the point of being excessively one-dimensional? Were things up to a point really like that back then? I have no survey or massive set of data points assembled to answer one way or another. What I do have are personal anecdotes; please take them as they are. Personal anecdotes only go so far, and yet, I have the feeling my two little tales will have resonance with those of others who lived through the Reformed and Conservative Judaism of the 1960s. If not, then apologies for the personal intrusion.

I am thirteen years old and in the confirmation class of my temple in Massachusetts. It is the 1960s, and mine is a Reformed/Conservative temple in the suburbs. The chief rabbi is a strict old man with a large Enrico Caruso collection of 78s, which he used to play for the students (who preferred Jefferson Airplane and owned the exact model of the radio Danny had confiscated in the film). His favorite sermon topic is who hated the Jews. It turns out Beethoven, Brahms, Goethe, Picasso, George Washington, and Fredrick Douglass were all antisemites. In short, everybody of consequence was (except Moses and Golda Meir). Today we are studying God. I ask, "If God is everything and everything includes evil why do we pray to God? Wouldn't that mean we are praying to evil?" He stares at me with disapproval, sizing me up. After a while he responds: "If you can scratch your nose with your hand, then why do it with your foot?" Many years later I think over what he said. I decide he meant something like: *Why make things difficult if you don't have to and anyway you are a smart ass boy who asks too many questions, at least have the grace to wait until the curse of Job hits you and then we'll talk . . . maybe.*

Years later my fiancée and I are in San Francisco and want to get married by a rabbi. Thirteen rabbis refuse us: this one is on study leave in Israel; this one requires that we pay up and join the congregation first (I recall his words on the telephone were: "Our life events are restricted to congregation members"); this one specializes in intermarriages and wants extra cash for a crash course in Judaism as part of the marriage deal, and won't reduce the cost after we explain that between the two of us we've done two lifetimes of Hebrew school and Jewish learning. Most won't marry us because one of us has been married before (to a Jew) and the rabbis require a GET which we won't get. Finally a clever woman rabbi, kinder and gentler than the rest, and smarter, says: *Let's play a game, when you were married was it under a proper canopy [Chupah], did you read out this, sing that, no, you didn't then you were never married and do not need a GET, I will marry you.* And so she did. Judaism can be a headache but its capacity for reasoning is marvelous; it can't finally help you (promising neither salvation nor explanation), but it can at least find a way to get you married, and without a GET. That is its consolation prize, its sponge cake.

Nevertheless it is crucial to restate the fact that postwar Judaism in America is structured around two points of certainty absent from the film: the Holocaust and Israel. These play a central role in giving the rabbis the authority they have even in this film. The Holocaust and Israel lent Judaism historical urgency and moral authority; they gave Judaism a mission, made it compelling. My uncle remained a Jew because of the Holocaust; in solidarity and defiance, my father supported the 1967 war with money as so many Reform and Conservative American Jews did, believing their heritage had finally found a secular realization in that new settler society. Between the resolute requirement of memory (*the world shall never forget*) and the commitment to Israel's survival, postwar American Judaism projected itself with fierce authority.

In the last quarter of the twentieth century, both of these magnets weakened. Israel's moral authority has been unhinged by its aggressive occupation politics. While the Holocaust will never disappear from the Jewish imagination, it has receded as a plank of Judaic sustainability. The Holocaust kept the likes of my uncle in the temple, but has less historical power to keep the children of the twenty-first century there. It is no longer a mission. And Rabbi Marshak is nowhere to be found. Already old in the 1960s, he was the last of his generation, the last of those bringing the Old World to the new. His aura, already anachronistic, has disappeared with him. Its power to compel was a combination of American immigrant nostalgia, old-world heritage, and the determination to preserve the last artifact of the ravaged world of European Jewry.

The patriarchy of the rabbis has weakened, leading to a kinder, gentler generation of the rabbinate for a twenty-first-century religious consumer and seeker of solace, tradition, and spiritual life. This reformation of Judaism continues. However, the sustainability of American Judaism has—without Marshak or magnets—become a serious matter.

Judith Butler (1956–)

BETWEEN ETHICS AND POLITICS

Bonnie Honig and John Wolfe Ackerman

> I began my philosophical career within the context of a Jewish education, one
> that took the ethical dilemmas posed by the mass extermination of the Jews
> in World War II, including members of my own family, to set the scene for the
> thinking of ethicality, as such.
>
> —JUDITH BUTLER, "ETHICAL AMBIVALENCE"

IN HER ESSAY "ETHICAL AMBIVALENCE," JUDITH BUTLER SAYS HER WORK IN PHI-
losophy can be seen as an extension of her early interest in Judaism, though it might
just as well be said that her early interest in Judaism was an extension of her interest
in philosophy. Punished as a teenager for misbehaving in Hebrew school, she was
sentenced, to her delight, to private tutorials with the rabbi, with whom she read
Spinoza, Buber, and more. Judaism and philosophy are thus inseparable for her.
Still, in later years, in her own academic work as a philosopher and theorist of sex/
gender, she was reluctant to turn to Jewish themes and hesitant, as well, to turn
to ethics. She overcomes her qualms about both in "Ethical Ambivalence." Here,
Butler thematizes her hesitation and moves, by way of Nietzsche, away from Hegel,
the continental philosopher who so influenced her early work, to Levinas, the Jewish philosopher of ethics with whom she had not earlier engaged.[1] Since turning to
Levinas, and to the topic of precarious life with which he is associated, Butler has
positioned herself as a Jewish thinker *and* as an active critic of Zionism. Indeed,
in the years since this essay was first written in 2011, Butler has become very well
known for her effort to develop a specifically Jewish critique of Zionism.

Judith Butler began her philosophical career as a critical but admiring reader
of Hegel in *Subjects of Desire: Hegelian Reflections in Twentieth-Century France*
(1986). She engaged issues of politics or identity, focusing not on ethnicity or religion but on sexual minorities. In *Gender Trouble: Feminism and the Subversion of
Identity* (1990), writing on behalf of gay, lesbian, and transsexual forms of subjectivity, she turned her critical attention to unjust heteronormative social structures.
She also criticized forms of feminist politics that contested male privilege but, at the

same time, resecured traditional sex-gender identities, thereby sidelining gay, lesbian, and transsexual forms of life. Mobilizing the resources of critical theory, continental philosophy, deconstruction, feminist theory, and psychoanalysis, Butler has since continued to mark, in books, essays, and lectures, the arbitrary and often coercive nature of identity, seeking to break down established divisions to enable new alliances and solidarities among marginalized groups.[2] She has also criticized the ideals of emancipatory politics, from the sovereign subject of the Enlightenment to universalism, humanism, and Zionism. Her critique of universalism typifies the sort of critique for which she has become famous. Some political and social critics, she says, want "to be able to use the language of universality without interrogating it," but their "rush to *decision-ism* and to strong normativity very often fails to consider what is meant by some of the very basic terms it assumes."[3] This is a hallmark of Butler's work: her commitment to relentlessly interrogate even our most cherished ideals.

After 9/11, Butler turned her attention most centrally to U.S. state-sponsored violence, specifically those actions that followed the attacks (from the military elements of the "war on terror" to the clandestine activities that accompanied them, from wiretapping to rendition and torture). This pressed her further into the role of public intellectual, reaching now to audiences beyond those in philosophy and the queer and feminist communities she had earlier addressed. By now a devoted reader of Levinas, she presented as "Jewish" but also as "humanist" the concern to stem violence and to mourn equally the deaths on all sides of political conflicts, and she called more fundamentally still for critical examination of the social ontologies that frame some lives as grievable and others as not, some deaths as losses and others as not. Movingly detailing her easy familiarity with someone like the murdered journalist Daniel Pearl, whose last name she notes is her middle name and whose European Jewish background is similar to hers, Butler highlights the importance of learning to say other names that are less familiar and to grieve the lives associated with them as well.

Most recently, and aiming to supplement Levinas who was not broadminded on the issue, Butler has turned her attention to Israeli-Palestinian politics and the challenge of what she calls "cohabitation." A member of the Executive Board of The Freedom Theater Foundation in Jenin, the Advisory Board of Jewish Voice for Peace, and the Board of Directors of Faculty for Israeli-Palestinian Peace–USA, Butler is also on the International Support Committee of the Russell Tribunal on Palestine and a vocal supporter of the Boycott, Divestment, and Sanctions (BDS) movement. She has given seminars and lectures at the Institute of Women's Studies at Birzeit University in Ramallah and is an increasingly frequent and sought-after activist voice of opposition to the Israeli occupation, as well as to discrimination against Palestinians and Arabs within Israel. Butler's book, *Parting Ways: Jewishness and the Critique of Zionism* (2012), makes the philosophical case for a Jewish ethics of nonviolence that should operate as a restraint on what can be done politically in the name of Judaism or Israeli security. Butler characterizes such work as Arendtian; she says it rekindles "an Arendtian tradition within Jewish thought" (*Parting Ways*, 179) and, indeed, Butler does follow in the footsteps of Hannah Arendt, the earlier, formidable critic of Zionism. But Butler also parts ways with

Arendt, joining the plural politics of "care for the world," as Arendt called it, with something Arendt—for better or worse—never sought to provide: the elaboration of an ethics by which to guide politics.[4]

Butler's Jewish ethics is built on what she sees as a paradoxically Jewish imperative to "part ways" from Judaism's ideology of "chosenness." Still, it is a Jewish ethics, and she sees it as a kind of transitional object for those Jewish supporters of Israel looking for a way to query or rework their inherited Zionism. This Jewish ethics is an instance of what Arendt, borrowing from the British parliamentary tradition, called "loyal opposition" (*Jewish Writings*, 393). Drawing on Arendt but also on Walter Benjamin, Primo Levi, Franz Rosenzweig, Franz Kafka, Levinas (tempered by Edward Said), and others, Butler finds an invitation in this mostly Jewish tradition of writers and thinkers to connect so-called friends and enemies. Her ethics of nonviolence, one that "binds the fate of the Jew with the non-Jew" (*Parting Ways*, 179), aims to provide the baseline for a new and different politics. This politics is guided by ethical hesitation, rejects sovereignty as ineluctably violent, and posits in place of sovereignty the shared trait of vulnerability and a norm of unchosen cohabitation that might ground the call, issued by Butler and others, for a possible right of return. This right of return is not just for Jews to Israel but also for Palestinians to Palestine. As she herself becomes involved in various political struggles in the West Bank and Israel, however, and as the situation in Israel/Palestine has arguably worsened in the last few years, with the Gaza war of 2014 constituting a particular nadir, the mutuality and vulnerability that Butler talks about in her writings have become more real and immediate, foregrounding aspects of quotidian interdependence that the state-centered face of the conflict sometimes obscures.[5] Butler's involvement in political activities has led her, increasingly, to a political position that, while still motivated by ethical responsibility toward ("non-Jewish") others, reaches well beyond ethical hesitation to the articulation of wide-ranging political claims.

Politics of Performativity

> I was drawn toward those kinds of readings that suspended the law, exposed its illegibility, its internal limits and contradictions, and even found Jewish authorization for those kinds of readings. I was also compelled to show that this kind of reading did not paralyze ethical or political action, to show that the law might be critically interrogated and mobilized at once.
>
> —JUDITH BUTLER, "ETHICAL AMBIVALENCE"

Mutuality and vulnerability have been important themes throughout Butler's work. In all her writing, Butler has examined the power and fragility of social norms, which both discipline and constitute subjects. We think we are governed by norms, and we are, but they are also dependent upon our daily reperformance of actions that conform to them. Thus, even very powerful norms can be altered, opened to ways of life previously foreclosed by the dominant social order.

In her best-known work, *Gender Trouble*, Butler argued that heterosexuality is not natural, but is rather the effect of heteronormativity, a normative ideology that may seem totalizing, natural, and irresistible but is actually reproduced through our own everyday performances of its demands. Butler cites practices of drag as just one instance of sex/gender's simultaneous strength and fragility: drag parodies conventional sex/gender roles and exhibits their artifice. Watching male drag performers put on femininity, we may come to realize that women do the same sort of thing. They teach themselves and their bodies femininity. Far from being natural, Butler concludes, sex/gender norms are performative, and they can be performed otherwise. In the daily reperformance of sex/gender norms, we can enhance or undermine reigning norms and even remake them. Indeed, those very norms, on which we seem to depend and by which we are constituted and constrained, actually depend on us for their vitality and power.

Some feminists criticized Butler's account of sex/gender performativity for suggesting that entrenched gender rules could be dissolved by way of a kind of individual voluntarism or posturing that does not address social injustice, which is systemic and impervious to individual actions.[6] Butler has come to concede elements of this critique and sought to remedy, first, her early work's "occasional voluntarism" and then, also, its "relentless activity," in her words, which she now offsets by calling attention not only to the need to interrogate and resist exclusions wrought by particular norms but also to respond to "the ethical claims of others."[7]

Uniting her earliest and latest work is Butler's vision of change as emerging out of a perfect storm of normative obligations, the desires they incite, and the possibilities for resistance that become available in the living and acting of the psycho-social positions they institute. In *Antigone's Claim: Kinship between Life and Death* (2001) and *Who Sings the Nation-State? Language, Politics, Belonging* (with Gayatri Spivak, 2007), Butler rejects both structuralist claims about the natural or law-like nature of patriarchal kinship as well as biopolitical claims about the vulnerability of the stateless to brutal subjection by sovereign state power. Butler champions those who not only contest sovereignty but also seek to enlist it, in altered form, on behalf of their cause. She admires Antigone's claim, in Sophocles' play, to a sovereignty that her antagonist Creon claims as exclusively his, and she endorses the public singing of the U.S. national anthem in Spanish by undocumented immigrants. Their performance, Butler notes, is a claim to equal participation under the very laws that proclaim the singers illicit or "illegal." Butler's aim here is to rework and reinhabit sovereignty so that it can be something other than the sole prerogative of a unitary and often arbitrary power.[8]

Sovereignty becomes more problematic for Butler, however, and less available for reinhabitation, when she focuses more centrally on ethics than politics. In *Precarious Life: The Powers of Mourning and Violence* (2004), *Giving an Account of Oneself* (2005), and *Frames of War: When Is Life Grievable?* (2009), Butler seeks out an ethics for her performative politics and theorizes a nonsovereign subject, constitutively dispossessed, vulnerable, and enmeshed in its relationships with others. In view of those entanglements, this ethical subject is hesitant to act, and is even, on occasion, instructed to refuse to do so (*Frames of War*, 184). Such inaction is a feature of the ethics of nonsovereignty (or of "ambivalence") that Butler promotes as a support for political resistance to the violence unleashed by sovereign states. Butler's effort to conjure a new Jewish (post)modernity capable of countering a hegemonic state Zionism is pursued under this ethical banner. This opens her politics to a new temptation, and Butler knows it. She sees that her post-Zionism must "overcome a sharp divide between ethics and politics" in order to avoid two perils: violence and withdrawal (*Parting Ways*, 9).[9]

Cohabitation: Ethical or Political?

[T]o "be" a Jew is to be departing from oneself, cast out into a world of the non-Jew, bound to make one's way ethically and politically precisely there within a world of irreversible heterogeneity.
—JUDITH BUTLER, *PARTING WAYS*

From this conception of the ethical relation follows a reconceptualization of both social bonds and political obligations that takes us beyond nationalism.
—JUDITH BUTLER, *PARTING WAYS*

Butler tethers her critique of nation-state Zionism to the claim that there is a distinctly Jewish obligation to cohabit the world with non-Jews. Butler traces this principle to Hannah Arendt's condemnation of Adolf Eichmann, whose real crime, Arendt said, was his refusal to share the world with others—"Eichmann thought that he and his superiors *might choose* with whom to cohabit the earth" (*Parting Ways*, 125)—and for this, Arendt found, he deserved to die. Butler borrows the violated norm of cohabitation, but she criticizes the voice in which Arendt passes sentence on Eichmann. That voice, Butler says, is the voice of sovereignty. When Arendt speaks as if *she* sentences Eichmann, she ventriloquizes the judges and inhabits without apparent discomfort and perhaps even with a certain pleasure, Butler discomfitedly notes, the subject position of sovereign power. Butler, who cringes in response to the death sentence and the sovereign voice in which it is uttered, dissociates herself from this and from the broader tendency toward sovereignty to which she thinks all political action is drawn. Butler reformulates Arendt's judgment into a universal ethical principle of cohabitation and self-dispossession less prone to slip into sovereignty.[10]

In this reformulation, as in her other recent forays into ethics, Butler is guided primarily by Emmanuel Levinas, in particular by his conviction (compatible with Butler's own account of how subjects are formed in response to social norms) that subjects are brought into being by way of address by an Other whose claims are prior and absolute. Butler is also drawn, however, to Levinas's wariness with regard to politics, which, he worried, drives subjects more toward sovereignty than plurality. As Butler sees it, the problem is that politics is incapable of cultivating its own necessarily plural and self-contesting ground. "Ethics," on the other hand, is able to undo presumptively preconstituted subjects and to sustain the plurality that politics must presuppose. It is in quest of such an ethics that Butler turns to Levinas as she turns to formulate a Jewish critique of (Israeli state) violence.

But Levinas is a somewhat unreliable contributor to this cause. Accepting the Zionist narrative of return, Levinas was not opened to the claims of Palestinians by his otherwise demanding ethics of the Other. Butler counters by revaluing Israel's historical dispersion, endorsing and not lamenting the fact that its departure from itself makes any unitary "Israel" impossible. Israeli state violence is not, on her account, a defensive necessity forced on it by friend/enemy politics; it is now cast instead as the unavoidable result of the impossible wish to fend off dispersal by way of a sovereignty-centered politics.

Butler finds in Edward Said, whom she dubs "a diasporic Levinas" (*Parting Ways*, 51), the politics that she thinks a Levinasian ethics ought to have provided but did not. She credits Said with recognizing the often painful lessons of exile that animate her vision. Like her, Said appealed to Jews to acknowledge experiences of displacement and dispossession as a basis for alliance with Palestinians. But Said's politics is also not enough, Butler suggests. It needs the supplement of the ethics she borrows from Levinas, which Said himself only began to provide late in the day: At the end of his life, Butler argues, Said too theorized a "constitutive ethicality" to be lived in the form of a binationalism involving "not 'two' nationalisms, but a joint effort to live to the side of a nationalist ethos," moving "beyond identitarianism and pluralism alike."[11]

Putting Levinas and Said together, Butler reads "dispossession as an exilic moment" that is not wholly negative: she offers us an "I" that has suffered, an "I" that has been "vacated" as self-sufficient and is "motivated" by its own suffering "to alleviate the suffering of others" (*Parting Ways*, 127; compare *Giving an Account of Oneself*, 136). The ethical subject is bound, "from the start," to "those who are not readily identifiable as part of 'one's community,'" whom one "never chose," and it is "dispossessed from sovereignty and nation" in response to their claims. This ethics takes us beyond nationalism, "beyond a sovereign claim" and toward "a challenge to selfhood that I receive from elsewhere" (*Parting Ways*, 9, 129–30; compare 23–25).

In sum, where she once admired efforts to reinhabit and revise sovereignty, from within, as part of an iterative, performative politics (modeled by drag performers, Antigone, so-called illegals in the United States), Butler now, in quest of a Jewish ethics of nonviolence, seems to move "beyond" sovereignty, and even seems to abjure sovereignty as per se corrupting and violent. Butler's embrace of Levinas leads her to argue that ethical politics must renounce sovereignty, not performatively subvert it. Arendt offers an important counter to that Levinasian view, one that is neither pro- nor antisovereign. She develops that view throughout her work, but it is especially in *Eichmann in Jerusalem*, in the text that Butler finds most unsettling, that Arendt's unique, iterative conception of sovereignty can be seen — especially if we approach that text through the lens of Butler's concept of performative politics.

Beyond Sovereignty?

> I'm not sure anybody wants to be *post*-sovereign.
> —JUDITH BUTLER, *WHO SINGS THE NATION-STATE?*

Butler sees Arendt's slip into a "sovereign" voice as a sign of how insecure is Arendt's grasp of the nonsovereign demand issued by Levinas. But we could also read Arendt's judgment of Eichmann as Butlerian parody, a performance of sovereignty in drag. On this reading, when Arendt passes sentence as she thinks it ought to have been passed — finding Eichmann guilty of crimes against humanity rather than, as the Jerusalem Court did, of crimes against the Jewish people — she speaks in the name of an alternative sovereignty, not that of the state of Israel but rather one that corresponds with the new international law, a sovereignty that does not yet exist but which would be needed to try the case properly in her view. Without that alternative sovereign form to anchor it, the Jerusalem Court risks looking like an arm of the state, not an instrument of justice. In quest of that new sovereignty, Arendt ventriloquizes it avant la lettre, as it were. Lonely sounding, seemingly sovereign in tone, her voice conjures further into existence the public and the new form of sovereignty that her death sentence presupposes.[12]

In her writings on Israel-Palestine, Arendt had gone even further and issued a call for sovereignty. The sovereignty she favored was not the old unitary form, which was in her view a relic of the nineteenth century, but a new practice of shared Jewish-Arab co-governance. The solution for Israel-Palestine was not to avoid sovereignty, but to renegotiate it into new, nonstatist forms. Her vision of alternate sovereignties importantly evidences Arendt's own mistrust of sovereign states as harbors for politics. The co-governance she proposed was to occur at the level of local councils and to be temporarily overseen by an international body. The institution that goes missing in her picture is the very one about which Butler also worries: the state. "Local self-government and mixed Jewish-Arab municipal and rural councils, on a small scale and as numerous as possible, are the only realistic political measures that can eventually lead to the political emancipation of Palestine" and thereby save the quest for a Jewish homeland, Arendt argued (*Jewish Writings*, 401).[13] Arendt also mentions the then proposed Jordan Valley Authority as a possible site of common cause (*Jewish Writings*, 399), as well as other forms of entrepreneurial activity. Although Arendt might not put it quite this way, we could say that she is here pressing for the generation of public goods (water, commerce) because these in turn generate the publics (not the friend/enemy divides) that politics and worldliness postulate. Profane practices like debating and administering shared and scarce resources give shape to a common world. The commitment to cohabitation is nurtured, on a daily basis, by diverse opinions and shared situations.[14]

Cohabitation, Butler's ideal, could be ethical and/or political, but co-governance, in the context of what Arendt called the "mutual refusal to take each other seriously" (*Jewish Writings*, 429), is ineluctably political. Butler does not discuss co-governance in *Parting Ways*, perhaps because the moment for that seems to have passed. In 2011, and even more so since, the ideal of co-governance has become even less realistic than in Arendt's day. Instead, Butler directs us to an ethics of equality that is not the fragile performative product of political action but the prior ethical condition of politics. She offers a norm of cohabitation to guide political actors and applauds examples of dissidence or indignation, not governance. In sum, Butler focuses on the critique of statist violence that she shares with Arendt, but treats Arendt's explicit brief for cohabitation in ethical rather than political terms. That said, there are, however, in Butler's political practice and in her writings intimations of an alternative notion of sovereignty that point beyond ethics to politics.

Co-Dissidence, Co-Governance, and How We Tell Their Stories

I am trying to imagine what might happen if two "traditions" of displacement were to converge to produce a postnational polity based

on the common rights of the refugee and the right to be protected
against illegitimate forms of legal and military violence.

—JUDITH BUTLER, *PARTING WAYS*

In *Who Sings the Nation-State?*, Butler approvingly notes Arendt's efforts to theorize politics as a mode of "shared governance" that involves "govern[ing] in common with those with whom we may share no sense of belonging at all." What Butler admires here is the institutionalization of "notions of social plurality that would diffuse sovereignty" (*Who Sings*, 25, 24). "Diffuse sovereignty" is a good term for Arendt's idea of a sovereignty other than the "spurious [sort] claimed by an isolated single entity." In its place, she suggests, a different sovereignty may assume "a certain limited reality," especially when we attend to politics as a site of plurality and mutuality, one that features "many men mutually bound by promises" (*Human Condition*, 245). As we have suggested until now, Butler's specific examples of unlikely collaboration among Jews and Palestinians today seem to attest more to the present possibility of nonsovereign co-dissidence than to any nascent efforts at a diffuse sovereignty of co-governance.[15] But, with Arendt's help, we may discern in Butler's political interventions intimations of a projective or "diffuse" sovereignty that tempers and perhaps even overcomes any ethical hesitations about sovereignty that Butler may harbor. For example, Butler lauds

> the activist weekly demonstrations at Bi'lin where many have suffered physical injury and death, the important triumph at Budrus to steer the wall away from the olive trees, the persistent rallying of support in Sheikh Jarrah for those threatened with the confiscation of their homes, and those whose homes have already been transferred to Jewish Israelis, the important engagement with *Ta'ayush* (Arabic for "living together") during the second Intifada when medical supplies were illegally transported into the West Bank, the Israeli feminist activism of Machsom Watch at the checkpoints dedicated to witnessing, chronicling and opposing harassment and intimidation of Palestinians, or the work of Palestinian and Jewish Israelis together at *Adalah* in Haifa (an organization surely worthy of receiving a Nobel), which has legally processed thousands of claims against Israel for the confiscation of Palestinian lands and the expulsion of Palestinians from their homes and their homeland. I would include among these the Boycott, Divestment, and Sanctions movement, which now has an Israeli version, which stipulates that co-existence requires equality and cannot take place under conditions where one party is subjected to colonial subjugation and disenfranchisement—an Arendtian view, to be sure.[16]

The value of these "forms of contact, adjacency, unwilled modes of co-habitation" that challenge inegalitarian proximity lies in their "activism," whether cooperative or solitary: "[T]hese are but a few of the many insistent and important ways of practicing and thinking about alliance, modes of working together, but sometimes working in separate venues against the illegal occupation and for Palestinian dignity and self-determination" ("Precarious Life and the Obligations of Cohabitation," 23). Butler's focus here is on dissidence, but such activisms depend on a possible future co-governance. This is almost always evident in Butler's writing, as when she imagines "a postnational polity based on the common rights of the refugee," as well as a "new concept of citizenship" that is not national but diasporic, never at home with itself, always in exposure to the other or, as Franz Rosenzweig might put it, the neighbor (*Parting Ways*, 16, 130).

Indeed, the stories Butler tells of cooperation across the Green Line, around the "separation barrier," and in defiance of the cordons traversing Israeli society are stories of individuals and groups taking political responsibility for a common world. When they do so, they project sovereignty and diffuse it. From time to time, Butler also tells stories that underscore the significance of "idealized moments" to revolutionary politics. For example, she describes how the 2011 demonstrators in Cairo's Tahrir Square established a sociality of "horizontal relations" as a practiced alternative to the regime, "so the social form of the resistance began to incorporate principles of equality that governed" the demonstrators' speech and actions, their methods of caring for and cohabiting with each other "incorporating into the very social form of resistance the principles for which they were struggling on the street" ("Bodies in Alliance"). Here she reiterates her arguments from *Gender Trouble* and *Bodies That Matter*, prizing the capacity to modify entrenched patterns of daily life by collectively and iteratively performing them otherwise.[17]

Telling stories alone is not enough to bring about new forms of co-governance, but incipient co-governance cannot be imagined or made real without such stories. And those stories require for their reality and realization ongoing exercises in co-dissidence and co-governance. Already existing political exercises in "diffuse sovereignty"—iterative, performative, diasporic—may be seen as responses to the call for "a new concept of citizenship." Without such ideals to illuminate their practice, dissidents and activists risk lapsing into old sovereign habits—whether into the violent sovereignty of unitary models of governance or the withdrawalism demanded by sovereign ethics of personal integrity. Each offers its own version of insulation from the true challenges of political life. Arguably for this reason, to help inoculate against such dangers, Butler moves beyond celebrating examples of resistance to call also for "a rethinking of binationalism in light of the racial and religious complexity of both Jewish and Palestinian populations, a radical reorganization of land partitions and illegal property allocations, and even minimally a concept of cultural heterogeneity that extends to the entire population and is protected rather than denied by rights of citizenship" (*Parting Ways*, 130–31).

Developing a post-Zionist Jewish ethics and politics of cohabitation, Judith Butler extends her earlier work on gender and performativity and makes clear her commitment not just to critique but to equality and the reconstruction of emancipatory ideals in practice. In this work, Butler has tended to incline more toward co-dissidence than co-governance.[18] The former instances her ethical commitment to cohabitation but may unfortunately also express her ethical reservations about risking implication in sovereignty, which is always to some extent complicit in the violence she wishes to combat, on Butler's Levinasian account. But the stories Butler tells about her ethics of cohabitation are illuminated, advanced, and perhaps even informed by a diffuse politics of sovereignty to which Butler's engagement with Arendt directs us. Butler's engagement with Jewish thought beyond Levinas and her involvement with and support for the BDS movement, for a Palestinian right of return, and even for new *state* structures in Israel-Palestine have eroded the divide between ethics and politics that once marked her work.[19] Butler's contribution to Jewish modernity is continuously taking further shape through her quest for a new politics of Israel/Palestine, one that she characterizes as "Jewish and not Jewish and, indeed, not restricted to that binary" (*Parting Ways*, 131). Butler's work is an important part of many efforts right now, some larger, some smaller, to shift the terms of cohabitation in Israel/Palestine in the hope of one day, maybe, remaking the current sovereign formations in the region.

Notes

1. Judith Butler, "Ethical Ambivalence," in *The Turn to Ethics*, eds. Marjorie Garber, Beatrice Hanssen, and Rebecca L. Walkowitz, CultureWork series of the Humanities Center at Harvard (New York, 2000), 15–28.

2. See, e.g., Judith Butler, *Frames of War: When Is Life Grievable?* (London, 2009), 135, as well as *Bodies That Matter: On the Discursive Limits of Sex* (New York, 1993); *Excitable Speech: A Politics of the Performative* (New York, 1997); *The Psychic Life of Power: Theories in Subjection* (Stanford, 1997); *Antigone's Claim: Kinship between Life and Death* (New York, 2000), and *Undoing Gender* (New York and London, 2004).

3. Interview with Gary A. Olson and Lynn Worsham, "Changing the Subject: Judith Butler's Politics of Radical Resignification" [2000], in *The Judith Butler Reader*, ed. Sara Salih with Judith Butler (2003), 356, 355. This is her response, first to Martha Nussbaum and then to Nancy Fraser, who calls on Butler to provide more normative guidance and less critique. Emphasis in original.

4. See Ella Myers, *Worldly Ethics: Democratic Politics and Care for the World* (Durham, NC, and London, 2013).

5. This can be witnessed in recent public presentations and political texts of Butler's, e.g., "Exercising Rights: Academic Freedom and Boycott Politics," lecture given at Birzeit University, Ramallah, February 8, 2010, published (in Hebrew) in *Mita'am* 24 (2011) (compare also "Israel/Palestine and the Paradoxes of Academic Freedom," *Radical Philosophy* 135 [2006]: 8–17); "Precarity, the Assault on Gaza, or Whose Lives are Grievable?," lecture given at Birzeit University, February 10, 2010; "You Will Not Be Alone," speech given at University of California–Berkeley, April 14, 2010, published on the *Nation* website, http://www.thenation.com/article/you-will -not-be-alone; "The Cultural and Academic Boycott," speech given at Israel Apartheid Week, Toronto, March 9, 2011; "The End of Oslo," LRB Blog, Sept. 25, 2011, http://www.lrb.co.uk /blog/2011/09/25/judith-butler/the-end-of-oslo; and "Self-Determination, Palestinian Statehood, and the Anarchist Impasse," lecture given at the Open University, Milton Keynes, UK, February 7, 2012.

6. See, e.g., Molly Anne Rothenberg and Joseph Valente: "[T]wo problems attend Butler's program, not only in *Gender Trouble* but throughout *Bodies That Matter*. First, Butler relies on a volitional politics even as she disavows volitionality in her model of subjectivity. Indeed, it is precisely Butler's own successful articulation of Derridean citationality with a nonhumanist, nonvolitional theory of subject formation that motivates our critique of the voluntarism of her political theory. Second, Butler's version of performativity stakes its claim to political efficacy upon an intentionalism so profound as to undercut the very social foundation of her project." "Performative Chic: The Fantasy of a Performative Politics," *College Literature* 24, no. 1 (1997): 296.

7. See Judith Butler, *Gender Trouble: Feminism and the Subversion of Identity*, 2nd edition (New York and London, 1999), new preface, xxv; and interview with Thomas Dumm, "Giving Away, Giving Over: A Conversation with Judith Butler," *Massachusetts Review* (2008): 97. Hannah Arendt was once subjected to a similar sort of critique by feminists who argued that her ideal of ancient Athens, in *The Human Condition*, reduced politics to the individualistic, "heroic" actions of posturing boys who sought glory, not justice. (See, e.g., Hanna Pitkin, "Justice: On Relating Public and Private," *Political Theory* 9, no. 3 [1981]: 327–52. On the limitations of this reading of Arendt, see John Wolfe Ackerman and Bonnie Honig, "Agonalität," in *Arendt-Handbuch: Leben—Werk—Wirkung*, eds. Wolfgang Heuer et al. [Stuttgart, 2011], 341–47.) Indeed, Butler herself criticizes Arendt on these very points, arguing that Arendt is too focused on "the 'act' in its singularity and heroism" and that she neglects social justice when she "adopts the internal point of view of the Greek polis on what politics should be, on who should gain entry into the public square and who should remain in the private sphere." "Bodies in Alliance and the Poli-

tics of the Street" (available at http://eipcp.net/transversal/1011/butler/en). (See also *Antigone's Claim*, 81–82; and Judith Butler, *Parting Ways: Jewishness and the Critique of Zionism* [New York, 2012], hereafter *PW*, 174–75; and compare *Frames of War*, 184, where Butler invokes Walter Benjamin to affirm the desisting from action [from voluntarism, from relentless activity] that her ethics would instead mandate: "Under such circumstances, when acting reproduces the subject at the expense of another, not to act is, after all, a way of comporting oneself so as to break with the closed circle of reflexivity, a way of ceding to the ties that bind and unbind, a way of registering and demanding equality affectively. It is even a mode of resistance, especially when it refuses and breaks the frames by which war is wrought time and again.") Butler finds more congenial Arendt's other work, in particular her writings on refugees and the pervasive condition of statelessness in the late modern world. These writings focus on the fragility of human experience and the need to share the world with others unlike ourselves.

8. See Bonnie Honig, *Antigone, Interrupted* (Cambridge, 2013), chap. 2.

9. Arendt, too, sees these as the two great perils of the Western political and philosophical tradition, and she associates *both* with the seductions of sovereignty construed as unitary: the violence of arbitrary domination and the withdrawal of "non-acting . . . as the only means to safeguard one's sovereignty and integrity as a person" (see Hannah Arendt, *The Human Condition*, 2nd edition [Chicago and London, 1998], 234). Both imperil politics, in her view.

10. See Butler, "Hannah Arendt's Death Sentences," *Comparative Literature Studies* 48, no. 3 (2011): 280–95. Most of this essay also appears in chapter 6 of *Parting Ways*, "Quandaries of the Plural: Cohabitation and Sovereignty in Arendt," which explores what Butler calls "the tension between sovereignty and cohabitation in Arendt" (*PW* 178). Interestingly, the essay version pulls back on Butler's condemnation of Arendt's slip into the sovereign voice, which is preserved in the book (see, e.g., *PW* 173–75, 177). At the end of the essay, Butler proposes an alternative that the book does not: "Does she elaborate a fictive position of sovereignty in order to condemn him to death within the fiction of her own making? Or does her voice split and counter itself in a theatrical enactment of an agonistic plurality?" Here, Butler seems to suggest that it cannot but do the latter; thus—beyond the inevitable dispersion of authorial voice posited in the book, but still despite itself—"it enacts a judgment in the name of a conjectured plurality," enacting that plurality too, as "unchosen, compelled, agonistic, and inconsistent" ("Death Sentences," 294–95). But it seems to continue to be the case that, for Butler, where sovereignty is dispersed into plurality, no sovereignty remains.

11. "Butler Live" (interview), in Vicki Kirby, *Judith Butler: Live Theory* (London, 2006), 156–57.

12. Arendt's presentation in effect parodies the very notion of a self-evidently sovereign nation-state; that she undertook this parody in the course of reporting on the trial of one of the administrators of the Final Solution more or less ensured that her parody would be missed. For complementary readings of Arendt's project, see Lida Maxwell, "Toward an Agonistic Understanding of Law: Law and Politics in Hannah Arendt's *Eichmann in Jerusalem*," *Contemporary Political Theory* 11, no. 1 (2012): 88–108; and Ariella Azoulay and Bonnie Honig, "Between Nuremberg and Jerusalem: Hannah Arendt's *Tikkun Olam*," *differences* 27, no. 1 (forthcoming, 2016).

13. In the 1940s and 1950s, Arendt argued that Zionism, a politics modeled on the nation-state, could not but produce a refugee problem—and she tracked this particular new nation-state-in-the-making's rapid production of a new minority problem, noting the Zionist leadership's official concession of minority rights to the Arab population in 1942, when Arabs were the numerical majority: "Proposed is an autonomous state based on the idea that tomorrow's majority will concede minority rights to today's majority, which indeed would be something brand-new in the history of nation-states" (Hannah Arendt, *The Jewish Writings*, eds. Jerome Kohn and Ron H. Feldman [New York, 2007], hereafter *JW*, 193; see also 429–30). The sovereign model of nation-statehood, she knew, was a symptom and support of the illusory vision of "autonomous Jewish politics" (*JW*, 57; compare 59) and its repeated failure to take seriously the "relationship of the Jews to other nations and peoples" (*JW*, 354), a critique she restated in *Eichmann in Jerusalem*, as well.

14. Arendt also discusses efforts from within the kibbutz movement to cultivate Jewish-Arab friendship—though she observes that the alternative economic structure of the kibbutzim, despite their strides toward "a new type of society in which there would be no exploitation of man by man," both reflected and fostered Jewish evasion of politics in Palestine and isolation in the region and the world. "In other words," she writes, "the alternative between federation and

Balkanization is a political one. . . . The task of a Near East federation would be to create a common economic structure, to bring about economic and political cooperation, and to integrate Jewish economic and social achievements" (*JW*, 349–51, 442, 450).

15. Like most political theorists, Butler tends to think of sovereignty as an all-or-nothing affair. When she talks about Arendt "institutionalizing notions of social plurality that would diffuse sovereignty," plurality is taken as an alternative to sovereignty—as it often is for Arendt too. Butler's differing readings of Arendt's sentencing of Eichmann are a good example of the tension in Butler's work between two ways of thinking about sovereignty—as intractably unitary or as possibly subject to pluralization or diffusion that does away with it (see note 9, above). But both obscure the third option, also discernible in Butler's work and actions, that we focus on here.

16. "Precarious Life and the Obligations of Cohabitation," public lecture given at the Nobel Museum, Stockholm, May 24, 2011, Ms., 23–24. Ms. available at http://www.nobelmuseum.se /en/nww-lecture.

17. While Arendt's theory guides us to actions in concert, her stories are often about great individuals. Indeed, she cites the Talmud's "thirty-six unknown righteous men who always exist and without whom the world would go to pieces" to justify the place of "quixotic morality in politics" (*JW*, 445). Butler, by contrast, calls attention to the activism of groups, even in dark times. These examples make real what others would miss or would cast as merely ideal and unrealistic. On the nonconflict between realism and idealism, or better on its unfortunate productivity in so-called realist thinking, see Bonnie Honig and Marc Stears, "The New Realism: From Modus Vivendi to Justice," in *Political Philosophy versus History?: Contextualism and Real Politics in Contemporary Political Thought*, eds. Jonathan Floyd and Marc Stears (Cambridge, 2011), 177–205.

18. In saying this, we do not mean to reprise deliberative democratic critiques of her work for being only critical and not normative—a distinction to which neither we, nor Butler, subscribe.

19. See, e.g, the 2013 interview "Willing the Impossible," https://www.opendemocracy.net/trans formation/ray-filar/willing-impossible-interview-with-judith-butler, and Butler's February 2013 talk at Brooklyn College on BDS, http://www.thenation.com/article/172752/judith-butlers-remarks -brooklyn-college-bds.

ACKNOWLEDGMENTS

IT IS A GREAT PLEASURE TO THANK ALL THOSE—INDIVIDUALS AND INSTITUTIONS— who helped in creating this book. First and foremost we are pleased to thank the Fondation Berma, Geneva, Switzerland. Without their generous support and confidence, this publication would not have been possible.

The University of Basel, Switzerland, provided a safe haven for the administration of this project. Here we encountered deep interest at various institutes and would like to thank Walter Leimgruber (Cultural Anthropology), Alfred Bodenheimer (Jewish Studies), and Ina Habermann (Center for Cultural Topographies).

Ulrich Schutz, editorial assistant, was essential to our progress. We are grateful for his support and superb professionalism. We wish also to thank Marc Koralnik of the Liepman Literary Agency in Zurich for his advice. Without the late Dr. Branco Weiss this book wouldn't have come into being. Béatrice Curty-Golay has been a patient companion on our long journey.

We thank our many contributors who addressed the intellectual adventures of their protagonists, as well as ours, with generous understanding. Working with so many brilliant people, of varied expertise, tastes, and intellectual temperaments, has been exciting, rewarding, fun, and sometimes even exasperating, but on the whole a wonderfully enriching experience, for which we are most grateful.

Translations from five languages were prepared by Catalina Girona, Sam Brody, Susann Codish, Amy Jacobs Colas, Catherine Diehl, Jeremy Gaines, Stephanie Galasso, Avner Greenberg, Patrick Hubenthal, Lisa Katz, Frances Kruk, David Nowell-Smith, Jeremiah M. Riemer, Batya Stein, and Catherine Temerson. Their careful and precise work is well appreciated.

This book has been made possible by the directors and the staff of Princeton University Press. We wish to thank Fred Appel, Natalie Baan, and Juliana Fidler.

Intellectual debts, unlike those associated with external goods, can be acknowledged but never repaid. We share a common interest in various topics with many friends: Yaron Ezrahi, Barbara Haering, Klaus Neumann-Braun, Arnau Pons, and Dan Rabinowitz. They all helped us with good ideas and advice.

THE EDITORS

CONTRIBUTORS

Editors

Jacques Picard is Branco-Weiss Professor for Cultural Anthropology and Professor for Modern Jewish History and Culture at the University of Basel. He is a co-director of the Institute of Cultural Studies and European Anthropology as well as the Center for Cultural Topography. He served as director of the Institute of Jewish Studies and as the Dean of research of the Faculty of Humanities. He was a member of the Independent Commission of Experts Switzerland—Second World War and served as its research director. Jacques Picard has widely published on the social and intellectual history of Jews in Europe.

Jacques Revel is director of studies (professor) at the Ecole des Hautes Etudes en Sciences Sociales, Paris. He served as the president of this institution between 1995 and 2004. He has also served as a professor of history at New York University and a visiting professor at the University of California at Berkeley and at Los Angeles, the University of Michigan, and numerous other universities worldwide. He is one of the editors of the journal *Annales: Histoire et Sciences Sociales*. Professor Revel's scholarship and publications center on two areas of study: the social and cultural history of Europe (sixteenth through nineteenth centuries) and the current trends of historiography.

Michael P. Steinberg is Vice Provost for the Arts and Professor of History, Music, and German Studies at Brown University. He served as founding director of Brown's Cogut Center for the Humanities and was a member of the Cornell University Department of History between 1988 and 2005. Educated at Princeton University and the University of Chicago, he has been a visiting professor at these two schools as well as at the Ecole des Hautes Etudes en Sciences Sociales in Paris and National Tsing-hua University in Taiwan. His main research interests include the cultural history of modern Germany and Austria with particular attention to German Jewish intellectual history and the cultural history of music.

Idith Zertal is an Israeli historian and essayist, who has taught at the University of Basel, at the Interdisciplinary Center Herzliya, and at the Hebrew University of Jerusalem. Professor Zertal has been visiting professor at the University of Chicago and the Ecole des Hautes Etudes en Sciences Sociales in Paris, and senior fellow at research institutes in Europe, the United States, and Israel. She is the author of many books and essays. Her book *Israel's Holocaust and the Politics of Nationhood* (originally *Nation and Death*) was published in Hebrew, English, French, German, Italian, Spanish, Catalan, and Polish. Professor Zertal is also the editor of a series of Hannah Arendt's books in Hebrew. Her own annotated translation of Arendt's *The Origins of Totalitarianism* was published in Israel in 2010.

Ulrich Schutz, photograph curator and editorial assistant of *Makers of Jewish Modernity*, is a co-worker of the Rector's Staff Unit at ETH Zurich, Swiss Federal University of Science and Technology. He graduated in History, Media, and Jewish Studies at the University of Basel.

Authors

John Wolfe Ackerman is a political theorist and Postdoctoral Researcher at Kent Law School, University of Kent at Canterbury, UK and visiting fellow at the University of Pennsylvania's Herbert D. Katz Center for Advanced Judaic Studies.

Robert Adler Peckerar is executive director of Yiddishkayt, the center for the study of European Jewish life.

Kevin B. Anderson is Professor of Sociology, Political Science, and Feminist Studies at the University of California, Santa Barbara.

Leora F. Batnitzky is Ronald O. Perelman Professor of Jewish Studies and Chair of the Department of Religion at Princeton University.

Nathaniel Berman is the Rahel Varnhagen Professor of International Affairs, Law, and Modern Culture at Brown University's Cogut Center for the Humanities. He also co-directs the Religion and Internationalism Project, an interdisciplinary forum.

Silvia Berti is Professor of Early Modern History at the Department of Philosophy at the University of Rome–La Sapienza.

David Biale is Emanuel Ringelblum Distinguished Professor of Jewish History and director of the Humanities Institute at the University of California, Davis.

Chana Bloch is a poet, translator, and Professor Emerita of English at Mills College, where she taught for many years and directed the Creative Writing Program.

Leon Botstein is President of Bard College and Leon Levy Professor in the Arts and Humanities.

Joseph Cohen is University Lecturer at the School of Philosophy, University College Dublin since 2007. He is also Researcher in Philosophy at the Karl Jaspers Center, University of Heidelberg.

Sidra DeKoven Ezrahi is Professor Emerita of Comparative Literature at the Hebrew University of Jerusalem and has been visiting professor at Duke, Princeton, Yale, Michigan, and Dartmouth.

Astrid Deuber-Mankowsky is Professor for Media Sciences at the Ruhr Universität Bochum.

Dan Diner is Professor for Modern History at the Hebrew University of Jerusalem.

Yaron Ezrahi is Professor Emeritus of Political Science and Political Philosophy at the Hebrew University of Jerusalem.

Lydia Flem is a psychoanalyst, a writer, and the author of a number of publications on Sigmund Freud. She lives in Brussels and Paris.

Ulrike Gehring is Professor for Modern Art History at the University of Trier. She has served as curator of art exhibitions at the Zentrum für Kunst und Medientechnologie at Karlsruhe.

Peter E. Gordon is Amabel B. James Professor of History and Harvard College Professor at Harvard University.

Ruth HaCohen is Arthur Rubinstein Professor of Musicology at the Hebrew University of Jerusalem, where she currently officiates as director of the Martin Buber Society of Fellows in the Humanities and Social Sciences.

Daniel Herwitz is Fredric Huetwell Professor of Comparative Literature, History of Art, and Philosophy at the University of Michigan, where for a decade he directed the Institute for the Humanities. He is also Honorary Research Associate at the University of Cape Town.

Hannan Hever is Jacob and Hilda Blaustein Professor of Hebrew Language and Literature and Comparative Literature at Yale University. He previously taught at the Hebrew University of Jerusalem, where he also served as the chair of the School of Literatures.

Ariel Hirschfeld is Professor of Hebrew Literature at the Hebrew University of Jerusalem.

Bonnie Honig is Nancy Duke Lewis Professor in the Departments of Modern Culture and Media (MCM) and Political Science at Brown University. She is also Affiliated Research Professor at the American Bar Foundation, Chicago.

Peter Hudis is Professor of Humanities and Philosophy at the Oakton Community College, Illinois.

Steven Jaron lives in Paris, where he works as a psychoanalyst and lectures on psychology at the Université Pierre et Marie Curie (Paris VI). His publications mainly consider both the literary and visual fields through the prism of psychoanalytic thought.

Bruno Karsenti is a philosopher and a director of studies (professor) at the Ecole des Hautes Etudes en Sciences Sociales, Paris. His work deals with the relationship between philosophy and the social sciences.

Pablo Kirtchuk is Associate Professor of Semitic Linguistics at the University Sorbonne (Paris IV).

Chana Kronfeld is Professor of Hebrew, Yiddish, and Comparative Literature at the University of California, Berkeley.

Martine Leibovici is a philosopher. She is a lecturer emerita at the Laboratoire de Changement Social et Politiques at the Denis Diderot University (Paris VII). She has published extensively on Hannah Arendt, Jewish modernity and totalitarianism.

Vivian Liska is Professor of German Literature and director of the Institute of Jewish Studies at the University of Antwerp, Belgium. She is also Distinguished Visiting Professor in the Faculty of the Humanities at the Hebrew University of Jerusalem.

Maud S. Mandel is Dean of the College and Professor of History and Judaic Studies at Brown University.

Yehudah Mirsky is Associate Professor of Near Eastern and Judaic Studies, and faculty member of the Schusterman Center for Israel Studies at Brandeis University.

Samuel Moyn is Jeremiah Smith, Jr. Professor of Law and Professor of History at Harvard University.

Jacques Picard, co-editor of *Makers of Jewish Modernity*, is Branco-Weiss Professor for Cultural Anthropology and Professor for Modern Jewish History and Culture at the University of Basel.

Griselda Pollock is Professor of Social and Critical Histories of Art, director of the Centre for Cultural Analysis, Theory and History, and one of the founders of the Centres for Cultural Studies (1985) and for Jewish Studies (1995) at the University of Leeds.

Arnau Pons is a Catalan poet, essayist, and translator. Since 2001, he has been a member of the hermeneutic Celan literature research group led by Jean Bollack in Paris. Pons has translated works by Paul Celan, Hélène Cixous, Dino Campana, Peter Szondi, and Hervé Guibert, among others, into Catalan and Spanish. As a publisher, he has published Hannah Arendt, Sarah Kofman, Idith Zertal, Mahmud Darwish, and Rachel Bespaloff, among others. In 2015 he received the National Prize of Spain's Ministry of Culture for his annotated translation into Catalan of Paul Celan's poem cycle *Atemkristall*.

Avi Sagi is Professor of Philosophy at the Bar Ilan University and Senior Research Fellow at the Shalom Hartman Institute in Jerusalem.

Christoph Schmidt is Professor of Philosophy and Religion at the Hebrew University of Jerusalem and Senior Research Fellow at the Van Leer Institute in Jerusalem.

Robert Schulmann is a German intellectual historian and Professor Emeritus of Boston University.

Galili Shahar is Professor for Comparative Literature and director of the Minerva Institute of German History at Tel Aviv University.

David Shneer is the Louis P. Singer Endowed Chair in Jewish History at the University of Colorado, Boulder.

Yuli Tamir is Professor of Philosophy and currently the president of the Shenkar College of Engineering and Design in Ramat Gan. She is a former Minister of Immigration (1999–2001) and Minister of Education (2006–2009) of Israel.

Galin Tihanov is the George Steiner Professor of Comparative Literature at Queen Mary, University of London. He was previously Professor of Comparative Literature and Intellectual History and founding co-director of the Research Institute for Cosmopolitan Cultures at the University of Manchester.

Enzo Traverso is Susan and Barton Winokur Professor in the Humanities at Cornell University.

Nelson H. Vieira is University Professor and Professor of Portuguese and Brazilian Studies and of Judaic Studies at Brown University.

Raphael Zagury-Orly is Researcher in Philosophy at the Karl Jaspers Center, University of Heidelberg and Guest Professor of Philosophy at the University of Rome–La Sapienza. He is also, since 2004, Professor of Philosophy at the Bezalel Academy of Fine Arts and Design, where, from 2010 to 2014, he directed the MFA program.

Raef Zreik is Co-academic Director at the Minerva Humanities Center, Tel Aviv University, and Associate Professor of Jurisprudence and Philosophy of Law at Carmel Academic Center, Haifa, Israel.

Moshe Zuckermann is Professor of History and Philosophy at Tel Aviv University.

ILLUSTRATION CREDITS

Chapter 2: Sigmund Freud in his summer cottage around 1932. Copyright © Ullstein Bild–Imagno.

Chapter 3: Émile Durkheim. Copyright © Picture Alliance/Leemage.

Chapter 4: Theodor Herzl at his desk in his study. Copyright © Ullstein Bild–Imagno.

Chapter 5: Simon Dubnow. Copyright © Ullstein Bild–Abraham Pisarek.

Chapter 6: Bernard Lazare. Copyright © Ullstein Bild–Roger-Viollet.

Chapter 7: Avraham Yitzhak Ha-Cohen Kook. Gift of Herbert A French to the Library of Congress.

Chapter 8: Aby Warburg: Courtesy of the Warburg Institute.

Chapter 9: Walther Rathenau. Photo copyright © Popperfoto/Getty Images.

Chapter 10: Else Lasker-Schüler. Copyright © Ullstein Bild–Abraham Pisarek.

Chapter 11: Rosa Luxemburg. Copyright © Ullstein Bild–Ullstein Bild.

Chapter 12: Arnold Schoenberg. Copyright © Hulton Archive/Getting Images.

Chapter 13: Martin Buber. Copyright © Paul Schutzer/The LIFE Picture Collection/Getty Images.

Chapter 14: Albert Einstein. Copyright © Popperfoto/Getty Images.

Chapter 15: Horace Kallen. Copyright © The New School Photograph Collection, The New School Archives and Special Collection, The New School, New York, NY.

Chapter 16: Franz Kafka. Copyright © Ullstein Bild–Imagno.

Chapter 17: David Ben-Gurion. Copyright © Arnold Newman/Getty Images.

Chapter 18: Franz Rosenzweig. Courtesy of the Leo Baeck Institute, New York.

Chapter 19: René Cassin. Copyright © Bill Ray/The LIFE Picture Collection/Getty Images.

Chapter 20: Shmuel Yoseph Agnon. Copyright © Pictorial Parade/Hulton Archive/Getty Images.

Chapter 21: Walter Benjamin. Copyright © bpk/IMEC, Fonds MCC/Gisèle Freund.

Chapter 22: Peretz Markish. From the Archives of the YIVO Institute for Jewish Research, New York.

Chapter 23: Gershom Scholem. Copyright © Ullstein Bild–Bunk.

Chapter 24: Leo Strauss. Courtesy of Jenny Strauss Clay.

Chapter 25: Yeshayahu Leibowitz. Copyright © Mondadori Collection/Getty Images.

Chapter 26: Theodor. W. Adorno, 1958. Copyright © Franz Hubner/Imagno/Getty Images.

Chapter 27: Mark Rothko. Copyright © Apic/Rue des Archives/PVDE/Getty Images. *Figure 1*: Rothko Chapel, Houston, Texas. Interior view with West triptych-Northwest-North triptych paintings. Photo by Hickey-Robertson. Copyright © 1998 Kate Rothko Prizel & Christopher Rothko / 2015 ProLitteris, Zurich. *Figure 2*: Mark Rothko, *No 27*. 1954. Oil on canvas, 205.7 x 220 cm. Private collection. Photo by Michael Bodycomb. © 1998 Kate Rothko Prizel & Christopher Rothko / 2015 ProLitteris, Zurich. *Figure 3*: Mark Rothko, *Untitled*. 1969. Oil on canvas, 92 x 78 7/8 in. (233.7 x 200.3 cm.) (5208.69). Collection of Christopher Rothko. Photo: Art Resource, NY. © Artists Rights Society, NY. © 1998 Kate Rothko Prizel & Christopher Rothko / 2015 ProLitteris, Zurich. *Figure 4*: Mark Rothko, *Untitled (Red, Orange)*. 1968. Oil on canvas, 233 x 176 cm. Fondation Beyeler, Switzerland. © The Beyeler Collection, Switzerland. Photo: Robert Bayer, Basel. © 1998 Kate Rothko Prizel & Christopher Rothko / 2015 ProLitteris, Zurich.

Chapter 28: Elias Canetti. Copyright © Ullstein Bild–Getty Images.

Chapter 29: Emmanuel Levinas. Copyright © Ulf Andersen/Getty Images.

Chapter 30: Hannah Arendt, 1949. Copyright © Fred Stein Archive/Archive Photos/Getty Images.

Chapter 31: Arnaldo Momigliano. Courtesy of the Centro Archivistico of the Scuola Normale Superiore, Pisa. Reprinted by permission of SNS. All rights reserved.

Chapter 32: Simone Weil. Copyright © Whiteimages/Leemage/Picture Alliance.

Chapter 33: Isaiah Berlin. Copyright © Gemma Levine/Getty Images.

Chapter 34: Nathan Alterman, 1961. Copyright © Micha Bar-Am/Magnum Photos.

Chapter 35: Saul Bellow. Copyright © Mondadori Collection/Getty Images.

Chapter 36: Primo Levi. Copyright © Archivio Mondadori/Getty Images.

Chapter 37: Paul Celan. Copyright © Ullstein Bild.

Chapter 38: Clarice Lispector. Copyright © Arquivo-Museu de Literatura Brasileira, da Fundação Casa de Rui Barbosa.

Chapter 39: Juan Gelman. Copyright © Ullstein Bild/Reuters/TOMAS BRAVO.

Chapter 40: Jacques Derrida, 2001. Copyright © APF/Joel Robine/Getty Images.

Chapter 41: Philip Roth, 2011. Copyright © Julian Hibbard/Contour by Getty Images.

Chapter 42: Dahlia Ravikovitch. Copyright © Dina Guna.

Chapter 43: Joel and Ethan Coen, 2008. Copyright © Richard Hartog/Getty Images.

Chapter 44: Judith Butler, 2012. Copyright © Target Presse Agentur Gmbh/Getty Images.

INDEX

NOTE: Page numbers followed by *f* indicate a figure.

Arendt, Hannah, 7, 115, 129, 415, 436–48, 527, 541, 603; Butler's engagement with, 644–45, 647–52, 652n7, 653–54nn10–17; on the disappearance of European Jewishness, 546; on Dubnow's Jewish nation, 63, 71–72; on Eichmann, 439, 444, 545, 647–49; on Herzl's theory, 50, 54; on Israel and Zionism, 448–49, 644; on Jewish identity in the modern age, 436–41; on Jewish literary tradition, 146; on the Jewish pariah, 444–48; on Lazare, 80–81, 87, 447; Lessing Prize of, 436; personal background of, 436–38; on Proust, 123n4; on secularism and the *Aufklärung*, 441–44; on worldlessness, 11

"Are We Still Jews?" (Simon), 366

Aristotle, 423

Arolosoroff, Chaim, 102

Arthur Aronymous und seine Väter (Lasker-Schüler), 147, 150

Asad, Talal, 356–57, 359–60

"Aspen Tree" (Celan), 547

The Assistant (Malamud), 603

Asturias, Miguel Angel, 567

"Atheistic Theology" (Rosenzweig), 352–53

Aufklärung movement. *See* Jewish Enlightenment (Haskalah)

An Autobiographical Study (Freud), 20

Auto da Fé (Die Blendung) (Canetti), 407, 409–14, 418

Avineri, Shlomo, 52, 56

Avishai, Bernard, 605

Bach, Johann Sebastian, 176–77

Bachmann, Ingeborg, 545

Baigell, Matthew, 395–96, 399, 401

Bakhtin, Mikhail, 417

Bakunin, Mikhail, 569

Balfour Declaration, 49, 100, 208, 210, 261, 264n17

Baron, Salo, 355

Barth, Karl, 352–53, 360, 374

Bassani, Giorgio, 461

Baudelaire, Charles, 1, 311, 313, 316, 496, 542, 569

Bauer, Felice, 233

Bauman, Zygmunt, 6, 119–20, 123n2

Baur, Rupprecht Slavko, 415

Beauvoir, Simone de, 553

Bebel, August, 163

"Before the Law" (Kafka), 246

Der Begriff des Politischen (Schmitt), 415–16

"Beheaded Heifer" (Ravikovitch), 622

Being and Time (Heidegger), 434n11

Bell, Richard, 469, 473–74

Bellow, Saul, 507–18, 603, 606; on conflict between traditional and modern Jews, 507–8, 512, 516–18; on individual complexity, 513–15; on Jewish humor, 516; on Jewish identity, 512–13; Nobel Prize for Literature of, 510, 514–15; personal background of, 508–10; translations of Singer by, 597; use of Yiddish by, 510–11

"Belonging" (Lispector), 552–53

Ben-Gurion, David, 96, 179, 215, 249–63; in Alterman's poetry, 501–2; cultivation of *mamlakhitiyut* by, 254–57; on Israeli Arabs, 201; legacy of, 261–63; political vision of, 251–54; as prime minister, 249–50; statesmanship of, 257–61, 502

Benjamin, Walter, 6–7, 108–10, 306–17, 342, 380, 386, 454, 472, 645; Adorno's response to, 314, 386–87; Arendt's response to, 445, 447–48; on art criticism, 316–17; on Baudelaire, 311, 313, 316, 496; on capitalism and the cult of work, 306, 309–13, 317–18nn2–3; on dialectic in standstill, 234, 247n2; on elimination of poverty, 314–15; on Goethe, 316–17, 544; on Lasker-Schüler, 157n3; on Nietzsche's superman, 311; nihilist world politics of, 317, 500, 613; on remembrance, 313–14, 526; on Schoenberg, 180; on Zionism and internationalism, 308–9

Bercovitch, Sacvan, 600

Berdichevsky, Micha Yosef, 10

Berg, Alban, 181

Bergelson, David, 326

Berger, Peter, 339

Bergson, Henri, 472

Berlin, Isaiah, 230n14, 253, 480–91; on freedom of thought and action, 484–85; on intellectual modesty, 483–84; on liberal nationalism and Zionism, 489–91; on moral agency, 480–82; personal background of, 482–83; on religious identity, 486–89

Bernard, Jean-Jacques, 476–77

Bernays, Isaac ben Ja'akov, 27

Bernays, Jacob, 454, 456, 463n19

Bernays, Martha, 26–28

Bernays-Heller, Judith, 18

Berryman, John, 510

"Be-shetef ir" (Alterman), 493

Bialik, Chaim Nachman, 65, 331, 495, 617

The Big Lebowski, 634–37

The Big Sleep (Chandler), 635

"Bildung und kein Ende" (Rosenzweig), 272–73

Biltmore Plan of 1942, 219n61, 261, 263

The Birth of Tragedy (Nietzsche), 117

Bjørnson, Bjørnstjerne, 294

Black Skin, White Skin (Fanon), 172n30